A COMPANION
TO
GREEK STUDIES

A COMPANION
TO
GREEK STUDIES

EDITED BY

LEONARD WHIBLEY, M.A.
Fellow of Pembroke College

FOURTH EDITION, REVISED

HP

HAFNER PUBLISHING COMPANY
New York and London
1963

Fourth Edition (Revised) published in 1931
by
Cambridge University Press

Reprinted by Arrangement

Printed and Published by
HAFNER PUBLISHING COMPANY, INC.
31 East 10th Street
New York 3, N.Y.

Library of Congress Catalog Card Number: 63-10743

Printed in U.S.A. by
NOBLE OFFSET PRINTERS, INC.
NEW YORK 3, N. Y.

PREFACE TO THE FIRST EDITION

THE *Companion to Greek Studies* was undertaken by the Syndics of the University Press with the intention of presenting in one volume such information (apart from that contained in Histories and Grammars) as would be most useful to the student of Greek literature. It differs in scope from other books of the same class; for besides a survey of Greek life, thought, and art in their different branches, it includes a chapter on the physical conditions of Greece, another containing Chronological Tables of politics, literature, and art, and a chapter on certain branches of criticism and interpretation. While each article has been entrusted to a writer who has made a special study of the subject, it has been the aim of the work to give the substance of our knowledge in a concise form. On this account the discussion of controverted points and technical details has been for the most part omitted. For the same reason sources and authorities have not usually been cited in the text, unless the reference has been necessary to establish an argument, to justify an important theory, or to remind the student of the *locus classicus* of the subject. It is hoped that the full table of contents and the indexes of proper names and Greek words will increase the value of the book for purposes of reference. Bibliographies have generally been appended to each article to help those who seek further information. Plans, views, and reproductions of ancient works of art have been carefully chosen and inserted in those articles in which illustration seems most necessary.

The principle which has been followed in the transliteration of Greek words coincides in the main with that adopted by the Society for the Promotion of Hellenic Studies. Names are presented in their familiar English or Latin form; but the diphthong ει is usually retained (*e.g.* Peisistratus, Cleisthenes), except in words which are as well established in English as Chaeronea and Alexandria. Greek words other than proper names, unless they are familiar in other forms in English, have usually been transliterated letter for letter (*e.g.* Plethron, Nike, Pentekostys).

While the book has been passing through the press, members of the Syndicate and other scholars have contributed much help in suggestion, in criticism, and in reading the proofs. Thanks are due to the following authors and publishers for granting the use of blocks or for permitting the reproduction of illustrations contained in works written or published by them; to Dr Arthur Evans, to Mr Cecil Torr for blocks from his book on Greek ships, to the Council of the Society for the Promotion of Hellenic Studies, to Messrs Longman and Co., to Messrs Macmillan and Co., to Mr John Murray, to the *Times*, and to Carl Gerold's Sohn Verlag.

L. W.

December 1904

PREFACE TO THE SECOND EDITION

A second edition having been called for within a year of publication, it has not been thought advisable to make changes of substance, but due note has been taken of criticisms, and corrections of detail have been made.

L. W.

March 1906

PREFACE TO THE THIRD EDITION

THE time that has passed since the book was first published allows and requires a fuller revision and more substantial additions than were possible when the second edition was produced. Some subjects are now discussed for the first time, such as Ethnology, Bronzes and Jewellery. Others, Fauna, Flora, Prehistoric Art, Terracottas, Finance and Palaeography, are treated by fresh writers. Professor Bosanquet has revised the article on Sculpture, which was undertaken in the earlier editions by Sir Charles Waldstein: the sections dealing with Archaic, Hellenistic and Graeco-Roman Sculpture have been rewritten: minor changes have been made in the sections dealing with the sculpture of the fifth and fourth centuries B.C. Mr Adcock has contributed a sketch of the development of early constitutions and has revised Mr Wyse's article on Law. Mr Wace has discussed the Prehistoric House. Sir John Sandys has kindly undertaken the revision of the contributions of the late Sir Richard Jebb and Professor A. S. Wilkins, and has made small additions or corrections in the articles on Literature, Education and Textual Criticism. Mr Gaselee has supplied a bibliography for the article on Metre.

There is scarcely an article that has not been revised. While it was not desired unduly to increase the size of the book, additions amounting to over 100 pages have been made and the number of illustrations has been increased by over fifty. The most considerable additions are connected with the fresh knowledge of the prehistoric age, which has supplied material for a discussion of the difficult problem of Ethnology and has made possible a fuller treatment of Prehistoric Art. Sir Arthur Evans, to whose excavations so much of our knowledge is due, has given generous help in reading Mr Wace's articles on Ethnology, Prehistoric Art and the Prehistoric House, and has made valuable suggestions. He also communicated his most recent conclusions as to the dates of Minoan civilization for the tables on pp. 80–81, which were compiled by the Editor.

To Sir Arthur Evans a further acknowledgment is due for permission to use illustrations of his finds, many of which have been reproduced from the Eleventh Edition of the *Encyclopaedia Britannica*. Acknowledgments are also made for the loan of blocks or the permission to reproduce illustrations or plans to the Director of the British Museum, the Council of the Hellenic Society, the Committee of the British School at Athens, Dr Wiegand, Mr Wace, Mr Ellis H. Minns and Mr Fisher Unwin.

L. W.

December 1915

b

PREFACE TO THE FOURTH EDITION

In the preparation of a new edition the purpose kept in view has been to submit the book to a thorough revision without increasing its length.

Since the first edition was published, more than twenty-six years ago, many of the original contributors have died and it has been necessary to replace or revise some of their articles. New articles have been written on Gems, Music, Money, and Metre: and the aid of other scholars has been sought to revise the articles on Flora, Literature, Philosophy, Weights and Measures, the Position of Women and Medicine. Other articles have generally been revised by those who contributed them to earlier editions, but Professor Gardner rewrote the account of the archaic period in the article on Sculpture, Mr Wace prepared new tables of the Earliest History of the Aegean and revised the account of prehistoric Constitutions, Dr Cary revised the articles on Population and Slaves and Slavery.

Additional illustrations have been inserted, and better blocks have been provided for some of the illustrations that were in the former editions. Thanks for permission to use additional illustrations are due to the Society for the Promotion of Hellenic Studies (40 a); the National Museum, Athens (14, 35, 36); the English Photographic Co., Athens (29, 32, 89); Metropolitan Museum of Art, New York (143); Berlin Museum (42); Fitzwilliam Museum, Cambridge (12, 87, 140, 145); Oxford University Press (43, 44); Messrs Macmillan & Co. Ltd. (13, 40a, 50, 142); Ernst Wasmuth A.-G., Berlin (18); E. Boccard, Paris (40); Alinari, Rome (30, 46); Brogi, Paris (45); and F. Bruckmann A.-G., Munich (39).

L. W.

29 *April* 1931

CONTENTS

CHAPTER I

GEOGRAPHY, ETHNOLOGY, FAUNA, FLORA

I. 1. GEOGRAPHY

By the late H. F. TOZER, M.A., F.R.G.S., *Honorary Fellow of Exeter College, Oxford*

I. 2. ETHNOLOGY

By A. J. B. WACE, M.A., *Deputy Keeper, Victoria and Albert Museum (formerly Director of the British School at Athens and Fellow of Pembroke College).*

I. 3. FAUNA

By D'ARCY W. THOMPSON, C.B., D.LITT., F.R.S., *Trinity College,*
Professor of Natural History in the University of St Andrews

A. MAMMALS

B. BIRDS

C. REPTILES AND BATRACHIA

D. FISHES

E. INSECTS

F. MARINE INVERTEBRATES

I. 4. FLORA

By the late Sir WILLIAM TURNER THISELTON-DYER, K.C.M.G., C.I.E., F.R.S., *Honorary Student of Christ Church, Oxford, Hon.* SC.D., *Cambridge, and* Sir ARTHUR FENTON HORT, BART., M.A. (*formerly Fellow of Trinity College*).

CHAPTER II

HISTORY

II. 1. CHRONOLOGY

By the late R. D. HICKS, M.A., *Fellow of Trinity College.*

CHAPTER III

LITERATURE, PHILOSOPHY, SCIENCE

III. 1. LITERATURE

By the late Sir RICHARD C. JEBB, O.M., LITT.D., *Regius Professor of Greek* and A. T. SINCLAIR, M.A., *Reader in Classics in the University of London* (*formerly Fellow of St John's College*)

III. 2. PHILOSOPHY

School of Aristotle by the late HENRY JACKSON, O.M., LITT.D., *Regius Professor of Greek* and R. HACKFORTH, M.A., *Fellow of Sidney Sussex College and University Lecturer in Classics* and **Later Schools** by the late R. D. HICKS, M.A., and R. HACKFORTH, M.A.*

A. PRESOCRATICS

B. SOCRATES AND THE MINOR SOCRATICS

C. PLATO AND THE OLD ACADEMY

D. ARISTOTLE AND PERIPATETICISM

* Mr Hackforth wishes to acknowledge the help which he received from Mr F. H. Sandbach, Fellow of Trinity College, in the revision of this article.

III. 3. SCIENCE

By the late JAMES GOW, LITT. D., *Headmaster of Westminster School*
(*formerly Fellow of Trinity College*)

A. THE HELLENIC PERIOD

CHAPTER IV

ART

IV. 1. PREHISTORIC ART

By A. J. B. WACE, M.A.

IV. 2. ARCHITECTURE

By the late F. C. PENROSE, LITT. D., *Honorary Fellow of Magdalene College,*
and E. A. GARDNER, LITT. D. (*formerly Yates Professor of Archaeology in
University College, London and Fellow of Gonville and Caius College*).

IV. 3. SCULPTURE

By the late Sir CHARLES WALSTON, LITT. D., *Fellow of King's College,*
and R. C. BOSANQUET, M. A., *Trinity College, formerly Professor of
Classical Archaeology in the University of Liverpool*

A. ARCHAIC PERIOD (*circa* 650–500 B.C.)

B. PERIOD OF TRANSITION (*circa* 500–460 B C.)

C. PERIOD OF MATURITY (*circa* 460–400 B.C.)

IV. 4. PAINTING

By F. R. E A R P, M. A., *Professor of Classics in the University of London*
(formerly Fellow of King's College)

IV. 5. VASE PAINTING

By A. H. S M I T H, C. B., M. A., *Trinity College, formerly Keeper of Greek
and Roman Antiquities in the British Museum*

IV. 6. TERRACOTTAS

By H. B. WALTERS, M.A., *King's College, Keeper of Greek and Roman Antiquities in the British Museum*

IV. 7. BRONZE-WORK

By H. B. WALTERS, M.A.

IV. 8. GOLD AND SILVER WORK

By H. B. WALTERS, M.A.

IV. 9. ENGRAVED GEMS

By H. B. WALTERS, M.A.

IV. 10. MUSIC

By R. P. WINNINGTON-INGRAM, M.A., *Fellow of Trinity College*

CHAPTER V

MYTHOLOGY AND RELIGION

MYTHOLOGY AND RELIGION

By E. A. GARDNER, LITT.D.

V. 2. RELIGIOUS INSTITUTIONS

CHAPTER VI

PUBLIC ANTIQUITIES

VI. 1. CONSTITUTIONS

Sections 429–434 by F. E. ADCOCK, M.A., *Professor of Ancient History*
Fellow of King's College
Sections 435–472 by LEONARD WHIBLEY, M.A.,
Fellow of Pembroke College

A. DEVELOPMENT OF CONSTITUTIONS

VI. 2. LAW

By the late WILLIAM WYSE, M.A., *formerly Fellow of Trinity College*, and F. E. ADCOCK, M.A.

A. EARLY LEGISLATION AND THE LAWS OF GORTYN

B. THE ATHENIAN JUDICIAL SYSTEM IN THE FOURTH CENTURY

VI. 3. FINANCE

By M. CARY, D.LITT., *Reader in Ancient History at University College, London*

c

VI. 4. POPULATION

By R. J. G. MAYOR, C.B., M.A., *formerly Fellow of King's College*

VI. 5. SLAVES AND SLAVERY

By R. J. G. MAYOR, M.A.

VI. 6. COLONIES

By the late H. J. EDWARDS, M.A., C.B., *Fellow of Peterhouse,*
and M. CARY, D.LITT.

VI. 7. COMMERCE AND INDUSTRY

By the late H. J. EDWARDS, M.A.

VI. 8. MEASURES AND WEIGHTS

A. MEASURES

By the late Sir WILLIAM RIDGEWAY, SC.D., and
F. N. PRYCE, M.A., *Assistant Keeper of Greek and
Roman Antiquities in the British Museum*

B. WEIGHTS

By the late Sir WILLIAM RIDGEWAY, SC.D., and H. MATTINGLY, M.A.
*Assistant Keeper of Coins and Medals in the British Museum
(formerly Fellow of Gonville and Caius College)*

VI. 9. MONEY

By E. S. G. ROBINSON, M.A., *Christ Church, Oxford, Assistant Keeper of Coins and Medals in the British Museum*

VI. 10. WAR

By Sir CHARLES OMAN, K.B.E., M.A., *Chichele Professor of Modern History in the University of Oxford*

A. ARMS AND ARMOUR

B. TACTICS

C. FORTIFICATION AND SIEGE-CRAFT

VI. 11. SHIPS

By A. B. COOK, LITT.D., *Laurence Professor of Classical Archaeology, Fellow of Queens' College*

VI. 12. THE CALENDAR

By the late JAMES GOW, LITT.D.

CHAPTER VII

PRIVATE ANTIQUITIES

VII. 1. A TABLE OF THE RELATIONSHIPS OF A MAN

By the late JAMES GOW, LITT.D.

VII. 2. RITUAL OF BIRTH, MARRIAGE, AND DEATH

By the late Miss J. E. HARRISON

VII. 3. EDUCATION

By the late A. S. WILKINS, LITT.D., *formerly Professor
of Latin in the Owens College*

VII. 4. BOOKS AND WRITING

By M. R. JAMES, O.M., LITT.D., *Provost of Eton College*

VII. 5. THE POSITION OF WOMEN

By the late F. WARRE CORNISH, M.A., *formerly Fellow of King's College*,
and Miss JANET BACON, M.A., *Girton College,
University Lecturer in Classics*

VII. 6. DRESS

Sections 668–669 by A. J. B. WACE, M.A.
Sections 670–679 by Lady EVANS, M.A.

VII. 7. DAILY LIFE, ITS SURROUNDINGS, EMPLOYMENTS AND AMUSEMENTS

By E. A. GARDNER, LITT.D.

A. TOWN LIFE

B. COUNTRY LIFE—AGRICULTURE, ETC.

C. FOOD AND DRINK, MEALS, COOKING, AND ENTERTAINMENTS

D. EXERCISE, GAMES, BATHS

E. TRAVELLING

VII. 8. HOUSE AND FURNITURE

Sections 702–709 by A. J. B. WACE, M.A.
Sections 710–713 by E. A. GARDNER, LITT.D.

VII. 9. MEDICINE

By the late Sir T. CLIFFORD ALLBUTT, K.C.B., M.D., F.R.S., *Regius Professor of Physic*, and C. SINGER, D.LITT., M.D., *Magdalen College, Oxford*

CHAPTER VIII

CRITICISM AND INTERPRETATION

VIII. 1. DIALECTS

By the late R. A. NEIL, M.A., *Fellow of Pembroke College*, and P. GILES, LITT.D., *Reader in Comparative Philology, Master of Emmanuel College*

VIII. 2. EPIGRAPHY

By the late E. S. ROBERTS, M.A., *University Lecturer in Epigraphy, Master of Gonville and Caius College*, and E. A. GARDNER, LITT.D.

VIII. 3. PALAEOGRAPHY

By E. H. MINNS, LITT.D., *Disney Professor of Archaeology, Fellow of Pembroke College*

VIII 4. TEXTUAL CRITICISM

By the late Sir RICHARD C. JEBB, LITT.D.

VIII. 5. METRE

By C. M. BOWRA, M.A., *Fellow of Wadham College, Oxford*

VIII. 6. HISTORY OF SCHOLARSHIP

By the late Sir JOHN SANDYS, LITT.D., *Public Orator*

LIST OF ILLUSTRATIONS

MAPS

I. GEOGRAPHY, ETHNOLOGY, FAUNA AND FLORA.

I. 1. GEOGRAPHY.

1. THE development of the Hellenic race, and the influence which it has exercised on mankind at large, were greatly affected by the position of the land which the Greeks inhabited, and by its peculiar characteristics. Greece was the most central country in the ancient world, or at least enjoyed more than any other the advantages which such a situation affords; for though in reality Egypt and Syria were more central, owing to their lying in closer proximity to the meeting-point of the three great continents, yet there were insuperable difficulties to prevent either of them from undertaking the part which was performed by Greece. The harbourless shore of Palestine precluded its inhabitants from holding communication by sea with other countries; and in the case of Tyre, which formed a marked exception to this rule, the narrow commercial policy which prevailed in that state was an effectual bar to hinder her from promoting human advancement on a large scale. Egypt, again, from being confined within the Nile valley, and being dependent on that river for her existence, was too self-centred to be desirous either of adopting ideas from abroad, or of imparting to others her long accumulated stores of knowledge. But Greece, while it lay on the threshold of Europe relatively to the eastern counties, was from its conformation eminently a receptive country. It occupied somewhat the same position in antiquity which England holds at the present day, as being the point of communication between the old world and the new, so that whatever ideas passed from the one to the other passed through it, and were liable to be modified by its influence. And the numerous bays and harbours which are found on its eastern coasts provided an easy access to traders from that quarter, while the islands of the Aegean, and especially the long line of Crete, facilitated their approach. On the other hand, Italy and Greece may be described as standing back to back to each other, for the outlets of the former of these countries are towards the west, and the eastern shores of the Adriatic are singularly destitute of good harbours. In consequence of this there was at first little intercourse between them,

Position of Greece.

G. A.

so that the nationalities which inhabited them were developed independently of each other, and it was not until Greek culture had reached its maturity that Italy was largely affected by it.

2. Few countries in the world possess characteristics so strongly marked as those of Greece. Its coast is indented in an extraordinary manner with numerous inlets, both large and small, so that its length is out of all proportion to the area of the country. This peculiarity becomes more striking as the land advances farther towards the south, for the shores of Epeirus and Thessaly present for the most part an unbroken outline, except where the land-locked Pagasaean gulf penetrates into the last-named district. To the southward of those provinces a waist is formed, where the Ambracian and Maliac gulfs approach each other from opposite sides; and from that point onward the coast becomes more varied, especially where it skirts the Euboic sea and the Corinthian gulf, until the Isthmus of Corinth is reached. There the peninsular formation of Greece is still more conspicuous, and its variety of outline culminates in the Peloponnese, which is pierced by the Messenian, the Laconian, and the Argolic gulfs. The mountains of Greece, also, which ramify through the whole country, and form a part of every view, are peculiar in their character. Though none of these rise above 8,000 feet—with the single exception of Olympus, which nearly reaches 10,000—yet their general elevation is very considerable, and many of them are covered with snow for several months of the year. As many as twenty-five are over 3,000 feet in height, and seven of these, among which are included the famous names of Parnassus, Taygetus, Cyllene and Erymanthus, are between 7,000 and 8,000 feet. These mountains are nowhere irregularly jumbled together, but are carefully grouped and delicately articulated, so that they possess the features to which the term 'classical' is usually applied. The hard limestone of which they are composed breaks in such a manner as to produce sharp outlines, and from the same cause their buttresses are subdivided into clearly cut ridges. The rivers, owing to the shortness of their courses, which prevents them from attaining any considerable volume, are nowhere navigable except for boats, and it is only the larger streams, such as the Peneus, the Spercheus and the Alpheus, which have a perennial supply of water. The remainder are torrents, which are only filled after violent storms, or during the winter season, and for the rest of the year display a white stony bed. The lakes also are a remarkable feature, for they all without exception have no outlet for their waters, except such as is provided by subterranean passages. Notable instances are found in the Copaic lake in Boeotia, and in those of Pheneus and Stymphalus in Arcadia. This phenomenon arises from the conformation of the inland basins, which are so hemmed in by mountains that no aperture is left for the escape of the water. The result is that, when the subterranean passage, or *catavothra*, is choked, as often happens, the level of the lake rises; but when the obstacle which closed it is

General characteristics.

removed, it falls, and sometimes the lake for a time disappears altogether. These changes, as might be expected, gave birth to numerous myths. The plains are in some cases upland levels, such as that of Mantinea, and sometimes maritime plains, like those of Athens and Argos, which are hemmed in on three sides by lofty mountains, and on the fourth are open to the sea. The variety of elevation which is illustrated by these instances is a characteristic of the whole of Greece, and had a marked influence on its climate. While the southern sun provided the element of genial warmth, the presence of the mountains and uplands furnished an inexhaustible supply of fresh breezes, and the temperature was everywhere rendered equable by the proximity of the sea. One more peculiarity remains to be noticed in the liability of the country to shocks of earthquake. This is explained by the circumstance that Greece lies close to a centre of volcanic agency, the exact locality of which is the island of Thera (Santorin). That volcano was famous in antiquity on account of the great eruption of 197 B.C., which Strabo has described, and it has been in activity within fifty years from the present time. On the mainland of Greece the mountain of Methana, on the coast of Argolis opposite Aegina, was formed by an eruption in 282 B.C. The occurrence of earthquakes is frequently mentioned in Greek history, and they seem in some measure to account for the disappearance of the monuments of antiquity throughout the country, many of which owing to their massive construction would otherwise in all probability have survived to our days.

3. Northern Greece is divided in two parts by the mountain chain of **Scardus** and **Pindus**, which forms a well-marked backbone, as it traverses the country from north to south, half-way **Northern Greece.** between the Adriatic and the Aegean. The districts by which it is flanked on either side form a strong contrast to each other, for while Macedonia and Thessaly present extensive plains with rich alluvial soil, the lands towards the west—Illyricum, Epeirus, and Acarnania—are occupied by a confused mass of rugged mountains, diverging in different directions. The range of Scardus rises far away towards the north, and separates Upper Macedonia from Illyricum, extending as far south as Lyncestis; at this point Pindus commences, and when it reaches the north-west angle of Thessaly, it rises conspicuously in Mount Lacmon. This is an important position, because the principal rivers and mountains of northern Greece radiate from it. Here are the sources of the Aous, the Arachthus, and the Achelous, which flow towards the western sea, and those of the Peneus, and in part also those of the Haliacmon, which enter the Thermaic gulf. Here also the Ceraunian mountains diverge towards the west, until they reach the Adriatic at the Acroceraunian promontory, while on the eastern side the Cambunian chain is the connecting link between Pindus and the mighty mass of Olympus. That mountain forms a bastion, by which the approaches to Greece are guarded at the north-eastern angle; and from it proceed, following the sea-coast, first the two other Mountains of the

Giants, Ossa and Pelion, together with the peninsula of Magnesia, and afterwards the line of summits which runs through Euboea, and is continued in the islands of Andros and Tenos, and others of the northern Cyclades. Again, at the southern termination of Pindus, near the head-waters of the Spercheus, and intermediate between the Maliac and Ambracian gulfs, stands the commanding summit of Tymphrestus, and from this the range of Othrys separates at right angles, overlooking the Maliac gulf, and extending as far as the straits of Artemisium and the entrance of the Pagasaean gulf.

4. **Macedonia,** though it cannot properly be called a Hellenic land, since its inhabitants were not reckoned as belonging to that race, yet calls for notice, both because of its importance as commanding the entrance to Greece from the north, and because it was the birthplace of the great monarchy, which was destined to subjugate that country. Its determining feature is the river Axius (Vardar), which divides it in two parts, flowing from north to south; for whereas its western portion is chiefly occupied by elevated plains, deeply sunk among the mountains, of which the plain of Pelagonia is the most important, on the eastern side the ground stretches away towards Thrace, and partakes of the wild and irregular character of that region. In this direction at an early period the boundary of the two countries was the Strymon; at a later time Macedonia extended its limits as far as the Nestus. Between those two rivers, in the interior, lay Mount Orbelus, and this was connected with Scardus by a lower range, which separates from that chain in the neighbourhood of Lyncestis. The ancient capital, Edessa, stood at the point where the passes from that district enter Lower Macedonia, and its position was worthy of the nursery of a great kingdom, for it is one of the most striking in Greece. It occupied a table of rock, which falls in front of it in steep precipices; and over these the river Lydias, which traverses the city by several channels, falls in numerous cascades. The later capital, Pella, was built on low ground nearer to the sea, on a site which had neither strength nor salubrity to recommend it. Thessalonica, the chief city under the Romans, was finely situated at the head of the Thermaic gulf, where it commanded the trade with the interior of the country; it was also the terminus of the western half of the Egnatian Way, which, starting from Dyrrhachium on the Adriatic, connected the two seas, and for many centuries formed the main line of communication between Rome and her eastern provinces. The coast, which extends from Thessalonica to the foot of Mount Olympus, was bordered by a rich plain, which is watered by the Axius, the Lydias, and the Haliacmon; and the northern slopes of that mountain, and also those which descend from its flanks towards the sea, formed Pieria, the home of the Muses before their worship was transferred to Helicon. Here the town of Pydna was situated, in the neighbourhood of which Perseus, the last king of Macedon, was defeated by the Romans. The mountains which bounded this region on the west, extending northward from Olympus, were called the Bermian chain.

5. The peninsula of **Chalcidice**, which projects from the coast of Macedonia into the north of the Aegean, bears a striking resemblance to the Peloponnese from the three promontories in which it ends; and even in the shape of its mountains and its vegetation it seems to belong rather to southern than to northern Greece.   It is not unnatural, therefore, that from an early time it should have been fringed with Greek colonies; these, as its name implies, were planted chiefly by settlers from Chalcis in Euboea. The easternmost of its three projections, which was called Acte, is joined to the continent by an isthmus about a mile and a half broad, where the remains of Xerxes' canal are still visible.   From this point it extends for about 40 miles, until at its extremity it throws up the vast conical peak of Athos, which is 6,400 feet in height.   This mountain, owing to its great elevation and its solitary position, has at all times been dangerous to navigators from its liability to attract storms, as the Persians discovered when the fleet of Mardonius was wrecked on its coasts.   The central peninsula of the three, Sithonia, though mountainous, is less so than Acte, while the third, Pallene, is comparatively level.   Near the end of Sithonia the town of Torone was situated, and close to the isthmus of Pallene, which is narrower than that of Athos, being only half a mile wide, lay the important Corinthian colony of Potidaea.   At no great distance from it, at the head of the Toronaic gulf, was Olynthus.   On the land side of the isthmus of Acte the city of Acanthus was situated, and at some distance to the north of it, at the point where the Strymon issues from the lake Prasias or Cercinitis, stood Amphipolis, with the port of Eion at the mouth of that river.

6. **Thessaly** was a semi-Hellenic country in respect of its population, and in its geography it partially resembled the districts which were occupied by the Hellenes.   Its inhabitants, though more closely related to the Greeks than were the Macedonians, were not of the pure Hellenic stock; and the land, though it presents a definite organisation, which is not to be found farther north, is neither maritime nor mountainous to the same degree as southern Greece.   Its vast plain is the most extensive that is found in the whole peninsula, and by the Greeks it was believed originally to have been a lake, until an escape was provided for its waters by the formation of the ravine of Tempe between Olympus and Ossa, which was created by a stroke of the trident of Poseidon the earth-shaker.   It is enclosed by well-marked mountain barriers: on the north by the Cambunian range, on the west by Pindus, on the south by Othrys, and towards the sea by Ossa and Pelion, which form a continuous chain—'mingling their roots with one another,' as Herodotus says—while Olympus rises to the northward of Ossa, and completes the line of circuit.   These mountains formed the outworks of the defences of Greece, but they could be traversed by passes at various points.   The most famous of these was **Tempe,** which, while it deserved the character of a beautiful and romantic vale which the poets have attributed to it, was at the same time a difficult and easily defensible passage.   It is a winding chasm, about four miles

and a half in length, flanked on either side by precipices of grey limestone, which rise in places to a height of from 500 to 1000 feet; but the features of the scene are everywhere softened by the copious stream of the Peneus which winds between, and by the luxuriant vegetation which accompanies it, and the glades that at intervals open out at the foot of the cliffs. The pass of Tempe, however, was of less importance than at first sight it appears to be, because it could be turned by another pass on the western side of Olympus from Petra in Pieria, which entered the Thessalian plain to the northward of Larissa; it was by this that Xerxes approached, and when the Greeks discovered the existence of this passage, they gave up all thoughts of defending Tempe. Again, towards the north-west, a pass led over Mount Lacmon from Epeirus, and followed the upper valley of the Peneus to Aeginium; by this route Caesar entered Thessaly before the battle of Pharsalia. Another, by means of which there was communication with the Ambracian gulf, passed over the Pindus chain to the southward of this, and descended into the plain at Gomphi. Finally, the great southern pass was that of Coela, which crosses Mount Othrys from the Maliac gulf nearly opposite Thermopylae; the importance of the town of Pharsalus arose from its guarding the approaches to it on the northern side. The whole of the wide area of Thessaly was drained by the **Peneus.** This river, after it has entered the plain at its north-west angle, describes an arc towards the south, and in this part receives the waters of a number of tributaries—the Enipeus, the Apidanus, the Onochonus and the Pamisus: the country which was drained by these was called Upper Thessaly, as being farther removed from the sea, while Lower Thessaly was the region between this and the slopes of Ossa and Pelion; they were separated from one another by a range of hills, which runs northward from Othrys in the direction of Larissa. After passing that city, and before reaching Tempe, the river at certain seasons of the year overflows the lower lands towards the south, and its inundations form the lake Nessonis; and, when that is full, they again escape, and pour themselves into the lake of Boebe. That lake has no outlet for its waters, for a watershed interposes between it and the Pagasaean gulf.

Politically, Thessaly was divided into four districts, Hestiaeotis, Thessaliotis, Pelasgiotis, and Phthiotis. Of these, Hestiaeotis occupied the north-western portion, with Tricca for its chief city, while Thessaliotis lay to the south-west. In the eastern portion of the latter of these, where the level ground runs up into an angle of the mountains, and is intersected by the stream of the Enipeus, was the plain of Pharsalia. Pelasgiotis was the eastern section, and contained the powerful cities of Larissa, Crannon and Pherae. Phthiotis, which occupied a position apart from the rest, in the south-eastern corner of the country, was a region of great importance in the heroic age, for Thucydides tells us that it was the original home of the Hellenic race, and from it the great Achilles was sprung. The Pagasaean gulf, also, on which it bordered, was celebrated in early story in connexion with the expedition of the Argonauts, for the pinewood of which the Argo was built was cut on the neighbouring slopes of Pelion, and the towns of Pagasae and Aphetae, which stood at the head and at the mouth of the gulf respectively, were regarded as the places where the vessel was constructed and from which it started on its voyage. The town of Iolcos, which was famous in the same connexion, lay under Mount Pelion, to the eastward of Pagasae; and close to it at a later period the city of Demetrias was founded by Demetrius Poliorcetes. This stronghold, which was of great importance as commanding the approach to Thessaly from this side, was called by Philip V of Macedon one of the three fetters of Greece, Chalcis and Corinth being the other two. The tribes which occupied the outlying portions of Thessaly were the Perrhaebi in the extreme north, the Magnetes along the range of Ossa and Pelion, and the Dolopes and Dryopes about the southern extremity of Pindus.

The history of Thessaly was influenced in a marked manner by its natural features. It was the temptation which the richness of its soil offered to invaders that induced the Thessalians to leave their home in Epeirus, and to expel from their early seats, first the Boeotians, and afterwards the Dorians, thus initiating the most important movements of the tribes to the southward of them. These broad acres also tended to foster aristocracy as the form of government, for they were in the possession of a few powerful families, such as the Aleuadae of Larissa and the Scopadae of Crannon, and were tilled for them by a serf population. And, as plains are specially suitable for the breeding of horses, the arm in which the Thessalians were strong in war was their cavalry, while the heavy-armed infantry, which in the rest of Greece was composed of the middle class, and was associated with free institutions, was excluded.

7. To the westward of Macedonia and Thessaly lay Illyricum and Epeirus, regions of bleak irregular mountains and upland valleys. The line of separation between them was formed by the Ceraunian chain, and Illyricum, which lay to the northward of it, was watered by several rivers, of which the Aous was the most important. At intervals along the coast were plains of some extent, and the exports which they afforded were the chief source of the prosperity of the neighbouring Greek colonies of Epidamnus (Dyrrhachium) and Apollonia. To the southward Epeirus extended as far as the Ambracian gulf, but the absence of harbours along its shores caused it to be for the most part an unknown land to the Greeks; indeed, its name Epeirus, or the Continent, implies that it was only known to them through the medium of the outlying islands. It comprised three regions: in the north-west Chaonia, which extended as far south as the river Thyamis; towards the east the inland district of Molottis; and to the south Thesprotia. Through Molottis flowed the chief river of the country, the Arachthus, which followed a course due south from its source in Mount Lacmon to the Ambracian gulf. Westward of this, in a valley of its own, lay the extensive lake Pambotis (Lake of Joannina), to

the south of which, at some little distance off, was the famous oracle of Dodona, the site of which has been recently discovered. It was probably the migration of the Thessalians from these parts which spread through the Greek world the renown of this oracle, and also that of the river Acheron, which flows through Thesprotia. The awe inspired by the deep and dark ravines, which that stream traverses in one part of its course, seems to have been the cause of its being associated with the infernal regions. At the point where it issues from these a large swamp called the Acherusian marsh is formed. To the north of the Ambracian gulf, within a bend of the Arachthus, the city of Ambracia was situated, and near its eastern coast that of Amphilochian Argos; but the most famous place in that neighbourhood was Actium, the scene of the great defeat of Antony and Cleopatra by Augustus, which commands the mouth of the narrow strait by which that gulf is entered.

8. The mountains of central Greece start from Mount Tymphrestus, which, as we have seen, marks the termination of the chain of Pindus. To the south-west diverge the irregular Aetolian ranges; while to the east the well-marked line of Oeta runs parallel to Othrys on the southern side of the valley of the Spercheus and the Maliac gulf, after which it is continued under different names along the coast of northern Locris and Boeotia, until it reaches Attica, and after throwing up the pyramid of Pentelicus sinks into the sea at Sunium. Beyond this point it rises again in the western Cyclades—Ceos, Cythnos, Seriphos and Siphnos. But the most lineal descendants of the main chain of northern Greece are those which take an intermediate course between the other two, and first as Parnassus and Helicon pass through Boeotia, and then as Cithaeron and Parnes separate the latter of those countries from Attica. Finally, an offshoot from Cithaeron runs off to the southward, and forms the important mountain of Geranea, which blocks the approach to the Isthmus.

Central Greece.

9. The districts which occupied the extreme west of this part of the country, Acarnania and Aetolia, exercised but little influence on the history of Greece. The most marked feature of **Acarnania** is the river Achelous (Aspropotamo), which on account of its abundant stream was famous in early Greek mythology. Owing to the amount of alluvium that it brought down, some of the Echinades islands, which lay off its mouth, were attached to the mainland; and the marshes which were formed at this point were the cause of the strength of the fortress of Oeniadae, which was situated about 10 miles from the coast. The chief town of Acarnania, Stratus, was built in a rich plain in the centre of the district on the right bank of that river. **Aetolia** also was intersected by a considerable stream, the Evenus, and between this and the Achelous lay an extensive lake, called Trichonis.

10. The district of **Malis** was situated between Mount Oeta and the south-western angle of the Maliac gulf. It was a small territory, but

To face p. 8.

of great importance to Greece, because it contained the pass of Thermopylae, through which lay the access to the lands farther to the south.
The road here ran between the foot of the mountains and the sea, so that
the passage could be defended by a small body of resolute men against
a much larger force. At the present day the deposit of the Spercheus
has advanced the coast-line so far that the pass no longer exists. To the
westward of the pass there is a deep gorge, through which the river Asopus
flows, and it was by this route that the Persians under Hydarnes commenced
their ascent to the mountains, which resulted in their taking Leonidas
and his followers in the rear. Directly to the south of Malis, but on the
opposite side of the range of Oeta, about the head-waters of the Cephisus,
was the little territory of **Doris**, which at one time was the seat of the
Dorian race. An important pass led through it from Amphissa near
the head of the Crisaean gulf to Thermopylae. At an early period the
whole of the country between the Corinthian and Maliac gulfs was
inhabited by the Locrian race, but they were broken up at the time of
the southward migration of the Boeotians, when that people was expelled from Thessaly by the Thessalians. After that period we find the
Epicnemidian Locrians occupying the heights of Mount Cnemis,
the easterly continuation of Oeta, and beyond them again, facing Euboea,
the **Opuntian Locrians**. Between the two a strip of Phocian territory
intervened, with a port at Daphnus. The other portion of the Locrian
tribe was the **Locri Ozolae**, who occupied the land that bordered on
the Corinthian and Crisaean gulfs to the south-east of Aetolia. Within
their territory lay the important town of Naupactus, which owing to its
strong position on the coast commanded the approach to the Corinthian
gulf.

11. Between the countries which have just been named and Boeotia lay
the land of **Phocis**. It was naturally divided into two parts, the upper
valley of the Cephisus and the vast mass of Parnassus. The former
of these was important because it was traversed by the route which led
from Thermopylae into southern Greece; this was commanded by the
city of Elatea, and the position of that place explains the consternation
which was felt at Athens on the announcement of its capture by Philip,
as described by Demosthenes in the *De Corona*. Parnassus was separated
from the Corinthian gulf by the chain of Mount Cirphis, and between
the two ran the valley of the Pleistus, which led to the Triodos, or meeting
of the three roads which there converged from Delphi, Daulis and
Thebes. In a steep position on the flank of Parnassus, overlooking the
Pleistus at a height of 1500 feet above the sea, stood **Delphi**, the
grandeur of the surroundings of which city increased the awe which was
inspired by the oracle. Behind it are two converging lines of precipices,
culminating in two summits, which are called by the poets the 'twin
peaks of Parnassus'; and at the angle which they form rises the spring
of Castalia, the stream from which descends to the Pleistus. At the back of

these precipices, in an upland region, lies the grotto which was called the Corycian cave, and far above this again is the true summit of the mountain. Delphi was regarded as the most central point in Greece, and thus, as Greece was considered to occupy a position half-way between the eastern and western extremities of the world, it received the name of the 'navel of the earth.' Between it and the head of the Crisaean gulf the Sacred Plain was interposed, at the head of which the guardian city of Crisa was built on a buttress of Parnassus, while the port of Cirrha was situated on the neighbouring coast.

12. **Boeotia** was singularly favoured in respect of its position, for it commanded the traffic between Phocis and Attica, and its coasts, which bordered on three seas, afforded great opportunities for the development of commerce—on the one hand towards the Corinthian gulf, from whence there was communication with Italy and Sicily, on the other towards the Euboic sea, the two bays of which, to the north and south of the Euripus, looked, the one in the direction of Macedonia and the Hellespont, and the other in that of Cyprus and Egypt. But these advantages were almost neutralised by the dull and heavy climate, which imparted a phlegmatic element to the character of the population. The entire area is naturally divided into a northern and a southern basin; the former of these, of which Orchomenus was the chief city, was the centre of supremacy during the heroic age, while the latter, which was presided over by Thebes, rose to importance in the subsequent period. The northern basin was completely surrounded by mountains; and as it received the waters of the Cephisus and other rivers, and afforded no outlet for them except underground passages which were easily blocked, the greater part of its surface was covered by the Copaic lake. At the present day this piece of water no longer exists, having been completely drained by a system of artificial canals and emissaries. The greatness of the resources of this region is shown by the names of the powerful cities which it contained—Orchomenus, Chaeronea, Lebadea, Coronea and Haliartus. The battle-field of Chaeronea lay in front of the city of that name, on the right bank of the Cephisus. The southern basin was for the most part drained by the Asopus, which flowed towards the Euboic sea from the neighbourhood of Plataea. That city stood on a northern spur of Cithaeron, and from it also a brook called Oëroë descended to the Corinthian gulf; the watershed between this stream and the Asopus was the scene of the battle of Plataea. To the northward of it lay Thebes in a valley of its own, into which the hill on which it was built projects, with the streams of Ismenus and Dirce flowing on either side of it. To the westward of Thebes stood the towns of Thespiae and Leuctra, and on this side of Boeotia also was Mount Helicon, the abode of the Muses, in the upper parts of which were the two famous fountains of Aganippe and Hippocrene. Near the course of the Asopus lay the towns of Tanagra and Oenophyta, and at no great distance from its mouth was the temple and sacred enclosure of Delium. The

amount of level ground which was comprised in Boeotia caused it to be the scene of numerous engagements. Several of these are associated with the names of Chaeronea and Coronea, while others are called up by those of Oenophyta, Delium and Leuctra.

13. The neighbouring island of **Euboea** was of great importance to Boeotia, both because it formed a breakwater to shelter its coast, and still more after it was joined to the mainland by a bridge in 411 B.C., because by that means it almost became part of that country. Previously to that date it had for a long time been one of the most valuable possessions of Athens, which city it had supplied with timber and corn, and with pasture for flocks. The Euripus, which was spanned by this bridge, was a narrow channel, somewhat more than 200 feet across, and was commanded by the city of Chalcis on the side towards the island. The changes of the tide in this strait, which occur several times in the day at irregular intervals, have been an object of wonder from the earliest times to the present day. On the Boeotian shore at no great distance off stood Aulis, the port from which the fleet of the Greeks sailed to Troy; and to the south-ward of Chalcis lay its rival, the city of Eretria. Euboea is intersected throughout its whole length by a range of steep mountains, which attains its greatest elevation in Mount Dirphys in the centre of the island. At its northern extremity it was separated from the Thessalian coast by the strait of Artemisium, while towards the south it ended in the two promontories of Caphareus and Geraestus. These were greatly dreaded by mariners on account of their storms, which was also the case with the rocks of Coela on the eastern side, where a portion of Xerxes' fleet was wrecked.

14. The triangular piece of ground which projected southward from Boeotia into the sea was the land of **Attica**. The two countries were divided from one another by the massive chain of Cithaeron and Parnes, which formed a continuous line from sea to sea. Three passes led over these mountains: in the centre, near their point of junction, that of Phyle, which was occupied by Thrasybulus at the time of the Thirty Tyrants; farther to the west that of Dryoscephalae, which crossed Cithaeron from Thebes by way of Plataea to Eleusis; and to the eastward that which led from Oropus over Parnes to Athens by Decelea, the usual route of the invading Lacedaemonians during the Peloponnesian war. The spurs which descend southwards from this chain divide Attica into a succession of plains from west to east. The first of these plains was the territory of **Megaris**, which originally, like the rest of the country, belonged to the Ionians, but passed into the hands of the Dorians when they invaded the land at an early period and established themselves there. The city of Megara was built about a mile from the Saronic gulf, on which it had the port of Nisaea, while it communicated with the gulf of Corinth by the port of Pagae. Its importance arose from its commanding the passes which led into the Peloponnese, one of which crosses Geranea, while the other skirts the foot

of that mountain, where the precipices of the Scironian rocks overhang the
sea. To the eastward of Megaris, and separated from it by the ridge of
Kerata, lay the plain of Eleusis, and opposite to this, on the farther side of
a bay, stretched the island of Salamis. It was in the strait by which this
bay is entered on its south-eastern side that the battle of Salamis took place.
Between the plains of Eleusis and Athens the line of Aegaleos intervened,
and it was in a depression in the ridge of this, between the two cities, that
the Sacred Way passed, which formed the route of the torchlight processions
in connexion with the Eleusinian mysteries. The plain of Athens was
watered by two streams, the Ilissus and the Cephisus. The former of these
flowed close to Athens, on its eastern side; but the Cephisus, the course of
which lay nearer to Aegaleos, was a much more important stream, and its
waters, which were drawn off into numerous channels for purposes of
irrigation, fertilised the groves of Colonus and the gardens of the Academy.
Mount Hymettus, which bounded this plain on the east, terminated in the
sea at the promontory of Zoster, but at its other extremity it does not join
the mountains towards the north, for it is separated by an interval of two
miles from the base of Pentelicus. At this point is the entrance to the
Mesogaea, an undulating plain, which was so called because it nowhere
touches the sea, being separated from it by the hills, which start from
Pentelicus and Hymettus respectively, and converge at Sunium. The strip
of fertile land, which followed the coast from Zoster to Sunium, bore the
name of the Paralia. The last of the plains of Attica, which remains to be
mentioned, was that of Marathon, in the north-east of the country; this was
enclosed on three sides by Parnes and Pentelicus, and on the fourth by the
Euboic sea. In the same direction, but on the northern side of Parnes, lay
the district of Oropus; geographically, this belonged rather to the territory
of Boeotia, but the Athenians carefully maintained their hold upon it,
because it facilitated their communication with Euboea. In consequence
of this Oropus was always a bone of contention between the two states.
The history of Athens, both external and internal, was materially affected
by the nature of Attica. Its light soil, which, though it favoured the growth
of the olive, was generally unremunerative to the cultivator, caused the
inhabitants to turn their thoughts towards the sea; and the length of the
seaboard, with the facilities which it afforded for communication with
foreign lands, led them in the same direction. Again, in the features of
the country which we have traced we discover the origin and character of
the three political parties of the early period. The Pedieis, who inhabited
the plains, were the great landholders, whose object was to retain the chief
power in their own hands; the Diacrii or Hyperacrii, who occupied the
sides of Pentelicus and Parnes and the ground in their neighbourhood,
were poor mountaineers, who had little to lose, and were consequently
disposed for political change; while the Parali, or dwellers on the sea-
coast, represented mercantile interests, and by their moderate views held
the balance between the others.

ATHENS

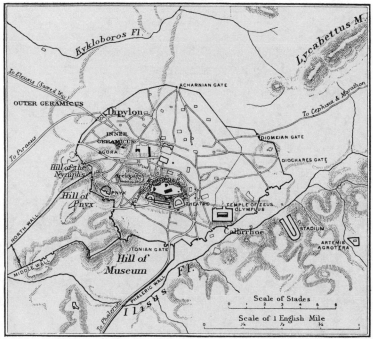

HARBOURS OF ATHENS

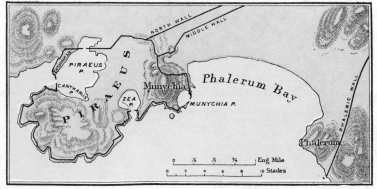

15. The site of **Athens** is on the eastern side of the Athenian plain, about four miles from the sea, where a number of craggy hills rise from the level ground. Conspicuous among these is the altar-shaped rock, on which stood the Acropolis, forming an irregular oval, about 1000 feet in length from east to west, and 500 feet in breadth, while its level summit was 350 feet above the plain : its sides are everywhere precipitous, except towards the west, where the ascent is somewhat more gradual. On this hill, and partly also on the lower ground to the south-ward of it, the original city was built; after a time this was gradually extended towards the north, but the line of the city walls was hardly more than half a mile distant in that direction. After the Persian wars the Acropolis ceased to be inhabited, and was reserved to be a fortress and a sanctuary, and was adorned with splendid buildings and works of art. The most famous among these were the Propylaea, through which it was entered at its western end, and within this, on the left hand of the spectator, the colossal bronze statue of Athena Promachos, and on the right the Parthenon, opposite to which, on the northern side of the area, stood the Erechtheum. To the westward of the Acropolis, at a lower elevation, and separated from it by a deep depression, in the neighbourhood of which was the space of ground called the Pelasgicum, rose the hill of the Areopagus. Under the north-eastern angle of this lay the famous cave of the Eumenides, with a fountain and temple ; while towards the south-east a stone staircase led to the summit, where a rock-hewn bench, running round three sides of a quadrangle, like a triclinium, formed the place of session of the great court of justice. Again, on the western side of the Areopagus, and following a direction from north to south, ran a line of hills—the Hill of the Nymphs, the Hill of the Pnyx, and the Hill of the Museum. The place of assembly on the Pnyx was an open space of ground, gently sloping towards the north-east, the lower part of which was supported by an ancient wall of massive construction : the upper part was skirted by a steep face of cliff, from the middle of which projected a solid rectangular block, forming the Bema, or platform, from which the orator spoke. The Dionysiac theatre lay near the south-east angle of the Acropolis hill, in the rocks at the foot of which its seats were partly excavated. Between it and the Ilissus stood the great temple of Olympian Zeus, and just below this, close to the bed of the stream, was the fountain of Callirrhoë. The Agora or market-place of Athens occupied an area to the northward of the Areopagus, including part of the quarter of the inner Cerameicus, which extended as far as the Dipylum, or north-western gate of the city. Mount Lycabettus, which lay outside the city walls towards the north-east, though it is by far the most conspicuous summit in the neighbourhood of Athens, is rarely mentioned by Greek authors.

16. The **Harbours of Athens** lay in the neighbourhood of the Hill of Munychia, which projected into the sea from the coast to the south-west of Athens. From its eastern side stretched

Athens.

Peiraeus, etc.

away the open roadstead of Phalerum, and under the hill itself, facing in
the same direction, were the small but safe inlets of Munychia and Zea.
To the west lay the Peiraeus, an almost ideal port, for it is safe, deep and
spacious, and its entrance is defended by a tongue of land called Eetioneia,
which projects to meet a corresponding prominence of the Peiraeic peninsula. This basin was again divided into two parts—the great harbour,
which was devoted to merchant vessels, and that called Cantharus, on the
southern side, which was reserved for ships of war. The latter haven, and
that of Zea on the opposite side of the peninsula, approached so near to
one another as almost to divide that piece of ground in two. The Long
Walls, which connected these harbours with Athens, were originally two,
one of which ran from the city to the Peiraeus, the other to the eastern
extremity of the bay of Phalerum; the third, which was added by the
advice of Pericles, was intermediate between these, and joined the eastern
part of the fortifications of Peiraeus to Athens, by which means the communication between the two places was rendered more secure.

17. The **Peloponnese** is compared by Strabo to the leaf of the plane-
tree, which it resembles in its broad surface and the variety of
its outline. The deep indentations of the coast which are
characteristic of Greece are here especially conspicuous.
The mountains which intersect it in several directions naturally subdivided it into a number of states, but at the same time its compactness
of form contributed an element of unity, which caused those states to
act in concert with one another when the occasion required it, and thus
facilitated the creation of the hegemony which was exercised by Sparta.
It may be regarded as the acropolis of Greece, being the inner fortress on
which the inhabitants of that country could fall back, when its outworks
had been taken by an invader. Its mountain system is independent of
that of central Greece. In the northern part of the country a massive
chain runs from east to west, separating Achaia from Arcadia, and reaches
a great elevation in three summits—Cyllene to the east, Aroanius in
the centre, and Erymanthus to the west. From this the other principal
chains diverge at right angles—on the eastern side of Arcadia the line of
Artemisium and Parthenium, which is continued as Parnon in the direction of Cape Malea; in the centre of the country, first Maenalus, and
afterwards Taygetus, the loftiest of all, which separates Laconia from
Messenia; while to the west the ranges are at first less definitely marked,
but as they advance southward attain a considerable height in Lycaeum,
and are continued by Mounts Ithome and Eva towards the promontory of
Acritas. The mountains of Argolis start from Cyllene, and follow a south-
eastern course through that country.

18. The **Isthmus of Corinth**, by which the Peloponnese was joined
to the rest of Greece, is about three and a half miles wide in its narrowest
part, and nowhere rises to any great height above the sea-level. Its
importance to the country may best be seen by comparing the correspond-

ing feature of the Italian peninsula. There the limb in which the organism terminates, Sicily, is severed from it by the Straits of Messina, and consequently that island never stood in the same intimate relation to Italy in which the 'Island of Pelops' stood to Greece. Immediately within the Isthmus the steep Oneian mountains barred farther progress, and the stronghold of **Corinth**, which stood at the western extremity of these, served as a warder to guard the passage into the interior. That city occupied one of the finest positions in Greece, for its lofty fortress, the Acro-corinth, was almost impregnable, and contained an inexhaustible supply of water in the fountain of Peirene; and it possessed two harbours, that of Lechaeum on the Corinthian gulf, and that of Cenchreae on the Saronic. It was enabled to communicate by sea for purposes of trade both with the far east and the far west; and this intercourse was facilitated by the Diolcos, a sort of roadway, by which vessels used to be drawn across the isthmus. At the same time it both commanded the lines of traffic between northern and southern Greece, and formed the most convenient station for the export of goods from the interior to foreign countries. The part which Corinth played in the politics of Greece was affected by these commercial interests, for they caused her on the whole to be in favour of the maintenance of peace, and to endeavour to preserve the balance of power between the other states.

19. About nine miles to the north-westward of Corinth, and two from the Corinthian gulf, stood the city of Sicyon, a place of importance in the early history of Greece, and for a long period a home of the fine arts. Beyond it commenced the district of **Achaia**, which extended as far as the promontory of Araxus, on the confines of Elis. It was a narrow strip of territory, being hemmed in between the mountains of northern Arcadia and the sea, and was for the most part composed of sloping fertile ground. Hence in Homer it is called Aegialus, or the coast-land. Its shores, however, are singularly uniform and destitute of harbours, in which respect they are strongly contrasted with those on the northern side of the Corinthian gulf, which are broken into numerous bays. The entire area is divided up into a number of valleys and small plains by gorges through which the torrents descend from the mountains; and owing to this conformation of the land the most natural political system by which the inhabitants could be held together was a federal union. The early confederation which was thus formed was afterwards developed into the famous combination which was called the Achaean League. The principal cities of Achaia were Pellene, Helice and Aegium on the gulf of Corinth, and Patrae (Patras) and Dyme beyond the straits at Rhium on the outer sea.

20. The north-west corner of the Peloponnese was occupied by **Elis**, a land not easily defensible, for it was largely composed of level ground bordering on the sea. On the edge of this lie two promontories, which probably were rocky islands before they were joined to the mainland

by alluvial soil—Chelonatas, the westernmost point of the Peloponnese, and Ichthys. It naturally fell into three divisions—to the north Hollow Elis, in the centre Pisatis, and to the south Triphylia. The first of these, Hollow Elis, comprised the western slopes of Erymanthus, and the valley and plains of the Peneus which flows from them. On its coast, at some distance northward of Chelonatas, was the port of Cyllene. Pisatis, which was separated from this by the spurs of Mount Pholoë, represented the lower valley of the Alpheus and its environs. That river rises at no great distance from the sources of the Eurotas, and after passing through western Arcadia, and receiving the waters of the Ladon and the Erymanthus, which flow from the northern part of that country, descends through an open valley to Olympia. That place, which from the Pan-hellenic character of the games which were celebrated there was almost as great a uniting force among the Greeks as the Delphic oracle, was situated on the northern side of the valley, on level ground which intervenes between the river and a conspicuous conical hill, Mount Cronius; while towards the west its area was bounded by the stream of the Cladeus, which here enters the Alpheus at right angles. The Altis, or sacred enclosure, contained the famous temple of Zeus with the chryselephantine statue of the god by Pheidias, and among other edifices the Heraeum, in which during the modern excavations of the place Praxiteles' statue of Hermes was found. The stadium and hippodrome lay without the Altis, on its eastern side. The third division of Elis, Triphylia, which owing to its position was easily dissevered from the rest of the country, was a narrow strip of coast-land between the mountains and the sea, extending as far south as the confines of Messenia, on which side the boundary was formed by the river Neda.

21. **Messenia** was a favoured country on account of its equably warm climate and fertile soil; but these very advantages were the cause of its misfortunes, because they acted as a temptation to its less favoured neighbours, and tended to enervate its inhabitants, so that they lost their power of resistance. It was divided into an upper and a lower plain, which were bordered by two ranges of mountains, which take their origin in Mount Lycaeum, and run, on the one side to Cape Acritas, on the other towards the chain of Taygetus. The upper plain was that of Stenyclerus, at the head of which stands the peak of Eira, the scene of the final struggle of the Messenian people, while at its exit rises Ithome, where the protracted defence under Aristodemus took place. This summit overlooks the lower plain, which extends to a greater width, and reaches to the head of the Messenian gulf. The city of Messene was founded by Epameinondas on the western side of Ithome, with the highest point of that mountain for its acropolis. The principal harbour in Messenia was that of Pylos (Navarino), a semicircular inlet, in front of which lay the long island of Sphacteria. The northern extremity of this island was separated by a narrow strait from the headland of Pylos or

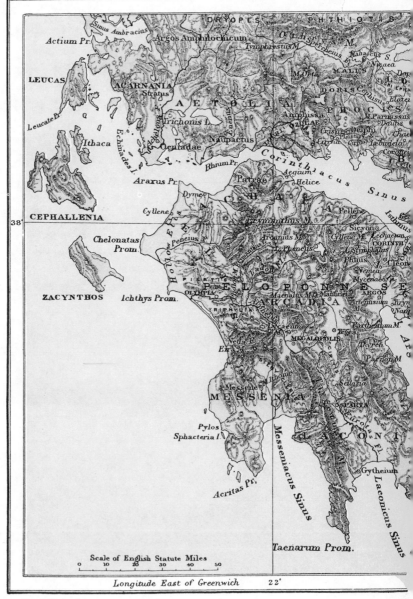

Scale of English Statute Miles
0   10   20   30   40   50

Longitude East of Greenwich   22°

Camb. Univ. Press

To face p 16

Coryphasium, which was occupied by the Athenians during the Peloponnesian war.

22. **Laconia** was separated from Messenia by the lofty range of Taygetus, while on its eastern side, towards the Aegean, ran the lower, but still elevated, chain of Parnon. In a deep depression between the two lay the valley-plain of Sparta, the 'hollow Lacedaemon' of the Homeric poems, which was eighteen miles in length by four or five in breadth; it was watered by the stream of the Eurotas, which rises on the confines of Arcadia, and ultimately finds its way into the Laconian gulf, after passing through a narrow defile called the Aulon. The site of Sparta, which was on the eastern side of the plain, and on the right bank of the Eurotas, in some respects resembled that of Rome, for it was built on a group of low hills by the side of a river. The strength of its position, owing to its seclusion and the steep mountains which surround it, explain how it came to pass that Sparta had no need of fortifications. The same features contributed towards the concentration of power in the hands of a limited number of citizens, and thus rendered it suitable for the maintenance of an aristocratic commonwealth. The plain and the best land in its neighbourhood were cultivated by the Helots, who occupied the position of serfs, while the mountainous and less productive parts were in the hands of the Perioeci, who, though free, had no share in the government. Of the passes by which the country could be entered, one led from western Arcadia by the upper valley of the Eurotas; to the eastward of this another, starting from Tegea, crossed the upland region of the Sciritis, and was afterwards joined by a third, which came from Argos through the border district of Thyrea. The two latter met at Sellasia, the scene of the great defeat of the Spartans by Antigonus Doson, and the valley which was thus formed descended on Sparta. Gytheum, the port of Sparta, was situated near the head of the Laconian gulf.

23. In the centre of the Peloponnese lay **Arcadia**, the only portion of the peninsula which did not anywhere touch the sea. It was in every respect a secluded land, being environed on all sides by mountains, and greatly elevated above the surrounding country, so that the plain of Mantinea is more than 2,000 feet above the sea. Its eastern and western regions, which are separated from one another by Maenalus and other mountains in the same range, in many ways differ from one another in their characteristic features. The western part, which is drained by the Alpheus and its tributaries, and had Megalopolis for its chief city, is an irregular hilly plateau; while that towards the east is occupied by a number of closed valleys, deeply sunk among the mountains, which have no outlet for their waters except by means of underground passages. Thus in some of them, such as those of Stymphalus and Pheneus in the north of the country, considerable lakes are formed; while others, like the great double plain of Mantinea and Tegea, are filled by alluvial soil. The last-named area, in consequence of its level character

and central position, became the great battlefield of southern Greece, so that not less than four great engagements were fought in it. From this neighbourhood three passes led to Argos: one from Tegea through Mount Parthenium; another, the most direct, called Prinos, from Mantinea through Mount Artemisium; and a third, called Climax, farther to the north. It was partly a result of the confined situation of Arcadia, and of the consequent difficulty of providing for the surplus population, that it supplied the Hellenic world with mercenary soldiers. Its inhabitants, both in their geographical position and their occupation, were the Swiss of antiquity.

24. The remaining province of the Peloponnese, **Argolis,** bore a strong resemblance to Attica in its shape and position, being a peninsula which started from a broad base and projected south-eastwards into the Aegean. In consequence of its long shore-line it was sometimes called the Argolic Acte. Its importance is shewn by the names of the cities that are found in it. On the northern coast lay Epidaurus, with its famous sanctuary of Asclepius, and Troezen, in front of which rose the strange volcanic peninsula of Methana; between this and the Peiraeus, in the middle of the Saronic gulf, was the island of Aegina, the position of which caused it to be regarded with jealousy by Athens, so that Pericles called it 'the eye-sore of the Peiraeus.' On the southern coast was Hermione. In the interior, towards the north-west, in an upland plain, were the sanctuary and temple of Zeus at Nemea, which were the scene of the Nemean games, and in its neighbourhood stood the cities of Phlius and Cleonae. Through this region led the pass between Corinth and Argos, the narrowest part of which was known as the Tretos. Between it and the head of the Argolic gulf, hemmed in on three sides by steep mountains, extended the Argive plain, which in the early period of Greek history was the chief seat of the civilization of the country. On the sea-coast was Nauplia, the chief sea-port for the Argolid, at first an independent state, and a member of the amphictyony of Calaureia. About the time of the Second Messenian War it became subject to Argos. A little distance inland, on a crust of rock which rises out of the level ground, stood Tiryns, a fortified citadel, the massive walls of which still testify to its strength. These walls, which are from twenty-five to fifty feet thick, are traversed by galleries or passages. The oblong area which the city occupied is divided into two enclosures of about equal size—an upper one towards the south, and a lower one towards the north. The main entrance, which is on the eastern side, has a great gateway flanked by towers, and also an inner gateway. On the western side there is a postern gate. The surface of the southern enclosure is covered by the remains of a prehistoric palace, in which may be traced the plan of an extensive court with an altar, and two separate sets of apartments (see § 707). On the western side of the plain lay Argos, with its imposing citadel of Larissa, and at its head Mycenae was placed, the wealth and primitive grandeur of which capital has also been attested

by the investigations of Dr Schliemann. Before his time the principal
gate, or Gate of Lions, as it was called from the figures of two lions sculptured in low relief by which it is surmounted, was a familiar object to
travellers; as was also the subterranean building, shaped like a bee-hive,
which was known as the Treasury of Atreus. These and other buildings
in their neighbourhood he explored; but his most remarkable discovery
was that of five prehistoric tombs, immediately within the Gate of Lions,
which he found by digging at a depth of from twenty-five to thirty-three
feet beneath the present level of the soil. Within these were contained
the remains of human bodies, some of which had their faces covered by
massive golden masks, and their breasts with golden breastplates; and
along with them lay an immense quantity of treasures, which were for the
most part of gold, elaborately wrought in a highly primitive style of art.
A sixth tomb, similar in character to these, was subsequently excavated.

25. Of the islands on the western side of Greece, the northernmost was
Corcyra (Corfu), which on account of its proximity to the
heel of Italy formed a convenient point from which that   The Islands.
country might be reached. Owing to its great fertility it has often been
identified, though without sufficient reason, with the Homeric Phaeacia.
Its capital city was situated in the middle of the eastern coast, facing the
mainland of Epeirus. To the southward of the mouth of the Ambracian
gulf lay Leucas or Leucadia (Santa Maura). This island was originally a
peninsula, having been joined to the coast of Acarnania by a sandy isthmus
at its northern extremity, which was pierced by a canal constructed by
the earliest Greek settlers. The headland of Leucate, which formed its
southern extremity, was famous as the scene of the Lovers' Leap. Then
followed the small island of Ithaca, with its conspicuous summit of Neritos,
which was separated by a narrow channel from Cephallenia. Finally,
opposite the headland of Chelonatas in Elis, lay Zacynthus (Zante).

26. The islands to the eastward of Greece—to omit those in the immediate neighbourhood of the coast, which have been already mentioned—
were important because they served as stepping-stones to join the lands on
either side of the Aegean. At the southern extremity of that sea a link
was formed by Crete, which was connected by Cythera with the Peloponnese, and by Casos, Carpathos and Rhodes with Caria. Farther to the
north a similar bridge was formed by the Cyclades, which were so called
because they formed a circle round the sacred isle of Delos. We have
already seen that the northern row of these islands—Andros, Tenos and
Myconos—forms a continuation of the mountains of Euboea, while those
towards the west—Ceos, Cythnos, Seriphos and Siphnos—stood in the
same relation to those of Attica. A link between the extremities of these
chains was formed by Paros and Naxos, and to the southward of the whole
group lay the volcanic islands of Thera and Melos. Delos itself, which is
less than three miles in length, is separated from the sister island of
Rheneia by a narrow strait, which forms an excellent harbour. In the

north of the Aegean is another group, consisting of Lemnos and Imbros, off the mouth of the Hellespont, which for a long period were occupied by Athenian colonists; Samothrace, with its sanctuary of the Cabeiri; and Thasos, which was famous for its gold mines. In the interval between the two last-named groups, to the eastward of Euboea, lay Scyros, the island of the great Achilles.

27. The western seaboard of **Asia Minor,** which from an early period was fringed with Greek colonies, in many respects resembled that of Greece, being distinguished by great variety of outline, and forming innumerable bays and harbours. Its chief headlands were Lectum, to the southward of the Troad, where the range of Mount Ida sinks into the sea; Mimas, a promontory noted for its dangerous storms, which was interposed between the bay of Smyrna and the island of Chios; Mycale, the scene of the famous battle, which lay opposite Samos; and the Triopian promontory, on the extremity of which the town of Cnidus was built. The climate of this region was temperate, and its soil extremely fertile, being watered by four rivers—the Caicus, the Hermus, the Cayster and the Maeander. The Greek colonies here fall into three groups, corresponding to the three chief Hellenic races. Those of the **Aeolian** stock were scattered over the northern portion of the coast, extending from Sigeum, at the mouth of the Hellespont, to Cyme, between the Caicus and the Hermus, and including the island of Lesbos, with its important cities of Mytilene and Methymna. The central portion, which bordered on Lydia, was occupied by the **Ionians,** who formed a confederation of twelve cities, or Dodecapolis, to which a thirteenth, Smyrna, was afterwards added. The chief among these were Phocaea, Ephesus and Miletus. Towards the south lay the **Dorian** colonies—Halicarnassus, Cos and Cnidus, together with the three cities in the island of Rhodes, Lindus, Ialysus, and Cameirus. These at first were combined into a Hexapolis, but after a time this was reduced to a Pentapolis by the exclusion of Halicarnassus. This portion of the coast was fringed by numerous small islands, of which Calymna and Cos were the chief.

The Greek Colonies.

28. Beyond the limits of the Aegean the colonies of the Greeks were gradually extended over a very wide area, both to east and west. The **Propontis,** which was the vestibule of the Euxine, was guarded by Cyzicus; and at its further end, on either side of the mouth of the Bosporus, stood Byzantium on the European, and Chalcedon on the Asiatic shore. On the southern coast of the **Euxine** the Milesian colony of Sinope was founded, and farther to the east its daughter city, Trapezus (Trebizond); while on the northern coast the opportunities for trade afforded by the rivers of Scythia encouraged the establishment of others in that inhospitable region, chief among which were Olbia, which commanded the mouths of the Hypanis (Bug) and Borysthenes (Dnieper), and Panticapaeum (Kertch) on the Cimmerian Bosporus at the entrance of the Palus Maeotis. In the eastern part of the Mediterranean others arose in

AEGEAN SEA & COAST OF ASIA MINOR

Scale of Miles
0 20 40 60 80 100

Camb. Univ. Press

Cyprus, especially Salamis, on the coast facing Syria, and Paphos at the opposite extremity of the island.   On the African coast, where it approaches nearest to the southern extremity of Greece, the Theraeans founded the colony of Cyrene, which in turn became the parent of Barca and other cities.   In **Egypt** the Greeks were not permitted to found colonies, but after a while they were established as settlers at Naucratis, which became an important trading station.   After the foundation of Alexandria, that great metropolis was the chief centre of Hellenic civilisation in the East.

29.   On the side of Europe, the rich island of **Sicily** afforded an inviting field for colonisation.   Though a considerable portion of its surface was mountainous, and the eruptions of Etna possessed an element of destructiveness which found no parallel in Greece, yet for the most part it was singularly fertile, and was specially suited to the growth of corn.   Of the two races by whom it was inhabited, the Sicanians, who occupied the western regions, and according to Thucydides were of Iberian extraction, were a hardy and warlike people ; but the Sicels, who dwelt in the eastern portion, were more akin to the Greeks in race, and readily yielded themselves to Greek influences.   The eastern coast, which looked in the direction of Greece, was naturally the first to attract settlers from that land. Here Naxos was founded at the foot of Aetna by the Chalcidians, and Megara Hyblaea by the Megarians ; but the most important was the Corinthian colony of Syracuse, which rose to great prosperity, chiefly in consequence of its magnificent harbour.   This was formed by an inlet of the sea, which intervened between the two headlands of Achradina and Plemmyrium, and was guarded on its outer side by the island of Ortygia. The site of this island was admirably suited for a maritime city, and the rocky heights which stretched to the northward of it provided a defensible position when its area required to be extended.   The river Anapus, which flowed into the innermost part of the harbour, furnished a means of communication with the interior of the country.   The harbour itself became famous in history as the scene of the sea-fight between the Athenians and Syracusans, which determined the momentous question whether the Athenian power was to become predominant in Sicily.   In the neighbouring districts the towns of Catana and Leontini were founded by Naxos, and those of Acrae and Casmenae by Syracuse ; but some time elapsed before the tide of emigration reached the southern coast.   This was due partly to the promontory of Pachynus, which had a forbidding character in the eyes of Greek sailors, like that which was presented by Malea in the south of Greece ; and partly to the presence of the Phoenicians, who occupied the most defensible positions.   At last, in the course of years, Camarina, Gela, Acragas and Selinus arose, among which the most important was Acragas or Agrigentum, the conspicuous remains of the temples of which city are still to be seen, crowning the elevated table of rock on which it was built. The Phoenicians now withdrew farther towards the west, but it was long before they were finally expelled from their stronghold on Mount Eryx, and from the important station of Panormus (Palermo). The only considerable settlement that was established on the northern coast of the island was Himera.

30. In **southern Italy** the Greek colonies multiplied so rapidly, that at last that district obtained the name of Magna Graecia. On that part of its shore which intervenes between Greece and Sicily, the Achaeans of the Peloponnese planted Sybaris and Croton, cities which were notorious from their feuds, which resulted at last in the destruction of Sybaris. Locri Epizephyrii also was founded on this coast by the Locrians; while in the innermost angle of the deep bay which lies between the heel and the toe of Italy stood Tarentum, a colony from Sparta. This place was famed for its temperate climate, for the suitableness of the soil in its neighbourhood for the growth of the olive, and for the fisheries of its extensive inner harbour, which was separated from the outer sea by the peninsula on which the city was built. The passage of the Fretum Siculum (Straits of Messina), by which the Tyrrhenian sea was entered, was guarded by Rhegium on the Italian shore and Messana on the Sicilian: and the coast to the northward of this was studded by a succession of towns, the remotest of which was Cumae. The fame of that place, which was the earliest in date of all these settlements, was ultimately eclipsed by that of its offspring, Neapolis (Naples), which arose in the neighbouring bay. Finally, the Phocaeans of Ionia made the farthest advance of all, and penetrated to the coast of Gaul, where they founded Massilia (Marseilles). The last-named place may be regarded as a typical instance of the positions which the Greeks selected by preference for their colonies; for the conditions which they desired were a safe harbour in the recesses of a bay, with a steep height close to it which might serve for an acropolis; and in the neighbourhood of this a moderate extent of cultivable land, backed by an extensive area in the interior of the country, from the inhabitants of which articles for export might be obtained. In this respect the colonists enjoyed greater advantages than the occupants of the parent states, for whereas the latter were bound to their original settlements whether they were advantageous or otherwise, the emigrants had an open field before them, from which to choose such sites as were best fitted for agricultural or mercantile purposes. In consequence of this it was in their power to accumulate wealth more rapidly; and the leisure which this wealth procured caused the fine arts to be more early developed among them than in the mother country—a fact, to which both their public buildings and their coins bear witness—and also gave birth to independent schools of philosophy, such as the Eleatic and the Pythagorean.

Leake, *Travels in Northern Greece*, 4 vols.; *Travels in the Morea*, 3 vols.; *Peloponnesiaca*; E. Curtius, *Peloponnesos*, 2 vols.; Bursian, *Geographie von Griechenland*; Lolling, *Hellenische Landeskunde und Topographie*; Struck, *Zur Landeskunde von Griechenland*; Frazer, *Pausanias's Description of Greece*, 6 vols., 1898; Neumann-Partsch, *Physikalische Geographie von Griechenland*, 1885; Cvijic, *Péninsule Balkanique*; A. Philippson, *Mittelmeergebiet*, 4th ed., 1922; Maull, *Griechische Mittelmeergebiet*, 1922; Newbigin, *Mediterranean Lands*, 1924; Stählin, *Das hellenische Thessalien*, 1925.

Bibliography.

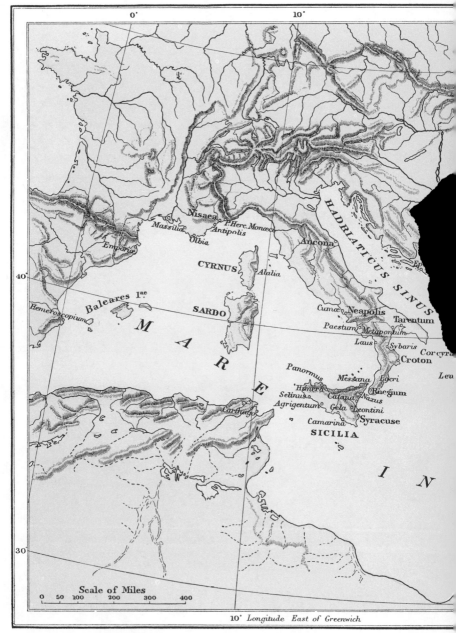

Nisaea
Massilia
P.Herc.Monaco
Antipolis
Olbia
Emporiae
HADRIATICUS SINUS
Ancona
Ep
CYRNUS
Alalia
40°
Hemeroscopium
Baleares I.ae
SARDO
MARE
Cumae
Neapolis
Tarentum
Paestum
Metapontium
Laus
Sybaris
Corcyra
Croton
Leu
Panormus
Messana
Locri
Himera
Catana
Nazus
Rhegium
Selinus
Agrigentum
Gela
Leontini
Syracuse
Carthago
Camarina
SICILIA
30°
I N
Scale of Miles
0   50 100   200   300   400

10° Longitude East of Greenwich

To face p. 22.

I. 2. ETHNOLOGY.

31. THE ethnology of Greece is one of the most complicated of all classical problems. The accounts given by the Greeks themselves are confused and contradictory. In one of the few *Difficulty of problem.*
instances, however, in which an ancient author uses archaeo-
logical methods, Thucydides (1. 8) arrives at a conclusion as to the original inhabitants of the Cyclades which accords with current ideas. Formerly all accounts of Greece before the Dorian Invasion were dismissed as legendary and fictitious. In more recent times archaeology and especially the discoveries of Schliemann and Evans have provided fresh material. Every prehistoric discovery and every new piece of literary criticism, on the Homeric question, gives a fresh turn to the shifting currents of opinion on Greek ethnology.

32. The area in which the Greek race developed is not large; it comprises the Greek peninsula south of Thessalonica and
the Acroceraunian promontory, with the adjacent islands *Area of Greek civilization.*
in the Ionian and Aegean seas and Crete. This territory
looks mainly to the south-east. This is the more fertile and the less rugged side, is better provided with harbours, and enjoys a warmer and drier climate than the north-west. The natural tendency of the Greeks in historical times was always eastwards, and was noted by Hippocrates who says (*de Aere*, 3 ff.) that cities which face east have the best, those that face west the worst climate. Bearing this division of Greece in mind we may separate it into the following districts. To the south-east there are Crete, the Aegean islands, and the plains and gulfs of Messenia, Laconia, Argolis, and Attica. To the north-west lie the north-western part of the Peloponnese, the Ionian islands, Aetolia and Epeirus. The north-eastern portion of Greece (Thessaly, Phocis and Boeotia) at first occupied an intermediate position, but as civilization spread northwards, naturally, owing to the south-eastern aspect of its gulfs and plains, became assimilated to the south-eastern group.

33. Anthropological opinion about early man in Europe and the home of the Indo-European stock is in such a state of
flux that any arguments based on it are insecure, especially *Sergi's theory.*
since craniological and similar data from Greece are scanty. It was once believed that the neolithic men of Europe were a dark, long-headed (dolichocephalic) race who were overrun by a fair, broad-headed (brachycephalic), Alpine race invading central Europe from Asia. Both of these were later subdued by the Indo-European races, who coming from Asia, the home of Sanskrit, imposed their languages on the peoples that they con-

quered. The most popular modern theory, that of the Mediterranean Race, was advanced by Sergi. He holds that the neolithic men of Europe came from Africa and were of a dark dolichocephalic type. Of this so-called Eur-African race one division remained in Africa and became the ancestor of the North African tribes. Another branch crossed into Europe and became Mediterranean Man inhabiting the northern shores and islands of that sea. A third branch also entered Europe, but pushed to the north and so produced the dark Nordic race. This Mediterranean race, which did not speak an Indo-European tongue, achieved a comparatively high civilization and was later overrun by the Indo-Europeans from Asia who were a fair, brachycephalic, barbarous people and gave their language to the races that they subdued. The loin cloth worn by Minoan and Mycenaean men is said to support this view, for it is believed to prove that they once lived in a much warmer climate. Another point relied on by Sergi is the supposed existence in some Celtic tongues of words not Indo-European. Some recent views tend to discredit the theory of the Eur-African race, though the evidence of skull types shows that the early Cretans were dolichocephalic. The home of the Indo-Europeans, which is placed by Sergi and others in Asia, is now put in eastern Europe, and the zoological theory of the variation of type in animals according to environment has been applied by Ridgeway to Mediterranean Man. The colouring of animals often depends on climate varying with the conditions of their life. The Arctic hare is white in winter, but blue in summer. Similarly the striping and colouring of the different species of zebras depends on the latitude in which they are found. If this is true of other animals there is no reason why it should not be true of man as well. Thus the men of a cold and northern climate or of a mountainous region will be fair, but those who live in a warm climate will be dark and sallow. This is similar to the Greek idea that the Aethiopians were dark because they lived nearer the sun than other races. Consequently the physical likeness seen amongst the various peoples of the Mediterranean basin can be held not to be due to a similarity of race, but to similarity of environment. Likewise the difference between northern and southern Europeans would be due not so much to a diversity of race as to a difference in climate.

According to Sergi's theory of the Eur-African race the primitive people of Greece were a branch of that race and did not speak an Indo-European language. At a later date they were overrun by 'Achaean' invaders from the north who introduced Greek. The later stage of this mixed race is represented by Homer and the final supremacy of the Greek language was established during the great migration, of which the Dorian Invasion was one incident. Linguistic support for this is found in the presence in Greek of words ending in -nth- and -ssos (e.g. ἀσάμινθος, Παρνασσός), which are accepted by Fick as pre-Greek. Probably the early inhabitants of Crete were not Indo-Europeans. Herodotus (1. 173) indeed says that all Crete was once occupied by barbarians. It received some colonists from Egypt in the early Bronze Age; and the survival well into historical times at Praesus in east Crete of a language written in Greek characters, which is certainly not Greek, makes it very probable that the earliest Cretans did not speak a Greek dialect. Till, however, the Minoan script can be read we cannot determine whether the 'Minoans' were Indo-Europeans or not.

34. Ridgeway divided the population of Greece into three layers, Pelasgian, Achaean and Dorian. The Pelasgians, the in-habitants of Greece from neolithic times, developed the Minoan and Mycenaean culture. They were a dark race and spoke an Indo-European tongue, Greek. Later they were conquered by a tall, fair race of Celtic affinities which the Greeks called Achaean. These came from the north, settled like Norman barons in the strongholds of the earlier race and adopted their civilization and language. The flourishing period of their domination is that represented by Homer and was the great age of heroic adventure. They were overthrown by the Dorian Invasion, after which Greece gradually settled into the division of states which prevailed in classical times. The strong points of this view are many. There is abundant proof that the Minoan culture developed in the Aegean area, in Crete. Neither history nor archaeology has revealed that any other language than Greek was ever spoken in Arcadia, the heart of the Peloponnese, which no invader conquered. Further if the Achaeans, an Indo-European race, settled among an alien race and imposed their language upon them, it would be contrary to most historical experience. The Normans in England, the Visigoths in Spain and the Franks in France did not impose their languages on those they conquered, for the conquered race nearly always absorbs the conquerors. The main exception to this rule is the case of Latin in the western provinces of the Roman Empire. But there are two weak points which are serious. To hold that the Pelasgians, as Greeks themselves asserted, were aborigines and that they produced and developed the Mycenaean culture, because wherever tradition says there were once Pelasgians, Minoan and Mycenaean remains are found, is to disregard some important archaeological evidence. Thessaly was traditionally one of the Pelasgian districts; excavations, however, have shown that the Minoan civilization did not develop there, but had its origin in Crete and reached northern Greece at a comparatively late stage. Again Greek tradition has no record of such an invasion of fair-haired northerners as this Achaean theory postulates. To accept as true the Athenian story that Attica was peopled by a pure autochthonous race and to disregard the tradition that the Achaeans were equally autochthonous in the Peloponnese seems un-reasonable. The probable existence of a third racial type, broad-headed, but not blond, called "Armenoid," also affects the problem.

Ridgeway's theory.

35. The latest general treatment of the question is that of Myres who examines in turn regional environment, anthropology, com-parative philology, archaeology, and tradition. The Greeks believed themselves of one blood, one language, one religion, and one

Myres' theory.

culture, but modern analysis and criticism reveal that, if the Greeks united, it was a union of many strains moulded together in the Aegean area. The geographical environment enables the dominant race to remain approximately thoroughbred in spite of alien admixtures; this applies also to the language and the culture. Indo-Europeans first arrived with Minyan ware, and further migrations and transitions followed between 1400 and 1000 B.C. during which "various profound changes went on collaterally, and not necessarily in causal connection." Thence emerged the nascent Hellenic race. "The general conclusion is that the Greeks never wholly were 'one people,' but were ever in process of becoming; that they achieved such unity as they enjoyed in their 'great age,' under austere regional controls eliminating, selecting, fostering qualities, faculties, and aspirations, in an originally diverse and heterogeneous population."

36. We must take the Greek tradition and see if it can be reconciled with the archaeological evidence. The earliest authority is Homer, who gives in two passages most valuable information about the early peoples of Greece. The first is the Catalogue in the second book of the *Iliad*. It used to be generally held that the *Iliad* is a comparatively late compilation of many different lays and that the Catalogue, which is condemned as inconsistent, is one of the latest additions. Latterly, however, opinion has turned in the opposite direction and many prominent scholars have declared themselves believers in the substantial unity of the *Iliad*. Recent archaeological and geographical research too has shown that the once despised Catalogue is a document of great value. Naturally it is inconsistent with classical Greece, for it describes prehistoric Greece; and Agamemnon's confederacy almost exactly coincides geographically, but not culturally nor chronologically, with the area occupied by the Mycenaean civilization at the time of its widest diffusion. The Trojan Catalogue has similarly been rehabilitated. It may be assumed that the Homeric Catalogue is an old geographical document the origins of which may be referred to a date as early as 1200 B.C. This means not that it was composed then, but that it represents the political geography of the Greek area about that time. The tradition of the distribution of peoples in that age was preserved—in what form we do not know—and was used by Homer at a later date.

The most important Homeric passage to be considered is the oft quoted one in the *Odyssey* (XIX. 175 ff.) about Crete:

ἐν μὲν Ἀχαιοί,
ἐν δ' Ἐτεόκρητες μεγαλήτορες, ἐν δὲ Κύδωνες,
Δωριέες τε τριχάικες, δῖοί τε Πελασγοί....

The Eteocretans, whose principal city was Praesus, were probably the aborigines of eastern Crete, and the Cydones similarly the first inhabitants of western Crete. The Praesus inscriptions, already referred to, if they are Eteocretan, show that they probably did not speak Greek. This conclusion would imply that the authors of the Minoan civilization were not Hellenes; and this is supported by the statement of Herodotus about barbarians in Crete. There are still the Achaeans, the Pelasgians and the Dorians to be considered.

37. The Greeks of the classical period themselves believed that the Pelasgians were the aborigines of Greece and with them they grouped Carians and Leleges. In Homer the Pelasgians The Pelasgians. appear in the list of Priam's allies and apart from the mention of them in Crete, their home seems to be about the Hellespont. It is in this very region and along the Aegean littoral of Thrace that we find them mentioned by Herodotus and Thucydides, at Placie and Scylace, at Antandrus, in Creston, in Acte, and in the islands of Lemnos, Imbros and Samothrace (Hdt. I. 57, II. 51, IV. 145, V. 26, VII. 42; Thuc. IV. 109). Both authors call them barbarians and so far all accounts of them agree. But as early as Homer there seems to be another use of the word Pelasgic, although the Pelasgi are a tribe with a fixed seat. The shrine at Dodona, which Hesiod calls Πελασγῶν ἕδρανον, is said to be that of Pelasgic Zeus, and Achilles' realm is called Pelasgic Argos. Apparently the Greeks came to use the adjective 'Pelasgian' to describe the primitive population of Greece, and this use is common in Herodotus who often mentions these hypothetical 'Pelasgians.' He calls Athenians, Argives, Aeolians, Arcadians and Dodonaeans Pelasgians, and it is quite likely that if the Achaeans had not been forced by the Dorian Invasion to change their position, he would have called them Pelasgians too. But he confuses the hypothetical Pelasgians with the true Pelasgi in Thrace whom he knew, for he argues that the Pelasgians were barbarians because those in Thrace were. This would make the autochthonous Athenians barbarians, and then it becomes exceedingly difficult to explain how they and their Ionian kinsmen changed their barbarian tongue for Greek. But Herodotus' confusion and Thucydides' suggestion (I. 6) that the primitive Hellenes must have been once in a similar stage of civilization to that of barbarians shows the basis of the Greek fallacy. Their argument seems to have been, the Pelasgians are barbarians, Greece was once barbarous, therefore the Greeks are Pelasgians. These hypothetical Pelasgians appear very frequently in later authors such as Strabo and Pausanias, but apparently they owed their great popularity to Ephorus, who attempted to reduce Greek history to a system and held that the Pelasgians originated in Arcadia, the most primitive part of Greece. The presence of Pelasgians in Attica and in Crete is explained by the possibility that the true Pelasgi, being mariners (one interpretation of their name is ' The People of the Sea'), like the Danes, made piratical raids and settlements on the Greek littoral. Hellanicus (*F.H.G.* I. 45) says that the Pelasgi were expelled by the Greeks, changed their name to Tyrseni and went to Italy. The Tyrseni are placed both by Herodotus (I. 57) and Thucydides (IV. 109) as neighbours of the Pelasgi in the north-west Aegean. This can be supported by the tale of Herodotus (I. 94) that the Etruscans came from

Lydia and the fact that in Lemnos, one of the islands where Pelasgi lived, a mysterious inscription of an Etruscan type has been found.

38. The Achaeans are considered by many modern critics to have **The Achaeans.** been the first northern invaders of whom we have any knowledge to enter Greece. They are assumed to be a fair people of the Celtic type and are credited with the introduction of the long sword, the round shield, amber, and the safety-pin brooch, which all make their appearance either in Homer or in the latest phase of the Mycenaean civilization which is taken to be the Homeric. The relation of Homeric civilization and armament to the Mycenaean cannot be adequately discussed here. That long swords, body armour, greaves and amber are found in the last phase of the Mycenaean culture is undeniable, but that the Achaeans were responsible for the change in armament is not certain. Such a change of armament need not necessarily have been caused by a new people, but could be reasonably explained by the gradual supersession of bronze by iron. But while it is quite likely that such improvements did come into fashion when the Achaeans, as Homer represents them to be, were the most powerful people in Greece, tradition nowhere records that the Achaeans were invaders. In Homer the name 'Achaeans' is used in two senses and in neither application is there any indication that they are new-comers; nor does Homer show any knowledge of the alleged Phrygian origin of the Pelopids. First in the *Iliad* and *Odyssey* the name Achaeans (as well as Danai and Argives) is used to describe comprehensively the Greek army at Troy or the Greeks in general. Secondly the Achaeans appear with the Myrmidons and Hellenes as making up the population of Achilles' kingdom in the Spercheus valley (*Il.* II. 681). The name appears to be originally tribal, comparable to other names such as Argives, Locrians, Boeotians. But because the Achaeans were apparently the most powerful of the Greek tribes, the name Achaeans is used to include generally all the tribes in Greece. Similarly when we speak of England and the English we do not mean that the country is inhabited exclusively by Angles, for it is well known that the population includes, besides Angles, Celtic, Saxon, Danish, and Norman elements. So when Homer uses the name Achaeans (or Argives or Danai) to describe Agamemnon's host he does not mean that it consisted entirely of one tribe; he merely uses the name of one prominent tribe as a convenient abbreviation for the whole body. The Achaeans have been considered to be invaders, formerly because the Greek tales about the Pelasgian aborigines of Hellas were accepted as true, and latterly, since the discovery of the great Bronze Age culture of the Aegean, because of the difficulties experienced in any attempt to reconcile the accounts of the Homeric civilization with the remains of the Mycenaean. But Herodotus (VIII. 73) and Pausanias (V. I. I) both state that the Achaeans were as autochthonous as the Arcadians, and that on the Dorian Invasion the so-called Ionian Migration took place from the Peloponnese which all tradition is unanimous in calling the chief seat of the Achaean power. It seems probable that the 'Ionians' who migrated were 'Achaeans' from the Peloponnese and possessed the Late Helladic III culture. Herodotus indeed says that the Cynurian Arcadians, who lived between the two old Achaean districts of Argos and Laconia, seemed to be Ionians who had become Dorianized. It does not seem necessary to disregard tradition and to consider the Achaeans as northern invaders. It is true that there were Achaeans in Northern Greece according to Homer, and the land round Mount Othrys close to the home of the great Achaean warrior Achilles was known in classical times as Achaia. But there is no tradition that these Achaeans were invaders from the north.

The tales of Danaus, the eponymous founder of Homer's Danai, Cadmus, Cecrops and other foreign settlers in Greece could be referred to the coming of 'Minoans' to the Mainland. The legendary dates agree well with the archaeological dates for the rise to power of Mycenae, Orchomenus and other cities. The downfall of Cnossus and the succession of Mycenae to supreme power in the Aegean which occurred about 1400 B.C. (the archaeological evidence is given in §§ 288, 291, 294) are reflected in Homer's mention of Achaeans in Crete and in the tale of Theseus. The Egyptian records of the defeat of the Akaiwasha and their allies in 1220 B.C. and the laconic statement of Rameses III that the isles were restless in 1190, together with the legend of the Trojan War between 1192 and 1183, might well be regarded as an echo of the political disturbances that followed the break-up of the Aegean thalassocracy. The restlessness was probably augmented by pressure from the north which culminated in 1124 and 1104 B.C. with the Thessalian and Dorian Invasions.

39. The Dorian Invasion was a constant tradition in Greece, and there seems no reason to reject it, as Beloch does. He argues that the evidence for it is late, the earliest being Tyrtaeus (ap. Strabo 362), and Homer does not mention it. Race names, he says, are late and there is no real break between the end of the Bronze Age and the beginning of the classical period. The Greeks invented a catastrophe whereas the penetration of northern races was gradual. But if Homer does not mention the Dorian Invasion, neither does he record the Ionian Migration which was one result of it, and if the latter be accepted the former should be. What Homer gives is a picture of pre-Dorian Greece during the transition from the Bronze to the Iron Age. Races may exist separately, though the names applied to them may be late. The mere fact that the racial name 'Greek' is late (not earlier than Aristotle) does not imply that Greeks never existed. There is an archaeological break between the Bronze Age and classical Greek civilization, or rather a period of transition which is not yet fully clear, but its archaeological confusion can be attributed to the disturbance caused by invaders. Archaeological evidence confirms the broad outlines of Greek tradition, and if tradition is good evidence, it would be

Dorians, Thracians, Macedonians, Phoenicians.

especially good when it relates to so great an upheaval. One can compare the tales of the great Celtic Invasion in 279 B.C. The Dorians always considered themselves as invaders, and the antagonism between Dorian and Achaean at Argos (Herodotus v. 83; Aristotle, *Pol.* 1303ª) and Sicyon (Herodotus v. 68, 69) points to the Dorians being alien conquerors. The various forms of the tradition hint that the invasion was not one big movement of a uniform race, but several separate invasions of mixed bodies. This is shown by Herodotus' tale (1. 56) of the wanderings of the Dorians, the crossing from Naupactus into the Peloponnese, the earlier date given to the Thessalian Invasion and the legend that the Corinthians were the latest comers (Pausanias v. 1. 1). It is possible that the earliest Dorians came by sea down the east coast of Greece. Thucydides (IV. 42) tells the story of Solygeius, the grave of Temenos was on the coast near Argos (Strabo 368), and Andron says that the Dorians reached Crete from Thessaly (*F.H.G.* II. p. 349, 4). There is a kind of pottery found in Thessaly, Attica, Argolis, the islands and Crete which stands midway between the last Late Helladic III wares and the earliest true geometric fabrics, and this can be quoted in support of such a theory. The home of the Dorians is given as Epeirus, and since there is no reason for rejecting this, it is quite likely that they were a north Greek race with some Illyrian affinities. Herodotus (1. 56) connects the Dorians with the Macedonians, and it is quite probable that the ruling race in Macedonia was akin to the Thessalian, a point which seems to be confirmed by linguistic evidence. The legend that the Argead kings of Macedonia (Herodotus VIII. 137; Thucydides II. 99) came from Argos is explained by Appian (*Syr.* 63) as referring to the Argos in the land of the Orestae about the sources of the Haliacmon. Herodotus says that the Argead kings came from the west and settled as lords at Aegae while the princely houses of Elimiotis and Lyncestis were akin to them. They are said to have driven the Thracian Bottiaeans and Pierians eastwards, and Strabo says (330, fr. 25) that the original inhabitants of Aegae were the Bryges or Phryges who on the Argead conquest moved into Asia Minor. If the Macedonians were a mixed race with a Greek-speaking aristocracy settled as overlords among a Thracian and Illyrian population it would explain Strabo's statement (327) that the peoples of Upper Macedonia were δίγλωσσοι. One of the languages was certainly Greek, and the other was most probably a Thracian or Illyrian tongue. Thus Demosthenes (*Olynth.* 3. 16, 24; *Fals. Leg.* 19. 327), since Philip was not of pure Greek race (probably the Macedonian aristocrats intermarried with their subjects), could call the Macedonians barbarians. Similarly Aeschines (*Fals. Leg.* 439) and the Hellenizing Macedonians, such as Alexander I, would call them Ἑλληνικώτατοι.

That the Thracians once extended further to the south-west than they did in historical times seems to be correct on the whole. Tradition (cf. C. O. Müller, *Orchomenos*, pp. 206, 213, 370) records that Thracians once dwelt in Phocis and Thessaly, and this can be supported by archaeological evidence. The Abantes, who in Homer appear in Euboea, were said to be Thracians. It is possible that they and the Perrhaebi, Magnetes and similar tribes were the remains of the old population of north-eastern Greece who had been overrun by their more civilized neighbours from the south-east. Tradition and archaeology both support this.

The connexion of the coming of the Macedonians with the movement of the Thraco-Phrygians to Asia Minor is quite possible. The invasion of the Macedonians, Thessalians and Dorians over the passes of Tymphrestus and Pindus and the Thracian and Ionian migrations to Asia Minor would all be part of a general movement in the Southern Balkans from west to east. A minor incident of this racial displacement would have been the Aetolian crossing into Elis. These may have been the migrations which drove the Pelasgo-Tyrsenians to Italy and they may have been originated by some pressure in the Northern Balkans, perhaps due to Celtic disturbances.

Ancient authorities assigned to the Phoenicians a large part in the origin of Greek civilization. In none of the places where Phoenicians are said to have settled have any definite signs of Phoenician occupation been found. It has been suggested that by Phoenicians the Cretans were meant, although the great age of Crete is considerably older than that of Phoenicia. A recent theory which would agree with the date when the Phoenicians were powerful at sea is that they were the bringers of art and culture to Greece at the beginning of the historical period, but this attempt to rehabilitate the Phoenicians has not met with much approval.

40.   Thus no satisfactory conclusion about the origin of the Greek race can be reached from linguistics, literature, history, or anthro-pology. Either the evidence is too scanty as in the case of craniology or the results are confusing because it is not known *Archaeological evidence. Conclusions.* what the ancient writers meant or indeed whether they knew what they meant. Recourse must be had to archaeology, and here, owing to recent excavations on the Mainland, definite suggestions can be made. The answer must be sought on the Mainland, for brilliant as they are the results from Crete alone are insufficient. In Crete from Neolithic times to the close of the Bronze Age civilization developed unbroken. Apart from Egyptian colonies during the Early Minoan Age there is no foreign admixture. The 'Minoans' were probably akin to the people of south-western Asia Minor and perhaps of Caucasian stock. Crete is full of the well-known pre-Hellenic place names and contained even in historical times some non-Greek inhabitants (§ 34). The people of the Cyclades were akin to the Cretans, and remained untroubled except for contacts with the Mainland in Middle and Late Helladic times which were strongest after 1400 when Mycenae succeeded to the supremacy of Crete. Their origin in south-western Asia Minor would agree with Thucydides' identification of the islanders as Carians. On the Mainland the earliest racial stratum is the Neolithic, reaching from the Peloponnese to Macedonia and possibly akin to the

Neolithic peoples of the Danube and Carpathians. In Southern Greece the Neolithic tribes were overrun at the beginning of the Bronze Age by a people of the same stock as the inhabitants of the Cyclades and Crete. The area over which their settlements extend coincides with the area in which the non-Greek place names occur, and the Early Helladic people were of the same race as those of Crete and the Cyclades. With the beginning of the Middle Helladic Period, about 1900 B.C., a new element entered the Mainland, the people who made and used 'Minyan ware' (see § 291). Its occurrence in Melos suggests intercourse with the Mainland, but its extreme rarity in Crete and the almost equal rarity of Kamares ware on the Mainland suggest a severance of relations between Crete and the Mainland. At the close of the Middle Helladic Period about 1580, when the XVIIIth Dynasty arose in Egypt, the people of the Mainland came into close touch with Crete and henceforward adopted the Minoan culture, art, script, and dress, with marked differences. Mycenae which had been first settled at the beginning of the Bronze Age became a powerful state under successive dynasties, the Shaft Grave and Beehive Tomb kings. On the fall of Crete about 1400, when the XVIIIth Dynasty decayed in Egypt, Mycenae became politically supreme in the Aegean. It was a period of amazing architectural activity there and at Tiryns, and also of great overseas enterprise as the pottery spread far and wide about the Levant proves. Evans holds that about 1580 the Cretans forcibly colonized large portions of the Mainland and imposed their culture on the population, and that this Minoan colonial empire lasted after the fall of Cnossus down to an Achaean invasion shortly before 1200 B.C. This view finds a break in the cultural evolution of the Mainland in the middle of the Third Late Helladic Period and regards the later pottery of this period as Achaean. Meyer and most archaeologists hold that the spread of the Minoan culture to the Mainland was the act of the Mainland population whose receptivity and vigour made them the most active agents in its expansion. Neither view admits any intrusion about 1580 other than that of the Minoan culture. Meyer believes that from 1580 onwards the culture of the Mainland through a transfusion of Minoan elements gradually transformed itself into the Late Helladic III civilization. The process can be traced in the pottery, and Nilsson has pointed out where the essential latent strength of the Mainland stock breaks through the Minoan veneer. The situation may be compared to that of the Etruscan culture which is strongly Hellenic with many vital differences, but no one suggests that Greeks conquered and colonized Etruria. The effort to find a break in the Third Late Helladic Period for the introduction of the Achaeans is based primarily not on the archaeological evidence but on the assumption that the Achaeans must have entered Greece before 1200 B.C. There is nothing in the culture of the Late Helladic III Period to suggest the intervention of an alien race. The family tombs continue in use from Late Helladic I and II through Late Helladic III without a break, and the difference between the early and late pottery of Late Helladic III is far less than that between Middle and Late Minoan pottery. The destruction of Mycenae took place early in the 12th century. The Iron Age then begins. The style of the pottery gradually becomes geometric and new elements appear. This disturbance just after the traditional date for the Trojan War is generally assumed to agree with the Greek tradition of the Dorian Migration. The Dorians entered a Greece already inhabited by Greeks, who must therefore have arrived previously. If the first arrival of Indo-Europeans were reflected in the archaeological evidence it should coincide with one of the breaks at the beginning and end of the Early Helladic Period. If the Neolithic folk were allied to the Danubian and Carpathian tribes they might have been Thracians and so bear out Greek tradition. The Early Helladic people akin to the Cretans and islanders and non-Hellenic could be called Pelasgians, Carians, and Leleges. The only place available for the first Indo-Europeans is at the beginning of the Middle Helladic Period, and they would then be the makers and users of 'Minyan ware,' though of course not Hellenes in the full sense of later times. The classical Greeks then would have been a blend of the three strains, the primitive Neolithic folk, the artistic and elegant Cretans, and the adventurous and creative Middle Helladic people.

On the Dorian Invasion the Achaeans, Minyans and Ionians wandered across the Aegean and settled along the Anatolian sea-board, and even as far afield as Cyprus. They carried with them a tradition of culture which under the influence of the neighbouring oriental peoples absorbed fresh ideas. Then as the Dorians began to establish themselves in the lands they had conquered and Greece enjoyed peace again, the Ionian colonists sent back the civilization they had preserved. This artistic tradition received fresh energy from the new comers in Greece and so produced a renaissance, the classical age of Greek culture. The island bridge in the south formed by Melos and Thera or Crete, Carpathus, Rhodes, Nisyrus and Cos was the great Ionian trade-route. This was the way across known to Homer (*Il.* II. 654, 671, 676), and along it were planted the first Dorian colonies which, according to legend, included a large proportion of Achaeans and Minyans (Herodotus IV. 145 ff., VII. 99; Polyaenus VII. 94; Strabo 683; Pausanias VII. 5. 2, 57. 3).

After all in Greece the history of civilization is more important than pure ethnology. Race is hard to define, and one language and one art may embrace more than one people. Civilization in the Aegean originated in Crete, and in spite of the changes which passed over the Greek area the Cretan tradition remained. Even if the power of the people that developed it was conquered, the race itself survived, for it is almost impossible entirely to destroy a civilized race. Cretan civilization was the forerunner of Hellenic, and reached its greatest expansion through an Indo-European people who, if tradition can be trusted, had long been settled in the Peloponnese. This gifted race, assimilating other elements, created the greatness of Mycenae and of Athens.

T. W. Allen, *The Homeric Catalogue of Ships*, 1921. J. Beloch, *Griechische Geschichte²*, 1912. C. W. Blegen and J. B. Haley, *The Coming of the Greeks*, American Journal of Archaeology, 1928, p. 141 ff. C.W.
Blegen and A. J. B. Wace, *Middle Helladic Tombs*, Symbolae Osloenses, 1930, p. 28 ff. C. D. Buck, *The Language Situation in and about Greece*, Classical Philology XXI, 1926, p. 1 ff. J. Burnet, *Who was Javan?* Proceedings of the Classical Association of Scotland, 1911–1912. V. G. Childe, *The Aryans*, 1926. A. J. Evans, *Palace of Minos*, I–III, 1921–1930; *Scripta Minoa*, 1909. Feist, *Kultur, Ausbreitung und Herkunft der Indogermanen*, 1913. A. Fick, *Vorgriechische Ortsnamen*, 1905. E. Forrer, *Vorhomerische Griechen in den Keilschrifttexten aus Boghazköi*, Mitteilungen der deutschen Orient-Gesellschaft, 63, 1924, p. 22.
C. M. Fürst, *Zur Anthropologie der prähistorischen Griechen in Argolis*, 1930. H. R. Hall, *The Civilization of Greece in the Bronze Age*, 1929. H. Hirt, *Die Indo-Germanen*, 1905-7. O. Hoffmann, *Die Makedonen, ihre Sprache und ihr Volkstum*, 1906. P. Kretschmer, *Einleitung in die Geschichte der Griechischen Sprache*, 1896. A. Lang, *The World of Homer*, 1910; *Homer and His Age*, 1906. W. Leaf, *Troy*, 1912; *Homer and History*, 1915. E. Meyer, *Geschichte des Altertums²*, Vol. II, Part I, 1928. K. O. Müller, *History and Antiquities of the Doric Race*, 1830. J. L. Myres, *Who were the Greeks?*, 1930. M. P. Nilsson, *The Minoan-Mycenaean Religion*, 1927. A. W. Persson, *Schrift und Sprache in Alt-Kreta*, 1930. F. Poulsen, *Der Orient und die frühgriechische Kunst*, 1912. W. Ridgeway, *The Early Age of Greece*, 1901; *Who were the Dorians?*, 1907; *Minos The Destroyer*, 1909. W. Z. Ripley, *The Races of Europe*, 1900. G. Sergi, *The Mediterranean Race*, 1901. A. J. B. Wace and M. S. Thompson, *Prehistoric Thessaly*, 1912.

I. 3. FAUNA.

41. THE fauna of Greece differs little, so far as is known, from that of Spain and Southern Italy: that is to say, it is part of the 'Mediterranean province,' in which the 'palaearctic' fauna of Europe is supplemented by southern forms common to the two sides of the Mediterranean. The birds, for instance, are for the most part those familiar to us at home, with the notable additions of vultures, hoopoes, bee-eaters, flamingos and pelicans. The reptiles, on the other hand, contain a much larger proportion of unfamiliar species, and the African element is here especially strong.

Greek writers, travellers and others, introduce us to many foreign animals whose home was in Egypt, Libya or the East. In poetry especially, fable, folk-lore and a refined mythology blend, often inextricably, with the plain tales of the naturalist; and in such allegories as that of the Labours of Hercules, the lion, the bear, the hydra and the crab are drawn from the ancient picture-book of the stars.

A. MAMMALS.

42. Apes (πίθηκοι), which still linger in Europe at Gibraltar (*Macacus inuus*), were in all probability met with by early Greek mariners at the Pithecusae, a group of Italian islands of which Ischia is one. The πίθηκος of Aristotle was this same Barbary ape. It was probably the common pet monkey (καλλίας, μίμω) of the Athenians, mentioned first by Archilochus (*circa* 750 B.C.). **Apes.**

The squeaking bat (τρίζουσαι νυκτερίδες, *Od.* XXIV. 6), a bird but not a bird (Plato), was recognised as a mammal (Arist.). The large fruit-bats of Egypt and Asia Minor are perhaps alluded to by Aristotle as the flying foxes (ἀλώπεκες), and even possibly by Homer (ποτὶ μακρὸν ἐρινεὸν ὑψόσ' ἀερθείς, *Od.* XII. 432). **Bats.**

43. Our common insectivores, hedgehog (ἐχῖνος) and shrew-mouse (μυγάλη), were known to the Greeks. Mycenaean warriors wore prickly caps of hedgehog-skin; and the skins came also **Insectivora.** into the Athenian market (Aristoph.), probably to be used in the combing or carding of wool. The hedgehog knew a thing or two, πόλλ' οἶδ' ἀλώπηξ, ἀλλ' ἐχῖνος ἓν μέγα. The ἀσπάλαξ, proverbial for its blindness (τυφλότερος σπάλακος), and commonly translated *mole*, means in most, if not in all cases, the root-feeding blind-rat (*Spalax typhlus*), the 'mole' also of Levit. vi, 19, 30.

44. The rabbit (λαγίδιον, ἡμιλάγος, κόνικλος), a native of Western Europe, was unknown to the classical Greeks, but the hare **Rodents.** (λαγώς, δασύπους, *Sicil.* λεπορίς) was the chief object of ancient sport. Xenophon mentions several varieties (ἐπίπερκοι, ἐπίξανθοι, ἕλειοι, ὀρεινοί, πεδινοί), and a smaller, longer-eared species was known from Egypt. At the present day, in the Archipelago, certain islands have only rabbits and others only hares.

The squirrel (σκίουρος, καμψίουρος (Hesych.), M. Gk βερβερίτσα) is described by Oppian, the dormouse (ἐλειός, *Myoxus glis*, and *M. nitela*) by Aristotle. The porcupine (ὕστριξ) exists in Greece, and is common in Africa (Hdt.); dogs were trained to draw it from its burrow (Callim.). *Spalax typhlus*, the blind-rat (M. Gk τυφλοπόντικος), is often confused with ἀσπάλαξ, the mole.

The beaver (κάστωρ, λάταξ, σαθέριον, σατύριον), unknown in Greece, was common in Pontus and Scythia (Hdt., Arist.). Neither the brown rat nor its forerunner the black rat had come to Europe till long after classical times. The latter was known in the middle ages as μῦς ὁ ποντικός (M. Gk ποντικός), but the animal so called by Aristotle is not to be identified. In the Cyclades, *Mus tectorum* is the only rat found by Erhard. Mice (μῦς, σμίνθος) were all too plentiful. The field-mice (ἀρουραῖοι) sometimes amounted, as now-a-days, to a plague; it was Apollo Smintheus who, like Baal the Phoenician Sun-god, sent them and protected them. Tame white mice were kept in Apollo's temple at Hamaxitos in the Troad.

45. The African elephant was known to Herodotus; the Indian was

Elephant. first seen in Babylon by Ctesias (*c.* 420 B.C.), and the Indian elephants of Darius fought at Arbela. The ivory trade was of far greater antiquity (cf. Homer and the excavators of prehistoric sites).

46. The horse (ἵππος, ἄλογον (Diod. Sic.), M. Gk ἄλογον, ἀλογάκι)

Ungulata. and the ass (ὄνος, M. Gk γάϊδαρος) were known from the earliest times. Africa (ἱππόβοτος Λιβύη, Oppian), and Cyrene in particular, were celebrated for their horses; as were also Thrace, Thessaly and Argos (cf. *Il.* II. 287; Pind. *P.* I. 717). Anacreon credits the Mysians with the first breeding of mules (ὀρεύς, ἡμίονος). Various species of wild ass (ὄνος ἄγριος, ὄναγρος) were known—Libyan (Hdt.), and Syrian or Mesopotamian (Xen.). The hippopotamus of the Nile (Herod.) probably got its Greek name, ἵππος ὁ ποτάμιος, by a strange corruption of an Egyptian word, which reappears in the Hebrew *Behemoth.* The wild boar (ὗς ἄγριος, ἀγριόχοιρος) was celebrated throughout antiquity, and is still common in Greece; domesticated pigs (ὗς, σῦς, χοῖρος, κάπρος, etc.) were known from the dawn of history. The ox (βοῦς, ταῦρος) was known to, and domesticated by, all the civilized nations of antiquity, and many varieties and races are recorded. Epeirus had a gigantic breed, yielding an amphora of milk daily (Arist.). The Thracian βόες ἄγριοι of Herodotus were probably the great Auerochs (*Bos primigenius*), the *urus* of Virgil and of Caesar. Βόνασος (Arist.) was the European bison, which survives in Lithuania and the Caucasus. The sheep (ὄϊς, ἀρνός, κριός) had also many varieties. The Mycenaean sheep, with long outspread horns, is said by Keller to have been derived from an African race, and Libya is called πολύμηλος in Pindar. The fat-tailed Syrian sheep are described by Herodotus and by Aristotle. A Libyan wild-sheep (κριὸς ἄγριος), described by Herodotus, is *Ovis tragelephas*, which figures on a Mycenaean ornament; its European ally, the Moufflon (*Ovis musimon*), is described from Sardinia by Pausanias. The goat (αἴξ, τράγος, χίμαιρα) was likewise domesticated from the earliest times. Its flesh is eaten in the *Iliad*, and its milk and cheese were, and are, a staple of Greek diet. The wild goat (*Capra aegagrus*) or Grecian ibex is still common, as in antiquity, in Crete. The three common European deer were well known: ἔλαφος including the red and fallow deer, and πρόξ denoting the little roe; in modern Greek the roe is ζορκάδι, *i.e.* δορκάς. The fallow deer, *platyceros* of Pliny (M. Gk πλατῶνι), is often recognisable in descriptions by its dappled hide (βαλιός). A few stories are told of the reindeer (τάρανδος) as an inhabitant of Scythia; and of the elk (ἄλκη) as a native of the Alps (Polybius), and of the country of the Kelts (Pausanias). The camel (κάμηλος) is first mentioned by Archilochus, and Aristotle has much to say of it, distinguishing the Bactrian from the Arabian species.

47. That the lion (λέων, λῖς) was found in Northern Greece 'between

Carnivora. the Achelous and Nessus,' is gravely stated by Herodotus, Aristotle, Pausanias, and others, but is yet hard to believe;

the Lion of Nemea is merely the solstitial sign of Leo, which the Lion Gate
of Mycenae and similar monuments likewise represent. Ctesias brought
strange tales of the tiger (τίγρις), under its Sanskrit (or Persian) name of
μαρτιχόρας, the 'Man-slayer'; and King Seleucus sent a tiger to Athens.
The leopard (πάρδαλις), common in Asia Minor, was known to Homer.
The lynx (λύγξ, M. Gk ῥῆσος, a Slavonian word) includes several species,
F. caracal, the African and Indian species, and the European species
(*F. pardina* and *F. lynx*) which Euripides, Xenophon and others speak of
as a native of Greece. The cat (αἴλουρος) is mentioned by Aristophanes,
doubtless as a wild cat, whose skins were brought to market by Boeotian
pedlars; and Herodotus had told of the sanctity of the cat in Egypt
(*F. maniculata*). The dog (κύων) was man's servant and comrade long
before the dawn of Hellas, and house-dogs, watch-dogs, sheep-dogs and
hounds were distinguished in Homer's time. Oppian (*Cyneg.* i.) describes
a great number of breeds; and some of these, such as the great Molossian
and Laconian hounds, and the little Μελιταῖα κυνίδια, or Maltese terriers,
are familiar in literature. Athens would seem to have had, like Constantinople, its pariah dogs (Aristoph.), but they were excluded from the
Acropolis. The wolf (λύκος) is still the dread of Greek shepherds, whose
fierce dogs, probably little different from the old Molossian breed, are
trained to attack it. The jackal (θώς, M. Gk or Turkish τσακάλι), *Canis
aureus*, is exactly described in Homer, as crowding round a wounded stag,
then flying when the lion comes, and again returning to what the lion
leaves; it is the yellow wolf (λύκος ὁ ξανθός) of Oppian, and is still found
in Greece. The fox (ἀλώπηξ, M. Gk ἀλωποῦ) was always a type of cunning,
and, like the wolf and the bear, a theme of fable and of folk-lore; a small
species (βασσάριον, Eg. *basar*) mentioned by Herodotus, was the Fennec
fox of Syria and Egypt. The domestic 'cat' of the Greeks (γάλη, γάλη
κατοικίδιος, Arist. *Pax*, 1079, etc.) was a sort of large weasel, probably
the white-breasted marten (*Mustela foina*). Γάλη ἄγρια or ἰκτίς was the
wild marten (*Mustela foina* or *martes*), and a larger species, described
in Aristotle as fond of honey and destructive to the hive, was probably
M. boccamela. In M. Gk the marten is called κάλια, i.e. γάλη, or ἀτσίδι,
i.e. ἰκτ[ισ]ίδιον, or κουνάδι, i.e. κυνίδιον, whence an early Greek printer of
Venice, Andrias Counades, adopted it as his emblem. The γάλη ἄγρια
and κατοικίδιος were wild and tame weasels or ferrets (*M. furo*). In
Aesop the weasel appears as νυμφή, the bride, which is still (νυφίτζα) its
popular Greek name; the name is euphemistic (cf. Theophr. *Char.* XVI.).
It is possible that Aristotle's 'white Pontic mice' were ermines. The otter
(ἔνυδρις, M. Gk σκυλοπόταμον) was valued for its fur, which, like so many
others, was brought to Athens from Boeotia; Herodotus speaks of the
otters in Scythia, and apparently also (but by mistake or confusion) of
otters in the Nile. The bear (ἄρκτος), the king of European beasts, was
familiar to the Greeks, but chiefly, as to ourselves, through folk-lore and
fable. It lived, according to Pausanias, on Taygetus and Maenalus, and
is still to be found in the mountains of Macedonia and Epeirus.

48. Seals (φώκη) are described by Homer, and figure on the coinage

Seals.

of Phocaea. A single species only, *P. monachus*, unknown to our own seas, inhabits the Mediterranean ; of its habits but little is known. The sealskins mentioned by Herodotus as used by dwellers on the Araxes were skins of *Phoca caspica*.

49. Dolphins (δελφίς) of various species are very common in the Medi-

Cetacea.

terranean ; a small species, φώκαινα, mentioned by Aristotle, may or may not have been the common porpoise. The dolphin's love of music is an interesting, but non-zoological myth. Κῆτος includes, besides the whales, any great monster of the sea. Φάλλαινα, a whale in Aristophanes (M. Gk μπαλαίνα), is a byword for the bloated Cleon.

B. BIRDS.

50. The Greeks distinguish many species, and even classes, of

Raptores.

rapacious birds, vultures, eagles, hawks and owls ; but the larger vultures and eagles were often confused. Thus in *Ag.* 138, στυγεῖ δὲ δεῖπνον ἀετῶν, Aeschylus is speaking of the carrion diet of the vultures. Four vultures occur in Greece : the great Läm- mergeier (*Gypaetus barbatus*), the Griffon (*Gyps fulvus*), the rarer black vulture (*V. cinereus*), and the small Egyptian vulture, or Pharaoh's hen (*Neophron percnopterus*), ὁ μικρὸς καὶ ἐκλευκότερος (Arist.), in M. Gk 'the cuckoo's horse' (κούκκου ἄλογον). The generic name, γύψ, includes all these. The various terms, αἰγυπιός, ἅρπη, περκνόπτερος, νέρτος (an Egyptian word), τόργος (Lycophron, probably also Egyptian), and φήνη, are not safely to be ascribed to separate species, though in particular passages their specific meaning is often clear. In later Greek, Dionysius (*de Avibus*) describes the Lämmergeier accurately, under the name ἅρπη ; it was probably the αἰγυπιός of Homer (*Il.* XVII. 460, etc.). It has a habit, shared with some eagles, of dropping its prey from a height to shatter it, especially when it feeds on tortoises ; and so Aeschylus, according to the legend (Ael. VII. 16, etc.), is said to have met his death. The griffon (M. Gk ὄρνεον, σπανίτης) is generally the 'eagle' of Scripture, the eagle-headed god Nisroch of the Assyrians, the banner of the Persian armies. Of eagles, many species occur plentifully in Greece, and of old they were doubtless still more abundant. Ἀετός is generic.

51. Of owls many species occur in Greece and three are very common.

Owls.

The great eagle owl (*Bubo ignavus*) is common in all moun- tainous parts, and is usually, but very doubtfully, identified with the κύμινδις or χαλκίς of Homer ; it is more certainly the βύας of Aristotle and later writers, the *Bubo* of Virgil (M. Gk μποῦφος). Ὠτός is another and smaller horned owl (*Asio otus* or *brachyotus*, especially the latter) ; αἰγοκέφαλος was probably the long-eared owl. Σκώψ is the little horned owl (*Scops giu*), well described by Alexander the Myndian

(Athen. IX. 391 B), and by Aelian (xv. 28); its monotonous cry is alluded to by Aristotle. Γλαῦξ is especially the little owl, *Athene noctua* (M. Gk κουκκουβάγια), everywhere resident in Greece, living among ruins, down wells, and in hollow olive trees, strictly nocturnal, concealing itself during the day. It was the bird of Athena and of Athens, the city's crest, the type of Athenian coinage (γλαῦκες Λαυριωτικαί) to the last days of the independence of the city.

52. Of the Passeres, or perching-birds, though some 150 species at least exist in Greece, few are mentioned in literature, and very few before Aristotle. Κίχλη (M. Gk τσίχλα) is the **Passeres.** generic name for the thrush-tribe, from Homer downwards; κόσσυφος or κόψιχος is the blackbird, of which a white variety was said, or perhaps fabled, to live on Mount Cyllene; I am half inclined to suspect an ancient joke, or a dialectic misunderstanding, as to the white *pinnacles*, κορυφαί, of the mountain. Κίχλη, in Aristotle, includes, besides the song-thrush, the migratory fieldfare and redwing; ἰξοβόρος is the missel-thrush, which remains to breed. ἀηδών, the nightingale, is probably applied, as in modern Greek, to various warblers. The singing nightingale was usually spoken of as female, as Shakespeare has it; Aristotle, like Milton, makes both male and female sing. The robin is a common resident in Greece, and ἐρίθακος is probably, but not certainly, to be identified with it. Other warblers are μελαγκόρυφος, the black-cap (or perhaps the marsh-tit); ἐλεᾶς, probably the reed-warbler; φοινίκουρος, the redstart; ὑπολαΐς, a bird in whose nest the cuckoo lays, is supposed to be the wheatear. Ὀρχίλος or τροχίλος (in late Greek, τρωγλοδύτης), is the wren, also known as βασιλεύς, the 'king of all birds'; it was hostile to the eagle, in ancient as in modern folk-lore. Σίττη is the nuthatch, a good omen to lovers; κύανος, a name that has been very diversely identified (though Aristotle gives a detailed description of the bird), is probably the rock-nuthatch, *Sitta neumayeri*, a bird almost peculiar to Greece and the Archipelago. Αἰγίθαλος is a titmouse, of which Aristotle distinguishes three species, the great tit (σπιζίτης), the long-tailed tit or a very similar form, and the little kind which includes the tomtit and its allies, of which *P. lugubris* is the commonest in Greek (M. Gk καλόγηρος, κλειδῶνας). The swallow, χελιδών, is the subject of innumerable poetic references, from Homer downwards. Aristotle informs us that μία χελιδὼν ἔαρ οὐ ποιεῖ. Athenaeus hands down to us the Rhodian swallow-song, ἦλθ', ἦλθε χελιδών, καλὰς ὥρας ἄγουσα, which the children sang on a certain day in spring: as they still sing a version of it in Greece, and as in Ireland and elsewhere they sing the wren's elegy on St Stephen's day; there are many fragments or echoes of the swallow-song in Greek poetry. Κωτίλας (Anacreon, etc.) was a poetic or perhaps a Boeotian word for the swallow. While χελιδών included the house-martin as well as the swallow, κύψελος may be identified as the sand-martin. Ἄπους is the swift, and δρεπανίς, a rare variety, is perhaps the large Alpine swift, *Cypselus melba*. Of the finch tribe, few are named in the early classics. Στρουθός, the sparrow, is

used by Homer (*Il.* ii. 308) and others, of small birds generally; in Aristotle (ix. 7) it is definitely the house-sparrow (M. Gk σπουργίτης), for the black chin of the cock-bird is unmistakably described. Πετροκόσσυφος in M. Gk, and probably λαιός in Aristotle, are names of the blue-thrush (*Petrocichla cyanus*), which was probably Lesbia's sparrow, and the στρουθίον μονάζον of the Psalms. Φρυγίλος may be rendered finch, but was perhaps just a familiar name for a sparrow. Χλωρίς (M. Gk φλῶρι) was the greenfinch; πυραλλίς (M. Gk πυρροῦλας) was probably the bullfinch. Χρυσομίτρης and ἀκανθυλλίς (It. Scanzlin) were names for the goldfinch. Σπίζα (M. Gk σπῖνος) and ἀκανθίς (Lat. carduelis), commonly translated 'linnet,' appear to have meant the siskin. Τύραννος, in Aristotle, is the tiny goldcrest, μικρῷ μείζων ἀκρίδος, φοινικοῦν λόφον ἔχων; but it is doubtless mixed up with the common wren, under such names as βασιλεύς, βασιλίσκος, ὀρχίλος. Κεβλήπυρις may be translated redpoll, or we may follow Tristram in rendering it goldcrest : the word occurs only in *Av.* 303. Of larks (κορυδαλλός) several species occur, the commonest being *A. cristata* : it is the crest of this species which is often alluded to, and through its crest the lark comes into mythological relation with the solar hoopoe. Ψάρ, or ψάρος (M. Gk ψαρόνι), is the common starling, always coupled in Homer with the jackdaw (κολοιός) : its eastern ally, the beautiful rose-coloured pastor, is described in later Greek and in Latin under the name of σελευκίς. This bird is well known in northern Greece, where it is called ἀγιοπούλι on its spring migration, when it destroys the grasshoppers, and διαβολοπούλι in autumn, when it devours the grapes. The raven (κόραξ) was very common : it was the messenger of Apollo, and, with his laurel-twig, figures on the coins of Delphi. Κορώνη, the crow (including the carrion and hooded crows), was also very common; it was hostile to the owl, and detested by Athena. There was a crow-song, as there was a swallow-song, and an echo of it is perhaps heard in Aristophanes (*Pax*, 1126). Σπερμολόγος was in all probability the rook, μαλθακὴν ἱέντα γῆρυν (Ar. *Av.* 233): it is a resident in northern Greece. Κίσσα, the jay, abounds in the olive-groves : the magpie (M. Gk καρακάξα) is not mentioned by the older writers. Κορακίας is mentioned by Aristotle, and identified by its epithet φοινικόρυγχος as the chough; the Alpine chough is common, the Cornish chough scarcer, in Greece. The golden oriole (? χλωρίων, M. Gk κιτρινοπούλι) is not uncommon.

53. Six woodpeckers occur in Greece, four of them common. Δρυοκολάπτης is in Aristotle the generic word, and he distinguishes

Woodpeckers and Parrots. three species, of which one is certainly the great black woodpecker. Πελεκᾶς is another name of general application. Κελεός (Arist.) is the green woodpecker; and the other common forms are the greater and lesser spotted woodpeckers, which may be the two smaller kinds of δρυοκολάπτης referred to by Aristotle. Ἴυγξ, the wryneck (*Iynx torquilla*), was sacred in Greece, as in Egypt and Assyria. It is admirably described by Aristotle. It figures often as a love-charm, the *locus classicus*

being Theocr. II.; and it was undoubtedly used in lunar rites. Its mythology is characteristically Greek, and not Latin. With the woodpeckers
Aristotle mentions κνιπολόγος, the little tree-creeper (ἐστὶ δὲ καὶ τοῦτο
ξυλοκόπον). The parrot (ψίττακος or ψιττάκη, βίττακος (Ctesias), σίττακος
(Nearchus)) is mentioned by Ctesias and by Aristotle, and frequently by
later authors, such as Pausanias, Arrian and Athenaeus.

54. Two kingfishers (ἀλκυών, M. Gk βασιλοποῦλι), very different in habit
and appearance, are common. The pied or Smyrna kingfisher
(*Ceryle rudis*), found generally on the sea-coast, has been Kingfishers.
identified with κήρυλος, which latter word, however, seems to be, like
ἀλιπορφυρίς, but a poetic equivalent of ἀλκυών. The myth of the halcyon
days (ἀλκυονίδες ἡμέραι) 'when birds of calm Sit brooding on the charmed
wave,' the exaggerated or mythical descriptions of the halcyon's plaintive
song (cf. *Il.* IX. 563 ; Eur. *I.T.* 1089), and the story in Aelian and Plutarch
of the female carrying the old male on her back, are mysteries not to be
explained by the zoologist.

55. Another bird of most ancient and complicated mythology is the
hoopoe (ἔποψ, M. Gk τζαλοπετεινός), a passing migrant in
southern Greece, but very common in northern Greece, as it Hoopoe.
is in Spain. Under Turkish rule it was reverently protected, as in ancient
Egypt. From its rayed crest it was of old a solar emblem, and its mythological relations, including the obscure and curious Tereus legend, are
manifold. Its note resembles that of the cuckoo, with which bird it is
associated or compared, as in German folk-lore (der Kuckuck und sein
Küster): and the Aeschylean or more probably Sophoclean fragment in
Aristotle (IX. 49 B), which describes the metamorphosis of the hoopoe (as
of the cuckoo both in Greek and English folk-lore) into a hawk, is connected with the cuckoo's singular resemblance to the latter bird. Κουκούφα
(Horapollo) was the old Egyptian name for the hoopoe.

56. Κόκκυξ, the cuckoo, was a harbinger of spring (Hes. *Op. et D.*,
489, etc.). Its singular habit of laying in an alien nest was
well known, and is described by Aristotle. A second and Cuckoo, etc.
larger species of cuckoo in Greece, *Coccystes glandarius* (M. Gk κράνος),
lays in the nests of the jackdaw, jay, and crow: but accounts in Aristotle
(*H.A.* VI. 7) of a cuckoo which builds its own nest, and in the pseudo-
Aristotelian 'Book of Wonders,' of one which lays in the nests of doves
and turtle-doves, are not to be explained The bee-eater (μέροψ, M. Gk
μελισσοῦργος) is one of the most beautiful and abundant of summer visitors,
as is the roller (*Coracias garrula*, M. Gk χρυσοκαρακάξ, χαλκοκορώνη) ; but
neither bird is mentioned in the early classics. Αἰγοθήλας, the nightjar or
goatsucker (M. Gk [αἰ]γιδοβύστρα, νυκτερίδα), had the reputation which its
name implies, and which it still everywhere bears.

57. Three pigeons, besides the domesticated varieties, are recognised
in Greek literature, the wood-pigeon (*C. palumbus*), the rock-
dove (*C. livia*), and the turtle-dove. The last, τρυγών, is Pigeons

a summer visitor, while the others are resident. Πέλεια, the Epic word, is in Homer the wild rock-dove, ἥ ῥά θ' ὑπ' ἴρηκος κοίλην εἰσέπτατο πέτρην, χηραμόν. Φάψ or φάσσα is usually the wood-pigeon or ring-dove, with which the stock-dove was compared; φάττα φάττῃ is Plutarch's version of 'as like as two peas.' Οἰνάς, often translated stock-dove, is a word of Semitic origin (Heb. *jonah*, a dove). Περιστερά is more or less generic, but is chiefly used for the domestic bird, περιστερὰν ἐφέστιον οἰκέτιν τε (Soph. fr.). Carrier pigeons were early known, as in the pretty Anacreontic, ἐρασμίη πέλεια. White pigeons, the sacred race of Babylon, were first seen in Greece near Mount Athos, during the Persian wars (Athen. IX. 394). Decoy pigeons were in common use, and were usually blinded (*H.A.* IX. 7). Dove-cotes (περιστερεών) are mentioned by Plato (*Theaet.* 197 c), and elaborately described by later writers. The dove is associated with Aphrodite, as with the Syrian Ashtaroth, but not in the earliest Greek: its later Christian symbolism is frequent in the Fathers. Deucalion's dove in Plutarch, ἐκ τῆς λάρνακος ἀφιεμένην, is drawn from a very ancient apologue.

58. Ἀλεκτρυών, ἀλέκτωρ, the barn-door fowl (ἀλεκτορίς, a hen, ὀρτά-
Fowls and Game-birds. λιχος, a chick), often mentioned simply as ὄρνις, a fowl (as in M. Gk πετεινός, a cock, ὄρνιθα, a hen), is a native of India, very early domesticated in the east; it was long spoken of as the 'Persian Bird.' It is first mentioned by Theognis and Pindar, by the former as the 'cock that crows in the morn,' ἆμος ἀλεκτρυόνων φθόγγος ἐγειρομένων. In Plato, likewise, we have 'at cock-crow,' ἀλεκτρυόνων ᾀδόντων. Many breeds were known in antiquity; among others the fighting-cock; and Themistocles instituted an annual cock-fight at Athens. The cock is represented on coins of many Greek states, and the oldest representation, on coins of Himera and Dardanus, closely resembles the wild *Gallus ferrugineus* or *bankiva* of Northern India.

The pheasant, φασιανός, or later τέταρος (the latter a Median word), was introduced from Asia Minor before the time of Aristophanes. Aristotle describes the eggs as spotted, and this is said actually to be the case with wild pheasants in the Caucasus. Ταώς, the peacock (Arab. *tawus*, etc., M. Gk παγώνι), was known in Athens in the time of the Peloponnesian wars (Athen. IX. 397 c). It was sacred to Hera, and its first home in Greece was probably in her temple at Samos. Μελεαγρίς, the guinea-fowl, was a sacred bird, kept in the Acropolis, and in various temples. The Greek and Italian birds (*Gallina afra* or *numidica*) differed, the latter having a red wattle, the former a blue. This suggests that the μελεαγρίς had sprung from the species now found in Abyssinia (*N. ptilorhynchus*) and had come to Athens by way of Egypt; while the *afra avis* was *N. meleagris*, a Numidian or West African bird. Ἀτταγᾶς, the francolin, a famous dainty, is now extinct and rare in Greece, and said to be fast disappearing in Asia Minor. Πέρδιξ, the partridge, is often named, and two species are distinguished by their notes: οἱ μὲν κακκαβίζουσιν, οἱ δὲ τρίζουσιν (Arist.). The latter is probably our common partridge, the former is *P. graeca* or *saxatilis*, a bird very like the Indian *chukar*. Ὄρτυξ, the quail, the most abundant of the game-birds, was captured in nets and often decoyed by a mirror : it was trained to fight, as still in Eastern Asia. The bustard, ὠτίς, is still common in Greece. Xenophon tells of its capture by coursing, with horse and dog.

59. The crane, γέρανος (M. Gk λελέκι), still breeds in Macedonia and Asia Minor. Its lofty flight, οὐρανόθι πρό, and clanging cry are described by Homer and Hesiod, and its regular migrations by Aristotle and many writers. The fight with the pygmies (*Il.* III. 6) is an ancient tale, extant also in India (Ael. XVI. 22). The stork, πελαργός, is a summer visitor. It was reverenced, as by the Egyptians, for its piety. It was common in Greece before the War of Independence ; but, no longer protected by the piety of the Moslems, it has become almost extinct. Various herons are included under the generic ἐρωδιός, *e.g.* ὁ πέλλος, the common heron, ὁ λευκός, the egret (*A. alba* and *A. gazetta*) (including also λευκερωδιός, the spoonbill, M. Gk κουλιάρι, *i.e. cuillère*), and ἀστερίας, the bittern (Arist.). It was a symbol of Athena on various coins, *e.g.* of Corinth and Ambracia, and was her messenger in the *Iliad*.

Crane, Stork and Heron.

Herodotus mentions two species of ibis, the white or sacred ibis (*I. aethiopicus*), and the black, or glossy ibis (*Plegades falcinellus*). The ibis was sacred to the moon, and to Thoth or Hermes, as in a hymn of Pherecydes, ὦ Ἑρμῆς ἰβίμορφε (cf. also Plat. *Symp.* IX.).

60. Many waders are mentioned, more or less casually. Κρέξ, though often mentioned, is difficult to identify ; the common identification with the corn-crake rests mainly on the assumption that the name is onomatopœic. Ἐρυθρόπους, the redshank, is common in Greece in winter. Χαραδριός is generally taken to be the stone-curlew (*Oedicnemus crepitans*), but its fabulous attributes are mixed up with eastern tales of the stork (Heb. *chasad*). The τροχίλος of Herodotus, which picks leeches (βδέλλας) out of the crocodile's mouth, is the Egyptian or black-headed plover, *Pluvianus aegyptius*. Φοινικόπτερος, a flamingo, is now rare in Greece, but abundant in Egypt and Asia Minor. The purple coot or gallinule (πορφυρίων), *Porphyrio hyacinthus*, a large and very beautiful bird, is or was lately found, according to Erhard, on Lake Copais and Lake Dystos in Euboea. The common coot is abundant, and retains its ancient name, φαλαρίς, φαλαρίδα.

Waders, etc.

61. The common or mute swan, κύκνος (*Cygnus olor*), is a common bird in the Levant, and was first brought to England from Crete during the Crusades. From Homer downwards, it is frequent in poetry, and Euripides would seem to have had a predilection for the bird. The swan's song, especially its dying song, is continually alluded to, and Socrates spoke of it at the last. It is a myth, and a very beautiful myth, and is not to be explained, as some would have it, by the loud trumpet-call of the northern whooper (*C. musicus*). Geese

Swans and Ducks.

(χήν) are mentioned by Homer, wild geese in the *Iliad* (ii. 460) and tame in the *Odyssey* (*e.g.* xv. 161). Χηναλώπηξ was the Egyptian goose (cf. Ael. x. 16), and both this name and πηνέλοψ are perhaps corruptions of one and the same Egyptian word. Many wild ducks occur in Greece. Νῆσσα is the generic word, and the common name for the domestic duck. Βόσκας or φασκάς (Athenaeus) is a small kind, probably including the teal and garganey (*Anas crecca* and *querquedula*). Γλαύκιον (Athenaeus), a duck with yellow eyes, may very well be the golden-eye (*A. clangula*), a winter migrant to Greece.

62. The gulls, λάρος (M. Gk γλάρος, γλαρόνι), are not discriminated.
Gulls and Terns. The κορῶναι εἰνάλιαι (*Od.* v. 66) or θαλάσσιοι were probably shearwaters, *Puffinus anglorum*, which abound in the Aegean. These noisy nocturnal birds, dwelling in labyrinthine burrows, were the Birds of Diomede (ἐρωδιοί, Ael. *N.H.* i, 1); sacred to Athene, they were probably also the ὄρνις ἀνοπαῖα of *Od.* i. 140.

63. Κόραξ, spoken of as a sea-bird (*H.A.* viii. 3), is the cormorant, and κολοιός the little cormorant (*Phalacrocorax pygmaeus*).
Cormorants and Grebes. Πελεκῖνος, the pelican (M. Gk σακκᾶς, the Turkish for a water-carrier), is still common on the coasts of N. Greece. Κολυμβίς is a grebe, especially the little dabchick (*Podiceps minor*, M. Gk βουτηκτάρα), very common in Greece, and ἀρνευτήρ (*Il.* xvi. 742) was perhaps a larger species of diver or grebe.

64. The ostrich, στρουθὸς ὁ μέγας, in later Greek στρουθοκάμηλος, is
Ostrich. mentioned by Herodotus from the Persian Gulf or the country of the Bedouin: and Xenophon met with it near the Euphrates. Aristophanes alludes to its beautiful white plumes (*Ach.* 1118), and Aristotle and Oppian describe many points in its appearance and structure.

C. REPTILES AND BATRACHIA.

65. The group of reptiles consisted, for the Greeks, of serpents (ὀφέων γένος) and oviparous quadrupeds (τετράποδα ὠοτόκα), the latter including the tortoises, crocodiles, lizards and frogs. Reptiles are abundant in Greece: and some of the islands especially (*e.g.* Myconos), barren and treeless, are very nests of snakes and lizards. Of African species there are not a few, and common European snakes (*e.g. Coronella laevis*) grow to twice their usual size.

66. The common land tortoises (χελώνη, M. Gk ἀχελῶνα), *Testudo graeca*
Tortoises. and *marginata*, are extraordinarily abundant in Greece; and so also are several species of the little fresh-water tortoise, ἐμύς. The turtle, χελώνη ἡ θαλαττία (*Thalassochelys caretta*), is not uncommon. All were well known to Aristotle, who carefully described their

habits and reproduction. The tortoise or turtle figures on the coins of
Aegina, one of the oldest coinages of Greece: whence the proverb τὰν
ἀρετὰν καὶ τὰν σοφίαν νικᾶντι χελῶναι.

67. Κροκόδειλος (Eg. χάμψα) usually distinguished as κρ. ὁ ποτάμιος,
is described by Herodotus. Κρ. ὁ χερσαῖος is a lizard,
especially the large Egyptian *Varanus niloticus*, but in   Crocodiles
M. Gk κροκόδειλος is the common *Stellio vulgaris* (cf. Herod. and Lizards.
II. 69). Σαῦρος (M. Gk σαυράδα) is the generic term for the smaller lizards,
of which many species occur in Greece. A large poisonous species,
Tropidosaurus algira, is dreaded in modern Greece (M. Gk κωλόσσαυρος).
᾽Ασκαλαβώτης or γαλεώτης is the little climbing gecko (*Hemidactylus
turcicus*, *Tarentula mauretanica*, and allied species). The chameleon,
χαμαιλέων, is common in Asia Minor; there is but a single, doubtful,
record of its capture in Greece.

68. Ὄφις is generic for a serpent, of which about a dozen species are
found in Greece. There are three poisonous vipers (ἔχις,
ἔχιδνα), *V. aspis, ammodytes,* and *lebetina.* The horned   Serpents.
serpents of Thebes (*H.A.* II. 1) are *Cerastes cornutus*, the dangerous horned
viper of the desert. ᾽Ασπίς is applied to various venomous snakes, among
others to the Egyptian cobra, *Naja haje.* Ὕδρος or ὕδρα is a harmless
colubrine snake, such as *Tropidonotus natrix* (M. Gk νερόφιδον), but the
Hydra of Lerna is mythological. Δράκων is some very large serpent, drawn
perhaps from outlandish stories of the python, like Aristotle's tales of the
immense serpents in Libya (*H.A.* VIII. 8), or Strabo's of those in India;
but legends of gigantic snakes, dwelling in neighbouring caverns, are still
rife among the Greek peasantry. The large serpents kept in temples, and
depicted on the coins of Croton and elsewhere, were probably *Elaphis
quadrilineatus* or perhaps *Coluber longissimus.* Another large but harmless
Greek serpent is *C. acontites* (*Zamenis gemonensis*) (M. Gk λαφίτης), which
grows to six or even eight feet long, and has an unpleasant habit of unprovoked
attack. The sea-serpents of the Indian Ocean (*e.g. Hydrophis pelamys*) are
mentioned by Aelian, who describes their flat, rudder-like tails.

69. Βάτραχος, the frog, was a favourite topic of the fabulist and of the
comic writers, as Aristophanes' Βάτραχοι and the *Battle of the
Frogs and Mice* testify. Four species are common in Greece,   Frogs and
R. temporaria, R. esculenta, Discoglossus pictus, and the little Toads.
green tree-frog, *Hyla arborea.* Φρύνη, the toad, is represented by three
species, *Bufo vulgaris* and *B. viridis,* and *Bombinator igneus.* It is
especially the last (Lat. *rubeta*) that is an enemy to bees, and is detested
by the bee-keeper (*H.A.* IX. 19). It was doubtless the green tree-frog, a
celebrated weather-prophet, of which Hesychius speaks: μάντις· ὁ ἐν τοῖς
κήποις βάτραχος. The salamander, σαλαμάνδρα (*S. maculata* or *atra*), had
the singular reputation of immunity from fire. Γύρινος is a tadpole, and
κορδύλος was probably the large gill-bearing tadpole of a salamander
or newt.

D. FISHES.

70. The fishes of the Mediterranean are very numerous, but for the most part strange to our eyes. While the Mediterranean species come more or less sparingly to our shores, our own staple food-fishes, such as herring, cod, haddock, whiting and plaice, are northern fishes which reach the Mediterranean rarely or not at all. Our food supply is drawn from a few fishes such as these, while that of the Mediterranean countries is drawn from a much larger variety, mostly of the ' spiny-finned fishes,' among which none greatly predominate.

71. The eel, ἔγχελυς (M. Gk χέλι), is the only fish specifically mentioned by Homer, who indeed contrasts it with all other fishes. Its

Sea-fishes.

generation was long obscure, and Aristotle speaks of it as produced from γῆς ἔντερα, the name still given, under another form, in Sicily (*casentule*) to the actual larvae (Leptocephali) of the eel. Ἐγχέλεις θηρᾶσθαι was a proverb (*Eq.* 864)—'to fish in muddy waters.' There were tame eels in the fountain of Arethusa (Ael. VIII. 4). The conger (γόγγρος, M. Gk μονγγρί) was also well known. The μύραινα (*Muraena Helena*) was a delicacy. Of the herring family, ἐγκρασίχολος, the anchovy, was the chief; σαρδῖνος (Athenaeus) was probably the true sardine, or young pilchard. Ἀφύη, μεμβράς, were small worthless fish, or 'sprats,' the fry or the smaller species of the herring tribe. The bright-coloured, shore-dwelling, nest-building family of the wrasses (Labridae) are known throughout the Mediterranean as the 'thrushes' (*tordi, grive*), or by other bird-names; they appear in Greek as κίχλαι, κόσσυφοι, etc.; and their nest is described by Aristotle. Σκάρος, the parrot-wrasse (*Sc. cretensis*), was celebrated for its habit of chewing the cud, a habit which has not been re-observed.

Among the mackerel family (Scombridae), we have the tunnies, θύννος (M. Gk τουνῖνα), the largest and most important food-fishes of the Mediterranean. Their routes of migration were attentively studied, and they were caught, much as pilchards are in Cornwall, in nets, watchers or 'hooers,' θυννόσκοποι, being stationed in watch-towers or on high places ashore: but in the nets, the great fish were harpooned with a τρίαινα or θρῖναξ. Ἀμία, πηλαμύς, and ὄρκυς, were other species of tunny or bonito; and πριμάδες and σκορδύλαι were the young of the same fish. Ξιφίας, the sword-fish, is often captured in the tunny-nets. The smaller mackerels (σκόμβρος, κολίας) were also valued, and were, and are, especially important in the Black Sea. Ἐχενηίς, the sucking fish (*Echeneis remora*), which attaches itself by the head to floating objects, was believed to have the power of stopping or delaying vessels: the phenomenon of 'dead-water,' by which a vessel may be so arrested in her course, is now known to be due to a curious action of submarine waves. The flying-fish (*Dactylopterus volitans*) was known as χελιδών. Various gurnards (κόκκυξ) were known, and Aristotle mentions the sound which they produce. The family of Sparidae or sea-breams contains many important food-fishes, e.g. *Cantharus lineatus* (κάνθαρος), *Pagrus vulgaris* (φάγρος), *Dentex vulgaris* (συναγρίς), *Box boops* (βῶξ), *Chrysophrys auratus* (χρύσοφρυς), and Sargus sp. (σάργος). The fish κάλλιχθυς, or καλλιώνυμος, is often mentioned, as is the ἀνθίας, both being sacred : the identification is uncertain. Grey mullets (κεστρεύς, κέφαλος, μίξων, περαίας, χελών) were abundant and esteemed. The red mullet is τρίγλη, which name it retains in modern Greek and in Italian (*triglia*). Among the sea-perches are λάβραξ (*Labrax lupus*), the bass, a much prized fish, and ὀρφώς, a large species, probably *Polyprion cernuus*, but also applied (in modern Greek) to *Serranus gigas*. Χάννα and ἐρυθρῖνος are two curious fishes, among which, according to Aristotle, only males and no females exist; they belong to the genus Serranus, which is known to be herma-phrodite : χάννα being *S. scriba* or *S. cabrilla*, and ἐρυθρῖνος the brilliantly coloured *S. anthias* or *Anthias sacer*. Of the flatfishes (Pleuronectidae) the most prized was ψῆττα, the turbot, and βούγλωσσον (M. Gk γλῶσσα), the sole. Βελόνη is the little pipe-fish (*Syngnathus*), with whose singular method of reproduction Aristotle was acquainted; the name is also applied to the garfish, *Scombresox saurus* (M. Gk βελονίδι). The angler, or fishing-frog (βάτραχος, ὁ ἁλιεύς), is often mentioned by Aristotle, who includes it among the selachians, or cartilaginous fishes.

72. Of the latter, sharks, dogfish, skate, many species were known, and Aristotle's knowledge of these was peculiarly detailed. He *Sharks.* knew, for instance, the remarkable viviparous reproduction, and the anatomical structure of the 'placenta,' in the smooth shark, *Mustelus laevis*, γαλεὸς ὁ λεῖος. Ἀκανθίας is the spiny dogfish, *Acanthias vulgaris*; σκύλιον, probably *Scyllium canicula*. Ἀλώπηξ is the fox shark, or thresher (M. Gk λαμία); καρχαρίας, a large species, such as the great blue shark. Βατίς is the skate or 'thornback,' and τρυγών is the dangerous sting-ray, *Trygon pastinaca*; νάρκη is the torpedo, whose power of shock is often referred to (Plato, etc.); very explicitly by Aristotle, who, speaking (according to an emended text) of τὸν τρόμον ὃν ἔχει ἐν τῷ σώματι, uses the very word that Réaumur uses (*tremblement*), in an early modern description.

73. Few fresh-water fishes are mentioned, besides the eel. The Salmonidae (salmon, trout, etc.), abundant in the Danube, are not met with in Greece, but Aelian has a charming *Fresh-water fishes.* account of fly-fishing in Macedonia, for certain 'speckled fish.' Κυπρῖνος is the carp, whose 'tongues' or rather fleshy palates were a delicacy, and βάλερος was perhaps the allied Prussian carp (*Carassius vulgaris*, It. *bulbaro*). Herodotus, Strabo and others mention several fishes of the Nile, whose Greek names in many cases hide Egyptian words (*e.g.* ἀβραμίς, ἀλαβής, ἀνθίας, βωρεύς, etc.). Herodotus also mentions the names of two fishes of the Macedonian or Thracian lake-dwellers, πάπρακες and τίλωνες: the former were probably perch, the latter (τίλων, s. ψίλων) may have been the great silurus or sheat-fish (German *Seilen*), which is the σίλουρος of

Aelian (xiv. 25). A close ally of the last fish is the γλάνις, whose care for its eggs and young (as in the allied American catfishes) is carefully described by Aristotle; this is a remarkable fish, peculiar to Greece, now known as *Parasilurus Aristotelis.* The sturgeons (ἔλλοψ, ἀκκιπήσιος, or γαλεὸς ἐκ 'Ρόδου, of Athenaeus), including the little sterlet, are important fishes of Northern Greece and the region of the Black Sea, migrating to the Aegean and Mediterranean.

74. The Greek fishermen still use much the same methods of fishing, by hook (ἄγκιστρον), spear (τρίαινα), net (δίκτυον), and trap

Fishing.

or creel (κύρτος), as are described by Oppian (*Halieut.* iii.). The nets, are of old, are of many kinds—μυρία δ᾽ αἰόλα τοῖα δολορραφέων λίνα κόλπων. Among these are the great tunny-nets (σαγήνη, M. Gk θυννί), the seine-nets (ἀμφίβληστρα, γρῖφοι), furnished with wings (πτερά), weighed with sinkers (μολυβδίδες, Soph., Plato, M. Gk μολυβῆθρες), and suspended from a headline or buoy-rope (σαρδών, σαρδόνιον, Xen., M. Gk σαρδούνας): sometimes they are attached by bridles (χάλινα) to a sort of otter-board (M. Gk σταλίκιον). A small casting-net (M. Gk πεζόβολος, Opp. πέζα, σφαίρων) is used from the shore. Drag-nets or dredges (γαγγάμη, Strabo, γάγγαμον, Oppian, M. Gk γαγγάβα) are used for oysters, sponges and sea-urchins.

Line-fishing is practised in various ways, *e.g.* with the rod (ἐκ δονάκων), with a single weighted line (καθετή), or with 'long-lines' (ὁρμιαὶ πολυαγκίστροι, Arist., Opp.) (M. Gk παραγαδία). The scarus and mullet are caught by using the female as a decoy (cf. Opp. *Hal.* iv. 40). The octopus, clinging to the rock, or to its nest (θαλάμι), is still compelled to leave go by help of the Aristotelian κόνυζα, or of a modern substitute, tobacco.

E. INSECTS (ἔντομα).

75. Μέλισσα, the bee (κηφήν, a drone), was known and domesticated from very early times, and its economy was well understood,

Bees and
Wasps.

save that the ancients took the queen-bee for a king (βασιλεύς, ἡγεμών). The hive-bee of Greece is the 'Ligurian' bee, a little smaller and lighter coloured than our own. The 'flowery hill Hymettus' is still celebrated for its thyme and for its bees. Enemies of the bee are κλῆρος, a little beetle (*Trichodes apiarius*), and the wax-moth, πυραύστης, the *tinea* of Virgil (*Galleria mellonella*), whose caterpillars were called τερηδόνες. Of other Hymenoptera, βομβύλιος is a bumble-bee (*Bombus*), of which many species are common. Σφῆξ, ἀνθρήνη, σείρην and τενθρηδών, are species of wasps, or hornets: an ἀνθρήνη which catches flies, cuts off their heads and carries their bodies home (Arist.), is *Bembex rostrata.* The ἰχνευμών, or 'hunting-wasp,' which kills spiders, is probably *Pelopaeus spirifex.* A mason-bee (*Chalicodoma muraria*) is described by Aristotle. Ants (μύρμηξ) are very numerous : they lay up food in summer, and do not (as in colder climates) become torpid in winter.

76. The butterfly (ψυχή) is conspicuous by its absence from the poetry of Greece. Aristotle describes its metamorphosis, in **Butterflies.** the case of a common 'cabbage white,' through caterpillar (κάμπη) and chrysalis to perfect insect. Πηνίον (spindle) and ὕπερον (pestle) are chrysalids of moths, such as the common currant-moth (*Abraxas grossulariata*). Σής is a clothes-moth (Tinea sp.); ξυλόφορος is the singular caddis-like larva of the moth Psyche. The true silk-worm was unknown until the age of Justinian ; but Aristotle describes a kind of silk-worm from the island of Cos, producing cocoons (βομβύλιος, νεκύδαλος). This was a large moth, probably *Lasiocampa otus,* a relation of our oak eggar.

77. Of beetles (κολεόπτερα, κάνθαροι) the most celebrated were κάραβος, the stag-beetle, μηλολόνθη, a species of cockchafer or (in Arist.) a dung-beetle (*e.g. Ateuchus sacer*), the sacred Scarab **Beetles.** of the Egyptians. Λαμπυρίς or πυγολαμπίς is a glow-worm.

78. Next to the bee the most celebrated of Greek insects is τέττιξ, the cicada, of which several species exist, some more vocal **Cicadas.** than others. The chief singer is probably *C. plebeia,* Scop. The τεττιγόνιον is a small species, *e.g. C. orni.* The male cicada (ἠχέτης) is alone vocal.

79. Ἀκρίς is a grasshopper or locust, of which three or four migratory and destructive species occur in Greece. Various names occur, **Grasshoppers,** many of these foreign, and some referring to the larva rather **Flies, etc.** than the perfect insect (*e.g.* ἀττέλαβος, πάρνοψ, τρωξαλλίς, etc.). Ψήν is the celebrated fig-insect (*Cynips psenes,* L.), by which the caprification, or cross-fertilisation, of the fig-tree is effected.

Of flies (μυῖα) many species are mentioned, *e.g.* μύωψ, a horse-fly (Tabanus), and οἶστρος, a gad-fly (*e.g. Oestrus rufibarbis*) : but the οἶστρος of the tunny is a Crustacean parasite, probably *Cecrops latreillii,* while that of the sword-fish is *Pennella filosa.* Of a certain gnat (ἐμπίς), Aristotle describes the aquatic larva (ἀσκαρίς); this is the common 'blood-worm,' the larva of Chironomus.

Among small and offensive insects, not rare in Greece, are φθείρ, the louse (*Pediculus*), κόρις (*Cimex*), the bug, and ψύλλα (*Pulex*), the flea.

80. Of spiders (ἀράχνια), several species are described. Φαλάγγια are large venomous species, *e.g. Galeodes araneoides.* Ψύλλα is **Spiders.** a jumping kind, probably *Attus scenicus.* The most skilful spiders, whose webs Aristotle describes minutely, are such as *Epeira diadema.* *Scorpio europaeus* (σκορπίος) is common in Greece. A curious little allied, but tailless, form, found in books, is mentioned by Aristotle (σκορπιῶδες ἐν βιβλίοις, *Chelifer cancroides,* L.). Ἴουλος and πολύπους are centipedes and millipedes.

F. MARINE INVERTEBRATES.

81. Crustacea (μαλακόστρακα) are extremely numerous and abundant in the Mediterranean, and many forms are mentioned by (*e.g.*) Aristotle and Athenaeus. 'Aστακός is the common lobster (*Homarus vulgaris*), now rare in the Aegean, and κάραβος (Lat. *locusta*) is the much more abundant sea-crayfish or 'langouste,' *Palinurus vulgaris*; but the names seem to have become interchanged in modern Greek. The καρίδες are shrimps of various kinds, the κύφαι, or hunchbacks, corresponding to the prawns (*Palaemon*). Κράγγων is the modern genus *Squilla*. Καρκίνιον and κύλλαρος are hermit-crabs. Καρκίνος is, generically, a crab, and various species are distinguished, such as πάγουρος (M. Gk καβοῦρι), *C. pagurus*; μαῖα, probably *Maia squinado*; ἵππος, the 'horseman crab,' *Ocypoda cursor*; ὁ ποτάμιος, *Thelphusa fluviatilis*. Πιννοτήρης is the celebrated *Pinnotheres veterum*, the guardian of the pinna-shell.

Crustacea.

82. The cuttle-fishes (μαλάκια) are an important article of food in the Mediterranean, and were studied by Aristotle in great detail. Τεῦθος and τευθίς are large squids, or calamaries, the latter probably *Loligo vulgaris*, and the former *Todarodes sagittatus*. Σηπία is the common *Sepia officinalis* and its near allies; σηπίδιον, the little *Sepiola rondeletii*. Πολύπους is the octopus; ἐλεδώνη, ὄζολις and βολίταινα, the allied *Eledone aldrovandi* and *E. moschata*. Ναυτίλος is *Argonauta argo*, sacred to Aphrodite (cf. Callim. 1. 6).

Cuttle-fishes.

83. The molluscan shell-fish (ὀστρακόδερμα), includes the univalves (μονόθυρα, στρομβώδεις), and the bivalves (δίθυρα). Of the former the purple-shell (πόρφυρα) is the most important; *Murex brandaris*, *M. trunculus*, and *Purpura haemastoma* were the species chiefly employed. All are found in heaps at Tyre and Sidon; and Monte Testaceo, near Tarentum, is said to be built of the first, which appears also on Tarentine coins. Νηρίτης includes large species (*e.g. Ranella gigantea*), and the small Trochi (It. *naridole*). Κῆρυξ or σάλπιγξ is probably *Tritonium nodiferum*, still used as a horn or trumpet by Sardinian, and possibly by Greek, shepherds; it is one of the species which lays its eggs in a sort of honey-comb (κηριάζειν). Αἱμορρροίς (s. ἀπόρραις) probably includes, with *Aporrhais pespelicani*, the large Pteroceras. Στρόμβος includes such large forms as *Voluta*. Athenaeus and others mention the large Indian στρόμβοι and χοιρίναι (*i.e.* cowries, M. Gk γουρουνάκι). Λέπας is a limpet, *Patella*, and θαλάττιον οὖς, the common sea-ear, *Haliotis*. Κόχλος is more or less generic, as is κοκάλια (It. *quecciole*) for the smaller kinds. Κοχλίας is a snail, *Helix*, of which various kinds are referred to, *e.g.* πωματίας, *H. pomatia*. Σέσιλος is a smaller snail, *e.g. H. arbustorum*. The Laconian σέμελος, a snail, is a Semitic word. Among the naked Gastropods is λαγὼς ὁ θαλάττιος, the celebrated sea-hare, *Aplysia depilans*.

Gastropoda.

84. Among the bivalves, or Lamellibranchs, κόγχη is generic. Ὄστρεα
is the common oyster, but the meaning of λιμνόστρεα is
uncertain. Κτείς includes *Pecten Jacobaeus* and allied species.   Lamelli-
branchiata.
Σωλήν is the razor-fish, *Solen* sp. Χήμη includes such forms
as Venus, and also Spondylus (χῆμαι.βασιλικαί, s. πελωρίαι). Μῦς, μυίσκα is
the common mussel, *Mytilus edulis*. Πίννα is the great *Pinna nobilis*, celebrated for its βύσσος, still spun into a fabric at Tarentum, and celebrated
also for the little crab which is domiciled in its shell (πιννοτήρης).
85. Τήθυον is an Ascidian, or sea-squirt, eaten in the Mediterranean.
Aristotle mentions two species, a red and a pale one, probably *Cynthia
papillosa* and *Phallusia mammillata*. Of the Echinodermata, ἀστήρ is a
starfish, *e.g. A. rubens*. Ἐχῖνος ὁ ἐσθιόμενος is *E. esculentus*. Other
species are ἐχ. ὁ λευκός, ἐχινομήτρα, βρύσσος, σπάταγγος, none of them
to be identified with certainty. Among the Coelenterata, the chief is the
precious coral, *Corallium rubrum*, κοράλλιον, λιθόδενδρον (Diosc.): it is
probably alluded to in Pindar, λείριον ἄνθεμον ποντίας ἐέρσας. Ἀκαλήφη is
a sea-anemone, *Actinia*, of which certain species were, and are still, eaten
in the Mediterranean: κνίδαι are probably similar, but inedible forms.
Πνεύμων appears to be a jelly-fish or Medusa. Several species of sponge
(σπόγγος) are mentioned by Aristotle and others, *e.g.* τράγος, ἀπλυσία, etc.
The fine-textured sponge of Achilles, used for lining or padding armour,
is probably the Turkey sponge.

    Aristotle's *Historia Animalium* sums up the scientific zoology of the Greeks.
The chief annotated editions are those of J. G. Schneider (1811),
Aubert and Wimmer (1868), and the recent Oxford translation   Bibliography.
(1911). The works of the older naturalists, from Albertus Magnus, through
Aldrovandi, Gesner, Belon, Rondelet, Jonston, Turner, Willoughby, to the days
of Linnaeus and Cuvier, teem with references to Aristotle. While allusions to
natural history run through the whole of Greek literature, the works of Herodotus,
Aelian (who transmits many fabulous and mystical tales, especially from Egypt),
Athenaeus and Oppian of the *Halieutica* and his Syrian imitator are of particular
interest to the zoologist. Among lost works, of which small fragments remain
in Athenaeus and elsewhere, two are above all others to be regretted, the
Ornithology of Alexander the Myndian, and the περὶ Ὁμοίων of Speusippus.
    O. Keller's *Antike Tierwelt* (two vols., Leipzig, 1909, 1913) is the best account
of ancient Natural History, especially from the side of art and archaeology; an
earlier work, *Die Thiere des classischen Alterthums* (1887), is still useful. Imhoof-
Blumer and Keller's *Thiere und Pflanzenbilder auf Münzen und Gemmen* (1889)
is a good compendium of coin-types.
    Among many other books and papers on classical Natural History, the
following are noteworthy: Apostolides et Yves Delage, *Les Mollusques d'après
Aristote*, Arch. de Zool. Exp. et Gén., IX. 1881; Aubert, *Cephalopoden des
Aristoteles*, Z. f. Wiss. Zool., 1862; J. M. Boraston, *The Birds of Homer*,
J.H.S. XXXI. 1911; Buchholz, *Die drei Naturreiche nach Homer*, Leipzig, 1873;
Cuvier, *Espèces d'écrevisses connues des anciens*, Paris, An I.; Dedekind,
Purpurkunde, Berlin, 1898; Th. Gill, *The remarkable story of a Greek Fish,
the Glanis*, Washington, 1907; Groshans, *Fauna Homeri et Hesiodi*, Lugd.

Bat., 1839–43; Hoffman and Jordan, *Catalogue of the Fishes of Greece*, Pr. Ac. N.S. Philad., 1892; W. Houghton, *Natural History of the Ancients*, London, n.d.; Koerner, *Homerisches Thierwelt*, Berlin, 1880; Lacaze-Duthiers, *Mém. sur la Pourpre*, Ann. Sc. Nat., (4) XII. 185; Lenz, *Zoologie der alten Griechen und Römer*, Gotha, 1856; Locard, *Hist. des Mollusques dans l'Antiquité*, Lyon, 1884; T. E. Lones, *Aristotle's Researches in Natural Science*, London, 1912; Lorentz, *Die Taube im Alterthume*, Warzen, 1886; E. von Martens, *Die classischen Conchyliennamen*, Stuttgart, 1860; Joh. Müller, *Die Haien des Aristoteles*, Berlin, 1839–42; Oder, *Der Wiedehopf in der griechischen Sage*, Philol. 1888; Pischenger, *Das Vogelnest bei den gr. Dichtern*, München, 1907; Rolleston, *Domestic Cat of the Ancients*, J. Anat. and Phys., 1868; Schlieben, *Die Pferde des Alterthums*, Leipzig, 1867; J. G. Schneider, *Die Krebsarten des Aristoteles*, Berlin, 1807; Sundevall, *Thierarten des Aristoteles*, Stockholm, 1863; D'Arcy W. Thompson, *Glossary of Greek Birds*, Oxford, 1895; *Egyptian Fish-names used by Greek Writers*, Jl. Egypt. Archaeol., 1928; John Young, *Malacostraca of Aristotle*, Ann. Mag. N. H., 1865; Klek u. Armbruster, *Bienenkunde des Aristoteles*, Leipzig, 1919; A. W. Mair's 'Loeb' edition of Oppian, 1928.

The following works constitute the chief part of our scanty modern literature on the zoology of Greece: Geoffroy St Hilaire, *Expédition scientifique en Morée* (vol. III.), Paris, 1832–35; Edward Forbes, *Mollusca and Radiata of the Aegean*, Br. Ass. Rep. (13), 1843; Von der Mühle, *Ornithologie Griechenlands*, Leipzig, 1844; Erhard, *Fauna der Cycladen*, Leipzig, 1858; Lindermayer, *Die Vögel Griechenlands*, Passau, 1860; Krüper, *Zeiten des Gehens und Kommens der Vögel Griechenlands*, Schleswig, 1875; Heldreich, *Faune de la Grèce*, Athènes, 1878; Apostolides, *La Pêche en Grèce*, Athens, 1907.

I. 4. FLORA.

86. THE Mediterraneo-Oriental is one of the best defined of botanical regions. It is bounded on the north by the high-lands which extend from the Pyrenees to the Hindu-Kush, on the south by the deserts which continue from the Sahara to Baluchistan. It has been the cradle of successive civilizations which have transmitted westward the plants they had domesticated and the products they had utilised. A so-called prehistoric stream had flowed north of it from Central Asia carrying its primitive food-plants and penetrating into the Mediterranean peninsulas.

Three continents contributed to the material equipment of Greece. Asia gave its cereals and the vine already developed for wine-making, Africa the olive and flax and Europe its own pulses. But it possesses little land available for grain and the necessity of importing it in exchange for wine and oil demanded the command of the sea for which its forests supplied the material. A widespread maritime commerce brought the luxuries and refinements of urban life. The food of the rural population was as frugal as it still is in Southern Europe; that of the Arcadians was proverbial; every possible native plant was used for food, and the fact that some were only eaten in time of famine tells its own tale. Incidentally a knowledge was acquired of other properties possessed by native plants and an empirical medicine was built up which has descended to our own day.

Necessity made the Greeks botanists; they possessed a name for every conspicuous Greek plant, and the majority of these names have come down to us. It may be due to a difference of national temperament but nothing of the kind has survived from the Romans, if it ever existed. Our knowledge of Greek botany begins with Theophrastus. A pupil and friend of Aristotle he occupies a unique position in the history of science. He stands alone without successor for two thousand years; his method was essentially modern and when the study of botany was resumed in the middle ages it advanced simply from the point where Theophrastus left it. His writings have the air of lecture-notes to be expanded on delivery; he appealed to an interested and instructed audience, for in enforcing a point he cites strings of mere names which must have been familiar. Alexander like Napoleon took scientific experts on his expedition; their reports are lost except what Theophrastus and Arrian have preserved; their description of the citron was borrowed by Virgil. Theophrastus reveals himself as an accomplished gardener with little to learn from modern horticultural practice; and he was keen to investigate its underlying principles. Market-gardening was an important industry in the neighbourhood of cities.

On the revival of learning it was assumed that the secrets of remedial medicine were to be discovered in the writings of Dioscorides alone. Vast commentaries were devoted to the identification of the plants he described, as the thread of tradition had been wholly broken. The result was vitiated by the attempt to find them in Western and Central Europe, the flora of which has little in common with that of the Mediterranean region. The difficulty has continued to the present day. But Halacsy has now given us a scientific enumeration of the native plants of Greece, and we can at any rate do something to wed a Greek name to a plant actually Greek.

In the following pages plants of more than scientific interest are enumerated with brief comments and identifications.

87 Oak, in a wide sense, δρῦς, which originally simply meant 'tree'; δρῦς is opposed to pines, πεύκη and πίτυς, in Homer, who thus recognises the distinction between broad- and needle-leaved trees (κωνοφόρα); the different species (δρυὸς γένη) received distinctive names:—Valonia oak, φηγός, *Quercus Aegilops*, sacred to Zeus (ὑπὸ φηγῷ πεφυκυίῃ Διὸς ἱρόν, Hdt. II. 56); the name was probably first applied to the acorns, which were, as they still are, eaten roasted (φηγοὺς σποδιοῦσι πρὸς τὸ πῦρ, Plat. *Rep.* 372 C) and thence transferred to the tree; βάλανος (whence Valonia is derived) was 'acorn' indiscriminately, in Homer the food of swine, but the Pythian oracle called the Arcadians βαλανηφάγοι, and according to Galen they continued to feed on acorns when all other Greeks were using cereals: Turkey oak, called ἄσπρις in Macedonia, αἰγίλωψ in Anatolia, *Quercus Cerris*; yielded bitter acorns and worthless timber: Holm oak, πρῖνος, *Quercus Ilex*; the acorns (ἄκυλοι) were fed to swine in Hom.

(Margin note: Trees, δένδρα, (a) broad-leaved.)

(*kalin* is Armenian for acorn): True oak, ἐτυμόδρυς, *Quercus Robur*; extended to Macedonia, and afforded food for swine: Scrub oak, πλατύφυλλος, *Quercus lanuginosa*; the prevalent species on both Aegean shores; modern experience confirms the statement of Theophrastus, πρὸς τὴν χρείαν τὴν οἰκοδομικὴν χείριστον: Cork oak, φελλός, *Quercus Suber*; first described by Theophrastus but now almost extinct in Greece and probably never plentiful; Pausanias found it in Arcadia without a name: ἀλίφλοιος, *Quercus Pseudo-suber* (?); Mt Ida: Gall oak, ἡμερίς, *Quercus infectoria*; described by Theophr. as from Mt Ida, but is not native to Greece; it produces 'Aleppo Galls,' κηκῖδες, which were and are still used in tanning. Poplar: Black Poplar, αἴγειρος, *Populus nigra*; literally 'wool-tree' from the fluffy seeds; formed the ἄλσεα Περσεφονείης of Homer, and grew with elms (Theoc. VII. 8): White Poplar (Abele), λεύκη, *Populus alba*, sacred to Heracles (Theoc. VII. 8), and hence used for wreaths (Ar. *Nub.* 1007): Aspen, κερκίς, *Populus tremula*; the name, meaning primarily a shuttle, was applied to the tree on account of its swaying leaves. Elm, πτελέα, *Ulmus glabra*; the species characteristic of S.E. Europe and W. Asia (Ar. *Nub.* 1008, Theoc. VII. 65). Plane, πλάτανος, *Platanus orientalis*; an Asiatic tree reaching its Western limit in Greece; often planted (ἐν ἀγορᾷ δ' αὖ πλάτανον εὖ διαφυτεύσομεν, Ar. *Fr.* 162). Beech, ὀξύη; a northern tree, not found south of Thessaly. Ash: Ash proper, βουμέλιος, *Fraxinus excelsior*; only in Macedonia: Manna Ash, μελία, *Fraxinus Ornus*; used for spear-shafts in Homer. Maple, ζυγία, *Acer campestre*: σφένδαμνος, *A. monspessulanum*. Hop-Hornbeam, ὀστρύα, *Ostrya carpinifolia*. Silver Lime, φιλύρα, *Tilia argentea*; ἔχον φλοιὸν ἐξ οὗ τοὺς στεφάνους πλέκουσι, Phot. Nettle Tree, λωτὸς τὸ δένδρον, *Celtis australis*; identified by Pliny with the λωτὸς τῶν λωτοφάγων; the wood was used for flutes (Eur. *Tro.* 544), statues, furniture and costly doors. Willow, ἰτέα: μέλαινα, *Salix amplexicaulis*: λευκή, *S. alba*: ἰτέαι ὠλεσίκαρποι, Hom., being supposed to shed their seed prematurely; primitive wicker shields were made of willow (σακέεσσι ἰτείνοισι, Theoc. XVI. 79): crack willow, ἐλίκη, *S. fragilis*. Alder, κλήθρη, *Alnus glutinosa*; grew in Calypso's isle. Judas Tree, σημύδα, *Cercis Siliquastrum*. Storax, στύραξ, *Storax officinalis*; yielded a fragrant resin still used for incense (Hdt. III. 107). Terebinth, τέρμινθος, *Pistacia Terebinthus*; yielded τερεβίνθινον ἔλαιον, the original oil of turpentine, whence the name; the wood, said by Theophrastus (*H.P.* v. 3. 2) to be blacker than ebony, was used for knife-handles, the galls (ibid. III. 15. 4) for tanning.

88. Pine: Corsican Pine, πεύκη or πίτυς in Homer, *Pinus Laricio*; called
Trees, Corsican, because the finest trees grew in Corsica (Theophr.
(*b*) Conifers, *H.P.* v. 8. 1); used for ship-building (Hom. *Il.* 13. 390):
κωνοφόρα. Stone Pine, πίτυς κωνοφόρος, πεύκη ἥμερος, *Pinus Pinea*; probably of Asiatic origin and cultivated; supplied crowns for Isthmian games; the Bacchic θύρσος bore the cones, the seeds, πιτυίδες, were eaten, hence the inducement βάλλει δὲ καὶ ἁ πίτυς ὕψοθε κώνους, Theocr. v. 49: Aleppo Pine, πεύκη παραλία, *Pinus halepensis*: Oriental Spruce, πεύκη Ἰδαία, *Picea orientalis*; yielded ψάγδας (*pix Idaea*), used for flavouring wine: Silver Fir,

ἐλάτη, *Abies pectinata*; supplied masts for ships (Hom. *Od.* II. 424); it was the tall ἐλάτη of Ida (Hom. *Il.* XIV. 288), and Strabo's καλὴ πεύκη; it furnished the material for the Trojan Horse (Virg. *A.* II. 16, *secta abiete*). Cypress, κυπάρισσος, an Asiatic tree early introduced into Europe; the fragrant wood (Hom. *Od.* v. 64) was used for ship-building, chests and coffins (Thuc. II. 34); it was exported from Crete, where it was thought to be indigenous (ἡ δε καλὴ Κρήτη κυπάριττον τοῖσι θεοῖσι, Hermipp.). Cedar, κέδρος, *Juniperus excelsa*, a tree of W. Asia reaching 100 ft.; used in Syria for ship-building (Theophr. *H.P.* v. 7. 1); (had the Greeks known the so-called 'Cedar of Lebanon,' they would have called it πεύκη): Prickly Cedar, ὀξύκεδρος, *Juniperus Oxycedrus*, a shrub; the fragrant wood is useless except for fuel; it is the θύον of Hom. *Od.* v. 60: Phoenician Cedar, ἄρκευθος, *Juniperus phoenicea*, a shrub of which the wood was used in Egypt for embalming: Juniper, κεδρίς: Savin, βράθυ. Yew, μῖλος; its poisonous qualities were recognised.

89. The rocky shores of the Mediterranean are clothed with a shrubby aromatic vegetation called *maquis*; its principal constituents are:—Myrtle, μυρσίνη and μύρτος: Mastick, σχῖνος: Rosemary, λιβανωτίς: Cistus, κίσθος: French Lavender, στοιχάς: Heath, ἐρείκη, *Erica arborea*; the *bruyère* of the 'briar' pipe: φιλυρέα, *Phillyrea media*: ἀσπάλαθος, *Calycotome villosa*; a spinous shrub which replaces our gorse, and which Plato (*Rep.* 616A) describes as the torment of tyrants in Tartarus. Over these shrubs scramble Smilax, μῖλαξ, used for garlands, and ἀσπάραγος, *Asparagus acutifolius*, the young shoots of which were eaten, as were those of Butcher's Broom, μυρσίνη ἀγρία, *Ruscus aculeatus*—as they are still in Sicily. Myrtle (not mentioned in Homer) was sacred to Aphrodite; the manufacture of wreaths in her honour was an industry (Ar. *Thesm.* 448); at the festival of Europa in Corinth a myrtle wreath, ἑλλωτίς, 20 cubits in circumference, was carried (Ath. 678A). Laurel, δάφνη, was sacred to Apollo and worshippers carried branches (Eur. *Ion* 422); the wood was found the best to make a fire-drill, τρύπανον, for producing sacrificial fire (Theophr. *H.P.* v. 9. 7): Alexandrian Laurel, δάφνη ἀλεξανδρεία, *Ruscus Hypoglossum*. Ivy, κισσός; sacred to Dionysus; the thyrsus was wreathed with it (ἀνὰ θύρσον τε τινάσσων κισσῷ τε στεφανωθείς, Eur. *Bacch.* 80). Chaste Tree, ἄγνος and λύγος, *Vitex Agnus-castus*; ὃν ἐν τοῖς θεσμοφορίοις ὑπεστρώννυντο αἱ γυναῖκες, Schol. Nicander, *Theriaca*, 71. Oleander, νήριον and ῥοδόδενδρον. Box, πύξος; wood used for mule-yokes (Hom. *Il.* 24. 269), and writing-tablets (Ar. *Fr.* 671). Dane-wort, χαμαιάκτη. Goat Willow, ἐλέαγνος, *Salix Caprea*; literally 'marsh-lamb' from the woolly seed catkins (hence 'Lamb's tails'); grew on the floating islands in Lake Copais (Theophr. *H.P.* IV. 10. 2). Christ's Thorn, παλίουρος, *Paliurus australis*. Alaternus, φιλύκη, *Rhamnus Alaternus*. Tamarisk, μυρίκη. Honeysuckle, περικλύμενον, *Lonicera etrusca*. Rest-harrow, αἰγίπυρος and -ον, *Ononis antiquorum*; a weed (*Anth. Pal.* app. 120). Mistletoe, ὕφεαρ, *Viscum album*: ἰξός, *Loranthus europaeus*

Shrubs, θάμνοι.

90. Few plants with attractive flowers are noticed in Homer and there
is no trace of their cultivation. The later Greeks had a keen
eye for them, and Theophrastus (*H.P.* vi. 6) enumerates a
large number used for garlands, many of which must have
been grown for the purpose:—Cabbage Rose, ῥοδῆ and ῥόδον, *Rosa centifolia*;
of Asiatic origin; the name is a Semitic loan-word, it only occurs in Homer

Coronary
plants,
στεφανώματα.

Fig. 1.   Fig. 2.

Fig. 1. The ὑάκινθος of Homer, reduced from nature.   Fig. 2. Inflorescence
of ὑάκινθος γραπτά (Theocr.), reduced from nature; the detached petal is
drawn nearly natural size and inverted to show markings.

in epithets; first mentioned in Archilochus (25); subject to mildew (ἀλμᾷ
νοσηματικῶς, Theophr. *C.P.* vi. 10. 5). Lily, κρίνον λευκόν, λείριον, *Lilium
candidum*; of oriental origin, represented on a Minoan vase; name probably
a Semitic loan-word; in Homer only the adj. λειριόεις, meaning merely
'white': Turk's Cap Lily, κρίνον πορφυροῦν, *Lilium chalcedonicum*: Martagon
Lily, ἡμεροκαλλές, *Lilium Martagon*. Violet, ἴον μέλαν and ἰωνιά; only once
in Homer (*Od.* v. 72). Gilliflower, λευκόϊον, *Matthiola incana*. Narcissus,
νάρκισσος; ἔσωθεν πορφυροειδές (Diosc.), *Narcissus poeticus*: καλλίβοτρυς,
Narcissus Tazetta; ἀρχαῖον στεφάνωμα to Demeter and Kore (Soph. *O.C.*

682); also called λείριον. Hyacinth (Fig. 1), ὑάκινθος, *Scilla bifolia*; found
by W. Leaf on Mt Ida; in the fifth-century Codex of Dioscorides at Vienna
the figure represents the Anatolian *Scilla cernua*; there was therefore a
continuous tradition that *v. ἀγρία* of Theophrastus was a blue *Scilla*; as
early as Columella the name was given, without great violence, to the nearly
allied *Hyacinthus orientalis*, whence are derived our garden hyacinths; the
cult of Hyacinthus transferred the name to the blue Larkspur (Fig. 2),
Delphinium Ajacis, *v. σπαρτή* (Theophr. *H.P.* VI. 8. 2), and, because the
petals were marked with AI, γραπτά (Theocr. x. 28). Crocus, κρόκος: the
Greeks included under the name the golden-flowered species; that of
Mt Ida, which 'brake like fire' (Tennyson), is *C. gargaricus*; the κ. χρυσαυγής
in Soph. *O.C.* is *C. Olivieri*, or *C. aureus*; Eur. *Ion* 890 refers to *C. chrys-
anthus*, a mountain species; see also Saffron. Corn Flag, ξιφίον, *Gladiolus
segetum*. Rose Campion, λυχνίς, *Lychnis coronaria*. Wall-flower, φλόξ,
φλόγινον. Carnation, διόσανθος,
Dianthus inodorus; in Minoan
fresco in Crete. Anemone, ἀνεμώνη
λειμωνία,*Anemone coronaria*. Gold-
flower, ἐλειόχρυσος, *Helianthe-
mum siculum*. Drop-wort, οἰνάνθη,
Spiraea Filipendula. All these were
used for floral garlands, but others
were made of aromatic plants.
Such were :—Lavender, ἴφυον:
Water Mint, σισύμβριον: Thyme,
ἔρπυλλος: Calamint, ἐλένιον: Worm-
wood, ἀβρότονον. Some other
plants which were not coronary
may find a place here:—Asphodel
(Fig. 3), ἀσφόδελος, *Asphodelus
ramosus*; the most conspicuous
feature in Greek meadows and so
of the Elysian fields (Hom. *Od.*
XI. 539); ἀνθέρικος was the flower-
stalk; the tuberous roots were
eaten by the poor with mallow
(νήπιοι, οὐδ᾽ ἴσασιν, ὅσῳ πλέον
ἥμισυ παντός, | οὐδ᾽ ὅσον ἐν μαλάχῃ
τε καὶ ἀσφοδέλῳ μέγ᾽ ὄνειαρ, Hes.
Op. 41). Epimenides is said to
have lived on these; they were
planted on graves for the benefit

Fig. 3. Asphodel, very much reduced,
reproduced from Bodæus à Stapel,
Theophrastus, 871.

of the dead. Water-lily, σίδη, *Nymphaea alba*. Peony, γλυκυσίδη. Primrose,
δωδεκάθεον. Bear's-foot, ἄκανθος, *Acanthus mollis*; origin of a famous
decorative pattern (Theocr. I. 55). Black Bryony, βρυωνία, *Tamus com-*

munis; the young shoots were eaten like asparagus. Grass-wracks, φῦκος (Hom. *Il.* IX. 7), *Zostera marina* and *Cymodocea nodosa* (ὅμοιον τῇ ἀγρώστει, Theophr. *H.P.* IV. 6. 6). Duckweed, φακὸς ὁ ἐπὶ τελμάτων (Diosc.), *Lemna minor*. Of Ferns there were:—Maiden-hair, ἀδίαντον and πολύτριχον: Oak-fern, δρυοπτερίς, *Asplenium Onopteris*: Polypody, πολυπόδιον: Male-fern, πτερίς, a vermifuge: Bracken, θηλυπτερίς: Milt-waste, ἡμιόνιον, *Asplenium Ceterach*: Hart's-tongue, σκολοπένδριον: Water-wort, τριχομανές, *Asplenium Trichomanes*. Other flowerless plants were:—Horse-tail, ἵππουρις, *Equisetum maximum*: Liverwort, λειχήν, *Marchantia polymorpha*: Tree moss, βρύον, *Usnea barbata*, used for bedding (Theocr. XXI. 7). Of marine algae the Greeks distinguished about a dozen; as Oyster Green, βρύον θαλάσσιον, which is ubiquitous: φῦκος φοῖνιξ, *Delessaria laciniata*: φῦκος θαλάσσιον τὸ πλατύ, *Padina mediterranea*.

91. The cultivation of the wheats, barley, oat and millets was pre-historic; that of spelt recent research has shown to be modern; it was unknown to the Greeks. Of wheats there were three kinds, all of Asiatic origin:—(i) Wheat κατ' ἐξοχήν, πυρός, *Triticum vulgare*; no plant has played so large a part in the destiny of mankind; two races were distinguished, winter wheat, χειμόσπορος, σίλιγνις (*siligo*), of Roman origin, and spring wheat, τρίμηνος and σητάνιος; words have preserved the successive stages by which wheat was made available for food; the primitive practice was to rub the grain, χῖδρα, from the ear, ἀθήρ, by hand; it was roasted, πεφρυγμένα, to make it more palatable, a still surviving Eastern practice; the use of a mortar produced wheat-groats, ἀλείατα, but it required a mill to grind a coarse meal, κρίμνον, meal, ἄλευρον, and flour, σεμίδαλις, which was a Syrian export (Hermipp. *Phorm.* I. 22); from the latter bran, πίτυρον, was separated by 'bolting'; this was made into a sort of bread, πιτυρίας, of little nutriment; paste, κόλλα, was made from σεμίδαλις for mending books; κρίμνον was eaten in frumenty or porridge, πόλτος; bread in various forms was a later development and was never the food of the populace: (ii) Rice-wheat (Fig. 4 *a*), ὄλυρα, δίκοκκος (ζέα), *Triticum dicoccum*, played an important part in antiquity, though since little grown except in Germany for the manufacture of starch; it is now identified as the Roman *far* (*primus antiquo is Latio cibus*, Plin. XVIII. 83); it was an important cereal in Egypt, where according to Pliny it was made into a fine flour, ἀθάρη, *ador*; bread made from it was thought less nutritious than from ordinary wheat; coarsely ground it was eaten as a frumenty; ptisans were made from it, τράγος, and, when decorticated, χόνδρος; this was an export from Italy (Hermipp. *Phorm.* I. 6); it was produced of good quality in Megara, that of Thessaly was inferior; (iii) one-grained wheat (Fig. 4 *b*), τίφη, ἁπλῆ ζέα, *Triticum monococcum*; now extends in a wild state from Achaea to Mesopotamia, but is little cultivated anywhere; Schliemann found it at Troy; used much as Rice-wheat; it was the *Kussémeth* of the O.T., wrongly translated 'spelt' in R.V. Darnel, αἶρα, was a harmful weed amongst wheat, as its grain was κεφαλαλγής. Barley,

[margin note:] Cereals, σιτηρά.

κριθή, ἀκοστή; of W. Asiatic origin; the chaff is adherent to the grain (γυμνόκριθον was a naked kind): to make this friable it was roasted, κάχρυς, like American pop-corn, in a φρύγετρον, and then reduced to groats, ἄλφιτα; from these was made with water and olive oil a frumenty or porridge, μᾶζα, which, seasoned with salt and other condiments, was the common food of the people; Plato calls such τροφή γενναία; Pliny notices the distinction between the ordinary food of the Roman and Greek peoples (*videtur tam puls ignota Graeciae fuisse quam Italiae polenta*, *N.H.* XVIII. 84); barley yielded a fine flour, πάλη, but it was thought inferior to wheat for bread; beer, ζῦθος and κοῦρμι, was made from it (οἶνος ἐκ κριθέων, Hdt. II. 77). Rye, βρίζα, native of S. Russia, yielded an ill-smelling black bread in Thrace and Macedonia. Oat, βρόμος, native of E. Europe; eaten in porridge; in Mysia only used as a famine food, but fed to draught-cattle; the name also includes the wild oat, *avena*, a weed of cultivated ground, *Avena barbata*. Rice, ὄρυζα (hellenized from an Indian loan-word), became known through Alexander's expedition; it found its way to Greece, but was dear and only used for a ptisan (*ptisanarium oryzæ*, Hor.); ὀρίνδης ἄρτος (Soph. *Fr.* 532) reflects Old Persian *vrinda* and refers to rice by vague report. Millet, κέγχρος, *milium*, *Panicum miliaceum*,

Fig. 4 *a*.
Rice-wheat.

Fig. 4 *b*.
One-grained wheat.

(From Engler and Prantl, *Nat. Pflanzenf.* vol. ii. part 2, p. 84.)

conjectured to be of Arabian and Egyptian origin: Italian Millet, ἔλυμος and μελίνη, *panicum*, *Setaria italica*; their culture, of great antiquity, only persisted among more northern races such as the μελινοφάγοι in Thrace; they are only available for porridge and were displaced in Greece by more valuable cereals, the Lacedaemonians alone continuing to eat ἔλυμος; both are important food grains in India. (Ragi, βόσμορος, *Eleusine Coracana*, a staple food of the poor in India, was imported into Europe at the beginning of the Christian era: Guinea Corn, *Sorghum vulgare*, though of African origin spreading eastward, was unknown to the Greeks; but Theophrastus mentions a cereal which poisoned their horses in India, and this Guinea corn is apt to do when green.) Sesame, σήσαμον and σησαμῆ; apparently of African origin spreading eastward; it is *the* oil plant of India; with the Assyrians it supplied the place of olive oil (Hdt. I. 193); thence it found its way westward again, but, though its name is a Semitic loan-word (*semsem*), it was unknown to the Hebrews; the seeds were sprinkled on cakes (Ar. *Pax* 869). Opium Poppy, μήκων; of Mediterranean origin; seeds used for bread (Diosc.), but only like *sesamum* (Galen).

92. Pulses serve as meat-substitutes and are an important food for southern peoples; mostly of local origin their use is of great antiquity. Bean, κύαμος; eaten in various ways, roasted (Theocr. VII. 66) or boiled, especially green and immature; *Pythagoricae sententiae damnata, quoniam mortuorum animae sint in ea,* Plin. XVIII. 118; (ὁ Αἰγύπτιος κύαμος was not a leguminous plant, but *Nelumbium*, allied to water-lilies; the edible seeds are buried in a broad receptacle, κιβώριον): Pease, πίσος; not mentioned in Homer but in later ages used like the bean; pease porridge was popular (Ar. *Eq.* 1171): Lentil, φακός; not mentioned in Homer, but much cultivated (and improved) from a remote time in Egypt and an important food in Greece; φακῆ (also φακοί) was a dish of lentils, which shows they were eaten whole; but they were the food of the poor (Ar. *Pl.* 1004); Pherecrates objects τοῦ στόματος ὄζει κακόν, steeped in vinegar they may have been more tolerable; φακοπτισάνη was a lentil soup: Chick-pea, ἐρέβινθος; coupled in Homer (*Il.* XIII. 589) with κύαμοι, whence Hehn identifies with πίσος, but Plato does the same (*Rep.* 372 C), and from Theophrastus onwards the identification is certain; eaten boiled with salt or roasted (Ar. *Pax* 1136), but not in porridge: Calavance, δόλιχος and φασίολος, *Dolichos sinensis*; of Asiatic origin, now cultivated in all warm countries; the pods were eaten whole with oil, either raw or cooked: Vetch, ὄροβος, *Vicia Ervilia*; grown for fodder, but seed only (found at Troy) used for famine food; the ὀρόβινον ἄλευρον was however medicinal: Lupine, θέρμος; Galen calls it πολύχρηστος; the seeds were eaten boiled with a sharp sauce: Fenugreek, τῆλις, βούκερας; seeds eaten like lupine.

Pulses,
χέδροπα.

93. Dog's tooth grass, ἄγρωστις, *Cynodon Dactylon*; ubiquitous in Greece: Lucerne, μηδική; introduced apparently from Asia Minor; the most important cultivated fodder crop (ὅλη τῇ πόα χρῶνται οἱ κτηνοτρόφοι ἀντὶ ἀγρωστέως, Diosc. II. 147); its familiarity is shewn by Ar. *Eq.* 606, ἤσθιον δὲ τοὺς παγούρους ἀντὶ ποίας μηδικῆς: Tree medick, κύτισος, *Medicago arborea*; a native shrub; Amphilochus the Athenian wrote a treatise on it, which only survives in Pliny's summary, *miris laudibus praedicatur pabulo omnium* (XIII. 130): Trefoil, λωτός (τρίφυλλος), *Trifolium fragiferum*; grew in hayfields (Diosc. IV. 111); (λωτός is a name applied to a number of widely differing plants, but the idea of edibility seems to underlie them all): Carob, κερωνία; native of W. Asia; the pods, κεράτια, were fed to swine in Syria (Luke XV. 16), and

Fodder Plants,
βοσκή.

imported into Greece; Galen, finding them indigestible, wishes they had not been.

94. Vine, ἄμπελος; of W. Asiatic origin; Theophrastus knew that it grew in the Hindu-Kush (*H.P.* IV. 4. 11); neither the Greeks nor the Romans had any distinctive name for it; both ἄμπελος and *vitis*, like 'vine' in English, were applied to other climbing plants; whatever may be said of *vinum*, οἶνος is a Semitic loan-word, *yāyin*, which apparently always meant wine, but οἶνος was used for fermented drinks generally (οἶνος ἐκ κριθέων, beer, Hdt. II. 77); the vine was grown in Europe in the age of bronze, and widely in Greece in the Homeric age; the wild stock, *Vitis silvestris*, has probably always existed in S. Europe; it is more or less diœcious, and the flowers of the barren form, οἰνάνθη, were dried and used as a perfume; the cultivated grape-vine and its product travelled west from Asia and found their way independently into the Italian and Greek peninsulas; in the Eastern Mediterranean the vine was not supported (but χαμῖτις), though sometimes grown up trees (ἀναδενδράς): Oleaster, κότινος, *Olea Oleaster*; native of E. Mediterranean shores; the wild stock of the olive (τὸ ἄγριον τῆς ἐλάας, Theophr.), on which in later practice it was grafted; used for crowns in Olympic games (Ar. *Pl.* 586): Olive, ἐλαία; the traditions point to its being an introduced tree and not developed culturally from the oleaster; Schweinfurth traces it to S. Nubia (Αἰθιοπικὴ ἐλαία, Diosc.); fabled to have been first planted by Athena on the Acropolis, whence the propagated descendants were μορίαι, cuttings: Fig; native of E. Mediterranean countries; the wild stock, ἐρινεός, simply mentioned by Homer; its fruit, ὄλυνθος and ἐρινόν, was worthless (ἀχρεῖος ὢν ἐς βρῶσιν, Soph. *Fr.* 190); the cultivated fig, συκῆ, came from Asia not earlier than Archilochus; it bore two crops in the year (διφόρου συκῆς, Ar. *Eccl.* 778), the earlier called πρόδρομοι; it is bisexual, and figs without fertilisation do not mature seeds and cannot be dried; to effect this, ἐρινάζειν, branches of the ἐρινεός were hung near; the fig-wasp, ψήν, which lives in its fruit, carried the pollen to the σῦκον; dried figs, ἰσχάδες, supplied an important food to the Athenians: Plum-tree, κοκκυμηλέα, *Prunus domestica*; of Asiatic origin; the Damson-plum, δαμασκηνόν, was the finest; the Bullace, προύνη, and sloe, βράβυλος, are European: Bird-cherry, κέρασος, *Prunus Avium*; a native forest-tree: Cornel, κράνεια, *Cornus mas*; native; wood used for spear-shafts and bows; the berries fed to swine in Homer: Pomegranate, ῥόα and σίδη (= σίβδη); of Asiatic origin (σίδη = Persian *sêb*), first mentioned in Empedocles, fifth century (the passages in Hom. *Od.* are suspect); the flower was κύτινος and βαλαύστιον: Citron, μῆλον μηδικόν; Asiatic; Dioscorides calls it κεδρόμηλον; the fruits imported into Greece (where they were not eaten but used to preserve clothes from moths), were supposed to be produced by the κέδρος; the word became *citrus* in Latin, which returned to Greece as κίτριον: Quince, κυδωνέα; native of W. Asia, first cultivated in Crete, whence the name; fruit ἑσπερίδων μῆλα, κυδώνιον and στρούθιον: Pear, ἄπιος, ὄγχνη (Hom.); European; pears

Fruits,
καρποφόρα.

were exported from Euboea (ἀπ᾽ Εὐβοίας ἀπίους, Hermipp. *Phorm.* I. 17):
Wild Pear, ἄχερδος, *Pyrus amygdaliformis*; native of S. Europe; a spinous
shrub or tree (Hom. *Od.* XIV. 10); (κοίλη ἀ. is a landmark in Soph. *O.C.* 1596);
ἀχράς is the fruit (τῶν ἀπίων μοχθηρά, Theophr.); Aristophanes (*Eccl.* 355)
jokes about its astringency: Apple, μηλέα; native of S. shores of Black Sea,
but naturalised in the Mediterranean region in prehistoric times: Sorb, ὄη
and οἴη, *Sorbus domestica*; a tree of S. Europe with an austere fruit, which
was split, dried and ground into meal: Mulberry, συκάμινον, later, μορέα,
Morus nigra (Galen scoffs at the use of names 600 years old); native
south of the Caspian, finding its way west through Syria; often confused on
account of resemblance of leaves with συκόμορον, which is a fig; both names
have a common origin in Hebrew; the white mulberry was not known to
the Greeks; μόρον seems used indiscriminately for the fruit of mulberry and
blackberry; Aeschylus and Sophocles (in Ath. 51 D) describe the successive
colours of the latter. Nothing in the way of *agrestia poma* apparently came
amiss to a Greek peasant: μέσπιλον stood for several nearly related trees,
as Medlar, ἐπιμηλίς: Oriental thorn, ἀνθηδών, *Crataegus orientalis*: Blackberry, βάτος (Hom. *Od.* XXIV. 230), *Rubus ulmifolius*: Raspberry, βάτος
Ἰδαία: Strawberry-tree, κόμαρος, *Arbutus Unedo*; a native tree; Galen speaks
contemptuously of the mawkish fruit, μιμαίκυλον, and Dioscorides says it is
unwholesome: Dog-rose, κυνόσβατος, *Rosa canina*; a shepherd in Theocr.
(v. 92) thought it could not compete with the rose of gardens; Galen says
that peasants got a poor nutriment from the 'hips': Strawberry was native,
but no name for it has come down to us.

95. Chestnut, Διὸς βάλανος; a tree of Pontus which has spread westward to the Mediterranean; its fruit was καστανικὸν κάρυον
Nuts, κάρυα.
and Σαρδιαναὶ βάλανοι; that it was introduced is inferred·
from neither tree nor fruit having any vernacular name; in its unimproved
condition it was little esteemed as a source of food; a superior sort was
exported from Pontus (τὰς δὲ Διὸς βαλάνους Παφλαγόνες παρέχουσι, Hermipp.):
Walnut, καρύα, fruit κάρυον; W. Asiatic, doubtfully native in Greece; the nuts
were little appreciated as food, but yielded an oil: Hazel, καρύα ἡρακλεωτική;
a native shrub; Galen says that it afforded a better food than the walnut;
τὰ ποντικά were probably larger nuts (filberts) than the native Greek: Almond,
ἀμυγδαλῆ; a native of W. Asia; the name supposed to be of Semitic origin;
the Greeks had μύκηρος; the nut was ἀμύγδαλον and κάρυον in LXX: Date-
palm, φοῖνιξ; native from the Euphrates to N. Africa, but fails to ripen fruit
on the northern Mediterranean shores; it is not mentioned in the *Iliad*,
but the φοίνικος νέον ἔρνος at Delos of the *Odyssey* (VI. 163) seems to have
made the fortune of the island, and its leaves became the symbol of victory;
Cicero says that the tree was still shown in his day; Herodotus knew, as
did the Assyrians, that the date required artificial fertilisation; the fruit was
φοίνικος βάλανος (Hdt. I. 193); δάκτυλος, whence 'date,' only occurs once
in Aristotle (*Meteor.* I. 4. 10), and is an Arabic loan-word; καρυῶτις
according to Galen was a fine kind which grew about Jericho; from βάϊς, a

palm-branch, we get through *badius* the colour of a 'bay'-horse; φοῖνιξ Θηβαικός, also κόϊξ, is the Doum Palm of Egypt, *Hyphaene thebaica*: φοῖνιξ χαμαιριφής is the Dwarf Palm, *Chamaerops humilis*, which is frequent on the Western Mediterranean coasts but wanting in Greece; the 'heart' of the leaves, or terminal bud, ἐγκέφαλος, was eaten, as it still is, hence the Italian name *cefaglioni*; so also was that of the date (Xen. *An*. ii. 3. 16).

96. The Greeks were largely vegetarians and they ate even the young shoots of wild plants, called indiscriminately ἀσπάραγοι; the more palatable were improved by cultivation and the proverb ὅσῳ διαφέρει σῦκα καρδάμων marks the range from a generous to a meagre diet; Aristophanes (*Ach*. 478) jests on the mother of Euripides being a greengrocer who palmed off an inferior thing. Cabbage, ῥάφανος, later κράμβη, *Brassica cretica*; οὔλη was a crisped sort like our savoy; little valued as a food but eaten as a relish; κραμβασπάραγος was 'sprouting broccoli'; μὰ τὴν κράμβην was a form of oath; it was also called μάντις (Nicander), perhaps from use in divination: Turnip, γογγυλίς; γογγυλο- σπάραγον, 'turnip-tops'; Navew, βουνιάς; the turnip of the South; Arum, ἄρον, *Arum italicum*; the tubers eaten like turnips: Radish, ῥαφανίς; Parsnip, ἐλαφόβοσκον: Carrot, σταφυλῖνος, later καρωτόν, a Latin loan-word: Grape hyacinth, βολβός, *Muscari comosum*, a common bulbous plant: Beet, τεῦτλον: Monks' rhubarb, λάπαθον, *Rumex Patientia*: Orache, ἀνδράφαξυς (ἀδράφαξυς in Theophr.): Blite, βλίτον (Galen calls the last two ἄποια): Mallow, μαλάχη, later μολόχη: a common food among the poor (σιτεῖσθαι δ᾽ ἀντὶ μὲν ἄρτων | μαλάχης πτόρθους Ar. *Pl.* 543–4): Charlock, λαμψάνη: Wild chervil, σκάνδιξ, *Scandix Pecten-Veneris*, and ἔνθρυσκον, *Scandix australis*: Samphire, κρῆθμον: Asparagus, ἀσπάραγος, *Asparagus acutifolius*: Purslane, ἀνδράχνη: Stinging nettle, ἀκαλήφη, only a famine food. Galen records that the young shoots of various thistle-like plants were eaten by peasants, as they still are: such were Cardoon, κινάρα, and Golden thistle, *Scolymus hispanicus*. Of cucurbits were cultivated:—Cucumber, σίκυος; native of N. India; the name is a Sanskrit loan-word; in later Greek it was called ἀγγούριον, a word of Slavonic origin, whence 'gherkin': Melon, πέπων; not without doubt but possibly of late introduction from India (the African Water-melon did not reach Europe till the middle ages): Pumpkin, κολόκυνθα; of African origin. While pot-herbs were cooked and eaten with a sauce, γάρος, or vinegar, others like our salads were eaten raw; such were:—Lettuce, θρίδαξ; it was thought insipid and the next two were eaten with it; Celery, σέλινον: Rocket, εὔζωμον: Chicory, κιχόριον: Endive, σέρις: Cress, κάρδαμον, *Lepidium sativum*; native of Persia, where Xenophon found it eaten with bread; the name is an Arabic loan-word; its pungency was stimulating, hence the proverb ἔσθιε κάρδαμον (Ar. *Nub*. 236, ἡ φροντὶς ἕλκει τὴν ἰκμάδ᾽ εἰς τὰ κάρδαμα): Water-cress, καρδαμίνη.

Pot Herbs, λαχανηρά.

97. Tree-fungi, ἀγαρικόν, except the poisonous Fly Agaric, τὸ μέλαν: Ground fungi, βωλίτης: Fairy rings (*champignons*), ἀμανῖται: Puff Ball, πέζις: Truffle, ὕδνον and ἴτον.

Mushrooms, μύκητες.

98. A vegetarian diet such as that of the poorer Greeks taxed diges-
tion, and copious use was made of ingredients to stimulate
it; as amongst all Southern peoples, alliaceous plants held
a first place:—Onions, κρόμμυον (κρόμυον ποτῷ ὄψον, Hom. *Il.*
xi. 630); largely grown at Megara, hence Μεγαρέων δάκρυα, 'crocodile's
tears': Leek, πράσον; the bulb was κεφαλωτόν, the shredded leaves (*sectile
porrum*) καρτόν; ἀμπελόπρασον was the wild form: Garlic, σκόροδον; γέλγις
was a head of garlic, φύσιγξ its membranous investment, ἄγλις an individual
'clove'; it was largely grown at Megara (Ar. *Ach.* 526): Shallot, ἀσκαλώνιον,
also γήτειον; a 'clove,' γηθυλλίς. Others can only be briefly enumerated:—
Mint, ἡδύοσμον and μίνθη, *Mentha viridis*: Pennyroyal, γλήχων: Marjoram,
ὕσσωπος, a Hebrew loan-word: Sweet Marjoram, ἀμάρακος and σάμψουχον,
Origanum Majorana; native of N. Africa: Dittany of Crete, δίκταμνον, *Origanum Dictamnus*: Basil, ὤκιμον, *Ocimum basilicum*; Asiatic: Costmary,
βάλσαμος, *Chrysanthemum Balsamita*; W. Asia: Savory, θύμβρα, *Satureia
Thymbra*: Sage, ἐλελίσφακον: Rue, πήγανον: Black Cummin, μελάνθιον,
Nigella sativa; W. Asia: Mustard, σίναπι. The 'seeds' (really fruits) of
various umbelliferous plants were used:—Dill, ἄνηθον: Anise, ἄνησσον: Cara-
way, καρώ; the roots were also eaten: Coriander, κόριον; W. Asia: Ajowan,
ἄμι, *Carum copticum*; native of India, came to Greece from Egypt: Cummin,
κύμινον; W. Asia; the name is a Hebrew loan-word; κύμινον and κάρδαμον
seem to have been the cheapest in each category, and supply Aristophanes
with a portmanteau word for a skinflint, κυμινο-πριστο-καρδαμο-γλύφος, a
fellow who would split cummin and stint cress, *Vesp.* 1357; cf. Theocr. x.
55: Fennel, μάραθον.

Condiments,
ὄψα.

99. Little has come down to us about Greek gardens or gardening.
But it is clear that the cultivation of coronary plants and
'vegetables' must have been a considerable industry. Theophrastus shows an intimate practical acquaintance with
gardening methods. Ἀδωνίδος κῆποι were small flower-pots (ὄστρακα), in
which fennel, lettuce, wheat and barley were sown, and withering quickly
symbolized the death of Adonis. Similar flower-pots were used for plants
which required care in raising them from seed. Baskets and larger pots
(κεράμια) were used for growing cucumbers and pumpkins, and for early
roses, which were forced with the aid of hot water. Aristotle gave his
Botanic Garden at Athens to Theophrastus, who improved it with the help
of a wealthy friend, finally bequeathed it to trustees, and desired to be
buried in it. He no doubt cultivated in it the exotic plants with which he
shows familiarity.

Gardening,
κηπευτικά.

100. The Greek Pharmacopoeia was almost coextensive with the
vegetable kingdom and cannot be epitomized. But the constant recurrence of εὐστόμαχος and εὐκοίλιος in Dioscorides tells
a story of δυσπεψία in no way surprising. Like all Southern
nations the Greeks clung to purgatives; the most violent was *herba terri-
bilis* of the middle ages, still in vogue in the south, which was euphemistically

Drugs,
φάρμακα.

called ἄλυπον, *Globularia Alypum*: Squirting cucumber, σίκυς ἄγριος and ἐλατήριον, *Ecballium Elaterium*, was a no less violent purge. The treatment of wounds unconsciously anticipates Lister; Dittany, βελουλκός, *cum tergo volucres haesere sagittae* (Virg. *A.* XII. 415), facilitated their extraction, being antiseptic, and κολλητικὰ τραυμάτων acted not mechanically but by excluding 'germs': Squill, σκίλλα, *Scilla maritima*, a plant with a large bulb still used in medicine, σχῖνος in Attic, hence Pericles was called σχινοκέφαλος on account of the shape of his head; it was planted on graves; the bulbs were hung before doors as a charm, and thrown by Arcadians at the statues of Pan if the God was unpropitious (Theocr. VII. 107): Moly, μῶλυ, *Allium nigrum*; Theophrastus (*H.P.* IX. 15. 7) states that the Greeks identified the Homeric plant with one which grew in Arcadia, had a bulb like an onion and leaves like a squill, and was used πρός τε τὰ ἀλεξιφάρμακα καὶ τὰς μαγείας, but could be dug up without difficulty. A characteristic feature of the Mediterranean flora is the occurrence throughout its entire range of Umbellifers producing odoriferous gums; amongst these were:—All-Heal, πάνακες, *Opoponax hispidus*; the gum was ὀποπάναξ, which smelt of crushed ivy leaves (it had in recent times a temporary vogue as a scent): of σίλφιον there were two kinds, the African and the Asiatic; the trade in the former, *Ferula tingitana*, was so important that the plant figured on the coins of Cyrene; the dried stems were exported (Antiph. δυσέρ. 1); Βάττου σίλφιον was proverbial for something costly; in Pliny's time it had been exterminated by sheep: the Asiatic plant was an *Asafoetida* (the σίλφιον found by Aristobulus on the Hindu-Kush was *Ferula alliacea*); the gum, ὀπός (often used alone), had a strong garlic flavour, hence called σκορδολάσαρον in late Greek; it was eaten with grated cheese (Ar. *Av.* 1579): Ammoniacum, ἀμμωνιακόν, *Ferula marmarica*; a bitter gum obtained from the N. African plant, used as a θυμίαμα, as still by Mahomedans.

101.   Hemlock, κώνειον (εὐθὺς γὰρ ἀποπήγνυσι τἀντικνήμια, Ar. *Ran.* 126):
Thorn-apple, πέρσειον, *Datura Stramonium*; native of Persia;

Poisons, φθαρτικά.   owing to confusion with περσαία, *Mimusops Schimperi*, an African tree cultivated by the Egyptians, the myth arose that this had been brought from Persia, where it was originally poisonous: Wolf's Bane, ἀκόνιτον, *Aconitum Anthora*; native of Pontus, not found in Greece: Mandrake, μανδραγόρας, *Mandragora officinarum*; a narcotic (Plat. *Rep.* 488 c); given as an anæsthetic before operations: Belladonna, στρύχνον μανικόν, *Atropa Belladonna*: Opium Poppy, μήκων; native of W. Asia and cultivated for its seed (Hom. *Il.* VIII. 306); hence sacred to Persephone (Theocr. VII. 157); it was doubtless early discovered that the juice of the whole plant, μηκώνιον, was soporific, but the collection of the drug, ὀπός, in Asia Minor from incised poppy-heads only dates from about the beginning of the Christian era; its use was spread by the Arabs, to whom it was a substitute for forbidden wine: Autumn Crocus, κολχικόν,

Colchicum latifolium (κτείνει κατὰ πνιγμόν, Diosc.): Black Hellebore, ἑλλέβορος μέλας, *Helleborus officinalis*: White Hellebore, ἑλλέβορος λευκός, *Veratrum album*.

102. Skins were first made into leather with fat; oil is now used; dyeing

Tanning and Dyeing Plants. βυρσοδεψικά and βαφικά.

the skins probably led to the discovery of tanning materials. The most important was Sumach, ῥοῦς, *Rhus coriaria*: the dried leaves were and still are largely used (the fruits, ἐρυθρόν, were an ὄψον); the rind, σίδιον, of the pomegranate was also used. Of vegeable dyes the most important were:—Madder, ἐρευθέδανον and ἐρυθρόδανον, *Rubia tinctorum*; the roots were used for dyeing wool and leather: Kermes, κόκκος βαφική; the female *coccus* of the Kermes Oak (Theophr. *H.P.* III. 7. 3), *Quercus coccifera*, native of N. shores of the Mediterranean; a *crimson* dye for wool and leather, now displaced by cochineal; it was called ὕσγινον from ὕσγη, the Galatian name for the shrub: Litmus, φῦκος, *Roccella tinctoria*; a cosmopolitan rock-lichen; used for dyeing wool, also as rouge for women (Theocr. xv. 16): Alkanet, ἄγχουσα, *Anchusa tinctoria*; the colour in the root, ῥιζίον, dissolved in oil was used as rouge: Saffron, κρόκος, *Crocus sativus*; the flowers are pale purple, the dye-stuff consists in the orange-coloured styles and stigmas: Woad, ἴσατις, *Isatis tinctoria*: Indigo, ἰνδικόν; imported from India, probably only known to the later Greeks.

103. The identification of the plants which supplied fibres for various

Textiles and Rope-materials, ἱστουργικά.

purposes is not free from difficulty: the following are fairly clear:—Flax, λίνον, *Linum usitatissimum*; a W. Asian annual plant cultivated for linen from remote antiquity in Syria and Egypt; the material for sails made maritime commerce possible; Hermippus (fifth cent. B.C.) describes Egypt as supplying the world (Herm. I. 12): Perennial Flax, βύσσος, *Linum angustifolium*; the prehistoric flax of Europe, still used in Russia; Pausanias distinguishes it from λίνον (Ἑβραίων) as a textile in Elis, where it still grows; the name is a Hebrew loan-word and was used for any fine fibre; σινδὼν βυσσίνη (Hdt. II. 78) was linen mummy cloth: Hemp, κάνναβις; of Central Asiatic origin and only cultivated in northern latitudes; it was unknown to the Egyptians and Hebrews and to the Greeks till late; it was used for a coarse cloth in Thrace, and Hieron II of Syracuse obtained it from Gaul for his rigging: Hemp-mallow, κάνναβις ἀγρία, *Althæa cannabina*; a native plant, used εἰς πλοκὴν σχοινίων (Diosc.); the absence of a vernacular name implies that its use was not early: Mallow, ἀμόργη, *Malva silvestris*; a widely spread European plant, which yields a fine fibre; its identity is fixed by εἶδος βοτάνης πορφυρᾶς (*Etym. Mag.*): Spanish broom, σπάρτος, *Spartium junceum*; a common shrub of S. Europe, σχοινοπλοκική (Strab. III. 160); the fibre was λευκαία and λευκόλινον; a cloth is still made from it in the S. of France: Palm-fibre, βύβλινος; while βύβλος was Papyrus, of which the pithy stems supplied writing material, its obvious want of tensile strength led Eustathius and Wilkinson to reject its use for ropes; the earliest Homeric rigging was made of twisted leather; the opinion of Pliny's day (XIX. 25) that σπάρτα (*navium armamenta*)

were like the sails made of flax was no doubt correct; but a coarser material
would be used for a cable; we further learn from Pliny (XIX. 31) that the
Date-palm was early used by the Greeks for the purpose, and rope made
from it has been found in an Egyptian tomb; Pliny adds that it improved
by lying in the water (XVI. 89); it might well be used for the ὅπλον βύβλινον
of Hom. *Od.* XXI. 391, and for the Egyptian cable of the Hellespont bridge
of Xerxes, which was only half as strong as λευκόλινον: Cotton thistle,
ἀκάνθιον, *Onopordon Acanthium*; τὰ ἀκάνθινα were cloths made in Cappadocia
from the down stripped from the leaves.

104. Giant Fennel, νάρθηξ, *Ferula communis*; one of the most striking
of the characteristic umbelliferous plants; the tough stems
were used by schoolmasters as 'ferules,' and carried by　Reeds, etc.,
Bacchantes, ναρθηκόφοροι; Prometheus brought in it from　καλάμινα.
heaven the spark (Aesch. *Prom.* 109): Pole reed, δόναξ and κάλαμος, *Arundo
Donax*: of W. Asiatic origin, early introduced into Mediterranean countries:
used for flutes (αὐλητικός), arrows (τοξικός), pens (Diosc. I. 114) (κάννα
was a Hebrew loan-word): Reed, φραγμίτης, *Phragmites communis*; native,
used for fences (χαρακίας): Distaff-thistle, ἀτρακτυλίς, *Carthamus lanatus*;
Theocr. (IV. 52) refers to the prickles; the leafless flower-stems were used
for distaffs.

105. Commerce supplied the luxuries of urban civilisation mostly from
the East. Unguents, μύρον, were of home manufacture, but
the more costly were imported from Syria and Egypt; the　Imports,
name is a Hebrew loan-word. The basis was oil, which has　ἐξωτικά.
the property of extracting vegetable scents, ἀρώματα; they were believed to
keep better if thickened with some powdered material, στῦμμα, such as the
root-tubers of κύπειρος, *Cyperus rotundus*. Βάκκαρις was Asiatic (μύρον
Λύδιον, Hes.); what plant, if any, was its basis cannot be conjectured, but
it was not βάκχαρ, Virgil's *baccar*, which was Cyclamen, a coronary plant:
Spikenard, νάρδος, *Nardostachys Jatamansi*, Himalayan, was a root-stock
clothed with fibrous leaf-remains resembling roughly a bearded wheat-ear,
hence ναρδόσταχυς ('spike-nard'): Malabathrum, μαλάβαθρον, is hellenized
Sanskrit, *tamālapattra*, the leaves of *Cinnamomum Tamala*, also called
φύλλον ἰνδικόν; there is no foundation for the absurd suggestion of Salmasius
that it was *betel*, or for attributing to the Greeks indulgence in the Indian
vice: Pepper, πέπερι, from the Malabar coast is mentioned by Hippocrates
and Theophrastus, but must have been too costly for general use; the most
important of all digestive stimulants, its commerce played a great part in
the middle ages; it was even used as a substitute for currency (hence our
'peppercorn' rent); incidentally it led to the discovery of the Cape of Good
Hope and the consequent decay of Venice.

The literature is extensive but it is mostly obsolete from the want of accurate
knowledge of the indigenous plants of Greece and of neighbouring
Bibliography.　Asia. This has now been remedied by E. de Halacsy, *Conspectus
Floræ Græcæ*, Leipzig, 1901–4; and Edmond Boissier, *Flora Orientalis*, 1867–

88. Of modern works the following may be consulted : Victor Hehn, *Kultur-pflanzen...in ihrer Uebergang aus Asien*, ed. 8 (revised by O. Schrader and A. Engler), Berlin, 1912; F. A. Fluckiger and D. Hanbury, F.R.S., *Pharmacographia*, ed. 2, London, 1879; Alphonse de Candolle, *Origine des Plantes Cultivées*, Paris, 1883; Theodor von Heldreich, *Die Nutzpflanzen Griechenlands*, Athens, 1862; and *Chloris Homerike*, Athens, 1896; Karl Koch, *Die Bäume und Sträucher des alten Griechenlands*, Berlin, 1884; C. C. Lacaita, *Etymology of the words Crocus and Saffron*, Appendix to George Maw, *A Monograph of the Genus Crocus*, London, 1886; James Yates, *Textrinum Antiquorum*, London, 1843. *Theophrastus*. Enquiry into Plants, with an English translation by Sir Arthur Hort. London, 1916.

Romer, Gotha, 1859, is useful for the summaries of the passages in classical authors, but the botany is taken second hand from C. Fraas, whose *Synopsis Plantarum Floræ Classicæ*, ed. 2, Leipzig, 1870, is uncritical and badly edited ; it borrows largely from Julius Billerbeck, *Flora Classica*, Leipzig, 1824, which is in turn based on Kurt Sprengel, *Historia rei herbariæ*, Amsterdam, 1807 ; K. Sprengel's edition of Dioscorides in the *Medicorum Græcorum Opera*, Leipzig, 1829–30, with a commentary, is indispensable as a summary of the work of previous authors, but the text is superseded by that of Max Wellmann, Berlin, 1906–7. Galen, *De Alimentis*, is invaluable and it is surprising that there is no available separate edition ; the great commentary of J. Bodæus a Stapel on Theophrastus, Amsterdam, 1644, is a treasure-house of citations relating to plants from classical authors, and the *Plinianæ Exercitationes* of C. Salmasius, Utrecht, 1689, is useful in the same way.

II. HISTORY.

II. 1. CHRONOLOGY.

106. THE Greeks themselves believed they possessed sufficient materials for constructing chronological tables of their history from the earliest times. Eratosthenes of Cyrene (about 276— 194, head of the Alexandrian library 235 B.C.) aimed at creating a science of chronology in his treatise περὶ χρονο- γραφίας. His investigations fixed the date of the principal epochs, on grounds which he considered sufficient, as follows : The fall of Troy 1184-3 B.C. : the Dorian migration 1104-3 : the Ionian immigration 1044-3 : the guardianship of Lycurgus 885—4 : the first Olympiad 776—5 : and so on to the expedition of Xerxes, the beginning and end of the Peloponnesian war, the battle of Leuctra, the death of Philip of Macedon and of Alexander the Great.

The conventional chronology.

The principles thus laid down were applied by Apollodorus of Athens, who dedicated to Attalus II of Pergamum a metrical work, *Chronica*, in four books ; this became the popular handbook on the subject; the chief events from 1184 B.C. to 144 B.C. were strung together in comic iambics. Though the works of Eratosthenes and Apollodorus are lost, much of their contents has been recovered, chiefly through the Christian writers Africanus, Eusebius, Jerome and Syncellus, who borrowed from them in order to synchronize profane and Old Testament history. The received chronology rests primarily upon Eusebius and Suidas, but in the main it doubtless reproduces the conclusions of the great Alexandrine authorities, although we are often left in uncertainty as to the grounds upon which a given date was fixed.

Sextus Iulius Africanus, a presbyter at Athens in the third century of our era, included in his πεντάβιβλον χρονολογικὸν the entire history from the Creation, 5500 B.C., to A.D. 221. To this work Eusebius was indebted for the table of Olympic victors, Ὀλυμπιάδων ἀναγραφαί. Eusebius Pamphili was bishop of Caesarea in Palestine A.D. 314 to 340. His *Chronica* consisted of two parts: (1) a short outline of universal history, mostly excerpts, to serve as materials for (2) the second part or Canon, in which the various eras were synchronized and the dates down to A.D. 324 brought under the era of Abraham, 2017 B.C. Only a few fragments have reached us directly: the great task of restoring the contents of the work, begun by Scaliger and only completed in the nineteenth century, starts from (1) an Armenian translation, (2) a Syriac epitome, (3) Jerome's Latin version (continued to A.D. 378 with Roman dates added), and (4) ἐκλογὴ χρονογραφίας of Georgius Syncellus (about A.D. 800), which was derived, though not directly, from Eusebius. These various sources do not always agree; even different manuscripts of Jerome sometimes differ as to a given date. Hence a new source of uncertainty wherever Eusebius is our sole authority. **Suïdas**, in the tenth century A.D., included in his comprehensive lexicon an epitome of literary history derived from Hesychius of Miletus, who compiled his ὀνοματολόγος ἢ πίναξ τῶν ἐν παιδείᾳ ὀνομαστῶν from good sources in the sixth century under Justinian.

107. An examination of the earlier and exclusively poetical literature (Homer, Hesiod, the Epic Cycle, the oldest lyric poets) yields hardly anything which will serve as a basis for chrono-logy. When prose-writing began, it followed the example which the poets had set in the narration of legends and pedigrees, but an attempt was made to rationalize the old stories by reconciling conflicting versions and supplementing what was incomplete. Without contemporary records chronological accuracy is impossible. The oldest documentary evidence in Greece, going back perhaps in some cases to the eighth century B.C., consisted of official lists, especially lists of local magistrates, priests, and victors in the games. These were inscriptions; for to inscribe some-thing in writing in a public place was always the official, and for long the only, mode of publication. When brief notices of events came to be appended to the names of magistrates there grew up annalistic local chronicles, such as Charon's 'Annals of Lampsacus,' technically called ὧροι, ὡρογραφίαι: a branch of literature particularly prolific at Athens, where the Ἀτθίδες (*i.e.* town-chronicles of Athens) begin with Hellanicus in the fifth century, while the most famous, that of Philochorus, was written in the third century, B.C.

Methods of dating.

Throughout the historical period the Greeks dated events by the local official for the time being: at Athens the first archon, at Sparta the first ephor, at Argos the priestess of Hera, chosen for life. This may be observed in the official designations of the years 432–1, 422–1, 412–1, in documents cited by Thucydides v. 19; VIII. 58, cf. II. 2 and schol. The names of the ephors are said to have been recorded from 757–6 B.C., of the annual archons at Athens from 683–2 B.C.: the list of the Argive priestesses of Hera was published by Hellanicus. Occasionally striking natural phenomena, eclipses or volcanic eruptions, served as landmarks in the dim past. Family registers were carefully kept. About 500 B.C. Hecataeus of Miletus traced his descent in 16 generations to a god. Hippocrates of Cos, the father of medicine, born about 460, claimed descent from Asclepius at 18 removes.

The method of dating by local officials must have been highly incon-venient from the great number of independent states and the amount of elaborate calculation and synchronism required to ensure accuracy: see Polybius XII. 11, Diodorus v. 1. For literary purposes a common basis was ultimately found in the Olympic festival, certainly used as an epoch in the third century B.C. by Timaeus of Tauromenium, and later by Polybius, Diodorus Siculus, Dionysius of Halicarnassus: indeed generally amongst Alexandrine *writers*. It never came into use in ordinary life, though it is found on a few, chiefly Olympic, inscriptions.

The festival month at Olympia was the 8th of the Eleian calendar, answering to Metageitnion, the second Attic month; hence at Athens the four-year period, called an ’Ολυμπιάς, was adjusted to begin with the new-year's day of the Attic year in which the games fell, *i.e.* with the first of Hecatombaeon (the first new moon after the summer solstice, approximately July). Thus Ol. 1. 1 covers the twelve months beginning about July, 776, and ending about June, 775 B.C. Hence the rule for converting Olympiads into modern dating B.C.: multiply the number of the Olympiads by four and if this can be subtracted from 780, the remainder gives the year B.C. when the *first* year of the given Olympiad begins: for the second, third, and fourth years respectively 1, 2, and 3 must be added before making the subtraction; for a date within the Christian era 779 should be subtracted from four times the number of the Olympiad, *e.g.* Ol. 75 begins in the middle of 480 B.C. (780 – 4 × 75 = 780 – 300 = 480): while Ol. 293 begins in the middle of A.D. 393 (4 × 293 = 1172 and 1172 – 779 = 393). The first day of the Attic year, *i.e.* the new moon after the summer solstice, falls about eleven days earlier each year than the preceding year until the arrival of the intercalary year: the intercalated month makes it about eighteen days later than the year before. It has been computed, on such data as we have, that between 432 and 263 B.C. the first of Hecatombaeon fell as early as June 22, and as late as August 9, but in the great majority of years in July.

Two modern dates are required in order to include *the whole* of any Attic, or Olympic, year mentioned by our authorities: *e.g.* Ol. 75. 1 = 480–479 B.C. Wherever in the following tables a single modern year is given as an equivalent of an Attic year, this is an abbreviation; the following year must be mentally supplied. Events within a given Attic civil year, however, can repeatedly be referred with certainty to the autumn and winter, on the one hand, or to the spring and early summer, on the other. This is, from the nature of the case, comparatively easy in military operations. An ordinary campaign would begin before and end after midsummer, thus running into two official years. Herodotus reckons campaigns from spring to spring: Thucydides ignores the official dating and, as he himself explains (v. 20), divides his year into a long summer, (*i.e.* the period favourable for military operations; including spring and autumn about 8 months from the middle of March to the middle of November) and a short winter (the four months about the winter solstice). Ostracism was decreed in the sixth or seventh prytany, February or March, the performance of a play at Athens took place in the spring; the Isthmian games about April: accordingly each of these events must be referred to the latter of the two years B.C. which make up a given archon's year. When there are no indications of the season, the double B.C. dating, though clumsy, is approximately correct. It is indeed the only effectual way of guarding against the false impression, which so many chronological tables produce, that the Attic civil year (like the English civil year since A.D. 1752) began on the 1st of January.

108. In the tradition of the earliest times the main thread was genealogical. The religious rites and other privileges attach-

Pedigrees.

ing exclusively to the members of a priestly family (γένος)
or clan (φρατρία) were bound up with the belief in relationship through
a common ancestor, after whom the family or clan was called. This
ancestor was sometimes a god, more often a hero celebrated in story. All
over Greece in historical times such patronymics are found; Aleuadae in
Thessaly, Branchidae at Miletus, Butadae at Athens, Asclepiadae at Cos
and in many other places. The pedigrees of the ruling families at an
earlier time were traced back to some famous founder, Cadmus at Thebes,
Cecrops at Athens, Inachus at Argos, Dardanus at Troy (occasionally to a
woman, as Aegina for the Aeacidae), while the Pelopidae descended from
Tantalus, a Lydian. The heroes described by the poets as taking part in
the Argonautic expedition, the Theban or Trojan war, or the return of
the Heracleidae must be considered contemporaries. Hence the divergent
genealogies could be brought into connexion, and chronologers were not
slow to avail themselves of the hint. Theoretically it is possible, at any
stage, to convert the family-tree into a history 'in skeleton outline' of the
period elapsed since the eponymous ancestor. We find this done tentatively in Homer (*e.g. Il.* VI. 152 sqq.), more consciously in the Hesiodic
Catalogue and *Eoeae* (a list of famous heroines, each account beginning
ἢ οἵη): the process is carried still further in the genealogies presumed
or recounted by Pindar and Herodotus. A few of the leading families are
here presented in tabular form.

(I)

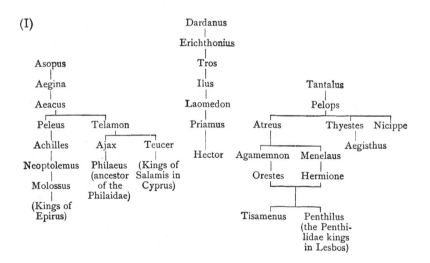

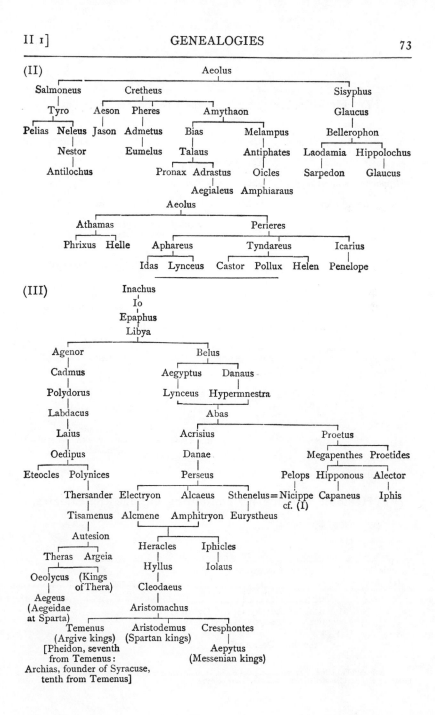

(IV) Heracleidae (other than the descendants of Hyllus).

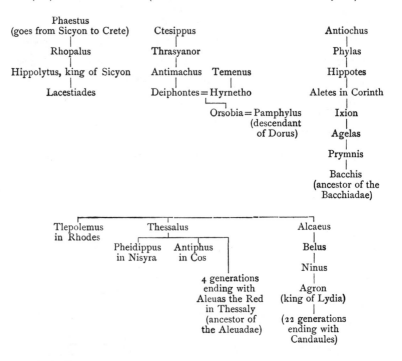

```
Phaestus
(goes from Sicyon to Crete)    Ctesippus                          Antiochus
         |                        |                                   |
      Rhopalus                 Thrasyanor                           Phylas
         |                        |                                   |
Hippolytus, king of Sicyon   Antimachus  Temenus                   Hippotes
         |                        |       |                           |
      Lacestiades            Deiphontes = Hyrnetho              Aletes in Corinth
                                     |___,                            |
                                Orsobia = Pamphylus                  Ixion
                                        (descendant                   |
                                         of Dorus)                  Agelas
                                                                     |
                                                                   Prymnis
                                                                     |
                                                                   Bacchis
                                                               (ancestor of the
                                                                 Bacchiadae)
```

```
    Tlepolemus          Thessalus                      Alcaeus
    in Rhodes       Pheidippus  Antiphus                 Belus
                    in Nisyra   in Cos                    |
                                                        Ninus
                                     4 generations        |
                                     ending with        Agron
                                     Aleuas the Red    (king of Lydia)
                                     in Thessaly          |
                                     (ancestor of      (22 generations
                                     the Aleuadae)      ending with
                                                        Candaules)
```

(V) Hesiodic Scheme for combining various Genealogies.

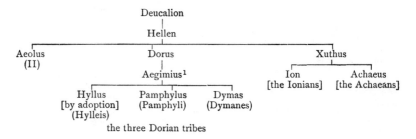

```
                            Deucalion
                                |
                             Hellen
                                |
 Aeolus              Dorus                         Xuthus
 (II)                  |                       Ion        Achaeus
                    Aegimius¹               [the Ionians]  [the Achaeans]
          Hyllus       Pamphylus    Dymas
      [by adoption]   (Pamphyli)  (Dymanes)
        (Hylleis)
              the three Dorian tribes
```

¹ It is doubtful whether any good authorities made Aegimius the son of Dorus, but it is the only way to bring the Heracleidae and Dorian families into the scheme.

(VI) The Kings of Sparta to the Persian Wars.
(Her. VII. 204, VIII. 131.)

Agiads	Eurypontids
Eurysthenes	Procles
Agis	[Soüs]
Echestratus — Lycurgus [according to some]	Eurypon
Labotas	Prytanis
Doryssus	Polydectes[1]
Agesilaus	Eunomus
Archelaus[2]	Charilaus — [Lycurgus guardian according to Plutarch and others]
Telecles	Nicander
Alcamenes[3]	Theopompus[3]
Polydorus	Archidamus [never reigned] — Anaxandridas
Eurycrates	Zeuxidamus — Archidamus
Anaxander [perhaps c. 651—620]	Anaxidamus — Anaxilaus
Eurycratidas	Archidamus — Leotychidas
Leon	Agesicles — Hippocratidas
Anaxandridas	Ariston — Agesilaus
Cleomenes c. 520—489, Dorieus, Leonidas †480, Cleombrotus	Demaratus 510—491, Menares
Pleistarchus[4] †458, Pausanias †469	Leotychidas[5] 491—469

[1] So Her. VIII. 131, but Simonides made Eunomus (and Lycurgus) sons of Prytanis, see Plutarch, *Lyc.* 1: and Polydectes is the son of Eunomus in Paus. III. 7. 2. In the conventional chronology of Apollodorus Polydectes is dropped altogether, or identified with Eunomus.

[2] According to some, a Menelaus reigned between Agesilaus and Archelaus.

[3] The first Olympiad, 776 B.C., falls in the tenth year of Alcamenes and Theopompus, according to Apollodorus. But Theopompus is the conqueror of Messenia according to Tyrtaeus.

[4] The remaining Agiad kings are: Pleistoanax 458—445, Pausanias 445—426, Pleistoanax *reinstated* 426—408, Pausanias *reinstated* 408—394, Agesipolis 394—380, Cleombrotus 380—371, Agesipolis II 371—370, Cleomenes II 370—309, Areius I 309—265, Acrotatus 265, Areius II 264—256, Leonidas II 256—243, Cleombrotus II 243—240, Leonidas II *reinstated* 240—236, Cleomenes III 236—223, Eucleidas 236—223, Agesipolis III 221.

[5] His grandson Archidamus, who succeeded him, took part in the Peloponnesian war and died about 427. The remaining Eurypontid kings are: Agis II 427—399, Agesilaus 399—361, Archidamus III 361—338, Agis III 338—331, Eudamidas I 331—?, Archidamus IV c. 296, Eudamidas II ?—244, Agis IV 244—240.

(VII) Attic Kings.

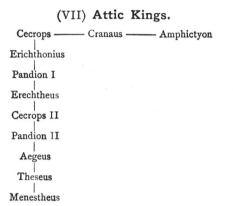

Cecrops ———— Cranaus ———— Amphictyon
|
Erichthonius
|
Pandion I
|
Erechtheus
|
Cecrops II
|
Pandion II
|
Aegeus
|
Theseus
|
Menestheus

109. The Marmor Parium, an inscription (C. I. G. 2374) which gives dates for various events from the earliest times, places Cecrops 1318 years before 264–3, the archonship of Diognetus, *i.e.* 1582–1 B.C., and makes the capture of Troy fall in the 22nd year of Menestheus, or 1209–8 B.C. The marble follows a scheme of its own, older than, and independent of, Eratosthenes. Philochorus assuméd 397 years between Cecrops and the Trojan era, and likewise 397 years between the Trojan era and the accession of the first archon for ten years (752 B.C.), a coincidence which is the key to the construction of the table.

Later accounts, not earlier than Theopompus *circa* 350 B.C., made Cecrops an immigrant from Egypt, but this contradicts the universal belief of older Athens that her people were αὐτόχθονες. Cecrops, Cranaus, Pandion and Erechtheus are ancient figures in Attic traditions: the interpolation of Cecrops II, Pandion II, Erichthonius (variant of Erechtheus), which goes back to Hellanicus, was due to chronological requirements.

(VIII) Athenian Families.

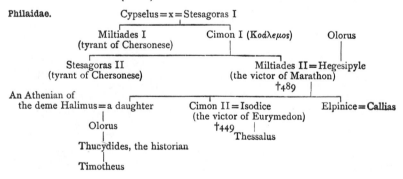

Philaidae.

Cypselus = x = Stesagoras I
|
Miltiades I (tyrant of Chersonese) — Cimon I (Κοάλεμος) — Olorus
|
Stesagoras II (tyrant of Chersonese)
Miltiades II = Hegesipyle (the victor of Marathon) †489
|
An Athenian of the deme Halimus = a daughter
Cimon II = Isodice (the victor of Eurymedon) †449 | Thessalus
Elpinice = Callias
|
Olorus
|
Thucydides, the historian
|
Timotheus

Eupatridae.

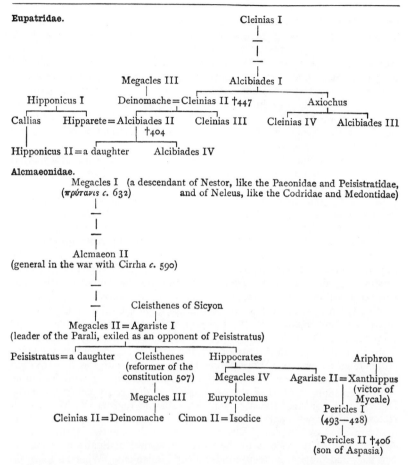

Cleinias I

Megacles III   Alcibiades I

Hipponicus I   Deinomache = Cleinias II †447   Axiochus

Callias   Hipparete = Alcibiades II   Cleinias III   Cleinias IV   Alcibiades III
                            †404

Hipponicus II = a daughter   Alcibiades IV

Alcmaeonidae.

Megacles I   (a descendant of Nestor, like the Paeonidae and Peisistratidae,
(πρύτανις c. 632)   and of Neleus, like the Codridae and Medontidae)

Alcmaeon II
(general in the war with Cirrha c. 590)

Cleisthenes of Sicyon

Megacles II = Agariste I
(leader of the Parali, exiled as an opponent of Peisistratus)

Peisistratus = a daughter   Cleisthenes   Hippocrates   Ariphron
                            (reformer of the
                            constitution 507)   Megacles IV   Agariste II = Xanthippus
                                                                                (victor of
                            Megacles III   Euryptolemus   Mycale)
                                                                            Pericles I
Cleinias II = Deinomache   Cimon II = Isodice   (493—428)

Pericles II †406
(son of Aspasia)

110. The account of the Theban, Argive, Spartan and Lydian kings in
Herodotus is instructive as illustrating the dependence which historians
placed on genealogies. From a comparison of v. 59 with IV. 147, it follows
that ten generations elapse from Cadmus to Theras, and Theras arrived in
Thera eight generations after Membliares, the Phoenician settler, whose
father Poeciles is obviously made to synchronize with Cadmus. Again,
seven generations separate Eurystheus and Procles from Amphitryon
(VI. 52), who is contemporary with Laius (v. 59). As the Argive list goes
back to Acrisius (VI. 53) and the Heracleidae continue to Leotychidas
(VIII. 131), a scheme of 26 generations is obtained. In the Agiad royal
family indeed there are 27, which is the reason why Ephorus and later
authorities inserted another king, Soüs, between Eurypon and Procles, of

whom Herodotus, *l.c.*, knows nothing. But when he gives his own date for the Trojan war as 'eight hundred years before my time' (II. 145) he is at variance with the twenty generations which he allows between Thermopylae and the return of the Heracleidae:—at least if we assume that 20 generations = 666⅔ years (II. 143), and that between the fall of Troy and the return only two more generations elapsed. At any rate, his date for Heracles is the key to his Lydian chronology: for Agron (I. 7) was the fifth in descent from Heracles, with whom was identified the Lydian Sandon, while Ninus, the father of Agron, is the eponym of Nineveh and the founder of the Assyrian dynasty.

III. All schemes based on genealogies have serious faults: they begin to reckon downwards, from the presumed ancestor, instead of upwards from known individuals: the number of links is not constant, tradition being susceptible of interpolations: the average of a generation is variously computed, as high as 40, or as low as 25 years. The main facts of Greek history, however, are firmly established, and the chronology from the time of the first contemporary historian (*i.e.* from the fifth century) can be ascertained, even with the imperfect means at our disposal, beyond all reasonable doubt. The mere existence of documentary evidence is indeed no guarantee that the facts attested must have taken place. For an inscription may be forged, as that bearing the names of Iphitus and Lycurgus upon the quoit at Olympia, or those seen by Herodotus (V. 59—61) upon tripods in the temple of Ismenian Apollo in Thebes. Or part only of a record may be historical. Thus there is an extant inscription, itself a copy of an earlier record, which enumerates the priests of Poseidon at Halicarnassus, with the years of their priesthood, from the foundation of the colony, beginning with Telamon, son of Poseidon, the first of sixteen names covering 504 years (C. I. G. 2165, Dittenberger, *Sylloge*[3] 1020). Even the valuable register of the Olympic victors, which goes back to 776 B.C., has not escaped suspicion. It was first published by Hippias of Elis, the famous sophist, in the fourth century. A similar list of the victors in the Carnean festival at Sparta from Ol. 26, 676 B.C., had previously been published by Hellanicus. What Hippias did was perhaps to reconstruct the Olympic register for the oldest time from such material, monumental or traditional, as he could find: at least this was the opinion of certain authorities known to Plutarch, *Numa* 1: τῶν Ὀλυμπιονικῶν...ὧν τὴν ἀναγραφὴν ὀψέ φασιν Ἱππίαν ἐκδοῦναι τὸν Ἠλεῖον ἀπ᾽ οὐδενὸς ὁρμώμενον ἀναγκαίου πρὸς πίστιν. Hence the necessity of submitting the materials to a rigorous criticism, a necessity fully recognized by Thucydides, the greatest of Greek historians. His conception of historical research may be gathered from the sketch of the earlier period (I. 1—23) which he has prefixed to his history. When the details can no longer be recovered we must be content, like Thucydides, with a general outline of social progress, to which inferences from institutions of a later time contribute no less than the critical treatment of tradition. If we are

Critical estimate.

now at all in advance of Thucydides it is in the recognition that much which passes for tradition is really the product of reflexion, the direct invention of a later and uncritical age, and by the great assistance rendered to history by a close study of the sources, literary and archaeological. The study of the literary sources has done much to reveal the basis for the traditions, statements, and tendencies found in later writers, especially compilers. Archaeology is the basis of our knowledge of prehistoric civilization. Epigraphy, comprising the publication of fresh inscriptions like the Lindian Chronicle and the re-editing of old, verifies or revises doubtful dates and occasionally gives new historical facts of the first importance. Our knowledge of the Athenian tribute and the financial administration of Athens depends on inscriptions, and recent epigraphical study has revolutionized the Athenian Calendar. Papyri found in Egypt continually furnish supplementary evidence, though great discoveries like Aristotle's *Constitution of Athens* are rare.

112. The racial origin of the Greeks is discussed elsewhere (§§ 31 ff.). The Greeks themselves believed in the unity of their race and appealed to their common language, religion, and **Divisions of Greek stock.** culture (Herod. VIII. 144). From an early time they recognised a division of the race into Aeolians, Ionians, and Dorians. This classification probably arose in Asia, as it best accords with the distribution of the Asiatic colonies. Hesiod's eponymous table of Hellen and his sons, Table (V) § 108, takes in the Achaeans as well. Obviously these four must have seemed the most important branches of the Greek race at the place and time at which the table was constructed. For the evidence of the dialects see §§ 724 ff.

Thucydides (I. 3) has pointed out the late and gradual application of the national name Hellenes in contrast to the name Barbarians for foreigners. In Homer, the Hellenes are merely the subjects of Achilles from Phthiotis in southern Thessaly: the terms Danaans, Argives, and Achaeans, more nearly approximate to a national designation. The term Graeci itself, by which the race was known in Italy, was a traditional name of the Hellenes when settled about Dodona in Epeirus (Arist. *Meteor*. I. 14, 352^b 2).

Partly from disparity of endowments, partly from their surroundings, the branches of the Greek race had a very unequal development. After the migrations Aeolian and Ionian immigrants made extraordinary progress in Asia, while European Greece was still backward and unenterprising: in later times the contrast is as striking between the great commercial centres at home and in the colonies, whether Ionian, Dorian, or Achaean, and the rude half-civilized tribes of the north and north-west, which do not emerge from obscurity until Macedonian times.

113. Archaeological evidence has enabled us to formulate a tentative chronology of prehistoric Greece. This is based on the archaeological sequence of the objects found in stratified **Prehistoric Chronology.** deposits at many sites in Crete, in the Islands, and on the Mainland. Greek chronology begins with the Neolithic Period, the beginning

of which is not known. In Crete about 3400 B.C. a Copper Age marks the transition to the full Bronze Age. The Bronze Age is divided into three main periods, Early, Middle, and Late, each of which is subdivided into two or more phases. The archaeological finds are further classified according to the district in which they are found, as Minoan for Crete, Cycladic for the Islands, and Helladic for the Mainland. The approximate dates of the various phases are furnished by the discovery of dated Egyptian objects in Crete and at Mycenae, and by the presence of Minoan and Helladic objects with definite stratigraphical context in Egypt where a definite chronology exists. Without this no actual dates by the Christian era could be given. Equally important, however, are the synchronisms provided by the finding of both Minoan and Helladic objects in Melos and of Melian objects at Cnossus. These and similar synchronisms based on the discovery of Helladic pottery in Thessaly determine the chronological relationship between the various archaeological sequences in the several districts, even though an actual dating by the Christian era is not possible.

114. THE EARLIEST HISTORY OF THE AEGEAN.

Approximate Dates B.C.	Crete	Greek Mainland	Egypt, Troy, etc.
STONE AGE From the earliest times to about 3400	*Neolithic* culture showing continuous development	*First Neolithic Period* in Thessaly, Central and Southern Greece	Analogies with Pre-Dynastic Egypt and with Macedonia
BRONZE AGE **Early** 3400—2800	*Early Minoan I* (Sub-neolithic)	*Second Neolithic Period* in Thessaly succeeded by	Troy, First City Egyptian settlement in
2800—2400	*Early Minoan II* Marked progress in all arts and crafts	*Early Helladic* culture in Southern and Central Greece First occupation of Mycenae Gradual development of civilization in contact with islands	Crete; early dynastic objects in Crete (Mesara, Cnossus, Mochlos)
2400—2100	*Early Minoan III* Pictorial and linear signs Circular ossuaries in Mesara		
Middle 2100—1900	*Middle Minoan I* First Palaces at Cnossus, Phaestus, and Mallia Hieroglyphic script A		
1900—1700	*Middle Minoan II* Kamares (Polychrome) ware Hieroglyphic script B Palaces at Cnossus and Phaestus destroyed	*Middle Helladic* First appearance of Minyan ware Kamares and Minyan ware in Melos	M. M. II pottery found in Egypt in XIIth Dynasty tomb XIIIth Dynasty statuette at Cnossus

Approximate Dates B.C.	Crete	Greek Mainland	Egypt, Troy, etc.
1700—1580	*Middle Minoan III* Rebuilding of Cnossus and Phaestus Great Age of Cnossus begins Linear script A Temple Repositories with faience figures Great earthquake First villa at Hagia Triada Restoration of Cnossus	Flying Fish fresco in Melos Melian vases in Temple Repositories at Cnossus Shaft Grave Dynasty at Mycenae begins	Inscription of Khyan (xvth Dynasty) at Cnossus 18th cent. B.C.
Late 1580—1500	*Late Minoan I a* Climax of Cretan power Destruction of Mallia	*Late Helladic I* Shaft Grave Dynasty at Mycenae Beehive Tomb Dynasty at Mycenae begins	
1500—1450	*Late Minoan I b*	*Late Helladic II* Tombs at Vaphio and Kakovatos (Pylos)	"Keftiu" and their offerings represented in Egyptian monuments c. 1500–1440 B.C.
1450—1400	*Late Minoan II* Palace at Cnossus remodelled Royal Tomb at Isopata Destruction of Cnossus		Troy, Sixth City Egyptian objects at Mycenae c. 1450–1350 B.C.
1400—1200	*Late Minoan III* Partial re-occupation of Cnossus	Supremacy of Mycenae *Late Helladic III* Treasury of Atreus. Palaces of Tiryns and Mycenae. Cyclopean fortifications Beehive Tomb at Dendra	Late Helladic III pottery at Tell-el-Amarna L. H. III pottery spread widely through the Levant Philistine pottery begins Egyptian Records c. 1288 B.C. Rameses II defeats *Kheta, Dardenui, Masa, Luka, Qalaqisa* c 1220 Merneptah defeats Libyans and allies *Akaiwasha, Tursha, Luka, Shardina,* 'Northerners from all lands'
IRON AGE **Early** 1200—1000		Trojan War Fall of Mycenae and Tiryns	c. 1190 'The isles were restless.' Rameses III defeats *Kheta* with allies *Pulesatha* and *Danauna*
	Gradual transition from L. M. III to geometric style	Geometric style develops from L. H. III pottery Dorian Migration Age of Epic Lays	Objects of xxth Dynasty at Vrokastro

115.　TRADITIONAL DATES OF LEGENDARY GREEK HISTORY

1466 Danaus	1229 Minos II	1124 Thessalian and Boeotian migration
1433 Deucalion	1225 Voyage of Argonauts	
1406 Minos I	1213 First Theban War	1104 Dorian migration
1313 Cadmus	1198 Second Theban War	1074—1066 Dorian Colonies
1283 Pelops	1192—1183 Trojan War	1054—1015 Aeolian Colonies
1261—1209 Heracles	1176 Colonies in Cyprus	1044 Ionian Colonies
1235 Theseus		

G. A.

116. Many invasions and displacements of earlier populations were

Migrations. dimly remembered in ancient Greece. The Dorians were always proudly conscious that they were a handful of invaders in Peloponnesus, holding down alien subjects by main force (Tyrtaeus, *Fr.* 2). Homer tells of Dorians in Crete (*Od.* xix. 177), but ignores them elsewhere; the times he is describing are anterior to the movements which determined the distribution of the population in historical Greece. In the tradition three invasions appear to be distinguished. (1) The Thessalians of historical times, coming from Thesprotia, conquered the country to which they gave their name, and the Boeotians, expelled by the Thessalians 'from Arne,' occupied the country called after them Boeotia. (2) The Dorians issued from northern Greece, overran Argolis, Laconia and Messenia, and colonized by sea Crete, Thera, Melos, Rhodes, Cos, Cnidus. This is the **Dorian migration.** (3) North-western Greece— Locris, Phocis, Aetolia, Acarnania—was overrun by invaders from Epeirus, part of whom crossed the sea into Iapygia, while an advanced guard seized Elis. The first two of these movements Thucydides (i. 12), following some accepted chronology, places 60 and 80 years respectively after the fall of Troy.

117. With these migrations the legends connect the first great wave of

Expansion of Greece. Greek colonization, by which the shores and islands of Asia Minor were overspread. The **Aeolian migration** is the establishment of settlers in Lesbos, Tenedos, and on the Mysian mainland under oecists (Gras, Penthilus, Cleuas and Malaus) who were said to be descendants of Agamemnon. Yet in historical times the affinities of the Aeolian and Lesbian cities lay rather with Boeotia and Thessaly. Next, according to the legend, came Ionians, originally the inhabitants of Aegialea, *i.e.* the later Achaia, in north Peloponnesus. They started, however, from Attica, and the most famous oecists, Neleus and Androclus, were sons of Codrus, tracing descent (like some of the Attic nobles) to Nestor. This is the **Ionian migration,** which occupied Chios, Samos, the Cyclades, and the central part of the Lydian and Carian coast of Asia Minor. Dorians again at various times settled in Crete, Thera, Melos, Rhodes, Cos, and on the Carian coast at Cnidus and Halicarnassus.

Earlier still in the traditional account were settlements on the Pamphylian coast at Aspendus, Perge, Selge, the oecists being heroes returning from the Trojan war :—in Cilicia, at Soli, Tarsus and Mallus, and at many points in Cyprus, the oecist of Paphos being Agapenor, an Arcadian. As the Cypriotes used a syllabary, their colonies were at any rate older than the introduction of alphabetic writing into Greece.

The standard work on the astronomical basis of chronology is L. Ideler,

Bibliography. *Handbuch der mathematischen und technischen Chronologie,* 2 vols., 1825/6, reprinted 1883 ; H. Fynes Clinton, *Fasti Hellenici,* 3 vols.,

1834/51 (3rd edition of Vol. II., 2nd edition of Vol. III.), needs revision. For a detailed bibliography see A. Schaefer, *Abriss der Quellenkunde der griechischen und römischen Geschichte, Erste Abtheilung, griechische Geschichte bis auf Polybios*, 4th edition, 1889, a good summary of the literary sources. For subsidiary sources consult E. L. Hicks, *Greek Historical Inscriptions*, 2nd edition, 1901, and G. F. Hill, *Sources for Greek History between the Persian and Peloponnesian wars*, 1897. As to the data of the literary chronology, see H. Diels, *Chronologische Untersuchungen über Apollodors Chronika* in *Rheinisches Museum*, Vol. XXXI., 1876, p. 1 ff., W. F. Wislicenus, *Astronomische Chronologie*. E. Cavaignac, *Chronologie*, 1925. W. Kubitschek, *Grundriss der antiken Zeitrechnung*, 1928. C. Blinkenberg, *La Chronique du Temple Lindien*, 1912. B. Meritt, *The Attic Calendar*, 1928. J. L. Myres, *Who were the Greeks?*, 1930. F. Jacoby, *Das Marmor Parium*, Berlin, 1904. J. D. S. Pendlebury, *Aegyptiaca*, Cambridge, 1930.

II 2. CHRONOLOGICAL TABLES.

A.   THE EIGHTH AND SEVENTH CENTURIES B.C.

118. THIS period is marked (1) by the growth of commerce and the foundation of colonies, especially in the Euxine and the west; by the rise of commercial cities—Miletus preeminently, other Ionian cities, Chalcis, Eretria, Aegina, Corinth. (2) Agriculture is still the staple industry, but is beginning to be supplemented by manufactures, as of woven cloth, pottery, armour. The coining of money is adopted from Lydia and quickly spreads all over Greece, working an economic revolution. The commercial rivalry of the Phoenicians in the eastern Mediterranean tends to abate. Egypt, now reviving under native rule (664), is at last open to Greek trade. (3) The constitution, once monarchy, has at the outset of this period in most cities become the rule of privileged noble families, which again is often overthrown, as trade and wealth increase, by a popular leader or 'tyrant.' (4) In Peloponnesus two military and agricultural states are conspicuous: **Argos**, long preeminent, subsequently to decline before the growing strength of **Sparta**, a state organized exclusively for war, which succeeds in conquering and holding down Messenia. (5) In intellectual progress the Ionians are the leaders. Writing began in Ionia; through Homer Ionic becomes the literary dialect. Along with the epic, various branches of lyric poetry flourish :—elegy, iambus, melos, and the choral ode.

Eighth and seventh centuries B.C.

There are scarcely any contemporary records. Of the dates preserved by tradition, more than half concern the foundations of cities (κτίσεις), sometimes conflicting, sometimes precise and consistent, as for Sicily (Thuc. VI. 1—4). The traditional data in the case of the Sicilian colonies must have been combined and harmonized by a systematizer, probably Antiochus of Syracuse. For the affairs of Asia Minor, Assyrian monuments (presumably contemporary) afford some aid. Thus Gyges, king of Lydia, appears on an inscription as a vassal of Assurbanipal about 660. Hence the date assigned to him by Herodotus, 716—678, must be given up. This affects the dates of some early poets (Callinus, Archilochus, Semonides) and of certain colonies which are vaguely referred to 'the times of Gyges.'

The principal Greek Colonies before the Persian War.

In the west (Italy and Sicily).

? Cyme[1] (Cumae) in Italy founded by Chalcis and Euboean Cyme Parthenope (Neapolis) by Rhodes

735 Naxos in Sicily by Chalcis and Naxos

734 Corcyra by Corinth, expelling earlier Eretrian settlers

734 Syracuse by Corinth (757 Parian Marble)

c. **730** Zancle by Cyme in Italy and Chalcis (757 Eusebius)

729 Leontini and Catana by Naxos in Sicily

728 Megara Hyblaea by Megara after a first settlement at Thapsus

721 Sybaris by Achaeans and Troezen

c. **717** Mylae by Zancle and Rhegium by Chalcis

710 Croton by Achaeans

708 Tarentum by Parthenii from Laconia

c. **700** Metapontum by Sybaris; Siris by Colophon; Locri Epizephyrii by Locrians; Caulonia by Achaeans; Poseidonia (Paestum) by Troezenians expelled from Sybaris

689 Gela by Rhodes and Cretans

664 Acrae by Syracuse

649 Himera by Zancle

648 Selinus by Megara

644 Casmenae by Syracuse

625–585 Ambracia, Leucas, Anactorium, Sollium, Apollonia, Epidamnus by Corinth

600 Massalia by Phocaea

599 Camarina by Syracuse

581 Acragas by Gela

579 Lipara by Cnidus and Rhodes (after a futile attempt to settle at Lilybaeum)

568 Alalia in Corsica by Massalia. (Other colonies of Massalia: Olbia, Antipolis, Nicaea, Agathe, Portus Monoeci, Rhoda, Emporiae, Alonae, Artemisium, and the most westerly Greek settlement Maenace.)

543 Hyele (Elea) by Phocaeans expelled from Alalia

In the north-east (Propontis and Euxine), the Aegean, and the south-east (Egypt and Cyrene).

770 Sinope by Miletus (re-founded after the Cimmerian invasion 631)

757 Cyzicus by Miletus (re-founded 676)

756 Trapezus by Miletus or Sinope (Cotyora and Cerasus by Sinope)

750–650 Many towns on the Thracian peninsula of Chalcidice (Torone by Chalcis; Mende by Eretria; Scione by Achaeans of Pellene; Acanthus(654), Stagirus(654), Argilus, Sane by Andros; Galepsus and Oesyme by Thasos)

712 Astacus by Megara

710 Parium by Miletus and Erythrae

696–2 Amorgos by Samos

689 Phaselis by Rhodes

677 Chalcedon by Megara

c. **680** Thasos by Paros

675 Abydus by Miletus

c. **670** Selymbria by Chalcedon

660 Byzantium by Megara

656 Istrus and Tyras by Miletus

c. **655** Acanthus, Stagirus, Argilus in Chalcidice by Andros

654 Abdera by Clazomenae (re-founded by Teians 545)

653 Lampsacus by Phocaea

c. **650** Milesian factory on the Bolbinitic arm of the Nile

647 Olbia (Borysthenes) by Miletus

633 Cyrene by Thera (Apollonia, its port)

601 Perinthus by Samos

c. **600** Panticapaeum and Theodosia in the Crimea by Miletus

c. **585** Tomi, Odessus and Apollonia in the Pontus by Miletus

before **585** Potidaea by Corinth

570 Naucratis (Miletus, Samos, Aegina and numerous cities represented in the Hellenion)

560 Amisus by Phocaea

c. **550** Barca by Cyrene (also Teucheira and Euesperides)

c. **545** Phanagoreia by Teos

538 Heracleia in the Pontus by Megara (and Boeotians)

510 Mesambria by Chalcedon and Megara

---

[1] The date given by Jerome, 1052, rests on a confusion with the Aeolian Cyme. Strabo makes it the oldest Greek city in Italy or Sicily, and this statement may come from Ephorus.

Civil Events[1]	Literature and Art
776/5 Ol. 1. 1 Coroebus, the first victor in the stadium at Olympia whose name is recorded.	**Epic poetry** flourishes.
752/1 Ol. 7. 1 Decennial archons at Athens.	**776**[2] Arctinus of Miletus: the *Aethiopis* and the *Sack of Troy*.
748/7 Ol. 8. 1 Pheidon, king of Argos, is said by Pausanias to have held the Olympic festival. (Herodotus says that he introduced the 'Pheidonian measures,' *i.e.* the Aeginetan standard. Ephorus attributed to him the first coining of money.)	**765**[2] Cinaethon of Lacedaemon: genealogical poems; *Heracleia* and *Oedipodeia* also ascribed to him by some.
744 *Tiglath-Pileser II, king of Assyria, at this time the greatest power in the East (—727).*	*c.* **750—700** Olympus, the founder of Greek music, composer for the flute (*i.e.* clarinet).
c. **725 Ol. 13. 4** The first Messenian war. In the twentieth year the Spartans under Theopompus enslave or expel the Messenians (Tyrtaeus).	**740**[2] Eumelus of Corinth: *Corinthiaca, Europia,* and *Bugonia.*
720 Ol. 15. 1 *First Assyrian invasion of Egypt by Sargon, the conqueror of Samaria.*	Other early epics; the *Cypria* (attributed to Stasinus or Hegesias), the *Returns* (Νόστοι) of the heroes from Troy (said to be the work of Agias of Troezen), the *Thebais* and *Epigoni* dealing with Theban legends.
709 *Seven Cyprian princes do homage to Sargon.*	
704/3 Ol. 19. 1 Ameinocles of Corinth builds triremes for the Samians.	
c. **700 Ol. 20. 1** War between Chalcis and Eretria for the Lelantine plain: Samos, Miletus and other cities take sides.	
693 Ol. 21. 4 *Midas, king of Phrygia, dies by his own hand in* the Cimmerian invasion of Asia Minor.	*c.* **690** Callinus of Ephesus, the earliest elegiac poet (he refers to the Cimmerian invasion).
683/2 Ol. 24. 2 Nine annual archons at Athens.	**676/5** The Carnean festival at Sparta at which Terpander is victorious. The introduction of the seven-stringed lyre attributed to him.
681 *Esarhaddon (—668). The Assyrians in his reign conquer Egypt which is held by twenty vassal princes.*	
679 *Esarhaddon defeats the Cimmerians under Tiuśpa.*	*c.* **670** Floruit Archilochus[4] of Paros, one of the colonists of Thasos: elegiac and iambic poet. Mentions an eclipse of the sun, *i.e.* April 6, 648.
670/69 Ol. 27. 3 Orthagoras tyrant of Sicyon (his family rules for 100 years).	
669/8 Ol. 27. 4 The Argives defeat the Spartans at Hysiae, Paus. II. 24. 8: Cynuria remains Argive.	*c.* **665** Thaletas of Gortyn in Crete: lyric poet and musician.
664/3 Ol. 29. 1 Sea fight between Corinth and Corcyra. *Accession of Psammetichus I, an Egyptian vassal prince, who with the aid of Greek and Carian mercenaries in time shakes off the Assyrian yoke (—610).*	
660 *Gyges, king of Lydia* (c. 680—660), *becomes a tributary of Assyria.*	
660/59 Ol. 30. 1[3] Zaleucus, legislator of (the Italian) Locri: author of the oldest written code.	
657/6 Ol. 30. 4 *Sardis taken by the Cimmerians.* About this time the Ephesian temple of Artemis burnt by the Cimmerians and Magnesia on the Maeander destroyed by the Treres.	

[1] Foreign events are printed in italics.
[2] On what data, or combinations, these figures of Eusebius rest is not known.
[3] Either in the 26th, 28th or 30th Olympiad the Pisatans are said to have wrested the festival from Elis and retained it 'many years.'
[4] The Parian Chronicle gives 681, Eusebius 665, as the ἀκμή of Archilochus.

Civil Events	Literature and Art

655/4 Ol. 31. 2 Cypselus, tyrant of Corinth (—625).
648/7 Ol. 33. 1 Myron, tyrant of Sicyon, victor in the chariot race at Olympia.

   c. **646** *Ardys, king of Lydia* (called Alyattes by Xanthus), *a vassal of Assyria. His reign perhaps* 652—615.

644/3 Ol. 34. 1 The Pisatans under King Pantaleon held the Olympic festival.
640/39 Ol.35.1 Cylon of Athens victor at Olympia[1]. About this time Charondas legislator of Catana.

   c. **640** The second Messenian war, in which Aristomenes took part[3].

631/0 Ol. 37. 2 Voyage of Colieus the Phocaean to Tartessus.

   626 *Death of Assurbanipal* (Sardanapalus). *Babylon recovers independence.*

625/4 Ol. 38. 4 Periander, tyrant of Corinth (Theagenes, tyrant of Megara, and Procles of Epidaurus his contemporaries).

621/0 Ol. 39. 4 Draco's written code at Athens.

   c. **620** *The Scythians* (Sacae) *invade Asia and weaken the Assyrian empire.*
   615 *Sadyattes, king of Lydia* (—604). He attacks Miletus but ultimately makes peace with its tyrant Thrasybulus.

612/1 Ol. 42. 1 Pittacus overthrows Melanchrus tyrant of Mytilene.

   610 *Necho becomes Pharaoh.*

c. **607/6** War between Athens and Mytilene for
Ol. 43. 2   the possession of the Troad. Pittacus slays Phrynon in single combat.

   606 Fall of Nineveh. *It was captured by Cyaxares the Mede and the Babylonian Nabopolassar.*
   605 Alyattes, king of Lydia (—560). He continues to encroach on the Greek cities.
   604 *Nebuchadnezzar* (—562).

c. **650** The *Little Iliad* (ascribed to Lesches of Lesbos) and the *Heracleia* (to Peisander of Rhodes). Also the earlier Homeric hymns (προοίμια): *e.g.* to the Delian Apollo and to Demeter.

640 Fl. Semonides[2] of Amorgos, iambic poet and satirist.

c. **640—623** Fl. Tyrtaeus of Aphidna, elegiac poet, who inspired the courage of the Spartans in the second Messenian war.

639 Birth of Solon.
Alcman (born at Sardis) migrated to Sparta where he composed hymns and paeans in Doric.

c. **630** The chest of Cypselus dedicated at Olympia (described by Pausanias v. 17—19).

c. **620** Mimnermus of Colophon flourished, elegiac poet: contemporary of Sadyattes[3] : mentions the defence of Smyrna against Gyges.
Rise of Melic poetry; introduction of new lyric metres. In Lesbos flourished Alcaeus, a leader in the opposition to Myrsilus the tyrant, and afterwards to Pittacus, author of στασιωτικά and συμποτικά (*c.* 610—595):
Sappho, famous for love poems and epithalamia (*c.* 610—565): and
Erinna, a minor poetess in the school, or circle, of Sappho.

c. **600** Arion of Methymna introduced 'cyclic choruses' (contemporary with Cypselus).

B. THE SIXTH CENTURY B.C.

119. (1) The Ionians reach the last stage of their development and begin rapidly to decline. All the Asiatic Greek cities pass

Sixth century. under the protection of Croesus; they entirely lose their independence to the Persians. In spite of the destruction of Smyrna and the emigration of the Phocaeans, material prosperity is as yet hardly impaired. (2) Further advance is made by the commercial cities.

---

[1] In a subsequent Olympic year (636, 632 or 628) Cylon attempted, by seizing the Acropolis, to make himself tyrant of Athens. His followers were massacred after surrendering and the Alcmaeonidae were tried and condemned for this breach of faith.
[2] The Parian Chronicle gives 665, Suïdas 640—610, as the ἀκμή of Semonides.
[3] The date adopted by Pausanias is 685—668. But, according to Plutarch (*Apophthegm. Epam.* 23), the restoration of Messene in 369 by the Thebans was 230 years after the conquest of the country.

The growth of manufactures and the introduction of a currency bring economic evils in their train ; loans, usury, mortgages and slavery for debt. These evils favour the rise of tyrants and occasionally of lawgivers (αἰσυμνῆ-ται): but at the end of the century the tyrants have all been deposed—except in Sicily and within the limits of the Persian empire. (3) The military state, Sparta, now at the head of a Peloponnesian confederacy, claims a vague headship of Greece and occasionally remonstrates with powers outside Peloponnesus. Argos is humbled, but Athens steadily increases in power. The Spartans about 600 B.C. are not yet stereotyped, but fresh and vigorous, in touch with foreigners ; a people fond of poetry, musical contests and art. (4) To epic and lyric poets must now be added the Ionian philosophers and prose writers, gnomic poets and fabulists, with the beginnings of tragedy. This century also saw the rise of plastic art in bronze and marble, and the foundation of the most archaic temples.

Herodotus, though writing *c.* 430, is the one invaluable and primary authority for this century. Additional information can be gleaned from the fragments of other historians and from Aristotle *On the Constitution of Athens* (of date 329 B.C.).

Civil Events	Literature and Art
595/4 Ol. 46. 2 **The first Sacred (or Cirrhaean) war** (—586/5), in which Cleisthenes of Sicyon and Solon took part[1].	The **Sculpture** of this century represented by the metopes of Selinus (? 600—580), the
595 *Psammetichus II* (—589). The Abu-Simbel inscription (Hicks, *G. H. I.* no. 3) by some of his mercenaries.	Apollo of Tenea and of Thera, the archaic female statues on the Acropolis. **Architecture** by the temples of Selinus.
594/3 Ol. 46. 3 **Legislation of Solon.**	The Artemisium at Ephesus re-
590/89 Ol. 47. 3 Pittacus, aesymnete of Mytilene. (Resigns 580, dies 570.)	built (Chersiphron of Gnossus).
589 *War between Lydia and Media* (ended by the eclipse of May 28, 585).	**596** Banishment of the Lesbian nobles: Alcaeus goes to E-gypt (his brother Antimenides serves under Nebuchadnezzar), Sappho to Sicily.
584 *Astyages, king of Media* (—550).	**592** 'Stesichorus' of Himera
582/1 Ol. 49. 3 Damasias, archon at Athens, in power for two years and two months.	(*c.* 610—550). He perfected the choral song with strophe,
First Pythiad[2]. The institution or restoration of the Nemean games.	antistrophe, epode: chose epic subjects for lyric treatment.
581/0 Ol. 49. 4 Psammetichus, the last tyrant of Corinth, expelled.	**582—78—74** Sacadas, poet and musician, victor with the 'flute' in the first three Pythiads.
c. **580** Civil strife at Miletus for two generations (—540).	**580** Rise of the Ionian school of natural philosophy. Thales of Miletus (*c.* 624—546) astronomer and physicist (φυσιολόγος).
	580/76 Dipoenus and Scyllis, Cretan sculptors, employed

[1] Thus the Amphictyony of Pylae must date from at least the seventh century.
[2] So the scholiast on Pindar, confirmed by the Marmor Parium and the table of Olympic victors in the *Oxyrhynchus Papyri*, Vol. ii. n. ccxxii. Cf. *ib.* pp. 85, 92. Others reckon the Pythiads to commence with 586 as the first, Pausanias x. 7. 3.
[3] Hence referred by Suïdas to Ol. 37, 632/28.

| | *Civil Events* | *Literature and Art* |

575/4 Ol. 51. 2   Smyrna destroyed by Alyattes.
572/1 Ol. 52. 1   Phalaris, tyrant of Acragas.
    570 *Rise of Amasis, Apries dethroned.*
    Egypt thrown open to Greek trade.
    Cyprus conquered by Egypt.
    Between **570** and **565** Nisaea captured
    by Peisistratus.

566/5 Ol. 53. 3   Games instituted at the Panathenaea.
561/0 Ol. 54. 4   Peisistratus tyrant of Athens. Expelled
    'not long afterwards.'
    560 Croesus, king of Lydia (—546).
    All Greek cities on the mainland
    reduced to dependence.
    c. **560** Tegea acknowledges the Spartan
    hegemony (Cheilon ephor 556).
    553 *Cyrus revolts from allegiance to
    Astyages.*
553/2 Ol. 56. 4   Camarina destroyed by Syracuse. (Not
    recolonized until 493/2.)
551/0 Ol. 57. 2   Peisistratus for a short time again
    tyrant, but, after a rupture with
    Megacles, expelled.
    550 *Overthrow of the Median empire
    by Cyrus.*
548/7 Ol. 58. 1   The temple at Delphi burnt.
    547 *Spring. Cyrus sets out on an ex-
    pedition against Lydia*[1].
546/5 Ol. 58. 3   **Capture of Sardis.** *The Lydian king-
    dom absorbed in the Persian empire.*
    545 *Spring.* The Argives defeated by
    the Spartans: Thyreatis conquered.
    Reduction of the Asiatic Greeks and
    the islands by Harpagus, the general
    of Cyrus. Bias of Priene advises
    emigration to Sardinia.
544/0 Ol. 59   The Phocaeans, driven from Ionia, settle
    first at Alalia in Corsica and then at
    Elea (Velia) in south Italy.
539/8 Ol. 60. 2   Return of Peisistratus 'in the eleventh
    year' of his exile[2].
    538 *October. Babylon taken by Cyrus.*

Literature and Art column:

upon marble and ebony statues
at Sicyon, Cleonae, Argos.
Archermus of Chios famous for
the oldest marble statues in
Delos or Lesbos.
Solon (*c.* 639—559) elegiac poet.
One of the **Seven Wise Men**
(with Thales, Pittacus, Bias
of Priene, Cheilon, Cleobulus
of Lindus, and Myson of Chen,
for whom Periander was substituted by others).
568/4 The *Telegonia*, an epic
poem ascribed to Eugammon
of Cyrene.
566 Glaucus of Chios fl., inventor of the process for weld-
ing iron: he moulds the stand
for the mixing bowl sent by
Alyattes to Delphi.
Anaximander of Miletus fl., pupil
of Thales, geographer and
map maker. Wrote *On Nature.*
556 Pherecydes of Syros (*c.* 596
—540) fl. Said to have been
the teacher of Pythagoras of
Samos. His treatise Ἑπτάμυ-
χος partly a theogony, partly
philosophical.
550 Aesopus fl. A slave, who
invented the type of fable in
which animals act. Lived at
the court of Croesus.
Bathycles of Magnesia fl. He
wrought the reliefs on the
throne of Apollo at Amyclae.
Statues of victors first erected at
Olympia (Ol. 59).
c. **540** Hipponax of Ephesus fl.,
author of bitter lampoons in
scazons, *i.e.* limping iambics.
540 Anaximenes of Miletus,
pupil and successor of Anaximander, fl.
540/36 Phocylides of Miletus,
gnomic poet: author of political and moralizing elegiacs.
536/2 Pythagoras of Samos fl.
Migrating to Croton in Italy,
in order to escape from Polycrates, he there founds a political and religious order: becomes
distinguished as mathematician
and physical philosopher.

[1] This date, which practically determines that of the fall of Sardis, is from a cuneiform inscription.
[2] There is a discrepancy in the authorities between the sum of the separate items and the total length
(17 years) which they assign to Peisistratus' tyranny.

	Civil Events	Literature and Art

533/2 Ol. 61. 4 Polycrates, tyrant of Samos, master of the sea.

529 Cambyses succeeds Cyrus on the Persian throne.

527/6 Ol. 63. 2 Hippias succeeds Peisistratus.

525   The Persians conquer Egypt.

524/3 Ol. 64. 1 A Spartan expedition against Polycrates unsuccessful. The Etruscans attack Cumae without success.

522 Death of Cambyses. The false Smerdis, a Magian, reigns for seven months, but is deposed and slain.

521 Darius, son of Hystaspes, becomes king, and suppresses various revolts in the provinces (521—519). He organizes the satrapies of the empire.

520/19 Ol. 65. 1 Cleomenes, king of Sparta (—489).

519/8 Ol. 65. 2 Plataea, by the advice of Cleomenes, seeks protection from Athens, 93 years before its destruction.

517 Conquest of Barca by the Persians.

514 Scythian expedition of Darius. Megabazus subsequently reduces Thrace and Macedonia. Histiaeus returns with Darius to Susa.

514/3 Ol. 66. 3 Murder of Hipparchus by Harmodius and Aristogeiton at the great Panathenaea (28th of Hecatombaeon, 514).

511/0 Ol. 67. 2 Destruction of Sybaris by Croton.

510 Spring. Harpactides archon. Expulsion of Hippias by the Spartans under Cleomenes. Hippias is settled at Sigeum.

c. 510 The Carthaginians expel a Spartan colony under Dorieus, half brother of Cleomenes, from the Cinyps in Libya.

508/7 Ol. 68. 1 Isagoras archon.

507 Spring. Cleomenes at Athens: he expels **700** families, but fails to overthrow the Council. After his departure Cleisthenes and his adherents are recalled. **Cleisthenes reforms the constitution of Athens, creating new local tribes with the trittyes and demes.** Athens applies to Artaphrenes, satrap of Sardis, for protection.

507/6 Ol. 68. 2 Alcmaeon (?) archon.

506 Spring. Peloponnesian invasion of Attica. Owing to Corinthian opposition and dissension between the kings, Cleomenes and Demaratus, the army retires. The Athenians defeat the Thebans and Chalcidians: 2000 cleruchs settled at Chalcis.

504 Aristodemus becomes tyrant of Cumae. (Hicks, *Gk Inscr.* 15.)

504/3 Acestorides archon.

536/520 Anacreon of Teos, lyric poet, and Ibycus of Rhegium fl. at the court of Polycrates. Besides love poems Ibycus wrote choral hymns on epic subjects.

534 Beginnings of Attic tragedy: Thespis.

536/20 Theodorus of Samos fl., one of the earliest to cast bronze. Also famous as an engraver of gems, and architect (with Rhoecus) of the temple of Hera at Samos.

c. **530** Xenophanes founder of the Eleatic school fl. Driven from Colophon to Zancle, Catana and Elea, he wandered 67 years over Greece, *Fr.* 24 (? 540—473). He wrote an hexameter poem *On Nature*, besides epics and elegiacs on a variety of subjects.

527—14 Onomacritus, an Athenian, at the court of Hipparchus fl. The Orphic theogony attributed to him.

525 Birth of Aeschylus.

523 Choerilus of Athens, tragic poet, begins to exhibit.

c. **522** Theognis of Megara, a bitter political partizan, fl. Author of elegies to Cyrnus. (Mentions events of 506 and 492.)

518 Birth of Pindar.

516/2 Gitiadas of Sparta architect of the temple of Athena Chalcioecus.

c. **504/0** Heracleitus of Ephesus, the last of the Ionian physical philosophers, wrote *On Nature* in a style proverbial for obscurity.

c. **504** Endoeus of Athens sculptor fl. (a ξόανον of Athena on the Acropolis).

C. THE FIFTH CENTURY B.C.

120.   The Ionians begin an ill-judged revolt which ends in the destruction of Miletus and the more complete subjugation of all

The Persian wars, 500—479.   Asiatic Greeks. Slight and ineffective aid had been given them by their kinsmen across the Aegean, who are next attacked. But Darius learnt to his amazement that the host which had sacked Eretria was no match on the field of Marathon for the Athenian hoplites charging with spear and shield. He did not live to carry out the grand invasion for which he was making elaborate preparations. Under Xerxes the whole resources of the Persian empire are pitted against the Greek nation, while Carthage lends aid by an invasion of Sicily. These attacks are repelled by the genius of Themistocles, the heroic self-sacrifice of the Athenians, and the large forces under the command of the Syracusan tyrant Gelon. In the struggle the Greeks are compelled, as never before, to unite, however imperfectly and reluctantly, for combined action, and to recognize a community of interest. The self-respect and enthusiasm of the victors receive a prodigious impetus.

Herodotus, V—IX, is the main authority for the period 500–479 (he was writing as late as 430).

	Civil Events	*Literature and Art*
500/499 Ol. 70. 1 Myrus[1]	Naxian oligarchs apply to Aristagoras of Miletus.	Architecture at the opening of the fifth century represented by
499/8 Ol. 70. 2	**499** Failure of the Naxian expedition. The Ionians persuaded by Aristagoras to revolt, contrary to the advice of Hecataeus.	the temple of Athena in Aegina: sculpture by the figures from the pediment. Contemporary schools of sculpture:
	The fleet at Myus won over: the tyrants, who were in command of it, expelled.	(1) at Aegina, Callon, *c.* 524—462: Onatas (the *Black*
	Winter. Aid sought in Sparta and Athens.	*Demeter* at Phigalia; at Olympia the colossal *Heracles of*
	498 *Spring.* Despatch of Athenian and Eretrian forces. Victory of the Ionian fleet off Pamphylia.	*the Thasians*, and votive offerings of the Achaeans and Hieron), *c.* 500—457:

[1] The names of the Athenian archons are appended to each year; the archons for the years **499/8, 498/7, 497/6, 486/5** are unknown.

The following archons of the fifth and fourth centuries belong to years omitted from the chronological table:

501/0	Hermocreon	**389/8**	Antipater	**350/49**	Apollodorus
475/4	Dromocleides	**388/7**	Pyrgion	**345/4**	Eubulus
442/1	Diphilus	**386/5**	Mystichides	**344/3**	Lyciscus
439/8	Glaucinus	**384/3**	Dieitrephes	**328/7**	Euthycritus
438/7	Theodorus	**382/1**	Evander	**320/19**	Neaechmus
436/5	Lysimachus	**381/0**	Demophilus	**315/4**	Praxibulus
434/3	Crates	**380/79**	Pytheas	**314/3**	Nicodorus
402/1	Micon	**377/6**	Calleas	**313/2**	Theophrastus
393/2	Demostratus	**374/3**	Socratides	**304/3**	Pherecles
392/1	Philocles	**351/0**	Theellus	**303/2**	Leostratus.

Lacrateides, a contemporary of Darius, archon in a year memorable for its severe winter, has been referred to one of the years 499–6.

Civil Events	*Literature and Art*
498/7 Ol. 70. 3 Sardis surprised and burnt. The Greeks defeated near Ephesus on the return march. Spread of the revolt from Byzantium to Cyprus, where Onesilus seizes Salamis. Athens refuses further aid.	(2) at Sicyon, Canachus (*Apollo with the stag at Branchidae*):
497 *Spring.* Operations of Daurises on the Hellespont.	(3) at Argos, Ageladas (*Zeus Ithomatas* for the exiled Messenians), *c.* 520—455.
497/6 Ol. 70. 4 The Ionian fleet off Cyprus. Defeat and death of Onesilus. Revolt in Caria: battle of the Marsyas. Flight of Aristagoras, who is slain near Myrcinus.	*c.* **500** Hecataeus of Miletus, traveller and geographer, and Dionysius of Miletus, historian, fl. Early Ionian prose-writers.
496 *Spring.* Capture of Soli. Suppression of the revolt in Cyprus.	*c.* **500** Lasus of Hermione, lyric poet and musician, teacher of Pindar.
496/5 Ol. 71. 1 Reduction of Aeolis. In Caria, battles of Labraunda and Mylasa. Histiaeus arrives from Susa, but is discredited at Sardis and flees to Chios.	*c.* **500** Pratinas of Phlius, tragic poet, the first to exhibit satyric dramas.
Hipparchus	**499** Aeschylus begins to exhibit at the age of twenty-five.
495/4 Ol. 71. 2 Cleomenes destroys 6000 Argives in the grove of Argos. The town defended by the women under Telesilla[1]. Battle of Lade.	**498** Pindar, *Pythian* 10.
Philippus	*c.* **496** Charon of Lampsacus, λογογράφος, early Ionian prose-writer, fl.
494/3 Ol. 71. 3 Siege and capture of Miletus 'in the sixth year of the revolt.'	*c.* **496** Birth of Sophocles.
Pythocritus	
493 *Spring.* The Persians reduce Chios, Lesbos, Tenedos.	**493** Phrynichus is fined for exhibiting at Athens the *Capture of Miletus.*
493/2 Ol. 71. 4 Themistocles begins the fortification of Peiraeus. Miltiades retires from the Chersonese. Artaphrenes regulates the affairs of Ionia, making a survey and fixing tributes.	*c.* **492** Parmenides of Elea fl. (? *c.* 520—455)[2]. A pupil of Xenophanes who reduced the Eleatic philosophy to a system, expounded in an hexameter poem *On Nature.*
Themistocles	
Hippocrates, tyrant of Gela, Anaxilaus of Rhegium.	
492/1 Ol. 72. 1 Expedition of Mardonius: the Persian fleet is wrecked off Mount Athos, but Thrace, Macedon and Thasos submit.	
Diognetus	
491 *Spring.* Envoys demand submission of the separate Greek cities. Aegina complies.	
491/0 Ol. 72. 2 Deposition of Demaratus at Sparta. Leotychidas his successor (—469).	**490** Pindar, *Pythians* 6 and 12. Simonides of Iulis in Ceos (556 —467) composed an epigram on the victors at Marathon (as later on Thermopylae, Salamis, Plataea). He lived at the court of Hipparchus, in Thessaly, and later in Sicily. Author of hymns, paeans, dithyrambs, elegiacs.
Hybrilides	Gelon tyrant of Gela. Ten Aeginetan hostages detained at Athens. Hence Aeginetan reprisals and ultimately war between Athens and Aegina (perhaps later 488/7).
490/89 Ol.72.3 A fresh Persian expedition under Datis and Artaphrenes having destroyed Naxos and Eretria lands in Attica, but is defeated at **Marathon** (*Sept.*).	
Phaenippus	
489 *Spring.* Miltiades attacks Paros without success.	*c.* **490** Panyasis, epic poet, uncle of Herodotus, author of a *Heracleia.*
489/8 Ol. 72. 4 Trial and condemnation of Miltiades, who dies in prison of his wound. Theron, tyrant of Acragas.	**488** Pindar, *Olymp.* 14?
Aristeides	

---

[1] These transactions are placed by Pausanias 'soon after the accession of Cleomenes.'
[2] Plato, *Parm.* 127 A. But Diog. L. IX. 23 places his ἀκμή in Ol. 69.

	Civil Events	*Literature and Art*
488/7 Ol. 73. 1 Anchises	487 *Spring.* Ostracism of Hipparchus, son of Charmus, the head of the Peisistratid party at Athens.	487 Chionides, comic poet, begins to exhibit 'eight years before the Persian war.'
487/6 Ol. 73. 2 Telesinus	Alteration in the appointment of archons: the lot applied to the candidates proposed by the tribes.	
	486 *Spring.* Ostracism of Megacles, nephew of Cleisthenes.	486 Pindar, *Pythian* 7.
486/5 Ol. 73. 3	The revolt of Egypt delays the preparations of Darius for an invasion of Greece.	*c.* 484 Epicharmus of Cos fl. He perfects Sicilian comedy
485/4 Ol. 73. 4 Philocrates	*Death of Darius. Accession of Xerxes* (—465). Gelon master of Syracuse.	and exhibits his plays at Syracuse shortly before the Persian war.
	484 *Spring.* Ostracism of Xanthippus.	484 Birth of Herodotus.
484/3 Ol. 74. 1 Leostratus	Egypt reconquered. Xerxes' preparations go on for four years (—480).	
483/2 Ol. 74. 2 Nicodemus or ? (Nicomedes)	Proposal of Themistocles to devote the profit of the mines at Maroneia to the building of 100 triremes. The war with Aegina (μέγιστος πόλεμος) continues (till 481)	
	482 *Spring.* Ostracism of Aristeides.	
481/0 Ol. 74. 4 Hypsichides	Xerxes winters at Sardis. Congress at the Isthmus of cities willing to resist. Envoys despatched to Argos, Crete, Corcyra, Syracuse.	481 Pindar *Nemean* 5 and Bacchylides 13.—Bacchylides (? *c.* 507—430 B.C.), a nephew of Simonides, competed with Pindar in the composition of
	480 *Spring.* Xerxes marches unopposed through Thrace and Macedonia into Thessaly, the Greeks having abandoned the defence of Tempe.	odes, paeans, dithyrambs. Other contemporary lyric poets: Timocreon of Ialysus in Rhodes, bitter enemy of Si-
480/79 Ol. 75.1 Calliades	Recall of ostracized and disfranchised Athenians. ARTEMISIUM, THERMOPYLAE (end of *August*), SALAMIS (*Sept.* 28). Xerxes withdraws with the fleet.	monides and his patron Themistocles: Corinna of Tanagra, and Telesilla of Argos. 480 Pindar, *Isthmian* 5 (6) (for
	Gelon and Theron defeat the Carthaginians at HIMERA.	Phylacidas). Birth of Euripides and of Antiphon.
	479 *Spring.* Attica reoccupied by the Persians. Athens burnt.	
479/8 Ol. 75. 2 Xanthippides	Battles of PLATAEA and MYCALE (*August*). Islands admitted to general Greek alliance. Ionians and Hellespontine Greeks allied with Athens. Siege and capture of Sestus.	

121.   Not content with the repulse of the invader, the Greeks resolve to continue the war and liberate their kinsmen in Asia from
The Pente-contaety, 478—431. the Persian yoke. Thus is formed a maritime league under Athenian headship which succeeds in its immediate object but gradually becomes transformed into the Athenian empire. As the Peloponnesian confederacy continues under Spartan headship, the national forces are divided. The two rival confederacies, at first united in enmity to Persia, become lukewarm, jealous, and at last bitterly hostile,

while the war against the barbarian is practically abandoned.　In Sicily
the moderate rule of a Hieron is followed by the revival of free government, while the career of Ducetius proves that the native Sicels are
assimilating Greek culture.

Throughout this period the Greeks put forth their full vigour in all
fields.　Art and literature rise rapidly to perfection.

Thucydides (I. 89—118) is almost the sole authority for the Pentecontaety, and
while he criticises the chronology of his predecessor Hellanicus it is remarkable that
he does not himself determine the *dates*, but only the *succession*, of events.　The Thirty
Years' Peace and the revolt of Samos are the only dates given by Thucydides: but the
death of Xerxes and the disaster at Drabescus may be determined from data which
he supplies, and for other events (*e.g.* Eurymedon or the earthquake at Sparta) the
margin of conjecture may be reduced to a few years.

A few dates, independent of Herodotus and Thucydides, may be gleaned from
Aristotle, *Constitution of Athens.*

	Civil Events	Literature and Art
	Winter. Themistocles at Sparta justifies the fortification of Athens.	**478** Pindar, *Isthmian* 7 (8). Pindar, Simonides, Bacchy-
	478 *Spring.* Pausanias in Cyprus.	lides, and after 472 Aeschylus
478/7 Ol. **75.** 3 Timosthenes	Hieron succeeds Gelon at Syracuse. Pausanias in Byzantium.　His arrogance and correspondence with Xerxes.	at the court of Hieron. Calamis of Athens active as a sculptor after the Persian wars.
	Winter. Recall of Pausanias on his trial for treason: he is acquitted.	His most famous work the *Sosandra*: admired for his
	477 *Spring.*　General disgust of the allies at Spartan headship.　Maritime confederation organized by Aristeides for prosecuting the war with Persia: Delos to be the treasury: ὁ πρῶτος φόρος ταχθείς.	rendering of horses.　Also Myron of Eleutherae, whose works, almost all in bronze, were distinguished for lifelike vigour and reality: *e.g.* the *Discobolus, Ladas,* the *Heifer,*
477/6 Ol. **75.** 4 Adeimantus	Dorcis is recalled and Sparta retires from the maritime war. Pausanias again in Byzantium.	afterwards taken to Rome. Pythagoras of Samos, from 496 resident at Rhegium, famous
	476 *Spring.* Leotychidas in Thessaly.	for his *Philoctetes* and for
476/5 Ol. **76.** 1 Phaedo	Leotychidas deposed: Archidamus king of Sparta.　Pausanias expelled from Sestus and Byzantium.　Cimon be- sieges Eion.	athlete statues, *e.g.* that of *Euthymus* after his third Olympic victory 472. Statues of the tyrannicides by
	Anaxilaus of Rhegium succeeded by Micythus.　Foundation of Aetna in place of the Ionian cities of Catana and Naxos.	Critius and Nesiotes set up in place of those carried off by Xerxes.
	475 *Spring.*　Capture of Eion.　The recovery of the Thracian coasts takes some years.　Attempt of Athens to plant a colony on the Strymon frus- trated by Thracians.	**476** Pindar, *Olymp.* 1, 2, 3, 10 and 11: Bacchylides 5.　The- mistocles choregus for Phry- nichus, who exhibits the *Phoe- nissae* in honour of Salamis. Simonides victor with the dithyramb.
474/3 Ol. **76.** 3 Acestorides	Hieron defeats the Etruscans in a sea fight off Cumae.	**474** Pindar victor with the dithyramb.　Pindar, *Fr.* 76— 78, *Pythians* 9 and 11.

| | *Civil Events* | *Literature and Art* |

473/2 Ol. 76. 4
Meno

Between **474** and **472** Conquest of Scyros. Ostracism of Themistocles. Anti-Spartan movement in Peloponnesus put down by a victory at Tegea over Arcadians and Argives.

472/1 Ol. 77. 1
Chares

Reduction of Carystus in Euboea by the Athenians. Treason and death of Pausanias.
Revolution in Elis. Death of Theron. Hieron deposes Thrasydaeus and annexes Acragas.
Between **471** and **469** Defeat of Arcadians by Lacedaemonians at Dipaea. The Argives reduce Tiryns.

471/0 Ol. 77. 2
Praxiergus

Outlawry of Themistocles who escapes to Corcyra and Epeirus. Συνοικισμὸς of Elis.

470/69 Ol. 77. 3
Demotion

Revolt and reduction of Naxos. Themistocles lands at Ephesus on his way to Persia.

469/8 Ol. 77. 4
Apsephion

468 *Spring.* Athenian expedition to Caria.

468/7 Ol. 78. 1
Theagenides

Autumn. Double victory of Cimon by land and sea on the EURYMEDON[1]. The Carian cities join Athens.

467/6 Ol. 78. 2
Lysistratus

Athenian decrees concerning Colophon and Erythrae: C.I.A. I. 9, 10, 11.
466 *Spring.* Death of Hieron. His brother Thrasybulus besieged in Ortygia and forced to capitulate. Syracuse a free state (—**405**). Downfall of tyrannies all over Sicily.

466/5 Ol. 78. 3
Lysanias

Cimon drives the Persians out of the Chersonese.
465 *Spring.* Projected colony of Ennea Hodoi on the Strymon. Revolt of Thasos. Disaster of Drabescus: the Athenian colonists cut off by the Edonians[2].

465/4 Ol. 78. 4
Lysitheus

Death of Xerxes. Artaxerxes I (—**424**).

464/3 Ol. 79. 1
Archedemides

Earthquake at Sparta. Revolt of Messenians. Occupation of Ithome.
463 *Spring.* Thasos capitulates 'in the third year.'

463/2 Ol. 79. 2
Tlepolemus

Cimon impeached by Pericles on his return from Thasos.
462 *Spring.* Expedition of Cimon, with 4000 men, to aid Sparta in the siege of Ithome.
Revolt in Egypt.

462/1 Ol. 79. 3
Conon

Fall of the Areopagus: its political functions restricted by the reforms of Ephialtes. State pay for dicasts instituted by Pericles.

Literature and Art

472 The *Persae* of Aeschylus. Pindar, *Olymp.* 6 (or 468) *Isthmian* 2 (or later). About this time comic choruses compete at the Great Dionysia and Lenaea.

?471 Thucydides born. Aeschylus in Sicily. The *Women of Aetna.*
The activity of Pheidias begins.
470 Hieron's victory at Delphi celebrated by Pindar, *Pythian* 1, Bacchylides 4.
Pindar, *Olymp.* 12 (or 468).
469 Socrates born.
468 Sophocles' first victory. Hieron's last Olympic victory: Bacchylides 3.
467 Aeschylus' *Seven against Thebes.*
466 Corax begins to teach rhetoric at Syracuse.
Between **472** and **465** Polygnotus, the celebrated painter, engaged in decorating the temples of the Dioscuri and Theseus, the Pinacotheca and other buildings at Athens. His most famous frescoes were the *Capture of Troy* in the Stoa Poecile and the *Lower World* in the Lesche of the Cnidians at Delphi. Micon and Panaenus also adorned the Stoa Poecile with frescoes of Marathon and the battle with the Amazons.
The temple of Zeus at Olympia is said to have been built with the spoil of the Pisatans, conquered by Elis before **470**. The sculpture of the pediments attributed to Paeonius of Mende and Alcamenes, a pupil of Pheidias (not finished before **457**).
464 Pindar, *Olymp.* 7, 9 and 13, *Fr.* 107.
462 Anaxagoras of Clazomenae, physical philosopher, comes to Athens. Pindar, *Pythians* 4 and 5.

[1] The battle is *after* the reduction of Naxos and *before* the revolt of Thasos.
[2] This was 29 years before the foundation of Amphipolis.

	Civil Events	Literature and Art
	Return of Cimon from Messenia, the Spartans having dismissed his contingent. Breach with Sparta: alliance of Athens with Argos and Thessaly.	*c.* **460** Noted painters of the Pentecontaety were Pauson, whose forte was caricature, Agatharchus and Dionysius of Colophon.
	461 *Spring.* Ostracism of Cimon. Assassination of Ephialtes.	
461/0 Ol. 79. 4 Euthippus	**460** *Spring.* Capture of Naupactus by the Athenians.	*c.* **460** Pindar, *Olymp.* 8. Hippocrates born. Democritus
460/59 Ol. 80. 1 Phrasycleides	**459** *Early.* Capitulation of the Messenians[1], who are settled by the Athenians in Naupactus. Megara joins Athens.	born. Fl. Magnes, a comic poet. **459** Thrasymachus born.
	The Persian army invades Egypt.	
	Summer. Battle of Papremis.	
459/8 Ol. 80. 2 Philocles	The Egyptian expedition decreed. The Athenian fleet under Charmantides moves from Cyprus to Memphis.	
	458 *Spring.* Battle of Halieis and naval battle off Cecryphaleia (Hicks, 19) between Athens and Corinth.	**458** Aeschylus, *Oresteia.*
458/7 Ol. 80. 3 Habron	Battle off the Aeginetan coast between Athens and Aegina. Aegina besieged by the Athenians.	
	Battle in the Megarid between Athens and Corinth.	
	Law permitting zeugitae to become archons.	
	457 *Spring.* The Peloponnesians in Phocis: they defeat the Athenians at TANAGRA. Recall of Cimon. The Athenians conclude an armistice with Sparta.	**457** A shield dedicated by the Lacedaemonians as acroterion of the temple at Olympia in honour of Tanagra.
457/6 Ol. 80. 4 Mnesitheides	The Athenians defeat the Boeotians at OENOPHYTA. Submission of Boeotia and Phocis. Capitulation of Aegina. Mission of Megabazus to Sparta from the Persian court.	**456** Aeschylus dies at Gela. Pindar, *Olymp.* 4 and 5?
456/5 Ol. 81. 1 Callias	Completion of the long walls to Peiraeus and Phalerum. Capture of Troezen by the Athenians. Megabyzus undertakes to reduce Egypt.	
	455 Expedition of Tolmides round Peloponnesus: Gytheium burnt.	**455** Euripides' *Peliadae.*
455/4 Ol. 81. 2 Sosistratus	The Athenians besieged in the island of Prosopitis.	
	454 *Spring.* Athenian expedition to Thessaly in favour of Orestes.	
454/3 Ol. 81. 3 Ariston	The custody of the common funds removed by the Confederation from Delos to Athens.	
	Annihilation of the Athenian army on the Nile and loss of relieving squadron.	

[1] ' In the fourth year' reading τετάρτῳ for δεκάτῳ, Thuc. I. 103. If δεκάτῳ, which Diodorus read, is right the revolt must have begun in 468, the date given by Philochorus. For the surrender of Ithome must have preceded the battle of Tanagra.

Civil Events	*Literature and Art*

Treaties made by Athens with Phocis
and Egesta: C.I.A. IV. pp. 8, 58.
Pericles in Sicyon and Acarnania.
Achaia joins Athens.

453/2 Ol. 81. 4 Law reviving local justices (οἱ κατὰ
Lysicrates δήμους δικασταὶ) at Athens.

452/1 Ol. 82. 1 Annexation of Aethalia by the Syra- **452** Bacchylides 6, 7
Chaerephanes cusans. Ducetius at the head of the
Sicels defeats the Acragantians and
Syracusans.

451/0 Ol. 82. 2 Law limiting the Attic franchise. **451** Ion of Chios begins to ex-
Antidotus Peace for 30 years between Sparta and hibit tragedies.
Argos.
Defeat of Ducetius who surrenders to
Syracuse.

450/49 Ol. 82. 3 Truce for five years between Athens **450—420** Rise of Sicilian Rhe-
Euthydemus and Sparta. Assessment of tribute. toric. After Corax and Teisias
[Recurs 446 and 439. Probably also the first authors of a handbook,
429 and 425.] Gorgias of Leontini became
449 *Spring.* Cimon's last expedition: eminent as a teacher and
to Cyprus. writer.
Treaty between Athens and Miletus: *c.* **450** Leucippus, founder of
C. I. A. IV. p. 6. the atomic theory, fl. (earlier

449/8 Ol. 82. 4 Death of Cimon. than Melissus and Diogenes
Pedieus **448** *Spring.* ? The Greeks invited to of Apollonia).
a congress at Athens with a view to **450—423** Cratinus nine times
restoring the temples destroyed by victorious with comedies. He
the Persians and securing the peace- attacked Pericles and Aspasia
ful navigation of the sea. and eulogized Cimon.
Lacedaemonian expedition to Delphi. **449—425** Crates, a comic poet.
Ducetius establishes himself at CaleActe.
War between Syracuse and Acragas.

448/7 Ol. 83. 1 Pericles restores to the Phocians the *c.* **448** Birth of Aristophanes.
Philiscus care of the Delphian temple.
447 *Spring.* Cleruchies in Cherso- **447** The building of the Par-
nesus, Euboea, Naxos, Andros, Lem- thenon commenced, Ictinus
nos. About this time a convention and Callicrates architects.
concluded with Persia (cited by the
orators as the Peace of Callias, or
of Cimon).

447/6 Ol. 83. 2 Revolt in Boeotia: the Athenians de-
Timarchides feated at Coronea.
446 *Spring.* Revolt of Euboea and **446** Pindar, *Pythian* 8.
Megara.
Peloponnesian invasion of Attica by
Pleistoanax.

446/5 Ol. 83. 3 Retreat of Pleistoanax. Recovery of
Callimachus Euboea.
Winter. The Thirty Years' Peace:
Athens renounces her land empire,
giving up Nisaea, Pegae, Troezen
and Achaia.
445 New Sybaris founded. Middle **444** Empedocles of Acragas fl.
wall at Athens (after **445**). Projected He was active in the over-
colony at Brea in Thrace (between throw of Thrasydaeus and of
446 and 443, Hicks and Hill 41). the One Thousand. Author

445/4 Ol. 83. 4 The Sybarites expelled from New of philosophical poems *On
Lysimachides Sybaris found a city on the Traeis. Nature* and *Expiations.*
Present of corn to Athens from Egypt.

Civil Events	Literature and Art
444/3 Ol. 84. 1 Foundation of Thurii. Praxiteles Ostracism of Thucydides, the son of Melesias. **443/2** Ol. 84. 2 **443** *Spring.* Lysanias	**443** Herodotus of Halicarnassus, the historian, one of the colonists of Thurii. The last event noticed in his history (VII. 137) is of date 430.
	442 or 441 Sophocles' *Antigone.*
441/0 Ol. 84. 4 **440** Revolt of Samos. Help refused Timocles by the Peloponnesian confederacy. **440/39** Ol. 85. 1 Battle off Sphagia: partial successes of Morychides the Samians. Investment of the town. **439** Capitulation of Samos after nine months' siege.	**441** First victory of Euripides. Cratinus, *The Thracian Women.* **440** Melissus, general of the Samians in the revolt, the last Eleatic philosopher. **440/39** Prohibition of personal attacks in comedy (μὴ κωμῳ-δεῖν ἐξ ὀνόματος). Repealed in 437/6. **438** Euripides' *Alcestis.* Completion of the Parthenon and of the chryselephantine Athena of Pheidias who goes to Olympia, where he receives a commission for the statue of Zeus.
437 About this time Phormio takes Amphilochian Argos (Thuc. II. 68).	**437** Pherecrates, poet of the old comedy, victorious. The *metrum Pherecrateum* called after him.
437/6 Ol. 85. 4 **436** Foundation of Amphipolis. Euthymenes About this time the expedition of Peri- cles to the Pontus. Athenian colonists at Sinope and Amisus. **435/4** Ol. 86. 2 Quarrel between Corinth and Corcyra. Antiochides Corinthian defeat off Actium. **433/2** Ol. 86. 4 Alliance between Athens and Corcyra. Apseudes Battle of Sybota (*May* 432). **432** Revolt of Potidaea. **432/1** Ol. 87. 1 The Megarians excluded by a decree Pythodorus from commercial intercourse with Athens and her allies. A Congress of allies at Sparta resolves upon war (*October*). Prosecutions of Aspasia, Pheidias and Anaxagoras.	**436** Commencement of the Propylaea: Mnesicles architect. Birth of Isocrates. **432** Publication of Meton's cycle. Diogenes of Apollonia, almost the last physical philosopher (alluded to in the *Clouds*, 423). Archelaus, pupil of Anaxagoras. Protagoras of Abdera (481—411) the most famous of the professional lecturers and teachers, called Sophists: and Prodicus of Ceos, moralist and orator, active about this time.

122.   The Athenian empire by seeking to impose a partial unity upon Greece had only provoked more and more the jealousy,   The Peloponnesian suspicion, and alarm of the Peloponnesian confederacy.   ponnesian The struggle between these rival powers widened into a   war: 431—404. conflict of race between Ionians and Dorians, and a party warfare between democracy and oligarchy, in which the resources of Greece were shattered, until by a disgraceful alliance with Persia and by the zealous partizanship of Cyrus, Sparta secured the final decision in her favour.

G. A.   7

The prosperity of the Sicilian Greeks was seriously impaired: the Athenian expedition was repelled at a heavy cost to the victors; the Carthaginian invasion destroyed five of the most flourishing states. Syracuse survived, but it passed under the tyranny of Dionysius.

Meanwhile the intellectual development proceeded apace. Tragedy had not yet passed its prime when the old comedy shot up to maturity; close upon the natural philosophers pressed the humanists and rhetoricians, the body of professional educators called sophists. In architecture, sculpture and painting, a succession of great artists became famous.

For the years 431—411 Thucydides is a contemporary authority of the first order: from 411 onwards Xenophon's *Hellenica*, I, II is a meagre supplement. Andocides' account of the events of 415, given in 399, must be received with caution.

	Civil Events	Literature and Art
	431 *Spring.* The Thebans attempt to surprise Plataea (*March*).	431 Euripides' *Medea.*
431/0 Ol. 87. 2 Euthynus	War begins *May* 25th. First Peloponnesian raid into Attica (repeated in 430, 428, 427, 425). First annual raid of the Athenians into the Megarid (repeated every year until 424), and cruise of the fleet round Peloponnesus. The Aeginetans expelled from their island and settled at Thyrea.	Sculpture represented by Polycleitus of Sicyon, pupil of Ageladas, who settled at Argos and decorated the Heraeum after the fire of 423, and was architect of the theatre at Epidaurus—most famous works: a *Doryphorus, Diadumenus, Amazon, Zeus Meilichius* (418), and chryselephantine *Hera.* Architecture represented by the temple of Apollo Epicurius at Bassae near Phigaleia : architect Ictinus.
430/29 Ol.87.3 Apollodorus	430 **Plague at Athens.** *Winter.* Potidaea capitulates. 429 *Spring.* Siege of Plataea. *Summer.* Trial and fine of Pericles.	
429/8 Ol. 87. 4 Epameinon	Phormio gains two naval victories in the Corinthian gulf. *Autumn.* Death of Pericles. 428 *Spring.* Mytilene and most of Lesbos revolt.	430 Hermippus comic poet fl. 429 Eupolis (*aetat.* 17) exhibits his first comedy. 428 Euripides' *Hippolytus.* Anaxagoras dies at Lampsacus.
428/7 Ol. 88. 1 Diotimus	*Autumn.* Blockade of Mytilene by the Athenians. *Winter.* Escape of 212 Plataeans.	
427/6 Ol. 88. 2 Eucles	427 *Summer.* Surrender of Mytilene: execution of the ringleaders: confiscation of the land. Alcidas crosses the Aegean with a Peloponnesian fleet. Surrender of Plataea. Faction at Corcyra. 426 *Spring.* An Athenian fleet in Sicilian waters.	427 Embassy of Gorgias of Leontini to Athens. Plato born (or 429). The *Banqueters* of Aristophanes.
426/5 Ol. 88. 3 Euthynus	Foundation of Heraclea in Trachis by the Lacedaemonians. Demosthenes, repulsed in Aetolia, with aid of the Acarnanians defeats the Ambracians and a Spartan auxiliary force at Olpae and Idomene. (The war in this part of Greece virtually terminated.)	426 Aristophanes' *Babylonians.*

Civil Events	Literature and Art

425 *Spring.* Fortification of Pylos by Demosthenes: the Spartans attack it, occupying Sphacteria. Proposals for a peace refused by Athens on the advice of Cleon.

425 Aristophanes' *Acharnians.* Painters of this time (431—404): Apollodorus of Athens (σκια-γράφος);
Zeuxis of Heraclea: an *Helen* for the temple of Lacinian Hera: he also decorated the palace of Archelaus of Macedon (413—339);

425/4 Ol. 88. 4
Stratocles

Capture of Sphacteria and 292 Spartans by Cleon and Demosthenes.
Massacres at Corcyra: the oligarchs exterminated.
Tribute of the Athenian allies raised.
Darius II succeeds to the Persian throne (—405).

Parrhasius of Ephesus: the *Demos of Athens*;
Timanthes of Cythnus: the *Contest for the arms of Achilles* and the *Sacrifice of Iphigenia.*

424 *Spring.* Conference at Gela. General pacification of Sicilian Greeks.

424 Aristophanes' *Knights.*
Thucydides the Athenian general in command of Thrace: on the motion of Cleon he is banished.
He is collecting materials for his history until the close of the war [Xenophon] *De Rep. Ath.* (not later than 424).

424/3 Ol. 89. 1
Isarchus

Capture of Cythera and Nisaea by the Athenians.
Brasidas marches through Thessaly: Acanthus revolts to him. He captures Amphipolis and Torone.
Winter. The Athenians invade Boeotia and are defeated at Delium.

423 *May.* Armistice for a year between Athens and Sparta.

423 Aristophanes' *Clouds.* The prize obtained by Cratinus with the *Wineflask.*

423/2 Ol. 89. 2
Amynias

Brasidas in the service of Perdiccas of Macedon.

422/1 Ol. 89. 3
Alcaeus

422 *Summer.* Cleon recaptures Torone. Cleon is defeated and he and Brasidas slain outside Amphipolis.
Winter. Negociations for peace.

422 Aristophanes' *Prelude* (Προαγών), *Wasps.*

421 *April.* Peace of Nicias and alliance for fifty years between Sparta and Athens.

421 Eupolis' *Flatterers* (first prize) and *Maricas*: Aristophanes' *Peace* (second).

421/0 Ol. 89. 4
Aristion

The terms refused by the allies of Sparta: they mistrust Sparta and try to form a new league.

c. **421—417** Antiphon *On the death of Herodes.*
421 or **420** Euripides' *Suppliants.*

420/19 Ol. 90. 1
Astyphilus

420 Athens enters into alliance with Argos and with Elis and Mantinea, recalcitrant allies of Sparta.

420 Birth of Isaeus.
c. **420** Hellanicus of Mytilene fl., author of an *Atthis* and other historical works.

419/8 Ol. 90. 2
Archias

419 Heraclea seized by the Boeotians. Alcibiades in the Peloponnese.

418/7 Ol. 90. 3
Antiphon

418 The Spartans invade Argolis and defeat the new formed alliance at **Mantinea**. They recover the prestige lost at Sphacteria. Oligarchies established in Argos and Sicyon.
417 *Spring.* Ostracism of Hyperbolus.

Fl. Democritus, the greatest Greek natural philosopher (460—351). He developed the atomic theory of Leucippus.

417/6 Ol. 90. 4
Euphemus

417 Popular rising at Argos against the oligarchy set up by Sparta. Renewal of the alliance with Athens.

417 Agathon wins the prize for tragedy.

416/5 Ol. 91. 1
Arimnestus

416 An Athenian expedition conquers Melos.
415 *Spring.* Envoys from Egesta, asking aid against Selinus, determine the Athenians to intervene in Sicily.
Summer. Mutilation of the Hermae.
Andocides banished from Athens under the decree of Isotimides.

c. **415** Strongylion, sculptor in bronze: the *Wooden horse* and *Artemis Soteira.*
Pupils of Pheidias:
Agoracritus of Paros: the *Nemesis* at Rhamnus;

	Civil Events	*Literature and Art*
415/4 Ol. 91. 2 Charias (C.I.A. II. 1250 Add.)	The Athenian expedition sails for Sicily. Alcibiades is recalled, escapes, is condemned in his absence. **414** *Spring.* Siege of Syracuse. *Summer.* Death of Lamachus.	Colotes: chryselephantine *Athena* at Elis; Theocosmus of Megara: a *Zeus* in the Olympieum; Alcamenes: *Aphrodite in*
414/3 Ol. 91. 3 Tisander	Gylippus, having landed at Himera, defeats the Athenian army besieging Syracuse and saves the city. **413** *Spring.* The Lacedaemonians renew the war with Athens, and occupy Decelea (—404). Εἰκοστή substituted for φόρος.	*the gardens*: *Hecate triformis*: *Heracles* (for Thrasybulus 403). Also of the Attic school, Callimachus: *Hera* at Plataea and *Laconian Caryatides.* **414** Aristophanes' *Birds,* second to the *Revellers* of Ameipsias.
413/2 Ol. 91. 4 Cleocritus	*September.* Total destruction of the Athenian forces in Sicily, including the relieving expedition under Demosthenes. Probouloi appointed at Athens to supervise the administration.	**413** Hegemon's *Gigantomachia.*
412/1 Ol. 92. 1 Callias Σκαμβωνίδης	**412** Revolt of Chios, Miletus and other allies of Athens. Alliance between Persia and Sparta. **411** *Spring.* Blockade of Chios, revolt of Rhodes. *May.* Subversion of democracy at Athens by the Four Hundred. Negociations opened with Sparta.	**412** Lysias and Polemarchus driven from Thurii to Athens. Euripides' *Helena.* **411** Aristophanes' *Lysistrata* and *Thesmophoriazusae.*
411/0 Ol. 92. 2 Mnesilochus (for two months) Theopompus	The army and fleet in Samos faithful to the democracy. Revolt of Euboea. Naval defeat of the Athenians off the island. *September.* Fall of the Four Hundred. A moderate constitution set up. *Winter.* Battles of Cynossema between Athenian and Spartan fleets. **410** *Spring.* Battle of CYZICUS: destruction of the Spartan fleet.	Antiphon (480—411), the most eminent speech-writer of the day and head of a rhetorical school, executed for his share in the Revolution of the Four Hundred.
410/9 Ol. 92. 3 Glaucippus	**410** (*July* probably). Restoration of full democracy at Athens. **409** Pylos and Nisaea retaken. Hannibal's invasion of Sicily: destruction of Selinus and Himera.	*c.* **410** Hippias of Elis—polymath (rhetor, sophist, mathematician, astronomer, poet, painter, sculptor and critic) fl. **410** Andocides, *De Reditu.*
409/8 Ol. 92. 4 Diocles	**408** *Spring.* Selymbria, Chalcedon, regained for Athens; Byzantium taken after a long siege.	**409** Sophocles' *Philoctetes.* **408** Euripides' *Orestes,* Aristophanes' *Plutus.*
408/7 Ol. 93. 1 Euctemon	**407** *Spring.* Thasos reduced. Alcibiades returns (*May*) to Athens. He is reappointed general. Death of Hermocrates of Syracuse.	Hippodamus of Miletus, architect and political theorist, lays out the new town of Rhodes. **407** Plato, *aetat.* 20, comes under the influence of Socrates.
407/6 Ol. 93. 2 Antigenes	Battle of Notium: Lysander defeats the Athenians. Alcibiades deposed. **406** *Spring.* Second Carthaginian invasion of Sicily. Acragas invested.	**406** Death of Euripides and of Sophocles.
406/5 Ol. 93. 3 Callias Ἀγγελῆθεν	Callicratidas defeats Conon and shuts up the Athenian fleet in Mytilene. *Autumn.* Battle of ARGINUSAE. *November.* Trial and condemnation of six of the Athenian generals. *Midwinter.* Acragas taken by Hannibal.	**405** Aristophanes' *Frogs.* Phrynichus second with the *Muses.* Other poets of the Old Comedy: Plato Comicus (fragments of 30 plays): Telecleides: Strattis: Theopompus.

Civil Events	Literature and Art

405/4 Ol. 93. 4
Alexias

405 The Athenian fleet surprised and destroyed by Lysander at AEGOSPO-TAMI (? *Aug.*). Blockade of Athens. Fall of Gela and Camarina. Dionysius, tyrant of Syracuse, makes peace with Carthage.

404 *April.* Surrender of Athens and end of the war. Destruction of the Long Walls, restoration of exiles, surrender of the fleet.

D. THE FOURTH CENTURY B.C. TO THE BATTLE OF CHAERONEA.

123. The Spartans, who had professed at the outset of the Peloponnesian war to be liberators of Greece from the 'tyrant city,' used their victory so selfishly that their allies were quickly disgusted, and within ten years a coalition was formed to break up their power.   The attempt did not succeed, though it was favoured by the Persians whose fleet destroyed the maritime supremacy of Sparta at the battle of Cnidus.   But Persia changed sides, and the king's peace re-established Sparta in her old supremacy by land and enabled her to oppress the weaker states with impunity until Thebes, at first allied with Athens (now at the head of a new confederacy), stoutly resisted, defied, and at Leuctra overthrew the oppressor.   In the west Dionysius I extended his power both in Sicily and Italy and waged several wars with Carthage.

Supremacy of Sparta: 404—371.

Xenophon's *Hellenica*, II—VI, is still our main authority.   While his impartiality has often been assailed—and he is an avowed champion of Sparta and Agesilaus—he is after all a contemporary, and his sins are mostly sins of omission.   The speeches of Lysias throw light on the condition of Athens under the Thirty and for some years afterwards. Diodorus Siculus is, in this century, the chief authority for Sicilian history.

As regards intellectual progress, we note the beginnings of the Middle Comedy, but verse is becoming less important than prose; oratory and philosophy develop side by side.   In art there is undiminished activity; even greater technical perfection and a mellower loveliness are attained in this century than in the last.

Civil Events	Literature and Art

404/3 Ol. 94. 1
(ἀναρχία as Pythodorus was not recognized)

404 *May.* The Thirty in power at Athens.
Excesses of the Thirty.   Execution of Theramenes, the advocate of moderation.
Winter. Thrasybulus with a band of exiles occupies Phyle and advances to Peiraeus.   The Thirty fortify Eleusis.

404 Critias of Athens, who died 403, poet and critic (elegies, tragedies, political pamphlets). Contemporaries of Lysander were Antimachus of Colophon, epic and lyric poet: author of a *Thebais* and of *Lyde*, a mythological poem: Timotheus of Miletus (447—357), the reformer of music and dithyrambic poet: one νόμος extant, *The Persians*: and

Civil Events	Literature and Art

403/2 Ol. 94. 2
Eucleides

403 Civil war in Attica. Critias slain. The Thirty deposed and succeeded by the Ten. Peace restored at Athens by the intervention of the Spartan King Pausanias. General amnesty (Boedromion *September* the 12th). Restoration of democracy.

401/0 Ol. 94. 4
Xenaenetus

Expedition of Cyrus. His victory and death at Cunaxa. Return of his Greek mercenaries to Trapezus. (400, *February.*)

Sparta makes war upon Elis (—399). Between **403** and **401** Dionysius subdues the Ionic cities Naxos and Catana and the Sicels.

400/399
Ol. 95. 1
Laches

War between Sparta and Persia (lasting till 386). Thimbron in Asia Minor.

399/8 Ol. 95. 2
Aristocrates

399 *Spring.* Accession of Agesilaus. Dercylidas recovers the cities of Aeolis. Conspiracy of Cinadon at Sparta.

398/7 Ol. 95. 3
Euthycles

397 *Spring.* Dionysius declares war with Carthage.

397/6 Ol. 95. 4
Suniades

Dionysius takes Motye.

396/5 Ol. 96. 1
Phormion

396 *Spring.* Agesilaus in Asia. Naval victory of Magon over the Syracusans off Catana. Himilcon besieges Syracuse: pestilence decimates the Carthaginian army.

395 *Spring.* Tithraustes, the successor of Tissaphernes, through Timocrates of Rhodes invites Thebes, Corinth, Argos and Athens to form a coalition against Sparta. Spartan attack upon Haliartus: Lysander slain.

395/4 Ol. 96. 2
Diophantus

Deposition of King Pausanias at Sparta.

394 *Spring.* Recall of Agesilaus from Asia. **The Corinthian war** (—386).

394/3 Ol. 96. 3
Eubulides

Victory of Sparta over the Corinthians and their allies at NEMEA (*July*). Naval victory of the Persian fleet under Pharnabazus and Conon off CNIDUS over the Spartans under Peisander (end of *July*). The islands and Asiatic cities relieved of Spartan harmosts. Agesilaus defeats the Boeotians at CORONEA (*August* 14).

393 *Spring.* Cythera taken by Pharnabazus and Conon. The long walls of Athens restored by the help of the Persians.

391/0 Ol. 97. 2
Nicoteles
390/89
Ol. 97. 3
Demostratus

390 *Spring.* Destruction of a Spartan mora by the peltasts of Iphicrates.

390 War between Evagoras of Cyprus and the Persians (—380).

389 *Spring.* Expedition of Thrasybu-

Choerilus of Samos, epic poet, author of a *Perseis*: resident at the court of Archelaus of Macedon (413—399) as Agathon and Euripides were.

403 Lysias' speech *Against Eratosthenes*. Proposal to give Lysias the Athenian franchise defeated by Archinus.

401 Lysias, *Or.* 32, *Against Diogeiton*.

c. **400** Lysias, *Or.* 25, *Defence on the charge of subverting the democracy*. Sophocles' *Oedipus at Colonus* represented.

399 Socrates condemned and executed on a charge of impiety and corrupting youth, brought by Anytus, Meletus and Lycon. Andocides *On the Mysteries*. [Lysias] *Against Andocides*. Lysias, *Or.* 30, *Against Nicomachus*.

398 Ctesias of Cnidus, court physician of Artaxerxes, brought down his *Persica* to this year. Lysias, *Or.* 13, *Against Agoratus*.

397 Isocrates, *Or.* 16, *De bigis*.

c. **396** Lysias, *Or.* 18, *On the confiscation of the property of Eucrates*.

395/4 Lysias, *Or.* 14 and 15, *Against Alcibiades*.

c. **393** Polycrates' *Accusation of Socrates*. Followed by Xenophon's *Memorabilia* and (perhaps) Plato's *Apology*.

392 or **389** Aristophanes' *Ecclesiazusae*. Gorgias' *Olympic Oration*.

Between **392** and **378** Isocrates active as teacher of rhetoric.

c. **391** Isocrates, *Busiris*, and *Against the Sophists*.

392/1 Andocides, *De Pace*.

390 Birth of Lycurgus.

c. **389** Birth of Aeschines and Hypereides.

389 The activity of Isaeus as a speech-writer commences (—353): *Or.* 5.

Civil Events	Literature and Art

	lus : Thasos, the Chersonese, Byzantium, Chalcedon recovered for Athens.	*c.* **388** Lysias, *Or.* 28 and 29, *Against Ergocles*, and *Against Philocrates.* *Or.* 33, *Olympiacus.*
	Between **391** and **387** Dionysius makes conquests in Italy including Locri, Rhegium, and Croton.	
387/6 Ol. 98. 2 Theodotus	Antalcidas with his fleet master of the Aegean : the Athenian corn-supplies threatened.	**388** Aristophanes' *Plutus* (second edition).
		387 Lysias, *Or.* 19, *On the property of Aristophanes.*
	386 *Spring.* **The King's Peace or Peace of Antalcidas** concluded between Persia and Sparta, and between Sparta and the coalition. Autonomy of the Greek cities proclaimed.	Plato (*aetat.* 40) first visits Sicily. **386** Plato begins to teach in the Academy.
385/4 Ol. 98. 4 Dexitheus	Mantinea broken up into four villages by the Spartans.	**385/4** Antiphanes first exhibits at Athens (he wrote 260 comedies and gained 13 victories).
383/2 Ol. 99. 2 Phanostratus	A Spartan garrison occupies the Cadmea at Thebes.	**385** Plato's *Symposium* not earlier than this year.
	The Spartans make war on Phlius and Olynthus (—379) and break up the Chalcidian federation.	**384** Demosthenes and Aristotle born. **381/0** Lysias' latest extant speech, the fragment *For Pherenicus.*
379/8 Ol. 100. 2 Nicon	*Midwinter.* Liberation of Thebes by Melon and Pelopidas. The Spartans expelled and democracy set up.	**380** Isocrates' *Panegyricus.* About this time the death of Gorgias, Lysias, Aristophanes, and Philoxenus of Cythera, the dithyrambic poet. Birth of Ephorus of Cyme and Theopompus of Chios.
	378 *Spring.* Spartan invasion of Boeotia (repeated in 377 and 376). Sphodrias attempts to surprise Peiraeus. Athens makes an alliance with Thebes.	**378** Prominent orators at Athens : Cephalus, Callistratus, Thrasybulus of Collytus, Leodamas, Aristophon.
378/7 Ol. 100. 3 Nausinicus	Financial reform at Athens. **377** *Spring.* Confederation, under Athens as president, formed to resist Sparta.	**376—351** Second period of Isocrates' school.
376/5 Ol. 101. 1 Charisander	The Athenians under Chabrias defeat the Spartans at sea off NAXOS (*September*).	**376** Death of Antisthenes. Anaxandrides, of Cameirus in Rhodes, victor at Athens [perhaps with the *Protesilaus*, in which the marriage of Iphicrates to a Thracian princess is celebrated]. He was author of 65 comedies, and gained the prize ten times.
	375 *Spring.* Chabrias wins adherents to Athens in the Aegean. Timotheus sails round Peloponnesus, secures the support of Corcyra and defeats the Spartans off Alyzia.	
375/4 Ol. 101. 2 Hippodamas	Some Boeotian towns reduced by the Thebans. Battle of Tegyra in which Pelopidas defeats the Spartans.	
373/2 Ol. 101. 4 Asteius	Spartan expedition against Corcyra repulsed before the arrival of Iphicrates and his relieving fleet. **Destruction** of Plataea by the Thebans.	**373** Isocrates' *Plataicus.* About this time *Or.* 2 and 3 addressed to Nicocles (successor of Evagoras in 374).
372/1 Ol. 102. 1 Alcisthenes	Jason tyrant of Pherae reduces Pharsalus and becomes tagus of Thessaly. **371** Congress at Sparta. Peace concluded (*June*), from which Thebes is excluded.	
371/0 Ol. 102. 2 Phrasicleides	Battle of LEUCTRA (*July*). Jason negotiates the retreat of the surviving Lacedaemonians.	

124. After the sudden and complete fall of Sparta the cause of oligarchy gave way in many states before a new democratic move-
The great-ness of Thebes and the rise of Macedon: 370—338. ment. In the Peloponnesus itself the genius of Epameinondas dealt Spartan power fatal blows by the union of Arcadia and the restoration of the Messenians. For the time Theban arms were irresistible. But deprived of her incomparable leader, and unable to retain the allegiance of discontented allies, Thebes, like Sparta, soon lost the prestige she had so suddenly acquired. Meanwhile a new power was growing in the north. Philip of Macedon, after repelling foreign invasion, enforcing military service, and expelling the Athenians from the Macedonian seaboard, was prepared to interfere, as opportunity presented, in central and southern Greece. He overran Thessaly, destroyed Olynthus, invaded Phocis. In peace and war alike, by intrigue and violence, he laboured incessantly to disarm and overcome all opposition, until the victory of Chaeronea secured the fruits of a policy which had raised up a Philippizing party in half the Greek states. What Athens, Sparta, and Thebes had attempted in vain—the unity of Greece—was now effected, in spite of their opposition, under the headship of a rude and only half Hellenic northern neighbour.

In the west the military monarchy which Dionysius I had founded in Sicily is lost by the incompetence of his successor. After a period of dissension and deplorable anarchy Timoleon, sent from Corinth with a relieving force, liberates Syracuse, expels the Sicilian tyrants, and decisively defeats the Carthaginians who had taken advantage of Sicilian troubles to resume their encroachments.

In this period prose style was perfected: oratory and polite letters preeminently flourished. The middle comedy is still prolific. The progress of science—mathematics, astronomy, natural history, biology—is remarkable. Sculpture in Scopas and Praxiteles attains to new perfection; every branch of art is assiduously cultivated.

To the year 362 Xenophon, *Hellenica* VI 5 and VII, is hardly better than a Peloponnesian chronicle, so numerous are the omissions. Diodorus XV, XVI (from 362 the only connected narrative) is most unsatisfactory: Plutarch (*Agesilaus, Pelopidas, Demosthenes, Dion, Timoleon*), even Justin and Nepos, may be used as supplements. In marked contrast to these late narratives the speeches of Demosthenes and Aeschines and the pamphlets of Isocrates are invaluable first-hand authorities.

Civil Events	Literature and Art
370 *Spring.* Ferment in Peloponnesus. Scytalism at Argos: 1200 oligarchs massacred. Disturbances at Tegea, Phlius, Phigaleia, Corinth, Sicyon. The walls of Mantinea rebuilt. Assassination of Jason of Pherae.	Sculpture in the fourth century represented by Cephisodotus of Athens (*Eirene and the infant Plutus, c.* 371):
370/69 Ol. 102. 3 Dysnicetus	The Arcadian League founded. *Winter.* First Theban invasion of Peloponnesus. Megalopolis founded. Messene restored.	Scopas of Paros (394—349?), architect of the temple of Athena Alea at Tegea: Praxiteles of Athens (the *Aphrodite of Cnidus, Eros, Satyr* and extant *Hermes*):
369 *Spring.* Alliance between Athens and Sparta.	Silanion of Athens, Damophon of Messene. Fl. Eudoxus of Cnidus, astronomer and philosopher.
369/8 Ol. 102. 4 Lysistratus	Second Theban invasion of Peloponnesus: Sicyon and Pellene detached from Sparta. Dionysius I sends 20 triremes to aid the Spartans.	
368 *Spring.* Pelopidas in Thessaly. Alliance of Macedonia with Thebes: Philip a hostage.	
368/7 Ol. 103. 1 Nausigenes	Defeat of the Arcadians by Archidamus and the mercenaries of Dionysius at Midea (the tearless battle). Congress at Delphi.	
367 *Spring.* Epameinondas in Thessaly procures the release of Pelopidas who had been taken prisoner by Alexander of Pherae. Death of Dionysius I.	**367** Dionysius I gains the tragic prize at Athens. Plato visits Sicily. Philistus of Syracuse (*c.* 435—356) becomes the adviser of Dionysius II. He left a *Sicilian History* in two parts (going down to 363/2).
367/6 Ol. 103. 2 Polyzelus	Envoys sent by the principal Greek states to Susa: Pelopidas from Thebes. *Winter.* Congress at Thebes. Peace on the terms of the King's rescript refused.	Aristotle, *aetat.* 17, comes to Athens as a student.
366 *Spring.* Epameinondas invades Peloponnesus for the third time. The adhesion of Achaia secured. Oropus occupied by a Theban garrison.	**366** The assumed date of Isocrates' *Archidamus* (perhaps not published before 356). Fl. Anaximenes of Lampsacus, rhetorician and historian (380 —320).
366/5 Ol. 103. 3 Cephisodorus	Alliance between Athens and Arcadia. Assassination of Lycomedes. Corinth makes a separate peace with Thebes.	
365 *Spring.* Timotheus conquers Samos. Cleruchies assigned in Samos and the Chersonese.	*c.* **365—360** Deinarchus born at Chalcis.
365/4 Ol. 103. 4 Chion	Outbreak of war between Elis and Arcadia.	
364 *Spring.* A Theban fleet sent out under Epameinondas. Byzantium joins the Theban alliance.	
364/3 Ol. 104. 1 Timocrates	Death of Pelopidas in a battle with Alexander of Pherae at Cynoscephalae (shortly after *July* 12). The Arcadians exclude the Eleans from the Olympic festival. Destruction of Orchomenus as a punishment for alleged disaffection to Thebes.	**364/3** Demosthenes' suit against his guardian Aphobus, *Or.* 27, 28, 29.

Civil Events	Literature and Art

363 *Spring.* A fresh Theban expedition to Thessaly : Alexander of Pherae is defeated and deprived of all his possessions except Pherae.

363/2
Ol. 104. 2
Charicleides

Division in Arcadia: the Ten Thousand refuse to appropriate the sacred treasures of Olympia to the payment of the troops.

Tegea now Theban, Mantinea Spartan.

362 *Early Summer.* Theban invasion of Peloponnesus. Surprise of Sparta attempted. Battle of MANTINEA : victory and death of Epameinondas (12 Scirophorion, beginning of *July*).

362/1 Plato's last visit to Sicily, in the interests of the banished Dion.

Xenophon's *Hellenica* closes with the battle of Mantinea, having begun from 411.

362/1
Ol. 104. 3
Molon

Peace concluded, from which Sparta is excluded by her refusal to recognise the independence of Messenia.

Demosthenes, *Or.* 30, 31, *Against Onetor.*

Revolt of satraps in Asia Minor : Datames, Ariobarzanes, Maussollus of Caria and Orontes (—359).

Apollodorus sues Timotheus (Dem. *Or.* 49).

361/0
Ol. 104. 4
Nicophemus

Death of Agesilaus on his return from Egypt, where he had served as a mercenary for the native kings Tachos and Nectanebis.

360/59 Theopompus of Chios, pupil of Isocrates, commenced his history, the *Philippica* in 58 books, with this year (—336).

360/59
Ol. 105. 1
Callimedes

359 *Spring.* Accession of Philip II in Macedonia.

359/8
Ol. 105. 2
Eucharistus

358 *Spring.* Assassination of Alexander of Pherae. Accession of Darius Ochus in Persia (—337).

359/8 Demosthenes trierarch. He writes, *Or.* 41, *Against Spudias*, and *Or.* 55, *Against Callicles.*

358/7
Ol. 105. 3
Cephisodotus

357 *Spring.* Euboea recovered from Thebes by the Athenians under Timotheus. Expedition of Chares to the Chersonese : Sestus recaptured from Cersobleptes.

Celebrated painters, *c.* 360 :
    Aristeides of Thebes (fl. 380 —340) :
    Euphranor of Corinth, also a sculptor (he painted the cavalry fight before Mantinea in which Gryllus, Xenophon's son, fell) :
    Nicias of Athens, contemporary with
    Praxiteles : also the school of Sicyon, Pamphilus, Melanthius, and Pausias, famous for encaustic.

357/6
Ol. 105. 4
Agathocles

Philip captures Amphipolis and Pydna. He forms an alliance with Olynthus. War between Athens and Philip (—346).

Expedition of Dion to Syracuse to expel Dionysius II.

Outbreak of the Social war. Death of Chabrias.

356 *Spring.* Dion, master of Syracuse, besieges Ortygia. Philip captures Potidaea.

Poets of the Middle Comedy :
    Alexis of Thurii, credited with 245 plays (392—286) :
    Eubulus, Ararus, Archippus and Amphis.

356/5
Ol. 106. 1
Elpines

Outbreak of the Sacred war (—346). Philomelus occupies Delphi.

Foundation of Philippi. Birth of Alexander.

Chares fights without success against the revolted Athenian allies off Embata. For their conduct in this battle Iphicrates and Timotheus are impeached and the latter fined.

356/5 Isocrates, *aetat.* 80, publishes *Or.* 8, *De Pace.*

355/4 Isocrates' *Areopagiticus.*

Demosthenes, *Or.* 22, *Against Androtion*, *Or.* 20, *Against Leptines.*

355/4
Ol. 106. 2
Callistratus

An ultimatum of Ochus causes the Athenians to recall Chares and make peace, recognizing the independence

Xenophon, *On the Athenian revenues.*

Civil Events	Literature and Art

	Civil Events	Literature and Art
	of Chios, Cos and Rhodes: Lesbos and Corcyra about the same time secede.	
354/3 Ol. 106. 3 Diotimus	Eubulus in power at Athens. Philomelus slain in battle against the Thebans at Neon.	354/3 Demosthenes, *Or.* 14, *De Symmoriis.*
	353 *Spring.* A Theban force under Pammenes sent to support the revolted satrap Artabazus. Onomarchus takes Orchomenus. Dion assassinated by Callippus.	
353/2 Ol. 106. 4 Thudemus	Philip in Thessaly: he is defeated by Onomarchus but takes Pagasae. Onomarchus captures Coronea and defeats the Thebans at Hermaeum. 352 *Spring.* Philip again in Thessaly: Onomarchus defeated and slain, Pherae taken. Philip's advance southwards checked at Thermopylae by an Athenian force. A Theban force under Cephision supports Megalopolis against Sparta.	353/2 Isocrates, *Or.* 15, *De Antidosi.* Isaeus, *Or.* 7, probably his latest extant speech. Demosthenes, *Or.* 16, *For the Megapolitans, Or.* 24, *Against Timocrates, Or.* 15, *Pro Rhodiorum libertate.* 352/1 Demosthenes, *Or.* 23, *Against Aristocrates* and (351 *Spring*) *Or.* 4, *First Philippic.*
352/1 Ol. 107. 1 Aristodemus	Philip in Thrace: submission of Cersobleptes.	*c.* 350 In the contest for eloquence instituted by Artemisia in honour of Maussollus Theopompus defeats Theodectes and Naucrates. Theodectes was victorious in tragedy.
349/8 Ol. 107. 4 Callimachus	Philip at war with Olynthus. Expeditions sent by Athens under Chares and Charidemus to its relief. 348 *Spring.* In Euboea Eretria, Chalcis and Oreus revolt from Athens. Phocion narrowly escapes defeat at Tamynae. An Athenian detachment captured at Zaretra.	350/49 Demosthenes, *Or.* 36, *For Phormion.* 349 *Autumn.* Demosthenes, *Or.* 1—3: the *Olynthiacs.*
348/7 Ol. 108. 1 Theophilus	*Autumn.* Fall of Olynthus before the third expedition under Chares arrives.	348/7 Demosthenes, *Or.* 39, *Against Boeotus.*
347/6 Ol. 108. 2 Themistocles	346 *Spring.* Peace of Philocrates. Ten Athenian envoys sent to treat with Philip. The terms agreed upon accepted by the assembly (*March*) and the envoys despatched to take the oaths from Philip and his allies return (*June*) a few days before Philip reaches Thermopylae. Phalaecus retires under a convention.	347 Death of Plato. Aristotle and Xenocrates leave Athens for Atarneus. 347/6 Demosthenes, *Or.* 21, *Against Meidias* (not delivered). 346 *April.* Isocrates, *Philippus.* *August.* Demosthenes, *De Pace.* 345 *Spring.* Aeschines, *Or.* 1, *Against Timarchus.*
346/5 Ol. 108. 3 Archias	The Amphictyons decree the destruction of Phocis as a state. Philip presides at the Pythian games. Dionysius II recovers Syracuse.	344/3 Demosthenes, *Or.* 6, *Second Philippic.*
343/2 Ol. 109. 2 Pythodotus	Alliance of Megara with Athens. Expedition of Timoleon to Syracuse. Dionysius II capitulates: Ortygia dismantled.	343/2 Hegesippus (?) *De Halonneso* [Dem. *Or.* 7]. Demosthenes, *Or.* 19, and Aeschines, *Or.* 2, *On the Embassy.*
342/1 Ol. 109. 3 Sosigenes	Philip occupies Oreus. Alliance of Chalcis with Athens. *Winter.* Philip in Epeirus: Arybbas dethroned, Alexander his successor. Diopeithes active on the Hellespont.	Aristotle at the Macedonian court as tutor of Alexander (—340/39). 342/1 Birth of Menander and of Epicurus (*Jan.* 341).

Civil Events	*Literature and Art*

341/0
Ol. 109. 4
Nicomachus

340/39
Ol. 110. 1
Theophrastus

339/8
Ol. 110. 2
Lysimachides

338/7
Ol. 110. 3
Chaerondas

341 *Spring.* Philip in Thrace, Cersobleptes dethroned.
Oreus and Eretria liberated by Athens and her allies.
340 *Spring.* Philip attacks Perinthus and Byzantium.
War declared by Athens. The siege of Byzantium raised. Demosthenes reforms the trierarchic system.
339 *Spring.* Expedition of Philip against Ateas, the Scythian king.
May. Timoleon gains a signal victory over the Carthaginians under Mago at the Crimesus.
Philip, as general of the Amphictyonic League against Amphissa, occupies Elatea. Panic at Athens.
The Theoric Fund diverted to war purposes.
338 Alliance of Athens and Thebes.
September. Philip's victory at CHAERONEA.
Macedonian garrison in the Cadmea.
Peace of Demades. Archidamus falls in Italy fighting for Tarentum against the Lucanians.

341 *Spring.* Demosthenes, *Or.* 8, *On the Chersonese,* and *Or.* 9, *Third Philippic.*
341/0 Demosthenes, *Or.* 10, *Fourth Philippic.*
The *Universal History* of Ephorus of Cyme was carried as far as this year. Diyllus continued it to 336.
c. **340** Anaximenes (?) *Rhetoric* [among Aristotle's works: *Rhet. ad Alexandrum*].
339 Isocrates' *Panathenaicus* [begun in 342, *aetat.* 94]. Xenocrates succeeds Speusippus in the headship of the Academy (—314). Heracleides of Pontus, a prominent member of the school and prolific author, was also a candidate.
338 Death of Isocrates.

E. THE END OF THE FOURTH AND OPENING OF THE THIRD CENTURIES B.C.

125. Greece was now a dependency of Macedonia : its fortunes were swallowed up in the broad stream of universal history.

Fall of the Persian empire : foundation of the Hellenistic kingdoms : 338—280.

Alexander destroyed the Persian empire, extended his conquests as far as India, and founded numerous Greek cities. After his death, as no strong central authority arose to keep his dominions together, the chief satraps of the provinces, *e.g.* Ptolemy in Egypt and Cassander in Macedonia, assumed the title of kings. Antigonus and his son Demetrius, the last aspirants to universal rule, were successively overthrown by a coalition of their rivals. Their fall paved the way for the ultimate establishment of three great powers, Macedonia itself and the Macedonian kingdoms of Ptolemy in Egypt and Seleucus in Asia, to whom fell the lion's share of the Persian empire.

In literature the last efforts of oratory, the development of the New Comedy, together with much activity in philosophy and history, belong to this period. In art, sculpture, painting and engraving upon gems are represented by celebrated works of undiminished excellence.

Arrian, who used the contemporary writers Ptolemy, Aristobulus, Nearchus, is the chief authority for Alexander's reign ; Curtius, Plutarch and Diodorus being subsidiary. Afterwards we depend upon Diodorus XVII—XXI (unabridged as far as the year 301 B.C.), with scanty and irregular supplements from Plutarch (*Phocion, Eumenes, Demetrius, Pyrrhus*), Justin, Pausanias and Strabo.

	Civil Events	*Literature and Art*
337/6	Death of Timoleon.	Artists contemporary with Alex-
Ol. 110. 4	Assassination of Philip. Accession of	ander :
Phrynichus	Alexander (—323) and of Darius III	Lysippus of Sicyon, cele-
336/5	Codomannus (—331).	brated for his statues in bronze
Ol. 111. 1	335 *Spring.* Alexander's expedition	(the *Apoxyomenos*, the colos-
Pythodelus	against the Triballi and Illyrians.	sal *Zeus of Tarentum*, the
335/4	*Autumn.* Revolt and destruction of	*Poseidon of the Isthmus*) and
Ol. 111. 2	Thebes.	for portrait statues of Philip
Euaenetus	334 Macedonian invasion of Asia	and Alexander: the painters
	Minor. Battle of the GRANICUS.	Apelles of Colophon (*Aphro-*
334/3	The Greek cities in Asia welcome	*dite Anadyomene*) and Proto-
Ol. 111. 3	Alexander, who sets up democracies.	genes of Caunus (*Ialysus, Satyr*
Ctesicles	Storm of Miletus: siege and capture	*with double flute*) and Pyrgo-
	of Halicarnassus.	teles, engraver on gems.
333/2	Alexander the Molossian in Italy as an	336/5 [Demosthenes] *Or.* 17, *On*
Ol. 111. 4	ally of the Tarentines (—330).	*the treaty with Alexander.*
Nicocrates	333 *Nov.* Battle of ISSUS.	335 Aristotle settles at Athens
	332 Submission of Phoenicia except	and teaches in the Lyceum
	Tyre and Gaza.	(—323), his philosophical
332/1	*Nov.* Capture of Tyre after seven	works being closely connected
Ol. 112. 1	months' siege.	with his activity as a teacher.
Nicetes	331 Capture of Gaza. Foundation of	
	Alexandria. March to Nineveh.	
331/0	Battle at GAUGAMELA, 30 miles west	
Ol. 112. 2	of Arbela (*Oct.*).	330 Lycurgus' *Or. Against Leo-*
Aristophanes	Babylon, Susa, Persepolis occupied.	*crates.*
330/29	Darius slain by Bessus.	*Autumn.* The case of the Crown
Ol. 112. 3	Rising in Peloponnesus. The Spartans	heard at Athens: Aeschines,
Aristophon	defeated by Antipater and Agis slain	*Or.* 3, *Against Ctesiphon*, and
	in Arcadia.	Demosthenes, *De Corona.*
	Alexander marches from the Caspian to	330/29 Callippus published his
	Paropamisadae [Cabul].	astronomy.
329/8	Alexander invades Bactria and Sogdiana	
Ol. 112. 4	[Bokhara] crossing Paropamisus	327 First victory of Philemon,
Cephisophon	[Hindu Kush].	poet of the New Comedy (359
327/6	Invasion of India. Defeat and sub-	—262). To him 97 plays were
Ol. 113. 2	mission of Porus.	attributed.
Hegemon	Dearth at Athens.	Death of Callisthenes of Stagirus,
326/5	Alexander returns from the Hyphasis	relative of Aristotle, who had
Ol. 113. 3	[Sutlej] and marches along the Indus	accompanied Alexander as his-
Chremes	to the Indian Ocean.	torian and was accused of con-
325/4	Land march, with heavy loss, through	spiracy.
Ol. 113. 4	Gedrosia [Baluchistan]. Voyage of	326/5 [Dem.] *Or.* 34, *Against*
Anticles	Nearchus to the Persian gulf.	*Phormion.*
324/3	Decree for return of the Greek exiles	324 Death of Lycurgus. Dein-
Ol. 114. 1	announced at the Olympic games.	archus' and Hypereides'
Hegesias	Flight of Harpalus, satrap of Baby-	speeches against Demosthenes
	lon, with treasure to Athens.	in the affair of Harpalus. Con-
	323 Death of Alexander (*June*), aged	demnation of Demosthenes
	32 years and 8 months.	and Demades. Exile of De-
323/2	First settlement: Perdiccas regent for	mosthenes.
Ol. 114. 2	Alexander's heir.	323 Epicurus, *aetat.* 18, comes
Cephisodorus	Revolt in Greece headed by Athens	to Athens.
	and Aetolians. Antipater shut up in	322 *Oct.* Death of Hypereides
	Lamia. **The Lamian war.** Ophelas	and Demosthenes. Death of
	established in Cyrene.	Aristotle at Chalcis. Theo-
	322 *Spring.* The insurgent Greeks	phrastus succeeds him in the
	defeated by Antipater at Crannon.	Lyceum.

	Civil Events	Literature and Art
	Victory of Cleitus over the Athenian fleet off Amorgos.	
322/1 Ol. 114. 3 Philocles	Change of constitution at Athens: the poorer citizens disfranchised and deported. **321** *Spring*. Resistance to Perdiccas and Eumenes offered by Antipater, Antigonus, and other satraps. Death of Perdiccas in Egypt.	**321** Menander's first play. (He is said to have written 105 in all.) His contemporary Diphilus of Sinope also wrote 100 plays.
321/0 Ol. 114. 4 Archippus	Second settlement at Triparadeisus in Syria. Antipater regent: Antigonus commander of the forces against Eumenes.	
319/8 Ol. 115. 2 Apollodorus	Death of Antipater. War between his son Cassander and his successor Polyperchon.	**319** Execution of Demades, the most fluent orator of the Macedonian party.
318/7 Ol. 115. 3 Archippus	Polyperchon declares the Greeks free. **317** Cassander recovers Athens. Death of Phocion (*April*).	
317/6 Ol. 115. 4 Demogenes	Demetrius of Phalerum in power at Athens (—307): further changes in the constitution. Arrhidaeus, nominal ruler, put to death by Olympias. Agathocles becomes tyrant of Syracuse.	
316/5 Ol. 116. 1 Democlides	**315** *Spring*. Eumenes betrayed and slain. Coalition of the other satraps for war against Antigonus (—311). Thebes rebuilt by Cassander, now master of Macedonia.	**315** First victory of Menander. **314** Death of Aeschines and of Xenocrates. Zeno of Citium, *aetat.* 22, comes to Athens and commences the study of philosophy. Polemo head of the Academy (—276).
312/1 Ol. 117. 1 Polemon	Battle of Gaza; Ptolemy defeats Demetrius Poliorcetes, son of Antigonus. Seleucus returns to Babylon. Era of the Seleucids. **311** The satraps make peace with Antigonus. The freedom of the Greek cities recognized.	**312** Timaeus of Tauromenium, the historian of Sicily (345—249), removes to Athens, where he settles until 262. c. **312** Theocritus born probably in Cos.
311/10 Ol. 117. 2 Simonides	Hamilcar lands in Sicily and defeats Agathocles at Ecnomus near the river Himera. Siege of Syracuse.	c. **310** Timon of Phlius born. c. **310** Birth of Callimachus of Cyrene. **307** Deinarchus of Corinth, last of the ten orators, retires to Chalcis (—292).
310/9 Ol. 117. 3 Hieromnemon	Agathocles invades Africa (*Aug.* 15, 310) and captures Tunes and Hadrumetum.	**307/6** Law of Sophocles of Sunium against the philosophers (rescinded the next year).
309/8 Ol. 117. 4 Demetrius	In Sicily Hamilcar is captured and slain. Ophelas of Cyrene murdered: his troops join Agathocles.	**306** Epicurus, having taught since 314 in Asia, returns to Athens and opens a school.
308/7 Ol. 118. 1 Charinus [or Caerimus Mar. Par.]	Utica taken by Agathocles who returns to Sicily, leaving his son Archagathus in command. Magas seizes Cyrene and maintains his power till his death (—258). **307** Demetrius Poliorcetes drives out Cassander's garrison and 'liberates' Athens 25 Thargelion (June).	**306** Megasthenes, envoy of Seleucus at Palibothra, the court of Sandracottus, *i.e.* Chandragupta (—298). Rhinthon of Tarentum, author of burlesques (hilarotragoedia).

	Civil Events	*Literature and Art*

307/6
Ol. 118. 2
Anaxicrates

Agathocles, unable to raise the siege of Tunes, abandons his son and his army and escapes to Sicily. End of his African invasion.

300/299 Epicurus completes Book XV of his great work *On Nature* (and four years later Book XXVIII).

306/5
Ol. 118. 3
Coroebus

The 'four-years war' between Demetrius and Cassander for the possession of Greece (—302).
Great naval victory of Demetrius over Ptolemy off Salamis in Cyprus.
Antigonus and his rivals assume the title of kings.
Agathocles makes peace with Carthage, and after defeating Deinocrates at Torgium admits him to a share of power.

297 Death of Euhemerus of Messene, author of a rationalist explanation of the myths (ἱερὰ ἀναγραφή).

295 Philetas of Cos (340—285), elegiac poet, tutor of Ptolemy Philadelphus (—292).

294 Zeno begins to teach in the Stoa at Athens.

305/4
Ol. 118. 4
Euxenippus

Demetrius lays siege to Rhodes.

293/2 Fl. Hieronymus of Cardia (360—260), historian of the Diadochi and Epigoni (Alexander's successors of the first and second generations).

302/1
Ol. 119. 3
Nicocles

Second coalition of the other kings against Antigonus and Demetrius.

292/1 Death of Menander.

288 Poseidippus of Cassandreia exhibits his first play. Contemporary dramatists Apollodorus of Carystus ; Philippides of Athens, author of 44 plays ; and Machon of Corinth or Sicyon, who lived and wrote at Alexandria.

301/0
Ol. 119. 4
Clearchus

Antigonus defeated and slain at IPSUS in Phrygia.
Seleucus and Lysimachus, the victors, divide his possessions.
Agathocles conquers Corcyra.

297/6
Ol. 120. 4
Antiphates

Death of Cassander.

288/4 Death of Theophrastus ; Strato of Lampsacus head of the Peripatetic school (—270).

296/5
Ol. 121. 1
Nicias

Lachares tyrant of Athens.

287 Birth of Archimedes at Syracuse.

295/4
Ol. 121. 2
Nicostratus

294 Demetrius, having expelled Lachares, enters Athens in triumph (*March*). He conquers the Spartans and wins Megara and most of Peloponnesus.
Pyrrhus made king of Epeirus.

285 Fl. Herophilus of Chalcedon and Erasistratus of Ceos, eminent amongst the ancient physicians for their anatomical discoveries.

294/3
Ol. 121. 3
Olympiodorus

Demetrius becomes king of Macedonia (—287). He holds Athens with a garrison.

At the court of Ptolemy Philadelphus flourished Callimachus, elegiac poet, and Theocritus. Alexander the Aetolian, elegiac and tragic poet, Sosiphanes of Syracuse, Sositheus of Alexandria in the Troad, Homer of Byzantium, Lycophron of Chalcis, Philiscus of Corcyra and Dionysius of Mallus (or Tarsus) were tragic poets known as the constellation, ἡ Πλειάς. Hermesianax of Colophon, elegiac poet, Gotades of Maroneia in Crete.

289/8
Ol. 122. 4
Aristonymus or Telecles (?)

Death of Agathocles.

287/6
Ol. 123. 2
Diocles

Demetrius driven by Pyrrhus from Macedonia.
(Ultimately Demetrius becomes a prisoner of Seleucus and dies in 282.)
Administration of Demochares, the nephew of Demosthenes (—270).

286/5
Ol. 123. 3
Diotimus

Lysimachus defeats Pyrrhus and expels him from Macedonia.
Ptolemy Philadelphus succeeds his father in Egypt (—247).

281 Aristarchus of Samos, originator of the heliocentric hypothesis, makes astronomical observations at Alexandria.

281/0
Ol. 124. 4
Urius

Lysimachus is defeated and slain at the battle of Corupedium by Seleucus, who proceeds to Macedonia where he is murdered by Ptolemy Ceraunus.
Pyrrhus is invited by the Tarentines to aid them against Rome.

The *Histories* of Duris of Samos (*c.* 340—260) which began with 370 went as far as this year. He also wrote a history of Agathocles.

F. THE THIRD AND SECOND CENTURIES B.C.

126. The invasion of the Gauls was successfully repelled from Delphi.

Federal Greece to the battle of Sellasia: 280—220. Macedonia, which had suffered more from their ravages, was gradually consolidated under the rule of Antigonus Gonatas, who in the Chremonidean war, in spite of the vigorous resistance of Sparta and Athens, reduced Greece once more to complete dependence. Meanwhile the Achaean League had grown from small beginnings to prosperity, and the prudent policy of Aratus sought to extend it over Peloponnesus. But in the struggle with Sparta, under the reforming king Cleomenes, it was defeated. Thereupon Aratus called in Macedonian intervention, and Antigonus Doson crushed the Spartan power at Sellasia.

In the west, Pyrrhus of Epeirus had hoped to found a kingdom, either in Italy or Sicily. He nearly succeeded in driving the Carthaginians from the island, but by his return to Italy forfeited his influence with the Sicilian Greeks. After the failure of his enterprise Rome completed the conquest of Magna Graecia; the Mamertines possessed themselves of Messana and the Carthaginians reconquered the west and north of Sicily, but Syracuse and the east coast enjoyed comparative prosperity under Hieron II.

This is the Alexandrian age in literature: the Rhodian and Pergamene schools of sculpture become famous.

For this period Plutarch (*Pyrrhus, Agis, Cleomenes, Aratus, Philopoemen*), Justin, Diodorus XXII—XXV, Polybius, in the introduction to his own special period, Books I—III, and the *Epitome* of Livy XII—XX, are the more important among numerous fragmentary sources of information.

	Civil Events	Literature and Art
280/79 Ol. 125. 1	The Achaean League revived by the union of Dyme, Patrae, Tritaea and Pharae. The Gauls in Macedonia and Thrace: Ptolemy Ceraunus slain: anarchy. Pyrrhus in Italy defeats the Romans at Heraclea.	280/79 Chrysippus born. 278/7 Chares of Lindus head of the Rhodian school of sculpture: the Colossus his work. 277/6 Death of Metrodorus of Lampsacus, pupil of Epicurus.
279/8 Ol. 125. 2	Irruption of the Gauls into Greece: Brennus defeated before Delphi. Apollodorus tyrant of Cassandreia. Pyrrhus sails for Syracuse.	Aratus' *Hymn to Pan.* Theocritus at Cos writes *Id.* 7. 275/4 Birth of Eratosthenes of Cyrene and Euphorion of
278/7 Ol. 125. 3	Victory of Antigonus Gonatas over one Gallic troop at Lysimacheia. Other tribes of Gauls cross into Asia, where they enter the service of Nicomedes, king of Bithynia.	Chalcis (Ol. 126). Timon of Phlius (*c.* 320—230) settles at Athens where he writes philosophical satires in the form of epic parodies (Σίλλοι).
277/6 Ol. 125. 4	Antigonus Gonatas becomes king of Macedon (—239).	272/1 At the court of Antigonus Gonatas flourish Antagoras of
275/4 Ol. 126. 2	Return of Pyrrhus to Epeirus.	Rhodes, epic poet, Aratus, author of the *Phaenomena*;
272/1 Ol. 127. 1	Death of Pyrrhus at Argos. Milo surrenders Tarentum to the Romans.	Persaeus, favourite pupil of Zeno, and Menedemus of Ere-

Civil Events	Literature and Art

tria, philosophers. Theocritus at Alexandria, *Id.* 14, 15, 17, *c.* 273—269; afterwards he returns to Syracuse, *Id.* 16.

271/0 Death of Epicurus (*Jan.* 270). On the death of Strato (Ol. 127) Lyco becomes head of the Lyceum (— 226). About this time Zenodotus of Ephesus librarian at Alexandria prepares an edition of *Homer*. Sosibius the Laconian historian flourished under Ptolemy I and II.

270/69
Ol. 127. 3

Hiero II king of Syracuse (—216).

270/69 Death of Polemon who is succeeded in the Academy by Crates and shortly afterwards by Arcesilas, founder of the Middle or Sceptical school. Bion of Smyrna, idyllic poet in Sicily.

266/1
Ol. 128. 3
—Ol. 129. 2

The Chremonidean war. Macedon suppresses a revolt in Athens and Megara, which was supported by Areus of Sparta and by Patroclus, admiral of Philadelphus. Siege of Athens which capitulates to famine 261 (Spring) and receives a Macedonian garrison (removed 255).

262/1 Philochorus of Athens brings his *Attic History* in 17 books down to this year, the accession of Antiochus Theos. He is shortly afterwards executed.

259/8

At Cyrene on the death of Magas Demetrius the Fair rules until his murder (some date this 250/47).

261 (after July) Death of Zeno of Citium. Cleanthes of Assos succeeds to the headship of the Stoic school (—232).

251/0
Ol. 132. 2

Aratus, *aetat.* 20, liberates Sicyon and unites it to the Achaean league.
c. **250** Rise of Arsaces and the Parthian kingdom.

251/0 Death of Timaeus of Tauromenium. Manetho of Sebennytus, the Egyptian historian, and (?) Herodas or Herondas of Cos, author of *Mimiambics*, flourish.

247/6
Ol. 133. 2
243/2
Ol. 134. 2

Accession of Ptolemy III Euergetes (—222). Cyrene joined to Egypt.
Corinth and Megara join the Achaean League. The Macedonian garrison expelled from Acrocorinthus.

247/6 Nymphis of Heraclea brought his history of Alexander and his successors down to this year. Menippus of Gadara, Cynic philosopher, and author of satires in prose and verse.

242/1
Ol. 136. 3

Agis IV attempts to restore the Lycurgean constitution at Sparta, and deposes his colleague Leonidas, who is banished.

241/0
Ol. 134. 4

Return of Leonidas. Death of Agis: his reforms are abrogated. At Pergamum accession of Attalus I (—197). End of the first Punic war: Carthaginian Sicily ceded to Rome.

245/4 Callimachus of Cyrene, long resident at Alexandria is engaged upon the compilation of the Πίνακες in 120 books. Apollonius (*c.* 280—200), author of the *Argonautica*, had probably already left Alexandria for Rhodes in consequence of his quarrel with Callimachus.

239/8
Ol. 135. 2
233/2
Ol. 136. 4
232/1
Ol. 137. 1

Accession of Demetrius II of Macedon (—229).
Lydiadas resigns his tyranny. Megalopolis joins the Achaean League.
Illyrian raids in Epeirus and Acarnania. Corcyra occupied by Demetrius of Pharus.

243/2 Death of Persaeus.
241/0 Death of Arcesilas of the Middle Academy.

229/8
Ol. 137. 4

Accession of Antigonus Doson, guardian of Philip V of Macedon (—221). Athens liberated by Aratus. Rome makes war on the Illyrians.

c. **240**? Neanthes of Cyzicus,

	Civil Events	*Literature and Art*
228/7 Ol. 138. 1	Submission of Teuta, the Illyrian queen. Adhesion of Argos, Hermione and Phlius to the Achaean League.	rhetor and historian, fl. He wrote *Hellenica*, a *Chronicle of Cyzicus* (ὧροι) and a biographical work (περὶ ἐνδόξων ἀνδρῶν).
227/6 Ol. 138. 2	The Romans admitted to Hellenic games and festivals. Cleomenes III king of Sparta.	**235/4** Eratosthenes librarian at Alexandria (—195).
226/5 Ol. 138. 3	Cleomenes removes the ephors and carries out the Lycurgean reforms at Sparta. A new division of land among 4000 hoplites.	**232/1** Chrysippus head of the Stoic school (208—4 : Ol. 143). **227/6** Sphaerus of Bosporus, sent by Cleanthes to Ptolemy III, aids Cleomenes in his reforms.
225/4 Ol. 138. 4 **224/3** Ol. 139. 1	Victory of Cleomenes over the Achaeans at Dyme. Continued success of Cleomenes : capture of Pellene and Argos ; secession of Cleonae, Phlius and Corinth from the Achaean League. Earthquake at Rhodes.	**226/5** Antigonus of Carystus, sculptor, art critic, and biographic historian of philosophy at the court of Attalus I, publishes his *Lives* about this time.
223/2 Ol. 139. 2	Cleomenes besieges Acrocorinthus and Sicyon. Aratus negotiates with Antigonus Doson who sends a force into Peloponnesus.	**222/1** Rhianus of Bene in Crete published a new edition of *Homer*, and wrote antiquarian epics, *e.g. Messeniaca.*
222/1 Ol. 139. 3	Antigonus conquers Tegea, Orchomenus, Mantinea. Cleomenes destroys Megalopolis. Accession of Antiochus III Epiphanes.	**221/0** The *Memoirs* of Aratus ended with 220 : Phylarchus of Naucratis wrote a history in 28 books, beginning at 272 and also ending with this year.
221/0 Ol. 139. 4	Utter defeat of Cleomenes by Antigonus and the Achaeans at Sellasia. Death of Antigonus Doson. Accession of Philip V (—178).	

127. The Achaean League, now the dependent ally of Philip V of Macedonia, was assisted by him against the Aetolian League in the Social war. The war came to an end because both sides wished to be free to wait upon events in the second Punic war. Syracuse and Tarentum both fell into the hands of the Carthaginians and were afterwards retaken by the Romans. Philip having made a treaty with Hannibal, Rome replied by raising up enemies against him at home—the Aetolians, Rhodes, Pergamum. After Zama, when their hands were free, the Romans humbled Philip : at Cynoscephalae the phalanx gave way before the legion. While Macedonia was in any sense formidable, Rome treated the states which from time to time were allied with her—Aetolians, Achaeans, Rhodes, Pergamum—with consideration and occasionally with generosity. When the final victory over Perseus was gained at Pydna, these allies were no longer wanted. Rome made no scruple to invade their rights and interfere with their domestic affairs on any pretext. In the case of the Achaeans this policy at last provoked the senseless outbreak of the Anti-Roman party which ended in the destruction of Corinth and the dissolution of the League.

The Roman domination: 220—146.

This is the classical age of Alexandrian and Pergamene scholars and critics.

Our chief authority for this period, directly or indirectly, is Polybius: Livy in the Greek sections of XXI—XLV usually follows him; so also does Appian. Subsidiary sources are Plutarch's *Lives of Philopoemen, T. Quinctius, Cato the Censor,* and *Aemilius Paulus,* together with Justin and Diodorus XXVI—XXXII, as before.

	Civil Events	Literature and Art.
220/19 Ol. 140. 1	The Social war: the Aetolian League with Elis and Sparta against the Achaean and Boeotian Leagues, and Philip of Macedonia.	220/19 Polybius' history begins here.
218/7 Ol. 140. 3	Philip sacks Thermum. [*Hannibal marches into Italy.*]	
217/6 Ol. 140. 4	Peace made between the Leagues. [*Trasimene.*]	
216/5 Ol. 141. 1	[*Cannae.*] Philip's treaty with Hannibal (215).	
	212 Fall of Syracuse.	212/1 Death of Archimedes.
211/0 Ol. 142. 2	**First Macedonian war** (—205). Rome, the Aetolian League, and Attalus of Pergamum against Philip and his Greek allies.	*c.* 210—206 Birth of Polybius. Death of Chrysippus between 208 and 204 (Ol. 143). Zeno of Tarsus the next head of the Stoic school.
205/4 Ol. 143. 4	The Aetolians make peace with Philip. 202 [*Zama.*]	202/1 Birth of Nicander of Colophon, didactic poet.
200/199 Ol. 145. 1	Philip captures Abydos. **Second Macedonian war** (—197).	200/199 Fl. Hermippus of Smyrna, biographer.
198/7 Ol. 145. 3	The Achaean League now allied with Rome against Philip and the Aetolians.	
197/6 Ol. 145. 4	Flamininus defeats Philip at CYNOSCEPHALAE. Peace made. The freedom of the Greek cities proclaimed at the Isthmian games (196). Eumenes II succeeds Attalus I at Pergamum.	197/6 Attalus dedicated four sets of figures (Giants, Amazons, Persians, Gauls) on the Acropolis at Athens to commemorate his victories over the Gauls (by Epigonus, or copies of his work).
195/4 Ol. 146. 2	Rome and the Achaeans make a joint campaign against Nabis, tyrant of Sparta.	195/4 Death of Eratosthenes. Aristophanes of Byzantium librarian at Alexandria.
192/1 Ol. 147. 1	Murder of Nabis. Sparta is won for the Achaeans. Antiochus, at the invitation of the Aetolians, crosses the Aegean and winters at Chalcis. Outbreak of the Syrian war (—189). The Syrians are defeated at Thermopylae and evacuate Europe.	
190/89 Ol. 147. 3	After the battle of Magnesia the Romans make peace with Antiochus, who is confined to his dominions east of Mount Taurus. Rhodes and Pergamum, the allies of Rome, rewarded with territory.	190/89 The Pergamene school of sculpture under Eumenes and Attalus II: Apollonius and Tauriscus of Tralles; the *Farnese Bull.* Between 183 and 174 the great marble altar at Pergamum with the Gigantomachia.
189/88 Ol. 147. 4	The Aetolians forced to accept heavy terms.	
188/7 Ol. 148. 1	Discontent in Sparta; Philopoemen abolishes the last remains of the Lycurgean Constitution.	
186/5 Ol. 148. 3	Roman interference with the Achaeans.	
183/2 Ol. 149. 2	The Messenians under Deinocrates revolt against the Achaean League:	

Civil Events	*Literature and Art*

	death of Philopoemen. Messene is reconquered by the Achaeans.	
180/79 Ol. 150. 1	The Romans insist on the restoration of the Spartan exiles: embassy of Callimachus, the younger Aratus and Lydiadas to deprecate this measure.	180/79 Death of Aristophanes: Aristarchus of Samothrace, the grammarian, librarian at Alexandria. Contemporary geographer and antiquarian,
179/8 Ol. 150. 3 177/6 Ol. 150. 4 172/1 Ol. 152. 1	Death of Philip V and accession of Perseus (—168) in Macedon. Gradual interference of the Romans with the Rhodians. **Third Macedonian war** (—168).	Polemon of Ilium. Sotion's history of the philosophers (between 200 and 170).
171/0 Ol. 152. 2 169/8 Ol. 157. 4 168/7 Ol. 153. 1	Success of Perseus. Licinius defeated near Larissa. PYDNA (Midsummer 168). End of the Macedonian kingdom. In consequence of the Roman victory Macedonia subdivided, Epeirus depopulated, Eumenes humiliated, Rhodes commercially ruined. One thousand Achaeans, on suspicion of Macedonian sympathies, are deported to Italy.	171/0 About this time Crates of Mallus grammarian and critic at Pergamum. A younger Neanthes of Cyzicus must be assumed to have written the history of Attalus I (241—197). Perhaps also a treatise against the Asian school of rhetoric (περὶ ζηλοτυπίας).
156/5 Ol. 156. 1	Raid of the Athenians upon Oropus. Embassy of Carneades, Critolaus and Diogenes to Rome on behalf of Athens (155).	167/51 Polybius the historian at Rome becomes acquainted with the younger Scipio and Panaetius the Stoic. c. 155 Carneades (213—129)
151/0 Ol. 157. 2 149/8 Ol. 157. 4	The survivors of the deported Achaeans released. War of the Achaeans against Sparta, which appeals to Rome. Insurrection in Macedonia in favour of a pretended Philip.	was the head of the New or Sceptical Academy. Diogenes of Seleucia 'the Babylonian' was head of the Stoics, and Critolaus of the Peripatetics. 151/0 Demetrius of Scepsis, antiquarian, flourishes.
147/6 Ol. 158. 2	L. Aurelius Orestes sent by the Roman Senate to Greece to authorize secession from the Achaean League. Subsequent mission of S. Iulius Caesar: Critolaus, at the head of the anti-Roman party, induces the League to declare war nominally with Lacedaemon, really with Rome. Metellus defeats the Achaeans at Scarphea. Mummius, his successor, arrives and destroys Corinth. Polybius after the defeat exerts himself to procure for his countrymen the best terms possible.	147/6 End of Polybius' history.

III. LITERATURE, PHILOSOPHY, SCIENCE.

III. 1. LITERATURE.

A. EPIC POETRY.

128. THE Homeric poems, with which the literature of Greece and of Europe begins, are works of a matured poetical art. Little is known concerning the earlier and ruder stages in the Greek development of that art. But three forms, at least, of primitive Greek poetry are traceable.

Primitive Greek poetry.

(1) There were old folk-songs, connected with the natural phenomena of the seasons, in which the yielding of spring to summer, of summer to autumn and winter, was symbolised by the death of a beautiful youth, such as Linus, Hylas, Ialemus, Hyacinthus or Adonis. Their origin appears to have been Semitic; but they were congenial to that early phase of the Indo-European mind which in India is represented by the Vedic hymns, and in which religion was largely a sense of divinity in the forces of external Nature. The local legends as to the personal relationships of the youth who had perished show the distinctively Greek element.

(2) Then there were legends of early bards,—shadowy names of ancient but vague renown, to which later composers attached their own work. Among these we can distinguish: (*a*) a Thracian group, associated with the Muses, the goddesses of memory or record, whose cult spread from the northern coasts of the Aegean to the district of Pieria in the north-east of Thessaly, and thence southward to the Boeotian Helicon and the Phocian Parnassus. To this group belonged Orpheus and his disciple Musaeus, who was said to have passed from Pieria into Boeotia; also three bards associated with a mystic cult of Demeter,—Eumolpus (at Eleusis), Pamphos (in Attica), and Philammon (at Delphi). Thamyris, 'son of Philammon,' figured as the latest of the Pierian poets; legend linked him with Delphi, and sent him into Messenia. (*b*) A group devoted to Apollo, and indicating a stream of influence which passed from Asia Minor, through the Aegean islands, to Greece Proper. To this belonged the Lycian Olen ('Ωλήν), famed at Delos, and Chrysothemis of Crete.

The cult of the Muses and the cult of Apollo thus represent the two main currents of primitive religious poetry in Greece. That sacred poetry took the form of *hymns* invoking and praising the deities. Apollo's worship must have given the larger scope to progress in metrical and musical art: his was the cithara; and his servant Olen was said to have 'invented' the hexameter. The hymn to a god gave type and model for the earliest lay in praise of a hero.

(3) Certain allusions in the Homeric poems point to the existence of a varied literature the ultimate origins of which may go back for some centuries. (1) The lays of Demodocus and κλέα ἀνδρῶν, *Il.* IX. 189 etc. These narrative poems, the forerunners of the Epic proper, are described as sung to the lyre. In Hesiod's time, and probably in Homer's too, narrative poetry was no longer sung, but was recited to the accompaniment only of a wand (Pind. *Isth.* III—IV. 37—39). (2) The Achaeans sing a psalm to Apollo (*Il.* I. 472—474) and other forms of song are mentioned (e.g. θρῆνος, *Il.* XXIV. 721) or alluded to (hyporcheme, *Il.* XVIII. 571, marriage song, *ib.* 492).

129. The idea of 'Epic' poetry, as the Greeks understood it, is most clearly expressed by Aristotle. It may be defined, in the first instance, by its differences from 'lyric' (or 'melic') and 'dramatic.' It was distinguished from lyric, as poetry which was recited, not sung to music. As distinguished from 'dramatic,' it was poetry which merely narrated (ἡ διηγηματική, *Poet.* xxiii), and 'imitated' life by means of verse only (ἐν μέτρῳ μιμητική, *ib.*), without help from action (τὸ πράττειν). Aristotle calls Epic poetry ἡ ἐποποιία (the making of ἔπη as distinguished from that of μέλη or δράματα): he does not use the word ἐπικός, which became current only in later times. In an epic poem, Aristotle demands (1) a dignified theme, (2) organic unity, and (3) an ordered progress. The events must form a connected series, and must all conduce to the end. To Aristotle, Homer is at once the earliest of poets and the most finished of epic artists.

The Epic.

130. In approaching the *Iliad* and the *Odyssey*, it is well to have in mind the general plan of each poem, as it now exists. The *Iliad* (15,693 lines) derives its unity, not simply from the person of the central hero, but from his wrath (μῆνιν ἄειδε, θεά). The story falls naturally into three chapters. (1) Books I—IX: Achilles is affronted by Agamemnon, and withdraws in sullen anger from the war; the Greeks are discomfited, and finally sue to Achilles, who remains inexorable. (2) Books X—XVIII: after much fighting and varied fortune, the Greeks are again reduced to extremities; Patroclus takes the field in the armour of Achilles, and, after driving the Trojans from the ships, is slain. Achilles is stricken with sore grief; at the prayer of his mother Thetis, the god of fire, Hephaestus, fashions new armour for him. (3) Books XIX—XXIV: Achilles renounces his wrath, returns to the warfare, and slays Hector: Priam, led by the god Hermes, ransoms the corpse of his son from the victor, and takes it back to be mourned and buried at Troy.

The Iliad and the Odyssey.

The *Odyssey* (12,110 lines) derives its unity from the person of Odysseus (ἄνδρα μοι ἔννεπε, Μοῦσα); and that unity is of a stricter kind than exists in the *Iliad*. The epic may be divided into groups of four books. (1) I—IV. The adventures of Telemachus. (2) V—VIII. The adventures of Odysseus, after leaving Calypso's isle, till he reaches Phaeacia. (3) IX—XII. The previous adventures of Odysseus. (4) XIII—XVI. Odysseus at the hut of Eumaeus in Ithaca. (5) XVII—XX. The return of Odysseus to his house. (6) XXI—XXIV. The vengeance on the suitors, and the hero's re-establishment in his realm.

131. The *Iliad* is an epic of warfare and debate, full of energy, of splendour, and of tragic pathos: the *Odyssey* derives its charm from narrative of wondrous adventure, and from description of social life; in respect to each, it moves in a *Character of Homeric poetry.* region almost wholly foreign to the *Iliad*; it is picturesque, rich in fancy, fertile in scenes of a tender and delicate beauty. But, with all their differences, these two great epics have, in the larger sense, a common stamp, which broadly separates them from all other compositions. They are akin in their way of presenting ideal human types, such as Achilles and Odysseus; they are akin in their way of blending divine with human action. And they are, further, inseparable in respect to certain qualities of form and style, which no other poetry unites in the same manner or the same degree.

This distinctively Homeric character consists, on the one hand, in a certain freshness and simplicity which (for us, at least) represent the poetical aspect of a primitive age; and, on the other hand, in a complete immunity from the defects which belong to the primitive stage in literature. The best traits of the best old ballads are here, but without . their frequent rudeness of form, their occasional lapses into grotesque or ignoble modes of speech, their want of sureness in the equable maintenance of a high level. Here, also, are the dignity and the finished eloquence of the literary epic, but without its artificialism, its besetting monotony, and its sometimes slow movement. This was the character which Matthew Arnold well summed up, when he said that the Homeric style has four ever-present 'notes': it is rapid; plain in thought; plain in diction; and noble.

The difficulty of uniting these qualities, as Homer unites them, is illustrated by some of Homer's translators. Cowper fails to be rapid; Chapman, Homeric in many things, is too much imbued with the 'conceits' of his age to be plain in thought (*e.g.* he renders ὅταν ποτ' ὀλώλῃ Ἴλιος ἱρή, 'When sacred Troy shall shed her tow'rs, for tears of overthrow'); Pope fails to be plain in diction; William Morris misses the Homeric nobleness, when he renders the first words of the *Odyssey* by, 'Sing me, O Muse, of the shifty.' The Homeric nobleness, it should be observed, is a far more flexible and versatile quality than the majesty of the literary epic; it is as much at home, as unfailing, and as appropriate, in the homeliest scenes of the *Odyssey* as it is in any passage of the *Iliad*.

132. There is no instance on record in which the educative power
of national poetry over a national mind has been so direct
or so large as in the case of the Homeric poetry. Homer,
says Plato, was described by his admirers as 'the educator
of Hellas.' And there was a good deal of literal truth in the claim. In
Xenophon's *Symposium* (3. 5) one of the guests,—a fair type, it may be
supposed, of the ordinary Greek of his class and age,—is made to say :—
'My father, anxious that I should become a good man, made me learn all
the poems of Homer.' In another chapter (4. 6) of the same piece we
read, 'Homer, the prince of poets, has treated almost all human affairs.
If any one of you, then, wishes to become a prudent ruler of his house,
or an orator, or a general, or to resemble Achilles, Ajax, Nestor, or
Odysseus,' let him study Homer. The Greeks of the classical age were
accustomed, indeed, to regard all poetry more or less from a didactic
point of view. To them, the poet was especially a teacher. Aristophanes
often expresses this view of his own work, and is true to orthodox Greek
sentiment when he enumerates the lessons, in one or another province,
which may be learned from the oldest poets (*Frogs* 1030 ff.). 'Homer,'
oldest and foremost of poets, was also the greatest of the teachers.
The Homeric influence is not only all-pervading in Greek literature, but
enters also into every part of Greek life.

Influence of the Homeric poems.

Herodotus (II. 53) speaks of Homer and Hesiod as having created the
Greek theogony. The Homeric poems traced types of divine character
which had an enduring influence on the Greek imagination. They also
presented old legends about the gods in a form from which an artistic
instinct had purged away the grossest elements. And by that beauty and
majesty with which Homeric poetry often invests the greater deities, it did
the Greeks an inestimable service ; it made them conscious that their own
religious sense was higher than their mythology.

Further, it should not be forgotten that, for the Greeks of the classical
age, Homer was an historian. Such a view of him is common to minds so
different as those of Herodotus and Thucydides. Appeals to the historical
authority of Homer are not infrequent in Greek literature.

133. Besides the two famous epics, many other poems were commonly
attributed to 'Homer.' Callinus (*circa* 660 B.C.) believed
Homer to have composed the epic *Thebais* (Paus. IX. 9. 5).
Herodotus leaves it an open question whether Homer is or
is not the author of the *Epigoni* (IV. 32). Homer's name, apparently,
could easily be attached to any epic of sufficient merit, especially if it
concerned Troy or Thebes. But this was not all. The hymn to the
Delian Apollo is regarded by Thucydides as the work of Homer. The
satirical poem *Margites* is ascribed to Homer by Aristotle. The parody
called the *Batrachomyomachia* (probably written *c.* 490 B.C.) also passed as
Homer's. To him, too, were ascribed the *Epigrams*,—16 short pieces or
fragments, of various classes and ages, in hexameter verse ; the places

Works as-cribed to Homer.

mentioned in them (except Arcadia in no. 16) all belong to the west coast of Asia Minor. The opinion that the *Iliad* and the *Odyssey* are the only genuine works of Homer dates only from the Alexandrian age, and perhaps did not become fixed before the time of Aristarchus.

134. The ancient notices of Homer's life appear to have been founded on poems attributed to him. This is clearly so as to the legends about his birth-place; *e.g.* the claim of Colophon rested on the *Margites*, and that of Chios on the Delian hymn. The extant Βίοι ʽΟμήρου are in no case older than the Christian era : that in Ionic, which bears the name of Herodotus, is a biographical romance, written probably in the second century A.D. The earliest recorded reference to Homer is that which occurred in a lost poem of Callinus, as reported by Pausanias (above, § 133). The earliest mention in extant work is by Xenophanes, who settled in Italy *c.* 530 B.C. The earliest quotation is by Simonides of Ceos (fr. 85, *Il.* 6. 148). *Notices of Homer's life.*

The term ʽHomeridae' occurs first in Pindar, *Nem.* 2. 2, ʽΟμηρίδαι ῥαπτῶν ἐπέων ἀοιδοί, referring to Homeric rhapsodists; where, however, the scholiast says that ʽoriginally the name was given to descendants of Homer, who sang his poetry in hereditary succession.' The logographers Acusilaus (*c.* 500 B.C.) and Hellanicus (*c.* 440 B.C.) spoke of them as a clan in Chios named from Homer (Harpocration *s.v.* ʽΟμηρίδαι): so also Strabo XIV. p. 645. They are mentioned by Plato as depositaries of the apocryphal poems (τῶν ἀποθέτων ἐπῶν) ascribed to Homer (*Phaedr.* 252 B), and as upholders of his fame (*Rep.* 599 E, *Ion* 530 D); by Isocrates (or. 10, § 65), as knowing esoteric traditions of his life. *Homeridae.*

135. ʽHomer' had been a subject of philosophical or rhetorical disquisition in Greece before any properly critical study of the poems began. Theagenes of Rhegium (*circa* 525 B.C.) is mentioned as the earliest of the allegorizing interpreters, who excused Homer's imputations on the conduct of his deities by explaining Hera as the air, Aphrodite as love, and so forth. Anaxagoras attempted a like process; the Homeric Zeus, he said, is mind, the Homeric Athena is art. These allegorizers are ʽthe old Homerists' (οἱ ἀρχαῖοι ʽΟμηρικοί) of whom Aristotle says that ʽthey see small resemblances, but overlook large ones' (*Metaph.* 13. 6. 7). Rhetorical and sophistical ingenuity, such as that of Protagoras or of Hippias, also found ample material in the Homeric text. Again, there were students of Homer whose aim was to reduce his narrative to plain historical fact. Thucydides (I. 9—11) shows a leaning to a ʽrationalizing' treatment of the Homeric narrative of the Trojan war. *Greek interpreters of Homer.*

136. But it was at Alexandria that Homer first became a subject of critical study. The great library contained texts (ἐκδόσεις) of Homer, which sometimes bore the name of the editor, *Alexandrian criticism.*

e.g. 'the text of Antimachus,'—(αἱ κατ' ἄνδρα); or the name of a
city, as 'the text of Massalia' (αἱ κατὰ πόλεις). Besides these, there
were 'common' or 'popular' texts (κοιναί, δημώδεις). All these were
probably derived from an older vulgate text, of which the sources are
unknown. This is a reasonable inference from the apparently narrow
limits of textual divergence. The Alexandrian critics refer to various
readings in particular verses, and to omissions or additions of a small
kind, but do not indicate large discrepancies or dislocations. And those
fragments of Homer which have recently been found in papyri of the third
century B.C. (or of a somewhat later but still early date) contain nothing
which invalidates this view.

The earlier Homeric criticism of Alexandria (from about 270 to
150 B.C.) is associated with the names of Zenodotus, Aristophanes, and
Aristarchus.

Zenodotus of Ephesus, who became librarian of the Alexandrian
Museum in the reign of Ptolemy Philadelphus (285—
Zenodotus.   247 B.C.), published a recension of Homer, and a Homeric
glossary (Ὁμηρικαὶ γλῶσσαι). He appears to have been a gifted man,
with a critical aim, but without an adequate critical method. Relying
too much on his own instinct, he made arbitrary changes in the
Homeric text; but he was a pioneer, and the effect of his work was, to
some extent, lasting. Aristophanes of Byzantium (*circa* 195 B.C.), a pupil
of Zenodotus, brought out a recension of Homer which
Aristophanes.   seems to have been sounder than his master's, inasmuch
as he had more respect for the evidence of manuscripts. His reading
seems also to have been wider. A story characteristic of the two men
has come down. Anacreon describes a fawn as forsaken κεροέσσης ὑπὸ
ματρός. Zenodotus wrote ἐροέσσης, on the ground that only the males
have horns. Aristophanes vindicated κεροέσσης by showing that poets
(Pindar, Sophocles and Euripides) ascribe horns to hinds as well as to
stags.

Aristarchus of Samothrace (a pupil of Aristophanes, and his successor in the headship of the Library) flourished *c.* 180—
Aristarchus.   145 B.C. He published (1) συγγράμματα, treatises on special
questions connected with Homer: (2) ὑπομνήματα, continuous commentaries on the Homeric text: and (3) ἐκδόσεις, editions of the text
itself. Two such editions came from his hand; the second seems to
have closed his labours on Homer. Previous grammarians had dealt
chiefly with rare or archaic words (γλῶσσαι): Aristarchus studied also the
Homeric usages of more familiar words. In forming his text, he gave due
weight to manuscript evidence. He also commented on the mythology,
the archaeology, and the topography of the poems. His recension was
never adopted in its entirety as a standard text, but had much more
influence than that of any other single authority. He was the best
Homeric critic, and the greatest scholar of antiquity.

Almost all that is now known about the lost works of Aristarchus comes through Didymus, a laborious grammarian of Alexandria, who, *circa* 30 B.C., wrote a treatise on the Aristarchean text of Homer (περὶ τῆς Ἀρισταρχείου διορθώσεως). The work of Didymus is itself known only through the 'Epitome,'—a series of extracts from Didymus and three other writers on Homer (Aristonicus, Herodian and Nicanor), compiled *circa* A.D. 200—250 by some unknown hand. In the tenth century, a transcriber of the *Iliad* copied this Epitome into the margin of his manuscript. That MS. is the famous Codex Venetus A, now in the Library of St Mark at Venice.

The division of the *Iliad* and the *Odyssey* into 24 books each seems to have been firmly established at Alexandria as early as *circa* 250 B.C., but its origin is unknown. Writers of the fifth and fourth centuries B.C. indicate passages of Homer merely by mentioning the persons or events prominent in them : thus verses are cited as occurring ἐν νεῶν καταλόγῳ (*Il.* book 2), ἐν Διομήδους ἀριστείᾳ (bk. 6), ἐν λιταῖς (bk. 9): ἐν Ἀλκίνου ἀπολόγῳ (*Od.* 8. 521), ἐν τοῖς νίπτροις (*Od.* 19. 386 ff.). *The division into books.*

137. The library founded at Pergamum in Mysia by Eumenes II, early in the second century B.C., became a rival to that at Alexandria; and a rivalry in Homeric criticism followed. Crates, of Mallus in Cilicia, who was librarian of Pergamum in the time of Aristarchus, wrote on Homer, and his emendations of the text are sometimes mentioned. In the view of Crates, Homeric criticism ought to include a mass of problems, philosophical, historical, and physical, which Homer suggested. The Pergamene school was rather inclined to despise the accurate grammarians of Alexandria; its own efforts were pretentious and sterile. *The Pergamene school.*

138. The most important scholia on the *Iliad* are those in the tenth century Codex Venetus A, and come mainly from two sources, viz. (1) the Epitome already mentioned (§ 136), and (2) a body of commentary compiled later than the time of Porphyrius (*circa* A.D. 270), whose 'Homeric Problems' were used. The most valuable scholia on the *Odyssey* are those in the Codex Harleianus (13th cent.), no. 5674 in the British Museum. *Ancient commentaries.*

Eustathius, archbishop of Thessalonica in the second half of the twelfth century, compiled Παρεκβολαὶ εἰς τὴν Ὁμήρου Ἰλιάδα καὶ Ὀδυσσείαν, *i.e.* 'Excerpts' bearing on Homer, which are taken from a very large number of writers, and illustrate both the language and the subject-matter.

139. The Alexandrians had decided that the *Iliad* and the *Odyssey* were the only authentic works of Homer. But their scrutiny into the authorship of the poems virtually stopped there. From a few casual mentions we learn that in the Alexandrian age there were, indeed, some persons who ascribed the *Iliad* alone to Homer, and the *Odyssey* to a different author. These were the *The Chorizontes.*

'Separaters' (οἱ χωρίζοντες). Aristarchus wrote against this 'paradox,' which never had any vogue in the ancient world.

140. A modern student of the *Iliad* and the *Odyssey* is at once struck with two broad facts about them. (1) Each shows finished poetic art. And Greek literature begins with these master-pieces. We have no samples of the ruder work which must have gone before. There is no parallel for such a phenomenon in the history of any other literature. (2) Each forms, in a large view, an organic and artistic whole. Yet each contains matter which on various grounds has been considered irreconcilable with the belief that one poet composed the entire epic. These two problems have been the basis of 'the Homeric question.'

The 'Homeric question.'

141. The critical study of the Homeric question began with Abbé d'Aubignac (born in 1604) whose *Conjectures Académiques* was published posthumously in 1705. D'Aubignac attempted to show that Homer never existed and that the *Iliad* was little more than a *corpus* of poems cleverly put together about the time of Lycurgus. More attention was paid to F. A. Wolf's *Prolegomena ad Homerum* (1795). Wolf sought to prove four main points. (1) The Homeric poems were composed, about the tenth century B.C., without the aid of writing, which then was either wholly unknown to the Greeks, or not yet in use for literary purposes. The poems were handed down by oral recitation only, and in that process suffered some changes. (2) The poems were for the first time written down about 550 B.C., in the time of Peisistratus. They then underwent some further changes at the hands of 'revisers' (διασκευασταί), or learned critics. (3) That artistic unity which belongs to the *Iliad* and (in a yet higher degree) to the *Odyssey* is not mainly due to the original poems, but has been superinduced by artificial treatment in a later age. (4) The original poems, out of which our *Iliad* and our *Odyssey* have been put together, were not all by the same author. But there was *one* poet, of commanding genius ('Homer'), who made 'the greater part' of the songs afterwards united in the two epics.

D'Aubignac and Wolf.

Wolf's theories were developed and modified by many scholars in the nineteenth century. The poems were subjected to a close analysis, and the analysis led to conclusions in sharp conflict with one another. Some scholars saw in Homer a primitive poet, author of an original sketch of one or both poems (*Ur-Ilias, Ur-Odyssee*), which formed the stocks on which later poets grafted new material. Others regarded Homer as a compiler, who combined old lays, unwritten and independent of one another, into single poems. There was no agreement in the application of this theory: Köchly, for example, dissected the *Iliad* into sixteen, and Christ into forty such lays.

Developments of Wolf's theory.

While there were thus two theories irreconcilable with each other, and the adherents of each arrived at widely different conclusions, a new criterion was derived from the excavations at Troy, Mycenae, and other places. The evidence of archaeology was applied.

Evidence of Archaeology.

Some hailed the *Iliad* and *Odyssey* as 'pure Mycenaean' on the grounds that many of the elements of Mycenaean culture, bronze weapons, Nestor's cup, boar's tusks on a helmet etc., are present in the Homeric poems. But such a position could not be maintained in its entirety, since there are allusions also to things and peoples of later times, geometric ware, Phoenicians. So the poems were analysed in such a way as to make the Mycenaean elements form one stratum, the later elements another. But the attempt failed; the elements were inextricably mingled, and the Homeric poems could not be made a mirror of contemporaneous cultural development. Attempts to correlate the archaeological with the literary analyses made the confusion worse, since the so-called oldest literary strata were often found to contain the latest cultural elements.

142.   With such inconclusive results it is not surprising that scholars sought another method of approach to Homer. They assumed the artistic unity of the two poems, and abandoned **Modern opinion.** the attempt to divide them into strata. Some, however (P. Cauer, C. Robert, Wilamowitz-Moellendorff, E. Bethe), while professing to reject the conclusions of Wolf, were still impressed by what they regarded as discrepant elements in the poems. They recognised what they regarded as 'accretions,' which they proposed to cut away from what they regarded as the work of the original author. This method again led to divergent results with no generally accepted conclusions.

Other scholars (*e.g.* F. Blass, J. W. Mackail, C. Rothe), starting from the presumption that each of the poems was the composition of a single poet, argued that the contradictions which had been found in different parts of the epics were no proof of divided authorship. The arguments that the two last books of the *Iliad* (as well as books II and X) and the conclusion of the *Odyssey* were later additions have been met (T. W. Allen, A. Shewan, E. Drerup, J. A. Scott). Furthermore, reasons based on linguistic evidence, the supposed ignorance of writing at the time when the poems were composed and the part played by the commission of Peisistratus were discredited. But disciples of unity have for the most part been disposed to allow that interpolations may have taken place, certainly before Aristarchus and probably after. But clearly, unless there is some measure of agreement about the interpolations, we shall be no better off than we were in the morass of the analysts. Some interpolated verses can be identified, but there is a wise reluctance to reject whole books or passages merely on the ground that they do not fit a particular theory. Again some scholars (*e.g.* G. Finsler, W. Schmid) have regarded Homer as the author of the *Iliad* but not of the *Odyssey*. They show some reasons for supposing that the *Odyssey* was written later than the *Iliad*, but no sufficient reason has been shown why it should not be the work of the same poet at a later period of his life. On the whole, modern opinion tends to accept the view that Homer, who was acquainted with writing, was the author of both the *Iliad* and the *Odyssey* substantially in the form in which they have come down to us.

143. There is no complete agreement, even among those who accept
Place of this opinion, about the place and date of composition of the
Composition, poems. Homer being rehabilitated, it was natural to look
Language. again to the ancient traditions about his life. Of the many cities
which laid claim to being his birthplace, Chios (Giles, Allen) and Smyrna
(Finsler) have the best credentials. Here enters the question of language.
The Homeric dialect is a mixture of old Ionic with Aeolic; hence T. W.
Allen chose Chios, an early Ionic settlement not far from Aeolic influence. It
is, however, unlikely that Homer wrote as he spoke. For the Homeric language
is a highly artificial *Kunstsprache*, so adapted to hexameter verse that it remained wedded thereto ever after. The mixture of dialects need not surprise
us; at all periods of classical Greek Literature poetic diction indulged freely
but by no means haphazardly in 'dialectal' words and forms. Still, the mixture
of Ionic and Aeolic serves to show that the ancients did not err in putting
Homer on the eastern side of the Aegean.

To assign a date to the composition of the poems is most difficult. It
is a matter of conjecture between somewhat wide limits (1000–
Date. 800 B.C.). It is possible that Herodotus was not far from the
truth when he referred to Homer and Hesiod as having lived 'four hundred
years and no more before my own time' (II. 53). If so Homer may have
lived about 800 B.C.

All that could be attempted here was to mark some of the salient points
Present in modern Homeric criticism. Recent studies have restored
position of the Homer to his position as the first and greatest epic poet, but
question. there is still great divergence of opinion about the extent of
his debt to the past, a debt which every poet owes in some measure. About
predecessors in the same field we know nothing; his material was drawn
from very old stories. To amplify this bald statement, to define the form
and language of these stories, seems an almost impossible task, but further
archaeological discoveries and further comparisons with 'epic material' of
other nations may yet shed some light[1]. For there is still a 'Homeric
question,' but it is not the same as that which puzzled our fathers.

144. The heroic saga of Troy, which furnished the material to the
Homeric poems, was also the source of several other epics, so
The Epic planned as to form preludes or sequels to the story of the
Cycle. *Iliad* and of the *Odyssey*. The Ἐπικὸς κύκλος was a body of
epic poems by various hands, arranged in the chronological order of the
subjects, from the origin and warfare of the Titans, down to the slaying
of Odysseus by his son Telegonus. When this Epic Cycle was first put
together, is unknown. The earliest notice of it is by a grammarian named
Proclus, whose date is uncertain, but may probably be placed about A.D. 140.
He wrote a Χρηστομάθεια γραμματική, or 'Manual of Literature,' in which
he gave prose summaries of the poems comprised in the Epic Cycle.

1. Meanwhile the works of C. M. Bowra, *Tradition and Design in the Iliad*, 1930
and W. J. Woodhouse, *The Composition of the Odyssey*, are of special value.

Extant fragments of the manual give his summaries of the poems in one part of the Epic Cycle,—viz. that which concerned the Trojan war. Arranged in the order of events, the series is as follows:—

1. Κύπρια: 11 books. Origin and earlier part of the Trojan war. Ascribed to Stasinus of Cyprus.

2. The Homeric *Iliad*.

3. Αἰθιοπίς (so called from the Aethiopian Memnon): 5 books. The Amazons at Troy. Exploits and death of Memnon. Death of Achilles. Contest for his arms.— Ascribed to Arctinus of Miletus.

4. Ἰλιὰς μικρά: 4 books. From the contest for the arms of Achilles down to the capture of Troy.—Doubtfully ascribed to Lesches of Mytilene.

5. Ἰλίου πέρσις: 2 books. Incidents attending the capture: story of Laocoon: withdrawal of Aeneas to Ida.—Ascribed to Arctinus of Miletus.

6. Νόστοι: 5 books. Adventures of heroes returning from Troy: Menelaus in Egypt: murder of Agamemnon.—Ascribed to Agias of Troezen.

7. The Homeric *Odyssey*.

8. Τηλεγονία: 2 books. The slaying of Odysseus in Ithaca by Telegonus, his son by Circe; and what ensued thereafter.—Ascribed to Eugammon of Cyrene (*circa* 565 B.C.).

Of the Κύπρια we have about 49 verses in all, preserved in quotations: the earliest citation is by Plato (*Euthyphr.* p. 12 A); but Herodotus (II. 117) mentions τὰ Κύπρια ἔπεα, denying that the epic can be Homer's, since it contradicts a notice in *Il.* 6. 289 ff. Of the Ἰλιὰς μικρά there remain 21 lines in all; one of these is preserved by Aristophanes (*Eq.* 1056 f.). Of the Ἰλίου πέρσις we have but 12 lines in all, and of the Νόστοι only 3. Nothing remains of the Αἰθιοπίς or of the Τηλεγονία.

These Cyclic poems imply a knowledge of the Homeric epics, and help to fix a lower limit for their age. Stasinus, Arctinus, Agias and Lesches are obscure names, of uncertain date. But the *Cypria*, the *Aethiopis* and the *Iliupersis* were probably as old as *c.* 775—700 B.C. The *Little Iliad* and the *Nosti* can scarcely have been later than 700—600 B.C.

145. The fame of Hesiod, as an ancient epic poet, dates at least from the early part of the seventh century B.C. From the literature of the fifth and fourth centuries B.C. we can see that he was then regarded as a great primitive teacher of practical and religious lore, not unworthy, on this ground, to be named along with Homer. The name Ἡσίοδος, like Ὅμηρος, became the symbol of a school, and was attached to compositions of diverse origin. But there is no reason to doubt that there was a poet named Hesiod, whose father emigrated from Cyme, a town of Aeolis in Asia Minor, to the village of Ascra, near Mount Helicon in Boeotia. The extant poems which bear Hesiod's name are, the *Works and Days*, the *Theogony*, and the *Shield of Heracles*. The first two of these are the poems with which Hesiod's name was chiefly associated throughout Hellas.

1. The Ἔργα καὶ Ἡμέραι is the poet's most characteristic and most famous work. It is a strange medley, evidently not written at a sitting, but consisting of the gathered observations of a shrewd observer. Its composition seems to have been prompted by a quarrel between the author and his younger brother Perses, who had cheated him of part of his patrimony, and having the ear of the rulers of the land (βασιλῆες) attempted to rob him further. Hence the poem opens with an exhortation to Perses to seek wealth, without

which man is a poor creature, not by unjust litigation, but by honest hard work. Hard work is inseparable from the lot of man as is shown by the history of the human race (Prometheus and the Five Ages). The primary source of wealth is the land, and a large part of the poem (383-694) is devoted to agriculture. The outline of a year's work on a farm is followed by notes, admittedly amateurish, on sea-faring. The remainder of the poem consists of further examples of Hesiod's teaching, the right thing to do and the right time and way to do it. The groundwork of many of these γνῶμαι must be far older than Hesiod, especially the religious and superstitious beliefs—a collection of the traditional lore of a farming community. The final part (765-828) of these precepts deals with lucky and unlucky days, whence the second word of the title.

2. The Θεογονία is in three principal sections. (i) 1—115. An introduction, in which a hymn to the Muses (36—67) has been inserted. (ii) 116—962. *Theogony* proper: including (*a*) 1—452, Cosmogony: how the visible universe arose out of chaos. The eldest dynasty of gods, Oceanus, Cronus, etc. (*b*) 453—880. The struggle between the dynasty of Cronus and that of his son Zeus: defeat of the Titans, and victory of Zeus. (*c*) 881—962. The supremacy of Zeus; the Olympian gods and their offspring. (iii) 963—1022. Goddesses who have wedded mortals, and their children. The last four verses form a prelude to a κατάλογος of illustrious women, piecing it on, for purposes of recitation, to what precedes.

3. The Ἀσπὶς Ἡρακλέους, a short epic of 480 verses, tells how Heracles (for whom Hephaestus made a shield) slew the robber Cycnus, son of Ares, at Pagasae in Thessaly. In its present shape, it commences with 56 verses concerning the birth and previous life of Heracles. This prelude begins with the words ἢ οἵη, 'Or such as was...' the hero's mother Alcmena. It came, then, from the Ἠοῖαι—an enumeration of illustrious women which was ascribed to Hesiod, and was so called because each heroine was introduced by the words ἢ οἵη. The *Shield of Heracles* is certainly of a later age than the *Works and Days* or the *Theogony*. But it may be as old as *c.* 600 B.C. Numerous other poems were ascribed to Hesiod, *e.g. Catalogue of Women*, appended to the *Eoiai*, *Precepts of Chiron*, the *Great Works*, but these like the *Shield* should rather be assigned to a Hesiodic or Boeotian School than to Hesiod himself. Our knowledge of this school has been increased by the discovery of papyrus fragments, the longest of which deals in an amusing way with the Wooing of Helen.

Hesiod is second only to Homer as an educator of the Hellenic race. The technical instruction of the *Works and Days* was doubt-

Hesiod as a thinker.

less valuable but hardly original. The religious instruction of the *Theogony*, sanctioned by Delphi, was of immense importance in Greek Religion. But Hesiod's chief title to fame is that he is the earliest moral philosopher of Europe. At a time when monarchical institutions had crumbled and power had fallen into the hands of greedy nobles, Hesiod like an Old Testament prophet seeks to recall princes and people to the paths of justice and avoidance of ὕβρις. If men act wrongly they will surely perish at the hand of Zeus, all powerful and all seeing, who has already destroyed other races of men. But Hesiod has faith that those who spend their lives in honest unceasing work will be rewarded with sufficient wealth to live, which is all that they may ask in this cruel age.

146. A collection of 34 pieces in hexameter verse has been handed down with the title, 'Hymns or Preludes of Homer and the

The Homeric Hymns.

Homeridae.' Rhapsodists usually prefaced an epic recitation by an address to some god; Pindar speaks of such

'Homeridae' as beginning Διὸς ἐκ προοιμίου (*N.* 2. 3). Most of these pieces were meant to serve as προοίμια, as is shown by the formula at the end, where the reciter says that now he will pass from the god to another theme. The hymn εἰς Ἀπόλλωνα is composed of two originally distinct poems, viz., one to the *Delian Apollo* (vv. 1—178), and one to the *Pythian Apollo* (179—546). The other hymns on a similar scale are those to *Hermes* (Hymn III), to *Aphrodite* (IV), and to *Demeter* (V). Each of these five longer hymns is a small epic poem (though each could be used as a προοίμιον),—narrating, with picturesque detail, some legend of the deity. There are many passages of great beauty, especially in the *Delian Apollo*, the *Demeter* and the *Aphrodite*. The Ionian epic style is fairly well maintained, and sometimes recalls the *Odyssey*; but the Homeric spirit and impetus are lacking. Much of the work may be referred, probably, to the sixth century B.C. (or the later part of the seventh). Didymus of Alexandria (*c.* 30 B.C.) thought that the hymn to the *Delian Apollo*, which Thucydides undoubtingly gave to Homer, was by the rhapsode Cynaethus of Rhodes (*c.* Ol. 69, 504 B.C., acc. to schol. Pind. *N.* 2. 1); but this is unlikely. It may be as old as the seventh century.

Next in interest to the five great hymns may be placed no. VII, on Dionysus taken by robbers (59 verses), and no. XIX, to Pan (49),—both, probably, Attic, of the fifth century. Some of the smaller pieces in the collection are mere scraps of inferior work. The short hymn to *Ares* (no. VIII) shows Orphic influences, as do also XIV (*Mother of the Gods*), XXX (*Earth*), XXXI (*Sun*), XXXII (*Moon*).

147. Epic verse continued to be written after the great age of Ionian epos was over. The Homeric model was followed by such men as Peisander of Rhodes, who (in the sixth century B.C. ?) wrote an epic on Heracles; by Panyasis, the uncle of Herodotus, who celebrated the same hero; by Choerilus of Samos, the historian's friend, who took the Persian invasion as the subject of the earliest historical epic on record; by Antimachus of Colophon, Plato's contemporary, who wrote a *Thebais*; and by many others. The Hesiodic tradition, too, was continued, in genealogical lore, by those dim figures of the seventh century, Carcinus of Naupactus, Asius of Samos, Eumelus of Corinth. Then there was a mystic epos, imbued with the Orphism of the sixth century. A philosophical epos, preluded by Xenophanes, is represented by Parmenides and Empedocles. (The Alexandrian and post-Alexandrian epics will claim a separate, though brief, mention.)

The later Epos.

But, in tracing the development of Greek literature as a natural growth and as the expression of a national mind, it is correct to say that the epic period was closing when the lyric period began. The Greek epic, as a chapter in the evolution of Greek poetry, is represented by the age of creative activity in that kind. Its typical works are the Homeric poems.

B. ELEGIAC, IAMBIC, AND LYRIC POETRY.

148. The Ionians, who had created epos in its highest form, were also
the leaders in developing the species of poetry which arose

**Elegiac
poetry.**

next after it. ἔλεγος (a word which has been conjecturally
referred to an Armenian origin) was used from early times by
the Asiatic Greeks to denote a dirge for the dead, accompanied by the flute.
Phrygia, the home of early flute-music, seems to be the country from which
the *elegos* came to the Ionians of the coast.   But flute-music was not only
funereal, and by the side of the funeral 'elegy,' festive or martial flute-songs
arose, to which the name 'elegy' was extended.   A new metre for such
songs was invented by Ionian poets familiar with the epic hexameter.   This
was the 'elegiac' couplet (ἐλεγεῖον),—an hexameter followed by a pentameter.
A continuous flow of hexameter verse sweeps the mind onward with it : in
the elegiac couplet, the effect of the pentameter is to give a meditative
pause, a moment of reflection,—inviting our thought to return upon itself.
Epic poetry moved in an ideal region of heroic life.   Elegiac poetry was
an utterance of the new age which was beginning for Hellas, and especially
for Ionia, in the eighth and seventh centuries,—an age of gradual transition
from monarchy to democracy, an age of enterprise and discovery, of
colonization and commerce, when fresh interests and widening experience
stimulated individual thought and feeling.

Greek elegiac poetry was universal in its range of theme: it could give
utterance to patriotic exhortation, to tender sentiment, to

**Its range and
duration.**

social gaiety, to the thoughts of the statesman or the philosopher, and to mourning for the dead.   In *martial* elegy, we
have a few verses from Callinus of Ephesus (660 B.C.), the first elegiac poet
on record, who urges his countrymen to repel barbarian invaders ; and the
stirring 'exhortations' (ὑποθῆκαι) of Tyrtaeus (*c.* 640) to the Spartans, in
the time of the Second Messenian War.   *Erotic* elegy has its earliest
exponent in Mimnermus of Smyrna (*c.* 620 B.C.).   *Gnomic* elegy is represented in the sixth century B.C. by Solon, with his thoughts on Attic politics
and on life at large ; by Phocylides of Miletus, with his moral precepts ;
and by Theognis of Megara (the only Dorian elegist of note) in those
counsels, based on the maxims of Dorian aristocracy, which he addresses
to his young friend Cyrnus.   *Funereal* or *commemorative* elegy is illustrated,
early in the seventh century, by Archilochus ; in the next, by Sappho
(fr. 119) ; and in the time of the Persian Wars, by Simonides of Ceos.   In
the fifth and fourth centuries B.C. elegiacs were occasionally written by
many great masters of Attic verse or prose.   No other form of Greek
poetry lived so long.   It was still cultivated with ingenuity and elegance in
the reign of Justinian.

149. Iambic poetry, like Elegiac, was an Ionian creation, and first comes into view at the same period, viz., *circa* 700—650 B.C. The word *iambus* has been connected with the Greek ἰάπτω ('to dart' or 'shoot'), as the metre of early satire: but **Iambic poetry.** another view makes it non-Hellenic and of Phrygian origin (H. Flach, *Gr. Lyrik*, p. 222). Elegiac and Iambic poetry may be regarded as, in a sense, companion forms, alike characteristic of the period which followed that of the great epos. Both alike were fitted for the utterance of individual thought and feeling on any subject; and neither demanded, of necessity, any high poetical gift. But there is also a difference between their aptitudes. The elegiac measure, derived from the epic, always suggests a circle of listeners: even when one person only is ostensibly addressed, the tone is social. The iambic measure, (the nearest, as the Greeks thought, to the cadence of every-day speech,) being more colloquial, is more suitable when the utterance is more personal, as in satire, or in controversy. Solon writes of his reforms both in elegiacs and in iambics: but the iambic form is that which he prefers for keen self-defence in detail. *Satire* was more especially the purpose to which iambic verse was applied by its earlier masters, as Archilochus (*c.* 650 B.C.), Semonides of Amorgos (*c.* 640), and Hipponax of Ephesus (*c.* 540), the inventor of the 'scazon.' This side of the iambic tradition was continued in Attic Comedy. The satirical vein was not, however, the only one in which these writers used iambic (and the kindred trochaic) metre. Solon's iambics, already mentioned, have an energy and a dignity which render them a worthy prelude to the iambic verse of Attic Tragedy.

150. Elegiac poetry and iambic poetry were both, in their earliest days, lyric, *i.e.* were wholly or partly sung to music; but before the fifth century B.C. their connexion with music was relaxed **Lyric poetry.** or lost. Greeks of that century would have designated elegiacs or iambics as ἔπη. The lyric proper, inseparable from music, was called μέλος: a lyric poet was μελοποιός. (λυρικός occurs first in the second century B.C.) The rise of Greek melic poetry was necessarily preceded by some progress in music. (1) The Phrygian Olympus, *c.* 750—700 B.C., developed flute-music, αὐλητική. (2) Terpander of Lesbos, *c.* 710—670, improved the cithara. The story that he gave it seven strings instead of four is now rejected: it was already a heptachord; it is more probable that by the addition of one string (νήτη) at the top of its compass he turned the former heptachord into an octachord, giving the Dorian mode, the kernel of the Greek musical system. He developed the art of singing to the cithara, κιθαρῳδική, and wrote νόμοι for it, sacred hymns to be sung by one voice.

Greek melic poetry had two main branches, the Aeolian and the Dorian. The Aeolian was *monodic*, for one voice, and was essentially the utterance of the singer's own feelings. The Dorian was *choral*, and dealt largely, though not solely, with themes of public interest, especially with those suggested by acts of public worship.

Terpander established in Lesbos a school of κιθαρῳδοί. The lyric
poetry which grew from these beginnings took its colouring
The Aeolian
lyric.   from the Lesbian temperament, in which Aeolian fire and
passion were joined to a fine sense of grace and beauty in
nature and in art.

These qualities find unique expression in the fragments of Sappho
(*c.* 610—565), which combine intensity of feeling with exquisite melody.
She was the head of a school or group of pupils in Lesbos, maidens whom
she trained in the lyric art, and much of her poetry seems to have been
connected with events in their lives. Additional fragments discovered in
Egypt are lamentably mutilated and can only be made intelligible by conjectural restoration. Her slightly older contemporary Alcaeus appears, in
the little that survives of his work, as a brilliant Lesbian noble, tried by
war and exile, cheered by love and revelry; a man of original force in
language and metre, possibly the inventor both of the 'alcaic' and of the
'sapphic' stanza,—fitting measures for lyrics to be sung by one voice,
in social gatherings. Sappho and (at an interval) Alcaeus are the great
names of the Aeolian lyric: there is no third. In matter and form,
Anacreon of Teos (*c.* 550—500 B.C.), the Ionian poet of pleasure, is akin
to the Aeolians, but, instead of their passion, he has only a certain grace
and sweetness. His metrical forms were largely of his own invention.
The spurious *Anacreontea,*—some 60 short pieces, all in 'iambic dimeter
catalectic' metre,—probably range in date from *c.* 200 B.C. to *c.* A.D. 400
or 500.

151. The Dorian choral lyric first took an artistic shape at Sparta.
Terpander had brought thither his citharodic art. A little
The Dorian
choral lyric. later, Thaletas of Crete (*c.* 670—640 B.C.) had brought the
paean, the 'dance-song' (ὑπόρχημα), and the choral dances of
the Cretan Apollo-cult. Alcman (*c.* 640—600 B.C.), who is said to have
come to Sparta from Lydia, is the first recorded poet of the choral lyric.
His best-known pieces were *parthenia* (odes for choruses of maidens): one
fragment, found in 1855, contains about 100 verses. Among his other
works were hymns, paeans, hyporchemes, and banquet-songs (σκόλια).

Stesichorus of Himera in Sicily (*c.* 640—555 B.C.) is the chief representative of the Dorian lyric in its earlier period. Heracles, Orestes, the
Atreidae, Odysseus, Helen, and other persons of epos, were taken by him
as subjects for hymns,—a form of poem previously reserved for gods or
demigods. He was, in fact, a lyric interpreter of epic tradition; his
dialect was epic, with a Dorian tinge. It was he who established the
tripartite structure in *strophe, antistrophe* and *epode* as the norm for the
choral lyric: but whether he was the first to add the epode is uncertain.
Further, he broke new ground by his lyric treatment of love-stories in his
poems entitled *Daphnis, Rhadina* and *Calyca*—precursors of the Greek
novel.

Ibycus (*c.* 550 B.C.) passed the first part of his poetical career at his native Rhegium in Italy, and wrote choral lyrics in the epic style of Stesichorus. He afterwards went to the court of Polycrates tyrant of Samos (533—522 B.C.), and there wrote love-poetry of an almost Aeolian fire. He is the only poet who has this kinship with both the great branches of the Greek lyric.

Simonides of Ceos (born in 556 B.C.), an Ionian, but of the Attic type, took the Dorian choral form for his lyrics. Others had sung of gods and heroes; he is the first who is known to have won the ear of Greece for ἐπινίκια, odes on victors in the national games. He also wrote lyric ἐγκώμια on notable men. His hyporchemes, too, were famed. Excelling in pathos, he made the dirge (θρῆνος) an accepted form of lyric song. A lyric epitaph on the defenders of Thermopylae, and some lines on Danaë, show the finish and charm of his versatile art. His elegiacs have already been mentioned (§ 148). He died in or about 467 B.C., probably at Syracuse.

152. Pindar was born near Thebes probably about 518, and survived the year 446. His fragments represent almost every form of lyric poem,—(1) hymns to deities, (2) paeans to Apollo, (3)   **Pindar.** dithyrambs to Dionysus, (4) *prosodia*, or processional songs, (5) *partheneia*, choral songs for maidens, (6) *hyporchemata*, choral dance-songs, (7) *encomia* in praise of eminent men, (8) *scolia* for banquets, and (9) dirges. Some of these fragments are magnificent. Parts of nine paeans discovered in Egypt were published in 1908. The paean was a hymn in honour of Apollo or Artemis, and is usually a prayer for help or a thanksgiving. Of Pindar's nine fragmentary paeans, nos. 8 and 9 are doubtfully so called; they resemble *hyporchemata*. The rest are to Apollo, Pythian or Delian etc., and are written to the order of various cities, Abdera (2), Ceos (4), Athens (5). No. 4 is the poem referred to in *Isthm.* 1. 6 ff. Some fragments have also survived of hymns to Zeus and other gods. But the forty-four odes of victory, ἐπινίκια or ἐπίνικοι,—14 Olympians, 12 Pythians, 11 Nemeans, and 7 Isthmians,—are the poems by which moderns best know him. The choral ἐπινίκιον was usually sung after the victor's return to his home, either in a procession (*Olymp.* 14); or, as more often, at a banquet (*O.* 1); or at the doors of the victor's house (*Nem.* 1. 19): rarely at the scene of the victory (*O.* 8).

Like all Greek lyrics, Pindar's odes had an instrumental accompaniment, —that of the lyre (which he calls λύρα or φόρμιγξ, and once κίθαρις), or of the flute (αὐλός), or both combined. The general character and tone of the ode decided the choice of the musical ʻmodeʼ (ἁρμονία) in which it was to be set. (1) The *Dorian* mode was grave, strong, majestic; as Pindar himself says (fr. 67 Bergk⁴), Δώριον μέλος σεμνότατον. (2) The *Aeolian* mode was joyous, animated, festal, breathing the spirit of chivalry; hence it is associated with the ἵππειος νόμος (*Ol.* 1. 101) and with the Καστόρειον (*Pyth.* 2. 69). (3) The *Lydian* mode, suited to the αὐλός, was tender and plaintive.

These musical modes have their respective affinities with certain metrical rhythms. The rhythms chiefly used by Pindar are the following. (1) The *dactylo-epitrite*, based on the dactylic prosodiac, $- \cup \cup - \cup \cup - (-)$, and the epitrite, $- \cup - -$. This grave and equable rhythm, sometimes called 'Dorian,' is naturally suited to the Dorian musical mode, with which it is associated in *Olymp.* 3. It is found in about one-half of the forty-four odes. (2) The Aeolian rhythm, based on the combination of trochee, $- \cup$, and dactyl, $- \cup \cup$, in different relations. Having a brisk and airy movement, this rhythm is congenial to the Aeolian mode, with which it is joined in *Olymp.* 1, *Pyth.* 2, *Nem.* 3. The Lydian mode is thrice connected by Pindar with the Aeolian rhythm (*Olymp.* 5 and 14, *Nem.* 4), but only once with the dactylo-epitrite (*Nom.* 8). (3) The *paeonic* rhythm, based on the paeon, $- \cup \cup \cup$, and kindred cretic, $- \cup -$. This occurs only in *Olymp.* 2 (the best example), *Olymp.* 10, and *Pyth.* 5.

Pindar's choice of mode and rhythm has, again, a certain influence on the colouring of his dialect. The basis of his dialect is that which Stesichorus adopted when he set the first example of treating heroic themes in lyric form. It is the epic, a composite dialect gradually shaped by poets, and not exactly corresponding with any spoken idiom. But Pindar tempers this with a certain infusion of non-epic Aeolisms and Dorisms, in proportions varying with the musical and metrical character of the poem.

Two general types of structure appear in the odes. (1) Thirty-seven of the forty-four are written in *triads*. The triad consists of strophe and antistrophe, with an epode. The number of triads in an ode ranges from one (as in *Olymp.* 4) to thirteen (*Pyth.* 4), but is usually three, four, or five; there is no ode of two triads. Some, at least, of the odes written in triads were accompanied by rhythmical dancing. (2) Seven of them are written, not in triads, but in a series of uniform strophes (*Olymp.* 14, *Pyth.* 6 and 12, *Nem.* 2, 4, and 9, *Isthm.* 7). These were processional.

As to arrangement of subject-matter, Pindar's normal scheme is (1) a proem, relating to the particular victory which he is celebrating, (2) a myth, which has some connexion with the victor's family or city, and (3) an epilogue, in which he returns to his immediate theme. But there is nothing mechanical in his method, which is of infinite flexibility and variety. His transitions are sometimes boldly abrupt, sometimes delicately skilful; *e.g.*, in *Olymp.* 1 the relative τοῦ (v. 25) is the link between proem and myth, as ἵνα (v. 95) between myth and epilogue. The first condition of understanding a Pindaric ode is to study it as a symmetrical whole.

Pindar's general characteristics are, splendour and swiftness of fancy and of language,—linking of present with heroic past by myths,—wise counsel, as of Delphi,—and panhellenic range of imagination. He had a matchless power of shaping magnificent phrases, and giving them their right setting in the spacious framework of the Dorian choral lyric. He has the keenest sense of what is grand or beautiful in nature. When he is epic (as in *Pyth.* 4), he brings out chosen moments with more than epic vividness, but curtails the story with more than epic boldness. His pictures of the heroes, so full of brilliant life, are in the spirit of Olympia, and of the generation which had repelled the Persians.

153. Bacchylides of Ceos (*c.* 507—430 B.C.?), nephew of Simonides, known till lately by a few fragments only, is now repre- Bacchylides. sented by nineteen poems or parts of poems, found in Egypt in 1897 : the date of the papyrus is probably *c.* 50 B.C. Of the thirteen epinikia in this collection, three (III—v) are for Hieron of Syracuse. The other six poems are hymns about divine or heroic persons, collectively called διθύραμβοι in the large Alexandrian sense. Two of these, both relating to Theseus, are of especial interest: viz. XVI [XVII], a paean for the Delian Apollo, to be sung by a Cean chorus ; and XVII [XVIII], a unique example of a dithyramb in the form of a dialogue. Bacchylides was an elegant and facile poet, with a special gift for picturesque detail.

154. A yet more recent addition to the literature of the Greek lyric illustrates the last stage of its decline. Timotheus of Miletus (*c.* 447—357), musician rather than poet, was a popular composer of 'nomes,'—not grave hymns, like Terpander's nomes, but of a more florid and dithyrambic type. A papyrus found near Memphis in 1902 contains 253 verses, in free rhythms, from his nome called the *Persae.* Here we have 214 lines from the middle part of it (ὀμφαλός),—which describes the sea-fight at Salamis,— and the end (σφραγίς), in 39 lines, where he names himself. It is the oldest extant Greek MS. (*c.* 320—290 B.C.?).

C. DRAMA.

155. The origin of tragedy is discussed elsewhere (§ 424). The 'dithy-ramb,' first mentioned by Archilochus (*c.* 650 B.C.), was a festive song in honour of Dionysus. The name seems to be a com- Early development. pound of δι- (the root of δῖος, cp. διπόλια) with a modified form of θρίαμβος (*triumphus*), a word used by Cratinus (*c.* 448 B.C.), denoting some kind of hymn to the wine-god. The dithyramb was one of the elements which lie behind Attic Drama. Its literary history is associated chiefly with Arion of Lesbos (*c.* 600 B.C.), who produced dithyrambs at Corinth which were sung by a chorus, probably of 50 persons. Further, the chorus of Arion was a τραγικὸς χορός. This meant 'a chorus of satyrs,' the attendants of Dionysus: Aeschylus uses τράγος in the sense of 'satyr' (fr. 207). The 'goat-chorus' may originally have been connected with an Arcadian cult of Pan; but from Arion's time, if not from a still earlier date, it was associated with Dionysus (cp. Herod. v. 67). The dithyrambic chorus, personating satyrs, became a principal feature of the Dionysia at Athens in the second half of the sixth century B.C.

But neither the literary dithyramb nor the chorus of satyrs make drama. It is probable that a simple but solemn drama of some kind in which the chorus were men existed in Attica and that Greek Tragedy is a fusion of different elements. At all events Thespis, a native of Icaria, produced at the Dionysia of 534 B.C. a chorus, pro-bably of men, whose leader held a dialogue, not with the chorus but with a person appointed for that purpose, who was called the *answerer* (ὑποκριτής, afterwards the word for 'actor'). There was now a *dialogue*, there was narrative of action, and comment; but there could be as yet no *drama*. Here matters rested in the space between Thespis and Aeschylus. The foremost name of that interval is Phrynichus. One of his pieces was the *Capture of Miletus* (on the disaster of 494 B.C.): another, the *Phoenissae* (476 B.C.), on the Greek victories of 480—79. In the latter piece, the scene was at the Persian court: the chorus represented the wives of the king's Phoenician sailors. Phrynichus, as we know from Aristophanes, was famed for the simple sweetness of his lyrics,— 'native wood-notes wild,' which he warbled as if the birds had taught him. To the same period belong Choerilus, an Athenian, and Pratinas, a Dorian who came to Athens from Phlius. Both made their mark in the development of the satyr-chorus, but little is known about them.

(3) Aeschylus, born in 525 B.C., is said to have first come forward as a poet about 500, and to have gained his first victory at the Dionysia in 484. His development of the choral τραγῳδία which he had received from Thespis and Phrynichus is thus described by Aristotle (*Poetics* iv. 13):—'Aeschylus first introduced a second actor; he diminished the importance of the Chorus, and assigned the leading part to the dialogue.' Aristotle had studied the history of Greek drama; writing at Athens *circa* 330 B.C., he had access to the whole literature, and to those records of the performances which he used in his lost Διδασκαλίαι. No fact in Greek literary history rests on firmer authority than his statement just quoted. Yet it has recently been alleged, without evidence, that the addition of the second actor cannot have been the work of Aeschylus, but must have been the official act of the State. The archon was paymaster; but the idea must have been the poet's. The general ordering of the Dionysia was, indeed, subject to the State. But in those early days, when the originally lyric τραγῳδία was being developed, each step in the development was due to the free initiative of the poetical artist. Arion took one step, at Corinth; at Athens, Thespis took a second step; Aeschylus took a third, the most important of all, and thereby created drama. Instead of the single actor, not a member of the chorus, with whom its leader held a dialogue, there were now two actors, both separate from the chorus. An actor might take more than one part. Thus in the *Supplices*, for which Aeschylus used only two actors, there are three parts, Danaus, Pelasgus, and the Herald,—the first and the third being played by the same person. A story could now be told in action.

156. The words τριλογία and τετραλογία cannot be traced back beyond the Alexandrian age, but the things date at least from Aeschylus. A tragic poet, competing at the Dionysia, produced a 'tetralogy,' or group of four plays, viz. three tragedies (a 'trilogy'), and a satyr-play. The number of the tragic chorus was at first 12: and the origin of 'tetralogy' is probably traceable to the

Aeschylus.

Trilogy and Tetralogy.

fact that four such choruses approximately represented the old dithyrambic
chorus of 50. The collective tribute to Dionysus thus remained roughly
the same, but gained variety and interest by being made in four separate
parts, of which the last (the σατυρικὸν δρᾶμα or σάτυροι),—a παίζουσα
τραγῳδία,—directly recalled the old τραγικὸς χορός. The 'tetralogy' was
the regular form of tragic competition down at least to the close of the
fifth century, and perhaps longer. The year 340 B.C. is the earliest for
which a departure from the rule can be proved; in that year the competitors produced two tragedies each.

157. Among the seven extant plays of Aeschylus, the *Supplices* has the
most marked affinity with the earlier time when the τραγῳδία
was essentially lyric. Its date is unknown, and has been
placed as late as 461, or as early as 492 : it must be older, at
least, than 472; possibly of 491 or 490. The distinctive feature is the
great importance of the Chorus, representing the fifty daughters of Danaus,
who have fled to Argos to avoid marrying their cousins, the sons of
Aegyptus. It was the first play of a trilogy; in the second (Αἰγύπτιοι, or
Θαλαμοποιοί?) the victorious pursuers forced on the marriage, and in the
third (Δαναΐδες) Hypermnestra was tried and acquitted for disobeying her
father Danaus by sparing her husband.

The *Persae* (472 B.C.), also largely lyrical, seems to have been prompted
by the *Phoenissae* of Phrynichus; it was the second piece of a trilogy
which began with *Phineus* and ended with *Glaucus*; and it is the earliest
play taken from contemporary history by a poet who had shared in the
deeds which he celebrated. The *Seven against Thebes* (467 B.C.), that
δρᾶμα Ἄρεως μεστόν (Ar. *Ran.* 1022), breathes the soldier-spirit which
appears in the poet's epitaph on himself at Gela (Athen. 627 C), but is
not one of his best plays: it was the third piece of his Oedipus-trilogy,
following a *Laius* and an *Oedipus*. The *Prometheus Bound* (probably
later than 468) is an immortal masterpiece of creative imagination, moving,
with Titanic power, amidst supernatural beings and elemental forces, yet
presenting that vast and weird spectacle with unfailing obedience to the
Hellenic instinct for clearness and for measure. It was followed by a
Προμηθεὺς Λυόμενος: whether the Πυρφόρος was first piece or third, is
doubtful.

In the *Oresteia* (458 B.C.), the only extant trilogy, each play is a whole,
within a larger unity; the Erinys of the house prompts the murderess in
the *Agamemnon*, menaces the avenger in the *Choephori*, and is reconciled
with the spirit of mercy in the *Eumenides*. The character of Clytaemnestra,
—the vision of Cassandra,—the presentment of the Furies in bodily shape,
announcing and interpreting their own dread prerogatives,—these are
among the things which best illustrate the sublime force of the poet's
genius. The total number of plays written by Aeschylus is given by Suidas
as 90, by others as about 70: the lower figure, so far as we can judge from
ascertained titles, is nearer the mark. This would represent the work of

Plays of
Aeschylus.

some 44 years, from *circa* 500 to 456 B.C., when he died in Sicily, at Gela. We have about 451 fragments.

Aeschylus uses iambic verse with equal mastery for vigorous narrative, as in describing the battle of Salamis; for declamation, as in the stately speech of Athena; for invective, as when Apollo expels the Furies; for controversy, as in the trial of Orestes; or for descriptive passages of quiet beauty, as when Prometheus depicts the change which he wrought on the primitive life of man. The poet's lyric style, again, is altogether his own; it has an epic tone, of Homeric nobleness; it is boldly imaginative, with an almost Pindaric rapidity in the succession of images; and it is reflective, not in Pindar's gnomic or didactic manner, but in a way that suggests a deeply-brooding mind, tinged with mysticism, grappling with dark problems of life and fate.

But his dominant thoughts, at any rate, stand out in grand, simple lines. He had seen ὕβρις overthrown in battle by the jealousy of the gods; he was an ardent lover of the freedom which he had helped to win; but it must be a freedom based on order, and secured against ὕβρις: his ideal is τὸ μήτ᾽ ἄναρχον μήτε δεσποτούμενον. Sin will be expiated by suffering (δράσαντι παθεῖν): but Zeus has shown men the way to wisdom, and has ordained that by suffering men shall learn. Zeus, 'whosoe'er he be,' is a power in harmony with reason, and working for righteousness.

158. The great founder of Attic drama was defeated at the Dionysia of 468 by a competitor some thirty years his junior, Sophocles of Colonus (born *c.* 496), who then gained the earliest of many victories. Ancient writers connect Sophocles with some improvements in the external form of tragedy. He added a third actor (Arist. *Poet.* iv. 15); and raised the number of the chorus from 12 to 15 (auct. vit., and Suidas). It was he, too, according to Aristotle, who first employed the art of the scene-painter (σκηνογραφία). We do not know how much this means. But one thing is evident. Aristotle names σκηνογραφία and 'the third actor' as the two inventions distinctive of Sophocles. Athenian tradition, then, which Aristotle had the amplest means of knowing, must have clearly associated Sophocles with some marked advance in the mode of producing plays.

More important, perhaps, than any matter of that kind was the change which Sophocles made in the method of tragic composition. The trilogy of Aeschylus consisted usually (if not invariably) of three tragedies connected in subject, so as to form three chapters of one story: and the satyr-play which completed the tetralogy had also (as a rule) some bearing on that theme. Sophocles introduced the practice of writing a trilogy in which the three tragedies had no link of subject with each other or with the satyr-drama which made up the tetralogy. This change suited the bent of his genius and the stamp of his art. The linked trilogy was a fitting instrument for Aeschylus, a dramatist of spacious imagination, who loved to express character by great strokes of action, and to trace the gradual working of nemesis up to some goal of divine reconciliation. But the unconnected trilogy was more congenial to Sophocles. The moral interest is the central one in his plays. When the single tragedy has a final unity of its own, that more limited framework invites the spectator to concentrate his attention on the finer touches of ethical portraiture.

The *Antigone*, which may probably be referred to the year 442 or 441 B.C., is the earliest of the extant plays, as is indicated by some points of internal evidence; *e.g.* it is the only one of the seven which contains no instance of ἀντιλαβή (the division of an iambic verse between two speakers), or of an anapaest in the first place of the trimeter. This beautiful tragedy is typical of its author's method. A play of Sophocles always involves some central issue so contrived as to prove the characters of the chief agents to their depths. In the *Antigone*, that issue is the conflict between the heroine's resolve to obey the unwritten law of the gods, and the resolve of Creon to enforce his edict. The march of the drama is in unison with the strength and clearness of the central conception; every incident, every speech, contributes to the progress; at each step the tragic interest rises towards the climax. The *Antigone* well illustrates, too, the Sophoclean use of the Chorus, which with him is less active than with Aeschylus, yet always directly assists the development. It does so by attuning the thoughts of the spectators to successive moods in sympathy with the action. In the *Antigone* there are six choral odes, and each of them has a direct bearing on the dramatic moment at which it occurs.

The *Ajax*, though its date is uncertain, clearly comes next in age to the *Antigone*; the parodos is of the early type found in the Aeschylean *Supplices*, *Persae*, and *Agamemnon*,—an anapaestic march followed by a lyric ode. Ajax dies at v. 865, and then more than a third of the play concerns the question whether he shall be buried. Athenians, familiar with the cult of Ajax, would find the true climax of the play, not in his death, but in the decision that he should receive funeral honours,—the necessary preliminary to his consecration as a ἥρως.

The *Oedipus Tyrannus*, of uncertain date (perhaps *circa* 429—420), has justly been regarded, from Aristotle onwards, as a model of excellence in the construction of a tragic plot; it contains, too, scenes of unsurpassed tragic power,—*e.g.* the abrupt exit of Iocasta, who sees the worst before it is seen by her lord. The *Trachiniae* (written probably between 420 and 410) has an imperishable charm in its Deianeira, one of the most exquisite portraits in all drama. Heracles, when he comes on in the last third of the piece, is less effective. The *Electra* may also be placed, on internal evidence, among the later plays (*circa* 420—414?). The avenging Orestes of Aeschylus and of Euripides is menaced by the Furies: the Sophoclean Orestes acts in calm reliance on Apollo, and there is no hint of trouble to come. The vengeance is regarded, as by

Athena in the *Odyssey*, in the light of a simply righteous deed; and in this sense the Sophoclean treatment of the story is characteristically Homeric.

In the *Philoctetes* (409 B.C.), a theme treated by the two other dramatists, the distinctive invention of Sophocles lay in associating the young Neoptolemus with Odysseus, and thus providing a new source of moral interest. No Greek play is superior to this in subtle character-drawing or in pathos. The *Oedipus at Colonus* was first brought out, after the poet's death, by his grandson and namesake, in the archonship of Micon (402—1), at the Dionysia in March, 401. It is a patriotic play, intensely Attic in feeling, with scarcely any plot, but of the highest interest and charm: the passing of Oedipus, at the sacred Colonus, is of a sublime beauty. A fourth actor is employed; this, and the choice of subject, are the only clear hints of date; but there is no doubt that the play was one of the poet's latest works. Aristophanes of Byzantium is said to have known 130 plays ascribed to Sophocles, and to have been allowed 113 as genuine. About 109 titles of lost plays are extant, and about 1012 fragments. A large part of a satyr-drama, the *Ichneutae*, has been recovered.

According to Plutarch (*Mor.* p. 79 B), Sophocles spoke of his own style as having passed through three successive phases. (1) In the first, he had imitated the majesty, the pomp,—ὄγκος,—of Aeschylus. (2) The second was marked by τὸ πικρὸν καὶ κατάτεχνον,—'incisiveness' (the 'sting' of style, not 'harshness'), and artificialism—an art which too little hid itself. (3) The third was ἠθικώτατον λέξεως εἶδος,—the kind of diction which is most expressive of character,—καὶ βέλτιστον, and there-fore best for his purpose,—fittest to make the persons of drama seem real. (We do not know whence Plutarch got this: possibly it was from Ion of Chios.) Our earliest play, the *Antigone*, is 26 or 27 years later than the date at which Sophocles gained his first victory; and it is not surprising, then, if we find no clear trace of the first, or Aeschylean, phase. But in the *Antigone* there is more of visible and masterful art in language,—τὸ κατάτεχνον,—than (*e.g.*) in the *Philoctetes*, where we certainly find τὸ ἠθικώ-τατον. In his later years, Sophocles was influenced by Euripides in some details of language and versification. But, in all essentials, the style of Sophocles and the general character of his work remained, to the end, thoroughly distinctive, and totally unaffected by the younger poet, to whom, indeed, he everywhere presents a contrast. Thus the prologue of the *Trachiniae* is Euripidean only in so far as it is historical; it is totally unlike the typical prologue of Euripides in being dramatic.

Aeschylus was a great creator; Sophocles, pre-eminently a great artist. He took the legends, and presented them in a harmonious and beautiful form, suitable to the material, and intelligible to all men. Piety and sympathy conspired to interest him in character,—in the motives and feelings of men, and the effects on them of the discipline administered by the gods,—and he had seen that suffering might be a blessing. Sophocles is essentially an Athenian of the age of Pericles. The impress of that age appears in his manner of reconciling consecrated tradition with newer and larger thoughts. He invests the conceptions of the popular religion with a higher spiritual and intellectual meaning. And the artistic side of the age is expressed by him in poetry, much as in architecture and sculpture it is interpreted by the remains of the Parthenon : there is the same sanity and wholeness of work; power joined to purity of taste; self-restraint; and a sure instinct of symmetry.

159. Euripides, born in 480 (16 years after Sophocles), began his career as a tragic poet in 455, and gained his first victory at the Dionysia in 441. Excluding the *Rhesus*, which is now generally allowed to be the work of some inferior hand (probably of the fourth century B.C.), we have 18 of his plays. Earliest among these is the *Alcestis* (438 B.C.), which stood as fourth play of a tetralogy in the place usually held by a satyr-drama (with which, in vv. 747—802, the revelling Heracles gives it a touch of kinship). To the same tetralogy belonged the lost *Telephus*, in which the poet broke with tragic convention by presenting that hero in the guise of a wandering beggar. The *Medea*, one of the greatest and perhaps the most faultless of its author's works, appeared in 431. The *Hippolytus* (428 B.C. ?),—distinguished as στεφανηφόρος (in allusion to a wreath offered by the hero to Artemis) from an earlier form of the play which had offended Athenian feeling,—is notable for the psychology of Phaedra, and the skill which conciliates a certain sympathy for the sinning woman with pity for the innocent youth whom she brings to death. In the *Andromache* (probably earlier than 425 B.C.), Hector's widow, now the concubine of Neoptolemus, and her son Molossus, are rescued by Peleus from the malice of Hermione and Menelaus, while her lord is slain at Delphi through the intrigues of Orestes: a poor play, mechanically closed by the intervention of Thetis. The *Heracleidae* (also of the earlier period) is a patriotic piece : the sons of Heracles, persecuted by the Argive Eurystheus, are received and sheltered at Athens by Demophon, son of Theseus.

The *Hecuba* (earlier than 423 B.C.), in which the widowed queen of Priam wreaks her vengeance on the Thracian Polymestor, lacks unity of design, but has a cleverly woven plot. The *Supplices* (421 or 420) is, like the *Heracleidae*, patriotic, and commendatory of an Athenian alliance with Argos. Creon king of Thebes has refused burial to the Argive warriors slain there. Their widows come as 'suppliants' to Eleusis. Theseus demands funeral rites from Creon, who is obdurate; the Athenians vanquish the Thebans in fight, and the Argive dead are brought to rest in Attic earth. Like the last two dramas, the *Mad Heracles* (*circa* 420—416) tends to exalt Athens,—the home to which Theseus brings the afflicted hero, to seek pardon from the gods for the deeds done in his Hera-sent frenzy. In the *Ion* (not later than 412), picturesque beauty and ingenious plot are combined with a severe treatment of Apollo. Ion, the young temple-servant at Delphi, proves to be the god's son by Creusa—the child whom he had left to perish. Athena decrees that Ion shall be king of Athens, and progenitor of the four Attic tribes. The *Troades* (415) depicts the sufferings of Trojan dames, Hecuba, Andromache, Cassandra, after the fall of Troy. It is scarcely a drama, but rather a series of pathetic scenes.

The *Electra* (413) is a notably original work, unsuccessful as a tragedy, but deeply interesting as a characteristic treatment of a theme handled by both the elder masters; here, too, the criticism of Apollo is unsparing. The *Helena* (412) is based on the legend that the real Helen went to Egypt, and only her wraith to Troy. Menelaus rescues her, by a ruse, from the Egyptian Theoclymenus, and brings her back to Greece. Some of the lyrics are fine; but the subject was ill-suited to tragedy, as the comic poets did not fail to see. The *Phoenissae* (*c.* 411—409) concerns the same subject as the *Seven against Thebes* (which is glanced at in vv. 751 f.),—the war of Polyneices, supported by the Argives, against his brother Eteocles. The 'Phoenician maidens' of the chorus are supposed to be on their way from Tyre to Delphi, and to have been detained at Thebes by the outbreak of the war. The play is not impressive as a whole, but there are brilliant passages and effective scenes. The *Orestes* (408) deals with a sequel to the slaying of Clytaemnestra and Aegisthus,— the madness of Orestes,—his peril, and Electra's, from the wrath of the Argive assembly,—their final deliverance,—and, at the close, the rescue of Helen by Apollo from the sword of Orestes. Despite much that is inartistic or even absurd, this play enjoyed great celebrity.

Iphigenia among the Tauri (brought out probably between 418 and 412) is excellent both in plot and in character-drawing. Goethe's *Iphigenie* is at least its equal in the latter quality, and has a more effective close; but the Greek poet was bound by the motive of the myth to end with the founding of the Artemis-cult at Brauron. The *Iphigenia at Aulis*, produced after 406, a beautiful play which the poet left unfinished, forms, in subject, a prelude to the other: Artemis rescues the maiden, the betrothed of Achilles, from the altar at Aulis, and carries her to the Tauric land. The genuine play ends at 1508; a spurious epilogue, of wretched workmanship, has been tacked on to it. The *Bacchae* (finished, though not acted, before the poet's death in 406) was written at the court of Archelaus, and designed for performance in Macedonia, to whose traditions of orgiastic worship the subject was congenial. In picturesque splendour the play has no Greek rival. It is unique in its sustained glow of Dionysiac enthusiasm, to which keen irony lends the force of contrast, and in its sense of natural beauty lit up by fancy.

The *Cyclops*, the only extant satyr-drama of Euripides, is founded on the *Odyssey* (book 9); though not a strong piece, it has the interest of showing that the *genre* which it represents was not farce, but παίζουσα τραγῳδία. Of 92 plays current under the name of Euripides, 75 (including

8 satyr-plays) were held genuine by the Alexandrians. We know about
50 titles of lost plays, and have about 1106 fragments.

The genius of Euripides was at discord with the form in which he
worked. He received tragedy with its primary conditions fixed:—three
actors; a chorus; and, for material, the heroic legends. Aeschylus and
Sophocles had felt, each in his own way, that the treatment must be ideal;
i.e. a certain nobleness (of that Homeric kind which Eumaeus shares with
Achilles) must be preserved to the persons of the heroic saga. Euripides
broke this convention (1) by often making his persons the exponents of
modern subtleties, sometimes of his own thought; (2) by touches of
'sophistic,' and of the new rhetoric; (3) by realism in the treatment of the
myth, *e.g.* by presenting Telephus in the guise of a wandering beggar.
Taking the ideal tragedy as his norm, Aristophanes insists in the *Frogs*,
and quite truly, that Euripides had robbed *that* tragedy of τὰ μέγιστα
(v. 1494), *i.e.* of its idealism. On the other hand, Euripides brought in
new elements of romance and melodrama, which have constituted one
of his charms for later ages.

In his technical method three points claim notice. (i) His choral
odes often have nothing to do with the action. The chorus of the two
elder masters was an organic part of the drama; between their dialogue
and their lyrics there was continuity of thought and tone. Such continuity
ceased to be possible when the myth was treated in a more realistic and
modern spirit. Euripides could not get rid of the chorus; he was right,
then, from his own standpoint, in making it a free lyric adjunct, a source
of variety. Further, he admitted in his later lyrics the more florid music
which was coming into vogue; and he also introduced solos of that stamp
(μονῳδίαι) for actors. (ii) He made the *prologue* serve, like a play-bill, to
tell who the persons were, and where the story began. Though sometimes
inartistic, this was useful in days when fewer people were at home in the
myths; especially when he took them into the by-paths of legend. (iii) He
made a large use of the θεὸς ἀπὸ μηχανῆς to close the play. The device
is sometimes effective (as in the *Hippolytus* and *Bacchae*), sometimes
clumsy (as in the *Andromache* and *Orestes*).

Certain thoughts on religion, conduct, and society pervade his work.
He resented the popular mythology which made gods immoral. He was
not, however, a mere agnostic or a pure rationalist. He recognised supernatural forces. He recognised human instincts and emotions above, as
well as below, reason. Welcoming moral nobleness wherever he found it,
in ruler, in virgin-martyr, in peasant, or in slave, he was troubled by
the drift towards wrong and folly which he saw in public and social life.
Mental loneliness and unrest are felt in him. Shrinking from no problem,
and striving to reach the core of every situation, he makes his persons
throw out such sayings as ἡ γλῶσσ' ὀμώμοχ', ἡ δὲ φρὴν ἀνώμοτος, or τί δ'
αἰσχρόν, ἢν μὴ τοῖσι χρωμένοις δοκῇ; These were seized on as immoral.
And his influence on the multitude in his own day was perhaps, on the

whole, not good; for he blurred those Hellenic ideals which were the common man's best without definitely replacing them. The charge of misogyny brought against him, the Greek poet who has treated women with most sympathy and insight, is a gauge of the extent to which he was popularly understood. But his human pathos has a universal appeal; he is, as Aristotle says (*Poet.* xiii. 6), τραγικώτατος, the most moving of poets. Though as a metrist he is inferior to both the elder masters, some of his lyrics are unsurpassed in splendour of fancy (*e.g. Bacch.* 135—169), and in dreamy charm (*e.g. Hippol.* 732—755). In language he is an exquisite artist who can veil his art. He was the idol of later antiquity; and is the favourite of countless modern readers who care less for the ideal drama of Aeschylus or of Sophocles.

160. After 400 B.C. tragedy declined: there were many tragic writers, but no new master arose. Already in the fourth century the work of Aeschylus, Sophocles, and Euripides was classical, and it was prescribed that some one piece of theirs should always be acted at the Dionysia along with the new plays. Athens remained the metropolis of tragedy till about 300 B.C.; then Alexandria became so, and in the reign of Philadelphus (285—247 B.C.) could boast of its seven poets known as 'the tragic Pleiad.' In A.D. 217 the edict of Caracalla abolished theatrical performances at Alexandria.

Decadence of Tragedy.

161. Tragedy sprang from the dithyramb; Comedy from the songs at rustic festivals of vintage and harvest, where the reproductive forces in nature, of which Dionysus was one type, were the objects of a rude symbolic worship. [Arist. *Poet.* iv. § 12 ἡ κωμῳδία...ἀπὸ τῶν τὰ φαλλικὰ (ἐξαρχόντων).] Thus Comedy, like Tragedy, had an original kinship with the Dionysiac cult; as, on the other hand, the earliest Tragedy, like the earliest Comedy, was largely an improvisation (αὐτοσχεδιαστική, Arist. *l.c.*). But there was also a vital difference. Tragedy sprang from a form of lyric poetry which was already artistic, and already a recognised part of Dionysiac ritual at public festivals. The germ of Comedy was a kind of mirth-making which had no similar pretensions. Starting with this advantage, Tragedy preceded Comedy by some 30 or 40 years in attaining its mature Attic shape.

Origin of Attic Comedy.

Dorians, who had a turn for rough satire and broad drollery, were the earliest comic entertainers. Megarian 'comedy,' first associated with the name of Susarion (*circa* 580—562 B.C.), seems to have dealt in jests of an order which Attic wit soon learned to scorn. At Syracuse, in the first half of the fifth century, Epicharmus advanced from the crude farce to a riper comic drama, drawn sometimes from common life, and sometimes from mythology. It is not known whether he used a chorus. The prose μῖμοι of his Syracusan contemporary Sophron were scenes from everyday life, classed, according to the sex of the persons, as ἀνδρεῖοι and γυναικεῖοι.

At Athens the course of development is supposed to have been somewhat as follows. (1) After the institution of the 'Great' or 'City' Dionysia

(perhaps *c.* 475 B.C.), a merry procession called a κῶμος had become a
feature of that festival. A troop of mummers marched into the sacred
precinct, to the accompaniment of flute and pipe, and sang a song in the
god's honour: after which, one of their number addressed the audience
in a humorous speech, turning on topics of the day. This *comus* was at
first voluntary and unofficial. (2) Somewhat later, but probably before
460, the *comus* began to be organised with aid from the State: there was
now a χορηγία for Comedy. (3) Between *c.* 465 and 431 B.C. the form
of Attic Comedy, as we know it, was evolved by a process of which the
details are unknown. κωμῳδία is thus 'the song of the κῶμος,' and presumably a term of Attic mintage; though the Dorians, according to
Aristotle, supported their claim to the invention by maintaining that it
was 'the song of the κώμη' (their equivalent for the Attic δῆμος: Arist.
Poet. iii. § 3). Tragedy furnished the general model of the development.
Cratinus (*c.* 450) is said to have limited the number of comic actors to
three, and that number suffices for every play of Aristophanes (allowance
being made for the assignment of small parts to 'supernumeraries' who
are not required to be absolutely mute). The number of the Chorus,
however, which in Tragedy was 12, and afterwards 15, was in Comedy
24 (as may be verified by the list of birds in Ar. *Av.* 297 ff.). In the
fifth century Comedy was the chief feature at the Lenaea (held in Gamelion, at the end of January or beginning of February), but was acted
at the Great Dionysia also. The number of competing poets in the comic
ἀγών was then three, but was raised in the fourth century to five. Each
poet exhibited only one comedy.

162. First among his predecessors, Aristophanes names Magnes (*flor.
c.* 460), who catered for the public with choruses of harp-
players,—of birds,—of frogs,—of Lydians, and what not, but   Poets of the
failed to keep their favour. Then came Cratinus (*c.* 450—   Old Comedy.
422),—the real founder of the Old Comedy,—who lived to defeat the
Aristophanic *Clouds* with his *Wine-flask* (Πυτίνη),—boldly inventive, im-
petuous as a torrent,—once the rage, and at last a poor unheeded dotard.
Next Crates (*c.* 449—425),—who turned from aggressive satire to more
elaborate character-drawing (*Poet.* v. 3),—distinguished by his 'dainty
conceits' and delicate style; but he had only a wavering success.
Pherecrates (*c.* 438—410) imitated the manner of Crates, but without
wholly renouncing political satire. Eupolis (*c.* 429—411), the contemporary and rival of Aristophanes, united a singular elegance of fancy
and diction with fierce and bitter satire, such as he levelled in his Βάπται
against Alcibiades, and in his Μαρικᾶς (Ar. *Nub.* 553) against Cleon.
Cratinus, Eupolis and Aristophanes formed the representative Alexandrian
triad for the Old Comedy. Among its minor poets may be named Phrynichus (*c.* 429—400), who preferred literary or imaginative themes (thus
his Μονότροπος, or 'Solitary,' depicted a sort of Timon): and Plato comicus
(*c.* 420—390), who was mainly a political satirist; his *Hyperbolus* was
brought out in 415.

163.   Aristophanes, born *c.* 448, began his career with three plays exhibited in the names of other persons.   The *Banqueters*

Aristophanes.

(Δαιταλεῖς, 427) is a satire on the New Education, followed in 426 by the *Babylonians* (subject-allies of Athens whom Cleon sets to grind, like foreign slaves, in his mill).   The *Acharnians* (425) is a plea for the peace-party.   Undeterred by the angry men of Acharnae, Dicaeopolis makes peace with Sparta on his own account, and forthwith presents an enviable contrast to the warlike Lamachus.   In the *Knights* (424),—the first piece which the author brought out in his own name,—Nicias and Demosthenes, faithful slaves of Demos, extricate their master from the clutches of his rascally Paphlagonian steward (Cleon); the onslaught on the demagogue shows the Old Comedy in its most reckless mood of unsparing satire.   The *Clouds* (a revised form of a play first produced in 423) is an attack on the new spirit of intellectual inquiry and culture rather than on a school or class,—'sophist' being used in a sense which would comprehend (*e.g.*) Heracleitus and Anaxagoras no less than Protagoras and Prodicus,—and Socrates is taken as the type of the entire tendency.

The *Wasps* (422), Racine's model in *Les Plaideurs*, is a satire on the average citizen's delight in being paid to serve on the huge juries of the law-courts, and the mad hunger for victims which it bred in him.   The *Peace* (421) resumes the purpose of the *Acharnians*.   Trygaeus, a woebegone Athenian, soars to heaven on a beetle, and finds the gods pounding the Greek states with the pestle and mortar of war.   He frees the goddess Eirene from a well in which she is imprisoned, and marries one of her handmaids.   In the *Birds* (414), two Athenians ('Plausible' and 'Hopeful') persuade the birds to build a city in the clouds, to which, having found wings, they migrate.   The gods, cut off from earth by the new settlement, send envoys to treat for peace, and 'Plausible' marries Basileia ('Royalty') daughter of Zeus.   The play is essentially a flight of free fancy, an escape from the troubles of earth.   It is a triumph of imagination and of lyric melody.

The *Lysistrata*, brought out at the Lenaea of 411, shortly before the Revolution of the Four Hundred, is reticent on politics, but interprets the popular desire for peace.   The women take the question into their own hands, occupy the acropolis, and force the men to capitulate.   The *Thesmophoriazusae* appeared a little later, at the Great Dionysia of 411, when the oligarchic conspirators had established a terrorism, though they had not yet struck their blow.   The play eschews politics.   Euripides is tried and condemned by the women at their festival, the Thesmophoria.   In the *Frogs* (405), produced soon after the death of Euripides and of Sophocles, Dionysus goes to Hades to bring back a poet: Aeschylus and Euripides contend in the shades for the tragic throne, and the god's choice falls on Aeschylus.   The play is of unique interest as a contemporary criticism of Attic Tragedy by a poet who thoroughly understood it, but was detached from it.   In the

Ecclesiazusae (392) the women, disguised as men, make their way into the ecclesia, and decree a new constitution, disfranchising the other sex. The *Plutus* (388) shows how Asclepius restores eyesight to the blind god of wealth, who thereupon enriches the good and impoverishes the unjust. The Chorus has no lyrics, but merely takes part in the dialogue.

The παράβασις was a characteristic feature which the Old Comedy inherited from the comus. At some moment of pause in the action,— usually towards the middle of the play,—the Chorus turned round so as to face the spectators, and 'came forward' a little towards them (hence 'parabasis'),—when the coryphaeus addressed the house in the poet's name, setting forth his merits, his grievances, or his views on things in general. The *Acharnians, Knights,* and *Wasps* have the parabasis in its most complete and elaborate form. The *Lysistrata, Ecclesiazusae* and *Plutus* have no parabasis. The full vigour of the Old Comedy (of which the parabasis is a symbol) did not much outlive 420 B.C. In his political satire Aristophanes scarcely affects to portray the real men; he gives a few of their superficial traits; but, for the rest, his Cleon and his Socrates are almost as much types of tendencies as his personified Ἄδικος Λόγος. It was his bent of mind, indeed, to clothe the abstract with a concrete form; and this is a mental link between the rollicking satirist of the *Knights* and that poet of brilliant and delicate fancy who soars in the *Birds*.

164. The Alexandrians distinguished between 'Old' and 'New' Comedy: from the age of Hadrian a further distinction was drawn between 'Old,' 'Middle' and 'New.' The Old Comedy becomes less pungently political in the middle period of Aristophanes (414—405), betraying the pressure of circumstances which imposed caution and reticence (we hear of laws, short-lived or futile, μὴ κωμῳδεῖν ὀνομαστί). The 'Old' political Comedy ceased when the Chorus (with its parabasis) dwindled and perished. The *Middle* Comedy (to which the *Ecclesiazusae* is akin, and to which the *Plutus* distinctly belongs) covers the period from *c.* 400 to 336. Political and personal satire has well-nigh vanished. The comic poet deals with types of characters or callings, which furnish his titles (*e.g.* ὁ Δύσκολος, ὁ Στρατιώτης), criticises philosophy or literature, parodies serious poetry, or travesties the myths. Scurrility (αἰσχρολογία) has given place to innuendo (ὑπόνοια: Arist. *Eth.* iv. 8. 6). The representative names of this period are Antiphanes and Alexis.

Comedy after Aristophanes.

The *New* Comedy (vigorous from *c.* 336 to 250) is an offspring of Euripidean tragedy even more than of *Old* or *Middle* Comedy. The metre and the comic atmosphere remain, but instead of satiric wit we have humour, plot and character-drawing. The diction also often recalls Euripides. But the characters are 'modern,' not drawn from legend; and the picture is one of the everyday life of the time. The predominant interest is in human beings, their loves and their hates, their meanness and their nobility. Hence the New Comedy made a universal appeal and could easily be adapted to other peoples and other tongues.

New Comedy.

Not only Plautus and Terence, but through them Shakespeare, Molière and the Restoration dramatists, indeed all writers of straight comedy, are indebted to Menander, Philemon, Diphilus, Apollodorus, Poseidippus. The most famous is Menander (342–290). He has long been known to us by numerous short and pithy fragments preserved in literary texts, but until 1905, when large portions of five plays were discovered in Egypt, our judgment of his work was dependent largely on the Latin adaptations. Even now we have no complete play, but there are three of which enough is preserved to allow us to understand his fame and to endorse Quintilian's admiration for his skill and sympathy in depicting character. The three are (1) Ἐπιτρέποντες (*Arbitrants*), (2) *The Girl from Samos*, (3) Περικειρομένη (*The Shorn Girl*). There are also considerable fragments of *The Farmer*, Γεωργός, and lesser remains of some eighty-five plays.

D. HISTORICAL PROSE.

165. The earliest traceable Greek prose, in the sixth century and the first half of the fifth, is that of chroniclers who put together the local records of cities; compilers of myths or genealogies; writers on the geography and traditions of countries outside of Hellas; and speculative thinkers, who sought briefly to set forth their views on the origin of the physical world. These earliest prose-writers were mainly Ionian; but our knowledge as to most of them is very scanty. Cadmus of Miletus (*c.* 550 B.C. ?), said to have written a κτίσις Μιλήτου, is a wholly obscure name. Eugeon of Samos (*c.* 510?) wrote annals of his island (ὧροι Σαμίων). Charon (*flor. c.* 470) did a like work for his native Lampsacus (ὧροι Λαμψακηνῶν), besides writing on Greek and on Persian history (Ἑλληνικά, Περσικά), and on the origins of cities (κτίσεις). Xanthus, a Lydian (*flor. c.* 450), wrote on the history of that country (Λυδιακά). Pherecydes of Leros (*flor. c.* 450 B.C.), called an Athenian because Athens became his home, compiled a large work on mythology. Acusilaus (*flor. c.* 500), a native of Argos in Boeotia, wrote 'genealogies' in which he drew on the Hesiodic poems. Among the early Ionian thinkers who committed their views to written prose were Anaximander of Miletus (*c.* 611—547), his follower Anaximenes, and Heracleitus of Ephesus (*flor. c.* 500). In quasi-historical prose-writing before Herodotus, the two most prominent names are those of Hecataeus and Hellanicus. Hecataeus of Miletus (*c.* 550—478), who wrote a Περίοδος γῆς, long remained an authority on geography: he was also a compiler of genealogical and other legends. The Lesbian Hellanicus lived *c.* 482—397: he compiled (1) local myths, (2) works descriptive of countries, as Περσικά, Ἀργολικά, and (3) lists of victors in games, etc. Thucydides (I. 97) mentions his Ἀττικὴ ξυγγραφή (the earliest *Atthis*), finding fault with its chronology.

The early prose.

In contradistinction to the ἐποποιός, or maker of verses, the writer of prose narratives was called λογοποιός, as Hecataeus is termed by Herodotus (II. 143), or λογογράφος, the name by which Thucydides (I. 21) describes the earlier chroniclers generally.

These writers, with all their varieties of subject and treatment, had, as regards form, one trait in common. They made no pretension to charm of style. With them, the business of the ψιλὸς λόγος was strictly practical,—to instruct. Hecataeus began his work on genealogies thus :— Ἑκαταῖος Μιλήσιος ὧδε μυθεῖται· τάδε γράφω, ὥς μοι ἀληθέα δοκέει εἶναι· οἱ γὰρ Ἑλλήνων λόγοι πολλοί τε καὶ γελοῖοι, ὡς ἐμοὶ φαίνονται, εἰσίν (Demetrius *De elocut.* § 12). Dionysius, in his general estimate of the 'logographers' (*De Thuc.* 5), notes also that they simply compiled, without sifting or criticising.

166.   Herodotus of Halicarnassus (born *c.* 484 B.C.) fought to free his city from the tyranny of Lygdamis ; fled to Samos, but returned after the tyrant's fall ; then went forth on wide travels, in- **Herodotus.** cluding a visit to Egypt (between 449 and 445) ; found a welcome at Athens, where he became the friend of Sophocles, perhaps of Pericles ; and finally made himself a new home in Magna Graecia with the Athenian colonists at Thurii (443).   He was again at Athens after 432, if, as is generally assumed, προπύλαια in v. 77 are the Propylaea completed in 432.   He alludes to the surprise of Plataea by the Thebans (VII. 233), and the expulsion of the Aeginetans by the Athenians (VI. 91), in 431 : to the execution at Athens of the Spartan envoys bound for Persia (VII. 137), in 430 : and to the devastation of Attica by the Lacedaemonians (IX. 73).   It is certain, then, that the History was under his hands till about 429 or 428.   He probably died *c.* 425, leaving book IX unfinished.   The present division into books (perhaps older than the naming after the Muses) is a good one, showing insight into the structure, but is certainly not the author's own.   When he wants to say that he will mention something further on in his work, he uses such phrases as ἐν ἄλλῳ λόγῳ (VI. 39), ἐν τοῖσι ὄπισθε λόγοισι (v. 22): and it is in this general sense that we should understand ἐν τῷ πρώτῳ τῶν λόγων (v. 36), referring back to I. 92.

The History derives its unity from the idea of collision between East and West, between Asiatic and Greek, culminating in the Persian wars. The first six books are, as it were, prefatory, leading up to the last three, in which the work reaches its climax. Book I is the career of Cyrus, the founder of the Persian Empire. Book II, opening with the accession of Cambyses, describes Egypt ; in book III, the new king conquers the Nile-land, dies, and is succeeded by Darius. Books IV and V give the Persian campaigns in Scythia and Thrace, with an account of those countries ; the Persian expedition to Libya, with some notices of that region and its Greek colonists ; and the Ionian revolt to 498. Book VI, after finishing the Ionian revolt, relates the Persian expedition against Greece of 492, and that of 490, repelled at Marathon. Then comes the crown of the work—

the great narrative of τὰ Μηδικά in books VII, VIII, IX, from the invasion of Xerxes in 480 to the retreat of Mardonius, and the capture of Sestos by the Greeks, in the winter of 479/8. It is possible that these last three books were the first which Herodotus planned and finished, and that he afterwards wrought his other material into the form of a large and varied proem to the Μηδικά. However that may be, the History, in its present shape, has a true unity,—not marred by book II, the part most obviously suggestive of an independent origin.

The sources used by Herodotus were manifold and various;—such records (chiefly monuments and inscriptions) as were accessible in cities or in temples, especially at Delphi; oracles; popular oral tradition; particular facts learned from specially informed persons (*e.g.* III. 55, IV. 76, VIII. 65, IX. 16); Greek writers, whether poets or λογοποιοί (VI. 52, 55, 137, etc.). He went about inquiring (ἱστορέων), and tried to make out what was the truth. When there are two versions of a story, he sometimes gives both, either with an indication of his preference (III. 9), or without it (III. 47). He is perfectly fair, without personal or national prejudice or malice: see, *e.g.*, his remarks on the charge of medism against the Argives (VII. 152). If in parts of the Μηδικά (*e.g.* the story about the Corinthians at Salamis) he has reflected the Athenian feelings of his day, that proves nothing against the man's own temper of mind, as seen in his whole work. The treatise ascribed to Plutarch, περὶ τῆς Ἡροδότου κακοηθείας—which includes (§ 12) the amazing charge that he was φιλοβάρβαρος —is aptly characterised by Stein:—'These assaults by an inordinately vain patriotism—which had no conscience in regard to historical fact— prove in the most significant manner the uncorrupted and undaunted integrity of Herodotus.' He never pretends to an accuracy or certainty which he knew to be unattainable. In Egypt he had to rely chiefly on priests and local guides, and this is his warning to his readers (II. 123):— 'The stories told by the Egyptians can be adopted by anyone to whom such things are credible. As for myself, my principle throughout the history is this,—that I record as I heard it what was told on each occasion.' Such warnings occur elsewhere also. When he criticises, the test is usually subjective,—his own sense of probability or fitness (οἰκός). He is pious; he treats the temple-legends with respect, often, too, with caution and reticence. He hints that men can know nothing of τὰ θεῖα (II. 3): but he clearly believes that supernatural agencies are potent over mankind; indeed, he relies on them overmuch to explain what mortals do or suffer.

The painstaking good-faith of Herodotus—manifest on every page—is indisputable. But he was not, of course, a critical historian: in his materials, fact was mixed with myth and folk-lore in varying proportions, and he was not competent to sift them. In regard to credibility, his History cannot be judged as a whole: every separate statement must be tried on its own merits. Akin to the Ionian writers of his own or an earlier day in describing countries geographically and socially, he is novel in the massive epic-like unity of his plan, in the dramatic life of his narrative, and also in the desire to amuse while he instructs, as seen in his admirably-told stories. He is the earliest artist in his kind, the Homer of European prose.

167. Thucydides, son of Olorus, an Athenian whose family was con-nected with that of Cimon, and derived wealth from gold-mines at Scaptesyle in Thrace, was born, according to one **Thucydides.** account, in 471 B.C.; but some think a date nearer to 460 more probable. He is said to have been the pupil of Anaxagoras and of the rhetor Antiphon; he was at any rate a disciple of the new intellectual movement, with its scepticism of tradition, its cultivation of a popular dialectic, and its study of rhetorical style. In the autumn of 424, when holding a military command on the coast of Thrace, he failed to save Amphipolis, and (probably to avoid a death-penalty) went into banishment. During twenty years of exile, he visited Peloponnesus, Sicily and Magna Graecia, and perhaps the court of Archelaus in Macedonia. In 404 he returned to Athens. He seems to have passed the last years of his life in Thrace. A conjecture regarding the date of his death has been founded on his silence in book III, ch. 116, as to an eruption of Etna which occurred in 396.

Throughout the Peloponnesian war, from its beginning in 431, he was collecting and sifting material for his work,—doubtless, too, gradually writing the first draft of it. But there is internal evidence that the History did not take its present shape until after 404. His plan was to carry it down to the capture of Athens in 404 (v. 26); but book VIII breaks off shortly after the Athenian victory at Cynossema (411). The Βίος, of composite authorship, which bears the name of Marcellinus (4th or 5th century A.D.?), says (§ 58), τὴν μὲν πραγματείαν αὐτοῦ οἱ μὲν κατέτεμον εἰς τρεῖς καὶ δέκα ἱστορίας, ἄλλοι δὲ ἄλλως, adding that 'the current and re-ceived division' (ἡ πλείστη καὶ ἡ κοινή) into eight books 'has prevailed.' If Thucydides had divided his work into eight books, the division into thirteen, and the 'other' arrangements here mentioned, could scarcely have found vogue. The division into eight books was presumably Alexandrian.

Book I opens with an outline of Greek history from the earliest times (1—23), designed to bring out the incomparable magnitude and signi-ficance of the war in which all Hellas (practically) was enlisted on the side of Athens or of Sparta. Despite the inevitable attempt to rationalise myth into history, this ἀρχαιολογία shows an insight and a grasp un-matched in the writings of the age. A survey of the πεντηκονταετία (479—431) fills book I. 89—117. The 'Archidamian' or ten-years' war (431—421) is concluded in books II—v. 24. The rest of book v (25—116) opens the story of the years of nominal peace (421—413), carrying it from the spring of 421 to the autumn of 416. The formula in c. 26 marks the author's sense that this is a distinct chapter of the war (γέγραφε δὲ καὶ ταῦτα ὁ αὐτὸς Θουκυδίδης), and announces that the history will go down to 'the capture of the Long Walls and the Peiraeus' (in 404). Events in

Greece Proper between the autumn of 416 and the autumn of 413 are incidentally noticed from time to time in books VI and VII. Had the author lived to finish his work, these notices would perhaps have been incorporated, with additions, at the end of book V, which is incomplete. The narrative of the Sicilian expedition in VI and VII, which has a unity of its own, may have been written before V; thus it is noticeable that Alcibiades, who figures largely in V, is introduced in VI. 15 as if mentioned for the first time. Book VIII contains the events of about two years (Nov. 413—Sept. 411),—the beginning of the Δεκελεικὸς πόλεμος or 'Ionian' war (413—404). It ends abruptly in the middle of chapter 109. The unrevised state of book VIII may be inferred from various small defects of style, but is less conspicuous than it has sometimes been represented. The absence of speeches in VIII cannot safely be regarded as a proof of incompleteness.

In contrast with λογογράφοι who compiled uncritically and wrote for effect, Thucydides claims that his history rests (a) on his own knowledge as an eyewitness and hearer, and (b) on laborious and accurate research. His ruling principle has been strict adherence to carefully verified facts (I. 21). We have only his results; but the lucid, judicial, severely earnest mind which is seen in the History makes it easy to accept his own account of his method. His use of official documents is noteworthy. In nine instances he gives the text of a treaty. Two of these affect Peloponnesian States only, and belong to the year 418 (V. 77, 79): to these he may have had access, as an exile, through Sparta or Argos. One (V. 47) is a treaty between Athens and the Argive confederacy, which he may have seen at Athens after his return in 404. Three are agreements between Sparta and Persia in 412 (VIII. 18, 37, 58), which neither power would have cared to publish; how he obtained these, it is hard to say, unless (as has been suggested) Alcibiades was the channel. The remaining three, agreements between Athens and Sparta, are of the years 423 (IV. 118) and 421 (V. 18, 23). These last three, it is assumed, he must have consulted at Athens after his return in 404: though it is not evident why he should not have seen them at Sparta. On the ground of some apparent discrepancies of a small kind between these three documents and his narrative, it has been supposed that the latter was composed first, and that the documents were inserted in a revision made by him after 404. The important point is that he desired to incorporate the evidence of the documents themselves. That marks an approach to the idea of critical history which places a wide interval between him and his predecessors.

With regard to the speeches, which constitute between a fourth and a fifth part of the History, he tells us (1) that he never introduces such a speech except when he had reason to know that one had been made; (2) that he does not pretend to give the exact form; but (3) that he has faithfully reproduced the speaker's general line of argument, the purport and substance of his speech, whenever it could be ascertained. With Thucydides, a speech or debate reported in the direct form always signalises a noteworthy point in the inner or mental history of the war, as distinguished from the narrative of its external facts. It brings into relief those thoughts and arguments which the writer wishes to make distinct and vivid in their bearing on some political or strategic moment. The style of Thucydides, most elaborate in the speeches, reflects the rhetoric of the day in its verbal artifices, such as antithesis and the discrimination of synonyms: so far it resembles the style of Antiphon. But it expresses Thucydides himself in its most characteristic features,—the eager crowding of thought on thought within one distended sentence, and the indifference to strict grammar so long as the idea is forcibly brought out. A theory has been put forward that the present complexion of the text is due to wholesale interpolation in late times, and that the real Thucydides was far more lucid, almost a Greek Macaulay. This view demands a violent and unscientific handling of the text; nor has it any support from external testimony. There has been, no doubt, some interpolation, but not in this sense or to this extent. A papyrus of the first century A.D. lately found in Egypt contains Thuc. IV. 36—41; and the text is substantially the same as that of our MSS., varying from it only in small details.

The genius of Thucydides is seen especially in the vivid power with which he interprets the tempers, motives, and policies of states and leading men. It is characteristic of him (in contrast, e.g., with Herodotus) that supernatural agency finds no place in his work: the causes with which he deals are rational and moral. Joining experience of war to grasp of principles, he illustrates the military art on land and sea. Intellectually and politically he is the greatest historian of the ancient world.

168. Xenophon, born about 431 B.C., of a good Athenian family, came as a young man under the influence of Socrates. In the spring of 401 he went to Sardis, on the advice of his Boeotian   Xenophon. friend Proxenus, and there joined an expedition, including upwards of 10,000 Greek mercenaries, which the young Persian prince Cyrus was about to lead inland,—nominally to Cilicia, but really into Persia, for the purpose of overthrowing his elder brother, Artaxerxes II. In a battle fought at Cunaxa, about 50 miles from Babylon, Cyrus was killed (September, 401). Soon afterwards the Greek leaders were treacherously seized by the satrap Tissaphernes, at a parley to which he had invited them, and put to death. The Greek troops, left leaderless, were in dismay, when Xenophon (hitherto neither officer nor private soldier, but merely an unattached volunteer) put heart into them by a spirited speech, and caused new generals to be chosen, of whom he himself was one. Fighting their way along the Tigris northward, past the site of Nineveh, and then through the mountains of the Carduchi (Kurds), in the fifth month (early in 400) they heard their vanguard cry, '*the sea, the sea !*' From Trapezus (Trebizond) on the Euxine, they made their way to

Byzantium. After two months' service with the Thracian chief Seuthes, the remnant of the Ten Thousand was incorporated at Pergamum with the army of the Spartan harmost Thibron. There, in March 399, Xenophon left them. If he then visited Athens, it was probably before the death of Socrates in May. Later in 399 he was again on the coasts of Asia Minor. In 396 he took service in Asia Minor with Agesilaus, and was present at Coronea (394), when his favourite hero defeated the allied Athenians and Thebans. Not long afterwards he was sentenced at Athens to banishment and confiscation of goods, as the penalty of 'Laconism.' The Spartans gave him an estate at Scillus in Elis, about two miles from Olympia, where, for many years (*circa* 387—371), he passed his life in country pursuits (especially hunting), and writing. This was his great literary period. Soon after the Spartan defeat at Leuctra (371), he was driven from Scillus, and settled at Corinth. After the new alliance between Athens and Sparta in 369, the Athenian sentence on Xenophon as a 'laconizer' was rescinded. His two sons then went to Athens, and served in the Athenian cavalry at Mantinea (362), where one of them (Gryllus) was killed. Xenophon's literary labours were continued at Corinth, and partly, perhaps, at Athens. He probably survived the year 355.

The writings of Xenophon may be classed as I. historical and political; II. ethical or philosophical; and III. technical.

I. The *Hellenica*, in seven books, takes up the history of Greece at the point in 411 where Thucydides breaks off, and continues it down to the battle of Mantineia in 362. The first part of the work (1—11. iii. § 10) completes the design of Thucydides by carrying the narrative of the war down to the capture of Athens in 404. This part has certain traits which mark it off from the rest of the *Hellenica*, viz. (1) the Thucydidean arrangement of events by years, (2) the absence of reference to sacrifices before and after battle, (3) the abstinence from criticisms of a personal kind, (4) the annual summary of Sicilian affairs. Dionysius (*Ep. ad Cn. Pomp.* iv), and Marcellinus (*Vit. Thuc.* § 45) speak of Xenophon's supplement to Thucydides as a distinct work, to which he pieced on his Ἑλληνικὴ ἱστορία. The part of Book 11 which begins at iii. § 11 forms a connecting link. The rest of the *Hellenica* falls into two chief portions, the first ending with the Peace of Antalcidas (v. i). The supplement to Thucydides was doubtless written first; the two subsequent portions were probably separated both from it and from each other by an interval; Xenophon was still working on the latter portion in 358. The History is full of instructive and picturesque detail. It has not, however, the higher unity either of art or of systematic thought. We miss the political insight and the intellectual grasp of Thucydides. The chronology, too, is often obscure. But the most serious defects appear referable to the writer's prejudices (especially in favour of Sparta, and, above all, of Agesilaus). Thus the Theban revolution of 379 is narrated without a mention of Pelopidas (v. v).

Neither he nor Epameinondas is named in connexion with the battle of Leuctra (v. iv. § 3). The foundation of Megalopolis passes unnoticed (VI. v).

The *Anabasis* comes chronologically between *Hellenica* II and III, and accordingly in III. i Xenophon refers us, for that expedition, to the account 'written by Themistogenes of Syracuse.' This account is no other than his own *Anabasis*, which was first published, it is clear, under the name of the Syracusan. His motive may have been to avoid the appearance of self-praise. In the *Anabasis* Xenophon is at his best; he tells his thrilling story with that freshness which a man of action often commands where a literary artist might fail; the style is plain, fairly concise, never rising much, but full of lively detail. It is a memorable book; that march opened the eyes of Greece to the inner weakness of Persia, and prepared the way for Alexander's invasion. The *Agesilaus*, a panegyric on the Spartan king, is largely put together from the *Hellenica* (books III and IV), and has been suspected as spurious, but without convincing reason. The essay on the *Lacedaemonian Polity* commends the institutions ascribed to Lycurgus, while admitting (c. xiv) that in modern Sparta they have broken down. The Περὶ πόρων, suggesting means for enlarging the revenues of Athens, is probably genuine. As appears from c. v. § 12, it was not written before 355.

II. The Ἀπομνημονεύματα (*Memorabilia*), recollections of Socrates, exhibit him chiefly in the aspect which impressed the writer's practical mind, as one who did moral and mental good to his associates. All the principal features of the master's thought and method are brought out. Xenophon, a Boswell, is probably truer to the life than Plato. The *Apology of Socrates*, seemingly meant to supplement or correct Plato's piece of the same name, is, if genuine, scarcely worthy of Xenophon. In the interesting *Oeconomicus*, Socrates exchanges views with a typical Athenian καλὸς κἀγαθός as to the management of his household and land. In the *Symposium*, a suggestive picture of an Athenian supper-party, Socrates discourses on the higher and lower ἔρως. There are parallelisms with Plato's dialogue, but the question of priority is doubtful. The *Cyropaedia* describes the education and life of the elder Cyrus, regarded as an ideal ruler; it is Socratic in tone, and highly finished in style, with a romantic colouring (as in the episode of Abradates and Pantheia, the first love-story in European prose). The *Hieron* is a dialogue in which Hieron, tyrant of Syracuse, dwells on the advantages of a private station, and the poet Simonides on the possible beneficence of a τύραννος.

III. The treatises on *Horsemanship* (Περὶ ἱππικῆς), the *Cavalry Officer* (Ἱππαρχικός), and *Hunting* (Κυνηγετικός) are practical manuals rich in the interest of technical detail. But the *Hunting* cannot, in its present form at least, be Xenophon's. The style in some parts (as in i. 1—17) is not his.

In the wide range of subjects covered by Xenophon he appears as an Athenian of practical bent and shrewd common-sense, familiar with many phases of non-Attic Hellas, a man who had seen and done much; a writer without rhetorical ambition, but too genuinely simple to affect simplicity; not wholly free from narrow prejudices, but of honest and pure aims, and with a plain Attic charm of his own.

169. The short and mutilated Ἀθηναίων Πολιτεία, in three chapters,

Treatises on the Polity of Athens. wrongly ascribed to Xenophon, is by an unknown author, who wrote *circ.* 424—420 B.C. It is thus the oldest extant piece of literary Attic prose; in style not rhetorical, but colloquial, terse and pointed. The writer dislikes democracy, but does not see his way to a change, and argues, with much candour and lucidity, that the Athenians, having adopted democracy, take the right means to maintain it.

The Ἀθηναίων Πολιτεία found in Egypt in 1890, and first published in 1891, has a preponderance of evidence in favour of its Aristotelian origin, whether its present shape is due to Aristotle or to an editor. It contains (I) a sketch of Athenian constitutional history to the restoration of the democracy in 403 (cc. 1—41), and (II) a description of the constitution existing in 328—325 B.C., under the heads of (1) franchise, (2) legislature, (3) administration, and (4) judicature (cc. 42—63). The first part raises several problems, where it differs from other authorities; the entire trustworthiness of the second part is unquestionable; and the historical interest of the whole can hardly be overrated.

170. The earlier Greek historians had been travellers, soldiers, men of

Literary compilers of history. affairs; in the second half of the fourth century we hear of bulky histories compiled by purely literary men, whose forte was rhetoric. Ephorus wrote a history of Greece (from the 'Return of the Heracleidae' to 340 B.C.), which was freely used by Diodorus Siculus. Theopompus wrote *Hellenica* in twelve books, dealing with the years 411—394; and a colossal *Philippica* (with Philip of Macedon for its central figure) in fifty-eight books, covering the period from 362 (where Xenophon leaves off) to 336. The period covered by his *Hellenica* was also chosen by another continuator of Thucydides, Cratippus. Little has survived of the work of these three historians. The Rise of Alexander brought more attractive themes than the squabbles of the early fourth century. But they were extensively used by later writers, Polybius, Plutarch and Diodorus Siculus, and much of our traditional knowledge of fourth-century history goes back to them. Theopompus and Ephorus were of the school of Isocrates and may have studied under him. Theopompus's style is certainly Ἰσοκρατικός. Ephorus is a sluggish writer needing the spur rather than the rein. To him is probably to be ascribed the *Hellenica Oxyrhynchia*, which was discovered in 1907 (*P. Oxy.* 842). This is a valuable account of the years 396—5. Its general agreement with Diodorus and its heavy style are in favour of regarding it as the work of Ephorus.

E. RHETORIC AND ORATORY.

171. The earliest Greek writer on the art of rhetoric was Corax of
Syracuse (*c.* 466 B.C.), whose Τέχνη λόγων was primarily
meant to help the plain citizen in speaking before a law-
court. He divided a speech into five parts,—proem, narrative, arguments (ἀγῶνες), subsidiary remarks (παρέκβασις), and peroration.
He also illustrated the topic of general probability (εἰκός), showing its
two-edged use: *e.g.* if A, a puny man, is charged with assaulting B, an
athlete, he can say, 'Is it likely?' If B is charged with assaulting A, he
can say, 'Is it probable that I should have done so, when my superior
strength was sure to create a presumption against me?' This topic of
εἰκός (says Aristotle, *Rhet.* 2. 24. 11) was the staple of the *Art* of Corax.
It was further developed in the τέχνη of his disciple Tisias (cp. Plat.
Phaedr. 267 A), who led a wandering life, and is said to have taught
Lysias at Thurii and the young Isocrates at Athens. Gorgias of Leontini,
when he visited Athens in 427 as an envoy from his fellow-citizens,
captivated the Athenians by his oratory, which had a poetical character,
and was especially marked by florid antithesis. It is doubtful whether he
wrote an 'Art': diction (λέξις), not invention or arrangement, was his
chief study. While the Sicilian school thus developed the technicalities or
graces of rhetoric, the Sophists of Greece Proper dwelt especially on the
minute proprieties of language; as Prodicus on the discrimination of
synonyms (ὀρθότης ὀνομάτων, Plat. *Euthyd.* 277 F.), and Protagoras on
correct grammatical forms (ὀρθοέπεια, id. *Phaedr.* 267 C).

172. Antiphon, the earliest of the ten Attic orators in the Alexandrian
canon, was born *c.* 480 B.C., and put to death in 411 by the
restored democracy, on account of the part which he had
taken in organizing the oligarchy of the Four Hundred. His work as a
theorist and teacher of rhetoric is represented by three Τετραλογίαι, each
consisting of four skeleton-speeches in an imaginary trial for homicide
(α and γ by the accuser, β and δ by the defendant). Of his three extant
speeches in real causes, the most important is a defence for a man
charged with the murder of an Athenian, Herodes, in Lesbos (περὶ
τοῦ Ἡρώδου φόνου, *c.* 421—417 B.C.): another, a defence of a choregus on a
charge of homicide, arising from the death of a youth in training for a
chorus (περὶ τοῦ χορευτοῦ): the third, a speech in which a young man
charges his stepmother with poisoning his father (κατηγορία φαρμακείας).
Antiphon is the earliest professional writer of forensic speeches (λογογράφος). He represents the 'austere' or 'rugged' style of early prose
(αὐστηρὰ ἁρμονία), as distinguished from the 'smooth' (γλαφυρά) of
Isocrates, and the 'middle' (μέση) of Demosthenes (Dionys. *De comp.
verb.* 22—24). It is dignified, weighty, slow in movement, and prone to
contrasts of single words (*e.g.* γνωρισταί, δικασταί, δοξασταί, κριταί, *De caede*

*The early
Rhetoric.*

Antiphon.

Herod. § 94).   The 'periodic' structure of sentences (λέξις κατεστραμμένη) is seen in the earlier and stiffer phase of its development from the 'running' style (εἰρομένη) in which clauses are simply strung together.

173.   Andocides, born *c.* 440 B.C., gave evidence in 415 as to the muti-
Andocides.   lation of the Hermae; was sentenced in the same year to partial disfranchisement for alleged acts of 'impiety'; and went to Cyprus.   Revisiting Athens in 411, during the oligarchy, he was imprisoned; returned to Cyprus on being released after the fall of the oligarchs; and again coming to Athens in 410, addressed the ecclesia in the extant speech *On his Return* (περὶ τῆς ἑαυτοῦ καθόδου), praying for the removal of his 'atimia.'   His appeal was rejected, and then he spent some years in visiting various parts of Hellas.   The general amnesty of 403 finally enabled him to return to Athens.   In 399 he was brought to trial for 'impiety,' on the ground that he had attended the Mysteries at Eleusis though disqualified by 'atimia' from doing so, and defended himself in the most important of his extant speeches, *On the Mysteries.* He was acquitted.   In the winter of 391—390, during the Corinthian war, he was one of the Athenian plenipotentiaries sent to treat for peace at Sparta, and in 390 made at Athens his extant speech *On the Peace with Lacedaemon,* urging that the terms offered by Sparta should be accepted. His advice was not taken.   According to the pseudo-Plutarch (*Lives of the Orators*) he was again banished.   The speech *Against Alcibiades* which bears his name is a late rhetorical forgery.   Andocides is a vigorous speaker, generally plain in style and method, and relying but little on rhetorical arti-fice.   The best example of his excellence in lively and graphic narrative is afforded by *De Myst.* §§ 34—69.

174.   Lysias, a native but not a citizen of Athens, was the son of a
Lysias.   Syracusan named Cephalus, who had settled there as a μέτοικος on the invitation of Pericles.   The date of the orator's birth is uncertain: ancient authorities place it in 459/8; but recent critics, *circ.* 450—440: his extant work belongs to 403—380. After his father's death, he left Athens, while still a boy, for Thurii, where he passed his youth and early manhood.   Driven from Thurii after the Athenian reverse in Sicily, he returned to Athens in 412, with his brother Polemarchus.   In 404 the comparative wealth of the brothers marked them out for plunder by the Thirty Tyrants, who put Pole-marchus to death.   Lysias escaped; and returning in 403 with Thrasybulus and the exiles, settled down to work as a writer of forensic speeches.   His industry seems to have been great.   Upwards of 230 compositions bearing his name were recognised as genuine by the Augustan Atticists.   We have 34 speeches (3 fragmentary, and 8 more or less mutilated), of which, however, six are spurious, viz. the *Epitaphios* (or. 2), *Against Andocides* (or. 6), *To his companions* (or. 8), *For the soldier* (or. 9), the *second* speech *Against Theomnestus* (or. 11), and the defence *For Polystratus* (or. 20).   Of the 28 genuine pieces, the most important and brilliant

is the speech *Against Eratosthenes* (or. 12), spoken in 403 by Lysias himself against the man (formerly one of the Thirty Tyrants) who had been chiefly instrumental in the murder of Polemarchus. The peroration, on the crimes of the Tyrants (§§ 92—100), was famous. Next in historical interest stands the speech *Against Agoratus* (or. 13, *c.* 399/8), an informer who had slandered away the lives of many citizens during the tyranny in 404. The defence *For Mantitheus* (or. 16, *c.* 392) is a good example of the skill with which Lysias could adapt a speech to the ἦθος of the person who was to speak it—in this case, a high-spirited young Athenian. The 'deliberative' oratory of Lysias is represented only by a fragment of a speech written for delivery in the ecclesia, a *Plea for the Constitution* (or. 34 περὶ τοῦ μὴ καταλῦσαι κ.τ.λ., 403 B.C.): and his 'epideictic' oratory, only by the brilliant fragment of his *Olympiacus*, spoken at Olympia (388 B.C.).

The qualities for which Lysias was especially admired by the best ancient critics were, a delicate mastery of Attic, subtle expression of character (ἠθοποιία), vivid description (ἐνάργεια), and a certain flexibility of mind which gives him almost unfailing tact and charm (χάρις). Technically, he represents the 'plain' style (ἰσχνὸς χαρακτήρ, λιτὴ or ἀφελὴς λέξις, *tenue* or *subtile genus dicendi*), as opposed to the 'stately' (μεγαλοπρεπής) and the 'middle.' He was the first rhetorical writer who reconciled literary finish with the Attic idiom of ordinary life.

175. Isocrates, born in 436 B.C., lost his patrimony in the later years of the war, and after teaching rhetoric at Chios for about a year (404—3), became a professional writer of forensic speeches at Athens. This period of his activity (403—393) is represented by six extant orations, among which the *Aegineticus* (or. 19, 394—3) is the best. In his later writings he speaks slightingly of such work for the law-courts,—evidently regarding it as a mere accident of his early life. His true career began in or about 392, when he opened a school at Athens near the Lyceum. The nature of the discipline which he sought to impart is best gathered from his discourse *Against the Sophists* (or. 13, *c.* 391 B.C.), and from the speech *On the Antidosis* (or. 15, 353),—the latter being an *apologia* ('an image of his mind and life,' § 7), thrown into the shape of a forensic speech against a man who had challenged him to undertake the burden of the trierarchy or submit to an exchange of properties (*antidosis*). The art which he professes to teach is, briefly, that of speaking or writing on large political subjects, considered as a preparation for advising or acting in political affairs. This is ἡ τῶν λόγων παιδεία,—his φιλοσοφία, or theory of culture, as he sometimes calls it (*Antid.* § 50). He distinguishes this art (1) from all studies which have no direct bearing on the higher political life, and (2) from studies which, though practical, are narrow in scope (*e.g.* forensic rhetoric). Censuring teachers who claim too much for their method (*Adv. Soph.* § 10), he emphasizes the need of natural aptitude (φύσις) and of hard work in the learner. His aim was to develope the faculty of his pupils through their own efforts (*Antid.* §§ 186—191). Many of them stayed with him three or four years (*Antid.* § 87). His school was famous throughout Hellas. Monographs have been written on the 'disciples of Isocrates,'— a long and varied list of eminent names, including Timotheus, Leodamas of Acharnae, Lycurgus, Hypereides, Isaeus, and the historians Ephorus and Theopompus.

Twenty-one speeches or discourses (besides nine letters) bear the name of Isocrates, and all are probably genuine. Six (as noticed above) are forensic. Nine may be classed as scholastic; viz., three hortatory letters or essays (*To Demonicus, To Nicocles*, and *Nicocles*, oratt. 1—3); four 'epideictic' pieces (*Evagoras, Encomium on Helen, Busiris, Panathenaicus*, oratt. 9—12); and the two essays on education already mentioned (*Against the Sophists*, and *Antidosis*, oratt. 13 and 15). The remaining six pieces are political. Two of these concern the relations of Greece with Persia. The *Panegyricus* (or. 4, 380 B.C.) urges the Greek states to unite in an invasion of Asia: this is the author's masterpiece, on which he is said to have spent ten years. The *Philippus* (or. 5, 346 B.C.) exhorts Philip of Macedon to lead a Panhellenic war against Persia. The other four political discourses deal with the internal affairs of Greece. The *Plataicus* (or. 14, 373) is a Plataean appeal to Athens for aid against Thebes. The speech *On the Peace* (or. 8, 355) exhorts Athens to abandon dreams of empire (ἀρχή), and content herself with ἡγεμονία of a free league. The *Archidamus* (or. 6, 366) purports to be spoken at Sparta by Archidamus III, in protest against the Theban proposal that Sparta should recognise the independence of Messene (restored by Epameinondas in 370). The *Areopagiticus* (or. 7, prob. 355) contrasts the Athens of the fourth century with that of Solon and Cleisthenes,—dwelling much on the old power of the Areopagus.

Isocrates died in 338, at the age of ninety-eight, just after the battle of Chaeroneia. He is said to have starved himself to death. If that is true, the cause can scarcely have been Philip's success: rather, perhaps, the breach between Philip and Athens. But in *Epist.* III, purporting to be written after the battle, Philip is still his hope for Greece. If that letter be a forgery, it is a skilful one.

The work of Isocrates was to establish a standard type of literary rhetorical prose. His style is marked by a smoothness due to studied avoidance of 'hiatus'; *i.e.* a vowel at the end of the word must not be followed (as a rule) by a vowel at the beginning of the next (φωνήεντα μὴ συμπίπτειν). In the *rhythm* proper to prose (εὐρύθμως καὶ μουσικῶς εἰπεῖν, or. 13, § 16) he was the earliest artist, as Cicero, his disciple in this, recognises (*Brut.* § 32). His *period* is not rigid, like that of Antiphon, nor terse and compact, like that of Lysias, but ample and luxuriant (ὑπαγωγική, 'leading one on,' like a winding river, Dionys. *Dem.* 4). The Isocratic prose had had a wide influence on Greek writing in his own day, and later; it contributed to mould the style of Cicero (cp. *Ad Att.* II. 1); and through him, or directly, it has influenced modern literature.

176. Isaeus, born probably *c.* 420 B.C., was a professional writer of speeches for the law-courts, chiefly in private causes. The
branch in which he chiefly excelled is represented by the　　Isaeus.
eleven extant κληρικοὶ λόγοι,—speeches connected, directly or indirectly, with will-cases. These are of great interest for the history of Greek testamentary law. There is also a large fragment of a twelfth speech, belonging to a different class,—a case of appeal (ἔφεσις) from arbitration to a jury. These belong to the period *c.* 390—353 B.C. The eighth speech, περὶ τοῦ Κίρωνος κλήρου, is the most characteristic, both in narrative and in argument, and shows Isaeus at his best. He is the earliest master, not, indeed, of forensic rhetoric, but of close forensic argument. His art is not, like that of Lysias, an art which conceals itself, but open, vigorous, and confident. There is no reason to doubt that the young Demosthenes studied with him (*c.* 366—363). 'The oratorical power (δεινότης) of Demosthenes took its seeds and beginnings from Isaeus,' says Dionysius (*Isae.* 20). This is probably true in the sense that Demosthenes was indebted to Isaeus for hints (1) in versatile arrangement, (2) in elaboration of systematic proof, and (3) generally, in the method of grappling with an adversary's case point by point.

177. Demosthenes, born in 384 B.C., the son of a well-to-do Athenian, was left an orphan in childhood. His guardians, false to
their trust, handed over to him when he came of age　　Demosthenes.
only a fraction (some £50 or £60 a year) of his patrimony. In 363 he brought an action against one of them (Aphobus) and obtained a verdict, but not the money; and, after some more fruitless proceedings, set about making his living as a λογογράφος for the courts. His political career was preluded by four speeches in public prosecutions, which are as many pleas for a high standard of public life (*Androtion* 355, *Leptines* 354, *Timocrates* 353/2 and *Aristocrates* 352). Of these the *Leptines* alone was spoken by Demosthenes himself: the other three were written for clients. The speech *Against Meidias* (347), who had assaulted him, was never delivered, and remains a mere sketch. Addressing the ecclesia during the same period, he propounded a scheme of naval reform in his speech *On the Navy Boards* (354); spoke *For the Megalopolitans* against Sparta (353/2), and *For the Rhodians* (352 or 353?) when they sought the help of Athens to throw off the Carian yoke.

His nine speeches against Philip of Macedon fall into two groups. The earlier group consists of the *First Philippic* (351) and the three *Olynthiacs* (349), spoken when Philip was still a foreign foe, threatening Greece from without. The second group comprises the speeches made after Philip had become a Greek power by admission to the Amphictyonic Council (346); viz., *On the Peace* (346), the *Second Philippic* (344), *On the*

Embassy (343, a forensic public speech), *On the Chersonese* (341), and the
Third Philippic (341). In 336 Ctesiphon proposed that Demosthenes
should receive a golden crown from the state. Aeschines then gave notice
that he would proceed against Ctesiphon for having proposed an unconstitutional measure, but took no action till 330, when he delivered his
speech *Against Ctesiphon*, an attack on the whole public life of Demosthenes. Demosthenes gained a decisive victory for himself, and for the
honour of Athens, in the most finished, the most brilliant, and the most
pathetic oration of antiquity, the speech *On the Crown*. In 322 he was
one of the patriots whose surrender was demanded by Antipater. He fled
to Aegina, and thence to the islet of Calauria, on the coast of Argolis,
where he was found by his pursuers, and took poison.

The traditional collection of Demosthenic speeches, probably founded
at Alexandria in the third century B.C., contains 61 pieces (including the
Letter of Philip, no. 12). There is a large proportion of spurious matter;
but in regard to many particular pieces the critics are much divided.
Among the συμβουλευτικοὶ λόγοι ascribed to him, the following may be
rejected :—*On Halonnesus* (or. 7), the work of Hegesippus, 342 B.C.: *On
the Treaty with Alexander* (or. 17), 335 B.C., by some unknown contemporary: and three rhetorical forgeries of later date,—viz., the *Fourth
Philippic* (or. 10), *On Financial Organisation* (περὶ συντάξεως, or. 13), and
the *Answer to Philip's Letter* (or. 11). [The *Letter of Philip*, printed as
or. 12 among the Demosthenic writings, may be genuine.] Among the
δικανικοὶ λόγοι, the following in public causes (δημόσιοι) are spurious :—
Against Neaera (or. 59, *c.* 343—339 B.C.), *Against Theocrines* (or. 58, *c.* 340),
and the two speeches *Against Aristogeiton* (or. 25, 26 —rhetorical forgeries).
The following speeches in private causes (ἰδιωτικοί),—arranged in the alphabetical order of the names of those against whom they were spoken,—are
spurious, but all or most of them were probably written between 369 and
322 B.C. :—*Apaturius* (or. 33), *Boeotus* II (40), *Callippus* (52), *Dionysiodorus*
(56), *Euergus and Mnesibulus* (47), *Lacritus* (35), *Leochares* (44), *Macar-
tatus* (43), *Nicostratus* (53), *Olympiodorus* (48), *Phaenippus* (42), *Phormio*
(34), *Polycles* (50), *Stephanus* II (46), *Timotheus* (49), *Zenothemis* (32).
The two ἐπιδεικτικοὶ λόγοι, *Epitaphius* (or. 60) and *Eroticus* (61), are
spurious. Quintilian (X. i. 107) knew letters of Demosthenes which he
thought genuine. The extant six letters (or some of them, especially nos.
2 and 3) have had defenders, but seem to be forgeries. The 56 προοίμια,
exordia or sketches for political speeches, have been compiled from Demosthenes or other classical models by various hands and at various
dates.

Demosthenes is the greatest artist in Greek prose, commanding all the
resources of technical rhetoric, and blending the best traits of earlier
styles in new combinations, without a trace of conscious effort. He has a
great variety of tones, and no less diversity in his arrangement of topics,
which (in the political speeches especially) is often intricate, yet always

leaves an impression of organic unity. He does not allocate one section
of his speech to narrative, another to argument, a third to emotional
appeals, and so on; they are skilfully intermingled; facts are connected
with principles; thought is penetrated by feeling; and the whole is fused
together by the fire of a powerful and ardent mind. Like Burke, he is a
representative of impassioned reason. No orator is more sparing in the
use of ornament for its own sake: in all his work it would be hard to
find a 'purple patch.' As John Bright found a well-spring of eloquence in
the plain and noble diction of the Bible, so Demosthenes uses the
simplest language without loss of distinction, and gains a persuasive
naturalness without falling into commonplace.

One of his characteristic qualities (in which he resembles but excels
Isaeus) is his manner of grappling with his adversary in close argument,
animated by lively question and answer, pointed with incisive irony, and
driven home with cogent vehemence. His pathos is of that austere and
reticent kind which marks the seventh book of Thucydides, a writer with
whose genius study and nature had placed him in the most intimate
sympathy. Demosthenes on the desolation of Phocis (or. 19, §§ 65, 66)
might be contrasted with Burke on the devastation of the Carnatic. It
would not be easy to surpass the indignant irony of the *Third Philippic*
(§§ 65, 66), or the restrained sarcasm which marks the earlier part of
the speech *On the Chersonese;* and there are occasional touches of grim
humour, as when, in the speech *On the Crown*, he compares Aeschines to
a physician who prescribes after the funeral. His perorations are usually
quiet, in that Attic taste which preferred that a speech, like a Tragedy,
should close calmly; and he often concludes with a wish in which the
final word is εὔφημον,—as in the *First Philippic*,—νικῴη δ᾽ ὅ τι πᾶσιν ὑμῖν
μέλλει συνοίσειν.

The 'private' forensic speeches—which he occasionally wrote, amidst
the stress of his political career, down to at least 345 B.C.—are nearly all
for plaintiffs; and he puts forth his strength in attack with the open art
of Isaeus. It is but seldom that, as in the speeches *Against Conon*
and *Against Callicles*, he portrays, like Lysias, the *ēthos* of the 'plain
citizen' who delivers the speech.

Laborious premeditation was his rule (cp. or. 21, § 191 ἐσκέφθαι—
μεμελετηκέναι—μεριμνήσας). Careful composition is indicated by the
Isocratic avoidance of hiatus, though this rule is less strict in the later
speeches; and by the unique rhythm governing those subtle harmonies
which modern criticism has sought to analyse. We may accept the
tradition that he rarely extemporised,—distrusting, perhaps, his own
impetuosity. Of his deliberative speeches, none would have taken
much more than an hour to speak: a limit which is natural, seeing
that they were to be spoken in the open air, and to an audience of
many thousands. It is possible that the written speech was sometimes
amplified in delivery: but in one instance, at least, which can be roughly

tested—the speech *On the Embassy*, as compared with the reply of Aeschines—the written text must be nearly that which was spoken.

The form of Demosthenic oratory is inseparable from the spirit of the man and the statesman. His aim was to revive public spirit at Athens, to purify the administration at home, and to invigorate the foreign policy. Athens was to him a noble but wayward person, of a generous character, with some dangerous faults (τὸ τῆς πόλεως ἦθος, or. 20, § 13). A statesman must be sincere, fearless in speaking out, and mindful that he is responsible (ὑπεύθυνος) to the state. The only stable national power is that which rests on truth and justice (or. 2, § 10). 'Beware not to exhibit as a nation conduct which you would shun as individuals' (or. 20, § 136). The struggle against Philip, which Demosthenes maintained, almost single-handed, for thirteen years, must not be judged in the light of events which he could not foresee. He was right, on every ground, in holding that Athens should stake her existence, as the champion of Greece, in defending the best thing that Greeks had known, the life of the free city. To fail in that cause was better than not to have striven (or. 18, § 208); not merely because, in the event, Athens fared better than the cowards and traitors (*ib.* § 65), but because the Athenians had been true to themselves and to Greece.

178. Aeschines, an Athenian born in 390 or 389 B.C. (as or. 1, § 49

Aeschines. shows), began life in narrow circumstances, and was for a time a tragic actor,—a calling for which he had the qualifications of a fine appearance and a magnificent voice. He afterwards became clerk (γραμματεύς) to the Ecclesia. In 346 he was twice an envoy to Philip. His speech *Against Timarchus* (345) aims at showing that this man—who was about to charge the orator with misconduct on the embassy in 346—was disqualified by an infamous life from speaking in the Assembly. The speech *On the Embassy* (343), a defence against his fellow-envoy Demosthenes, is extremely able, and contains some admirable passages of narratives; it just won him an acquittal. The speech *Against Ctesiphon*, attacking the whole career of Demosthenes, was an ignominious failure. He then withdrew to Ephesus, and afterwards opened a school of rhetoric at Rhodes. The date of his death is unknown. Aeschines had brilliant natural gifts for eloquence. In the art he was deficient; his style is uneven, and can fall low: but it often exhibits the 'splendour' which both Dionysius and Cicero recognise. He can be edifying or lively; his attack is vigorous and adroit; he has wit and pathos. It is the ἠθικὴ πίστις that is lacking; he fails to inspire trust.

179. Lycurgus (born *c.* 390), a member of the noble priestly clan of

Lycurgus. the Eteobutadae, served Athens from 338 to 326 B.C. as minister of finance and of public works; the precise title of his office (or offices) is uncertain. His only extant speech is that *Against Leocrates* (*c.* 331), who had fled from Athens after Chaeronea, and is indicted as a traitor. It is a solemn and lofty protest on behalf of public spirit, blending the luxuriance of Isocrates (the author's master in composition) with something of the archaic stateliness of Antiphon.

180. Hypereides (born *c.* 389 B.C.), also a pupil of Isocrates, is now represented by portions of six speeches, found in Egypt Hypereides.
between 1847 and 1890. 1. *Against Demosthenes*, in the
Harpalus affair (324); a fragment, much mutilated: papyrus of second century A.D., found in 1847. 2. *For Lycophron* (before 338); a fragment of the earlier part, much mutilated: same MS. 3. *For Euxenippus* (*c.* 330—324); almost entire: same MS. 4. *Against Philippides* (*c.* 336); the latter part: papyrus of first century B.C., found in 1890. 5. *Against Athenogenes* (*c.* 328—326); the greater part, but the beginning is lost: papyrus of second century B.C., found in 1888. This typical speech is coupled by the author of the treatise 'On the Sublime' (ch. 34, § 3) with the orator's defence of Phryne as an example of his fine tact and skill. 6. *Epitaphios* (322) on Leosthenes and his comrades who fell in the Lamian war; imperfect at the end (but partly supplemented by Stobaeus *Flor.* 124. 36): papyrus of late first or early second century A.D., found in 1856. Hypereides unites the most varied qualities; a smooth fluency, joined to force, rapidity and fire; keen wit and sarcasm; a diction now lofty and now colloquial; the subtlest art, veiled by an easy grace. He was not a statesman, nor a man of estimable character; but a supremely brilliant and versatile Athenian.

181. Deinarchus (born *c.* 365—360), a native of Corinth who lived at Athens as a μέτοικος, wrote speeches for the law-courts, of Deinarchus.
which three remain,—those against Demosthenes, Aristo-
geiton, and Philocles, when they were accused of taking bribes from Harpalus (324 B.C.). He was called (according to Hermogenes) a κρίθινος Δημοσθένης, perhaps because his coarse imitation was to the original as beer to wine. His name completes the Alexandrian decade of Attic orators.

182. From about 300 to 280 B.C. the new settlements in Asia Minor were the places where the study of oratory chiefly flourished. 'Asianism'
The old eloquence had been a fine art; the new was little versus
more than the practice of set declamation, with a bent 'Atticism.'
towards bombast or forced point. This tendency has been called 'Asianism,' in contrast with the classical Atticism. A reaction in favour of the Attic standards began towards the close of the second century B.C. The maturity of the 'Attic revival' is represented at Rome, in the Augustan age, by the best literary critic of antiquity, Dionysius of Halicarnassus.

F.　PHILOSOPHICAL PROSE.

183.　Philosophical prose-writing began in Greece with the Ionian monists of the sixth century, Thales, Anaximander, Anaximenes, Heracleitus.　Their views, and the later developments of Greek Philosophy, are set forth in another section of this book.　Here we have only to note the relation in which Plato and Aristotle respectively stand to the literature of Greek prose.

184.　Plato (born *c.* 429—427, died 347) is the greatest master of the

Plato.

Dialogue, as he is also the earliest whose work survives. Three chief aspects of his style may be distinguished. (1) His mode of representing *conversation* is easy, flexible, urbane, with a lightly playful wit and a delicate irony; shades of character and of manner in the persons are often marked with subtle skill.　Some of the best examples occur in the opening scenes of dialogues (*e.g. Phaedrus, Gorgias, Protagoras, Republic*).　(2) Another phase is seen in passages of *continuous exposition*.　Some of these, especially such as speak of the philosophic life (*e.g. Theaetetus* pp. 173—175), or of the soul in its relation to the quest of truth (*e.g. Symposium* 201 D—212 A), exhibit his style in its highest elevation; the language is remarkably copious, sometimes, indeed, verging on redundance (see *e.g. Sympos.* 211 B—C); it flows on in a stream of eloquence which is never rhetorical, though at times of a poetical cast; an intense earnestness, a certain glow and rapture, can be felt in it.　(3) Then there are the passages of *narrative* or *description*. The chief examples are the four longer myths, concerning the destiny of the soul after death (*Gorgias* 523 A—527 A, *Phaedo* 109 A—114 C, *Republic* 614 A—621 B), or its experience before birth (*Phaedrus* 246 A— 250 C).　In these we note the strength and clearness of the sublime imaginative vision; the great simplicity of language; and the use (in a manner resembling Dante's) of homely images to render particulars distinct.　Plato's power as a literary artist can, however, be adequately appreciated only by studying one of his dialogues (*e.g.* the *Phaedo*) as an organic whole.　His prose is unique; partly because he alone conveys a notion of the manner in which intellectual Greeks of that age talked among themselves; and partly, again, because his style so often moves in a borderland between prose and poetry (μεταξὺ ποιήματος...καὶ πεζοῦ λόγου, as Aristotle said, according to Diogenes Laertius III. 37).

185.　Aristotle (384—322), in his treatises as they have come to us,

Aristotle.

shows small care of literary form.　It is indeed probable that (in many cases at least) they are merely sketches for lectures, or summaries based on notes taken by hearers.　They are examples of a strictly scientific prose, in which the first aim is precision of statement.　A marked characteristic of Aristotle's writings is the frequent use of philosophical terms (such as ὕλη, οὐσία, τὸ τί ἦν εἶναι, ἐντελέχεια, δύναμις, etc.), either invented or made technical by himself. There are, indeed, passages which are impressive in a literary sense, though more by the thought than by the form (*e.g.* that on the θεωρητικὸς βίος in *Ethics* x. vi): there are also many striking sentences or phrases (*e.g.* the precept ὅσον ἐνδέχεται ἀθανατίζειν in *Eth.* xII. vii). In his lost Dialogues (written perhaps *c.* 362—347), which were of an 'exoteric' or popular character, he is said to have used the embellishments and graces of literary art. This is attested by Cicero (*Acad. Prior.* II. 38. 119, *veniet flumen orationis aureum fundens Aristoteles*), Dionysius (*Vet. Script. Cens.* IV. 1), Quintilian (x. 1. 83), Themistius (or. 26, p. 385), and others. The tradition is illustrated by at least one extant fragment (no. 40, p. 1481) from Aristotle's dialogue entitled *Eudemus*.

Two of his works have a direct bearing on Greek literature.

1. In the *Rhetorica* (composed *c.* 330), he treats that art as the popular branch of dialectic. It is the method of 'discerning in every case the available means of persuasion'; and these are of two classes. (1) There are the 'proofs external to the art,' ἄτεχνοι πίστεις, such as depositions of witnesses, or documents. (2) Then there are the proofs furnished by the art itself, ἔντεχνοι, which are of three kinds; (i) λογικὴ πίστις, proof, or seeming proof, by argument; (ii) ἠθική, when the speaker persuades the hearers that he is trustworthy; and (iii) παθητική, when he works upon their emotions. Books I and II concern the method of providing these proofs (εὕρεσις). Book III begins with remarks on delivery (ὑπόκρισις), regarded chiefly as management of the voice. It then deals with expression (λέξις, diction and composition), and arrangement (τάξις). Aristotle fixed the main lines on which Rhetoric was treated by most of the later technical writers.

Rhetorica.

2. The present form of the *Poetica* is incomplete. The first book (in 26 chapters) alone is extant, and its text has been much disturbed: of the second book, which dealt with Comedy, only fragments remain. Imitation (says Aristotle), μίμησις, is the principle common to Poetry with Music, Dancing, Painting and Sculpture. All these arts are imitative, while the means, objects and manner of imitation differ in the several arts, as also in the several branches of Poetry (i—iii). Tragedy and heroic epos imitate the nobler aspects of life; satire and comedy, the lower (iv, v). Poetry can generalise; it can express the universal through the particular (*e.g.* Achilles is a typical or 'ideal' hero): and therefore 'Poetry is a more philosophical and a higher thing than History' (ix. § 3), which tends to express only the particular. Tragedy is defined and analysed, with profound insight (vi—xix). The function of Tragedy consists in 'effecting, through pity and fear, the proper *purgation* (κάθαρσις) of these emotions' (vi. § 2). The metaphor is medical: Tragedy excites pity and fear; and, in doing so, affords a wholesome outlet to those emotions, attended by a pleasurable sense of relief: in the words of Milton's comment (preface to *Samson Agonistes*),

Poetica.

it tends 'to temper and reduce them to just measure with a kind of delight.' Some critics, from the sixteenth century onwards, found in Aristotle
a doctrine of the so-called 'Three Unities.' But this was incorrect.
Organic *unity of action* is the only dramatic 'unity' enjoined in the
Poetics (viii, ix). The sole reference to a unity of *time* is in v. § 4:
'Tragedy endeavours, as far as possible,' to confine the duration of the
action to one day of twenty-four hours: *i.e.* this was the ordinary practice,—
sometimes, however, neglected (as by Aeschylus in the *Agamemnon* and
Eumenides). As to unity of *place*, there is not a word: that, too, was
usually observed on the Greek stage, but not always. From Tragedy the
treatise passes to the subject of poetic diction at large (xx—xxii; here
there has been a good deal of interpolation): and closes with a briefer
treatment of Epic Poetry, chiefly in its relation to Tragedy. Fragmentary
though the work now is, it is a contribution of lasting value to the theory,
not only of Poetry, but of Fine Art in general.

G. LITERATURE OF THE ALEXANDRIAN AND ROMAN AGE.—POETRY.

186. The latter part of the fourth century B.C. is the moment at which
the best period of Greek literature,—that which is more
especially called 'classical,'—may be considered to end.
Down to that time Greek literature had been creative.
No pre-existing pattern guided the great artists who first shaped the
epos, the elegy, the various forms of iambic or lyric poetry, and the
Attic drama; no tradition prescribed the form adopted by the first
great historians and orators. From 'Homer' to Demosthenes, every
one of these men was a true 'maker.' And this creative literature,
throughout the course of its spontaneous and natural growth, was in
touch with life. Epic poetry was heard in the halls of Achaean chiefs, or,
later, by the crowds that thronged around the rhapsode. Elegy, iambic
verse, and the Aeolian lyric, were social. The choral lyric had its place
at religious festivals and at the national games. Drama belonged to the
cult of Dionysus in his theatre. The orator addressed himself to the
jurors in the law-court or to the public Assembly. The historians, such
as Herodotus, Thucydides or Xenophon, were men who drew on their
own practical experiences, and whose most attentive readers would be
men of action, fain to gather lessons useful in politics or in war. The
great literature of Greece was animated by the political freedom, the
popular faith, and the social interests of the Greek city.

There is thus a twofold justification for the line commonly drawn
between the Hellenic and the Alexandrian period. First, all the principal
types of literature had been created before the earlier period closed.
Secondly, all the conditions of literary production were changed. The
Athenian poet of the fifth century, composing for the benefit of his

[marginal note:] Character of the 'classical' period;

fellow-citizens at the Dionysia, was in a totally different case from the poet writing at Alexandria, with its motley and polyglot population of 800,000. The Alexandrian was a man of letters, usually dependent on patrons, or on the favour of some literary clique among 'the reading public.' The Alexandrian litera-ture never makes on the modern imagination that special demand which is made by the Hellenic; one has not to conceive, as inspiring and welcoming it, a form of civic life that has vanished. It is a literature of the study. *and of the Alexandrian.*

187. But, while there are these plain grounds for drawing a line between Hellenic and 'Hellenistic,' it is all the more needful not to misapprehend or undervalue the later Greek literature. It was a prolific and a versatile literature, which lived on for some seven centuries, producing a marvellous amount of permanently valuable and interesting work. It was, in the main, imitative and repro-ductive, not creative. But there was still abundant scope for personal originality, for the expression of individual genius, for the exercise of taste and humour in modifying the traditional forms of poetry or prose by local colouring or characteristic style. Originality, in the sense thus defined, appears from age to age in almost every branch of the later literature. It is enough to name four writers, in each of whom the distinctive excellence is of an original stamp,—Theocritus, Polybius, Plutarch, and Lucian. *Value of the later Greek literature.*

The course of the later literature from about 300 B.C. to A.D. 500 or 600 might be treated as consisting of two principal periods, between which the opening of the Augustan age is the point of division; but, however convenient as an aid to memory, such an arrangement does not correspond with any break of continuity. For the purposes of a sketch like the present, it is better to take simply (1) the literature of verse, and (2) the literature of prose, and to trace each from the beginning of the Alexandrian age to the later times of the decadence.

188. Callimachus (*c.* 260 B.C.), a learned critic and scholarly poet, is our best representative of the prevailing Alexandrian taste in his day. His hymns to *Zeus, Apollo, Artemis, Delos,* and his *Calathus of Demeter* are pedantic and frigid. The elegiac Λουτρὰ τῆς Παλ-λάδος is his best extant piece (it relates the blinding of the seer, so splendidly told in Tennyson's *Tiresias*). Catullus translated his *Lock of Berenice*, with fidelity as is shown by fragments discovered in 1928 (*C.R.* 1929). Ovid imitated his *Ibis,* and took hints for the *Fasti* from his Αἴτια ('origins' of sacred tradition and usage). The Αἴτια remained unknown in the original until 1905 when considerable fragments were discovered at Oxyrhyn-chus and published five years later (*P. Oxy.* 1010). They contain (1) the final part of the love story of Acontius and Cydippe, (2) part of the fourth and last book of the *Aetia* in which Callimachus bids farewell to poetry, and resolves to devote himself to prose. In the same group of papyri are long but muti-lated portions of Callimachus' *Iambi.* Further long fragments of the *Aetia* (introduction and Book II) were discovered and published in 1927 (*P Oxy.* *Poetry of the third and second cen-turies B.C.— Callimachus.*

2079—2080). Part of his *Hecale* (an idyllic epic) was recovered in 1893. On the whole the papyri allow us to form a more favourable estimate of Callimachus than the extant *Hymns*. He shows variety and skill in narration. Some of his 74 epigrams are good; one of them, on the death of Heracleitus, is familiar to English readers through William Johnson (Cory)'s version, which in beauty comes near to the original. His ideal was the short, highly-polished poem,—in his own phrase, πίδακος ἐξ ἱερῆς ὀλίγη λιβάς, ἄκρον ἄωτον.

189. The proverbial μέγα βιβλίον μέγα κακόν was his saying,—a pointed allusion to the *Argonautica*, in four books, by his younger contemporary, Apollonius of Rhodes, who found his motive (one can hardly say his model) in Homeric epos. Apollonius uses an imitative epic diction; in place of the old epic life and fire, he has elaborate picturesqueness, many touches of true observation, and sometimes a vein of dreamy pathos. His mingling of these with an epic manner produces much the same sort of effect as the blending of medieval with classical elements in William Morris's *Jason*. The *Argonautica* seems to have been coldly received; but it lived to be studied by Virgil.

190. Theocritus, born at Syracuse, to which he returned in his later years, flourished at Alexandria in the reign of Ptolemy Philadelphus (285—247). His bucolic idylls, the oldest extant examples of pastoral poetry and the patterns of nearly all later work in that kind, are inspired by a true feeling for the rural life and scenery of his native Sicily. There was, doubtless, in Sicily some bucolic folk-poetry to build on; the ancient, like the modern, shepherds of Greece must have had their songs. Then the Dorian Sicilians Epicharmus and Sophron had dramatised little scenes from real life, some of them, probably, rural. The idylls of Theocritus are not sham pastorals, of the kind which 'royal goatherds in silk and lace' sang and danced in the seventeenth century; they are not even conventional in the sense of Virgil's *Eclogues*: they make one breathe the air of the Sicilian uplands and coasts, and the rustics in them, even if somewhat idealised, are alive.

The word εἰδύλλιον was used to denote a cabinet-picture in verse, a short poem with local colour and pretty detail. When it came into use, we do not know: Pliny was familiar with it ('*sive idyllia sive eclogas*,' *Ep.* IV. 14). Some think that it meant merely 'style,' a qualifying epithet being added; *e.g.* a pastoral piece might be headed βουκολικὸν εἰδύλλιον: but, in that case, it would be strange that the distinctive epithet should have been dropped, and the colourless word used with a specific meaning. The collection of 'idylls' bearing the name of Theocritus includes pieces of various classes. Five, at least, to judge by internal evidence, are not his; viz. XIX, XX, XXI (beautiful in itself), XXIII, and XXVII.

The famous *Adoniazusae* (XV) is a scene from common life which approaches to the character of a μῖμος: the same might be said of XIV. There is a group of poems in which some phase of love is the leading

motive; including the two lyric pieces in the Aeolic dialect, modelled on
Alcaeus (xxviii, xxix). Then there is a series of short poems in which
the material is epic or mythological (Heracles, Hylas, Pentheus, Dioscuri,
etc.); where Theocritus is seen more under the influence of Alexandrian
taste, yet nearly always rising above the tame pseudo-epic method by a
certain alertness of fancy and vivacity of treatment. Of the epigrams
ascribed to him, several are pretty, but some at least are spurious:
nos. 7, 9, 11, 15, 16, 20, 21 are attributed in the Anthology to 'Leonidas
of Tarentum *or* Theocritus,' or to the former alone. Theocritus is the last
genuinely inspired poet of Hellas, a fresh and living voice in an age of
literary mannerism; one of the most beautiful and lovable of the world's
poets.

191. The *Europa* of Moschus of Syracuse (*c.* 150 B.C.) is a little gem
of descriptive poetry, genuinely Alexandrian where it shows
its indebtedness to some painting of the maiden riding the   Moschus
bull (verses 125—129). Bion of Smyrna (*c.* 100) is now best   and Bion.
represented by his brilliant but rather florid *Lament for Adonis* ('Ἐπιτάφιος
Ἀδώνιδος). His death (*c.* 80) is mourned by an anonymous pupil in the *Lament
for Bion*, once ascribed to Moschus, a piece of exquisite music and pathos.
Moschus and Bion are always classed as 'bucolic'; but, so far as their remains show, they would be better described by the more general term 'idyllic.'

192. Here may be noticed two characteristically Alexandrian productions, one akin to tragedy and the other to comedy.
The Ἀλεξάνδρα (= Κασσάνδρα) of Lycophron, a tragic poet   Lycophron.
(*c.* 260 B.C.), is a monologue by Cassandra in 1474 iambic   Timon.
trimeters, prophesying all that would come of her brother Paris going to
Sparta. It is a display of recondite learning in diction and mythology.
Every device which can darken language, metaphor, and allusion is concentrated in this prodigy of exulting pedantry. Timon of Phlius (*c.* 280),
a disciple of the sceptic Pyrrhon, satirised the non-sceptical schools of
philosophy in poems called σίλλοι. Lucian uses the word σίλλος in
the sense of 'squinting.' As applied to satire or lampoon, the term may
have arisen from the notion of presenting a subject in a humorously distorted view. These σίλλοι were in three books of hexameter verse, of
which II and III took the form of a satiric Νέκυια, where Timon spoke with
the shades of the wise. Only fragments (about 140 verses) remain.

193. Aratus of Soli in Cilicia (*c.* 270 B.C., or perhaps somewhat later)
has left two poems, (1) Φαινόμενα, in 732 hexameters, an
unscientific and inaccurate description of the constellations   Didactic and
and the circles of the sphere, versified from a prose work by   learned poetry.
Eudoxus of Cnidus (*c.* 360 B.C.); and (2) Διοσημεῖα, in 422 verses,—a
supplement to the former,—*Prognostics* of weather, which he seems to
have taken chiefly from Hesiod and Theophrastus. Cicero and other
Romans translated Aratus. St Paul quoted at Athens τοῦ γὰρ γένος ἐσμέν
from *Phaenom.* 5 (Acts xvii. 28).

Nicander of Claros, a physician (*c.* 150 B.C.), wrote (1) Θηριακά, in 958 hexameters, on venomous animals and the wounds which they inflict, and (2) Ἀλεξιφάρμακα, in 630 vv., *Antidotes* to poison; works noteworthy for some points of zoological or old medical lore.

Akin to these are the much later poems which bear the name of Oppian (*c.* A.D. 180), viz. (1) Ἁλιευτικά, an epic in five books, of which I and II deal with the natural history of fishes, and III—v with the art of fishing; (2) Κυνηγετικά, an epic on hunting in four books,—inferior to the other as a composition, but of some interest for zoology. It has been held, not without strong reasons, that these two poems are of different authorship; but the personality of Oppian is utterly obscure. A third epic which bore his name, but is now known only through a prose paraphrase of part of it, is Ἰξευτικά (*Fowling*).

There was also a learned epos of mythology and of history, represented by Rhianus (220 B.C.) in his lost Ἡράκλεια, Ἀχαικά, Μεσσηνιακά, etc.; and by Euphorion of Chalcis (*flor. c.* 235 B.C.), also an elegiac poet, one of whose epics, called Μοψοπία (an old name of Attica, according to Suidas), dealt with various Attic myths.

194. After the second century B.C. the graver and more ambitious **The later heroic or mythic epos.** forms of Greek poetry almost cease. Quintus of Smyrna (formerly called *Calaber*, because first known to modern scholars through a MS. found at Otranto) cannot be placed much before 400 A.D., and was possibly somewhat later. His Τὰ μεθ᾽ Ὅμηρον, a sequel to the *Iliad* in fourteen books, carrying the story to the capture of Troy, is smooth and tame,—but not without antiquarian interest and value. Nonnus (*c.* 425 A.D.?), an Egyptian Greek, wrote an epic *Dionysiaca*, in forty-eight books, on the adventures of the god. Chaotic in matter and turgid in style, it is curious for some metrical peculiarities in the structure of the hexameter which seem to indicate that the older Greek 'pitch-accent' had become (or was tending to become) the modern 'stress-accent' as seen in the Byzantine πολιτικοὶ στίχοι. Orphic mysticism, too, is represented by poetry which may probably date from the second or third century A.D., and may have been the work of Egyptian Greeks; viz. (1) τὰ Ὀρφέως Ἀργοναυτικά, in 1384 hexameters, making Orpheus, bard, prophet and enchanter, the central figure of Jason's world; (2) the Λιθικά (768 vv.), on the talismanic virtues of rare or precious stones; and (3) the eighty-seven 'Orphic' hymns, with which the eighth 'Homeric' hymn (to *Ares*) is not unreasonably classed by Hermann.

195. The 'mimes' of Herodas (first published in 1891, from a **Minor forms of poetry.** papyrus containing seven nearly complete poems, besides fragments) represent a species of composition which was, no doubt, popular, but of which we had hitherto possessed no example. They are little scenes from common life, dramatised in choliambic dialogue (μιμίαμβοι); 'The Schoolmaster'—'A jealous woman'—'A visit to Asclepius,' etc. The realism is sometimes rather repulsive, but there is rare dramatic skill, much humour, and some pathos. Nothing is known about their author. He was familiar with the island of Cos, which is the scene of at least two mimes (ii and iv); and probably lived *c.* 300—250 B.C. [See the edition by J. A. Nairn, 1904, p. xv.]

Babrius (an Italian, to judge by the name), who is now generally placed *c.* A.D. 100, turned into choliambic verse 137 fables, mostly of the 'Aesopic' kind,—using, probably, some late collection in prose. These μυθίαμβοι Αἰσώπειοι are of much literary and linguistic interest, but the naïve spirit of the old Greek beast-fable (αἶνος) is overlaid with modern scepticism and 'sophistic.'

196. One modest rill of poetry runs through the entire course of the later literature, beginning before Alexandrian days, and long outlasting the fall of the Western Empire. This is the elegiac,—descended, without a break, from the age of Callinus and Mimnermus. Erotic elegy more especially flourished in Macedonian and Roman times. Hermesianax of Colophon (*c.* 320 B.C.) was one of its exponents, but far less famous than his younger friend Philetas of Cos (*c.* 300 B.C.), whom Ovid imitated, and whom Propertius preferred to Callimachus. Other elegists of note were Asclepiades of Samos (*c.* 290 B.C.); Euphorion of Chalcis (*c.* 235 B.C.); Antipater of Sidon (*c.* 100 B.C.); Meleager of Gadara (*c.* 60 B.C.); Crinagoras of Mytilene (*c.* 20 B.C.); Palladas of Alexandria (*c.* A.D. 400); Paulus 'Silentiarius' (*c.* A.D. 540, chief of the *silentiarii* or secretaries of Justinian); and Agathias (*c.* A.D. 580). *Continuity of elegiac poetry.*

197. The short ἐπίγραμμα of from one to four couplets was the favourite form of elegiac composition. These 'epigrams' are of various classes, such as the amatory (ἐρωτικά); convivial (συμποτικά); satirical (σκωπτικά); dedicatory, especially inscriptions on works of art or votive offerings (ἀναθηματικά); hortatory (προτρεπτικά); sepulchral (ἐπιτύμβια). *The 'epigram.'*

Collections of ἐπιγράμματα (chiefly of inscriptions on ἀναθήματα) were made in the Alexandrian age, the earliest on record being that of the geographer Polemon (*c.* 190 B.C.). The first collection of epigrams on all subjects was the 'Garland' (Στέφανος) of Meleager (*c.* 60 B.C.), which represented forty-six poets, from the earliest times onwards. The title Ἀνθολογία seems to have been first used by Philip of Thessalonica (*c.* A.D. 110?). The next important collection was the Κύκλος ἐπιγραμμάτων by Agathias (*c.* A.D. 580), in seven books. Using these and other materials, Constantinus Cephalas (who appears to have flourished *c.* 920 A.D.) put together the great *corpus* (representing upwards of 320 writers) now known as the *Palatine Anthology*, because it was found in the Palatine Library at Heidelberg by Salmasius (Saumaise), about the year 1606. The *Planudean Anthology*, in seven books, was compiled by Maximus Planudes, a monk of Constantinople (*c.* 1300), who appears to have done little more than abridge and re-arrange the work of Cephalas. *Anthologies.*

198. The foregoing sketch will have served to show that the Greek poetry written after *c.* 300 B.C. attains to excellence only in one form,—that of elaborate finish, with beauty or prettiness of detail, within a small framework. This excellence is raised to its highest level by the genius of Theocritus. But the general conditions are the same in the hymns or epigrams of Callimachus, in the mimes of Herodas, and in the various phases of elegy from Philetas to Agathias. In the epics, on the other hand, whether heroic or didactic, art fails to compensate for the lack of inspiration.

Summary.

H. PROSE OF THE ALEXANDRIAN AND ROMAN AGE.

199. Meanwhile, in contrast with this narrowly limited sphere of merit in verse, the Greek prose literature of the Alexandrian and Roman age is full of varied energy. It finds scope in almost every branch of knowledge and every form of composition. A general view of this literature can best be given by taking separately the main lines of development, and indicating some of the principal works in each.

Prose Literature.

200. For Greek mathematics and astronomy the third and second centuries B.C. were almost such a period as the fifth century B.C. had been for literature,—a time of original work by men of genius. These men are dealt with in a separate section of this book. But one of them, Eratosthenes (*c.* 234 B.C.), the successor of Callimachus in the headship of the Alexandrian Library, was eminent in letters as well as in science. In addition to his mathematical writings, he was the author of poetical, philosophical, historical and critical works, thus meriting the title of ὁ πένταθλος. His treatise *On the Old Comedy*, in at least 12 books, seems to have dealt with every part of the subject,— theatres, scenery, actors, dresses, poets, their themes and their styles.

Science and Learning.

201. The labours of the Alexandrian critics were fruitful in revised texts (ἐκδόσεις) of the best Greek writers, especially the poets, and in commentaries (ὑπομνήματα) upon them. The older of the extant scholia on Homer, Pindar, the dramatists, Theocritus, Thucydides, Demosthenes, Plato and Aristotle are largely indebted to these labours, and are now the principal sources from which some idea of their scope and method may be gleaned. Reference has already been made (§ 136), in connexion with Homer, to the work of Zenodotus (*c.* 280 B.C.), Aristophanes of Byzantium (*c.* 195 B.C.), and Aristarchus (*c.* 180—160 B.C.). The poet Callimachus (*c.* 260 B.C.), who succeeded Zenodotus as head of the great Library at Alexandria, was best known as a critic by his catalogue, in 120 books, of the chief writers in every branch of literature (πίνακες τῶν ἐν πάσῃ παιδείᾳ διαλαμψάντων καὶ ὧν συνέγραψαν). The enormous industry of Didymus (*c.* 30 B.C.), the latest of those

Criticism and exegesis.

Alexandrian scholars whose writings were a mine for the scholiasts, seems to have been largely employed in digesting and abridging the work of his predecessors. [Cp. *De Demosthene commenta*, ed. 1904.]

202.   Besides endeavouring to discriminate authentic from spurious writings, the eminent Alexandrian critics of the third and second centuries B.C. exercised a kind of censorship by selecting the best writers in each kind from the enormous mass of literature, good, bad, and indifferent, which had come down to them.   Thus they chose out four heroic poets (with Homer at the head), three iambic, four elegiac, nine lyric; nine historians, ten orators, and so on.   The term for including an author in one of these select lists was ἐγκρίνειν: *e.g.* the orator Deinarchus is described by Suidas as τῶν μετὰ Δημοσθένους ἐγκριθέντων εἷς. Quintilian renders this term by *in numerum redigere* (X. 1, § 54), or *in ordinem redigere* (I. 4, § 3).   As each writer so selected was, in his way and degree, a norm of excellence (κανών), the select lists themselves were called κανόνες.   Aristophanes and Aristarchus probably bore the chief part in framing these lists, so far, at any rate, as the poets were concerned (*poetarum iudices*, Quint. X. 1, § 54). These 'canons,' while merely confirming the fame of great authors whose popularity was already secure, doubtless had some influence in condemning to relative obscurity such lesser writers as the critics ruled out (*exemerint numero*, Quint. I. 4, § 3), and, so far, must have affected their chances of survival.   The definite line thus drawn by the Alexandrians between writers who are, and who are not, of the first rank is the earliest expression of the idea involved in the later phrase, a 'classic.'   But that term (it may be noted in passing) has nothing to do with lists or classes formed by the Alexandrians.   Roman citizens of the first *classis* in respect to property were distinctively called *classici*, while all others were *infra classem.*   Hence the term was transferred to literary rank.   This metaphor occurs first in the *Noctes Atticae* of Gellius (*c.* A.D. 150): *classicus adsiduusque* (= *locuples*) *scriptor, non proletarius* (XIX. c. 8: cp. VI [VII] c. 13).

The Alexandrian κανόνες.

203.   The Alexandrian study of mythology, which has left its impress on the Alexandrian poetry, was represented in prose by Apollodorus of Athens (*c.* 140 B.C.), a pupil of Aristarchus.   He wrote a work 'On the gods' (Περὶ θεῶν) in 24 books, a survey of traditions and opinions concerning them, treated from the Stoic point of view.   He was also the author of 'Annals' (Χρονικά), in 4 books of iambic trimeters, beginning from the fall of Troy.   These works are now known only from fragments.   The extant Βιβλιοθήκη in 3 books (now supplemented by an epitome found in codex Vat. 950), wrongly ascribed to him in the MSS. and by Photius, is a concise handbook of mythology, compiled under the Empire, probably from a lost manual of the first century B.C.

Mythology.

204.   The attention bestowed at Alexandria on textual criticism and on exegesis naturally led to the gradual development of systematic grammar.   Dionysius Thrax (born 166 B.C.) wrote a

Grammar.

Τέχνη γραμματική which seems to have been the first work of its kind, and was certainly the first to find wide acceptance ; it remained in use down to the Renaissance. Apollonius Dyscolus (*c.* A.D. 130), surnamed ὁ τεχνικός, and designated by Priscian, some three centuries later, as ' grammaticorum princeps,' was the founder of a systematic syntax. Two of his treatises survive, viz., περὶ συντάξεως τῶν τοῦ λόγου μερῶν, and περὶ ἀντωνυμίας (' on the pronoun '). His son, Aelius Herodianus, was the author of the once celebrated Καθολικὴ Προσῳδία, or ' General System of Accentuation,' in 20 books,—the chief source used by later Greek writers on the subject. It is lost, and what we know of it is derived from a corrupt and mutilated epitome (made perhaps by the grammarian Arcadius, *c.* A.D. 200), a few extracts preserved by Porphyry, and the numerous references of the scholiasts. The epitome was adopted by Chandler as the basis of his work on Greek Accentuation.

205. Along with grammar, lexicography was much cultivated. Julius

Lexicography. Pollux, a Greek of Naucratis, compiled an Ὀνομαστικόν of which the approximate date is fixed by the dedication prefixed to each of the ten books (Ἰούλιος Πολυδεύκης Κομμόδῳ Καίσαρι χαίρειν), since the young Commodus received the title of Caesar in A.D. 166, but the higher title of Augustus in 177. The work is of great value as a storehouse of words and technical terms (often illustrated by quotations) relating to various branches of knowledge. Valerius Harpocration (whose date is doubtful between such wide limits as *c.* A.D. 150 and 350) is the author of λέξεις τῶν δέκα ῥητόρων, an alphabetical list of words and proper names used by the orators, with explanations which are often valuable, especially in regard to legal (or other technical) terms. From Moeris (Μοῖρις), known as the Ἀττικιστής (*c.* A.D. 200 ?), has come down a list of Attic words and phrases, with their equivalents in other dialects (chiefly in the κοινή), entitled λέξεις Ἀττικῶν καὶ Ἑλλήνων. Each article is simply a brief entry ; *e.g.* ἀροῦν Ἀττικοί· ἀροτριᾶν Ἕλληνες (*i.e.* the κοινὴ διάλεκτος). Other noted lexicographers, whose works have perished, were Pamphilus (*c.* A.D. 50 ?), and Diogenianus (*c.* A.D. 130). All this material, and much more of a similar kind, was available for the later compilers of comprehensive dictionaries, such as Hesychius, the author or authors of the *Etymologicum Magnum*, and Suidas.

The study of metre is represented by Hephaestion (*c.* A.D. 150),

Metre. whose chief work, Περὶ μέτρων, in forty-eight books, is lost. But we have his own epitome of it, Ἐγχειρίδιον περὶ μέτρων, which was thenceforth the standard manual on the subject, and which indeed is of permanent value, not only for the information which it contains, but also for its citations of poets.

206. Geography, on its mathematical side, profited by the progress of

Geography. Greek science. Eratosthenes (*c.* 234 B.C.) was the first who approximately measured a geographical degree. Hipparchus (*c.* 120 B.C.), the astronomer, invented the method of determining position by latitude and longitude. Ptolemy (Claudius Ptolemaeus, *c.* A.D. 150) was the author of a Γεωγραφικὴ Ὑφήγησις, long the standard text-book on the subject, in which latitude and longitude were used to determine the position of many thousands of places. Meanwhile the literary treatment of geography had been continued in works of which the general type was derived from earlier writers such as Hecataeus. Scylax (*c.* 350 B.C. ?) was the author of a Περίπλους, still extant, describing parts of Europe, Asia and Libya. Scymnus (*c.* 80 B.C.) wrote a Περιήγησις which is lost : the extant poem in nearly a thousand iambic verses which bears that title, and which was formerly ascribed to him, is of unknown origin.

207. A new method and aim distinguish the Γεωγραφικά of Strabo, who lived under Augustus, and in the earlier part of the reign of Tiberius. The reader whom Strabo had in view was the educated Roman, more especially the Roman who might be called upon to bear some part in provincial administration. Such a man ought to know, at least in outline, the physical and political geography of each country, and the principal events in its history. This is the knowledge which Strabo seeks to furnish, while omitting, as a rule, descriptive or local detail of the minuter kind. Of his seventeen books, the first two are introductory, dealing with the principles and science of geography. Eight books are then given to Europe; six to Asia; and one to Egypt and Libya. At the end of book VII, the part which dealt with Macedonia and Thrace is lost; and for that part we have to rely on a meagre epitome of the whole work made probably towards the close of the tenth century. The permanent value of Strabo is in respect to history no less than to geography.

208. Pausanias, a native of the region about Mount Sipylus in Lydia, wrote his Ἑλλάδος περιήγησις in the latter part of the second century. One clue to the date is given by the latest event noticed, viz., the incursion into Greece of the Κοστόβωκοι (X. 34, § 5), a Sarmatian tribe, which occurred somewhere between A.D. 166 and 180 (perhaps in 176). The work is in 10 books: I. Ἀττικά, with Megara: II. Κορινθιακά, with Sicyonia, Phliasia and Argolis: III. Λακωνικά: IV. Μεσσηνιακά: V. and VI. Ἠλειακά: VII. Ἀχαϊκά: VIII. Ἀρκαδικά: IX. Βοιωτικά: X. Φωκικά. It is a guide-book, combining a record of memorable traditions with a description of notable objects. For the historical part, the writer has consulted a large range of Greek literature, both verse and prose, besides occasionally using inscriptions or other documents. As to the descriptive part, he states in several instances that he has seen the things which he describes; and, generally, he gives it to be understood that his account rests on personal inspection. Nor is there the slightest reason to doubt this. A theory has, indeed, been set up that Pausanias slavishly copied a much earlier 'periegete,' Polemon of Ilium (*c.* 170 B.C.). Hence, it is said, (1) he describes things which, in his own day, no longer existed; and (2) ignores monuments subsequent in date

Strabo.

Pausanias.

to Polemon. But the first charge has never been proved; and the second is untrue. For example, Pausanias describes the new Corinth, which dated only from 44 B.C.: he also describes works produced in the reign of Hadrian, as the Olympieion at Athens and its works of art (I. 18. 6—9); and the images dedicated by Herodes Atticus in the temple of Poseidon at the Isthmus (II. 1. 7—9). The fragments of Polemon (Müller III. 109 ff.), so far from supporting the accusation, indicate that Pausanias either did not know the writings of Polemon, or else disregarded and sometimes tacitly controverted him. The extant monuments of Greece are the best proof that Pausanias described Greece as he saw it. Thus his accuracy has been confirmed by excavations made in 1895 at the sanctuary of the Δέσποινα at Lycosura in Arcadia. [See J. G. Frazer's *Pausanias*, vol. I. pp. lxxxix ff., and vol. V. p. 622.]

209. Polybius of Megalopolis was born towards the close of the third century B.C. (probably *c.* 210—206), and lived to the age of eighty-two. The son of Lycortas, one of the leading men of the Achaean League, Polybius was in youth the political disciple of his father's friend and colleague Philopoemen, whose ashes he carried to the grave in 183 B.C. In early manhood he was himself a magistrate of the League. From 167 to 151 he was a political prisoner at Rome, living in the house of Aemilius Paulus, whose two sons, Fabius Maximus Aemilianus and Scipio Aemilianus (Africanus minor), were his pupils and friends. He was present with Scipio Aemilianus at the destruction of Carthage in the spring of 146 B.C. Later in the same spring, he was at Corinth, either during or just after the sack by Mummius. When the Roman province of Achaia had been organized, the Roman commissioners assigned to Polybius (in 145) the duty of visiting the several cities and arranging the local details of the new settlement.

History. Polybius.

The subject of his History (Ἱστορίαι, usually called by him πραγματεία), as originally planned, was the period from the beginning of the Second Punic War to the conquest of Macedon (219-167 B.C.). But he afterwards enlarged this plan, continuing his narrative to the fall of Carthage and the final subjugation of Greece (146 B.C.). He also prefixed an introductory sketch (books I and II) of the events from 264 (where the Sicilian History of Timaeus ended) to 221 B.C., including the First Punic War (264–241 B.C.) The History was in forty books. Only the first five (going down to 216 B.C.) have been preserved entire: but of the remaining thirty-five we have extracts, made by various Byzantine compilers, and fragments. The ruling idea of the work is the recognition that the power of Rome is irresistible; and that this central, all-subduing power has given unity to the history of the Mediterranean States. His subject is ἓν ἔργον, ἓν θέαμα (III. 1).

The period from 220 to 146 B.C. 'corresponds,' he says, 'partly with our own days, and partly with those of our fathers;...some of the events happened before our eyes, and of the rest we heard from those who had seen them' (IV. 2). Polybius spared no trouble in visiting sites and examining documents; nor did he fail to use earlier writers where they could help. He was a careful student of laws, institutions and customs. His chronology, as Cicero noted (*De off.* III. 32), is exact. Above all, he is a man of large mind, thoughtful and fair. He is not a first-rate writer. He has not the grasp, the piercing insight, or the literary force of Thucydides. But he is a historian of the same class, a man at once of action (both political and military) and of research. Nor can Thucydides himself be placed above Polybius in respect to complete equipment of knowledge, or to those moral qualities which assure the value of narratives and judgments.

210. The history of Rome, or universal history with Rome for its centre, employed a number of learned compilers from the Augustan age onwards. Their idea of scope and scale was taken, not from the example of Herodotus or Thucydides, but from the forty books of Polybius; and their writings have shared, more or less, a like fate. Few copies were in circulation; Byzantine readers had recourse to epitomes or excerpts; and the original works have reached us, for the most part, only in a fragmentary form. *Compilers of Roman History.*

211. The Βιβλιοθήκη Ἱστορική of Diodorus Siculus (*c.* 40 B.C.) is a general history of the world, grouped around that of Rome, and carried down to Caesar's conquest of Gaul. It was in forty books, of which we have only the first five (the mythical history of Egypt, Assyria, Aethiopia, and Greece), and books XI—XX (480–302 B.C.), with some fragments. Diodorus was essentially a compiler, without much critical faculty, and he certainly is not a lively writer; but we owe him a debt for the facts which he has preserved. *Diodorus Siculus.*

212. Dionysius of Halicarnassus (*c.* 25 B.C.)—whose excellence as a literary critic has already been noticed (§ 182)—composed a Ῥωμαϊκὴ Ἀρχαιολογία in twenty books. This was an 'Early History of Rome' to 264 B.C., meant to form an introduction to Polybius. We have books I—X (complete) and XI (imperfect), going down to 441 B.C.; also excerpts from XII—XX. Polybius had said that Τύχη, in giving empire to Rome, had been 'an honest umpire'; and Dionysius develops this thought by tracing Roman dominion to the inborn abilities and virtues of the race. Moreover, the Romans, he argues, are not 'barbarians,' but of Greek descent. Dionysius was evidently painstaking in research; he did not understand the constitutional history of Rome; but he gives us a great deal of useful information. He is a literary man of alert and graceful mind, with certain ideas which he wishes to work out in a historical form. His style is good; and the fictitious speeches in his history are sometimes excellent of their kind. *Dionysius of Halicarnassus.*

213. Appianus of Alexandria (*c.* A.D. 140) wrote a general history of Rome (Ῥωμαϊκαὶ Ἱστορίαι) from the earliest times to the accession of Vespasian (A.D. 70), in twenty-four books. *Appian.*

Book I, entitled Βασιλική (sc. ἱστορία), treated of the regal period. The
wars of Rome were next narrated as follows, each book (as a rule) taking
its title from the country concerned:—II. Ἰταλική (Wars in Italy other than
the Samnite) : III. Σαυνιτική (Samnite wars) : IV. Κελτική : V. Σικελικὴ καὶ
νησιωτική : VI. Ἰβηρική : VII. Ἀννιβαϊκή (Second Punic War) : VIII. Λιβυκή
(beginning with a general sketch of the Punic Wars) : IX. Μακεδονική :
X. Ἑλληνικὴ καὶ Ἰωνική : XI. Συριακή : XII. Μιθραδάτειος. Nine books
(XIII—XXI) then dealt with the civil wars (Ῥωμαϊκὰ Ἐμφύλια) from the
times of Marius and Sulla to the battle of Actium (31 B.C.). Book XXII
(Ἑκατονταετία) covered the century from 30 B.C. to 70 A.D.: XXIII (Ἰλλυρική)
and XXIV (Ἀράβιος) comprised the Illyrian and Arabian Wars. We have
(1) excerpts and fragments from books I—V and IX : (2) the whole of
books VI—VIII ; XI ; XIII—XVII (the Civil Wars, to 34 B.C.,—the most
valuable among the extant parts of the work) ; and XXIII. Books X,
XVIII—XXII, and XXIV are wholly lost. Appian was a compiler pure
and simple ; he is weak in geography and chronology, but writes a plain,
clear style.

214. Dion Cassius (c. A.D. 200) wrote a Ῥωμαϊκὴ ἱστορία from the
Dion Cassius. foundation of the city to A.D. 229 (the seventh year of
Alexander Severus). It was in no less than eighty books.
The first thirty-five of these are now represented only by a considerable
body of excerpts and fragments (filling about 98 8vo. pages in Bekker's
edition). Books 36—60 are extant in a practically complete state. The
last 16 chapters of book 60 however (cc. 29—35) have come down to us
only in the abridged form given to them by John Xiphilinus, a Byzantine
scholar in the eleventh century. These twenty-five books (36—60)
comprise the period from the campaign of Lucullus against Mithradates in
68 B.C. to the death of the Emperor Claudius in A.D. 54. For the series of
books from 61 to 80 (inclusive) we have only the epitome of Xiphilinus,
occasionally supplemented by excerpts, or fragments of other abridgments.
These books cover the period from A.D. 54 to A.D. 222. The distinctive
merit of Dion Cassius consists in his familiarity with the details of Roman
administration. The son of a senator, he had himself filled the offices of
quaestor, aedile, praetor, and consul. He is equally at home, as Niebuhr
observed, in constitutional or legal matters and in military tactics. So
far as can now be judged, he possesses the merit which he claims (frag. 1.
2) of having used his sources with discrimination and care. His chief
model in method and treatment was Polybius ; he was also a student of
Thucydides ; and he seeks, in their spirit, to trace causes and motives.
He is a valuable authority, especially for events in or near his own time.

215. Herodian (c. A.D. 240) wrote a history of the Emperors from
Herodian. Commodus to Gordian III (A.D. 180—238). Taking the
death of Marcus Aurelius (180) as his starting-point, he
called his work Τῆς μετὰ Μάρκον Βασιλείας ἱστορίαι, and divided it into
eight books, which have come down entire. The period of fifty-eight years
comprises fifteen reigns. His narrative is clear and vivid. This history

was made popular in the later times of the Renaissance by Politian's Latin version (1493).

216. Apart from the Greek compilers of Roman history, two remarkable men enriched the historical literature of the Greek language in the Imperial age. Flavius Josephus (*c.* A.D. 80), a Jew of noble descent, wrote a 'History of the Jewish War' (Περὶ τοῦ Ἰουδαϊκοῦ πολέμου) in twelve books, from the capture of Jerusalem by Antiochus Epiphanes in 170 B.C. to its capture by Titus (at which he was present) in A.D. 70. A statesman and a soldier, Josephus has so far a certain kinship with the classical historians of an earlier time. The Greek into which he translated his work from the Hebrew in which he first composed it is often marked by a certain graphic liveliness (ἐνάργεια): but, in styling him 'the Greek Livy,' St Jerome did less than justice to his solid historical merits. He wrote also an 'Early History of the Jews' (Ἰουδαϊκὴ Ἀρχαιολογία), in twenty books, going down to A.D. 66. His aim here was to do for his nation what Dionysius of Halicarnassus had attempted for Rome.

Josephus.

217. The literary activity of Arrian (*c.* A.D. 150) was curiously dominated by the idea of a parallel between his own relation to his master in philosophy, the Stoic Epictetus, and that of Xenophon to Socrates. One portion of his works formed a manifold counterpart to the *Memorabilia*. He edited the 'Lectures' (Διατριβαί) of Epictetus (in eight books, of which the first four are extant): compiled his 'Discourses' (Ὁμιλίαι) in twelve books, now lost; and, besides a Life of the master (also lost), the extant 'Manual' (Ἐγχειρίδιον) or summary of his teaching, which was much read alike by pagans and by Christians. Then at the side of Xenophon's *Anabasis* he placed his own Ἀνάβασις Ἀλεξάνδρου, also in seven books, of which we have the whole, except a passage lost at the end of VII. c. 12. Setting out from Philip's death in 336 he goes down to Alexander's in 323. Arrian is a critical historian, who has carefully sifted his documents. He has also the merit of clearness in describing military matters. His extant Ἰνδική (or τὰ Ἰνδικά) forms a kind of appendix to his *Anabasis*. It is a description of parts of India, based, so far as the interior of the country is concerned, on Megasthenes (*c.* 300 B.C.) and Eratosthenes, while in regard to the coasts he used the Παράπλους of Alexander's admiral Nearchus. The treatise is written in Ionic, like the Ἰνδικά of Ctesias (*c.* 400 B.C.),—for whose work, however, he had small esteem (*Anab.* v. 4, § 2). As if to complete his claim to be called ὁ νέος Ξενοφῶν, Arrian wrote a treatise on hunting (Κυνηγετικός), a sort of supplement to that which passes as Xenophon's.

Arrian.

218. Plutarch, who was born at Chaeronea in Boeotia not later than A.D. 50, and probably died soon after 120, is chiefly famous as the author of the Βίοι. In the extant collection there are two elements. (*a*) A series of Βίοι παράλληλοι. Plutarch narrates the life of an eminent Greek; then the life of an eminent Roman who in some way resembled him; and subjoins a short comparison

Biography. Plutarch.

(σύγκρισις). There are twenty-two such couples. In one instance, he takes a pair of Greeks (Agis and Cleomenes), and sets them over against a pair of Romans (Tiberius and Gaius Gracchus), adding a collective 'comparison.' There are thus forty-eight Parallel Lives in all. In four instances (Themistocles and Camillus; Pyrrhus and Marius; Alexander and Julius Caesar; Phocion and Cato minor) the σύγκρισις is wanting. (*b*) There are also four single lives :—Artaxerxes II (Mnemon); Aratus (the founder of the Achaean League) ; and the emperors Galba and Otho. These were originally independent pieces.

As a biographer, Plutarch may be said to have three principal traits. (1) He sharply distinguishes biography from history. ' I am a writer of lives,' he says, ' not of histories....A small matter, a saying, or a jest, often brings out character (ἔμφασιν ἤθους ἐποίησε) better than battles...or sieges' (*Alex.* 1). Hence he often passes lightly over events important in themselves, particularly when they have been well told by others. (2) His aim being vivid moral portraiture, the authorities which he consulted were especially such as could supplement the greater historians by supplying personal details. The historical value of the *Lives*, so far as it can now be tested, has been justly estimated by Heeren :—Plutarch generally went to the best sources available ; he used them with intelligence and fidelity ; and his standard of biographical work was a high one. (3) As he is strong on the ethical side, so is he weak on the political. He seems to have no measure of the difference between the conditions of life in the free Greece of the fifth century B.C. and in the dependent Greece of a later age. Thus the 'liberty of Greece' proclaimed by Flamininus in 196 B.C. rouses in him an enthusiasm (*Flamin.* c. 10 f.) which Trench has justly contrasted with Wordsworth's truer estimate of it, as ' A gift of that which is not to be given.' In the Roman Lives (*e.g.* those of Sulla and Cicero) the lack of political insight is especially apparent.

The Ἠθικά (*Moralia*) form a collection of some eighty pieces, many of which are essays on points of conduct, while others relate to questions of history, antiquities, letters, or science. In the miscellaneous and delightful gossip of these pieces Plutarch appears, to use Joubert's phrase, as the Herodotus of ethics. The natural piety of the man, his moral dignity, and his geniality are felt throughout. It is good to know, through him, another aspect of his age than that depicted by Suetonius, Juvenal and Tacitus. As to mere style, Plutarch is one of the very few popular writers who have more to gain than to lose from a good translation ; he was too fond of long compound words and involved sentences.

219. Diogenes Laertius (whose date is uncertain, but may perhaps be placed *c.* A.D. 200—250) wrote a work on the lives and opinions of philosophers, which is quoted by various titles, as Σοφιστῶν Βίοι (Eustathius), Φιλόσοφοι Βίοι (Photius). The first seven of his ten books contain the philosophers of *Ionia*, beginning with Thales. Under this head he includes the Socratic schools,

Diogenes Laertius.

which he divides into three groups: (1) Plato and the Academics; (2) Aristotle and the Peripatetics; (3) the Cynics and the Stoics. He then devotes his last three books to the philosophers of *Italy* (and their followers); beginning with Pythagoras and ending with Epicurus. The work is a mere compilation, uncritical, and somewhat careless: the author's main object was to collect entertaining anecdotes. But it is of immense value for the history of philosophy: about forty writers, now lost, are quoted in it.

220.   The name Philostratus was borne by a series of 'sophists' who came from the island of Lemnos.   I. The first of these, said by Suidas to have lived in Nero's reign, is obscure. Some critics ascribe to him the dialogue Νέρων which has come down among Lucian's writings.   II. Flavius Philostratus (*c.* A.D. 210), known as 'the Athenian,' was the author of Βίοι Σοφιστῶν,—sketches of rhetoricians and orators, as well as of some men who might 'lay claim to philosophy,' from the days of Protagoras to his own.   The chief value of the work is for the later history of rhetoric.   He also wrote Τὰ εἰς τὸν Τυανέα Ἀπολλώνιον, a Life of that wandering Pythagorean and mystic (born *c.* 4 B.C.), whom many then regarded as a supernatural being. III. A third Philostratus, called 'the Lemnian,' nephew and son-in-law of the second, was 24 years old in Caracalla's reign (A.D. 211—217 : *Vit. Sophist.* II. 30).   His Ἡρωικός is a dialogue on the heroes of the Trojan war, largely indebted to the cyclic and tragic poets, and censorious of Homer, especially for exalting Odysseus at the expense of Palamedes. In his Γυμναστικός he exhorts an enervated age to revive athletic contests. But his most popular work was the Εἰκόνες.   In these he purports to describe a variety of pictures in a portico at Naples.   IV. A fourth Philostratus (*c.* A.D. 300?), the maternal grandson of the third, wrote another set of Εἰκόνες (of which only part remains), in avowed imitation of the earlier series, but with inferior grace and spirit.   Elegant description, in which language vied with the works of the painter's or sculptor's art, was a literary fashion of the time.

221.   Rhetoric had been placed on a new footing by Aristotle, who had laid down principles or general rules, and so con- structed an intelligent art (see § 185).   Hermagoras of Temnos (*c.* 110 B.C.), whose works are lost, treated the subject in a manner less abstract than Aristotle's, but more scientific than that of the pre-Aristotelian writers, who had dealt mainly with the practical requirements of the law-courts.   Hermogenes (*c.* A.D. 170), building partly on Hermagoras, made a complete digest of rhetoric, which is contained in five extant treatises.   He is clear and acute. Among other extant works, once popular, may be mentioned the 'Art of Rhetoric' by Cassius Longinus (*c.* A.D. 260); the 'Exercises' (προγυμν- άσματα) of Aphthonius (*c.* A.D. 315), long a standard text-book, which again came into use at the Renaissance; and the 'Exercises' of Aelius

Marginal notes:

The Philostrati.

Rhetoric after Aristotle.

Theon (*c.* A.D. 380).   The remarkable essay on the sources of ' Sublimity '
(περὶ ὕψους)—meaning what we should rather call ' impressiveness in
style ' generally—is ascribed in the oldest MS. to ' Dionysius [of Halicar-
nassus] *or* Longinus,'—showing that the authorship was doubtful.   The
internal evidence points to a date earlier than that of Longinus ; perhaps
to the first century A.D.

222.   During the first four centuries of the Empire there was an
extraordinary demand for rhetorical accomplishment.   The
arts of panegyric and of adulation played a prominent
part in every phase of public life.   Forensic speech had
an enlarged scope, especially in the provinces.   Rhetoric, as the most
useful, became the most popular form of Greek culture.   The name
σοφιστής, which Isocrates had accepted for himself, now became a quasi-
professional title.   Under Hadrian and the Antonines, the ' sophists '
reached a high degree of dignity and influence.   Marcus Aurelius established at Athens a school of Philosophy, with four Chairs (θρόνοι),—
Platonic, Peripatetic, Stoic, and Epicurean ; and, at its side, a school
of Rhetoric, with two Chairs,—the Sophistic (in the theory and art
of rhetoric), and the Civic (πολιτικός, concerned chiefly with forensic
speaking).   The ' sophistic ' Chair held the superior rank.   Similar posts
existed in many of the greater cities, and were objects of strenuous
ambition.

The New Sophistic.

223.   The abundant examples of ' sophistic ' literature which have
come down to us contain much that is tedious and inane,
but also not a little that is interesting and curious.   Dion
Chrysostom (*c.* A.D. 100), who enjoyed the favour of Nerva
and Trajan, has left a collection of discourses (λόγοι) which are partly
orations, partly essays on philosophical, political, or literary themes.
In his best-known piece, the Ῥοδιακός, he censures the custom, adopted
in Rhodes, of inscribing ancient statues with new names, and then erecting
them as memorials of modern men.   Dion's style is easy and pleasant.

Dion Chry- sostomus.

Publius Aelius Aristeides (*ob. c.* A.D. 180) represents the
rhetoric of display at the zenith of its glory : in the opinion
of his age, and in his own, he was at least the equal of Demosthenes.
His most ambitious λόγοι are in praise of cities (*e.g.* his *Panathenaicus*, on
the model of Isocrates), or of deities (as his Εἰς Δία).   His six ἱεροὶ
λόγοι relate to incubations in temples of Asclepius.

Aristeides.

224.   Three noteworthy sophists belong to the fourth century.   Libanius of Antioch (born *c.* A.D. 314) was more than a successful
rhetorician.   His Life of Demosthenes, and his ὑποθέσεις to
the orator's speeches, have a lasting interest.   Among his
Letters are some which he wrote to Basil and to John
Chrysostom (his pupils), to Athanasius, to Gregory of Nyssa,
and to the Emperor Julian.   Themistius (*c.* A.D. 360), a
student of Aristotle (on whom he commented), and in style an imitator of

The fourth- century sophists.

Libanius.

Themistius.

Plato, had a great reputation for eloquence, but, unlike most of the
sophists, disclaimed the power of extemporary speech.   Himerius.
Himerius, after becoming eminent as a teacher of rhetoric
at Athens, was invited by Julian to Antioch in A.D. 362. In his extant
λόγοι, which are largely 'displays,' he often imitates Aristeides, not without
ingenuity and spirit. Gregory of Nazianzus and Basil were among his
pupils.

The Emperor Julian (born A.D. 331, died 363) has a link with the
'sophists' through his encomia on Constantius and on   Julian.
Eusebia, his discourses on pagan deities, and other
rhetorical compositions. These are, however, less distinctive than his
two satirical pieces. The Καίσαρες ἢ συμπόσιον is a witty dialogue on his
predecessors, among whom Marcus Aurelius fares best. When Julian
visited Antioch in 362, the streets resounded with insolent songs, which
(as Gibbon says) 'derided the laws, the religion, the personal conduct,
and even the *beard* of the emperor.' In his Ἀντιοχικὸς ἢ μισοπώγων
he retorts by castigating the manners of that dissolute city. But it is the
large collection of his Letters which gives the best and most interesting
view of his genius, his character, and his tastes.

225. The study of rhetoric, by cultivating expression as an art, encouraged those lighter forms of literature which depend   Lucian.
mainly on style. Lucian, a Syrian of Samosata (*c.* A.D. 120—
200), began life as an itinerant sophist, visiting Ionia, Greece Proper,
Italy, and Gaul. Settling at Athens when he was about forty, he gave
himself to the literary work which made his fame ; in later years he was an
official of a law-court in Egypt. A sceptic and a wit, placed in an age of
shams, Lucian has at least a negative zeal for truth : he does not
believe that man can know, but he is a vigorous enemy of pretence in
religion, philosophy, and literature. The Δὶς κατηγορούμενος intimates his
distinctive claim ; he is the founder of *satiric* dialogue. Rhetoric there
upbraids the 'Syrian' with forsaking her, his first love, for 'the bearded
Dialogus'; while Dialogus complains that the Syrian has dragged him
from his philosophical heaven to earth, and given him a comic instead of
a tragic mask. Lucian's dialogues blend an irony, which he had studied
in Plato, with an Aristophanic mirth and fancy. His satire ranges over
the whole life of his time ; but among his more conspicuous butts are the
Olympian deities (as in Ζεὺς τραγῳδός, Θεῶν διάλογοι, etc.), the philosophers
(as in Ἑρμότιμος, Βίων πρᾶσις, Ἁλιεύς), and the pedantic stylists (Λεξιφάνης,
Σολοικιστής). In thought, he is of no school, but chiefly admires Epicurus,
who to him, as to Lucretius, is the great emancipator from superstition.
Lucian makes us feel, not (as Aristophanes often does) that he is modern,
but rather that he is a detached observer of the ancients : this is due
to his mental separateness from his time, and to a certain tone which
suggests that he wrote for the few, or to please himself only ; here he
sometimes resembles Swift. He has furnished some prototypes of later

work (*e.g.* the ’Aληθὴς ἱστορία, relatively to ‘Gulliver,’ and like books; the Νεκρικοὶ διάλογοι, to Landor's ‘Imaginary Conversations’). As to his purely artificial Attic Greek, it is easy to find blemishes in the grammar; but as a whole, in general texture and in spirit, it is the most remarkable and the best-sustained *tour de force* ever achieved,—not to say by a foreigner (καὶ ταῦτα βάρβαρος αὐτὸς εἶναι δοκῶν, *Bis Accus.* § 34),—but by any post-classical writer of the language.

226. The composition of fictitious letters (such as the ‘Epistles of **Letters.** Phalaris’) was a favourite exercise. From Alciphron (*c.* A.D. 200—220?) we have three books of such letters, supposed to pass between Athenians of an earlier time; they are little sketches of common life, drawn largely from Comedy. The imitative Attic dialect shows in some traits a study of Lucian.

227. The stores of literature in the greater libraries invited discursive readers to compile extracts illustrative of their favourite **Miscellanies.** subjects. Athenaeus, of Naucratis in Egypt, wrote at the **Athenaeus.** end of the second or early in the third century A.D. The date must be subsequent to the death of the Emperor Commodus in 193 (p. 537 F). But the Ulpian whose peaceful death is noticed at p. 686 c cannot be the jurist, who was murdered by the soldiery in 228. Athenaeus has thrown his collections into the form of a conversation among twenty-nine erudite guests who meet at dinner on several successive days. The title of this work (in fifteen books), *Deipnosophistae*, would more naturally mean ‘connoisseurs in dining,’ but is intended to signify ‘learned men at dinner.’ The talk rambles over a wide field,—the pleasures of the table, and everything connected with them,—literature, music, natural history, medicine, grammar, the usages of public and social life. The compilation is a mine of antiquarian lore; in particular, it is a rich source for fragments of Greek poetry (especially Comedy). Quoting upwards of five hundred authors who would otherwise be unknown, Athenaeus gives us a glimpse into the wealth of the Alexandrian Library which he used.

228. Claudius Aelianus (*c.* A.D. 220) has left a large budget of anecdotes on various subjects (Ποικίλη ἱστορία), in fourteen books; and **Aelian.** a mass of notes or stories about the characteristics of animals **Polyaenus.** (Περὶ ζῴων ἰδιότητος). Polyaenus, a Macedonian (*c.* 170 A.D.), is the author of Στρατηγήματα, in eight books, a series of stories describing the stratagems of famous men (and of some women), chiefly in war, but partly also in civil affairs. He writes well, and the work is of considerable interest for history and biography.

229. Stobaeus (John of Stobi in Macedonia) is a compiler to whom we owe no small debt. Two works (parts of one plan) bear **Stobaeus.** his name: (1) Ἐκλογαὶ φυσικαὶ διαλεκτικαὶ καὶ ἠθικαί,—extracts from prose-writers in several branches of philosophy; and (2) Ἀνθολόγιον,—a collection of extracts both in prose and in verse, arranged

under topics. Many precious fragments, especially of poetry, are known
through him alone. As he quotes the Neoplatonist Hierocles (*Ecl. Phys.*
c. 7), who wrote in the latter part of the fifth century, he may be referred
to the end of that century, or to the earlier part of the sixth.

230. Galen (Claudius Galenus) was born at Pergamum in A.D. 130,
and is said to have survived the accession of Caracalla (211).
He was not merely a great physician, but a man learned in   Medicine
all the philosophy and science of his age. One of his   and Philo-
distinctive aims (as seen especially in his treatise on the   sophy.
'Opinions of Hippocrates and of Plato') was to correlate   Galen.
medicine with psychology. 'The best physician,' he held, 'is also a
philosopher.' The compass of his writings was very large. He seems to
have written at least five hundred treatises, of which more than eighty
(excluding spurious or doubtful pieces) are extant. His commentaries on
Hippocrates (the founder of Greek medicine, *flor. c.* 410 B.C.) have been
invaluable to all later students.

231. Sextus Empiricus (*c.* A.D. 220?) was a physician,—his surname
denoting that he belonged to the sect of physicians called
ἐμπειρικοί, who insisted on practical experience as the   Sextus
paramount guide in medicine. Two of his works are extant.   Empiricus.
(1) In one he gives 'outlines' of the Sceptic philosophy of Pyrrhon
(*c.* 320 B.C.): Πυρρώνιαι ὑποτυπώσεις ἢ Σκεπτικὰ ὑπομνήματα. (2) The
other work is a refutation, in 11 books, of all non-sceptic teachers, who
are collectively called μαθηματικοί, as representing various positive μαθή-
ματα (grammar, rhetoric, geometry, arithmetic, astrology, music; logic,
physical philosophy, ethics). The title is, Πρὸς τοὺς μαθηματικοὺς ἀντιρρη-
τικοί. Sextus is valuable as an authority on the Sceptics, and also for the
light incidentally thrown on other systems or disciplines.

232. For the rise and progress of Neoplatonism, and a notice of its
chief exponents in the third and fourth centuries (Plotinus and Porphyry),
the reader may be referred to the section on Greek Philosophy (§ 277).
Stoicism, the other school of thought which was mainly influential
in this period, has as its chief representatives Epictetus (*c.* A.D. 110) and
the Emperor Marcus Aurelius Antoninus (A.D. 131—180). How the Stoic
teaching of Epictetus was recorded by Arrian, has already been mentioned
(§ 217). The *Meditations* (Τὰ πρὸς ἑαυτόν) of Marcus Aurelius
were written, amidst the labours of court or camp, in a   Marcus Au-
private journal, and were first published in 1550 from a MS.   relius.
now lost. His chosen master is Epictetus, whom he follows in fixing his
attention upon practical ethics. The point of view is, throughout, that of
the station which defined his sphere of duty,—the Emperor's. This 'most
human of all books' (as Renan called it) is a complete picture of the
man's inner life. Remembering the character of the age in which Marcus
lived,—remembering also the nature of the trials, public and domestic,
which he endured,—we shall not think Matthew Arnold's estimate of him

exaggerated: 'he is one of those consoling and hope-inspiring marks
which stand for ever to remind our weak and easily discouraged race how
high human goodness and perseverance have once been carried, and may
be carried again.'

233. We have now traced the development of Greek prose literature
from the Alexandrian age down to the period of its decline. The more
prominent works in each of the principal departments have been indicated. But, before concluding this sketch, a brief notice

The Greek romance-writers. is due to a form of composition, slight indeed in its early
essays, and even actually a symptom of decadence, yet of
much interest for literary history, as being the prototype of
the novel. The Greek writers of prose romance in the Imperial age are
called ἐρωτικοί, because the romance was uniformly the story of a hero and
a heroine, the chief motive being love, and the next, ad-

Literary pedigree of the Greek novel. venture. The oldest Greek examples of such stories were
supplied by some lyric poems, now lost, of Stesichorus
(see § 151). In Greek prose the earliest love-story is that
of Abradates and Pantheia in Xenophon's *Cyropaedia*. The Greek writers
of romance under the Empire took much of their scenery, sentiment,
and imagery from the pastoral poets and love-elegists, Greek or Latin:
in plot and situations they gave free rein to their fancy, unchecked by
regard for probability. Parthenius of Nicaea (*c.* 30 B.C.) compiled a little
treatise (extant in an epitome) Περὶ ἐρωτικῶν παθημάτων,—thirty-six short
love-stories, all tragic, dedicated to Cornelius Gallus, and intended as
material for elegiac poetry.

234. Photius, writing in the ninth century, has preserved (*cod.* 94 and
166) outlines of two compositions which were, no doubt,

The first recorded novelists. among the earliest specimens of the Greek prose romance.
Iamblichus (*c.* A.D. 110),—not to be confused with the
Neoplatonist,—was the author of a love-story called Βαβυ-
λωνιακά, which Photius describes as a δραματικόν, *i.e.* a tale of action, with
dialogue. Antonius Diogenes (of uncertain date, but probably earlier
than A.D. 300) wrote 'The marvels beyond Thule' (Τὰ ὑπὲρ Θούλην
ἄπιστα),—in which Deinias met the heroine, Dercyllis, in Thule, and
shared with her many wondrous adventures.

235. The extant representatives of the pre-Byzantine romance are
five in number. (1) Xenophon of Ephesus (probably not

Xenophon of Ephesus. later than A.D. 250) is the author of Τὰ κατὰ Ἀνθείαν

Heliodorus. καὶ Ἁβροκόμην,—the scene being laid at his native city.
(2) Heliodorus (*c.* A.D. 275) is the author of Αἰθιοπικά,—
the adventures of Charicleia, a priestess of Delphi, and the Thessalian
Theagenes, with whom she flies to Egypt, and to whom she is finally married
in Aethiopia. Though inferior in poetic fancy to Longus, Heliodorus is on

Longus. the whole the best of these writers. (3) Under the name of
Longus, we have Τὰ κατὰ Δάφνιν καὶ Χλόην,—a pastoral

romance of much grace and beauty; the scene is in Lesbos. Nothing is
known of the writer, but on literary grounds it may be conjectured that he
lived before A.D. 300. (4) Achilles Tatius, who sometimes
imitates Heliodorus, and lived not much later than A.D. 300, Achilles Tatius.
wrote Τὰ κατὰ Λευκίππην καὶ Κλειτοφῶντα. In tone and taste Chariton.
he is inferior to the three preceding authors. (5) A similar
remark applies to ' Chariton of Aphrodisias ' in Caria,—probably a name
assumed by a writer of the fifth century. The scene of his story, Τὰ κατὰ
Χαιρέαν καὶ Καλλιρρόην, is laid at Syracuse, towards the end of the fifth
century B.C.,—the heroine being the daughter of the Syracusan statesman,
Hermocrates.

236. At the period when feeling and fancy which had once inspired
drama, and then pastoral or elegiac poetry, thus found an
enfeebled utterance in prose romance, the life of Greek Conclusion.
literature was rapidly waning. During the fourth and fifth centuries that
process was hastened by two principal causes. The divergence of
colloquial from literary Greek was becoming more marked. The estrange-
ment of Christians from those Hellenic writings which they associated with
paganism was also progressive; though, even then, not a few of their own
greatest teachers were among the foremost masters of Greek style and
eloquence. In A.D. 529 the edict of Justinian closed the schools of heathen
philosophy. A hundred years later the stream of Greek literature, which
for some fifteen centuries had been practically continuous, might be said
to have ceased. Hellenism gave place to Byzantinism. But the work of
that creative mind, first revealed in the *Iliad*, which had moulded the great
monuments of Hellenic thought and imagination, was to remain as a
permanent inheritance of mankind. After a long age of partial obscuration
or oblivion, the intellectual and spiritual forces which ancient Hellas had
transmitted to Rome were revived in Europe at the Renaissance. By
helping humanity to find itself again, and by diffusing ideas which are still
fruitful in every field of knowledge, those forces determined the transition
from the medieval to the modern world.

W. Christ, *Gesch. der Griech. Literatur*. To the age of Justinian. 6th ed.
1912-1924.—W. Schmid, *Griechische Literaturgeschichte*, I. I Bibliography.
(Epic and Lyric), 1929.—U. von Wilamowitz-Moellendorff, *Die
griechische Literatur des Altertums*, 3rd ed. 1912 and *Hellenistische Dichtung in
der Zeit des Kallimachos*, 1924.—A. and M. Croiset, *Histoire de la littérature
grecque*, 1887-99.—J. Geffcken, *Griechische Literaturgeschichte*, I (before Plato),
1926.—*Shorter Histories*. A. and M. Croiset, *Manuel*. 1900.—Gilbert Murray.
3rd ed. 1917.—Mahaffy, 3rd ed. 1890.—W. C. Wright and H. W. Smyth, 1910.
—P. Legrand, *La Poésie alexandrine*, 1924.—J. U. Powell and E. A. Barber,
New Chapters in the History of Greek Literature, 1921, and 2nd series, 1929.
Further bibliographical details in P. Masquéray, *Bibliographie pratique de la
littérature grecque*, 1914 and in the Bibliographies of the *Cambridge Ancient
History*, Vols. II, IV, V, VII.

III. 2. PHILOSOPHY.

A. PRESOCRATICS.

237. At a time when Central Greece had not yet won itself the leisure necessary for intellectual development, philosophy, the study of first causes or principles, was already cultivated in the colonies of the East and the West. As early as 600 B.C. the Greeks of Ionia asked themselves 'What is this world in which we live?' and as early as 500 the Greeks of Italy and Sicily echoed the question: but it was not till about 450 that the mother-cities, now prosperous at home and abroad, began to interest themselves in speculative inquiry. Thenceforward, until A.D. 529, when the schools were closed by Justinian, philosophy found a congenial home at Athens. Early in the sixth century B.C. certain legis-

The Ionians. lators, rulers, and statesmen—Thales, Solon, Periander, Cleo-
bulus, Cheilon, Bias, Pittacus—were styled in recognition of their practical ability the seven wise men (σοφοί). One of them, **Thales** of Miletus (c. 624–546), was celebrated also for his mathematical attainments, as well as for a theory of the primary stuff or material of the universe. On the strength of this physical speculation he was known to after ages as a philosopher (φιλόσοφος)[1], that is to say, 'a lover of knowledge for its own sake.' Assuming that the various sorts of matter are modifications of a single increate and imperishable substance, but making no attempt to explain why and how the single substance variously modifies itself, he affirmed that all things are water. Next, **Anaximander** of Miletus (born 610/9), accepting Thales' assumption, took for his primary stuff the boundless or indefinite (ἄπειρον), that is to say a substance which, not being any of the four kinds of matter commonly recognized, nor yet a mixture of them, was capable of giving rise to them by 'separating out' (ἐκκρίνεσθαι), and again of re-absorbing them in unending alternation. A generation later **Anaximenes** of Miletus, abandoning this conception of a neutral substance, chose for his primary stuff air, from which the other forms of matter arise by rarefaction and condensation. The Ionian succession ended about 500 with **Heracleitus** of Ephesus, who, protesting against the static conception of reality implied in his predecessors' doctrine of a permanent stuff persisting behind its modifications, held that all things are in flux (πάντα ῥεῖ), that is to say that each sort of matter is constantly changing into another. The world lives in and through change, resting on

---

[1] The word is however said to have been first used by Pythagoras, probably with reference to the distinction of the Three Lives, those of the φιλόσοφος, the φιλότιμος, and the φιλοκερδής.

a give-and-take or 'harmony' of the primary opposites, Hot and Cold, Dry and Moist. In its purest form the stuff of the world is Fire (πῦρ ἀρχή), a substance which though extended in space is not conceived as purely material, but identified with the divine Reason (λόγος) which controls the universe. In a sense, therefore, the four Ionian thinkers named may be grouped together as monists, who, postulating a single primary stuff, took severally for their respective principles, Thales, water modifying itself; Anaximander, a neutral ἄπειρον giving rise to the four commonly recognized sorts of matter by separation; Anaximenes, air giving rise to the other sorts by rarefaction and condensation; Heracleitus, fire passing perpetually into the other sorts in a recurrent cycle.

Ionian monism.

238. Meanwhile, after Anaximenes, but before Heracleitus, **Pythagoras** of Samos, who about 530 removed to Croton in Italy, was preparing the way for new developments. Pythagoras presents a rare combination of qualities as mathematician, philosopher and religious reformer. The school or sect which he founded was closely allied to the Orphic cult-societies already known in South Italy, but its importance lies chiefly in the fact that in place of, or side by side with, the ritual purification of abstinence and taboo was set the inward purification attained by contemplation (θεωρία) of the true nature of the universe as a harmonious cosmos or world-order. This cosmos is a system of numbers or ratios which concrete objects are said to 'represent' (μιμεῖσθαι) in the same sense as later, in Platonism, things represent the Forms; the doctrine apparently originates in Pythagoras' discovery that the concordant intervals of the musical scale are expressible as, or constituted by, numerical proportions. Furthermore the elements of number are Limit (πέρας) and the Unlimited (ἄπειρον), and in the Pythagorean cosmology these are identified with Light (or Fire) and Darkness (or Air) respectively. The blank void of Air or Darkness is ordered or limited by the luminous points of Fire, the heavenly bodies; and the 'harmony of the spheres' (as it afterwards came to be called), which results from the intervals at which they are set, reproduces the ἁρμονία or attunement of the musical scale. Hence numbers are, to use Aristotelian terminology, the 'formal cause' of the universe. Another, and in all probability a later, form of the number-doctrine makes numbers the material cause, the actual stuff of which physical objects consist: the mathematical unit or monad is a point having magnitude, and geometrical solids are identified with physical bodies. For reasons which cannot here be discussed, it is probable that this 'number-atomism,' as it has been called, is later than the Eleatic criticism which next claims our notice.

The Pythagoreans.

In the early years of the fifth century **Parmenides** of Elea embodied his teaching in a poem called *Nature*, which is divided into two parts, *Truth* and *Opinion*. In *Truth*, rejecting alike the dualism of Pythagorean cosmology and the attribution by the Ionians of change or modification to a primary stuff asserted to be the sole, homogeneous content of reality, Parmenides affirms, in the epigrammatic formula

The Eleatics.

the ent (ὄν) *is, the non-ent* (μὴ ὄν) *is not*, the distinction between the One which is and the Many which become or are not. The ent, excluding all variety and change, is the only object of knowledge, increate and imperishable, whole, sole, immovable, determinate, neither past nor future, but ever present; a homogeneous all, one, and continuous, like to a well-rounded and evenly-balanced sphere[1]. These propositions, resulting from thought, not sense, are the objects of knowledge. In *Opinion* he propounds a cosmological theory, Pythagorean in general outline, resting on the assumption of a duality of elements, Light or Fire and Dark or Earth, of which phenomenal things consist, and from which they derive their characteristics. Parmenides' purpose in writing the second part of his poem, the premisses of which patently and avowedly contradict those of the first part, is probably to be explained, following Aristotle, as due to the need felt by the author to 'follow appearances' (ἀκολουθεῖν τοῖς φαινομένοις), that is, to give some account of the world of sense though it be only apparent and unreal.

The task of Parmenides' pupil **Zeno** (born about 489 B.C.) was to furnish indirect support to the monistic doctrine of his master by demonstrating the impossible consequences of a pluralistic hypothesis. His arguments, of which the most famous are certain paradoxes of space, time and number (including the familiar 'Achilles and the Tortoise'), are directed primarily against the later form of Pythagoreanism mentioned above. It is probable that this doctrine of number-atomism was propounded with a view to meeting Parmenides' criticism by building up reality out of numbers regarded as spatial, each possessed of the characteristics of the Parmenidean One.

239. It was indeed this same need to meet the Eleatic criticism that called forth the remaining pre-Socratic systems, those of **Empedocles** of

The Pluralists.   Agrigentum, **Anaxagoras** of Clazomenae, and **Leucippus** of Abdera, all contemporaries of Zeno. Common to them all is the recognition that the change and motion banished from the universe by Parmenides can only be restored, or in other words the world of our experience can only be explained, on a hypothesis which starts not from the One but from the Many. 'The corporealist hypothesis had proved unable to bear the weight of a monistic structure' (Burnet); but it was still possible to 'follow appearances' by explaining the things of sense, their generation and destruction, and their changes, in terms of the combination and separation of a plurality of Parmenidean 'reals.' Further, the systems of Empedocles and Anaxagoras both recognize the need of postulating a cause of motion. In the old Ionian philosophies the primary stuff had been credited, whether explicitly or implicitly, with the property of self-motion, but Parmenides' denial of motion to the Real had, as one of its effects, led

---

[1] Xenophanes of Colophon (born c. 565), a satirist who attacked anthropomorphic polytheism, had asserted the unity of God, or the world, in a pantheistic sense. But he was not a philosopher, and the traditional view that he founded the Eleatic School seems to have originated in a misunderstanding of Plato's allusion in *Sophist* 242 D.

to a more strictly corporealistic conception of 'dead matter,' which needs
an external cause to move it. Accordingly first **Empedocles**   Empedocles.
asserts that the four commonly recognized sorts of matter, fire,
air, earth and water, are 'elements' in the sense of irreducible constituents
of reality; in his own words they are the the 'roots of all things' (τέσσαρα
τῶν πάντων ῥιζώματα); and the universe is governed by two moving causes,
alternately predominant, namely Love or attraction, and Strife or repulsion.
Love, when it ousts Strife, produces a complete aggregation of the interspersed elements in a unity called the sphere (σφαῖρος). Strife, when it
ousts Love, separates the four elements the one from the other. In the
intervals between these crises, Love and Strife by their joint action give
rise to cosmic or particular existences. At the beginning of our own epoch,
when Strife returned and brought about the disruption of the sphere, first
air, fire, earth and water discovered themselves; then trees; then 'whole-
natured' (οὐλοφυεῖς) animals, without distinction of sex or species; reproduction, and the differentiation into species, follow when Strife has
gained further mastery. Bone, flesh, muscle and blood—which last is the
seat of intelligence—consist severally of elements united in determinate
proportions. The organ of sensation, receiving into appropriate pores films
or effluvia given off by the object, apprehends the elements of the object by
means of the corresponding elements contained in itself; for like is known
by like. The evidence of the senses cannot be implicitly trusted, but they
are the only source of knowledge. One of the most important contributions
to science made by Empedocles was the proof that atmospheric air is a
distinct substance, not to be identified either with empty space or with
vapour or mist.

The teaching of his religious poem, the *Purifications*, expounds the
Orphic doctrine of the dual nature of the human soul and its possible
liberation from the 'wheel of birth,' whereby it may attain divinity and immortality. This teaching is not inconsistent with that of the scientific poem:
for while the embodied soul is compound of Love and Strife and interfused
with the bodily elements, it is not a mere function of those elements: when
they perish the soul survives, either to migrate into another body or, finally,
to be purged of Strife and recombine as Love with all Love in the unity of
the sphere.

Secondly, **Anaxagoras** of Clazomenae who, though born a few years
before Empedocles, was later in his intellectual activity, is uninfluenced by
such religious preconceptions, and approaches philosophy   Anaxagoras.
from a purely scientific standpoint. He rejected the Em-
pedoclean hypothesis of 'four roots' on the ground that neither change nor
the infinite variety of matter known to experience can be accounted for by
their combinations. Thus, in the case of animal tissues, flesh and bone were,
according to Empedocles, composed of the four elements combined in
different proportions. But this seemed to Anaxagoras to amount to asserting
that flesh comes from what is not-flesh, and so to violate the implications

G. A.   13

of the Parmenidean doctrine of being. On the other hand, we do observe, in the case of nutrition, flesh and the other bodily tissues somehow built up out of bread, water, etc. The solution must be that every kind of natural substance is composed of particles or seeds (σπέρματα) which themselves contain all the sensible properties of matter. These properties, however, are not yet conceived of as adjectival, as qualities or attributes of a subject, but as things: hence the formula 'there is a portion of everything in everything.' But these quality-things have no existence apart from the seeds, whose various natures they constitute through their quantitatively different combinations. Thus a piece of flesh is not divisible into elements other than flesh, however far division is carried: but it is constituted, whatever its size, by the same indefinite number of quality-things as a grain of wheat or as a piece of any other sort of natural substance. This explains not only nutrition, but every other sort of change known to experience.

In the beginning, when the seeds were indiscriminately mixed, there was a chaos wholly destitute of perceptible form or quality. Then Mind (νοῦς), the rarest and finest of things, external to the formless chaos and independent of it, communicated to it a motion of rotation (περιχώρησις). Thereupon like seeds came together in appropriate regions and produced perceptible aggregates; and so the orderly universe began. Plato and Aristotle agree both in commending Anaxagoras for making his moving cause intelligent, and in censuring him for limiting its activity to the communication of an initial impulse. But it is plain that the teleological system which they desiderate is foreign to Anaxagoras' νοῦς, the operation of which is deliberately so limited, since his aim is to formulate a purely mechanistic system.

Thirdly **Leucippus**, a contemporary of Anaxagoras and Empedocles, propounded a thorough-going atomism, which his successor **Democritus** (born about 450 B.C.) developed and enforced. The elements of things are, they said, the full (πλῆρες, ναστόν) and the empty (κενόν, μανόν), the full being an infinity of immutable atoms (ἄτομα, ἄτομοι), differing from one another in shape and size, while the empty is the vacuum or space[1] without which motion would be impossible. The eternal motion of the atoms is a given fact, calling for no external cause. Moving in all directions atoms impinge upon one another, and vortex motions, resembling the rotation of Anaxagoras, are set up, each of which is the beginning of one of the innumerable worlds. The smaller atoms tend to the circumference, the larger to the centre, and those alike in shape and size come together, forming groups to constitute perceptible bodies. Sensation and knowledge are explained by Democritus on purely materialistic lines. Sensations such as hot and cold, sweet and bitter, are affections which the object produces in the subject. Soul or mind, like fire, consists of atoms which, being fine and spherical, are conspicuously mobile. There are two sorts of knowledge: genuine knowledge which has

The Atomists.

---

[1] Empty space is μὴ ὄν in the sense that it is not Being in the Parmenidean sense: but it nevertheless exists.

for its objects the atoms and the void, and dark knowledge which has for its objects the impressions of sense. Thus whereas Anaxagoras attributed to his seeds all the qualities which we find in things, Democritus tried to express the qualities of things in terms of atoms and void: and whereas Anaxagoras ascribed the creative impulse to an external mind, Democritus conceived the universe as the necessary and accidental (that is to say, undesigned) result of the motion of atoms through space. The work of Democritus does not appear to have become known at Athens until the time of Aristotle; Plato never refers to him, but at a later period Epicurus was glad to borrow his science, and to graft it upon his own unscientific, unphilosophical system.

240. Towards the middle of the fifth century, a spirit of criticism and scepticism succeeds the dogmatism of these pre-Socratic systems. This was natural: in the first place, philosophy had reached the limit of its advance along the line pursued; 'Leucippus had answered the question of Thales in the sense in which Thales had asked it' (Burnet); secondly, the picture of the universe presented was *Philosophy superseded by Humanism.* so unlike that known to the senses that it aroused the profound mistrust of the average man; thirdly, the rapid development of democracy, particularly in Athens and in Sicily, had brought about an urgent need of practical education with a view to public service, a need which men of intellectual ability sought to satisfy. Thus philosophy fell into disrepute; and under the guidance of certain professional teachers, commonly called **Sophists**, who, frankly abandoning the pursuit of truth as elusory, claimed to communicate culture, accomplishments, and aptitude for *Sophistry.* affairs, the intellectual energies of Greece took the direction of Humanism. Amongst the earliest sceptical pronouncements are those of the two most famous sophists, **Gorgias** of Leontini (who visited Athens as an elderly man in 427) and **Protagoras** of Abdera (circ. 500–430). 'Nothing exists' said Gorgias; 'if it did, we could not know it; if we could know it, we could not communicate our knowledge of it to others': so he turned to the study and teaching of rhetoric. 'Man is the measure of all things, of what is, that it is, of what is not, that it is not' said Protagoras, meaning that truth is relative to the individual: so he turned to the study and teaching of literature. Sophistry flourished for about a hundred years; two lines of descent, and five phases or varieties may be discriminated. In the one line, (1) the sophistry of literature, begun by Protagoras and continued by Prodicus and others, gave rise to (2) polymathic sophistry, professed by Hippias, which sought to popularize literature, learning, science and art, and from this again sprang (3) the eristic sophistry of Euthydemus and Dionysodorus, which claimed to teach an art of disputation applicable to all subjects. In the other line (4) the sophistry of forensic rhetoric, beginning at Syracuse with Tisias and Corax about 467, and brought to Central Greece by Gorgias, was succeeded in the early years of the fourth century by (5) the sophistry of political rhetoric, which, ably represented by Isocrates (436–338),

13—2

was in possession of the field when Plato in the character of an educational reformer returned to Athens and established the Academy. In the course of their teaching questions of individual and political morality often arose, and indeed many of them professed to teach 'goodness' (ἀρετή). They were not conspirators against morality: if, as it would seem, they sometimes preached disregard of the current code, it was for the most part the pose of the clever speaker who likes to shock his audience; nevertheless the exclusive study of style and method, and the persistent practice of oratory and debate, may well have encouraged both in teacher and in learner a dangerous disregard of truth.

B. SOCRATES AND THE MINOR SOCRATICS.

241. As Gorgias and Protagoras, despairing of philosophy, had betaken
Socrates: life themselves, the one to rhetoric, the other to literature, so
and person- **Socrates** under like circumstances devoted himself to the
ality. study of conduct. Born at Athens about 470, he was the son
of a sculptor. He served with distinction at Potidaea in 432—429, at
Delium in 424, and at Amphipolis in 422. He gave conspicuous proof
of independence and resolution in his refusal to bend before the demos
in 406 and in his contemptuous defiance of the Thirty in 404. An out-
spoken critic of democracy, he was brought to trial and put to death
in 399 by the restored democrats, who disliked, not so much his supposed
heterodoxy in religion and education, as rather his reactionary politics, which
at this juncture were all the more dangerous because they were not extreme.
Socrates' outward appearance, which was grotesque and even repulsive,
contrasted strangely with the moral virtues and the intellectual gifts
which warranted Plato in pronouncing him 'of all whom he had known,
the best, the wisest, and the justest.' His perfect self-control did not make
him self-righteous, nor his amazing powers of endurance, censorious.
He was scrupulous in his performance of duties to his God, to his
country, to his fellow-men. He was a genial companion and a faithful
friend. Naturally observant, acute, and thoughtful, he had acquired a
remarkable tact in handling questions of practical morality, and in the
course of a life-long war against vagueness of thought and laxity of
speech, had made himself a singularly apt and ready reasoner. In
the humorous affectation of dulness which his contemporaries knew as
'Socrates' accustomed irony,' there was nothing ill-natured, nothing
insincere. He was truthful in deed, in word, and in thought. In
pursuance of what he accounted his divine commission, Socrates spent
his days in the market-place, the streets, the gymnasia, cross-examining
all comers about their affairs, their occupations, their principles of
action, and convincing them of an ignorance which mistook itself for
knowledge. For himself, he was, perhaps, as the oracle had said, wiser

than others, but only in so far as, whilst they, being ignorant, supposed themselves to know, he, being ignorant, was aware of his ignorance. Of his hearers many, regarding his curious questionings with indifference or irritation, shunned Socrates as a bore or worse. Others, seeing in the society of so acute a disputant a good preparation for public life, attached themselves to him temporarily as they might have attached themselves to any ordinary sophist. To others he was a wise counsellor and a perfect ensample of civic and domestic virtue. Finally there was a little knot of intimates who, having something of his enthusiasm, entered more deeply into his principles, and in due course transmitted them to the next generation. Yet even those who belonged to this inner circle were united not so much by a common doctrine as by a common admiration for their master's character and intellect.

242.   The truest account of Socrates' life and activity is not that given in the *Memorabilia* of Xenophon, who was ill fitted to appreciate and expound his fundamental principles, but his own account in the *Apology* of Plato. What Socrates there tells his judges implies a philosophy of life to which Plato remained a constant adherent; and a great part of Plato's own work, at least in the earlier part of his life, was to interpret that philosophy both to himself and to others. How much of his own Plato added in this process is a question on which opinions differ, and will always differ. British scholarship in the last twenty years has inclined   Plato's towards the complete identification of the Platonic with the   Socrates. historical Socrates; nevertheless the evidence of Aristotle appears decisive against this view: the metaphysical basis for Socratic ethics provided by the theory of Forms (Ideas) is Platonic, and the Pythagorean and Socratic influences which combined to suggest it are independent of one another. Nevertheless we should not hesitate to interpret and amplify the testimony of the *Apology* in the light of the ethical doctrines put forward in the earlier dialogues, particularly *Euthyphro, Laches, Charmides, Protagoras* and *Gorgias*.

Socrates tells the court that his one concern has been to help his fellow-citizens to 'care for their souls' ($\psi v\chi\hat{\eta}s$ $\grave{\epsilon}\pi\iota\mu\epsilon\lambda\epsilon\hat{\iota}\sigma\theta a\iota$). By this phrase he meant the cultivation of a way of life based on rational moral insight, which should determine all human activities and pro-   The 'Care of vide a standard for the valuation of external so-called goods,   the Soul.' these being in fact good only in so far as they are rightly employed, in virtue of moral insight or wisdom, in the furtherance of man's spiritual well-being. Wisdom is to be attained both by training of the character, and by clarification of our moral judgments; and these two processes are really one and inseparable, since a right moral judgment must necessarily find its expression in right action. Hence Socrates declared that 'Goodness is Knowledge'—a formula widely current in his   'Goodness day and often in the mouths of the Sophists, but one to which   is Knowledge.' he gave a deeper and truer meaning—and that 'No one does wrong voluntarily'—which is another way of putting the same thing. Further, seeing that the knowledge expressed in right moral judgments is not that of obligations externally imposed but that of our own good, the good that the ignorant pursue inconsistently and waveringly, it is the only source of Happiness or well-being (εὐδαιμονία). Finally, Goodness is a unity, not a sum of virtues which can be possessed apart from one another: for knowledge must necessarily determine every part of our conduct alike.

Socrates had no ready-made system of morals to inculcate: he disliked the term 'disciples' used to describe his associates, and he asserts in the *Apology* that he never taught anyone anything. Each man must find the truth for himself; this conviction arose partly from a genuine humility, which is one side of the Socratic 'irony' (εἰρωνεία or self-depreciation), and partly from a profound distrust of the Sophistic pretensions to 'teach virtue,' as though it could be summed up in rules and precepts. All that Socrates could do was to help men to think for themselves; and so in the *Theaetetus* Plato makes him compare himself (with an allusion to the calling of his mother, Phaenarete) to a midwife. It followed that 'Dialectic,' question

Dialectic.

and answer, was the only method open to him in the performance of his divinely-appointed duty as a physician of souls: and incidentally we may believe that the more a Platonic dialogue conforms to this procedure, the more genuinely Socratic is its content. Most frequently the object of a Socratic conversation was the definition of an ethical term, such as Justice, Temperance, Courage. In the application of the dialectical method two processes are distinguishable, the destructive process by which the worse opinion was eradicated, and the constructive process by which the better opinion was induced. In the former, the so-called ἔλεγχος, taking his departure from a seemingly remote principle to which the respondent readily assented, Socrates would draw from it some unexpected but undeniable consequence inconsistent with the opinion impugned. In this way the respondent was brought to pass judgment upon himself. If, as often happened, having been thus reduced to a state of doubt or perplexity (ἀπορία), the respondent at this point withdrew from the inquiry, something had been gained, inasmuch as he was now more or less conscious of his ignorance. If however he was willing to make a further effort, Socrates would direct him to suitable instances, and so help him to frame a generalized opinion which did not depend upon the passions and the prejudices of the moment. In this constructive process, though the element of surprise was no longer necessary, the interrogative form was carefully retained, because it secured at each step the conscious and responsible assent of the interlocutor.

243. Plainly Socrates had no pretension to be the founder of a school: and it is now commonly recognized that the connexion of the so-called 'Socratic schools' with him is only indirect. These are three in number,

'Socratic schools.'

the Cynics, the Cyrenaics and the Megarians. The **Cynics** are said to have derived their name from the gymnasium of Cynosarges, where their reputed founder, Antisthenes of Athens, was in the habit of teaching. But an alternative derivation is from the nickname 'dog' (κύων) given to **Diogenes** of Sinope, who was the real originator of the Cynic way of life. It is true that the germ of their anti-social and negative morality can be found in the Antisthenes of Xenophon's *Symposium*, and Diogenes was very likely in-fluenced by him; but the tracing back of Cynicism to Socrates through Antisthenes is the product of a much later age. For Aristotle the 'Anti-stheneans'—he never calls them Cynics—are concerned only with logic: they maintained that nothing can be called by any name but its own, and denied the possibility of definition other than an enumeration of parts, of predication which is not identical, of falsehood, and of contradiction. Cynicism proper is not a philosophy in the sense of a body of doctrine, but a way of life exaggerating or caricaturing the simplicity of Socrates, and ostentatiously denying the elementary duties and the ordinary decencies of civilized society. Plato is said to have called Diogenes 'a Socrates gone mad.' In pronounced contrast to this movement is that of the **Cyrenaics**, who have more claim to the title of philosophers; but it is very doubtful whether the school originated with the **Aristippus** of Cyrene known to us as an intimate of Socrates, or existed at all in the early fourth century; for they are unknown to Aristotle. More probably their real founder was a grandson of the same name, who has been confused with the elder Aristippus. The Cyrenaics found the end of existence in the pleasure of the moment. Happiness is the aggregate of such pleasures. Virtue is good in so far as it is a means to them. One pleasure is as good as another; nevertheless, the wise man will so enjoy that he shall never be the slave of enjoyment: he will use pleasure, but he will not be carried away by it. With this ethical scheme was connected the psychological theory that pleasure is a smooth movement, discomfort (πόνος) a rough one. Finally, the **Megarian** school is certainly derived from Socrates in the sense that its founder, **Eucleides** of Megara, was an intimate of Socrates, to whom Plato and other Socratics resorted after the master's death. The school, however, was commonly regarded as continuing the Eleatic doctrine, and though Eucleides seems to have made some attempt to interpret the Socratic doctrine of Goodness in an Eleatic sense, asserting 'that the Good is the One, though called by many names,' his followers appear to have devoted themselves to the dialectical method of controversy originated by Zeno, with the consequence that they are known to us mainly as 'eristics' abounding in sophistical fallacies.

The Cynics.

The Cyrenaics.

The Megarians.

Whatever parts of Socrates' teaching were inherited by these three schools, they were no more than broken fragments. On the other hand **Plato**, 'the complete Socratic,' accepting it as a whole and developing it harmoniously, was led to formulate a comprehensive system of metaphysical and ethical philosophy.

C. PLATO AND THE OLD ACADEMY.

244. Plato, son of Ariston, was born in or about the year 428, and belonged to an Athenian family of distinction, especially on his mother's
Plato's family. side. His two elder brothers, Glaucon and Adeimantus, are the interlocutors of Socrates in the *Republic,* and his mother's brother Charmides and her cousin Critias, afterwards one of the Thirty, were also closely associated with him. Through these relatives it is highly probable that Plato came to know Socrates as a boy; but from the terms in which he speaks of him in the Seventh Letter we may infer that he was not among Socrates' closest associates, unless perhaps in the last
Plato's youth. few years before 399. As a young man in his twenties his main interest was not in philosophy, but in practical politics: his ambition to enter on a public career was, however, quenched by the misgovernment both of the oligarchs in 404 and of the restored democrats. The execution of Socrates by the latter finally convinced him that the whole fabric of society was unsound, and that politics, alike in Athens and in other Greek states, lacked all principle. Hence his main purpose throughout the remainder of his life was to impress upon men the need of applying first principles to the task of government. His passionate conviction of this need finds its clearest expression in his greatest work, the *Republic,* where he puts it into the mouth of Socrates in almost the same words[1] as he himself uses in the seventh *Letter*. This proves clearly, if proof were needed, that he accepted Socrates' fundamental precept of the paramount importance of knowledge in human life.

245. We know little of the details of Plato's life, with the exception of his two visits to the Syracuse of Dionysius the Younger, in 367 and 361; but of these we have an account from the best source possible, namely his
Visits to Syracuse. own letters. It is enough here to say that they represent an attempt, rendered fruitless chiefly thanks to the character of Dionysius, to apply in practice the conclusions which he had reached by middle life in regard to the education of a ruler. Earlier, in 388-7, he had visited the court of the elder Dionysius; the story goes that the tyrant became offended with him, and caused him to be sold as a slave at Aegina; but there is no mention of this in the *Letters*. It is probable that before this first visit to Sicily, he had travelled to Egypt, Cyrene, and Magna Graecia. On his return to Athens he established the school or college[2]

[1] In the seventh *Letter* (326 A) he says "Finally I saw clearly that the system of government in all states now existing is bad......The human race will not see better days until either the kind of men who follow philosophy rightly and genuinely acquire political power, or else those who have political power be led by some dispensation of Providence to become real philosophers." Cf. *Rep.* v. 473 D.

[2] The school, which in the eye of the law was a religious brotherhood ($\theta i\alpha\sigma o s$), was a foundation for the encouragement of education, study and research. In addition to directing the studies of the members, the head, and perhaps some of the seniors, delivered formal lectures. A picture of a discussion-class in the Academy is given by the comic poet Epicrates (Frag. 11, Kock).

known as the Academy, of which he remained the active head until his death in 347. It is generally believed that the programme of higher education described in *Republic* VI–VII was the programme of the school; if so, the studies pursued were mainly mathematical, *The Academy.* leading up to the 'greatest study' of Dialectic or Philosophy. Biological studies also were undertaken, though perhaps this was a later development. It is certain, moreover, that social and political science were not neglected: for Plato's ultimate object was to train students to be statesmen and legislators, not pure scientists out of touch with practical life: their scientific and philosophical training was a means to an end. That the Academy won a high reputation as a school for legislators is evident from the fact that several Greek cities applied to it for help in organizing their constitutions or drawing up codes of law (Plutarch, *Adv. Colotem*, 1126 C): it is illuminating to learn that Eudoxus, the famous mathematician and astronomer, did such work for Cnidus, and Aristotle for his native Stageira.

246. What has been said of the Academy is an indication that, alongside of the primary impulse, derived from his own experience and his memory of Socrates, towards the reformation of society, there existed *Practical and* in Plato another impulse, distinct though not ultimately con- *philosophical* flicting, towards the attainment of philosophical truth. On *interests.* this side he is the successor of Ionian science, of Eleaticism, and of Pythagoreanism. Aristotle tells us that from early manhood he had associated with Cratylus the Heracleitean, and we may believe that metaphysical and scientific interests were strong in him in the formative years of adolescence, before they were swamped by the experiences of social and political rottenness in his middle twenties, and that they re-asserted themselves in later life.

247. With the exception of the *Apology of Socrates*, all Plato's writings take the form of dialogues. At the outset this was a natural and appropriate form, due partly to the desire to preserve the external character of Socratic conversations, partly to the fact that he had no dogmatic system to propound. Later, when Plato's own philosophy had grown more definite, exposition rather than search for truth was required, and the dialogue form often, not always, becomes less appropriate and less real. The order of the dialogues cannot be certainly established, important though it is for tracing the development of Plato's thought. But there is good ground for regarding the *Laws*—said to have been left unfinished at the *Order of the* author's death—as the latest, and stylistic tests, initiated by *dialogues.* Lewis Campbell in 1867 and perfected by C. Ritter, have convinced scholars that *Sophist, Politicus, Timaeus, Critias, Philebus* and *Laws* form the latest group, probably separated by some years from those which precede them. The present writer accepts Ritter's further conclusions, which distinguish a middle group, consisting of *Republic, Phaedrus, Parmenides* and *Theaetetus*, and an early group embracing all the rest. Internal evidence dates the *Theaetetus* with great probability in 368-7. Beyond this there is much diversity of opinion, but it seems reasonable, on grounds both of content and of form, to regard the slighter dialogues, of which the most important are *Euthyphro, Charmides, Laches*, together with the *Apology*, as preceding the large-scale dialogues in which Plato's powers as a literary artist are shown at their height, viz. *Gorgias, Symposium, Phaedo*. The *Protagoras*, a master-piece of dramatic art, is usually held to precede the three last-named, though Prof. A. E. Taylor puts it after the *Gorgias*. Further than this it is not possible to go with any degree of probability.

248. Modern scholars are agreed that the conception of an 'earlier' and a 'later' Platonism, in the sense which implies a radical reconstruction in certain dialogues of doctrines put forward in others, is mistaken. On the other hand, Aristotle knows of a latest form of Platonism, in which the Forms are identified with numbers, that is not represented but only fore-shadowed in the latest dialogues. In the dialogues themselves we see not reconstruction, but development; some scholars see more development, some less, and it must be realized that the view taken in this sketch, where space precludes argument, would not meet with universal acceptance.

On the basis of what has been said above it will be convenient, if not strictly exact, to speak of four groups of dialogues. In the first

First Group.

of these the characteristic procedure is the search for a de-finition of an ethical term, such as Piety (*Euthyphro*), Temperance (*Charmides*), Courage (*Laches*). No conclusion is reached, but the Socratic equation of Goodness with Knowledge is regularly accepted as conditioning the search, and the inadequacy of common opinions is brought out. These dialogues are often called 'Socratic,' but in fact they are not merely descriptions of Socrates' conversations, real or imaginary: they should rather be regarded as partly apologetic, in the sense of being a further revelation of the per-sonality of Socrates sketched in the *Apology*, partly as Plato's thinking out on paper of the implications of Socrates' principles. The *Protagoras*, which

Protagoras.

is here regarded as closing this group, has a more positive con-tent. Whereas the first dialogues had approached the problem of explaining the Socratic equation from the side of particular virtues, Good-ness is now viewed as a whole of inseparable parts, and tentatively explained as identical with Knowledge in the sense of a 'measuring art' which estimates pleasures and pains with a view to attaining the maximum nett amount of pleasure or good. Although Socrates is made to express doubt of this hedonistic conclusion almost as soon as it is uttered, it may be taken to represent Plato's temporary view.[1] The dialogue, which confronts Socrates with the greatest of the Sophists, is further designed to display the un-reality of the Sophistic claim to 'teach goodness,' though the social theory put into the mouth of Protagoras seems to contain hints for an ethical

---

[1] The interpretation of the *Protagoras* here given has been often put forward, but is rejected by Taylor and others. It is of course incompatible with the belief that a constant ethical doctrine, that of Socrates himself, is expounded in all dialogues down to the *Republic*.

doctrine to follow later in the *Republic*. Other dialogues in which the pretensions of Sophistry are exposed are the *Euthydemus* and *Hippias Minor*, both probably close to the *Protagoras* in date.

249. The *Gorgias* may be placed on the border-line of the first and second groups. The ideals of pleasure and political power are here subjected to an examination which shows their worthlessness in contrast with the ideal of Socrates, who is the only true statesman of Athens, since her so-called statesmen have always pursued material, not moral and spiritual, ends. The feature that connects this dialogue with the second group is a tinge of asceticism and 'other-worldliness,' which probably reflects the awakening of Plato's interest in the religious side of Pythagoreanism. Moral goodness is now for the first time conceived in Pythagorean fashion, as a balance between opposing factors in the soul, a κόσμος corresponding to the κόσμος of the universe (506–7).

Gorgias.

In the dialogues of the second group Pythagorean influence is prominent, and combines with Socraticism to shape a definite ethical and political doctrine based on a metaphysical foundation. We are told by Cicero (*Tusc. Disp.* 1. 32), who is here thought to be following Poseidonius, that Plato went to Italy to become acquainted with the Pythagoreans, and the same writer elsewhere (*De Finibus*, v. 87) says that he undertook this journey 'now that he had drawn his picture of Socrates, in order to add thereto the doctrine of the Pythagoreans and to learn about those things which Socrates rejected.' This testimony seems to preserve a valuable truth: about the year 387 Plato's thought began to take a wider sweep: his old interest in 'the nature of things' as expounded by the Heracleitean Cratylus was re-awakened, and he was led to ask where, if there is no stable reality in this flux of things, we can find an object of knowledge. The procedure of Socrates, in his search for definitions of ethical terms, implied that such an object is to be found; it must therefore be found not in the things of sense but in a higher order of reality to which the law of πάντα ῥεῖ does not apply. This higher order is a world of eternal, immutable Forms (εἴδη or ἰδέαι). Here and there in the dialogues of the first group there are hints of an attribution of independent existence to the 'universals' of Socratic definition: but it is only now that the doctrine (commonly known as the Theory of Ideas) becomes prominent and clearly defined. Moreover, in the *Phaedo*, where it finds its fullest presentation, we can see clearly that it is shaped under Pythagorean influence. The Forms are not merely the common element in the particulars grouped under them regarded as existing apart from those particulars: they are perfect, and sensible things approximate to them, represent them inadequately, or strive to reach their perfection. They are, in fact, like the concepts of the mathematician, whose straight line and triangle are objects of reason, but unknown to sense: they are the models (παραδείγματα) of which sensible things are imperfect copies (εἰκόνες). In the *Symposium* they are described in a passage of exalted imagery as the objects of mystical contemplation.

Second Group: Pythagorean influence.

Theory of Ideas or Forms: Phaedo.

In the *Meno* and *Phaedo* the doctrine is associated with the Orphic-Pythagorean doctrines of Reminiscence and Rebirth: the Forms are known by the discarnate soul, but this knowledge is lost at birth and only gradually recoverable through the 'suggestions' found in imperfect sensible copies; it is significant that in the *Meno*, where the Reminiscence doctrine first appears, it is the *a priori* character of *mathematical* knowledge that is thus accounted for.

The nature of the relation between Forms and particulars is expressed in a variety of ways: the inadequacy of them all is admitted later in the *Parmenides*, and it is doubtful whether Plato ever reached a satisfactory solution of this problem: he does not appear to do so in the dialogues. Sometimes the Form is immanent in the particulars, sometimes the element in particulars which makes them copies of the Forms is something distinct from the Form itself; sometimes the relation is indicated only by the vague terms μίμησις (imitation, representation), μέθεξις[1] (participation) and κοινωνία (communion).

250. In this earliest presentation of the Theory of Forms its ethical application is for the most part only implicit; it is in the *Republic*,[2] which opens the third group of dialogues, that Plato uses it as the foundation of a comprehensive ethical and political system, re-interpreting in its light the demand of Socrates that society should be governed by statesmen possessed of knowledge. The knowledge of the philosopher-rulers is to be nothing less than a complete survey of reality, that is of the Forms seen in their mutual relations and dependent on the supreme Form of the Good, the absolute principle which gives both reality and intelligibility to the universe. Guided by such rulers, human society and human conduct will reproduce the order of nature or true being. In the scheme of education designed for the ordinary 'guardians' (afterwards called 'auxiliaries,' ἐπίκουροι, to distinguish them from the 'perfect' guardians or rulers) righteousness (δικαιοσύνη) is interpreted as a proper functioning of the three parts of the soul, Reason, Temper and

Third group: Republic.

---

[1] The metaphysical theory is bound up, or confused, with a logical theory in which μέθεξις means the relation of a subject (particular) to a predicate (universal).

[2] The content of this great dialogue is so rich and varied that any brief outline must necessarily omit much of importance. Its formal thesis is that 'Righteousness is better than Unrighteousness.' The principal argument—which includes descriptions of the ideal state and its degradations, together with the theory of philosophic virtue—occupies books II—IX. The tenth book consists of two appendices, (*a*) on imitative poetry, supplementary to what has been said about μουσική in the third book, (*b*) on rewards and punishments in a future life, a matter expressly left out of account at the beginning of the second. The ideal state is an aristocracy, in which there are three classes: (1) the artisans and husbandmen, who have no share in the administration; (2) the auxiliaries, who, having been selected in infancy, and trained to philosophy under the eye of the state, act, from the age of thirty-five to that of fifty, as commanders in war, and subordinate magistrates at home; (3) the guardians, who, continuing at the age of fifty to be distinguished in knowledge and in action, rule their country, their fellow citizens, and themselves, in accordance with the good.

Appetite, in a concord to which corresponds the concord between the three classes of the State. In this doctrine of a tripartite soul and a concord or harmony of its parts Plato is again drawing on a Pythagorean source.

In the *Phaedrus* the mystical apprehension of the Forms is presented as in the *Symposium*, but the doctrine of Reminiscence is now rationalized into a discernment of the Form as a unity 'gathered together by reasoning from many acts of perception' (δεῖ γὰρ ἄνθρωπον ξυνιέναι κατ᾽ εἶδος λεγόμενον, ἐκ πολλῶν ἰὸν αἰσθήσεων εἰς ἓν λογισμῷ ξυναιρού-μενον (246 B). This gives the first dim apprehension of the Form, and requires to be followed by the clarifying process of Dialectic, which employing Collections (συναγωγαί) and Divisions (διαιρέσεις) will determine the true content of a Form by setting it in the context of the totality of Forms. Plato is here partly concerned with providing a classificatory scheme for the study of 'natural kinds,' an interest which became more prominent in the Academy, we may suppose, about this time. Parallel with the re-interpretation of Reminiscence is a new conception of the soul as self-moving substance and cause of all physical movements: its immortality is a necessary consequence of this, and is no longer rested, as in the *Phaedo*, only on a reasonable faith.

251. The *Parmenides* begins by a string of criticisms directed by the founder of the Eleatic school against the theory of 'participation.' The purpose of these has been variously understood, but the most likely explanation is that they were originated by the Megarians, the contemporary representatives of Eleaticism, who refused to allow any reality whatever to the sense-world. Seeing, however, that the criticisms take the form of asserting, not so much that 'participation' is impossible, as that it is a term susceptible of various meanings none of which is satisfactory,[1] it is reasonable to suppose that the Megarian criticism had suggested to Plato the need for a fuller and more exact account of the relation between Forms and particulars than had been given in the *Phaedo* and *Republic*. If this is so, no such account is to be found in the dialogues; it has been suggested that it was contemplated in the *Philosophus*, a projected but un-written dialogue which was to complete the trilogy begun by the *Sophist* and *Politicus*. Plato gives no hint in the *Parmenides*, nor indeed anywhere else, that the Theory of Forms is to be reconstructed, or that the Forms are to be limited to 'natural kinds.'[2]

The main purpose of the *Theaetetus* is, by a refutation of empiricist theories of knowledge, to provide indirect support for the thesis that knowledge is of the Forms alone. The relativist doctrine of Protagoras is refuted both in regard to sensation, where Plato interprets it as resting on the flux-doctrine of Heracleitus, and in regard to judgment. The carefully elaborated theory of sensation here given, whatever its origin, is to be understood as accepted by Plato himself.

Phaedrus.

Parmenides.

Theaetetus.

---

[1] 133 A ἄλλο τι δεῖ ζητεῖν ᾧ μεταλαμβάνει.

[2] For a conjectural explanation of Aristotle's statement in *Met.* 1070 A 18, which seems to limit Forms to natural kinds, see Ross's edition of the *Metaphysics*, Introduction, p. 2.

252. The contents of the latest group of dialogues can be here only
very briefly indicated. The *Sophist* is mainly occupied with
logical problems, suggested perhaps by Antisthenes and the

Fourth group: Sophist.

Megarians: the possibility of significant negative predication
is established, and the combination of Forms with one another (κοινωνία
εἰδῶν), implied already in the *Republic*, is shown to be a necessity of thought.
The *Politicus* discusses the merits of political constitutions from a less idealistic

Politicus.

standpoint than the *Republic*: the rule of the philosopher-
king is still the best, but in default of his appearance society
must rest on sound laws. The purpose of the dialogue is, as Burnet says,
'to determine the provinces of realism and idealism in politics,' and Plato's
general attitude is close to that adopted in the advice given to the followers

Philebus: the latest Platonism.

of Dion in the Seventh and Eighth Letters. In the *Philebus* the
'mixed life' of Knowledge and Pleasure is advocated as con-
stituting the good for man; but Pleasure is the inferior in-
gredient, and whereas all kinds of knowledge are admitted only certain
'pure' types of pleasures are sanctioned. The dialogue contains, moreover,
what seems an adumbration of the latest Platonism, known to us from
Aristotle, in which the Forms are identified with numbers. Aristotle says
(*Met.* 988 A 8 sqq.) that both sensible things and Idea-numbers were analysed
into a material and a formal principle, and that while the material principle
for both alike was 'the great and small' (τὸ μέγα καὶ τὸ μικρόν), the formal
principle of things was the Idea-numbers[1], and the formal principle of these
latter was the One. The *Philebus*, in an analysis of πάντα τὰ νῦν ὄντα ἐν τῷ
παντί, declares that all things are a mixture of πέρας and ἄπειρον, and the definitions and illustrations here given of these two elements warrant us in regarding
them as in principle identical with the numbers and the great-and-small
respectively. The mixture thus effected is termed μικτὴ καὶ γεγενημένη οὐσία,
and is said to be the work of νοῦς. Here we find a point of contact with the

Timaeus.

Timaeus, which must be close to the *Philebus* in date. The
Timaeus takes the form of a cosmological myth, in which the
elements of rational philosophy, on the one hand, and of poetical fancy
and religious faith on the other cannot be disentangled, because they are
consciously blended in the writer's mind. The 'divine artist' (δημιουργός)
working with a given material fashions the universe, a living creature compound of soul and body, on the model of the eternally existent Forms. The
analysis of physical objects reproduces the *Philebus* doctrine of πέρας and

---

[1] The general purport of the Idea-number doctrine is well given by Ross (*op. cit.*
p. lxviii): 'In describing the Ideas as numbers, as successive products of the One and the
Great-and-small, he may have seemed to himself to be stating in the clearest way the fact
which is so often expressed in the later dialogues, that in the ideal world itself there is
multiplicity as well as unity. And the series of the numbers produced successively by the
One seemed to him to express most clearly the hierarchy of the Ideas—linked through
fewer or more intermediates with the supreme Idea—which was in his thoughts as early
as the *Republic*.'

ἄπειρον: the constituents of the 'four elements' are four of the five regular geometrical solids, themselves built up out of two types of elementary triangle, which 'inform' or limit *Space*, the formless ὑποδοχή or 'receptacle' of all Becoming. To attempt to rationalize or explain away the δημιουργός would be a mistake; the fact is that Plato, in his later years, advanced more and more towards a theistic metaphysic.[1] It was doubtless in this direction that he turned to find an answer to the question why and how things come to participate in Forms: it is, in fact, God that brings it about.

253. In the *Laws*, his latest work, Plato is insistent on the necessity of religious belief as the foundation of social morality, and puts forward a proof of Divine Providence resting on the doctrine of soul previously announced in the *Phaedrus*. There are good souls and bad: but amongst the good there must be a supreme soul which controls all the movements in the universe. The tenth book, in which this argument occurs, is notable as the earliest attempt to expound philosophical theism. For the rest, the *Laws*, which takes the form of drawing up a code of law for an imaginary colony, contains much of Plato's ripest thought on the practical problems of education and of jurisprudence.

The Platonic authorship of the *Epinomis*, an appendix to the *Laws*, was questioned in antiquity, but the tendency of modern scholarship is to accept it. Its chief point of interest is certain astronomical arguments which seem to imply Plato's acceptance of the late Pythagorean theory of the earth's diurnal revolution, not round the sun but round an invisible 'central fire.' Unfortunately for the history of science, the opposed view of a stationary earth at the centre of the universe, advocated by the Platonist Eudoxus, received the countenance of Aristotle.

254. Plato's successors as heads of the School merit little attention. The first was his nephew **Speusippus**, who, in ethics, refused to recognize any kind of pleasure as good. In regard to the number theory, whereas Plato, we are told, had recognized mathematical numbers as intermediate between idea-numbers and sensible things, Speusippus discarded the idea-numbers and retained the mathematical as the primary entities. We also learn that he postulated independent originative principles for different sorts of substances, 'thus' says Aristotle 'making the universe episodic, like a bad tragedy.' He was succeeded in 339 by **Xenocrates**, who identified the idea-numbers and the mathematical, a doctrine which seems to make havoc of Plato's and which is rightly pulverized by Aristotle. His successor, **Polemo**, appears to have confined himself to Plato's ethical teaching, disregarding its metaphysical basis. With **Crates**, who succeeded Polemo in 270, the so-called Old Academy ended.

---

[1] As Prof. Taylor well says 'The *Republic* is permeated by religious faith, but Theism as a principle of metaphysical explanation only makes its appearance in Plato's latest dialogues.'

D. ARISTOTLE AND PERIPATETICISM.

255. Born in 384 at Stageira in Chalcidice, **Aristoteles**, son of Nicomachus, came to Athens in his eighteenth year, and entering
Aristotle's
life. the Academy, was attached to it as learner and teacher for at
least twenty years. After the death of Plato in 347, Aristotle
spent three years at the court of Hermeias of Atarneus. A visit to Mytilene
followed. In 343 or 342 he was called to Macedonia to undertake the
education of Alexander, and there he remained until his pupil was about
to start upon his expedition into Asia. In 335 or 334 Aristotle returned to
Athens and established in the Lyceum the so-called Peripatetic school.
Twelve years later, having been accused of offences against religion, he
retired to Euboea, where he presently died in 322.

Both Plato and Aristotle wrote works intended for the reading of the
educated public as well as lectures for their schools. In the
Dialogues and
Lectures. case of Plato it is the former class of writings that have
survived in the dialogues: but Aristotle's published dialogues,
which had a reputation for literary excellence, are lost to us save for
fragments: what we possess represents his lectures, being for the most part
his own notes, or memoranda of lectures delivered, which were posthumously
edited by his pupils. The principal treatises, under their medieval titles,
may be classified as follows:

i. logic: the *organon*, including *categoriae, de interpretatione, analytica
priora, analytica posteriora, topica, de sophisticis elenchis.*

ii. metaphysics: *metaphysica.*

iii. physics: *physica, de caelo, de generatione et corruptione, meteorologica.*

iv. biology: *historia animalium, de partibus animalium, de incessu animalium, de generatione animalium, de anima, parva naturalia.*

v. ethics and politics: *ethica Nicomachea, ethica Eudemia, politica.*

vi. literature: *rhetorica, poetica.*

256. It has been seen that biological studies, based on a classification
of fixed natural species, became an important feature of the
Natural
kinds. Academy's activity in Plato's later years. In the Platonic
system this classification was part of Dialectic, that is to say
of the general articulation of the totality of Forms in a single comprehensive,
philosophical survey. Aristotle, rejecting the ideal of a single body of knowledge, and repudiating the doctrine of Forms as existent apart from the
particulars, addressed himself to the development of the theory of fixed
species. There are, he held, in nature certain determinate kinds of animate
existence, namely, animal and vegetable species (*metaphysics* Z ii etc.).

Apart from accidents or attributes which are not common to
Material and
formal causes. all the members of a kind, each of its several members is, in
thought, though not in fact, resolvable into two constituents,
or has two *causes* (αἴτια), namely, *matter* (ὕλη), recipient of form, and *form*
(εἶδος, μορφή), determinant of matter. Of these, matter—out of which, by

combination of the primary qualities, hot and cold, wet and dry, the four elements are developed (*de gen. et corr.* B ii, iii)—is, in the last analysis, a purely indeterminate substratum or potentiality; form is the sum of the characteristics which distinguish the member of the kind as such. Hence, while it is in virtue of its matter that the particular exists in time and space and that it becomes perceptible, it is in virtue of its form that it is what it is and that it is known. From this point of view the specific form is spoken of as τὸ τί ἦν εἶναι, *the being what it always was* or real essence of the particular.

257. But beside the material cause and the formal, which together constitute the particular (τόδε τι) or composite (σύνολον), Aristotle required, to complete his conception of animate existence, a moving cause (ἀρχὴ κινήσεως) and a final cause (οὗ ἕνεκα). For these he looked, proximately, to a previous member of the species, which member as moving cause, having the continuance of the species for its final cause, transmits the specific form to its offspring (*metaphysics* Z viii); for 'man generates man' (ἄνθρωπος ἄνθρωπον γεννᾷ): and, ultimately, to the *prime unmoved mover* (πρῶτον κινοῦν ἀκίνητον), namely God, who, existing apart as pure form or complete reality without any element of matter or unrealized potentiality, has, or rather *is*, an eternal activity of thought in which the distinction of thinking subject and object of thought is transcended. He is said to move the universe as being the object of its desire (κινεῖ ὡς ἐρώμενον, *metaphysics* Λ vii): that is to say, the orderly motions of the heavenly bodies and the orderly succession of animal and vegetable life on earth are due to an attraction, which causes all things to approximate, in the different degrees possible to them, to the perfection of the eternal divine thought. Hence the government of the universe is monarchical: so Aristotle asserts, but his account is vitiated by two defects: in the first place, his doctrine of God's activity as one of self-contemplation alone precludes any real divine government or providence; secondly, the relation to God of the other unmoved movers—the 'Intelligences,' as the Schoolmen called them—which Aristotle's astronomical theory needs to cause the movements of the planetary spheres, is left unexplained.

Moving and final causes.

258. By soul (ψυχή) Aristotle means 'the first actuality of a natural organized body': that is to say, the activity which, whether displayed or not, is implicit in the living body, and distinguishes it from the body which is lifeless (*de anima* B i, ii). In plants soul is nutritive. In animals it is at any rate nutritive and sensitive, and may be appetitive and motive also. In man alone it is not only nutritive, sensitive, appetitive, and motive, but also intellectual. Sensation—in which sense receives the form of sensible objects without their matter, as wax receives the impress of a seal—implies a ratio between object and subject, and requires an intervening medium (*de anima* B iii—xii). Beside the five special senses, of which touch is primary, Aristotle recognizes a common or central sense, which (1) is conscious of sensation, and (2) distinguishes the impressions received by one special sense from those received by another (*de anima*

Psychology.

Γ i, ii: *de somno* ii: *de iuventute* iii). The 'common sensorium,' the seat of consciousness, is the heart. Intellect is explained on the analogy of sense: as the senses receive the forms of sensible objects, so intellect receives intelligible forms, *i.e.* universals. The mind, until it actually thinks, is a mere capacity or potentiality of thought, and when active is one with its object. To account for the transition from potentiality to actual thinking, Aristotle finds it necessary to postulate an 'active intellect' as an efficient cause: this intellect is always operative, and is said to create the objects which the 'passive intellect' receives. This doctrine is left by Aristotle in great obscurity, and its interpretation is uncertain: he appears to indicate an impersonal thought, which is not part of the human soul but is a necessary presupposition of our thinking. To identify this with God, as Alexander did, is natural: nevertheless the identification seems incompatible with the doctrine of *metaphysics* Λ: God has not *our* knowledge, but knows only himself.

259. What is it then that Aristotle holds to be primarily existent (πρώτως ὄν)? It is not Plato's transcendental idea. It is not the *universal* (καθόλου), the common characteristic or characteristics by which species are combined in a genus, or particulars in an artificial group. It is not the purely receptive substratum called matter. It is not the particular in which form and matter are conjoined. It is the form, and nothing but the form. That is to say, the primarily existent is the sum of the specific characteristics of the particular, in contradistinction to its recipient matter and to attributes which accidentally belong to it: and these specific characteristics of the particular, in so far as they are available for purposes of classification, constitute the object of knowledge. Thus what exists and can be known is *species*. But the species exists only in its members, and therefore it is in them that it must be studied. Such is the doctrine explicitly stated in *metaphysics* Z. Nevertheless, in the *categories*, an early work of Aristotle, but certainly genuine, primary existence is ascribed to the particular or composite of form and matter. This terminological discrepancy does not however imply inconsistency of thought. For the primarily existent form, of which we hear in the *metaphysics*, is form immanent in a particular: and the primarily existent particular, which is spoken of in the *categories*, is the particular in so far as it represents the species to which it belongs, and no further.

First existence.

260. When he had settled his philosophical position and his relations to Plato, Aristotle was free to address himself to his proper function, that of making sciences; and accordingly his extant writings deal, not with metaphysic only, but also with logic, physics, biology, psychology, ethics, politics, and literature.

Sciences.

Of all Aristotle's achievements, the greatest perhaps was the invention of logic. The group of treatises generally known as the *organon* includes an enumeration of categories or heads of predication; a study of the quality, quantity, and conversion, of propositions; a detailed investigation of the syllogism and its figures;

Logic.

a summary discrimination between *induction* (ἐπαγωγή) or generalization from known particulars in regard to those particulars, and *example* (παράδειγμα) or inference from known particulars in regard to unknown particulars, effected by means of a *general* more or less perfectly certified; a theory of scientific research; a treatise on disputation; and a classification of fallacies. In dealing with these matters, Aristotle distinguishes between *dialectical debate*, by which the premisses of demonstration are provisionally justified, *demonstration*, the true method of Science, which deduces universally valid propositions from primary and immediately known premisses, and *sophistry* or *eristic*, pursued, irrespectively of truth, with a view to argumentative success. In the main, logic still is what Aristotle made it. In physics and biology his work has been superseded: for, here at any rate, πάντων εὑρετὴς χρόνος. But his physical speculations occupied the field for more than eighteen centuries: and modern biologists speak with respect of his insight and his powers of observation.

Natural sciences.

261. Three treatises on ethics are included in the Aristotelian canon: (1) the *Nicomachean ethics*, said to have been so called because edited by Aristotle's son Nicomachus, (2) the *Eudemian ethics*, now generally acknowledged to have been edited, not composed, by his pupil Eudemus of Rhodes, (3) the *magna moralia*, a comparatively short compendium of Aristotelian ethics based on the treatises just mentioned and compiled probably early in the third century[1]. It was probably given the name it bears because each of its two books or volumes is considerably larger than each of the ten books and the seven or eight books into which the *Nicomachean ethics* and the *Eudemian ethics* are respectively divided. Books v, vi, vii of the *Nicomacheans* are word for word the same as books iv, v, vi of the *Eudemians*. Recent investigation has shown that these books cannot originally have formed part of the *Eudemians*, since they belong not to the earlier stage of Aristotle's ethical doctrine, when speculative wisdom (σοφία) and practical (φρόνησις) had not yet been distinguished, but to the later stage when they were sharply contrasted, as in the *Nicomachean Ethics*. It is however not certain that they originally belonged to the latter treatise either.

Ethical treatises.

262. Aristotle's ethical teaching had for its aim, not to establish the distinction between right and wrong, nor to investigate the means by which right and wrong may be discriminated, nor to formulate moral rules, nor to improve moral rules already existing, but—on the assumption that current morality, whether capable of improvement or not, justifies itself theoretically and explains itself in practice—to ascertain what scheme of life is, for an individual duly qualified by nature and by circumstances, the most desirable and the best. According to the *Nicomachean ethics*, man's highest good (ἀνθρώπινον ἀγαθόν) or well-being (εὐδαιμονία) consists in the discharge of his appropriate function, and is

Ethics.

---

[1] It has been attributed by W. Jaeger to Dicaearchus, a pupil of Aristotle.

therefore to be found in an activity of soul characteristic of the best and completest of virtues, such activity being sustained throughout a complete period of existence (I. vii. 15): whence it follows that external goods are not parts of well-being, but, in so far as they are necessary to the display of the activity aforesaid, conditions of it. Now virtue is of two sorts, moral and intellectual. Moral virtue—the virtue of the semi-rational division of soul, that is to say, of the appetites and emotions, which results when that division is obedient to the rational division—is 'a permanent state of the soul which chooses the mean relatively to ourselves, a mean defined by judgment in such manner as a man of practical wisdom would define it' (II. vi. 15). The chief moral virtues are courage, temperance, liberality, munificence, magnanimity, self-respect, gentleness, justice. The intellectual virtues are, practical judgment, the virtue of that subdivision of the rational division which controls the semi-rational division, and speculative wisdom, the virtue of that purely intellectual subdivision of the rational which may perhaps be called reason (νοῦς). Since reason is obviously the best part of the soul, its virtue, speculative wisdom, which has for its appropriate activity contemplation (θεωρία), is the best of virtues. Whence it follows that the highest good attainable by man is to be found in the life of contemplation or philosophy, the practical life of moral virtue ranking second to it. Nevertheless, the philosopher will loyally do his duty as a member of society. The highest good, being an activity, brings with it the highest pleasure.

263. Such being the question proposed, and such the answer returned to it, it remains to enumerate briefly the subjects dealt with in the several parts of the *Nicomacheans*. In Book I, having stated his subject and settled preliminaries, Aristotle formulates in general terms his conception of human happiness, and indicates a popular psychology sufficient for his immediate purpose. Book II defines moral virtue and enumerates the moral virtues. The voluntary and the involuntary are investigated in III. i—v, so far as is necessary for the understanding of the term 'deliberate,' used in the definition of moral virtue. In III. vi—xii, IV, and v, the conception of moral virtue as a mean is justified by a detailed examination of the moral virtues and of the corresponding vices or formed habits of excess and defect. Book VI has for its subject the intellectual virtues, and concludes with an emphatic assertion of the intimate relationship which subsists between moral virtue and practical wisdom. In Book VII are included, first, an account of the imperfect moral states called continence and incontinence, and secondly, a treatise on pleasure and pain, which are respectively identified with unimpeded and impeded activity. Books VIII and IX deal with friendship, which is entitled to consideration both because friendliness is a social virtue, and because friends are the most important of external goods. Under this head Aristotle handles the relations of the citizen to his neighbour, a matter which does not fall directly within the scope either of the *ethics* or of the *politics*. Book X contains (1) a theory

The *Nico-macheans ethics.*

of pleasure, which is here regarded as the concomitant of an activity, (2) the interpretation, in the light of results obtained, of the general formula propounded at I. vii. 15, to the effect that the contemplative and practical lives rank respectively first and second, and (3) a disquisition upon the relations of private well-being to public institutions, which serves to connect the present treatise with the *politics*.

264. As in the *ethics* Aristotle is concerned with the well-being of the individual, so in the *politics* he treats of the well-being of the community. The city or state (πόλις), as opposed to the horde **The *politics*.** (ἔθνος), is a complex organism developed out of the village (κώμη), which again springs from the family (οἰκία). The city is then the end or consummation of society, and man is a civic or political animal. Within the family there are three principal relations—master and slave, man and wife, father and children—which relations subsist each for the benefit of its correlative members. The first book, which deals with these matters, and the second, in which certain polities, ideal and real, are criticized, together form a sort of introduction to the work. In Book III Aristotle propounds his theory of polity. The best of cities would be one in which absolute power was exercised for the benefit of all the citizens by one person, or more persons than one, superior to the rest in mind and in body. But this is an unattainable ideal. In default of it, right polities (ὀρθαὶ πολιτεῖαι) are those in which the sovereign (κύριον), whether one, few, or many, rules for the benefit of the community: perversions (παρεκβάσεις) are those in which the sovereign, whether one, few, or many, uses its power for its own advantage. Of the right polities—aristocracy, monarchy, and polity proper—aristocracy is the best (III. xv. 1286, but compare *ethics* VIII. xii. 1160), because the aggregated virtue of several is better than the solitary virtue of one: and polity proper (πολιτεία), in which all rule and are ruled in turn, is the least good. Of the perversions—democracy, oligarchy, and tyranny—democracy, which has the smallest power for evil, is the least bad, and tyranny, which has the greatest power, is the worst. Two principles hold for all the right polities. First, neither birth nor wealth nor virtue has a claim to the exclusive possession of power: all the excellences which operate in the state are entitled to consideration: and consequently all free men must be admitted to a share in the administration. Secondly, irresponsible authority is too great a temptation even for the best of men; and therefore, whether in aristocracy or in monarchy or in polity proper, the sovereign must submit itself to the 'passionless intelligence' of law. In Books IV (VII) and V (VIII) we have the scheme of a perfect or ideal state, in which the virtue of the man and the virtue of the citizen are identical. The life of the perfect state is one of practical action. But practical action does not imply aggression and conquest. For the perfect state, the end is not war but peace, just as for the best man, the end is not business but leisure. Unlike Plato, Aristotle did not hope to realize his ideal: but an impracticable scheme may carry practical lessons, and accordingly Aristotle proceeds to plan the institutions of a

new Callipolis. Unluckily this part of the treatise is incomplete: but at
any rate we learn what he had to say in reply to Plato about the use and
the abuse of music in education and otherwise. The investigation of (1) the
ideal state, is then theoretical or speculative. In the three books which
remain Aristotle addresses himself to practical applications, and on the
strength of a careful study of the several known forms of polity proper,
democracy, oligarchy, and tyranny, inquires (2) what is the best of practicable constitutions, (3) what sorts of constitution are suitable to given
sorts of people, (4) how a constitution may be established and maintained
in accordance with given assumptions or conditions, (5) what is the best
constitution for the generality of states, (6) what circumstances tend to
change, to overthrow, and to maintain, the several sorts of constitution.
Polity proper, in which, as all rule and are ruled in turn, the middle class
is influential, is, he thinks, not only the most stable of constitutions, but
also for the generality of states the best, being indeed inferior only to
the unattainable ideal. For its maintenance he would rely, as Athens did
and the United States do, upon supreme or constitutional laws (νόμοι),
unalterable, or alterable only with special formalities; to which constitutional laws, upheld by courts of justice, all ordinary enactments
(ψηφίσματα) must conform. The eight books of the *politics* are commonly
read in the order I, II, III, VII, VIII, IV, VI, V: but it is clear that there was no
original order, the work being a compilation of separate treatises. Aristotle's
learning, tact, and wisdom, are nowhere seen to greater advantage than in
this masterly treatise.

265. It is a familiar paradox that, whilst Plato and Aristotle are
commonly regarded as 'the two poles of human intelligence,' Cicero speaks of Academics and Peripatetics as
'agreeing in fact, differing only in appellation.' There
is truth in both appreciations. The two philosophers
started from different standpoints: for, to the metaphysician Plato, that
which is actual in time and space was *ipso facto* unreal, whilst, to the
physicist Aristotle, that which is actual in time and space was the only
reality. But for both alike knowledge is of the Form, the permanent
universal, not of the mutable, transient particular. And, when the followers of Plato abandoned the theory of Ideas, and the followers of
Aristotle lost something of their master's eagerness in the study of nature,
the difference between the two schools was inconsiderable, especially in
ethics, the subject of which Cicero was principally thinking. The greatness
of Aristotle was not fully understood until the middle age, when the whole
of civilized Europe acknowledged his intellectual supremacy, and rightly
saw in him 'the master of those who know.'

266. Aristotle's successor was **Theophrastus**, head of the school
from 323 until about 288, author of numerous treatises in
almost every department of inquiry. Of these there are
extant two botanical works and fragments of a valuable

Academicism and Peripateticism.

The Peripatetics.

history of physical opinions, a storehouse upon which subsequent epito-
mators have drawn largely: also a fragmentary discussion of metaphysical
problems and the graphic sketches known as the *Characters*. **Eudemus**, to
whom the *Eudemian ethics* was once ascribed, rivalled Theophrastus in erudition. Both these philosophers showed little independence in speculation,
adhering to the main lines of their master's system. But **Strato** of
Lampsacus, who was for eighteen years head of the Lyceum, in succession
to Theophrastus, made an attempt to carry physical research farther and to
develop Aristotle's cosmology into a system of naturalism. He rejected
the transcendent deity as the first cause of motion, and accounted for all
phenomena by the operation of natural necessity. In psychology he
ignored the distinction between intellect and the sensitive soul. He
referred all sensation to the central principle of the soul (ἡγεμονικόν), which
he located in the brain. After Strato the Peripatetics popularized ethics or
devoted themselves to historical, rhetorical, and philological studies to the
comparative neglect of logic, physics, and metaphysic. When Andronicus
of Rhodes had published a new edition of Aristotle's writings, *circa* 70 B.C.,
the arrangement and exposition of the master's doctrine generally became
the occupation of the school. Alexander of Aphrodisias (*circa* A.D. 198—211)
was the most celebrated expositor: his commentaries on the *topica, meteorologica, de sensu,* and parts of the *analytica* and *metaphysica* are preserved,
together with dissertations of his own on many disputed points of doctrine.

E. LATER SCHOOLS: EPICUREANS, STOICS, SCEPTICS.

267. By this time the original impulse of curiosity in Greek inquirers
was well-nigh exhausted. The organization and growth of   Characteris-
the sciences which had proceeded so vigorously in the fourth   tics of the
century were followed by a marvellous development, particu-   Later Schools.
larly of mathematics and astronomy, in the Alexandrian age: but the great
men of science, even when adherents of this or that school of philosophy,
for the most part troubled themselves little about metaphysics, so en-
grossed were they with their own special investigations.   Political and
social changes, the loss of Greek freedom, the opening of the East to
Greek culture under Alexander's successors, the decay of patriotism,
similarly tended to discourage speculative thought. Philosophy, to obtain
a hearing, must offer the individual what he most needs, and just then
the search for truth had less attraction than the search for happiness.
In the accepted threefold division of philosophy, practical *ethics* on a basis
of reasonable certainty was held to be more important than the other two
sciences, viz. *logic* and *physics* (including cosmology and psychology).
In all three departments the later schools make free use of the ample
materials which their predecessors had accumulated, and as a rule decline
to hazard a new solution of the old problems. Materialism, in one or

other of its phases, was the prevailing tendency. Whatever exists acts and
is acted upon, but to the thought of the age action through contact was
alone conceivable. Thus the corporeal nature of mind and mental phenomena became a presupposition of their reality.

268. Born in 341, son of an Athenian schoolmaster who had settled as
a colonist in Samos, **Epicurus** began early the study of
philosophy under Nausiphanes, a Democritean. In after
days he boasted that he had been self-taught, and was a
merciless critic of all other philosophers. Having made disciples in
Mytilene and Lampsacus, he removed in 306 to Athens and there founded
a school. The scene of instruction was his garden: the society which met
there was united by close friendship and veneration for the master: it
resembled a church rather than a philosophical school. In this peaceful
retirement Epicurus wrote some 300 separate treatises, the most important
a work *On Nature* in 37 books, which had reached Book xv in 300/299,
while Book xxviii was finished in 296/5. A voluminous writer, he dis-
dained for the most part the embellishments of style, and aimed at clearness, not always successfully. He died in 270. His doctrines were passed
on almost unaltered from generation to generation by his followers, of
whom the Roman poet Lucretius alone has any claim to distinction. An
epitome of his system is extant in three epistles preserved by Diogenes
Laertius, two of which are certainly from his own hand; we have also a
collection of some 42 excerpts, known as the *Fundamental Tenets* (κύριαι
δόξαι).

Epicurus. Life and writings.

To this eminently practical thinker, the one thing needful was wisdom
for the conduct of life; experience was the only basis of
certainty and the study of nature desirable only in so far
as it freed men from superstitious terrors. Hence Epicurus
headed a reaction against science. The logic and metaphysic of Plato
and Aristotle he distrusted as dealing with words, not things. For
logic he substituted 'canonic,' an inquiry into the Canon, or test of truth.
The exact sciences, mathematics and astronomy, rested, he thought, on
unproved assumptions. Historical and literary studies were superfluous
intellectual luxuries. 'Keep clear of all liberal culture' is his advice to
a young friend. Sick of the verbal logomachies of his predecessors, hostile
to *a priori* argument and suspicious of abstract terms, he appealed to the
common sense of the plain man. He made sensation the standard of
truth. Internal feelings and the perceptions of sense are
always true and trustworthy. Even beyond momentary im-
pressions, certainty extends to 'preconceptions' (προλήψεις), *i.e.* the general
notions or mind-images resulting from repeated identical sensations, and
further to what are called 'apprehensions of the mind' (ἐπιβολαὶ τῆς
διανοίας), by which the mind cognizes certain images, such as those of the
gods, directly, without the intermediacy of sense. For whatever we feel to
affect us—our minds or our senses—must be real in virtue of so affecting us.

General As-pects.

Canonic.

The senses, then, are infallible. Scepticism is self-contradictory. What possible means have we of checking the evidence of sense? One sense cannot convict another, for they all have different objects. Reason cannot be invoked as umpire, for reason depends for its data upon the senses. Thus Epicurus is forced to explain error as the result of mental activity: opinion and fancy, movements in the mind consequent upon and distinct from the movement of sensation, mix false with true: our judgment is often deceived, our senses never. Yet even in everyday life, much more in physical inquiries, it is necessary to go beyond the direct testimony of the senses and frame opinions respecting the unknown. Epicurus had grasped the problem of inductive logic, that what we do not see has to be explained on the analogy of what we do see, the unknown by familiar and observed fact. Here a new canon is required. An opinion or explanation, he holds, is true if it is supported by observed facts and not contradicted by them; if unsupported or contradicted by facts, it is false.

269. In the belief that ignorance and superstition were the chief obstacles to happiness, Epicurus aimed at presenting such a physical theory as would exclude divine interference and render absurd the supposition of design in the arrangements of the world. Accordingly he reproduced the atomism of Democritus. But there is an enormous difference in the spirit of the two systems: for Epicurus was supremely indifferent to the accuracy of scientific results so long as his practical object was attained. In regard to celestial phenomena, such as thunder and eclipses, he refused to be restricted to one out of several admissible conjectures. When he has suggested possible causes which involve no supernatural intervention, enough has been done: in the painstaking research of the 'system-mongers,' in truth for its own sake, he took no interest (he called it ἰδιολογία and κενὴ δόξα). Again, while in general appropriating Democritus' principle that 'every event has a necessary cause,' a principle indispensable if divine interference is to be excluded, Epicurus spoiled the consistency of his system by a violent protest against invariable natural necessity. 'It were better,' he says, 'to believe the tales concerning the gods than be the slaves of inexorable fate.' The protest is apparently intended to justify (1) freedom of the will (cf. τὸ παρ' ἡμᾶς ἀδέσποτον), which he in some sense assumed, and (2) the spontaneous deflection (παρέγκλισις) of the falling atom so that it swerves slightly out of the perpendicular, an expedient to account for collisions of the atoms and world-making which would otherwise be in his view inexplicable.

However, in spite of these inconsistencies, Epicurus deserves credit for preserving faithfully the main outlines of the atomistic theory. All is either body or empty space; everything real is corporeal, the properties of bodies having no independent existence and time itself being an 'accident of accidents' (σύμπτωμα συμπτωμάτων). The atoms are immutable, although possessed of parts which are mentally distinguishable; the changing properties of bodies are due to the motion of their atoms. Soul

is a corporeal thing, a compound of fragile delicate atoms kept together by
the body enclosing them, to which they in turn transmit sensation. Besides
a nameless substance, which is the seat of sensation, atoms of air, fire and
wind combine to constitute soul: irrational soul (*anima*, which feels), if
spread all over the frame, rational soul (*animus*, *mens*, thought, passion, will),
if close packed in the breast. Perception and imagination are due to the
impact, in the one case upon the senses, in the other upon the material
mind, of the films or husks (εἴδωλα) which are continually thrown off from
the surface of bodies (στερέμνια). It is a corollary of this doctrine that the
mental images of the gods have real causes, and hence is inferred that the
gods are immortal and perfectly happy beings, constituted of the finest
atoms and dwelling in the lucid interspaces between the worlds (μετα-
κόσμια): with the working of that 'vast automatic mechanism,' the universe, they have nothing to do.

From such a school scientific discoveries could hardly be expected;
it is, however, surprising to find with what wonderful imaginative insight
Lucretius, following doubtless in the footsteps of his master, has sketched
the earlier stages of human progress and the origin of language and the
arts.

270. Epicurus held that pleasure is the sole good, pain the sole evil.

Ethics.

This was a necessary consequence of his epistemological
position: for the only good and evil known to the senses are
pleasure and pain. By pleasure may be understood (1) the exciting 'pleasure
of motion' (ἡ ἐν κινήσει), or (2) the calm 'pleasure of equilibrium' (ἡ κατα-
στηματική). But since every pleasure of the first kind is conditioned by a
painful want which it removes, Epicurus pronounces it inferior to the second
kind; it is indeed to be sought for, but not beyond the limit at which it
ceases to conduce to the second. This latter he conceived not merely
negatively, as absence of pain, but as a positive harmony of body and
mind. The body is the original source of all pleasant sensation—nor
could Epicurus conceive of a good wholly independent of sense: but
mental pleasures are of higher value as extending into the past and
future by memory and expectation. Actual bodily pains, however severe
(and experience shows that the pains of disease, if chronic, are tolerable;
if violent, do not last long), may be allayed and outweighed by ideal
mental pleasures recalled or anticipated. This was one consideration
making for the attainment of happiness. Another was the inculcation
of an almost ascetic plainness of living: the simplest and easiest satisfaction
of 'natural and necessary' desires, the neglect of the 'natural but not
necessary' wants to which luxury ministers, and the extirpation of those
other vain desires 'unnatural and unnecessary' which rest on a mere sentiment. Virtue again, though not an end in itself, is valuable as a means
to pleasure: no one can live pleasantly without living wisely, well and
justly. To explain the origin of civil society Epicurus falls back upon the
fiction of the social contract. Natural justice is a compact of expediency

for the prevention of mutual injury, and the wise man is a gainer by observing the compact. The great deterrent from wrong-doing is the alarm and sense of insecurity attending it. A high value is attached to friendship, which, although in theory only desirable on utilitarian grounds, is yet spoken of as in itself life's greatest blessing.

271. The Stoic school took its name from the fact that its founder, Zeno (perhaps 336/5 to 264/3), lectured in the στοὰ ποικίλη, a colonnade of the Agora at Athens adorned with the frescoes *Stoics.* of Polygnotus. His native town, Citium in Cyprus, contained Phoenician as well as Greek inhabitants, but there is no real evidence that he was of Phoenician descent. Attracted to Athens by his taste for philosophy, he studied under Crates the Cynic, Stilpo the Megarian, and the Academics Xenocrates and Polemo, before he opened a school of his own. He was held in great respect in his later years by the Athenians and by Antigonus Gonatas, King of Macedon. His successor in the headship of the school was Cleanthes of Assos who died in 232/1; to him succeeded Chrysippus of Soli in Cilicia (*circa* 280—Ol. 143, 208/4), who completed and consolidated the Stoic doctrine, adding largely on the logical side, and surpassing even Epicurus in the number of his treatises or 'articles,' more than 700. Of these three philosophers only fragments survive, except the *Hymn to Zeus* of Cleanthes. The Stoics were preeminently moral philosophers, proud to be reckoned among the Socratics. Zeno began as a Cynic[1]; and indeed the Cynic mode of life, though not inculcated in the *Relation to predecessors.* school, was always tolerated as a justifiable protest against prevalent corruption. In the end, dissatisfied with Cynic contempt for theoretic knowledge and culture, Zeno came under other influences. From the Old Academy he took the conceptions of 'natural objects of desire' and 'life according to nature.' The Peripatetics he followed in a mass of physical details and, with a difference, in his distinction between active force and passive, inert matter. But Pantheism, the chief feature of Stoic physics, was learnt not from Aristotle but from Heracleitus, whose own doctrine of Logos or Reason has been completely obscured for us by its transference to the later system. Out of these multifarious elements Zeno and Chrysippus endeavoured, with more success than their contemporaries, to construct a comprehensive theory of being and knowledge as the basis of conduct.

272. Their system also included formal logic, in which they differed fundamentally from Aristotle. Instead of taking the proposition *S* is *A* to express a relation between a particular subject *Logic.* and a universal, they regarded it as expressing an *event in S*. Every significant proposition expresses an event occurring in a physical body: it is known as λεκτόν, for only the states and the acts of physical bodies can be

[1] The main ideas of Cynicism which Zeno adopted are, the self-sufficiency of virtue, the strength of the moral will, the distinction of things good evil and indifferent, the ideal of the wise man, and cosmopolitanism.

the objects of discourse and reasoning. Conformably to this analysis of propositions, the Stoics appear to have discarded the Aristotelian categorical syllogism, and substituted a form of the hypothetical and the disjunctive in which neither of the premises nor the conclusion contains a universal. In fact they regarded science as consisting, not in the establishment of general laws, but in a chain of singular propositions concerned with individual subjects. Not only universals, or abstract general notions (ἐννοήματα), and λεκτά are unreal, as being incorporeal, but time and space also. Again innovations were made in the treatment of the categories. Aristotle, whose object was to tabulate the various predicates attaching to a given concrete subject (a σύνολον of form and matter), framed ten 'heads of predication' (γένη, or σχήματα, τῶν κατηγοριῶν): these might be reduced to four, substance, quantity, quality, and relation (which the other six illustrate), or in the last resort to two, substance and attribute: further, Aristotle made these heads of predication all coordinate. The Stoics replaced this coordination by a succession. The four highest genera (γενικώτατα) are special determinations of the widest conception, Something (τὶ), each in turn being more precisely determined by the next. They are (1) substratum or subject-matter, ὑπο-κείμενον, (2) essential quality, ποιόν, (3) mode or accident, πὼς ἔχον, (4) relation or relative mode, πρός τί πως ἔχον. The subordination of all to a single substratum, implicit in each, indicates a definite view as to the general formal relations of real existence.

273. With the Epicureans the Stoics maintain that the corporeal alone is real, since only that which can act and be acted upon really

Physics.

exists. Hence the qualities of bodies (conceived as forms or shaping elements) and mental states (τὸ ἡγεμονικόν πως ἔχον) are necessarily corporeal. But while the Atomists hold that the qualities of organized matter—life, sense, intelligence—are absent from atoms, and conceive motion as obeying rigid mechanical laws, the Stoic affirms the adaptation of means to ends and takes the teleological view of nature as the outcome of intelligence. His fundamental tenet is the unity of the world, which is not an aggregate of unrelated existences—not a fortuitous concourse of atoms—but a living thinking being, an organic whole animated and informed by reason, its parts united by 'sympathy' and its development proceeding by an inner necessity according to unalterable law. Various lines of argument converge in demonstrating the existence and perfection of this great First Cause, and the absolute dependence of all particular things upon it. This one reality is known, in its various relations, by various names: Zeus, Nature, Providence, Destiny, Reason, Law, Fire, Aether, Breath (πνεῦμα). Analysis discloses, it is true, *two* factors or principles (ἀρχαί) in all existence: that which is active, or God; that which is acted upon, matter void of quality (ἄποιος ὕλη). But since they are inseparable they must not be regarded as coordinate, but as the two-fold aspect of the one reality. Matter—extended, continuous (not discrete, like the atoms), infinitely divisible—is taken in a positive sense, as the material *out of* which particular things are shaped: it is also called substance (οὐσία). Thus it stands in sharp contrast to Plato's 'receptacle of generation, *in which things become*' (*Timaeus*) and to Aristotle's potentiality, which so long as it is indeterminate is sheer negation (στέρησις). The active principle or moving cause (the sole cause which the Stoics recognized, and necessarily corporeal) has the all-important property of tension (τόνος), which is manifested in different grades in the different classes of particular things: as a principle of continuity (ἕξις) in inorganic bodies, of growth in plants (φύσις), as the vital principle of animals (ψυχή) and the reason (λόγος) of man. The properties of things depend upon the tension of air-currents penetrating their substance, and entirely commingled with it (κρᾶσις δι' ὅλων). Here, it should be observed, Aristotle's specific forms are materialized and the axiom that two bodies cannot simultaneously occupy the same space is denied. The life of the universe recurs in a never ending series of cycles, each exactly reproducing its predecessors. At first Zeus and the world were identical. Out of his eternal substance (conceived, with a distant anticipation of the nebular hypothesis, as a mass of fiery vapour or warm breath) the orderly universe was evolved by successive stages, the four elements separating from the homogeneous mass and proceeding on their 'way up and down' in Heracleitean phrase (ὁδὸς ἄνω κάτω). The world and all its parts are stages in the transformation of the primitive substance: as they have grown up, so they will decay; and the end is a general conflagration (ἐκπύρωσις) when the world is reabsorbed in Zeus. While upholding the unity of the divine nature, the Stoics felt free to ascribe divinity to its manifestations: thus they accepted, and rationalized, the popular mythology, usually assigning a physical interpretation to the legends, and defended the belief in omens and the practice of divination.

274. Man is a microcosm; his soul is an emanation from the soul of the universe. This fiery breath appears in its greatest refinement in the ruling part (ἡγεμονικόν), or inner self. All soul, as such, has the faculties of perception and activity. The human soul has also an intellectual faculty (διάνοια, νοῦς). In the ruling part, or centre of the soul's life, the psychic functions first become actual. What are called 'parts' of the soul—the five senses and the powers of speech and reproduction—are better regarded as functions of the one central soul: they are defined as means of communication (πνεύματα νοερά) between the ruling self and the sense organs. By the possession of reason even the lower faculties of perception and desire, which man shares with the brutes, are raised to a higher level, and become rational faculties; in perception man is self-conscious; his activity is self-determined. All vital processes, thought included, are physically conditioned by exhalation from the blood (ἀναθυμίασις). The soul survives death, but in the most favourable case only until the end of the present cycle. Thus the Stoics reject absolutely the Platonic assumption of irrational faculties. The unity of the soul is

Psychology.

their main tenet—in fact, the key to their psychology: man feels, knows, wills with the whole soul.

Such a psychology favours an empirical theory of knowledge. Perception is conditioned by the presentation (φαντασία) of an external object, upon which the percipient subject has then to pass judgment. Cleanthes crudely explained this presentation as an imprint (τύπωσις), like that of a seal upon wax: Chrysippus preferred the vaguer term modification (ἑτεροίωσις) of mind, which, be it remembered, is material. The content of sensation is not always valid: here the Stoics joined issue with Epicurus and sought to lay down the conditions of possible hallucination. The criterion is found in καταληπτικὴ φαντασία, i.e. a presentation which directly involves, or leads to, κατάληψις or 'apprehension' by the mind of the object presented to sense: it is the peculiar clearness and distinctness of such presentations that causes the mind to give its assent (συγκατάθεσις) to them as being true images of the object, provided the percipient be sane and in good health. We are told that Chrysippus recognized perception (αἴσθησις) and preconception (πρόληψις) as criteria, as well as the καταληπτικὴ φαντασία: what is probably meant is that these are two kinds of κατάληψις, the former applying to sense-presentations, the latter to presentations of reason, that is to say to notions (ἔννοιαι) derived from sense-experience, the common notions spontaneously and uniformly developed in all men. Under the pressure of controversy with the sceptics of the New Academy, further conditions were accepted as necessary; otherwise the perception is not of the true kind which involves 'apprehension.' In perception as such no knowledge is contained: the mind's activity by tension and assent converts sensation into apprehension (κατάληψις) and knowledge. In Zeno's simile φαντασία, κατάληψις and ἐπιστήμη correspond to the open hand, the bent fingers, and the clenched fist.

Here it is convenient to notice two sections of Stoic ethics, treating (1) of desire or 'impulse' (ὁρμή), (2) of emotion, whose importance is mainly psychological. As the unity of the soul was emphasized by the denial of a division into rational and irrational parts, so under the single head of desire were included all springs of action, animal instincts as well as impulses of reason or passion. The Stoics contended, against Epicurus, that the original impulse of all sentient creatures is not to pleasure but to self-preservation, the maintenance of the organism unimpaired. This appetite is anterior to, and presupposed in, all desire of particular pleasures. In rational beings desire, moulded by reason, is directed to that order and harmony of nature and of human society, which is moral good (καλόν, honestum).

As the Stoics recognized no irrational faculty and attributed to the one inner self all mental processes, even impulses from which vicious acts proceed must be functions of reason, although of reason perverted. Such impulses are the emotions or passions (mental pain and pleasure in the present, fear and vicious desire in regard to the future). They may be roughly described as unnatural, irrational movements of soul, or more precisely as impulse in excess (ὁρμὴ πλεονάζουσα). The excess is due to a false or over-hasty judgment (δόξα πρόσφατος): hence, by a confusion (which Zeno himself is said to have anticipated and avoided) of intellectual error with its effects, emotion was sometimes said itself to be false judgment, *e.g.* fear to be the belief that an impending misfortune is an evil. Holding these views the Stoics were unable to acquiesce in the mere regulation of emotion, and demanded its entire suppression. As false judgments are under our control, so also are their effects the emotions. Nevertheless certain 'right emotional states' (εὐπαθείαι) are allowed, viz. rational joy, rational cautiousness, and rational wishing. The Stoics were firm in upholding human responsibility: Cleanthes expressly excepts from divine agency the evil wrought by men through their own folly. On this question the Stoics tried to harmonize opposing tendencies. Their physical principles made everything determined, human action being a link in the chain of causality. In their ethics, however, they assume that man can of himself realize happiness: all things obey the law of the universe; it is for him to comprehend it and to cooperate with it by willing obedience. His freedom consists in and is restricted to this.

275. On the basis of Stoic physics was constructed a moral idealism, remarkable for rigid consistency and absolute severance   **Ethics.** from everyday life. The end which as a rational being man chooses for his proper good, is activity and not mere passive feeling, is consistent and harmonious, is further a life in agreement with nature (ζῆν ὁμολογουμένως τῇ φύσει). Here (1) the nature of the universe, or (2) the individual nature of man may be intended; on either interpretation the agreement of part with whole can only mean the subordination of the individual to the order of the universe: the Greek conception of good to be pursued making way for that of law to be obeyed, though a law of which man himself as a rational being is the giver. Good then is moral good alone, decried by opponents as an abstraction or chimera, but to the Stoic an ideal to be realized in a life of moral virtue. Virtue is good in itself, apart from all consequences, an indivisible whole which we possess entirely or not at all, incapable of increase or diminution; an abiding condition (διάθεσις) of soul, not a temporary attribute (ἕξις); inalienable, so long as reason lasts; one and the same, however various the circumstances under which it is manifested. While each virtue is defined as knowledge of a particular region of fact, yet so closely are they connected that where one exists, the rest are also to be found. Right intention, the essential characteristic of all, may be described as force of will due to the tension or bracing of soul-substance. These principles imply a revaluation of objects and of the actions directed to their attainment. There is no mean between rational and irrational, virtue and vice, good and evil: all vice and all vicious persons are at an infinite remove from virtue, as he who is a hand's-breadth beneath the surface and he who is a hundred fathoms down will alike be

drowned. While moral good and moral evil stand thus apart, the world of
intermediate objects, which are means, not ends, still admits of classification
according as they are relatively natural (κατὰ φύσιν), or unnatural (παρὰ
φύσιν), the former being preferred in comparison with the latter, e.g. health
is desired and not sickness, though neither is in itself a good. Zeno expressed
this by calling the one class 'promoted' and the other 'degraded' (προηγμένα,
ἀποπροηγμένα), and by ascribing to them value, positive and negative (ἀξία,
ἀπαξία) respectively. So too with conduct: besides truly virtuous action,
technically called righteousness (κατόρθωμα), its opposite, vice, being sin,
Zeno recognized a wider sphere of natural and proper conduct, for which
he coined the term καθῆκον, very inadequately rendered by external or relative duty. This was variously defined as that which admits of rational
defence, an action appropriate to our natural constitutions, or as congruity
in life: apparently it included acts of prudent self-regard (e.g. the care of
health) and the superficial observance of other elementary moral rules. This
at any rate is true of intermediate 'duty' (μέσον καθῆκον): duly performed,
with full knowledge and right intention, this becomes perfect duty which is
indistinguishable from righteousness.

Ethical doctrine assumes a concrete form in the description of the wise
man, who is alone free and happy, never led into error or hurried into
emotion, endowed with true wealth and beauty, in no way inferior to Zeus
himself, since length of time cannot increase the perfect happiness he realizes
by right conduct. In contrast with this picture is the universal depravity of
the actual world, where none are righteous and sin is folly and madness.
Applied ethics, recognizing the real condition of mankind, endeavours to
alleviate and remedy it. Later Stoics urged men to set out upon a progress or
pilgrimage to virtue. The moral improvement of individuals and the cure of
souls diseased became ever more important aims. Stages of progress were
distinguished and the highest stage approximated to the unattainable ideal.

While respecting the independence of the individual and holding the
wise man self-sufficient, the Stoics taught that men are born for society.
We are all members one of another, citizens by birth of that universal state
the city of God, of which families and canton states are adumbrations, with
a single government and mode of life for all the world, where is neither
Greek nor barbarian, bond nor free. Cherishing such aspirations, which
even the Roman empire mocked rather than satisfied, the Stoics could hardly
take a hearty interest in the politics of small Greek communities. But if
the ties of patriotism were loosened, the obligation to justice, universal
benevolence, and humane treatment of slaves was enlarged and enforced.

276. Widely as the two systems differed, Epicurus and the Stoics agreed
in regarding philosophy as essentially a practical pursuit and
happiness as its end. The same practical aim was followed
by the Sceptics: negative conclusions and renunciation of the search for
truth were to them only means of attaining peace of mind. **Pyrrho** of Elis
(circa 365—275), the first in the Sceptical succession, propounded quietism

Sceptics.

empirically from observation of the contradictions in sense perceptions and in opinions and customs. Of the nature of things we can know nothing: our attitude therefore should be a cautious suspension of judgment (ἐποχή), whence results mental calm, freedom from passion (ἀπάθεια), and absolute indifference (ἀδιαφορία) so far as outward things are concerned. In the affairs of life the Sceptic should follow custom; whenever in so doing he pronounces an opinion, it is with the mental reservation that this opinion is *not more* (οὐδὲν μᾶλλον) true than its opposite. Pyrrho left no writings: his views are known from a satirical poem (Σίλλοι) of his follower **Timon** of Phlius. Of later Pyrrhonists **Aenesidemus**, who reduced the sceptical arguments to ten heads or tropes (τρόποι), and **Sextus Empiricus** (*circa* A.D. 200) are the most important. The works of Sextus which have come down to us are the *Pyrrhonean Hypotyposes* in three books and *Against the Mathematicians* in eleven books, of which the first six are concerned with the different branches of a liberal education, grammar, rhetoric, geometry, arithmetic, astronomy and music, while the other books VII—XI deal with philosophy proper. These writings present not merely a complete exposition of the sceptical argument but also a mass of invaluable information respecting contemporary schools of dogmatists. Meantime Scepticism had gained an independent footing in the Academy, where **Arcesilas** of Pitane in Aetolia (*circa* 315—240) engaged in vehement controversy with the Stoics and their head. The question at issue between them was chiefly the basis of certitude, and Academic scepticism retained this polemical and dialectical character throughout with consequences profoundly affecting all contemporary schools. Arcesilas used to argue both sides of every question: he contended (1) that for every true presentation of sense there is a corresponding false one which cannot be distinguished from it: (2) that for conduct a reasonable probability is as safe a guide as knowledge. This last suggestion received its full development from **Carneades** of Cyrene (214—129), the ablest of all the Post-Aristotelians, and the only philosopher of any originality in the four centuries after Chrysippus. His acute and persistent criticisms forced many Stoics to modify their doctrine. His contributions to a positive theory start with the observation that perceptions do not occur in isolation, but that each perception forms part of a group, the members of which may be separately investigated. Hence he distinguished three grades of probability. A perception may be (1) probable in itself: or (2) it may derive support from the probability of the other perceptions, occurring along with it. If all the concomitants are present, this is so far a guarantee of truth. Or (3) not satisfied with testing a single perception we may examine each member of the group to which it belongs: the absence of contradiction throughout will lend a cumulative effect to the probability of each. Thus Carneades was careful to distinguish the subjective from the objective standpoint: for the Stoic division of objects into cognizable and incognizable he substituted one into probable (*i.e.* apparently true) and improbable. Without relaxing the rule that we must suspend **our** judgment he could allow probable opinions to be formed, and claim for a high degree of probability that for all practical purposes it was as useful as the certainty of the dogmatists.

277. For centuries the four leading schools, Academics, Peripatetics,

Eclectics. Epicureans, and Stoics, continued to teach and to dispute. The result of their controversies was in the end insensibly to modify opposing views. After 156 B.C. the study of philosophy was introduced at Rome, and changes were made to suit the needs of the ruling class, keenly interested in literary culture and willing to make acquaintance with the new subject for which they had little or no aptitude themselves. **Panaetius** of Rhodes (185—110) and **Poseidonius** of Apamea (130—46) took an active part in popularizing Stoicism for the Romans. Neither was orthodox: Panaetius denied the general conflagration, and disbelieved in divination: Poseidonius gave up the unity of soul by admitting an irrational faculty: both were students and admirers of Plato; the latter was a man of great learning in many fields: he seems to have attempted a unification of all science, and has been called 'the last great intellectual force which Hellenism, untouched by Rome, produced' (W. W. Tarn). Stoic influences in turn encroached upon Peripatetic physics and ethics. Nor did the Academy, which had offered such vigorous opposition, maintain its independence. After **Philo** of Larissa (*circa* 88 B.C.) had admitted that in their own nature things are cognizable, although not by the Stoic criterion, **Antiochus** of Ascalon (*circa* 78 B.C.) terminated the long controversy by accepting nearly all the distinctive Stoic doctrines and boldly asserting, in defiance of plain fact, that they had always been doctrines of the Academy and had originally been borrowed by Zeno. Antiochus thus professed to restore the Old Academy; about the same time arose a school of Neo-Pythagoreans who professed with no greater truth to have revived the teaching of Pythagoras. But the most famous of these revivals and the last strange vicissitude in the fortunes of Plato's foundation, was the rise of Neo-Platonism. **Plotinus,** an Egyptian (*circa* A.D. 250), who never succeeded in writing Greek idiomatically, once more resumed the consideration of the metaphysical problems which had long been persistently ignored. Fifty-four of his tracts were collected by his pupil Porphyry and have come down to us arranged in six Enneads or sets of nine. He began with a refutation of materialism and substituted for it an idealistic theory of the universe, systematically elaborated; although incorporating much from Plato and something occasionally from Aristotle he was in the main original. He defended the freedom of the will, distinguished three grades of virtue, of which the lowest was cathartic or moral virtue, and defined the end which the philosopher should realize as the union of the soul by ecstasy with the divine. The acumen and sobriety of their founder did not long satisfy the Neo-Platonists, who ran riot in fantastic speculation as they grew more absorbed in magic and oriental superstition, until in A.D. 529 Justinian closed the school at Athens and a small band of recusant philosophers took refuge with Chosroes of Persia.

Each of the later schools stands not merely for a body of reasoned doctrine, but primarily represents a certain mental attitude or theory of life. The Epicurean ideal includes much more than Epictetus—
M. Aurelius. the contented enjoyment of tranquil pleasure. There is the elation which springs from conscious enlightenment and the sober mind freed from prejudice, that greatest bane of our peace. The Sceptic found congenial occupation in the examination of intellectual problems and the refutation of all possible knowledge; Carneades, like Hume, conducted a fruitless inquiry into every phase of opinion, with the keenest logical subtlety. The Stoics on the other hand. with unwavering faith in reason, claim for the actual order of things the distinctively religious emotions of men. Such, at least, is the teaching of the two great Stoics whose works have come down to us. **Epictetus** of Hierapolis (*circa* A.D. 90), first a slave and afterwards a freedman, was an earnest teacher of morality whose life was an embodiment of his doctrine. He wrote nothing himself, but from his disciple the historian Arrian we have four books of the *Discourses of Epictetus* and the *Encheiridion* or manual of excerpts. They inculcate the autonomy of the will, the duty of absolute submission to the divine order of nature. Man's fellowship in the rational system of the universe implies a privileged position of sonship, whereby he can grow into the mind of God and make the will of nature his own. The great aim of life should be the formation of right judgments, universal benevolence, endurance and apathy, 'to bear and forbear.' The famous meditations of the emperor **Marcus Aurelius Antoninus** (A.D. 120—180) *To himself*, Tὰ εἰς ἑαυτόν, in twelve books, breathe the same spirit tempered at times by eclectic tendencies, passing doubts and tender melancholy.

J. Burnet, *Early Greek Philosophy* (3rd edition, 1920): *Greek Philosophy, Thales to Plato*, 1914. E. Zeller, *Die Philosophie der Griechen*, five volumes, 1879–1923. T. Gomperz, *Griechische Denker*, 3rd edition, Bibliography. 1922. (Four volumes of the former and the whole of the latter have been translated into English.) H. Ritter et L. Preller, *Historia Philosophiae Graecae*, 9th edition (E. Wellmann), 1913. H. Diels, *Die Fragmente der Vorsokratiker*, 2 vols., 4th edition, 1922. F. M. Cornford, in *Cambridge Ancient History*, Vols. IV, V, VI. A. E. Taylor, *Plato, The Man and his Work*, 1926. W. D. Ross, *Aristotle*, 1923. H. Diels, *Doxographi Graeci*, 1879. H. Usener, *Epicurea*, 1887. C. Bailey, *The Greek Atomists and Epicurus*, 1926. *Epicurus*, 1926. A. C. Pearson, *Fragments of Zeno and Cleanthes*, 1891. H. von Arnim, *Stoicorum veterum fragmenta*, 3 vols., 1903–5. R. D. Hicks, *Stoic and Epicurean*, 1910. For a detailed bibliography, see *Cambridge Ancient History*, Vols. IV–VII.

III. 3. SCIENCE.

THE history of Greek science falls into two periods, which may be divided, with sufficient accuracy, at the year 300 B.C. In the first, which may be called the Hellenic period, science was ancillary to speculative philosophy, and some knowledge of its progress is necessary for understanding the philosophical literature of the time. In the second, which may be called the Alexandrian period, science passed into the schools, and was studied for its own sake, and its history is recorded in many books written by professors for the students of their faculty, and unreadable to anybody else. In a manual such as the present, it seems proper to give more space to the first period than to the second, and to say more of geometry, the Greek science *par excellence*, than of the other sciences. Arithmetic requires a few preliminary lines to itself.

278. The Greeks never at any time possessed a good set of arithmetical symbols. When writing became a common art, they used

Practical arithmetic (λογιστική).

for 5, 10, 100, 1,000, 10,0000 the initial letters of the names of those numbers, viz.: Π (πέντε), Δ (δέκα), Η (ἑκατόν), X (χίλιοι), M (μύριοι). Upright strokes indicated units under 5, and there were compendia, ⊓, Ϝ, Ϝ for 50, 500, and 5000. Thus MXXXΓΗΗ⊓ΔΠΙΙΙΙ stood for 13,768. These symbols were used, at least in public inscriptions, for some centuries after the alphabetic signs, with which we are more familiar ($a = 1$, $\beta = 2$, $ς = 6$, $ι = 10$, $κ = 20$ etc.), were invented. The latter are found first on Ptolemaic coins and papyri of the third century B.C. They are not, as is frequently said, of Phoenician origin, and seem to have been the invention of some Alexandrian *savant*, who knew the proper places of the obsolete letters F and Q, but not that of ૧. Both these sets of symbols are excessively clumsy for actual operations in arithmetic, as anybody can see who attempts to multiply ΜΗΔΠ by ΜΜϜ, or ͵αριε΄ by βφ΄, and it is probable that all sums were done on the ἄβαξ, ἀβάκιον, or 'reckoning-board,' which was divided into columns for units, tens, hundreds etc., while, in each column, the digit (so to say) required was represented by so many beans or pebbles (not exceeding nine). Obviously, with such a table, operations in all the four rules can be managed, though multiplication and division must have been very awkward, especially if the multiplier or divisor were high numbers. Fractions were a standing difficulty, and the Greeks did not operate with them until they had reduced them to a series of submultiples (*i.e.* fractions of unity). Thus the fraction $\frac{23}{32}$ would be treated, in calculation, as $\frac{1}{2} + \frac{1}{8} + \frac{1}{16} + \frac{1}{32}$. Hence, no doubt, for astronomical purposes, sexagesimal fractions (our *minutes* and *seconds*) were used (as in Babylonia), for 60 is divisible by 2, 3, 4, 5, 6, 10, 12, 15, 20, 30; so that a fraction of which the denominator is 60 can be easily reduced to submultiples. But if a fraction was very difficult to handle, some convenient

approximation was used instead, for great nicety was seldom required.
Calculation was taught in Greek schools as early as there were any schools
at all, and it was a favourite subject of the sophists, among whom Hippias
of Elis was the most eminent professor of it. It is probable that merchants
and bankers were assisted in their calculations by a complicated finger-
symbolism, but clear references to this do not occur before the Christian
era. (See Mayor on *Juvenal* x. 249.)

A. THE HELLENIC PERIOD.

279. Investigations into the nature of number were undoubtedly introduced into Greece by Pythagoras, who, finding that many
qualities, *e.g.* form, size, stability, beauty, harmony, depended   Theory of
on arithmetical relations, conceived that possibly all qualities   Numbers
might depend on subtle combinations of numbers, and hoped   (ἀριθμητική).
to find, in arithmetic, the key to the universe. His father was a lapidary,
and Prof. Ridgeway has ingeniously suggested that he was first led to
mathematical enquiries by the observation of crystals. He lived some
time in Egypt, and here probably the particular bent of his studies was
determined : for the Egyptian priests had long been familiar with some
facts to which he afterwards attached great importance. They knew, for
instance, that the circumference of a circle is about $3\frac{1}{7}$ of the diameter :
that a triangle of which the sides are in the ratio 3 : 4 : 5 must contain
a right angle, and that the square on the hypotenuse of (at least some)
right-angled triangles was equal to the squares on the sides. Pythagoras
discovered for himself, apparently, that the fifth and the octave of the note
given by a string can be produced by stopping the string at $\frac{2}{3}$ and $\frac{1}{2}$ of its
length respectively : and possibly he was led to the study of proportion by
its obvious utility in architecture. From these beginnings it became the
favourite pursuit of the Pythagoreans, and, through them, of other philosophers, to classify numbers according to their properties, to find numbers
which satisfy given conditions, to find arithmetical analogues for geometrical
facts and *vice versa*, and to discern all the other symmetries which are
implied when three given magnitudes are in the proportion (ἀναλογία)
$a : b :: b : c$. From Plato, who was profoundly impressed by Pythagorean
learning, and from Aristotle and later writers we learn a great deal about
Pythagorean nomenclature and theories; and Euclid in his *Elements*
(στοιχεῖα) has preserved all the best discoveries of his predecessors. A few
specimens must suffice here. Numbers were classified as *even* (ἄρτιοι), or
odd (περισσοί): numbers which have no factors but unity are *prime*
(πρῶτοι) : products of three numbers are *solid* (στερεοί), and some of these
are *cubes* (κύβοι) : products of two numbers are *plane* (ἐπίπεδοι), and some
of these are *squares* (τετράγωνοι), the rest *oblongs* (ἑτερομήκεις or προμήκεις).
The odd numbers, being the differences between successive squares, were
also called *gnomons* (γνώμονες). A *triangular* number (τρίγωνος) was half

the product of any two successive numbers. The root of a square number was called its *side* (πλευρά), the root of any other number was itself *inexpressible* (ἄρρητος), but both the root and the square were sometimes called the δύναμις of each other. Those numbers are *perfect* (τέλειοι) which are equal to the sum of their factors, and two numbers are *amicable* (φίλιοι) to one another when each is the sum of the factors of the other. It was known that a right-angled triangle could be constructed by taking sides in the ratio of 3 : 4 : 5. Pythagoras and Plato invented other arithmetical formulae for the construction. Pythagoras, beginning with an odd number, gives the sides as $2n + 1$ and $2n^2 + 2n$, the hypotenuse as $2n^2 + 2n + 1$. Plato, beginning with an even number, gives the sides as $2n$ and $n^2 - 1$, the hypotenuse as $n^2 + 1$. Almost all the propositions of Euclid's 2nd Book are geometrical proofs of arithmetical equations : his 5th Book deals with proportion in all magnitudes : in his 6th Book, propositions 28 and 29 are geometrical solutions of quadratic equations to which Plato alludes in the *Meno* : his 7th, 8th and 9th Books treat of numbers specially; and incidentally he shows how to find the G.C.M. and L.C.M. of two or more numbers (VII. 2, 3, 36, 38), and how to sum a geometrical series (IX. 35). His 10th Book is devoted to the great mystery of incommensurables (ἀσύμμετρα); and here especially the great advantage of geometrical symbols appears, for the diagonal of a square is always incommensurable with the sides, and hence any incommensurable quantity can always be represented accurately by such a diagonal. The facts that the diagonal of a square is incommensurable with its side and that the square root of 2 is an inexpressible number were among the earliest secrets of the Pythagorean school : but the further investigation of incommensurables seems to have begun with Theodorus of Cyrene, Plato's mathematical teacher.

280. An elaborate history of geometry before Euclid was written by Eudemus, the pupil of Aristotle, about 330 B.C. This work is lost, but is frequently cited by later historians and scholiasts, and Proclus, about A.D. 450, gives what appears to be a summary of it. The summary begins : 'Geometry is said by many to have been invented among the Egyptians, its origin being due to the measurement of plots of land. This was necessary there because of the rising of the Nile, which obliterated the boundaries appertaining to separate owners.' It goes on to name the chief geometers, in the following order : Thales, Mamercus, brother of the poet Stesichorus, Pythagoras, Anaxagoras, Oenopides of Chios, Hippocrates of Chios (who first wrote an 'Elements'), Theodorus of Cyrene, Plato, Leodamas of Thasos, Archytas of Tarentum, Theaetetus of Athens, Neocleides, Leon (author of an 'Elements'), Eudoxus of Cnidus, Amyclas of Heraclea, Menaechmus, and Deinostratus his brother, Theudius of Magnesia (also author of an 'Elements'), Cyzicenus of Athens, Hermotimus of Colophon, Philippus of Mende. Some hints as to the services of each of these geometers are given by Proclus, but none of their works is

Geometry.

now extant.   Many isolated proofs and solutions, however, have survived, and these have been carefully discussed by Bretschneider and Dr Allman. There is evidence to show that the Greek geometers arrived with some difficulty at *general* proofs.   Thus we are told that the proposition, that the interior angles of a triangle are equal to two right angles, was at first proved separately for the equilateral, the isosceles and the scalene triangle, and that the sections of the cone were at first obtained from three different sorts of cones : it is probable also that the Pythagorean theorem (Eucl. I. 47) was known for isosceles triangles (in which it might have been suggested by a tiled pavement) long before Pythagoras proved it for all right-angled triangles.   The propositions expressly attributed to Thales and Pythagoras would seem to show that, before the time of the Sophists (say 450 B.C.), the main contents of the first two books of Euclid and part of the 5th and 6th were known.   The orderly statement of enunciations and proofs is ascribed to Pythagoras, and the various στοιχεῖα, issued from time to time, are not to be regarded as mere 'elements,' but as 'systematic arrangements' of the whole subject.   It is true that Euclid, in his στοιχεῖα, omits much that was known in his day; but his book was not 'elementary' when it was written, and his omissions are mainly due to the fact that he confines himself to the use of the ruler (κανών) and compasses (διαβήτης).   Plato certainly seems to have favoured this limitation, though he is said to have invented a machine for the solution of the duplication-problem (to be presently mentioned).   The geometry of the circle was not much studied by the Pythagoreans, but was a favourite study in Athens.   And here it should be said that Eudemus and Proclus, an ardent Platonist, seem to be unfair to the sophists, of whom the summary names only one, Hippocrates of Chios. There is reason to believe that Hippias of Elis, Antiphon and Meton, if not more, were excellent mathematicians.   The progress of geometry in Athens was largely due to the absorbing interest of three problems, viz. quadrature of the circle, trisection of an angle, and duplication of the cube. These led to the invention of new methods of proof and of new mechanical contrivances, and also to the investigation of many new curves and to the geometry of *loci*.   For instance, Menaechmus, a contemporary of Plato and the founder of the geometry of conic sections, invented solutions of the duplication-problem in which both the parabola and the hyperbola were used.   It was apparently in regard to methods of proof that Plato made his chief contributions to geometry.   He added to the legitimate processes the method of analysis, of which the *reductio ad absurdum* is a particular form.   The method had no doubt been used before, but Plato seems to have examined it thoroughly, distinguished its types and pointed out its defects.   The oldest definition of *Analysis* as opposed to *Synthesis* is appended to Euclid XIII. 5, and was perhaps framed by Eudoxus (*ob.* 355 B.C.), to whom that proposition is attributed.   It states that 'Analysis is the obtaining of the thing sought by assuming it, and so reasoning up to an admitted truth : Synthesis is the obtaining of the thing sought by reasoning up to the inference and the proof of it.' In other words, the synthetic proof (of a theorem) proceeds by showing that certain admitted truths involve the proposed new truth : the analytic proof proceeds by showing that the proposed new truth involves certain admitted truths : but there are some necessary differences between analysis applied to theorems and analysis applied to problems. The steps of the analysis taken backwards should constitute a synthetic proof, and the Greeks always gave the synthesis after the analysis, lest some condition should have been overlooked or some proposition should not be convertible. Again, a problem may be under some conditions impossible, and this fact is likely to be overlooked in analysis. Hence to the synthetic solution, the Greeks added, if necessary, a *diorismus* or statement of the conditions under which the problem is possible. The invention of the *diorismus* seems to be ascribed, by Eudemus, to Leon the Platonist, but Plato himself uses a kind of *diorismus* in the *Meno* (86 D—87 A), and it is certain that he imparted his discoveries freely to his pupils. Thus he gave the method of analysis to Leodamas of Thasos, and may well have given the *diorismus* to Leon, who merely illustrated it by copious examples. The introduction of the method of analysis is regarded, by competent judges, as one of the greatest advances in the history of mathematics.

281.   Next after geometry, the science to which the early Greeks contributed most was astronomy. Here they were assisted by a considerable collection of observations made by the Chaldaeans, who had discovered, for instance, the period of 18 years (or 223 lunations) which brings round the order of eclipses. Thales, who knew of this discovery, is said to have known also the following facts : that the solar year is 365 days, that the intervals between the equinoxes are not equal, that the moon is illuminated by the sun, and that the earth is spherical. The Pythagoreans are said to have held that the earth revolved round the sun, and Leucippus that the earth had a rotatory motion, though he also held that the sun revolved round it. Other astronomical speculations may be read in Aristotle's book περὶ οὐρανοῦ. The actual work done seems to have lain chiefly in observations with a view to obtaining more exact measurements of time and space. The credit of inventing a rude sundial is shared between Anaximander and Anaximenes. Eudemus, the pupil of Aristotle, whose history of geometry was alluded to in the last section, wrote also a history of astronomy, in which the inclination of the ecliptic was given as 24°, but it is not known who made this measurement. Pytheas of Massilia is said to have made observations on solstitial gnomons in various places, and to have concluded that Massilia and Byzantium are on the same parallel of latitude. Several other attempts at exact measurement are also recorded, but the chief interest lay in the estimation of the exact length of the solar year and the lunar month, and the invention of cycles in which the years and the months should finally coincide. The most celebrated of these cycles are those of Meton of Athens (*circa* 430 B.C.) and Callippus of Cyzicus (*circa* 330 B.C.). Meton calculated 19 solar years

Other sciences.

= 235 lunar months = 6940 days. This cycle was found, by the time of Callippus, to be slightly erroneous. He therefore improved it by correcting the solar year to $365\frac{1}{4}$ days, and inventing a cycle of 76 solar years = 940 lunar months = 27,759 days. (This is merely the quadruple of Meton's cycle, less 1 day.) Observation of the stars led also to observation of the weather, and most of the weather-lore of antiquity is derived from the Φαινόμενα, a lost work of Eudoxus. There are some signs also of the study of mechanics. The lever and the wedge had been known from a very remote age. Archytas is said to have invented the screw (κοχλίας) and the pulley (τροχιλαία). Aristotle appears to have had some notion of the theory of the lever and of the parallelogram of velocities. Some very careful observations must also have been made in optics, for the architecture of the Parthenon and other temples shows many exact optical corrections, and there was sufficient interest in the subject to induce Euclid to write a book (still extant) about it. In the inductive sciences, apart from medicine, the chief work was done by Aristotle and his pupil Theophrastus, whose treatises on natural phenomena (μετεωρολογικά) and zoology and botany have come down to us. In these subjects very little further advance was made for about 1,800 years.

B.   THE ALEXANDRIAN PERIOD.

282. Alexandria was founded, in B.C. 332, by Alexander the Great, who, in pursuance of his plan for breaking up nationalities, deported into it a mixed population of Egyptians, Greeks and Jews. On Alexander's death, it fell to the portion of Ptolemy Lagi (322 B.C.), who founded the famous library and schools. These continued to exist till the city was taken by the Arabs in A.D. 640, and almost every scientific man of any note in the intervening centuries either was a professor or had been a student in Alexandria. A rival school, with an excellent library, was founded by Eumenes II (*circa* 197 B.C.), in Pergamum, but this school was never distinguished for original research, except perhaps in medicine. The first *savants* whom Ptolemy invited to assist him were Demetrius Phalereus, a distinguished Athenian, and Euclid, whose native place is unknown. Demetrius was succeeded, in the management of the library, by Zenodotus, Callimachus, Eratosthenes, Apollonius, Aristophanes, Aristarchus. Of these, only Eratosthenes, a man of many talents, and Apollonius were distinguished in mathematical sciences. The rest were philologers, devoted to textual criticism, the preparation of commentaries and lexicons, and the determination of grammatical nomenclature. The first complete Greek grammar was written by Dionysius Thrax, a pupil of Aristarchus, about 120 B.C. The mathematical school founded by Euclid was continued by Conon of Samos, who added Berenice's Hair to the named constellations: Eratosthenes of Cyrene, who measured a geographical degree, and probably invented the four-year cycle that we now use with the Julian calendar: Apollonius of Perga, who exhausted the geometry of conic sections. In the second century B.C. the best known mathematician is Hypsicles, who added a 14th Book (on the regular solids) to Euclid's Elements: but there were others, Nicomedes, Diocles and Perseus, who wrote on various new curves, and Zenodorus, who wrote on figures of equal periphery. Archimedes, the greatest mathematician of antiquity, lived in Syracuse (*ob.* 212 B.C.), but he corresponded with Conon and Eratosthenes, and there is other evidence which makes it probable that he was once a student of Alexandria. A large collection of his works is extant, comprising treatises on statics and hydrostatics, on a symbolism for very high numbers, on the quadrature of the circle and other curvilinear areas, and on the cubature of the sphere, the cylinder, and other solids. He was busy also with astronomy and with many ingenious mechanical contrivances, of which the water-screw is still in use. But the greatest astronomer, before the Christian era, was Hipparchus, and the greatest mechanical engineer was Heron, both of whom lived about 120 B.C. Hipparchus, who worked perhaps at Rhodes and not at Alexandria, is known to us from his commentary on the Φαινόμενα of Aratus and from many allusions to him in Ptolemy's *Almagest.* He invented, among other things, trigonometry, both plane and spherical, the method of stereographic projection, and the method of determining the position of places by reference to latitude and longitude: and he discovered, among other things, and estimated very nearly, the precession of the equinoxes. Very little advance was made on his learning till the time of Copernicus and Kepler. Heron of Alexandria was perhaps an Egyptian by birth, but he wrote in Greek on arithmetic and mensuration, on the *dioptra,* a sort of theodolite, and its uses in civil engineering, on the simple machines (lever, wedge, screw, pulley and windlass), on engines of war and on many ingenious contrivances, mostly toys, in which the pressure of air or water was utilised. One of his inventions, now called Barker's mill, is still in use. After the first century B.C. only a few names are worth recording. Nicomachus of Gerasa and Theon of Smyrna wrote on the theory of numbers, in the Pythagorean manner. Serenus of Antissa (date unknown) and Menelaus (*temp.* Trajan) faintly adumbrated some of the most recent developments of geometry. Claudius Ptolemaeus, who certainly observed in Alexandria in A.D. 139, produced later the Μεγάλη Σύνταξις (afterwards called *Almagest* by the Arabs), the exposition of that famous astronomical theory which remained unchallenged for 1400 years. It contains, of course, incidentally a great deal of geometry and trigonometry; and Ptolemy's merits, as a mathematician, are thought by the best judges to entitle him to rank with Euclid, Archimedes and Apollonius. At the end of the next century (*circa* A.D. 300) lived Pappus of Alexandria, author of *Mathematical Collections* (συναγωγή), a professorial work of great interest, containing notes on all the mathematical books then studied. Theon, who edited Euclid, and his daughter, the famous Hypatia (*ob.* A.D. 415), are the last important mathematicians of the Alexandrian school. One only remains to be mentioned, Diophantus of Alexandria, a writer of uncertain date, who seems to belong to the third century. He is the author of a work called Ἀριθμητικά, which is a series of exercises in the solution of algebraic equations. He does not say that his algebraic symbols were new or that he himself contributed anything to the methods that he uses, but the book is unique among Greek mathematical works, and Diophantus will always have the credit of being the inventor of algebra. The work in geography and chartography begun by Eratosthenes and Hipparchus was continued (though not in Alexandria) by Poseidonius (*circa* 80 B.C.), who had clear notions on tides; by Strabo (*circa* 20 B.C.) and others; and culminated in the celebrated map and index of Claudius Ptolemaeus, in which latitude and longitude were assigned (not correctly, of course) to every considerable place in the inhabited world. The Alexandrian school of medicine was admirably equipped, and remained, in the fourth century of our era, the most famous and fashionable. The study of medicine involved some study of botany and of the art of distillation (in the ἀμβίκα, whence *alembic*); but zoology remained where Aristotle left it. The fact is that the inductive and applied sciences, except in so far as they were ancillary to medicine, do not seem to have been subjects of the lecture-room but to have formed part of the traditional lore of the professions that required them. We can judge of their progress not by the aid of specific treatises but only by inference from isolated and incidental remarks of writers who are dealing with some other subject. The treatment of ores, for instance, and the making of alloys and of glass, perhaps led to some theory of heat and of chemical combination, but there is no extant work on these subjects; nor, though the Greeks were certainly acquainted with the magnet and with the electrical properties of amber, is there any evidence of a profounder study of these phenomena. Similarly, there are indications of some careful study of forestry, and Aelian's book (*circa* A.D. 150) is testimony to some continued interest in zoology; but the facts known are insufficient for the construction of a history, still less of a summary account, of progress in these sciences.

Abundant references will be found in the following works: (*a*) On the whole subject: S. Günther in Iwan von Müller's *Handbuch der Klass. Altertumswissensch.* Band v. Abth. 1. (*b*) On mathe- **Bibliography.** matics: G. Friedlein, *Die Zahlzeichen der Griech. u. Römer*: M. Cantor, *Vorlesungen über die Gesch. der Math.* Vol. I.: J. Gow, *Short History of Greek Mathematics*: J. G. Smyly on *Greek Arithmetic* in *Mélanges Nicole*: Sir T. L. Heath's full studies of *Diophantus, Euclid, Apollonius*, and *Archimedes*. (*c*) On Plato's Mathematics, B. Rothlauf, *Die Math. zu Platons Zeiten*; and S. H. Butcher in *Journal of Philology*, XVII. p. 219. (*d*) On Astronomy, R. Wolf, *Geschichte der Astronomie* and Sir T. L. Heath's *Aristarchus of Samos*. (*e*) On Geography, Sir E. H. Bunbury, *Ancient Geography*, and H. F. Tozer's smaller book with the same title. (*f*) On Mechanics and Physics, R. Poggendorff, *Geschichte der Physik*. (*g*) On Mineralogy, Lenz, *Mineralogie der alten Griechen*. (*h*) On Botany, E. Meyer, *Geschichte der Botanik*. (*i*) On Zoology, Corus, *Geschichte der Zoologie*, and Höfer's works in French on the history of the Sciences.

IV. ART.

IV. 1. PREHISTORIC ART.

283. OUR knowledge of Prehistoric Greece is comparatively recent.
Schliemann, who worked from 1870 to 1890, with ardent
Excavations. Chronology. faith in the historical basis of Greek legends, gave us the
first glimpse of early Greece and Asia Minor by his famous
excavations at Mycenae, Troy and Tiryns. Later Sir Arthur Evans and
Dr Halbherr revealed the Minoan civilization in Crete, whence Schliemann
suspected light on the origin of Mycenaean culture would come. Following
them a host of scholars have investigated the beginnings of Hellenic art.

Since, as is only natural, the development of civilization in the Greek
area was not uniform it is better to take the several districts separately.
The districts in which prehistoric remains have been found are Crete, the
Cyclades, Southern, North-Central (Thessaly, Phocis, Boeotia), and Western
Greece, Macedonia, and the Trojan area. Of the material remains of the
prehistoric period the pottery takes first place, because in most excavations
more fragments of pottery are found than of any other class of object. For
this reason the history of an inhabited site, if properly excavated, should be
read in its pottery. The comparison of the pottery sequences from the
different sites has made it possible for archaeologists to sketch broadly the
main lines followed by the development of civilization in the Aegean
basin.

The history of Greek culture begins with the Neolithic Period (later or
polished stone age), for few remains of the Palaeolithic Period (older stone
age) have yet been found.

The Bronze Age is divided into three stages, Early, Middle, and Late,
which in Crete are called Minoan, on the Mainland Helladic, and in the
islands Cycladic. Each stage can be subdivided into two or more phases,
e.g. Middle Minoan I, II, III, etc.; but it must be remembered that the
periods in the different districts were not absolutely contemporary. For
the principal synchronisms between them and their approximate dates see
§ 114 above.

284. Our principal knowledge of the neolithic period in Crete is
derived from the deposits below the foundations of the
Crete. Neolithic Age. palaces at Cnossus and Phaestus. The earliest remains are
those of coarse hand-made household vessels, basins, bowls,
and plates. They have wide mouths and simple flat bottoms; there are
neither long narrow necks nor elaborate bases. The ware was polished by
hand both within and without. Later, as some progress was made in the
rudiments of civilization, this pottery was decorated with simple geometric

patterns incised in the clay and filled with white pigment. In pottery not so decorated a certain refinement was obtained during the polishing process by rippling the surface, which naturally increased the glitter of the burnishing. With this pottery figurines of clay or stone, tools such as polished stone axes (celts) and chisels, and bone pins and awls are found, while flakes of obsidian, imported from Melos or Istros (Giali), served as knives and razors. It is of course impossible to define the chronological limits of the neolithic period; but from about 3400 B.C. there was a gradual transition from the use of polished stone to bronze which began to be adopted for cutting instruments, though, since bronze was rare and valuable, the use of heavy stone hammers and axes and obsidian knives was not immediately abandoned.

In the first phase of the Early Minoan period, the pottery was still of a primitive type. The heavy polishing and the decorative incisions of the Neolithic Period were abandoned; and the *Early Minoan.* shapes of the vessels showed more conscious design. We find vases with wide bodies and narrow necks, fitted with caps or lids and provided with small knobs so pierced that the vessels could be hung up. A goblet with a tall foot is also evidence of the same tendency towards more careful design, but in fabric all the vases are rough and hand-made. The first advance in technical skill seems, as often, to go hand-in-hand with a decrease in the desire for decorative effect. In the second phase of this period there first appears one of the two methods of painting pottery which were alternately dominant in the Cretan Bronze Age, the dark-on-light and the light-on-dark styles. The former, which is the earlier, is represented by vases with dark geometrical designs on a hand-polished buff ground. With this is found a peculiar type of ware covered with a hard paint of good quality which, owing to the firing, has a mottled surface varying in colour from orange-red to black. In the third phase this mottled ware still continued, but it was gradually replaced by a light-on-dark style in which geometrical patterns in white were applied to a ground of blackish glaze paint. Here spiral and curvilinear elements begin to appear in the designs. In all these fabrics the vases are on the whole well made and well designed, for there is a great variety of shapes, among which jugs with tall beaks and bowls with long side spouts are common. The last two phases also show a distinct and rather sudden advance in civilization. Typical of them are beautiful stone bowls which present a charming variety in material, size, design and colour. The skill and good taste which they show foreshadow the later artistic excellence of Minoan Crete. Much gold work in a simple but delicate style has also been found. Sprays of leaves, pendants, beads, decorative strips, pins with daisy-shaped heads and similar ornaments in this metal occur in tombs and with them gems, beads and seals in ivory, steatite, crystal, and other precious stones. The use of bronze is attested by the discovery of short leaf-shaped daggers and double axes. Signs of the pictographic script are to be recognised on some seals of the period which are the earliest traces of any form of writing yet found in Greek lands.

Since at the close of the Neolithic Age Crete had made no greater advance in civilization than any of her neighbours, one might well enquire how it was that she so soon outdistanced them. The answer is simple. The main impulse, which generated the Minoan culture, as evidenced by the difference between Neolithic and Early Minoan Crete, came from early dynastic Egypt. The stone vases from Mochlos find their best analogy in those from the tombs of Naqada, and it is possible that during the troubled times, which marked the beginning of dynastic Egypt, some of the older population, then expelled, may have settled in Crete.

Fig. 5. Polychrome vase of Middle Minoan II style.

285. In the Middle Minoan age the dark-on-light style of pottery survived continuously, but is rare and latent, for the light-on-
Crete. Middle Minoan. dark style was dominant. This latter style culminates in the second phase with the beautiful polychrome cups of egg-shell fabric. Some vases imitate vessels of metal or bowls of veined and coloured stone; others have a decoratively roughened surface (barbotine). The decoration is painted in white, yellow, cherry-red, and deep red on a ground of black glaze paint. This light-on-dark polychrome ware—often known as Kamares from the scene of its first discovery—reaches a very high level of artistic excellence both in technique and design (Fig. 5). The patterns are mainly curvilinear, very often floral and strongly naturalistic. The fine fabric, the polychrome technique and the free and original naturalistic motives combine to make it one of the most striking of pre-historic wares. As might be expected from the refinement of the pottery, this age, especially in the last two phases, showed great progress in all the arts that increase the comfort or luxury of life. The architecture of the earlier part of the Middle Minoan age is represented by the first palaces at Cnossus, Mallia, and Phaestus which perished in a general catastrophe at

the end of the second Middle Minoan period. To the succeeding phase (M. M. III) belong the later palace at Phaestus and large parts of that at Cnossus, including the original plan of the domestic quarter. The walls of the palaces were adorned with brilliant polychrome frescoes. The charming painting of a boy gathering crocuses from Cnossus is the earliest example (M. M. II). The use of hard stones for seals and gems becomes common and the designs have a naturalistic character, especially in the treatment of animals, and stone lamps and vases are found. In metal work a great advance is made. The bronze swords or rather elongated daggers are more effective weapons than those of the earlier period. Objects in precious metals are scarce, but a few specimens have been found (for instance a silver vase from Gournia), which give the metal prototypes of some of the egg-shell pottery. The workers of this and the Late Minoan period were trained crafts-

Fig. 6. Faience plaque from Cnossus.

men and almost all materials were alike in their skilled hands. Their carving in ivory and crystal was as delicate as their painting. Examples of their modelling are votive terracotta statuettes from hill-top shrines at Petsofa near Palaikastro (see Fig. 140) and on Giouchtas near Cnossus. These, which fall in the first phase (M. M. I), with their quaint polychrome decoration, are important as showing the male and female costumes of the age (§ 668). But the most remarkable objects are the faience figurines and plaques from the repositories of the palace shrine at Cnossus (M. M. III). The art of making faience was obviously learnt from Egypt, but it became firmly established in Crete. Moulds for making figures in faience have been found in the island, and the designs and technique are typically 'Minoan' and not Egyptian. The most striking of these figurines are the Snake Goddess (see Fig. 144) and her votaries and other ritual objects, such as sea-shells, flying fish, flowers and fruit, belonging to her shrine. One plaque (Fig. 6) represents a wild goat with two kids. In its fresh and delicate naturalism it is unsurpassed by any monument even of the great age of Greek art. The Snake

Fig. 7. Filler (*rhyton*) of Late Minoan I *b* style.

Goddess herself and a series of crocus buds are most realistically modelled with little if any regard for conventional artistic designs. Other objects in the same material include a large series of tesserae, perhaps intended to form a mosaic with crystal, representing the façades of houses, which are interesting as showing the types of the houses of the age. The script developed also and the pictographic signs became more and more conventional and from them arose a linear system.

286. The next phase, Late Minoan I *a*, continues the transition begun, after a check by an earthquake, in Middle Minoan III and some objects once called Late Minoan I are now assigned to Middle Minoan III. The style of the pottery changed from light-on-dark to dark-on-light. In the second phase, Late Minoan I *b*, the climax of Cretan greatness was reached. At first naturalistic patterns continued, and favourite designs included lilies, sprays of ivy and simple scrolls. Then marine motives came into fashion, and prevailed in the next phase (L. M. I *b*). On the vases are rocks covered with waving sea-plants and among them are seen octopuses, sea-urchins, anemones, molluscs, and various kinds of fish (Fig. 7). The decorated vessels are elegantly designed, even the large store jars. Graceful jugs and long fillers or libation vases (*rhytons*) are two of the most characteristic shapes. Naturalism, however, was not confined to painting for the decoration of pottery; the art of fresco painting was highly developed. The cat fresco from Hagia Triada is in this respect perhaps unsurpassed (M. M. III). This represents in a masterly manner a cat crawling stealthily through waving plants in order to spring upon an unsuspicious pheasant. Typical too are the cup-bearer (L. M. I *a*) and the portrait of a girl (L. M. II) from Cnossus (see Figs. 142, 143) which give us likenesses of the men and women of the race which produced this civilization. Animation of style is shown in some scenes illustrating bull-baiting and others in which a number of fashionably dressed ladies of the court are attending some great function. This belongs to a series of slightly *rococo* miniature frescoes (M. M. III–L. M. I *a*), some of which are remarkable for their representations of shrines (cf. Fig. 22). In addition to the painting of figures in life-size, as in the great frescoes, there are similar figures in high relief in painted stucco and others in lower relief like the bull's head (Fig. 8) which represent the highest achievements of Minoan art. Fragmentary as the remains are, they give indications of groups and of friezes on a vast scale. The knowledge

Fig. 8. Bull's head in relief in painted stucco from Cnossus.

of anatomy displayed would be wonderful in any age or country. Equally striking are the carved steatite bowls—originally probably covered with gold-leaf—representing a harvest home, warriors, boxers and similar subjects. The low relief, the complexity of some of the scenes such as the harvest home, and the comparatively small size of the vases thus ornamented, combine to emphasize the skill of the artists in depicting such

Fig. 9. Ivory figurine from Cnossus.

subjects in detail with strength and spirit. Well-carved bowls and lamps of stone prove that the lapidaries of the period were also accustomed to combine practical utility with decorative art. The delicate ivory figurines, with their graceful and flowing movement of the limbs, like the diving boy from Cnossus (Fig. 9), display both elegance and strength. Other carvings, the ivory Snake Goddess at Boston or the marble statuette at Cambridge, in their careful anatomical detail, reflect the skill and observation of the artists. On the other

Fig. 10. Seal impressions of Minotaurs from Zakro.

hand gem-cutting was on the same high level as the carving of the steatite bowls. Favourite motives of this same transitional M.M. III–L.M. I *a* period were fantastic animals such as the Minotaur types from Zakro (Fig. 10), and pairs of heraldic animals, especially lions (Fig. 11). Metal working is illustrated by a series of spirited impressionist statuettes and by fine bronze bowls and ewers. Masterly workmanship in the decorative arts is well represented by the royal gaming board with its elaborate mosaic of crystal, ivory, gold, silver, and blue glass-paste. The pictographic script was now definitely replaced by the linear signs which indicate a great advance in the art of writing. During the fifteenth century B.C. (L.M. I *b*–L.M. II) Minoan art

Fig. 11. Seal impression with heraldic animals from Crete.

after a final flourish of naturalism became conventional and *rococo*, as seen in the last stages of the palaces at Cnossus and Phaestus and in tombs like the vaulted tomb at Isopata.

287. At the end of the second Late Minoan period in Crete the palace of Cnossus was sacked and burnt, and the same fate overtook the other great centres of art and civilization in Crete. In spite of this the culture of the next and last phase (Late Minoan III) was the same, for there is no break in its development, and the old sites continued to be inhabited, but as might be expected this phase was artistically degenerate. Its character is well shown by the various objects found in the tombs of Cnossus. The long bronze swords, often with delicately engraved decoration, show that the metal workers' skill was

Crete. Late Minoan III.

devoted to the arts of war as well as to those of peace. But the ivory plaques carved in low relief, the finely engraved gems, the gold jewellery and many other similar minor objects of art, indicate that the Cretan tradition was still alive. Typical of this period are the terracotta sarcophagi painted with interesting scenes or symbols. The most important is the famous example from Hagia Triada which is of soft limestone covered with a thin coat of stucco. On this are painted ritual scenes. A terracotta specimen from Palaikastro is of the house type with a gabled roof and may have been influenced by wooden chests brought from Egypt. It is painted with various symbols, amongst which a double axe erected between the horns of consecration is conspicuous. Such sarcophagi show that the tradition of painting continued, but on the pottery, though the dark-on-light style was preserved, the fine marine designs became stylized and conventional. The octopus, no longer treated naturalistically, is converted into a conventional decorative pattern, and the same fate befalls lilies and other floral motives. The 'close style' of vase painting shows how weakness of design was masked by covering as much of the surface as possible with ornament. Much in use was the so-called stirrup vase or false-necked amphora, a round-bodied vase of moderate size with a small narrow neck which is, however, closed at the top. Instead of this closed mouth there is on one side on the shoulder a small circular projecting spout. Attached to the false neck on either side are loop handles which together have the appearance of a stirrup. Towards the close of the period another new shape appears, a wide two-handled crater characteristic of the final stages of Minoan culture. The 'Shrine of the Double Axes' at Cnossus and the corresponding one at Gournia, both of this age, are of great importance for the history of religion. The streets and houses of Palaikastro and Gournia similarly give a picture of social life. The period closes with a transition to the Early Iron Age well illustrated by sites like Vrokastro, and here the age verges on the historic.

288.   Little is known of the Stone Age in the Cyclades and the history
Cyclades.   of civilization begins with the Bronze Age, which as far as we can judge seems to have been contemporaneous with that in Crete. But, while Crete is a large and fruitful island, the Cyclades are small and most of them have not sufficient soil to be fertile, for they are the tops of a primeval mountain chain now submerged in the Aegean. From this lack of natural advantages we should not expect the prehistoric culture of the Cyclades to be so flourishing as that of Crete. Melos and Thera, which seem to have reached a higher level than the others, are the nearest to Crete and possess natural volcanic products which were very valuable to primitive man. Melos is rich in obsidian, which is the best material for making cutting tools when bronze is rare. Naxos, Siphnos, and Paros, more fertile islands, are rich in marble and they consequently seem to have been more civilized than some of their neighbours. The publication of the recent discoveries in Samos and future exploration in Andros and Euboea should throw more light on Cycladic culture and its connections.

In the Early Cycladic period the pottery was at first of a simple type made and polished by hand and decorated with elementary linear patterns incised in the clay. Then followed a dark-on-light painted ware with simple geometric designs in matt black, and the dark-on-light style remains dominant in the Cyclades, although from time to time we find attempts at a light-on-dark style. Of the early incised ware the most striking vases are those shaped like frying-pans, with elaborate patterns of spirals, fish and primitive boats on the outside. Of the dark-on-light ware a common type at the end of the period was a tall jug with a beaked spout and two small breast-like projections on the upper part of the body. Some of the vases of this period, which are covered with a thin semi-lustrous paint shading from black to chestnut, may be akin to the mottled ware of Crete. But, as in Crete, the most striking objects of this period are the well made and polished marble bowls, some with tall bases and thin sides. With these are found small figurines, also of marble, which usually represent women (Fig. 12). Many of these are of the rudest type, being flat fiddle-shaped figures; others are definitely carved into the likeness of the human figure, but the legs are not separated (in all the arms are folded across the chest), and there are others of a more developed style, for the legs are separated and fairly well modelled. All the figures however are flat and the heads are elongated with only a rough representation of a face. In addition there are a few exceptional specimens such as those of men playing a double flute or seated on a stool playing harps. Though all are primitive, yet the obvious attempts in some cases at delicate carving and the clear desire of the maker to find expression in a material which was not yet thoroughly mastered, are exceedingly interesting, for these are the earliest examples of marble sculpture found on Greek soil. Bronze was scarce and is represented only by a few small knives, chisels and double-edged axes, but lead seems to have been known, for models of boats in this metal have been found. Of gems there are a few rudely cut examples in steatite and other soft stones, and gold work is rare and of an elementary type.

Fig. 12. Marble fig-urine from the Cyclades.

Cyclades. Early Period.

289. In the Middle Cycladic period the islands fell definitely under the influence of Crete. The native dark-on-light style con-tinued and curvilinear designs, which began to appear at the end of the last period, now became common. The tall beaked jugs and small cups with decoration confined to a panel on the front were

Cyclades. Middle Period.

typical shapes, as well as low shallow bowls with a small spout. But, as the islands came under the influence of Crete, the native potters began to imitate the naturalistic designs of Middle Minoan ware, and lilies, crocuses and other floral motives were popular. Further in Melos, at the very end of the period, vases occur with well drawn floral patterns in red-brown and black, in imitation of the polychrome Middle Minoan ware, and many of these, except for the inferior technique, almost deserve to rank with the best products of Crete. The native clay, especially in Melos, is soft and porous, and ill-adapted for fine pottery or good painting. With these local fabrics are found many specimens of the typical light-on-dark ware of Crete,

Fig. 13. Fresco of flying fish from Phylakopi in Melos.

and *vice versa* some Melian jugs have been found in the temple repositories at Cnossus, and the close relations between Crete and Melos are thus demonstrated. At this same time Middle Helladic pottery is found in Melos together with Cycladic imitations of it, a remarkable fact in view of the extreme rarity of Middle Helladic pottery in Crete. Lack of material makes it impossible to attempt to estimate the advance in culture made in other respects, but the pottery is enough to show that for artistic taste and a true appreciation of nature the Cyclades were worthy neighbours of Crete.

In the first two phases of the Late Cycladic period the same dependence on Crete is noticeable in the pottery, for the best productions of the Melian potters are imitations of Late Minoan I and II

Late Period.

vases. A bronze statuette from Phylakopi in Melos and some fragments of ivory point in the same direction. The painted frescoes found in the ruins of the earlier palace at Phylakopi, especially the splendid flying fish (Fig. 13) with their brilliant colouring and fine naturalism, suggest that they were made by Cretan artists. The Cyclades were also in touch with the Mainland, for the contemporary pottery of Late Helladic I and II is found in Melos by the side of the local and of the Cretan styles. Finally on the destruction of the Cretan palaces Cretan influence in the islands seems to have vanished, for henceforward in Late Cycladic III only Late Helladic III pottery was imported, probably from Argolis. Similarly the local wares, which continued, were imitated from Mainland and not from Cretan examples. Minor objects of art are not common except seal stones bearing the usual Minoan or Mycenaean devices, and in Melos the artistic tradition which produced these gems seems to have lasted through the early Iron Age into the first phase of archaic Greek art. The end of the Bronze Age in the Cyclades is marked by some disturbance which overthrew the old seats of civilization although it did not entirely destroy the tradition. The city at Phylakopi was ruined at the end of this period and never again inhabited, and the centre of life in Melos was transferred to the site of the classical city.

290. According to recent research the area which had decisive influence on the formation of the Greek race and art was that which includes Phocis, Boeotia, Attica, and the Peloponnese. The earliest inhabitants were of the same race as the people of the First Neolithic Period in Thessaly and enjoyed a similar culture, which is quite distinct from that of Crete. Soon after the end of this period (about 3000–2800 B.C.) these parts of the Mainland were overrun by a bronze-using people who seem to have come from south-western Asia Minor and to have been akin to the early Bronze Age folk in Crete and in the Cyclades. The invaders' settlements extend as far north as Othrys with plentiful remains of houses, pottery, and other household gear. They buried their dead in ossuaries or caves. Their houses are described in § 706 below. The first pottery was primitive and hand-made with a reddish polished slip and simple incised patterns of a geometric type like those of the Cyclades. Later it was covered with glaze paint which varies in colour from red-brown to black. Sometimes the firing mottles the black with reddish blurs as in the contemporary ware from Vasiliki in Crete. Characteristic shapes are a broad-mouthed flask (*askos*) and a bowl of a sauce-boat type with a long spout, recalling contemporary shapes in Crete and in the Cyclades. Towards the close of the age some vases, especially tankards, were decorated with simple linear patterns in bands on the natural colour of the clay. Other vases had similar patterns rendered in white on the black glaze, again suggestive of the light-on-dark (E. M. III) pottery. Simple figurines and seal impressions in clay, some small implements of bronze, and some gold ornaments in Berlin, and a gold sauceboat in the Louvre hint that these people were not behind their kinsmen in the islands.

291. Some little time after the beginning of the Middle Minoan I phase
in Crete a new element entered the Greek Mainland typified
Middle
Helladic. by a new style of pottery, the so-called 'Minyan' ware. This, a
good fabric of a peculiar grey colour, is often wheel-made and
in its shapes recalls metal work. Less fine varieties in pale brown and a
yellowish colour also occur, and some have plain decoration by incisions or
thin painted lines. Together with this pottery a matt painted ware which may
be descended from the patterned Early Helladic pottery was in use. Of the

Fig. 14. Goblet of "Minyan" ware.

grey ware characteristic shapes are a goblet on a tall ringed stem (Fig. 14), the
forerunner of the Mycenaean kylix, and a kantharos with high swung handles.
Of the matt painted ware typical shapes are large pithoi and small cups with
panel decoration, a shape known also in Melos and in Crete. The patterns
were at first linear, but tended to become more free, and later running
spirals were popular. At the end of the period, together with a few pieces
which show curvilinear designs in white on black and reflect the influence of
Kamares ware (M. M. II–III), there appear a considerable number of vases

with designs of birds and fantastic animals in a polychrome technique on a reddish ground. These vases recall the contemporary bird vases of Melos, examples of which were found in the temple repositories at Cnossus (M. M. III). This style is best represented in the Sixth Shaft Grave, the oldest of the royal graves of Mycenae. The graves were small shafts lined with slabs, small stones, or crude brick, and in some cases the body was covered by part of a pithos ; but they are poorly furnished and consequently except for the Sixth Shaft Grave at Mycenae there is not enough to give a good idea of the culture of the period, which to judge by the character of the pottery must have been at least on a level with that of Melos. (For the apsidal houses of the M.H. Period see § 706.)

Towards the end of the Middle Helladic age Cretan influence made itself felt on the Mainland. Some indications of it were visible before in the Kamares sherds at Aegina and Asine, but from the beginning of the six-teenth century it comes in full force. Some think it is the result of a direct and wholesale conquest and colonization of the Mainland by the rulers of Cnossus. Others think that from this time on the people of the Mainland, conscious of their growing strength and the increasing weakness of Crete, which declined with the decay of Egypt, began to raid Crete and bring back rich spoils and slaves, who were craftsmen skilled to exercise their art for the benefit of the rulers of Mycenae, Tiryns, Thebes, and Orchomenus. The truth probably lies between the two theories. Some adventurers or refugees probably came from Crete to Greece, and the rising powers of the Mainland, attracted by the culture of Crete, seized every opportunity to enjoy it and adapt it to their purposes.

292. The first phase of the new era, Late Helladic I, is that of the Shaft Grave kings at Mycenae. The amazing treasures found in those graves by Schliemann are an epitome of the culture of the period.

Late Helladic I.

Bronze work is plentiful; there are huge bronze pots and bowls and a splendid series of long swords, many of which have engraved blades and hilts made of ivory, gold and inlaid work. The dagger blades are inlaid with designs in different metals such as gold and silver. One scene represents panthers hunting aquatic birds on the banks of a stream full of fish and edged with lotus. On another hunters armed with spears and protected by large shields are seen attacking three huge lions. Gold work is exceedingly plentiful; there are thin discs decorated with the nautilus, cuttle-fish or bees, personal ornaments such as pins, one with an elaborate head representing a woman beneath a palm tree, and thin plates embossed with spiral and lily patterns used to encase wooden boxes. In all such work motives drawn from nature were employed for decorative purposes. The siege scene on a silver libation vase shows that metal chasing was not confined to gold. Here a band of slingers and archers posted on broken ground be-low a city wall defend themselves with desperation, while on the walls a group of women is seen encouraging them. There is also a graceful flagon of silver and a bull's-head libation vase (*rhyton*) of the same metal with

Fig. 15. Reconstructed Vase of Late Helladic II from Mycenae.

Fig. 16. The gold cups from Vaphio in Laconia.

horns of gold. A remarkable piece of goldsmith's work is the ring representing a cult scene (Fig. 17). On this the goddess, whose emblem, the double axe, is placed near her, is seated under her sacred tree receiving women who come to bring her offerings. In the sky above are the sun and the crescent moon. The exquisite work on such a small scale, the detail of the women's costumes and the interest of the cult scene render this one of the most important of the treasures of Mycenae. Some of these treasures are of Cretan origin and others show analogies with objects from Asia Minor, but many must have been made by craftsmen working on the Mainland. The stelae carved in low relief which stood over the graves show the influence of Cretan decorative patterns but the scenes of war and of the chase which recur in the frescoes and on the seal stones of the Mainland show another feeling, a manly and vigorous creative spirit. The pottery shows two strains, one an imitation of the contemporary Cretan Late Minoan I *a* ware, and the

Fig. 17. Gold ring from Mycenae.

other a continuation of the Middle Helladic tradition which was modified under Cretan influence. Ultimately the two strains were united in the well known Mycenaean pottery of Late Helladic III in which much of the ornament was based on the Minoan. Floral motives were popular and also fine decorative designs of spirals and waving lines.

To the next phase, Late Helladic II, belong the famous cups from the tomb at Vaphio (Fig. 16). The scenes on them show men catching wild bulls, probably for bull baiting such as is figured in the frescoes of Cnossus and Tiryns. The spirited designs

Late Helladic II.

and the naturalistic execution make them masterpieces of prehistoric art. The same style is seen in the gold vase from the royal beehive tomb at Dendra in Argolis, which is of Late Helladic III date but contained some treasures of earlier times. This shows a seascape of octopuses swimming above a rocky floor with dolphins sporting on the surface. The marine designs fashionable on Cretan pottery appear also on the Mainland, but the most charming vases of this age are graceful stemmed goblets with two handles, a refinement of the Minyan goblet (Fig. 14) of Middle Helladic times. They show pleasing floral or marine designs on a yellow buff ground. Characteristic too are the big 'palace style' amphoras (Fig. 15), a type which in Crete was apparently peculiar to Cnossus but on the Mainland was popular in every important centre. The best series of these comes from the beehive tombs at Pylos in Triphylia. One or two rings of iron indicate that iron though known was precious, and there are many minor objects of art in amethyst, amber, faience, ivory, and glass, and decorative stones like steatite and alabaster. Some of these materials point to trade with Egypt and the East, while amber shows contact with Central Europe. The introduction of the beehive tomb at Mycenae suggests the advent of a new dynasty.

293. With the downfall of Crete and the collapse of Egypt soon after
Late Helladic 1400, the Mainland, as shown by fortress palaces like Mycenae
III. and Tiryns, became the centre of the Aegean culture which
its vigorous possessors spread far and wide over continental and insular Greece and the Levant, from Macedonia to Palestine and Egypt, and even as far west as Sicily. Rhodes and Cyprus were flourishing centres. To this age belong the great monuments of architecture, the finest beehive tombs, the Lion Gate at Mycenae with its imposing sculpture, and the cyclopean structures of Tiryns. It was a period of bold overseas enterprise. Art became conventionalised and the floral and marine patterns on the pottery are stereotyped or shorthand versions of earlier designs, but the fabric of the pottery is excellent and the wares seem to have been produced on a large scale. Most characteristic of this stage are the stirrup vase, the tall graceful Mycenaean kylix, and a wide two-handled crater. The frescoes of Mycenae, Tiryns, and Thebes which began in the preceding phase developed bolder and more comprehensive, if less artistic, designs. The boar hunt from Tiryns is a spirited composition. The friezes of women from Tiryns and Thebes (the latter is the earlier) have grace and elegance. The battle and chariot scenes from Mycenae and Tiryns show motives repeated on some of the large vases. The use of the human figure in vase paintings, as on the famous Warrior Vase from Mycenae (Fig. 18), is a striking variation from the Cretan custom, and in religion, in houses, and in burial customs the people of the Mainland, though they had borrowed much of their art and their script from the Cretans, show a fundamental racial difference from them. Characteristic of the age are the female terracotta figurines with bird-like faces and horn-like projections for arms. Ornaments of gold are common, but substitutes of glass covered with gold leaf were popular. Ivory is more in evidence than before and tombs at several sites have yielded innumerable plaques and other objects carved with a variety of designs including women, lions, and sphinxes. Bronze weapons were still in use, and safety-pin brooches (*fibulae*) of bronze made their first appearance at the end, but iron did not come into ordinary use till after the fall of Mycenae.

Fig. 18. Scene on the Warrior Vase from Mycenae.

Fig. 19. Vase of red on white ware from the Spercheus valley.

Towards the end of the Bronze Age, about the beginning of the twelfth century, the culture shows signs of decline. Art tends to become an industry, the natural feeling for design weakens and even before the fall of Mycenae the first traces of the geometric style can be seen.

294. In North-Central Greece we have more evidence for the Neolithic Age than in other districts of the Mainland, largely because in Thessaly the Stone Age seems to have continued when the rest of Greece, for the most part, was already in the Bronze Age. This was probably caused by the isolation of Thessaly, which seems to have been surrounded by a forest belt. The Prehistoric Age in Thessaly may be divided into four periods; the first and second are Neolithic, the third is the transition from the Stone to the Bronze Age, and the fourth, which is approximately contemporary with the three Late Helladic periods, is the full Bronze Age. In the first Neolithic Period the remains of the rude hamlets which are found about the plains of Thessaly, Phocis and Boeotia are characterized by an abundance of good hand-made ware with rather elaborate linear designs in red on a white ground (Fig. 19). There are many local varieties of this ware, but its essential features remain the same throughout the whole region. Some of the pottery, especially a plain red ware, is thin, well made, and highly polished. With it are found stone implements of the usual types, axes, hammers and chisels, and pins and awls of bone.

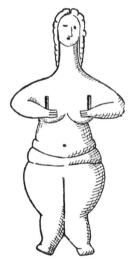

Fig. 20. Reconstructed drawing of steatopygous statuette from Thessaly.

The only sign of contact with the outside world is shown by the presence of knives and flakes of Melian obsidian. The statuettes, which are usually female, although primitive and steatopygous, by their painted decoration and rude modelling indicate a desire to render the human form (Fig. 20). The presence of cereals in some of the settlements and the bones of sheep and the antlers of deer, show that the people lived a simple agricultural and pastoral life, varied by the pleasures of the chase. The culture of the Second Thessalian Period is confined to the regions north of Mt Othrys, for Phocis and Boeotia seem to have been overrun by the bronze-using newcomers of the Early Helladic Age. The original inhabitants do not seem to have been entirely driven out, for in Phocis and even in the Peloponnese, pottery typical of the Second Thessalian Period has been found. In Thessaly itself the culture is no longer as uniform as in the first period. In Eastern Thessaly a new class of pottery appears, which has marked analogies with the early wares of Moldavia, Bukovina, and Podolia. This is decorated with complicated patterns, comprising both linear and spiral elements, painted in dark brown on a cream ground. The vases, which are well polished and of a simple open type, are not of quite so good a fabric as the earlier wares. In Western Thessaly the pottery shows by its patterns that it is developed from the red-on-white ware. These are now usually painted in brown-black on a polished ground that varies from red to buff. But in both regions the most striking vases are those decorated with geometrical and curvilinear designs in brown-black and orange-red on a cream ground. Apart however from the changes in the pottery, the character of the culture seems to have remained much the same. The Third Period is marked by a distinct artistic degeneration, for the bulk of the pottery is coarse and unpainted. A monochrome black polished ware, sometimes decorated with simple geometric patterns in white or with incisions, made its appearance and some of this ware is well made. There are also many vases of a coarse fabric which are painted or rather crusted with thick, dusty-white or pink paint. The technique is unsatisfactory, but some of the spiral patterns are elaborate. The same degeneration is visible in the terracotta statuettes. These have long flat stone heads painted with rude representations of a human face, tapering to points which were inserted in formless bodies of clay. A few figurines all of stone have also been found, which are not so rude as the terracotta figurines with stone heads. In this period the use of bronze seems to have been first introduced, though few actual traces of it have been discovered. In the Fourth Period the degeneration of the local culture is even more apparent, for the pottery is very coarse, thick and rough, so that an advance in technical skill shown by the introduction of bronze is accompanied by an artistic decline. Two male seated figurines in terracotta show improvement in modelling, for their execution, though rough, is not without spirit (Fig. 21). Now there are definite signs of outside influence at work in Thessaly. Hitherto the only signs have been the Melian obsidian and some sherds of Early and Middle Helladic wares. The beehive tomb at Kapakli near Iolcus has yielded pottery, gold work and similar objects of the Second Late Helladic Period, and there are other examples from tombs at Pagasae and in Perrhaebia. In the Third Late Helladic Period towards the end of the Fourth Thessalian Period the Mycenaean culture spread thinly all over Thessaly, but without displacing the old local culture, which continued in a degenerate form. This invasion of the Mycenaean culture and perhaps the intrusion of some geometric type of

Fig. 21.　Terracotta statuette from Thessaly (Fourth Period).

ware from the north-west combined with the local tradition to produce a
geometric style of pottery of a peculiar character. Wares of a similar character
are found also in Attica, the Cyclades, Argolis and Crete, and mark the
transition from the Bronze to the Iron Age.

295. In Western Greece the Neolithic Age is best represented by painted
West Greece.   sherds from a cave in Leucas which seem to be contemporary
with the Second Thessalian Period. In the same island and
in Ithaca Early and Middle Helladic wares have been found and Cephallenia
is rich in tombs of Late Helladic III date. In Aetolia and Acarnania
Middle Helladic pottery is known at Thermus and Late Helladic III
pottery has been found at many sites.

296. Macedonia had a neolithic culture similar to that of the Second
Macedonia.   Period in Thessaly. With the Bronze Age an Early Macedonian civilization was brought in by people akin to those of
Crete, the islands and Southern Greece. They possibly came from the
Trojan area. After 2000 B.C. in Middle Macedonian, Chalcidice was
occupied by a branch of the same people who introduced 'Minyan' ware
into Greece, while in Central Macedonia the older race developed independently perhaps under the influence of Danubian incursions. In Late
Macedonian the two districts reunited with a common culture resulting
from a fusion of the two racial elements. In the last phase after 1400 B.C. the
culture was much affected (especially in Chalcidice) by contact with Late
Helladic centres like Mycenae. Finally about 1150 Central Macedonia was
overrun by a Danubian tribe and the Iron Age began though the metal had
been known in the country as early as 1600 B.C.

297. The last area which can reasonably be brought into this context
Troy.   is the Trojan, although the prehistoric Trojan culture, except
that of the Sixth City, lay on and not within the boundary of the
Aegean sphere and is more akin to finds in Phrygia and Thrace. Troy had
relations with Macedonia in the Early Bronze Age and later geographical
factors made it a natural link between Asia and Europe. The First City at
Troy, which dates from about 3000 B.C., probably belongs to the very
beginning of the Bronze Age. The walls of the houses are rudely built of
small stones and the pottery is of a rough fabric decorated with incised
lines. The second city, which dates from the second half of the third
millennium B.C., was much more imposing, and to judge from the evidence
of buildings, which had undergone alterations, was in existence for a long
time. The fortifications are strong and the walls of the houses consist of
crude brick and timber, laid on a foundation of stones. Thus constructions
as well as plans strikingly resemble early Aegean architecture. In this city
much pottery was found, and some of the vases were made to resemble the
female figure with quaint faces, breasts, and rough arms. Bronze was in
common use as is shown by the finds not only of bronze vessels, knives and
axes, but also of moulds for casting them. The figurines in stone are flat
and shapeless, with owl-like faces; and the culture of this city, apart from

the richly decorated axes and the gold work, does not seem to show a very high stage of art. The gold and silver vases of the great treasure, called by Schliemann Priam's Treasure, although it is doubtful if it belongs to this city, shows in its spiral ornamentation on bracelets, pins and the like, a resemblance to jewellery from the later Shaft Graves of Mycenae. Here and in some pottery and implements there are suggestions of connections with the Aegean, Greece, and Macedonia, but other objects such as pottery and knives of Cypriote type and the famous axe of white jade point to relations with the east. Further, the material used for arrowheads and small knives is flint and not Melian obsidian, and the ordinary pottery finds its nearest analogies in Phrygia. The fourth and fifth settlements at Troy were small and of no importance. To them succeeded the sixth city, which was fortified with strong walls well built of worked stone. It was contemporaneous with the last two phases of the Mycenaean age, as is indicated by the finding of Late Helladic II and III vases, but the typical culture of Troy is not Mycenaean. The bulk of the pottery is of local manufacture and among it is a number of vases similar to the Middle Helladic fabric called Minyan ware, but later in date. The seventh city stands at the beginning of the Iron Age, and in it were found a number of weapons, especially axes of bronze which have a striking likeness to finds from Serbia and the Danubian area, and such finds may possibly reflect a Thraco-Phrygian invasion.

298. There is much that is striking in the architecture of prehistoric Greece, but, as might be expected, so technical an art remained in rather a primitive condition. The most interesting remains are the palaces at Cnossus, Mallia, and Phaestus in Crete and at Tiryns and Mycenae, and those of the houses in the different regions. These are described briefly in Ch. VII. 8.

Architecture.

Prehistoric temples or shrines do not exist except for the shrine of the double axes at Cnossus (L. M. III), which is a small chamber six feet seven inches long by four feet eleven inches wide, and similar chapels at Gournia (L. M. III) and Asine (L. H. III). The so-called temple in the sixth city at Troy, if it is a temple, can hardly be called Greek. Some fragmentary frescoes from Cnossus (Fig. 22), together with a gold model from the fourth Shaft Grave at Mycenae, give us the probable appearance of the façade of a Minoan temple. There seems to have been a high foundation of good masonry, on which stood the shrine itself with three portals. The temple consisted of a main chamber with smaller chambers as wings on either side; an arrangement that recalls that of Etruscan temples as described by Vitruvius. The roof was flat, but in the model an altar of the typical Minoan type is seen above the central portal. In each of the chambers and visible through the open doorways are sacred pillars (baetyls) with the horns of consecration. The buildings shown in these illustrations do not seem to have been large and should perhaps be called shrines rather than temples. The foundations of a shrine similar to that shown in the reconstructed fresco (Fig. 22) have been recognised on the

Temples and Shrines.

west side of the central court at Cnossus, and in this the wings were open.

299. The walls of the cities do not show any particular features unlike those of early fortifications elsewhere. The only exceptions are the great underground galleries (late L. H. III) in the thickness of the walls at Tiryns with a series of side chambers attached, which were probably used as storerooms. The walls show two main styles;

Fortifications.

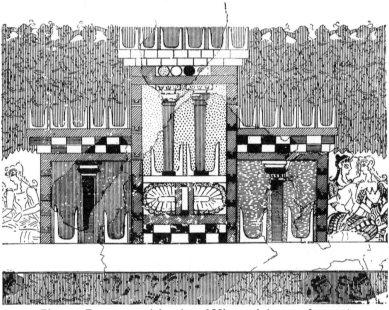

Fig. 22. Reconstructed drawing of Minoan shrine on a fragment of fresco (L.M. I *a*) from Cnossus.

the Cyclopean style with huge blocks of stone roughly fitted together, and ashlar work with blocks hewn into a more or less rectangular shape. The ashlar work is seen at its best in the walls of the Cretan palaces, where the friable gypsum is used for covered walls and limestone for walls exposed to weather, and in the later beehive tombs at Mycenae (L. H. II and III). Both Mycenae and Tiryns have two gates, a main entrance and a small postern. The main gate at Tiryns is set obliquely so that those who approached it had the wall on their right or shieldless sides. At Mycenae the approach to the Lion Gate has the city wall on the left, and on the right just in front of the gate a strong bastion is thrown out to help to guard the entrance. This had the effect that anyone who attacked the gate would find

himself enclosed in a small court barely thirteen feet square and exposed
on three sides to missiles from the citadel. The Lion Gate itself is slightly
over ten feet high and between nine and ten feet wide. The sockets for the
double gates are still visible in the threshold, and behind the gates a strong
wooden beam ran into sockets in the gate-posts. The gate is roofed with
a massive lintel and over the centre is a triangular relieving space to lighten
the weight on the lintel, which is filled with the lion relief. The postern
gate was built on the same principle. At Troy the walls of the sixth city
have a scarped substructure six to seven feet high to carry the perpendicular
upper walls. Three gates can be made out clearly: two of these are on the
same principle as the Lion Gate, and the third runs at right angles through
the wall with a big square tower overlooking it on the left. The large

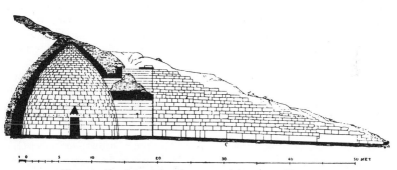

Fig. 23. Section of the Treasury of Atreus at Mycenae.

square towers at Troy, of which three can be seen clearly, are a feature
which has so far not been recognised at Tiryns, Mycenae, or any other
Mycenaean site.

    300. The most remarkable monuments of prehistoric architecture in
Greece, the beehive tombs of the Mainland, show three stages
of progressive development (L. H. II—L. H. III). The   **Beehive**
most famous examples are the so-called Treasuries of Atreus   **Tombs.**
at Mycenae and of Minyas at Orchomenus (both L. H. III). These tombs
are built in an excavation cut in a sloping hillside, so that the tomb proper
must be approached by a cutting which runs straight into the hill. The
Treasury of Atreus is the best preserved (Fig. 23). The approach is twenty
feet wide and one hundred and fifteen feet long, and at the door of the
tomb the depth of the cutting, which is faced with ashlar masonry, is about
forty-five feet. The door of the tomb is twenty feet wide, is three inches
short of eighteen feet high, and in width varies from eight feet nine inches
at the bottom to eight feet one inch at the top. The lintel is composed of
two gigantic slabs, one (29 ft. 6 by 16 ft. 6 by 3 ft. 4) being estimated to weigh

one hundred and twenty tons. Over the lintel is the usual triangular relieving space, once masked by ornamental slabs of reddish stone, and before the door on either side stood two columns of green marble sculptured with zigzag and spiral patterns. The columns, which like all Mycenaean columns are thinner at the bottom than the top, rest on simple square plinths At the top is a carved capital of a simple torus shape separated from the shaft by a neck ornamented with a lotus leaf pattern. Above the columns there seems to have been a carved cornice. The door was double, to judge by the socket holes still visible. Within is a great chamber shaped like a beehive, fifty feet high and formed of thirty-three horizontal courses. Each of these courses is a circle superposed one upon another corbel fashion and supported by counter weighting. Bronze nails in the interstices of the courses show that the walls were once decorated with rosettes or similar ornaments in bronze. The tomb proper is a square rock-hewn room, intended to be lined with masonry but unfinished, and connected with the beehive by a double door about ten feet high. A pit in the floor of this side chamber was probably the burial place. At Orchomenus the wonderful stone ceiling, with its beautiful decoration of spirals and rosettes, was the roof of the square side chamber of the tomb Such side chambers are not a constant feature and seem only to occur in the larger and more elaborate examples. In others the interments took place in pit graves in the floor of the beehive.

Bibliography. C. W. Blegen, *Korakou, Zygouries, Gonia* (Metropolitan Museum Studies III); C. W. Blegen and A. J B. Wace, *Middle Helladic Tombs* (Symbolae Osloenses, 1930); H. T. Bossert, *Alt-Kreta*; H. Boyd-Hawes, *Gournia*, British School at Athens, *Phylakopi*; H Bulle, *Orchomenos* I; *Cambridge Ancient History*, Vols. I, II and Volume of Plates I; F. Chapouthier and J. Charbonneaux, *Mallia*; W. Dörpfeld, *Troja und Ilion, Alt-Ithaka*; A J. Evans, *Palace of Minos, Prehistoric Tombs of Knossos, Scripta Minoa, The Shaft Graves and Bee-Hive Tombs of Mycenae*; D. Fimmen, *Kretisch-Mykenische Kultur*; F Halbherr, L. Pernier and others, *Scavi della Missione Italiana* (Mon. Ant. XII ff.); E. H. Hall, *Vrokastro*; H R. Hall, *The Civilization of Greece in the Bronze Age*; W. A Heurtley, *Prehistoric Macedonia* (Antiquity, Sept. 1929); G Karo, *Schachtgräber von Mykenai*; A. D. Keramopoullos, Θηβαϊκά ('Αρχ. Δελτίον III); M. Nilsson, *Minoan-Mycenaean Religion*, J. Pendlebury, *Aegyptiaca*; *Egypt and the Aegean* (Journal Egypt. Arch. XVI); A. W. Persson, *Fouilles d'Asinè* (Bull. Soc. R. Lettres Lund 1922—23, 1924—25); G. Rodenwaldt and K. Müller, *Tiryns* II and III; H. Schliemann, *Mycenae, Tiryns*, R. B. Seager, *Mochlos, Pseira, Pachyammos*; C. Tsountas and J. L Manatt, *Mycenaean Age*; A. J B. Wace, *Excavations at Mycenae* (Annual British School at Athens, XXIV, XXV); A. J B Wace and M. S. Thompson, *Prehistoric Thessaly*; S. Xanthoudides, *Vaulted Tombs of Mesarà*.

IV. 2. ARCHITECTURE.

[For prehistoric architecture see §§ 298 ff.; for theatre buildings § 425;
for fortifications §§ 683 ff.; for the architecture of houses §§ 702 ff.]

301. The later and more complete architecture was to a great extent
evolved from the works of the primitive period. The Greek genius was
indeed ever ready to adopt new ideas, yet when once a recognised type had been formed, the new ideas were brought into   Survival of
                                                              the wooden
harmony with the old: for instance, the stone architecture   type.
of the Greeks demonstrates to a very great extent that its
decorative features were founded upon the type of wooden construction.
That they recognised this fact themselves is evident from Vitruvius (IV. 2),
who drew his information, as he continually tells us, from Greek sources—
but it is also capable of being proved from modern investigations. The
Lycian tombs, and some which have lately been discovered in Cyprus,
show in the plainest manner that forms proper only to timber have been
copied by way of ornament in stone. This imitation can be followed
through the whole of the entablature, that is, the upper horizontal members
of a Greek façade of the complete period. It can hardly be doubted that
the timber type grew out of the real construction of this primitive period.
Not only do the columns and entablature prove this, but it may also be
seen in the wooden casing provided for doors, etc., even in marble buildings
of the fifth century, a survival from the time when inferior materials, such
as unbaked brick, made such an arrangement necessary. The extensive
use of terracotta facing in Greece and Sicily, sometimes even on stone
buildings, is evidently derived from a wooden structure.

302. The Dorian immigration, traditionally attributed to the eleventh
century B.C., introduced many new elements into Greek architecture,
especially, in all probability, the gable form of roof; the Mycenaean
buildings seem to have been flat-roofed. But other elements
of the Doric order seem to be influenced by Mycenaean   Development
                                                        of Doric
models. The date of the earliest Doric buildings has not   order.
indeed been determined, but it was probably subsequent to
the Dorian invasion of the Peloponnesus. It may also be affirmed that
on the whole this species of architecture largely prevailed in the colonies
attributed to the Dorians, whilst the rival and contemporary Ionic order
was the favourite on the eastern side of the Aegean. There were, however,
sufficiently numerous exceptions to prove that these two orders did not
show an absolute line of demarcation between the states of Dorian and
Ionian extraction. The earliest Doric building in Greece is the Heraeum
at Olympia. Its walls are an example of the Mycenaean practice of
building only the lower portion of the wall in stone, and the upper
of mud-brick and timber. In its colonnade we can trace the gradual

substitution of stone columns for the wooden tree-trunks that had originally
served the same purpose; for the varying sizes of the shafts and profiles of
the capitals show that they were set up in succession, at considerable
intervals of time. In the Opisthodomus, Pausanias records that one of the
columns was of oak—doubtless the last survivor of the original wooden
ones.

The earliest Doric columns are fluted, as were also the stone columns
at Mycenae. The origin both of this practice, and of the essential form
of the column, is very obscure. The column is made extremely effective,
both structurally and aesthetically, by the contrivance of a projecting abacus
connected with the circular shaft of the column by a conoidal echinus.
The profile of this echinus is bulging, almost bowl-shaped, in early
examples, and gradually becomes flatter, with so great regularity of development that a temple can be approximately dated from it. The shaft
of the column diminishes upwards, in contrast to Mycenaean examples,
which diminish downwards. Even in the earliest examples which have
been discovered it is found to be a very accurate conic section, elliptic
or sometimes parabolic in the earlier, and hyperbolic in the later and more
refined examples.

303. Another beautiful refinement is the very slightly curved outline of
the shaft called the ἔντασις. This is found even in the early
Doric columns now standing in the temple of Corinth, which
date probably from the sixth century B.C. There are, however, remains of fallen columns probably of a still earlier
date, from which by careful measurement the existence of an entasis can
be deduced. The Doric order at its first introduction was very solid, both
as regards the shaft of the column and the proportionate height of the
entablature; but it gradually became more slender. The height of the
Doric columns of the temple at Corinth was about three and a quarter
times the breadth of the abacus and four and a quarter times the diameter
of the shaft at its base: in the Parthenon the height was five times the
breadth of the abacus and five and a half times the diameter of the shaft.
So long as it retained its massive character the simplicity of its detail
harmonized admirably with the general effect. The long series of refinements, culminating in the Parthenon, which is by overwhelming authority
admitted to have exhibited the highest rank of architectural achievement,
took place before it lost the qualities for which it is most admired; but
when afterwards it became attenuated, not only in the slenderness of the
column but also in the massiveness of the capital, as in the Portico of
Philip in the island of Delos, and some other late examples, the result no
longer satisfied the eye, and the order was found to be ineffective and
ill-adapted for the recovery of what it had lost in dignity of form by the
introduction of further enrichment. In many early temples the wooden
entablature was covered by painted terracotta mouldings, of which many
beautiful specimens have been found in Sicily, at Olympia, and elsewhere.

Refinements in the Doric order.

304. There is no reason to suppose that the **Ionic order** was developed later in time than the Doric. It has this much in common with the Doric, that the entablature exhibits a *Parallel development of the Ionic.* wooden origin. The most conspicuous early remains are those of the huge temple of Hera, at Samos, and those of the equally huge early temple of Artemis, at Ephesus, but these enormous temples had many precursors of smaller size; and it is not unreasonable to hope that when circumstances shall allow of the investigation of sites in the Turkish provinces as complete as has taken place in Greece and the Grecian sites in Italy, more of these earlier essays may be found. Unlike the Doric, there is no evidence that the Ionic column of the earliest examples was more massive than those of later times. In Ionic columns of early period the height is ten times the diameter. The origin of the Ionic capital has been much discussed. Dr Puchstein, in his treatise on the Ionic capital, points out that while volute capitals are known in Assyrian and other oriental architecture and decoration, the essential feature of the Ionic order, the combination of the volute with a cymatium or torus, belongs exclusively to Greece. And from whatever quarter its elements were derived, its extreme elegance was due to its treatment at the hands of the Ionian Greeks. The peculiarity of the Ionic fluting is the adjustment of a fillet separating the flutes. The two orders under discussion met one another on common ground, at Athens, which had been spared by the Dorian invasion, and so retained more of the old civilization than any other important city in Greece proper.

305. The invention of the **Corinthian order** is traced by some from the palm-leaf-capped columns in Egypt, although the resemblance between such columns and those of the Corin- *Derivation of the Corinthian order.* thian order is extremely slight. The modern habit of rejecting traditions, justifiable no doubt in many cases, is often carried too far, and we may accept the statement of Vitruvius (IV. 1) that Callimachus was led to the invention by seeing an acanthus plant which had twined itself round a basket of sepulchral offerings, particularly as the date of the building of the temple at Bassae, where the earliest known example of such a capital was found, accords perfectly well with the era of Callimachus. It may also be remarked as favourable to the theory of its being a personal invention, that the new feature seems to have taken its place in architecture very gradually, and it was not until the Doric had become so attenuated as to have lost its character for sublimity, and the Ionic had been so frequently repeated as to have led to the desire for some novelty, that the Corinthian order obtained general acceptance. Probably the first great work in which it took the prominent place was the Olympieum at Athens. It had been used in subordination with Doric and Ionic, as already related, at Bassae, and about the same time or very shortly afterwards with Doric in the Tholus at the Hieron of Epidaurus and in the great Milesian Ionic temple at Didyma. It had also, according

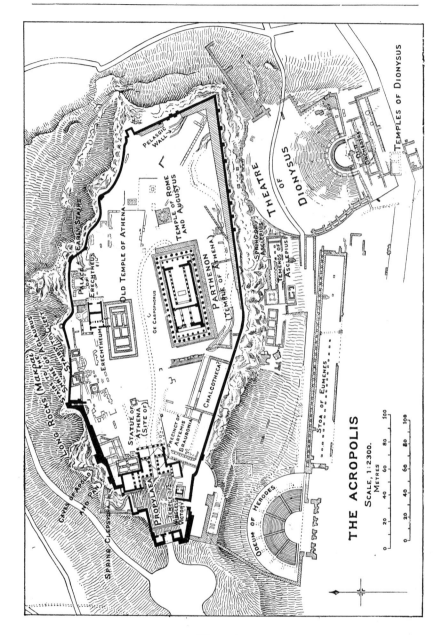

Fig. 24.

to Pausanias, been combined with both the more ancient orders at Tegea. In Roman times the Corinthian and the modifications derived from it were used almost exclusively.

306. The essential parts of a completed Doric building may be seen upon the accompanying diagram. The whole structure usually rests upon three steps, *aaa*, of which the uppermost is called the stylobate (στυλοβάτης). These steps always show a slightly curved convex surface, sloping towards the

Architectural members of a Doric building.

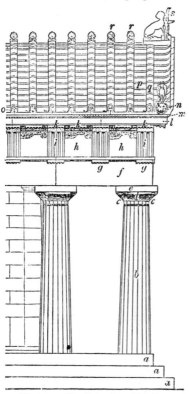

Fig. 25. Doric order (Aegina).

ends and the sides. Directly upon this stylobate, with no intervening base, rests the shaft of the column, *b* (στῦλος or κίων); this shaft is either monolithic or composed of drums (σφόνδυλοι); it is fluted (ῥαβδωτός), the top and bottoms only of the flutes being finished before the column was set up; in unfinished temples the rest of the shaft remains unfluted, as at Segesta. Doric flutes intersect at sharp angles. The neck of the column, *c* (ὑποτραχήλιον) is usually surrounded by fillets (Lat. *annuli*). On this rests the curved echinus, *d* (ἐχῖνος) forming a transition to the square abacus, *e* (πλίνθος). These members, *c*, *d*, *e*, together form the capital (κιονόκρανον or κιόκρανον). The upper part resting on the columns, *f—m*, is together called the entablature (ἐπιβολή). Its lower portion is the plain architrave, *f* (ἐπιστύλιον). The frieze is divided into triglyphs, *i* (τρίγλυφοι), so called because they are divided into three bands by two vertical channels, and metopes, *h* (μετόπαι), or holes between the triglyphs. It is generally supposed that the triglyphs represented the ends of the horizontal beams in a wooden prototype. Either some or all of the metopes might be

Fig. 26. Ionic column (Priene).

decorated by sculpture. Below the triglyphs come the regulae with guttae, *g*. There is usually one triglyph over each column and one over each intercolumniation. Above the frieze is the cornice (γεῖσον), *l*, crowned by the sima (κῦμα, κυμάτιον), *m*; its under surface has, over each metope and triglyph, a modillion or mutulus, *k*, with guttae, which probably represents a slanting beam of the gable roof. The roof itself was covered with tiles (κέραμοι) either of pottery, or more often, in large temples, of marble; they were in alternate rows of flat tiles with raised edges, *p* (σωλῆνες), and ridge-tiles, *q* (καλυπτῆρες): the ridges terminated below in antifixes (ἀνθέμια), *o*,

and above, on the ridge of the roof, in coping tiles (ἡγεμόνες), r; lions'
heads, n, usually served the purpose of gargoyles. The gable end or
pediment (ἀετός) was often filled with sculpture; and it also had acroteria,
s, above it whether figures or conventional ornaments, on the centre and
at each end.

The Ionic order differs from the Doric both in column and entablature.
The Ionic column is of two kinds, the Ionic proper and
the Attic (see the diagrams); both alike have a base   Architectural
(σπεῖρα), and a volute capital; but the base in the Ionic   members of an
Ionic building.
consists of a torus, u, resting on a lower member divided
by two channels (τρόχιλοι), t, while the Attic base has an upper and lower

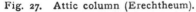

Fig. 27. Attic column (Erechtheum).

torus, uv, divided by one channel, t; the upper torus is often fluted. In
early examples, the base varies considerably in form. The base sometimes
rests upon a square plinth, s, but this member is often omitted, especially
in the Attic form. The shaft is fluted, but the flutes do not intersect,
being separated by flat fillets. The neck of the Attic column is enriched
by a band of honey-suckle ornament (ἀνθέμιον). The capital consists of a
torus or echinus, w, surmounted by a channel, x, which ends on either side

in volutes, *y*, and a low abacus, *z*. In the Ionic form the channel is plain ; in the Attic it is divided by a deeply profiled incision. The Ionic form may be seen in most of the temples of Asia Minor, and the Propylaea and Temple of Nike Apteros at Athens ; the great example which gives the name to the Attic form is the Erechtheum. The entablature has an architrave divided into three bands or fasciae ; above this, in what is usually regarded as the normal form of the order, is placed a continuous frieze (ζωφόρος), not divided into metopes and triglyphs, but often adorned with sculpture. The frieze is, however, omitted entirely in several of the best-known examples from Asia Minor, and the cornice comes immediately above the architrave. Below the cornice is a row of dentils in the Ionic, but not in the Attic form ; modillions also are found ; but where they occur they are always below the dentils, not above them as in Roman architecture. The Corinthian order is identical with the Ionic in everything except the capital.

307. The earliest temples were probably simply shrines, consisting of four walls, carrying the roof, with a doorway usually in the eastern wall. This simplest type was followed by a succession of structures, the classification of which, according to Vitruvius (who evidently uses Greek sources), was as follows :

Classification of temples.

1. In **the temple in Antis** (ἐν παραστάσιν, Fig. 27ᵃ, 1, 1 *a*) the walls of the cella were prolonged a little beyond the doorway and terminated each with a pilaster. Between these antae as they were called might be placed two columns, so that a porch having three entrances was thus formed in front of the door. The roof, with its shallow gable or pediment, rose above this, supported by the two columns and the antae. Sometimes a similar porch was added at the back also.

2. The **Prostyle temple** (Fig. 27ᵃ, 2) marked a considerable advance on the temple in Antis. Two columns were added, one in front of each of the antae, and these with the columns between them formed a portico in front of the entrance.

3. In the **Amphiprostyle temple** (Fig. 27ᵃ, 3) the prostyle portico of the front was reduplicated at the back. A familiar example is that of the elegant little temple of Nike Apteros, near the entrance to the Acropolis at Athens. The front porch so formed was called the Pronaos and that in the rear the Opisthodomus or Posticum.

4. The **Peripteral temple.** (Fig. 27ᵃ, 4, 4 *a*.) According to the definition of Vitruvius this form was developed from the Amphiprostyle temple ; but in the great majority of extant examples it appears as an adaptation of a temple formed of a cella, with a porch at each end like that of the temple in Antis. Round this centre was built a complete colonnade, forming a covered ambulatory on each side of the cella. This arrangement, which marked an enormous advance on the amphiprostyle temple, was probably an invention of Greek architects. In Egypt there were open courts with

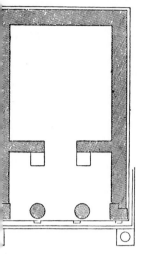

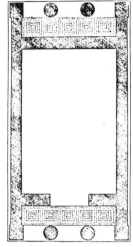

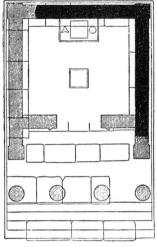

Temple in Antis (smaller temple at Rhamnus).

1 a.　Temple in Antis with posticum (Temple of Artemis at Eleusis).

2.　Prostyle temple (Temple at Selinus).

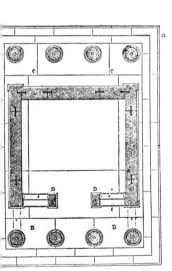

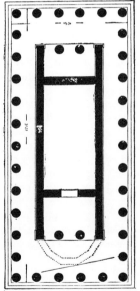

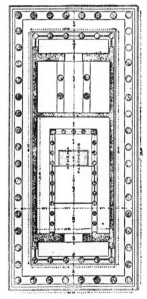

Amphiprostyle temple (Temple of Athena Nike at Athens).

4.　Peripteral temple in Antis (Theseum).

4 a.　Peripteral temple, Amphiprostyle (Parthenon).

Fig. 27ᵃ.　Plans of Temples.

colonnaded ambulatories against the external walls, but the effect of these was so different from that of the Greek temples that they could hardly have been taken as models. The Greek form appears to have been a native development, and was probably invented very early, since it appears in the Heraeum at Olympia, but remained in favour to the very last.

5. The **Dipteral temple** required a double range of columns round the cella. A variety of this class, called by Vitruvius the Pseudodipteral, omitted the inner row of columns on the flanks but retained its space, the cella wall ranging with the second column from the corner. The great temple at Selinus is pseudodipteral.

6. The **Hypaethral temple** was identical with the Dipteral, except that it had an entrance at each end, and in the midst a kind of open court surrounded by a portico of two ranges of columns, one above the other. Vitruvius' example of this is the Olympieum at Athens. But it should be observed that the plan of this temple as derived from excavation does not closely agree with the definition; the great Milesian temple at Branchidae is its best representative.

Vitruvius takes four as the normal number of columns at each end of an amphiprostyle temple; the normal peripteral, formed by placing a colonnade round such a tetrastyle temple, is hexastyle, and the dipteral or pseudodipteral octastyle. But where the amphiprostyle temple itself is hexastyle, of course its peripteral form is octastyle, as in the case of the Parthenon; Vitruvius says that the normal Hypaethral is decastyle; but the example he quotes is octastyle. For the peripteral temple with six columns in the front, he gives 11 as the usual number for the sides, and, for an octastyle temple, 15; but in this respect the temples varied considerably, the earliest temples being usually the longest in proportion to their width : the Parthenon had 17.

308. Of the monuments of Greek architecture, few have come down to us in a condition calculated to exhibit their original beauty, but imperfect remains and particularly underground foundations exist to a great extent. Much has already been found, and fresh additions to our knowledge are being continually made. Of the works left standing in a more or less perfect state, temples and theatres supply the largest list. Temples have in several instances been preserved to us in consequence of their having been converted into churches. At Athens this circumstance has preserved to us the Parthenon, the Erechtheum, the Theseum, and the larger portion of what now remains of the Olympieum. The temples at Paestum have been saved by the insalubrity of the site. Theatres have been protected partly by their prolonged use during the early centuries of our era and partly by the extreme solidity of the masonry of their enclosing walls. A similar condition has in many cases preserved to us important remains of ancient fortifications, to which end their lofty sites have often contributed—a

Existing remains of Greek architecture.

Fig. 28.   Temple of Olympian Zeus at Athens.

favourable condition shared by some of the finest temples, such as the temple in Aegina, and the temples at Sunium and Bassae. Of strictly secular buildings, the Thersilion, or 'Hall of the Ten Thousand,' at Megalopolis, excavated by the British School of Archaeology in 1890—1893, though recovered in plan only, is too important not to be specially mentioned. The Treasuries exhumed at Olympia and Delphi are also valuable recoveries. Private houses have also been found, especially at Delos and at Priene; for these see § 710.

309. The principal site on which **Doric** temples are to be seen is Athens, where the Parthenon and Theseum represent the architecture of the best period. The date of the Parthenon is well known: it was dedicated in 438 B.C. The architectural features of the Theseum seem to indicate a slightly earlier date. At any rate it exhibits all the refinements of beauty and skill of the best period. The **Propylaea**, coeval with the Parthenon, is a building belonging mainly to the Doric order in its most perfect period, while the gate called that of the new Agora, dated about the beginning of our era, exhibits the same order in its decadence. The proportion of the height of the column to the diameter in the former of these two is about the same as in the Parthenon, namely $5\frac{1}{2}$, in the latter it is a little more than 6, but the chief sign of inferiority is seen in the contour and want of projection of the capital. There are also, at Athens, important fragments of Doric structures of a much earlier period, in particular one which has the appearance of being the most archaic that has yet been discovered. Its discovery in a city which claimed chief relationship with the Ionians goes to prove that employment of this order was not exclusively a question of race. The next most complete and important example of the Doric order is the Temple of Poseidon at Paestum, which preserves the whole of its peristyle complete. It is a magnificent building, of archaic character, possibly belonging to the sixth century B.C. It is the only instance remaining of what was probably not an unusual form, having in the interior two ranges of colonnades, one above the other, for the purpose of supporting the roof. It is known by written records that this was the case in the Parthenon, and by unmistakable fallen fragments that it was so in the temple at Aegina. In the temple at Paestum the capitals are larger in proportion than they are in the Parthenon, being intermediate between the latter and the example at Corinth. Two other ancient buildings form a group with the Temple of Poseidon, but are in themselves of greatly inferior interest, one called the Temple of Ceres and the other, which may be a secular building, called the Basilica. They are still standing, with their peristyles complete, on an unencumbered site, and the effect produced by them is very striking. Next to the remains at Athens and Paestum, Acragas (Girgenti), and in a lesser degree Syracuse, present the most important examples of Doric temples. There are numerous ruins at Selinus, Olympia, Delphi and Delos, which furnish valuable material for study.

(margin note: Existing remains of Doric temples.)

310.   The most refined and beautiful examples of the **Ionic order**
are at Athens.   Of the complex and elegant Erechtheum on
the Acropolis substantial remnants exist, and that exquisite   Existing re-
mains of Ionic
temples.
gem, the Temple of Nike Apteros, is still preserved; both of
these have been to a great extent reconstructed out of the
original materials; but the memory of the small temple which formerly
existed on the banks of the Ilissus, not far from the gigantic columns of
the Olympieum, is only preserved to us in the carefully executed plates
of Stuart (vol. I.).   The internal Ionic architecture of the temple at Bassae

Fig. 29.   Temple of Nike Apteros.

should be also specially mentioned.   As regards size, the palm must be
assigned to the temples of Asia Minor.   Some of these are enormous, and
amongst them are the two oldest known to us, the Temple of Hera, at
Samos, and that of Artemis, at Ephesus.   The excavations at the latter
place disclosed different layers of foundations.   The uppermost and latest
foundations belong to the time of Alexander the Great, when the earlier
temple, of the time of Croesus, had been destroyed by fire.   The latest
was 342 feet in length and 163 feet in width, and the sixth-century temple
was nearly the same size.   The temple at Samos was very nearly as large.

Fig. 30.   Temple of Poseidon at Paestum.

The temple of Artemis at Sardis had columns 60 feet high, and was 340 feet long and 150 feet wide; but the largest temple of all was the temple at Didyma, near Miletus, which has been already mentioned.   In addition to the above there were Ionic temples of great beauty and importance at Magnesia, Priene, Teos, and the Smintheum in the Troad.   The Ionic order, though much rarer in Magna Graecia than the Doric, was not unknown there.   The temple built by the Locrians near Gerace was of this order, as was the small temple 'of Empedocles,' at Selinus.   Mention

should also be made of the fine internal columns of the Propylaea at Athens, and various elaborate tombs, especially the Nereid Monument and the Mausoleum at Halicarnassus.

311.   The invention of the **Corinthian order** by Callimachus has already been spoken of, as well as its first employment at Bassae and Epidaurus.   A very beautiful and early example remains to us in the Choragic monument of Lysicrates, at Athens (date about 335 B.C.), now sadly mutilated but for-

Existing examples of the Corinthian order.

18—2

tunately seen and recorded by Stuart when in a fairly perfect state. The capitals of the example from Epidaurus are well preserved. For a long time this order was used with much reserve, but after its employment by Antiochus Epiphanes, about the year 174 B.C., as the ruling order in the great temple of Olympian Zeus at Athens, it became almost exclusively used both in religious and secular buildings.

312. Finally, the characteristics of these orders may be thus stated. The Doric on account of its gravity and simplicity is by far the most solemn : it received from Greek architects great refinements, of a scientific and artistic character, particularly in the mathematically adjusted profiles of the mouldings and the curvatures of the main vertical and horizontal lines applied as delicate corrections of an optical nature, together with a rigorous but very practical scheme of proportion, which undoubtedly contributed to the perfection of the works of the best period. These principles had indeed been long applied in a greater or less degree before they reached their climax in the Theseum, Parthenon, and the Athenian Propylaea, but afterwards they were gradually neglected, and the Doric order in its last representations having become flat and degenerate, went out of favour and almost ceased to be practised. The Ionic order of the best time partook of all or most of the refinements which were applied to the Doric, and had the same beauty of outline and the same studied accuracy of proportion. It admitted of more ornament than the Doric, but when subsequent fashion demanded still more elaborate decoration, it was of too pure a nature to admit it with advantage, and it yielded its place to its successor the Corinthian, which was ready to accept from the hands of the Romans all the superabundant enrichment which they looked for.

Character-istics of the three orders.

313. As the **Parthenon** (Fig. 27ª, 4*a*) may be taken as the type of all Greek temples in their full development, a general notion of the appearance and object of such structures may be obtained from a short description of that building. The main purpose of a temple was to enshrine the statue of the deity to whom it was dedicated, and this function was performed by the ναὸς or cella. The statue was placed looking towards the east, in the central axis of the temple ; and care was taken in this shrine, as in most other temples, that there should be an unobstructed view of the local horizon ; in this case the ridge of Mt Hymettus was seen through the lofty eastern door. The object of this arrangement was that on certain particular days of the year the rising sun, and on all occasions the first bright eastern glow, might lighten up the statue, and there can be but little doubt that when the temple was first founded the orientation was so chosen that on the principal feast day at least it should be illumined by the rising sun. On the occasion of festivals the main body of the worshippers stood without; the interior was not intended to receive a congregation, as except in the early morning the light there would have been obscure. Apart from the great doors, a certain amount

The Parthenon.

Fig. 32.　The Parthenon.

of light would reach the cella through the semi-transparent marble tiles of the roof. It has been suggested that there were other arrangements in the larger temples to introduce some light from the roof; but there seems no necessity for anything of this kind in the Parthenon. The ναὸς in the Parthenon was about 100 feet in length, and so it was able to inherit from the earlier temple that it replaced its official title of the Hecatompedon. The total interior breadth was 63 feet, divided into three aisles by colonnades, the central division being 34 feet wide. The flanking colonnades were returned on the west, but the eastern end was almost entirely occupied by the great entrance doorway. There were no galleries, but the two ranges of Doric columns were connected by architraves, the architrave of the upper range giving support to the roof. The statue stood at 60 feet from the entrance. At the back, that is westward of the ναός, another apartment 63 feet north and south by 43 east and west, was formed; the name Parthenon, in official documents, belongs to this chamber only, though it is often loosely applied to the whole building. The chamber had originally no door of communication with the ναός. Its ceiling was supported by four lofty columns in the middle of the apartment, and it was entered from the west by a door of the same size as that which entered the ναὸς from the east. Each of these doors was faced with a portico of six Doric columns. The eastern porch was called the Pronaos, the western the Opisthodomus. Thus these two chambers with their porches formed a complete amphiprostyle temple. The whole was then surrounded by an ambulatory called the peristyle, supported by forty-six Doric columns. Both pronaos and opisthodomus were furnished with gratings reaching from floor to roof between the columns; and so all the compartments of the building were suitable for storing precious offerings and treasures; we have many inventories of their contents. The opisthodomus and Parthenon were used as treasuries. The total length on the upper step, called the stylobate, which carried the columns of the peristyle, was 228·14 English feet, and the breadth, also on the upper step, 101·33. It will be seen that this forms very nearly the proportion of 9 to 4 [it would be exact if the breadth had been 101·395]. It was almost invariably the case that a Greek temple was so planned that the length and breadth of the stylobate formed with each other a ratio in low numbers (it was not always the upper step that was taken, but one of the steps of the stylobate, which were generally three in number). There is scarcely an exception to this rule of proportion. This is not the only instance of proportion in low numbers found in contiguous portions, both horizontally and vertically, in this temple; but the subject would be too extensive to follow here in detail. The total height of the temple to the apex of the roof, measured from the bottom of the stylobate, was 65 feet, to which the columns contribute 34·25. This temple, built entirely of white marble, was also very richly adorned with sculpture. At the two ends the triangular spaces enclosed between the horizontal cornice and the sloping lines which indicated the roof, were filled with magnificent sculptures. There were also other important sculptures in the metopes under the great cornice, and in the frieze which surmounted the cella wall, and these were carried round its whole extent, within the peristyle. For these sculptures, of which the greater part are now in the British Museum, see § 324.

The chamber called the Parthenon is almost if not quite peculiar to this building; in the more usual form the cella with its pronaos and opisthodomus and external peristyle would complete the temple. There is also some evidence of decorative painting, but the scantiness of this evidence is consistent with the view that colour, which was applied largely to temples built of soft stone and coated with a fine stucco, was used with great reserve on marble structures, being employed only in details and on narrow mouldings, while the broader surfaces were left plain.

W. B. Dinsmoor. *The Architecture of Ancient Greece.* Revised and rewritten from Anderson and Spiers, *Architecture of Greece and Rome*; Perrot and Chipiez, *Histoire de l'Art dans l'Antiquité*, vol. VI. **Bibliography.** *Grèce primitive—Architecture*; Borrmann and Neuwirth, *Geschichte der Baukunst*; D. S. Robertson, *Handbook of Greek and Roman Architecture*; B. Fletcher and B. F. Fletcher, *History of Architecture* (useful for its numerous diagrams); Penrose, *Principles of Athenian Architecture*; Marquand, *Greek Architecture.* See also the publications, too numerous to quote, of different sets of monuments, such as those of Olympia, Delphi, Athens, Sicily, Asia Minor, etc.

IV.   3.   SCULPTURE.

A.   ARCHAIC PERIOD (*circa* 650—500 B.C.).

314.   The origin of sculpture in Greece cannot be traced back with any certainty beyond the end of the seventh century B.C. **Origins and early development.** Before this time there existed decorative work in metal, gems, and pottery which reached back to the traditions of Cretan and Mycenaean times. Such traditions of handicraft and even of formal representation were doubtless of great service to the earliest attempts of the sculptor. Sculpture may from the first be divided into two classes, decorative or architectural and free. The first of these often represents figures or groups in action, and makes considerable use of early decorative forms; it is found in the metopes of Doric temples, the continuous frieze of Ionic temples, and in the groups which may adorn the pediments or gable

ends of either order. Sculpture in the round, on the other hand, offered many difficulties to the primitive sculptor. Early images of the gods made very little attempt to represent the human figure; numerous statuettes, made of terracotta, bronze or stone, have been found on early sites; an imitation of such figures in marble may be seen in Fig. 33. The first improvements

Fig. 33. Marble statue dedicated by Nicandra, from Delos.

in the rendering of the human figure were attributed to **Daedalus**, to whom many early statues surviving into later time were attributed. But, even if he is not an entirely mythical character, his association with Minos in Crete implies a date long before the beginnings of sculpture in Greece. On the other hand various traditions attributed the invention of sculpture in marble to **Melas, Micciades,** and **Archermus** of Chios, or to **Dipoenus** and **Scyllis,** Cretan Daedalids, who made statues of gods in the Peloponnese and elsewhere in Greece, and who worked in wood and ivory.

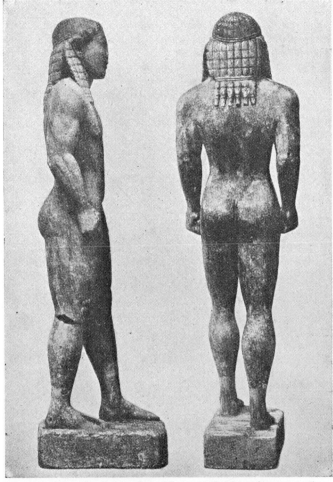

Fig. 34. Statue by Polymedes of Argos, one of a pair representing Cleobis and Biton, found at Delphi.

The invention of sculpture in bronze was attributed to **Rhoecus** and **Theodorus** of Samos. All these appear to have been historical characters, the names of some being recorded in inscriptions. The sculpture of the sixth century B.C. consists mostly of nude male and draped female figures, standing in rigidly frontal pose, with the left foot advanced and the arms close to the side. This pose is clearly borrowed from Egypt; the style and proportion of the figure can be distinguished as characteristic of certain early schools, such as those of the Peloponnese, Boeotia, Attica, Ionia, and the Aegean islands. How much such statues may differ from one another may be seen by comparing the work of an Argive sculptor, the statues of Cleobis and Biton (Fig. 34), whose sturdy proportions and exaggerated muscles foreshadow the athletic ideals which were to characterize the Argive school of the fifth century, with the comparatively slim and graceful figure of the Apollo of Tenea, an example probably of the art of the Aegean islands (Fig. 37).

315. The exploitation of marble quarries, first in Naxos and afterwards in Paros, which yielded a much finer quality, gave a great impetus to the insular schools and carried their products to all parts of the Greek world. A colossal sphinx on a high Ionic column, dedicated by the Naxians at Delphi, shows how a decorative type, borrowed from the East, could be adapted to a monumental use. A figure of a winged Victory, dedicated by Archermus of Chios, is said to have been the first example of the type.

Ionian sculpture outside Ionia.

In the second half of the sixth century the Ionian style in sculpture enjoyed a vogue almost as wide-spread as Ionian commerce. It took root in Lycia (reliefs of the Harpy Tomb) and penetrated to Cyprus, where it modified but failed to break down the conservative local tradition; it was carried to the shores and islands of the northern Aegean, to Black Sea colonies, to Etruria, and even to Spain, where it helped to produce the hybrid Iberian style exemplified in the Elche head (now in the Louvre). Ionian artists executed important commissions on the mainland, such as the Throne of Amyclaean Apollo made for the Spartans by **Bathycles** of Magnesia and known to us through Pausanias' description, and a series of Treasuries at Delphi, dedicated by Siphnos, Cnidus and Phocaea, of which we have extensive remains—exquisite miniature temples with porches borne by caryatids and friezes in which a variety of subjects, including a Gigantomachy and groups of seated deities, are treated with growing mastery of composition and high technical skill. The pediment of the Siphnian Treasury represents Apollo and Heracles in dispute over the tripod; Athena stands between them, Artemis and other figures at either side; next the chariots of the two rivals, and in the angles first a kneeling and then a recumbent man. Here for the first time we have several of the motives which were used in the great pediments of the fifth century. On the other hand the pedimental sculptures of an early sixth-century temple, recently brought to light in Corfu, are neither coherent in subject nor harmonious in scale—in the centre a bogey-like Gorgon flanked by her children Pegasus and Chrysaor and by two couchant panthers, and at the sides, where they seem puny by comparison, two detached groups of gods in battle with giants; this may be Peloponnesian work.

316. It is on the Acropolis at Athens that the interaction of various schools can best be studied, owing to the preservation of much early sculpture in the layers of débris buried after the sack of the citadel by the Persians. They must have found there a veritable museum of works of art dating from the seventh century onwards, and our own generation has succeeded in piecing together

Athens: architectural sculptures in poros.

Fig. 35. Kore of Attic workmanship on the Acropolis.

many of the statues which they wrecked. An earlier stratum yielded sculptures in poros (local limestone), mostly remains of stiffly composed groups in high relief which adorned the gables of early temples—chiefly combats of heroes and monsters, among them the so-called Typhon, whose three human bodies spring from a coil of snaky tails. There are also some life-sized groups of lions tearing bulls. The gay colouring of the poros sculptures pays no regard to nature, and their effect must have been somewhat barbaric. None seem to be earlier than about 575 and all must have been discarded before the

Fig. 36. Kore showing Ionic influence.

beginning of the earlier Parthenon about 508 B.C., since they were found under a terrace formed at that time.

Although marble did not replace limestone for architectural sculpture until late in the century (*c.* 530), it had long been in use for single statues. The earliest specimens of Attic marble-carving are primitive images of the seventh century, and a numerous series of Korai

Marble Korai.

and other works enables us to follow its growth down to about 540, when under the rule of Peisistratus Ionian art came into fashion and the simple native handiwork (Fig. 35) was eclipsed by imported statues of Parian and Naxian marble. The school of Chios supplied some of these exotic models; the signature of Archermus occurs on a base on the Acropolis, and figures of flying Nikai have been found there which resemble the Delian figure mentioned above. The imported Ionian Korai are fine ladies, tall and slender, in clinging transparent dresses which are gathered up in the left hand and drawn tight round the lower part of the body. The complexity of the dress, enriched with painted borders and sprinkled patterns, and the self-conscious beauty of the face with its expressive, inlaid eyes and smiling lips, mark a great technical advance and justify the ancient fame of the Chian school. The Attic sculptors copied and varied the type, learning much in the process (Fig. 36); but they did not lose their independence and vigour. One of the best of the Korai fits a base bearing the signature of the Athenian **Antenor**; after the fall of the Peisistratids the same sculptor made a bronze group of the Tyrannicides, of which, however, no copy survives. Thenceforward Ionian influence receded and Attic art became more virile. In the opening years of the fifth century it rendered nude male figures, horses and hounds, with a truthful simplicity and a delicacy of modelling which foreshadow the achievements of the Pheidian age.

B.　PERIOD OF TRANSITION (*circa* 500—460 B.C.).

317. The second half of the sixth century B.C. had done much to emancipate art from archaic traditions. The splendour-loving tyrants, from Polycrates of Samos to the Sicilian rulers, were the patrons of artistic enterprise. Peisistratus above all was conscious of the forces at work and eager to direct them. Religion followed and expressed the movements of the time: sculpture was employed to realise the ideals of mythology. The development of architecture introduced the adornment of metopes and pediments, which helped the sculptor to free himself from the trammels of hieratic tradition. The decoration of interiors by means of paintings taught the sculptor to attempt and the public to appreciate a more natural treatment. This emancipation from artistic conventions was most directly encouraged by the custom of erecting statues in commemoration of athletic victories at the great games. The first of these statues, carved in wood, were erected, as Pausanias tells us, to Rhexibius and Praxidamas, about 536 B.C., and the custom was henceforth universal. The sculptor aimed at representing the perfect development of the human body; the palaestra became his school and supplied him with models. The artists of the transitional and all subsequent periods were influenced by this naturalism in the treatment of ideal subjects, such as the gods and heroes of the temple statues which attained perfection in the works of Pheidias and the other sculptors of the Periclean age.

318.   The artists of the period of transition made advances in three
directions: in acquiring greater freedom of technique, in
establishing types of beauty, and in informing their works
with ideal grandeur. The advance in technical skill may be

*The nude
male type.*

Fig. 37. 'Apollo' of Tenea.

realised by comparing one of the more advanced Kouroi, the 'Apollo' of
Tenea (Fig. 37), which though found near Corinth seems to be the work of an

Ionian sculptor, with the Choiseul-Gouffier Athlete in the British Museum.
In the Tenea 'Apollo' the feet are close together, one advanced before the
other: the body rests on them in mechanical equilibrium, each half of the

Fig. 38. The Choiseul-Gouffier Athlete.

figure being identical with the other: the neck is erect; the head manifests
the same mechanical balance and the arms hang symmetrically at either side.
On the other hand in the Choiseul-Gouffier statue (Fig. 38), which is a copy of

a statue of about 450 B.C., the weight of the body is thrown upon one leg, while the other is lightly bent; the body and the legs are naturally joined, the head is inclined slightly downwards to one side, and the arms are freely extended. Some small bronzes of an early date, representing a discobolus, furnish a striking illustration of the advance made in this period,

Fig. 39. The Discobolos of Myron.

if they are contrasted with the Discobolos of Myron, which shows the greatest freedom in the rendering of a complex pose.

319. A similar improvement is marked in the modelling of the surface and in the truer anatomy of the human figure. In the early Kouroi the structure of the body, the appearance of the muscles, the elasticity of the surface are incorrectly or inadequately rendered: the later types manifest a most accurate knowledge of

Anatomy and drapery.

the body and great freedom in treating pose or movement. The Choiseul-
Gouffier athlete and the Discobolos of Myron (Fig. 39), in spite of their
faint suggestions of archaic convention, rank very
high as examples of perfect modelling.

In the treatment of drapery we may contrast the series
of draped figures from the temple of the Didymean
Apollo (now in the British Museum) with the
draped figures from the pediments of the temple
of Zeus at Olympia. In the former the folds of
drapery are indicated by the mechanical incision
of a few straight grooves, which scarcely suggest
the body beneath: in the latter statues we find that
variety of planes and lines which enabled the Greek
artist successfully to represent softness and pliancy
of texture. The statues already mentioned will
serve to illustrate the growth of the
sense of beauty. The earlier and late   Sense of
metopes from Selinus illustrate the   beauty.
same process. One of the best instances illustrating
the last stages in this transition to the highest and
freest art is the Charioteer from Delphi (Fig. 40),
whose date would fall about the year 470 B.C. To
the same period or a little later must be assigned
the magnificent bronze figure of Zeus or of Poseidon striding vigorously forward and wielding
thunderbolt or trident. This was found in the sea
off Cape Artemisium (Fig. 40 a).

320.   The schools of sculpture which effected
the emancipation from the trammels of archaism
were those of Argos with Ageladas as the chief
artist, Sicyon with Canachus, Aegina with Onatas,
Rhegium with Pythagoras, and
Athens with Critius and Nesiotes,   Schools of
Hegias, Myron and Calamis. Argos   Argos, Sicyon,
and Sicyon were closely related to   Aegina.
one another. The sculptors of Argos were con-

Fig. 40. The Charioteer,   servative and 'practised Art as it had been handed
from Delphi.   down to them.' The fame of **Ageladas** rests
on the tradition that he taught the three greatest
sculptors of his time, Myron, Pheidias and Polycleitus. His own works,
which included statues of Zeus, of Heracles and of Olympian victors, are
not especially praised by ancient authors. **Canachus** of Sicyon worked
in gold and ivory as well as in wood, bronze and marble. His famous
Apollo at Miletus is probably reproduced on a Milesian coin as well as in
the small Payne-Knight bronze in the British Museum. Still greater

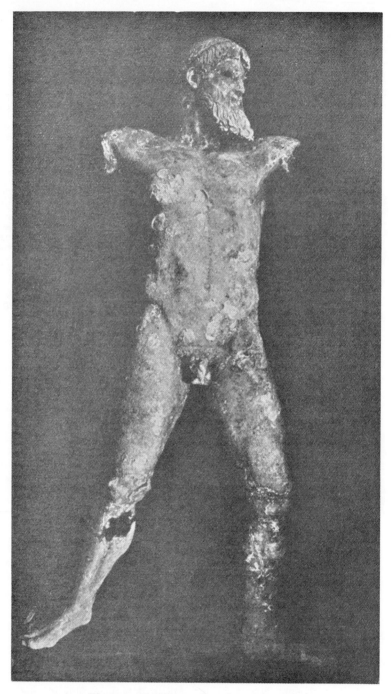

Fig. 40 a.   Poseidon or Zeus from Artemisium.

importance attaches itself to the school of Aegina, of which **Onatas** was the chief representative. He executed numerous bronze statues, some of them in groups, and probably contributed to the advance of sculpture in freedom of attitude and of modelling: qualities which distinguish the famous pediment sculptures from the temple of Aphaea at Aegina (now in Munich). This temple, built soon after the Persian wars, was thrown down by an earthquake when the colouring of its sculptures was still well preserved, so that it has been possible to recover the colour-scheme as well as the grouping of the figures. In both gables there was a battle-scene, with Athena in the centre, groups of combatants *The Aegina pediments.* at either side, kneeling archers and fallen men in the angles. Each figure is an independent marble statue, worked in the round and so balanced as to need no extraneous support. The sinewy forms and energetic attitudes may reflect the style of the Aeginetan bronze-workers. Although the two pediments have much in common, they seem to have been designed by different artists, one more advanced than the other, and a comparison of their work illustrates in a vivid way the speed with which the art of this age progressed and the sense of beauty grew. In the west pediment the faces are distorted by the so-called 'archaic smile,' in the east they are set and serious; again, the attitude of the wounded man is cramped and grotesque in the one, movingly lifelike in the other.

321. The most important work produced at Athens in the decade after Salamis was the second group of Tyrannicides, made by *Schools of* **Critius** and **Nesiotes** to replace Antenor's, which Xerxes *Rhegium and* had carried off. The two colossal figures survive in a marble *Athens.* copy at Naples, which can be completed from other sources. The heavy expressionless face of Harmodius with its exaggerated chin show little advance upon the fine statue of an ephebus from the pre-Persian *stratum* on the Acropolis, but there is a new energy in the movement and greater skill in the handling of the robust muscular forms. The statues of athletes, as we have seen, promoted a freer and truer treatment of the human body; and in this branch of art **Pythagoras** of Rhegium and **Myron** of Eleutherae had attained a high level of excellence before the middle of the fifth century. Although Pythagoras won praise for some heroic statues, and Myron's groups of gods, and above all else his famous heifer, are celebrated by ancient authors, the fame of both artists rests chiefly upon their statues of athletic victors: the most noted of these are the boxer Euthymus and a Pancratiast by Pythagoras, and those of the famous runner Ladas and a Discobolos (several copies of which are extant) by Myron. Pliny tells us that Pythagoras *primus nervos et venas expressit capillumque diligentius,* Diogenes Laertius speaks of him as πρῶτον δοκοῦντα ῥυθμοῦ καὶ συμμετρίας ἐστοχάσθαι, and these passages confirm the impression gained from his works that in the modelling of details as well as in the freedom and balance of his figures Pythagoras marked a new departure. Myron's Ladas was invoked as ἔμπνοε Λᾴδα, and Quintilian, in exemplifying the freedom and variety of pose in statues, says of the Discobolos, *quid tam distortum et elaboratum, quam est ille discobolus Myronis?* These testimonies, confirmed by the extant copies of the Discobolos, show how successfully Myron emancipated himself from archaic constraint in the treatment of the nude male figure. In the Disc-thrower the moment chosen is one of arrested movement. This

(i)　　　　　　　　　　　　　　　　　(ii)

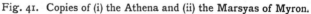

Fig. 41. Copies of (i) the Athena and (ii) the Marsyas of Myron.

is also true of the bronze group representing Athena and Marsyas, which can be reconstructed since both figures survive in marble copies. The story ran that Athena invented the flutes, but threw them away because her face was distorted in the act of playing; thereupon Marsyas picked them up. Athena has dropped the flutes and is moving away, but turns to wave the satyr back (Fig. 41 (i)), while Marsyas (41 (ii)), checked in his advance, stands poised on tiptoe between desire and dread. Myron made his Athena a slim girl, thus heightening the contrast with the satyr.

Calamis of Athens, whose Hermes Criophorus and Sosandra are possibly extant in reproductions, seems to have made some progress in representing the draped figure. The beautiful bronze statue of a charioteer from Delphi (Fig. 40) is ascribed to him by some authorities, by others to

Fig. 41 a. Apollo, from Olympia.

Pythagoras. This figure and some finely modelled fragments of horses are all that remains of one of those groups commemorating a chariot-victory which were much in fashion at the time. The sculptures of the temple of Zeus at Olympia were made about 460 B.C. They consist of two pediments, representing the preparations for the chariot-race of Pelops and Oenomaus and the fight between Lapiths and Centaurs, and metopes representing the labours of Heracles. By their dignity and originality of composition and the mastery of their execution, especially in the male figures, they are among the finest of architectural sculptures. Pausanias attributes them to **Paeonius** and **Alcamenes**; but most archaeologists reject this statement as irreconcilable with their style, which clearly belongs to the time between the Persian Wars and the Parthenon. The finest single figure is the Apollo (Fig. 41 a) from the centre of the west pediment.

C. PERIOD OF MATURITY (*circa* 460—400 B.C.).

322. The predecessors of **Pheidias** had gradually surmounted the technical difficulties which impeded freedom of artistic exe-

Pheidias: his achievement.
cution. It was his great achievement to attain the perfection of art by effecting a complete harmony of form and matter. He applied the sculptor's materials to express the greatest and deepest ideas and emotions of man. The perfection of physical beauty in a healthy and normal type was already established as the artistic ideal. This ideal he adapted to represent the gods and heroes of Hellas, developed through centuries of time by the imagination of a people at once simple and artistic, fixed in type by the epic poets and made more real by the great tragic poets. Through Pheidias Greek Art received those permanent qualities, described by Winckelmann as 'the noble *naïveté* and quiet grandeur of the Greek statues.' Pheidias was thus heir to all the artistic advances made by his predecessors. Born about 500 B.C., he was in the age of greatest receptivity when the victories over the Persians thrilled the hearts of the Greeks. The unity of feeling evoked by the common danger was strengthened by the intercourse between the citizens of different states, refugees from Ionia and the islands as well as Greeks of the mainland. And the Attic people after the great victories, 'forced, as it were, to recolonise their own country,' were moved to give to their city the most splendid adornments of art. It was in accordance with the character of the Periclean age that Pheidias informed his statues with the grandeur and sublimity which all ancient writers ascribe to them.

On the description of these writers we are obliged to rely for our ideas of his greatest works[1]. No adequate reproduction of the

The Athena Parthenos.
colossal gold and ivory statue of Athena Parthenos has come down to us: the various statuettes (the Lenormant, Varvakeion Athenas, etc.) are late Roman copies. The coins of Elis do not enable us to realise his masterpiece, the figure of the seated Zeus at Olympia, the work which moved Quintilian to say that Pheidias had added something to the received religion. This statue of gold and ivory, rising over forty

[1] Furtwängler's suggested recognition of the Lemnian Athena by Pheidias in the statue at Dresden combined with the Bologna head remains an hypothesis.

feet high, represented Zeus as seated upon a throne, every available part
of which was adorned with smaller statues in the round or filled with
large designs of *repoussé* relief in gold. The colour in the
gold enamels and the soft ivory tones of the nude flesh, The Zeus of
Olympia.
the paintings on the base, had effects of their own, which
were yet subordinated to the overpowering unity of the sublime figure of
the god. To form our impression of the artistic spirit in which Pheidias
worked we must turn to the sculptures of the Parthenon. We must
remember that in them we have, not great temple statues, but parts of
a scheme of architectural decoration. Even so we are not justified in
ascribing these works to the hand of Pheidias with absolute certainty,
though we can at least claim for them that they represent Attic sculpture
of the time when it was guided by the genius of Pheidias.

323. We can distinguish the earlier from the later works of Pheidias.
The first were probably executed to Cimon's orders, when
Pheidias had not fully and independently developed his Earlier and
later periods
of Pheidias.
genius. They included the thirteen figures dedicated at
Delphi in honour of Marathon, Miltiades in the centre,
flanked by Athena, Apollo and a row of tribal heroes, a monument
reminiscent of the Argive school. An Athena of gold and ivory at Pellene,
another Athena at Plataea, the colossal bronze statue of the same goddess
on the Athenian Acropolis (called on doubtful authority Πρόμαχος), also
belong to the artist's earlier period, none of them perhaps falling later than
460 B.C. About the later period of Pheidias' life there is considerable
uncertainty, as there are contradictory accounts of the prosecution for
sacrilege directed against him by the enemies of Pericles. It seems most
probable that he had already finished his great statue of Athena, which was
dedicated in 438 B.C., and was supervising the work on the Parthenon
when the prosecution took place. He then went to Elis and made the
statue of Zeus for the temple of Olympia in 438 and the following years.
To the years of his absence from Athens must be ascribed the statue of
Aphrodite Urania at Elis and the Anadumenos at Olympia, and to uncertain periods of his life the beautiful Lemnian Athena, a Hermes at
Thebes, the figure of an Amazon at Ephesus, and other works which Pliny
saw at Rome.

324. The sculptures of the **Parthenon** consist of metopes in high
relief, a frieze in low relief, and pediment sculptures in the
round. No works of classical antiquity represent more fully Sculptures
of the
Parthenon.
the blending of monumental repose and simplicity with
vitality and grandeur, whether we regard the composition of
the entire frieze and pediments or take the individual figures one by one.
The metopes, representing a variety of subjects, among which the battle
with the Centaurs and the taking of Troy can be distinguished with
certainty, are the earliest in date. In the pediments there is no uncertainty
of touch, no trace of early influence. The compositions in both pediments

Fig. 42. 'Theseus' from the East Pediment of the Parthenon.

Fig. 43. The Fates, or Hestia, Gaia and Thalassa, from the Parthenon.

make Athena the centre of interest. In the east pediment the birth of the
goddess, in the west pediment the struggle with Poseidon, are represented.
The figures on either side in each pediment have been identified by some
archaeologists with divinities or Greek heroes; others regard them as
personifications of nature and of localities. The groups are full of varied
life and movement, while they are harmonious and restful in their unity
and concentration of idea, as well as of design. The single figures, the
so-called Theseus (or Olympus, or Dionysus) (Fig. 42), the Fates (or
Hestia, Gaia and Thalassa) (Fig. 43) from the east pediment, the river-god
Cephissus from the west pediment, are instinct with life in their natural
pose, in the modelling of the nude and of the flowing draperies; at the
same time they are simple and grand in execution. They are types of
human life, which will ever remain, through all changes of fashion or taste,

Fig. 44. Horsemen, from Frieze of the Parthenon.

the classical instances of sculpture. The frieze which ran round the outer
wall of the *cella* or nave of the temple was 524 feet in length and represented the Panathenaic procession (Fig. 44). The technique of low relief,
in which two and three layers of figures are shown one above the other,
the rise from the background never exceeding 2½ inches, marks the highest
skill. In the western frieze the horsemen are preparing to mount or slowly
moving off; the north and south sides give the procession of horsemen,
chariots, lyre-players, men and maidens with offerings, the hecatombs of
cows and sheep dedicated to the goddess by Athens and the colonies.
The eastern frieze, over the entrance of the temple, represents the ascent
to the Acropolis in the presence of the assembled deities to whom the
hecatombs are to be offered. The central scene shows preparations within
the temple; the priestess receives two stools, like those on which the deities

sit, from girl attendants, and a priest aided by a boy folds the old peplos, removed from the image to make room for the new robe which is to be brought by the procession.

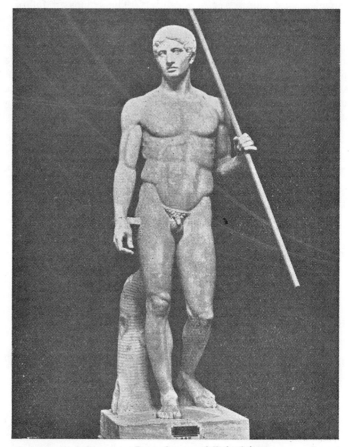

Fig. 45. Doryphoros of Polycleitus.

325. Polycleitus of Argos, whose activity falls in the second half of Polycleitus. the fifth century B.C., though his work did not attain the sublimity characteristic of the masterpieces of Pheidias, rivalled him in grandeur and simplicity. While continuing the traditions of Argos, he was strongly influenced both in spirit and technique by the work of the Attic school. The criticisms of ancient authors and the works ascribed to him combine in presenting him to us in two contrasted aspects.

On the one hand he appears as the 'academic' artist, whose Doryphoros establishes a canon of human proportion, and whose works, at once severe and large in character, incline towards monotony and merit the title of Classical in the restricted sense of that term.   His canon of proportion is massive (*quadrata signa*), not lithe and graceful, and his choice of poses is restricted, according to Pliny—*proprium eius est uno crure ut insisterent*

Fig. 46. Diadumenos of Polycleitus.

signa excogitasse. Quintilian quotes the opinion that his deities lacked majesty, and that even in his ideal representation of human forms he avoided those ages in which character was most manifest.   On the other hand, ancient criticisms and extant works testify to the exceeding beauty as well as to the high finish in the modelling of his statues.   These

contrasts can best be reconciled if we assume that the more sober and
restricted character belongs to the works of his earlier period, when the
influence of the Argive school was dominant, while the beauty and finish,
variety and softness, mark a later period, when Attic models had impressed
him. The Doryphoros (Fig. 45), with square massive body, broad modelling, and oblong head with close mass of finely-carved hair, represents the
first period; the Diadumenos, especially as it appears in the replica
recently discovered at Delos (Fig. 46) and in a head now in the British
Museum, has a more graceful pose, a more detailed modelling, a freer
treatment of the hair, and represents the second period. The same
characteristics appear in the vigorous attitudes and the supreme finish
of the metopes from the temple of Hera at Argos. These, as well as
the female head, probably from a pedimental statue of Hera, bear the
same relation to Polycleitus as the Parthenon sculptures do to Pheidias.
The gold and ivory statue of Hera, which Polycleitus made for the
temple of that goddess built in place of the older temple burnt down
in 423, enjoyed a fame in antiquity second only to that of the masterpieces of Pheidias. We hear also of his statue of Hermes, and that he
was victorious over three competitors, Pheidias, Cresilas and Phradmon,
with an Amazon statue for the temple of Artemis at Ephesus. Polycleitus
appears to have fixed the type of the Amazon which exists in so many
replicas in the museums of Europe. Some of the other works ascribed to
this artist should probably be adjudged to the younger Polycleitus, who
flourished nearly a century later.

326. Both Pheidias and Polycleitus were succeeded by important
schools. **Alcamenes** was employed on many important
commissions in Athens; and **Paeonius,** who came from
Mende in the Chalcidice, made the graceful figure of a
flying Nike set up on a lofty basis at Olympia by the
Messenians and Naupactians, about 420 B.C. The influence of Pheidias
can be traced also in the frequent reproduction of types of Zeus and
Athena, as well as in the Attic sepulchral reliefs, which follow in style
between the age of Pheidias and the great revival of Art under Scopas
and Praxiteles in the fourth century B.C. A typical work of this period
is the statue of the goddess Eirene with the infant Plutus (Fig. 47), the
work of **Cephisodotus,** who was probably the father of the great
Praxiteles. The statue stood in the Agora of Athens, and may be
associated with the worship of the goddess Eirene, instituted after the
battle of Leucas (375 B.C.). A replica of this work is probably to be
recognised in a statue now in the Munich Museum, and it admirably
represents the transition. The pose of the figure, the simple and almost
severe folds of the robe, suggest the art of the fifth century; while the
subject, the goddess carrying the infant son on her arm, like a Madonna
with the Saviour, and the downward turn of her head toward the child,

Transition to the fourth century masters.

mark the introduction of a sentiment which belongs to the fourth century and which found expression again in the Hermes with the infant Dionysus of Praxiteles.

Fig. 47. Eirene with infant Plutus.

D. GREAT SCULPTORS OF THE FOURTH CENTURY
(*circa* 400—320 B.C.).

327. The leading masters of the fourth century, Scopas, Praxiteles and Lysippus, substitute for the majesty and sublimity of the Periclean age more graceful and familiar aspects of art which appeal to human sympathies and emotions while they succeed better in portraying individual characteristics.

Schools of the fourth century.

This tendency, natural in the development of all arts, traceable in the literature and philosophy of the period, was furthered by the change in the social and political spirit of the age. In sculpture the change can be distinguished both in subject and in treatment. In the choice of religious subjects for sculpture Zeus, Hera and Athena make way for Apollo, Aphrodite and Artemis, and in these deities the youthful and almost passionate side is accentuated. Other deities such as Dionysus and Hermes (hitherto bearded) are represented as types of attractive youth and thus lose their aspect of divine reverence and grandeur. New deities are developed out of older forms or evolved from some quality of an existing god (Nike, Eirene, Plutus): and the minor deities or attendants on the great gods (Eros, Maenads, Satyrs) form the subjects of single statues. The influence of the drama, more especially the greater freedom of comedy, and the development of painting, encouraged naturalism and individualism in sculpture, characteristics which find expression in the grave-monuments alluded to above. This class of sculpture served to bridge over the transition from religious to domestic art, as it represented in solemn and religious form figures and scenes and ideas of actual life (Fig. 48). Thus attitudes suggestive of sentiment, the expression of various moods and the appeal to emotion in the spectator, were introduced into sculpture. With the technical advance of painting in colour and form, light and shade (§§ 350 f.), the sense for finer work in texture and modelling was increased in the sculptor, and the art of colouring statues was carried to its highest perfection. Thus subject and treatment combine in producing, not the severe grandeur of Pheidias, but the exquisite beauty of form and charm of expression which are found in the Aphrodite or the Eros of Praxiteles.

Choice of subjects.

328. The chief artists of the period, Scopas and Praxiteles, show a difference in their treatment of individual sentiment. Scopas expressed passion and movement by obvious physical methods; Praxiteles suggests feeling by subtler and less direct appeals. Scopas was a native of Paros, probably the son of the sculptor Aristander, who gained some repute as a worker in bronze and was also employed on a group which the Spartans dedicated at Amyclae to commemorate the victory of Aegospotami. Polycleitus is also said to have taken part in executing this group, and we may perhaps infer a direct connexion between the Argive school as represented by Polycleitus and the artists of Paros. The artistic activity of Scopas falls within the period from 394 to 349 B.C. The pediments of the temple of Athena at Tegea, the eastern representing the hunting of the boar of Calydon, the western the battle between Telephus and Achilles in the plain of the Caïcus, were executed from the designs of Scopas, if not by his hand. Fragments of the eastern pediment have been excavated: and two male heads (Fig. 49) show the qualities of pathos, which we regard as characteristic of that artist. The faces are turned on one side and looking upwards. Details of modelling and

Scopas.

Fig. 48. Sepulchral monument of Hegeso at Athens.

expression confirm the effect of violent emotion. The cheekbones and brows are accentuated by the deep furrows round the nose and mouth: the forehead is not smooth, but shows bumps and depressions: the upper eyelid of the eye is drawn up, and is scarcely visible in profile, while the hollow ridge under the lower eyelid is deeply sunk. Thus in the pose of the head and in the elaboration of details alertness and vigour are suggested. One of the most important works of Scopas, which the rhetoricians delighted to describe, was his raving Maenad, of which a mutilated copy and various adaptations exist. The Maenad was represented in the height of Bacchanalian frenzy: her head thrown back with flowing hair, her drapery blowing in the wind, and her hand holding part of a mangled kid. The effect of movement was intensified by the expression of the face. We have no means of distinguishing with certainty the individual work of the four

Fig. 49. Heads from Tegea.

artists (Scopas, Bryaxis, Timotheus and Leochares), who worked together on the famous Mausoleum of Halicarnassus, the remains of which are now in the British Museum. But the figure of the charioteer from one of the smaller friezes, with the massive drapery flowing back and the body inclined forward, seems eminently characteristic of the art of Scopas. His most ambitious composition, a vast group of sea-gods and sea-monsters, was transported to Rome. It represented the apotheosis of Achilles, Poseidon and Thetis escorting him with a train of Nereids riding on dolphins, hippocamps, Tritons and many other creatures of the sea: a masterpiece of tempestuous movement, echoed in many later designs. Other works of Scopas from their subject or character may not have possessed this quality of movement or passion. Such were the Apollo Smintheus, the Apollo at Rhamnus, the statues of Asclepius and Hygieia, the Hecate at Argos, the

Leto and Ortygia, and the famous Aphrodite, which Pliny preferred to the Cnidian Aphrodite of Praxiteles. In the Aphrodite Pandemos, riding on a goat, which is reproduced on coins of Elis and in other works of minor art, the typical style of Scopas may have found expression. If we assign that masterpiece of ancient sculpture, the huge drum from the temple of Artemis at Ephesus, now in the British Museum, to Scopas (and one of the pillars was ascribed to him by Pliny), we have an instance of more subdued sentiment, approaching the character of the work of Praxiteles, though the upward gaze in the nude Thanatos and in the Hermes reminds us of other works of Scopas.

329. The sculptors associated with Scopas in the decoration of the Mausoleum were themselves of high repute in antiquity. **Timotheus**, we learn from inscriptions, was appointed to make models for sculptures at the temple of Epidaurus, and we may therefore recognize his work in some interesting sculptures found at that site, representing Nereids, Victories and Amazons. A group of Leda sheltering the swan, preserved in Graeco-Roman copies, resembles them in the bodily forms and the clinging draperies. **Leochares** was a famous sculptor of Athens, employed by the general Timotheus to make the statue of Isocrates and by Philip of Macedon to produce the gold and ivory portraits of his family for the Philippeum at Olympia. Statues of Zeus and of Ares were also attributed to him; while his bold attempt to represent Ganymede carried off by the eagle, a replica of which can be recognised in the Vatican, shows that he was an artist of originality. (For **Bryaxis**, see § 333 below.)

Timotheus and Leochares.

330. In **Praxiteles**, the younger contemporary of Scopas, the art of the fourth century finds its fullest expression. The more sentimental and sensuous character of his work is revealed in his choice of subjects; ten of the forty-one works associated with his name by ancient authorities represent human figures, while among the divinities whom he represented neither Zeus nor Asclepius occur: Hermes and Poseidon only once. Of the male gods, Apollo and Dionysus were most frequent, conceived no doubt in their more youthful and sensuous aspect; while the boy Eros was represented in three of his most famous statues. Among the goddesses Artemis appears four times either in groups or singly; but Praxiteles' fame was founded above all on his five statues of Aphrodite, which served to found the type of nude female beauty in Greek art. Praxiteles showed also a preference for figures from the Dionysiac cycle, maenads and satyrs, and in the two groups, the one representing Agathodaemon and Agathe Tyche, the other Peitho and Paregoros, he shows the tendency of his age towards allegorical art. In choice of subject Praxiteles is thus in marked contrast to the sculptors of the fifth century, who represented the great divinities in severe and impressive style. The contrast is made more manifest when we consider the artistic qualities of his work, as revealed in the description of ancient authors or in extant

Praxiteles.

monuments. His statue of the Cnidian Aphrodite, for which king Nicomedes offered to cancel the public debt of Cnidus, was set in a small temple. Coins of Cnidus show us the position of the figure, and marble copies at

Fig. 50. Aphrodite of Cnidus, Vatican.

Munich and in the Vatican (Fig. 50) give some idea of pose and outline. The goddess was represented as completely nude and about to enter the bath. The flesh was delicately tinted, the eyes and the hair and the drapery by her side were coloured by encaustic painting, a process which Praxiteles applied to all his marble statues and in which the famous Attic painter Nicias frequently cooperated with him. The exquisite beauty and

Fig. 51. Hermes with infant Dionysus by Praxiteles.

the perfect finish of the work gained the unbounded praise of the ancient world. The group excavated at Olympia, Hermes carrying the infant Dionysus (Fig. 51), enables us to appreciate the delicacy of his modelling, which is so inadequately represented in the copies of his works and which cannot be reproduced even in a cast from the original. The wonderful indication of texture, the treatment of the hair and of the drapery hanging over the tree stump, combine with the soft grace of outline and the gentle pose and expression of the face to show us the qualities on which rested the fame of Praxiteles. A fortunate discovery of the French excavators at Mantinea has given us three slabs, representing Apollo, Marsyas and the Muses, which are described by Pausanias as decorating the base of statues by Praxiteles. With their help we may claim for his school certain draped figures of tall and dignified women which inspired some of the best Tanagra

**Draped fe-
male statues.** figurines and were imitated by portrait-sculptors down to Roman times. The *flens matrona*, mentioned by Pliny, may have been a monumental statue like the Mourning Lady recently acquired by the British Museum from the Trentham collection. Of his Parian Eros we gain some impression from a coin of Paros as well as from the copy at Dresden and a torso in the Louvre. His Apollo Sauroctonos and his Satyr are also represented in copies. All his works have in common a softness of outline and repose in expression ; and we may generally notice a downward droop of the head and a downward glance of the eye, in contrast to the upturned gaze in the works of Scopas.

331. Lysippus, who became the favourite sculptor of Alexander,
Lysippus. owned no master; but his native place, Sicyon, had a well-established artistic tradition and was the seat of a progressive school of painting (§ 350), in which his colleague at Alexander's court, the painter Apelles, had studied. Lysippus was one of the most prolific artists of antiquity: Pliny's statement that he completed 1500 works in his lifetime is doubtless exaggerated, but he worked almost exclusively in bronze, and the casting of bronzes did not of course demand so much labour on the part of the artist as the carving of marble. The passion and sentiment, predominant in Scopas and Praxiteles, are not manifest in Lysippus. Though the individual element in art reaches its height in his portrait statues of Alexander, yet the greatness of his subject invests his work with a healthy idealism, and raises it to a plane in which personal passion and introspective sentiment have no place. In choice of subject Lysippus approaches the spirit of the fifth century. Aphrodite is not found among his works, but Zeus was represented four times. His statue of that god, made for Tarentum, was a colossus (sixty feet in height). It is probable that the stern-browed type of Zeus with wavy hair, shaggy beard and a naturalistic treatment, such as we see in the Zeus of Otricoli and other copies, owed its origin to Lysippus. Lysippus also delighted in the representation of the heroic world. He represented Heracles five times, in the colossal statue at Tarentum as well as in the statuette of Heracles Epitrapezios. Probably most of the statues of Heracles in the museums of Europe were derived from the type established by Lysippus.

332. He represented Alexander in so many statues that he almost
created an ideal type. We are told that he succeeded in
combining the lion-like energy of the great monarch with a
certain languid softness of the eye. We cannot identify any
of the extant busts of Alexander with the work of Lysippus,

*Portraits of
Alexander:
statues of
athletes.*

Fig. 52. Apoxyomenos, attributed to Lysippus.

but the busts in the Louvre and the Capitol may reflect his influence.
Lysippus also represented the king on horseback, with his generals, in a

great group illustrating the battle of Granicus. In collaboration with Leochares he represented Alexander at a lion hunt. It is probable that the beautiful marble sarcophagus found at Sidon and now in Constantinople contained the body of one of Alexander's officers, and that the reliefs were directly influenced by the groups mentioned above. The statues of athletes, mentioned as the work of Lysippus, were probably faithful portraits. We learn that his brother Lysistratus, in his desire for truthful rendering, took plaster casts from the faces of his sitters. The bronze head of a pugilist found at Olympia seems to illustrate the characteristic treatment of athletic statues in this age. The Apoxyomenos (Fig. 52), the nude youth scraping from his arm the oil and dust of the palaestra, represented for us by a marble now in the Vatican, is sometimes regarded as a type in which Lysippus embodied his canon of art as Polycleitus embodied his in the Doryphoros[1]. In contrast to the square and massive proportions of the earlier artist, Lysippus, we are told by Pliny, 'made the head smaller, the body more lithe and dry, so that the slimness of the figure appeared greater': and 'whereas the ancient sculptors represented figures as they were, Lysippus represented them as they appeared to be.' This indication points to an improvement in technique as well as to the influence of painting, which reached its highest development in this age.

E.   HELLENISTIC PERIOD (*circa* 320—31 B.C.).

333. The commissions executed by Praxiteles and Scopas in Asia Minor foreshadow the change that was brought about by Alexander's conquest. Athens retained her prestige and produced original work for a time, but her artists became more and more retrospective, and finally, under Roman domination, occupied themselves mainly with the commercial production of copies or imitative works. After the division of Alexander's empire the centres of progress shifted to the Hellenistic kingdoms, which enlisted the best workers of the day. **Bryaxis**, one of the sculptors of the Mausoleum, made temple-images for two of the new capitals: an Apollo for the famous sanctuary of Daphne near Antioch, and a Serapis for the artificial cult which Ptolemy Soter established at Alexandria. Of the pupils of Lysippus, **Eutychides** broke fresh ground

---

[1] The question has been complicated by the discovery at Delphi of a marble statue, the ideal portrait of Agias, a famous athlete, which is thought to be a contemporary copy of the bronze statue of Agias made by Lysippus and set up in Thessaly. Its proportions recall those of the Lansdowne Heracles and other statues hitherto assigned to Scopas, and it lacks the advanced anatomical knowledge shown in the Apoxyomenos. We may either suppose that the Agias was an early work and that during Lysippus' long life he developed new methods, which is quite likely: or we may post-date the Apoxyomenos and regard it as a work of one of Lysippus' followers who had benefited by the anatomical studies which were first undertaken in the Museum of Alexandria.

with his bronze Tyche of Antioch, which survives in small copies, showing
the city-goddess enthroned on a mountain, and the river Orontes, personified as a strong swimmer, at her feet.   Another, **Chares** of Lindos,
made the bronze Helios at Rhodes, which was over 100 feet high, and even
after its overthrow by an earthquake was reckoned one of the Seven Wonders.
The noblest work of this age which has come down to us is the Nike

Fig. 53. Niobid in the Vatican.

of Samothrace, which probably commemorated the naval victory of
Demetrius (306). The colossal marble figure stood on the prow of a
galley, her draperies blown back by the wind, a trumpet raised to her
lips; and the effect was enhanced by the romantic scenery in which she was
placed. In the same way the famous group of Niobe and her children,
preserved for the most part in enfeebled Roman copies, was designed for

exhibition in wild natural surroundings. We possess a Greek version, perhaps the original, of one superb figure, and can understand why Roman critics thought the work worthy of Scopas or Praxiteles (Fig. 53).

334. The most important centres of Hellenistic art were Pergamum and Rhodes. Before describing the works of these and minor schools it will be convenient to deal with some general characteristics.

The majestic types of the Olympians had been fixed by fifth-century art. The fourth century, pushing characterisation further, distinguished the mild Asclepius from the stern-browed Zeus, and Zeus from his brother of fickle moods, Poseidon; and touched the goddesses with a human tenderness which is seen at its best in the Demeter of Cnidus. It remained for the Hellenistic age to invest these divine figures with a pomp of drapery and attribute analogous to those which distinguished the deified rulers of earth from their subjects. The sculptor of the Belvedere Apollo shuns the muscular athletic type which had contented democratic Greece, and substitutes slender aristocratic proportions and a theatrical pose of conscious authority. To enhance the splendour of rich draperies, the Pergamene sculptor insists that they are new by indicating the creases, crossing one another at right angles, that would be left in a freshly unfolded mantle. Phases of baroque extravagance alternated with returns to classic simplicity. Sometimes the imitation or modification of older types, combined with a heightened mastery of technique, resulted in such a masterpiece as the Aphrodite of Melos; the unknown sculptor of this type of noble womanhood, working as late as the second century, drew his inspiration from the grand style of two or three hundred years before.

The gods in Hellenistic Art.

Where all else is shadowy, one maker of colossal temple-images stands out as a distinct personality—**Damophon** of Messene, who worked in his native city, at Megalopolis, and in Achaia, during the brief spell of freedom which followed the downfall of Sparta (191 B.C.). We have considerable remains of an ambitious group, seen and described by Pausanias, which almost filled the little temple of Despoina near the modern Arcadian village of Lycosura: four colossal figures about fourteen feet high, Despoina and Demeter seated, two others standing, The modelling of the bodies, built up in many pieces, does not bear a close inspection, but the boldly chiselled heads have a breadth and grandeur which at one time led good judges to assign them to the early years of the fourth century.

335. Most of the Greek portraits in our museums are copies made for decorative purposes in Hellenistic and Roman times. Their usual form is that of the herm, in which the head and upper part of the chest rise from a square shaft; the bust was evolved by Roman art; but it must be remembered that in most cases the original was a complete statue, and that much of the character expressed in pose, gesture and dress, is lost in the abridgement. The series opens in the fifth century with helmeted heads of Attic strategi. That of Pericles is

Progress of Portraiture.

probably derived from the bronze statue by Cresilas which stood on the Acropolis; only the turn of the head and slightly parted lips suggest the energy of the complete statue. Another Attic work of this time, the Anacreon Singing, exists both as statue and herm. The fourth century witnessed a gradual advance. In the well-known Sophocles (Fig. 154) we have the conventional, idealised exterior of a somewhat pompous citizen; the sculptor has not penetrated beneath the surface to reveal the poet's soul. The head of Plato, ascribed to **Silanion**, is a literal transcript from life; a later age found this and the cognate head of Socrates insipid and recast them in a more dramatic mould. We have already noted the portraits by Lysippus and Leochares, and the greater realism introduced by Lysistratus. Their influence may be seen in the life-like head recently identified as Aristotle, and the somewhat later Menander. The Demosthenes of the Lateran is an important landmark, for it almost certainly reproduces a statue by **Polyeuctus** set up in the agora at Athens in 280. It has gained in impressiveness through the discovery that the hands, formerly restored as holding a roll, were tightly clasped, in a pose expressive of failure and resignation. The realism of the worn, mobile face prepares us for later masterpieces of characterisation, such as the so-called 'Seneca' of the Naples Museum, the head of a literary recluse, haggard and unkempt. The sculptors of this period represented the sorrows of old age with special insight and sympathy, as in the Euripides, now at Copenhagen, whose deep-sunk eyes and cheeks tell of a sensitive nature long buffeted by the world, or the blind Homer, haunting in its pathological realism.

Very different are the portraits of men of action, for which the Lysippian heads of Alexander set a fashion; the leonine brow and clustering locks, the turn of the head and challenging upward gaze, became royal insignia among the Diadochi. Two bronze statues in the Museo delle Terme may be Hellenistic originals. One represents an unknown dynast in heroic nudity, leaning on a spear, the other a boxer of singularly brutal type, who sits resting after a bout.

336. The reliefs of preceding centuries, other than architectural pieces, were for the most part grave-reliefs, representing the dead person often attended by kinsfolk or servants, or votive reliefs, representing deities either alone or approached by worshippers. The rich series of Attic grave-reliefs was cut short by a sumptuary law, passed under Demetrius of Phalerum (317—307), at a moment when sculptors were beginning to introduce a personal note, individualising the features and allowing freer play to emotion. The development of the votive reliefs was in the same direction; localities are more fully indicated and particular incidents recorded. It was only a step to the landscape and *genre* reliefs, akin in subject and treatment to the cabinet-pictures designed for private houses, which are common in Hellenistic and Graeco-Roman sculpture. The subject might be mythological or

drawn from real life, but in both cases the treatment was idyllic and there was often a landscape background. These rural scenes with their rocks and fountains, old gnarled trees and quaint roadside shrines, are the counterpart of the pastoral poetry which became popular in the third century. They have been claimed as Alexandrian, but there is at least as much reason to connect them with Asia Minor. Nor is it easy to distinguish the genuine Hellenistic examples from works in the same spirit executed in Campania or Rome in the first two centuries of the empire.

337.   Pergamum is better known to us, thanks to excavation, than any other Hellenistic city except Delos. From 283 B.C. onwards the genius and wealth of its princes transformed a petty hill-fortress into a splendid capital. Sculptors were attracted

School of Pergamum.

Fig. 54.   The Dying Gaul.

from Athens and elsewhere to execute monuments of which we can form a good idea both from remains on the spot and from copies found in Italy. Attalus I (241—197 B.C.) adorned the city with bronze groups commemorating his victories over the Gauls, who for a generation had exacted blackmail from the states of Asia Minor. Some of them survive in excellent, perhaps contemporary, marble replicas; such are the Dying Gaul (Fig. 54), now in the Capitol, and the group representing a chieftain killing his wife and himself, now in the Museo delle Terme. They are marked by an insight into racial characteristics and a sympathy for the heroic qualities of a barbarous foe which are new in Greek art. Attalus also dedicated a series of smaller bronzes on the Acropolis at Athens which showed the overthrow of the Gauls as the climax of successive struggles between civilization and barbarism. Copies of a dozen of these figures have been recognised in various museums; the subject is always a defeated Giant, Amazon, Persian, or Gaul, resisting with fiery energy or prostrate in death. Pliny names four sculptors as responsible for these groups, the most notable being **Antigonus**, who was also a pioneer in art-criticism; for the Attalids formed a collection of sculptures and paintings by great masters, which encouraged the critical study of art, just as the famous library fostered literary research. Among other works which may be assigned to the Pergamene school of the third century is a reconstructed group representing the punishment of Marsyas, who is shown hanging by his arms from a tree, while Apollo sits waiting and a slave sharpens the knife. This Scythian knife-sharpener, now in Florence, is treated with the same ethnological realism as the Gaulish warriors. The Marsyas, of which there are various replicas, is a masterpiece of anatomical detail; but the later versions betray that morbid interest in bodily pain which sometimes mars Pergamene and Rhodian sculptures.

338. The most important works of Hellenistic sculpture that have come down to us are the two friezes, now in Berlin, of the Great Altar built by Eumenes II (197—159 B.C.) on the acropolis of Pergamum. The principal frieze, from the exterior of the podium, represented the war of the gods and giants in high relief and on a very large scale, the height of the slabs being $7\frac{1}{2}$ feet, and the combined length about 350 feet, of which nearly three-quarters are preserved. The traditional episodes of the saga are woven into a crowded battle-piece of surpassing energy. The allied forces of heaven include the Olympians and many lesser deities, Rhea and Cybele with their lions, furies and gorgons, nymphs and satyrs in the train of Dionysus, Sun and Moon and other powers of the sky, the gods of the sea led by Poseidon and Oceanus, even the hounds of Artemis and the eagles of Zeus. Of the giants some are youths of superhuman beauty and strength, some winged, some semi-bestial with head of lion or bull, but most have human bodies with snakes in place of legs. The sculptors used to the full the opportunities offered by the varied forms and equipment of the combatants, the steeds and chariots and heavy robes of the gods, the spreading wings and scaly coils of the giants. The swift free movements of the victors are contrasted with the impotent writhings of the earth-born. One of the best-preserved groups (Fig. 55) shows Athena triumphant over Alcyoneus, whom she drags by the hair; Victory hovers beside her and from the ground Earth raises her head in piteous appeal for her children. The key-note of the whole is the victory of mind over brute force. From this

breathless scene of vengeance the spectator passed up a great flight of steps to the actual place of sacrifice, enclosed by a screen-wall on which the lesser frieze unfolded the story of Telephus, reputed founder of Pergamum, in a series of calmer scenes, enriched with suggestions of landscape.

339. The influence of Pergamene art was felt far beyond the limits of the kingdom. The Attalids undertook costly public works at Athens and sent gifts to the great Hellenic sanctuaries.

Minor Asiatic schools.

At Cyzicus, the native place of the wife of Attalus I, a temple built in her memory contained famous reliefs illustrating filial piety, which are described in the Anthology. Otherwise we know little of art at Cyzicus and can only suspect its influence in the Thracian and Euxine area; certain Hellenic types, current there at this time, afterwards passed by way of Danube and Rhine into the common stock of Roman provincial sculpture.

Fig. 55. From the Frieze of the altar of Pergamum.

Bithynia produced a native sculptor in **Doedalsas**, who worked in the latter part of the third century. His Zeus Stratios, the chief cult-image of Nicomedia, is only known through coins, but his Bathing Venus has been identified in the well-known statues of the goddess crouching as though under a fountain; there is a good copy in the Louvre. Another Bithynian, Boethus, will be discussed among the sculptors of Rhodes, since he seems to have settled there.

340. The arts as well as the sciences were encouraged at the splendid court of the Ptolemies, and we have evidence of original achievements in painting, mosaic, and lapidary's work. But our ancient authorities have less to say of sculpture, and the specimens found in Egypt are for the most part works of modest scale, suitable for the decoration of private houses. They include marble statuettes,

Sculpture at Alexandria,

remarkable for the liquid softness of their modelling, and some bronzes and terra-cottas which treat *genre* subjects with a realism verging on caricature. The colossal figure of the Nile, now in the Vatican, may reproduce a public monument of Alexandria ; the bearded river-god reclines in tranquil meditation, one arm propped on a sphinx, seemingly unconscious of the swarm of children, personifying the sixteen cubits of the Nile-flood, who sport about him or climb over his body (Fig. 56). A broader humour animates the reliefs on three sides of the base, which show the adventures of pygmies among hippopotami and crocodiles.

Mention has been made above of works executed by Bryaxis and Eutychides for Antioch. The kings of Syria were more dependent for the embellishment of their realm upon Greek art than were those of Egypt, where a monumental native art already held the field ; and the contributions of Syrian Hellenism to early

and at Antioch.

Fig. 56.   The Nile.

Christian architecture and sculpture were not less important than those of Alexandria.   But until Antioch and other Seleucid cities have been explored, we cannot trace the early stages of this development.

341.   From the second century onwards the chief centre of Hellenistic art was south-western Asia Minor and in particular the republic of Rhodes. The wealth of sculpture which adorned both the capital and the old sanctuary of Athena at Lindos is attested by Pliny and Dio Chrysostom and by numerous inscriptions.   A native artist, **Philiscus** (second century B.C.), produced a group of Apollo with Leto, Artemis and the Nine Muses, which was afterwards in Rome.   For his Muses he originated types which became popular in later antiquity.

School of Rhodes.

They appear for the first time on a relief by Archelaus of Priene, the Apotheosis of Homer, now in the British Museum. **Boethus** of Chalcedon, who worked at Rhodes in the first half of the second century, produced *genre* works such as the boy wrestling with a goose, of which several versions exist. The same playful spirit appears in an archaistic bronze herm, bearing his signature, recently discovered in the sea off Tunis; it is crowned with a loosely knotted scarf, which is treated with the utmost naturalism so as to form a piquant contrast to the solemn bearded face of the old god. About many of these works there is a fluent, almost *rococo*, elegance which links them with the contemporary terracotta figurines of Asia Minor. A different spirit was brought into Rhodian art by sculptors trained in the Pergamene school. The group called the Farnese Bull, representing the vengeance taken by Amphion and Zethus upon Dirce, is derived from one carved by **Apollonius** and **Tauriscus** of Tralles; their adoptive father, Menecrates, seems to have worked on the Pergamene frieze. The extant group, found in the Baths of Caracalla, is a free copy of the Antonine age. It is pyramidal in composition, skilfully built up on a rocky background, but overloaded with accessory figures; the original was certainly simpler and more effective. We possess the original of another group, removed from Rhodes to Rome, representing the death of Laocoon and his sons (Fig. 57); it was the joint work of **Agesander, Athanodorus, and Polydorus**, members of an artist-family mentioned in several Rhodian inscriptions, and may be dated about 50—30 B.C. This, the last great achievement of independent Greek art, portrays the extremity of physical and mental anguish with every refinement that the accumulated craftsmanship of generations could suggest. The marvellous technique and profound if exaggerated anatomical realism go far to justify its fame.

342. On the mainland the sculptor's art tended to become hereditary. Sons and pupils carried on the traditions of the Lysippian school at Sicyon and the Praxitelean at Athens. Both devoted themselves to portraits (see § 335 above), for which there was an increasing demand even in impoverished states, and furnished versatile recruits to the Asiatic capitals where there was work to be done on a larger scale. The Sicyonians produced athlete statues for Olympia and can be traced far into the third century, down to Xenocrates, whose treatise on sculpture was one of Pliny's sources. The Athenian school preserved a certain continuity of academic tradition until the second or third century after Christ, resisting the extravagant tendencies of the Pergamenes and Rhodians, and transmitting to the Roman world an accurate knowledge of older styles. A sculptor-family, in which the names Eubulides and Eucheir alternate, can be traced for five generations (*circa* 300—150 B.C.); fragments of a colossal group by Eubulides III have been found at Athens. In the same way **Polycles** and his descendants are known for four generations as makers of portraits and temple-statues (*circa* 200—80 B.C.); members of this family made images of Jupiter and Juno for the Greek temples built by

Continuity of the Athenian school.

Q. Metellus Macedonicus in Rome, at some time between his triumph in 146 and his death in 115. It is mainly to Athenian sculptors that we owe the wonderful series of portraits of philosophers, men of letters, and other worthies

Fig. 57.   Laocoon.

which were used to adorn Hellenistic and Roman libraries.   Athens in the last century before our era was at once a centre of literary pilgrimage and a market for works of art, where copies, sometimes called Neo-Attic, were turned out in great variety. Attic work of this age is seen at its best in the famous Belvedere torso, signed by Apollonius, son of Nestor, a colossal seated figure of surpassing force and technique, which many good judges regard as an original. The Farnese Heracles, signed by Glycon of Athens, and the marble vases by Sosibius and others are typical of the commercial side of the industry, which adapted and combined older themes. For altars, well-heads, candelabrum-stands and similar pieces, on which archaic designs were thought appropriate, Neo-Attic art evolved a bastard hieratic style, afterwards transplanted to Rome, where it diverged still further from its prototypes and was often employed for statues of the gods.

343. The Romans first became familiar with Greek art from Etruscan Greek sources, then by direct intercourse with Sicily and Magna sculpture Graecia, which was intensified by the conquest of Campania. in Rome. The bronze Wolf of the Capitol is an Ionian work of the later sixth century, and we hear of Greeks modelling figures in terracotta for the temple of Ceres in 493. As Rome brought under her sway the cities of the Greek world, she seized their accumulated treasures. The spoils of Syracuse (212 B.C.), Tarentum (209), and Eretria (198), were followed by the collections of Pyrrhus (187) and Perseus (168). Mummius in 146 plundered Corinth and Thespiae, Sulla shipped many masterpieces from Athens and other cities in 84. What the conquerors left was gleaned down to the close of the Republic by governors of the stamp of Verres. Even before the acquisition of the Pergamene kingdom in 133, statues by Pheidias, Scopas, Praxiteles and Lysippus were to be seen in public places in Rome. Romans of the governing class began to pride themselves on Greek culture and to form collections under the advice of Greek experts. Hitherto Roman buyers had sent their commissions to Athens. The Tunis Museum has recovered from a wreck of about 80 B.C. what may have been a typical cargo, perfunctory copies of statues in marble, decorative marble vases, some relics of an earlier age looted from temples near Athens, fine bronzes and miscellaneous furniture. But a few years afterwards some eminent Greek sculptors had their studios in the capital. **Arcesilaus,** the friend of Lucullus and Varro, whose group of Cupids playing with a lioness is praised by Pliny, received enormous prices even for his sketches in plaster. **Pasiteles,** at once a sculptor and writer on art, *qui et quinque volumina scripsit nobilium operum in toto orbe,* modelled all his works in clay, as is the modern practice, and made conscientious studies from life. We may perhaps recognise his influence in the marvellously life-like modelling of the later Republican portraits, and may certainly credit him with raising the standard of connoisseurship. An extant work signed by 'Stephanus, pupil of Pasiteles,' is an accurate copy of a Peloponnesian athlete-statue of the early fifth century.

F.   GRAECO-ROMAN PERIOD (31 B.C. *onward*).

344.   Under Augustus the stream of classical art divides.   On the one hand it enters a new region, leaving academic traditions behind, and broadens out to mirror the life of the new empire in that Roman imperial sculpture which excelled in portraits and historical reliefs[1]. On the other hand there is an increased

The academic tradition under the Empire.

Fig. 58.   Marble Relief of Antinous.

[1] The independent development of Roman Sculpture is treated in the *Companion to Latin Studies*, § 835 ff.

production of copies and imitative works; extant replicas of popular
pieces, such as the Satyr of Praxiteles, which were in demand for the
decoration of houses or gardens, can be counted by the dozen; and the
admiration felt for works of primitive style continued to inspire 'archaistic'
imitations. The copyist's art was at its best under the Julio-Claudian
house and gradually deteriorated. There was a brief revival under Hadrian;
some of the numerous sculptures which record the beautiful melancholy
features of Antinous have a dignity and grace worthy of Hellenic traditions
(Fig. 58). The leading sculptors were still men of Greek or Asiatic
blood, and it was in the old seats of Hellenistic culture that Christian art
was destined to have its birth.

Text-books: E. A. Gardner, *Handbook of Greek Sculpture*, and *Six Greek
Sculptors*; H. B. Walters, *The Art of the Greeks*. Longer works:
Bibliography. M. Collignon, *Histoire de la Sculpture Grecque*, 2 vols.; A. Furt-
wängler, *Masterpieces of Greek Sculpture*; W. Klein, *Geschichte der Griechischen
Kunst*, 3 vols. G. Dickins, *Hellenistic Sculpture*; A. W. Lawrence, *Classical
Sculpture*, and *Later Greek Sculpture*. Illustrations: Brunn-Bruckmann, *Denkmäler griechischer und römischer Skulptur* (over 700 large photographs, in
progress, the recent parts with critical text); J. Warrack, *Greek Sculpture*;
G. F. Hill, *One Hundred Masterpieces of Sculpture*; Hirth, *Der schöne Mensch*,
Part I. *Altertum*, with critical text by Bulle; S. Reinach, *Répertoire de la Statuaire
grecque et romaine* (small outline drawings forming an index of almost all known
statues), and *Répertoire des Reliefs grecs et romains*; Conze, *Die attische Grab-
reliefs*; Th. Schreiber, *Die hellenistische Reliefs*; A. Hekler, *Greek and Roman
Portraits*; J. J. Bernoulli, *Griechische Ikonographie*, 2 vols.; R. Delbrück, *Antike
Porträts*. For the sculptures found at Delphi, Olympia and Pergamum the
official reports on the excavations should be consulted. For Athens, G. Dickins,
Catalogue of the Acropolis Museum; A. S. Murray, *Sculptures of the Parthenon*;
Sir C. Walston, *Essays on the Art of Pheidias*; and the British Museum
publications. A useful survey of the sculpture in the Roman Museums is given
in H. Stuart Jones' *Classical Rome*; see also the same writer's *Catalogue of the
Sculptures of the Museo Capitolino*, and W. Amelung, *Die Sculpturen des
Vaticanischen Museums*. The ancient authorities are collected in Overbeck, *Die
antiken Schriftquellen zur Geschichte der bildenden Künste*, and H. Stuart Jones
Ancient Writers on Greek Sculpture.

IV. 4. PAINTING.

345. As we possess no first-rate examples of Greek painting, our knowledge of the subject is chiefly derived from the statements
Sources of
knowledge.   of ancient writers, of whom Pliny is the most important.
His short sketch of its history (*N. H.* xxxv) is supplemented
by incidental notices in the works of other writers, such as Pausanias and
Lucian, who is perhaps the best of ancient critics. The statements of
these authorities are, however, supplemented and corrected by certain
existing works of art, which, though they belong to the humbler forms of

painting, often give valuable evidence. Of these the most important are Greek vase-paintings and Roman and Etruscan wall-paintings. Vases, since many of them date from the best period of Greek art, are our most trustworthy witnesses, but for obvious reasons their evidence is restricted to matters of composition and drawing. In these the best of them are inimitable, but of colour they tell us nothing, and for this reason their value decreases with the advance of painting; and after the fifth century they diverge too far from independent painting to be safe guides. The Roman wall-paintings, on the other hand, are remarkable for their colouring, and as they follow Greek traditions, and often reproduce, with more or less freedom, Greek originals of an earlier period, they offer useful evidence for the study of pure Greek painting. Besides these two classes there have lately been discovered a number of portraits on Egyptian mummy-cases, which are Greek in style, though, like the Pompeian paintings, they belong to the Roman period, most of them probably to the second century A.D. Many of these are encaustic, and give us a high idea of the capabilities of that process.

Finally our materials have lately been increased by the discovery of a large number of painted *stelae* at Pagasae in Thessaly. Nearly a hundred of these retain considerable traces of painting and many are well preserved. They apparently belong in date to the third century B.C. and are executed in encaustic directly upon the marble. In subject and composition they reflect, with some modifications, the sculptured monuments of Attica, and therefore can hardly be taken as direct representatives of independent painting, even though their discoverer believes, on the evidence of the subjects represented, that some of them may be derived from works of the Sicyonian school mentioned in literature. Their artistic value in most cases is not great, but they furnish fresh evidence as to the nature of the encaustic process. In them the paint appears to have been laid on with a spatula, not with a brush. In style and treatment they appear, when allowance is made for their monumental character, to confirm the conclusions reached from other sources. But a final judgment is not possible till they have been more adequately published.

346. The Greeks appear to have employed three methods of painting, fresco, tempera, and encaustic. The first of these, fresco, or painting on wet plaster (which fixes the colours when it dries without the aid of any other medium), was employed for the decoration of walls. There are many examples of it at Pompeii and elsewhere which show a degree of skill in the manipulation of this difficult process fully equal to that of the mediaeval Italian painters. The date at which this process was discovered is however uncertain. The existing remains of the fifth century (*e.g.* the Lesche at Delphi) are executed on the dry plaster, and after that encaustic is the method usually employed. Nevertheless the skill of the Greco-Roman painters shows that the fresco process was no new invention. The usual process for easel pictures appears

Technical methods.

to have been tempera. The practice of ancient painters in this process probably differed in detail from the mediaeval, but was essentially similar, in that both used a sticky medium, such as yolk of egg, and not oil. The encaustic process is no longer employed, and its nature is uncertain. Its peculiarity was that the colours were mixed in wax, which sometimes at least was heated before application to render it fluid. Besides the brush an instrument called a 'cestrum,' probably a kind of spatula, was used for laying on the stiff pigment. This process appears to have been slow and difficult, but it had the advantage of depth and richness of colour, and may in some measure have filled the place of modern oil-painting. The earlier Greek painters used few pigments, but by the time of Apelles they possessed a very adequate palette. Taking all the evidence together, we cannot place their technical resources very much below those of the great painters of the Renaissance.

The history of Greek painting may for convenience be divided into five periods, (1) the Primitive, before 500 B.C., (2) the Polygnotan, to the time of the Peloponnesian War, (3) the Transition, about the last quarter of the fifth century, (4) the Fourth century, (5) the Hellenistic period. The reasons for this division will be apparent later.

347. The first of these periods may be dismissed briefly. The so-called Mycenaean period was until lately represented by fragments of wall-paintings at Tiryns and Mycenae, executed in several colours on a white ground. The best of these, representing a man catching a bull, is spirited, in spite of incorrect drawing. But recent excavations at Cnossus in Crete have revealed several frescoes more perfectly preserved than any on the mainland. They embrace a variety of subjects, and are said to show a naturalistic freedom even more remarkable than that of the other works of this period. Unfortunately they have not yet been reproduced in an accessible form. Then comes a gap in our records only filled by vases and a few terracotta plaques and some shadowy names of artists. None of the latter appear to have lived earlier than the seventh century B.C., and the stories told of them are untrustworthy. In all probability their work differed little except in size and finish from vase-paintings, and through vases we may trace the gradual advance to the freer style of Polygnotus, in whose great works painting first took rank with sculpture as an independent art.

Primitive period.

348. Polygnotus, whose father Aglaophon was himself a painter, was a Thasian by birth, but came to Athens in the time of Cimon. Here he adorned the walls of several public buildings with paintings of mythological subjects, among others a Sack of Troy in the Stoa Poecile, and a Rape of the Leucippidae in the shrine of the Dioscuri. But his most famous works were two in the Lesche at Delphi, the Sack of Troy, and Ulysses in the Underworld. These were large compositions, each containing at least seventy figures, and probably covered the walls of the building. There was in these no

Second period. Polygnotus.

complete landscape background to the scene, but only slight indications of locality, such as a rock, a tree, a house, or the like; and the unity of effect depended therefore on the balance of groups and single figures, which were arranged with careful symmetry. The conception was grave and serious as befitted the subjects and the monumental character of the work. The greatest advance made by Polygnotus was in the treatment of the human face, which he freed from the rigidity of earlier Art, giving it for the first time life and expression. In this he anticipated sculpture, and there can be no doubt that he and the other great painters of his time strongly influenced the sculptors of the succeeding Periclean period. His skill in the treatment of the face enabled him to become a master in the expression of character, for which he is praised by Aristotle and other writers beyond

Fig. 59. Vase illustrating the style of Polygnotus.

all other painters. His colouring was simple and without any play of light and shade, but must have been skilful, for Lucian selects for special praise the complexion of Cassandra in the Sack of Troy; he was also admired for his refined and studied treatment of drapery, a trait which is illustrated by many vases of the period. The two most famous contemporaries of Polygnotus were **Micon and Panaenus**, the brother of Pheidias, for whom he executed the paintings **Micon and Panaenus.** on the throne of Zeus at Olympia. Micon and Panaenus seem to have shared the painting of the famous Marathon of the Stoa Poecile. In the same place Micon executed alone an Amazonomachia, in which the Amazons appeared on horseback. In style these painters probably resembled Polygnotus, but in the opinion of all critics he stood alone in grandeur of conception. All of them however were inspired by the patriotic enthusiasm which was called forth by the Persian Wars (Fig. 59).

349. About the end of the fifth century there was a transformation in the character of Greek painting. Large monumental composi-

Third period.
Transition.

tions gave way to easel pictures, and with this change came a great advance in the treatment of colour and chiaroscuro. The figure was given relief by means of light and shade, and the study of perspective made possible a more natural treatment of the landscape background. Thus the painter was able to attain to a much closer imitation of natural effects. There was also a change in spirit. Mythological subjects still predominated, but the artist's first aim was no longer to tell the story but to produce a beautiful picture from the elements which it offered. The way had been prepared for this change by previous artists, notably by Apollodorus of Athens, but the first great masters of the new manner were

Zeuxis and
Parrhasius.

Zeuxis of Heraclea and **Parrhasius** of Ephesus, who lived at the time of the Peloponnesian War and probably till the early years of the fourth century. Both alike showed the characteristics of the new school, but Zeuxis was noted more especially for the novelty of his conceptions and the wonderful beauty of his female figures; Parrhasius for his fine drawing, his exquisite care in the treatment of the face, and his power of rendering the emotions. The Helen of Zeuxis in the temple of Hera at Croton, which was famous for the incomparable beauty of the nude figure, is characteristic of his art. No less so is the 'Centaur Family' described by Lucian (*Zeuxis*). Among the works of Parrhasius the picture of the Athenian people was admired for the skill with which the artist had expressed in the single figure of Demos all the conflicting qualities of that inconstant personage. The subjects of his other pictures, *e.g.* The Madness of Ulysses, Philoctetes, Prometheus, offered scope for the subtlety of expression which marked his art. A

Timanthes.

contemporary and rival of these painters was **Timanthes** of Cythnus (or possibly of Sicyon), who on one occasion carried away the prize from Parrhasius. His masterpiece was the sacrifice of Iphigenia, a work highly praised by ancient writers for the wonderful expression of different degrees of grief in the faces of the spectators. It is possibly the original of a picture discovered at Pompeii.

350. This period is not sharply distinguished from the preceding, but

Fourth period.
Fourth cen-
tury.

is marked by the rise of separate schools which in different ways developed the new manner and added to the stock of technical knowledge. These schools were the Sicyonian, Attic, and Ionic. In painting, as in sculpture, the Sicyonian school was

Sicyonian
School.

marked by the careful study of the theoretical and technical parts of Art. It was founded by **Eupompus** at the beginning of the century. His pupil **Pamphilus**, celebrated for his varied attainments and particularly for his profound study of artistic theory, was the teacher of three great masters, Apelles, Melanthius and Pausias. Only the two latter belong properly to the Sicyonian school, and of

Melanthius we know little. Pausias was an encaustic painter and excelled in small pictures, especially of flowers and children. His strength lay in colouring and chiaroscuro, and the most famous example of his skill in this was the black bull in a picture of a sacrifice. It stood facing

Fig. 60. Painting on marble from Herculaneum, signed by Alexander the Athenian. Probably after an original of about 400 B.C.

the spectator, but in spite of this and the added difficulty of its colour, he succeeded perfectly in giving it due relief. He seems to have sought out such problems, and no doubt the encaustic process, of which he was

the first great master, helped him in their solution. He is noteworthy as
the first painter of *genre* pictures. Pausias left several pupils, of whom we
know little, and the Sicyonian school maintained its reputation till the
time of Aratus in the middle of the third century. Its continuity of
tradition and the solid technical training, which Plutarch describes by the
word χρηστογραφία, preserved it from decay longer than the rest.

As our authorities are not explicit on this point there is a doubt

Attic School. whether all the painters now to be mentioned belong to one
school, but they possess certain qualities in common which
makes it convenient to treat them together. Ancient writers ascribe many
paintings to a painter **Aristeides**, but as they appear to have confounded
two painters of this name, of whom one lived at the beginning of the
fourth century, the other in the time of Apelles, we can form no distinct
idea of either. One of the pictures so ascribed however deserves notice.
It represented the sack of a town, and the leading motive was the figure of
a dying woman with an infant at her breast. The choice of such a subject
is characteristic, and shows that the love of a dramatic situation, manifested
already by Parrhasius and Timanthes, grew more powerful in the fourth
century. **Nicomachus**, son and pupil of the elder Aristeides, was a
painter of repute about the middle of the century. He seems to have
preferred mythological subjects, especially those which offered scenes
of vigorous action, *e.g.* the Rape of Persephone. He was celebrated for
rapidity of execution. Another pupil of Aristeides, equally famous in
sculpture and in painting, was **Euphranor**, who is constantly cited as the
type of versatile genius. It is remarkable at this date that his most famous
works were wall-paintings. They were in the Stoa of Zeus Eleutherius at
Athens, and represented Democratia and Demos, the Twelve Gods, and
the cavalry battle before Mantinea. Plutarch praises the last highly for its
vigour and life. Euphranor said of his Theseus, who appeared in the first
of the series, that he was fed on beef, whereas the Theseus of Parrhasius
was fed on roses, a remark which illustrates the increased realism of the
time. Of Euphranor's many pupils we know little, but one of them,
Antidotus, was the teacher of **Nicias**, an Athenian and one of the greatest
painters at the end of the fourth century. He excelled in female figures, and
two of his paintings of mythological heroines, an Io and an Andromeda,
are perhaps reproduced in various Pompeian frescoes, which give us a
high idea of the grace and refinement of their original. He also painted,
like Polygnotus, the Underworld, but his treatment was doubtless very
different, especially as we hear that he was a master of chiaroscuro. It is
to be observed that the painters of this school showed a preference for
mythological and dramatic subjects. So much may be inferred from the
lists of their works furnished by Pliny and others. Moreover the praises
accorded to them by ancient critics relate chiefly to qualities of expression
rather than technique. In these two points lies their difference from the
painters of the Sicyonian school.

351.   The two chief painters of the Ionic school were Apelles and Protogenes. **Apelles,** the greatest of all ancient painters, was born at Colophon, probably between 370 and 360 B.C.   He   Ionic School. Apelles. studied first at Ephesus under Ephorus, and later at Sicyon under Pamphilus.   It was no doubt here that he acquired that perfection of execution which was one of the charms of his work, but he was not confined by the rules of any single school, but took from each what was needed for his development.   The subjects of his pictures mark a new departure, for most of them were portraits, a branch of painting little cultivated before.   It became popular now through the influence of the Macedonian court, the chief members of which he frequently painted. These appear, however, rarely to have been simple portraits, but received an additional dignity and interest from the introduction of artistic motives. Apelles was fond of placing his figures on horseback, and in his portraits of Alexander he often presented him in the company of divine persons or personifications.   Thus he painted him with the Dioscuri, and riding in triumph with War in chains beside him, and again wielding the thunderbolt ; the wonderful relief of the hand which held the bolt was specially admired.   He seems to have had a taste for allegory and personification, which he carried far in the elaborate picture of Calumny described by Lucian.   Herein he anticipated the taste of the next age.   His mythological pictures were few, but his Aphrodite Anadyomene was by far the most famous picture of antiquity.   Its motive is uncertain, but its charm lay in the beauty and grace of the nude Aphrodite, who was wringing from her hair the water of the sea from which she had just risen.   It seems to have resembled in spirit the Cnidian Aphrodite of Praxiteles. The distinctive qualities of Apelles' work appear to have been perfection of finish combined with the perfect ease which came of absolute mastery of technique, and above all a certain grace and charm peculiar to himself.   This quality of χάρις was claimed by Apelles himself as his peculiar merit, and his judgment was confirmed by critics.   He does not seem to have been remarkable for creative imagination and cannot therefore be called the greatest of painters in quite the same sense that Pheidias was the greatest of sculptors.   Indeed it was impossible for any painter to combine the highest technical skill with the highest imaginative qualities, for painting only reached technical completeness when the creative power of Greek Art was already declining.   **Protogenes,** a painter of the same period and also a native cf Asia Minor, was declared by Apelles equal to himself in all but ease of execution.   He worked chiefly at Rhodes, and his masterpiece was a picture of Ialysus, the eponymous hero of the Rhodian city, on which he is said to have spent seven years.   Another picture equally famous presented a satyr leaning at ease against a pillar with a shepherd's pipe in his hand, a pose which recalls the satyr of Praxiteles, the so-called 'Marble Faun.' He also painted portraits, including an Alexander with Pan.   His work was extremely lifelike and marked by extraordinary finish, but the intense

care he spent upon it rendered the effect somewhat laboured. If we may
trust the story which connects him with Demetrius Poliorcetes, he must
have lived at least to the end of the fourth century.

352. The great age of Greek painting ended with Apelles, but there
were some interesting developments in the time of the
Diadochi. We notice the beginnings of these in the work
of **Antiphilus**, a painter whose tendencies connect him
with this period, though he seems to have lived earlier, for
he painted portraits of Philip and Alexander. He worked both in encaustic
and tempera and was versatile also in the choice of subjects, for he painted
mythological scenes, portraits and *genre*. One instance of the latter was
a picture of a boy fanning a fire, the light illuminating his face and the
room about him. In another picture he painted women spinning. These,
and a picture of the death of Hippolytus, a somewhat sensational subject,
mark his connexion with later artists. He was remarkable for facility of
execution. **Theon** of Samos, called also Theorus, was famous for pictures
of a highly realistic and sensational character, which were called φαντασίαι.
One of these represented a hoplite charging, and before exhibiting it the
painter always caused a trumpeter posted near to sound the charge, upon
which the curtain was suddenly withdrawn. This desire to produce
illusion by a sudden and overpowering effect was new in Greek Art, but we
find the same spirit in the sculpture of the later period, especially in the
Pergamenian frieze of the Gigantomachia.

(marginal note: Fifth period. Hellenistic painting.)

Another characteristic of this period is the development of *genre*, the
popularity of which is attested by many Pompeian paintings based on
Greek originals. Of the artists who practised it the best known is
Peiraeicus, who painted 'barbers' and cobblers' shops, asses, eatables
and the like,' and was called 'rhyparographus,' a malicious perversion of
ῥωπογράφος. These humble subjects, which must have owed their attraction mainly to the execution, mark an increased love of realism, when
compared with those of the earlier *genre* painters, Pausias and Antiphilus,
whose subjects had an interest apart from the treatment. But even so
Greek painters, to judge from existing remains, never lost their love of
representing the type, rather than the individual, and thus differed from
later realists.

These were the two most important new growths in later Greek
painting. Even as late as the early Roman Empire painters retained
a high degree of technical skill, but they did little more than vary
the motives of earlier artists. Two painters only deserve mention.
Timomachus of Byzantium, whom Pliny ascribes to the age of Julius
Caesar, though some modern writers would place him earlier, seems to have
reverted to the severer spirit of the painters before Alexander. His masterpieces were pictures of Ajax after his madness, and of Medea meditating
the murder of her children, in which he seems to have expressed powerfully
the dramatic and psychological interest of the subjects. The Medea is

probably reproduced by a picture at Pompeii, one of the finest discovered there. The subject is treated with much restrained power. All centres in the highly expressive face and pose of Medea, who stands quietly with her hands painfully pressed together. Besides these and other mythological pictures, Timomachus also painted portraits. Another painter, **Ludius** (or perhaps Tadius), a contemporary of Augustus, deserves a passing mention. He introduced a new style of decorative landscape for the adornment of walls. The subjects of these were 'villas, porticoes, gardens, groves, hills, lakes, harbours,' and similar scenes. These were mingled together in profusion and enlivened by the addition of figures, the whole producing a light and cheerful effect. The many examples of such scenes in Pompeian painting perhaps reflect his style. They are pleasing

Fig. 61. Woman's head from the Crimea. Late fourth century B.C.

and effective as decoration, but show little regard for truth to nature and none for perspective. Landscape had already been employed for a similar purpose by the Greeks, and we do not know wherein Ludius' innovation lay. The earlier Greek style of decorative landscape is probably represented by the fine paintings of scenes from the *Odyssey* discovered in a house in the Esquiline. These and some of the landscape backgrounds in pictures after Greek originals show a considerable knowledge of natural effect, but the Greeks seem never to have cultivated landscape as an independent art.

Any account of an art based, as that of Greek Painting must be, chiefly upon literary records, is inevitably unsatisfactory; for it cannot enable the

reader to visualize the works described.   Yet the records here summarized,
when compared with the monuments, suggest certain conclusions which
it will be useful to collect.

We see in the first place that Greek Painting followed the same course
of development as Sculpture.   It is at first, in the hands of Polygnotus and
his contemporaries, monumental, dealing with heroic and mythological
subjects, usually on a large scale, but relying for its effect on the beauty
and dignity of the individual figures, with at most a linear symmetry, as on
a relief.

The figures, though ranged at various altitudes and not merely in
rectilinear rows, and though sometimes overlapping, or partly concealed by
the background, are still virtually conceived on one plane.   The principle of
composition is not yet truly pictorial; there is no serious attempt to express
a third dimension; the background is quite subordinate, and effects of light
are unknown.   It is still coloured drawing; probably of great delicacy and
dignity, but not different in principle from sculpture in relief.

In the next period we have the beginnings of a more pictorial style.
It is clear that Zeuxis and Parrhasius, in their innovations, though some of
these, as Sculpture shows, were dictated by the spirit of the times, were in
part guided by artistic motives.   They desired to give relief to their pictures;
they become conscious of light, and of a third dimension.   Colouring
becomes more naturalistic, and the background and accessories more
important.   And these characteristics are carried further by Pausias and
later painters.   It is probable that even they, to the modern eye, would
seem a little sculpturesque.   The human figure always predominated, and
its beauty or expressiveness is the chief theme of praise; light and atmosphere
and landscape are usually subordinate.   But on the other hand literary
records and monuments, so far as they go, alike prove that before the period
of decline Greek Painting had developed beyond the stage of coloured
drawing.   The knowledge of perspective, linear and atmospheric both, is
still incomplete, but the principle of composition is now more truly pictorial.

The painter attempts to give his picture depth and conceives it in a
definite light.   Light and space, in other words, become positive elements
in composition.   It would even appear that in some cases the painter's
interest centred rather in light and colour than in form.   Some modern
writers indeed believe that this stage was not reached till late in the Greco-
Roman period, but the evidence seems to prove conclusively that the Greek
painters of the fourth century were already more conscious of light and
colour as living elements in a picture than any painter of the Italian
Renaissance before Leonardo, though in scientific knowledge of perspective
they may have been inferior.   The change of style, here ascribed to the
fourth century, is illustrated to some extent by a comparison of Figs. 60
and 61.   The characteristics of the later period are still better illustrated
by the Pagasaean *stelae*, of which no good reproductions are accessible.

The most complete and systematic account of Greek painting is contained in M. H. Swindler's *Ancient Painting*, 1930, which is well illustrated and contains an exhaustive bibliography. The clearest idea of the artistic achievement of Greek painters is given by E. Pfuhl's *Greek Masterpieces of Drawing and Painting*, translated by J. D. Beazley, 1926. For the Pompeian paintings Helbig's *Wandgemälde der verschütterten Städte Campaniens*, 1868, is still the most complete account, but the excellent study by L. Curtius, *Die Wandmalerei Pompejis*, 1929, which contains the results of modern research, should be read. The best reproductions of Greek paintings are to be found in Hermann and Bruckmann's *Denkmäler der Malerei*, 1906— . Upon questions of technical processes *Greek and Roman Painting*, A. P. Laurie, Cambridge, 1910, may be consulted.

Bibliography.

IV. 5. VASE PAINTING.

353. MYCENAEAN art and culture decayed and died out, at an uncertain period, about 1000 B.C. The traces of an artistic tradition surviving into later times are doubtful and local (as at Tiryns and Salamis), and on some sites there is evidence of a continuous occupation.

Geometric Art.

Fig. 62. Pyxis of Geometric Ware.

The period of change and political disturbance, represented by the Dorian Migration, was followed by a new development of art. In pottery the new style is known as Geometric, since the predominant decoration is of a linear and geometric character. In particular, it is rich in variations of the Maeander (or Greek Key) pattern, which does not occur in Mycenaean art. The surface of the vase is apt to be closely covered

Fig. 63. Vase of Geometrical Style. Subjects: a funeral procession and mourners. A procession of chariots.

with rich designs, arranged in panels, symmetrically disposed (Fig. 62). Vases of the style in question were first found in numbers near the Dipylon gate at Athens, and are hence called Dipylon vases.

In the later examples of the group there is a gradually increasing use of human and animal figures, at first in panels and afterwards in bands. The figures are mechanically drawn, according to a conventional system, the heads and bodies being little better than triangles, and the limbs black strokes. The highest level of achievement is represented by certain large vases, with scenes of funeral processions and mourning (Fig. 63). The geometric style is believed to have survived as late as the eighth century B.C. In its later development (known as the Phalerum style, because examples were found on the road from Athens to Phalerum) the geometric ornament becomes subordinate, and preference is given to figures of animals, and the like.

354. Oriental influence had before this date begun to have its effect on Greek art. In part by the agency of the Phoenicians (whose activity has been underestimated by some recent writers) and in part through those communities that were most in touch with the East, such as Ionia, Cyprus and Rhodes, oriental

Oriental
types.

Fig. 64. Corinthian Pottery.

types were introduced. We meet with winged figures and animals such as Chimaeras, Gryphons, Pegasi, and Sphinxes. To some extent these types, especially Gryphons and Sphinxes, had been familiar also to the artist of the Mycenaean period. How far historical Greece inherited them, and how far it borrowed them afresh from the East cannot yet be stated with certainty.

It was also characteristic of many of the early vase painters that these types, together with panthers, lions, cocks and the like, were combined in closely packed friezes, in which the interspaces of the field are filled up with rosettes, wheels, lotus buds, and other decorations. An explanation of this system of decoration has often been sought in the supposed designs of oriental embroidery.

In its extreme form, this style is represented by the 'Corinthian' wares

(Fig. 64). This name has long been given to a well-defined group of pottery, of which some leading examples were found in the neighbourhood of Corinth. But a similar tendency towards irrelevant decoration is also found in other early wares such as the early Attic 'Vourva' ware, the Rhodian wares (Fig. 65) and in the so-called Proto-Corinthian group, which is rather a series parallel to the Corinthian wares, though earlier on the whole.

Fig. 65.　Rhodian Plate.　Subject: Winged Gorgon.

As these vases develop in style the oriental element recedes: they approach in character the black-figure vases, and thus form a transition to the vases of fully-developed historical art.

355. During the seventh century B.C., the potters of many different localities were working on independent lines. They were gradually attaining to a fuller power of expressing the human figure, and of representing incident. They also began to

Rise of Attic School.

connect their artistic types, many of which had been inherited in an impersonal form, with subjects derived from the epic poems or mythology. At some period which cannot be exactly dated, but probably about the beginning of the sixth century B.C., the Athenian and Corinthian potters introduced a series of improvements, and by degrees the Attic school took the lead.   Hitherto it had been one school among many rivals, whose mutual relations are singularly difficult to trace, but it now assumed an easy supremacy.   The various local schools became insignificant, while the Athenian export trade increased.   It was only at a much later time, when Athenian industry began to decay, that the manufacture was seriously taken up in South Italy and other outlying districts.

356.   The material improvements, fully developed by the Athenian potters, were two.   They introduced the use of the fine   **Black-figure** clay, coloured to the familiar tint intermediate between red   **Style.** and orange; and they perfected the equally characteristic   **Methods.** lustrous glaze, rich black at its best, but sometimes tending towards olive green or brown.   With the introduction of the brilliant glaze came the careful study of lines engraved with a sharp metal point in the black glaze so as to show the ground colour below.   Occasionally in older wares, especially in those of Corinth (Fig. 64), the lines are incised in the dark figures to add internal details, or to define parts of the outline.   For the most part, however, though there are some notable exceptions, the incised work is singularly rough and hasty.   The Athenian painters began to practise the use of a point, worked with the careful precision of an engraver, and acquired both the skill of draughtsmen, and the power of expressing minute details in the internal drawing of the black figures.   Other colours were also added after the firing of the black, and were fired at a lower temperature, for which reason they have often disappeared.   White was freely used for such objects as linen garments, etc., and especially for the flesh colour of women.   For while the artist was ready to accept the convention of black, marked with incised lines, for the male figures, he seems disinclined to use it for the women.   Finally, a ruddy purple was freely used for helmets, draperies, etc., and in a quite conventional manner for hair, beards, and parts of animals (compare Fig. 66).

357.   The productions of the Athenian black-figure potters may be briefly described as belonging to the following classes: **Black-figure** (1) a period of archaic simplicity; (2) a period of com-   **Style.** parative freedom, followed by (3) alternatively, an affected   **Subdivisions.** conventionalism, or an attempt at freehand treatment, of which neither the artist nor his methods were capable.   In (1) the draperies and figures are alike conventionally treated.   Especially the women's dresses hang in stiff straight lines to the feet, without creases.   The figures are either in profile or straight to the front.   The composition is elementary, with numerous small figures.   In (2) there is greater freedom in the action, and considerable power of representing the nude male form in varied and

vigorous position. The draperies reflect something of the movement of the figures. The composition is less mechanical. At the same time it becomes simpler and more dignified, with a reduced number of figures represented on a larger scale. In (3), which appears to represent the

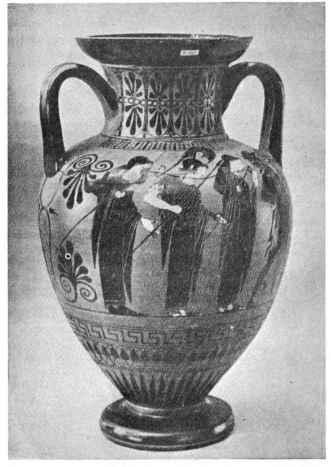

Fig. 66. Black-figure Amphora. Subject: Hermes leading the goddesses to Paris.

latest period, two tendencies are at work. Either there is an affected formality which seems to reflect the earliest period, combined with an extraordinary elaboration of small details expressed by the incised line (compare especially the vases of Exekias); or the execution becomes careless and rough. In part this occurs on small vases of slight and hasty work, but in part it seems to be due to a school seeking freedom by a wrong path.

358. In one considerable class of vases, namely the Panathenaic amphorae, the conservative influence of religious custom preserved the use of the black-figure style for more than 150 years after it had ceased to be practised for ordinary purposes. These vases, which contained the oil won by victors in the Panathenaic games, were of a fixed type. On the one side were an archaic figure of Athena, standing, usually between two Doric columns, and the inscription, written columnwise, τῶν ᾿Αθήνηθεν ἄθλων. On the other side is an agonistic scene. Some of the vases are genuinely archaic, but others can be dated between the years 367 and 313 B.C. by the names of the Archons, which are also inscribed.

Panathenaic vases.

359. The range of subjects represented on the black-figure vases is not large, when considered in relation to the number of vases, on account of the frequency with which the painters repeated the established types. The subjects include figures of deities singly or in groups, especially Dionysus and his following; special myths connected with deities, such as the birth of Athena; the labours and adventures of Heracles, and his final apotheosis, all rigidly following the typical schemes; certain episodes connected with the Trojan and Theban cycles; also numerous scenes of combat, often over the body of a fallen warrior, presumably an epic hero, but not definitely named. Of scenes of daily life, the most common are those connected with athletic games and the exercises of the palaestra. Scenes from the life of women are less common, but they are occasionally represented bathing or at the well. Scenes of trade, industry and agricultural operations occur, but only rarely on the black-figure vases.

Black-figure Style. Subjects.

360. The Greek potters who practised the black-figure style of painting succeeded in reaching a considerable height of artistic achievement. The story from mythology or the epic poems is told with vivacity and directness. Attention is concentrated on the essential points by a singular economy of all accessories independent of the figures. Thus in the language of the vase painters a single column may stand for a temple, and a tree or a plant may show that the scene is out of doors, while a dolphin or a fish may represent the sea. At the same time much of the drawing is strictly conventional, and a certain amount of grotesqueness is always present, being inseparable from the method employed of black silhouettes. The vases of this class have that interest which always attaches to the productions of a primitive or early art. Owing however to the inherent limitations of the method, which led to its abandonment, the black-figure vases do not reach the highest level. The release of vase painting from its shackles could only be effected by the introduction of another and freer style.

Black-figure Style. Artistic capabilities.

22—2

361. Towards the close of the sixth century B.C. a complete reversal
was effected in the system of vase painting, when the artists
seem to have become aware of the advantages of leaving the
figures in the ground colour of the vase, standing out upon
the dark glaze. The illustration (Fig. 67) shows part of a vase at Palermo of
the transitional potter Andocides. By a whim, the artist has painted the two
halves of the vase in the two styles. By the new method the grotesqueness,
which seems inseparable from the black-figure vases, was eliminated, and the
changes of technique made advances in drawing possible. The methods
employed in the new style were the following. While the clay was still
somewhat soft, the artist made a sketch of his design with a blunt point,
lightly marking the clay. The figures are thus sketched out, sometimes

*The Red-
figure Style.
Methods.*

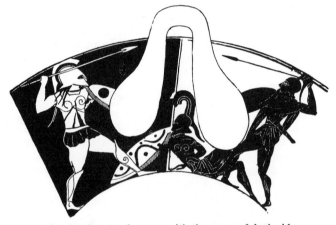

Fig. 67. A part of a vase with the name of Andocides.

after repeated trials, the draped figures being sketched in the nude, and the
draperies afterwards added. Next a stripe of black glaze, about an eighth
of an inch wide, is carefully drawn round the outside of the figures for
which vacant spaces are thus left. The background is filled up by painting
over the interstices which are bordered by the broad stripes, but, nearly
always, in such a way that the stripe can be distinguished if examined
with oblique light. The interior details of the figures are next drawn
with fine lines of the glaze, and freehand drawing takes the place of the
incised lines of the preceding style. For special portions, such as the
profiles, a thin black line is often drawn along the boundary of the subject
in order to give it better definition and fineness of outline. Occasionally some of the interior details, such as the abdominal muscles, are
drawn with the glaze thinned out to a light brown, and are only faintly

visible. In rare cases this lighter glaze is also used as a local wash. To separate a black piece of the figure, such for instance as the hair, from the background an incised line is first used; later a space of light ground was left along the margin of the black part of the subject. Accessories which overlap the glaze are sometimes painted in red. Nor did the practical-minded Greek craftsman omit to use such mechanical aids as he found suitable. Circles, such as those that frame the **Mechanical aids.** interior of a kylix, are drawn while the vase revolves on the wheel. Straight lines, as for instance for a spear, are drawn with the aid

Fig. 68. Red-figure Kylix. Subject: Young warrior.

of a flexible ruler. Small circles are struck with a pair of compasses (cf. Fig. 68).

362. Excavations on the Acropolis of Athens have established, contrary to what had previously been supposed, that the red- **Red-figure** figure style was fully developed at the time of the Persian **Style. Begin-** war. Countless fragments of pottery were found in the **nings.** strata of rubbish levelled for the purpose of rebuilding the Acropolis temples, and among them were numerous signed fragments by well-known masters of the greatest period of red-figure painting, such as Hieron,

Chachrylion, and perhaps Euphronius. Since the red-figure style had been brought to perfection by the time of the second Persian invasion, it follows that, as some years, perhaps a generation, must be allowed for its development, the introduction of the style cannot have been later than the latter part of the sixth century—say 525 B.C. On the other hand, the excavations that have been made in the tumulus of Marathon yielded numerous black-figure vases, but only one red-figure fragment. We thus obtain definite evidence that about 490 B.C. the black-figure fashion still prevailed for funereal usages although the red-figure vases must have been coming into common use for dedications in the temples of the Acropolis. For a certain time, which cannot at present be accurately defined, the two styles were practised simultaneously, in some cases by the same persons. A small group of potters is known (Nicosthenes, Andocides (cf. Fig. 67), Hischylus and Pamphaeus) who produced vases in each of the two styles, and also used both styles on the same vase, either for its inner and outer surfaces, or for different parts of the same surface.

363. The flourishing period of Attic red-figure painting seems to have fallen between about 525 and 400 B.C. The painters of this century and a quarter have been divided into groups, described as (1) Earliest, (2) Ripe Archaic and (3) Free. These groups again have many subdivisions.

1. The earliest painters, known as the groups of Andocides and Epictetus, developed the new technique. Artistically they continued to work in the spirit of the black-figure schools, carrying on its stiff mannerism, not refreshed by a renewed study of nature. 2. The 'Ripe Archaic' (formerly known as the 'strong') style is represented primarily by the group of Euphronius, composed of a series of masters whom we know to have been active about 480 B.C. The drawing becomes large and ideal, and the artist obtains complete mastery of the human form. Other names associated with this section, as potters or painters, are Phintias, Euthymides, Brygos and Duris. 3. The later Athenian masters worked in what was formerly known as the 'fine style.' It is now described as the 'free' or 'classic' style, and subdivided into 'early' and 'ripe.' The leading artist of the 'early free' style is Polygnotos (not to be confused with the painter). The chief representative of the 'ripe free' style is Meidias. The works of the group are marked by freedom in the treatment of the figure, and elaborate systems of composition, with occasional suggestions of landscape.

364. With the introduction of the red-figure style, the range of subjects represented becomes wider, and instead of repeating the accepted type of a particular incident, such as one of the labours of Heracles, the artists seek to vary their treatment of a subject. Theseus becomes prominent on the vases at the same time that his cult was being developed at Athens. Subjects from daily life become more frequent, and scenes occur from life in the

Red-figure Style. Subjects.

palaestra, the banquet-room, the street, the school, and the women's apartments.　Towards the close of the period children are also introduced.

365.　A frequent addition to Athenian vases whether black- or red-figured is an inscription such as καλός, or more fully ὁ παῖς καλός, or with a proper name as Λέαγρος καλός.　In such cases the painter has followed the current Athenian custom, Names with καλός.

Fig. 69.　Red-figure jar (Stamnos).　Subject: Combat of
Horseman and Foot-soldier.

by which lovers and admirers thus wrote the names of the objects of their admiration.　Aristophanes, *Vesp.* 97, alludes to the custom

> καὶ νὴ Δί᾽ ἢν ἴδῃ γέ που γεγραμμένον
> υἱὸν Πυριλάμπους ἐν θύρᾳ Δῆμον καλόν,
> ἰὼν παρέγραψε πλησίον "κημὸς καλός."

Where the name is given, it is doubtful in some cases whether the person named was specially related to the potter, or whether he was of conspicuous station, and well known to the Athenian public. Several attempts have been made on the latter hypothesis to identify the καλός-names with those of known persons, and thus to obtain fixed points in the chronology of vase painting, but in most cases such identifications are extremely doubtful. In another direction, the καλός-names are important, since they point to a synchronism of the artists who use the same name, and in some cases suggest the author of an unsigned vase. Occasionally, but not often, the inscription is feminine (as ἡ παῖς καλή). In certain cases it applies to figures on the vase, probably in a sense equivalent to Bravo! a humorous expression of admiration for the figure.

366. With the decay of the Athenian potteries at the close of the fifth century, the manufacture of the red-figure vases passed to other places, especially to the Greek districts of South Italy. The vases of this period are often very large and highly ornate, but the treatment becomes conventional. The range of subjects is narrower, and such themes as a woman at her toilet accompanied by Erotes (cf. Fig. 70), become more numerous than any others. When mythological and heroic subjects are introduced, the painter makes conscious reference to works of literature, and there is no longer an independent system of traditional types handed down in art. In several cases the designs are directly borrowed from plays of Euripides. There is also a tendency to introduce farcical subjects, and a considerable number of the South Italian vases represent scenes from unknown comedies.

Red-figure Style. Italian Schools.

367. At the beginning of this period it is hard to distinguish between vases produced at Athens and at Italian centres under Athenian inspiration. Later the Italian works become more distinct in their technique. There is a growing use of white, which occurs but little on the Athenian vases. Upon the white there is an attempt to show shade and detail with yellowish brown. The palmette and other ornaments under the handle become large and coarse. The red-figure style probably died away in Italy in the third century B.C. About the time that it came to an end an attempt was made to produce a somewhat similar effect by simpler means. There is a class of vases which are covered all over with black glaze and have the figures painted in white upon the glaze. In another class of vases figures are altogether abandoned and the decoration consists of subjects moulded in relief. In some cases copies of coins are thus inserted, while in others we have subjects which are known to recur in silver.

Red-figure Style. Italian technique.

The end of the Red-figure Style.

368. Through all the earlier periods of vase painting, side by side with the conventions of the black- and red-figure styles, there had existed schools of painting whose technique consisted in figures drawn in outline upon a light ground, the space

White Athenian Vases.

within the outlines being filled in with washes of colour. These methods
had been practised at Naucratis, Rhodes and Sparta, and, to a certain
extent, at Athens during the time of the black-figure vases. They
became important however at Athens at the beginning of the fifth century
with the introduction of the red-figure style. We have a series of fine
vases, one of which is signed by Euphronius, with figures thus drawn in
delicate line upon a white ground. But the most familiar use of this

Fig. 70. Late Red-figure Amphora, Apulian shape. Subject:
Toilet scene.

method is upon the numerous class of vases known as the White Athenian
Lekythoi. These we know to have been painted for the use of persons
making offerings at a tomb. The only reference in Greek literature to the
vase painters concerns this group. Aristophanes (*Eccl.* 995) speaks of

τὸν τῶν γραφέων ἄριστον
ὃς τοῖς νεκροῖσι ζωγραφεῖ τὰς ληκύθους.

The subjects are for the most part connected with the tomb. Sometimes the tombstone is shown, and sometimes mythological scenes connected with the tomb, such as a meeting between the deceased and Charon. Sometimes scenes from daily life are represented in a manner corresponding to that of the marble reliefs (cf. Fig. 71). As regards technique the vases are usually of red clay with glazed necks and feet, while the body is covered with a fine coating of white. After a preliminary marking, the subject is

Fig. 71. White Athenian Vases.

drawn in fine lines, at first of black glaze, later of glaze thinned to a golden brown, and finally with dull red lines. The surfaces of the figure and draperies may then be covered with washes of colour usually transient and therefore often lost or difficult to trace. Many of these vases are very beautiful, and all are pervaded by that feeling of placid and gentle melancholy which marks the sepulchral reliefs. Dealing, however, almost exclusively with the tomb and its surroundings, the vases, like the reliefs,

lack variety, and, when they are examined in masses, the treatment of the
later vases is felt to be monotonous.

For a general account see H. B. Walters, *History of Ancient Pottery, Greek,
Etruscan and Roman, based on the work of Samuel Birch*. The
best introduction to the subject is a study of a catalogued collection, **Bibliography.**
e.g. The British Museum, catalogued by C. H. Smith and H. B. Walters; the
Ashmolean Museum, *Catalogue of Greek Vases*, by Percy Gardner; the Fitzwilliam
Museum, *Catalogue of the Greek Vases*, by E. A. Gardner. General collections
of vase paintings: Furtwängler and Reichhold, *Griechische Vasenmalerei*; the
Journal of Hellenic Studies and other archaeological periodicals. Books on
special classes: Graef, *Die antiken Vasen von der Akropolis zu Athen*;
A. S. Murray, *White Athenian Vases in the Brit. Mus*. A re-issue of vases,
published before 1892, is supplied by Reinach's *Répertoire des Vases peints, grecs
et étrusques*. A large and continually growing number of vases is illustrated and
described in the *Corpus Vasorum* of the Union Académique Internationale.
[The Parts for Great Britain include the British, Ashmolean, and Fitzwilliam
Museums.] Many attributions and groupings of unsigned vases will be found
in the works of J. D. Beazley, especially *Attic Red-figured Vases in American
Museums* (1918) and *Attische Vasenmaler des rothfigurigen Stils* (1925).

IV.   6.   TERRACOTTAS.

369. WORKS in Terracotta or baked clay have been preserved to us
from all periods of classical antiquity.   For the most part
such objects are of small size and were originally of trifling **Extensive use of clay.**
value.   While the ease with which clay could be obtained
and worked favoured copious production, its fragility and want of value
made it unsuited for the permanent and serious work of the sculptor.
Clay was widely used by the Greeks for many artistic purposes, in architectural decoration and in sepulchral monuments as well as in the
manufacture of terracotta statuettes.

It has been shown above (§§ 286, 295) that the use of clay for
sculptured images, albeit of a very rude kind, was well known
in primitive times, and besides stiff conventional representa- **Statuettes, seventh century.**
tions of deities we also find clumsy figures of human beings
and animals.   The use of the word πλαστική for sculpture
points to the practice of modelling or moulding (πλάσσειν) in wet clay as
one of the earliest methods in this art.   The earliest clay statuettes found
in Greek tombs of the historic period, as in Cyprus, Rhodes, and Boeotia,
are of two types, corresponding to the principal types of primitive statues:
they are either flat like boards (σανίδες) or columnar in form (κίονες).
They date from about the seventh century B.C.; the limbs are hardly
modelled, and they are often decorated with red and black paint, like the
contemporary vases.

They are followed in the sixth and fifth centuries by statuettes, archaic
but showing more development in style, with modelled limbs
Sixth and fifth centuries. and drapery, of which two types almost exclusively prevail.
These are the *standing and seated female figures*, which
again present a close analogy to the contemporary types of Greek statues.
Such figures were probably intended to represent deities, especially those
of the underworld, Demeter and Persephone; but the same types appear
to have been used indiscriminately for votive offerings in temples and for
funeral purposes. In the latter case they were originally regarded as
embodiments of the souls or ghosts of the departed, as well as representations of the protecting deities of the nether world; a confusion of the

Fig. 72. Greek Statuettes from Rhodes and Sicily (Archaic period).

deity with his worshipper was a common feature of primitive Greek beliefs,
and finds frequent reflection in early art. Another favourite type is the
funeral mask or bust, usually feminine; a type probably derived from
Egypt, where the upper part of the coffin was often modelled in the form
of the deceased. The Greeks converted these into busts, hollowing out
the back, and adding a veil and the high cylindrical head-dress which
typified the underworld deities. Archaic terracottas of another class are
obviously only children's playthings, buried in their tombs for their use in
a future existence. These comprise dolls with jointed limbs, figures of

horsemen, animals, and even fruit. An epigram in the Greek Anthology tells how Timarete dedicated to Artemis her dolls and other playthings of her childhood. Here the word used for doll is κόρη, 'girl' or 'maiden,' a word in general use for the terracotta figures of girls in later Greek times. The contents of the tomb of a girl, dating from the fifth century B.C., recently acquired by the British Museum include a figure of the deceased seated in a high chair or throne, as if deified, surrounded by a pair of shoes or boots, a spinning implement, a bridal vase, and other objects.

It has often been remarked that Greek terracottas do not exhibit, like other branches of art, a continuous and gradual development from archaism to perfection, followed by a similar decadence, but that there is an abrupt break in the fifth century during which this art is almost un-represented. At the same time the Tanagra figures are sufficient evidence that there was a 'finest period' for Greek terracottas, but as they date from the latter half of the fourth century and the first half of the third, they are widely separated from those of the archaic period which have already been described. In the tombs excavated at Tanagra, terracotta statuettes are commonly found in those of the sixth century, but in those of the fifth they are almost entirely wanting; the fourth-century tombs which yielded so many thousands are dated by means of the plain black-glazed pottery which they contained. This seems to indicate that at Tanagra at least there was a fashion in tomb-furniture, and that in the fifth century, as always at Athens, painted vases had the preference. But in Rhodes and other places where terracottas have been found in large numbers, it is probable that another influence was at work. This was the hieratic tendency so often manifested in Greek art; the terracottas conform to an archaic style for religious reasons. In Rhodes archaic terracottas were often found with fifth-century red-figure vases. On the other hand some sites, such as Athens, and Larnaka in Cyprus, have yielded terracottas of distinctly fifth-century style; but these are exceptional.

370. In order to know the characteristics of the best Greek work in terracotta, we must therefore turn our attention to the Tanagra statuettes of 350—250 B.C. In comparison with those of archaic or hieratic style we are now confronted with *Tanagra figures.* a startling change. The seated and standing feminine types are still in a majority, but it is their meaning that has changed. In short they are no longer mythological but *genre* figures; they are no longer suggestive of religious beliefs, but only of secular daily life. The change however must be considered to be due to artistic rather than to religious development; the art-types became secularised, and conceptions originally religious were adopted almost unconsciously for subjects drawn from daily life. Hence we find an almost unlimited variety of feminine standing types. All with-out exception wear the long tunic or *chiton* and the mantle or *himation* which with the addition of a large shady hat formed the typical dress of the Greek girl or matron. They usually hold a fan, a mirror, or a ball, or their hands are simply employed to hold together their draperies; the seated types are similar, but more rare, and are usually placed on a rocky base to add picturesqueness to the composition.

The place which these figures occupy in the history of art certainly corresponds rather to the conceptions of the Hellenistic Age than to those of Praxiteles and his contemporaries. It is not improbable that the true source of their inspiration is to be sought in painting rather than in sculpture; and it may be recalled that during the fourth century there was an influential local school of painters in Boeotia, which chiefly devoted itself to *genre* subjects. In the terracottas of Myrina in Asia Minor, which

Fig. 73. Greek Statuettes from Tanagra (third century B.C.).

in artistic merit stand next to those of Tanagra, Hellenistic characteristics are even more strongly marked. These figures break more completely with tradition, and are hardly earlier than the second century B.C. There is a much greater variety of subject, and figures of Aphrodite and Eros, Dionysus, Victory, and other deities are of frequent occurrence, as are also comic and grotesque subjects. But the influence of Tanagra is also apparent, and in fact the Tanagra types are found repeated, with varying success from an artistic point of view, all over the ancient world. In Asia Minor, in Cyprus, North Africa, and Southern Italy a large proportion of the terracottas found on each site are mere repetitions of the favourite

poses and motives.   Generally speaking, the terracottas found in different
parts of the Greek world exhibit strongly-marked differences, each having
their peculiar local features.   In Rhodes and Cyprus, for instance, the
terracottas are mainly archaic or hieratic in style; at Myrina in Asia Minor
and in the Cyrenaica nearly all date from the Hellenistic Age.   Large
numbers of votive terracottas were found by Sir Charles Newton at Cnidus
and Halicarnassus; at the former, in the precinct of Demeter and Persephone, they were packed in layers in a subterranean chamber, 'assorted
like articles in a shop.'   They usually represent the goddesses to whom
they were dedicated.   At Naucratis in the Egyptian Delta and in the
Fayûm numerous terracottas have been found which manifest Egyptian
influence both in style and subject; these belong mostly to the Ptolemaic
period.   The terracottas of Sicily show a marked individuality, and a
quite independent development, from the richly-coloured votive figures of
the archaic period found at Selinus to the Erotic and Bacchic types of the
Hellenistic Age, often coloured with a peculiar enamel-glaze of various
hues.

371.   These statuettes and other small objects in terracotta are, as
has been noted, obtained from tombs, or less often from the
shrines of divinities.   Though in earlier times the original **Use and purpose of the statuettes.**
intention may have been to bury them as substitutes for
better offerings for the use of the dead or as votive offerings
to the gods below, in later times such a purpose must have been almost
forgotten.   The dainty and playful statuettes which have been found in
great numbers in the cemeteries of Tanagra in Boeotia and elsewhere, can
only be supposed to have been regarded as part of the accustomed
furniture of a grave, without special religious or other significance.   Terracottas obtained from shrines are of a votive character, consisting of figures
of the divinity or of representations of acceptable offerings.   Plato alludes
to the practice of hanging up small figures (κόραι) in shrines, but other
passages in classical authors speak of 'makers of clay figures for the
market' or of those who 'make little images of clay for children.'   Thus
we see that many of these figures can only be regarded as children's toys.
Doubtless, too, the figures found in tombs had already served their purpose
in this way, or as household ornaments.   While the terracottas of the
archaic period are mainly votive or religious in character, the later ones
show by their illimitable variety of subject, pose, and conception, that no
special meaning was intended; and the transformation of hieratic types
into mere *genre* creations was brought about partly by the growth of artistic
taste, partly by the general rationalising tendency of religious beliefs.

372.   The principal methods employed for the production of terracotta
figures are as follows.

(1)   Figures of horsemen and the like of a rough ap- **Methods of production.**
pearance are produced by rolling and pinching soft clay
with the fingers.   Such figures are found chiefly in Cyprus, but also occur

elsewhere.   They are primitive rather than archaic, since the same methods would at any time produce the same results.

(2)   Statuettes and reliefs are worked directly in the soft clay, with the ordinary modelling tools.

(3)   Subjects are cast in clay, from clay moulds.   Most of the smaller terracottas were made thus, and numerous moulds are extant (Fig. 74).   From the original figure, which might be in wax or clay, a mould was prepared, by pressing soft clay upon the front of the figure.   This mould was baked,

Fig. 74. Mould for terracotta statuette

and could then be used for the production of copies.   As a rule only the front is moulded, the back being hastily shaped by hand.   In rare cases moulds are also found for the back.   The figure thus prepared was painted and fired.

In the manufacture of an ordinary terracotta statuette five distinct processes were usually employed: (a) the preparation of the clay; (b) moulding and modelling; (c) retouching and adding details; (d) baking; and (e) colouring and gilding.   The earlier terracottas are usually produced by one of the two methods described above, i.e. by modelling by hand or with tools; but subsequently the use of a mould became invariable. Although a whole series of figures might be cast from one mould, there were many devices for avoiding monotony, by varying the pose of the head or the position of the arms, or again by different attributes or variety ot colouring, all this being achieved in the process of retouching. The colours employed to decorate the figures are usually red and blue, laid on a creamy-white slip, with which the whole figure was coloured. These pigments are usually applied to the drapery, black or deep yellow being employed for hair, features, and other details, and gilding for ornaments.

373. The use of terracotta for architectural or structural purposes also forms a very important branch of the subject. In early times unburnt or sun-dried brick was in general use for building purposes; but burnt brick, though universally em-ployed at Rome, was rarely used in Greece, owing to the abundance of marble and good building stone. On the other hand terracotta orna-mentation for buildings was in general use down to the end of the sixth century B.C. Except in Sicily and Italy, however, its employment became gradually more restricted, and in the more important buildings its place was taken by marble for tiles and architectural ornaments. Terracotta was generally used for roof-tiles, which were of two kinds—flat and covering-tiles, for cornices and the rows of water-spouts along the eaves, and for the *antefixae* or ornamental terminations of the covering-tiles along the gables and sides of the building. Among the last-named we find many choice examples of decoration in relief at all periods. In the sixth and fifth centuries these terracotta ornaments were usually adorned with bright colours, such as red and blue, and numerous painted specimens have been found at Olympia and elsewhere. In Sicily and Italy it was a common practice to nail slabs of terracotta over the stone-work, and these were either painted or decorated with patterns in relief. The *antefixae* or terminal roof-tiles played a large part in the decoration of temples, and were adorned with all kinds of subjects in relief; they were especially popular in the archaic period. Pausanias mentions early specimens which he saw in Athens, representing Theseus slaying Sciron and Eos carrying off Cephalus. Two similar groups were found in Delos on the site of a fifth-century temple. Terracotta was also largely used for coffins and sarcophagi, of which the most remarkable examples, covered with painted decoration, have been found at Clazomenae in Asia Minor; and for sepulchral urns and large vases made for placing in the tomb.

374. Apart from the architectural terracottas just described, relief-work in this material is comparatively rare; a remarkable exception however is formed by the so-called 'Melian' and 'Locrian' reliefs, and others from the Acropolis of Athens. The Melian reliefs, many of which have been found in Melos and on neighbouring sites, are usually of open-work, cast in a mould and often repeated; they date from the end of the archaic period, about 480 B.C. The subjects are

[margin note: Terracotta in architecture.]

[margin note: Reliefs.]

usually mythological, such as Perseus slaying Medusa or Bellerophon and the Chimaera (Fig. 75). On the other hand the reliefs found at Athens and Locri (in Southern Italy) are votive in character, with figures of the deities to whom they were dedicated or other appropriate subjects; they are in the form of rectangular plaques, intended for hanging against a wall.

Fig. 75. Archaic relief from Rhodes (about 480 B.C.).

Pottier, *Les Statuettes de Terre cuite dans l'Antiquité*, Paris (Hachette), **Bibliography.** 1890. C. A. Hutton, *Greek Terracotta Statuettes*, London (Seeley), 1899. *Brit. Mus. Catalogue of Terracottas* (1903). R. Kekulé, *Die antiken Terrakotten*, 1880, etc. (Stuttgart). Vol. III. *Typen der griechischen Terrakotten*, by F. Winter (1903). Walters, *Art of the Greeks* (1906), chap. X.

IV. 7. BRONZE-WORK.

375. Although to a great extent partaking of the nature of sculpture and bound up with its history, Greek bronze-work is sufficiently important for separate treatment. Not a few of **Extensive use of bronze.** the great sculptors, notably Lysippus, worked exclusively or mainly in bronze, and there are a few existing masterpieces, such as the Charioteer at Delphi (Fig. 40), in that material. But nearly all the great statues in bronze have perished, or are only represented by heads and other fragmentary remains. On the other hand there are extant innumerable specimens of decorative art in bronze, and there was no material on which the Greeks lavished so much skill and attention. It is difficult at the present day to realise the extensive use of bronze in antiquity, even after the introduction of iron. The ancients always employed bronze for locks and keys, knives and other tools, and for defensive armour and weapons, where we now use iron or steel. It was also largely used for furniture, such as chairs or couches, for mirrors and toilet articles, and for vessels of all kinds where we should employ wood, glass, clay, and other materials. Bronze moreover is a material which easily lends itself to decoration, by means of modelling, chasing and engraving, and thus gave ample play to the marvellous decorative instincts of the Greeks. Many of the bronze objects in our museums take high rank as works of art; and we have besides an enormous number of bronze statuettes, used for adorning domestic shrines or for attachment by way of ornament to articles of furniture, which are often of great merit, or of interest as copies from masterpieces, though hardly of sufficient importance to call for notice in a history of Greek sculpture. Greek bronze-work may be considered under two heads, for each of which distinct technical pro- **Different processes.** cesses were required : (1) Statuary, produced either by solid casting, by riveting together beaten plates, or by the hollow-casting process known as *cire perdu*. The two former processes are practically confined to the earliest periods, and hollow-casting is almost universal from the sixth century onwards. (2) Decorative work, ornamented with chased, engraved, or *repoussé* designs.

All the earliest bronze statuettes are cast solid, and for smaller objects this process was always retained, but the waste of valuable material and inconvenient weight of larger figures soon brought about the introduction of hollow-casting from Egypt. The alternative early process of riveting beaten plates together (σφυρήλατον) was often applied to the ξόανα or primitive cult-statues when it was desired to cover them with a representation of drapery. It was also largely used for decorative work, ornamentation and figures in relief being produced by beating up from behind with a blunt instrument, and the details being engraved with a sharp point in front. Of this kind of work the best examples are a series of early reliefs from Olympia, the Acropolis of Athens, and other sites. They date from the seventh century B.C., and are variously attributed to a Corinthian or Argive, and to a Chalcidian school. Chalcis in Euboea was the only town in Greece possessing copper-mines of importance, and was a great commercial centre in the seventh and sixth centuries B.C., but so far no remains of early art have been found here.

The attribution of the invention (or rather introduction) of hollow-casting to Rhoecus and Theodorus of Samos about 600 B.C. may be not without a germ of truth. They probably learned the art in Egypt and introduced it into the Peloponnesus. They were probably also the first to utilise clay figures as material for bronze statues. Pausanias mentions a

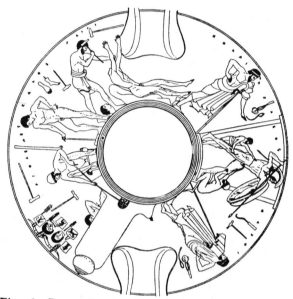

Fig. 76. Bronze foundry, from a vase-painting at Berlin.

statue of Night by Rhoecus at Ephesus as the earliest hollow-cast statue. The *cire perdu* method which henceforward became customary was in the main identical with that in use at the present day. The name refers to the manner in which a wax model was disposed of and replaced by molten bronze; its essential features were the clay or plaster model roughly reproducing the whole conception with which the sculptor began to work, and the thin coating of wax laid over it in which all the details were accurately executed. Over this an outer mould of clay was employed, and the wax being melted in a furnace ran out through holes, the molten bronze being introduced in its place. Finally the surface of the bronze was prepared by touching up or by such adornments as colouring, lacquering, or gilding. A vase-painting in the Berlin Museum (Fig. 76), dating about 500 B.C., represents a bronze foundry with statues in process of completion; it shows that the casting was often done in several pieces, the parts being afterwards welded together.

376. Existing Greek bronze statuettes of the archaic period are mostly of small size, and reproduce the types familiar from the larger works of the period, such as standing male or draped female figures. Of the fully-developed style of the fifth century there are comparatively few examples in bronze, though the art of Pheidias and Polycleitus is reflected in some statuettes of later date. When we reach

Extant works.

Fig. 77. Bronze relief from the river Siris.

the fourth century the reproductions of famous sculptures become more numerous, and this period seems to have been the golden age of the art in Greece, not only for the statuettes, but also for decorative bronze-work. Among the most remarkable bronze works of this period are two in the British Museum, the colossal head of Aphrodite from the Castellani collection which reflects the spirit of Scopas, and the lovely head of Hypnos in which Praxitelean qualities are most apparent. The great worker in bronze of this century was the sculptor Lysippus, and there are many existing bronzes which belong to his school, notably the exquisite heroic figure from the Lake of Bracciano in the British Museum, in some respects the finest bronze in existence. It is cast solid with a flat back, having been attached to a piece of furniture, and therefore belongs rather to the category of reliefs than to that of figures in the round. Equally reminiscent of the style of Lysippus are the famous Siris bronzes, from the shoulder-pieces of a cuirass, which from a technical point of view are a truly marvellous piece of work (Fig. 77). The figures are beaten out from behind in *repoussé* work, and are hammered out to such a degree of fineness that they are almost in the round, and the bronze is hardly thicker than paper. The details are worked with extraordinary care and delicacy. The influence of Lysippus is also apparent in another group of bronzes in the British Museum, found at Paramythia near Dodona; they represent various deities, and date from the third century B.C.

The tendency of the Greeks to lavish decoration on ordinary articles of household use is nowhere better exemplified than in their mirrors and mirror-cases, which were invariably of bronze. The archaic form of the Greek mirror was that of a circular polished disc, often with a handle sculptured in the form of a figure, such as Aphrodite. The back of the disc was sometimes engraved with a group of figures, but the Greeks for some reason did not favour this method of decoration, and it was left for the Etruscans to bring it to perfection. Many of these archaic mirrors have been found on the Acropolis at Athens and elsewhere in Greece; but they were supplanted about the end of the fifth century B.C. by plain circular discs without handles, enclosed in flat boxes or cases with hinged covers. The outside of the cover was usually adorned with a relief (ἔμβλημα) attached separately. Many of these designs, which cover the period 400—200 B.C., are exceedingly beautiful, the *repoussé* work being often most elaborate. The subjects are very varied, many being mythological or from heroic legend. One of the most beautiful, representing Aphrodite and Anchises, was found with the Paramythia bronzes mentioned above; among the engraved designs which are occasionally found on the backs of the mirrors themselves, the finest is a group of personifications of the city of Corinth and the island of Leucas. Another in the British Museum represents Pan and Aphrodite playing with knucklebones (Fig. 78); the drawing is very fine and the conception is of great beauty. But the style of the reliefs is by no means uniform, some being of very inferior workmanship.

Although engraving on bronze was never so popular in Greece as in Etruria, and seems to have gone out of fashion entirely by the end of the fifth century, there are yet sufficient examples of fine work in this style to call for mention. Its history can be traced from the Geometrical period (eighth century B.C.) when large brooches (*fibulae*) were made in Boeotia, to the bow or foot of which large flat pieces of metal were attached, engraved with elaborate designs, of animals, ships, etc. One in the British Museum actually has a mythological subject, the slaying of the hydra by Heracles. The style is however rude and conventional. As a specimen of sixth-century work we have a bronze cuirass found at Olympia, engraved with the subject of a lyre-player and chorus, Sphinxes, and various animals. The style is somewhat affected, and recalls that of some black-figured vases of the period. The transition from the archaic to the 'fine' period is well illustrated by two bronze discs, one in the British Museum, the other at Berlin, dating about 500—480 B.C. In both cases the subjects engraved are single figures of athletes engaged in the contests of the πένταθλον; the style corresponds to that of the earlier red-figured vases and may be a reflection of the work of the sculptor Myron. Of the later instances of Greek engraving in bronze the best are those on the mirrors already

Fig. 78. Greek mirror with engraved design.

described. Allusion has also been already made to some of the most noteworthy examples of Greek bronze-work in *repoussé* relief, both of the archaic and of the fine period. The archaic period is best represented by the reliefs from Olympia and Athens, the later by the mirror-cases. An interesting specimen of the transitional period of 500—480 B.C. is a curious little figure of Athena found on the Acropolis at Athens, which is formed of two reliefs placed back to back, so as to show both sides of the figure. The style though archaic is full of grace, and may be compared with that of the female figures in marble found on the same site.

Bibliography.—*Brit. Mus. Catalogue of Bronzes* (1899). W. Lamb, *Greek and Roman Bronzes* (1929). See also *Bibliography of Sculpture*, p. 322.

IV. 8.   GOLD AND SILVER WORK.

377.   GREEK ornamental work in metal includes work in gold or silver
as well as in bronze, and the former may be considered under two heads :
Jewellery or personal ornaments of all kinds, such as finger-rings, earrings,
necklaces, or pendants; and Chasing, which includes vessels of gold and
silver or ornaments of furniture, etc.   Ornamental work in the precious
metals appears at a very early stage, as has been noted above (§§ 285 ff.), and
that at quite an advanced stage of technical development.   In the later
products may be traced the whole development of Greek art down to
Roman times.   The ordinary Greek term for gold and silver
Τορευτική.
work was τορευτική, though in strict accuracy this word
denotes chasing, as opposed to ἐμπαιστική or work in *repoussé*.   It may
however be employed as a general term for all processes of stamping,
chiselling, or engraving, which could be applied to metal, with the exception of casting and moulding, which belong to the art of πλαστική or
sculpture, and γλυπτική or engraving of gems and coin-dies.

During the period of the dawn of Greek history there is a gap of
several centuries after the decadence of Mycenaean art, during which the
jeweller's art is at a very low ebb, and specimens of metal-work hardly
exist; although the contemporary series of 'island-gems' shows that the
gem-engraver's hand had not lost its cunning.   We are forced to turn for
the metal-work of this period to literary records, such as they are, and to
seek in the descriptions of the shields of Achilles and Heracles the achievements of the goldsmiths and silversmiths of this age.   The less mythical
chest of Cypselus, in which the decoration was largely plated with gold, is
also instructive for our purpose.   The method of decoration, if not the
technique, of the Homeric shield may be reflected in a series of bronze
and silver bowls found in Cyprus and Italy, which belong to the eighth
and seventh centuries B.C. (Fig. 79).   They are unquestionably of
Phoenician workmanship, richly ornamented with engraved designs of
hunting-scenes, pastoral scenes, and decorative patterns; but they must be
regarded rather as influencing Greek art than as actually illustrating its
development.   Some gold plaques found at Cameirus in Rhodes, now
in the British Museum, which date from the seventh century B.C., have
quasi-Oriental *repoussé* designs of the Asiatic Artemis, Centaurs, and
similar subjects.

The metal-work of the archaic period is really better illustrated by the
products of Etruscan art; the processes employed by these
Etruscan
work.
people were largely identical with the Greek, and their
achievements hardly inferior in style or technical merit,
while gold ornaments have been found in the richest profusion in Etruscan

tombs of the sixth and fifth centuries. Towards the end of the seventh century B.C. a great wave of Oriental and Greek influence swept into the country, and in this we may possibly find a verification of the tradition that when Demaratus was expelled from Corinth in 665 B.C. he took with him a body of craftsmen who introduced various arts into Italy. Traces both of Greek and Oriental influence are to be found in the contents of the Polledrara tomb at Vulci, which included a bronze bust with reliefs of Greek style round the pedestal, and a richly-embossed gold diadem. The contemporary Regulini-Galassi tomb at Cervetri was very rich in gold

Fig. 79.　Phoenician metal bowl.

ornaments. Silver is always much rarer, but the series of reliefs found at Perugia form a notable exception. In point of style these may be compared with the Ionic Greek vases of the sixth century; and it is probable that much of what has hitherto passed for Etruscan metal-work must have been actually imported from Greece, and especially from Ionia. The art of the Etruscan goldsmith manifests itself in various forms; in necklaces, brooches, earrings, and diadems, often richly ornamented with filigree or granulated work; but these soon degenerate into pretentious vulgarity or hasty fragile work only produced for funeral purposes.

It is therefore to Etruria that we must chiefly look for information as
to the achievements of Greek workers in metal down to the fifth century.
Even when the technique is of purely native origin the Etruscan jewellery
of this period is largely inspired by Greek feeling and Greek ideas.   This
rarity of early Greek jewellery in Greece is the more remarkable, because
although Greek taste would at all times have avoided any tendency to
vulgar display of ornament, yet statues, vase-paintings, and other works of
art give evidence that jewellery and ornaments were worn by Greek women
throughout the period.   We know from the description of Pausanias that
the statue of Athena Parthenos was adorned with much jewellery.   Otherwise the goldsmith's art can only be illustrated by a few finger-rings or
pairs of earrings, or by the quasi-Oriental objects found in profusion in
the tombs of Greek cities in Cyprus, such as Amathus, Curium, and
Marion.

378.   In the fourth century B.C. the goldsmith's art in Greece reached
a pitch of magnificence and beauty, combined with delicacy
Greece. and fertility of invention, which has never been surpassed.
Fourth century. In no class of ornaments is it better illustrated than in the
wonderful treasures obtained in the excavations of the
Russian government in the Crimea and along the northern coast of the
Black Sea.   The chief finds have been made at Kertch, the ancient
Panticapaeum, a remote outpost of Hellenic civilization in the Cimmerian
Bosporus; it was a colony of Miletus, and had close commercial relations
with Athens in the fourth century.   A tomb explored in 1831 at Koul-Oba
contained a rich array of gold ornaments, silver vessels and other furniture.
A woman's skeleton was adorned with a diadem of electrum embossed
with monsters and floral patterns, and on her breast were two large gold
medallions representing the head of Athena Parthenos, evidently copied from
the famous chryselephantine statue by Pheidias (Fig. 80).   Her companion,
a male, wore a gold tiara, a torque ornamented with figures of Scythian
horsemen, and bracelets, and his armour was plated with gold.   From the
sumptuous contents of this tomb it has been supposed to contain the remains
of a local ruler and his queen.   In 1862 the tomb of a Scythian ruler was
excavated at Nicopolis; it contained a silver-gilt amphora (Fig. 81) which
has been described as the finest extant specimen of Greek *repoussé* work in
this material.   The body is ornamented with birds and floral patterns and
on the shoulder is a frieze of Scythians grooming or breaking in horses.
The composition is extremely spirited and life-like.   Besides this the tomb
contained many gold ornaments, including gold-plated scabbards and bow-
cases with reliefs.   In 1864 the remains of a priestess were found at
Bliznitza, her ornaments forming a treasure of richness and beauty beyond
description.   They include frontlets, necklaces, bracelets, and a huge pair
of earrings or rather pendants hung over the ears, the last-named ornamented with medallions representing nymphs with the armour of Achilles.

The contents of these tombs may be dated about 350—320 B.C., and the series of ornaments has generally been regarded as forming the finest extant specimens of ancient jewellery.   The gold is wrought with exquisite

Fig. 80.   Gold ornaments from the Crimea.

delicacy and mastery of modelling.   It is an open question whether they are of local workmanship or importations from Athens; but it is probable

Fig. 81. Silver chased vase from the Crimea.

that in the fourth century many Athenian artists migrated to the Crimea, where they found a favourable opening for carrying on their trade among an opulent and friendly people.

Fine gold-work of the fourth century is not however confined to these regions. The British Museum possesses very beautiful specimens of necklaces and earrings from Melos and other sites round the Aegean Sea, in which the principle of decoration is a combination of elaborate chain-work with pendants modelled in the form of Cupids, Sirens, or Victories, or of simpler forms. Some of the finger-rings of the period are also engraved on the bezel (which is plain without any stone setting) with designs of great merit. In all this Greek gold-work of the finest period the guiding principle is to regard the workmanship as of more importance than the

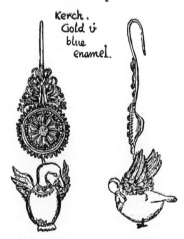

Fig. 82. Greek earrings from Kertch.

material, as is also the case with engraved gems. In the succeeding century the delicacy of workmanship preserves almost the same high level, but simplicity of taste gives way to over-elaboration.

379. Greek work in chased silver is comparatively rare, at least in comparison with that of the Roman period; but the fact appears to be that it was little used for works of art before the Hellenistic Age. That was the time when painted vases began to go out of favour, and with the increase of wealth and luxury vases of metal came into general use for domestic and decorative purposes. Thus a new industry arose, and in Asia Minor there sprang up an important school of *caelatores* or silver-chasers, of whom Pliny gives some account. The first place he assigns to Mentor, a silver-worker of about 350 B.C., who made two cups for which the orator Crassus paid four hundred pounds. Other famous names were Acragas, Boethus, and Mys, who made

cups decorated with mythological subjects, which were preserved at Rhodes. There were also famous cups with scenes from heroic legend, made by Zopyrus and Pytheas. After the conquest of Asia in 189 B.C. Lucius Scipio carried off gold and silver-chased vases of the respective weight of fifteen hundred and fourteen hundred pounds.

Besides chased vases there are some good extant examples of statuettes in silver, among which may be mentioned a group of a boy **Silver statuettes.** and goose in the British Museum, dated by coins found with it, about 240 B.C. Its interest lies in its being a reproduction of the well-known *genre* types associated with the sculptor Boethus of Carthage. Greek silver vases are distinguished by the simple refinement of their form and the delicate chasing of the ornaments. The Romans were great collectors of such objects, and closely imitated them. Hence in the vases of the famous Bosco Reale and Hildesheim treasures (at Paris and Berlin respectively) we see the spirit of the Hellenistic Age reflected as faithfully as in the Pompeian wall-paintings.

Three methods of decoration are employed in the silver vases with reliefs. Either the figures are in *repoussé*, which is the general rule, or they were chiselled out like sculptured reliefs; sometimes these two methods are combined. Or thirdly, they were made separately and soldered on, like the Siris bronzes, in which case they were known as ἐμβλήματα (*crustae*). The great silver vase from the Crimea described above is an example of the chasing process, except for the heads of animals which were made separately in *repoussé*.

Brit. Mus. Catalogue of Jewellery (1911). E. H. Minns, *Scythians and* **Bibliography.** *Greeks*, Cambridge, 1913. E. Fontenay, *Les Bijoux Anciens et Modernes*, Paris (1887). Daremberg and Saglio, *Dict. des Antiqs.*, *s.v.* Caelatura. Walters, *Art of the Greeks* (1906), chap. XIII.

IV. 9. ENGRAVED GEMS.

380. Until recent years the number of engraved gems known to the **Minoan and Mycenaean Period.** archaeological world which belonged to the prehistoric civilizations of the Mediterranean era was exceedingly small. We may except the Egyptian scarab, which can be dated as far back as 2200 B.C., and perhaps also the Babylonian cylinder. This, however, although it was used for similar purposes, is not strictly an engraved gem. The silence of the Homeric poems had led scholars to assume that gem-engraving was an art of later birth, and no distinction was made between the few remains of Minoan or Mycenaean art and those of the degenerate post-Homeric period, which from their frequent occurrence in the Aegean islands were termed 'Island-stones.'

The researches of Sir Arthur Evans in Crete have enabled us to trace the evolution of the engraved gem from a mere lump of clay marked with linear devices for sealing purposes to the rank of a real work of art.

This development took place during the period known as 'Middle Minoan' (2100—1580 B.C.). The earliest stones mark the transition from the pictographic to the hieroglyphic method of writing; an object is first represented by a picture of it, and then the sign comes to represent an idea, as for instance a gate stands for 'guardian,' a leg for 'leader.' Other gems of the Middle Minoan period have representations of vases, ships, and marine animals, such as the cuttle-fish (Fig. 83). The Late Minoan gems (1580—1200) are not easy to distinguish from those found on other Greek sites, and usually known as Mycenaean; in style they show a remarkable uniformity, their naturalism and feeling for life contrasting strongly with the conventionality of Eastern art (see Fig. 84). The mainland gems show a preference for deities, monsters, and human figures, and a more developed technical skill. The attempts to achieve perspective, and the feeling that the field must be well filled, sometimes lead to the most curious distortion of the figures. These gems are nearly always glandular (shaped like a sling-stone) or lenticular (bean-shaped).

Fig. 83. Minoan gem.   Fig. 84. Mycenaean gem.

381. The downfall of the Minoan and Mycenaean civilisations, which was completed about the end of the eleventh century B.C., caused a general set-back to culture, which is exemplified in the gems of the geometrical period. The subjects are almost *Seventh and Sixth Centuries.* entirely confined to marine animals or monsters, and there is a general absence of life or imagination. Soft, opaque, and easily-worked stones such as steatite become popular, and though the glandular and lenticular forms are still prevalent, others such as the Oriental cone-shaped seal are now introduced, this form being the prototype of the early Greek scarabaeoid which prevails in the sixth century. The island of Melos seems to have been the chief centre of gem-engraving at this time, and in its products we find either a survival or a recrudescence of the Mycenaean art-tradition, combined with a style which approximates to that of archaic Greek art. These are probably not earlier than the seventh century B.C.

In the seventh and sixth centuries we find on such sites as Cameirus in Rhodes and Tharros in Sardinia gems of strongly Orientalising character, due to Phoenician influence. Importations of Egyptian scarabs were also common, as at Amathus in Cyprus. Even in gems of purely Greek type, the scarab-form is general, but subjects of Oriental type, whether Egyptian or Assyrian, vie in favour with the ordinary themes of early Greek art. These gems bridge the gap between the lingering influences of Mycenaean civilisation and archaic Greek art. In the sixth century however the conventionality of the geometric period was replaced by the free imagination and naturalism which seems to be the result of Mycenaean traditions preserved in Ionia. The earlier gems of the archaic period are of distinctly Ionian or 'east-Greek' type, and the island of Samos appears to have been the head-quarters of Ionian engraving. We are thus reminded of the names of the two famous Samian gem-engravers recorded by ancient writers, Mnesarchus and Theodorus, and the story of the ring of Polycrates, engraved by the latter, who was also a famous sculptor.

The art of the mainland in this period is chiefly represented by scarabs or scarabaeoids, found in Etruria, but undoubted importations from Greece. Small details of treatment enable us to distinguish the scarabs from the local Etruscan products. The scarabaeoid, derived as we have already seen from

Fig. 85. Greek scarab of the sixth century B.C. of the finest archaic style : *one and a half times the real size.*

Fig. 86. Gem of the fifth century B.C.: *one and a half times the real size.*

the East, is similar in outline, but has a plain convex back, and is not modelled like a beetle. This latter form gradually worked its way into favour in Greece, and in the succeeding 'finest' period tended to oust the scarab altogether. In the earlier sixth-century gems there is a great uniformity and conventionality of treatment, and the varieties of positions and motives are limited; kneeling and running figures are popular as conforming with the desire to fill all the available space. In the execution of the gems there is a remarkable minuteness and precision, combined with the deliberate restraint characteristic of all archaic work. One of the finest examples we possess is the Satyr with drinking-cup (Fig. 85). The British Museum contains another fine gem with the signature of the artist Syries, who was probably an Ionian.

382. In the fifth century the materials for study are surprisingly scanty; exports to Etruria are rare, because the Etruscans were now producing excellent work of their own. The scarabaeoid becomes the typical form, in which the Greek spirit of design is presented with an admirable breadth and simplicity, the usual subjects being a single figure from daily life or a finely-executed animal subject (Fig. 86). Chalcedony was the favourite material, and in the fourth century

Fifth and Fourth Centuries.

coloured glass pastes became common. We have very few names of engravers during these two centuries, either recorded or on actual signed gems.
The outstanding name is that of Dexamenus of Chios, whose signature
occurs on four existing gems, one being in the Fitzwilliam
Museum at Cambridge (Fig. 87): a bluish chalcedony with
the subject of an Athenian lady seated at her toilet, to
whom an attendant offers a wreath and a mirror. Of the
others, two are in the Hermitage, and one at Boston; two
more gems in the British Museum have been assigned to
him on grounds of style. In the British Museum is also
a fine fourth-century gem signed by Onatas, with the
subject of Victory erecting a trophy. The paste intaglios
of the fourth century remind us of the σφραγῖδες ὑάλιναι
of which so many are recorded as having been dedicated
in Greek temples about this time (as for example in the

Fig. 87. . Dexa-
menus gem.

Parthenon and the temple of Apollo in Delos). Although we know nothing
of his work, we must not omit to mention here the famous fourth-century
engraver Pyrgoteles, who rose to such fame that Alexander the Great ordered
that he alone should engrave the royal portrait.

382a. The Hellenistic period of Greek Art which extends from the
death of Alexander to the taking of Corinth (323–146 B.C.)
shows a general widening out in the stream of Greek art.   **Hellenistic
Period.**
The gems of the period illustrate this development, and in
actual fact approach closely in many respects to the work of the Graeco-
Roman period, with which they have almost more in common than with
Greek gems of the best period. The scarab and scarabaeoid disappear entirely,
and are replaced by the flat unpierced ringstone, or by an elongated oval
and convex form. The favourite materials are the carnelian, sard, jacinth,
and garnet. The style of the gems is characteristic of
the art of the period, with its fondness for expressing
passion or pathos. Figures of deities are common, especially Apollo, Aphrodite, and Dionysus; some gems
appear to reproduce well-known works of art. Another
notable development is in the direction of portraiture,
of which Fig. 88 may serve as an example; this is probably due to the influence of the coins with their portraits
of the Diadochi and of Oriental rulers. We have also   Fig. 88. Fine por-
representations of Alexander the Great, typical rather   trait gem of the
than contemporary; one in the British Museum bears   third century B.C.:
the signature of an artist Pheidias. A few other authentic   *real size.*
engravers' signatures are found, such as Apollonius, Daedalus, and Onesas.

Furtwaengler, *Antike Gemmen* (1900); British Museum *Catalogue of Engraved
Gems* (1926); Beazley, *Lewes House Gems* (1920); Sir A. Evans,
Bibliography.   *The Palace of Minos at Knossos* (1921, 1928, 1930); J. H. Middle-
ton, *Engraved Gems of Classical Times* (1891).

IV. 10. MUSIC.

383. OUR fragments of Greek melody are short, mutilated, and of dates
General Character-istics. Har-mony and Grace. often unknown but certainly widely differing; and it is impossible to judge a nation's music merely from theory. Nor can we give a clear account even of the theory of Greek music, since the practice alone could make some parts of it intelligible. About certain general characteristics, however, there is little doubt:

(*a*) Greek music was in the main non-harmonic. The Greeks were aware of the effect of simultaneous harmony and used consonances and perhaps dissonances, though not between voices. But it is likely that the accompaniment, which we are informed was above the voice part, was only an ornamental elaboration and not a second part in counterpoint.

(*b*) Purely melodic music often makes great use of embellishment by grace-notes. It seems that the Greeks cared little for this, as their great desire was to prevent the sense of the words from being obscured.

384. (*c*) The spoken language with its pitch-accent was, as Aristoxenus
Melody and Accent. says, λογῶδές τι μέλος. It is not surprising therefore to find that in the majority of extant vocal melodies the movement either follows the pitch-accent or avoids contradicting it; and that, further, this agreement is much closer in the Delphic Hymns of the second century B.C. than in the Hymns of Mesomedes of the second century A.D., by which time the pitch-accent was breaking down.

385. (*d*) Rhythm was determined by the quantities of the spoken
Rhythm. language to a much greater extent than melody by the accents. It is really impossible to distinguish between the rhythm of Greek music and the metre of Greek poetry. While the quantities which syllables had in ordinary speech may sometimes have been modified, such modifications are as much the concern of the metrist as of the musician. Metre is treated elsewhere (see §§ 786 ff.); and two points only shall be mentioned here that are of particular musical interest. (i) There seems to have been little or no ictus on "the first of the bar." Indeed the conception of "bar" is almost inapplicable to the less simple lyric metres, where the unit was the phrase rather than the foot. Within the same phrase may be found long syllables separated now by one, now by two short syllables, and there is no reason to believe that the theses (not "stresses") were necessarily equidistant in time. (ii) Recent writers have shown how the Greek sense of form operated in the use and combination of rhythmic phrases and have discovered connections between subject and rhythm analogous to the Wagnerian *leit-motiv*. It would appear that Form in Greek music was more a matter of rhythmical than melodic structure.

386. While the foregoing sections might suggest that the position of
Status and Variety. music was merely ancillary, the art was in fact considered of the very greatest importance,—not only Μουσική in the wider sense, but music as we understand the word. Plato

and Aristotle both thought it desirable to regulate musical education and practice in their ideal states; and, though the idea is strange to us, it seems to have been popularly held that individual modes and rhythms possessed specific moral characters and educative influence. Such views were not unchallenged and probably belonged more to the philosophers than to the musicians. (See also "Education," § 645.)

Further, the existence of purely instrumental music must not be forgotten. Alongside vocal solos accompanied by aulos or cithara (αὐλῳδία and κιθαρῳδία), and choral lyric of various kinds, there existed from the oldest times solo aulos-playing (αὐλητική). In origin associated with Asia it became in the sixth century a feature of the Pythian games; the "Pythian nome" celebrated Apollo's victory over the serpent and contained an element of "programme-music." Solo cithara-playing came later and never attained great importance.

387. The principal instruments of professional music were the cithara and the aulos. The cithara was an elaborate form of the lyre, which was the amateur's instrument. The strings, whose number was from time to time increased, were plucked and their tone could not be sustained. The aulos was a wind instrument of varying material, played with a single reed, like our clarinet. Apparently it was usual for auloi to be employed in pairs, but the manner of this is doubtful. The aulos developed by the addition of holes and by various obscure devices. We know the names of many other instruments, among which the barbitos, the lyre of Sappho and Alcaeus, may be mentioned.

Instruments.

388. Our modern scales, as found on the pianoforte, consist of tones and half-tones. Among the Greeks three main types (γένη) of scale may be distinguished, diatonic, chromatic and enharmonic. Aristoxenus illustrates these genera from a group of three intervals making a perfect fourth ($2\frac{1}{2}$ tones), as it might be E F G A in the diatonic. He mentions six nuances (χρόαι): διάτονον σύντονον, $\frac{1}{2}$ 1 1: διάτονον μαλακόν, $\frac{1}{2}$ $\frac{3}{4}$ $1\frac{1}{4}$: χρῶμα τονιαῖον, $\frac{1}{2}$ $\frac{1}{2}$ $1\frac{1}{2}$: χρῶμα ἡμιόλιον, $\frac{3}{8}$ $\frac{3}{8}$ $1\frac{3}{4}$: χρῶμα μαλακόν, $\frac{1}{3}$ $\frac{1}{3}$ $1\frac{5}{6}$: ἐναρμόνιον, $\frac{1}{4}$ $\frac{1}{4}$ 2; and implies a diatonic: $\frac{1}{2}$ $1\frac{1}{8}$ 1, and a chromatic: $\frac{1}{3}$ $\frac{2}{3}$ $1\frac{1}{2}$. It will be seen that he assumes that six tones make an octave, and that the tone can be bisected. With these evaluations we can compare the more scientific formulae of a number of researchers from Archytas (fourth century B.C.) to Ptolemy (second century A.D.), who express their intervals by mathematical ratios; and the truth is likely to lie where Aristoxenus and the mathematicians support one another. In the *diatonic* we may distinguish two main types: $\frac{16}{15} \times \frac{9}{8} \times \frac{10}{9}$ (approximating to $\frac{256}{243} \times \frac{9}{8} \times \frac{9}{8}$—"Pythagorean" intonation), and $\frac{28}{27} \times \frac{8}{7} \times \frac{9}{8}$. The latter with its septimal tone is given by both Archytas and Ptolemy and agrees with the diatonic implied by Aristoxenus. The surest points about the *chromatic* and *enharmonic* are that the highest interval was a minor third for the former, a major third for the latter. In both cases the two smaller intervals (known as the πυκνόν) were perhaps approximately equal, though, as the chromatic implied by Aristoxenus lies closely between that of Archytas

Types of Interval.

24—2

and the "soft" variety of Ptolemy $(\frac{28}{27} \times \frac{15}{14} \times \frac{6}{5})$, there may have been a chromatic with middle interval about double the lowest.

389. No connected history of the Greek scales can be written. We only
Structure of
the Scale
System.
have glimpses at certain stages. The one fixed point is the system described by Aristoxenus (end of fourth century B.C.) and writers who follow him. It consists of thirteen keys (later fifteen) a semitone distant from one another. Each key (τόνος) was a similar scale two octaves in length, with diatonic, chromatic and enharmonic variation. In the diatonic form it covered the range A—a′ on the white notes of the pianoforte. This scale, known as the Greater Perfect System (σύστημα τέλειον μεῖζον) can be analysed in two ways.

(i) It can be regarded as consisting of a number of similar tetrachords either joined by a common note (συναφή) or separated by a tone (διάζευξις). The diagram gives the names of notes and tetrachords.

A* B* c d e* f g a* b* c′ d′ e′* f′ g′ a′*

It will be realised that only those notes marked with an asterisk are un-affected by the variations of the genera. There was also a supplementary tetrachord, a b♭ c′ d′ (συνημμένων), which provided in effect a modulation to a key a fourth lower. A—a, plus this tetrachord, is called σύστημα τέλειον ἐλάττον. As the greater system is based on the octachord e—e′, so is the lesser on a heptachord e—d′, both primitive elements in Greek music.

(ii) The System contains in itself the seven species of the octave (εἴδη τοῦ διὰ πασῶν)—B octave (Mixolydian), C (Lydian), D (Phrygian), E (Dorian), F (Hypolydian), G (Hypophrygian), A (Hypodorian). Seven of the τόνοι also bear these names, though the order is reversed. It seems that the τόνος got its name from that octave-species which it brought into the middle of the total gamut.

Similar names are also used by fifth- and fourth-century writers, notably Plato and Aristotle, of certain ἁρμονίαι (e.g. ἡ Δώριος ἁρμονία, ἡ Δωριστί). This word is probably rightly translated "modes," for the opinion of Monro who equated them with the τόνοι has not won acceptance. It does not follow that they were identical with the species, though the species are probably descended from the modes. It is necessary to go behind Aristoxenus' system.

390. Apparently Asia as well as Greece provided material for Greek music. There was a struggle, but the system of Aristoxenus **The Develop-** represents in theory at least an Hellenic victory. The details **ment of the** of this process of centuries are quite obscure. The native **Scale System.** music of Greece was probably diatonic; perhaps from a primitive tetrachord developed the aforementioned heptachord and octachord. The names Phrygian and Lydian betray an Asiatic origin. Legend connects both with a certain Olympus, a vague figure who is also credited with the Spondeion scale. This in its original form was as: e f̄ a b c̄' (the bar indicates a quarter-tone sharp). By division of the lowest interval it became enharmonic, though the simpler style also survived. The only other evidence for early scale-forms is provided by Aristides Quintilianus (A.D.) in a list of six scales which go back at least to the fifth century B.C.

> Dorian: d e ē f a b b̄ c' e'   Syntonolydian: e ē f a c'
> Phrygian: d e ē f a b b̄ c' d'   Ionian: e ē f a c' d'
> Mixolydian: B B̄ c d e ē f b
> "Lydian":   ē f a b b̄ c' e' ē'

Three points in particular should be observed, the variation in compass, the gaps in the series, the combination of the enharmonic quarter-tones in some with the d that belongs strictly to the diatonic; even the Dorian has it. The "Lydian" has a late look and is probably spurious. Elsewhere we hear also of a second Ionian, of Aeolian, Locrian and other modes.

Out of such heterogeneous material the tidy system of Aristoxenus was made. Details can only be guessed. An important stage must have been the recognition that the enharmonic, first characteristic of Asia, the chromatic, which probably arose in imitation of it, and the diatonic could all be reduced to terms of a tetrachord. The Dorian, at first diatonic, took, as we see, an enharmonic form also; similarly, the enharmonic Lydian would find a dia-tonic shape, and so on. Later, as instruments developed, several modes could be played on one instrument, and a composite scale arose. As this basic scale was extended, so was the analysis by tetrachords. Eventually the double-octave was reached, seven of the modes survived in the form of octave-species, the three genera were separated. But much of this was a matter of theory rather than practice; for not only in the fragment from Euripides but in the post-Aristoxenian second Delphic Hymn we find combina-tions of diatonic and enharmonic similar to those in the modes of Aristides.

391. Ptolemy wrote in the second century A.D., and his system differs in important respects from that of Aristoxenus. He reduced the "keys" to seven, but his τόνοι are not pitch keys at all, **Tonality.** but the seven species of the octave extended into species of the double-octave. Does this represent a radical change in practice? Or is it another way of looking at the same musical phenomena? If we knew anything definite about the tonality of Greek melodies at any period, we might be able to answer these questions.

There is no ancient theory of tonality. There are certain passages which may be interpreted as attributing the function of a tonic to the note μέση. To the μέση of the Perfect System? Or the μέση which by another nomenclature was the fourth note from the bottom of any octave-species? The theories of Westphal, Gevaert, Monro, Macran are all unproved guesses and open to grave objections; in no case can they be applied without difficulty to the unsystematised ἁρμονίαι. Only in the case of the Dorian can we be tolerably certain that the tonic of its E—E octave was A, μέση by both nomenclatures. Had the systematisation imposed a Dorian tonality upon the old modes? The existence of pure pitch keys suggests it, but the fragments give no support. On either side of Aristoxenus the scales of Aristides and the "keys" of Ptolemy both suggest modal variety. But is there strict continuity between them? There are surely likely to be considerable differences between music written in gapped enharmonic scales and the diatonic which was normal in Ptolemy's time. If some of the later diatonic fragments suggest certain modalities, it does not follow they are the modes of Pindar or even of Timotheus.

392. The following are the remains of Greek melody (the clue to their notation is given by Alypius, ed. Jan): (i) a papyrus fragment of Euripides, *Orestes* 338–44, apparently in one of the old ἁρμονίαι. (ii) A short tragic fragment found among the Zenon papyri (250 B.C.) [*J.H.S.* 1931]. (iii) Fairly extensive portions of two Pæans of the second century B.C., found engraved on stone at Delphi. Despite certain anomalies they illustrate well the Aristoxenian analysis by tetrachords. (iv) The Aidin Inscription, or Epitaph of Seikilos, a brief diatonic melody of uncertain date. (v) A papyrus, now at Berlin, containing vocal and instrumental fragments of unknown dates, including part of a Pæan and part of what may be a tragic lament. (vi) Three manuscript hymns—the Hymn to the Muse of uncertain date, and two hymns probably by Mesomedes (second century A.D.), to the Sun and to Nemesis. (vii) A Christian hymn, not later than the third century A.D.

The main ancient authorities are Aristoxenus (ed. Macran, 1902), Aristotelian Problems (Gevaert et Vollgraf, 1903), Ps.-Plutarch, De Musica (Weil et Reinach, 1900), Ptolemy's Harmonics (Düring, Göteborg, 1930), Aristides Quintilianus (Jahn, 1882). Aristoxenus and Aristides are contained in Meibom's Antiquae Musicae Auctores Septem (Amsterdam, 1652) along with some shorter treatises. v. Jan's Musici Scriptores Graeci (Teubner, 1895) contains these latter, the Aristotelian problems and excerpts from Aristotle.

On the fragments Jan's Supplementum, Reinach's La Musique Grecque (1926) and J. F. Mountford in New Chapters in Greek Literature, 2nd Series (1929), may be consulted. The Delphic Hymns may also be found conveniently in Collectanea Alexandrina (J. U. Powell, 1925).

More or less comprehensive works on the subject are: Westphal, Die Musik des griechischen Alterthums, 1883; Gevaert, Histoire de la Musique de l'Antiquité, 1875-81; Monro, Modes of Ancient Greek Music, 1894; Riemann, Handbuch der Musikgeschichte (3rd ed., 1922). Reinach's brilliant summary quoted above contains a useful bibliography. See also Bursians Jahresbericht, CIV, CXVIII, CXLIV, CXCIII.

V. MYTHOLOGY AND RELIGION.

393. THE religion of Greece, though in its essential character it was intimately connected with the nature of the Greek people, was also, especially in details, greatly influenced by political con- *Introduction; local varia-* ditions. Just as every little state had its own independent *tions.* constitution, so also it had its own recognised cycle of gods, and its own manner of worshipping them. There was indeed a common basis of custom and belief underlying most of these varying rites; many groups of states met in religious confederations at a common shrine, and a few centres of worship came to be recognised and attended by all of Hellenic race. But these tokens of unity, however conspicuous, were the exception, not the rule. In a comprehensive account of Greek religion it is often necessary to speak as if there were a common and uniform system of mythology or of worship throughout Greece; but it must always be remembered that any such system or arrangement, however true in its application to Greece as a whole, would not apply in all its details to any one of the little states into which the country was divided.

394. There have been and there probably will be much controversy and many opinions as to what part of the religion of Greece was brought by the Greeks as their version of the common Aryan *National and local elements* inheritance, and what part they adopted from the earlier *in religion.* inhabitants of the lands, or borrowed from foreign neighbours. It is generally admitted that the Greeks were not the first inhabitants of their country; and immigrants or invaders are usually influenced by the religion of those whom they drive out or subjugate. The notion of the omnipresence and omnipotence of a deity is usually unknown in an early stage of belief; the power of any god often has local or tribal limitations; and it is natural, under such circumstances, for the invaders to credit the aborigines with a more intimate knowledge of the nature and worship of the gods of the land, and accordingly to adopt many of their beliefs and customs. The same thing happened again, though in a less degree, when the various successive waves of Greek immigrants supplanted their predecessors, and also whenever a Greek colony was established among barbarians. The methods and degrees of adoption *Methods of adopting new* vary. Sometimes the ancient cults remain as popular super- *divinities.* stitions, receiving no recognition from the official religion of the ruling caste, yet often resorted to when that official religion has failed in its function of maintaining friendly relations with the local gods, and plague or disaster has followed. Often the power of effecting a reconcilia-tion lies with the survivors of the earlier race, who however are regarded as sorcerers rather than as priests. More frequently, however, the necessity for such special measures was averted by the formal adoption of the earlier gods and their worship into the State religion of the immigrants; this might be done in two ways; either the local god was officially added to their pantheon, as a new god with a new name; or, more often, he was identified with some god whose worship was already recognised, and whose name was perhaps amplified with a new title, while new customs were incorporated with his official ritual. The consequent concretions and modifications can alone explain how, for example, two conceptions so apparently incompatible as the 'queen and huntress, chaste and fair' of the usual mythology and the many-breasted mother-goddess of Ephesus were both called Artemis by the Greeks, while on the other hand, the identical myth and ritual ascribed in one place to Zeus is ascribed elsewhere to Dionysus. In the first case, the goddess, without changing her name, has absorbed the nature and attributes of another goddess, who, though in many respects dissimilar, yet had enough resemblance in her functions to suggest the identification; in the second a ritual, probably identical in origin, has been adopted by different families or amid different surroundings, and has consequently been assigned to the official province of different gods. Thus there was a constant tendency for all the various local cults to be absorbed into the worship of a limited number of recognised gods and goddesses, into whose personality the various local divinities were merged. And it was natural that the gods chiefly worshipped by each state or race should absorb the greatest share of these various accretions, and so extend almost without limit their attributes and their functions. On the other hand, there was a contrary tendency, inspired by the feeling of a common nationality, encouraged by the oracles and other centres of common worship, and influenced by a common literature and art, to introduce system into the chaos, and to assign to each deity his province, not so much in the patronage of a special city or race, as in the fostering and protection of certain physical, intellectual, or moral qualities or attainments.

395. The main difficulty in the study of Greek religion does not, however, lie so much in local variations as in the various strata of ritual and of belief which we find side by side, not only in sporadic survivals, but also as part of the official worship of various cities. At first sight this variety is obscured by the prevalent custom of affiliating all kinds of ritual to the worship of the official gods of the state, and incorporating many primitive customs in their regular festivals. When we come to examine in detail the local cults of any state, we find that they include many elements which cannot readily be explained in relation to the worship of the Olympian gods, as distinguished by the anthropomorphic imagination of the Greeks, but find an easy explanation in relation to more primitive beliefs and customs. For example, the Anthesteria at Athens, officially connected with the worship of Dionysus and the opening of the wine-jars, is evidently concerned to a great extent with the tendance or exorcism of ghosts; and the dramatic performances in honour of the same deity, whether we assign their origin to the commemoration of dead heroes or to the orgiastic cult of the year-spirit, or to other primitive sources, probably have no original

Various stages of belief and ritual.

connexion with the god of the vine. Again a festival such as that of the Bouphonia or Dipolia at Athens, with its ritual murder of the ox, its condemnation of the axe, and its simulated resurrection of the victim, finds an analogy in many primitive rites that have nothing to do with the Hellenic Zeus. Such ceremonies, and the beliefs or superstitions that underlie them, can only find more or less accidental mention in a systematic account of the state worship of the Olympian gods; and in that worship they often acquire a meaning as far removed from their original intention as in the case of pagan customs or ceremonies adopted by the Christian Church. For example, magic rites, intended originally to promote the fertility and growth of the crops, seem to have become associated, at Eleusis and elsewhere, with the belief in immortality and in communion with the gods. In such cases it is the acquired meaning which is of chief interest to the scholar, as helping him to understand Greek literature and thought. But at the same time it is often necessary to go back to the original intention of a rite in order to understand much that would otherwise seem incongruous or incomprehensible.

It is often suggested or implied by writers on Greek religion that there were in it two main strata, roughly classified as the chthonic 'Chthonic' and and the Olympian, the religion of fear and the religion 'Olympian' religion. of service, and that these two belong respectively to indigenous or primitive inhabitants, and to a conquering or immigrating race. At the other extreme is the theory stated by Herodotus, and commonly held by the Greeks themselves, that it was Homer and Hesiod who first assigned to the gods their names and their functions. This last view is held in a modified form by some modern mythologists, who think that the great change from a consciousness of mysterious powers in nature to a belief in certain definite and personal gods, from fetishism or polydaemonism to polytheism, was not due to any immigration or foreign influence, but to a development in Greece itself of the anthropomorphic imagination which finds expression in the Homeric poems. It is not to be supposed that these poems represent the religion of the common people; this doubtless preserved many primitive elements that later came to be adopted into official cults; but the predominance and human character of the Olympian deities, which we find in Homer, is also the main characteristic of later religious beliefs. It is also probable that the artistic representations of the gods, based on this anthropomorphic imagination, reacted very strongly on the beliefs of the people.

395 a. The worship of sacred stones and trees is found in Greece as well as in other neighbouring countries; it is especially Worship of attested by Cretan and Mycenaean gems and by survivals stones and trees in historic times. Stones, said to have fallen from heaven, may have been of meteoric origin; the Dioscuri were worshipped as two beams at Sparta, and Dionysus at Thebes as a log, later plated with bronze. Probably such stocks and stones were originally regarded as having some magic properties in themselves, and later came to be regarded

as the seat of a superhuman power or the symbol of a deity. A familiar example of sacred trees is offered by the oaks of Dodona; at Temnos the image (ἄγαλμα) of Aphrodite consisted of a growing myrtle (Paus. v. xiii. 7). The worship associated with rocks, springs, and trees survived throughout the country in the cult of Pan and the Nymphs; river-gods also were worshipped as givers of fertility to mankind as well as to the fruits of the earth.

We find many traces of sacred animals. Mythologists still hesitate to

of animals allow that there is evidence for anything like a totemistic system of beliefs and practices in Greece, though some tribal names suggest it. Nor is there any record—apart from the horse-headed Demeter at Phigaleia—of any Greek deity being worshipped in a wholly or partly animal form. But epithets such as γλαυκῶπις, βοῶπις, may be significant survivals, and so may the animals who are often associated with some god as his peculiar attribute, the owl with Athena for example, and the eagle with Zeus; a similar origin may underlie the tales of the various transformations of gods into animals, Zeus into a bull or eagle or cuckoo, Poseidon into a horse, and so on. There were also rites in which the worshippers were called animals or imitated their shapes, as in the bear dance of Athenian maidens for Artemis Brauronia, or the men called ἵπποι in the worship of Dionysus. The snake, too, was often regarded as an embodiment of chthonic deities or heroes, for instance, of Asclepius and of Erichthonius at Athens.

The cult of ancestors, or of the dead generally, is to be seen not only

of the dead in the recognised custom of offerings at the tomb, but also in survivals which vary from the worship of heroes to magic rites for the exorcism or propitiation of ghosts. The latter is most conspicuous in the Attic festival of the Anthesteria, where it is strangely mingled with a Dionysiac festival. Hero-worship is sometimes preserved in a simple form, as in the case of the founder (οἰκιστής) of a colony; but frequently ancient local divinities come to be degraded to the rank of hero, as in the case of Trophonius at Lebadea, and in this case they often came to be associated with the worship of an Olympian god. On the other hand, heroes such as Amphiaraus and Asclepius sometimes attained almost divine honours.

It is clear from what has already been said that we must expect to find Greek mythology and ritual compounded of elements belonging to various strata of religious belief and custom. In the most primitive stage, a god

survivals. is actually identified with some sacred object or animal, or even a human being; he must naturally require peculiar care and observances, and may be amenable to direct punishment by human agency if he fail in his duties. Even when religious ideas have reached a higher plane, and the god is regarded as having an independent existence, but becoming incarnate or immanent in his sacred emblems, the same ritual would be applicable. But the almost infinite subdivision of the divine power, by which each divinity was restricted to a very narrow class of objects or functions, yielded by very slow degrees to the generalising tendency which developed polytheism out of polydaemonism. With a higher and more worthy conception of deity the interpretation of rites and customs would also be given a higher meaning, and this might in time affect the rites themselves. A sacrifice, at first regarded as an actual meal provided for the god, would next become an offering of which only the more ethereal portion, the savour, was actually received by him; and finally would be regarded as a symbolical dedication to him of what was useful to the life of man, and so acceptable as homage, though not necessary for his sustenance. And again, those arts of sorcery and magic, which in an earlier stage were employed by men to force or persuade their god to do their will, gave place to the art of divination, by which men tried to learn the will of the god in order to conform to it. In Greek religion we find side by side traces of all these various stages, some of them probably surviving from the primitive inheritance which they brought with them from their original home, some adopted or borrowed from those whom they conquered or with whom they came in contact, some due to the development in Greece itself of new religious conceptions, mainly under the influence of poetic imagination.

V. 1. MYTHOLOGY.

396. THE origin of myths has always been a matter of keen and often unprofitable controversy; it is now generally admitted that no one system of interpretation is universally applicable, but that Greek mythology was derived from many different sources.

Various systems of interpretation of myths.

Many religious customs and ceremonies exist of which the true meaning and origin are either entirely forgotten or preserved only by a vague and uncertain tradition. Stories naturally grow up to explain the reason of such ceremonies, which then come to be explained as derived from the myth which has grown out of them. For example, because the mystae wandered about fasting in the dark at Eleusis, it was said that Demeter herself had done the same. This is a principle of very wide application; but where the Greeks themselves had lost all knowledge of the origin and meaning of a custom, we cannot expect to arrive at any satisfactory results by mere conjecture. Here the comparative method of study is invaluable. When we find similar customs prevalent among all European peoples on certain occasions, such as spring or harvest, we are justified in concluding that the meaning and origin are probably in all cases the same; and it is very often possible to find some examples among primitive or conservative peoples which show that meaning with a transparent simplicity. We may safely apply this interpretation to more complicated ceremonies also, and to the myths which have grown out of them. And sometimes, even when no such direct relation or influence can be assumed between similar ceremonies among

1. Myth as interpretation of ritual.

different peoples, the ceremonies of a civilised race may be explained on the analogy of those observed by a primitive or savage one. But this principle must be applied with the utmost caution: it rests on the justifiable assumption that the working of the human mind is usually similar under similar conditions; great care must however be taken in investigating every particular case, to make sure whether the nature and intention of the ceremony are really analogous.

Ceremonies connected with human employments, such as seed-time and harvest, are dependent on the course of nature, and thus the

2. Myth derived from natural symbolism. myths belonging to them also reflect the succession of the seasons or of other natural phenomena. But there is another class of myth derived more directly and obviously from these natural phenomena; the clearest case is that in which some natural object is actually personified; for example, Helios (the sun), or river-gods. This principle of interpretation has been applied by some mythologists with so little discrimination as to have brought it into undue discredit; the solar myth, in particular, has become almost a byword from its unlimited use to explain almost every kind of story. Great caution is necessary in this case also; we must especially avoid attributing to primitive religion fanciful interpretations such as belong to a later age. Here too the comparative method is a help. It is safer to investigate how other primitive peoples speak of the powers of nature, than to exercise our ingenuity in imagining how the ancestors of the Greeks may have conceived of those powers. And while we may rarely be able to place the fundamental conception of any of the chief Greek deities in a mere impersonation of a natural object or phenomenon, we may yet admit that an association with such objects or phenomena has had a considerable influence upon their character and attributes.

There is another system of explanation of which an extreme application was made by the philosopher Euhemerus (about the end of

3. Myth as transformed historical tradition. the fourth century B.C.), who suggested that the gods were merely men who had been accorded divine honours for their exploits or beneficence; thus even Zeus was merely a great conqueror, who died and was buried in Crete, and afterwards came to be deified. Few, if any, would now apply such a system as this to the interpretation of all mythology, although some mythologists regard ancestor-worship as the most important element in early religion. But the line between gods and heroes is clearly marked in Greece, although some individuals seem to hover between the two categories; and although many heroic legends, such as those of the siege of Troy and the return of the Heracleidae, doubtless contain a nucleus of historical fact, the same origin cannot often be assigned to the mythology of the gods. In some cases, however, the stories told about a god may be influenced by the history of his cult; thus the wanderings of Apollo or Dionysus are often thought to reflect the route by which their worship had spread.

The extreme theory that 'myth is a disease of language' would hardly now meet with much acceptance, and even the stock example that Apollo's association with the wolf is due to a misunderstanding of the epithet λύκιος or λύκειος cannot be allowed. But there are doubtless many instances in which an attempt to explain some name or epithet has either led to the existence of a myth or modified its form : the various explanations given by ancient authorities of the epithet τριτογένεια suffice to show how this might happen.

4. Myth derived from verbal resemblances.

Artistic types had a considerable influence on Greek mythology, at least in its later, classical, form. In an early stage, Art is very rarely original, except in detail, and is most conservative in the repetition of a limited number of fixed types, both for the figures of the gods and for the representation of mythical scenes. And where a mythical person or scene had no recognised artistic type, it was very common for some other accepted type to be modified and adapted to fit it. Thus various myths influenced one another through their artistic representations ; and sometimes a type, at first almost fortuitously chosen, came to meet with wide acceptance. Thus the Sphinx and the Sirens, for example, owe their form in later myth to their being first rendered in Greek Art by purely decorative forms borrowed from the East.

5. Myth due to representations in Art.

Elaborate and fanciful allegories, such as may be seen in the myth of Cupid and Psyche, are not earlier than the Hellenistic age. But a simpler and more direct kind of allegory is to be traced in earlier mythology. The personification of moral forces, such as Ate and the Erinyes, partakes to some extent of this nature. But we must guard against such excessive appeal to allegory as was used by the Neo-platonists in the interpretation of myths.

6. Myth derived from allegory.

397. Besides the sources of mythology, we must also notice a classification which, though it cannot be followed systematically, we must not altogether overlook. This classification depends to a great extent on the class of the population to which certain myths especially belong, and also has a relation to the circumstances which have led to the preservation of so much of Greek myth as has been recorded. We may divide mythology into (1) **popular**, (2) **official**, (3) **poetical**, and (4) **philosophical**. The first is of course the basis of all the others, and if we could get at it directly, our study would be greatly facilitated. But mere folk-lore was not often likely to be preserved in its natural state, either by literature, inscriptions, or art; and so we are usually obliged to deal with its indirect reflexions, according as it is taken up into the system of organised State religion, or made a basis for the imaginative tale of the poet, or for the allegorical application of the philosopher. Sometimes, however, a myth may happen by some accident to have been recorded in its popular and primitive form ; more often that form can be inferred from the official or literary version, by comparison

Classification of myths.

(1) Popular.

with similar rites or stories preserved to the present day either in Greece or
among other peoples. **Official** mythology, as recognised

(2) Official.

by the various cities of Greece, has naturally been recorded
to a great extent both by literature and inscriptions, though not always in
such a way as to allow us to distinguish the purely local myths from those
which were more generally accepted; later compilers have done much to
increase the confusion. **Poetical** mythology is what we

(3) Poetical.

always speak of first when we speak of Greece; within it
there are many degrees of relation to popular mythology, on which it also
had a decided influence.   Homer has been called 'the Bible of the
Greeks,' and although the works known under Homer's name did not claim
any special divine sanction or infallibility in matters of ritual and belief,
their universal acceptance had a great influence on Greek religion, and
even on the popular conception of the gods.   In later writers we meet with
every variety in the treatment of myth, from attempts to arrange and to
record the true mythical tradition to poems in which the mythological
names are mere pegs on which to hang studies of contemporary life and
character   In reading ancient mythologists we must be on our guard
against an apparent uniformity and system which is often introduced by
the compiler rather than inherent in his subject.   The **philo-**

(4) Philo-
sophical.   **sophical**, and especially the mystical form taken by some
myths, mostly in later times, is really outside the domain of
mythology, and is not likely to mislead a cautious student.

398.   The conception of a god existing before the world and creating
it is entirely foreign to the mythology of the Greeks.   To

Cosmogony,
Theogony, etc.   them Zeus and his Olympian colleagues, the present rulers
of the universe, had not existed from the beginning, but had
predecessors.   In Greece the myths of the origin of the world and of the
earlier divinities are of a very complex nature.   Some of them represent
crude physical theories as to the origin of the universe; others may refer
to the earlier inhabitants of the country and their deities, who were actually
superseded by the Greek pantheon.   The miscellaneous and heterogeneous
elements were gathered together and brought into an apparently consistent
system by works like the Theogony of Hesiod; a good deal of this system
must be regarded as the theory of professional mythologists rather than as
genuine mythology.

Homer makes Ocean the origin of all things, including the gods.
According to Hesiod, Chaos was the first of things; then

Origin of the
gods.   came Earth, Tartarus, and Eros—a conception clearly embodying some early philosophical speculations like that
parodied by Aristophanes, who joins Eros with such primaeval abstractions
as Chaos, Night and Erebus in the origin of the universe.   In the Hesiodic
system Erebus and Night follow as the children of Chaos, and from this
pair proceed Aether and Day.   Earth produces Heaven; and then from
this pair, Uranus and Gaia, comes the brood of the Titans, the

youngest of whom is Cronos. Gaia stirs up her children against their
father, and provides for Cronos the sickle with which he mutilates Uranus.
Where his blood fell on the earth, arose the Giants, and the Erinyes;
from that which fell into the sea proceeded Aphrodite. Cronos and his
sister Rhea are the parents of Hestia, Demeter, Hera, Hades, Poseidon,
and Zeus. Cronos swallowed all his elder children, but when the turn
of Zeus came, Rhea substituted a stone. The rest of the principal Greek
gods were the children of Zeus;—Athena, Apollo, Artemis, Hephaestus,
Ares, Hermes, and Dionysus. Zeus and the other children of Cronos
fought long against the Titans, and prevailed finally by
the help of the Hecatoncheires, monsters which Gaia had   Overthrow
borne to Uranus, and which their father had bound beneath   of the Titans
the earth. The story of this contest has left but few traces in literature and
art; but another variation on the same theme, the battle
between the gods and the giants, which cannot be traced   and of the
back in mythology beyond the sixth century B.C., gained   Giants.
a much greater hold on popular belief, and is one of the commonest
subjects for art in all periods. It was regarded as typical of the triumph of
Greek over 'Barbarian,' of civilization and culture over brutality and
violence. The Titanomachy and Gigantomachy were not unnaturally
confused by the Greeks themselves in later times, even the names of the
combatants sometimes being transferred from the one to the other. The
prevalence of order in nature over destructive or irregular powers
was also associated with this myth, and it was accordingly localised in
regions noted for rugged scenery or volcanic phenomena, such as Pallene,
earlier called Phlegra, or the Phlegraean plains near Cumae in Italy. All
the gods, including Heracles, took part in the fight; Poseidon hurled the
island of Cos (or Nisyros) upon his opponent; according to another tale a
Giant or Titan was buried beneath Etna.

The most interesting among the Titans are the family of Iapetus; the
stories about them have to do with the origin or earliest
history of mankind. His wife was a daughter of Ocean,   Origin of
either Asia or Clymene, and among his children were Atlas,   mankind.
who held up the sky above the earth, Prometheus, and Epimetheus.
Prometheus, according to Hesiod, took the part of men, cheated Zeus over
his share of sacrifices, and stole fire from heaven. To requite him, the
gods fashioned Pandora, who was the first woman. The origin of mankind is here left in confusion. It was a common belief that the human
race had arisen from the earth, especially in the case of 'autochthonous'
races or heroes, or had proceeded from rocks or trees; some families
claimed direct descent from the gods and from nymphs. According
to the most accepted genealogy, Deucalion was the son of Prometheus;
he and his wife Pyrrha were the sole survivors of the Flood; after it
they cast stones behind them which became men and women—a myth
which evidently attempts to reconcile the two versions. Deucalion's
son was Hellen, who was the ancestor of all the Greeks through their

eponymous ancestors Aeolus, Dorus, Achaeus, and Ion. The belief that men were made out of clay by the gods seems to be found in the fifth century; later it is Prometheus who thus moulds both men and beasts.

399. In any organised system of polytheistic mythology, it is almost necessary that a certain limited number of gods and god-
The principal gods; their number. desses should be recognised as the principal divinities. These were often grouped together in certain definite num-bers, such as the triad of the often-recurring Homeric formula, Ζεὺς τε πατὴρ καὶ Ἀθηναίη καὶ Ἀπόλλων, and each state usually had its special group that was invoked in oaths and solemn ceremonies. The recognition of twelve as the proper number of the chief divinities seems to be early and widespread: but there were great discrepancies among the Greeks themselves as to what gods should be included in the number. On an archaistic altar of later period, which however may go back to an Attic original, we find, grouped in pairs, Zeus and Hera, Poseidon and Demeter, Apollo and Artemis, Hephaestus and Athena, Ares and Aphrodite, Hermes and Hestia (Dionysus being omitted). But the twelve deities on the Parthenon frieze, consisting of seven gods and five goddesses, imply a different selection. The altar of the twelve gods at Olympia included Cronos, Rhea, Alpheus, and the Graces; and in groups of the gods upon vases, even where the number twelve is found, it is sometimes made up of pairs of consorts, such as Poseidon and Amphitrite, Dionysus and Ariadne; so that the selection often seems arbitrary. Except Hades, all the rest seem to be regarded as habitually present at the court of Olympus, to which Heracles was also formally admitted, though he does not usually appear there in artistic representations, except in those which refer to the occasion of his admission.

400. The monarchical system of government was prevalent among the Greeks at the time when their mythology was settling into its
1. Zeus, su-preme god, accepted form; and hence it was no violation of their polytheistic beliefs to acknowledge one supreme ruler over gods and men. Such a supremacy was generally attributed to **Zeus** by all the Greeks, even in states where some other deity was the chief object of worship, as Athena was at Athens; and thus he came to absorb into himself all the essential characteristics of the supreme god, which often varied greatly from place to place.

(*a*) As supreme ruler of all above the earth, Zeus has control over the
ruler of heaven, weather: the thunder is his sign; the rainbow (Iris) and the eagle are his messengers; he is νεφεληγερέτα, ἐρίγδουπος, and also οὔριος and εὐάνεμος.

(*b*) In relation to mankind, he is the giver of victory, irresistible in battle whether waged by gods or men. Beside the thunder-
lord of man-hood and battle, bolt, the aegis is his peculiar attribute in this capacity; he lends it to Athena and occasionally to Apollo; but Zeus is peculiarly αἰγίοχος. This aegis was said to be the skin of the goat Amalthea; but an association with the word καταιγίς (ἀΐσσω),

early affected its symbolism (see also § 402). Zeus is also the god of prowess in battle and of all manly excellence (ἄρειος, σθένιος); hence two out of the four great athletic festivals of Greece were in his honour, the Olympian and the Nemean, besides many others, such as the Sthenia at Argos and the Arcadian Lycaea.

(*c*) Zeus, as supreme ruler, is the source of all moral order; in this capacity his consort is Themis, and he delivers the θέμιστες, those universal and unwritten laws of right and wrong which are the origin of all human law and custom. of moral order, He is therefore the punisher of guilt, especially blood-guilt, and also the purifier (ἀλιτή-ριος and καθάρσιος or μειλίχιος); he is the especial protector of suppliants (ἱκέσιος). To find out his will as a guide to conduct is the object of oracles and of divination.

(*d*) As king and father of gods and men, Zeus presides over all social and political ties and organisation. The altar of Zeus ἑρκεῖος stood in the court of every house; as τέλειος he presided over marriage, and as κτήσιος over the prosperity of political and
social order, of the household. Passing beyond the family to the clan, he is φράτριος, and as βασιλεύς he is head of the State. The king rules not only as his priest but as his representative, often by hereditary descent; a symbol of this power was the sceptre, sometimes, as at Chaeronea, itself an object of worship. As governments became more democratic in form, they still owed their sanction in council and assembly to Zeus, βουλαῖος and ἀγοραῖος and ὅρκιος. He is especially the common god of all of Greek race, as Ἑλλήνιος or Πανελλήνιος, and in an even wider sphere, as ξένιος, he enforces the universal rights of hospitality. He was worshipped as σωτήρ and ἐλευθέριος, especially after a great deliverance like the Persian wars.

(*e*) Lastly, to those who had advanced to a monotheistic stage of belief, Zeus was the name of the one god, the beginning and end of all things; in mystic, pantheistic philosophy he becomes a mere abstraction, as in the Orphic poems. monotheistic
conception.

The Greeks themselves attributed the origin of the worship of Zeus, like that of the Hellenic race, to Thessaly; and Mount Olympus was his chosen home. The Olympian cult came to be universally recognised as the orthodox form of the worship of Zeus; it found a centre at Olympia in Elis, which in later Origin of
cult, Thessaly.
Olympian
worship. times almost superseded its original home in northern Greece.

Dodona possessed the oracle already famous in the time of Homer, who attributes it to the Pelasgian Zeus, and mentions the service of the primitive priestly race, the Σέλλοι. See § 426. Dodona.

In the Peloponnese we find the worship of Zeus established, in a primitive form, upon several conspicuous mountains. Chief among them is Lycaeum, which also had the name Olympus. Worship on
mountains. We are but imperfectly informed as to the ritual at this place; it seems to have been very primitive and probably to have included human sacrifice.

The worship of Zeus in Attica also preserves many primitive features.
He was worshipped as πολιεύς on the Acropolis, and there
was also an altar of Zeus ὕπατος near the Erechtheum, of
which the foundation was attributed to Cecrops.   A primitive sacrifice to Zeus (probably at the threshing season) was at the Dipolia
or Buphonia; this was no common sacrifice but a murder (φόνος), for
which the axe used was ultimately condemned and banished; the hide
of the bull sacrificed was stuffed and set up again.   The worship of Zeus
Olympius at Athens cannot be traced back beyond the time of Peisistratus,
who, however, probably founded the Olympieum on the site of an earlier
temple of Zeus.

*Attic wor-
ship.*

The legends of the birth and childhood of Zeus, which are generally
adopted in later mythology, appear to belong in their origin
to Crete, where also their scene is usually placed, though
the Cretan Ida sometimes gives place to the Phrygian
Ida, which seems in many ways to be closely connected
with it in mythology.   In a cave on mount Ida, or elsewhere in Crete,
the infant Zeus was concealed by his mother Rhea, with the help of the
Curetes, whose dance in armour, interpreted as a device to drown the
cries of the child, was probably in its origin intended as a more direct
defence against dangerous powers.   The death of Zeus was also a theme
of Cretan legend, and was quoted by Euhemerus in support of his famous
theory, though it need cause us no surprise in the case of a god so closely
identified with the powers of nature.

*Cretan tales
of birth of
Zeus.*

Hera was generally acknowledged in later organised mythology as
the consort of Zeus.   But in some early centres of his
worship we find another consort, Dione, for example, at
Dodona and at Athens; and Leto seems to claim also the
position of a legitimate wife.   Apart from allegorical unions, such as those
with Mnemosyne, mother of the Muses, or Themis, mother of the Hours
and Fates, we also find many tales of the love of Zeus for nymphs or for
mortal women.   These stories occupy a very prominent part in literary
mythology, on account of the scope they offer for poetical description.
Their origin is not in all cases similar.   In some instances the nymph
was the chief goddess of the place, and has sunk into a subordinate position
before the jealousy of Hera, of which she often is the victim in the story;
in others, the ancestress of a heroic race is merely a genealogical invention,
and her union with Zeus is the result of the ambition, common to so many
of the princely families of Greece, to derive their lineage in a direct line
from 'the father of gods and men.'

*Consorts of
Zeus.*

Zeus is represented in Art as the ideal of ripe manhood, bearded,
with a face full of majesty and benignity.   In early times he
is often represented standing or advancing, with a thunderbolt in his hand; but this conception of his power was
superseded by the more dignified conception of the god enthroned, which,
after the great statue made by Pheidias at Olympia, came to be so

*Represen-
tation in Art.*

universally accepted that it was difficult for a Greek to conceive of Zeus under any other form. In earlier Art the thunderbolt is his usual mark of identification; and, especially in later times, he is frequently accompanied by the eagle.

401. Hera is in orthodox Greek mythology the legitimate consort of Zeus, and this conception seems to underlie all her functions. She represents the female principle in nature, as Zeus does the male; hence the popular spring festival of universal occurrence, which celebrates the union of the two as essential to the continuation of life in plants and animals, finds its obvious recognition in the ἱερὸς γάμος of Zeus and Hera. She presides over the life of women as Zeus over that of men, and is in particular the goddess of marriage (γαμηλία, τελεία) and of childbirth; in this last capacity she is εἰλείθυια, or Eileithyia, sometimes the Eileithyiae, her daughters, are associated with her. The classical worship of Hera seems also to have absorbed the worship of a primitive goddess worshipped in the form of a cow—a worship of which we may notice many survivals in her cult and myth, especially in the Homeric epithet βοῶπις, and in the Argive legend of Io, who is transformed into a cow by the jealousy of Hera, and is probably to be regarded as a mythical double of the goddess herself.

In Homer (*Il.* IV. 51) Hera claims Argos, Sparta, and Mycenae as her especial cities; and it seems probable that the earliest centre of her worship in Greece was the Heraeum which lies between Argos and Mycenae, nearer to the latter. Hence her worship appears to have spread to Samos, and to the Lacinian promontory near Croton in S. Italy, both of which became especially famous for it, as well as to many other sites in Greece. The most prominent festival in the majority of these places seems to have been the ἱερὸς γάμος, and it is connected with other ceremonies easily paralleled in popular custom, such as the carrying of the image of the goddess down to the seashore, hiding it in a bush, seeking for it, and conducting it back in festal procession when found. In the case of Hera, these ceremonies were especially associated with the bridal bath and the marriage procession; in the spring of Canathus, at Nauplia, she yearly renewed her virginity. Games of prowess, especially races, for girls only, were held in honour of Hera at several places, especially at Olympia, where her temple was of very ancient foundation. To this Olympian festival women only were admitted, as men only at the games in honour of Zeus. Hera appears also as the protector of heroes, especially in the legend of Jason and the Argonauts, but her association with a Minyan tale is curious, for little early evidence of the cult of Hera has been found in Northern Greece. Like all divinities whose cult is closely connected with the changes of nature, she also had an offended or sullen aspect; at Stymphalus she was worshipped as virgin, wife, and widow; the darker side of her worship was developed in poetical mythology in the various tales of her quarrels with Zeus and her jealousy of his other

2. Hera, character.

Local cults.

consorts, which may also represent in some degree the jealousy of the orthodox worship of Hera against other local goddesses who took her place as consort of the chief god.

In Art Hera appears either as a dignified matron or queen, or in her more youthful aspect as the bride of Zeus; in either **Representation in Art.** capacity her special attributes are a high decorated crown (στεφάνη or πόλος) and full rich drapery; she usually carries a sceptre, often a pomegranate; in the Heraeum at Argos her seated statue by Polycleitus, in gold and ivory, was the most famous of all; her sceptre there was surmounted by a cuckoo, because Zeus was said to have visited her in that form. Among the earliest remains of Greek sculpture is a colossal head from the temple statue in the Heraeum at Olympia; the Farnese head at Naples, and others in the Ludovisi collection at Rome are the best known examples of her type. Her sacred bird, the peacock, stood in her temple, and is reproduced on coins of Argos.

402. Athena appears in early times as the chief deity of many places, giving increase to the fruits of the field and of trees and also to **3. Athena, character.** the youth of her people, and bestowing prowess and victory in war and skill in the arts of peace. In later times the brighter and more intellectual side of her character came into prominence, and, especially as the patron goddess of Athens, she came to be regarded as representing the pre-eminence of the Greek genius in art, literature, and science. Athena was said to have been born from the head of Zeus, with the help of an axe-stroke given by Prometheus or Hephaestus **Myth of birth, etc.** (Zeus, according to some legends, having previously swallowed her mother Metis, daughter of Ocean, because of a prophecy that her offspring would be stronger than its father). Many places claimed to be the scene of her birth, especially such as had a river or lake Triton or Tritonis (cf. τριτογένεια). She is often spoken of as κόρη Διός, and she alone shares many of his functions and powers; her special attribute is the aegis, in which is set the head of the Gorgon, which she either slew herself (according to the Attic legend) or by the instrumentality of Perseus (the Argive version). Her commonest epithet is γλαυκῶπις, of which the exact force is doubtful, though it cannot be dissociated from the owl, which constantly appears in Athens and elsewhere as the companion or the symbol of the goddess. Her poetical name Pallas is not easy to explain; it may probably be associated with her worship in the Attic district Pallene, and also with Pallas, a giant or Titan whom she slew; some etymologists derive it from πάλλω. Her name in Epic Greek is Ἀθήνη, Ἀθηναίη; in Attic, Ἀθηνᾶ.

The worship of Athena in her chosen city, Athens, was of predominant influence: in connexion with this two stories are **Attic cult.** most prominent—that of the birth of Erechtheus (or Erichthonius) and that of the contest of Athena and Poseidon for the land, when Athena produced as her symbol the sacred olive tree in the Erechtheum, and Poseidon either the salt spring in the same building or the horse. In honour of Athena the Panathenaic games were celebrated at Athens; they included athletic, musical, and warlike sports; the chief ceremony of the whole festival was the dedication of the peplos, woven for the goddess by maidens and women in her service. Her statue was also taken down to the sea and bathed once a year, in early summer, at the plynteria.

The more warlike aspect of the goddess was prominent in Athena Itonia, worshipped in Boeotia and Thessaly, and was not unknown in Athens. Thus too she is the protector of heroes in war ($\sigma\theta\epsilon\nu\iota\acute{a}s$, $\acute{a}\rho\epsilon\acute{\iota}a$); she is Athena $\nu\acute{\iota}\kappa\eta$ or $\nu\iota\kappa\eta\phi\acute{o}\rho os$; {Other local cults.} she is also the tamer of the horse ($\dot{\iota}\pi\pi\acute{\iota}a$, $\chi a\lambda\iota\nu\hat{\iota}\tau\iota s$), and she teaches men how to make ships, especially the ship Argo. In her more peaceful aspect she is $\kappa o\nu\rho o\tau\rho\acute{o}\phi os$, $\dot{\nu}\gamma\acute{\iota}\epsilon\iota a$, and presides over the city at Athens and elsewhere, as $\pi o\lambda\iota o\hat{\nu}\chi os$, $\beta o\nu\lambda a\acute{\iota}a$. As Ergane she is the patroness of all kinds of crafts and handiwork, especially weaving ($\ddot{\epsilon}\rho\gamma a$ $^{\prime}A\theta\eta\nu a\acute{\iota}\eta s$). She protects agriculture, and especially the olive, and is honoured by musical and orchestral performances; she invented the flute. Especially she is the goddess of enlightenment, of reason and thought, and so of art and science, and in her own Athens the clearness of the air and of the intellect were associated with and attributed to her. In later Greece she represented Attic culture, and her statue was set up in libraries.

In the earliest representations Athena is represented as fully armed and striking with raised spear, sometimes with a distaff in the other hand as representing the other nature of the goddess. {Representation in Art.} Her most famous statues at Athens were the colossal gold and ivory statue within the Parthenon and the colossal bronze statue (sometimes wrongly called $\pi\rho\acute{o}\mu a\chi os$) outside it, both by Pheidias.

403. Apollo, as familiar to us in his poetical and artistic representations, is the god of light (Phoebus) and youth and music, often too the god of the sun, and sometimes consciously identi- {4. Apollo, character.} fied with Helios. But, though this side of his character is most prominent in historical times, and especially in literature, it is a mere perversion of ingenuity to attempt to derive from it all his mythological functions. Apollo was the chief god of several divisions of the Greek race, and as such was the protector of youth ($\pi a\tau\rho\hat{\varphi}os$, $\kappa o\nu\rho o\tau\rho\acute{o}\phi os$), the leader of colonies ($\dot{a}\rho\chi\eta\gamma\acute{\epsilon}\tau\eta s$), the fosterer of flocks and herds ($\nu\acute{o}\mu\iota os$), the guardian of streets ($\dot{a}\gamma\nu\iota\epsilon\acute{\nu}s$), and especially the god of expiation and purification, and the lord of oracles. Several of his festivals are clearly of primitive origin, and celebrate the renewed vigour of the spirit of vegetation in spring.

Leto, the mother of Apollo and Artemis, was associated with them in worship in many places. She wandered long before their birth, and according to a Boeotian legend was changed into {Delian myth of birth and origin of worship.} a wolf; a cause was found by later mythology in the jealousy of Hera, as the legitimate consort of Zeus. The wandering island of Delos was fixed, and became the birthplace of the god, who was born the seventh day of the month, therefore sacred to him. Such was the Delian myth, which came to be universally accepted, and even the Delphic worship was said to have been founded by the god after a journey from Delos, though many other places claimed his birth by ancient legend. Many places have the legend of the ἐπιδημία and ἀποδημία of the god, who spends his summers among his worshippers, his winters elsewhere, usually with the Hyperboreans.

Apollo, though worshipped by the Dorians, does not belong exclusively to them in origin. Miletus and Delos were Ionian, **Local cults.** and his earliest Peloponnesian worship at Amyclae, where he was associated with Hyacinthus, is earlier than the Dorian immigration, though adopted by the Spartans as their national cult. The Hyacinthia, a festival of three days in the middle of summer, included mourning over the death and rejoicing in the revival of Hyacinthus. The Carneia at Sparta were musical and military games. The Peloponnesian rites as celebrated by the Dorians were doubtless influenced by the Delphic worship which was also predominant in the north of Greece. At Delphi, the return of the god in spring was celebrated at the Theophania; in the following month, at the Theoxenia, Apollo **Delphic cult.** was entertained with a sacred banquet by the Delphians, and received the other gods as his guests. The greatest of the Delphic festivals, the Pythia, were held in summer every fourth year, and celebrated the victory of Apollo over the Python. The worship of Apollo Pythius, derived from Delphi, is found throughout Greece. In or near the Delphic temple was the navel of the earth (ὀμφαλός), and here too the oracles were given by the Pythian priestess. Apollo had many other oracular shrines, notably those at Miletus (Branchidae), at Abae in Phocis, and at Mt Ptous in Boeotia. Every eight years—probably at every other celebration of the Pythia—the death of the dragon Python and the blood-guiltiness and flight of Apollo were commemorated in the σεπτήριον; a boy representing the god had to fly to Tempe; there he was purified, crowned with the sacred bay, and escorted back in the δαφνηφόρια to Delphi. The great Apolline festivals at Athens were the θαργήλια on the first day of which two men, the φαρμακοί, were led out as if to be sacrificed as an expiation; and the πυανέψια, a rejoicing over the first-fruits of the harvest, which were carried round on a branch called εἰρεσιώνη. The time of the Theoria or sacred embassy to Delos was also regarded as a specially sacred season in Athens.

Special forms of Apollo which appear to be of a primitive nature are λύκιος or λύκειος, sometimes associated with Lycia, but **Association with animals.** evidently implying that the god took the form of a wolf, as in Argive myth and on Argive coins. Epithets like σμινθεύς and παρνόπιος find a more plausible explanation in the warding off of pests such as field-mice and locusts. Apollo was frequently invoked as the sender and consequently also the stayer of plague (ἀλεξίκακος), and the giver of sudden death. As healing god (παιήων, παιώνιος) he is the father of Asclepius. He is especially the god of suppliants seeking purification, as in the case of Orestes.

In early times he is often represented as bearded; later he is the ideal type of youth and was set up with Hermes and Heracles in gymnasia; the effeminate type of later Art is a mere degradation. His constant attributes are the bow and **Representation in Art.** the lyre; the tripod and bay are especially connected with his Pythian worship, the gryphon with his journey to the Hyperboreans.

404. Artemis figures in later mythology and art as the feminine counterpart of Apollo, the virgin huntress and type of vigorous maidenhood, and also as goddess of the moon; but here more than in any other case the name was used to include **5. Artemis, character.** many different and even inconsistent conceptions. Many ancient local goddesses were either identified with Artemis, or associated with her as attendant nymphs. She shares with Apollo the myth of her birth, but it was said to have happened in Ortygia, a name assigned in this connexion to various cities, such as Ephesus and Syracuse, and later to Delos. She also shared the worship of Apollo in most of his sacred places: but her separate cult is evidently more primitive. She appears as the goddess of free and wild nature (ἀγροτέρα) especially in connexion with mountains, groves, and springs. Thus in Arcadia Megisto and Callisto, the ancestresses of the Arcadian race, were forms of the goddess herself; with the name Arcas we may compare the bear-dance performed in honour of the Brauronian Artemis at Athens. She gives increase to all wild creatures and protects their young (πότνια θηρῶν); and extends the same protection to flocks and herds and to mankind: in this connexion, and as a lunar goddess, she is especially the goddess of women, their protector in childbirth (λοχία), and the giver of life and death. Maidens frequently made offerings of dress to her before their marriage (χιτώνη, λυσίζωνος). She was the patroness of hunting and hunters, and honoured with gifts of the chase (δίκτυννα in Crete, λαφρία in Calydon). Human sacrifice to her seems preserved in the tale of Iphigenia (herself a form of the goddess) and in the scourging of Spartan boys till their blood ran on the altar of Artemis Orthia. The Tauric Artemis, whose worship was said to have been brought with her image from Thrace by Orestes and Iphigenia, was also propitiated with human sacrifice; her name seems to imply a connexion with herds. Artemis appears also as the protectress of civil and political life (εὔκλεια, σωσίπολις).

Several other goddesses seem to be regarded as little more than varying names for Artemis; such are Bendis in Thrace, Britomartis in Crete, and others. Hecate is the goddess of roads **Identifications.** and passages, and her image was set up at places where three ways met (τριοδῖτις = trivia); her triple form is said not to be older than

Alcamenes (end of fifth century). She is the goddess of night, of goblins and of magic, and of the underworld; also of the moon and of other functions of Artemis. Nemesis, or Upis, of Rhamnus, was also regarded as a form of Artemis. The name Artemis was also given to some of the great mother-goddesses of Asia Minor, notably at Ephesus, where her many-breasted image shows a conception far indeed removed from the ideal Greek huntress.

In early Art, Artemis is often represented with a high crown or
Represen-
tation in Art. πόλos on her head, and grasping a wild beast, leopard or lion or stag, in one or in each hand; this is clearly an imitation of oriental models, but survives traditionally even till late times: in statues she appears either in full flowing drapery, or in short chiton and often hunting boots; she carries the bow and quiver; sometimes also a torch, especially as Hecate.

405. It was the current notion of **Hermes**, from the time of Homer,
6. Hermes,
character. that he was the herald and messenger of the gods (διά-κτορος). But he has another aspect as a giver of increase, especially to flocks and herds. As such he was especially worshipped in Arcadia, where his mother, Maia, bore him in a cave on Mt Cyllene. His image, here and elsewhere, was the symbol of generation in its crudest form; and this character was constantly present in the conventional images of the god (Hermae). The Homeric hymn to Hermes represents him as the inventor of the lyre and as the thief of Apollo's cattle; in both tales there may be a reflexion of the rivalry between the early cults of two similar deities, and their partition of functions in orthodox mythology; the two were often worshipped side by side. Both alike are patrons of youth (κουροτρόφος) and of the palaestra; both protect flocks and herds (νόμιos), and Hermes ἐνόδιos, like Apollo ἀγυιεύς, has his statue in roads. Rude statues of Hermes were constantly set up also as boundaries, over which he especially presided. In the Argive legend, Hermes was sent to slay the many-eyed giant Argus, the guardian of Io when transformed to a cow; hence his constant epithet ἀργειφόντης; he beguiled Argus with music, and then cut off his head with the ἅρπη, the same weapon, which, with his winged sandals, he lent to Perseus to slay the Gorgon. In Boeotian legend, he gave the flying golden ram to Phrixus, and the lyre to Amphion, who drew beasts and stones by its power. At Tanagra, where his birthplace was claimed by Mt Cerycion, there was an annual ceremony in honour of Hermes κριοφόρος, when a youth representing the god bore a ram on his shoulders round the town. This was said to be in memory of a plague he stayed. As god of wayfarers, Hermes was represented by rude or unwrought stones along the roads; he was the god of commerce, and also of all cunning and even theft; and also of luck and treasure-trove (ἐριούνιos). As herald, he gave skill in speech, and he was also the conductor of wayfarers on their last journey to Hades (χθόνιos, ψυχοπομπός).

Besides the rude images already mentioned, we find Hermes usually represented in early Art as a bearded man; later, as beardless. The herald's staff (κηρύκειον) is his constant attribute, and he also has wings on his feet, or winged sandals, and a winged cap. In later Art he is usually the swift messenger of the gods; sometimes the god of commerce, with the purse, or, represented as speaking, the god of oratory (λόγιος). Calamis made a statue of him at Tanagra as Criophorus, and Praxiteles as carrying the infant Dionysus at Olympia. In the beautiful Naples bronze he sits ready for flight.

Representation in Art.

406. **Dionysus or Bacchus** is in later poetical mythology the giver of wine and of its pleasures, the leader of the rout of maenads and satyrs, and the patron of the drama. This is however only one side of his real mythological character ; more than in the case of any other Greek deity, the worship of Dionysus is bound up with primitive and popular customs and ceremonies, in which he is worshipped as the god of vegetation (δενδρίτης); and even the orgiastic dances in his honour are not so much the results of intoxication as magic invocations of the god at critical periods. Dionysus is barely mentioned in Homer; his official and poetical recognition belongs to a later time. His introduction from abroad is a constant feature in myth; but although some of the orgies celebrated in his honour may be traceable to Thrace or Phrygia, his worship is not entirely of foreign origin, and even his name appears to be Greek, and must probably be connected with Nysa, the mountain where he was brought up ; but the original Nysa was shown in innumerable places, including Naxos, Euboea, Thessaly, Thrace. Thebes was the chief centre of the myths concerning Dionysus in Greece. Here his mother, Semele, one of the daughters of Cadmus, was burnt up owing to her rash prayer to see her lover Zeus in his divine glory ; Zeus took her son, yet unborn, and sewed him up in his thigh, whence he issued in due time. Hence the epithets μηρορραφής, διμήτωρ, δισσότοκος. Hermes took the child Dionysus, and gave him to the nymphs of Nysa. These nymphs, the satyrs, and the old Silenus, or the Sileni, guarded his youth, and after became his attendants. The stories of the opposition to his orgiastic worship by kings like Lycurgus of Thrace and Pentheus of Thebes, who attacked the maenads and met an evil fate at the hands of the god, probably preserve in part a tradition of official opposition to the cult. But they also contain elements borrowed from the ritual itself; such as the tale that Pentheus was thought to be a wild beast and torn to pieces. Such wild hunting, ending often in the destruction of the god or his victim, and often showing traces of human sacrifice, is almost universal as one side of the worship of Dionysus (Ζαγρεύς, Ἀγριώνιος, Λαφύστιος, Ὠμηστής), it is contrasted with the milder aspect of the god (Μειλίχιος, Λύσιος). Dionysus in this connexion often appears in the form of a bull or a goat (ταυρόμορφος, Μελαναιγίς). In the Aegean islands Dionysus was worshipped not only as a god of vegetation and

7. Dionysus, character,

origin and myths.

of the vine, but also as a sea god, for example in the story of the Tyrrhenian pirates whom he changed to dolphins. In Naxos his consort was Ariadne, associated with Theseus by Attic legend. His expeditions to the far east appear early; after the time of Alexander they were extended to India. One of the commonest scenes in early Art is that in which Dionysus brings Hephaestus back to Olympus. (For the Attic festivals and the drama see § 425.) At Athens every spring the marriage of Dionysus with the Basilinna, wife of the Archon Basileus, was the official recognition of a common country ceremony.

Dionysus is represented in early Art, and often later, as bearded and in rich drapery; later he is usually represented in a youth-
**Represen-
tation in Art.** ful and somewhat effeminate type. His early images were often mere masks, affixed to posts or to trees. His rout of satyrs and maenads was a favourite subject at all times, but was treated with especial skill by Scopas. His great gold and ivory statue at Athens was by Alcamenes, who made him bearded and enthroned, with a wine cup in his hand. His special attributes, beside this, are the thyrsus, the ivy-wreath, and the panther.

407. Demeter and Persephone were worshipped together in many temples throughout Greece as the Great Goddesses (Μεγάλαι
**8. Demeter
and Perse-
phone.** θεαί or simply τὼ θεώ, also Σεμναί, Πότνιαι); Persephone was frequently called simply κόρη, sometimes Ἁγνή or Δέσποινα. According to the generally accepted legend, Persephone was the daughter of Demeter by Zeus; while she was gathering flowers with her companions, she was seized by Pluto and carried off to his realm below. Her mother wandered in search of her, and was unconsolable; in her anger no corn or fruit was brought forth by the earth: at length a reconciliation was effected, on condition that the daughter should divide her time between her husband below and her mother on earth. Such is the main outline of the story, though there are many variations in its details The scenes of its episodes were claimed by many places. According to an Arcadian version, the father of Persephone was Poseidon; Demeter was changed into a mare, and her anger was for the violence done to herself not to her daughter. Hence she was called Ἐρινύς, Μέλαινα. Homer knows none of these stories, but refers to the union of Demeter with the mortal Iasion in a new-ploughed field. All these tales are clearly derived from primitive popular rites connected with harvest and seed-time, such as are still found throughout Europe. They were most fully developed in connexion with the Eleusinian legend as recorded in the Homeric hymn to Demeter. Mother and daughter alike are impersonations of the corn spirit. Accordingly, Demeter is represented as the giver of corn, through her favourite Triptolemus; in this connexion also she is κουροτρόφος. As Thesmophorus, in Attica, she appears also as the guardian of civil life, especially marriage, worshipped by matrons only at the Thesmophoria. The sacrifice of pigs, there and

at the Eleusinia, was explained from the enmity of the pig to crops.   For
the mysteries see § 428.

Persephone was united with **Pluto** as ruler of the realm below
and of the dead.   Pluto or Hades has no very distinct
mythological personality, except in connexion with his
consort, and most of his duties are deputed to others.

> 9. Hades.

408.   **Poseidon** is the god of the sea and of water generally; this
restriction of his functions is generally recognised (though
the first part of his name means simply 'lord'); what is
preserved to us of his mythological character is more than usually tinged
with the poetic conception, which here seems often to coincide with
the popular one.   As god of the sea, Poseidon lives in his palace
beneath the waves at Aegae, a mythical locality; the name suggests
the Aegean; he rides over the waves in his chariot drawn by horses or
sea-horses, accompanied by his consort Amphitrite, his son Triton, and the
monsters of the deep.   He is also the god of springs and rivers; in this
character he is conceived of under the form of a bull, as river-gods often
are; and he gives the moisture necessary for vegetation (φυτάλμιος).   The
sea-god is also thought of as the holder of the earth and the shaker of
it in earthquakes (γαιήοχος, ἐννοσίγαιος).   He is also ἵππιος, god of horses
and of chivalry.   The great centre of the worship of Poseidon in historical
times was the Isthmus of Corinth, where the Isthmian games included
not only athletic contests and horse and chariot races, but also races for
ships.   The temple at Calaureia was also the centre of an early amphictyony
in his honour.   In Arcadia, he was the god of horses, especially in his
union with the horse Demeter.   At Athens his early worship is preserved
in the tale of his contest with Athena for the land, when he produced the
salt spring on the Acropolis, or the horse.   But he became identified with
Erechtheus and sank to the position of a mere *protégé* and attendant of
Athena.   As ἵππιος he still retained his position at Colonus.   Sacrifices,
especially of horses, were cast into the sea for him in several places.
Poseidon no less than Zeus was regarded as direct ancestor by many
princely families.   Poseidon is usually represented in art as standing, with
trident and dolphin or tunny.   He frequently in later times has one foot
raised on a rock or other support.   In gigantomachies he usually hurls
the island of Cos or Nisyros on his opponent.   His train of Nereids and
Tritons was a favourite subject with Scopas and later artists.

> 10. Poseidon.

409.   It is generally admitted that the worship of **Aphrodite** in
Greece has been influenced to an exceptional degree by
various oriental cults; but these have been so thoroughly
assimilated by Greek mythologists and poets that it is impossible to distinguish them from what is really of Hellenic or local
origin.   She is the goddess of love and sexual. passion, alike in the
highest and in the lowest form.   Her worship and that of her constant
attendant Eros served alike as a ratification of the ordinance of marriage, as

> 11. Aphro-
> dite.

a pretext for unbridled licentiousness, and as a subject for philosophical speculation about unions and affinities; she is the giver of all grace and beauty, especially to women. She also has a connexion with the growth of vegetation which is found in oriental cults such as that of Adonis, and in the corresponding Roman goddess Venus. She was also worshipped as a goddess of the sea and giver of fair weather (εὐπλοία).

There are two distinct and inconsistent accounts of her birth; according to Homer and others she was the daughter of Zeus and Dione; according to Hesiod she was the product of the mutilation of Uranos by his son Cronos, and was born out of the foam of the sea, whence she arose and landed at Cythera or at Paphos in Cyprus (Κυθηρεία, Κύπρις; the Greeks connected the name Aphrodite, rightly or wrongly, with this legend). Her worship, in its oriental form, was spread from Cyprus and Cythera, and from Eryx in Sicily; it also had a centre in Corinth. Much confusion has been caused by the varying use of the epithets Urania and Pandemos. Originally Aphrodite Pandemos was probably the Greek goddess of marriage, and Aphrodite Urania corresponded to the Syrian Astarte, queen of heaven, who was worshipped with licentious rites. But Plato and later mythologists inverted the relations of the two by associating them respectively with 'heavenly' and 'earthly' love. At Elis the symbol of Urania was the tortoise and that of Pandemos was the goat, in statues made by Pheidias and Scopas respectively. At Corinth and Sparta Aphrodite was represented as armed, and she was the legitimate consort of Ares (ἀρεία) at Thebes and Argos. The blending of this tradition with the other common myth regarding her as the consort of Hephaestus led to scandalous stories like that sung by Demodocus in the *Odyssey*. The identification of Aphrodite with various goddesses, mostly of oriental origin, leads to much confusion. Upis, or Nemesis, at Rhamnus was sometimes identified with her, and the statue is actually said to have been designed originally as an Aphrodite. Venus and Adonis, originally Syrian, find a counterpart in a similar pair throughout the East, Cybele and Attis in Phrygia, Aphrodite and Cinyras or Cyris in Cyprus. The 'garden of Adonis' and his festival generally take a prominent place in late Greek worship, especially at Alexandria. Aphrodite was from the earliest times recognised in statuettes of oriental workmanship; but the Greek goddess was usually draped until the fourth century; and even then Praxiteles found in the bath a pretext for her nudity, which later became normal, though the severer and more dignified aspect of the goddess was continued in works such as the Venus of Melos.

410. Hephaestus is the god of fire, whether elemental, as in volcanic phenomena, or applied to human use, especially for metal-work and handicraft generally. He was the son of Zeus and Hera, and was hurled down from heaven either by his father or his mother; he fell in the sea, where he was brought up by Thetis and Eurynome, or else into Lemnos; his lameness, appropriate to the smith, is given either as the cause or the effect of this fall.

12. Hephae-
stus.

His consort is Charis in the *Iliad*, probably following the Lemnian mythology ; in Hesiod, Aglaia, youngest of the Charites ; in the *Odyssey*, Aphrodite.   In early Attic myth he was associated with Athena in the parentage of Erichthonius ; but the worship of the virgin goddess modified the legend.   He was worshipped at Athens with Prometheus and Athena at the χαλκεῖα and other festivals, especially as the god of artificers, and torch races were held in his honour ; in this connexion he was associated too with Daedalus, possibly originally identified with him.   Lemnos was the great centre of his worship ; here the Sinties, a people specially devoted to him, had received him on his fall; he had his smithy under the volcano Moschylus ; Cedalion was his instructor and henchman.   Every year there was an expiatory rite, when all fires had to be extinguished in the island for nine days, till fresh fire was fetched from Delos.   He was also associated with Dionysus, especially in the tale of the chair with invisible fetters which he sent to his mother. Dionysus made him drunk and conducted him back to Olympus with his satyrs and maenads, the scene forming a favourite subject in art.   In the west his workshop was assigned to Aetna or Lipari, and he was associated with the Cyclopes.   Many mythical works of art were assigned to him, such as the necklace of Harmonia, which brought ill-luck.   In Art, he is represented in the guise of a smith, with conical cap, hammer, and pincers, and with a limping gait.

411. **Ares** was the god of war and sometimes of pestilence, and has the special functions assigned to many other deities as ἄρειος or ἀρεία; he was worshipped in Thrace, but the Greeks often   13. **Ares.** looked on him as a barbarian, and he had no very honoured place in their pantheon.   He was consort to Aphrodite in Thebes, Athens, Argos, etc. He had a temple on the Areopagus at Athens, which was by some accounts founded in his honour by the invading amazons ; according to another version, he was tried by the court of the twelve gods there for his murder of Halirrhothius, son of Poseidon, who had done violence to his daughter by Agraulus, Alcippe.   His son Oenomaus at Elis was conquered by Pelops, as others of his sons elsewhere were destroyed by Heracles or other more popular heroes.   He appears usually as an armed warrior, and the spear and the torch are his symbols.

412. **Hestia** has a more important position in cultus than in myth. She was sister of Zeus, and chose perpetual virginity.   She is the goddess of the hearth, whether of the house or of the   14. **Hestia.** city, like the Roman Vesta; she receives the first and last offering at every feast.   Her symbol is the hearth, ἑστία, in the house, and the κοινὴ ἑστία in the Prytaneum.   She is often associated with Hermes, typifying the life of the family within, as he its communication with outside.   At a sacrifice to Hestia, nothing might be taken or given away.   In Art she is seated or stands in rich drapery, usually veiled, and often leads the procession of the gods.

Minor and attendant deities.

413. Of minor deities not even an enumeration can be attempted here, but an indication may be given of the classes into which they fall.

1. Olympian.

First we may mention the attendants and messengers of the gods, such as Iris, Nike, goddess of Victory, Hebe, Ganymede, Eileithyia, the Graces, the Horae, etc. Some are cup-bearers or attendants, others either communicate directly the will of the gods to men, or are mere personifications of the favours and functions of the deities they accompany.

2. Of earth.

Next come the nymphs, satyrs, and sileni, whom we have already met as the attendants of Dionysus and other gods. **Pan** was an Arcadian god, the son of Hermes and protector of flocks; he was essentially the god of the country, but was introduced into Athens, where he was worshipped in a cave under the Acropolis, because he was supposed to have helped the Athenians at Marathon by casting 'panic' terror into the Persian ranks. He invented the pan-pipes, or syrinx, which was personified as a nymph; Echo also, as well as other nymphs, were his companions. He appears in Art either as a youthful shepherd, with λαγωβόλον and syrinx, or in the more familiar form with goat-legs and goatish face and horns. **Priapus** was especially the god of vegetation and gardens, and his image symbolised in the coarsest manner the reproductive energy in nature. The centaurs, who in origin offer many analogies to the satyrs, are also country creatures; most of them are typical of wild and unbridled savagery; a few, such as Cheiron, are the trainers of heroes, skilled in medicine and country lore.

3. Of water.

Beside the recognised dynasty of Poseidon, his consort Amphitrite, and his attendants, we find many other deities of the water. Oceanus, and his consort Tethys, is little more than an abstraction. Nereus is the father of fifty daughters, the Nereids, among whom Amphitrite and Thetis are the most conspicuous. Leucothea and her son Melicertes were identified with Ino the daughter of Cadmus and her son Palaemon. Proteus, more than any other, is typical of the power of sea-creatures to transform themselves into various shapes. Glaucus is another demigod of popular myth. Triton, sometimes the son of Poseidon, is also the 'old man of the sea,' with whom Heracles wrestles. All these and many others are merely variations on the same conceptions. Every river has its own god; but Achelous is the chief of all. Helios plays a part, usually a subordinate one, in several myths;

4. Meteorological personifications.

he was especially worshipped at Rhodes; he has rarely a clear mythological character apart from Apollo; a similar statement may be made as to Selene, especially in purely Greek myth. Eos, in her pursuit of Cephalus, and her union with Tithonus, seems to have a clearer personality. The stars, the winds, and other phenomena are also personified; and Aeolus, father of the winds, is familiar to us from Homer.

Some ethical personifications, such as Themis and Nemesis, have a distinct cultus and are sometimes identified with other deities; we also find temples to the Erinyes, or Furies, who are more than a mere allegory. Death, Sleep, the Fates, Fortune were all represented in Art, and even a conception like Αἰδώς or Ἔλεος had an altar. Eirene and her child Plutus are a transparent allegory, as are many others that could be mentioned. The fortune of cities was a favourite form of personification in Hellenistic times, as in the well-known statue called 'Antioch.'

5. Ethical personifica-
tions.

Many foreign deities have already been spoken of as identified with recognised Greek deities; others who retain a separate individuality are Rhea Cybele, the Phrygian mother of the gods, the Cabiri, the Egyptian Isis, Serapis, and others, and Mithras and other oriental deities in later times.

6. Foreign deities.

414. The worship of the dead, and the offerings made at the tomb, formed a prominent feature of Greek ritual. Some demigods or heroes were represented as of mortal origin, especially those connected with healing, such as **Asclepius**, whose position is intermediate between gods and heroes; some others, such as **Amphiaraus**, who had oracles where they were consulted, had been seers in life. Even the **Dioscuri** and **Heracles** were regarded as men who were deified, though Heracles only was admitted to Olympus. But practically any man, when he died, might be said to become a hero, though the word was not so generally applied until comparatively late times. Conspicuous examples are offered by the oecists of the various colonies, and the heroic honours given them.

Heroes.

V. 2. RELIGIOUS INSTITUTIONS.

415. THE various stages in the growth of belief and of ritual which have been noticed in the general introduction to this section have left their traces throughout Greek religious institutions. It is however impossible, in the present state of our knowledge, to treat the subject in a strictly historical manner, though in some cases it may be possible, within certain limits, to distinguish the more primitive rites from their later modifications. We must also remember that there are many intermediate steps between popular tradition and custom on the one hand, and the official and recognised ritual of great centres of worship on the other; and that what is preserved to us, especially in the former case, depends often on doubtful or indirect evidence, or on fortuitous and often isolated records.

Introduc-
tion; various
stages in
ritual.

For convenience in systematic treatment, we may classify the subject according to the following table, which must not be regarded as scientifically complete or accurate, since some cross divisions are possible.

Classifica-
tion of the
subject.

Ritual
{
A. Ordinary
{
1. Persons
2. Places
3. Manner
4. Times
}

B. Extraordinary
{
a. in celebration (Festivals)
{
1. Athletic
2. Musical
3. Dramatic
}

b. in manifestation
{
1. Oracles
2. Healing
3. Mysteries.
}
}

416. In the ordinary ritual of daily life no priest was necessary as an intermediary between men and gods. Alike in the

A. Ordinary ritual.

1. Persons employed in worship.

Head of family or State.

time of Homer and Hesiod and in historical Greece, everyone could make sacrifice and prayer for himself on ordinary occasions. Such functions naturally belonged to the head of the family, and were performed at the hearth; similarly, when they were performed on behalf of the State at the common hearth of the city, they devolved upon the head of the State—the king in early times; under republican institutions they either belonged to the chief political magistrate, or to another officer, sometimes given the special title of 'king,' who was the head of the State for this purpose, but held none the less an essentially political office, and was eligible under the same conditions as a civil magistrate.

Thus Aristotle *Pol.* VII. (VI.) 8 refers to the officers who perform θυσίας τὰς κοινὰς πάσας, ὅσας μὴ τοῖς ἱερεῦσιν ἀποδίδωσιν ὁ νόμος, ἀλλ᾽ ἀπὸ τῆς κοινῆς ἑστίας ἔχουσι τὴν τιμήν, and says they are variously called ἄρχοντες, βασιλεῖς, or πρυτάνεις. The right to share in such common State sacrifices was a privilege exclusively belonging to citizens, and aliens were excluded from them. On the other hand there were many religious ceremonies,

Priests.

whether for the State or for individuals, which required certain skill or knowledge beyond those of the ordinary layman, and which therefore had to be performed by a special priest; and others which only the members of a certain family, or persons possessing peculiar qualifications, were privileged to perform. This was particularly the case with oracles, mysteries, etc. (§§ 426, 428); but also with more ordinary public priesthoods; for example, the chief priestess of Athena and the high priest of Erechtheus at Athens were always from the sacred family of the

Family cults.

Eteobutadae. In many instances also a family or clan kept up a special worship, in which other citizens did not participate, but which nevertheless was recognised as part of the official religion of the State; such were the rites of the Clytidae at

Religious associations.

Cos. In later times associations for religious purposes became very common (θίασοι, ἔρανοι); they admitted all classes to membership, including women and slaves; sometimes they were devoted to the worship of a recognised deity of the State; more often to the celebration of foreign rites, frequently of an orgiastic character.

Though there was no distinct priestly caste in Greece in early times, priesthoods were often hereditary; some remained so; others, in common with other political offices, came to be elective or decided by lot. In later times they were very commonly sold. The perquisites of the priest of a frequented shrine were fixed by law or custom; he often had, for example, a certain prescribed share of all victims, including the skin. A considerable revenue resulted from the sale of these proceeds of sacrifice, which in some cases went to the State; the custom of selling priesthoods was virtually a part of the system of farming taxes and revenues. Often too, in more private cases, the founder of a shrine retained certain privileges, often as priest, in dedicating it to a god for public use. But the State always kept a control over such dedications, and at Athens and elsewhere it was illegal to introduce the worship of any foreign divinity without the express sanction of the people.

Appointments and privileges of priests.

417. Although a sacrifice or other religious service might be offered anywhere, it is obvious that in all stages of religious belief certain places would be regarded as either more pleasing to the gods or more likely to attract their attention. The two main causes which led to the selection of such places were physical and social; to these may be added, though much less frequent, historical.

2. Places of worship.

Physical conditions would vary with the stage of belief; thus in a primitive stage, conspicuous trees or springs or other natural objects would be regarded as the abode of a special deity, if not as his embodiment, a notion which survived to later times in the local shrines of Pan and the nymphs throughout the country; it was an advance towards generalisation when Poseidon or other marine deities were invoked by the sea-shore, or even at a river; sacrifices to Poseidon continued to be thrown into the sea in many places. When heaven was regarded as the abode of the gods, it was natural to get as near to them as possible in high places, such as the tops of mountains; many gods were so worshipped as ὕπατος, ἄκραιος, etc. Extraordinary phenomena also naturally evoked worship; thus Hephaestus was specially worshipped in volcanic Lemnos.

Physical reasons for sanctity.

Among social conditions the first and most universally prevalent was the necessity for a recognised centre for the worship of the family and of the State. Every house had its hearth (ἑστία) in its midst, the seat of the ἐφέστιοι or μύχιοι θεοί, and also its altar of Zeus Ἑρκεῖος, the protector of its enclosure, in its fore-court. When the king was, for religious purposes, the head of the State, it was natural for the hearth of his palace to be the centre of worship for the State. Thus the house of Erechtheus at Athens was identical, according to Homer, with the earliest temple of Athena. Usually in later times the common hearth of the town had a separate existence, in

Social reasons for sanctity.

connexion with the Prytaneum, the centre of State hospitality in the Agora; often this hearth was represented by a tholos of round shape, recalling the hearth of an early house; of such a nature was the temple of Vesta (Ἑστία) at Rome. The temples of the gods of the agora, the ἀγοραῖοι θεοὶ who presided over the political and commercial activity of the State, were naturally in the most crowded parts of the city, near the centre of civic life. Other temples were usually placed in conspicuous positions in the town, sometimes on sites hallowed by old associations, and perhaps originally consecrated from physical causes, though it was the growth of the town that occasioned their importance. Socrates indicates the ideal arrangement of historical times when he says (Xen. *Mem.* III. 8. 10) ναοῖς γε μὴν καὶ βωμοῖς χώραν ἔφη εἶναι πρεπωδεστάτην, ἥτις ἐμφανεστάτη οὖσα ἀστιβεστάτη εἴη· ἡδὺ μὲν γὰρ ἰδόντας προσεύξασθαι, ἡδὺ δὲ ἁγνῶς ἔχοντας προσιέναι. Such conditions were perfectly fulfilled by the temples on the Acropolis of Athens, which, while visible from every part of the city, could only be approached by a devious ascent.

Historical conditions also in some instances determined the site of a dedication; the commonest examples were the tombs of heroes and the trophies set up on fields of battle; but it was usual for the memorials of great victories to be set up not on the spot where the event had occurred, but within the precinct of some deity to whom the glory was ascribed; thus, although trophies were set up at Marathon, Salamis, and Plataea, the real memorials of the defeat of the Persians were to be found at Athens, Olympia, and Delphi.

Historical reasons for sanctity.

In a place set apart for the worship of the gods (ἱερόν), the essential thing was an altar (βωμός, ἐσχάρα) for sacrifice, and an enclosure or precinct (τέμενος); to these might be added a temple (ναός), which was regarded as the abode of the god, and contained his image or symbol. The temple was in no case regarded as a place of assembly for worshippers; they met in the temenos outside; most sacrifices too were offered at the altar which stood outside the temple, usually in front of it, though a small altar, mostly for incense or symbolical offerings, might be placed inside it. In course of time other buildings came to be added. A temple could possess property, consisting of dedicated objects, of slaves, of money in specie, of money invested, and of real property; this was administered and audited by officials appointed by the State, and we possess numerous inscriptions recording such administration, or giving inventories of the possessions of the god. From temple funds came the money expended on keeping up sacred buildings, on performing the regular sacrifices and other acts of public worship, and on the salaries of officials. A special privilege possessed by some temples was that of asylum, which often extended to a considerable distance around, as at Ephesus; this privilege was especially used by slaves to escape from the cruelty of their

Sacred places and buildings, precincts, altars, temples.

Property of temples.

Right of asylum.

Fig. 89. The Acropolis at Athens, from the S.W.

masters. Some temples were in particular repute for political offenders; for example, the temple of Athena Alea at Tegea.

418. Sacrifice, actual or symbolical, was the central and essential point of all acts of worship in Greece; prayers and hymns, curses, oaths, and purifications are all inseparable from it. We may divide sacrifice into three kinds, tributary, piacular, and mystic, though it is often impossible to draw a rigid line between them, and their signification is often confused in historic times.

3. Manner of worship; sacrifice.

Tributary sacrifice is natural as soon as worship is differentiated from sorcery, and the gods are regarded as higher powers, and on friendly terms with mankind; the tribal or national god is honoured with gifts just like an earthly king. At first sacrifice is regarded as a contribution to his actual needs; he consumes the offering, or, if it is burnt, he at least imbibes its savour; and even in a more advanced stage of thought, the notion of a pleasing service is never lost. All kinds of human food may thus be offered, whether bloodless, fruits, milk, honey, wine, etc., or the flesh of animals.

Tributary sacrifice.

Piacular sacrifice is due to the notion that if an offence is committed the god requires a life in atonement; if the criminal himself cannot be slain, then the whole people is under a curse till a substitute is found. This is not only the case with special and discovered offences, but with such constantly recurring offences or pollutions as are unavoidable, and must be atoned for by a periodical sacrifice. A survival from a primitive belief in malignant powers, which must be propitiated in order that they might leave the worshipper alone, also led to similar rites. In such cases the victim was not eaten in a sacrificial banquet by the worshippers, but was completely consumed, thrown into a sacrificial pit, or cast out, sometimes into the sea; or, in some cases, consumed by the priests only.

Piacular sacrifice.

Mystic sacrifice is not intended to please the god or to avert his anger, but to have a certain magic effect upon his personality; thus it belongs to the earliest stage of religious belief, and its original meaning is often lost or obscured in historical times. Its motive lies in the belief that the god is incarnate in some person or animal, upon whose physical vigour his activity depends; it is therefore necessary that this person or animal should not be suffered to decline gradually with age, but should be slain while in full vigour, so that his powers may be transmitted unimpaired to his successor. This notion is especially prevalent in connexion with spring or harvest festivals throughout Europe, and distinct traces of it can be found in Greece; the god who is also victim is regarded as embodying or typifying the spirit of vegetation and natural reproduction. The chief characteristics of this kind of sacrifice are mourning, often succeeded by rejoicing, on the part of the people, blood-guiltiness on the part of the sacrificer, a pretended resurrection or re-incarnation of the god, and a solemn sacramental banquet in which his flesh is eaten by his votaries; or, if the sacrifice is regarded as an atoning

Mystic sacrifice.

one, his blood is sprinkled over them. Sacrificial rites have been explained
by some modern mythologists upon totemistic principles; but as it is not
yet proved that the Greeks or any Aryan people ever had
totemism, it is safer to avoid such explanations. The victims   Totemism
or offerings proper to different gods varied from place to   doubtful for
place; as a general rule we may expect the offering of like   Greece.
to like; for instance a female victim to a female deity, a black sheep to
chthonic deities, etc.; but no universal rules can be made.
The local ritual and offerings were usually prescribed in   Appropriate
detail in each shrine, and are often recorded in inscrip-   offerings.
tions.

The proceedings at the actual sacrifice were usually the same.   First
came the preparations; garlands were worn by priests and
by the victim, whose horns were often gilded. Then it   Ritual of
was led to the altar; if it struggled, the omen was bad; if it   sacrifice.
bowed or shook its head, the omen was good. Next a bowl of water was
sanctified by plunging in it a torch from the altar, and all present were purified with it (χέρνιβα νέμειν), and the altar sprinkled. In the sacred silence
which followed (εὐφημία) came the prayers. Then came the sprinkling, on
and around the victim, of the οὐλοχύται (grains of barley) brought in a flat
basket (κανοῦν), which was therefore among the essential implements of
sacrifice. After this began the sacrifice itself; first some hair was cut from
the victim and thrown in the fire (κατάρξασθαι); then it was stunned with
an axe or club; its throat was cut, and the blood caught in a vessel, the
head being turned down for Chthonian gods, upwards for others; the blood
was poured on the altar, or sprinkled over the worshippers if the rite was
piacular. During these proceedings was kept up an ὀλολυγμός, or, in later
times, flute-playing. Then the victim was skinned and cut up; the entrails
were inspected for the purpose of divination (§ 426), and the portions
set apart for the god were burnt on the altar. Usually they were the
thigh-bones and fat, and portions of each joint, and the tail. The rest
was cooked on spits, and divided among those present.

Prayer, as an accompaniment of regular sacrifice, usually followed
a set formula known to the priest; or of course any special
petition might be introduced, especially if the sacrifice were   Prayer.
made for the purpose. When separate from sacrifice, prayer often referred
to past offerings, or was connected with a vow promising future sacrifice.
The Greek worshipper prayed standing, with his hands raised, palm
upwards, to heaven; if he addressed the gods below, he might stretch his
arms downward, stamp on the ground to call their attention, or kneel to
touch the ground with his hand; but kneeling in prayer, except with this
motive, was regarded as barbarian and unworthy of a free man. Kissing
the hand to the god (προσκυνεῖν) was not unusual. Prayer was usually
made aloud (εὔχεσθαι) unless there was some special reason for conceal-
ment. Curses (ἀραί), which are clearly only a form of
prayer, are especially addressed to the gods below; they,   Curses.

more often than other prayers, were written and attached to an image,
dedicated in a shrine, or buried; they were used as a means of private
revenge or a protection against injury, and were especially inscribed on

Oaths.

tombs. **Oaths** owe their force to the curse implied or expressed in case of their violation, and so are regularly made
over sacrifice (καθ' ἱερῶν τελείων, ἐπὶ τομίων ὀμνύναι, ὅρκια τέμνειν, etc.), the
person swearing touching the victim, the altar, or the symbol of the god;
they were the regular confirmation of treaties and of all responsible
political offices. Zeus ὅρκιος was the special president over such oaths;
but every State had its prescribed list of deities whose names made an oath
especially binding; and certain shrines were regarded as giving a peculiarly
inviolable sanction to an oath.

419. Religious observances and ceremonies entered into almost
every act of the daily life of a pious Greek. We have already

4. Times of worship.

seen that no meal was eaten without offering some portion
of meat and drink to the gods—a custom equivalent to
the modern practice of saying grace before and after meat. A special
sacrifice would be held in a private house on festival days. Sacrifice and
prayer were also necessary at the beginning of any important enterprise,
and on the occasion of any of the chief events in the course of life. Thus
birth, marriage, death, each was accompanied by its peculiar rites (see
§§ 632 ff.); and sacrifices were held at the opening of any public function,
such as an assembly, council, or law-court (εἰσιτήρια).

420. If we include all festivals, small as well as great, we shall find that
they make up a considerable proportion of the year; and

B. Extra-ordinary ritual. (a) Festivals.

most of them were probably kept as holidays; they
appear to have occupied about 70 days in the year at
Athens. The Greeks regarded these holidays much as we
regard our days of rest; thus Plato (*Laws* II. p. 653 D) says that 'the
gods, pitying the laborious nature of men, ordained for them, as a rest
from their labours, the succession of religious festivals.' The proportion of
holidays to working days was not very different from what it is with us; but
their irregular intervals and grouping together round the great festivals
must have caused them to interfere more with the routine of daily life.

Beside the division of festivals already indicated (§ 415) we may

Civic festivals.

also classify them as civic, confederate, and national. Of
civic festivals we may get a notion from our comparatively complete knowledge of the Attic calendar. The majority of these
were probably in some degree common to all Greeks, especially spring
and harvest celebrations, and others which depended on the course
of nature, though varying in their official recognition and their dedication to a particular deity. They did not however coincide in time
at various places, chiefly owing to the erratic nature of the Greek
calendar, which usually adopted some device, such as three intercalary
months in an eight-year cycle, to reconcile the solar year with the period of
twelve lunar months, and consequently often varied considerably in its

relation to the seasons (see § 630). Such devices varied from place to place in their application, and so the correspondence of the local months and their festivals varied also. Certain days of the months were observed, varying locally; thus at Athens it appears that the third and seventh days were sacred to Athena and Apollo respectively.

The Panathenaic games, which were celebrated with especial magnificence every four years, and were, if not in religious significance, in pomp and fame, the greatest of all Athenian festivals, were essentially of a civic character. The Great Panathenaea, celebrated in the third year of each Olympiad, occupied six to nine days. The great procession and sacrifice, and the offering of the peplos, took place on the 28th of Hecatombaeon (τρίτη φθίνοντος). It was preceded by games which included not only musical and athletic contests, but also warlike exercises, and competition in εὐανδρία, between the tribes. There was also a torch-race, and boat races at the Peiraeus on the last day. The prizes accorded to competitors consisted of jars of the oil of the sacred olives, varying in number from 140 to one; ornamental vases, with a figure of Athena on one side and a representation of the special contest on the other, were also given.

The Panathenaic games.

421. Confederate festivals were common in early Greece; a group of states, either connected in race or neighbours in position, joined in a common worship of some divinity, usually at a centre which had no independent political existence; well-known examples of such amphictyonies, as they were called, were those which united in the worship of Apollo at Delos, and of Poseidon at Calaureia, and the greatest of all, which met at Anthela near Thermopylae in honour of Apollo, and was afterwards transferred to Delphi. The description of the Delian festival in the Homeric hymn gives the best notion of such an assembly in early times, telling how the long-robed Ionians gathered themselves together, with their children and their wives, to celebrate in honour of Apollo contests in boxing and dancing and song. As national festivals there were four canonically recognised in Greece, the Olympian, the Pythian, the Isthmian, and the Nemean. It is very difficult to understand how these four, and no others, came to be selected for such special honour. The Pythia originated in the meetings of the Delphic amphictyony, and the famous oracle of Delphi doubtless led to their universal recognition. Olympia had a primitive shrine and oracle, and came early to be recognised as the chief centre of the worship of the Olympian Zeus in Greece. The Isthmia and Nemea probably owe their celebrity to the early importance of Corinth and Argos, which respectively presided over them. The recognition of all these four games as national or Hellenic cannot be traced back beyond the sixth century; the Olympian indeed claim an uninterrupted celebration from 776 B.C., as well as an earlier mythical origin; but the name Hellanodicae, and the recognition

Confederate festivals.

National festivals; the four great games.

of Hellenic sanction which it implies, are probably not earlier than the
seventh century; and the historical foundation of the Pythian dates only
from 586 B.C., of the Isthmian from 582 B.C., and of the Nemean from
573 B.C.   It seems likely that their recognition as a bond of union among
all of Hellenic blood was not so much of spontaneous growth as due to the
encouragement of far-seeing politicians, especially the enlightened tyrants
of Argos, Corinth, Athens, and other cities.   There is no doubt that both
by the close relation of athletic to military prowess, and by the feeling of
Hellenic unity which they fostered, they contributed very materially to the
result of the great struggle between Greeks and barbarians at the beginning
of the fifth century.

422.   These great games, though differing as to various details in the
nature and manner of their contests, were in the main conducted upon the
same principles; it will therefore suffice here to describe in more detail one
of them only, the Olympian.   The Olympic tradition, which attributed
a mythical origin to the games, and regarded any innova-
Athletic festivals; Olympia; institution of games.   tion as a revival of a forgotten practice of primitive times,
claimed continuous celebration from 776 B.C. for the stadium
alone, and stated that all the other contests had been added
to it by degrees.   The judges, who were called Hellanodicae,
were at first two in number; in later times the normal number seems to
have been ten.   The administration of the games originally belonged to
Pisa, but was transferred to Elis in historical times.   Most of the events
for open athletic competition are said to have been instituted by the
beginning of the seventh century, except the pancratium, which was not
introduced till 648 B.C.   Towards the end of the same century were
instituted the various competitions for boys.   The hoplite race was not
added till 520 B.C., and then probably with a distinct military purpose.
Four-horse chariot races were introduced in the 25th Olympiad (680 B.C.),
and ridden horses in 648 B.C.   Various other experiments, such as mule
chariots, were introduced and dropped again in the fifth century.   Colts ran
after 384 B.C.   A contest of trumpeters and heralds was introduced in the
96th Ol. (396 B.C.).

The Olympian festival was held every fourth year; the sacred month,
in which it was celebrated, was alternately the second or the
Order of celebration.   third after the summer solstice, a season when the extreme
heat must have been trying both to competitors and to
spectators.   The games themselves took place in the middle of the month,
so that the sacred truce (ἐκεχειρία) would last a fortnight before and after
them, and enable visitors to travel in safety to Olympia and home again.
Its beginning was proclaimed throughout Greece by the σπονδοφόροι,
heralds sent out from Elis.   An immense concourse gathered together
from all Greek towns and colonies; the festival was not only religious
and athletic, but afforded a fair for commerce, and an opportunity for
emulation in display among the θεωρίαι or sacred embassies sent to

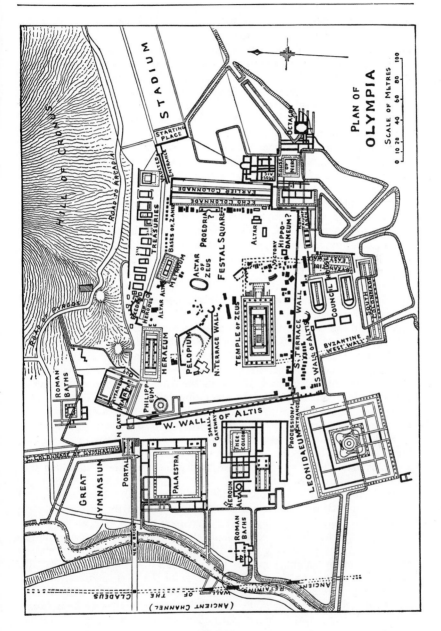

Fig. 90.

represent the various states, as well as among individuals. It gave an opportunity for the publication to as wide an audience as possible of literary productions, such as the history of Herodotus, which is said to have been read there; and also of addressing the assembled Greeks upon some topic of vital interest, as in the Panegyric orations of Lysias and Isocrates. The

The Altis at Olympia. sacred precinct of Zeus at Olympia was situated on a piece of level ground at the junction of the Cladeus with the Alpheus; it was called the Altis; since the excavation of 1876–81, its plan is completely known to us. It was surrounded by a wall with several entrances; in the southern part of it stood the great temple of Zeus, containing the gold and ivory statue of the god by Pheidias, and ornamented by the sculptures now in the Olympian museum. N. of the temple was the Pelopium, or grave of Pelops. N. of this again, just at the foot of the hill of Cronos which overhung the Altis, was the Heraeum, the most ancient of the temples that still partly survive. Near the Pelopium was the great altar of Zeus, made of the ashes of victims. Further east, on a terrace cut out of the hill, was a row of treasuries, built to testify to the glory of the various cities which dedicated them, and to hold the offerings which they made to the god. In front of them stood the Zanes, a set of statues made from fines inflicted on athletes for violation of the rules. In addition to other buildings, the whole space was filled with altars, dedications, and statues, mostly of victors, of which many of the bases still remain, and the enumeration of which occupies the best part of two books of Pausanias. At the N.E. corner of the Altis was an arched passage leading into the stadium, where the starting-place and goal of the athletes may still be seen. S. of the stadium was the hippodrome, where the chariot races took place, and all around the Altis were grouped the houses for priests and officials, and for the entertainment of official or distinguished guests, porticoes to house the crowd of ordinary pilgrims, a gymnasium for the competitors, and the prytaneum, bouleuterium, and other public buildings connected with the games. Women were not admitted to the great festival of Zeus, but had a separate one of their own in honour of Hera; a peplos was offered to the goddess, and games were held in which the competitors were girls.

A victory at the Olympian games was the highest honour which a

Qualifications, rewards and competitors. Greek athlete could desire, and formed the culmination of all his training. Every competitor was obliged to prove that he was of Hellenic parentage, that he suffered under no political or moral disqualification, and that he had undergone ten months training; in later times he had also to train for a month in the gymnasium at Elis, under the eyes of the Hellanodicae. When he formally entered as a competitor, he and his relatives had to take a solemn oath over the sacrifice of a boar-pig at the altar of Zeus ὅρκιος in the bouleuterium at Olympia that he had complied with the conditions, and would keep the rules of the contest. After this he was not allowed to

withdraw, and any unfair proceeding or breach of the rules was punished
by a fine. No official prize was given to the victors, except a crown of
wild olive (κότινος) and a palm-branch and the right to erect a statue in
the Altis.

The absence of any prizes of intrinsic value distinguished the four
great national games as στεφανῖται from others, like the Panathenaea; at
Delphi the crown or garland (στέφανος) was of bay, at the Isthmus of pine,
or earlier of parsley; and at Nemea also of parsley. But the victor's
friends and his city added to these honours many others, some of a more
substantial nature; they celebrated his victory both at Olympia and on his
return home with festal procession and song; it was for such occasions as
these that Pindar wrote the odes that have proved 'a monument more
lasting than bronze.' At Athens, the victor was awarded, by the law of Solon,
a sum of 500 drachmas and food in the prytaneum for the rest of his life;
everywhere he had the place of honour in war and peace; and, at Sparta,
the right to a place in battle near the king. Such honours testify to the
belief in early times that a victorious athlete was not only a man specially
favoured by the god in whose service he had distinguished himself, but
that his physical prowess proved his qualification for the highest services
to his country, and was a sign of the most perfect manhood. But,
about the end of the fifth century, a change came about for the worse.
It was found that the healthy and abstemious diet and
all-round development which had so far distinguished the   Decline of
Greek athlete could not hold their own, in actual contest,   athletic
against a heavy meat diet and a special training; and   honours.
from that time athletes tended more and more to become a special class,
with muscles developed at the expense of their brains. Still, the honour
given to victors was by no means omitted in later times, and the
greatest ambition of an athlete, to be a victor at all the four games
(περιοδονίκης), always remained a distinction which was held in the highest
honour.

The programme of the Olympian games is said to have been got
through in a single day in the earlier period; in later
times it was spread over five days. The stadium was the   Programme
first event to be decided, and its victor gave his name   of games.
to the Olympiad. The Olympic stadium can be exactly measured, as
the starting and finishing line are both preserved; the
length of the course is just over 210 yards; there is of   The sta-
course a free space beyond at each end. It follows that   dium; run-
the δίαυλος was very nearly equivalent to the quarter-mile;   ning.
the exact length of the δόλιχος is not known for certain; probably it
was between two and three miles. At the starting-point a line of
stone slabs was let into the ground, which contained sockets for posts,
to mark off the space assigned to each runner, and also two shallow
grooves adapted for him to get his toes into for the start; as these

two grooves are only about six inches apart, it seems clear that the Greek runner must have started with his feet close together, a position which

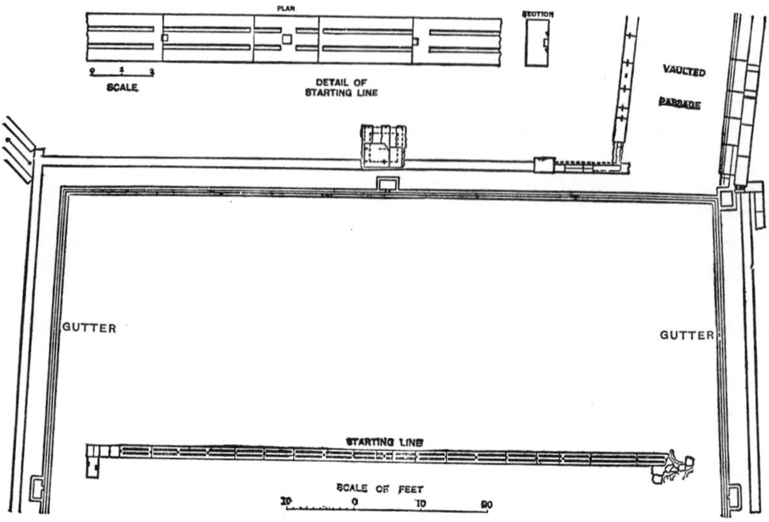

Fig. 91. Starting-place in Stadium at Olympia.

must have been prescribed in order to secure a fair start. The posts must either have served to stretch the lines along the course to divide the tracks assigned to the various competitors or else to act as guides to the runners in the broad course. No arrangement for a curved turn was found, so that it seems probable that in the δίαυλος the athlete had to turn sharply and come back after turning the post assigned to him. In the long race a different arrangement may have been made. In the hoplite race each competitor carried a shield, and it is clear from vases that the skill of the runner consisted in swinging this so as to aid his start and turn. In earlier times this contest may have been a race in full armour, and training in it may explain the Athenian charge at Marathon. It was a δίαυλος.

The pentathlon, or contest of five events (ἅλμα, ποδωκείην, δίσκον,

ἄκοντα, πάλην), consisted of contests in the long-jump,

The pentathlon. throwing the disc, throwing the javelin, running and wrest-

ling; the first three of these appeared only in the pentath-lon, while the last two existed also as separate contests. The way in which the victory in these five events taken together was decided is not recorded. In the ἅλμα, or long jump, weights like dumb-bells (ἁλτῆρες) were held in

Jumping. the hands; from the pictures on vases, the jump appears to

have been preceded by a few steps; the swing of the weights was used, as now sometimes, to assist the spring, the arms being thrown forward as the jumper took off, and swung far back before he alighted. A 'garden' (σκάμμα ; τὰ ἐσκαμμένα is probably identical, not, as L. and S. say, to be distinguished) or piece of dug earth was prepared to show the marks of the jump and to break the jar of alighting.   The use of weights is known by modern practice to increase considerably the distance that can be covered ; but it is quite inadequate to explain a record such as that of Phayllus, whose jump of 55 feet rests on no good authority.   As to the method of throwing the disc we are well informed by vase-paintings and statues, especially the copies of Myron's famous discobolus ; the competitor took his stand with the right foot slightly in   Throwing advance and the disc in his left hand ; then he transferred it   the disc. to his right, swung it back as far as possible, and discharged it by an underhand throw, bringing all the weight of the body into play, at the same time bringing the left foot forward so that his weight rested on it at the moment of throwing.   The throwing of the javelin, which was thrown either by the hand alone or by the help of a thong wound round the shaft and held in the fingers so as to impart a revolving   Throwing motion to the throw, was apparently at Olympia for distance   the javelin. only ; elsewhere throwing at a mark was also practised.

In Greek wrestling three throws were necessary for a victory (τριαγμός). It took place on prepared ground, to give foot-hold and   Wrestling. break falls (σκάμμα).   The competitors were free to get their grip as they could, and much of their skill was devoted to this object.

Boxing, in earlier times, was not considered unworthy of gods and heroes, and was practised by men of high rank ; the ἱμάντες   Boxing. μειλίχαι then used consisted merely of thongs of leather wound round and round the fists, as constantly represented on vases. These were totally different from the brutal instrument made of solid leather which was used in later times (ἱμὰς ὀξύς, μύρμηξ, Lat. cestus) when professional boxers were a special class.   The pancratium was a contest in which fighting of any sort was allowed; this and boxing went on until one of the competitors acknowledged him-   Chariot races. self as beaten.   These contests were all, probably, held in the stadium ; in the hippodrome the chariot and horse races took place.

423. Musical festivals were not usually held separate from athletic festivals, but formed a part of them.   At Olympia, indeed, the musical contests either did not exist at all or took a very   Musical subordinate position ; but in the Panathenaea, at Delphi,   festivals. and elsewhere, they formed a prominent part of the games.   There were usually four principal kinds of contest in what we should call music ; lyre playing, flute playing, and singing to the accompaniment of the lyre or flute (κιθαρισταί, αὐληταί, κιθαρῳδοί, αὐλῳδοί); to these may be added competitions between ῥαψῳδοί, men who recited the Homeric poems.   At Delphi singing

to a flute was early abolished, as being too wild and melancholy in character. The great feature of the Delphian musical festival was the Pythian strain (Πυθικὸς νόμος), which was what we should call a piece of programme music, representing in five movements the fight of Apollo and the Python, the death of the monster, and the triumph of the god. It is evident that here narrow limits were laid down within which the art of the composer and the executant (who were apparently the same) must be confined. Closely allied to these musical contests were those in choric singing and dancing, for both men and boys, which formed part of many festivals; these continued to exist in many places, side by side with the more elaborate form which had been developed from them, the drama. Of choric singing without dancing we have no record; but dancing without singing was common, as well as the combination of the two.

424[1]. Dramatic Festivals.—The most conspicuous development

Dramatic festivals.
Origin of drama.

of the drama in Greece was in connexion with the worship of Dionysus; but δρώμενα, or ritual actions, which occurred in the cult of other gods, were more or less dramatic in character; for example, in the Eleusinian mysteries. Similar customs occur in many places as a part of the magic rites associated with the year spirit, with the death and revival of vegetation, or with human activities at seed-time, harvest, vintage, or other seasons; these survive in the performances of mummers or their equivalent in many parts of Europe, notably in Thrace. Wherever such rites came to be regarded as the dramatic repetition of a myth, it was natural that they should develop into drama, and that they should be used to commemorate other myths than those originally associated with them. It was not uncommon for the participants in these rites to masquerade as animals. It is an obvious suggestion that the 'tragic' chorus originated in such a dance of goat-men; but the satyrs who form the rout of Dionysus have more characteristics of horses in early art. The origin of the various forms of play, tragedy, satyr-drama, and comedy has been the subject of endless theorising from the time of Aristotle to the present day; but the facts about the early development of these various forms are extremely obscure, and it is impossible now to trace with certainty their relation to the primitive rites or dances from which they were respectively derived. It is even uncertain how far the difference between them is essential, how far due to more or less artificial differentiation. It has been suggested that the origin of drama, especially of tragedy, is rather to be sought in the commemorative rites performed over the tombs of dead heroes, as in the case of the tragic choruses commemorating the 'sufferings of Adrastus' at Sicyon, which Cleisthenes transferred to the service of Dionysus. But even if we admit that some characteristic elements of Greek drama may be traced to such

---

[1] For the literary history of the drama see § 155 to § 164.

a source as this, it is not therefore necessary to derive all dramatic performances from it.

425. The conventional forms taken by tragedy and comedy at Athens were developed in the sixth century B.C. from local Attic celebrations which, whatever the origin of some of their ele- ments, were at that time dedicated to Dionysus; and it is this *Development in Athens.* brilliant development at Athens to which dramatic festivals owe their chief interest. The two festivals in Athens at which plays were performed were the Great or City Dionysia (Διονύσια τὰ ἐν ἄστει), about the end of March, and the Lenaea (ἐπὶ Ληναίῳ ἀγών) about the end of January. At both alike the plays were performed in *Great Dionysia and Lenaea.* the great Dionysiac theatre. The Great Dionysia formed one of the chief festivals of Athens; they were held at a time when the city was full of strangers as well as citizens, and were celebrated with great pomp and magnificence. They appear to have included a festal procession and sacrifice, and also choric dances in honour of the god; the festival of Lenaea was probably of earlier foundation, and of a similar nature, though in the days of the drama it had sunk to a subordinate position, and was only a local festival of the Athenians. Tragedies seem to have been performed in Athens before the middle of the sixth century, though their state recognition at the Great Dionysia did not take place until some years later. It is uncertain when tragedies began to be introduced into the Lenaea; it was probably not long after the middle of the fifth century; but the festival was never on the same footing as the Great Dionysia in this respect. In the fourth century and later, when it was recognised that the great days of tragedy were past, it was customary to add to the dramatic contests of the Great Dionysia, after the Satyric play, and of the Lenaea also, a revival of an old tragedy; and the new plays to be performed came to be less in number. Comedy was not adopted so soon as tragedy into the religious festivals recognised by the State. New plays were brought out both at the Lenaea and at the Great Dionysia; especially at the latter, if they were tragedies; but in the case of purely political satires, such as the *Acharnians*, the Lenaea offered an opportunity for addressing the Athenian citizens alone, without holding them up to the ridicule of their neighbours (αὐτοὶ γάρ ἐσμεν οὑπὶ Ληναίῳ τ᾽ ἀγών *Ach.* 504). New comedies continued to be produced at both festivals throughout the fourth and probably the third century, while the 'middle' and 'new' comedy were flourishing. In the second century we find that the same custom had come in as in the case of tragedy; the representation opened with an old comedy by a well-known poet, before the new ones were brought on. Such revivals were, as was to be expected, mostly from the 'new' comedy of Menander and Philemon; the 'old' comedy, with its political allusions and ephemeral jests, did not interest the later Greeks, at least on the stage.

The celebration of the Dionysiac festivals was, of course, like all other religious ceremonies, under the control of the State; the arrangements were presided over at the Great Dionysia by the Archon Eponymus, at the Lenaea by the Basileus. The production of plays, the hire of the chorus, the provision of dresses and accessories, formed one of the chief liturgies in the fifth and fourth centuries, and was discharged by the richer citizens in turn; it was called choregia, and the man who undertook it was called a choregus. After the fourth century the wealth or the public spirit of the Athenian citizens had so far decreased that the system of choregi had to be given up; the State undertook the expense of production and an agonothetes was appointed to administer it. The audience consisted of both Athenians and visitors; special places were reserved for priests and officials, the central one of the front row being assigned to the priest of Dionysus Eleuthereus. Common people had to pay for their seats, but the fee was provided by the State for needy citizens. There is no satisfactory evidence that any distinction of class or sex was made in the right of admission. It has been much disputed, on grounds of probability, whether women were admitted, especially at comedies; but the evidence seems to show conclusively that they were.

Order of celebration.

The tragic actor's dress and make up was confined in later times to a limited number of recognised types; though the descriptions we have of these are of late date, it is probable that they were stereotyped in accordance with the practice of the earlier period. All alike wore high buskins ($\kappa\acute{o}\theta o\rho\nu o\iota$) to increase their apparent stature, and huge masks with a wig surmounting a conical erection above them ($\acute{o}\gamma\kappa o\varsigma$) enclosing the whole head; their bodies were also padded in proportion. The masks and dress of comic actors were taken from ordinary life, and conformed, at least in later times, to a certain number of easily recognised types. The masks, however, in this case, were more grotesque and exaggerated in expression, even in the 'new' comedy of manners where they seem to us so much out of place.

Dress of actors.

The theatre buildings of the Greeks are known to us not only from the descriptions of Vitruvius and other writers, but also from many extant examples which, on the whole, confirm those descriptions. In no case, however, have we any satisfactory evidence of the arrangements as they existed during the fifth century, when the extant plays of the great dramatists were written. These must therefore be inferred from the evidence supplied by the plays themselves, by extant remains of later date, and by various other literary records. In the earliest times choric dances in honour of Dionysus were held on any convenient spot, usually in or near his sacred precinct. When an actor was introduced, he is said to have mounted

Theatre buildings.

Origin.

on a table or a cart so as to be visible over the heads of the chorus to the surrounding spectators. The first improvement was probably a low and rough platform or stage for the actors, and a booth (σκηνή) to serve as a dressing and property room; the stage would naturally be placed close to this booth, which would also serve as a background; and the spectators would group themselves on the further side of the dancing-place, ὀρχήστρα, which would be chosen, if possible, in such a position that a natural slope of a hill would enable a crowd to see and hear well what was going on. Such are the essential parts of a Greek theatre at all periods, though they were later given a permanent and elaborate architectural form. In early times it was customary in Athens for the actors to set up their booth and dancing-place in a part of the agora which History of the theatre at Athens. later retained the name of the orchestra; but the physical advantages of the great precinct of Dionysus south of the Acropolis soon led to its being preferred for all theatrical performances. Here an early circle of stones may still be traced, partly underneath the orchestra of the present theatre, partly under its stage buildings, which doubtless formed the border of the old orchestra on which, in the earliest period, the Attic drama was played; the booth and stage, and also the spectators' seats, were probably temporary erections of wood. It is said that the temporary structure of the theatre at Athens gave way in 499 B.C. when Aeschylus and others were competing; but the stone theatre which took its place was not completed until the time of Lycurgus, shortly before 330 B.C., so that all the plays we know must have been first performed in a temporary, or at least an unfinished theatre. The theatre of Dionysus, as completed by Lycurgus, consisted of an auditorium (θέατρον), partly cut out of the Acropolis rock, partly built on massive substructures and supporting walls. Its lines, especially in the lower part which bordered the orchestra, followed the shape of a semicircle prolonged towards the stage by tangents. It was, as in all other theatres, divided by a horizontal gangway (διάζωμα) and by staircases (κλίμακες) into wedges of seats (κερκίδες), and in the lowest row were thrones for priests and officials. Leading out of the orchestra on either side were the πάροδοι, by which the chorus entered. All that is left of the stage building is the foundation, consisting of a massive wall between two projecting towers: the space between these probably served for the erection of whatever stage or scenery was required. In later times a proscenium with a front consisting of short columns was substituted; such a proscenium is better preserved in other theatres.

At Epidaurus the theatre, designed by the younger Polycleitus in the fourth century, was a marvel of symmetry. The audi- Other Greek theatres. torium is almost elliptical in its curve, being drawn from three centres; it is well preserved, as also is the circle of the orchestra, bordered by a line of white stone. The stage buildings can be restored from the extant foundations and architectural fragments; it is, however, a matter of dispute whether they are contemporary with

the theatre; similar constructions, some of them better preserved, are found in many other Greek theatres, but none of them can be assigned with certainty to a date earlier than the second century B.C.   In all alike there was an oblong building, the σκηνή, at least two stories high, often, probably, considerably higher.   In front of this was a platform carried by a row of columns, the προσκήνιον or λογεῖον; it is usually about 12 feet high and 10 feet broad, and corresponds to the Greek stage as described by Vitruvius.   In some theatres, as at Sicyon and Megalopolis, there are indications that a wooden proscenium, probably of similar form, preceded

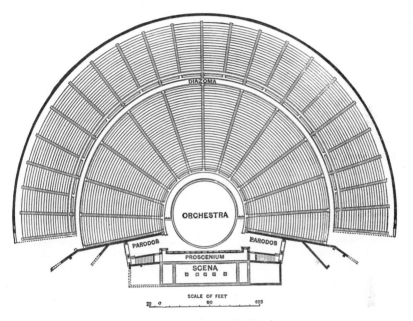

Fig. 93. Theatre at Epidaurus.

the stone one. The space between the columns was usually filled in with slabs of wood (πίνακες); and there were also, in most cases, doors leading between them on to the orchestra.   The top of the platform was approached by doors leading through the wall of the σκηνή; it was also accessible at each end, either by a door in a projecting tower (παρα-σκήνιον), a ramp, or a return of the platform round the side of the σκηνή.   These side-entrances had, both for actors and chorus, a con-ventional meaning derived from the position of the theatre at Athens; those entering from the west, on the actors' left, were supposed to come from the city or harbour, those from the east, the actors' right, from the country. Where this statement as to right and left is reversed, it is made

27—2

from the spectators' point of view. The stone σκηνή of later Greek times usually had an architectural decoration which served without modification or addition to represent the palace or other building in front of which the action took place. Illusory scene painting, such as exists on the modern stage, was not attempted; the scene painting for which Agatharchus was famous in the fifth century was probably a kind of architectural perspective which took the place later supplied by solid architecture. Changes of scene were indicated in a purely conventional manner by triangular prisms called περίακτοι, which could be turned so as to show different objects or symbols painted on their various sides. Other appliances connected with the σκηνή were the ἐκκύκλημα, a kind of movable platform or turn-table that could be revolved as a conventional manner of representing the interior of a building, the μηχανή, a sort of crane on which deities and others appeared suspended in the air, and the θεολογεῖον, a high platform for the appearance of the gods. The χαρώνιοι κλίμακες served for the entrance of infernal deities or ghosts, probably through a trap-door. It has been proposed to recognise them in the steps leading to the subterranean passages that have been found below the orchestra in some theatres; but as no such arrangement existed at Athens or Epidaurus, it cannot have been indispensable to the performance of a Greek drama.

It has hitherto been generally assumed that the proscenium served as a stage upon which the actors appeared, and that a raised stage was usual in the Greek theatre. This has, however, been disputed most cogently by Professor Dörpfeld, mainly on the following grounds:

The stage question.

(1) That a stage of such proportions, about 12 feet high and 10 feet broad, would be inconvenient and even dangerous for the actors.

(2) That actors on such a stage would be partly invisible to the nearer spectators in the lowest tiers of seats.

(3) That the extant dramas imply a ready communication, and even a possibility of actual contact, between actors and chorus, such as is precluded by a stage 12 feet high.

(4) That according to the old view the stage was at first low, then became higher in Hellenistic times, and lower again in Roman theatres; and that such a broken development is improbable.

It is accordingly suggested that the proscenium was a background, not a stage, and that the actors appeared on the orchestra level in front of it. In addition to avoiding the above objections, Professor Dörpfeld maintains that we thus obtain a continuous development. The table or cart, if it ever existed, was soon discarded, and the actors wore high cothurni instead, to raise them above the chorus. The προσκήνιον was merely an ornamental front to the σκηνή, and formed a background to the actors; the platform above it may have served as the θεολογεῖον. In the Roman theatres the actors remained in the same position, but half of the orchestra was sunk to a depth of five feet or so, leaving them on a low platform.

The objections to this view are very serious. The chief one is that it provides no adequate reason for the presence of the platform in front of the σκηνή in all extant theatres. The use of the θεολογεῖον was too rare to justify so universal an arrangement ; and, if not wanted for a stage, such a platform spoils the architectural form of the σκηνή, as representing a palace. We know, moreover, from inscriptions that its official name was not only προσκήνιον but also λογεῖον. This nomenclature also upsets the theory of continuity, for in the Roman as in the Greek theatre, the name proscenium or logeum is given to the platform, not to the ornamental front of the scena. The objections to the old view may be met as follows :

(1) A stage of similar height existed in the theatres of Asia Minor, where the actors certainly appeared, as Professor Dörpfeld himself admits, on the top of it; it cannot then be impossible for Greece.

(2) A high stage would be optically inconvenient only to the occupants of a very small number of seats, those at the ends of the front rows, probably minor officials ; and even they would lose very little of the action.

(3) The absence of communication between actors and chorus is far the most serious difficulty ; in extant plays such communication is certainly not uncommon, and it is difficult, if not impossible, to believe that the plays were written to be performed on stages such as are now extant. These, however, are all of a date much later than the plays; and it has been suggested that in the fifth century the stage was lower and more accessible from the orchestra. It must however be admitted that a stage of this description cannot be inferred from any architectural evidence. It is possible that the arrangements at Athens in the fifth century were quite different in character ; but even if the σκηνή was a temporary construction, it must have followed some conventional scheme ; for the intervals between the plays did not suffice for the erection of a special setting for each.

The raising of the stage and its separation from the orchestra is in conformity with the literary development, in which the chorus was either separated from the action of the drama or entirely suppressed. The later form of proscenium must, however, be considered in relation to the revival of earlier plays. Many of the plays in which a proximity between actors and chorus is required may never have been revived ; we have, for example, no instance recorded of the revival of a play of Aristophanes ; but when communication was necessary, we are informed that temporary steps like scaling ladders were used. Such a device may well have been tolerated in a revival of an old play.

(4) The development of the stage in the Greek theatre is continuous, if it became steadily higher. The Roman theatre need not be considered

in this connexion; it was a new arrangement to meet different conditions.

426. The second class of extraordinary ritual is that in which the essential thing is a revelation made by the god or a special exercise of his power for the benefit of the worshippers; the ceremonies practised by the worshippers on these occasions *Extraordinary ritual, (b) in manifestation.* are important not so much in themselves as for the sake of the immediate result which they produce, since the worshippers thereby acquire either a declaration of the will of the gods (Oracles of conduct), or a physical or moral change in their own nature (Shrines of healing and Mysteries).

In the most primitive stage of religion, we find various occult practices used by sorcerers and others so as to compel the gods to do the will of men; with a higher conception of the power and nature of the gods, their place is taken by the *Oracles; divination.* art of divination or soothsaying, of which the object is to find out the will of the gods, in order that men may act in accordance with it, or at least so govern their conduct as not to clash with it, in order to obtain what is good and to avoid evil. Hence it is especially employed when any calamity or plague shows the gods to be displeased, or when any project, of which the issue is doubtful, is contemplated. The foretelling of the future is often incidentally involved, but is not the essential thing. Calchas, best of seers, knew by his prophetic skill 'what is and what shall be and what was before.' There were many means of divination in Greece (μαντική); they may be divided into direct and indirect; and also into spontaneous and artificial (τεχνικόν). Direct divination comes in inspiration, usually accompanied by madness or phrensy, or in dreams; in some cases the meaning of this might be obvious, but more often it required skilled interpretation; and means are said to have been taken to induce it, such as inhaling mephitic vapour, chewing bay leaves, drinking blood, or sleeping under conditions likely to excite dreams. Indirect divination consisted in observing natural phenomena, the flight of birds and the proceedings of other animals, or in listening for chance utterances overheard. Here too the application might be obvious; but more often skilled interpretation was necessary, as it also was in the case of divination over sacrifice; both the state of the chief organs in the victim, and the manner in which the fire burned on the altar, were taken as an indication of the will of the god, and of his acceptance of the offering. One of the commonest forms of divination was by sacrifice; if the result was favourable, the ἱερά were said καλλιερεῖν, or the same verb was sometimes used of the sacrificer.

All these kinds of divination were used by the various oracles of Greece, though they might also be practised on any spot. Such oracles were numerous, though some of them came to exceed others in reputation, from the sanctity of their worship or the skill with which *Dodona.* they were administered. The best known of all were those

of Dodona and Delphi.   At Dodona the shrine seems to have been served
by the primitive and barbarous tribe of the Selli (called by Homer ἀνιπτό-
ποδες χαμαιεῦναι); the priestesses were called πέλειαι or doves.   In early
times the response was obtained by listening to the rustling of the sacred
oak-tree; later bronze caldrons were set up, which gave various sounds to
the wind; and a statue of a boy, dedicated by the Corcyreans, held in his
hand a whip with astragali, which hit against a caldron.   All these sounds
were doubtless interpreted after certain codes known to the priests.   Many
questions, written on sheets of lead, have been found at Dodona, but no
responses; they are of various nature, from questions of state policy, or of
the success of private commerce, to enquiries after lost property or a wife's
fidelity.

At Delphi the Pythia, after drinking of the sacred spring, delivered the
responses, which were recorded and interpreted by the pro-   Delphi.
phetes, who reduced the answer into hexameter verse, until
the time of Pyrrhus; later they were in prose.   The tale of the cleft and
its intoxicating vapour lacks early authority.   The influence of the Delphic
oracle was very great, owing in great degree to the skill with which it was
managed by the officials; it is not to be supposed that the whole system
was a pious fraud; doubtless the prophetes honestly attempted to make
sense and metre out of the ravings of the Pythia; but clearly a good deal of
discretion in editing was left to him.   When consulted on matters of fact
or future events, the oracle usually kept on the safe side, with the help of
obscurity or ambiguity; e.g. Κροῖσος Ἅλυν διαβὰς μεγάλην ἀρχὴν καταλύσει.
In matters of ritual or religion it was constantly referred to, and it probably
contributed in a great degree to the assimilation and systematisation of the
great mass of floating myths and customs which existed in Greece.   In
spite of a political bias which weakened its authority during the Peloponnesian war, Delphi continued to have an authority on religious matters,
which it shared with Dodona; few new departures in religion, even in
matters of detail, were taken without consulting some oracle of high
credit.

427.   Some of the places resorted to by invalids in search of health are
of the nature of oracles, and in that case cannot be rigidly   Healing
distinguished from oracles of conduct; such were that of   shrines.
Amphiaraus at Oropus and that of Trophonius at Lebadea.
In the Amphiaraeum the custom was for the person consulting the Hero
to sleep in his sanctuary on the skin of a sacrificed ram; the dream that
came to him was the response, and was interpreted by the priest.   Much
the same was the custom at Lebadea, where, however, the preliminary
ceremonies were more complicated and awe-inspiring, and where the
worshipper was let down into a hole in which he saw visions.   In both
cases the communication of the god was given to the worshipper himself
directly, not through a professional medium; this is the main distinction
from oracles such as Delphi.

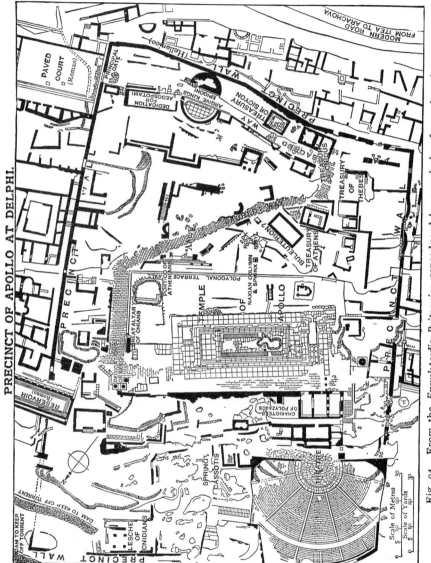

Fig. 94. From the *Encyclopaedia Britannica*, reproduced by permission from plans in *Bulletin de Correspondance Hellénique*, 1897, XVI, XVII.

Fig. 95. Delphi.

The cures worked by **Asclepius** at his especial precinct at
Epidaurus, and also at Athens and elsewhere, partake to
Epidaurus. some extent of the nature of these dream-oracles. The
patient always slept in a special building called at Epidaurus the
ἄβατον; and sometimes, especially in later times, the priestly interpretation of his dream may have amounted virtually to a medical
prescription. But in the lists of earlier cases the cure is almost always
represented as instantaneous. These lists are not contemporary with the
cures they record, but they are probably based to some extent on
dedicatory tablets and other documents, and are not entirely apocryphal.
Some surgical cases may be explained as a slight exaggeration of actual
operations; but many of the cases may well be perfectly authentic
'miracles,' such as those which are known to occur at Lourdes and at
Tenos at the present day. The cure effected usually follows the same
formula. The patient sleeps in the abaton; he sees an appropriate vision,
in which the god or one of his sacred animals, especially the snake, touches
the part affected; and in the morning he goes forth whole. An excellent, though burlesque, description of the scene in the portico where the
patients slept is to be found in Aristophanes' *Plutus*.

428. **Mysteries** were rites in which certain privileged worshippers
were admitted, after due preparation and under a bond of
Mysteries. secrecy, to certain sights and ceremonies which were
calculated to have a permanent effect on their character both on earth and
in the other world. Such mysteries existed in several places in Greece,
but the most important by far were the Eleusinian, which were imitated
elsewhere. Those of Samothrace were also of high repute. The source
from which the Eleusinian Mysteries were derived is a puzzle;
Eleusis; tradition attributed them to Thrace and to Orpheus. Like the
history of Olympian games, they are unknown to the composers of the
mysteries. *Iliad* and *Odyssey*; but we cannot imagine the Mysteries,
like the games, to be a purely Hellenic growth of later times. Their
foundation is assigned to Eumolpus, whose descendants always supplied
the Hierophant, or chief official of the Mysteries; he was assisted by
other Eleusinian officers : the Daduchi, or torch-bearers, from the family of
Triptolemus (to whom Demeter first gave the corn), the Herald, and others.
Probably in Solon's time the Eleusinia were taken into the recognised
State religion at Athens, and the Lesser Mysteries were founded at Agrae,
a suburb of the city. Under Pericles they were raised to a Panhellenic
festival, and their importance grew more and more as faith in the
State religion declined; they were especially encouraged by mystic
philosophers and others as a rival to the growing power of Christianity,
and therefore are much reviled by early Christian writers.

The first stage in initiation took place at the Lesser Mysteries at
Agrae, in Anthesterion (February); ˙in the following Boe-
Order of dromion (September) the worshipper was admitted to the
celebration. lesser initiation at Eleusis (μύησις); another year must elapse

before he was allowed full participation (ἐποπτεία).   New participants
had to be under the direction of a mystagogue.   The ceremonies of the
Eleusinia began in Athens on the 15th of the month, when the mystae
assembled at the Stoa Poecile (ἀγυρμός); on the 16th they bathed in the
sea (ἅλαδε μύσται) and also washed a pig which they sacrificed next day at
the Eleusinion at Athens.   On the 19th the great procession to Eleusis
started, and arrived after sunset.   There the mystae fasted, roamed about
the shore, and sat on the stone where Demeter mourned for her daughter
(ἀγέλαστος πέτρα).   When worked up to a state of religious excitement
by wandering in the dark and fasting, they were admitted to the brilliantly
lighted hall (τελεστήριον); then the final ceremonies of initiation were
performed, the sacred fast was broken, and the sacred drama was performed, on the nights of the 22nd and 23rd.   On the 24th followed games
and theatrical performances; on the procession back to Athens the mystae

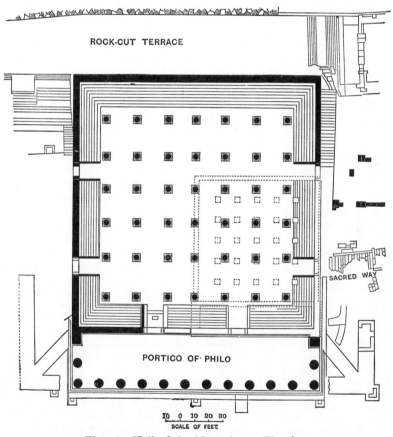

Fig. 96. Hall of the Mysteries at Eleusis.

were met by the rest of the people at the bridge over the Cephisus, and interchanged jests with them (γεφυρίζειν). Recent excavations at Eleusis

The Teles-
terion. have shown that the τελεστήριον was a great hall, surrounded by steps on which the mystae sat to observe the sights and sounds provided for their edification. As to what actually happened in the τελεστήριον, we are imperfectly informed; some have wondered that the Mysteries kept their secret so well; but in reality there probably was no secret to keep. The essential thing in the Mysteries was not the imparting of any doctrine or revelation of mystic truth, but the production of a certain mental state, induced by fasting and religious excitement, in which the partaking of the sacred food and drink, the handling of certain sacred objects, and the hearing and seeing of the sacred drama and chants (δρώμενα and λεγόμενα) made so great an impression on the excited imagination as to leave a permanent effect on the character. The drama doubtless represented scenes connected with the Great Goddesses of Eleusis, Demeter and Core or Persephone. In earlier times, as represented by the Homeric hymn to Demeter, it was probably the well-known tale of the sorrow of Demeter and her search for her lost daughter, and the return of Core. Dionysus and Iacchus were certainly prominent in the myth and ritual under Athenian administration, and in Hellenistic times the Zagreus story was introduced. The allegory of the death and resurrection of the corn, and its application to human life, was

Character
and influence
of the
Mysteries. probably never lost sight of. But what is most striking is the moral effect on the mystae, attested by so many of the greatest and most respected of classical writers, who always speak with the utmost reverence of the Mysteries though many of them are by no means slow to condemn what they think unworthy in the popular religion. In common belief, too, those who had been initiated had a happier lot after death. All the symbolism employed may not have been in accordance with modern notions of decency or dignity; but it cannot be doubted that the general impression produced on the worshippers was similar to that now attributed to the most sacred and solemn religious observances.

For Mythology and Religion:—M. P. Nilsson, *A History of Greek Religion*; H. J. Rose, *A Handbook of Greek Mythology*; A. B. Cook, *Zeus*; **Bibliography.** Farnell, *Cults of the Greek States*; Preller, *Griechische Mythologie* (4th ed., by Robert); Roscher, *Lexikon der griechischen und römischen Mythologie*; Harrison and Verrall, *Mythology and Monuments of Ancient Athens*; Frazer, *The Golden Bough*; *Pausanias*; J. E. Harrison, *Prolegomena to Greek Religion*. For Athletic Festivals:—E. N. Gardiner, *Greek Athletic Sports and Festivals*; E. N. Gardiner, *Olympia*. For the Theatre:—Haigh, *The Attic Theatre*; A. Müller, *Griechische Bühnenaltertümer*; Dörpfeld, *Das griechische Theater*; Puchstein, *Die griechische Bühne*; M. Bieber, *Denkmäler zum Theaterwesen im Altertum*; Sir W. Ridgeway, *The Origin of Tragedy*; F. M. Cornford, *The Origin of Comedy*. For Eleusinia:—Lenormant, in Daremberg and Saglio, *Dictionnaire des Antiquités*; Philios, *Éleusis*; O. Kern, *Die Griechische Mysterien der Klassischen Zeit.* For Epidaurus:—Cavvadias, *Épidaure et ses ruines.*

VI. PUBLIC ANTIQUITIES.

VI. 1. CONSTITUTIONS.

A. DEVELOPMENT OF CONSTITUTIONS.

429. THE origins of the political institutions of the Greeks are to be found in the different elements which made up the Greek race (see §§ 31 ff.). From the civilization which excavations have revealed in Crete and the islands and on the Mainland we *The earliest people.* can form some idea of political conditions. The rulers of Crete lived secure, fearing neither attack from without nor insurrection from within. Their fleets which held the seas protected their coasts, while within the islands they commanded the service of their subjects to produce great buildings, to develop to a high degree arts and crafts, to maintain peace between the great men of the land. As far as may be deduced from the material evidence, the idea of the State was triumphant over the resistance of the family unit, which retarded and at the same time strengthened the political growth of the Indo-European peoples. The dwellers in the islands lived in little towns which clustered under the shadow of palaces; their religion was of the race or state rather than of the family. The rulers were priests as well as princes. Government was almost bureaucratic, with careful accounts and regular officials. The nobles were courtiers rather than country barons; and in the little towns was found the centre of the people's social life and interests.

We have no means of judging how the Greek Mainland was ruled in Early and Middle Helladic times (see § 40) but after 1600 B.C., when the Middle Helladic people had absorbed the Minoan culture, we find the political conditions different from those of Crete. After 1400 B.C., when Crete collapsed, the palace citadels of Mycenae and Tiryns arose. Within them lived also the chief officers of state. The people dwelt in undefended communities. It was a well organized military power based perhaps on a feudal system. Roads were built and trade encouraged perhaps under monopolies. Labour was plentiful and cheap, half serf or slave, for no free labour could have piled up the great fortresses. While the Peloponnese was enjoying advanced material culture, Thessaly remained in a comparatively primitive condition, and no clear idea can be formed of its political institutions or of those of Macedonia.

430. Of the ending of this period we have no certain knowledge. The Middle Helladic newcomers (the first Aryans) about 1900 B.C. probably brought a system in which the family was all-important. In their wandering the members of a family had learnt to render absolute obedience to their head, and, when they settled down in the new land, this order continued. Moreover as newcomers they felt distinctly the bond of race which united them as much as it separated them at first from the older people. Their political life consisted of two forms of loyalty, to the head of the family and to the larger racial unit, the tribe ($\phi\nu\lambda\dot{\eta}$)—with the leader in war at its head. The incoming tribes moreover were not town-dwellers, and did not always occupy the towns of the older inhabitants but lived sometimes scattered in villages without elaborate fortifications. Even in historical times the Aetolians and some other peoples in Western Greece are described as living κατὰ κώμας ἀτειχίστους τῷ παλαιῷ τρόπῳ. The relations of the newcomers towards the older people varied according to the conditions of their settlement, but in general the older people, if they were not driven out, occupied a subject position. But from the very beginning the older people and the Indo-European newcomers began to be fused together, and there slowly arose a new form of society in which the ideas which were found strongly marked in the newer people guided the political development, while material culture was largely adopted from the older race of the mainland and islands. About 1400 B.C. the centre of power shifted from Cnossus to Mycenae which dominated the Aegean and the Levant, but at the end of the Second Millennium another people of Indo-European race entered Greece. Throughout the whole of the Aegean area there were movements of peoples, and the result of the dislocation thus caused was the collapse of the older civilization and social order, though the material culture rather waned than was extinguished. This fusion of people produced what we know as the Greek race (§ 40) and with the history of its political development begins Greek constitutional history.

The Invaders.

431. The main source of evidence for the early stages of this political growth is to be found in the Homeric poems, for the Greek Epic looks back to an Heroic Age, and this age seems to correspond to the early days when the fusion of races in the Greek peninsula was fairly complete and the political order was being developed. While the picture which the *Iliad* and *Odyssey* present is romantic in colouring, we receive from the poems a clear impression of political and social conditions. They show aristocracy established. The chiefs (βασιλῆες) settled in different districts in Greece, formed with their kinsmen a class of nobles (their rank implied in the use of such terms

Homeric Greece.

as ἄριστοι, ἀριστῆες) raised in dignity and power above the rest.   Many of
the chiefs had taken as their seats fortified castles (πόλισμα or πτολίεθρον),
which had been built for the rulers of the earlier people, and Homer
depicts a court life of wealth and lavish feasting and minstrels singing of
noble deeds.   The chiefs were foremost in battle, followed by their ἕταιροι
(who recall the *comites* of the Germans and the followers of the Macedonian kings).   Below the privileged class of chiefs and warriors come
the class called δημιοεργοί, craftsmen or small farmers cultivating their
own lot of land, and last of all the poor freemen (θῆτες) working for
hire.   Of slaves there were but few.   The heroic kingship is described
by Aristotle as heroic rule willingly accepted : the kings claimed divine
descent (διογενέες, διοτρεφέες) and were under the special protection of
Zeus.   Their powers, which included leadership in war, judgment of
disputes and mediation with the gods, were limited by the custom of
consulting other orders in the State.   Thus it was usual for the king to
seek the advice of a council, composed of certain chosen chiefs (called
γέροντες βουληφόροι though they were not necessarily old men); and the
commons might be summoned to the ἀγορά to learn the decisions or to
hear the discussions of their chiefs.   There they might express approval
or dissent by shouting, but they were powerless to alter the resolves of
their masters.   In the βασιλεύς, the βουλή and the ἀγορά we may recognise
the germs of later political authorities, magistrates, council and assembly.
The *Iliad* has for its scene the camp of an army on foreign soil in which
many princes, each the ruler of his own domain, are combined under
the leadership of Agamemnon, who enjoys a higher degree of kingly
rank implied in the titles βασιλεύτερος and βασιλεύτατος.   The *Odyssey*
represents a number of chiefs assembled in Ithaca, recognising no rule
in the absence of Odysseus and claiming equal dignity.   Telemachus
admits that in default of Odysseus another might be king, though he
claims lordship over his own estate and dependents.

The very character of the Homeric poems makes it certain that they
over-emphasise the difference between gentle and simple.   When allowance
is made for this it remains true that the idea of the personal dignity of
the freeman which has so large a part in the thought of Indo-European
races was potent from the beginnings of the Greek people.   The power of
this element was increased by the Dorian Invasion, referred to above, which,
apparently took place after the age reflected in the Homeric poems.   This
so-called invasion was the immigration of a new group of Aryan people
into the Greek world which caused much dislocation and scattering of the
Greek people. The newcomers gave a fresh vitality to the Aryan element
in Greek political life, while they destroyed or impoverished much of the
civilization which was carrying on the tradition of the older Aegean culture.
This crisis in the history of the Greeks is hidden from us, but to it is no
doubt due much of the difference which is seen when we turn from the
Greece of the Epic to the Greece of historical times.

432. When we are first able to trace the political institutions of the
Greeks at the beginning of the eighth century, they are
found to be based on organisations widespread throughout
the great mass of the people, and not limited to an aristocratic class. The most important factors in society were the sense of
solidarity of the family and the looser bond of the tribe (φυλή). In some
cases the tribes felt themselves part of a larger racial unit, thus the three
tribes of the Ἀπόδωται, Ὀφιονεῖς and Εὐρυτᾶνες were all Αἰτωλοί. The
larger national unit was called an ἔθνος, which in early times reflected rather
a distinction from surrounding peoples than any real inner organisation.
The true political boundary of the early tribal State is the point at which
the sense of the tribal bond becomes weak. Within these tribal-groups
there were families each with their headman : and one of these men was
the chieftain (generally called βασιλεύς) who led the tribesmen in war,
then almost the only business of a State. In general the βασιλεύς was
assisted by a Council of elderly experienced chiefs called γερουσία or
βουλή. With settled life in Greece and the islands smaller organisms
arose. The country of Greece is so broken up into little glens and
valleys, and the tendency to live in little villages was so strong, that
local needs and interests tended to produce smaller political unions.
Besides this the strong sense of the family-bond which the newcomers
brought with them caused a family solidarity more clearly felt than the
bond of common descent within the tribe. When both ties between prosperous and related families were sharply realised the result was a γένος or
clan; when the feeling of union rested rather on local solidarity and mutual
help in war the union took the freer form of the φρατρία or brotherhood.
These groups were not mutually exclusive, though both were usually local in
character. It must not be assumed that the larger political unit, the tribe,
was artificially built up of local units of village communities and the like.
Membership of a γένος or φρατρία bore a social meaning, the political
position of a man in the State rested on his birth within the tribe. Race,
not residence or clan-membership or brotherhood-membership, is the test.
Later Greek political speculation conceived of the primitive State as
arranged in concentric rings, beginning with the family and ending with
the tribe, but this artificial theory is not borne out by the historical
evidence. The Greeks conceived of common race as descent from a
common tribal ancestor and carried this idea of common descent into
unions where it could only be fictitious. Thus members of a φρατρία,
originally a free association for mutual help, began to regard themselves
as in a sense related and to worship a fictitious ancestor. Moreover, as
religion was to the Greeks the obvious sanction of all unions and the
Greek religion was in great measure ancestor-worship, the associations
took a religious form. Thus in the earliest days of the Greek race there
was the great political institution of the tribe (φυλή) sometimes forming part
of an ἔθνος, and the unit of the family (οἶκος), together with two forms

The Tribal State.

of association, the γένος and the φρατρία, all of these supported by the
sanction of religion and resting on real or fictitious ties of birth.

These primitive tribal communities were subject to influences, economic,
religious and military, which had varying effects in different
parts of Greece.   Many of the cities of the earlier people   Formation of
ceased to be centres of population after the great immigra-   the city State.
tions from the North.   But there were districts such as Boeotia where the
mixed race of newcomers and earlier people continued the city-life in the
old cities, and made them the home of such political life as they had.   But
throughout the greater part of the Greek world there was no real town-life.
The people lived in homesteads and villages (κατὰ κωμάς) over the face of
the country.   From the beginning however the inhabitants chose some
defensible spot where they might take refuge in sudden stress and partially
fortified it.   This place of refuge was a πόλις, and was often the seat of the
ruler of the tribal community.   In many cases it coincided with an old
town of the earlier people.   Gradually in many parts of Greece these πόλεις
exerted a powerful attraction and awoke an instinct for centralised political
life (συνοικισμός).   Where this was aided by other influences the result was
a city State in which keenly felt political association took the place of the
old dimly felt bond of race.

Thus in Lacedaemon the military need for union against the older
population, here hostile because not absorbed, led the Spartans to make
their political centre a city on the Laconian plain.   Economic reasons
were powerful in inducing the people of the Isthmus to form the city of
Corinth which grew up beneath the shadow of the old place of refuge.
A combination of causes, together with a strong political instinct led to
the formation of Athens, the greatest Greek city State.   The people of
Attica, while in great measure continuing to live scattered over the country,
made the city of Athens their place of government.   In these instances the
old tribal State based on common birth passed into the new city State
based on community of political life.   A member of the community is now
πολίτης, the man who shares in the πόλις.   This new institution found
expression in the colonies which were planted on the coasts of Asia Minor
and also in Sicily and S. Italy.   The colonists were crowded together on
the coast, hemmed in by enemies in the interior: in many cases they
were not all of one tribal stock but adventurous spirits from diverse tribes.
Thus none of the conditions of the old tribal State were fulfilled and
almost perforce the colonists formed themselves into city States.   And as
commercial intercourse became more and more common between the
colonies and the motherland, the colonies did much to quicken the growth
of the city State within Greece proper.

433.   The city States thus formed showed in a sense a renascence of
the town-life of the older people in the Second Millennium.
But there was found in them a vigorous political spirit which   Character of
was probably the heritage of the northern people.   The πόλις   the city State.

stood to the Greeks for freedom (ἐλευθερία) and the right to govern themselves as they would (αὐτονομία). As a πολίτης the Greek felt that he was a
member of the community with rights and a will of his own. That was the
principle of ἐλευθερία. By αὐτονομία was meant the right of the πόλις to
govern itself according to the will of the πολῖται; it was the extension of
the idea of ἐλευθερία in terms of the State. This right could only be
maintained by complete independence. No alien body must have the
least power over the πόλις. No form of coalition can be tolerated which
infringes the αὐτονομία of the State. The only thing which cities can have
in common is religion, for that is of the race. Such associations of States
as necessity enforced were regarded as religious associations, and thus
the complete political independence of the city State was never in theory
abandoned. This third principle, the safeguard of the other two, is the
principle of αὐταρκεία; the city must be self-supporting.

The result was that in those parts of Greece where the city State was
highly developed, the idea of citizenship, of membership of a community,
superseded the older ideas of race, or of residence. A man who lived at
Marathon or Sunium conceived of himself as a citizen of Athens rather
than as a man born of Attic parents within the borders of Attica, or as an
inhabitant of a particular village. It was now the common citizenship and
not the common ancestor in which the bond of union was found. The
head of the city State might still be a chief (βασιλεύς), his authority might
still rest on membership of some ancient family which seemed to be half-
divine. But the idea of the city State rested on the will of man; the
πόλις was to the Greeks a projection of the will of the πολῖται, and it soon
became clear that a πόλις could exist without a king. The tribal State, on
the other hand, needed a tribal head, for to the Greeks it appeared a family
on a large scale and the Greeks could not conceive a family without a single
personal head. For all these reasons Greek constitutional history is in the
main the history of the city State, which rested on the will of the πολίτης
guided by the rival or complementary tendencies of aristocracy, oligarchy
and democracy.

434. But there were large parts of Greece which either did not
develop a city State or retained much of the more primitive tribal institutions. Thus Elis remained through most
of the Classical period a tribal state. The Eleans were
immigrants and conquerors surrounded by people of the older race who
retained partial independence and among whom the Pisatans formed a city
State at Pisa. There was not sufficient reason, military or economic for
centralisation, for the subjects were not capable of rebellion and the country
was given over to agriculture and pasturage. Thus in the valley of 'Hollow
Elis' there remained an old-fashioned tribal State, the central point of which
was the great sanctuary at Olympia—a religious but not a political capital.
The true bond of union was a strong racial feeling which was reflected in
the dialect of the country which clung tenaciously to its northern character.

Survivals of the tribal State. Elis.

There were local units called δᾶμοι which had grown out of the need for some kind of local control, most probably for the management of common pasturage, but it was not till the fifth century B.C. that these δᾶμοι were correlated by any kind of strong central government.   At first the Eleans had been content to be led by a king, but monarchy was superseded by a kind of agricultural oligarchy of the men powerful in the δᾶμοι.   The social organisations of the old tribal State flourished in full vigour.   The free brotherhoods appear as πατριαί, the clans as γενεαί.   All free-born Eleans were fully privileged citizens; whoever was by birth ἀνὴρ ϝαλεῖος belonged to the community.   If he held any position of authority he was τελεστά, otherwise he called himself ϝέτας.   Had it not been for the fact that all Greece came to Olympia for the festivals, Elis might have remained for ever untouched by the political progress of the city States.   But there gradually grew up some of the forms of democracy and in the fifth century a kind of city State.

In Thessaly, where northern immigrants ruled over an earlier people whom they had reduced to serfs (πενεσταί) the country was **Thessaly.** divided by the mountain ridges into cantons (Thessaliotis, Pelasgiotis, Hestiaeotis, Phthiotis), and these formed tribal communities bound together by common race.   In general the cantons were quite in-dependent of each other, but important decisions affecting the whole of Thessaly were referred to a gathering of all free Thessalians (οἱ Θετταλοί, τὸ κοινὸν τῶν Θετταλῶν).   Also in time of war the Thessalians united their forces under a generalissimo (ταγός), appointed till the crisis was past by the whole people.   Thus in general Thessaly presented the ap-pearance of a tribal State of the old type.   But within the cantons there were cities, most of them the townships of the old people, now occupied by the conquering race.   These cities were self-governing, with a political life apart from the organisation of the cantons in which they were situated. Here then was presented the singular phenomenon of active city States planted like islands among the usually dormant institutions of the tribal cantons.

435.   In the position of the ταγός and τὸ κοινόν of Thessaly is seen a union of tribal communities.   Such unions were not so **Forms of** easily formed among city States jealous of their independ- **Union** ence.   But there are cases where, despite the formation of **between** cities, a sense of race kept alive a shadowy kind of union. **States.** Thus in the Argolid in the seventh century there was a league of cities united in the worship of Apollo Pythaeus, based on the sense of Dorian solidarity.   This league had no political capital, and broke up as the various city States developed their political life.   So too in Arcadia, where there was a mixture of city States such as Tegea and Mantinea with small tribal communities such as the Παῤῥάσιοι, a racial union existed which found a religious centre in the sanctuary of Zeus Lycaeus.   There was here too an early federal coinage but no definite political union. In Boeotia

28—2

also there was from early times a league of cities with a religious centre at
Onchestus. By the sixth century the political federation of the country
was definitely realised under the leadership of Thebes. This federation
was forcibly broken up in the fifth century but reconstituted after 445 B.C.
In the Oxyrhynchus fragment of a lost historian (§ 170) is an account of
the constitution which had been developed by the beginning of the fourth
century. The federal principle is shown systematically applied on a logical
basis of representation. The cities of Boeotia, some with smaller places
dependent on them (χώρια συντέλη), were divided into eleven units of
government (μέρη). Thebes and her dependencies formed four μέρη,
Tanagra one, Orchomenus and Thespiae, each with dependencies, two.
Other units were formed by the combination of three smaller States. Each
μέρος appointed one federal governor (Βοιωτάρχης), and contributed an
equal number of councillors and dicasts, equal contingents of troops, equal
taxes to the federal government. Political privilege rested on a property
basis. The chief organ of government was the Federal Council (κοινὸν
συνέδριον) of 660 councillors. From Thucydides (v. 38) we should assume
that this body was divided into four βουλαί on the principle applied to the
government of the single States (§ 438). The federation was broken up by
Sparta for a short time but was revived after Leuctra on a democratic basis.
Thebes was the place of meeting of the sovereign assembly (δᾶμος) and
from its general preponderance had a dominant position in the league.

436. Though the tribal State persisted in backward parts of Greece
and some cities united in federations, the main political
progress of the Greeks was shown in the development of
the independent city State. The formation of cities was associated both
as cause and effect with the institution of aristocratic government. The
transition to aristocracy meant nothing more than the transference to the
class of nobles of the sovereignty hitherto entrusted to one of their number.
Hence the change did not of necessity involve any break of continuity, it
was often gradual and, as the title of βασιλεύς might be retained for the
chief magistrate, it was sometimes imperceptible. In some cases special
causes contributed to lessen the kingly power. As kings were appointed
to lead in war, their failure in the field, or even an interval of peace
might weaken their authority. City life, which brought the nobles
together and fostered political discussion, must have had the same
effect, and in particular the union of smaller communities to form
cities abolished the monarchic powers of petty chiefs, who were compensated by the position assigned to them on an aristocratic Council.
Though the united State might still have a kingly head, his power was
modified by the rights gained by the nobles. Whatever the cause of
the transition to aristocracy, the constitutional changes involved were
neither many nor important. The king, if his privileges were not
entirely abolished, shared his power with others and became a magistrate
responsible and liable to render account. It was an essential consequence

Aristocracy.

that the Council should gain importance, for it was in the Council that the nobles expressed their will. On the other hand the commons usually suffered by the institution of many rulers in place of one, and the Assembly in an aristocracy rarely enjoyed serious consideration. Power became centred in a class; the nobles alone had a knowledge of law and religion; they were divided into clans (γένη) (§ 432) and this organisation generally served as the basis of political divisions. Sometimes the nobles married only within their own order, as Herodotus tells us of the Bacchiadae at Corinth. The land was held in great part by the ruling class, and in many States the possession of a lot of land was a necessary qualification for privilege. As special forms of aristocracy may be noted the aristocracy of the kingly family (as at Corinth and in some of the colonies), the aristocracy of landholders (as the γαμόροι at Syracuse), the aristocracy of knights (ἱππεῖς in Colophon, ἱπποβόται in Chalcis), the aristocracy of the conquering race (as in Sparta).

437. Aristocracy succeeded to the hallowed prescription which monarchy had enjoyed, but it could not permanently withstand the general progress of the race. The commercial activity of the Greeks, due in part to their expansion over the Aegean, and the introduction of money as the medium of exchange (see § 584) had political effects. Men of the lower classes rose to wealth and yet were excluded from the government. On the other hand the small farmers and labourers became indebted to the great landowners, and under the harsher application of the laws of debt forfeited their lands or their freedom. Thus great inequality of property resulted; and the nobles, who still strove to keep power in their hands, administered the laws, the krowledge of which was the secret of their class, in their own interest. A period of political ferment ensued; the social and political disorder called for reform or revolution. In some States lawgivers (αἰσυμνῆται) were appointed to revise and to publish the law (as in the seventh and sixth centuries B.C. Zaleucus at Locri, Pittacus at Mytilene, Draco and Solon at Athens). In many instances they broke the exclusive privilege of aristocracy, wealth took the place of birth, and the characteristic principle of oligarchy was introduced. Often, however, the discontent was so deeply seated that more violent remedies were required. The oppressive government of the nobles or the rich, the concentration of landed property in a few hands, and the consequent impoverishment of the peasants, the exclusion from all privileges of the artisans and traders, prepared the way for ambitious men to seize the tyranny.

In Greece tyranny began early in the seventh century, and the last tyrant was overthrown before the end of the sixth century (Hippias of Athens, 510 B.C.): but tyranny lingered later in some of the eastern and western colonies, where also it was revived in the fourth century. The Greek conception of a tyrant was that of a man ruling without law or responsibility, with a view more to his own interest than to that of his subjects. It was not essential to the idea that he should use his power

harshly or oppressively; later ages, reflecting on the evils of unconstitutional rule, associated with the early tyrants a character that was often un-
deserved. Some tyrants rose from the unprivileged classes, as Cypselus at
Corinth and Orthagoras at Sicyon; more of them were discontented nobles.
All gained their position by demagogic arts, by championing the people
against the nobles or the oligarchs. Their sway rested on force: they
were usually attended by a bodyguard, often employed mercenaries and
sometimes raised large armies and engaged in foreign wars. Generally the
constitution was suspended and the government was administered by the
tyrants. They used their power to break the ascendancy of the former
ruling class by banishment and taxation, while they fostered, to some
extent, the interests of the commons by colonies, great public works and
the encouragement of trade and industry. Tyrants were greatly influenced
by the progressive tendencies of the age: they broke with the past and
introduced innovations: they favoured new religious cults, in their desire
to break down the old worships of the nobles: they sought the sanction
and support of the great shrines, such as Delphi and Olympia. They
maintained brilliant courts, where artists, poets and painters were welcomed:
architecture and lyric poetry owed much to their patronage. The dominions
of their States were increased by colonies and foreign conquests. For
many reasons tyrannies were usually of brief duration: tyranny had no
prescription, the tyrant gained his position by his own efforts, maintained
it by force and put down opposition with violence. The Greek instinct
for lawful government resented such a negation of constitutional forms:
and the repeated expulsion of Peisistratus shows that even a paternal and
benevolent administration could not reconcile the citizens to usurpation.
The tyranny at Sicyon, it is true, lasted for a hundred years, but in most
places tyranny was of brief duration. In some States oligarchy was
restored. In others the liberal tendencies of tyranny had emancipated
and educated the lower classes and prepared the way for democracy.

438. Oligarchy, in its widest sense, is the government of a minority.
Most of the oligarchies of Greece made wealth the qualifica-
Oligarchy.
tion for political rights: but some States restricted privilege
to birth. Thus in Thessaly (§ 434) the different towns were governed by
predominant noble families, a narrow form of oligarchy called δυναστεία.
In Sparta, as in Crete, compliance with the course of training (ἀγωγή)
was required from those who were entitled by birth to citizenship. The
oligarchies of wealth varied in the assessment required and in the number
admitted to privilege. The constitution based on the hoplite census,
such as was instituted at Athens after the fall of the Four Hundred, differed
little from a moderate democracy and was sometimes denoted by the term
πολιτεία. The oligarchy of fixed number limited privilege to a definite
number of citizens, who themselves elected fresh members in case of a
vacancy occurring. The constitution of the Five Thousand, projected at
Athens but not realised, would conform to this type: and constitutions
of a Thousand existed in several of the colonies. Of the government of

the oligarchies we know but little.   Generally speaking the chief power
was vested in a Council (βουλή, γερουσία) composed of men who had the
highest qualifications of birth or wealth, appointed in some cases for life.
The cities of the Boeotian federation (§ 435) were governed by four βουλαί,
membership of which depended on a property qualification.   Each of them
in turn had the preliminary consideration of business, but the ultimate
decision rested with all the βουλαί, acting collectively.   In oligarchies
generally the magistrates, subordinate and responsible to the Council, were
entrusted with greater power than was usual in democracies and sometimes
enjoyed a longer tenure.   In States where an Assembly existed as a separate
institution it usually had a restricted competence.

439.   Democracy was the government of the people (ὁ δῆμος) in which
the many (οἱ πολλοί, τὸ πλῆθος) exercised political rights and
in which the voice of the majority was decisive.   Democracy   Democracy.
was of gradual development and varied with the qualifications required for
full citizen rights and with the powers directly entrusted to the people.   In
the moderate form all citizens were admitted to the Assembly, but a
property qualification was required for office, and the Assembly was limited
in its functions to the election of magistrates, the exercise of certain
judicial powers, and the decision of certain important questions.   In the
more advanced forms all free men of citizen descent had practically the
same privileges.   The principle of equality was asserted in the admission of
all citizens to most offices (some usually required a money qualification), in
the application of the lot to the less important offices, and in the provision
of pay for public services.   The cardinal principles of democracy were thus
equality (ἰσότης, ἰσηγορία, ἰσονομία) and liberty (ἐλευθερία) manifested in
the freedom of life and conduct, which was greater in democracies than
in oligarchies.   In the organisation of government the Assembly (ἐκκλησία)
was the most important element, and exercised a constant control over
administration and policy.   The direct powers thus entrusted to the
majority made oratory important and gave opportunity to the demagogues,
one of whom assumed a leading position as the champion of popular
rights (προστάτης τοῦ δήμου).   Usually the Assembly had not itself powers
of legislation, the ultimate decision on changes of law being reserved to
the law courts; and the democracy was then regarded as a government
under the reign of law.   Other powers also were, of necessity, delegated.
The preparation of business for discussion by the Assembly, the administration in detail, and in part the execution of the measures adopted by the
Assembly were left to a large popular Council (βουλή).   Democracy tended
to weaken the executive, except in the case of military magistrates.   Powers
of administration were subdivided among a number of officials, appointed
by lot, who were subject to popular control and responsible at the end of
their term.   The law courts were regarded, equally with the Assembly, as
the normal sphere for the exercise of collective power by the people.   Hence
their action was not subject to the revision of the Assembly: they were

regarded rather as the means by which the other elements in the State, including even the Assembly, might be compelled to act in accordance with the laws and to observe the principles of the constitution. But the popular constitution of the large jury courts disqualified them for the proper discharge of this function: they tended in fact themselves to override the laws, until there resulted the degenerate democracy, described by Aristotle, in which the many are sovereign and not the law. Of the character and development of democratic institutions Athens, as the leading democracy, forms the best example; and of democracies in other States we have little detailed information.

440. With the establishment of democracy at Athens began the conflict of oligarchs and democrats, not only between States, but between factions within single States, as in the signal instance of Corcyra. Sparta and Athens, the two great powers of Greece, opposed in character, policy and constitution, favoured and protected States in political sympathy with themselves, and sought by supremacy or confederation to advance the political principles which they professed. The overthrow of Persian rule and the rise of Athens to empire promoted the cause of democracy, and before the outbreak of the Peloponnesian War the States of the Delian confederacy were with few exceptions democratic, as the allies of Sparta were with equally few exceptions oligarchic. The war was, in great measure, a struggle between democracy and oligarchy. The decline of Athenian power in the Aegean was followed by the revolt of many allies and the institution of oligarchies in many States: and Lysander used his final victory to establish narrow oligarchies of his partisans (δεκαρχίαι) throughout Greece. With the reaction after Cnidus and Leuctra democracy regained ground, and for the time the accession of Thebes strengthened the democratic cause, but after the Social War many States of the Aegean reestablished oligarchy. If we may believe the philosophers, both democracies and oligarchies intensified their characteristics, and the extreme forms (ὀχλοκρατία or δημοκρατία ἐσχάτη and δυναστεία or ὀλιγαρχία ἄκρατος) were common. In Sicily the 'new tyranny' arose, a military government, based on military necessities, and in Thessaly, Epeirus and other backward States of Greece certain chieftains established a similar government. In Macedonia, where the vague powers of the king recalled the heroic monarchy, Philip established a domination which united his own land and brought Greece to subjection. The Macedonian monarchs were indifferent to the war of constitutions in the Greek States, but political considerations sometimes caused them to establish oligarchies or tyrannies in their own interest. The break-up of Alexander's kingdom resulted in the establishment of great monarchies, more or less oriental in character. Within Greece Macedonian ascendancy was maintained by tyrants in the different cities; to oppose this subjection, the smaller States sought to gain strength by uniting in confederations, and in the Achaean and Aetolian leagues something resembling federal govern-

Later development of Constitutions.

ment was developed. These leagues lasted until Greece was absorbed in the Roman Empire, after which time the Greek States lost their political importance and enjoyed little more than a municipal independence.

B. ATHENS: HISTORY OF THE CONSTITUTION.

441. Athens and Sparta are the only States of whose constitutions we have a detailed knowledge. Athens pursued a more normal course in the development of her government. Sparta was, in many respects, different in type from the other States of Greece and maintained her old institutions with a rigid conservatism.

The early history of the Athenian constitution is legendary. The Athenians, who counted themselves as belonging to the Ionian stock, claimed to have been undisturbed in their land, and it is probable that Attica escaped conquest by the invaders from the north. The early legends reflect the *Legendary history of Athenian Constitution.* gradual union of Attica, which was originally divided into a number of independent townships, under the sway of different families. Some of these communities combined in religious leagues, and with the name of Cecrops is associated the union of the inhabitants in twelve πόλεις. We may assume that at some early time smaller communities were grouped round fortified centres, each with its own government of chieftain and council, and that all recognised some common bonds of kinship, although the πόλεις were so far independent as to make war on each other. Ion, who was called in to help the Athenians, was said to have introduced the four Ionic tribes. If, as is probable, each tribe had a local unity, this measure further promoted the union of Attica. The different πόλεις were now grouped in four tribes (φυλαί), of which each was ruled by its φυλοβασιλεύς, while all recognised the authority of a single chief, whose seat was Cecropia, the original city of Athens. The final union of the country (συνοικισμός) was ascribed to Theseus, who put down the separate governments of the different πόλεις, induced the nobles to settle in Athens, and made that city the capital and seat of rule. Theseus was said to have divided the people into three classes, Εὐπατρίδαι, γεωμόροι (also called γεωργοί, ἀγροικοί) and δημιουργοί; classes which probably existed before in the separate πόλεις, and assumed political importance in the new constitution.

442. The four tribes into which the Athenians were divided, Γελέοντες, Ἀργαδεῖς, Αἰγικορεῖς and Ὅπλητες, were found in other Ionian states. Whatever the original meaning of the names we can trace no difference of privilege between the tribes, and pro- *Tribal organisation.* bably at an early date all Athenians were admitted to membership of them. Each tribe was divided into three φρατρίαι. The grammarians preserve traditions, which cannot be accepted, that there was a fixed number of γένη, thirty to each φρατρία and even a fixed number of members in each γένος. It is probable that the γένη and φρατρίαι (which had their origin in kinship) formed religious unions, at first open only to Eupatrids. But at some time before Solon the other classes seem to have gained admission, and the members of the γένος (γεννῆται) included both the original Eupatrid members (ὁμογάλακτες) and those admitted to share in the rites of the γένος (ὀργεῶνες). These conclusions are disputed; in any case the early social organisation was aristocratic; and political privileges were dependent upon birth.

443. Of the government in early times we have no detailed knowledge. According to the legends, the kingship, which gradually established its sway over Attica, was not strictly hereditary. Its powers were modified by the institution of other officers and by the συνοικισμός attributed to Theseus, by which the Eupatrids settled in Athens as a privileged class. The traditions of the transition from monarchy to aristocracy are not consistent. Aristotle who in some cases based his account on inferences from later institutions, says that the polemarch was appointed (on the coming of Ion) to share the duties of the king. The βασιλεύς still continued to be the head of the State and was chosen from the family of the Medontids. Later (according to the traditional chronology in 1090 or 1070 B.C.) the ἄρχων was appointed. At first all these magistrates were chosen for life, later in 753/2 their tenure was limited to ten years and in 683/2 to one year. Lastly the board of six θεσμοθέται was instituted, six magistrates, chosen like the rest from the rich Eupatrids, 'to record the judgments.' The nine magistrates did not form one college until a later time. The division of power among several magistrates of limited tenure led to the establishment of aristocracy. The Council, which met on the Areopagus, was composed of ex-magistrates sitting for life. It had vague and extensive authority, appointed the magistrates, directed all important matters of administration, exercised a censorship over the citizens, watched over the laws and exercised such judicial functions as were not expressly left to the magistrates. From the great powers thus entrusted to the Council, and from the influence which a body of ex-magistrates sitting for life must possess, we may assume that, as usually happened in aristocracies, the government of the State was centred in the Council. Of other magistrates the κωλακρέται were probably an early institution and the ναύκραροι are mentioned as existing in the seventh century.

Early government.

444. Naturally the nobles ruled in the interests of their own order and the classes excluded from the government were oppressed and discontented. The economic changes of the seventh century led to distress and injustice. Most of the land was held by a few rich men; the smaller landowners had fallen into debt and had mortgaged their land, while the poorer peasants were cultivating the land of the rich, and default in payment of the rent reduced

Draco and Solon.

them and their families to serfdom, as the debts were secured upon their
persons[1]. Meanwhile a commercial class must have arisen, excluded from
all share in the government. These elements of social and political discontent, and the divisions and rivalries between the great houses prepared
the ground for a tyrant. After the attempt of Cylon (between 636 and
624 B.C.) the nobles felt obliged to make concessions, and in 621 Draco
was appointed lawgiver. Aristotle (*Ath. Pol.* 4) describes an elaborate constitution as the invention of Draco. This is in conflict with his statement
in the *Politics* that Draco only drew up a code of laws, and on other
grounds it is doubtful whether the Draconian constitution should not be
regarded as the invention of a later age. It is described as entrusting
power to all hoplites, it anticipates in many institutions the work of Solon,
and contains arrangements of a complex and artificial character, which
seem unsuited to a primitive polity. In any case Draco drew up and
published a code of laws but made no attempt to heal the social disorders.
The necessity for drastic reform was as great as before, and in 594/3 B.C.
Solon was appointed διαλλακτὴς καὶ ἄρχων, with full power to relieve the
social distress and revise the constitution (§ 437). His social reforms
(σεισάχθεια) cancelled debts and thus cleared the land from mortgages and
set free debtors from serfdom; others, who had been sold as slaves, he
ransomed from abroad, and he enacted that for the future no one should
be allowed to pledge his liberty. Solon then proceeded to reconstruct
the constitution. There had already arisen three military classes of ἱππῆς,
ζευγῖται and θῆτες. He defined limits for membership of these in produce
of corn, oil and wine from their land, and further marked off from among
the ἱππῆς a first class of πεντακοσιομέδιμνοι. Only members of the first
three classes were eligible for offices of State, only members of the first
class for the highest offices. The Thetes, who were exempt from hoplite
service, were admitted to the Assembly and the Law Courts, but had no
other privilege. Aristotle attributes to Solon the appointment of magistrates by a combination of lot and election (κλήρωσις ἐκ προκρίτων). This
is difficult to reconcile with other evidence and with other parts of Aristotle's
narrative, and in itself it seems improbable. Solon instituted a new βουλή of
Four Hundred. The Assembly had the decision of war and peace, and
perhaps of some other important questions. Solon introduced the right of
appeal (ἔφεσις) from the sentence of the judicial magistrates to the law
court, and this was regarded as his most important democratic institution.
The people probably conducted the εὔθυναι of the magistrates (§ 453) in
the Assembly or the law court. The Council of the Areopagus was left in
possession of its extensive powers to watch over the laws and the constitution, to supervise the administration and to exercise a censorship over the
citizens. The Athenians remained as before divided into four tribes. Repealing
the laws of Draco with the exception of those relating to homicide (§ 491),
Solon drew up a comprehensive code of laws and founded the system of

---

1 They were called ἐκτήμοροι. There is a conflict of evidence and opinion as to
whether they paid one-sixth or five-sixths of the produce as rent.

private law. He encouraged trade by altering the system of weights, measures and coinage.

445. Solon was often regarded as the founder of democracy and he first gave political rights to the Thetes, but privilege was proportioned to wealth and the aristocratic organisation of the State left great influence with the nobles. His work was a compromise, which left most

Peisistratus. citizens discontented. Faction ensued, based on the local divisions of plain, shore and hill men (πεδιεῖς, πάραλοι, διάκριοι). Each of these divisions was headed by an ambitious noble and the field was open to a tyrant. After three intervals of anarchy Damasias, archon in 582, endeavoured to make his office into a permanent tyranny. On his fall ten archons were appointed, five from the εὐπατρίδαι, three from the γεωμόροι and two from the δημιουργοί. The disorders of the State continued until Peisistratus, the champion of the poor hill men, made himself tyrant in 560. Tyranny lasted, with two interruptions, until 510. After his second restoration Peisistratus established his power and ruled with a wise moderation. The constitution was not changed, but the tyrant took care that the chief offices should be held by his friends. He relied on the support of the commons and his reign was celebrated as the age of gold. He promoted agriculture, undertook great buildings, introduced new religious cults and festivals and secured the support of poets for his dynasty, and extended the power of Athens in the Aegean. Hippias succeeded his father in 527, and after the assassination of Hipparchus became a harsh and suspicious despot, until the Alcmaeonidae, who had been exiled by Peisistratus, gained the support of Sparta and overthrew the tyranny.

446. In the confusion which ensued Cleisthenes, the Alcmaeonid,

Cleisthenes. adopted the cause of democracy, triumphed over his rivals, and in 508/7 B.C. was given authority to revise the constitution. The tyranny had broken the power of the nobles and thus prepared the way for democracy, but the laws of Solon had in great part fallen into disuse. The aim of Cleisthenes was to give free play to the democratic elements in the constitution of Solon, to prevent the domination of the nobles or the usurpation of tyrants. To effect this end, he took measures to abolish the political importance of the old divisions of φυλαί, φρατρίαι and γένη based upon birth, and to substitute new artificial divisions, so arranged as to obviate the possibility of local factions. He enrolled the citizens in ten new tribes, which superseded the four Ionic tribes for political and administrative purposes. Further the whole of Attica was divided into thirty τριττύες, ten of which included the city and its neighbourhood, ten the coast and ten the interior. Each tribe was composed of three τριττύες, chosen one from each of these sections. Each τριττύς contained a number of townships (δῆμοι)[1]. Both tribes and demes had their own officers and administered their own affairs (§ 452).

[1] There is reason to doubt the statement of Herodotus (v. 69) that there were a hundred demes in all, ten to each tribe. In later times the number was certainly larger.

The tribes served for military purposes, each furnishing contingents of infantry and cavalry; and in the administration of the State, magistrates, appointed in general to form boards of ten, were appointed one from each tribe or one for each tribe. Solon's Council of Four Hundred was increased to Five Hundred, and fifty members were chosen from each tribe. A revision of the roll of citizens (διαψηφισμός) is said to have been carried out after the overthrow of the tyrants. Cleisthenes extended the bounds of citizenship by the admission of metics and freedmen. Ostracism (§ 460) was introduced to guard against tyranny (though within twenty years it was employed to remove politicians who had no designs against the constitution). It is possible that Cleisthenes made other changes of which we have no record. Aristotle tells us that in 501 the generals were chosen one from each tribe, and the organisation of the board of ten generals (under the chief command of the polemarch) may have been the work of Cleisthenes. The measures of Cleisthenes succeeded in breaking the power of the great families and of local factions, while the new tribes and demes encouraged the citizens to play their part in political life. But the constitution, based on the support of the middle classes, retained many restrictions on full democracy. Property qualifications were required for the higher offices and the Council of the Areopagus still exercised wide powers of control.

447. The victory over Persia, the rise of Athens as a power at sea, her relation to the confederacy at Delos, and the general development of trade and industry strengthened the force of democracy. In 487/6 a combination of lot and election was introduced for the appointment of the archons. This change must have greatly diminished the power and importance of the archons, and it may have been the occasion for the transfer of the chief command to the generals, who in the first half of the century ceased to be tribal officers and became the most important magistrates in the State (§ 456). The Council of the Areopagus was assailed in 461, and its powers were transferred to the Council of Five Hundred, the Assembly and the Law Courts. The γραφὴ παρανόμων may have been instituted to give to the law courts the duty of controlling legislation: in any case the popular dicasteries gained in power and importance: and, as the dicasts were recruited from all classes, it was natural that Pericles should institute pay for them. The democratic principle of payment for public duties, which tended to equality of privilege between rich and poor, was applied also to the Council, to many of the magistrates, and to citizens serving in the army and fleet. In other ways provision was made for the poorer citizens by the system of cleruchies (§ 548), and by public distribution of corn. In 458/7 the archonship, which had since Solon been opened to the second class, was opened also to the Zeugitae (the fourth class were never formally admitted to the office, but in later times their disqualification was ignored). It is possible that the introduction of the lot, without preliminary election of candidates, for the administrative (but not for the military) offices

dates from this time. All citizens were thus given an absolute equality of chance, though δοκιμασία (§ 453) was applied to exclude the incompetent. In some respects aristocratic traditions were maintained: men of family filled the boards of generals and played a leading part in politics; and in 451/0 those who could not show descent from citizens on both sides were excluded from citizenship. Pericles, at last left unopposed in the direction of policy and elected general sixteen years in succession, obtained so complete an ascendancy in the State that Thucydides describes the government as the rule of one man. With his death the conditions were changed: men of less ability and of lower social position competed for the favour of the people; the war intensified feeling, and political life became more violent and more vulgar. Cleon, the most prominent of the new demagogues raised the dicasts' pay to three obols, and was probably responsible for the tyrannous raising of the tribute in 425 (§ 513). After the disaster at Syracuse a reaction set in against the democracy. In 413 ten πρόβουλοι were elected to supersede, in part, the democratic Council. They prepared the way for the oligarchy of Four Hundred, instituted in 411 and overthrown after a few months' rule. For a brief time a government of mixed democratic and oligarchic elements, with the franchise limited to those who could serve as hoplites, held sway, but in 410 full democracy was restored, and boards of συγγραφεῖς and ἀναγραφεῖς were appointed to revise the laws. After the disastrous end of the war, the oligarchs with the support of Lysander procured in 404 the appointment of thirty legislators (συγγραφεῖς), who, neglecting the purpose of their appointment, established a reign of terror, which caused them in later times to bear the name of the Thirty Tyrants. They were overthrown by the democratic exiles and democracy was restored under the mediation of the Spartan king in 403. The archonship of Eucleides in this year marks an era. The revision of the laws then undertaken most probably involved the introduction of some institutions, which cannot be traced before this date, and the constitution, as revised, lasted without serious change until Athens lost her independence.

448. There is no doubt that in the fourth century the constitution, which was supposed to be a democracy, ruling in accordance with law, became relaxed in its working; that in the age of Demosthenes the people exercised an absolute power in the Assembly and the law courts. The principle of dividing the State revenues among the citizens was extended by the introduction of pay for the assembly and the increase of the theoric distributions (§ 512). The jealousy of the sovereign people was shown by the constant control of the magistrates exercised in the Assembly or the law courts. The responsibility of the individual citizen was enforced by the γραφὴ παρανόμων. The power of oratory increased; the demagogue and the professional accuser (συκοφάντης) gained in importance, while the citizens, disinclined for military service and relying on professional generals and mercenary armies, were not ready to make the efforts which the pursuit of an independent and

The constitution in the fourth century.

consistent policy demanded. Hence Athens fell inevitably before the organised strength of Macedonia.

449. The Athenians, after Chaeronea undisturbed in their government, provoked interference by revolt. Antipater occupied Munychia with a garrison and limited the franchise to those who had not less than two thousand drachmae. Twelve out of twenty-one thousand lost their political right. In *Athens under the Macedonians and the Romans.* 319 B.C. the Athenians rose and restored democracy, but next year they surrendered to Cassander, when the franchise was limited to those having not less than one thousand drachmae. Demetrius Phalereus, entrusted with the control of the city, allowed the forms of democracy to remain but instituted the important board of seven νομοφύλακες, who controlled the Council and Assembly as well as the magistrates, whose number and importance were diminished. He also reformed the judicial system and superintended the finances. In 307 Demetrius Poliorcetes delivered Athens and restored her democracy, but in 295 he found it necessary to control the Athenians by garrisons. Athens made several attempts to recover her freedom, and in 229 with the help of Aratus she got rid of the Macedonian garrisons, but refused to join the Achaean league, seeking support from Egypt, Pergamum and Rhodes. The relation of Athens with other powers was reflected in the honours paid to foreign monarchs. In 307 two new tribes were created called Antigonis and Demetrias, in honour of the Macedonian king and his son. It was probably after the liberation of Athens that a thirteenth tribe, the Ptolemais, was instituted in honour of the Egyptian king. When Rome took up arms against Macedonia in 200 the Athenians abolished the Antigonis and Demetrias, but instituted a twelfth tribe, the Attalis, in honour of the Pergamene king. Almost from the first the Athenians declared for Rome, and in 146 B.C. Athens became an autonomous *civitas foederata.* Her independence was however little more than municipal, and, though the forms of the democracy survived, Rome, provoked by the accession of Athens to Mithradates and later to the cause of Pompey, strengthened the aristocratic elements in the constitution. The στρατηγὸς ἐπὶ τὰ ὅπλα absorbed the powers of all the generals and, with the chief archon, ranked as an eponymous magistrate. His duties were connected with the peaceful administration of the State, the corn supply and the studies of the ἔφηβοι. The archons ranked as the highest officials. They were elected, and even foreigners such as Domitian and Hadrian held the office of ἄρχων ἐπώνυμος as a mark of honour. Four ἐπιμεληταὶ τῶν δικαστηρίων presided over the judicial administration. The Council (whose numbers varied at different times from three hundred to seven hundred and fifty) was appointed by lot. It was superseded in importance by the Areopagus, which, recruited from the elected archons, had an aristocratic character and was entrusted with wide powers. From the time of Hadrian an imperial curator (λογιστής) superintended the finances. The shadow of the old constitution lingered on and Archons and Areopagus survived the fall of the Roman Empire.

C. ATHENS: THE CONSTITUTION IN ITS DETAILED
ORGANISATION.

Aristotle's systematic account of the constitution ('Αθηναίων πολιτεία cc. 42 ff.) refers to the Athens of his own day, and our knowledge of constitutional details is generally fuller for the fourth century than for any other period. The following account deals therefore with the constitution in its fullest development, though many of the institutions doubtless dated from the reforms of Cleisthenes, and much that is said will therefore apply equally to the fifth century.

450. Besides citizens, the population of Athens included resident
Metics.　　　aliens and slaves (§§ 534 ff.). The resident aliens (μέτοικοι) were encouraged to settle in Athens, on account of the part which they took in trade and industry, and the service which they performed in the fleet. A metic had to register himself with a citizen as his προστάτης, who, in some degree, represented him in the law courts, and otherwise protected his interests. The metic paid a special tax of 12 drachmae a year (μετοίκιον), and was liable also to the taxes which fell upon citizens, to the εἰσφορά indeed at a higher rate. He might by special privilege be ranked with the citizens for purposes of taxation (ἰσοτελής) or even be granted the right, otherwise restricted to citizens, of owning land and houses in Attica (ἔγκτησις γῆς καὶ οἰκίας). The metics were liable to military service.

451. Citizenship was derived by birth or creation. Foreigners who
Citizens.　　had deserved well of the State might be given citizenship by vote of the Assembly (ποιητοί, δημοποίητοι). Citizenship by birth in the strict theory of the constitution required descent from citizen parents on both sides. This condition, relaxed in practice at different periods, was asserted by laws enacted or revived on several occasions, when a revision of the citizen roll (διαψήφισις) in accordance with this principle was carried out. The child was at an early age enrolled in his father's φρατρία. In his eighteenth year he was admitted to his father's deme and then enrolled in the ληξιαρχικὸν γραμματεῖον. For two years he ranked among the ἔφηβοι and went through a course of military training under the discipline of elected officers (σωφρονισταί and κοσμηταί). In his twentieth year he was enrolled on the πίναξ ἐκκλησιαστικός and entered on the full rights of citizenship (ἐπιτιμία), so far as these did not depend on conditions of age.

452. The old corporations, superseded politically by the reforms of
Religious and political corporations.　Cleisthenes (§ 446), continued to exist for religious purposes. The Ionic tribes, four in number, each headed by a φυλοβασιλεύς, retained a ceremonial character. The φρατρίαι, in which all citizens were enrolled, headed each by a φρατρίαρχος, held assemblies (ἀγοραί) and passed decrees. More important was the political

organisation of the State in demes and tribes. The demes were local divisions of the city or the country districts of Attica; some bore place-names (as Acharnae, Eleusis, Marathon), others patronymics (as Butadae, Cothocidae). Originally the residents in each deme were enrolled as members (δημόται); but as membership was hereditary a man might belong to a deme in which he did not reside. Men owning property in demes to which they did not belong were called ἐγκεκτημένοι and paid a tax ἐγκτητικόν. The deme had its own magistrates, of whom the δήμαρχος was the most important, and its assembly (ἀγορά), which maintained local cults, passed decrees and administered its property. The demes served also for various purposes of State: they formed the units from which the men for the army and the fleet were raised, and candidates for membership of the βουλή were chosen from the demes in proportion to their population. The demes were combined in thirty Trittyes, and each tribe (φυλή) was composed of three Trittyes. From the time of Cleisthenes to the year 306 B.C., there were ten tribes, which were named after Attic heroes and arranged in the following order: Erechtheis, Aegeis, Pandionis, Leontis, Acamantis, Oeneis, Cecropis, Hippothontis, Aeantis, Antiochis. Other tribes were instituted at later epochs in honour of foreign princes (§ 449). The eponymous heroes had their temples and special cults. The tribes were entrusted with self-government: at the head of each tribe were the ἐπιμεληταὶ τῆς φυλῆς, elected every year, who controlled the administration, managed the property with the aid of a ταμίας, and called assemblies of the tribe (ἀγοραί). These assemblies passed decrees, appointed χορηγοί and γυμνασίαρχοι, and elected magistrates such as τειχοποιοί and ταφροποιοί, who superintended the share of the public works that fell to each tribe. The tribes were important political divisions: the Council was formed of ten πρυτανεῖαι, one from each tribe, almost all magistrates formed boards of ten, appointed one from or one for each tribe. Each tribe supplied contingents of cavalry and infantry, commanded by φύλαρχοι and ταξίαρχοι.

453. The organs of government were the Magistrates, the Council of Five Hundred, and the People (exercising its power in the Assembly or the Law Courts). The principles of democracy were realised in the general rules affecting the magistrates. With few exceptions the administrative magistrates were appointed by lot and for a single year and a second appointment to the same office was forbidden. The multiplication of magistrates ensured at once the admission of a large number of citizens to office and prevented the officials from becoming too powerful. The control of the executive by the people was enforced by the scrutiny of candidates before they entered on their duties (δοκιμασία), by the review of their conduct while in office (ἐπιχειροτονία), and by the strict audit and account to which they submitted on retiring (εὔθυναι). The generals and other military officers, certain of the more important financial officers as well as the

Magistrates in general.

officials of the tribes and demes, were appointed by vote (χειροτονητοί or αἱρετοί), the rest were appointed by lot (κληρωτοί). Magistrates were appointed in the early spring, and entered office at the beginning of the Athenian official year in July. The interval allowed time for the δοκιμασία, which, in the case of the archons, took place first before the βουλή, then before a law court, and, in the case of other magistrates, before a law court only. The scrutiny was partly concerned with the formal qualification of the candidate, but it was open to any citizen to bring an accusation against a candidate and secure his rejection. On entering office the magistrates took an oath. During their term magistrates were liable to be suspended and deposed. At the κυρία ἐκκλησία of every Prytany (§ 460) a vote on the conduct of the magistrates was taken (ἐπιχειροτονία): if the vote were unfavourable (ἀποχειροτονία), the magistrate was suspended and brought to trial. On retiring from office all magistrates had to render account of any funds administered by them as well as to submit their official conduct to review (λόγον καὶ εὐθύνας διδόναι). The officials concerned with this examination were the λογισταί, συνήγοροι and εὔθυνοι, each board ten in number and appointed by lot. The magistrates had to receive their discharge from a jury court, where the process must have been summary and in most cases formal, but the λογισταί might lay a specific charge against them or any citizen might proffer an accusation, in which event a regular trial took place. Most of the magistrates formed boards of ten, and it was probably usual that one of their number should act as president (πρύτανις), whether by rotation or by special appointment. Subordinate officials, such as treasurers (ταμίαι), secretaries (γραμματεῖς), and heralds (κήρυκες), were attached to most boards. To enforce their authority and punish offences within their own sphere of duty magistrates generally were qualified to impose fines to a limited amount (ἐπιβολὰς ἐπιβάλλειν) or to bring the accused directly before a law court in which they presided (§ 482).

454. For the offices appointed by lot a preliminary selection was first

The Archons.

made by lot in each tribe among those who offered themselves as candidates, and from the men thus chosen the final appointment was made by lot. To provide for the death of a candidate or his possible rejection at the δοκιμασία reserve candidates were chosen (ἐπιλαχόντες). Of the administrative magistrates the nine archons were first in dignity and importance. With the secretary of the Thesmothetae they formed a board of ten and were chosen one from each tribe. At the end of their term they became members of the Council of the Areopagus (§ 459). Collectively they took part in the appointment of magistrates by lot and the allotment of dicasts to the δικαστήρια. For the most part the duties of the Archon, the King, the Polemarch and the Thesmothetae were separate, and were mainly judicial or religious. The chief archon (ὁ ἄρχων) was the formal head of the State, his name serving to date the year in muster rolls and decrees. He conducted the

Great Dionysia and some other festivals, assigning choruses and appointing χορηγοί. His judicial duties were connected with the law of the family (§ 482). The King (ὁ βασιλεύς) was the religious chief of the State, superintending the Mysteries, the Lenaea, and the torch race. His judicial duties included cases of a religious character and he presided over trials for homicide (§ 491). The Polemarch (ὁ πολέμαρχος) had lost his position as commander-in-chief. He conducted certain ceremonies and sacrifices, and presided over lawsuits in which non-citizens were concerned (§ 482). The duties of the six junior archons (οἱ θεσμοθέται) were exercised collectively and were almost exclusively legal or judicial. They had a general superintendence over the law courts, and they presided in many public and in some private trials (§ 483), and they were concerned with the revision of the laws.

455. The Eleven (οἱ ἕνδεκα), chosen one from each tribe with a secretary, were police magistrates, having jurisdiction over malefactors and looking after the prison. The duties judicial and administrative of the minor magistrates (all *Other administrative magistrates.* of whom were arranged in boards of ten) are sufficiently implied in their names, ἀστυνόμοι, ἀγορανόμοι, μετρονόμοι, σιτοφύλακες, ἐμπορίου ἐπιμεληταί. Of magistrates appointed to control public works (ἐπιστάται τῶν δημοσίων ἔργων) five ὁδοποιοί and ten ἱερῶν ἐπισκευασταί were appointed by lot, while the more important office of superintending the water supply was held by one man (κρηνῶν ἐπιμελητής) elected by the people, as were such extra-ordinary officers as the ἀποστολεῖς, who superintended the despatch of a fleet, σιτῶναι, who purchased corn for the State in time of famine, and the ζητηταί, commissioners to undertake a special inquiry, such as were appointed after the mutilation of the Hermae.

For religious duties there were many boards of magistrates such as the ἱερεῖς, the ἱεροποιοί and ἀθλοθέται, the ἐπιμεληταί τῶν μυστηρίων and the ἐξηγηταί, as well as many menials *Religious magistrates.* attached to the different temples.

For the financial magistrates see § 518.

456. The most important officers in the State were the ten generals (στρατηγοί). Appointed originally to command the contingents of the tribes, they were elected by the tribes, but when, *Military magistrates.* in the fifth century, the chief command passed to them from the polemarch they were elected from all the citizens, but with such regard to the tribes that there were rarely two generals elected from the same tribe. It does not seem likely that there was any regular division of duties or difference of rank between them in the fifth century, although it was usual for the assembly to nominate particular generals for each expedition and to determine which of them should hold the command-in-chief. The superior power thus given is implied in the phrases ὁ δεῖνα τρίτος... αὐτός or ὁ δεῖνα καὶ οἱ συνάρχοντες. Further one general might be given a position which raised him above all his colleagues (στρατηγὸς δέκατος αὐτός). Occasionally extraordinary powers were conferred on generals, which enabled them to act independently of their colleagues, or, to some extent, of the Council and Assembly (αὐτοκράτορες). It is thus obvious that there were means within the constitution of conferring great executive power on a magistrate, who gained the confidence of the Assembly. Pericles and Alcibiades are both described by Thucydides as entrusted with full power in the State. At some time in the fourth century a division of duties was introduced, and when Aristotle wrote, five of the generals had specific functions, the στρατηγὸς ἐπὶ τὰ ὅπλα holding the first place on the board and commanding on active service.

The normal powers of the generals were at all times great and extensive. They were not merely commanders-in-chief, they controlled the military and naval administration, provided for the defence of the land and the provisioning of the city. They conducted the levy, nominated trierarchs and superintended the raising of the property tax, and presided in suits connected with these duties as well as in trials for military offences. As the chief magistrates they took a prominent part in negotiations and in the ratification of treaties with other States. They had a right of access to the Council and could submit motions to be brought before the Assembly (γνώμη στρατηγῶν). They could get extraordinary meetings of the Assembly summoned by the prytaneis, and in all Assemblies they could claim precedence for their proposals. Subordinate to the generals were the ten ταξίαρχοι, each commanding the infantry contingent of his own tribe. Below them ranked the λοχαγοί. The cavalry was commanded by two ἵππαρχοι, with φύλαρχοι and δεκάδαρχοι subordinate to them. The ships of the fleet were each assigned to a trierarch, a rich citizen called upon to undertake the duty, who prepared the ship for service and commanded it in war (§ 516).

457.   The Council from the time of Cleisthenes contained five hundred
The Council of the Five Hundred. members, and its full official title was ἡ βουλὴ οἱ πεντακόσιοι. Every citizen over the age of thirty was eligible, but no one might serve on the Council more than twice. The councillors were appointed by lot, fifty from each tribe, and were so chosen that the demes composing each tribe had a number of candidates proportionate to their population. The Council was thus representative of the different districts of Attica, and the balloting for candidates in small communities like the demes left room for intrigue on the part of those who desired a seat on the Council. Reserve candidates were chosen (ἐπιλαχόντες). The councillors designate submitted to a δοκιμασία before the old Council: in case of rejection an appeal to the law courts was allowed. The councillors entered office just before the beginning of the official year and took an oath. During their term they were exempt from military service and received pay; and on leaving office they were individually liable to render account (εὔθυναι).

The numbers of the Council made it desirable to have some smaller body which would always be accessible. Hence the fifty councillors of each tribe formed standing committees (πρυτανεῖαι), each acting for a tenth of the year in an order settled each year by lot. The members (πρυτάνεις) met every day in the θόλος; they received foreign envoys, despatches from officials or foreign States, and informations of serious offences. They prepared business for the Council, and, by means of a written πρόγραμμα, summoned both Council and Assembly. A president (ἐπιστάτης τῶν πρυτάνεων) was chosen by lot every day to hold office for a single day and night, during which time he remained in the θόλος with a third of the prytaneis chosen by himself. He kept the keys of the State treasury and archives and the State seal, and in the fifth century he was the actual president both in Council and Assembly, the prytaneis helping to maintain order. In the fourth century a change (first traceable in 378/7 B.C.) was introduced. Before every meeting of either Council or Assembly the ἐπιστάτης τῶν πρυτάνεων drew by lot from the councillors of the nine tribes not forming the prytany nine πρόεδροι, who maintained order, brought forward business and counted the votes in the Council or Assembly. From their number one was chosen as president (ἐπιστάτης τῶν προέδρων). The Council, summoned by the πρόγραμμα, met on all days that were not festal or unlucky, usually in the βουλευτήριον. The sittings (ἕδραι) were usually public, but private citizens (and magistrates other than the generals) could only address the council if introduced or called upon to do so.

458. The Council had extensive powers, deliberative, executive and administrative, but alike from its constitution and from its real subordination to the Assembly, its independent authority was not great. As a deliberative body it pre- **Powers of the Council.** pared all business for consideration in the assembly (προβουλεύειν), and it was unconstitutional for any business to be submitted to the vote of the people, before it had been discussed in the Council and formally entered on the πρόγραμμα. As an executive body it had a limited power of fining and could pass decrees of honour, but the Assembly, after deciding on a course of action, often delegated the execution to the Council, which appointed special commissioners for the purpose. The administrative powers of the Council were most important. Aristotle asserts more than once that the Council shared with the magistrates the general administration of the State. It exercised some control over the magistrates, especially over those who had public monies ·in their hands ; it took part in the δοκιμασία of the archons and of the candidates chosen for the new Council. It looked after the building and the repair of the fleet, reviewed the cavalry, inspected public buildings, and took a most active and important part in financial business (§ 517). In the sphere of religion it had the supervision of sanctuaries, festivals and ceremonies. It gave audience to foreign envoys and swore to treaties and alliances. In the fifth century it was concerned also with the control of the Delian confederacy. It took part in legislation (§ 462), and it had certain judicial

functions (§ 489). Certain officials were appointed by the Council from its own members to discharge special duties, ten λογισταί to receive the accounts of magistrates in every prytany, a γραμματεὺς τῆς βουλῆς, and in the fourth century a second γραμματεὺς ὁ κατὰ τὴν πρυτανείαν, responsible for the drafting and inscription of decrees and the keeping of the archives, and two ταμίαι to look after the funds of the Council.

459. The Council of the Areopagus, officially termed ἡ βουλὴ ἡ ἐξ Ἀρείου πάγου, was composed of ex-archons, admitted on passing their εὔθυναι, and subject to a δοκιμασία before the Areopagus. Archons during their year of office seem provisionally to have been allowed seats on the Council. The members sat for life, but were liable to εὔθυναι. The sittings of the Council were private. In earlier times it had important political powers, which were taken from it by the reforms of Ephialtes and Pericles; it retained a certain supervision in matters of religion and important judicial duties (§ 491), and it was sometimes commissioned to conduct judicial investigations in the case of grave crimes (as after Chaeronea and in the affair of Harpalus). At particular crises it was given political authority, as at the end of the Peloponnesian War. From the end of the fourth century its powers were gradually extended, and in the time of the Roman supremacy it was an important organ of government.

The Council of the Areopagus.

460. The Athenian people (ὁ δῆμος, τὸ πλῆθος τῶν Ἀθηναίων) exercised a direct sovereignty. Administrative and executive functions were of necessity delegated to magistrates or Council, but both authorities were jealously controlled. The powers of the Assembly (ἐκκλησία) were indeed limited by the law courts, which exercised a final decision on changes of law and a power of revision over the decrees of the Assembly (§ 461): but this was no derogation from the supremacy of the people. For the dicasts were regarded not as magistrates but as citizens assembled for special duties, acting as irresponsibly as in the Assembly but with different procedure. With this qualification the Assembly had unlimited powers, and settled matters of policy or administration by discussion and vote. The decision of war, peace, treaties and alliances, the election of generals and other military officers, the assignment and despatch of forces, the conduct of military operations, the raising and the apportionment of funds, were all within its province.

The Assembly.

All citizens of age and in possession of their civic rights were qualified to take part in the Assembly: usually only a small proportion actually attended, composed in the main of the poorer classes living in or near the city. Four regular meetings were held in each prytany and extraordinary meetings (σύγκλητοι) were called, when they were required. In the fifth and fourth centuries B.C. the Pnyx was the usual meeting-place, except for νόμοι ἐπ' ἀνδρί, for which the ἀγορά was used. The meetings were summoned by the prytaneis, who for the ordinary meetings published a πρόγραμμα five days before. Extraordinary meetings were called in emergencies by a trumpeter. Six ληξίαρχοι, assisted by thirty συλλογεῖς τοῦ δήμου, controlled the attendance. Pay for the Assembly was introduced, probably early in the fourth century : at first one obol, it was soon raised to three, and in Aristotle's time it was actually one and a half drachmae for the κυρία ἐκκλησία and one drachma for the other meetings. At the first Assembly of each prytany (κυρία ἐκκλησία) the ἐπιχειροτονία of magistrates took place (§ 453), the provisioning and security of the State was considered, and formal notice of certain judicial proceedings was given. The business of the other three ordinary meetings was also prescribed.

The Assembly opened with sacrifice and prayer : the presidents brought forward the business on the πρόγραμμα. On each question the προβούλευμα of the Council (§ 458) was read out by the herald. The προβούλευμα might contain a definite proposal, might offer alternative courses or might serve simply to introduce the business for consideration. A preliminary vote (προχειροτονία) was taken to decide if the προβούλευμα should be accepted as it stood or discussed. If it were not immediately accepted the herald asked τίς ἀγορεύειν βούλεται; Naturally the proposal of the Council would find advocates, but anyone could propose to reject or amend it, or could make counter proposals. All proposals had to be put in writing. It was also open to a citizen to bring forward some subject which had not been considered by the Council. If the Assembly approved, the subject was referred to the Council, which was directed to prepare a προβούλευμα. When the discussion was concluded, the citizens voted by show of hands (χειροτονία). At the conclusion of the business of the day the Assembly was dissolved, in rare cases it was adjourned until the next day. In case of unfavourable signs from heaven (διοσημίαι), earthquakes, eclipses or even rain, the session was suspended. For νόμοι ἐπ᾽ ἀνδρί (ὀστρακισμός, εἰσαγγελία, ἄδεια and grant of citizenship) a quorum of six thousand was required, and voting took place by ballot. In the κυρία ἐκκλησία of the sixth prytany every year a vote was taken whether recourse should be had to ostracism. If the Assembly so decided, in the eighth prytany an extraordinary Assembly was called in the ἀγορά, when the citizens wrote on potsherds the name of the man they wished to ostracise. If six thousand voted in all, the man against whom a majority of votes was cast had to leave Athens for ten years. Although the preliminary vote was taken every year in the time of Aristotle, the last instance of ostracism recorded is that of Hyperbolus in 417 B.C.

461. Besides the purely judicial functions of the dicasts (§ 487) they had other duties, which, if judicial in form, had great consti-   Constitu-
tutional importance. Their control over the magistrates by   tional position
δοκιμασία, ἐπιχειροτονία and εὔθυναι has been already men-   of the law
tioned : they were also the ultimate authority in legislation.   courts.
Further, it was a principle of the constitution that the decisions of Council or Assembly should conform to the laws of the State, and so far as they did not do so they were liable to be quashed. The γραφὴ παρανόμων, the safeguard of the constitution in the fifth as well as in the fourth century,

could be brought against any law or decree, on the ground that it conflicted with some law still in force. The citizen bringing the suit made a ὑπωμοσία, which had the effect of suspending the force of the law or decree until the trial, which took place before the court of the Thesmothetae. Aristotle tells us that a law could be attacked merely as inexpedient, but, even in the case of decrees, although the legality of the form or substance was the issue, it was impossible to exclude arguments based on expediency, and the widest license was allowed in practice.

462. The Assembly was competent to pass decrees (ψηφίσματα), which must conform to the existing laws (νόμοι), but a special
Process of legislation. procedure was adopted for legislation. In earlier days lawgivers such as Solon and Cleisthenes were appointed to draft reforms, which were presumably accepted by the Assembly. In the fifth century legislative commissions (συγγραφεῖς) were, on occasion, appointed to frame proposals, which were then referred for ratification to the Council and Assembly. In the fourth century we find a formal and elaborate procedure in force, the clearest idea of which we gain from Demosthenes *in Timocratem* §§ 20—33. Once a year in the κυρία ἐκκλησία of the first prytany (which was always held on the 11th Hecatombaeon) the laws were passed in review (ἐπιχειροτονία νόμων). If any laws were challenged and if the assembly voted provisionally for reform, definite proposals were drafted by the citizens interested, published (with a copy of the existing law) and handed in writing to the γραμματεὺς τῆς βουλῆς to be read to the Assembly. At the fourth assembly of the prytany, after consideration by the Council, the Assembly voted for the appointment of νομοθέται, who seem usually to have been a thousand in number and were chosen by lot from the dicasts. The assembly appointed five σύνδικοι to defend the existing laws. With the νομοθέται, presided over by πρόεδροι with an ἐπιστάτης, as if they were a deliberative body, the final decision lay. After speeches on both sides the πρόεδροι put the question whether the old law should stand, or the new law supersede it (διαχειροτονία), and the vote of the majority decided the issue. Even if the new law was carried, it was liable to the γραφὴ παρανόμων, not merely on grounds of informal procedure, but even on the broad issue that it was inexpedient. Apart from the proposals of private individuals, it was the duty of the Thesmothetae every year to see whether there were contradictions or other anomalies in the existing laws, and if they so determined, to propose and publish amendments, which were submitted in the same manner to the vote of the νομοθέται.

D. THE SPARTAN CONSTITUTION.

463. While Athens presented in her constitution a type of rapid and complete development, Sparta was celebrated for her conservative adherence to old traditions. Secluded from the rest of Greece, untouched by the influences which elsewhere produced Hellenism, Sparta maintained for centuries her primitive order. Her institutions, based on the domination of a conquering race, had some parallels in other States: in some respects, and above all in her long continuance of the military system and of her empire, Sparta was unique. While other Greeks admired the stern consistency of her traditions, they knew little of her constitution in its working, and as Sparta had no literature, we have to rely on the vague idealisations of writers like Xenophon and Plutarch, corrected by the less favourable account of Aristotle in the *Politics*.

The legends traced the origin of the State to the invasion of the Dorians, a hardy race of warriors from the north, who *History of* conquered the previous inhabitants. The struggle was *the constitu-* protracted, until in the eighth century B.C. the conquered *tion.* were reduced to submission and the rulers concentrated themselves in Sparta, an unfortified city in the plain of the Eurotas, from which, as from a camp, they ruled their dominions and extended their conquests. Tradition from the time of Herodotus made Lycurgus the author of the constitution. Diverse accounts of his descent and of his date have led some modern writers to disbelieve in the reforms or even the existence of Lycurgus, but it is not improbable that in the long struggle the Dorians found in Lycurgus a leader who reorganised their military power, perhaps introduced their peculiar system of training and society (κόσμος), and adapted their existing polity to the necessities of sovereignty over a subject population. Plutarch quotes the so-called ῥήτρα, which Lycurgus is said to have received from Delphi. It is an archaic ordinance, which enumerates the different elements in the Spartan constitution, the ἀρχαγέται, γερουσία and ἀπελλά, and asserts the sovereignty of the δᾶμος. Two changes were ascribed to the reign of Theopompus (*c.* 750 B.C.): the first, by an addition to the ῥήτρα, diminished the powers of the Assembly by giving the kings and the Senate power to set aside any 'crooked' decision of the people: the other instituted the ephors, but this tradition is doubtful, and their origin is attributed by Herodotus to Lycurgus. Archaeological evidence shows an arrest of culture and the introduction of a fixed and ordered system of life which culminated by the middle of the sixth century and followed a military reorganisation. With this may be associated the rise to importance of the ephors (§ 469). These institutions survived unchanged long after they had ceased to correspond to the real forces or needs of the State: and to this cause we may trace the rapidity of Sparta's fall, after the first impulse was given.

464. The division of classes was a result of the original conquest. The

Classes of
population.
Perioeci.

population consisted of Σπαρτιᾶται, the ruling class, περίοικοι, a class free but in political subjection, and Εἵλωτες, serfs attached to the soil (§ 532). Foreigners were hindered from settling in Lacedaemon by ξενηλασίαι, and bought slaves were rare. The perioeci, who must have far outnumbered the Spartiates, dwelt in the small towns of the uplands and coast districts of Laconia and Messenia. Besides cultivating their own land they carried on trade and industry, which were forbidden to the Spartiates. They served in the Lacedaemonian armies as heavy armed troops, and in the fleet, and were sometimes entrusted with the command of divisions. They paid tribute from their lands to the kings (βασιλικὸς φόρος), and though they were probably left free in the administration of their towns they had no political rights, and were subject to the arbitrary control of the ephors (who could put them to death without trial), and perhaps also to the supervision of Spartan officials called ἁρμοσταί. Their feelings towards their rulers tended to an increasing dislike and disloyalty.

465. The ruling class bore the name of Σπαρτιᾶται to distinguish them

Spartiates.

from their subjects, while οἱ Λακεδαιμόνιοι (used sometimes to include Spartiates and perioeci) denoted the State. Originally the Dorian invaders had taken possession of the fertile plain of the Eurotas, and are said to have divided it in lots (κλῆροι). Plutarch's statement that there were after the conquest of Messina nine thousand lots, is the invention of a later time (§ 527). The lots, which were cultivated by Helots, formed at once the privilege and the qualification of citizenship: for the revenue from his κλῆρος enabled the Spartiate to contribute to his mess and perform his duties in peace and war. The sale of the lot was forbidden. The theory of the State implied equality of property among the Spartiates, but from early times there were rich and poor among the citizens, and the law forbidding the possession of gold and silver was broken and ignored. It has been thought that there was a class of nobles, but the καλοὶ κἀγαθοί (§ 467) seem to have been men superior in dignity rather than privileged by birth. Citizenship required, besides descent from citizens, participation in the system of training and contribution to the messes (§ 471). Those who fulfilled these duties were called 'peers' (ὅμοιοι), while those who failed to do so and lost their political rights seem to have been called ὑπομείονες. The division of the citizens is obscure. It is usually assumed that the Spartiates were divided into the three Dorian tribes (Ὑλλεῖς, Δυμᾶνες and Πάμφυλοι), which were found in other Dorian States as well as in Spartan colonies, and the twenty-seven φρατρίαι mentioned by a late writer may have been subdivisions of these tribes. There were also five local tribes, taking their name from the five villages, which made the town of Sparta, subdivided into ὠβαί.

466. The constitution recalled the heroic age in the division of authority

between kings, Council and Assembly. It had, however, special characteristics of its own. Ancient writers were in doubt how to describe it, as
it was regarded as combining different elements—monarchic, aristocratic
and democratic. In the spirit of its administration and in the real powers
exercised by the Spartiates in the Assembly, or by means of their representatives the ephors, we must rank the constitution as an aristocracy
of birth.

From the earliest times there were two kings (ἀρχαγέται), from the two
dynasties of the Agiadae and Eurypontiadae, each of which
traced descent from Heracles. The origin of the double kingship, ascribed by legend to the division of authority between the twin
sons of Aristodemus, may have been due to the rival claims of different
houses, or possibly to the union of two Dorian communities, in which both
chieftains, like Romulus and Tatius, retained their sway. The kingship
bore an heroic character, and originally the kings must have enjoyed the
dignity of the Homeric monarchs as priests, judges and generals. In
the sphere of religion the kings offered sacrifice for the State and held
certain special priesthoods, while each selected two Πύθιοι, as envoys to
the Delphic oracle, which was always in close sympathy with Sparta. In
judicial affairs most of the civil jurisdiction had passed to the ephors, but
Herodotus tells us that the kings decided disputes about heiresses, adoption,
and public roads. The kings commanded the army in the field, and
originally they could make war on whom they wished, and the command was shared between them: from the end of the sixth century the
right of declaring war passed to the Assembly, and it was ordained that
only one king should take the field. The king's power of command was
absolute, but he was usually accompanied on a campaign by two ephors,
and he might subsequently be called to account. The kings had seats on
the Senate, and probably at first presided in both Senate and Assembly,
until the duty passed to the ephors. Special honours and privileges were
accorded to the kings and certain revenues and perquisites assigned to
them. The kingship involved more honour than power. Aristotle describes their office as an absolute generalship held for life : their authority
was limited by the other powers of State, such as the Senate and the
ephors, with whom they had to exchange oaths every month (§ 469).

Further, their power was weakened by division. One king could not
act against the veto of the other, and it was regarded as salutary to the
State that the kings should be at discord. Naturally the influence of a
king depended in great part on his individual character. Agesilaus directed
the policy of Sparta throughout his reign ; but the State was fearful of
tyranny, and retained the power of controlling and deposing the kings.

467. The kings were assisted in the government by a Council of elders
(γερουσία). This Senate consisted of the two kings and
twenty-eight members over sixty years of age, who held
office for life and were irresponsible. They were chosen from the

καλοὶ κἀγαθοί (§ 465) by a process, in which the shouts of the people in the Assembly decided the election. As the method of their appointment left room for intrigue, so their irresponsible tenure made them liable to corruption. The two kings, if absent from the meeting, could vote by deputy. The ephors probably presided. The Senate deliberated on all important business and prepared questions for the consideration of the Assembly, whose decisions it was competent, in conjunction with the kings, to set aside. It acted also as a criminal court, before which even the kings could be brought to trial. In general it had large and probably undefined powers, and Plutarch says it checked at once the absolutism of the kings and the independent action of the Assembly.

468. The Assembly (ἀπελλά), which resembled in functions and procedure the Homeric ἀγορά, in accordance with the ῥήτρα,
Assembly. met every month between Babyca and Cnaceum (within the precincts of Sparta). All Spartiates over thirty years of age might attend. Originally the kings, later (before the fifth century) the ephors, summoned and presided over the meetings. The Assembly was only competent to express its opinion on proposals previously considered by the Senate or the ephors, and discussion seems to have been usually limited to kings, ephors and senators. Votes were given by shouting, in case of uncertainty by formal division. The Assembly elected magistrates and senators, decided disputed succession to the throne, voted on peace, war, alliances and other questions of foreign policy, determined which king should take the field on a campaign, and decreed the emancipation of Helots. No doubt any proposed change of law was submitted to the assembly, but legislation was rare at Sparta. The authority of the Assembly was diminished by the addition to the ῥήτρα, empowering the kings and Senate to set aside any of its decisions: but the Spartiates at any rate enjoyed greater influence than the commons in the Homeric assembly, and they were further compensated by the powers wielded by the ephors, whom they elected to represent them.

469. The legends are at variance about the origin (§ 463) and the original duties of the ephorate; the institution was at least
Ephors. as early as the eighth century B.C., and probably from the first the ephors had important powers. The ephors, five in number, were elected yearly from all Spartiates (by a 'childish' process, perhaps similar to that employed for the choice of senators), and entered office at the beginning of the Spartan year (about the autumn equinox). They had a common dwelling-place, and acted collectively in accordance with the votes of the majority. One of their number presided over the board and gave his name to the year. On entering office they issued a proclamation to the Spartiates, κείρεσθαι τὸν μύστακα καὶ προσέχειν τοῖς νόμοις. The archaic character of this proclamation makes it likely that from the first the ephors were concerned with the maintenance of discipline over the Spartiates;

they seem moreover to have represented the rights of the Spartiate body
as against the kings, at whose expense their powers were subsequently
increased.   In conjunction with the Senate they had practical control of
the government : it was a tradition that when the kings were at variance,
the ephors should decide.   They wielded the most important executive
authority in the State : they summoned and presided in Senate and
Assembly, in foreign affairs they negotiated with the envoys of other States
and introduced them before the Assembly, whose decrees on war, peace
or alliance they carried into effect.   In the event of war, the ephors called
out the troops ($\phi\rho\rho\nu\rho\grave{a}\nu$ $\phi\alpha\acute{\iota}\nu\epsilon\iota\nu$), stating the years required for service, and
ordered the despatch of the army.   Two ephors accompanied the king in
the field to observe and report on his conduct.   As the maintainers of
the State discipline ($\kappa\acute{o}\sigma\mu\sigma$) the ephors had supervision not only over
Helots and Perioeci, but also over Spartiates.   They superintended the
education of the young, and they had general powers of control and
punishment over the citizens, which extended to other magistrates and
even to the kings.   They could suspend, arrest and bring to trial the
other magistrates, who were also accountable to the ephors at the end of
their term.   The limitation of the kingship was expressed in the oaths
exchanged between kings and ephors every month, the kings swearing
to observe the laws and the ephors guaranteeing their power on this
condition.   The kings were bound on the third summons to appear before
the ephors, who had a general right of control over their life and conduct.
They presided in State trials before the Senate, where even the kings might
be prosecuted, and they executed the sentence.   They had general powers
of civil jurisdiction.   Their direction of policy, their control of all ranks,
their executive power gave the ephors a position, which, modified though
it was by the limitation of their tenure and the liability to render account
to their successors, made the ephorate the dominant element in the
constitution.

   470.   There were no other civil magistrates of importance.   The $\pi\alpha\iota\delta o$-
$\nu\acute{o}\mu\sigma$ superintended the education of the young, the $\dot{a}\rho\mu\acute{o}\sigma\nu\nu o\iota$
supervised the conduct of the women.   There were doubtless   Other magis-
many minor officers, such as the $\dot{\epsilon}\mu\pi\acute{\epsilon}\lambda\omega\rho o\iota$, stewards of the   trates.
markets, of whom we know nothing more than the name.   In the army
there were many officers subordinate to the king, while, when Sparta
undertook operations at sea, the $\nu\alpha\acute{\nu}\alpha\rho\chi\sigma$ had to be entrusted with independent command, which gave him almost the position of another king.

   471.   More important than the formal institutions of government was
the system of education and discipline to which the Spartans   Education
submitted.   The Spartan State owed its origin to conquest :   and
its preservation required the subjection of the conquered.   discipline.
Hence, as Aristotle says, their whole system was directed only to efficiency
in war, and their city was like a standing camp.   The State regulated the
whole life of its citizens, who from the age of seven began their course of

training (ἀγωγή). The boy was entered in a βοῦα (each βοῦα being sub-divided into ἴλαι). The members were called παῖδες (7 to 18 years old), μελλίρανες (18 to 20) and ἴρανες (20 to 30). From the ἴρανες the βουαγοί and the ἴλαρχοι were chosen, and at the head of the system was the παιδονόμος. The education was mainly physical: with a minimum of learning the youths were trained in discipline, endurance and courage, suffering privations in food and clothing. From the age of twenty the Spartans became liable to military service, and entered military messes (συσσίτια, called in Sparta ἀνδρεῖα or φιδίτια), to which the members (about fifteen in number) contributed their share of food and wine and money, as a necessary condition of citizenship.

The Spartan ideal was narrow. The State demanded the sacrifice of the family as of the individual. While the system ensured a living to the Spartiate and leisure to train himself for war, it put the most galling restrictions on his liberty; he was forbidden to engage in any trade or art, forbidden to leave his country without permission, forbidden to own property, while he passed his life in a training school and his manhood in a barrack. The ideal was impossible of attainment: the system was hollow and effete long before the corruption and decay were revealed by the fall of Sparta's power.

472. The long wars of the fifth century which culminated in the final struggle with Athens, service in foreign lands, the influx of wealth, the introduction of luxury, threatened the old order, while the same causes led to the decline of population (§ 527) and the disfranchisement of many citizens, who could no longer fulfil their obligations. The kingship had been weakened during the Peloponnesian War, when Agis had to submit to the advice of the σύμβουλοι. The power of the Ephors had increased; the ambition of Lysander aimed at tyranny; the attempt of Cinadon revealed the internal corruption of the State. Agesilaus by skilful policy revived the power of the kingship and the prestige of the state, but the attempt of Sparta with Persian support to dictate to the rest of Greece was shattered in the disaster of Leuctra, which broke her power for ever. Messenia regained her independence, and the loss of this fruitful domain must have deprived many Spartiates of their κλῆροι and increased the inequality of property. Other causes contributed to the same result. At some time in the fourth century a law of the ephor Epitadeus gave the Spartiate liberty to dispose of his κλῆρος, which had hitherto been regarded as State land allotted for individual use; and landed property came into the hands of a few, two-thirds of it in Aristotle's time being held by women. Apart from the serious decline of popu-lation, many, who would have been qualified by birth for citizenship, must have lost their rights through lack of property. By 250 B.C. in a total of seven hundred Spartiates only one hundred were still in possession of land. The corruption of the State led two kings in succession to attempt a revo-lution. With the pretext of restoring the Lycurgean institutions, Agis III

Decline of Sparta and revolution.

(244 B.C.) proposed to create new citizens by granting privileges to perioeci and foreigners, to make a fresh distribution of land and to introduce again the old training and discipline.　He was opposed by the ephors, whose domination was threatened, and who represented the vested interests of the few Spartiates still possessed of citizenship, and he met with a violent death. Cleomenes III (237—222 B.C.), a king of the rival dynasty, resumed the aims of Agis.　Seeing the necessity of supporting his policy by force, he created an army of mercenaries and carried out a revolution.　The ephorate was abolished (the ephors being replaced by πατρονόμοι), the land re-distributed and the number of Spartiates increased to four thousand. Cleomenes ruled as a tyrant and made his brother the other king.　His military ambition brought him into conflict with the Achaean league, and his defeat at Sellasia led to his flight from Greece.　His reforms were annulled and the old corruption restored.　Lycurgus, a Spartiate not of Heraclid birth, was raised to the kingship, and after expelling the other king reigned as a tyrant.　Other tyrants succeeded, and after Nabis had been conquered by the Romans (195 B.C.), the coast towns were organised as a separate federation (τὸ κοινὸν τῶν Λακεδαιμονίων).　Sparta was forced to join the Achaean league and later received the position of a *civitas foede-rata* in the Roman province of Achaia.　The kingship was abolished, the πατρονόμοι becoming the chief magistrates.　In other respects old forms were maintained, and even the Lycurgean institutions were supposed to survive.

The best text-books dealing with the subject as a whole are G. Busolt and H. Swoboda, *Griechische Staatskunde* (fully documented and complete), Munich, 1920–26; K. F. Hermann, *Lehrbuch der griechischen Staatsaltertümer*, sixth edition, part III, which gives an excellent account of constitutions in general and the principal leagues, edited by H. Swoboda, Tübingen, 1913; B. Keil, *Griechische Staatsaltertümer* in Gercke and Norden's *Einleitung in die Altertumswissenschaft*, vol. III, second edition, Leipzig, 1914; G. Gilbert, *Handbuch der griechischen Staatsaltertümer*, vol. I, second edition (on Athens and Sparta) translated into English, London, 1895; A. H. J. Greenidge, *A Handbook of Greek Constitutional History*; G. Glotz, *The Greek City and its Institutions*, London, 1929. Other books which may be consulted are F. W. Newman, *Politics of Aristotle*; J. E. Sandys, Aristotle's *Constitution of Athens*, second edition; L. Whibley, *Greek Oligarchies*.

Bibliography.

VI. 2. LAW.

A. EARLY LEGISLATION AND THE LAWS OF GORTYN.

473. THE Homeric poems reveal surprisingly little about the character
of the unwritten customary law of early Greek communities
under the rule of kings. The king was judge in peace as
well as captain in war; 'to thee Zeus has entrusted (says
Nestor to Agamemnon, *Il.* IX. 99) σκῆπτρόν τ' ἠδὲ θέμιστας,' *i.e.* the symbol
of political power and the knowledge of law, θέμιστες being apparently the
various concrete manifestations of θέμις, Right, and embracing both judicial
sentences and established usages. The king, however, was not the only
judge. A scene on the shield of Achilles (*Il.* XVIII. 497 sqq.) showed
'elders' (γέροντες) sitting in the agora 'on polished stones in the holy
circle,' to give judgment in a dispute about the 'price of a man slain.'
Judges were conceived as upholding Right and Justice by divine commission (see *Il.* I. 238, XVI. 385 sqq., *Od.* XIX. 109 sqq.); but jurists search
in vain not only the *Iliad* and *Odyssey* but even Hesiod to discover the
forms and conditions under which justice was sought and obtained, and the
accepted rules of right in particular relations, *e.g.* as regards succession or
debt or the taking of life. Although we read of the duty of avenging
a slain kinsman (*Od.* XXIV. 433), of homicides driven to fly their country
(*Od.* XXIII. 118), of the acceptance of blood-money (*Il.* IX. 631), it is not
possible to define the law of murder and the attitude of the community
and its organs towards the blood-feud.

Customary law.

474. Law was first written and published in the seventh century B.C.,
after the downfall of monarchy, in the course of the political
and economical struggle between nobles and commons, land-
owners and serfs, rich and poor; and probably by the opening
of the sixth century there was no considerable Greek State, Sparta excepted,
which had not advanced beyond the stage of unwritten usage (ἄγραφα
νόμιμα) and absolute (αὐτογνώμονες) judges. The change in each case was
carried out by a legislator (νομοθέτης; note that the word νόμος is first found
in Hesiod), some distinguished man, not necessarily a citizen, commissioned
with absolute authority to draw up and issue a code, which was accepted
by the community without modification. The demand for definite rules
binding judge and magistrate seems to have been first successful in the new
communities of the West, which had developed rapidly, and were not
restrained by traditional reverence for an ancient landed aristocracy.
The laws made by Zaleucus for Epizephyrian Locri about the middle of
the seventh century B.C. were traditionally regarded as forming the earliest
Greek code. Charondas of Catana, called by some authorities a disciple

Early legislators.

of Zaleucus, was lawgiver not only for his native town but also for the other Chalcidian cities of Sicily and Italy. In later ages both Zaleucus and Charondas enjoyed a high reputation, at any rate with thinkers of a conservative bent, but little is recorded of the details of their legislation. Ephorus asserts that Zaleucus' principal 'innovation' was to limit the arbitrary caprice of judges by stating in his laws the punishment for each offence. According to Aristotle, Charondas introduced the procedure called ἐπίσκηψις, and recognised in his laws Courts of Judges, to which poor men as well as rich were admitted (see *Pol.* VI (IV). 13. 1297 a 23). Other ancient legislators were Aristeides of Ceos, Pheidon of Corinth (Arist. *Pol.* II. 6. 13), Philolaus of Corinth, who made laws for Thebes, and in particular laws regulating adoption (νόμοι θετικοί), 'to preserve unchanged the number of the lots of land' (κλῆροι, Arist. *Pol.* II. 12. 10), and Androdamas of Rhegium, who legislated for the Chalcidians in Thrace and was the author of laws about homicide and heiresses (ἐπίκληροι). More light falls on the development at Athens. The laws framed by Draco in 621 B.C. were a concession wrung by the discontented classes from the governing oligarchy. The Athenian nobles (εὐπατρίδαι) were the sole depositories of the secrets of *ius* and *fas*, civil law and religious precept, then hardly distinguishable, while the nine Archons drawn from their ranks were, at any rate in civil disputes, the sole administrators of justice, controlled, if at all, by nothing better than the intervention of the Council of the Areopagus composed of ex-archons. It is doubtful whether Draco did more than formulate and put in order existing practice; he did not meddle with land-tenure and the hard law of debt, although these were the main sources of trouble. Still it was a great advance to substitute a public code with fixed penalties in place of a mysterious body of custom interpreted and applied by the nobility. The only part of this code that is now known is the law of murder and homicide. The rest was abolished or absorbed by Solon in 594 B.C. in his vast attempt to reform the economy, constitution, and laws of his country. Even in the age of Demosthenes, after all the changes of the fifth and fourth centuries, it was Solon, not Draco nor even Cleisthenes, whom Athenians revered as the founder of their legal and judicial system.

475. The development of law and jurisdiction is better shown by the archaic inscriptions found on the site of the Cretan city Gortyn than by literary tradition. The older of these in-scriptions are separated by peculiarities of alphabet and writing into two groups, belonging to two distinct periods. The fragments assigned to the first period cannot well be regarded as older than the fifth century B.C. Fines are estimated in 'cauldrons' (λέβητες) and in 'tripods,' while the obol (ὀδελός) occurs only twice in a newly-found fragment. It was supposed that the reckoning in cauldrons and tripods points to a time when coined money was as yet unfamiliar, but in fact coins of the fifth and fourth centuries bearing a small badge of a cauldron or a tripod have been

Laws of Gortyn: 1st period.

found in Crete, and so the reckoning may be referred to these coins. Other considerations combine to make the fifth century the most probable time for this first code. The early legislator or legislators of Gortyn, as the broken stones reveal, did not omit to deal with the powers of the magistracy (the Cosmi) and the observances of religion. Thus we have the remains of a calendar for public offerings. But most of the fragments are concerned with details of private law, *i.e.* inheritance and succession, adoptions, dowries, blood-money, rural offences, barter and sale. There are also some rules for funerals. Unfortunately these laws are too fragmentary for us to form any clear idea of their scope and their underlying principles. A scale of fixed penalties was clearly a feature of this legislation as of the code of Zaleucus, and the motive may have been the same in both cases. It is probable that all these early laws were engraved on the walls of the temple of the Pythian Apollo, on the site of which the fragments were discovered.

476. The most important relic of the second epoch is that famous monument of ancient law, which has been given the somewhat misleading title of the Twelve Tables of Gortyn. This inscription was originally engraved on the round interior wall of some kind of court-house in the market-place of the city. Besides the Twelve Tables there are remains of other collections of legal inscriptions, including a group, seven columns in length, which clearly once belonged to a connected whole. There are also many separate fragments, both of laws and of decrees of the Assembly, which throw some light on the laws and their administration. These various inscriptions may be grouped together to represent the second period of Gortynian legislation. But there are at least one hundred years between the earliest and the latest of them. The most important seem to fall within the limits of the fourth century B.C. The matter of the laws is a strange amalgam of barbarism and civilization, of old institutions and new ideas. The principle that the State should supersede the private action of the individual had been realised at Gortyn to a greater extent than at Athens even in the fourth century; on the other hand there are traces of ancient procedure which had vanished from Athenian practice. In fact Crete, like Sparta, is a type of arrested development, the social and political organisation of its cities abounded in archaic survivals even in the age of Ephorus and Aristotle. The Gortynian legislators of the first period are not likely to have dealt with property and the family in a revolutionary spirit; they were content, we may guess, to collect and publish the ancient rules and customs of Gortyn. The laws attributed to the second period look like a restatement, with additions and amendments, of articles and chapters of the prior code; they allude to an existing body of written law, and prescribe occasionally that this or that provision shall not be retrospective. But the foundations on which the new laws rest are gone. The nature and extent of the innovations cannot be fixed with precision, and the aims of the reformers are unknown.

Laws of Gortyn: 2nd period.

477. An Athenian of the Periclean age would have scoffed at the old-fashioned and simple procedure. It is entirely oral, yet free Laws of from the punctilious formalism and technical incumbrances Gortyn: often found in primitive law. Documentary proofs are not Procedure. used. There is no written record of the verdict, and a past judgment is proved by the testimony of the judge and his 'remembrancer' (ὁ μνάμων). The 'remembrancer' still speaks from memory: in the age of Aristotle the title had come to denote a 'registrar.' Oaths and testimony are the only forms of proof. Ordeal has vanished, but the oath, in origin a kind of ordeal, retains much of its primitive significance. At Athens the 'challenge to an oath' (πρόκλησις εἰς ὅρκον) degenerated into a piece of chicanery. At Gortyn the oath of purgation is sometimes prescribed by law; it is final, and binds the judge. There is one instance of the use of oath-helpers, the 'Eidhelfer' of early Germanic law, men who swear not to a relevant fact, but to support the oath of the principal party by sharing the perils of perjury, 'four for a freeman, two for an ἀπέταιρος (probably a freeman degraded from his ἑταιρία), the lord (πάστας) for a serf (Ϝοικεύς).' Kinsmen as 'oath-helpers' in trials for homicide seem to have survived at Cyme in the fourth century B.C.; Aristotle confusing them with witnesses cites the practice as absurd. The fragments of the first period preserve their title, ὀμωμόται, 'co-jureurs.' Witnesses proper (μαίτυρες) are either ceremonial or evidential. In general they only make a declaration (ἀποπωνίοντι), but cases are distinguished in which their statement must be fortified by an oath. The number and quality of the witnesses required for the valid performance of certain processual and contractual acts are fixed by law. In some cases the law determines that if both parties affirm their contention on oath, the plaintiff's oath shall prevail against the defendant's oath (ὀρκιότερον ἤμην).

478. The large tribunals, so eloquent of the Greek fear of corruption and intimidation and found in oligarchies as well as in demo-cracies, have not yet invaded Gortyn, at any rate in civil Laws of Gor- suits. All cases mentioned in these laws are tried before a tyn: Judges single judge, but the judge differs according to the suit. and Arbitra- tors. Thus we find 'the judge of the ἑταιρίαι' and 'whosoever judges concerning pledges' (ὅς κα τῶν ἐνεκύρων δικάδηι), and in more general terms, 'The complainant shall plead where it is proper, before the judge, as is written for each case.' The classification of actions and jurisdictions is not preserved, nor is it stated how the judges were selected. It is possible that in some cases they were executive magistrates, members of the College of Cosmi, who at Gortyn had taken the place of the king. We see that one of this body, ὁ κσένιος κόσμος, had jurisdiction in disputes affecting the status of freed-men, as the Polemarch had at Athens; and Aristotle asserts that the power of the Cosmi in Crete was identical with that of the Ephors at Sparta, who certainly had judicial functions. If the judges were really members of the executive, Gortyn was at the same stage as Athens in the years between the

legislation of Draco and the reforms of Solon, when the archons were
bound by a code but had not ceased to be judges with full powers.
However this may be, the growth of written law has not entirely effaced
the features of the early 'doom-giver.' In part the Gortynian judge
has become only the mouthpiece of the law, obliged to *give judgment*
(δικάζειν) according to the witnesses or the oath of purgation, wherever the
law prescribes these forms of proof, but he still retains a province in which
he has great latitude of decision, where he '*takes oath and decides*' (ὀμνὺς
κρίνει) '*in view of the contentions of the parties*' (πορτὶ τὰ μωλιόμενα) as distinguished from '*the declarations of the witnesses*' (τὰ ἀποπωνιόμενα), where,
in short, he combines the freedom of the *arbiter* with the dignity of the
iudex, 'not necessarily affirming or denying the respective pretensions of
the parties, but deciding according to his solemn conviction of what is
right in the circumstances.' Judgment generally takes the form of an
award of damages, calculated either in money (στατῆρες, δάρκναι, ὀδελοί) or
according to the value of the property in dispute (the double, the triple,
etc.). The judge can also declare a right and issue an order to act or
abstain, but contempt of such a sentence does not provoke of necessity
the immediate intervention of the executive; the sanction is again a fine,
proportional or progressive, and payable to the injured party. The
period within which sentence must be given is occasionally specified, and
the penalty for refusing to give judgment seems to have been confiscation
of the estate of the recalcitrant judge. Appeal from a judgment is not
mentioned, and execution is apparently left to the energy of the successful
litigant, who, within certain limits, may enforce his rights by seizing not
only the goods but the person of his adversary.

Arbitrators appear on one mutilated fragment, from which we discover
that they were sometimes required under penalties to pronounce the award
within three days from the appearance of the parties. Their name and
their place in the general system are unknown.

479. In surveying the contents of the laws the archaic elements, as is
natural, seize first the attention of the reader. Rape and
adultery are regarded simply as matters for private compensation, and the law lays down a graduated tariff of compositions. The treatment of adultery is a particularly instructive example of
the caution with which in rude societies the State interferes to check private
vengeance and self-redress. The composition for adultery is still the
Homeric μοιχάγρια, i.e. the ransom of an offender caught in the act and
detained by the injured family. The exposure of infants appears a matter
of course, of which the law takes notice only in order to protect the rights of
the father, if the child is free, or of the lord, where serfs are concerned. The
law of debt is primitive, though apparently milder than that of early Roman
history. At Gortyn, though it is unlawful to arrest before trial a slave whose
ownership is disputed, or a freeman whose status is in question, a special
clause guarantees the rights of the creditor: '*the man convicted in court* (ὁ

*Laws of Gor-
tyn: archaic
elements.*

νενικαμένος, who has some resemblance to the Roman *addictus*) *and the man whose person is pledged* (ὁ κατακείμενος, the *nexus*) *may be arrested with impunity.*' The debtor is conceived as in temporary custody, bound to work at the mandate of the creditor to whom he has pawned himself (ὁ καταθέμενος). He may still be sued, like any other citizen, for injury done to a third person, and cast in damages, but '*if he has not the means to pay,*' the successful prosecutor and the creditor who holds the man as security, have to come to some arrangement, the particulars of which are lost. On the other hand, if the debtor suffer wrong, the creditor must sue for him, and claim the indemnity due to a freeman, which, when recovered, is to be shared equally between the two. The rights of the creditor are also protected by a law that acts of gift are not valid if they conflict with the claims of a creditor.

480. The law of the family which includes the law concerning slaves is comparatively modern in principle. In a sense the family at Gortyn is the antithesis of the family at Rome. *Patria potestas* is unknown. Sons can hold property of their own acquired either by their own exertions or by inheritance, and the father is not responsible for their debts. The separate rights of women and of children are recognised to a degree which neither Attic Law nor Roman Law ever reached. So in the case of married women the husband has only the usufruct of his wife's estate. When she dies he has no right of inheritance. If there are children, the property is theirs. If there are not, her heirs at law recover not merely '*the goods she brought with her,*' into the marriage, but also half of the '*fruits*' of the property, and half of all '*that she has woven in the house.*' A like principle obtains, when marriage is ended by the death of the husband or by divorce. On the other hand, testaments are unknown, even in the rudimentary form introduced at Athens by Solon. The code seems to be combating the tendencies which produce the testament; it seeks to protect heirs at law by fixing a maximum for gifts (apparently *donationes mortis causa*) by a husband to a wife or by a son to a mother. The order of succession resembles in the main that at Athens. One remarkable innovation, foreign to ordinary Greek practice, deserves notice; daughters are conceded a right of inheritance by the side of sons. The aim, however, of this reform is apparently rather to limit dowries than to protect daughters; it is also provided that a dowry must not exceed the daughter's proper share of the estate. As parts of the estate the law specifies houses in the city, cattle, and '*goods*' (κρήματα). Land is not mentioned; perhaps the territory of Gortyn consisted of common pastures, over which the citizens had grazing rights and of inalienable '*lots*' of arable land, which were occupied and cultivated by the serfs. These lots apparently remained undivided, but probably the eldest son acted as lord (πάστας) over the serfs. The slave is regarded as an integral part of the family and comes under the protection of the law, which shows a tendency towards an increasing recognition of his right. Thus the slave is protected from injury

Laws of Gortyn: new tendencies.

by a third party though the right to recover damages is vested in his master.
Even against his master the slave can claim protection from outrage and
even proceed at law against him.   The slave may own property and may
contract a legally recognised marriage.   Some clauses in laws of the second
period regulate the position of children born of the marriage of a slave and
a freewoman.   The children are free if the slave goes to live in the house
of the freewoman, they are unfree if the freewoman goes to the slave.
A later decree does away with this distinction and makes the children of
any freewoman free.   Children born of a free man and a slave woman
were already regarded as free.   So, too, the position of freedmen is defined
and legally protected.   They are placed under the especial care of officials
called τίται.   The elaborate provisions made to secure the proper marriage of
an 'heiress' (πατρωιῶκος) have travelled far from the primitive conception of
the sacred duty of the kin to raise up a son of the blood of her father.   It
is plain that the pecuniary interests of the relatives overshadow their obligations to the 'heiress' and her father's house.   Thus the law forces an
unmarried girl, if an 'heiress,' either to marry e.g. her oldest paternal uncle,
if he profess willingness, or to indemnify him by the surrender of part of
the estate.   But the estate might be little or nothing.   The law does not in
this case force any relative either to take the girl or provide a dowry, as was
the rule at Athens, and yet it still holds to the old principle that married
she must be, and with speed.   Adoption, again, is an example of an old institution in a state of transformation and decay.   The procedure is of antique
simplicity, the act being public and oral, as the name denotes (ἄνπανσις, announcement).   *Announcement shall be made in the agora, when the citizens
are assembled, from the stone from which speeches are made.   And the adopter
shall give to his ἑταιρία a victim and a pitcher of wine.'   There is no hint
that the citizens are anything but witnesses, that the ἑταιρία can refuse to
admit the new member to their fellowship.   The original design of the
practice was to supply the want of a male heir in the direct line and to
secure the continuance of the family with its *sacra*, and this view is the
source of the Athenian rule that a father of children cannot adopt.   It is
not clear that this restriction survived at Gortyn.   The main concern of the
law is to depose the artificial son from a position of equality with natural
heirs.   In the presence of children he is not permitted to inherit more than
the portion of a daughter.   Here too the Athenian law keeps closer to the
primitive idea; at Athens, if after the adoption children were born to the
adopter, the adopted heir still retained the full rights of a son.   Moreover
the bond is easily dissolved; the son may be 'renounced' (ἀποϝειπεῖν) by a
declaration from the stone in the agora before the assembled citizens,
receiving as consolation a gift of ten staters' formally delivered by the
'remembrancer of the Cosmus of strangers' (ὁ μνάμων ὁ τῶ κσενίω).

B. THE ATHENIAN JUDICIAL SYSTEM IN THE FOURTH CENTURY.

481. The system of jurisdiction developed under the Athenian democracy had its origin in the legislation of Solon. Before Solon the nine Archons exercised full judicial power, not merely receiving plaints and examining the parties, but pronouncing final judgment. Solon (Arist. 'Aθ. Πολ. 9) introduced '*the reference to the dicasterion*' (ἡ εἰς τὸ δικαστήριον ἔφεσις) : in other words, he allowed an appeal from an Archon's sentence to a court of judges, which represented the nation, and, in theory at any rate, included members of every class, even the poorest. At first this court was probably a meeting of the δῆμος, like the ecclesia, without any elaborate organisation. It is not possible to fix a certain date for the beginning of that elaborate organisation of dicasteries which is reflected in the literature and inscriptions of the fourth century. Such a system with magistrates dependent on it presupposes constructive legislation, and of this no record survives. We only know that Pericles introduced the practice of paying these judges, and so the dicasteries became effective democratic organs.

Development of the Democratic Courts.

482. The remarkable feature of the system is the sharp distinction between a court of judges (δικαστήριον) and a president of such a court (ἡγεμὼν δικαστηρίου). All magistrates, not merely those whose duties were primarily judicial, but executive officials like the Eleven or the Generals, and even Financial Boards such as the Receivers-General (ἀποδέκται), might act as ἡγεμόνες δικαστηρίων. Two cases must be discriminated. On the one hand magistrates retained from an earlier and non-democratic age the right of punishing offences within the sphere of their administrative activity by the imposition of fines (ἐπιβολαί); but the maximum of such fines was fixed by law and, though no doubt varying with the office, was never large, so that officials had no independent power of dealing with acts of contumacy or illegality, when the legal fine was inadequate. They could, if they chose, lay a 'denunciation' (εἰσαγγελία) before the Council or Assembly, but probably the ordinary course was to bring the offender before a court. We do not know the rules of procedure in such a case. It is not likely that the magistrate was both president and prosecutor. The charge may have been delegated to a deputy. The second and more important case was when a magistrate did not come before a court of his own motion, but introduced plaints and claims of private persons concerning matters which belonged to his special department. His rôle resembled that of a court officer. He received the charge, saw that legal rules were observed, prepared the materials on which the judges had to decide, settled with the Thesmothetae the day of trial, presided in court, and sometimes was responsible for execution of the

ἡγεμονία δικαστηρίου.

sentence. The law and practice of the constitution left him small authority during the preliminaries of a trial and no influence at all on the judgment. This separation of judicial and ministerial functions followed in the main a simple and intelligible principle. An executive magistrate was not competent to entertain charges unconnected with the laws he had to apply and enforce. His 'hegemony' was defined by his office. As the First Archon (ὁ ἄρχων) guarded the interests of orphans, heiresses, and widows, so he had cognizance concerning the family rights of citizens. A charge of murder or sacrilege had to be presented to the Second Archon (ὁ βασιλεύς), who retained both the name and the religious duties of the primitive king. The old military functions of the Third Archon (ὁ πολέμαρχος) explain why he received a variety of actions, public and private, affecting freedmen and resident aliens. A prosecution, however, for a military offence, e.g. falling out of the ranks in battle (λιποταξίου), was brought before the Generals, because the control of the Army and Navy had passed to this board. If merchants were suspected of not conveying from the port to Athens the prescribed proportion of a grain cargo, the Superintendents of the Emporium (οἱ ἐπιμεληταὶ τοῦ ἐμπορίου) were the proper persons with whom to lodge an information (φάσις).

483. This principle of distribution, which is easily applied to administrative posts, fails us when we come to the magistrates whose work was primarily or entirely judicial, i.e. the Thesmothetae (the six Junior Archons acting as a College), the Forty, and the Introducers (εἰσαγωγεῖς). Roughly stated, the difference between their provinces is that the last two boards received nothing but private actions, the Thesmothetae little save public actions. As administrators the Thesmothetae were answerable for the annual revision of the laws, the arrangement of the time and place of trials, and the ratification of the international compacts (τὰ πρὸς τὰς πόλεις σύμβολα) which sometimes regulated the conduct of suits between foreigners and citizens. Their 'hegemony' embraced a few private actions, e.g. mining cases (δίκαι μεταλλικαί, in which the State as lessor of the mines often had an interest), 'mercantile' cases and 'treaty' cases (δίκαι ἐμπορικαί and δίκαι ἀπὸ συμβόλων, one of the parties in the first kind of suit being frequently, and in the second necessarily, an alien), but their principal task was to preside over public actions, and especially actions to punish crimes directly assailing the constitution or administration of the State, e.g. 'denunciations' (εἰσαγγελίαι), 'presentments' (προβολαί), 'informations' (ἐνδείξεις), indictments of the presidents of the Council and Assembly (γραφαὶ προεδρικαὶ καὶ ἐπιστατικαί), indictments for illegal proposals (παρανόμων), prosecutions of officials for taking bribes (δώρων), and for other offences, e.g. wrongfully entering a name on the list of State-debtors (ψευδεγγραφῆς), prosecutions of aliens for usurping the rights of citizens (ξενίας), and of citizens for false citation (ψευδοκλητείας). Further, they prepared for trial some public actions of a different kind, in which the individual, not the State, was

οἱ θεσμοθέται.

immediately injured, *e.g.* γραφαὶ ὕβρεως, but the principle on which these were selected is not now apparent; why, for example, did Athenian legislators assign prosecutions for adultery (γραφαὶ μοιχείας) to the Thesmothetae rather than to the First Archon, the protector of the family?

484. The Forty were more prominent in the ordinary life of Athenians than they are in the records of literature and inscriptions. The office seems a democratic creation, being the descendant οἱ τετταρά-κοντα. of the thirty itinerant judges (δικασταὶ κατὰ δήμους), established in 453/2 B.C. Their number after the fall of the thirty tyrants (403 B.C.) was raised to forty, four members being drawn by lot from each tribe. They were divided into ten sections, according to their tribes, and each section received suits brought against members of its own tribe. This was the tribunal that had jurisdiction in the bulk of private suits, particularly suits about rights of property, sales, debts, contracts, leases, etc. The Forty were to some extent real judges; their sentences in disputes involving less than 10 dr. were final. Further, unlike the magistrates hitherto considered, they did not prepare for trial the more important actions which they were not permitted to settle on their own authority, but selected by lot a public arbitrator and remitted the case to him.

485. These public arbitrators (οἱ διαιτηταί) were an organised body, composed of all Athenians in their sixtieth year, *i.e.* the οἱ διαιτηταί. last year of military service. The individual appointed by the Forty was compelled to discharge the task allotted on pain of disfranchisement (ἀτιμία), unless in that year he held another office or happened to be abroad. Any complaint brought against an arbitrator by an aggrieved suitor was heard by the whole body in session, and the legal consequence of an adverse verdict was disfranchisement, though the condemned arbitrator was allowed an appeal to a δικαστήριον. The first duty of the arbitrator was to seek to effect a compromise. If this proved impossible, after due hearing of the arguments and evidence he gave his award on an appointed day (ἡ κυρία, sc. ἡμέρα) and confirmed it by a solemn oath at the 'stone of swearing' in the agora. If the litigants acquiesced, the suit was ended. If, however, either side 'appealed to the court' (ἐφιέναι εἰς τὸ δικαστήριον), the arbitrator placed in two caskets (ἐχῖνοι), one for each party, the depositions, oaths, challenges, in short all the material on which his sentence was based, attached a written note of his decision, and gave the caskets under seal to that section of the Forty from which he had received his commission. These then brought the case before a court, and presided over the trial. The judges were 201 in number, if the sum involved was under 1000 drachmae; 401, when the amount was larger. In the pleadings it was not permitted to appeal to any depositions or laws or challenges except those contained in the caskets and already used before the arbitrator.

The public arbitrators are one of the most interesting products of Athenian democracy. The design of the institution was excellent, to procure the settlement of private suits by experienced and impartial men whose first aim was to make peace. How far it was successful, and what amount of business was terminated without an appeal, cannot now be discovered. The arbitrator was designated by the chance of the lot, and the weight of his judgment with the litigants and the court must have varied according to his personality. But in appreciating the democracy it is important to remember that in a large number of disputes the constitution did not compel two quiet citizens to face the ordeal of a trial in court, but provided a cheap and simple and reasonable means of getting justice.

486. The 'Introducers' (οἱ εἰσαγωγεῖς) were a special board in charge of certain actions in which a speedy decision was desirable. They were five in number, one for two tribes, and were appointed by lot. All suits assigned to them were ἔμμηνοι, *i.e.* were brought to trial in a court within a month from the reception of the plaint, but their 'hegemony' did not cover all 'monthly' suits; thus δίκαι ἐμπορικαί were ἔμμηνοι, as were various actions brought by and against the Tax-farmers (τελῶναι) before the Receivers-General (ἀποδέκται). They prepared actions for the recovery of a wife's dowry, actions against certain classes of debtors, actions for assault (αἰκείας: so 'Αθ. Πολ. 52, but in 346/5 B.C., according to Dem. XXXVII. 33, these cases went before the Forty), actions to recover what were called ἔρανοι, *i.e.* loans not bearing interest and consisting of joint-contributions from friends associated *ad hoc* by the borrower or some other person (δίκαι ἐρανικαί), actions in which bankers and partners were concerned (δίκαι τραπεζιτικαί, κοινωνικαί), actions arising out of a trierarchy.

οἱ εἰσαγωγεῖς.

487. The all-powerful judges of the democracy, οἱ δικασταί or οἱ ἡλιασταί (an archaic name, rare in the Orators and of uncertain origin), whose courts controlled the appointment and conduct of the executive and eventually curtailed even the authority of the Assembly, were nothing but a body of ordinary citizens, over thirty years of age and not in any way disqualified, *i.e.* not in debt to the State and not under sentence of Atimia. No record survives of the manner in which this body was recruited and subdivided during the fifth century. As to its size we have no better evidence than Aristophanes who, writing in 422 B.C. (*Wasps* 661), sets down 6000 as a maximum that had never been exceeded, and Aristotle ('Αθ. Πολ. 24) who, in describing the results of the imperial and democratic policy of Athens after the Persian wars, mentions 6000 judges as an item in a total of more than 20,000 citizens who received pay from the State. The pay, introduced by Pericles (probably soon after the overthrow of the Areopagus in 462/1 B.C.), was increased by Cleon in 425/4 B.C. to 3 obols (τριώβολον) for a day's sitting, and this rate was retained throughout the history of the institution. Little is known about the organisation of the judges even in the fourth century, until we reach the age of Aristotle. The *Ecclesiazusae* and *Plutus* of

οἱ δικασταί.

Aristophanes show that in the first quarter of this century they were drafted into ten sections, marked by the letters A to K. The system cannot be reconstructed from a comedian's allusions, but it is different from that described by Aristotle in the *Constitution of Athens*. Even Aristotle's account contains obscurities which are not entirely due to the imperfections of the MS. Here only the leading features can be noticed. Appointment to the office of judge must be carefully distinguished from appointment to serve at a particular trial. As to the first we learn that the judges were distributed into ten sections, numbered from A to K, and that each section contained approximately the same number of members, and included representatives from every tribe; but we are not told how or when judges were chosen, nor whether there was a fixed number. Each judge on appointment received a ticket (πινάκιον) of boxwood, on which were inscribed the letter of his section and his full style as a citizen, *i.e.* his own name together with the names of his father and of his deme. The process of forming a court (δικαστήριον) to hear a case was singularly elaborate. The Thesmothetae determined what trials should be taken, and what court-houses used, on a given day, the lot deciding between the competing claims of magistrates who had business ready. The aggregate of judges required was easily made out by the authorities, since the law or special decrees (ψηφίσματα) determined the number that should sit in each suit. Early in the morning the judges assembled at the allotment-chambers (κληρωτήρια), one for each tribe (not, as might have been expected, one for each section), and the nine archons and the Secretary (γραμματεύς) of the Thesmothetae proceeded to the sortition, each presiding over his own tribe. The first business was to settle who among the judges present were to serve that day, the number to be drawn in each allotment-chamber being one-tenth of the total needed. The peculiarity of the process or sortition consisted in the ingenious arrangements directed to ensuring the selection of representatives from each of the ten sections into which each tribe was divided. Why such pains were taken Aristotle does not explain. The next task was to allot to the various trials the judges who had been nominated for the day. The Thesmothetae chose the court-houses to be used, and marked each by a letter from Λ onwards, assigned by lot. Moreover the door of each court-house bore on its lintel (σφηκίσκος) a distinguishing colour. Let us suppose that only two courts were to sit, one of 200 judges, one of 400, and that Λ was allotted to the green court (τὸ βατραχιοῦν), M to the red court (τὸ φοινικιοῦν). Then in each allotment-chamber twenty acorns (βάλανοι) marked Λ, forty marked M were deposited in an urn (ὑδρία), and twenty green batons (βακτηρίαι), forty red batons were placed at the entrance. The sixty judges already selected were called up one by one and drew an acorn from the urn. The acorn determined each man's court. A judge who drew Λ was given a green baton, and armed with acorn and baton went off to the green court. Before entering he probably gave the acorn to an official, and received in return a ticket (σύμβολον) which he had to present at the end of the day in order to get his three obols. Pay was not distributed by tribes but by sections. The aim of this complicated system was to prevent bribery, intimidation, and packing. Accident alone determined where an individual would sit, and no man could get admission to a court to which he had not been allotted. Further, each court was made an image in miniature of the nation, containing an equal contingent of judges from each tribe.

Courts of 201, 401, 500, 700, 1001, 1,500, 2000, 2,500 are mentioned by authorities of the fourth century. A court of 6000 occurs once only, in Andocides, *Myst.* 17, but the text is justly suspected. The even numbers in the authorities, such as 500, 700, etc., are probably inexact and mean courts of 501, 701, etc. Courts of 1001 and more are only found in great political trials.

The judges were sworn once a year, possibly when appointments were made and the sections recruited. The entire oath cannot be reconstructed, but the following clauses can be recovered from scattered references in the Orators. ' I will vote according to the laws and according to the decrees of the Athenian People and the Council of the 500, and where there are no laws, according to my most honest judgment, without favour or animosity.' 'I will vote on nothing but the matter of the charge.' ' I will hear impartially both the prosecutor and the defendant.'

488. The democratic theory that it was the duty and privilege of every citizen to take part in the work of government was every-
Character of the courts. where applied by the Athenians with excellent logic and much fertility of contrivance, but nowhere with more thoroughness and ingenuity than in the constitution of their tribunals. The complex organisation we have described rests on two very simple ideas, that law ought to be intelligible to the average man, and that the common sense and moral instincts of large bodies of ordinary citizens are the best guarantees of a pure administration of justice. There is no evidence that the Athenian judges were often bribed or terrorised or intentionally dishonest. Neither did the discretion granted them in the absence of a statute become an instrument of oppression. This danger, though real enough, was diminished by the number and representative character of the judges, who were not likely to treat as criminal acts tolerated by public opinion. But the speeches of the Orators are a convincing proof, if proof be needed, of the vices inherent in such a system. The amount of injustice done cannot now be estimated, but it is sufficient condemnation of the courts that appeals to passion and political prejudice, insinuating sophistry, and outrageous misrepresentations of law were judged by shrewd and experienced observers suitable means to win a verdict. No development of law was possible; nothing excited the suspicion and mistrust of the judges so much as a display of legal subtlety. No body of precedent to supplement or interpret the written

code could be formed from recorded judgments. The conclusions of a court were bare affirmations or negations, not discriminating between law and fact, applicable only to a particular case, and based on reasons, which were known only to the individual voters, and perhaps not always to them. And these decisions, such as they were, could not bind another court, for in theory and practice the courts were equal and independent, each being a committee of the Sovereign People, supreme and irresponsible.

489. The steady growth of the authority of these courts left ultimately little room for judicial activity on the part of the Council and the Assembly. There was a time (probably not before the curtailment of the prerogatives of the Areopagus in 462/1 B.C.) when the Council of 500 could not only fine and imprison, but even inflict capital punishment. In the fourth century we find the supremacy of the dicasts definitely established by statute. The Council was only empowered to imprison traitors and conspirators against the democracy, and defaulting tax-farmers with their sureties and collectors. It could not impose a fine above a certain amount, apparently 500 dr., and was compelled to refer to the courts all grave offences brought under its notice. The judicial functions of the Council, like those of a magistrate, were of two kinds. It was an administrative as well as a deliberative body, and was responsible for the proper conduct of certain branches of the public service, *e.g.* finance and the navy. In this capacity it could intervene *ex officio* to investigate, and punish or get punished, offences within its province. But it had another and a wider sphere; the bulk of the 'denunciations' (εἰσαγγελίαι), whether brought by a magistrate or private citizen, were laid before the Council. If the Council voted that the charge should be investigated, the Presidents (πρυτάνεις) arranged a time for trying the case and had power to imprison, or hold to bail, the accused according to the gravity of the alleged defence. If after hearing both parties the majority voted for acquittal, the accused was released and the business ended. If on the contrary he was declared guilty, the Council had next to decide whether a fine, such as it was competent to inflict, was an adequate punishment, or whether the matter should be referred to a body with greater judicial powers.

Jurisdiction of the Council and Assembly.

εἰσαγγελία.

Denunciations might also be submitted to the People at that Assembly in each Prytany which was called ἡ κυρία. The people first voted by show of hands (χειροτονία) whether the information should be accepted or not. The acceptance of a denunciation brought about the same position as the preliminary investigation by the Council. In either case it was possible for the Assembly to act as a court and try the case on its own reference or at the instance of the Council, or for the Council or Assembly to refer the matter for trial to a dicastery. At the beginning of the fifth century it seems to have been the practice to refer all such cases to the Assembly.

From about the middle of the fifth century to the first decades of the fourth century these cases were sometimes submitted to the Assembly, more often to a dicastery, from early in the fourth century onwards always to a dicastery. The Thesmothetae acted as Presidents of the court in these matters and there were legal provisions to ensure a speedy trial.

The offences which might properly be prosecuted by an εἰσαγγελια were not clearly defined until a point about the middle of the fourth century. Before that date the εἰσαγγελία was used to enforce an ancient law which punished with death anyone who deceived the people with false promises. So also treason (προδοσία), whether in its widest sense or in particular, the betraying of a fortress, etc., might be made the object of a 'denunciation.' In fact the εἰσαγγελία was used to punish political defeat as was impeachment in English politics, except that at Athens the procedure was simpler and much more commonly employed. Also the Council might entertain a 'denunciation' on any subject over which they exercised a general superintendence, e.g. finance.

About the middle of the fourth century, however, when the εἰσαγγελία had become no more than a means of bringing an offender before a dicastery and the part played by the Council or Assembly was little more than a formality, the offences for which a 'denunciation' was the proper procedure were strictly defined and grouped together in a νόμος εἰσαγγελ-τικός. The offences in question were (1) an attempt to overthrow the democracy, (2) the betrayal of a city or army or fleet to an enemy, or any treasonable dealings with an enemy, or (3) corrupt bad advice given by an orator to the people (ἐάν τις ῥήτωρ ὢν μὴ λέγῃ τὰ ἄριστα τῷ δήμῳ τῶν Ἀθηναίων χρήματα λαμβάνων). According to Hypereides prosecutors sought to bring very various offences within the scope of this law and irregularities were permitted, but the law itself was clear. These political εἰσαγγελίαι should be distinguished from two other kinds of 'denunciation.' (1) εἰσαγγελίαι κακώσεως (maltreatment of parents, orphans, heiresses, or widows) which were laid before the First Archon and always tried by a dicastery, (2) εἰσαγγελίαι διαιτητῶν. The use of the term in these cases is due to the general sense of 'denunciation' in the word before the procedure was appropriated for definitely political offences.

490. A 'presentation' (προβολή) was a criminal information laid before the people. On certain fixed days citizens could present to the Assembly the names of sycophants (not more than six at a meeting) and of persons who had deceived the demos by false promises or, like Meidias, violated the sanctity of a festival. The procedure did not aim at securing a trial either conducted or commanded by the people, but at testing public opinion as a preliminary to an action in court. The people heard the charge and the defence, and a show of hands was taken on the guilt of the accused. If the decision was against the complainant, it was injudicious, possibly illegal, for him to go further. If the accused was condemned, the assailant profited by the moral effect

of the vote, if he went before a court, but he was not obliged to bring an action, and if there was a trial, the judges were in no way bound by the verdict of the Assembly.

491. Only one domain escaped to some extent the encroachments of the popular courts. The Athenians were singularly conservative in their treatment of homicide. The prin- **Trials for** **homicide.** ciples and rules of Draco's code were still venerated in the age of Aristotle, after three centuries of profound change. The law abolished the blood-feud and blood-money, and discriminated degrees of guilt, but never, as at Rome, came to rank the taking of human life with other offences against the community. Plato's *Laws* prove the vitality of the old religious conception of bloodshed, that the murderer was polluted and spread pollution, that the angry spirit of the victim called on his kindred for vengeance. The part of the State at Athens was to control and regulate the methods of this vengeance, and to prescribe the conditions on which the offender should receive the 'forgiveness' (αἴδεσις) of the avengers and be purified of the stain of blood. Trials for bloodshed were held at five different places, always in the open air: on the Areopagus, at the Palladion (a **The five** sanctuary of Pallas on the E. side of the city outside the **courts.** walls), at the Delphinion (a sanctuary of Apollo Delphinios, also on the E. side of the city and outside the walls), in Phreatto (a tongue of land overlooking the sea near the harbour of Zea), and at the Prytaneum, the official residence of the First Archon, on the N. slope of the Acropolis. It is supposed that the first three places were originally refuges where the shedder of blood found asylum.

Cases of voluntary homicide (φόνος ἑκούσιος or ἐκ προνοίας), of wounding with intent to kill (τραῦμα ἐκ προνοίας), of arson (πυρκαϊά), and of poisoning (φάρμακα) were heard on the Areopagus. The judges were the ex-archons, who composed the Council of the Areopagus. The penalty of murder was death and confiscation of property; of malicious wounding, banishment and confiscation.

In the age of Draco and Solon fifty-one judges called ἐφέται sat at the Palladion, the Delphinion, and Phreatto. The significance of the title is unknown, and all that is handed down to us about the mode of appointment is that ἐφέται were 'chosen according to merit' (ἀριστίνδην, *i.e.* not by a property qualification, πλουτίνδην, and not by lot). Whether this ancient institution survived at all under the developed democracy is doubtful; at any rate early in the fourth century it seems to have disappeared, for examples are found of large courts (*e.g.* 700) of dicasts trying cases of involuntary homicide, which Draco's laws assigned to the ἐφέται.

The court at the Palladion took cognisance of involuntary (ἀκούσιος) homicide, of conspiracy (βούλευσις, procuring or counselling another to wound or kill), and of the killing of a slave or resident alien or foreigner. The punishment of unintentional manslaughter was banishment for a limited period without confiscation. Apparently, if the next of kin granted 'forgiveness' according to certain rules, the exile could return before the expiry of the legal terms.

The court at the Delphinion heard those who confessed to homicide, but pleaded that it was lawful (δίκαιος). The principal cases exempted from punishment, but not from ceremonial purification, were these : if the deed was done in self-defence, if the slain man was an adulterer taken in the act, if a competitor in an athletic contest or a comrade in war was killed unintentionally.

The court in Phreatto cannot have sat very often. It was required if a man, already banished for unintentional homicide, sought to clear himself of a further charge of murder or malicious wounding. The exile was obliged to conduct his defence from a boat that he might not pollute the soil of Attica, and the judges heard him from the shore.

The proceedings at the Prytaneum were even more archaic. Here the King (the Second Archon) and the Tribe-Kings (φυλοβασιλεῖς) solemnly tried and sentenced undiscovered murderers, and animals or inanimate objects that had caused the loss of human life. The condemned objects were cast beyond the bounds of the State.

492. The magistrate to whom all prosecutions for homicide were

Procedure.

brought was the King, the representative of the State-religion. None but the next of kin were entitled to prosecute. A murderer was secure from molestation, if he received the pardon of his victim. A person accused of homicide was not arrested, but on receiving the plaint the King issued a proclamation (πρόρρησις) forbidding him to enter the agora or sacred places. Even after the beginning of the trial the defendant could escape the death-sentence by withdrawing from Attica. Once outside the country he was guaranteed from violence on condition of avoiding the Panhellenic games and the Amphictyonic festivals; it was unlawful to pursue or arrest him across the frontier.

493. The distinction between public and private wrongs was recognised

Public and private actions.

in the code and judicial practice of Athens as early as the age of Solon. In the fourth century actions were classified as either public (ἀγῶνες δημόσιοι, δίκαι δημόσιαι, or simply γραφαί) or private (ἀγῶνες ἴδιοι, δίκαι ἴδιαι, or simply δίκαι) according to the nature of the offence or matter in dispute; but the line of division between crimes and civil injuries was naturally not the same as that drawn at Rome in the days of Gaius, or in England at the present time; and of course there were occasions when an Athenian had the option of proceeding either 'publicly' or 'privately.' Moreover, if the archaic rules of δίκαι φονικαί be set aside, no essential difference can be discovered between civil and criminal procedure. In both the preliminaries conducting to a trial were generally the same, a summons (πρόσκλησις) and a statement of the charge before some magistrate. In the trial, it is true, there might be a difference, for all public actions (except certain δίκαι φονικαί, and such εἰσαγγελίαι as were decided in the Council or Assembly) were carried at once before dicasts, whereas many (but not all) forms of private action went in the first place to a public arbitrator, and probably were often settled without an appeal to the supreme tribunal. The principal peculiarities of a public suit sprang from the absence of a Public Prosecutor and showed themselves in the position and liabilities of the person bringing the action. (1) Any Athenian in possession of the full rights of a citizen was entitled, although not directly wronged or injured, to institute any public action, provided it was not one of the δίκαι φονικαί; in a private suit the plaintiff could be no one but the person whose rights were immediately affected, or the legal representative (κύριος or προστάτης) of such person, if a woman or minor or resident alien. (2) In public actions the punishment or fine was regarded as satisfaction due to the State, and there were only a few public actions, e.g. φάσις and ἀπογραφή, in which the prosecutor received any portion of the pecuniary penalty awarded on condemnation; in nearly all private actions the object in dispute or the compensation went to the plaintiff; we know in fact only three forms of private action in which the State exacted a penalty over and above the private damages, i.e. δίκαι βιαίων (forcible seizure of chattels and rape of a free person), ἐξούλης (ejectment), ἐξαιρέσεως (uindicatio in libertatem, when the plaintiff claimed a person as his slave and the defendant maintained that the alleged slave was free). (3) In a public action the prosecutor incurred a fine of a thousand drachmae (αἱ χίλιαι), and a modified ἀτιμία, forfeiting the right to bring a similar public action in the future, if he either withdrew before a trial or failed at the trial to obtain a fifth of the judges' votes; in private suits the State, as the system of arbitration indicates, did its best to encourage compromises out of court and peaceful settlements. In certain private actions (e.g. δίκαι ἐμπορικαί and παραγραφαί) a litigant, generally but not always the plaintiff, failing to obtain a fifth of the votes incurred an additional penalty, being condemned to pay to his successful opponent one obol for every drachma of the sum at issue, i.e. one-sixth of the whole (ἡ ἐπωβελία). (4) In private suits in which the damages were estimated at more than 100 dr. both parties paid court-fees (πρυτανεῖα), 3 dr. for damages from 100 to 1000 dr., 30 dr. for higher sums. A deposit (παρακαταβολή) of a tenth part of the amount claimed was required from a person laying claim to a disputed inheritance, a deposit of a fifth from a person asserting rights in property confiscated by the State (ἐνεπισκήπτεσθαι). In a public action the prosecutor generally paid nothing but a trivial fixed sum called παράστασις (a drachma?), and even this was not always demanded, e.g. in εἰσαγγελίαι κακώσεως, but if the action was a φάσις or an ἀπογραφή, in which success brought pecuniary profit to the prosecutor, court-fees on the usual scale were obligatory.

494. Another division of actions, into δίκαι πρός τινα and δίκαι κατά
τινος, is to be distinguished from the preceding classification,
δίκαι πρός and has in view only the punishment or non-punishment of
τινα and κατά the defeated party. Nearly all public actions are obviously
τινος.
δίκαι κατά τινος, but a γραφὴ παρανόμων brought against
the author of a law at a time when he was no longer liable to penal
consequences, was ranked among δίκαι πρός τινα ; hence the speech written
by Demosthenes against Leptines' law (or. xx) bears the title πρὸς Λεπτίνην,
whereas Aeschines' indictment of Ctesiphon's ψήφισμα is inscribed κατὰ
Κτησιφῶντος. Among private actions, a suit to recover damages for breach
of contract or injury to property (δίκη βλάβης) is a good illustration of
a δίκη κατά τινος, a διαδικασία of a δίκη πρός τινα : in a διαδικασία the parties
were properly neither plaintiffs nor defendants, but rivals and competitors,
and the proceedings were a contest either to shift the responsibility for
a public burden such as the χορηγία, or τριηραρχία, or a State-debt, or to
secure a right or privilege, as when several persons claimed an inheritance,
or when families or individuals claimed a priesthood (ἱερωσύνη), or its
honours and emoluments (γέρα).

495. Again, all actions were either ἀγῶνες ἀτίμητοι, i.e. not requiring
τίμησις or assessment of penalty or damages by the judges,
ἀγῶνες ἀτί- or τιμητοί, requiring such assessment. There were two
μητοι and classes of ἀγῶνες ἀτίμητοι. (1) In some actions, public and
τιμητοί.
private, the penalty (τίμημα) was determined before trial,
either by law or by special decree (ψήφισμα), or in consequence of covenant
between the parties, e.g. when proceedings were on a contract to which
were annexed penalties for non-performance. (2) In many private actions,
e.g. in recovery of debt or to establish title to property, no τίμησις was
necessary after award of judgment on the fact or right.

496. Ἀπαγωγή, ἐφήγησις, ἔνδειξις. These actions were distinguished by
Some special two peculiarities of procedure. (1) The prosecutor was not
forms of public obliged to summon his opponent to appear before the com-
action.
petent authority on a certain day, but either himself seized
the criminal and carried him before the magistrate, as in ἀπαγωγή, or conducted the magistrate and his officers to the spot where the culprit was to
be found, as in ἐφήγησις, or lodged with the magistrate a written information
(ἔνδειξις), leaving him to effect the arrest. (2) The magistrate took steps
to secure the presence of the prisoner at the trial either by committing him
to gaol or by requiring three sufficient sureties (ἐγγυηταί) for his appearance.
The law only permitted such an invasion of the liberty of a citizen in the
case of certain gross and notorious offences. Ἀπαγωγή was allowed
(1) against 'malefactors' (κακοῦργοι) in the technical application of the
term, i.e. against thieves (κλέπται), clothes-stealers (λωποδύται, specially
active in the gymnasia), cut-purses (βαλαντιοτόμοι), house-breakers (τοιχω-
ρύχοι), kidnappers (ἀνδραποδισταί, formidable in a slave-holding society);
(2) against persons labouring under any kind of disfranchisement (ἀτιμία),

if detected exercising the rights from which law excluded them; (3) against persons banished either for homicide or political crimes, if they unlawfully returned to the country (κατιέναι). Probably ἀπαγωγή was not strictly legitimate, unless the offender was caught *flagrante delicto* (ἐπ᾽ αὐτοφώρῳ). 'Malefactors' who confessed before the magistrate were executed without a trial. The Eleven had jurisdiction over classes (1) and (2), the Thesmothetae over class (3). It is noticeable that attempts were sometimes made to use ἀπαγωγή as a swifter and easier method of prosecuting for murder, the accused person being apprehended on a charge of violating law by trespassing on public or sacred places when stained by bloodshed; but we have no means of determining how far this interesting innovation was supported by law or public opinion. So, too, in moments of public excitement the Athenians were very ready to have recourse to this summary form of procedure to punish offences quite outside its original scope, *e.g.* to punish metoecs who left Athens at times of public danger. Little is known about ἐφήγησις. It could be employed against thieves, and probably was sometimes necessary, for a private citizen was not allowed to enter forcibly another man's house, even in pursuit of a criminal, and ἔνδειξις was apparently not applied to 'malefactors.' The range of ἔνδειξις was thus narrower than that of ἀπαγωγή. In our authorities we only read of its use against the second and third class of offenders enumerated above. An 'information' was given either to the Eleven or to the Thesmothetae.

497. The distinctive feature of φάσις and ἀπογραφή was the reward accruing to the prosecutor (for a possible exception see below), and the court-fees required in consideration of this advantage.   φάσις.

Procedure took the normal course of summons by the prosecutor and appearance of the parties before some magistrate. A φάσις could be instituted (1) against those who infringed the laws regulating export and import, the customs, the corn-traffic, the silver mines of Attica; (2) against guardians mismanaging wards' estates (φάσις ὀρφανικοῦ οἴκου). The presiding magistrate varied according to the offence, *e.g.* cases concerning the mines and customs went to the Thesmothetae; offences against import and export laws to the Superintendents of the Emporium (οἱ ἐπιμεληταὶ τοῦ ἐμπορίου); while the First Archon protected the interests of orphans.

498. The application of the word ἀπογραφή to denote an action is derived from the meaning 'written inventory.' (1) Any citizen believing another to be in possession of State-property   ἀπογραφή.

could enforce either surrender or proof of title in court by submitting to the Eleven a 'specification' of the said property. (2) The process was extended to assist the State in recovering debts, particularly debts on judgments in court. A State-debtor was not only *ipso facto* ἄτιμος, but on failure to pay by a certain date (generally the 9th Prytany of the year in which the verdict was given) his debt was doubled and could be exacted by confiscation; at this stage any private person could help or stimulate the action of the executive by presenting an ἀπογραφή of property alleged

31—2

to belong to the debtor, but a trial only ensued when the articles of the inventory were contested wholly or in part, or the debt denied. A share of three-quarters was the recompense of the informers according to [Dem.] LIII. 2, but this seems a surprisingly large proportion.

499. The first task of a litigant was to catch his adversary in some

Normal course of an action, public or private.

public place and summon him (προσκαλεῖσθαι, καλεῖσθαι). A summons (πρόσκλησις, κλῆσις) at Athens was an oral request to appear at a stated time before the magistrate within whose province the suit lay, and was delivered by the plaintiff or prosecutor in the presence of witnesses, generally two (κλητῆρες). The regular interval between citation and appearance is thought to have been five days. An alien (but not a citizen) could be taken at once to a magistrate (the Polemarch) and either imprisoned or held to bail. If on the appointed day the defendant did not attend, and service of summons was duly attested, he was liable to suffer judgment by default (ἐρήμην ὀφλισκάνειν), which however might be reversed by successful prosecution of the κλητῆρες for false citation (γραφὴ ψευδοκλητείας). If both parties appeared, the magistrate had first to consider the plaint or bill of indictment (λῆξις, ἔγκλημα), which was submitted in writing. No doubt in theory Athenian magistrates had power summarily to dismiss an accusation for errors in form or law; but they were untrained men, with no special legal knowledge, and the danger of deposition during office and of prosecution on the expiry of their term made them apprehensive of the consequences of denying a suitor, or of appearing to trespass in any way on the prerogatives of the dicasts. They were naturally disposed to leave technical difficulties to be raised by the defendant at a later stage, and the cases, we may suspect, were not numerous in which to quash a suit was clearly safer than to entertain it. If the magistrate professed himself satisfied with the plaintiff's statement, he proceeded to require court-fees from the complainant —whether the defendant paid now or later is not known—or the παράστασις from a public prosecutor, or the deposit (παρακαταβολή), when this was necessary; and on payment made arrangements for the examination (ἀνάκρισις), in which the case on both sides was to be fully set forth and scrutinised. The Forty sent all suits within their jurisdiction to be examined by a public arbitrator, but otherwise the magistrate who admitted the plaint superintended the preparation of the case for trial before Heliasts. He also saw that the charge was copied out on a whitened board (σανίς, λεύκωμα), and exposed for public inspection in his office or some appropriate place. The appointment of a day for the examination ended the first stage of proceedings.

500. The ἀνάκρισις probably began with the parties taking oaths to

ἀνάκρισις : παραγραφαί.

the truth of their declarations (ἀντωμοσίαι, διωμοσίαι). The defendant, being called upon for his defence, handed in a written plea. If instead of meeting the charge by a direct

denial he alleged that the action was not maintainable (οὐκ εἰσαγώγιμος) on
grounds of law or fact, *e.g.* because the magistrate was not competent, or
because the time for legal proceedings had expired, or because the matter
had been already settled by a judgment of a court or an arbitrator's award,
or because a release and discharge (ἀπαλλαγή, ἄφεσις) had been given, the
objection raised, if not allowed by the plaintiff, was referred to a court of
Heliasts, thus giving rise to an action distinct from the original suit, which
was meanwhile suspended.　　An exception to the plaint might take the
shape of a παραγραφή or a διαμαρτυρία.　The παραγραφή, a written statement, as the name imports, was the more convenient form of special plea.
The burden of proof lay with the defendant, who at the trial of the issue
spoke first.　If he failed to convince the judges—and they were impatient
of formal and technical objections—the primary action was resumed ; if he
succeeded, the plaintiff was or was not barred from further proceedings,
according to the substance of the special plea.　In a trial on a παραγραφή
both parties were liable to the ἐπωβελία on failure to obtain a fifth of
the votes.

　　501.　A διαμαρτυρία was a more complex and certainly older procedure.
If the defendant pleaded that the action was not maintainable, the plaintiff had the prior right to produce a witness, 　ἀνάκρισις :
who deposed the contrary, that the action was maintainable, 　διαμαρτυρίαι.
for reasons specified.　The contest was then transformed into an action for
false testimony (δίκη ψευδομαρτυρίων), brought by the defendant against the
witness put forward by the plaintiff.　But it might happen that the plaintiff
did not choose to exercise his right.　It was then the turn of the defendant
to put forward a witness to testify that the action could not be brought into
court, and of the plaintiff to take the offensive and bring an action against
the defendant's witness.　The effect of this secondary trial on the original
suit depended, of course, on the character of the exception taken.　The
procedure was allowed both in public and private suits, but in our authorities is commonest in cases of disputed succession.　In these, however, it is
somewhat simplified.　When *e.g.* sons in possession of an estate (κλῆρος)
availed themselves of the διαμαρτυρία to shut out claimants alleging themselves to be the rightful heirs, there was strictly neither plaintiff nor
defendant.　The διαμαρτυρία always took the same form, the declaration of
the witness being that 'the estate cannot be claimed at law (οὐκ ἔστιν
ἐπίδικος), there being lawful sons.'　We find no example of a contrary
declaration emanating from the other side.　The burden of disproof fell on
the claimants.　And the consequences of the secondary action were more
decisive.　If the witness was acquitted, the claimants necessarily abandoned
their pretensions.　If he was convicted, the estate was as good as lost to
the sons, but not as yet secured by the claimants, who had still to establish
their own rights in court, and might in the end be ousted by new competitors.

502. If the defendant took the 'straightforward' course (εὐθυδικίᾳ
εἰσιέναι), denying the charge without demurrers and evasions,
the magistrate's work was to collect all the articles of proof
and see that they were in the proper shape, for nothing was
admissible at the trial that was not in writing and had not
been disclosed at the ἀνάκρισις. Law was proved by authenticated extracts
from statutes, decrees, and public records. Copies of bonds (συνθῆκαι,
συγγραφαί), wills, accounts, etc. had to be certified by witnesses. An action
was allowed to compel an adversary or any third person to produce
relevant documents (δίκη εἰς ἐμφανῶν κατάστασιν). All testimonial evidence
was presented in the shape of written depositions. It was usual, but not
necessary, to bring the witnesses to the office to confirm their declarations.
An oath, though common, was not obligatory, and was administered by the
parties, not by the magistrate. At the trial, however, no depositions could
be read to the Judges, unless the witnesses were present in court to signify
their assent. If a witness was abroad or ill, his statement was committed
to writing in presence of persons appointed for the purpose, who were
required to testify to the accuracy of the document (called an ἐκμαρτυρία)
before the evidence was admitted. A citizen was bound to give testimony
when requested; and reluctant witnesses could be compelled by a solemn
summons (κλήτευσις) either to depose or to take a public oath (at the stone
of swearing in the agora) that they knew nothing of the matter (ἐξόμνυσθαι);
the penalty for contumacy was 1000 dr. A witness who broke an engagement to attend in court was liable to prosecution (δίκη λιπομαρτυρίου).
Hearsay evidence (ἀκοὴν μαρτυρεῖν) was inadmissible, except the declarations of persons deceased. Women, minors, and disfranchised citizens
were incompetent to give testimony. Neither of the parties could be
witness in his own case; but they could cross-examine each other, and the
answers were taken down and used at the trial.

ἀνάκρισις: documentary proofs and witnesses.

503. The evidence of slaves could only be given under torture, and was
not admitted without the consent of both parties. Hence the
frequent use in legal proceedings of the 'challenge to torture'
(πρόκλησις εἰς βάσανον). Slaves were often in possession of
valuable information, and one of the regular artifices of litigants was to offer
to give up their own slaves for examination (παραδιδόναι, ἐκδιδόναι) or to
ask the surrender (ἐξαιτεῖν) of slaves belonging to their adversaries. A
formal document was drafted, stating the conditions and consequences of
the inquiry, *e.g.* whether the statement extracted should only decide some
particular point in dispute; or should be taken as a final verdict ending the
whole controversy and disposing of the necessity for a trial. Challenges
were not serious attempts to reach a settlement, but were designed to
influence the dicasts. The aim of a challenger was to construct such a
proposal as would be refused, in order to be able to denounce his opponent
in court for concealing the truth from fear of revelations; the opponent
sought to turn the tables by an inconvenient counter-challenge, and both

πρόκλησις εἰς βάσανον.

sides recited to the judges commonplaces on the use of torture as an instrument to elicit truth. It is not likely that freemen were in the habit of staking important interests on the word of a slave on the rack.

504. The 'challenge to an oath' ($\pi\rho\acute{o}\kappa\lambda\eta\sigma\iota\varsigma$ $\epsilon\grave{\iota}\varsigma$ $\acute{o}\rho\kappa o\nu$) was a relic of an ordeal. Trial by oath originally was an alternative to trial by witness. The Gortynian code sometimes directs that an oath of exculpation shall decide a cause. But at Athens in the fourth century this method of decision was not controlled by a magistrate, but had sunk to a matter of private arrangement between the parties. The challenge was a written proposal that the dispute should be settled, wholly or in part, by a peculiarly solemn oath to be taken, according to circumstances, either by the challenger himself or by his opponent or by some third person, who might even be a woman. Such offers were rarely sincere and rarely accepted. The risk was too great, and the 'challenge to an oath' generally indicated that the challenger had no witnesses or documentary evidence to produce. But if oratorical capital might be made out of a refusal, the recognised manœuvre was to devise a counter-challenge that would be rejected by the adversary.

$\pi\rho\acute{o}\kappa\lambda\eta\sigma\iota\varsigma$ $\epsilon\grave{\iota}\varsigma$ $\acute{o}\rho\kappa o\nu.$

Other challenges of various kinds might be made before the hearing in court, but the two described are most prominent in the Orators.

505. As soon as both parties had marshalled their proofs or exhausted their stratagems, the examination was closed, and the magistrate took over all the papers and kept them sealed and secure until the trial. The date was settled with the Thesmothetae. The law prescribed that some suits (*e.g.* all cognizable by the $\epsilon\grave{\iota}\sigma\alpha\gamma\omega\gamma\epsilon\hat{\iota}\varsigma$ and mining and mercantile suits received by the Thesmothetae) should be introduced into court within the space of a month from the lodgment of the plaint, whence the name $\acute{\epsilon}\mu\mu\eta\nu o\iota$ $\delta\acute{\iota}\kappa\alpha\iota$, but in general no limit was fixed, and a trial might be long delayed by the pressure of business on magistrates and dicasts, or by the success of a litigant in procuring adjournments of the $\acute{\alpha}\nu\acute{\alpha}\kappa\rho\iota\sigma\iota\varsigma$ and postponements of the hearing. The magistrate or magistrates who had superintended the examination (for examination before arbitrators see § 485) presided also at the trial, supported by police, heralds, clerks, etc., and were responsible for the orderly conduct of business. When the judges were in their places and all was ready, the president called on the parties to come forward. A suitor who did not answer the summons, whether plaintiff or defendant, suffered judgment by default, unless some satisfactory explanation of his absence, such as sickness, the death of a near relative, or public duties, was presented in proper form. A person unable or unwilling to appear procured a friend or agent to swear to the truth of the alleged excuse ($\acute{\upsilon}\pi\omega\mu o\sigma\acute{\iota}\alpha$) and pray for an adjournment; the other side was allowed to offer a counter-oath ($\acute{\alpha}\nu\theta\upsilon\pi\omega$-$\mu o\sigma\acute{\iota}\alpha$), denying the facts alleged and opposing the application, and the dicasts, after hearing arguments and evidence, voted whether the petition should be granted.

The trial: date and adjournments.

506. If both suitors were present, the clerk of the court read out the
plaint and the rejoinder, after which the parties were called
upon to address the judges, the plaintiff first, and after him
the defendant. In some cases each side spoke twice. Hired
advocates were expressly forbidden, every citizen being presumed by the
law capable of pleading his own cause. This was too hard a rule even for
Athenians, who generally had some familiarity with public affairs, and
whose law aimed at simplicity, and was certainly accessible. A nervous
and inexperienced speaker, after a few prefatory words, could get permission
from the judges to call a friend or relation to support him (συνηγορεῖν). But
these 'friends' never developed at Athens into professional advocates;
they had always to satisfy a suspicious audience drawn from a small society
that their only motive was personal feeling, even if it was nothing better
than hatred of the side they opposed; and to speak often branded a man as
a συκοφάντης. One profession only, and one peculiar art, was produced by
the Athenian system, the profession and art of the λογογράφοι, men who
made a business of composing speeches to be learned and delivered by
others, and who also, no doubt, gave advice on niceties of law and procedure. But the name was a reproach, and the perfection of the composer's
art was to mask his identity and disguise his legal learning. A fixed time,
varying of course according to the case, was allotted to the speeches, and
an official (ὁ ἐφ' ὕδωρ) checked the speakers by a water-clock (κλεψύδρα).
When the orator had occasion to appeal to his proofs, the clock was
stopped (ἐπιλαβεῖν τὸ ὕδωρ), while the clerk read out the deposition or
challenge or oath referred to, and the witnesses were called up. Witnesses
were never cross-examined, but a speaker could interrogate his adversary,
and the judges could interrupt and question the speaker.

The trial: speeches.

507. The speeches ended, officials distributed among the judges ψῆφοι
for voting. The nature and use of the ψῆφος differed at
different periods. The comedians of the fifth century speak
of shells (χοιρῖναι), and of a vessel of acquittal (καδίσκος
ἀπολύων) and of condemnation (ἀπολλύς). In the last quarter of the fourth
century, according to Aristotle, each judge received two bronze discs with a
cylindrical axis (αὐλίσκος) running through the centre. One had a hollow
axis, was called ἡ τετρυπημένη (ψῆφος), and was for condemnation; the
other, in which the axis was solid, was called ἡ πλήρης, and was for
acquittal. Two urns (ἀμφορεῖς) were set on a platform (βῆμα), one of
bronze, called 'the decisive urn' (ὁ κύριος), because the judge dropped into
it through a narrow slit the ψῆφος which expressed his verdict, the other of
wood, called 'the inoperative urn' (ὁ ἄκυρος), for the reception of the
second ψῆφος, which was nugatory. The aim of these arrangements was to
prevent frauds and ensure secrecy. It was impossible to put two ψῆφοι
into the same urn, and spectators could not detect how a judge voted.
The ψῆφοι in the bronze urn were publicly sorted and counted, and the
number of votes on each side was proclaimed by a herald. Victory went

The trial: the voting.

to the suitor who had the larger number; if the votes were equal, the defendant was acquitted. When the verdict was guilty and the case an ἀγὼν τιμητός, a second vote was necessary; the judges had to decide the penalty, personal or pecuniary (τιμᾶν τί χρὴ παθεῖν ἢ ἀποτεῖσαι). A penalty (τίμημα) was always named in the plaint, but a prosecutor after the announcement of the votes was sometimes induced by pity or policy to propose (τιμᾶσθαι) something more lenient. Thereupon the defendant made a counter-proposal (ἀντιτιμᾶσθαι), naming the punishment he was content to suffer, and the judges simply voted in the same way as before, for one or the other proposal. This unsatisfactory method of awarding justice was inevitable in courts constituted on the democratic model, in which the president was not a judge; if every judge out of a body of 200 or more had been allowed to suggest what he considered a reasonable sentence, the result would have been disputes, confusion, and waste of time. In a few cases the law gave the judges the discretion of imposing a specified additional penalty (προστίμημα), such as confinement in the stocks (ποδο-κάκκη) for five days and five nights, when a person had been found guilty of theft and condemned in damages, but here there was no difficulty; a judge moved to inflict the legal extra penalty, and the rest voted yes or no on the motion.

508. In public actions the punishments were either personal, *i.e.* death, selling into slavery (not used against citizens), deprivation whole or partial of civil rights (ἀτιμία), or pecuniary, *i.e.* fines   Penalties. and confiscation. Imprisonment was not used as a separate and independent punishment, though decreed as an additional penalty in a few cases, either to accelerate payment of debts due from tax-farmers (τελῶναι) and lessees of public property (οἱ μισθούμενοι τὰ δημόσια), or as a public stigma for petty theft. Athens had only one prison (τὸ δεσμωτήριον, in familiar language τὸ οἴκημα, 'the House'), and that not very secure; and to keep convicted criminals in confinement, unless they were to be speedily executed, would have seemed to Athenians expensive and superfluous. No public feeling against capital sentences existed, and disfranchisement, followed, if necessary, by confiscation, was ordinarily an effective way of coercing State-debtors.

Penalties in private actions were pecuniary only, with one exception; imprisonment could be added in 'mercantile suits' (ἐμπορικαὶ δίκαι) in which one of the parties was commonly a travelling foreign merchant (ἔμπορος), who, if defeated, might slip away to avoid payment, and, if victorious, could not be expected to stop at Athens to combat the delays of a fraudulent debtor.

509. In public cases the sentence was carried out by magistrates, *e.g.* the Eleven superintended executions, the πωληταί sold con-   Execution. fiscated estates, the πράκτορες registered and got in debts. In private cases the rule was self-help; no public officer gave assistance in execution of judgment. The court or the law named a period within

which the damages were to be paid or the property surrendered (ἡ προ-θεσμία sc. ἡμέρα). If the defendant did not comply by the appointed day, he was said to be ὑπερήμερος, and his adversary had the right to seize and, if necessary, sell movables (ἐνέχυρα λαβεῖν, ἐνεχυράζειν) in discharge of the debt, or to take possession of real property by formal entry (ἐμβατεύειν). A remedy against resistance was given in an action for ejectment (δίκη ἐξούλης). A judgment-debtor condemned in this action was treated as a public offender; he incurred a fine to the State equal in value to the damages or property the plaintiff was seeking to recover, and could escape the painful disabilities attached to a state-debtor only by satisfying both the plaintiff and the State. Some scholars think that an action for ejectment could also be brought as a substitute for proceedings by way of distraint or entry, non-payment being interpreted to constitute ejectment, and that this was the only course open, if no visible effects existed, execution against the debtor's person being unlawful.

510. There was no appeal from dicasts, for no superior jurisdiction existed. But their decision could be set aside on two pleas.

Reversal of judgment. (1) A litigant who had lost his case through non-appearance in court, might within two months apply for a new trial (τὴν ἔρημον ἀντιλαγχάνειν, but, when an arbitrator's award was assailed, τὴν μὴ οὖσαν ἀντιλαγχάνειν). (2) A judgment might be suspended and eventually annulled by prosecuting witnesses for false testimony (δίκη ψευδομαρτυριῶν), provided that notice of prosecution (ἐπισκήπτεσθαι ταῖς μαρτυρίαις, to 'denounce' the evidence) was given in court before the judges began to vote.

Bibliography. J. H. Lipsius, *Das attische Recht und Rechtsverfahren.* Leipzig, 1905–15 (the standard work). *Recueil des Inscriptions Juridiques Grecques,* by R. Dareste, B. Haussoullier, Th. Reinach. Paris, 1891–1904. *Histoire du Droit Privé de la République Athénienne,* by L. Beauchet. Paris, 1897. 4 vols. (A systematic exposition of the contents of the law.) *Das Stadtrecht von Gortyn und seine Beziehungen zum gemeingriechischen Rechte,* by J. Kohler and E. Ziebarth. Göttingen, 1912. G. M. Calhoun, *The growth of criminal law in Ancient Greece,* Berkeley, 1927. P. Vinogradoff, *Outlines of Historical Jurisprudence,* vol. II, *The Jurisprudence of the Greek City,* Oxford, 1922. Also articles in Pauly-Wissowa, *Real-Encyklopädie* and Daremberg et Saglio, *Dict. des Antiquités.* See also *A working Bibliography of Greek Law,* by G. M. Calhoun and C. Delamere, Harvard, 1927.

VI. 3. FINANCE.

511. It will be convenient to review the methods of Greek finance under the following heads: i. City States. II. Federations. III. Territorial monarchies. IV. Temples.

City States. General principles.

I. Although we do not know in detail the financial practice of any city State except Athens, the information supplied by Aristotle, by the author of the pseudo-Aristotelian treatise on *Economics*, and by a large and growing stock of inscriptions, makes it possible to assert certain principles which underlay the general usage of city State finance.

Except in a few States which maintained a large staff of paid officials, or a fleet in permanent commission, the normal expenses of government were small. These expenses, moreover, were frequently curtailed by the custom of transferring certain public obligations or liturgies from the State to individuals (see § 515). Hence the revenue required in ordinary times was inconsiderable. In view of the smallness of the sums involved, comparatively little care was bestowed in most city States on financial administration. It was an uncommon thing to appoint a special ministry of finance, or to take a general survey of income and expenditure in the form of annual budgets; and hardly any attempt was made to accumulate reserve funds against a time of crisis. The imposts were for the most part of a simple character, so as to offer no great difficulty in assessment or collection. A large proportion of the revenue was usually derived from indirect taxes such as market dues and customs. These were frequently, though not invariably, levied at a uniform low rate, $2\,^{\circ}/_{\circ}$ being a common figure. No distinction was ordinarily made for fiscal purposes between imports and exports, and differential tariffs for the protection of home industries were unusual. As a source of ordinary revenue direct taxation in the form of a land tax or of a general property tax was avoided, but percentages were frequently levied on the profits of trades. Some States also derived a large revenue from rents accruing from State properties, such as lands, houses and fisheries, and from royalties on the produce of mines. The collection of taxes was for the most part left to companies of contractors, to whom the right of collection was assigned by public auction, usually for the term of one year. On the other hand much care was bestowed on the keeping of accurate accounts, so that misappropriations of public money must in theory at least have been very difficult of execution.

There is no clear evidence of taxes being fixed at progressive rates, so as to place a relatively heavier burden on the rich. But it is probable that the poorest class of citizens at Athens and elsewhere were exempt from the general property-tax (§ 514). Moreover the liturgies which the wealthy had to perform, and the free contributions (ἐπιδόσεις) which they were expected to offer in times of special need, more than made up for the absence of progressive ratings. Additional burdens in the form of a poll tax or trade-licence were laid on foreigners. It will also be noticed that the selection of taxable objects was generally so contrived as to favour the small land-owners as against the traders. The payment of taxes in kind, which was still in use during the sixth century (as in the case of the 10 °/₀ impost levied by Peisistratus on the produce of Attica), had in the following century been generally superseded by money contributions.

Extraordinary expenditure, frequently necessitated by the fondness of the city States for war, and by their improvidence in not building up reserve funds, was sometimes met by the imposition of a general property tax (εἰσφορά). But recourse was often had to expedients which purchased a momentary convenience at the price of much ultimate harm. Of these devices the most reputable were a loan from another State or, more often, from a temple treasure (§ 521), an appeal for special subscriptions by rich citizens, or the creation of State monopolies. But the list of financial makeshifts also includes depreciation of coinage, compulsory loans, confiscations and other ruinous exactions.

512. Among Greek city States the finances of Athens are at once most important and best known. The principal charges upon the public purse were as follows:

Athens.
Expenditure.

(1) The maintenance of the army and navy. Although the upkeep of the warships was made a liturgy and so did not devolve upon the State, the provision of new vessels and the payment of the crews, which absorbed ½—1 talent for each ship in every month, constituted a heavy item of expenditure, even in times of peace (about 250 t. per annum in the time of Pericles). The army was a less costly institution, as only a small fraction of the total forces was permanently embodied. But the large sum of 40 talents was expended yearly on the horsemen. In times of war the cost grew disproportionately, owing to the high rates of pay (1—2 drachmas per day). The campaign of 440—39 B.C. against Samos is computed to have consumed 15—1600 t., and the siege of Potidaea (432—30 B.C.) absorbed 2000 t. (2) The upkeep of fortifications, harbours and other public works. Much care was bestowed on these even in normal times. The special expenditure of Pericles on new constructions was enormous: his buildings on the Acropolis alone cost over 2000 talents. (3) Payment for public service. In the fifth century wages were paid to 500 members of council, to 6000 jurors, and to 1400 public officials. About 390 B.C. a fee was also paid to citizens attending the Ecclesia. The amounts were at first small (1—3 obols a day for jurors), but the pay for attending the Ecclesia, which was the most considerable item, was raised to 6 and for some meetings to 9 obols. The expenditure eventually grew so high that one of the first measures of reform introduced after the Macedonian

conquest (321 or 317 B.C.) was the reduction of public salaries. (4) The celebration of public festivals. The outlay upon these was largely defrayed by means of liturgies (§ 515). But a serious expenditure was incurred in the distribution of pocket-money from the public purse to holiday-makers. In the days of Pericles, who introduced these 'theoric' bounties, payment was made at a low rate (2 obols a day) and was confined to the Dionysia, in the fourth century disbursements were made at most or all of the festivals, which were specially numerous at Athens. Thus Demosthenes (1. 19) could argue that the diversion of the 'theoric' funds into the war chest would constitute a decisive increment to the military resources of Athens. In 321 or 317 B.C. 'theoric' pay was abolished. (5) Minor expenses, which included the maintenance of 300—1200 public slaves as a police force; the payment of poor-law relief (2 obols a day; the $\delta\iota\omega\beta\epsilon\lambda\iota\alpha$ instituted by Cleophon c. 410 B.C. was a temporary expedient); and the graving of public inscriptions.

513. The ordinary items of revenue were:

(1) The royalties on the mines of Laurium, which were worked intensively since the time of Peisistratus and from **Athens. Revenue.** 483 B.C. contributed substantial sums to the exchequer. (2) The duties levied at Peiraeus on imports and exports, at a normal rate of 2°/ₒ ($\pi\epsilon\nu\tau\eta\kappa o\sigma\tau\acute{\eta}$). In 401—400 B.C. these brought in a net revenue of 30—36 t. But in periods of commercial prosperity the proceeds may well have stood at double or treble this amount. (3) Market dues ($\epsilon\pi\acute{\omega}\nu\iota\alpha$), usually at the rate of 1°/ₒ. The yield of this tax must have been considerable, for Athens in the fifth century had become an emporium for the produce of half the Mediterranean and of the Black Sea. (4) A harbour toll ($\epsilon\lambda\lambda\iota\mu\acute{\epsilon}\nu\iota o\nu$) of unknown amount. This impost must also have produced a large sum, for practically all the trade of Athens was water-borne. (5) An octroi ($\delta\iota\alpha\pi\acute{\nu}\lambda\iota o\nu$), probably levied at the gates of Athens. Perhaps this served as a substitute for customs duties on the land frontier. (6) Various minor imposts, such as the poll tax on resident aliens ($\mu\epsilon\tau o\acute{\iota}\kappa\iota o\nu$) at 6—12 drs., the fees paid by non-citizens for the right of trading ($\xi\epsilon\nu\iota\kappa\grave{o}\nu$ $\tau\acute{\epsilon}\lambda o\varsigma$), and the proceeds of judicial fines and confiscations. The yield of the $\mu\epsilon\tau o\acute{\iota}\kappa\iota o\nu$ stood in 309 B.C. at not less than 20 t., for in this year 10,000 aliens were officially registered, and this total probably comprises adult males only; the yield in the fifth century cannot be determined, but was probably not less. (7) Fines and confiscations must at times have produced a large revenue, and it is even alleged that Athenian juries dealt severely with prisoners in the hope of thus easing the public finances.

In addition to these sources of income, the Athenians during the second half of the fifth century had at their disposal the tribute from the members of the Delian League. The transference of the **Tribute.** federal treasury to Athens in 454 B.C. soon led to the fusion of imperial and Attic finances, and appropriations of federal-funds to Athenian purposes became a regular practice. The amount of the tribute, which in

477 B.C. is said to have been 460 t., subsequently fluctuated a good deal; but eventually it underwent progressive augmentations, and in 425 B.C. it was assessed at 1360 t. After a reduction in 421 B.C. it was raised in 417 B.C. to 12–1300 t. In 413 B.C. a system of indirect taxation was introduced in place of the tribute (§ 519) in the hope of increasing the income from the allies, but the gradual disruption of the League soon cut off this source of revenue. A further imperial impost may be found in the δεκατή, which was probably a tithe levied on all ships passing through the Bosporus. Taken altogether, these imperial exactions more than doubled the income of Athens.

514. In times of emergency the normal revenue was supplemented by various expedients. During the fifth century the commonest practice was to contract a loan from a temple treasure (§ 521).

Extraordinary Revenue.

Failing this resource, appeals were issued for free contributions, to which both Athenians and foreign sympathisers sometimes contributed. But the chief extraordinary source of income was the property-tax (εἰσφορά), the first levy of which is recorded in 428 B.C. (Thuc. III. 19), when a sum of 200 t. was collected by this means. In 378—7 B.C. improved arrangements were made for the assessment of the burden, which had hitherto been left to be settled between the individual tax-payer and a board of assessment commissioners (ἐπιγραφεῖς). A census of land, houses and other property in Attica was taken, so that the Ecclesia in fixing the amount of the Eisphora might know what percentage of the national wealth it was exacting, and so might save itself from imposing an excessive rate. The total declared value was 5750 t. (Polyb. II. 62. 7, confirmed by Dem. 14. 30). The property of the poorer citizens was probably not included in this valuation, and no doubt much wealth was concealed or undervalued. Furthermore the work of individual assessment was now made to devolve upon groups of tax-payers (συμμορίαι), 100 in number, each of which possessed an approximately equal aggregate of wealth and contributed an equal quota of the sum required. The members of each group were left to distribute the burden imposed upon it among themselves. For this purpose they appointed a president (ἡγεμών), usually their richest member, and a registrar (διαγραφεύς) who made out the amount due from each individual. The collection of the Eisphora, which at first had been in the hands of State officials (ἐκλογεῖς) was made over about 374 B.C., as a liturgy, to the 300 richest citizens, who paid in advance (προεισφορά) the full amount of the tax and recovered as best they could from the other members of their respective symmories. The list of the 300 was originally drawn up by the Council; subsequent alterations in it were probably effected by ἀντίδοσις (§ 515). In the fourth, probably also in the fifth century, both real and personal estate was taxed, and corporate property was also subject to the impost, but the poorer citizens were exempt. The question whether the Eisphora was a uniform or a progressive tax cannot be answered definitely. Probably differential rates were in force, and in the fifth century at least the

Solonian classes were no doubt used as a basis, but the method of differentiation is quite uncertain.

The total revenue of Athens amounted in 431 B.C. to 'not less than
1000 t.' (Xen. *Anab.* VII. 1. 27).   In 422 B.C. this total
had been nearly doubled (Ar. *Vesp.* 660).   By 346 B.C. the   Total revenue.
public income had sunk to 400 t. and in an unspecified year of the fourth
century only 130 t. were collected (Dem. 10. 37).   On the other hand in
338—326 B.C. not less than 1200 t. were levied annually, and in 317—
307 B.C. the same total was attained.   In times of war the revenues often
fell far short of requirements, but under normal conditions they covered all
necessary expenditure, and in the age of Pericles they usually provided a
handsome surplus.

515.   The various 'public services' (λῃτουργίαι) may be considered
under the head of revenues, in so far as they relieved the
exchequer of considerable expenditure.   The best known   The ordinary
liturgies.
regular 'liturgies' are χορηγία, γυμνασιαρχία, ἑστίασις, ἀρχε-
θεωρία.   The first was the obligation to collect, maintain, instruct, and
equip one of the many choruses needed for the dramatic and musical and
orchestic competitions at the great festivals.   For example, at the City
Dionysia 3 tragedies, 5 comedies, and 10 dithyrambs were performed, so
that 18 choregi had to be found.   The expense varied according to the
nature of the competition and the ambition of the choregus; we read of
3000 dr. spent on a tragic chorus, 1600 dr. on a comic chorus, 1500 dr.
and 300 dr. on a cyclic (*i.e.* dithyrambic) chorus.   The task of the γυμνα-
σίαρχος was to keep and train a team of men to represent his tribe in the
torch-races (λαμπαδηδρομίαι) associated with some festivals, *e.g.* the Panathenaea and the Hephaestiaea; 1200 dr. might be spent.   The ἑστιάτωρ
had to feast his tribe, doubtless on some religious occasion; what this cost
is not recorded.   The ἀρχεθέωρος was the head of a sacred embassy sent in
the name of Athens to some festival outside Attica, *e.g.* to Delos or Olympia,
or to consult the oracles at Delphi and Dodona.   The expense of such
embassies was partly borne by the State, but prominent men sometimes
spent lavishly to maintain the dignity of their country.   In the age of
Aristotle the choregi for tragedies and the ἀρχεθέωρος were appointed by
the Archon; the rest were nominated by their tribes.   These burdens were
only laid on men whose property was 3 t. or more.   No one could be
compelled to take more than one 'liturgy' in the same year, or the same
'liturgy' twice, or to serve in two successive years.   Anyone who thought
his nomination unfair had a remedy (called 'exchange' (ἀντίδοσις) from one
incident in the procedure), provided he could fix on some definite person
on whom the burden ought to have been imposed.   He could challenge
that person to take the 'liturgy' or exchange properties.   If no compromise
was reached, the dispute was taken before a court of judges, who heard
inventories and arguments, and assigned the burden to the party whom
they considered more fit to bear it.

516. The duties attached to the office of trierarch are a remarkable
illustration of the demands made by the Athenian democracy
on the patriotism of the rich. The State provided the ship
and all necessary equipment (τὰ σκεύη), and was supposed to
pay the crew and petty officers. The legal obligation of the trierarch was
to get the vessel launched and ready for service, to keep it efficient while
at sea, and on the expiry of his term to hand over everything, hull, fittings,
and tackle, in good condition, or pay damages, if he could not prove in
court some valid plea, such as storm or battle. In practice trierarchs
often did more, from ambition or public spirit, or because the State
failed in its duty. The responsibility and dangers of such a post were
serious enough in themselves, apart from the expense, which normally
ranged from 40 to 60 minae for a year's command. At the beginning of the
Peloponnesian war the Generals were able to nominate annually 400 men
rich enough to maintain one ship each for a year. After the Sicilian
disaster it became necessary to allow two persons (συντριήραρχοι) to divide
between them the service and the charges. In 357—6 B.C. the law of Periander adapted to the trierarchy the system of companies already used for
the εἰσφορά. The 1200 richest citizens were distributed into 20 companies
of 60 members each. The poorer members in each company were formed
according to their means into contributory groups (συντέλειαι) of 3, 5, 6 or 7,
each set of contributors (συντελεῖς) being responsible for one ship. The
actual commander was chosen from the group by the Generals in conjunction with 'The Twenty,' who were probably the superintendents (ἐπιμεληταί)
of the companies. The plan was a failure, according to Hypereides and
Demosthenes. The richer members, who had been put at the head of the
companies, arranged themselves in groups in their own interests, so that men
wealthy enough to undertake a ship by themselves escaped with a payment
which was only ⅙th or 1⁄10th of their proper share. Demosthenes in 340—
39 B.C. carried a law to remove this abuse, and to secure that each member
should contribute in proportion to his property, but the details of his scheme
are unknown. The census required for the trierarchy in its various forms is
nowhere stated. ἀντίδοσις was allowed, and in the fourth century no one
could be compelled to serve more than once in three years.

The trierarchy.

517. The administration of the finances was chiefly vested in the
Council. This body usually possessed no expert knowledge,
and owing to the annual changes in its membership it could
not ensure continuity of policy. But its duties called for
little exercise of discretion. The distribution of revenue was largely regulated by means of appropriations which in the fourth century at least were
established by law (I. G. II. 38, ll. 20—22), e.g. court fees and fines were
set apart for the payment of jurors. Since 435—4 B.C. surpluses were paid
automatically into the treasury of Athens (Hicks and Hill 49, ll. 49—51:
in spite of repeated attempts to assign this inscription to 420—417 B.C., the
date given above seems well established); in the fourth century they flowed

*Financial ad-
ministration.*

either into the theoric or (from 339 B.C.) into the military chest.   The chief
discretionary functions of Council were to adjudicate contracts to tax-
farmers, and to advise the Ecclesia about the levying of Eisphora and
about the disposition of unappropriated funds (ἐπέτεια).   On the other
hand its routine work was heavy, for it supervised the operations of all
financial officials and was ultimately responsible for the proper auditing of
all accounts (see § 458).   During the fourth century the control of finance
tended to pass into the hands of individual citizens who had made a
special study of the subject.   From 354 and probably on to 339 B.C.
Eubulus assumed a general supervision of the various financial officials
(Aeschines 3. 25), and from 338 to 326 B.C. Lycurgus wielded a similar
power.   Eubulus probably exercised this authority as a member of the
theoric board, and Lycurgus as a treasurer of the military chest, for the
holders of these offices possessed a co-ordinate control with the Council
over financial policy (*Ath. Pol.* 47, § 2 ; 49, § 3).   In 321 B.C. the control
of all finance was centralised under one or more magistrates ἐπὶ τῇ
διοικήσει, whose office survived into the second century B.C. (I. G. II. 453).
All the above-mentioned officials were appointed by election, and as their
term of office was frequently renewed, they were able to acquire a continuous
experience in administration.

   518.   The departmental officials, who were appointed by lot and therefore seldom consisted of specialists, were numerous and varied.
The collection of revenue was indeed largely left over to   Financial
                                                            officers.
tax-farmers, through whose agency all indirect imposts were
received, and the levying of Eisphora was eventually made into a liturgy
(§ 514).   On the other hand no attempt was made to reduce the financial
staff by the institution of a central exchequer in which all public monies
might be kept.   Each spending department possessed a chest of its own,
the keeping of which required a special official.   Hence the number of
departmental treasurers (ταμίαι) defies computation.   It will suffice here to
mention the most important of these functionaries.   Ten Hellenotamiae
received the tribute from the Delian League in the fifth century.   Ten
κωλακρέται collected the court fees of litigants.   Ten πράκτορες levied
the fines imposed by the courts.   Ten πωληταί received the rents and
royalties on the State property, and the instalments (καταβολαί) of purchase-
money from the tax-farmers.   The same officials also sold confiscated
property by auction.   The monies taken in by these and all other
collectors were paid over to ten receivers-general (ἀποδέκται), who
proceeded to apportion the revenue among the various departments according to the statutes on appropriations and the disposition of the
Council, which supervised the entire work of distribution.   Disbursements
from the departmental chests were made by the respective treasurers
according to standing orders, or by special authorisation of the Council
or Ecclesia.   The ταμίας τῆς βουλῆς and the ταμίας τοῦ δήμου defrayed
the petty cash expenses arising out of the meetings of these bodies.   The

theoric board paid the State contributions to the national holidays.
Military expenses were charged in the latter half of the fifth century
upon the Hellenotamiae; in the fourth century they seem to have been
paid by the ἀποδέκται until about 338 B.C., when a special keeper of
the war chest (ταμίας τῶν στρατιωτικῶν) became the paymaster of the
Strategi.

A remarkable feature of Athenian finance was the care bestowed
upon the control of accounts. Every official who handled
public money was required to keep a record of all his receipts
and expenses and to submit them to account (§ 453).

Control of accounts.

519. II. The finances of the federations were simpler than those of
the city States, for their expenditure could almost be comprised under a single head, the maintenance of armies and
navies. In the more rudimentary leagues, such as the Peloponnesian
League, no regular financial authority is found until the end of the fifth
century: presumably each federating State paid the expenses of its contingent out of its communal funds. In the Boeotian League of the fifth
century B.C. the federal government had acquired the right of imposing
taxes on the federating districts (§ 435).

Federations.

Peculiar conditions governed the finances of the Delian League.
Owing to the scale of its military operations it required a revenue of
exceptional size. Until 413 B.C. taxation took the form of a fixed
impost (φόρος) levied on all members of the League save a small and
diminishing number who contributed men and ships in lieu of money.
The rates of the tribute were determined in the first instance by the
general assessment of Aristeides; subsequently they were revised by special
commissioners (τακταί) appointed as a rule at intervals of four years. The
collection of the tax was left in the hands of the local authorities. In 413 B.C.
the φόρος was commuted into a 5 °/₀ duty on imports and exports, which
was levied by special federal officials (εἰκοστολόγοι) in the ports of the
various States (§ 513). At the foundation of the League the disposition of
this revenue rested with the federal parliament at Delos. But from the first
the assessment of tribute was in the hands of Athens, and the Hellenotamiae or treasurers of the federal chest were always Athenian officials.
After the transference of the treasury from Delos to Athens in 454 B.C.
control of the League's funds was usurped by the Athenian Ecclesia, by
whose decree henceforth all federal taxes were imposed and all payments
were made. Accordingly the Athenians were enabled without any constitutional hindrance to appropriate the handsome surpluses which eventually
accrued to the League (§ 513).

The finances of the second Athenian Confederacy in so far resembled
those of the first League that a common treasury was again established at
Athens. But the control of the funds and the assessment of contributions
(συντάξεις) was under the joint control of the Athenian Ecclesia and the
Congress of the allied cities. Moreover the effective revenue of the League,

barely sufficed to cover expenditure, so that appropriation of surpluses by Athens was no longer possible.

In the Achaean League a federal treasury was established for the maintenance of a permanent army. Considerable disbursements out of this chest are recorded (Polyb. v. i. 11), and mention is made of an Eisphora (Polyb. iv. 60. 4) and of fines as means of raising revenue. The method of collection was probably by requisition and not by direct levy, and it is doubtful whether any special financial magistrates were appointed except a board of Accountants (δοκιμαστῆρες).

520. III. The finances of the territorial monarchies in the post-Alexandrine age were on a far higher scale than those of the city States. The upkeep of large fleets with heavy **Monarchies.** tonnage, and of highly paid and well equipped armies, the maintenance of luxurious courts and the lavish patronage bestowed upon artists and men of learning, caused a great rise in expenditure. But the revenues more than kept pace with this increase. Antigonus Monophthalmus enjoyed an income of 11,000 t., and Ptolemy Philadelphus raised 11—14,000 t. yearly. The public income was derived from customs dues, rents from crown lands, which in the empires of the Seleucids and Ptolemies were very extensive, taxes or tithes on freeholds, royalties from mines (e.g. in Macedonia), and the sale of monopolies in all manner of industrial and commercial operations (in Ptolemaic Egypt). In the kingdoms of Syria, Pergamum and Macedonia regular contributions were also exacted from the dependent cities (φόρος, εἰσφορά, σύνταξις), and special levies were imposed for the conduct of wars (e.g. Γαλατικά) and the celebration of notable events. In Egypt petty imposts, direct and indirect, were established in great variety: some 218 different kinds of payment are recorded. Lastly, certain public obligations, such as the maintenance of canals and dykes, were met by 'liturgies' of compulsory labour. Little is known of administration, except in Egypt. Here the finances were under the supervision of a central διοικητής, one of the king's chief ministers. The officials under his control were not co-ordinated in many separate departments, but constituted a hierarchy of three grades, viz. village, district and county functionaries. Revenue, which was partly paid in kind, according to the old Pharaonic system, but consisted mainly of money payments, was collected by officials (οἰκονόμοι) or by tax-farmers under strict supervision. The money proceeds were paid over into the government bank or one of its numerous district branches, and this in turn paid out at the order of the central or district διοικητής. The central bank received all district surpluses and either paid them into the treasury (θησαυρός) or lent them out on interest. These operations were facilitated by the extensive use of money of account, which largely superseded cash payments. The movement of public monies was controlled by an elaborate system of audits. The revenue accounts of the farmers were overhauled by the οἰκονόμοι, and general accounts were drawn

up by a central ἐκλογιστής and by district officials of the same name. The king's 'civil list' (ἴδιος λόγος) was kept distinct from the government monies, and was administered by a special functionary.

521. IV. Many Greek sanctuaries derived a considerable income **Temples.** from domains, State subventions, dedications and offertories, and their funded wealth grew to such dimensions as to require a special board of administrators. As most Greek States exercised a right of borrowing from temple-monies for public purposes, the treasurers were commonly appointed by the community and stood under State control. But the accounts of the sacred funds were always kept separate. The discovery of many such accounts at Athens, Delphi, Delos and elsewhere has made it possible to study temple finance in detail.

At Athens vast wealth accumulated during the fifth century in the **Athens.** shrine of Athena Polias. The ordinary revenues of the goddess, which consisted of rents, fines and tithes of confiscated property, and amounted to some 50 t. yearly, were then greatly augmented by tithes of booty from the Persian Wars. From 454 B.C. Athena was endowed with $\frac{1}{60}$th part of the Delian League tribute ; about 435—4 B.C. she received 3000 t. (Hicks and Hill 49, l. 3), probably as a repayment from the League funds of loans previously made ; and from the same year she took on deposit the annual surpluses of tribute (ibid., l. 51) and (perhaps also since 435—4 B.C.) any other unallocated revenues (I. G. I. 188, l. 3). In 431 B.C. her treasury contained 6000 t. in specie alone (Thuc. II. 13). On the other hand Athena's funds were always liable to be diverted to profane purposes, for by means of a special vote of indemnity (ἄδεια) the Ecclesia could empower itself to borrow sums at a low rate of interest (the computations in Hicks and Hill 62 indicate an annual rate of 1·2°/₀). In the Peloponnesian War full use was made of these powers. Between 433—2 and 423—2 B.C. 4750 t. were borrowed (I. G. I. 273, fr. h.), and soon after 412 B.C. a special reserve of 1000 t. was exhausted. The failure of the Athenians to repay these loans, and the loss of her special revenues after the war, reduced Athena to comparative poverty. The finances of the goddess were administered by ten ταμίαι τῆς θεοῦ, who were appointed by lot out of the entire citizen body (Ath. Pol. 47, § 1).

The treasuries of the other gods of Athens, which were consolidated in 435—4 B.C. under a board of ταμίαι τῶν ἄλλων θεῶν (Hicks and Hill 49, ll. 12—18), were also well endowed, for between 433—2 and 423—2 B.C. no less than 768 talents were borrowed from this fund. The office of the ταμίαι τῶν ἄλλων θεῶν appears to have been merged after 343—2 B.C. in that of the ταμίαι τῆς θεοῦ. The sanctuaries of Eleusis contained a fund under the management of seven ἐπιστάται and two ταμίαι, who were elected by the Athenians for terms of four years. Towards the end of the fifth century 10 talents of coined money had accumulated.

At Delphi Apollo enjoyed a large revenue from the rents of pasture lands, from highway tolls (δεκάται), and above all from the offerings of pilgrims. The administration of the funds was entrusted to eight πρυτάνεις, who apparently acted as receivers and paymasters-general, subject to the control of the Council and Ecclesia of Delphi town. In 369 B.C. their functions were partly transferred to a board of ναοποιοί appointed by the constituents of the Amphictyonic synod. The chief duties of the ναοποιοί were to collect subsidies for the rebuilding of Apollo's temple and with part of the proceeds to construct and maintain the new shrine. From 339 to about 326 B.C. a further board of ταμίαι was instituted by the constituent cities in order to collect the fine imposed in 346 B.C. upon the Phocians, and to supplant the πρυτάνεις as paymasters-general. Thus the tendency at Delphi in the fourth century was for the temple finances to be emancipated from the control of the secular authorities.

The management of the treasury of Apollo at Delos is illustrated by a long series of inscriptions ranging from 315 to 166 B.C. These include inventories, contracts, departmental accounts and general balance sheets, and taken altogether afford a fairly complete conspectus of temple finance. The chief sources of Apollo's income were (i) rents of houses and plough land, amounting in all to 8700 drs. per annum; (ii) customs, harbour and fishing dues, which had been conceded by the city of Delos to the sanctuary and were farmed for the latter by τελῶναι; (iii) interest on numerous loans issued to public and private borrowers at a uniform rate of 10°/₀ for a five years' term; (iv) special subsidies paid from the municipal chest of Delos; (v) dedications by Hellenistic kings and others. The main items of expenditure were the upkeep of the temple, payment of salaries, the performance of sacrifices and the celebration of festivals. The treasury was also obliged to lend out money, apparently without interest, to the city of Delos, and although securities were exacted on this as on other loans, it is doubtful whether repayment could always have been enforced. But in normal years the revenue, amounting in all to 27,000 drs., exceeded the expenditure by 6000 drs. Hence we find that about 200 B.C. a fund of 60,000 drs. had accumulated. The administration of the chest, which in the fourth century had been under Athenian officials (Hicks and Hill 104), was entrusted from 315 to 166 B.C. to two Delian magistrates known as ἱεροποιοί, who were appointed, probably by election, for one year at a time. The business of the ἱεροποιοί was extensive, for they received and paid out all monies and had the sacred chest (which consisted of a number of earthenware jars) in their keeping. But their discretion was strictly limited. No money could be deposited or withdrawn by them except in the presence of their secretary, the Secretary of State, and the Council of State as represented by the Prytaneis. The Council sitting *in pleno* supervised the annual taking of stock and checked the accounts of the outgoing treasurers. The Ecclesia had the sole power of authorising disbursements not sanctioned by standing orders. In Delos, as in Athens, the 'sacred' and 'public' chests were kept apart for purposes of accounting, but in practice the sacred chest might be regarded as a State bank whose chief function was to lend its funds to the government in times of emergency.

Boeckh-Fränkel, *Staatshaushaltung der Athener* (Berlin, 1886); Riezler, *Über Finanzen und Monopole im alten Griechenland* (Berlin, 1907); **Bibliography.** Francotte, *Les finances des cités grecques* (Paris, 1909); Swoboda, *Über griechische Schatzverwaltung* (*Wiener Studien*, 1888, pp. 178–307; 1889, pp. 65–87); Guiraud, *Études économiques sur l'antiquité* (Paris, 1905), pp. 77–120; Gilbert, *The Constitutional Antiquities of Sparta and Athens*, pp. 328–76; Cavaignac, *Études sur l'histoire financière d'Athènes* (Paris, 1908); Kahrstedt, *Forschungen* (Berlin, 1910), pp. 207–33; Ed. Meyer, *Forschungen*, II (Halle, 1899), pp. 88–148; Wilcken, *Ostraka*, I (Leipzig, 1899), chs. 4–6; Grenfell and Mahaffy, *The Revenue Laws of Ptolemy Philadelphus* (Oxford, 1896); H. Maspero, *Les finances de l'Égypte sous les Lagides* (Paris, 1905); U. Wilcken, in Mitteis-Wilcken, *Grundzüge und Chrestomathie der Papyruskunde*, vol I, pt. I, chs. 4 and 5 (Leipzig, 1912); Bourguet, *L'administration financière du sanctuaire pythique* (Paris, 1905); Homolle, *Les archives de l'intendance sacrée à Délos* (Paris, 1887); and the accounts of the Delian Treasury in *Inscriptiones Graecae*, vol. XI. pt. 2 (Berlin, 1912) and in *Inscriptions de Délos* (Paris, 1926–9).

VI. 4. POPULATION.

522. It is not possible to form a very accurate estimate of the population of the ancient Greek States. The modern conception of statistics was unknown to them: such records of population as were kept had a practical, not a scientific aim: they showed how many persons in a given district were possessed of certain rights or liable to perform certain duties. We learn the numbers of fully qualified citizens or heavy-armed men in a particular State: but as to the numbers of the women and children, of the slaves, and of the free men not included under the heads mentioned, we get little or no reliable information. Again, a frequent cause of error is introduced by the Greek system of numerals, which was such as to lead easily to mistakes in copying (*e.g.* μ stood both for 40 and for 10,000, and δ, the symbol for 4, is apt to be confused either with δύο or with δέκα). Conclusions must therefore be based on the evidence as a whole rather than on particular passages: and any view which may be adopted will leave discrepancies in the authorities which cannot be satisfactorily explained. The nature of the evidence and the difficulties involved will appear from a statement of the question as to the population of Attica, with regard to which we have considerably fuller information than is forthcoming in the case of the other Greek States.

Nature of the evidence.

523. From at least the fifth century onwards official registers of various kinds were kept at Athens, as was no doubt the case elsewhere in Greece. The most important of these were (1) the φρατερικὸν γραμματεῖον, a register kept by the φρατρίαι, in which the names of all children born of citizen parents were inscribed soon after birth; (2) the ληξιαρχικὸν γραμματεῖον, a register kept by the officials of the demes, in which the names of all male citizens who had reached the age of 17 were inscribed, and from which was compiled the list of citizens entitled to vote in the assembly (πίναξ ἐκκλησιαστικός); (3) the κατάλογος, a register of the male citizens between the ages of 18 and 60 who belonged to one of the three higher property classes, and were therefore qualified by their wealth to serve in the cavalry or heavy-armed infantry. The statements made by Thucydides as to the military strength of Athens were derived no doubt from the κατάλογος, and other statements purporting to give the total number of male citizens may perhaps be referred back to the πίναξ ἐκκλησιαστικός. From the latter part of the fourth century onwards (4) lists were kept showing the number of ἔφηβοι, or youths of the wealthier classes who entered yearly on a course of preliminary military training. Considerable fragments of the lists of ἔφηβοι have been preserved, but these are of little use for determining the total population, as the proportion of citizens who underwent this special training is unknown, and probably varied from time to time. Finally it is recorded that under the rule of Demetrius Phalereus (317—307 B.C.) a census was taken which included not only the citizens and the metics, but also the slaves.

Official registers at Athens.

524. The census of Demetrius is said to have shown 21,000 citizens, 10,000 metics, and 400,000 slaves (Athenaeus, VI. p. 272 B). The number of citizens here given is in agreement with the statement of Plutarch that in 322 B.C., when the franchise was withdrawn from citizens possessing less than 2000 drachmas, 12,000 were disfranchised, while 9000 retained their rights. Other notices from the latter part of the fourth century agree in fixing the number of citizens at about 20,000, and this may be accepted as approximately correct. The number of Athenian citizens in the middle of the fifth century B.C. would appear to have been considerably larger. The most important evidence for this period is derived from Thucydides (II. 13), who states that at the opening of the Peloponnesian War the Athenian forces included 13,000 hoplites ready for service in the field, and 16,000 hoplites, consisting of the oldest and the youngest citizen-soldiers and of the metics, who were available for garrison duty in Attica. The number of the metics who served as hoplites was at this date about 3000 (Thuc. II. 31). It thus appears that Athens was able to provide from her own citizens a heavy-armed force of 26,000 men, divided into a field army and a reserve army of equal strength. If to these are added the cavalry, and the citizens of hoplite census who were engaged in garrison duty abroad, or were

Number of Athenian citizens.

exempt from military service through age or through physical infirmity, it would seem that the total number of male citizens of the three upper property classes may have amounted to about 35,000. The number of citizens of the lowest property class, the Thetes, can only be conjectured. It is probable however that they formed less than half of the whole population; and it has been suggested with some plausibility that a statement of Philochorus (quoted by the Scholiast to Arist. *Wasps*, 728, and Plutarch, *Pericles*, c. 37), according to which the total number of claimants to Athenian citizenship on the occasion of a distribution of corn among the citizens in 445 B.C. amounted to 19,000, should be interpreted as giving the generally accepted number of the Thetes at that date. The whole free male population of Attica of the age of 18 and upwards in 431 B.C. may thus be estimated at about 55,000 citizens, with an additional 10,000 or 15,000 for the metics. Some modern writers, however, estimate the number of Athenian citizens at the opening of the Peloponnesian War as 30,000 or 35,000. This number agrees with the loose statement now and then made that the number of citizens was 30,000 ($\tau\rho\iota\sigma\mu\acute{\upsilon}\rho\iota\omega$); but it can hardly be reconciled with the passage of Thucydides referred to above, or with his further statement that Acharnae, which was only one, though considerably the largest, of the Attic demes, was able to supply 3000 hoplites. The number of citizens was no doubt greatly reduced by the plague in 430 B.C. and the following years: and throughout the Peloponnesian War there was a heavy drain of men, and also a loss of wealth, which must have diminished the numbers of the richer classes in comparison with the Thetes. It is therefore conceivable that in 411 the number of male citizens able to provide a hoplite's equipment at their own expense was no more than 9000, as seems to be implied in the speech of Lysias for Polystratus (§ 13); though it is possible that in this number the citizens serving with the army in Samos are not included. It is at any rate probable that by the end of the war the number of male citizens had sunk to between 20,000 and 30,000, and that it remained at some such figure throughout the fourth century B.C.

525. We have no statements as to the numbers of women and children; these can only be estimated from the number of the adult males. Such evidence as is available appears to show that the men above the age of 18 probably formed about one-third of the population. At this rate the total free population of Attica (including metics) would have been about 200,000 at the beginning of the Peloponnesian War.

Women and children at Athens.

526. The census of Demetrius Phalereus referred to above is said to have shown a slave population in Attica of 400,000. This figure must be considered in connexion with a further statement made in the same passage of Athenaeus to the effect that Aegina at one time possessed 470,000 and Corinth 460,000 slaves. That Aegina, a barren island which was never of importance after the first

Slave population.

half of the fifth century B.C., should ever have contained 470,000 slaves, is quite impossible: the number given for Corinth is hardly less so: and both statements are now generally rejected. The statement as to Attica is less incredible: but doubt is thrown on it by its context, and economic considerations are so strongly against it as to make it probable either that the passage is corrupt, or that the number is a mere conjecture. It is not likely that the number of slaves in Attica can ever have exceeded 200,000, and the estimates given by most modern writers for the number of slaves in the fifth century are considerably smaller than this.

527. The evidence as to the population of Sparta is more scanty, and the various notices are again difficult to reconcile with one another. It is doubtful too whether statements as to *Sparta.* the number of Spartan citizens refer only to the ὅμοιοι (the fully privileged citizens) or include also the ὑπομείονες (the disfranchised citizens), but it is probable that in most cases the ὅμοιοι only are intended. According to the tradition which was usually accepted in later classical times, but which perhaps dates no further back than to the reforms of Agis in the middle of the third century, the Laconian territory was divided in early days into 9000 lots, one for each Spartan citizen, and 30,000 lots, one for each of the Perioeci. The number assigned to the Spartan citizens by this tradition agrees sufficiently with the statement of Herodotus that there were 8000 Spartan citizens at the time of the Persian War. But if these accounts are correct, there must have been a rapid decrease in the number of citizens during the fifth and fourth centuries. Xenophon states that at the battle of Leuctra 700 Spartiates were present. If, therefore, as is usually assumed, two-thirds of the Spartan army took part in this battle, it would seem that at this date the number of citizens (probably of the ὅμοιοι only) was about 1,500. Aristotle gives the number of Spartiates as less than 1000, and at the date of the reforms of Cleomenes it was reduced to 700. As to the number of the various subject-classes of Lacedaemonia we have no means of forming an estimate: but it seems clear that the Perioeci considerably outnumbered the Spartans, and that the numbers of the Helots were larger still.

528. A rough calculation as to the population of some of the other leading Greek States may be derived from the notices given as to the forces which they could put into the field. At the *Other Greek* end of the fifth century B.C. Argos appears to have possessed *States.* about 20,000 citizens, Thebes about 20,000, Corinth about 12,000. It has been estimated that the total population of the Greek mainland, including Macedonia, at the end of the fifth century may have amounted to 3,000,000, 2,000,000 of these being free and 1,000,000 slaves or serfs: but these figures of course rest very largely on conjecture. Many Hellenic States outside Greece proper were of considerable size: Syracuse was in the fifth century the equal of Athens, and in the fourth the largest of all Greek States. It is, however, useless to attempt any estimate of the population

of the colonies, as we have no means of learning what proportion the Greek population bore to the barbarian or semi-barbarian population in each case.

529. It is possible with somewhat more confidence to give a sketch of the general movement of population in Greece. That there was a rapid increase during the eighth and seventh centuries B.C. is shown by the number of colonies founded during this period, and in particular by the remarkably rapid growth of the cities of Magna Graecia. During the sixth and fifth centuries the colonizing movement became less active, largely no doubt because the best land available had already been occupied: but colonists were still forthcoming in large numbers whenever there was an attempt to found a new settlement. In the fourth century Plato and Aristotle felt it necessary to discuss remedies for the danger of overpopulation, and Isocrates advocated the conquest of Asia as an outlet for the expansion of the Greek race. The pressure felt was probably due not entirely to increase of population, but also in part to the replacement of free labour by slave labour, which was then in progress in many parts of Greece. It is, however, clear that Greece was still in a position to send large quantities of mercenaries and settlers to the East during the reigns of Alexander and the early Diadochi. But soon afterwards the tendency towards a decrease in the free population, which had made itself felt in Attica in the fourth century, began to spread through the rest of Greece. Polybius (c. 150 B.C.) is the first writer to notice the decrease, which continued with increasing force: under the early Empire the cities of Greece, with a few exceptions such as Athens and Corinth, had sunk to the position of villages, and Plutarch, writing in the first century A.D., estimates that the whole country could hardly produce 3000 hoplites.

Movement of population. (margin note)

Bibliography. The first attempt at a critical treatment of the question as to the population of the ancient world was Hume's *Essay on the Populousness of Ancient Nations*. The figures for Greece have been examined more in detail by Boeckh (*Staatshaushaltung der Athener*, Book I.), Wallon (*Histoire de l'Esclavage*, vol. I. pp. 221–83), and more recently by Cavaignac, *Histoire de l'Antiquité*, II. ch. I. The most comprehensive treatment of the subject is contained in Beloch's *Bevölkerung der griechisch-römischen Welt*. The numbers of the population of Attica are discussed by Wilamowitz-Moellendorff, *Aristoteles und Athen*, II. 9, and Meyer, *Forschungen zur alten Geschichte*, vol. II. pp. 149–89. A mention of the most recent estimates is to be found in Zimmern, *The Greek Commonwealth*, pp. 169–73, 393. For statistics of military strength, see Beloch, in *Klio*, 1905, pp. 341–74; 1906, pp. 34–78.

VI. 5. SLAVES AND SLAVERY.

530. SLAVERY is found in Greece under two different forms. (1) In certain districts there existed from early times a system of praedial slavery or serfdom, somewhat similar to that which prevailed in mediaeval Europe. Such serfs were members *Forms of slavery.* of a more or less organised subject community, were attached to the soil, and were recognised by the State as possessing certain rights against their masters. (2) The other form, which eventually became prevalent over the whole of Greece, was slavery of the Roman or modern type. The slave was regarded merely as a piece of property to be disposed of at pleasure, and stood in no relation to the State except through his owner. The word δοῦλοι is applied to both of these classes, but belongs more strictly to the latter: no generic word was used to describe the serfs, who were known by different names in different parts of Greece.

531. Personal slavery existed to some extent in the society known to us through the Homeric poems. Slaves (called δμῶες, οἰκῆες, or more rarely δοῦλοι) are found in the houses of *Slavery in Homeric times.* nobles, who obtained them by war or piracy or by purchase from Phoenician slave-traders. But slavery was not at this time general, and even in princely families much of the household work was done by the sons and daughters of the house. The master had no doubt absolute power over his slaves: still the relationship between master and slave as described by Homer is in many cases close and friendly. No trace of serfdom is found in the Homeric poems: for the θῆτες who are mentioned as the lowest class of society were free labourers working for hire.

532. At the beginning of historic times serfs are found existing in different parts of Greece, but so far as we know only in those States which are recorded to have been invaded and con- *Origin of serfdom.* quered by Dorians or other immigrants from northern Greece. It was generally believed by the Greeks, and is probably true, that the institution of serfdom was due to the Dorian migration and kindred movements, and that these subject-classes represented the descendants of the original population of the districts in which they were found. The most important of these serfs are the Helots (Εἵλωτες), who formed the subject-population of Laconia and Messenia. *Helots.* They were a Greek-speaking people, and are said to have been descended

partly from the pre-Dorian population of Laconia and partly from the
inhabitants of Messenia, who were successively conquered and enslaved
by the Spartans: we have no definite information as to their numbers,
but they certainly far outnumbered their Spartan masters. They were
attached to the landed estates (κλῆροι) of the Spartans, and were bound to
pay to the proprietors a yearly rent, which was fixed in early times at a
definite proportion of the total produce, and might not be increased. The
proprietor might not deal with his serfs in any way which involved their
separation from the estate, he might not either sell them or set them free
or put them to death. He had, however, a certain claim, not clearly
defined, on their personal services, which was probably not usually burden-
some, as the Spartans resided not on their estates but in the capital.
Subject to these conditions the Helots retained their property and family
rights: they kept for themselves what was left of the produce of the estate,
and must in some cases have been comparatively well-to-do: in the time
of Cleomenes 6000 were able to purchase their freedom at the price of
five minas (£20) apiece.

The Helot thus possessed considerable freedom as against his master,
but as regards the State his slavery was absolute. It was a custom for the
Ephors on entering office each year to declare war against the Helots, thus
expressing the fact that the State was bound by no obligation towards them:
they might be put to death without form of trial: and a special corps of
Spartan youths (κρυπτεία) was employed to keep watch on them and make
away with any who appeared dangerous. The State could also override
the rights of the individual Spartan proprietor, by emancipating the Helots
attached to his κλῆρος or withdrawing them for service in the army. It was
the practice from early times to employ Helots as light-armed troops, and
on the formation of a navy they were employed as rowers and marines:
sometimes, though not often, they served as hoplites. Helots who had
distinguished themselves in war were occasionally given their freedom:
such emancipated Helots were called νεοδαμώδεις, and received the status
of περίοικοι. The μόθακες or μόθωνες, children of Helot or half-Helot birth,
who had been brought up with Spartan children, formed another semi-
privileged class: they could, at any rate under certain circumstances,
rise to high office. Gylippus and Lysander both came from this class.
By this policy of either putting to death or promoting possible leaders of
revolt, the Spartans were able to maintain their rule, in spite of their small
numbers and the hatred with which they were regarded; and they had
only once to deal with a serious Helot revolt that was not encouraged
by foreign invasion.

533. Of the serfs existing in other parts of Greece much less is known,
but such information as we have seems to show that their
position was similar to that of the Helots. The Thessalian
serfs were called πενέσται: they cultivated the estates of the
Thessalian nobles, paying a fixed rent: their masters were forbidden to

Other classes
of serfs.

put them to death or sell them out of the country. In Crete again there was a Dorian aristocracy ruling over non-Dorian subjects, who were divided into μνῶιται, serfs belonging to the State, and ἀφαμιῶται or κλαρῶται, serfs attached to the estates of private individuals. Other subject-classes existed in early times in other Dorian States under such names as γυμνήσιοι at Argos and κορυνηφόροι or κατωνακοφόροι at Sicyon. Nothing is recorded of these but the names, and it is probable that in many States serfs ceased to exist as a distinct class at a comparatively early date. In Laconia serfdom continued until the third century B.C., when its abolition was begun by Cleomenes (240—220 B.C.) who enabled many of the Helots to buy their freedom, and was completed by Nabis (tyrant of Sparta, 207—192 B.C.).

534. Slavery in the stricter sense of the word existed to some extent, as has been said, in the Homeric period, but it did not become generally prevalent in Greece till much later. In historic times it is first mentioned in Ionia: Chios is named as the earliest centre of the slave-trade, and is said in the fifth century to have possessed more slaves than any other Greek State except Sparta. A law against keeping slaves is said to have been passed by Periander (tyrant of Corinth about 600 B.C.), and it would appear therefore that slavery was at this date practised to some extent on the Greek mainland, but was hardly a recognised institution even in the most advanced States. By the middle of the fifth century slaves were no doubt common in the most important cities, but even in these many forms of industry were still carried on by free men. Thucydides describes the Peloponnesians at the opening of the Peloponnesian war as αὐτουργοί: the expression can hardly be meant to apply to commercial towns like Corinth, but must mean that foreign slaves were not employed in the rural districts. Even in the middle of the fourth century slavery was not general in Boeotia, and was almost unknown in Phocis and Locris: but by the beginning of the third century it was probably prevalent all over Greece.

> Growth of personal slavery.

535. Slaves were occasionally of Greek, but more often of foreign race. It was a rule of Greek international law that prisoners taken in war became the property of the conquerors, but in the fifth and fourth centuries B.C. it was the almost universal practice to exchange prisoners of Greek race or to allow them to be ransomed: the treatment of the Athenian prisoners by the Syracusans is one of the rare exceptions. Instances are rather more common in which a captured city was destroyed and the whole of the inhabitants sold into slavery: this was allowed by Greek sentiment as a punishment for the revolt of a subject-city: it was occasionally practised in other cases (as at Plataea, Melos, Olynthus), but was then strongly condemned. Athenian law did not, at least from the time of Solon, allow enslavement for debt, nor the sale of children by their parents: in some other parts of Greece both were possible. The child of a free man by a slave woman took the position of a slave in

> Enslavement of Greeks.

Athens. Children exposed at birth became the property of anyone who cared to bring them up: and cases of kidnapping occasionally happened. It is not known how far the freedom of a Greek citizen was protected by States other than his own: but such an incident as the selling of Plato into slavery by the tyrant Dionysius was certainly exceptional. The proportion of Greek to barbarian slaves was small, and probably tended to diminish.

536. Barbarian slaves were drawn mainly from Western Asia (Lydians, Phrygians, Syrians, etc.), from Thrace, or from the tribes of South Russia, who were known by the generic name of Scythians. Aristotle defends the enslavement of both classes as natural, on the ground that the Orientals possessed intelligence without courage and the Northerners courage without intelligence. Barbarian slaves were obtained by means of a regularly organized slave-trade, of which Byzantium and Delos are named as centres. Slaves were occasionally home-bred (οἰκότριβες): but on the whole it was found more economical to buy them at maturity. The great majority of the slaves must have been adult males: those employed in the mines, agriculture, and other industries were naturally in most cases men, and men seem to have been more used than women even for domestic service. (For an estimate as to the total number of the slave population of Attica see § 526.)

Barbarian slaves.

537. Aristotle speaks of the slave as being merely a machine (ἔμψυχον ὄργανον, κτῆμά τι ἔμψυχον): and this was on the whole the view taken by Greek law and public opinion. A slave could be bought and sold at pleasure, could be given in pledge or taken in distraint, just like any other commodity. His family relations were not recognised by the law: he could not own property, and any money that he might earn belonged not to him but to his master. But as regards his personal position, Greek law, or at least Attic law, did not carry out its theory with the same severity as did the law of Rome. A freeman who assaulted a slave was liable, not only to an action for damages (δίκη βλάβης) on the part of the owner for injury to his property, but also to a criminal prosecution (γραφὴ ὕβρεως). A freeman who killed a slave was punishable for manslaughter, though not for murder. Even the owner's rights over his slave's person were limited by Athenian law: the slave might not be put to death, and in the case of gross ill-usage he might take sanctuary and demand to be sold to another master (πρᾶσιν αἰτεῖν). Slaves could not appear as parties in the law-courts, and at Athens their evidence was not as a rule admitted except under torture: in the fifth century the practice of torturing slaves seems to have been a reality, but in the fourth century, though frequently proposed in the law-courts, torture seems rarely to have been employed. Slaves could be manumitted, and in such an event the slave often paid a certain sum to the master as price of his liberty: he could not, however, claim the right to buy his freedom, as indeed the purchase money was in the eye of the law his master's property.

Legal position of slaves.

Since the slave could not enter into a contract recognised by law, manumission often took the form of a fictitious sale by the owner to some god :
registers of these sales were preserved in the temples, and many specimens
have been found at Delphi and elsewhere.　At Athens manumitted slaves
(ἀπελεύθεροι) received the privileges of μέτοικοι, but remained under the
obligation to regard their former master as their patron (προστάτης), and to
perform certain duties towards him : in case of neglect of these they
were liable to a δίκη ἀποστασίου, and might, if convicted, be again sold into
slavery.

　538.　The average price of an able-bodied unskilled slave such as would
be employed for work in the mines was about 2 to 1½
minas (£8 to £6).　Slaves possessed of special skill or　Price of
slaves.
personal qualities might of course fetch much higher prices :
the highest recorded is a talent (£240), which Nicias is said to have paid
for a mining overseer.　Demosthenes' father owned 32 swordsmiths, who
cost in all 190 minas (£760, or on the average £24 each), and 20 couch-
makers, who cost in all 40 minas (£160, or an average of £8 each).

　539.　As to the conditions under which slaves were employed, our
knowledge is almost confined to Attica.　Slaves were
employed by the Athenian State for several purposes.　A　Employment
by the State.
force of Scythian archers (Σκύθαι or τοξόται) was maintained
to keep order in the Assembly and public places : and slaves were also used
for the subordinate work of the government offices.　A writer of the fourth
century proposed that the State should purchase slaves to work the silver
mines at Laurium, but this plan was never carried out.　The Athenian
warships were rowed to some extent by slaves, who were not the property
of the State but were supplied by the trierarchs : but free men were
preferred for this service.　Slaves who had served with the fleet were
sometimes emancipated, or even enfranchised, as after the battle of
Arginusae.　A proposal was made to arm the slaves after Chaeronea,
but it was rejected, and Hypereides its mover was impeached for making it.

　540.　Slaves were employed by private owners (1) as domestic servants
and (2) as workers for profit.　It is not clear how far down　Employment
by private
owners.
in the social scale the employment of slaves for domestic
purposes extended, but it was probably confined to the richer
classes.　At any rate it was not the practice at Athens, as it was at Rome,
for a single individual to own a large number of slaves for purposes of
luxury.　Even in well-to-do households only about five or six slaves were
usually employed.　It would seem that in Attica in the fifth century the
small farmer was not a slave-owner, and that agriculture was mainly
carried on by free labour.　Slaves were, however, employed at this period
in various industries.　Inscriptions dealing with the payments made by
the State for the building of the Erechtheum in 407 B.C. show that slaves
worked as masons side by side with free labourers and received the same

wage. Again the names of several of the Attic vase-painters indicate that they were or had been slaves. In such cases as these the slave probably worked directly under the control of some small master-craftsman by whom he was owned. Another practice was for the owner to set up the slave as an independent worker in some business on condition of receiving regularly a stipulated payment (ἀποφορά) out of his profits. Slaves working on these terms were described as χωρὶς οἰκοῦντες. It was not uncommon for an owner to promise a slave his freedom at the end of a definite period in order to stimulate his energies. Slaves who were employed in business could sometimes attain to considerable wealth and importance; thus Pasion, who is referred to in several orations of Demosthenes, rose from being a slave to be an Athenian citizen and the leading banker in Athens, and on his death bequeathed his business to a former slave of his own. Cases such as this represent one end of the scale; at the opposite end we find the slaves who were employed in the silver mines at Laurium. The work here was carried on exclusively by slaves, owned by capitalists who had leased concessions in the mines from the State. The slaves were chained and worked underground in gangs under slave overseers; the labour was exhausting and incessant, and the death rate was high. It would seem that this was the earliest industry in which slave labour was employed on a large scale; we are told that Nicias, one of the richest Athenians of his day, had 1000 slaves engaged in these mines.

541. Slavery, as it existed at Athens in the fifth century, differed in some important respects from slavery as it was organised later in the Roman world. In the first place, Athenian society in the fifth century was still in the main a society of free workers, though slaves had begun to form a considerable element in the population. The view sometimes held that Greek civilization was fundamentally based on slavery does not correctly represent the facts as regards this period. Secondly, as a natural consequence of a state of things in which slaves and free men worked together at the same employments, the distinction between the slave and the free man, though sharply drawn by the law, was less marked in ordinary intercourse than it became in later times. It is noted by several writers as a feature of Athenian life that the slaves shared to some extent in the general liberty. They were not compelled to wear a special dress, and in appearance and manner they were often indistinguishable from the citizens. Access to the gymnasium and ecclesia was forbidden to them; but they were allowed to enter the temples and to take part in public and private religious rites. The Attic drama shows how intimate and human the relation between slave and master could sometimes be. The familiarity allowed the slave in Latin comedy represents the manners of the Athens of Menander rather than those of Rome; Plautus indeed mentions it as a peculiar feature in Greek society that the slaves were permitted a certain amount of

Development of slavery.

enjoyment and recreation. In the fourth and third centuries Greek slavery underwent no radical change. In the lands conquered by Alexander his successors retained existing systems of serf-cultivation (especially in Asia Minor and Egypt). On the other hand they did not introduce industrial slavery, save in mines and in a few royal factories at Alexandria and Pergamum. In the Greek homeland manumissions appear to have become more frequent in the third century, and at Delphi Apollo encouraged this practice under the form of a fictitious sale. On the other hand in the second century the trade in slaves received an impetus from the demands of the enriched classes at Rome, and Delos became the principal slave-mart of the Mediterranean. In the second and first centuries B.C. Attica and Greece in general became, like other parts of the Roman Empire, the scene of slave revolts and servile wars, which were unknown in earlier times.

542. Slaves were named at their master's pleasure. In general there seems to have been nothing to prevent slaves from bearing the same names as free men, though they usually received one of certain stock-names which came to imply a servile position. Among those commonly used were names expressing or implying the race of the slave, as Geta or Manes: names descriptive of personal appearance, as Xanthias or Pyrrhias: and names expressing some quality which the slave possessed, or which was thought desirable in a slave, as Dromon, Sosias. The name was often changed on manumission.

Names of slaves.

Wallon, *Histoire de l'Esclavage dans l'Antiquité*; Boeckh, *Staatshaushaltung der Athener* (3rd ed.), Book I. c. 13; Zimmern, *Greek Common-wealth*, Part III. c. vii, xv, xvi; Ed. Meyer, *Kleine Schriften* (2nd ed.), pp. 169–212; Sargent, *The Size of the Slave Population at Athens during the* vth *and* ivth *centuries* B.C.; Tod, in *Cambr. Anc. History*, v. ch. 1 (with bibliography).

Bibliography.

VI. 6. COLONIES.

543. THE first beginnings of Greek colonisation may be traced back to the last three or four centuries of the second millennium B.C., during which the later Hellenic immigrants, Achaeans and Dorians, entered the Greek homeland. In consequence of these invasions a movement of population away from Greece set in, which resulted in the occupation of the Aegean islands and of the west coast of Asia Minor with settlers of Aeolian, Ionian and Dorian stock.

Hellenic expansion.

This primary expansion was followed, throughout the Greek world, by a period of internal development, political and economic; until there ensued, by a natural reaction, a second age of expansion, which lasted from the middle of the eighth to the middle of the sixth century, and resulted in the foundation of some 250 colonies (ἀποικίαι), supplying an almost continuous circuit of Hellenic influence round the Mediterranean and the Euxine. The geographical distribution of these cities may be seen by a reference to § 27. Viewed chronologically, they fall into two main divisions: (1) those of the period 750—700, and (2) those of the period 650—550. To the former belong Corcyra, Sinope and Trapezus, and the chief colonies in Italy and Sicily, and in Chalcidice: to the latter the colonies of colonies, and such important foundations as Massilia and Agrigentum, Cyrene, Chalcedon and Byzantium, Olbia and Panticapaeum. In the first period the Ionian Chalcis and Miletus (herself the mother of 75 cities) were the leading colonists: in the second Miletus, Megara, Corinth and Phocaea, and among the later colonies themselves Syracuse and Massilia—all trading or manufacturing cities, be it noted.

544. The colonies of the second epoch were the results partly of necessity, partly of enterprise. Sometimes colonisation became necessary for political or economic considerations, as a relief from foreign or domestic tyranny, from deadlock between parties, from over-population, debt and slavery. More often, the enterprise of a person (Cypselus of Corinth) or of a State (Miletus) discerned in colonisation a means of commercial gain. The Italian and Sicilian colonies, many of which owed their origin to political causes, became agricultural and pastoral communities for the most part, though some gained an added importance from their situation (*e.g.* Sybaris) upon regular trade-routes between East and West: the colonies of the Propontis and the Euxine were distinctly commercial from the first.

Causes of colonisation.

545. In cases of enforced emigration the colonists were members or subjects of the same State (*e.g.* the Parthenii at Tarentum): whereas colonies of enterprise were often heterogeneous, including invited contingents from friendly States, and chance adventurers. In the original 'colonies' Ionians had sometimes combined with Dorians, and in the later foundations also, though nominally Dorian or Achaean, the Ionians often had a considerable share. It was usual to commit the whole expedition to the care of a 'founder' (οἰκιστής), entrusted with plenary powers and assisted generally by seers and surveyors (γεωνόμοι): his duty it was to lead the way to the selected region, to direct the apportionment of lands, and to frame the constitution of the colony. In most cases he would secure the authorisation of the Delphic Oracle; and without unduly magnifying its influence in this connexion, it is quite clear that the Oracle was sagacious enough to utilise the political and geographical resources of its intelligence department in the best

Procedure.

interests of a larger Hellenism, and its colonial policy justly redounded to its credit. The Oracle, in fact, confirmed rather than initiated; for the formal foundation of cities could only have followed the tentative efforts of explorers, whose successful traffic or piracy among unknown tribes encouraged more peaceful visits and more permanent settlements.

546. The relations of a Greek colony with its mother-city deserve attention, for though somewhat indeterminate, they could exercise no mean influence upon history, as a few prominent examples (*e.g.* Corcyra and Corinth) showed. Politically the colony was independent (Potidaea, with its Corinthian ἐπιδημιουργοί, is an exception), but the sentiment of filial loyalty was everywhere manifest. It appeared in a desire to reproduce the conditions of life in the metropolis (from whose πρυτανεῖον it was customary to carry fire to the colony); in the mission of representatives and victims to great home festivals, and in special honours shown to the representatives of the mother-city at colonial celebrations; in the request for an oecist from home when a colony wished to found a colony of its own; in a reference to the mother-city at seasons of distress, and in a general avoidance of war and misunderstanding with her. Sometimes a closer commercial connexion may be seen, as in the coinage of the Corinthian colonies, where one type was preserved, with the addition of an initial letter to mark each city; or in the Greek trading companies at Naucratis, which were in direct communication with their several parent-states; and to a less formal degree in the Milesian colonies, which served as trading agencies round the Euxine.

Character-istics of the colony.

Some Greek settlements (*e.g.* in the western Mediterranean, where considerable opposition was encountered) were never able to develop beyond the factory-stage; but as a general rule the conditions of a city-state were faithfully reproduced, for the Greek colonist, with all his love of travel, loved his home also. So in Sicily, in Italy, and along the Euxine sea-board, the settlers occupied first the spots most similar to the home-country—a country of bays and harbours, of citadel-hills, and clear natural boundaries. And as in topography, so in politics; colonies of co-citizens tended to become oligarchical, the original settlers forming the body politic, while communities of merchant-adventurers were often timocratic after their kind. As a general rule, political development in the colonies was more rapid than at home; thus the codes drawn up by Zaleucus of Locri and by Charondas of Catana anticipated those of Greece proper. In religion the imitative tendency was again apparent; but the worship of local deities (*e.g.* of Ammon in Cyrene) was frequently incorporated, and divine honours were paid after death to the oecist—or, if his name had been forgotten, to some god or hero (usually Apollo Archegetes or Heracles) chosen as official founder of the colony.

33—2

547. The colonial life had its shortcomings: successful trade led to
money-worship, and fiercer strife between rich and poor.

Effects.

But a distinctly Greek nationality was everywhere maintained,
and confirmed from time to time by participation in the great national
festivals, or by a renewal of filial obligations. Each colony taught the
'barbarians' around the lessons of a higher humanity, in private and in
public life, learning meanwhile those arts of accommodation to which the
Ionian temperament so readily lent itself. Where it rested upon trade, the
intercourse was usually of a peaceful nature: but the determined opposition
of Carthage in the West obliged the Greeks to show that they could fight
as successfully as they traded.

The history of Greece and of Europe repeatedly brought the colonies
into prominence: Syracuse and Byzantium have determined the fate of
nations. In literature, too, 'Greater Greece' deserved well; but it was in
philosophy and science that the colonial intellect found fullest expression.
After Pythagoras took up his abode at Croton Italy became the mother
of philosophers—Parmenides, Xenophanes, Zeno, Empedocles; Abdera
claimed Democritus and Protagoras, Sinope Diogenes, and Stageira Aristotle.
It is no exaggeration to say that the Greek colonies have been in large
measure responsible for the continuity of western civilisation, for the Greek
model of city-life, perpetuated by such examples as Neapolis, Byzantium,
and Massilia, became the foundation of much that is best in the civic
systems of to-day.

548. Though traditionally regarded as the metropolis of the Ionian
cities, Athens took no prominent part in the larger colonising
movements, preferring to concentrate her resources at home:

Cleruchies.

but under Pericles a few State colonies were sent out (*e.g.* to Brea and
Amphipolis in Thrace, and to Thurii), generally with the object of securing
some point of vantage in 'barbarian' territory. More often, however, the
Athenians relieved domestic distress, controlled their allies, and secured
their conquests, by means of κληρουχίαι. A party of citizens, chosen by lot
from all who offered, was conducted by a State official to a selected spot
in Greek territory, and was there established upon allotted portions after
the ejection (Scyros, Hestiaea) or subjection (Naxos, Andros) of the previous
inhabitants. The allotments were not regarded as private property, for the
State reserved the freehold; residence was compulsory, and the right to
sub-let required a special grant. As *propugnacula imperii* these State-organised
settlements practically corresponded to Roman colonies. The first certain
instance occurs in 506 at Chalcis, where 4000 lots (κλῆροι) were apportioned;
subsequently the same policy was adopted in Scyros, Lemnos, Imbros,
Lesbos, Chalcidice and elsewhere. The cleruchs retained their Athenian
citizenship; their votes might lapse by absence, but their names remained
on the registers of tribe and deme, and they were still liable for military
service. Constitutionally, the cleruchies were miniatures of Athens, with
local ecclesia, boule and magistrates; but all important lawsuits were re-

ferred to the Athenian courts, and a general control was exercised by an
ἐπιμελητής and (in the fourth century) by a στρατηγός from Athens. This
profitable system of occupation was naturally popular with the Athenian
democracy, but often oppressive for the subject States: indeed, its abuses
contributed to the downfall of the Athenian Empire in the Peloponnesian
War, so that we are not surprised to find 'no cleruchies' insisted upon as
one of the conditions of the Second Confederacy of 377 B.C.

548a. With the reign of Alexander a new era in Greek colonisation
began. In the territories conquered by him the great Macedonian founded, according to tradition, some seventy colonies,   Later
Colonisation.
whose object was to hold down the natives, to serve as centres
of trade, and to diffuse Greek civilisation. Alexander's colonial policy was
generally followed by his successors, and more particularly by the Ptolemies
and the Seleucids. The chief areas of later Greek colonisation were Asia
Minor, Syria, and Egypt; but new settlements were made in the Balkans,
in Iran and India, and in Somaliland. In size the Hellenistic colonies
ranged from royal capitals like Alexandria and Antioch, which became the
most populous cities of their day, to mere villages, as in the case of the
purely military foundations.

The military colonies (κληρουχίαι, κατοικίαι) comprised both active soldiers
and veterans. In Egypt and Asia Minor the soldiers mostly received from
20 to 60 acres of land. Not infrequently they were given waste land, with
obligation to improve by plantation; but in this case the rents due from
them were abated or remitted. In Egypt the κλῆροι, from being fiefs
dependent on military service, were gradually converted into heritable
leaseholds. The right to sub-let to natives was freely exercised.

Colonies with a considerable civilian population usually possessed all
the self-governing institutions of a Greek city. The military settlements
were either subordinated to the nearest city (as in the Seleucid monarchy)
or to the royal officials (as in Egypt), but they usually formed corps
(πολιτεύματα) with limited rights of self-administration. The native residents
were sometimes, but not in all cases, admitted as citizens.

Article *Colonia* in Daremberg and Saglio's Dictionary; articles *Katoikoi*,
Klerouchoi, in Pauly-Wissowa's Real-Encyclopädie; Busolt,   Bibliography.
History of Greece, chapter ii. §§ 6, 7; Zimmern, *Greek Common-*
wealth, part III. chapter vi; Hogarth, in *Cambr. Anc. History*, II. ch. 20; Myres,
ibid. III. ch. 25 (with bibliography); Tscherikower, *Die hellenistischen Städte-*
gründungen (*Philologus*, Supplement XIX, pt. I).

VI. 7. COMMERCE AND INDUSTRY.

549. THE heroes of Homer are represented as the lords of pastoral and
Pioneers of agricultural communities, wherein the merchant (ἔμπορος)
Mediterranean had no existence, and the craftsman (δημιουργός) compara-
commerce. tively little importance. Navigation was carried on with
considerable skill, but chiefly for hostile purposes : still, in the *Odyssey*,
we can trace the beginnings of more peaceful voyages. But as far
back as 3000 B.C. the Cretans seem to have sailed and traded in the
Mediterranean : much later—probably not before 1200 B.C.—came the
Phoenicians, establishing their factories and settlements along its shores.
There were other traders also, but not so enterprising or far-reaching,
Taphians, Carians, Lemnians, Phaeacians, Thesprotians, and Sicels. The
general method of traffic was probably barter. At first only a simple
exchange was practicable, but gradually some sort of currency came to be
arranged upon the basis of generally accepted units such as the ox, of
which the local units—such as the package of silphium at Cyrene, and the
tunny at Olbia and Cyzicus—could be conveniently reckoned as submultiples. The traders brought in their vessels, and set out on the beach
the attractive products and manufactures of the East—ivory, purple stuffs,
glass, metals, tools, weapons, jewellery; and took in exchange whatever
they could get—sheep and oxen, wool and hides, and corn (afterwards oil
and wine also). Slaves, too, were a staple commodity on both sides, and
in many cases the early traders were kidnappers also, so that their visits
were frequently regarded with suspicion.

550. But it was obvious that the Greeks, with their natural affinity for
the sea, their geographical advantages, and their imitative
Greek propensities, could not long remain merely passive partners
expansion. in these rough and ready transactions. The successive
expansions of Dorians, Ionians, and Aeolians over the peninsula of Greece,
the islands of the Archipelago, and the west coast of Asia Minor, began
a new chapter in commercial history, in which the Greeks were to play the
leading part. Slowly they ejected or subjected the previous occupiers,
and made the Aegean their own ; commerce abroad was sustained and
solidified by the development of special industries at home. But the era
of expansion was not at this stage complete : the Greek followed the
Phoenician all over the Mediterranean, especially northward and westward.
Greek colonies in the eighth and seventh centuries supplanted or supplemented Phoenician factories, until the whole sea-board was connected by
a chain of some 250 trading-centres, by which the products of the civilised
and uncivilised world were brought into circulation. In this commercial
development Aegina, Corinth, the cities of Euboea, Delos, Miletus, and

Megara were conspicuous.   In the sixth century B.C. the chief commercial
centres were Miletus, Samos, Sinope, Byzantium, Phocaea, the cities of
Rhodes, Ephesus, Aegina, Corinth, Athens, Chios and Corcyra: in the
fifth century Athens was indisputably the leader, though the Ionian cities,
with Corcyra, and Corinth, were still of first-rate importance.   The result
of the Peloponnesian War ruined at once the political and the commercial
pre-eminence of Athens.   Corinth still enjoyed a considerable prosperity,
and Athens recovered somewhat during the fourth century; but the conquests of Alexander, while they widened the sphere of commerce, and
brought East and West into closer relationship, diverted Greek trade to
fresh centres, Alexandria, Antioch, Seleucia, Rhodes and, for a time, Delos,
large towns of the modern type which held their own up to and during the
Roman supremacy.

551.   The chief commodities which formed the basis of the Greek
export-trade were the oil of Attica; the wine of Chios,
Naxos, Lesbos, and Thasos; the agricultural produce of   Trade-routes
Megara and Boeotia; the purple of Cythera and other   and centres.
coast-places; the copper of Euboea and Cyprus; the silver of Laurium;
the gold of Thasos; the iron of Laconia; and the tunny of Byzantium.
The chief manufactures for export were the woollens, purples, and carpets
of Miletus, Chios, and Samos; the metal-work of Corinth, Chalcis, and
Argos; the trinkets of Aegina; the pottery of Chalcis, Corinth, and
Athens.   The principal import was corn, obtained from the Black Sea,
Magna Graecia, Sicily, and Egypt: other articles shipped in large quantities
were salt, salt fish, wool, timber and skins.

552.   The positions of the Greek colonies enable us to determine with
fair accuracy the direction of the principal trade-routes,   Sea-routes.
since the ships of the Greeks (who were not more adventurous sailors then than now) commonly followed the coast-lines.
The most important route led northwards from Aegina, Corinth, and
Athens, by way of Euboea, Pagasae, Chalcidice, Thasos, Samothrace,
Imbros, Lemnos, Tenedos, Lampsacus, Cyzicus and Byzantium, to the
Black Sea.   Here the leading traders were Miletus and her sister-cities,
with Megara, Athens, and, later, Rhodes.   Another important route crossed
the Aegean to the north-east by way of Euboea, Chios and Lesbos,
and so reached Clazomenae and Phocaea; another, bearing eastward
by the Cyclades to Miletus and Ephesus, was associated with branch
lines connecting Athens and the Peloponnese with Crete, Rhodes,
Cyprus, Phoenicia, and Egypt.   To the west the most important route
circumnavigated the Peloponnese to Leucas and Corcyra, and thence
struck across to Italy, Sicily, and beyond.   (For the speed of merchant
vessels see § 625.)   The connecting agents between so many different
ports must have derived no little advantage from the carrying trade
alone, as we may gather from the importance to which Phocaea and

Sybaris attained. And the natural result of this inter-connexion appears also in the establishment of sound systems of coinage, weights and measures, in the improvement of ship-building (especially at Corinth and Phocaea), and the use of rowing as a surer method of transport than sailing, and generally in the growth of a certain consciousness of trade responsibilities.

553. On land, there was a network of roads intersecting the Greek peninsula; these, though perhaps intended primarily for religious ends, could be used for trade. Thus Sparta was connected with the coast east and south, and with the adjacent States west and north; Argos with its own coast, Mantinea, Orchomenus, Sicyon, and Corinth; and all the roads in the Peloponnese found a focus at Olympia. A highway ran from Corinth past Megara to Plataea and Thebes; and the latter was in its turn connected with the coast and with Delphi, Thessaly, and the north. Commercial intercourse between the Adriatic and the Euxine was maintained by land from the earliest times: and each of the chief Euxine cities represented the terminus of a land-route, Olbia from the north, Phasis from the east, and Sinope from the south, while in Ephesus the great caravan-lines from the east were concentrated.

Land-routes.

554. The chief centres of the wool-trade were Asia Minor (Miletus), Attica, Megara, and Magna Graecia (Tarentum). The wool in its rough state (ἔριον, πόκος, οἴσυπος) was first washed (πλύνω), then beaten (ῥαβδίζω), combed (ἕλκω), and carded (ξαίνω), after which it was ready for the dyer (βαφεύς). The next process was that of spinning (νέω, κλώθω), by which the natural thread was drawn off the bundle (τολύπη) on the distaff (ἠλακάτη), twisted in the fingers into a continuous thread (νῆμα, στήμων), either coarse (πυκνός) or fine (ἰσχνός, ἀραιός), and attached to the spindle (ἄτρακτος, ὄνος). Unevennesses were taken off with the teeth (κροκυδίζω), and the wool-bound spindle (κλωστήρ) was put into a basket (κάλαθος, τάλαρος). The question of weaving (ὑφαίνω) is complicated by difficulties, due to a confusion of two looms (upright and horizontal) and a different use of terms by different authors. The earlier Greeks employed the upright loom (ἱστός), with its two side-poles (ἱστόποδες, κελέοντες) and cross-piece: subsequently the horizontal loom, of similar design, was introduced, probably from Egypt. In using the upright loom the threads of the warp (στήμων) were laid on and fastened (διάζομαι, ἄττομαι) to the cross-piece, being kept vertically parallel (μηρύομαι) by heddles or loops (μίτοι) half-way, and by other loops (καῖροι), and weights (ἄγνυθες, λαῖαι) of stone or clay, at the bottom. The heddles were fastened alternately to two cross-rods (κανόνες), and the method of weaving consisted of drawing forward each set in turn, thus leaving a passage for the horizontal cast of the shuttle (κερκίς), which carried the

Export industries.
(a) Wool.

Spinning.

Weaving.

thread of the woof (κρόκη) wound into a bobbin (πηνίον). The Greeks wove downwards, and used a spattle (σπάθη) to pack (κρούω, σπαθάω) the woof upon the warp, and a comb (κτείς) to smoothe the texture and the surface before cutting out (ἐκτέμνω) the piece of work. The details of the horizontal loom are quite uncertain : in the hand-looms of later times pedals have been used to effect the raising of the alternate threads of the warp, and it is reasonable to suppose that the Greeks had some similar contrivance.

The products of Greek looms (ὕφασμα) eventually became celebrated for technical and artistic excellence, exhibiting every variety of colour and pattern (e.g. ῥαβδωτός, 'striped,' πολύμιτος, 'damask'), into which gold and silk threads were not infrequently woven (χρυσόπαστος). Spinning and weaving continued as in early times to be the special employment of female slaves (χερνῆτις) in large households : but the better methods of wholesale manufacture, and the special skill required for such operations as dyeing and cleaning, soon invested the woollen industries with a technical character. As was natural, some of the manufactories confined themselves to one branch of work ; for instance, one at Athens supplied χλάμυδες only, another at Megara ἐξωμίδες for workmen.

555. Wine and oil were important articles of export. The vine was probably a foreign introduction, and found a home in many of the islands, in Sicyon, Chalcidice, Asia Minor, and Magna Graecia. (For the cultivation of the vine and the *(b)* Wine and oil. manufacture of wine see §§ 686, 691.) The producers or wholesale merchants sold by sample (δεῖγμα) to retail dealers in the markets : for the purposes of carriage pitched skins (ἀσκοί) were used. The olive, which was probably indigenous in the Aegean area (there was an olive press in the Palace at Cnossus), early became associated with Attica : it was also cultivated at Cyrene, Cyprus, Massilia, Clazomenae, and Sinope. (For the manufacture of oil see § 686.)

556. Greek mining owes its introduction to the Phoenicians, who probably copied Egyptian methods : these were often irrational, from an ignorance of geology. The exacting labour of the mines (μέταλλα) was carried out by gangs *(c)* Metallurgy. *(1)* Mining. of slaves, by whom the ore (μεταλλεῖον) was extracted from the richest veins (φλέβες, ῥαβδοί) : from the pit's mouth (στόμιον) galleries (ὑπόνομοι, σύριγγες) were hewn out, pillars (ὅρμοι, μεσοκρινεῖς) being left for support. Hard by outside were furnaces (κάμινος, χόανος) and workshops (ἐργαστήρια), where the processes of crushing (τύπτω), washing (πλύνω), sifting (διασήθω) and smelting (ἕψω, ὀπτάω) were carried out, until the metal was freed of slag (κίβδος, σκωρία). Diodorus Siculus (III. 11 et seqq.) and Agatharchides (c. 24 et seqq.) have given vivid pictures of gold-mining in their own times ; and the other metals seem to have been similarly worked. Besides the simple metals various alloys were commonly used: *e.g.* of gold (ἤλεκτρον, ἀδάμας); of silver (λιθάργυρος, κέγχρος, καδμεία); of copper (χαλκός); while from iron a kind of steel (χάλυψ, κύανος, ἀδάμας) was made by tempering the red-hot metal in water.   Of the numerous metal-working centres Corinth attained a special pre-eminence by excellent

(2) Metal-work.   workmanship: the evidence of terminology shows us to what an extent this industry was elaborated and subdivided. Gold was principally used for jewellery; silver for the vessels of the table; bronze or copper for larger vessels, or works of art; and iron for general purposes.   The methods of working fall into three groups, according to the condition of the metal: (i) pliant, (ii) liquid, (iii) hard.   (i) To this class belong the processes of plating, turning, and punching: the oldest and commonest practice was to hammer (ἐλαύνω, σφυρήλατος) plates (λεπίς, πέταλον) of metal into the required shape, sometimes by means of a block, and to join them together afterwards; ornamentation in relief or the reverse was effected by the use of the punch.   (ii) When casting was invented is doubtful: tradition ascribes it to Rhoecus and Theodorus of Samos (flor. 600—550 B.C.), and iron-soldering (σιδήρου κόλλησις) to Glaucus of Chios (fl. 490), though in this case similar methods had long been in vogue, as is proved by the golden relics of Mycenae. Sometimes moulds and models (πρόπλασμα, λίγδος) were formed of clay alone, sometimes of clay and wax spread over a wooden core (κάναβος) with an envelope of clay, the molten metal eventually replacing the wax. (iii) The art of cutting and graving metal (τορευτική) was elaborately developed, till it included many varieties of chasing and damascening, chiefly employed in the manufacture of weapons.

557.   Under ceramic industries are included (1) bricks and tiles; (2) pottery, plain or ornamented; (3) statues and models.

(d) Ceramic industries.   (1) Bricks (πλίνθοι) were more often sun-dried (ὠμαί) than baked (ὀπταί): tiles (κέραμοι) were made either flat or curved.   (2) In the manufacture of earthenware (κέραμος, ὄστρακον) the clay was first kneaded and tempered (ἕλκω, ὀργάζω), next manipulated (ἐλαύνω) upon the wheel (τροχὸς κεραμικός), then dried or burnt (ὀπτάω); the soundness of the vessel was tested by knocking (κρούω), after which in most cases some form of ornamentation was added.   (For methods of vase-painting see §§ 353 ff.)   At first there was little specialisation among potters, but as time went on the development of taste and technique rendered this inevitable.   Individuality appeared in various ways: in the nature of the clay; in the shape of the ware; in the treatment of the groundwork; in the subjects chosen for the ornamentation; in a preference for outline, silhouette, or relief; in the addition of new colours, locally procured or admired.   (3) The works of art in which clay was used consisted of (i) statues large or small—the latter being the familiar terracotta figures manufactured in great numbers (especially at Tanagra) for purposes of religion or ornament (see §§ 369 ff.)—or (ii) clay reliefs, designed with or without the aid of moulds, for the external decoration of public and private buildings.   Moreover, artists in stone or metal commonly used clay models or designs : and the manufacture of clay dolls (κόραι) for children became a special branch of the potter's trade (κοροπλάθοι).

558.   The interchange of ideas and commodities which resulted from the increase of commerce raised the standard of comfort, and complicated the city life—a development which may be illustrated by a classification of the numerous arts, crafts, and trades of which there is evidence.   (*a*) The house itself implied quarrymen, brick and cement makers, stonemasons, builders, bricklayers, foresters, sawyers, carpenters and joiners, with a supervising ἀρχιτέκτων ; the manufacture of furniture and utensils occupied a host of workers in stone, clay, metal, wood, wool, glass, and other substances, with a terminology so complete that almost every article gave its name to a particular craft (*e.g.* κλινοποιοί, καδοποιοί, ληκυθοποιοί).   (*b*) The supply of food, drink, and household necessaries occupied flour-merchants, millers, bakers, bread-sellers, confectioners, butchers, fishmongers, poulterers, greengrocers, fruiterers, vintners, salt-boilers, spice-sellers, cooks, torch-makers, oil-merchants.   (*c*) Articles of apparel engaged spinners, weavers, dyers, tailors, fullers, cleaners, glovers, hosiers, hatters, tanners, leather-sellers, shoemakers.   (*d*) The manufacture of arms was a distinct industry, with special craftsmen after their kind (*e.g.* κρανοποιοί, ἀσπιδοποιοί).   (*e*) Under the head of conveyance may be included shipwrights, oar-, sail-, rope- and tackle-makers; horse-dealers and saddlers; cartwrights and wheelwrights.   (*f*) Personal luxuries were attended to by barbers, perfumers, and unguent-sellers; stick-, umbrella-, and camp-stool makers; goldsmiths, silversmiths, jewellers; workers in horn, bone, ivory, tortoise-shell, amber; paper and pen makers, booksellers: for entertainments and amusements there were flower and garland sellers, flute and lute players, jugglers and acrobats, trainers of game-cocks and quails, trained cooks, furniture-brokers, doll-makers, musical-instrument makers.

Lesser industries.

559.   Wholesale trade was developed comparatively late among the Greeks, but the progress of commerce and the verdict of society rapidly differentiated it from the retail business conducted by producers (αὐτοπῶλαι) and petty tradesmen (κάπηλοι), just as wholesale manufactories (ἐργαστήρια) were distinguished from the workshops of single craftsmen.   Wholesale traders (ἔμποροι) frequently did not confine themselves to one commodity, but shipped various cargoes for colonial ports; they would often accompany their goods in person (οἱ πλέοντες, συμπλέοντες), unless they had some authorised traveller, or agent abroad.   At most large ports a spacious hall (δεῖγμα) was provided at public expense for the purpose of displaying samples

Trade.
(a) Wholesale.

(δείγματα), while commission-agents and interpreters facilitated the relations of seller and buyer.   It was customary to purchase a return-cargo
with the proceeds of sale, as foreign moneys might involve a loss on
exchange at home : on the other hand it is to be noted that the coinage
of Athens was accepted everywhere.   At the ports of call on the voyage
merchants usually contrived to ascertain where the prices were best, and
sometimes they resorted to questionable artifices in order to rig the
markets.

560.   The centre of trade in each city was the market-place (ἀγορά),
(b) Retail   where most of the retail establishments were to be found,
trade.—   though shops were scattered over the rest of the city as
Markets.   well.   At Athens, which city we may take as a type,
business was carried on in permanent bazaars and colonnades (στοαί),
under the wicker roofs (γέρρα) of temporary booths (σκηναί, κληναί), or
under umbrellas (σκιάδεια).   Here the various trades and crafts were
grouped, so that the separate corners (κύκλοι) came to be called after the
articles sold—fish, meal, wine, pots, or slaves.   (Cf. the phrases εἰς τὰς
χύτρας, πρὸς τοὔλαιον, εἰς τοὔψον, ἐν τοῖς λαχάνοις.)   Special importance
attached to the monthly market, at which slaves were generally sold.   The
shops and show-rooms in the market were places of common resort for
the citizens during the forenoon (ἀγορᾶς πληθούσης) : hither it was customary
for the master of the house (or afterwards a special slave, ἀγοραστής) to
come and make the necessary purchases ; the presence of ladies or female
slaves as customers was not generally approved, though a good deal of
the selling was done by women (e.g. ἀρτοπωλίδες, λεκιθοπωλίδες).   Porters
(προὔνεικοι) might be hired to carry home purchased goods.   Besides the
regular markets, there were occasional fairs (πανηγύρεις), and the great
religious and athletic festivals incidentally furthered commercial transactions on a large scale.

561.   The control of all that went on in the Athenian market was
Regulation   entrusted to the ten ἀγορανόμοι, five of whom were assigned
of trade.   to the Peiraeus, and the ten μετρονόμοι, similarly distributed :
for the supervision of wholesale trade the ἐμπορίου ἐπιμεληταί
and σιτοφύλακες were appointed.   The legal processes (included among
the ἔμμηνοι δίκαι) for the settlement of trade disputes were various and
comprehensive (e.g. τραπεζιτικαί, μεταλλικαί, κοινωνικαί): how complicated
these suits might be, appears from the elaborate legal terminology contained
in the Private Speeches of Demosthenes.   So far as the State exercised any
control over matters of business it did so ostensibly in the interests of the
whole body politic (e.g. to secure the food-supply), and not in those of a
particular trade : it was this motive which prompted, for example, the
Athenian ordinances regulating the import of corn and the export of oil
and shipbuilding materials, and the prices of millers and bakers ; or forbidding tanners and cheesemongers to exercise their odorous callings in

the denser parts of the city. Harbour-dues, customs, and tolls, with so
many communities set so close together, must often have proved a heavy
burden on the trader, by sea and land : our information on the subject is
unsatisfactory, but we may form some idea of the general system from those
at Athens, of which the principal ones were: πεντηκοστή (2 p.c. on exports
and imports), ἐλλιμένιον (harbour-due, perhaps charged on passengers, not
on goods), ἑκατοστή (perhaps identical with the last), ἐπώνιον (1 p.c. on
sales), διαπύλιον (gate-money); and lastly, the δεκάτη imposed, when Athens
was strong enough, on all ships entering or leaving the Euxine.

562. Taken as a whole the most important commercial class were
the bankers (τραπεζῖται), whose functions were threefold:
(a) money-changing ; (b) money-lending ; (c) the receipt of   **Bankers in
deposits (παρακαταθήκη) for safe-keeping or for investment   business.**
in their own or other concerns.   (a) For the business of money-changing
and testing (hence δοκιμασταί, ἀργυρογνώμονες) they kept by them scales
(hence the nickname ὀβολοστάται), touch-stones (βάσανος), and a counting-
table (ἄβαξ): a small commission or agio (καταλλαγή, κόλλυβος) was
charged. (b) A loan might be friendly (χρῆσις), or formally contracted
(δανεισμός, δάνειον), the latter class being divided according to the security
(δάνειον ἔγγειον, ναυτικόν). With no rate of interest fixed, there was room
for abuse (hence ἡμεροδανεισταί, τοκογλύφοι) : for the calculation of interest
two methods were in vogue—by the first a certain fraction of each mina
lent was charged each month (so ἐπὶ δραχμῇ = $\frac{1}{100}$ per month, or 12 p.c.
per annum), by the second a certain fraction (e.g. τόκοι ἔφεκτοι) of the
whole sum lent became payable at the end of a year, or of a specified
period, and this was the method employed for ναυτικὰ δανείσματα. In
ordinary loans the commonest standards of interest were 12 and 18 p.c.
per annum, payable on the last day of the month to the creditor or his
representatives ; sometimes the place of payment and class of coin were
specified. In the case of a defaulter (ὑπερήμερος) the creditor had the
right to seize (ἐμβατεύω) the pledge (ἐνέχυρον) or mortgage (ὑποθήκη) on
which the loan was secured, with or without an action of ejectment (δίκη
ἐξούλης), according to the bond. In earlier times the temples (e.g. at
Delphi and Ephesus) had served as the principal storehouses of money
and valuables, but as business developed the bankers undertook this
charge, and such deposits frequently formed a large proportion of their
trading-capital (ἀφορμή). Again, bankers were constantly employed, like
our lawyers, as confidential intermediaries or guarantors (ἐγγυηταί) in
all money matters. Their accounts must have been carefully kept, by
themselves and a staff of clerks, chiefly freedmen and slaves : the details
would be copied down from memoranda (γραμματείδια) into day-books
(ἐφημερίδες) and ledgers (γραμματεῖα, βιβλίδια), in which credit and debit
accounts were shown on separate pages. Besides receiving deposits at
home, the bankers were often able, by means of agents or fellow-bankers

residing in distant places, to save their clients the trouble and risk of conveying large sums in cash; in such cases the banker's order authorizing the payment of the sum in question was accompanied by a proof of identity in the shape of a token (σύμβολον) or tally (σκυτάλη), and the payee, if not personally known to the banker on whom he drew, was required to produce a third party nominated in the original bond (συγγραφή). Drafts of this kind, though common enough between bankers and clients, never became so widely negotiable as the modern cheques and letters of credit, since there was no real 'fiduciary circulation' in Greek business.

563. Associations for religious, political (ἑταιρεῖαι), social and benevolent

Companies.

(ἔρανοι) objects were so usual in Greece that the formation of various mining and trading companies (οἱ εἰς ἐμπορίαν οἰχόμενοι) on the analogy of these was but natural. Some such companies existed in the fifth century, though the evidence as to their conditions and legal rights is very vague: the fourth century witnessed a considerable development, and companies were formed for privateering, for insurance (after Alexander's time), and other objects, but banking seems never to have been one of them.

564. As a general rule the Greek theory of capital was quite ele-

Loans.

mentary: indeed, as a modern scholar has remarked, 'dans ces sociétés on ne capitalise pas, on thésaurise.' Yet the principle of the loan was not uncommon among the Athenians—it was by this means that demes, phratries and temples disposed of their surplus of capital, and made it effective (ἐνεργός). The most frequent, and certainly the most lucrative method of investment was the bottomry loan (ναυτικὸν δάνεισμα, ἔκδοσις), which corresponds more or less to the 'pacotille' contract in the Middle Ages. The borrower made repayment conditional upon the success of his undertaking: in many cases therefore the loan answered the purpose of maritime insurance, but with greater risk to the underwriter than in our day. As a compensation for the risks involved, which were greatly increased by war, piracy, and unseaworthy vessels, a high rate of interest—e.g. τόκοι ἐπόγδοοι for a short voyage, ἐπίτριτοι for a longer one—was charged; the advance was made upon the ship, tackle, cargo, profits, conjointly or separately. As a precaution against depreciation, the borrower was bound to show goods of greater value than the loan (sometimes twice as great). If the money was lent only for the outward voyage (ἑτερόπλους), the lender would have a representative at the destination, or he would go himself, or send an agent: in this way it was convenient for merchants to advance money on a vessel in which they had occasion to travel themselves. In the case of a double voyage (ἀμφοτερόπλους) equivalent goods had to be loaded at the foreign port, as a security for final payment. The loan was a written contract (συγγραφή) in a formal style, with detailed

specifications, sometimes in duplicate: the terms of the bond gave the
capitalist the right, in case of non-payment, to distrain the property
offered in security, or, if that was inadequate, the remaining property
of the defaulter. The actions arising out of these contracts belonged
to the class called ἐμπορικαί: complications frequently arose from the
fraudulent action of shipowners and captains, by which the letter of the
charter-party was evaded for the sake of illicit gain.

565. We may distinguish three classes engaged in commerce and
industry, (a) citizens, (b) non-citizens, (c) slaves. (a) The
first class was in many cases diminished, in some altogether
non-existent, by reason of political prohibition or social
discountenance. The Dorian States especially hated the idea of manual
labour for their citizens, and the Spartiates were absolutely forbidden to
engage in agriculture, trade, or industry: on the other hand the Phocians,
as late as 360 B.C., complained that one Mnason, with his 1000 slaves,
was keeping an equal number of his fellow-citizens out of work. In the
mercantile and manufacturing cities also the proportion of burgesses
directly occupied in commercial and industrial concerns varied considerably, according to the degree of intellectual and artistic development
or of political pauperism. Misfortune or necessity often compelled
citizens to labour for a livelihood, as for example at Athens after the
Peloponnesian War, where in better days public business had afforded
both employment and remuneration. The commercial instincts of Greek
citizens more often found an outlet in indirect ways, such as the investment of money or slaves in mines, banks, or factories: and many leading
men derived their incomes from such sources. (b) The partial or complete abstention of the citizens from trade and industry left opportunities
which their so-called inferiors—whether conquered races, resident aliens,
or freedmen—were not slow to utilise; at Sparta the Perioeci, at Athens
the Metics, were intimately associated with all kinds of trade, and the
latter almost monopolised the business of banking: the most eminent
banker of Greek history was a metic, Pasion, whose credit was everywhere accepted, and whose public services eventually procured for
him the citizenship. At Athens, besides the poll-tax (μετοίκιον), metics
had to pay for the right of sale (ξενικὸν τέλος), while burgesses were
exempt. Freedmen fulfilled important duties as managers or chief
clerks for citizens or metics, or engaged in business independently with
slave-workmen. (c) But it was upon slave-labour, though more costly
and less productive, that Greek commerce and industry chiefly depended
from the beginning. (For the industrial employment of slaves see § 540.)

566. Although there seem to have been no proper guilds or
corporations of workmen until the Roman supremacy,
there were instances of association, whether local, such as
the settlement of similar workmen (συνεργοί) in distinct
quarters (e.g. Κεραμεικός), and the concentration of μέτοικοι at Peiraeus,

[marginal notes:]
Commercial and industrial classes.

Associations of workmen.

and of Jews at Alexandria; or commercial, such as the frequent combination of kindred trades, tanners and shoemakers, fullers and tailors, innkeepers and vintners. Except in certain cases (*e.g.* the heralds, cooks, and flute-players at Sparta) there was no obligation on the son to take up his father's trade or craft, though this would naturally be a frequent occurrence. Certain terms of apprenticeship obtained, for which a definite fee (δίδακτρον) was paid to a master of the craft (ὁ ἐπιστάτης τῆς ἐργασίας).

567. The cheapness of food-stuffs and the existence of slave-labour

Wages. combined to reduce the wages obtainable by free labourers. Some difficulty is involved in the study of this question, as it is often uncertain whether the wages recorded in inscriptions and elsewhere include rations or not. At Athens in the second half of the fifth century the unskilled labour of porters, scavengers, farm-hands, was paid at the rate of 3 or 4 obols daily: skilled citizens (whether citizen, metic, or slave) normally received 1 drachma; even an architect earned sometimes no more than 1 drachma a day, but this last was a regular stipend paid monthly. Single services were naturally paid for at a somewhat higher rate; for example, the porter in the *Frogs* demands 2 drachmae, and refuses 9 obols. A bath could be had for 2 obols, a cloak cleaned for 3: 20 or 30 drachmae were paid, according to size, for engraving an inscription, 110 for grooving a column. Far greater sums were realised by the State-physicians (and their trained slaves), artists of special repute, musicians, actors, and hetaerae: it is reported that Polycrates of Samos gave as much as 2 talents to secure the services of Democedes of Croton, and that Amoebaeus the actor was paid 1 Attic talent for each appearance. Teachers of the best class were able to obtain 500—700 drachmae yearly: a fencing-master received 300 drachmae for 2 months' instruction. Protagoras and Gorgias, the Sophists, charged 100 minae for a complete course of lectures; afterwards Sophists accepted less, even taking a fee (from 1 to 50 drachmae) for a single lecture, and we find that Isocrates learnt rhetoric of Evenus of Paros for 5 minae.

568. The Greeks cannot be considered an industrial race in the true

The status of Commerce and Industry. sense of the term, for history shows that as they advanced politically they severed themselves from direct industrial employment. In the Homeric age personal labour was considered no degradation for free men, and even rulers possessed more than an elementary acquaintance with such useful arts as house- and ship-building. But the spread of commerce and colonisation wrought a change: culture increased, but so also did slavery; the one depreciated trade, the other diminished the dignity as well as the market value of free labour. There were exceptions: at Corinth, for instance, the industrial class was respected—for on industrial activity depended the production of commodities for exchange in foreign trade, and for the purchase of necessaries—and the good understanding thus brought about was largely responsible for the long-continued prosperity of the city. The introduction of a money-economy in Greece, and the efforts of legislators like Solon, secured the traders and artisans political recognition, though still leaving abuses, which the tyrants readily turned to account: these in their turn, for reasons political and economic, deliberately favoured commerce and furthered industry by colonisation, public works, and other means. The prejudice against trades and handicrafts was most pronounced in Sparta: elsewhere, though the political disabilities might be reduced or removed, the social stigma was scarcely diminished—indeed, even the fullest development of democracy at Athens did but stereotype the conventional horror of hard work, and proclaimed leisure, and not labour, to be the citizen's privilege. The philosophers took the same view, branding as mean ($\beta\acute{\alpha}\nu\alpha\nu\sigma\sigma$) and unworthy of citizens the necessary, if humble, occupations on which society rests, and discountenancing the principle of loans.   Intellectual labour was hardly considered at all on its merits, and the artist often suffered with the artisan ; the marvel is that, amid all this depreciation, mechanical skill and artistic taste should have attained so high a standard of excellence. The capitalist was generally exempt from adverse criticism, but usury met with special disfavour: doubtless there was some justification for this in the unscrupulous methods and exorbitant percentages to which lenders sometimes had recourse, and often the natural animosity between citizens and aliens was the real cause ; but the truth remains that even the best-intentioned Greeks had no conception of the real significance of money and capital, and in their short-sighted superiority discouraged a free circulation, thus deliberately courting economic ruin.

Agriculture and other 'natural' branches of industry ranked somewhat better in social estimation: but even here the development of city-life tended to a disparagement of the countryman, so that $\dot{\alpha}\sigma\tau\epsilon\hat{\iota}\sigma$ became irreconcilably opposed to $\ddot{\alpha}\gamma\rho\sigma\iota\kappa\sigma$.   The consummation of the city-unit may have been brilliant, but it was hopelessly unbusinesslike: and against its literary, philosophic and artistic excellence has to be set a commercial and industrial system which rendered political economy an impossibility, and material prosperity a degradation.   Fortunately the conquests of Alexander the Great inaugurated a new order of things: in the large towns of the Hellenistic period society grew more tolerant, commerce more cosmopolitan ; and to Rhodes belongs the honour of establishing a system of mercantile law which has formed the basis of our modern codes.

H. Blümner, *Home Life of the Ancient Greeks*, chap. xiv, London, 1910; *Technologie und Terminologie der Gewerbe und Künste bei Griechen und Römern*, Leipzig, 1869 ; B. Büchsenschütz, *Besitz und Erwerb im griechischen Alterthume*, Halle, 1869 ; E. Meyer, *Die wirtschaftliche Entwicklung des Altertums* (in Kleine Schriften, vol. i.) Halle, 1910; A. Boeckh-   Bibliography.

Fränkel, *Die Staatshaushaltung der Athener*, Berlin, 1886; G. Glotz, *Ancient Greece at work*, London, 1926; A. E. Zimmern, *The Greek Commonwealth*, Part III, ed. 4, Oxford, 1924; H. Francotte, *L'Industrie dans la Grèce ancienne*, Brussels, 1900–1; Art. *Industrie und Handel* in Pauly-Wissowa, *Real-Encyclopädie*; E. Speck, *Handelsgeschichte des Altertums*, vol. II, Leipzig, 1901; J. Hasebroek, *Staat und Handel im antiken Griechenland*, Tübingen, 1928; J. Toutain, *The Economic Life of the Ancient World*, London, 1930; F. Oertel, Appendix in third edition of Pöhlmann's *Geschichte der sozialen Frage und des Sozialismus in der antiken Welt*, vol. II, Munich, 1925; O. Neurath, *Antike Wirtschafts-geschichte*, 2nd ed., Leipzig, 1918.

VI. 8. MEASURES AND WEIGHTS.

A. MEASURES.

569. THE ancients held that the simple measures (μέτρα), such as the finger, foot, palm, span, cubit, and fathom, were derived from the various parts of the human body (Heron Alex. tab. I., Vitr. III. 1, 5). Among primitive and unmixed races, where all live under the same conditions, there will be little variation in stature, and consequently a foot of average size will give a standard sufficiently accurate for practical needs. When, however, different races come into contact, or when different habits of life cause variation in stature among various classes of a single race or a single community, variations of the foot and cubit will naturally be found. As the progress of civilization demands greater exactitude, the inter-relations of various standards will be carefully ascertained by the use of some natural object of uniform size, such as the barley-corn of the English linear system. Lastly, with the advance of science efforts are made to get some general units fixed with greater accuracy, and to bring these into relation with the measures of capacity and standards of weight.

Origin of standards.

Measures of capacity are first obtained from natural products of a uniform size, such as the hen's egg used as their unit by the ancient Irish and the Hebrews, the small gourd now used at Zanzibar, and the joint of the bamboo, and the cocoa-nut employed by the Chinese and the Malays. The *cochlear* (from *cochlea*, a mussel-shell) is the smallest Roman measure, whilst it is not improbable that the Greek κύαθος originally meant a gourd. In measures so derived there are naturally many local variations, and universal standards, such as those established in this country in 1824, can only be set up by a strong central authority. In Greece we have two notable instances of such legislation : Pheidon of Argos fixed the standard measures used by the Peloponnesians, and Solon fixed the Attic standards of measures and weights. On such occasions it is possible that an attempt may be made to fix certain relations between the standards of length, capacity, and weight. From what has been said, there is no need to suppose that the Greeks had to go to Babylonia or Egypt, as has been held, to obtain a foot standard.

570. The foot measure is mentioned in Homer (ἑκατόμπεδος), but its exact length is unknown. Homer is acquainted also with some of the subdivisions and multiples of the foot which were used in the historic period, *palm* (δῶρον, probably = later παλαιστή), *cubit* (πυγών, πυγούσιος), *fathom* (ὄργυια), πλέθρον (πέλεθρον). Many foot standards were in use in historic Greece. The Olympic is said to have been taken from the foot of Heracles and was traditionally the largest standard known. Its length, as deduced from the existing measurements of the Stadion at Olympia, is 320·5 mill., but it may have originally been longer. It is surpassed by other standards, the Aeginetan, which was 333 mill. (as taken from the measurements of the Temple of Aphaea), and the Pergamene πούς φιλεταίρειος, named after King Philetaerus, which was 330 mill., while a Samian standard may have been as high as 350 mill. The Aeginetan and Pergamene feet are practically identical and correspond with the *pes Drusianus*, 330 mill., used in Gaul and Germany at the time of the Roman conquest; all three seem derived from a people of bigger build than the indigenous Athenians, as the Attic standard is only 295·7 mill. This Attic foot compares with the Roman of 296 mill. and with the English of 301 mill. The subdivisions of the foot are taken from parts of the hand, multiples from the arms, the smallest unit being the finger-breadth (δάκτυλος).

Standards of length.

2　finger-breadths = 1 κόνδυλος, middle joint of finger.
4　finger-breadths = 1 παλαιστή (Homeric δῶρον), hand-breadth or palm.
8　finger-breadths = 1 διχάς or ἐμιπόδιον, half-foot.
10　finger-breadths = 1 λιχάς, span of thumb and first finger.
12　finger-breadths = 1 σπιθαμή, span of all the fingers.
16　finger-breadths = 1 πούς, foot.
18　finger-breadths = 1 πυγμή, short cubit, elbow to start of fingers.
20　finger-breadths = 1 πυγών, short cubit found in Homer and Herodotus, elbow to end of knuckles, with the fist closed.
24　finger-breadths = 1 πῆχυς, the normal cubit, elbow to tip of fingers.
2½ feet = 1 βῆμα, pace.
6　feet = 1 ὄργυια, fathom, the stretch of both arms.
100　feet = 1 πλέθρον, originally the breadth of the γύης, acre, the space between the οὖρα or boundary stones; its square becomes the unit of land measure.

Of these subdivisions the cubit with its half, the full span, was probably taken over from oriental sources, but it entered the Greek system naturally as = 1½ feet.

571. For the higher measures of length convenience demanded higher denominations, one of which was regarded as a new unit, although continuity with the rest of the system was preserved by making it a multiple of the foot. These larger measures may be regarded as independent in origin; for as the smaller measures are based on natural objects, so the larger were derived from nature and from distances which occur in ordinary life. Homer expresses distances

Road measures.

by a stone-cast (*Il.* III. 12, cf. Thuc. v. 65; Polyb. v. 6), a quoit-cast (*Il.* XXIII. 431), a spear-cast (*Il.* XV. 358), by the distance which a man can reach with a spear (*Il.* X. 357), and by the still more indefinite phrase 'as far as man can be heard when he shouts' (*Od.* v. 400), and by standards derived from agriculture (*Il.* X. 352, the breadth of the acre-piece of ground ploughed in one day by mules). Time was made the measure of the longest distances (a method still much employed for measuring distances), *e.g.* a day's journey by an active traveller (εὔζωνος ἀνήρ), or a journey of a day and a night, or on horseback, or in a merchant-ship. The practice of measuring by stations (σταθμοί) falls under this head, as such distances were fixed with reference to the endurance of man and horse long before they were actually measured out by stades.

The normal unit of road measure, in later times the unit of astronomers and geographers, was the στάδιον. The Doric form σπάδιον (from σπάω) appears to indicate that this was the distance traversed in a single draught by the plough, *i.e.*, it was the length of the plough-gate, γύης, just as the πλέθρον was its breadth, corresponding to the English furlong. It is not necessary to suppose, as has frequently been done, that the Greeks went to the East to borrow a unit which arises so naturally from their own native system of agriculture. The *stadion* is also the length of the race-course, the distance that a runner can traverse at top speed, and from this come its multiples; the δίαυλος (or διστάδιον), so called from αὐλός (= αὖλαξ), the old name of the *stadion*, perhaps originally double furrow, later a course up and down the *stadion*; the ἱππικόν, the course for horses twice up and twice down; and the δόλιχος, the long-distance course, generally 12 stadia. The παρασάγγης, 30 stadia, was a Persian measure (mod. *farsang*), used by Greeks writing on Asia Minor.

The length of the *stadion* was invariably 100 ὄργυιαι or 600 feet, no matter what the length of the foot might be; and hence its exact length is often a matter of doubt. Distances in stadia as computed by the historians are apt to be discrepant and often indicate a very small measurement for the foot. It cannot be doubted that their figures are often based on faulty translation from foreign measures into stadia, or on rough calculations from length of march, or number of paces.

572. Measures of surface are necessarily employed in every community, as soon as it begins to cultivate land. Tradition says that from such a necessity geometry arose (Herod. II. 109). As with the itinerary measures, the original unit of the system was not a specific number of feet, but some natural quantity, which at a later date was harmonized with the smaller measures. These measures are essentially measures of surface, though often used as measures of length (e.g. *plethron*). A natural measure of this sort was a strip of land of considerable length and moderate breadth, being the amount ploughed in one day by a yoke of oxen (cf. γύης = 'plough' and 'acre,' and Lat. *iugum* = 'yoke' and 'acre'). The later Greeks used the square *plethron* = 10,000 feet, which was also the size of the Italian *vorsus*. The γύης of the

Land measures.

Heraclean tables probably represents a piece of land 5000 feet long and 100 feet broad, *i.e.* 50 *plethra*. In Sicily and Cyrene land was measured on a system common in various parts of the mediaeval and modern world. The *medimnus* as a land measure in each region represents as much land as could be sown by a medimnus of seed, but in each case the system was probably native and not introduced by the Greeks. In Egypt σωκάριον δεκαόργυιον, a term derived from the amount of seed required, = square of 10 ὄργυιαι.

573. The ancients distinguish dry measures of capacity from liquid; the lower units are common to both but otherwise the systems are different. Local variations are numerous, but the lowest unit is the κύαθος, supposed originally to have been a kind of gourd, which contains about ·04 litres = ·08 English pint. Both for wet and dry measures the table then runs:

Measures of capacity.

1½ *cyathi* = 1 ὀξύβαφον.
3 *cyathi* = 1 ἡμικοτύλιον.
6 *cyathi* = 1 κοτύλη in Attica (the word is used for a kind of cup); elsewhere τρύβλιον or ἡμίνα.
12 *cyathi* = 1 ξέστης (a loan word = Latin *sextarius*).

The systems now diverge. For liquid measures (ὑγρά) the table is:

6 cotylae = 1 ἡμίχους.
12 cotylae = 1 χοῦς (Lat. *congius*).
12 choes = 1 μετρητής.

The *metretes* is the measure of the large wine-amphoras and contained 864 *cyathi* = 38·88 litres (the contents of Panathenaic amphorae vary from 38·39 to 40·34 litres). The Roman *amphora* is much smaller, 576 cyathi.

For dry measures (ξηρά), the table is:

4 cotylae = 1 χοῖνιξ, at Athens a day's allowance of corn for a man.
4 choenices = 1 ἡμίεκτον.
8 choenices = 1 ἑκτεύς or μόδιος.
6 modioi = 1 μέδιμνος. The Attic medimnus is supposed to have contained 51·84 litres, the Spartan from 71·16 to 77·88.

B. WEIGHTS.

574. Like other peoples the Greeks based their weight-system on natural units,—their smallest being the barley-corn, $\frac{1}{12}$th of an obol in the Attic system. The smallest weights, however, meet us but seldom in our general reading. Of the weights with which we have most to do, the obol denoted originally the metal spit, the drachm the six spits, which can be grasped in one hand, later the silver equivalents of these. The mina, of foreign, probably Phoenician, derivation, denoted first a measure, only in the second instance a weight. At the head of the system comes the talent—the amount a man can carry in one load. But the

Origin of weight standards.

talent of Homer, we must note, was a much smaller unit, some 135 grains of gold, representing, in all probability, the value of a cow.

575. In Greece, as elsewhere, the first use of the balance and of weights was in connexion with the use of the metals, gold, copper, and, later, silver. To the question whether the standards used for these metals were identical with those in commercial use, no general answer can be given with any confidence. Solon, when he replaced the Aeginetic system by the Euboic at Athens, introduced a commercial standard, heavier throughout by one twentieth than the coin standard. Again, an Athenian decree of the second century B.C. fixes the commercial mina at 138, instead of 100, drachmae of the coin standard. This larger mina appears to be nothing more nor less than the Aeginetic mina, which, therefore, could continue in commercial use even in places where it was no longer used for coins. The actual weights, which have been found in many parts of Greece, are often difficult to fit exactly into the standards as theoretically determined by us.

Coin and commercial standards.

We must always be prepared, then, to find differences between coin-weights and the commercial standard, analogous to that between our own troy and avoirdupois. That other systems than the Attic and Aeginetic were in use is made probable at once by the existence of many varying standards of coin-weights in different parts of the Greek world, the Persic and Phoenician in the East, the Achaean and Campanian in the West, to take only a few examples. The conclusion is confirmed by the weights which have come down to us.

In the smaller denominations the coins are our chief source of knowledge. If we take the average weight of a sufficient number of well-preserved specimens and make a small allowance for average loss by wear, if we, then, check our result by a 'frequency table'—that is to say, by a ladder of weights, each rung of which represents a difference of, say, half a grain, on which each coin is marked on its appropriate rung, we can hope to obtain a close approximation to the true norm; for we may expect those rungs of the ladder to be most frequently marked which lie next below the norm, and, when this frequency mark coincides closely with the average, there can be small room for error.

576. It is impossible here to do more than indicate the standard weights of the two chief coin-standards, the Attic-Euboic and the Aeginetic. They were as follows:

Attic and Aeginetic standards.

Denomination	Attic-Euboic	Aeginetic
obol	11·09 grains (·72 grammes)	16·2 grains (1·05 grammes)
drachma (= 6 obols)	66·5 gms. (4·31 gms.)	97·22 grs. (6·30 gms.)
mina (= 100 drachmae)	6650 grs. (431 gms.) (nearly the same as a pound avoirdupois)	9722 grs. (630 gms.)
talent (= 60 minae)	399,000 grs. (25·86 kg.)	583,320 grs. (37·8 kg.)

Neither standard was absolutely steady and the weights of the Aeginetic in particular, which showed a lasting tendency to decline, must only be taken as approximate. The Aeginetic system, associated in its first stages with the great half-legendary name of Pheidon of Argos, was of predominant importance in early Greece. Solon substituted for it at Athens the Euboic system and the Attic-Euboic standard tended, in later times, to gain more and more at the expense of its rival. In the Greece of Alexander the Great and his successors it was the prevailing coin-standard, though, as we saw above, the Aeginetic sometimes existed beside it as an independent commercial standard.

Actual weights, as we have indicated, do not always correspond exactly with these standards. Of the Attic system the British Museum has, among others, the following: minae of 6639 grains (430·3 grammes), 6958 grs. (450·9 gms.), 7010 grs. (454.2 gms.), 7161 grs. (464 gms.), four-drachma pieces of 234 grs. (15·16 gms.), 253 grs. (16·39 gms.) and 261 grs. (16·91 gms.). The Aeginetic commercial standard is represented by a MNA ΑΓΟΡ. of 9970 grs. (646·05 gms.). Other pieces of the Aeginetic standard are a half-mina of 4823 grs. (312·52 gms.), a ten-drachma piece of 973 grs. (63·04 gms.), a five-drachm piece of 477 grs. (30.91 gms.). These weights are usually flat pieces of lead or bronze and frequently bear types, which may, in some cases, represent city badges,—tortoise, dolphin, amphora, crescent, caduceus, knucklebone—several of which we illustrate here in figures 97 to 100.

Fig. 97. Attic Half-mina (Roman period) belonging to the ἀγορανόμος ('Clerk' of the Market).

Fig. 98. Cyzicene Stater weight.

Fig. 99. Aeginetan Hemitet-arton (⅓ Mina).

Fig. 100. Cyzicene Half-stater weight.

577. It has been customary in recent years to derive Greek standards of weight from standards in use in Babylonia[1]—royal and land standard, gold and silver standard—each of the four, either at normal level or on any one of three enlarged scales. From so rich and varied a system any weight-standard could obviously be derived. But as the very existence of all these Babylonian norms is hotly contested and as the application of them to Greek metrology has involved a good deal of what we may call undue pressure, it is safest for the time to maintain a discreet scepticism on the whole question.

Origin of weight-standards.

Hultsch, *Reliquiae Scriptorum Metrologicorum, Metrologie*; W. Ridgeway, *Mensura*, and P. Gardner, *Pondera*, in *Smith's Dictionary of Antiq.*; Sir W. Ridgeway, *Origin of Stadion (Jour. of Hell. Stud.*, 1888), and *Origin of Metallic Currency and Weight Standards*; O. Viedebandt, *Antike Gewichtsnormen und Münzfüsse*; Daremberg-Saglio, *Dictionnaire des Antiquités grecques et romaines* (articles, *Mensura* and *Pondus*): British Museum, Dept. of Greek and Roman Antiquities, *Guide to the Exhibition illustrating Greek and Roman Life* (3rd edition, 1929; *Weights and Scales*, pp. 149 ff., *Measures and Instruments*, pp. 184 ff.).

Bibliography.

VI. 9. MONEY.

578. As soon as the community has passed the stage of mere barter and its individuals begin to specialise as farmers, smiths, etc., it must evolve a currency: some thing or things must be adopted which may serve at the same time as a medium of exchange, a measure of value and a means of accumulating wealth. At first goods in common use such as livestock or metal, worked and unworked, were generally chosen. Thus cattle were used among the early Teutonic peoples and bronze tools in China. But currency to perform its threefold function efficiently must be as compact, indestructible and unvarying in quality and as constant in supply as possible. Therefore the metals which especially answer these requirements soon tend to become its main, if not sole, instruments, and commodities, which may originally have been the main currency, are correlated with them. Pieces of gold, silver and copper of convenient shape and weight pass from hand to hand, but weight and purity must still be checked at each transaction. An extended commerce is possible with a currency of this kind. Such a reckoning in units of metal is implied by the clay tablets from Cnossus of the late Minoan Period which show pictographs of weights, ingots and scales in conjunction with numerical signs. Contemporary or somewhat later ingots in copper of the shape depicted have been found in Crete and Cyprus, in the sea off Chalcis, near Mycenae and elsewhere; some of these bear incised signs, an interesting

Minoan period.

---

[1] Herodotus III. 89, on the Persian tribute, tells us that silver was paid on the Babylonian standard, gold on the Euboic and that the Babylonian talent equalled 72 Euboic minae.

fact in view of the next stage, the development of coined money. The standards by which they are regulated appear to be of Egyptian origin. Besides copper, gold in rings, bars and slices of bars, and oval ingots has been found in graves of the same and succeeding periods. Some at least of these have been fashioned to definite weights usually representing a unit of about 135 grains which, like the copper unit, seems to have come from Egypt.

579. This then was the stage of development which money had reached when the Greeks entered the Aegean area, and we find it reflected in the Homeric poems, in the story of Glaucus ὃς τεύχε᾽ ἄμειβε χρύσεα χαλκείων ἑκατόμβοι᾽ ἐννεαβοίων (*Iliad* VI. 235–6). Though values were thus expressed in terms of cattle, metals *Homeric and transitional period.* must have been the usual medium of exchange. There is some ground for believing that Homer's gold talent was a piece of gold representing the value of this ox-unit and that it weighed roughly the same as the Mycenaean gold rings just mentioned and the common gold coin of classical times, the Euboic-Attic stater (see § 580); if so its name, τάλαντον, shows that it must also represent the value of a load of some bulkier commodity, which can only be the copper ingot used in Minoan times. In the dark ages which followed iron also takes its place as a means of currency, especially in the Peloponnese, where it survived in uncoined form in arrested Sparta as the official medium of exchange till the third century. Iron circulated originally in the shape of the "spit" (ὀβο(ε)λός) and perhaps its half the "cake" (πέλανος). "Spits" of copper were also in use. Six "spits" made a "handful," δραχμή, and both obol and drachm were carried over, as the names of denominations, into the currency of coined silver which followed. In more than one place the iron spits were dedicated in temples, perhaps on their supersession (e.g. the spits at Delphi said by tradition to be Rhodope's (Her. II. 135) and Pheidon's in the Argive Heraeum). Similarly the βοῦς (presumably represented by a given weight of metal) was still a currency unit in Attica at the time when the Draconian code was drawn up and as such its name lingered in popular speech long after the introduction of coined money, as in the proverb βοῦς ἐπὶ γλώσσῃ for suborned silence.

580. Towards the end of the eighth century the practice began of putting a stamp on pieces of metal intended for circulation and at length coined money came into existence. This momentous *Invention of coinage: form, types, etc.* innovation was made in the coastlands of Asia Minor, by the Lydians according to the sixth-century evidence of Xenophanes. By the end of the seventh century it had spread to the islands and mainland of Greece, by the sixth to Italy and Sicily. Every city of importance wished to issue its own money (to do so was a sign of autonomy) and the resulting coins are a characteristically varied reflection of Hellenic life. Here only the most important and typical coinages can be mentioned. As Aristotle says (*Pol.* I. A 9, 1257 *a* 41), the stamp was to show that the weight was true and to dispense with continual use of the balance. At first the type was stamped on one side only of the coin, the obverse, while the other, the reverse, showed a sinking

or incuse, the mark of the punch which drove the metal into the engraved die. In the later sixth and fifth centuries it became usual to engrave a

design on the punch as well, and thus the coin reaches its final form. The earliest types were probably the badges of individuals, perhaps Lydian kings or tyrants of cities, or even mere private merchants. Thus one Asiatic coin bears above the badge the explanatory in-

Fig. 101. Electrum coin of Phannes.

scription Φαννος εμι σεμα, "I am Phannes' badge" (Fig. 101). The theory that the coin often bore a type representing the superseded commodity previously used for currency, e.g. the axe at Tenedos, has not won acceptance.

Personal badges were naturally most numerous when coinage was still in the tentative stage in Asia Minor; otherwise the coin type was almost always the badge of the city. This badge might contain a punning allusion,

like the seal at Phocaea, or an-nounce some local product like the silphium of Cyrene (Fig. 102) but it usually represented a divinity with local associations. At first the representation was indirect, some sacred animal or attribute being employed, as Apollo's lyre at Delos.

Fig. 102. Coin of Cyrene.

Then, from the middle of the sixth century, with the development of religious ideas the god appeared in person. This innovation was encouraged by the growing use of the reverse type, one side often representing the god and the other his attribute. Inscriptions occur occasionally among the early coins of Asia Minor but the practice of regularly inscribing the community's name was slow of growth and does not become general before the fifth century. Here Corinth (end of seventh century) seems to have led the way. By the fourth century the practice was almost universal and as the ethnic inscription fulfils the same function as the city badge it allowed far greater latitude in the choice of types. The name was at first abbreviated to the initial letter or syllable only. When written at full length it usually appears in the genitive plural of the adjectival form, e.g. Συρακοσίων, (money) "of the Syracusans." In addition to the city type and ethnic inscription we find as early as the fifth century a subsidiary type (the so-called symbol), which was the badge of the officiating magistrate, sometimes accompanied by his name; from the fourth century onwards the presence of one or both was usual. Their object was to fix responsibility for the issue and so prevent fraud.

Weight standards in general have been dealt with elsewhere (§§ 569 ff.). Naturally the standards used for weighing the older bullion currencies con-tinued to regulate the weight of the new coined money. The talent and mina were still employed in reckoning large amounts with the difference that they usually connoted no longer a bar of metal but a number of coins: e.g. at Athens a mina in practice means twenty-five tetradrachms. The unit-coin within each series is called a stater or standard coin, whether didrachm, tridrachm or tetradrachm according to local usage. The Euboic-Attic standard, however, was in almost universal use for pure gold; therefore (except where χρυσοῦς is loosely used of electrum) the gold stater (χρυσοῦς) means in practice a didrachm of 133 grains or the slightly lighter daric (see § 582). It must be borne in mind that the normal scale of coin weights within a standard varied slightly between different cities using the same standard. Further all standards tend to fall in weight in course of time, owing to deductions made for expenses of striking, to worn coins being used as blanks for a new issue, to special financial straits and perhaps to official fraud. Thus in the fifth century the coins of Sicilian cities were actually 1 °/₀ or so heavier than the contemporary coins of Athens though struck on the same standard, and the gap between the latter and the later coins of the Hellenistic kingdoms and of second-century Athens herself was even greater. All Greek gold, electrum and silver coins are "value" coins, that is, the nominal value of the coin coincides in theory with its value as mere metal. The earliest coins were of denominations (mostly staters) representing a considerable purchasing power, but the growth of trade produced an increasing demand for small change and coins in the same metals representing small fractions came more and more into use. The inconvenience of such tiny coins led to the introduction of larger bronze coins of the same or even lower face values. These were "token" coins, that is their face value was considerably greater than their value as metal, and their acceptance depended solely upon convenience backed by the authority of the state. The earliest bronze coins are found in Sicily towards the end of the fifth century and a hundred years later their use is general. In the Peloponnese iron was also occasionally used in the same way.

581. We may now return to the primitive coinages of Asia Minor. The metal used was a natural alloy of gold and silver found in the river beds and known as ἤλεκτρον, λευκὸς χρυσός, or loosely as χρυσός. As the types are still mostly the badges of individuals, whether striking for the community or not, the coins cannot be distributed with any certainty among the different mints. One series, however, with a lion's head is plausibly assigned to the Lydian kings, and another, with a lion turning its head back, to Miletus (Fig. 103), where the same type occurs in later times. The variety of weight standards in use is bewildering: at least four may be distinguished, the Euboic, the Babylonian, the Phocaic and the Phoenician; the approximate weights of the stater in each are as follows: Euboic, 268 grains; Babylonic, 167 grains; Phocaic, 254–248 grains;

Early Asiatic coinages; Croesus.

Fig. 103. Electrum coin of Miletus.

Phoenician, 220–215 grains. To produce smaller values the stater was usually divided by three, though the half stater also occurs. The commonest subdivisions were the third, sixth and twelfth, the sixth (hecte) being most frequently met with, but the twenty-fourth, thirty-sixth, forty-eighth and even the ninety-sixth, a tiny coin not exceeding two grains, are also found. Electrum is an unsatisfactory metal from the monetary point of view. Where coins were made from the alloy in its natural form, the proportion of gold and silver and therefore the intrinsic value might vary considerably from piece to piece though the appearance remained the same, while the preparation of an artificial alloy offered great scope for fraud. There was, therefore, an increasing tendency to use either pure gold or silver. In the sixth century we find coins in silver of Miletus and one or two other cities of the Asiatic coast modelled in shape and weight on the staters of Aegina (see § 584). Next Croesus, refining the natural electrum of his rivers, introduced a

Fig. 104. Gold coin of Croesus.

simultaneous coinage in gold and silver, finally adjusting the weights so that a gold stater of 124·5 grains (Fig. 104) exchanged against twenty silver pieces of 82 grains. The ratio underlying this equation is one of $13\frac{1}{3}$: 1, the same as that given in round figures by Herodotus (III. 95), who elsewhere records the inauguration of this first bimetallic currency (I. 94).

582. Croesus' currency seems to have been accepted if not continued

Coinage of Persian Empire.

by his conquerors, for the specific Persian coinage, bearing the image of the Great King running with bow and spear, or dagger, was not introduced until the reign of Darius I and bears his name. It followed substantially the bimetallic standards of Croesus,

the gold piece (δαρεικός, Fig. 105) weighing 130 grains, and the silver (σίγλος, occasionally δαρεικός also), 86 grains. The weight of the daric was near enough to the Euboic standard to be treated by Herodotus as belonging to it; the silver standard he calls Babylonic (III. 89). The Persian coinage continued unchanged in form and weight, and with only minor variations in type, down to the time of Alexander. How long the government was able to maintain a true bimetallism within its borders, with twenty sigli exchanging against one daric, is a disputed point. Outside the Empire there was a steady tendency for the price of gold to fall in terms of silver during the later fifth and fourth centuries, and it is difficult to see how appreciation of the siglos as against the daric could be prevented. The passage in Xenophon (*Anab.* I. vii. 18) where Cyrus promises a reward of ten talents of silver and pays in darics is not quite conclusive, for it does not name the standard on which the silver was reckoned. This is most likely however to be the Babylonian and if so the original ratio was still in force at the end of the fifth century. Both gold and silver must have been struck in enormous quantities; Pythius, reputed the richest man in the Empire after Xerxes, is said to have possessed 2000 talents of silver (the equivalent of 12,000,000 sigli) and 4,000,000 darics (Herodotus VII. 28). The sigli appear to have been used principally in Asia Minor and are rarely found in other parts of the Empire. The daric had an international currency and is found also in Macedonia, Greece proper, Egypt and Sicily. In addition to the King's money we find two other classes of money struck within the boundaries of the Empire, by the satraps and by the Greek cities. In the fourth century, though not before, the great satraps, e.g. Pharnabazus, Spithridates, Datames etc., issued silver and occasional bronze with their own types and sometimes in their own names. Most of these issues were made in dependent Greek cities and intended for the payment of mercenaries. They imply a relaxation of the central control instituted by Darius I who treated a similar issue by Aryandes satrap of Egypt as an act of treason.

583. On the other hand the King seems never to have restricted the rights of the Greek cities to coin money in their own names, and Themistocles at Magnesia was even permitted to strike coins of Attic weight. After the Persian conquest most Asiatic cities coined in silver only, but electrum coinage of staters and hectae, of Phocaic weight and on the early model, was continued down to the time of Alexander by Phocaea in conjunction with Mytilene and by Cyzicus. The Cyzicene stater (Fig. 106) (248 grains) was struck in great quantities and became an international currency circulating up and down the Aegean and Black Sea; it varied considerably in alloy but usually consisted of 40—50 °/₀ of pure gold, the

Later Asiatic coinages: electrum and silver (4th—2nd cents.)

Fig. 106. Cyzicene stater.

remainder being silver with a little copper. In practice it passed at a fixed value and appears to have been equated with the daric. Athens, contrary to her usual policy towards her subject allies, seems to have encouraged its production and the constantly changing personal types (to which the civic badge, the tunny, is always added) sometimes reflect Athenian myth and story. Lampsacus also continued to strike electrum staters till the fifth century and sums of Lampsacene as well as of Phocaic and Cyzicene staters are often mentioned in Attic inscriptions. In the fourth century Lampsacus also began an important currency of pure gold of the same value as the daric which lasted until Alexander. The silver coinage of the Asiatic cities subject to Athens was considerably restricted in the fifth century though such mints as Samos and Chios were still at work. With the collapse of the Athenian empire there was a revival marked by a wide extension of the standard used at Chios to other cities. At this period Peloponnesian fleets and armies were constantly stationed in the Eastern Aegean and the rapid spread of the Chian (later and more generally known as the Rhodian) standard was probably due to the convenient relation in which its tetradrachm weighing 236—240 grains stood to the Peloponnesian currency. It is in fact the fortieth of the Aeginetan mina and under the name of τεσσαρακοστὴ Χία we find it used to pay the Spartan fleet under Mindarus (Thuc. VIII. 101). Throughout the fourth century the coinage of the Western Asiatic cities continued to be regulated principally on the Rhodian standard, the most important mints being Rhodes and Ephesus. After the Macedonian conquest this standard was largely replaced by the Attic which is represented in the issues of Alexander, Lysimachus, the Seleucids and the Attalids, and, after the defeat of Antiochus III, by the renewed issues of the liberated cities, Smyrna, Cyme, etc. About 200 B.C. a new coin, the cistophorus, with uniform types, the Dionysiac cista and the bowcase of Heracles with snakes, was introduced by the cities of the Pergamene kingdom. It weighed three Attic drachms but was itself divided into four drachms. In the course of the century, perhaps owing to its convenient relations with the Roman system, it largely replaced the coinage of Attic weight in this area and became the official currency of the province of Asia.

584. If we cross the Aegean to Greece proper we find a somewhat

Mainland Greece: Aegina, Corinth.

different picture: the coinage was from the first in silver and the weight standards were more uniform, while instead of the bewildering variety of personal badges we find almost always the unchanging badge of the city as type. The first coinage

is that of Aegina (Fig. 107). It began early in the seventh century and Pheidon of Argos was said by fourth-century tradition to have been its author. Herodotus tells us that he reorganised the measures of the Peloponnese; he also perhaps demonetised the old iron currency (§ 579); so that there is nothing inherently

Fig. 107. Stater of Aegina.

improbable in the story. The constant type is the tortoise (changed after the Peloponnesian War from the sea to the land variety) with a plain incuse reverse, and the coins, which were popularly called χελῶναι, formed the staple currency of the Peloponnese down to the fourth century. They are struck on the Aeginetic standard (see § 576), the stater, here a piece of 2 drachms, weighing 194 grains. For small change the half-stater (drachm), the hemidrachm or triobol, the diobol, obol and hemiobol were also issued. The influence of the Aeginetan coinage was far-reaching. The first silver coins issued in Asia Minor were, as we have seen, of this standard and the earliest coins of Greece proper and the islands, with the exception of Corinth, Athens and Euboea, conform to the Aeginetan pattern in make as well as weight. The standard was dominant in mainland Greece as far as the Macedonian border, in the islands and Crete down to Alexander's time, and reappeared in a diminished form in the coinages of the Achaean and Boeotian leagues of the third and second centuries. Aegina was soon followed by Corinth whose first money dates from the second half of the sixth century and was doubtless introduced by Cypselus (Fig. 108). The weight and divisional system are however quite different from the Aeginetic; the stater

weighed up to 133 grains and was divided by three into thirds (drachms), sixths (triobols), eighteenths (obols) etc. The same weight standard in doubled form, with the same division by three, is found in the earliest coinage of Chalcis and her colonies. It derived from Asia Minor

Fig. 108. Earliest Corinthian stater.

through Samos, which also used it in early times, when she stood in close relations with both Chalcis and Corinth. The type of Corinth was Pegasus, and, like the types of Aegina and Athens, it remained unchanged till the end, though a second type, the head of Athena, took the place of the incuse reverse in the sixth century. These Pegasus staters (πῶλοι) circulated freely up the Adriatic coast, in South Italy and in Sicily,

especially in the fourth century. The numerous coins of the Corinthian colonies are uniform in type and weight with those of the mother-city and were sometimes struck in her mint. Only Corcyra refused to conform; though using the same drachm she struck it in tetradrachms instead of tridrachms,

Fig. 109. Stater of Corcyra.

and with her own type, the cow and calf (Fig. 109).

585. Attica before the time of Solon did not coin its own money but used the Aeginetan. In the course of his reforms Solon reorganised the currency. The two accounts of his measures, Athens. Androtion's and Aristotle's (Plutarch, *Solon* xv and 'Αθ. Πολ. 10), differ in certain points but the general outline of his monetary reform is clear. By a measure of inflation he issued a new Attic silver coin weighing about 130 grains to replace the staters of Aegina weighing 194 grs. then in circulation; thus, since debts incurred in the old currency were payable in the new, he lightened the debtor's burden by a third. The new coin was of the same weight standard as the Corinthian stater and the earliest Euboean coinages (see § 584) but under Aeginetan in-

fluence it was divided into two not into three drachms. The variety of the types, owl, horse, wheel, trisceles etc., always with incuse reverse, suggests that like the early types of Asia Minor they were personal badges. This money continued until Peisistratus remodelled the coinage. He doubled the size of the standard piece, which is hence-forward a tetradrachm, weighing 267

Fig. 110. Tetradrachm of Athens. (4th cent.)

grains, and introduced an unchanging type on either side, Athena's head for the obverse and her owl for the reverse (Fig. 110). The form which he thus gave to the coinage was maintained in essentials until it was suspended in the troubles following Alexander's death; and the weight standard and divisional system as he left it is commonly known as the Euboic-Attic. Three periods may be distinguished, (1) down to the beginning of the Persian Wars, (2) from thence to the end of the Peloponnesian War, (3) from thence to the early third century. In the first the style is archaic, often of great beauty but sometimes so rough as to suggest that certain issues were struck in Peisistratus' Thracian lands. In the second the great extension of the workings at Laurium increased enormously the supply of bullion available for coining; the style becomes archaising and the types fixed to the smallest detail.

With the growth of the empire it became the policy of Athens to close the mints of her allies as far as possible and compel them to use her own money. A privileged position was however accorded to the Cyzicene electrum (see § 583) which owing to its high value supplemented rather than rivalled the silver tetradrachm. This general policy was so far successful that coinage in the islands practically disappeared and was considerably diminished in the Thraco-Macedonian and Asiatic coasts. At the end of the century, owing to the financial pressure of the Peloponnesian War, especially after the occupation of Decelea had restricted so severely the supply of bullion from Laurium, the gold Nikai in the Parthenon were melted down and coined into money, while bronze coins plated with silver were issued in place of the tetradrachms. Both events are referred to by Aristophanes in a passage in the *Frogs* (718 ff.) where the good old silver and new gold coins are contrasted with the base badly struck bronze. The gold pieces were the obol, diobol, drachm and didrachm (stater) and at the current ratio of 12 : 1 the gold stater (which is mentioned in an inscription though no example has come down to us) represented 6 silver tetradrachms. The last period begins with the resumption of the coinage of silver in 394/3. On the appearance of the new issue the old emergency coins of silvered bronze were demonetised, a proceeding which Aristophanes implies caused some hardship (*Eccles.* 819 ff.). The types of the new coins were unchanged though the style became careless and less archaistic. At a later period the temple treasures were requisitioned a second time and an abundant coinage of gold was struck by Lachares when defending the city against Demetrius Poliorcetes in 295/4.

The denominations may be presented in tabular form as follows:

Decadrachm*	= 10 drachms	Trihemiobol (= 1½ obols)	= 1/4 drachm	
Tetradrachm	= 4 ,,	Obol	= 1/6 ,,	
Didrachm*	= 2 ,,	Tritartemorion†		
Drachm	= 1 drachm	or Tritemorion	= 6/8 obol	
Pentobol†	= 5/6 ,,	Hemiobol	= 4/8 ,,	
Tetrobol†	= 4/6 ,,	Trihemitartemorion†	= 3/8 ,,	
Triobol	= 3/6 ,,	Tetartemorion	= 2/8 ,,	
Diobol†	= 2/6 ,,	Hemitetartemorion†	= 1/8 ,,	

    * in second period only   † in third period only

The inconvenience of the lower fractions of the obol is patent, the smallest weighing just over one grain. In the fourth century their place was filled by bronze coins, the χαλκοῦς being the equivalent of the hemitetarte-morion.

The Athenian coinage as reconstituted by Peisistratus became the most important international currency of Greece before Alexander. The mines of Laurium provided bullion for enormous quantities of coin and the tetra-drachms (γλαῦκες) of all three periods circulated freely East and West to the borders of the Greek world, while local imitations were produced in Syria and Central Asia, Arabia and Egypt. The Euboic-Attic standard established itself in Sicily in the fifth century while later its adoption by Alexander assured its dominance in the Hellenistic period.

Towards the end of the third century coinage was again resumed and continued until the Roman Empire. The coins of the "new style," as they are called, are broad and thin, in contrast to their bullet-like predecessors. The types were somewhat altered—the Parthenos now occupied the obverse, the owl with Panathenaic amphora and olive wreath the reverse; the elabo-rate system of officials' names etc. recorded not only the year but the month and the workshop in which the coin was struck. Tetradrachms, drachms and hemidrachms were the only denominations issued in silver, the others being supplied by bronze.

586. Macedonia and Thrace, especially the Pangaean range, produced abundant supplies of gold and silver. Coinage began there in the sixth century not only in the Greek cities but also among the semi-barbarous mining tribes of the interior, the Orrescii (Fig. 111), Edonians, Derrones etc. The influence of Asia Minor was much stronger here than in Greece proper (cp. the interest of the Milesian Histiaeus in Myrcinus, Herod. v. 11) and there was even a small early coinage of electrum on the Ionian pattern. The bulk of the coinage however is in silver. This travelled in large quanti-ties to the South and East where it occurs frequently in Egyptian hoards of the sixth century and occasionally

Macedonia and Thrace.

Fig. 111. Stater of Orrescii.

in Cyprus and even Mesopotamia. The weights of the coins are very variable; the Chalcidian colonies began by using the Euboic standard of their mother-city, while other cities and the mining tribes usually employed some form of the Babylonic standard which regulated some of the early Asiatic electrum and also the King's silver (§§ 581, 582). The remarkable fluctuations in these weights and a steady downward trend suggest a continual attempt to fix the value of the silver unit in terms of gold during a period when the supply of gold is steadily increasing, a groping towards bimetallism which finds complete expression in the simultaneous coinages in gold and silver of Philip and Alexander.

587. After the sixth century the expansion of the Athenian empire and still more that of Macedonia increasingly curtailed the native coinages. Philip II completed the absorption of the mining areas into his kingdom and with the product of their intensified exploitation launched a new bimetallic coinage. Like the Athenian war

Philip and Alexander.

Fig. 112. Gold stater of Philip.

coinage (see § 585) his gold stater is a didrachm of Attic weight (Fig. 112) and is the equivalent of 6 silver staters (tetradrachms). As however by this time, partly through his own mining activity, the ratio of gold to silver had sunk from 12 : 1 to 10 : 1, the new tetradrachm which he introduced is of the so-called Phoenician standard and weighs only 224 grains. Both reverse types are agonistic and refer to the Olympian victories of which he was so proud. Alexander's conquest of the East set free further enormous stores of bullion though it does not seem to have affected materially the relative values of the two metals. His coinage, like Philip's, was in gold and silver, and the same ratio of 10 : 1 was observed. It is however simplified by the adoption of the Attic standard for silver as well as for gold; on this footing the gold stater was the equivalent of 20 drachms of silver instead of 24 as in Philip's reckoning. The equivalent of 20 silver units to the gold piece had been established for centuries in the Persian Empire (see § 582) and this fact may have influenced Alexander in making the change. The types for the gold stater were Athena and Nike,

Fig. 113. Tetradrachm of Alexander.

for the silver tetradrachm (Fig. 113) Heracles and Zeus. The gold staters of Philip and Alexander and Alexander's silver tetradrachm remained among the most important currencies till Roman times. The gold passed freely west as well as east of the Adriatic; and Philip's staters (Φιλίππειοι) also circulated through North-Western Europe where they formed the model for the Celtic coinages of Britain, Gaul etc. Alexander's silver became the staple currency of the Eastern Mediterranean. He struck great quantities at mints like Tarsus and Babylon as well as in Macedonia, and all his successors except the Ptolemies continued to use the same standard. So great was the popularity of the Macedonian coinages that silver with types and name of Alexander and to a lesser extent gold with those of Philip continued to be issued from time to time by independent cities until the first century B.C.

588. In the West coinage begins in the middle of the sixth century. The pound of bronze (*litra* in Sicily, *libra* in Italy) appears to have been the native currency unit, but the Greeks used silver, supplemented later by bronze for small change, and by

The West. Italy and Sicily.

occasional gold in Sicily. The earliest coins of South Italy, and especially of the
Achaean cities (e.g. Sybaris,
Fig. 114), are remarkable
for their fabric, the type in
relief on the obverse being
reproduced on the reverse
in intaglio. Early in the
fifth century the normal
two-sided coin was intro-
duced.   The   prevalent
weight standard, except in
Campania, was akin to,

Fig. 114. Coin of Sybaris.

and perhaps derived from, the Corinthian form of the Euboic, for the stater
(νόμος), though appreciably lighter, is similarly divided into three not two
drachms. The standard of Campania with a drachm of 57–60 grains was
introduced by colonists from Phocaea in the sixth century and is important
as being that adopted by Rome for her first silver coinage early in the third
century. The further expansion of the Roman power in the following period
put an end to all individual coinages except that of occasional bronze.

The earliest coins of Sicily were struck by the Chalcidian colonies Zancle,
Naxos and Himera (Fig. 115), on the standard of the mother-city and consisted
of drachms (third-staters) of 89 grains. Later in the sixth century Syracuse

Fig. 115. Coin of Himera.   Fig. 116. Coin of Syracuse.

(Fig. 116) began to coin on the Euboic-Attic standard which spread rapidly
over the whole island and remained in use for silver by Greek and Semite
alike till the death of Agathocles. In the fifth century the strong government of the tyrants with their large military establishments resulted in an
abundant coinage; the types, reflecting the taste of the governing classes,
are mostly agonistic. In the fourth century perhaps owing to the effect of
the Carthaginian wars coinage was much scantier and the money in circulation consisted principally of Punic coins and Corinthian staters. The ease
with which the Attic replaced the original Chalcidian form of the Euboic
standard is probably due to the simple relation which it provided with the
native litra of bronze, for the Siceliots represented this unit by a silver coin
of 13 grains, a twentieth of the Attic tetradrachm, and gave the Corinthian
stater of 133 grains the name of δεκαλιτρὸς στατήρ. In the third century
Sicilian coinage became still scantier except for the important silver

35—2

currency based on the litra which Hieron II issued in the names of himself and his family; while after the Second Punic War, as in Italy, and for the same reason, only occasional bronze occurs.

Bibliography. E. Babelon, *Traité des monnaies grecques et romaines*; *British Museum Catalogues of Greek Coins* [by districts]; P. Gardner, *History of Ancient Coinage*; B. V. Head, *Historia Numorum*; G. F. Hill, *Handbook of Greek and Roman Coins*; *Historical Greek Coins*; W. Ridgeway, *Origin of Metallic Currency*.

VI. 10. WAR.

A. ARMS AND ARMOUR.

589. FROM the earliest times of which we have any knowledge the most important part in Hellenic warfare was played by the Hoplite. His equipment varied but little between the days when the Homeric poems were written and the days when Greece fell before the power of Rome. It consisted of helm, cuirass, greaves and shield, with spear and sword as offensive arms. The helm (κόρυς or κυνέη) was normally of bronze, though occasionally of leather. Its character varied somewhat at different epochs but we can distinguish three main forms. (1) The Corinthian helm when drawn down covered the whole head as far as the chin, and only showed the wearer's eyes through two eye-slits: it could however be worn tilted backwards when an engagement was not in progress, and then exposed the whole face. This form of headpiece was often destitute of crest or plume. (2) The Athenian helm was of a more open type: it left the face visible, though the cheeks were sometimes protected by moveable plates which could be turned up or down. It was usually furnished with a crest, consisting of a metal ridge in which was set a tall ornament of leather, horsehair, or feathers. The crest was occasionally triple, consisting of a larger decoration in the middle and two smaller ones on each side. (3) A simpler form of headpiece was a plain pointed steel cap (πῖλος) without any vizor, cheek-piece, or crest: it seems to have been specially common among the Spartans. We have no space for the description of the many minor varieties of helm. The cuirass (θώραξ) generally consisted of a breast-plate and back-plate of bronze, joined by thongs or by straps fastened by a buckle. The earliest form of body-armour was short, and only reached down to the hip-bone: to supplement it the warrior wore the μίτρα, a broad girdle of leather and bronze, which covered the stomach and hips, and was girt on before the cuirass was donned. From the fifth century onward the shape of the breast-plate and back-plate was improved, so that they came down lower and more adequately protected the lower parts of the body. For the μίτρα was substituted a single or double fringe of leather strips, strengthened with

Hoplite equipment.

Defensive armour.

metal studs or edging, called πτέρυγες, which hung down half-way to the knees. Warriors whose means were narrow often substituted for the cuirass a tight-fitting jerkin of leather (σπολάς) more or less strengthened with metal in its more important parts. We also hear occasionally of body-armour composed of linen quilted, or stuffed with felt. The greaves (κνημῖδες) were thin pliable plates of bronze adapted to the shape of the leg: they opened at the back, and when slipped on were fastened below the knee and above the ankle with thongs or straps. In arming himself the warrior first assumed his greaves, then his cuirass, and lastly his helm.

Fig. 117.　Hoplite with Corinthian helmet, and Boeotian shield.
Bronze statuette.

The hoplite's shield (ἀσπίς) was round or oval, and varied from three to five feet in length. It was composed of several thicknesses of leather, and had a metal rim and boss. In early days it was managed by means of a single strap grasped by the left-hand (πόρπαξ) and of a broad belt passed round the left shoulder (τελαμών), so as to throw much of the weight on the body and thus relieve the arm. In later days shields were generally somewhat smaller, and were managed

Shield.

by two handles (ὄχανα) instead of a belt and a strap, the left hand being thrust through the first so as to grip the second. Only the Macedonian phalangite, requiring both hands to manage his long pike, was compelled to hang his shield on his left arm by a single handle through which passed hand, wrist and forearm. The custom of painting devices upon the shield seems to have prevailed from the earliest times: in the fifth and fourth cen-

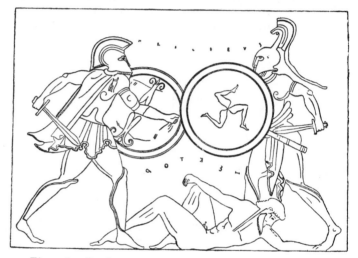

Fig. 118. Combatant warriors, from a fifth century vase.

turies the hoplite bore not his own personal cognisance but one chosen by the state, either the initial letter of its name or its regular badge. Thus the Sicyonian shield was blazoned with a large Σ, and the Theban with a club : the shield of the Macedonian infantry was painted in a peculiar concentric pattern of crescents and stars which is easily recognizable on coins and monuments.

590. The hoplite's lance (δόρυ) was a stout weapon about six feet long, employed mainly for thrusting : in the Homeric poems the heroes are often introduced casting their lances as missiles, but this practice was rare in historical times, when the weapon was generally used only as a pike for close combat. Very different from the normal Greek lance was the σάρισσα of the Macedonian phalangite, an enormous spear of eighteen feet in length, requiring both hands for its management. Owing to their vast size the heads of five sarissae projected beyond the front line of the phalanx, which seemed utterly impenetrable to the enemy as long as its order remained unbroken. The Greek sword (ξίφος) was a comparatively short and ineffective

Lance and sword.

weapon compared to the Roman *gladius*. It seldom exceeded 25 inches in length, and very often fell short of 20 inches. It was straight, acutely pointed, and double-edged for both cut and thrust work. The guard or cross-piece was small, in some of the ancient types almost non-existent. Occasionally a short curved sabre (μάχαιρα, κοπίς, δρέπανον), only fitted for hewing and not for thrusting, was used, but it was much less common than the straight sword. Spear and sword were the hoplite's only weapons : the axe, mace and halberd were essentially foreign weapons and never became naturalized among the Greeks.

591. The Greek horseman bore the same arms as the hoplite save that he very often dispensed with the use of a shield, needing his left hand for the reins. When the shield was carried it was round, and somewhat smaller than that of the foot-soldier. The lance was naturally used much more than the sword by cavalry : the latter weapon was too short for efficient employment on horseback. The lance was used both over-hand and under-hand, and was occasionally thrown as a missile. It was not a long weapon needing to be placed 'in rest' under the arm like that of the mediaeval knight. The only trace of the use of a lance of considerable length is found in the army of Alexander the Great, where there were certain 'σαρισσοφόροι ἱππεῖς.' The horseman had neither stirrups nor saddle, sitting on a mere ἐφίππιον of felt or skin, fastened round the horse's belly by a strap. The inefficiency of Greek horse is largely to be accounted for by their want of a sufficiently long lance, and by the fact that the shock of the individual rider was lessened owing to his being destitute of stirrups or saddle. His thrust was delivered with the force of his own arm alone, not with that of man and horse together, and was therefore less than that of a rider sitting tight in his saddle with his lance in rest. If a Greek horseman, depending on his balance and the grip of his knees alone, had delivered a charge with the same impetus as a mediaeval knight, he would have been carried backwards over his horse's tail when his lance struck his adversary. From the fifth century onwards the Greeks were acquainted with the use of light horse, destitute of armour and using the missile dart (ἀκόντιον) as their chief weapon. They seem to have been developed on the plains of Apulia and Sicily, being first heard of in the army of the Syracusan tyrant Gelon. The Tarentines were most noted for their strength in this arm, and from the fourth century mounted javelin-men were often called 'Tarentines,' whatever their nationality[1]. Horse-bowmen on the other hand were of distinctly barbarian origin, and only prominent in the armies of Alexander the Great and his successors.

---

[1] They are first mentioned in 316 B.C., but the Tarentine coins contain an admirable set of representations of them, armed with a large round shield and three darts, from about 420 onwards. These troops sometimes were furnished with two horses, and leapt from one to the other.

592. The arms of light infantry were the dart, bow and sling. They
wore no metal armour, being at the most protected by
leather or quilted jerkins, and wearing (in Northern Greece at
least) a broad felt hat (πέτασος). The javelin-man (ἀκοντιστής)
carried a small bundle of his weapons and a light shield: the darts (ἀκόντιον)
were light and ranged from three to five feet in length. The bow (τόξον)
was very short, sometimes not more than half the length of the English
six-foot weapon of the Middle Ages. It was made generally of an elastic wood,
but sometimes of two pieces of horn soldered into a central handle. Greek
archery seems never to have been very good or efficient: such as it was,
it flourished most in Crete. Its poorness is best shown by the fact that
those two very inferior weapons the dart and the sling continued to exist
alongside of the bow to the very last days of Greek history. Really
competent archery drives slingers and javelin-men out of the field. The
most famous employers of the sling (σφενδόνη) were the Rhodians and
Cretans, with some of the peoples of Northern Greece. Their most
common missile was an almond-shaped lump of lead, but pebbles and even
clay-balls were used in default of a proper provision of metal.

*Light
infantry.*

B. TACTICS.

593. The descriptions of battles in the Homeric poems must not be
taken as accurately reproducing any real stage of the Art of
War, either in the Heroic age or in the time when the poems
were composed. Objectless single combats in front of the
line, and protracted scuffles over the corpses of fallen heroes can never
have constituted the main part of an engagement. An army, whose solid
portion consisted of warriors heavily armed with helm, cuirass and shield,
must fight in more or less orderly array. The best description of a hoplite
force in Homer is that in *Iliad* XVI. 210—216, where the battle-line of the
Myrmidons is compared to a wall reared by a skilful builder, shield touching
shield all down the front. The exigencies of poetry cause the narrative to
neglect the main heart of the fight in order to describe the ἀριστεία of
chiefs. There is no reason to doubt that at an early stage of Greek warfare
the chariot was used in battle, as we see it employed in Egyptian or
Assyrian monuments. Corroboration of the native tradition on the subject
is supplied by representations of war-chariots in Mycenaean art. But in
the prehistoric days when they were employed by the chiefs, the main mass
of the host must still have consisted of half-armed and untrained retainers,
not of the hoplites described in the *Iliad*. The poet in short was mixing
the half-remembered tactics of antiquity with those of his own day.

*Homeric
warfare.*

594. Aristotle (*Politics* VI. (IV.), 13) is probably right in stating that in
the normal Hellenic state there was a time when the main
fighting force consisted of a cavalry furnished by the nobles.
Traces of the long lost predominance of the mounted chief

*Predomin-
ance of
cavalry.*

are to be found in the existence of a class known as ἱππεῖς in states which in historic days no longer employed cavalry. Athens had no organized force of the kind till the middle of the fifth century, but the 'knights' occur in the legislation of Draco and Solon. At Sparta the 300 who bore the name always served on foot as the body-guard of the kings. In the Greece of the fifth century the only region where the knightly class still retained its ancient preponderance both in politics and on the battle-field was Thessaly, where a cavalry composed of nobles was the ruling power, and the hoplite was only of secondary importance. In Boeotia, the only other land whose mounted force was in all ages very important, the heavy infantry was in historic times the main battle-force.

595. The day of the preponderance of cavalry came to an end when it was discovered that a solid body of mailed hoplites, standing shield to shield, without flinching, could turn back a charge of horse. Except in flat regions like Thessaly and Boeotia, the mounted arm disappeared for a space from the battle-field. The tactics of the hoplite-array which thus superseded the knighthood were very simple. Drawn up in lines generally about eight deep, the troops advanced with level front against their adversaries and tried to bear them down by the heaviness of their impact. The charge of the hoplite-array being the decisive point in a battle, the all-important aim was to keep the line unbroken, as its strength lay in its continuity, and gaps were fatal. The two things to be feared were that the line might be broken, or that it might be outflanked. The latter disaster had a tendency to happen upon the left wing of an army, for (as Thucydides remarks in describing the battle of Mantinea) the extreme right-hand man of every host was apt to edge away to the right, in order to avoid exposing his unshielded right side to the enemy. His comrades instinctively followed his example all down the line, each striving to get close under his right-hand neighbour's shield. Thus the extreme left-hand end of the line was drawn out of its original place as the advance continued, and if two arrays of exactly equal strength started precisely opposite to each other at a mile apart, it was found that each, at the moment of contact, would be slightly outflanking its enemy on the right and slightly outflanked by him on the left wing. It was of course unlikely that two armies would be precisely equal and show an identical length of front: where they did not, the host whose superior numbers enabled it to outflank the other had the better chance of victory. Hence came a tendency on the part of armies numerically inferior to their foes to choose for battle a position where there was some natural obstacle, covering one or both flanks, and preventing the enemy from turning the wings. In Greece, a land of passes and ravines, such positions abounded: the ideal one for a small force was a defile like that of Thermopylae, where it could draw itself up with both flanks safely protected, and so prevent the superior numbers of the enemy from telling.

Hoplite tactics.

596. Competent generals, though placing their main reliance on their hoplites, took bowmen, slingers and javelin-men into the field, because they knew that their adversaries would also be furnished with such troops, who would be able to annoy the hoplites from a distance, unless kept in check by bands armed like themselves. These formed a subsidiary force, 'furtive hoverers on the edge of battle,' as one ancient writer calls them. It is significant that in many engagements, where large numbers of light-armed troops were present (as at Plataea and Delium), there is little or no mention of their doings during the fight. The best-known instance of a victory won by light troops over hoplites in the fifth century took place in 426, when the Athenian general Demosthenes was routed by the Aetolians. Having advanced without any sufficient provision of archers or peltasts into a rugged region, his men were continually harassed from a distance by the evasive foe, till after severe losses they grew demoralized, turned, and fled for the coast. Hotly pursued by their nimble adversaries they only escaped with the loss of half their numbers. Battle-tactics remained almost unchanged down to the fourth century. The hoplites stood in the centre in a continuous line: the cavalry (if any was present) was drawn up on one or both flanks, while the light troops made play in front till the lines closed, and then drew aside. Ambushes were occasionally set, from which select detachments ran in on to the flank or rear of the enemy, *e.g.* by Demosthenes at the battle of Olpae in 426. There are few traces, if any, of some of the commonest military practices, such as the retention of a reserve, or the drawing up of a second line to support the first, or the 'refusing' of part of the battle-line by placing it where it could not be easily reached by the enemy. The last-named device was impossible so long as generals sacrificed all other advantages to the necessity of keeping a level front all down the line, and throwing in all their troops simultaneously. It often occurred, of course, that the fight did not open at the same moment on all parts of the field, (*e.g.* at Plataea and Delium), but this was the result of accident, not of design.

Use of light-armed troops.

597. The late development of tactics among the Greeks is all the more curious because professional soldiers were known from a very early age. The Spartans most certainly deserve that name, and it is equally applicable to the mercenaries, who are found serving in great numbers as early as the seventh and sixth centuries. But the Spartans seem to have excelled mainly in the handiness under arms which comes from perpetual drill, and in the power to make rapid and orderly movement which results from subdivision into small tactical units. Their array was stereotyped, and new military devices were not to be expected from such a conservative race. Their mobility came from the fact that they had a complete system of field officers and subalterns, forming a hierarchy down which orders were easily and rapidly passed. In an ordinary Greek state the host was divided only by 'tribes'

Drill and organisation of the Spartans.

or suchlike large divisions, and the command was passed down the line by the shouts of the general's herald.   Among the Spartans on the other hand the smallest unit, the *Enomotia*, was only some 32 or 36 strong: four of them made a *Pentekostys*, and four *Pentekostyes* made a λόχος of some 500 spears.   Each of these bodies had its officer (ἐνωμοτάρχης, λοχαγός, etc.), responsible to his superior till the Polemarch or King was reached at the top of the ascending scale of responsibility.   It is curious to find that not even a Spartan training could secure complete discipline in the field: the first battle of Mantinea (418) was almost lost by gross disobedience on the part of two officers, who neglected to move up to the left at the king's orders.

598.   The origin of mercenary troops in Greece is lost in the mists of extreme antiquity.   In the Homeric poems exiles and adventurers are often found hiring themselves out to serve as the   **Mercenaries.**
henchmen of warlike princes.   In a later age a large band of foreign spear-men was part of the necessary equipment of a tyrant.   Princes like Periander and Polycrates hired hundreds of such retainers, while the great Syracusan tyrants of the early fifth century counted their mercenaries by the ten thousand.   The more adventurous of the Hellenic soldiers of fortune went to the East or Egypt; King Apries and King Amasis in the last-named country are said to have maintained no less than 30,000 Ionian and Carian troops.   Nor did the Persian Satraps disdain in a later age to strengthen their disorderly hordes by a solid core of Greek hoplites.   By the fourth century we find permanent bands of mercenaries led by noted *condottieri*, ξεναγοί, wandering from land to land in search of employment.   The Athenians of Demosthenes' day suffered much trouble from their inveterate habit of employing these hirelings, instead of calling out their citizen levy. The mercenary chiefs, to whom they entrusted the conduct of their campaigns, preferred (as was natural) their private interests to those of their employers.   They were always set on plunder rather than on fighting, and often committed deeds of actual treachery.   Aristotle remarks that the mercenary kept his head better in situations of ordinary danger, but that he was quite incapable of the occasional acts of desperate devotion which were not infrequently to be found among citizen troops fighting for their own hearths and homes.

599.   The fourth century saw a profound modification of the methods of war, connected with the names of Iphicrates, Epameinondas,
and the two great Macedonian kings Philip and Alexander.   **Develop-**
The first-named officer somewhat improved the reputation   **ments in the**
of light troops by organizing a corps of peltasts who bore   **fourth**
century.
light body-armour of quilted linen, and carried not only
darts but also a spear and sword for close combat, so that they were able on occasion to join in hand-to-hand fighting.   His great achievement however, the destruction of a Spartan *mora* near Corinth in 391, was accomplished not by bidding his men close, but by pursuing the same

harassing tactics by which the Aetolians had routed Demosthenes in 426. The name of Epameinondas marks a much more important landmark in military history. The chief device which he invented was that of strengthening one wing for offensive purposes and 'refusing' the rest of his battle-line till the strong wing had already made a breach in the enemy's array and shaken his confidence. At Leuctra (371) he destined his left wing for the offensive, contrary to the ordinary Greek custom which placed the best troops on the right, the post of honour. Here he massed the Theban contingent in a solid column fifty deep, while his centre and right were composed of the other Boeotian levies drawn up in the usual line-formation. The Peloponnesians faced him in a continuous array twelve deep, the Spartans taking the right as was their wont. Epameinondas hurled the Theban column at the Lacedaemonians, while bidding the other Boeotians hang back and refrain from closing. In spite of the desperate resistance of king Cleombrotus and his men, the column broke right through them and split the Peloponnesian host in two. The allies who formed the left and centre of Cleombrotus' army would not stand firm when they saw their masters beaten and the king slain : almost before the Boeotians had come into contact with them they gave ground and retreated in good order to their camp. This is the first example of a deliberate advance *en échelon* in Greek military history. At Mantinea (362 B.C.) Epameinondas adopted the same order of battle (Fig. 119): he massed his Boeotian troops in a deep column on the left, flanking them with the best part of his cavalry, in order to prevent their being charged by the horsemen of the hostile right wing. His Arcadian, Argive and Messenian contingents on his centre and right were destined only to hold the enemy employed, while the Boeotians dealt the decisive blow. A detached body, mainly composed of light troops, was thrown out far to the right, to threaten the hostile left, and prevent it from delivering a counter-stroke. When the lines closed the result was much the same as at Leuctra, but the Spartans on the right wing of their host strove so desperately to hold their ground that Epameinondas had himself to lead the 'sacred band' to the head of his column to strike the final blow.   He broke the hostile line and won the fight, but was slain in the moment of victory.

600.   We are unfortunately very ill-informed as to the details of the battles of Philip of Macedon : we know enough however to be able to conclude that he owed his success to two main devices. He used his cavalry far more that any general before him, and he trained his infantry to work in very close and solid columns and to use far longer weapons than their enemies, so that they bore them down by sheer force of impact. His celebrated phalanx was armed with spears more than twice the length of those of the previous generation : when the pikes were brought down to the charge, those of the second, and perhaps even more ranks all projected in front of the men in the front line, and the thicket of shafts was so close as to

Tactics of Philip.

seem impenetrable. The Greek hoplites with their six-foot spears could not resist the far longer (at least 13 feet, perhaps later 18 feet) sarissae

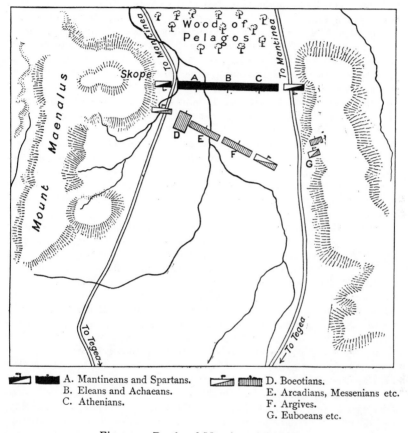

A. Mantineans and Spartans.
B. Eleans and Achaeans.
C. Athenians.

D. Boeotians.
E. Arcadians, Messenians etc.
F. Argives.
G. Euboeans etc.

Fig. 119. Battle of Mantinea (362 B.C.).

projecting in front of the Macedonian phalanx. The core of Philip's infantry was composed of the six τάξεις of native Macedonian foot armed with the sarissa, but he also employed many mercenaries equipped in the ordinary Greek fashion, as well as a large corps of ὑπασπισταί, whose main duty was to cover the flanks of the phalanx. They were a light form of infantry of the line, bearing shield and pike, but wearing only a broad felt hat instead of a helmet, and a linen or quilted jerkin instead of a cuirass. It was however by means of their cavalry, even more than by the sarissae of their phalanx, that Philip and Alexander won their victories. The native Macedonian horse was itself numerous, and to this after 344 Philip added the Thessalian cavalry, the most formidable body of the kind in Greece. It seems probable that the good service which he got out of an arm hitherto somewhat ineffective in Hellenic warfare was the result partly of using horsemen in larger bodies than had ever been seen before, partly of training the men to charge home in close order instead of endeavouring to perform feats of individual prowess. Perhaps he may have given them a longer lance than they before possessed, but this is uncertain. It is at any rate clear that Philip used his cavalry in masses for delivering flank attacks on the hostile line, while the phalanx assaulted it in front. We should gather that he was the first who relied upon it for striking the decisive blow in battle: Epameinondas seems only to have used it to drive the enemy's horse away and to cover the flanks of the hoplites. It would appear that in the armies of Philip and his greater son the cavalry generally formed a sixth or a seventh of the whole force, whereas in earlier days they seldom rose to a tenth or a twelfth.

601. The details of the battles of Alexander the Great are far better known to us than those of his father's victories. Alike at

Battles of Alexander. the Granicus, at Issus and at Arbela he concentrated his best cavalry on the right wing, which he headed in person, and with it delivered the decisive attack. The phalanx in the centre kept the enemy at bay with its long spears, while the left wing, composed of the Thessalian and mercenary cavalry, covered the flank of the infantry and maintained a 'defensive-offensive' attitude. At the Granicus, where the enemy was not possessed of any crushing numerical superiority, and at Issus, where the Persians threw away their advantage by cramping their host into the short two-mile front between the hills and the sea, Alexander's plan succeeded without much difficulty. But at Arbela (Fig. 120), where he was enormously outflanked on both wings on a treeless plain, he had to take special precautions. Preserving the general character of his array, he told off a considerable body of men to form flank and rear guards, in case the enemy might swing round his wings and try to attack him from the side. Thus he advanced with the army formed in a sort of hollow square, of which the front was solid, and destined for offensive work, while the sides and rear were weak, and intended only to hold off the enemy till the main line should have done its work. The outflanking movement, which Alexander had feared, actually took place and caused some confusion : moreover a body of Indian cavalry which slipped in between two of the brigades of the phalanx also did mischief. Nevertheless the attack of Alexander's right wing was so decisive that the Persian King saw his centre pierced and turned to fly. When he had departed his whole army, even those parts of it which had not been unsuccessful, melted from the field. Alexander may be styled pre-eminently a cavalry general. It was always with his horse-guards (ἄγημα), followed by the other squadrons of the native Macedonian horse, that he delivered the decisive blow. But he also knew thoroughly well how to handle his infantry, especially the 'Hypaspistae' and other light troops, and in mountain campaigns, where cavalry could not be employed, showed

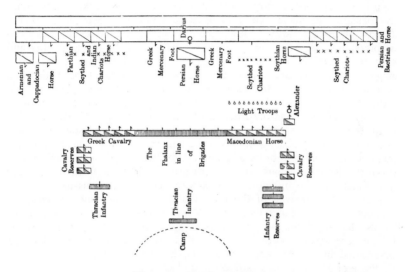

Fig. 120.   Battle of Arbela.

himself as brilliant a commander as at the Granicus or Arbela. In his last days he set on foot an experiment which was destined never to be carried into effect; he began to reorganize the phalanx, and to incorporate in it numbers of Asiatic archers and other light troops, who were to form its rear ranks, while the Macedonians bearing the long sarissa were to stand only four deep in front of them. Apparently the orientals were to sally out on the flanks, to cast their missiles, and then to take refuge behind the Macedonians when the enemy proceeded to charge, just as the arquebusiers of the sixteenth and seventeenth centuries were wont to take shelter behind their pikemen.

602. Alexander's successors led armies far inferior in military value to that of their great master: the contending generals after his death enlisted orientals in great hordes, sometimes allowing them to keep their own weapons, sometimes giving

Successors of Alexander.

them the Macedonian equipment of sarissa and shield. They fought with unwieldy masses of inferior troops rather than with the small but highly trained army which Alexander had used at Issus or Arbela. Their tendency to sacrifice quality to dead weight of numbers is well shown by the fact that they doubled the depth of the phalanx, thus making it a much more unwieldy weapon to handle. For some time after Alexander's death the normal battle consisted of an attempt by each side to break through or turn one of the hostile wings by furious cavalry charges, and then to roll up the infantry centre by attacks from the flank. In response the phalanx was made denser in order to be able to beat off all cavalry attacks by mere solidity. Under Philip and Alexander it had still some mobility, and its various τάξεις could act independently of each other and execute individual movements. But in the third century it became a single clump of spears of most unwieldy size, which could well maintain a passive defensive, but for offensive purposes could only move straight forward in a slow and lumbering fashion. Pyrrhus seems to have been the only general among the Epigoni who tried to keep the phalanx mobile: in his Roman wars we read that he drew it up in a row of small columns, not in one mass, placing bodies of Italian troops, armed in their native manner, between each of its brigades. After two victories he failed to wear down the Roman legions, whose superiority lay in their flexible array and in the fact that the individual legionary carried both the missile *pilum* and the broadsword instead of the unwieldy sarissa. Where he was beaten it was not likely that kings like Philip V and Perseus, who used the phalanx in its densest form, would succeed. Even more certainly doomed to failure were adversaries of Rome who, like Antiochus III, employed armies marshalled in the Macedonian fashion, but consisting of mere orientals destitute of Macedonian steadiness and obstinacy.

C. FORTIFICATION AND SIEGE-CRAFT.

603. Greece is a land of sharply-cut rocks and ravines, where fortification was easy and attack difficult. There are many isolated and precipitous hills, on which strongholds of a formidable kind might easily be constructed by building rude walls of unhewn stone, along the fronts most accessible from below. Hence the early type of fortress in Greece was a rocky citadel, like the Acropolis of Athens or of Corinth. Where a position entirely cut off from neighbouring high ground could not be found, the culminating point of a ridge or the end of a spur would be chosen, and only the 'saddle,' where the stronghold joined the rest of the high ground, would require elaborate fortification. Only a few places, such as Thebes, lay on the plain and required a firm and complete ring wall to form their primitive citadel. There is no reason to doubt the extreme antiquity of many of the Hellenic fortresses, of which Mycenae

Primitive citadels.

and Tiryns may serve as types. In them we find a hill crowned by a plateau, surrounded by a strong wall of large irregular blocks carefully fitted in with smaller stones. At the points most open to attack it was built of enormous thickness, and sometimes swells out into large bastion-like projections, some of which are hollow and contain casemates. Not infrequently the rock was scarped down outside the walls to make it more precipitous. There was only one gate, the approach to which was so contrived as to expose the assailants to the fire of missiles from the wall : and as it turned in to the right, anyone drawing near was compelled to present his unshielded side to the besieged.

604. As towns grew in size an unfortified lower city often grew up at the foot of the Acropolis. In case of invasion this would be abandoned to the enemy ; but the citadels, which offered a refuge to all the citizens, were practically impregnable, if proper watch against escalade were kept at the accessible points. Year-long blockade, which a citizen army has rarely patience or leisure to undertake, or treachery from within, could alone subdue them. When Greek colonisation spread to East and West, a favourite desire of the colonists was to seize a headland and fortify the neck by which it was joined to the mainland. The island city of Ortygia at Syracuse and the old town of Tarentum are examples of such strongholds. Walls round the sea-front were only needed when wars between the Hellenes themselves, in a later generation, exposed the cities to attack from the side of the water. The growth of wealth and population ultimately induced the Greeks to surround their lower-cities with walls, and not to trust merely to the strength of the Acropolis. The sixth century was the great period of such building, and the tyrants were often the undertakers of this serious task. With the attempt to render impregnable localities protected by no natural obstacles, and often situated on perfectly flat ground, scientific fortification began. Walls had now to be built of regular masonry : towers (generally quite small) projected from them at intervals, so as to give a flanking fire on the ground in front of the straight spaces of 'curtain' between them, and to prevent the close approach of the besieger. Where the character of the soil allowed, ditches were often cut round the foot of the walls. Stone was so easily procured in most parts of Greece that good ashlar masonry was generally employed : but where stone was scarce, or the city too poor to pay for it, bricks were sometimes used. Mantinea, it will be remembered, fell in 385 because the Spartans were able to turn the river Ophis against the face of a wall built of nothing more than sun-dried brick, which crumbled and fell when exposed to the moisture. Occasionally a mere ditch and earth-wall, topped by a palisade, was all that a small town could afford.

The fifth century saw the commencement of building on a really ambitious scale. Gelon's great wall round the mainland suburbs of Syracuse, and still more the Themistoclean fortifications of the Peiraeus and of the whole city of Athens were both enormous undertakings. They were

(marginal note: Fortified cities.)

thoroughly successful in their object—no serious attempt was ever made to breach them, and enemies who attacked Syracuse and Athens only tried to work by blockade or by suborning treachery inside the city. The Periclean 'Long Walls' from Athens to Phalerum and from Athens to Peiraeus were a further step in advance in the way of fortification: they included such a large extent of ground that the whole population of Attica with their belongings and probably their cattle (so far as it was not sent over to Euboea) could get within them. Syracuse again supplies the best parallel: the tyrant Dionysius by walling round the whole plateau of Epipolae enclosed a vast space, much of which was never covered with houses, and only served as a refuge in time of need for the inhabitants of the whole Syracusan territory. Attacked a dozen times this great entrenched camp (for such in fact it was) never fell by force (though it was often taken by treachery) till the day when it was stormed by the legionaries of Marcellus, nearly two centuries after its construction.

605. As the fifth century saw the development of scientific fortification, so also it witnessed the beginnings of scientific siege-craft.

Siege-craft. How primitive they were can best be judged by glancing through the numerous sieges detailed by Thucydides. It was still the rarest of events for a city to be taken by other means than starvation or treachery, but we begin to hear both of engineers (like the celebrated Artemon whom Pericles employed at Samos) and of μηχαναί or siege-machines. These seem to have been no more than the ram (ἐμβολή), the scaling-ladder, mantlets for the protection of men working near the walls, and sometimes no doubt peculiar devices like the great fire-machine with pipe and bellows, by which the Thebans burnt their way into Delium in 424 B.C. The best commentary on the effectiveness of such engines is supplied by the time taken by the Athenians (who passed as being skilled in siege-craft) to reduce Thasos (463), Samos (439) and Potidaea (429). These places, as well as Plataea which was besieged by the Thebans for nearly three years, were all reduced by famine. Thucydides gives a long account of the devices employed against Plataea. The attempts to build a mole overtopping the city wall, to take the city by a general attack with rams, to burn a way in by heaping faggots below the wall, were foiled by the counter-devices of the Plataeans: and the besiegers then built a double wall of circumvallation, strengthened with towers at intervals, round the whole city. After eighteen months they reduced the starving garrison to surrender.

606. Plataea was but a small place, its garrison was too weak to make sorties, and no attempt was made to relieve it from outside.

Siege of Syracuse. Far other was the case of the Athenians before Syracuse in 414—13: there the besiegers had to deal with a great city containing an army able to meet them in the open field, while they had at their backs many hostile communities which might at any moment endeavour to help the besieged by attacking the beleaguering force in the

rear. We note that the Athenians made no attempt to concentrate their
attention on one part of the Syracusan walls for the purpose of breaching
or escalading it. They simply sat down to starve out the place, by running
lines of circumvallation from sea to sea parallel to the city wall (see Fig. 121)

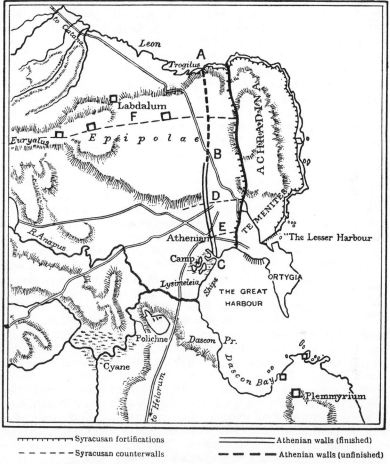

Fig. 121. Plan of Syracuse to illustrate the siege.

The Athenians landed on the north side of Epipolae, stormed the heights
by surprise, erected a fort at Labdalum, and set to work to lay out lines
across the plateau, on which they established their camp. The first reply
of the Syracusans was the building of a counter-wall (παρατείχισμα),
'enfilading' the direction of the projected Athenian circumvallation: it

ran out from Achradina below the Epipolae plateau at right angles to the
wall of the former [D]. This counter-wall was stormed by the besiegers,
who thus gained possession of the terrain south of the Epipolae plateau.
The besieged threw out another counter-wall [E] in the low ground by
the harbour, starting from the wall of the lower city. This wall also the
Athenians took after a hard-fought action, and now proceeded to build
their lines of circumvallation at leisure. The southern section [B, C] was
completed with a pair of walls facing inward and outward. The northern
portion [A, B] had not even a single wall completed when Gylippus
appeared with a relieving army, and as Nicias sent out no 'containing
force' he was able to enter Syracuse through the gaps in the Athenian
lines. Nicias shirked a general action, which alone might have enabled
him to re-occupy the northern part of their lines. Gylippus then stormed
the fort at Labdalum, encamped his whole army on the northern side of
Epipolae and threw out the third counter-wall [E]. The Athenians allowed
it to be completed, and made no attempt to storm it, standing on the
defensive in the southern part of their lines. The siege was now practically
impossible, since Syracuse had a free access to the open country behind
Gylippus's new wall. Nicias would have done well to sail home at once; but
he lingered on in his lines, with the disastrous result that we know. It is
curious to note how entirely the whole series of operations round Syracuse
had turned on the idea that a besieger, to have any chance of success,
must necessarily wall in his enemy for the purpose of starving him.

607. The ease and rapidity with which the Carthaginians a few years
later effected the capture of four great cities in Sicily, Selinus,
Himera, Agrigentum and Gela, marked a new era in the
history of Greek siege-craft. The predominance of the
defensive over the offensive, which had prevailed for so long,
seemed shaken by such catastrophes. The Carthaginians' success however
was largely due to the reckless expenditure of human life in which their
generals were able to indulge. They threw their mercenaries at the walls
with a disregard for loss of which no Greek citizen general would have
dared to dream. But they prepared the way for the stormers by keeping
down the fire of the besieged with thousands of archers and slingers, some
of whom they placed on wooden towers erected close to the walls; they
attacked many places in the *enceinte* simultaneously with the ram, and they
also practised mining at several points. When the walls were shaken, they
sent in their hordes with a rush, to attack every weak spot, and even to try
intact places with escalade. That great genius Dionysius the elder, on
whom the brunt of the Carthaginian attack ultimately fell, showed himself
quite able to deal with it. To him is due a great advance in Greek siege-
craft both offensive and defensive. He is perhaps best remembered for his
invention of the catapult (καταπάλτης), which in its original form was a
large crossbow for the shooting of heavy bolts, which would pierce shields,
mantlets, and palisading, and had a range of at least twice that of the
ordinary arrow. By a slight alteration of principle it could also be made

The Carthaginians and Dionysius.

to throw stones or lumps of lead heavy enough to smash battlements or walls that were not too solid.   At the siege of the Carthaginian fort of Motye in 398, we find Dionysius overwhelming the besieged by the concentrated fire of his catapults, which he mounted on towers of wood so as to command the walls.   His contribution to defensive siege-craft may be gathered from the construction of his great wall round Syracuse, whose projecting point at Euryelus is perhaps the strongest known Hellenic fortification.   This angular castle is protected by no less than three ditches, one behind the other; between the second and third is a strong 'horn-work' which has to be stormed before the main fort can be reached.   The latter is strengthened with bastion-like towers, and flanked by a high keep commanding the whole structure.   In short the system of 'successive interior lines of defence' is scientifically carried out.

608.   All through the fourth century the devices of attack and defence were steadily developing, any advance in the destructive power of one being rapidly answered by an improvement in the resisting power of the other.   By the time of the Philip and Alexander. Macedonian conquest the siege by blockade had been superseded by the siege with regular approaches, ending in the breaching of the wall by the action of rams, borers ($\tau\rho\acute{u}\pi\alpha\nu\alpha$) and mines ($\acute{o}\rho\acute{u}\gamma\mu\alpha\tau\alpha$), after the defenders' missile-discharge had been silenced by the use of catapults of all kinds playing either from the trenches or from moveable towers.   This method of procedure was often successful against places protected by nothing more than the simple ring-wall.   Philip and Alexander both achieved many victories by employing it: some of the sieges which the latter brought to a triumphant end were very notable for the difficulties overcome—and specially those of Tyre and Gaza.   In the case of the former the only approach to the island city was along an artificial isthmus, formed by a mole thrown out into the sea.   The Tyrians repeatedly stopped the mole and destroyed Alexander's machines and covered ways.   It was only when their attention was distracted from the main attack by naval diversions against the sea-wall, that, after seven months, the chief point of assault was breached and stormed.

609.   But improved methods of attack were always answered by improved methods of defence.   By the third century every fortress, except rocky fastnesses like the Corinthian acropolis Later developments. which could defy all the devices of ancient siege-craft, had · to strengthen itself.   Ditches were widened and deepened, and out-works ($\pi\rho\text{o}\tau\epsilon\iota\chi\acute{\iota}\sigma\mu\alpha\tau\alpha$) erected in front of the *enceinte*, which had to be taken before the main wall could be assailed.   They were composed, like the mediaeval 'lists' which served the same end, of banks topped with palisading.   Still more effective was the application of the new system of attack to the defensive, *i.e.* the concentration of quantities of catapults against the enemies' machines and covered ways, and the use of counter-mines against his mining.   When the besieger had erected wooden towers,

the besieged shot fire-arrows at them, or slung pots of burning pitch or oil
against them.   But if the structures were protected (as was commonly the
case) with raw hides or iron plates, the best chance of setting them on fire
was to make a sortie, and thrust combustibles below and behind them,
on their uncovered sides.   Another plan was to drive a countermine under
the track on which the moveable tower was advancing, and excavate a
hole two or three feet underground.   When the machine came over this
pit-fall it sank in, and became immovable, or better still, upset sideways.
The best remembered leaguer of the post-Alexandrine period was that
of Rhodes in 305 B.C. by Demetrius the son of King Antigonus, who won
from his skill in siege-craft the name of 'Poliorcetes.'   All the approved
methods of attack were used against the strongly fortified port.   The sea-wall
was battered by machines mounted on galleys lashed together, and over-
topped by towers built on rafts.   But the Rhodians beat off the attack and
the floating towers were sunk by a storm.   The prince then turned against
the land-wall, which he battered with numerous catapults, undermined, and
finally approached with an enormous 'Helepolis' or moveable tower of the
largest size, 150 feet high and garrisoned by 3,400 men.   Demetrius
twice got up to the foot of the walls and breached them, but the Rhodians
sallied forth at the critical moment and burnt his enormous tower.   After
repeated attempts to storm the breaches had failed, the assailant was
compelled to withdraw, after wasting nearly a year on the abortive undertaking.   Numberless other sieges could be cited from the times of the
Epigoni, but they only illustrate the details of the system of attack and
defence which had been already developed in the fourth century.   Nor
have we space to speak of the progressive improvements of the two sorts
of catapult ($\kappa\alpha\tau\alpha\pi\acute{\alpha}\lambda\tau\alpha\iota$ $\acute{o}\xi\upsilon\beta\epsilon\lambda\epsilon\hat{\iota}s$ and $\kappa\alpha\tau\alpha\pi\acute{\alpha}\lambda\tau\alpha\iota$ $\pi\epsilon\tau\rho\sigma\beta\acute{o}\lambda\sigma\iota$), the bolt-
shooting and the stone-throwing varieties, of which elaborate accounts are
to be found in the surviving works of the engineers Philo and Hero, to
which the reader may be referred for further information.

Rustow and Koechly, *Geschichte des griechischen Kriegswesens*, 1852; Droysen,
Heerwesen der Griechen, 1889; Delbrück, *Geschichte der Kriegs-*
Bibliography.   *kunst*, I. 1900; and J. Kromayer, *Antike Schlachtfelder in Grie-*
chenland, I–IV. 1903–19. J. Kromayer und G. Veith, *Heerwesen und Kriegführung
der Griechen und Römer*, 1928; Kromayer-Veith, *Schlachten-Atlas zur antike
Kriegsgeschichte*, 1926–29; W. W. Tarn, *Hellenistic Military and Naval Developments*, 1930.

VI. 11. SHIPS.

610. As early as the third millennium B.C., crescent-shaped ships with high prow and stern were common in the Aegean. The prow sometimes resembled an open beak, the stern forming a bifurcate tail. The single mast was supported by forestays and backstays. Ships were also equipped with oars and steering-paddles. Our knowledge of them is derived from Cretan seal-stones, etc. (Fig. 122).

Prehomeric ships.

Fig. 122. Ships on early Cretan seal-stones and on a 'Late Helladic' *pyxis* from Pylos.

Smaller craft too were used. In a grave at Palaikastro in eastern Crete dating from the 'Early Minoan' (*circ.* 3400—2100 B.C.) or 'Middle Minoan' (*circ.* 2100—1580 B.C.) period there was found a small-sized clay model of a flat-bottomed boat with a raised prow and the remains of two

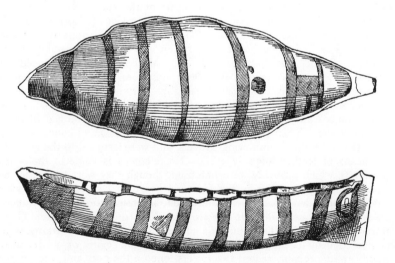

Fig. 123.   Terracotta boat (coracle?) from Phylakopi. (From *Excavations at Phylakopi in Melos*, London, 1904, p. 206, fig. 180.)

thwarts. During the 'Late Minoan' (*circ.* 1580—1200 B.C.) and sub-'Minoan' periods similar vessels were in use. The mast was stepped into a four-sided mast-box amidships, and could apparently be lowered into a large rowlock at the stern. There was a small decking aft for the steersman. The oars were attached to the gunwale by leather loops or bights; and at either end of the ship were hawse-holes for cables. These details we gather from models found in Cypriote tombs. The legend that Cinyras, king of Cyprus, promised a fleet to Menelaus, but sent clay boats with clay crews, is recalled by the fact that small terracotta ships and boats are frequent in the graves of Amathus. A terracotta boat from Phylakopi in Melos (Fig. 123) is of special interest. It is painted inside and outside with vertical black bands probably meant for wooden ribs. Its gunwale forms a series of short curves, perhaps to denote the sagging of hides stretched over the ribs (cp. Verg. *Aen.* 6. 413 f. cumba | sutilis, Plin. *nat. hist.* 24. 65 sutiles naves, Strab. 308 ῥαπτοῖς πλοίοις). It has also a painted eye on either side of the prow.

611. The Homeric poems are our main source of information about early Greek shipping. According to them ship-timber (δόρυ νήϊον) included oak, pine, fir, alder, poplar and white poplar. Masts and oars were usually of fir. The woodwork of the hull was erected on shipbuilders' stocks (δρύοχοι), and held together by pegs or trenails (γόμφοι) and dowel joints (ἁρμονίαι). The keel (τρόπις) thus laid down curved up fore and aft, so that ships were crescent-shaped (ὀρθόκραιραι, κορωνίδες). No mention is made of a separate stern-post, and the cut-water (στείρη) may have been merely the forepart of the keel. Ribs (σταμῖνες) covered with long planks (ἐπηγκενίδες) formed the sides (τοῖχοι) of the hull. From different statements in the *Iliad* and *Odyssey* it appears that the Homeric ship had either 20 or 50 oarsmen. Where a crew numbers 52, a couple of officers are perhaps included. More than 50 rowers need not be assumed: for the epithet ἑκατόζυγος describes proverbially a ship of unheard-of size; and, though Boeotian ships carrying 120 men apiece are mentioned in the *Catalogue*, we are not told that all were rowers. There is then no reason to suppose that the men rowing were arranged in more tiers than one. Their oars (ἐρετμά), with blade (πηδόν) and handle (κώπη), somewhat resembled winnowing shovels, and were fastened to the gunwale by means of leather loops (τροποί). No reference is made to thole-pins (σκαλμοί), which probably were not used, though they were known to the later Greeks and appear in the Homeric hymn to Dionysus. The view has been held that κληῖδες were tholes: but a consideration of the evidence leads to the conclusion that κληῖδες, like ζυγά, denotes thwarts. These thwarts served the double purpose of beams and seats—an arrangement commended by its simplicity and confirmed by the ζυγῖται of a later time. Each thwart probably seated two rowers, one on the port and one on the starboard side (cp. *Od.* XIII. 76 τοὶ δὲ καθῖζον ἐπὶ κληῖσι ἕκαστοι | κόσμῳ).

Homeric ships.

The compound εὔσσελμος means perhaps 'well-planked' rather than 'well-benched.' The hold (ἄντλος) below the beams was not decked, but there were raised deckings (ἴκρια) fore and aft. The forecastle could be used as a look-out post. The poop had space for the helmsman, and could accommodate a passenger for the night. In *Il.* xv. 729 Ajax, defending the stern of a vessel, quits the poop (ἴκρια) and retires θρῆνυν ἐφ' ἑπταπόδην. The word θρῆνυς elsewhere in Homer means 'a foot-stool,' and ἑπταπόδης in Hesiod means 'seven feet *long*,' not 'seven feet *high*.' Probably, then, the θρῆνυς ἑπταπόδης was a fixed stool or bench extending across the vessel at the forward end of the poop, in such a position that the helmsman (κυβερνήτης, κυβερνητήρ) as he sat on the poop working the handle (οἰήιον, οἰήια) of the large steering oar (πηδάλιον) could rest his feet upon it. A poop of this kind, with two steps or stages, actually appears on 'Dipylon' ware (Fig. 127, cp. Fig. 128). Over the poop towered the tail-piece (ἄκρα κόρυμβα) of the vessel, an ornamental prolongation of the keel at the stern, which seems to have been regarded as inviolable (ἄφλαστον from φλάω = θλάω): to cut off the enemy's tail-piece was to secure a trophy. This ornament began by resembling the tail of a fish (Fig. 122), but came to look more like that of a bird with an increasing number of plumes falling gracefully towards the poop (Fig. 125). On Egyptian ships it had the form of a lotus-bud or flower. The waist of the Homeric vessel, being much lower than forecastle or poop, was provided with wattled screens or bulwarks: these are shown on later vase-paintings (see the Rhodian *pinax* Fig. 125). When Odysseus made them for his craft, 'he laid much brushwood thereon,' so as to have a stout fence to keep out the spray.

The single mast (ἰστός) was probably stepped into the keel. Its heel was supported by a prop (ἰστοπέδη), which, to judge from the expression κοίλης ἔντοσθε μεσόδμης, was a box whence the mast could be lowered aft into a rest (ἰστοδόκη): the whole arrangement is seen in the 'Cypriote' models mentioned above. The mast was secured by two forestays (πρό-τονοι) and one backstay (ἐπίτονος). On it was a yard (ἐπίκριον) that carried a lugsail (ἰστίον, ἰστία perhaps because made of several pieces) of white canvas (σπεῖρον) or cloth (φάρεα). Halyards would be necessary for the operation of hoisting sail; and sail would be shortened by means of brailing-ropes (κάλοι). The ὑπέραι or 'upper ropes' are probably braces for moving the yard horizontally. The πόδες or 'lower ropes' are sheets attached to the lower corners of the sail. The ropes in general were made of twisted ox-hide or the fibres of the papyrus-plant. Ships were moored by cables from the bows and stern. Heavy stones (εὐναί) were cast out at the bows in lieu of metal anchors. And mooring-cables (πρυμνήσια, πεῖσμα, πείσματα) were run out from the stern to the shore, where they were attached to a rock or a holed stone. After mooring the ship the crew could disembark. If small boats were not used for the purpose—and there is no allusion to them—this may have been effected by reeving

a double rope through the mooring-stone (hence τρητὸς λίθος) at one end
and the anchor stones at the other: it would then be possible to haul in or
haul out either from the ship itself or from the quay. A long pole (κοντός)
would assist in the process. When beached, the vessel was supported by
blocks or shores of stone (ἕρματα μακρά, ἔχματα).

612. The characteristic feature of merchantmen was their breadth (*Od.*
IX. 323 φορτίδος εὐρείης). Odysseus' raft (σχεδίη) resembled
them in size and apparently also in structure. War-ships, on
the other hand, were distinguished by their speed (θοαὶ νῆες).
In sea-fights, bronze-shod pikes of enormous length, made of pieces of
wood glued together, were employed : cp. the huge spear on an Etrusco-
Ionian *krater* figured below (Fig. 133). Homeric epithets for ships refer to
their colour, form, speed, or skilful build. The tarred hulls (μέλαιναι) were
often painted at the bows with blue (κυανόπρωρος, κυανοπρώρειος), or crimson
(φοινικοπάρῃος), or vermilion (μιλτοπάρῃος). These colours, together with
their inevitably beautiful lines (κορωνίδες, ὀρθόκραιραι, and perhaps ἀμφιέ-
λισσαι), appealed to the eye. Their speed (θοαί, ὠκεῖαι, ὠκύποροι, ὠκύαλοι,
ποντοπόροι) and ingenious construction (γλαφυραί, κοῖλαι, εὐεργής, εὔσσελμοι,
εὔζυγοι) made a similar appeal to the imagination.

Details of Homeric ships.

613. The Hesiodic poems (*circ.* 700 B.C.) make use of the traditional
epithets and add a few practical directions. There are two
sailing seasons : the first and more risky one in spring after
the rising of the Pleiads; the second between midsummer and autumn :
between the two the northerly Etesian winds are blowing in the Aegean.
When the Pleiads set, the ship is to be beached and a stone fence built
about it to keep off the wind and rain : the plug (χείμαρος) must also be
pulled out lest the rain rot the bottom : tackle, sail, and steering-oar are to
be carefully stored at home till winter is over. The wise man will bestow
his cargo aboard a big merchantman, and will have nothing to do with
a little ship. This allusion to small craft and the phrase νῆας πήγνυσθαι
ἀραιάς recall the graceful little vessels depicted on Boeotian bronzes of the
'geometric' period (eighth or seventh century B.C.). A *fibula* in the British
Museum shows a ship of the sort handled by two men (Fig. 124). Besides
the high stem and stern, the small deckings fore and aft, the ἄφλαστον, and
the single mast in its step, there are several new features to be noted. The
horizontal timbers project at either end so as to form teeth; and there is
a substantial spur at the bows—an innovation (seen already on the *pyxis*
from Pylos, Fig. 122) that effectually changed the crescentic appearance of
the earlier hulls. Cabins of lattice-work are shown, and perhaps a lantern
at the mast-head. The steersman is plying the paddle over a rowlock with
the instep of his foot—a departure from Homeric custom which may be
witnessed in the Mediterranean to this day.

Hesiodic ships.

614. During the seventh and sixth centuries the prevailing types of
war-ship were fifty-oared vessels (πεντηκόντοροι) and long-boats.
The latter were called πλοῖα μακρά or νῆες μακραί as contrasted

Penteconters.

Fig. 124. Ship on a Boeotian *fibula*.

not with the former but with the πλοῖα στρογγύλα or νῆες στρογγύλαι,
'round' ships or tubs, *i.e.* merchantmen (γαῦλοι, ὁλκάδες) broad of beam.
We must not therefore assume that the penteconters were shorter than the
long-boats.   In all probability they were the direct descendants of the
Homeric ships of 50 oars—long vessels with small decks fore and aft,
carrying one tier of rowers 25 a side.   A good illustration of such a boat,
despite the deficient number of oars, may be found on a Rhodian *pinax*
now in the British Museum (Fig. 125).   It is approximately of the same
date as the Boeotian bronzes, but shows a much longer vessel.   The
curved keel is prolonged upwards at the bows and bears a fine ἄφλαστον
at the stern.   The hull terminates forwards in a formidable spur.   Small
decks or cabins are visible fore and aft, bulwarks of interlaced hoops
between them, a couple of steering paddles and eleven oars.   Another
vessel on a similar *pinax* has her bows shaped like a boar's head with
projecting snout.   According to Herodotus this form of prow was
characteristic of the Samian navy in the time of Polycrates (532—522 B.C.);
and Plutarch states that the Σάμαινα or ship of Samian build was invented
in Samos during his reign.   But it is probable that the boar's-head prow
was in vogue in the Aegean at an earlier date and was not confined to
Samian vessels: cp. Theseus' vessel on the François vase, which is of

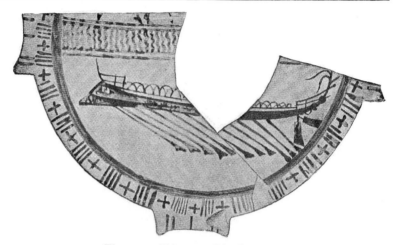

Fig. 125. Ship on a Rhodian *pinax*.

Fig. 126. Ship on the François vase.

Athenian fabric and dates from the first half of the sixth century B.C. (Fig. 126).

615.   Long-boats may be recognised in the war-galleys depicted on
Long-boats.   the 'Dipylon' ware of the eighth or seventh and on the
black-figured Attic vases of the sixth century. These classes of pottery enable us to trace an advance in ship-building. Of the fragments found near the Dipylon at Athens one represents a vessel much like the Rhodian penteconter, except that the foredeck forms two stages while the bows are marked with a wheel-shaped patch (cp. the later eye). Others give a view of both gunwales in primitive perspective (Fig. 127). The waist is fitted with a trellis-work of cross-bars, which served as row-locks, the oars being presumably attached to the vertical and passed beneath the horizontal bars. The mast, where present, carries an oblong sail; and the position of sheets, braces, and halyards working through hooks can be determined. Fragments that appear to show two distinct

Fig. 127. Ship on a 'Dipylon' vase.

tiers of rowers must not be taken to represent triremes, but long-boats
seen in the same crude perspective, the further set of rowers being figured
above the nearer set.   A large terracotta *lebes* found near Thebes and now
in the British Museum affords a very complete picture of such a galley
(Fig. 128).   Nineteen men on the one side and twenty on the other are
pulling their oars over a couple of horizontal rails connected with the
gunwale by means of uprights.   The oars are fastened to single thole-pins,
though the straps are not shown.   The artist has made the further oars
stop suddenly on reaching the nearer oars, presumably to avoid complica-
tion of lines.   The rail projects beyond the stem-post, thereby forming
a tooth, and the keel is similarly prolonged into a spur.   The ἄφλαστον is
simple and less decorative than the recurved ornament (? a horn) above
the cut-water.   A shield is slung on the poop, from which the helmsman
plies two large paddles; and it is a fair inference from the shield that the
expedition represented is one of a warlike character.   The captain, clasping
the wrist of his wife, is about to step on board.   An ivory relief from the
sanctuary of Artemis Orthia at Sparta (*circ.* 600—550 B.C.) represents a
war-ship of similar build using a sail instead of oars (Fig. 129).   Three warriors
are seated on deck; three sailors are occupied with the rigging; one man
fishes from the raised prow; another crouches on the long spur; the
steersman sits at his paddles; and the captain, as before, bids farewell to
his wife.

The black-figured vases attest a change.   In the 'Dipylon' galleys
(eighth or seventh cent.) the rowers were exposed to view (? ἄφρακτοι) and
plied oars attached to tholes.   In the 'black-figured' galleys (sixth cent.)
they row through ports and are no longer visible (? κατάφρακτοι); for the
space once covered by the cross-bars has become part of the vessel's side.
A vase by the painter Aristonophus (*circ.* 650 B.C.) marks the transitional
stage : the rowers, though still exposed to view, are rowing through ports.
Other details of the long-boats may be learnt from the black-figured vases, on
which they frequently figure.   The keel sweeps upwards in a gradual curve at

the stern, and sometimes ends in a goose-head ornament (later called χηνίσκος). As a rule there is no poop, because the waist of the ship has

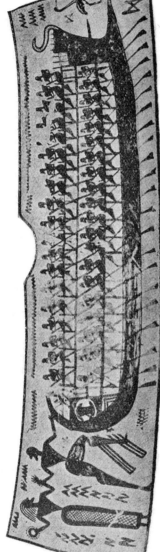

Fig. 128. War-ship on a *lebes* from Thebes.

Fig. 129. Ivory relief of a war-ship from Sparta.

(From *The Annual of the British School at Athens*, 1906—7, xiii. pl. 4, 2.)

been raised to the height of the former poop. A gangway or landing-ladder is sometimes slung aft; for it was by the stern that vessels were moored to the quay. Forward there is an elevated stem-post, which rises above a forecastle of considerable size. The forecastle is occasionally in two stages, and sometimes adorned with a diaper pattern. Below it projects a long spur, commonly shaped like the head of a boar or fish. Sometimes a large eye is added on the bows. Usually a railing of some sort extends as a bulwark from forecastle to stern. Where oars are shown, they are arranged sometimes in one tier starting from rowlocks on what is now the gunwale, sometimes in two tiers (cp. Aesch. *Ag.* 1617 f.) of which the upper starts from rowlocks on the gunwale, the lower from ports diagonally or vertically below the upper oars. The number of oars visible varies (*e.g.* 14 in one tier, or 9 + 9, 9 + 10, 11 + 12). One, or more often two, steering-paddles appear at the stern. There is always a mast and an oblong sail. But in vessels prepared for action they are cleared out of the way; or at least the sail is brailed up to the yard. The mast has sometimes halyard-hooks. The yard is formed of two pieces lashed together (hence κεραῖαι). And the rigging includes, as before, halyards, brailing-ropes, braces and sheets. A sample long-boat of about 500 B.C. may be seen on a *kylix* from Vulci now in the British Museum (Fig. 130).

Fig. 130. War-vessel on a *kylix* from Vulci.

616. In round-boats as contrasted with long-boats the waist was continuous with forecastle and poop. The prow, instead of being shaped into spur or snout, formed a curve roughly

Round-boats.

corresponding with that of the stern (Fig. 131). Sails were used in preference to oars, though a score of the latter might be carried for occasional
purposes. These differences are explained by the fact that the round-boat
was built for a cargo, whereas the long-boat was built for ramming the

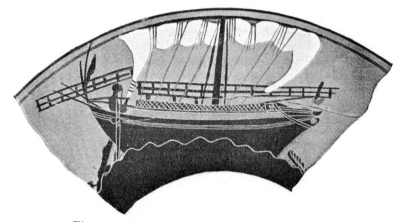

Fig. 131. Merchant-vessel on a *kylix* from Vulci.

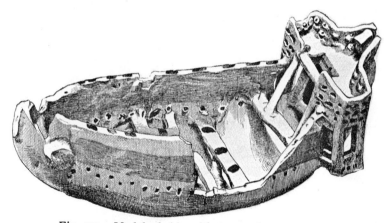

Fig. 132. Model of ship with turrets from Amathus.

enemy. On vases of the sixth century merchant vessels have bulwarks of
railings or lattices: later wooden walls (παραφράγματα) and turrets (πύργοι)
were used as a protection against pirates. These turrets, which projected
overboard, might be as many as eight in number and of considerable
height. The earliest evidence of them is a terracotta model (sixth cent.)

from Amathus, now in the British Museum, which has two near the stern
(Fig. 132). Merchantmen had a mast and sail of the usual pattern. In
addition to the foregoing there were doubtless many types
of vessels to be seen in Greek waters before 500 B.C. Small   Other types.
craft of all kinds (ἄκατοι, κέλητες, κέρκουροι, ἐπακτρίδες, etc.) must have
been very numerous. If the vase paintings found in Italy and Sicily may
be trusted, ship-builders affected more or less grotesque animal forms: the
whole boat was made to resemble a boar (Fig. 133), a shark (cp. later
πρίστεις), a bird (Fig. 134, cp. later κύκνοι), etc., and the outline was some-

Fig. 133.   Boar-shaped vessel on an Etrusco-Ionian *krater*.

times completed by awnings or by more permanent structures erected
on deck (Fig. 133).

Fig. 134.   Bird-shaped vessel on an Etrusco-Ionian *krater*.

G. A.   37

617. Clement of Alexandria preserves the tradition that the Sidonians were the first to invent a three-banked vessel (τρίκροτον ναῦν).

Origin of
triremes.

Herodotus says that triremes (τριήρεες) were used on the Mediterranean and the Arabian Gulf by Necos, who was king of Egypt in 600 B.C. They seem to have been adopted by the Greeks at an even earlier date, though a couple of centuries or more elapsed before they superseded all other types of vessels as men-of-war. According to Thucydides (I. 13), 'The Corinthians are said to have been the first to adopt something like the modern style of ship-building, and the oldest Hellenic triremes are said to have been constructed at Corinth. A Corinthian shipwright, Ameinocles, appears to have built four ships (ναῦς) for the Samians; he went to Samos about 300 years before the end of the Peloponnesian War.' If Pliny (*H. N.* VII. 206) was right in understanding Thucydides to assert that Ameinocles made four *triremes* for the Samians, we must suppose that the historian dated the introduction of triremes into Greece at about 700 B.C. This is usually regarded as an anachronism, but is by no means impossible. Thucydides goes on to mention the navies of Corinth and Corcyra about 664 B.C., that of the Ionians between 559 and 521 B.C., that of Polycrates between 546 and 538 B.C., and the Phocaean fleet that colonised Massilia a few years later than 600 B.C. 'These,' he continues, 'were the most powerful navies, and even these...appear to have consisted chiefly of fifty-oared vessels and galleys of war with but few triremes.' It is surely implied that here and there triremes were to be found as early as 664 B.C. If so, Ameinocles may have built four of them in 704 B.C. However that may be, Thucydides adds that about 490 B.C. the Sicilian tyrants and the Corcyraeans had triremes in considerable numbers at a time when the Aeginetan and Athenian fleets were small and composed mainly of penteconters. It was Themistocles who inaugurated (483 B.C.) the policy of maintaining a large permanent fleet by building one hundred triremes, which were used at Salamis ; and these triremes, unlike later triremes, were not decked throughout.

618. The word τριήρης means 'trebly-equipped' (√αρ of ἀραρίσκω,

Usual theory
of the trireme.

cp. the cognate τριάρμενος applied to three-decked sailing-ships) and does not itself denote that the vessel had three tiers or banks of oars. It is, however, commonly held that such was the case, the rowers of the lowest tier being termed θαλαμῖται, θαλάμακες or θαλάμιοι, because they sat in the hold (? θάλαμος), those of the middle tier ζυγῖται or ζύγιοι, because they sat on the beams (ζυγά), those of the highest tier θρανῖται, because they occupied benches analogous to the θρῆνυς of the Homeric steersman. This view, while satisfying the literary allusions, is supported partly by the *a priori* consideration that, just as the long-boat with two banks was an improvement upon the penteconter with one, so the trireme with three would have been an improvement upon the long-boat with two; partly by archaeological evidence,

which must be briefly summarised. A relief (Fig. 135) found on the
Acropolis at Athens and dating from about 400 B.C. shows part of a ship,
whose details have been explained (Torr, *Anc. Ships* p. 45, n. 109) as
follows. The hull is marked by five parallel bands. The two lowest
are waling-pieces (later ζωστῆρες), that is, projecting timbers forming

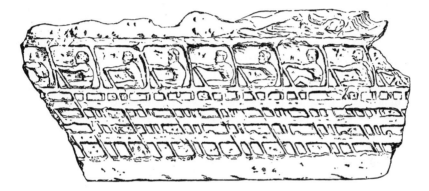

Fig. 135. Waist of a war-vessel on a relief from Athens.

horizontal lines round the vessel. Between them are the ports of the
θαλαμῖται. The third band is the gunwale: between it and the upper
waling-piece are the ports of the ζυγῖται. On seats raised slightly above
the gunwale the θρανῖται are represented rowing oars that are attached
to tholes and seemingly pass under the fourth band, which may be a
gangway (πάροδος). Above the θρανῖται is a structure resembling a modern
hurricane-deck supported on uprights. The same arrangement of waling-
pieces, gunwale, gangway and hurricane-deck recurs on coins of Cius in
Bithynia about 300 B.C. Again, a trireme on Trajan's column has three
tiers of oars, the θαλάμιαι coming through ports between two waling-pieces,
the ζύγιαι through ports just below the gunwale, the θρανίτιδες through
lattice-work above the gunwale. With regard to the internal arrangement
of θαλαμῖται, ζυγῖται and θρανῖται, it is held that each rower sat below
but a little to the rear of the rower above him, so that θαλαμίτης ζυγίτης
θρανίτης formed an oblique, not a vertical line: this would economise
space and facilitate their movements. Others think that the θαλαμῖται
sat close to the vessel's side, the ζυγῖται higher up were distant from it
the breadth of one thwart, the θρανῖται still higher were removed by the
breadth of two thwarts: the oar of each rower would then pass over the
head of the rower below.

619. The difficulties attached to all hypotheses based on the assump-
Another theory of the trireme. tion of *superimposed* tiers of oars become impossibilities when we advance from triremes to ships with 5, 10, 15, 20, 30 and even 40 banks of oars. In fact, the only escape from them lies in the direction of a very different theory. Col. Yule (*Travels of Marco Polo* I. pp. lx.—lxix.) remarks that the mediaeval fleets had galleys termed by Italian writers biremes, triremes and quinqueremes, the distinction between which depended on the number of rowers that sat on one bench pulling each his separate oar, but through one rowlock port. The system of grouped oars was in vogue down to the sixteenth century. The width of the galley was much increased by an outrigger deck projecting beyond the ship's side and supported on timber brackets. This framework was the rowlock upon which the oars rested and to which they were fastened by strap and thole pin. In the centre line of the deck ran a raised gangway clear of oars. Each galley had from 25 to 28 benches a side arranged as in the diagram (Fig. 136), where *a, b, c* mark the

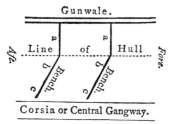

Fig. 136. Arrangement of rowers in a mediaeval trireme.

position of the three rowers. In front of each bench was another lower bench or stretcher: the stroke was given by the rower mounting upon his stretcher and letting himself fall back in a sitting posture on the rowing-bench. Mr H. F. Brown (*Academy*, Sept. 29, 1883, p. 219 f.) suggested that this arrangement of rowers might explain the Greek trireme. And Sir William Ridgeway inclined to the same view, adding that in all likelihood the traditional build of Greek and Roman galleys descended through the Byzantine fleets to those of Ravenna, Venice, etc. The Greek trireme on this showing had rowlock-ports, through each of which passed three oars plied by three men seated on one bench. We thus obtain for the first time an adequate explanation of Aeschylus' strange periphrases τρίσκαλμοι ναῦς, τρίσκαλμοι βάριδες (*Pers.* 679, 1075): a vessel with three tiers of oars *superimposed* could not be described as 'a threetholed barge' any more than a building with three stories as 'a three-windowed house'; but if each porthole had three thole-pins for its three oars, then the distinctive feature of the ship is well expressed by the word τρίσκαλμος.

As to the terms θαλαμίτης, ζυγίτης, θρανίτης, two possibilities present themselves. (1) On the one hand Mr W. W. Tarn, who accepts the system of grouped oars, argues well (*Journ. Hell. Stud.* 1905, XXV. 139 ff., *Class. Rev.* 1906, XX. 75 ff.) in defence of the view that these terms had nothing to do with the horizontal rows or banks of oars, but denoted three divisions or squads of rowers, the 'thranites' being astern, the 'zygites' amidships, the 'thalamites' in the bows. He contends that the 'thalamites' got their name from the θάλαμος or 'cabin' in the bows, the 'thranites,' as Prof. Ridgeway (*Class. Rev.* 1895, IX. 266) suggested, from the θρῆνυς or 'raised step' of the helmsman astern. This explanation is certainly tenable, though it does not agree with all the statements of the ancient scholiasts and lexicographers. (2) On the other hand, it may be held that the θαλαμίτης was the man who rowed nearest to the porthole (θαλαμίη Hdt. v. 33, cp. Ar. *Ach.* 553, *Peace* 1232); the ζυγίτης, he who sat next him originally on the beam (ζυγόν); the θρανίτης, he who worked the longest oar by rising on a stool (θρᾶνος) to gain force for his stroke. If we suppose that the rowers' bench was in three steps or levels, we can satisfactorily account for all passages cited in proof of superimposed rowers *e.g.* Schol. Aeliani quoted by Graser *de re navali* § 4 ἡ μονήρης καὶ διήρης καὶ ἐφεξῆς (λέγεται) κατὰ τοὺς στίχους τοὺς κατὰ τὸ ὕψος ἐπ' ἀλλήλοις, *Etym. Mag. s.v.* θαλάμιαι κῶπαι·...ὁ κατώτατος ἐρέτης θαλάμιος λέγεται, ὁ δὲ μέσος ζύγιος, ὁ δὲ ἀνώτατος θρανίτης. If again we suppose that the bench was bent aft as in the mediaeval galleys, we can understand such passages as Schol. Ar. *Ran.* 1074 θρανίτης οὖν ὁ πρὸς τὴν πρύμναν· ζυγίτης ὁ μέσος· θαλάμιος ὁ πρὸς τὴν πρῶραν, for *c* is nearer to the stern than *b*, *b* than *a*. The trireme would still be τρίκροτος ναῦς, propelled by three στοῖχοι of oarsmen; for if we stood at the prow and looked aft, we should see three ascending files of men on port and starboard side respectively[1].

Neither view excludes the employment of two tiers of rowers. Marino Sanuto (A.D. 1300—1320) speaks of two-deckers in which each deck was occupied by groups of three or four men to a bench. Similarly the acropolis relief may be taken to represent two tiers of θαλαμῖται with their oars, the lower tier rowing through ports just above the lowest waling-piece: the other sloping lines may be strengthening timbers of some sort, if not brackets supporting an outrigger-deck like that of the Venetian galleys. The vessel on Trajan's column has two

---

[1] See *Classical Review* XIX. 376 for the elevation and cross section of a model trireme arranged on this hypothesis.

possible tiers of oars rowed through port-holes in her side, and one
admittedly impossible tier rowed through lattice-bulwarks. In short, this
theory satisfies all the literary and archaeological evidence hitherto adduced.
It has also the great advantage of showing—as will be seen later on—how
the trireme-system developed into that of the many-banked vessel. It may
be added that in 1883 Rear-Admiral Fincati of the Italian navy made
practical experiments with Venetian barges arranged in the two conflicting
methods, the superimposed and the side by side. He found that, while
the former was almost unmanageable, the latter gave the surprising
speed of nine miles an hour.

620. Concerning Attic triremes of the fourth century valuable information is afforded by inscriptions containing inventories of
the Athenian dockyards between 373 and 323 B.C. (C.I.A.
II. nos. 789—812). From these we gather that triremes
commonly had as many as 200 oars, *viz.* 54 θαλάμιαι, 54 ζύγιαι, 62 θρανίτιδες, 30 περίνεω, though lower numbers also are found. Two questions
arise. Why more θρανίτιδες than θαλάμιαι or ζύγιαι? And what were
the περίνεω? To neither question can a certain answer be returned.
It is probable that, where the converging lines of the gunwale left
insufficient room for benches of three rowers each, a couple of θρανῖται,
seated one in front of the other, were accommodated on either side of
the vessel fore and aft: the space altogether beyond the oars at the
bows and stern was called the παρεξειρεσία. It is also probable that the
περίνεω were simply 'spare oars' for use in case of accident. The oars
were of no great size; for they could be shouldered and all on a
forced march. Thus the περίνεω measured only 9 or 9½ cubits in 373—
372 B.C. All the oars were worked against tholes (σκαλμοί), to which they
were fastened by leather loops (τροπωτῆρες, κωπητῆρες). The port-hole was
fitted with a leather flap (ἄσκωμα), probably to protect the woodwork from
friction. When a trireme was used as a transport for cavalry (ἱππηγός,
ἱππαγωγός) her oars were reduced to sixty in number, and the hold was
occupied by the horses. On either side of the bows one, or sometimes two
large eyes (ὀφθαλμοί) probably served as hawse-holes. Just behind these
were massive projecting cat-heads (ἐπωτίδες), which served a double purpose. From them the anchors (ἄγκυραι) of iron weighted with masses of
stone and lead, later of lead throughout, were slung; and, in ramming an
enemy's ship, the cat-heads would protect the oars from damage. They
were sometimes enlarged and strengthened by props (ἀντηρίδες) in order to
inflict injury on the hostile prow. Gunwale and gangway ended at the
cat-heads. The projecting spur carried a ram (ἔμβολος) with an auxiliary
ram (προεμβόλιον) above it. Rams had three teeth and were of wood
sheathed with bronze, they were sometimes twisted or torn off from the
trireme's nose (σίμωμα) by the shock of the collision. So great was this
shock that the timbers of the vessel ramming had to be secured from

Details of the trireme.

starting by means of two or more girdling cables (ὑποζώματα) passed horizontally round the entire hull.   Above the ram rose an elevated stem-post; and ship was distinguished from ship by a badge (σημεῖον), which might be a carved figure-head (ἐπίσημον) or a relief or painting on the bows (παράσημον).   The stern still terminated in a curved tail-piece: hence coins of Phaselis in Lycia show the hinder part of a war-ship with an ἄφλαστον bent towards the mast.   The stem and more often the stern ornaments (ἀκρωτήρια, later ἀκροστόλια) were lopped and kept as trophies.   The steering apparatus consisted, as before, of two large oars (πηδάλια, some-times πλῆκτρα) tied between two pegs just below the gunwale with a loop (ζεύγλη).   The term οἴαξ properly denotes the handle of a steering oar, but was also used of the entire paddle including the blade (πτέρυξ).   The two handles were perhaps connected by a tiller (Plat. *Politicus* 272 E πηδαλίων οἴακος ἀφέμενος, cp. Lucian, *navig.* 6 ὑπὸ λεπτῇ κάμακι τὰ τηλικαῦτα πηδάλια περιστρέφων).

Two kinds of sails, ἱστία μεγάλα and ἀκάτεια, were used on Athenian triremes about 400 B.C.   In prospect of a sea-fight the former were put on shore and the latter were hoisted.   Corresponding to these two types of sail, two types of mast (ἱστὸς μέγας, ἱστὸς ἀκάτειος) and yard (κεραῖαι μεγάλαι, κεραῖαι ἀκάτειαι) are entered on the inventories about 350 B.C. Many ships carried a mast and yard of each kind for alternative use.   Two timber supports (παραστάται) were employed for one or other of these masts.   The ropes (τοπεῖα) about 350 B.C. were ἱμάντες or halyards(?), πόδες or sheets, ὑπέραι or braces, ἄγκοινα or fore-stay(?), χαλινός or back-stay (?), κάλως or brailing-ropes (?).   Not long afterwards the second or lighter rigging was discarded in the Athenian navy; for the inscriptions show that in 330 B.C. and the following years triremes had simply mast (ἱστός), yard (κεραῖαι), sail (ἱστίον), and ropes (τοπεῖα): these last included μηρύματα καλωδίων or loops of brailing-ropes (?) in place of the earlier κάλως; but other details are wanting.   The sails were commonly of linen, and about 330 B.C. a finer and a coarser variety of sail-cloth were in use.   The ropes were mostly made from flax or papyrus-fibre.   Protective awnings of sail-cloth or horse-hair were spread over the open spaces on board before a fight.   Triremes in 406 B.C. carried παραρρύματα, in 405 and again about 377 παραβλήματα.   In 357—356 each trireme had two παραρρύματα λευκά, two παραρρύματα τρίχινα, one κατάβλημα, and one ὑπόβλημα.   In 325—324 triremes still had these four varieties, but by 323—322 the ὑποβλήματα had been dropped.   Some such coverings are carried on the poop of a black-figured long-boat now in the British Museum.   Gangways (ἀποβάθραι), ladders (κλιμακίδες, κλίμακες), and poles of various sizes (κοντοί) also formed part of a war-ship's equipment.   Attic long-boats and triremes were built of fir, or failing that of pine: for merchantmen pine was preferred.   Triremes had, however, a keel of oak, since they were frequently hauled ashore: merchantmen had a keel of pine, with a false keel of oak or beech.   The remains of the ship-sheds at Zea and Munychia, each built to contain one trireme, show that the sheds were originally about 20 feet broad by more than 144 feet long: the beam of an Attic trireme was therefore about one-seventh of its length.

621. Quadriremes (τετρήρεις) were first built by Dionysius I of Syracuse

Quadriremes and quinqueremes.

in 398 B.C. according to Diodorus, though Aristotle ascribed the innovation to the Carthaginians. Inscriptions of 330/329 and 325/324 B.C. mention quadriremes at Athens. The number and management of their oars is unknown. If triremes were rowed by three men to a bench, quadriremes were probably manned on the same principle, like the Venetian galleys of A.D. 1316 with four rowers to each bench. Quinqueremes (πεντήρεις) also were invented by Dionysius I in 398 B.C., if Diodorus is to be trusted: Pliny states that they originated at Salamis. Dionysius II had some in his fleet, and they appeared in the Athenian inventories in 325/324 B.C. At the battle of Ecnomus in 256 B.C. the Roman and Carthaginian quinqueremes carried about 300 rowers and 120 combatants apiece. In 212 B.C. we hear of 400 rowers aboard the quinquereme, and of the same number in A.D. 40. Of their distribution we know nothing. Mr Tarn holds that each oar was worked by a team of five men. But again the probability is that ancient, like mediaeval, quinqueremes were rowed by five men on each bench pulling five oars through one rowlock-port.

622. Throughout the latter half of the fourth and the whole of the

Vessels of exceptional size.

third century B.C. the kings of Sicily, Macedonia, Asia and Alexandria rivalled one another in constructing enormous men-of-war. Ships of 6, 7, 8, 9, 10, 11, 12, 13 and 15-fold equipment (ἑξήρεις, ἑπτήρεις, κ.τ.λ.) were successively multiplied. And even larger vessels were launched. Demetrius Poliorcetes in 288 B.C. built certain ἑκκαιδεκήρεις, which were regarded as portents. One of them, or one like them, in the Macedonian fleet of 197 B.C. was expressly mentioned in a treaty with Rome: she sailed up the Tiber in 167 B.C. and gave her name to one of the Roman docks. Archimedes is said to have built an εἰκοσήρης for Hieron of Syracuse, and Ptolemy Philadelphus to have possessed one εἰκοσήρης and two τριακοντήρεις. The existence of such gigantic craft is proved by an inscription from the temple of the Paphian Aphrodite in Cyprus, which commemorates the builder of a 20 and a 30-fold vessel. Finally a τεσσαρακοντήρης ναῦς was constructed by Ptolemy Philopator (222—204 B.C.). It has sometimes been regarded as mythical: but Athenaeus v. 37 cites the description of it given by Callixenus of Rhodes, a contemporary of Philopator, and Plutarch, *Demetr.* 43, probably draws upon the same source. According to them its length was 280 cubits. Its beam (from πάροδος to πάροδος) 38 cubits. The stem towered up 48 cubits above the water; the stern-ornament, 53. The draught was less than 4 cubits. It had a double prow carrying 7 rams, and a double stern. There were 4 steering-paddles 30 cubits long. The

oars (κῶπαι θρανιτικαί) were weighted with an equipoise of lead at the
handle end: the largest of them measured 38 cubits in length. Twelve
girdling cables 600 cubits long strengthened the fabric of the boat. It
held more than 4000 rowers, 400 sailors, 2,830 soldiers on the deck, besides
servants, stores, etc. Callixenus' account of this leviathan throws some
light on the other colossal vessels enumerated above. It could be floated
in a dock 4 cubits deep; it had high stem and stern; it was 280 cubits
long. These dimensions suggest comparison with a Nile-barge built by
Sesostris, which also had a length of 280 cubits (Diod. 1. 57). Probably
Philopator's boat was a similar flat barge with but one tier of oars. It is
noticeable that the τεσσαρακοντήρης, the τριακοντήρης, and one of the
εἰκοσήρεις, were built by kings of Egypt, and might therefore naturally be
modelled on the ordinary Nile-barge. The other εἰκοσήρης, the ἐκκαιδεκήρεις,
πεντεκαιδεκήρεις, τρισκαιδεκήρεις, δωδεκήρεις, ἐνδεκήρεις, δεκήρεις, and ἐννήρεις,
were all built either by the Ptolemies or by those who had come into
frequent connexion with them, so that they too may well have been barges:
the δεκήρεις under Antony at Actium are expressly said to have stood only
10 feet above water (Orosius VI. 19). The ὀκτήρης, ἑπτήρεις, ἑξήρεις in all
probability were of like pattern. We must not, however, suppose that these
exceptional vessels were rowed on the trireme system. Forty men on one
bench pulling forty oars through one port is only less absurd than forty
tiers of oars in a ship drawing four feet of water. The fact is that tiers of
oars superimposed would very soon become impossible; and even grouped
oars have a comparatively narrow range. The latter method which, as we
have seen, was practised during the Middle Ages was in the first half of the
sixteenth century superseded by the use of long sweeps plied by from 4 to
8 or even more men apiece. The Greek ἑξήρεις, etc. may have been rowed
on the same system. This explanation squares with all that we know of the
barges in question. Memnon, a historian of about Hadrian's time, describes
(ap. Phot. p. 226) an ὀκτήρης called ἡ Λεοντοφόρος, which belonged to the
fleet of Heraclea on the Euxine in 280 B.C.: he tells us that it carried
1,600 rowers, 1,200 fighting-men, and 2 steersmen; also that 100 men rowed
each file (στοῖχος). Now 100 rowers to each στοῖχος and 8 στοῖχοι on port
and starboard side respectively amount to 1,600 rowers all told. Similarly
the τεσσαρακοντήρης must have been a big barge with, say, 100 sweeps, each
worked by 40 men. Of these 40 it is probable that 20 pulled, while 20
pushed: Babylonian boats of very considerable size were propelled in this
manner (Hdt. 1. 134).

The ships termed ἡμιολίαι or τριημιολίαι from about 350 B.C. onwards
were presumably manned by 'once and a half' or 'thrice
half' their normal crew. This may have been managed by   ἡμιολίαι or
doubling the rowers abaft the mast, as was the case with the   τριημιολίαι.
fuste or lighter galleys of the Venetians, which had their oars in pairs from
the stern to the mast but singly from the mast forward.

623. It will be seen that three distinct stages can be traced in the evolution of the Greek war-ship. (1) The penteconter and long-boats had a single tier of oars, each oar being pulled by one man. Increase of motive power could as yet be secured only by lengthening the boat so as to accommodate more rowers. (2) Triremes, quadriremes, and quinqueremes made an advance by multiplying the number of rowers on each bench, the several rowers pulling their several oars through the same port-hole. (3) Ἐξήρεις κ.τ.λ. further multiplied the oarsmen, while they economised the oars, probably by employing a single tier of sweeps, each of which was worked by from 6 to 40 men. Mediaeval galleys were evolved in precisely the same way, every successive stage being the result of practical experience and experiment.

Evolution of war-ships.

624. The Greeks themselves distinguished between (a) an old and (b) a new method of naval warfare.

Naval warfare.

(a) The old method aimed at making the sea-fight resemble a land-fight. The vessels engaged had their decks crowded with hoplites and light-armed troops: these, as soon as they were within striking distance, attacked the enemy with spears, bows, etc., while the ships remained stationary; so that the issue was decided, not by the manœuvres of the rowers, but by the quantity and quality of the fighting men on board. This elementary method, which is illustrated by Figs. 133, 134, was still in use towards the close of the fifth century B.C. Thucydides describes the battle between the Corinthian and Corcyraean fleets off Sybota (432) as follows: 'The decks of both were crowded by heavy infantry, with archers and with javelin-men: for their naval arrangements were still of the old clumsy sort. The engagement was obstinate, but more courage than skill was displayed, and it had almost the appearance of a battle by land. When two ships once charged one another it was hardly possible to part company, for the throng of vessels was dense, and the hopes of victory lay chiefly in the heavy-armed, who maintained a steady fight upon the decks, the ships meanwhile remaining motionless.... Brute force and rage made up for want of tactics' (Thuc. I. 49). Later, such fighting was exceptional: *e.g.* Nicias' fleet in the harbour at Syracuse (413) were forced to contend ἀπὸ τῶν νεῶν πεζο-μαχίᾳ; and, when the Syracusans cut down their prows and strengthened their cat-heads (ἐπωτίδες) with additional timbers to increase the effect of their charge, the Athenians responded by the use of iron grapnels (χεῖρες σιδηραῖ) to prevent the ship which had charged from sheering off (Thuc. VII 62).

(b) The new method, brought to perfection by the Athenians in the course of the fifth century B.C., involved a wholly different principle. The customary weapons of land-warfare were almost entirely discarded. Instead, the trireme itself was now regarded as a missile to be launched with sudden

violence against the vulnerable parts of the enemy's vessel and again as
suddenly withdrawn by means of dexterous rowing. Especially characteristic of this method were the two manœuvres named διέκπλους and
περίπλους. The διέκπλους, practised *e.g.* by the Ionian fleet at Lade (494)
and mentioned in connexion with the Greeks at Artemisium (480), meant
that a single line of ships passed between the ships of the opposing line,
turned swiftly, and charged them from behind. The περίπλους consisted
in out-flanking the enemy ships so as to charge them beak to broadside.
It was in order to avoid the διέκπλους that the Peloponnesians in the Gulf
of Corinth (429) 'arranged their ships in the largest circle possible without
leaving an inlet, turning their prows outwards and their stern inwards:
within the circle they placed the smaller craft which accompanied them,
and five of their swiftest ships that they might be close at hand to row
out at whatever point the enemy charged them.' To meet this the
Athenians under Phormion 'ranged their ships in a single line and sailed
round and round the Peloponnesian fleet, which they drove into a narrower
and narrower space, almost touching as they passed, and leading the crews
to suppose they were on the point of charging' (Thuc. 11. 83 ff.). Both
the διέκπλους and the περίπλους involved making an ἐμβολή or charge with
the beak (ἔμβολον): but Athenian ships were too light in the bows for a
direct prow to prow charge (ἐμβολή ἀντίπρωρος). As distinguished from
these definite manœuvres a chance collision or unsystematic attack was
termed προσβολή.

625. The trireme was much faster than the merchantman; for, though
both were rigged alike, the former could supplement its
sailing powers by means of a large number of oars, whereas
the latter carried only a few for occasional use. Besides, the
lines of the trireme were designed with a view to rapid movement, those of
the merchantman with a view to storage-room. (1) Xenophon states (*an.*
VI. 4. 2) that it was a very long day's voyage for a trireme with the help of
its oars to go from Byzantium to Heraclea in Bithynia: the distance is at
least 120 nautical miles; and, reckoning 'a very long day' at 16 hours, we
thus obtain an average rate of at least 7½ knots. The same author elsewhere (*Hell.* II. 1. 30) says that Theopompus of Miletus, who brought the
tidings of victory from the Hellespont to Sparta in 405 B.C., reached his
destination on the third day: now from Aegospotami to Gytheium, where
he would land, is certainly not less than 330 nautical miles; Theopompus
must therefore, at the lowest estimate, have covered 110 nautical miles per
day. From Thuc. III. 36 ff. we learn that, on the voyage from Athens to
Mytilene (at least 186 nautical miles), it was possible for a trireme making
the passage at its topmost speed almost to catch up one that had started
about 24 hours earlier but was in no particular hurry. (2) According to
Apollonius Rhodius I. 601 ff., the distance from Mt Athos to Lemnos,
i.e. about 30 nautical miles, is as much as a well-equipped ὁλκάς could

(margin note: Speed of ancient vessels.)

traverse between dawn and midday: this gives about 5 knots as a good pace for a merchantman, and a total of some 60 per day. In Thuc. II. 97 it is asserted that 'the voyage round (from Abdera to the mouth of the Ister) can be made by a merchant vessel, if the wind is favourable the whole way, at the quickest in 4 days and as many nights': the distance in question is at least 460 nautical miles, *i.e.* 115 for each day + night. Herodotus observes (IV. 86) that a sailing-vessel (νηῦς) in the course of a long day can go 70,000 ὄργυιαι = a fraction over 69, and in a night 60,000 = a fraction over 59 nautical miles; nearly 130 in all, therefore, in a long day and a night. In Lycurg. *c. Leocr.* 60 we are told that from Athens to Rhodes was a four days' voyage: the distance is at least 264 nautical miles, which allows an average of 66 per day. A greater pace became possible in Hellenistic times. Pliny, *H. N.* XIX. *prooem.*, quotes some examples of exceptionally rapid passages. Arrian too speaks of traversing 500 stades, *i.e.* nearly 50 nautical miles, between sunrise and noon. In fact, ancient sailing records compare by no means unfavourably with the average rates of our own day.

For further details see A. Cartault, *La trière athénienne*, Paris, 1881, C. Torr, *Ancient Ships*, Camb. 1894, and in Daremberg-Saglio, *Dict. Ant.* Bibliography. s.v. 'navis' (Paris, 1904), pp. 24–40, W. Kroll, 'Schiffahrt' in Pauly-Wissowa, *Real-Enc.* II A, 408–419, A. Köster, *Das antike Seewesen*, Berlin, 1923, *id.* 'Das Seekriegswesen bei den Griechen' in J Kromayer-G. Veith, *Heerwesen und Kriegführung der Griechen und Römer*, München, 1928, pp. 163–208, W. W. Tarn, *Hellenistic Military and Naval Developments*, Cambridge, 1930, pp. 120–152, 162–166, also the same writer's able articles on 'The Greek Warship,' *Journal of Hellenic Studies*, 1905, XXV. pp. 137–56, 204–24, on 'The Fleets of the First Punic War,' *ib.* 1907, XXVII. pp. 48–60, on 'The Dedicated Ship of Antigonus Gonatas,' *ib.* 1910, XXX. pp. 209–22, and on 'Thranite, Zugite, and Thalamite' in the *Class. Rev.* 1906, XX. pp. 75–7.

*** The theory of the trireme here advocated will be found set out (with illustrations of a model made under the direction of Mr Wigham Richardson) in *The Classical Review*, Oct. 1905, XIX. pp. 371–7.

VI. 12. THE CALENDAR.

626. THE civil or calendar day (*i.e.* our day of 24 hours), called by the Greeks ἡμέρα, or, for more exactness, νυχθήμερον, was reckoned from sunset to sunset. The period of darkness, *The Day.* νύξ, was divided into ἑσπέρα, λύχνων ἀφαί, πρῶτος ὕπνος, μέσαι νύκτες, and ὄρθρος. The period of light, ἡμέρα in a restricted sense, was divided into πρωΐ (later ὄρθρος), μέση ἡμέρα or μεσημβρία, and δείλη. But πρωΐ is often contrasted (meaning 'early') with ὀψέ 'late,' and δείλη πρωΐα with δείλη ὀψία. The dawn, ἕως, was reckoned by Homer as part of the day, later as part of the night. These periods were never exactly defined. A more careful measurement of time was introduced when Anaximenes (about 520 B.C.) borrowed from the Chaldaeans the πόλος or γνώμων, a kind of rude sundial, in which a perpendicular staff threw its shadow on a measured table. The daylight was then divided into twelve equal parts (μέρη, afterwards ὧραι), which varied in length, of course, at different periods of the year. Another contrivance, which could be used in the dark, was the κλεψύδρα, a bronze cistern fitted with a tap which would emit a measured quantity of water in a given time. On a campaign, the night was divided into three or five equal φυλακαί, measured by a κλεψύδρα. As the nights and the φυλακαί grew shorter, the tap could be plugged to restrict the flow of water. Only astronomers regarded the day as a period of 24 equal hours (ὧραι ἰσημεριναί).

627. Occasionally the year was regarded as divided into two seasons only, θέρος and χειμών. In this case, θέρος is sometimes meant to cover the six months from the morning rising of *The Seasons.* the Pleiades to their morning setting (mid-May—mid-Nov.): but, more often, it is the 'open' season (March—Nov.) when campaigning and voyaging were possible. Generally, however, the year was divided into three seasons χειμών, ἔαρ, θέρος. The hottest part of the summer was called ὀπώρα, and (after 450 B.C.) a fourth season, called φθινόπωρον or μετόπωρον, our 'autumn,' was commonly admitted. Various dates were assigned for the commencement of spring, but, since the morning-rising of Arcturus was always regarded as the beginning of autumn, probably the evening-rising of the same star was the most generally recognised commencement of spring.

628. The natural duration of a month, or moon-period (μήν), is 29 days 12 hours 44 min. 3 sec. The Greeks, who never knew this measurement exactly, estimated the month at 29½ days, and *The Month.* avoided the fraction by assigning 29 and 30 days to alternate months. The month of 29 days was called 'hollow' (κοῖλος): that of 30 days 'full' (πλήρης). Each month was divided into three periods, δεκάδες, though in a 'hollow' month the last *decad* had only nine days. The periods were commonly named δεκὰς πρώτη or μηνὸς ἱσταμένου, δεκὰς δευτέρα or μέση or μηνὸς μεσοῦντος and δεκὰς τρίτη or μηνὸς φθίνοντος, ἐξιόντος, λήγοντος. But the error in the estimate of a lunation was so great that, in early times, the months cannot often have corresponded with the moon and there was little reason to adhere to any precise rule in the naming of the days. Hence, in Hesiod (*Op.* 765—828), the days are numbered sometimes continuously from 1 to 30, sometimes by their place in a decad. But, after Solon's time, the method of intercalation was such that the month did correspond pretty nearly with the moon and most days were named according to their place in a decad, those of the last decad (φθίνοντος) being usually counted backwards. Hence, in Attic writers, the names of the days are as follows : 1, νουμηνία. 2, 3, 4, δευτέρα ἱσταμένου, τρίτη ἱσταμένου, τετρὰς ἱσταμένου (κ.τ.λ.)—10, δεκάτη ἱσταμένου. 11, ἐνδεκάτη. 12, δωδεκάτη. 13—19, πρώτη —ἐνάτη μεσοῦντος or πρώτη ἐπὶ δέκα—ἐνάτη ἐπὶ δέκα. 20, εἰκὰς or εἰκάδες. 21, δεκάτη φθίνοντος or δεκάτη ὑστέρα. 22, ἐνάτη φθίνοντος or (in the 4th century) δευτέρα μετ᾽ εἰκάδας. 23, ὀγδόη φθίνοντος or τρίτη μετ᾽ εἰκάδας. 24, ἑβδόμη φθίνοντος or τετρὰς μετ᾽ εἰκάδας, and so on to 27, τετρὰς φθίνοντος or ἑβδόμη μετ᾽ εἰκάδας. 28, τρίτη φθίνοντος or ὀγδόη μετ᾽ εἰκάδας. 29, (in a full month) δευτέρα φθίνοντος or ἐνάτη μετ᾽ εἰκάδας. 29, in a hollow month, or 30, in a full month, τριακὰς or ἔνη καὶ νέα ('old and new moon'). The name δεκάτη προτέρα also occurs, but it is uncertain whether it refers to the 10th or the 20th. It will be observed that there was no δευτέρα φθίνοντος in a hollow month. Theoretically, the months consisted of 29 and 30 days alternately, but (owing to the neglect of the odd minutes in the true lunation) an extra (ἐμβόλιμος) day was required every 32 or 33 months. This day was apparently inserted as δευτέρα φθίνοντος in a hollow month, so that occasionally three months of 30 days each occurred together.

629. The natural duration of a year, *i.e.* of the revolution of the earth round the sun, is 365 days 5 hours 48 min. 48 sec. This period may be measured from a solstice or from an equinox. The Attic year began, theoretically, with the summer solstice, but the civil or calendar year began with the first day of Hecatombaeon, which fell always more or less near Midsummer. The following is a list of the Attic months :—

The Year.

1.	Ἑκατομβαιών (about July).	7.	Γαμηλιών (Jan.).
2.	Μεταγειτνιών (Aug.).	8.	Ἀνθεστηριών (Feb.).
3.	Βοηδρομιών (Sept.)	9.	Ἐλαφηβολιών (March).
4.	Πυανεψιών (Oct.).	10.	Μουνυχιών (Apr.)
5.	Μαιμακτηριών (Nov.).	11.	Θαργηλιών (May).
6.	Ποσειδεών (Dec.).	12.	Σκιροφοριών (June).

Different places had different names for the months and began the civil year at different times. Those Laconian months of which the names are known appear to stand in the following order : 6, Ἀρτεμίσιος (March). 7, Γεράστιος. 8, Ἑκατομβεύς. 9, Φλιάσιος. 10, Ἡράσιος. 11, Καρνεῖος (August). The names and order of the Delian and Delphian months are known and the names but not the exact order of the Boeotian months. In Delos, Elis and Boeotia the year began with the winter-solstice: in Sparta, Achaia and Aetolia with the autumnal equinox. Universally only 12 months were named and the intercalary month (to be presently mentioned) repeated the name of the month after which it was inserted.

630. Twelve months, of 29 and 30 days alternately, contain only 354 days, so that a twelve-month was short of a year by 11 days **Intercalation.** and a fraction, which fraction the Greeks never estimated exactly. The deficiency was supplied by inserting, every two or three years, an extra month of 30 days. In Athens, this month was inserted in winter after Ποσειδεών, and was called Ποσειδεών δεύτερος[1]. In a cycle of 8 years (ὀκταετηρίς or ἐνναετηρίς) three intercalary months were inserted, but so that there should never be thirteen months in two consecutive years. Eight years of 354 days contain 2,832 days, and three intercalary months of 30 days each raise this total to 2,922 days. This is equal to 8 solar years of $365\frac{1}{4}$ days. But 99 lunar months of $29\frac{1}{2}$ days contain $2,923\frac{1}{2}$ days, so that, by the end of 8 years, the νουμηνία fell $1\frac{1}{2}$ days before the actual new moon. Three intercalary days were therefore inserted every 16 years; but obviously these additional days, which made the months coincide with the moon, prevented the year from coinciding with the sun. The regulation of the calendar thus involved perpetual difficulties, and Meton, in 432 B.C., proposed a new and more satisfactory cycle of 19 years, in which there should be 7 intercalary months (see § 281). A modification of this cycle was introduced at Athens about 340 B.C., but afterwards the old ὀκταετηρίς was adopted once more. It should be observed that the importance of a correct calendar was brought home to everybody by the recurrence of certain fixed agricultural festivals. For instance, the προηρόσια, a festival which preceded the autumn ploughing, was fixed for a date in Boedromion, and the Panathenaea, a festival held on the conclusion of harvest, was fixed for a date in Hecatombaeon. It would have been absurd to hold these festivals on the given dates, if the dates did not coincide nearly with the agricultural operations thus celebrated. It may be inferred, therefore, that the charge of the calendar was committed everywhere to certain ἱερομνήμονες, whose duty it was to secure the regular performance of proper rites: but very little information is obtainable on this point (cf. Aristoph. *Nub.* 615—626).

The chief modern authorities are A. Mommsen, *Das Kalenderwesen der Griechen*, 1883; G. F. Unger in Iwan v. Müller's *Handbuch*, 1886; **Bibliography.** and Schmidt u. Rühl, *Handbuch der griech. Chronologie*, 1888. The main outlines of the subject, given above, are undisputed: but endless difficulties arise in the details. B. Meritt, *The Attic Calendar*, 1928.

---

[1] It is obvious that the insertion of this month would disturb the sequence of 29 and 30 days for alternate months, so that the same month might be 'hollow' one year and 'full' the next; moreover, the intercalary month was itself sometimes nominally 'hollow,' though it contained 30 days (in which case one day was treated as intercalary).

VII. PRIVATE ANTIQUITIES.

VII. 1. A TABLE OF THE RELATIONSHIPS OF A MAN.

§ 631.

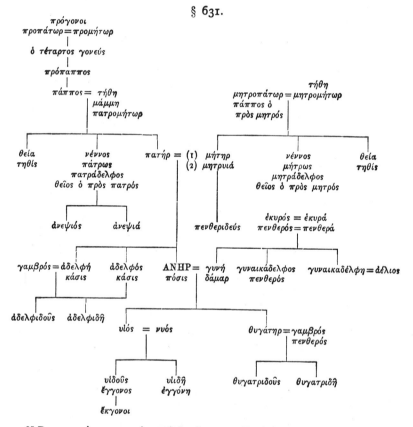

N.B. μητρυιός or πατρυιός *stepfather* is necessarily omitted from the above Table. κασίγνητος *brother*, κασιγνήτη *sister*, and compounds of these (as πατροκασίγνητος) are also omitted. Some terms are doubtful: *e.g.* Pollux (*Onom.* III. 16. 22) restricts νέννος to the *mother's brother* or *mother's father*. (See Liddell & Scott, *s.v.*)

It will be observed that a man's relations by marriage seem to be called indiscriminately πενθεροί or γαμβροί, but usually in prose πενθερός means 'father-in-law' and γαμβρός 'son-in-law.'

A woman had some special terms of relationship, viz. γάλως *husband's sister*, δαήρ *husband's brother*, εἰνάτηρ *brother's wife* or *husband's brother's wife*. It does not appear that *a man* had any special name for his *brother's wife*.

VII. 2. RITUAL OF BIRTH, MARRIAGE, AND DEATH.

632. THE Greek woman was attended in child-birth by a midwife (μαῖα, μαιεύτρια) or a female slave, not by a doctor. The birth of
a boy was advertised by the hanging of an olive wreath to the
Birth.
house door, of a girl—regarded as unlucky—by a woollen fillet. The new-
born child was laid on the ground to gain strength by contact with Mother
Earth and with its buried ancestors. The father, by lifting it up, acknowledged its legitimacy. The child was at once bathed in water or water mixed
with oil or (at Sparta) with wine. It was then swaddled in swathing bands
(σπάργανα), and laid in a λίκνον or winnowing basket for cradle. The usual
head-gear of a child was a pointed cap, and it was customary to hang about
its body βασκάνια or charms. As soon as practicable, *i.e.* on the fifth or seventh
day, the first formal rite was performed, the ἀμφιδρόμια. House, mother and
attendants were purified, and someone, probably the father, stripped of his
clothes (γυμνός), ran round the hearth carrying the child, a rite intended to
make the child walk and run quickly. The scholiast on Aristoph. *Lys.* 757
says that at the ἀμφιδρόμια the name was given, but this seems usually to
have been postponed to the more public ceremonial of the tenth day (δεκάτη),
to which relations and friends were bidden.   On this occasion took place
a sacrifice and feast, the guests brought presents (among them σηπίαι and
πλεκτάναι, to give the child a good grip of things), and the father, if such
was his intention, formally recognized the child.   A male child frequently
took the name of either paternal or maternal grandfather.   Public opinion,
except at Thebes, countenanced the occasional exposure (ἔκθεσις) of
children.   Mythological stories show that in heroic times it was not infrequent.   Tokens for recognition (γνωρίσματα) seem sometimes to have
been attached.   The duties of a well-to-do mother were shared by a nurse
(τροφός), sometimes by a wet-nurse (τίτθη), and the relation between child
and nurse seems to have been close and enduring.

633.   Marriage among the Greeks was arranged by the parents or near
relations, often with the help of a match-maker (προμνή-   *Marriage.*
στρια).   The necessary preliminary was the betrothal (ἐγγύησις or ἐγγύη), in which the woman was handed over by her κύριος, her
nearest male blood-relation.   If this ceremony were neglected or performed
by the wrong person, the marriage was null and the children illegitimate.
It was usual, though apparently not prescribed by law, that a dowry (προίξ
or φερνή) should be settled on the wife, a very necessary arrangement in
view of the great facilities for divorce.   The meaning of the term ἔδνα,
wedding-gifts, seems to have fluctuated, denoting in Homer gifts given by
the husband for his wife, and later wedding presents given as now by
the guests.   The month most in favour for marriage was Gamelion, and
certain days, *e.g.* the fourth day after the new moon, and the day of the

full moon, were regarded as specially lucky. As regards the actual ritual of marriage, the preliminary ceremonies to propitiate the gods (προγάμια) seem to have been separately performed by each family, and at no fixed date. Both bride and bridegroom propitiated the local gods (θεοὶ ἐγχώριοι) by some form of personal dedication, either by the offering of a lock of hair, or in the case of a river-god by bathing. The primitive meaning of the ceremony is placed beyond doubt by the formula in use among Trojan girls, Λάβε μου, Σκάμανδρε, τὴν παρθενίαν. The river-bath was later represented by the ante-nuptial bath in water brought from a sacred spring at Athens, Callirrhoë. The vessel used was called the Bath-Carrier (ἡ λουτροφόρος), and sometimes appears in effigy in the graves of those who died unmarried. A sacrificial feast (θοίνη γαμική) was given by the

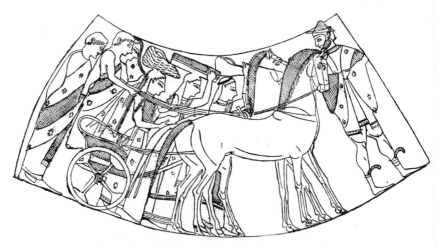

Fig. 137. Carrying Liknon in marriage procession, from a black-figured amphora.

bride's father, and probably at some other time another feast known as the γαμηλία was given by the father of the groom to his tribesmen. To this feast it was customary to subscribe (γαμηλίαν εἰσφέρειν τοῖς φράτερσι). At the θοίνη γαμική sacrifice was made to the household gods, and the sesame wedding-cake (σησαμῆ), made of pounded grain and honey, was eaten. Women were present with the bride, but sat apart. The bride was then taken home by the groom; she was veiled, and sat between the groom and his best man παράνυμφος or πάροχος, who drove the bridal chariot. She was accompanied by her mother, who bore torches lit at the father's hearth, and with them went a crowd of revellers and flute players. If we may judge from vase-paintings, the mother of the groom, bearing lighted torches, also awaited her at the door of her new home. In Boeotia the axle of the wedding chariot was burnt on the arrival of the bride. If the groom was not married for the first time the παράνυμφος alone brought the bride. At her entry into her new home the bride was greeted with a shower of grain, fruit and sweetmeats (καταχύσματα), and Solon prescribed that within the bridal chamber she should eat a quince with the groom. At Athens it was the custom at marriages that a boy, both of whose parents were alive (ἀμφιθαλὴς παῖς), should carry a λίκνον (Fig. 137) full of loaves, and then pronounce the words, Bad I have fled, better have I found (ἔφυγον κακόν, εὗρον ἄμεινον). At Athens the priestess of Athena at some time not stated carried the aegis into the house of the newly married. Festal hymns had probably accompanied the whole ceremony, but the actual epithalamia were sung by the bridesmaids outside the bridal chamber, those sung in the evening being known as the κατακοιμητικά, those in the morning as the διηγερτικά.

634. After death the eyes and mouth were closed by the relatives, and the head veiled. The women of the family washed the dead man and anointed him, clothed him in white, decked him with woollen fillets, and crowned him with flowers or vine-leaves. Aristophanes specially notes that the ὀρίγανος was in use. So decked he was ready for the πρόθεσις, or lying in state. He was placed on a couch, his face toward the door. In his mouth, where the Greek keeps his small change, was placed an obol, not originally as a fee for Charon (ναῦλον), but as a minimum precautionary sum for the dead man's use. Its connexion with Charon was a bit of popular myth-making, possibly due to the joke hazarded by Aristophanes. The honey cake (μελιτοῦσσα) placed in the dead man's hand, originally the normal offering to the underworld gods, was later in like manner associated with Cerberus. An oil flask (λήκυθος) was placed at the dead man's head, and friends and relations gathered round to say farewell, while a dirge was sung by hired mourners (θρηνῳδοί). A vessel of water was placed at the house door, that each departing guest might purify himself from ceremonial uncleanness contracted by contact with the dead. On the day after the πρόθεσις took place the actual funeral, the ἐκφορά, which had to be finished before sunrise. At Athens no woman under sixty years of age might enter the room from which the dead man had just been removed unless she were one of the next of kin, a regulation obviously due to a desire to keep the dead man's soul, released by death, in the family. The same desire explains the regulation that women relatives should walk behind the bier in its passage to the grave, to catch the soul should it flutter away. The body was laid on a bier and borne either on a car or on the shoulders of friends; hired mourners and flute-players as well as friends and relations accompanied it to the grave. The ceremonies at the grave varied of course according as the body was buried or burnt. Cremation was practised by the Northern immigrants, the Achaeans, inhumation and occasionally embalmment in honey by the indigenous primitive population. Cremation is therefore the uniform practice in Homer, but inhumation reemerges in

classical times, *e.g.* in Æschylus.   When the body was burned, a more
expensive and tedious process, a pyre (πυρά) had to be erected; as the
fire burned down, wine or water was poured on the ashes to extinguish
them, and the bones and ashes of the body were collected in a vase
(ὀστολόγιον).   In the case of burial, as the grave was filled up friends and
relations threw in vases, terracotta images and the like, not wholly out of
sentiment, but from fear that the dead man, if not pacified, might return to
claim his goods.   Save in the case of a public funeral, we hear of no
oration nor even of any spoken ritual, but the dead man was thrice saluted
by name in a loud voice (τρὶς ἀνακαλεῖν, βοᾶν), and the funeral proper
was over.   The funeral company went straight back to the house of the
nearest relative, where a feast (περίδειπνον) was given.   On the third and
ninth days sacrifices (ἐναγίσματα) were offered at the tomb (τρίτα, ἔνατα),
and again on the dead man's birthday, and the anniversary of his death,
also at the public festival of the νεκύσια, the All Souls' Day of the Greeks.
The dead man became a chthonic δαίμων, potent for good or evil.   His
natural symbol as such, often figured on tombs, was the snake.   Regulations
about suicides and unnatural criminals, *e.g.* fratricides, were based, then as
now, on the belief that they were potential vampires, and must so far as
possible be incapacitated.   The fear of the vampire-*revenant* grew with
the practice of burial in place of burning.

Fig. 138.   Scene at grave-mound surmounted by a stele, from
a black-figured lekythos in the Naples Museum.

635.   The funeral monument was ordinarily a mound (τύμβος) or simple
slab (στήλη), or column (κίων) to mark the place of burial

Funeral
monument.

(Fig. 138).   Occasionally it took the form of a hero chapel
(ἡρῷον).   Primarily, no doubt, the dead man was buried
within his own family precinct; later the custom arose of burying the

dead by the sides of public roads.　The inscription was ordinarily just so much as was needed for identification, *i.e.* the name, father's name, deme. At Sicyon no more than the dead man's name and that of his father appear ; at Sparta even the name was forbidden.　In later days eulogistic verses came into fashion, and the salutation χαῖρε, and when faith declined and sacrilege was dreaded, elaborate curses are invoked on the intruder.　When sculpture is used to adorn the tomb, the subjects represented are usually simple scenes of human life, but cast in somewhat hieratic mould; not unfrequently a mourning Siren is sculptured on a tomb; otherwise, save for the occasional appearance of Hermes Psychopompus, mythology is conspicuously absent. Cenotaphs were erected for those whose bodies had disappeared, and over the grave of a murdered man a spear was set up and watched by relations for three days.

Greek mourning usually prescribed black garments and close shaven hair; at Argos white was worn.　It was customary then as now to observe a certain amount of seclusion during the period of mourning.　This varied in various places; at Sparta it was only twelve days, at Athens and Argos thirty.

Pauly-Wissowa, *Real-Encyclopädie, sub voc.* ἀμφιδρόμια, etc. for Classical references; F. B. Jevons, 'Greek Burial Laws and Folklore Customs,' *Classical Review*, June, 1895, p. 247, for theories as to 　Bibliography. the origin of ritual and for many details ; Ridgeway, *Early Age of Greece*, 1901, Chap. VII. 'Inhumation, Cremation and the Soul'; Harrison and Verrall, *Mythology and Monuments of Ancient Athens*, 1890, sec. D ; Harrison, *Prolegomena to the Study of Greek Religion*, 1903, Chapter VII. ; E. Samter, *Geburt, Hochzeit, Tod*, Leipzig, 1911 ; A. Dieterich, *Mutter Erde*, Leipzig, 1905.

VII. 3. EDUCATION.

636.　FOR the time of Homer we have only slight glimpses at the methods and aims of the training of children.　Phoenix, we learn, taught Achilles μύθων τε ῥητῆρ' ἔμεναι πρηκτῆρά τε 　Homer, ἔργων, from which we see that the power of effective speech 　Crete and was even then made an object of education.　But for the 　Sparta. most part the intellectual training was limited to the use of the lyre and to singing.　Dancing, wrestling, swimming and other athletic exercises were practised, but no hint is given as to any general teaching of them.　The education of the boy in morals and religion was doubtless given by the father, and mainly by his example : while the girl learnt her household duties and the rules for her conduct in daily life from her mother.　The first trace of any educational institutions is to be found in Crete, where *gymnasia* existed at a comparatively early date, and are said to have been maintained by the State.　But these were not intended for youths under seventeen years of age (Hesych. *s.v.* ἀπάγελοι); up to that time they learnt at home reading, music and the laws of their country; it was only when they were taken from their parents' care, and placed under military discipline in ἀγέλαι, that the State training began: and though it included music and dancing, the aim was simply to make them the better soldiers. The same may be said of the famous Spartan discipline. The greatest care was taken to train boys in hardihood, and in skill in the use of weapons, as well as in obedience and good discipline. They perhaps learnt to read, and certainly were taught music and singing: but on the whole it was a physical and moral, not an intellectual, training which was given to the young Spartans.

637.   Schools, in the modern sense, appear first in the Ionian colonies of the islands and of Asia Minor, where first the use of writing **Schools.**   for literary purposes became general. Herodotus (VI. 27) tells us of a school at Chios, the roof of which fell in shortly before the battle of Lade (494 B.C.), crushing all but one of the 120 pupils who were assembled in it. A year or two earlier a similar mishap befell a school in the island of Astypalaea. Laws for the regulation of schools are ascribed to Solon (Aeschines *Tim.* §§ 9—11), and if these are genuine, schools must have existed at Athens early in the sixth century. The general prosperity which followed the Persian wars must have given them a large extension. But it is only at a later date that we find any traces of either State support or private endowment. The earliest instance of the former is when during the Persian occupation of Athens, the Troezenians, who had given shelter to the Athenian women and children, resolved that the latter should carry on their education in the schools of the town at the public cost. Later on we find endowment quite common: *e.g.* at Rhodes in 162 B.C. the State accepted a large donation of corn from Eumenes, 'that its value might be invested, and the interest devoted to pay the fees of the tutors and schoolmasters of their sons,' for which Polybius rather sharply censures them: and an inscription of the first century at Teos shows that there were there three salaried teachers of literature, two of gymnastics, and one of music, whose income was in part at least provided by endowment. But at Athens schools were entirely 'private ventures.' Nor was there any State control other than that secured by the laws. In some Dorian States there were officers called παιδονόμοι, who were charged with the oversight of the training of boys: but probably they did not concern themselves with anything but the gymnastic exercises. We read in Plato (*Crit.* 50) that the laws required parents to train their children in 'music' and 'gymnastics,' but we have no knowledge how these laws were enforced. Apparently the court of Areopagus had a general power of supervision, in the days when its functions were unrestricted. After the reforms of Ephialtes, it is probable that the Sophronistae, whom we find afterwards charged with educational duties, took up this office. Naturally the character of the schools varied greatly. Demosthenes taunts Aeschines with having been an assistant in a

school of no repute, kept by his father, where he discharged the humblest and most menial functions, while he himself had been going εἰς τὰ προσήκοντα διδασκαλεῖα.

638.　Up to the age of seven years children remained at home under the charge of their mother, or, in well-to-do houses, of a nurse (τροφός), who was almost invariably a slave. From her lips they would learn stories of the gods and heroes, and fables of animals; and sometimes tales of ghosts and hobgoblins, *Home training of children: games.* such as those which aroused the disapproval of Plato, to scare them into good behaviour.　Healthy occupation was found for their restless activity in many kinds of games, most of them such as are still familiar to our nurseries :—the rattle (πλαταγή or κρόταλον), an invention of the philosopher Archytas, 'in order that having the use of this, they may not break any of the things in the house, for little creatures cannot keep still' (Arist. *Pol.* v. 6. 2), toy carts, boats, beds, tables, cooking utensils, dolls of clay and wax, and dolls' houses.　Other recorded games were perhaps better suited to a later age, such as ball-playing (σφαῖρα), the hoop (τροχός), top (ῥόμβος), and swing (αἰώρα) ; blind man's buff (χαλκῆ μυῖα), the tug of war (ἑλκυστίνδα), and many others.　Especial favourites were knuckle-bones (ἀστράγαλοι), and jumping or standing on an inflated and well-greased wine-skin (ἀσκωλιασμός).

639.　The girls continued to receive at home such training as was thought needful, which doubtless varied greatly in different cases.　There are certainly instances in which Athenian women knew how to read and write : and there is a charming *Education of girls.* terra-cotta (not, it is true, of Athenian origin) which represents a girl seated on her mother's knee and learning from a roll which she holds.　Probably too they learnt dancing: music seems more doubtful among those of good repute: and few had any kind of intellectual training.　The newly-wedded wife of Ischomachus in Xenophon's *Oeconomicus* knows nothing but the labours of the loom, and habits of temperance, modesty and teachableness. She has been trained 'to see, to hear, and to ask as little as possible.' And when her husband takes her education in hand, it is limited to the duties of a good housewife.　It was one of the boldest of Plato's proposals that women should have the same training as men (*Rep.* v. 451 f.).　Teos is the only place where girls are spoken of as going to school along with boys, and even there the education of the former ceased at an early stage. In some Dorian States the girls were allowed to take part in gymnastic exercises and contests.　In Sparta the girls were thoroughly trained in athletic exercises, especially in dancing, running and wrestling; and whether they practised entirely naked, as some authorities imply, or only lightly clad in the short *chiton*, as seems more probable, their freedom is in striking contrast to the seclusion usual in most Greek States.　But the testimony, not only to the splendid vigour and beauty of the Spartan women, but also to their high tone of morality and their influence in the

State, proves that the perilous experiment under the existing conditions was by no means unsuccessful.

640. As soon as the boys were too old to be managed by their mothers or the nurses, they were placed under the care of παιδαγωγοί. These were invariably slaves, and too often slaves who were unfit from age or some physical defect for ordinary work. But though often rude and boorish (if we may argue from the way in which they are usually depicted in works of Art), they were, so far as possible, of high and trustworthy character. Their main duty was to look after the morals of the children. They kept them under constant supervision; taught them what was becoming in eating, drinking, dress, bearing and general behaviour; and corrected faults, at times with considerable severity. They regularly accompanied the boys to school, but took no part in the teaching. It is commonly said that they waited during the hours of lessons in a room called παιδαγωγεῖον. The principal objections to this view, which is strongly supported by the derivation of the word, are (1) that the school kept by the father of Aeschines, with reference to which we find this term used, was not one likely to have had anything but the barest necessaries; and (2) that on vases and the like παιδαγωγοί are depicted as present in the schoolroom itself.

The peda-gogues.

641. The purpose of education, especially in the earlier time, was not to stimulate or gratify intellectual curiosity, but to develop in the future citizen the physical, mental, and moral excellence which might fit him to do good service to the State. The religious element was, to our notion, singularly lacking: but it was to some extent provided, partly by the religious observances of the time, partly by the frequent public festivals in honour of the various deities, and mainly, so far as definite beliefs were concerned, by the study of the national poetry, especially the hymns. The two main branches of education were γυμναστική and μουσική. Plato lays it down that boys should begin with the former: but we have no definite information how far this was usual in practice. There are indications that they went on to some extent side by side, the latter naturally occupying the earlier part of the day, while the later hours were given to physical recreation. Gymnastics were taught by a παιδοτρίβης, in a παλαίστρα. There has been much discussion as to the precise distinction between a γυμνάσιον and a παλαίστρα: but two facts are clear. The term γυμνάσιον is never used with reference to education, until a very late date: and a παλαίστρα is often found as a term for a part of a γυμνάσιον. Hence it is safe to say that a παλαίστρα is either a training school for boys, or that part of a gymnasium specially devoted to wrestling (παλαίειν) and boxing. In the former sense it commonly bore the name of the owner or the original builder. The palaestra was an enclosed place, if possible near a running stream, and open to the air, that boys might be accustomed to bear the heat of the sun: ἐσκιατραφηκώς, like the Latin *umbratilis*, was a term of

Aim in education.

Physical training.

disparagement, as contrasted with ἡλιωμένος. In wrestling, skill and suppleness of limb were of not less importance than strength: and all kinds of tricks were encouraged (*e.g.* ὑποσκελίζειν): but we can hardly believe that the ferocious practices which marked some contests (λυγίζειν, τραχηλίζειν, ἄγχειν, ἐκκλᾶν τὸν δάκτυλον) were permitted to boys. In the πάλη ὀρθή a wrestler was vanquished if he was thrown thrice by his opponent (cp. Aesch. *Eum.* 589 ἐν μὲν τόδ᾽ ἤδη τῶν τριῶν παλαισμάτων): in the ἀλίνδησις or κύλισις the struggle was continued, as the wrestlers lay on the ground, until one confessed himself beaten. Boys wrestled naked, having first anointed themselves with oil, sprinkled with sand. After the contest, the oil, dust and sweat were scraped off with a στλεγγίς (*strigil*), and a cold bath was commonly taken, in the form of a plunge and a swim, if a river was near. Warm baths (βαλανεῖα) were not unknown, especially in the luxurious Ionian towns ; but they were always looked upon with some disfavour (Ar. *Nub.* 991). Next in importance to wrestling was running. We learn that at Olympia boys were only allowed to contend in the short race, a single course of the στάδιον (about 200 yards): it is probable therefore that school training was limited to this : and the distance may have been further graduated according to age. Leaping, both the high and the broad jump, with and without a run, and usually with the aid of weights (ἁλτῆρες), throwing the quoit (δισκοβολία) and the spear (ἀκοντισμός) were also practised. As to the place of boxing in the training of boys, we have little information ; but as there was a prize for boxing open to boys at Olympia as early as 616 B.C., it was probably not neglected, though it could hardly have held a prominent place.

642. In μουσική the first stage was the study of γράμματα, *i.e.* reading and writing, under the γραμματιστής. Dionysius of Halicarnassus (*De Comp. Verb.* c. 25) gives the following account of the method pursued in his time (1st cent. A.D.)
'First we learn the names of the elements of speech (στοιχεῖα τῆς φωνῆς), that is the γράμματα, then their several forms and values (τύπους καὶ δυνάμεις), the syllables and their modifications (τὰ περὶ ταῦτα πάθη), and finally names (ὀνόματα) and verbs (ῥήματα), and connecting particles (συνδέσμους) and the changes which they undergo (τὰ συμβεβηκότα τούτοις), contractions, expansions, acute or grave pronunciation, cases, numbers, inflexions, and the like. Then we begin to read and to write, at first syllable by syllable, very slowly, and the more rapidly, as we acquire some familiarity.' Some have supposed that Dionysius here describes the method of acquiring the power of reading, not by learning the names of the letters first, but by learning their powers, so combining them at once into syllables. But this is hardly consistent with his language, and is directly contradicted by a passage in Athenaeus, which tells how there was a kind of chant used in schools :—βῆτα ἄλφα βα, βῆτα εἶ βε, etc. A terracotta plate found in Attica, doubtless intended for use in schools, contains a number of syllables αρ βαρ γαρ δαρ ερ βερ γερ δερ κτλ. The

Reading and writing.

study of grammar which Dionysius describes was of course common only at
a later date, when the Sophists had brought this into fashion.   In learning
writing the pupil had to follow lines (γραμμαί) drawn by his master with a
stilus on a tablet : it seems to be uncertain whether these were straight
lines drawn to regulate the size and evenness of the letters as in our copy-
books, or letters to be traced over by him.   The former is the more natural
meaning for γραμμαί, but the latter course was known to and approved by
Quintilian (I. I, 27).   For writing they used at first boxwood tablets (πυξία)
covered with wax, on which letters were scratched with a *stilus* (γραφίς or
γραφίδιον, not στῦλος) : afterwards papyrus was employed, with a reed pen
(κάλαμος) and ink (μέλαν).   Tables or desks were never used in schools :
the tablet or paper was rested on the knees, as is usual still in
the East.

643.   Whether arithmetic was taught in the schools, as Plato would have it
taught in his ideal State (*Laws* VII. 819), seems doubtful.   It

Arithmetic
and drawing.

was never regarded as a part of παιδεία, but probably from
its practical value it was not wholly neglected.   Reckoning
on the fingers (ἐπὶ δακτύλων συμβάλλεσθαι, πεμπάζειν) or with the help of
pebbles (ἀπὸ ψήφων λογίσασθαι) or an *abacus* (ἀβάκιον) may have been
picked up at home, or as part of the ordinary business of life.   Later on,
when the educational value of mathematics was better understood, and
when the training of children was less exclusively directed to the development of character, some elementary teaching of arithmetic and geometry
became usual : but we cannot say whether this was given by the γραμματιστής, or by a special teacher.   We learn that drawing (γραφική) was made
a school subject, and to some extent combined with mathematics, first by
Pamphilus, the head of the Sicyonian school of painting, early in the fourth
century (Plin. *H. N.* xxxv. 76 f.).   The purpose of teaching it was partly to
train the eyes to the appreciation of beauty, partly to help in judging
works of Art, that, as Aristotle rather quaintly puts it (*Pol.* v. 3. 7), they
might not be cheated in the purchase and sale of household goods.

644.   Plato allows three years for the mastery of the rudiments of reading and writing, but doubtless before this was completely

Literature.

achieved boys began the study of the poets.   At first this
consisted mainly in learning verses by heart, and we find on
vases pictures of boys standing before the teacher, who is seated, and who
reads from a roll.   Afterwards the matter was more carefully explained, and
the poets served as manuals, not only for mythology and for morals, but
also for geography and history.   The chief text-book was Homer : it was
not uncommon for Athenian boys to know the whole of the *Iliad* and the
Odyssey by heart.   Hesiod and the cyclic poets were also studied ; and the
gnomic poets, Theognis, Solon, Mimnermus and Phocylides, as well as the
lyric poets like Tyrtaeus were learnt, mainly in selections and chresto-
mathies.   We have a very interesting specimen of the illustrations used in
teaching poets in the *tabula Iliaca* of Theodorus, now preserved in the

Capitoline Museum at Rome, which contains scenes from the *Iliad*, with
brief descriptions appended.

645.   For μουσική in the narrower sense there was usually a special
teacher called κιθαριστής, though there are instances of the
same master teaching both γραμματική and μουσική.   Boys   Music.
were taught at the same time to play on the lyre and to sing.
The instrument used was commonly the simpler λύρα, not the more
elaborate κιθάρα preferred by professional musicians.   The pipe (αὐλός)
was not unknown in schools, as we see from the instructive representation
of a school in the famous vase of Duris (Fig. 139); but it was in fashion at

Fig. 139. Vase-painting by Duris, on a cylix.

Athens only for a short time after the Persian wars, though it was always
much used in Boeotia.   It naturally could not be played by a singer: it was
supposed to disfigure the face, and its music was thought to be unduly
exciting.   Music was studied partly as a graceful accomplishment for hours

of leisure, partly as adding pleasure to festive gatherings, at which every-one was expected to play and sing in his turn, but especially for its influence upon the temper and character. The Greeks always attached immense importance to the moral effect of music, and distinguished the influence of the various keys or modes in a manner which our ignorance of the exact nature of Greek music precludes us from realising or appreciating very clearly. The Dorian mode, for example, was regarded as moral and manly, the Phrygian as orgiastic, the 'slack' Lydian and Ionic as suited only for drinking-songs, the Mixo-Lydian for lamentation (see § 389). Such of the Greek tunes as have come down to us seem to our modern ears very un-attractive. Undoubtedly the training in singing would be accompanied by a careful study of rhythm and metre, and also of pronunciation, in the widest sense, including τόνος, πνεῦμα, and χρόνος. Also the language of the lyric poets would suggest more thorough instruction in poetic diction and dialect, as well as in a wider range of mythology and history.

646. At the age of fifteen or sixteen γυμναστική claimed a greater part of the time of the pupil, though the attention which he con-
Gymnastics. tinued to give to μουσική would doubtless depend upon his own tastes and the social position of his parents. The earlier gymnastic exercises were probably (as Aristotle held that they should be) light and easy, such as might develop the grace and vigour of the body, without putting too great a strain on it. But three years or so after the date of puberty the time came for more severe training, both in diet and in exercises. Yet the wisest teachers always drew a sharp line between the training which made men vigorous and brave soldiers, and that which led to professional athleticism. The term 'trainer' (παιδοτρίβης) came to be distinguished in the later time from that of 'teacher,' and his profession was less esteemed. The difficulty of carrying out high intellectual training along with excessive physical exertion was recognised, and the brutalising effects of pure athleticism deplored (§ 422). Dancing was apparently but little practised by any but those who were in training for the chorus at public festivals. It was more general perhaps in the case of girls; and at Sparta it was usual for all, especially in the form of the warlike Pyrrhic dance.

647. A wide extension was given to the traditional basis of education by the influence of the Sophists. The common feature of
The Sophists. this class of teachers, widely as they differ in many respects, was a dissatisfaction with the narrow limits of the ordinary culture, especially as failing to satisfy the demands of a legitimate intel-lectual curiosity. They offered, to all who cared to pay their fees, instruction in subjects either entirely new, or largely developed by their efforts. Protagoras, for instance, taught systematic grammar, and correctness of diction (ὀρθοέπεια), Prodicus the distinction of synonyms, Hippias the rules of rhythm. Generally speaking, dialectics and rhetoric (as developed by Gorgias), the elements of physical science, mathematics and philosophy

were the subjects which attracted students of leisure from all parts of
the civilised world to Athens. But our limits prevent us from dealing with
these higher and purely voluntary studies. It is only needful to observe
how the extension which they gained must have had its influence on the
range and method of the work of the ordinary schools, so that we have to
be careful in applying the abundant information which we have as to the
first and second centuries after Christ to the fifth and fourth centuries B.C.

648. It may, however, be worth while to notice the origin of what has
been called 'University life at Athens.' From seven to
eighteen years of age, a boy learnt at Athens what his father's   The Ephebi.
wishes or means prescribed for him. But at the latter age
the State took the control of him for a period of two years. We learn
about the institution of ἐφηβεία mainly from inscriptions (§ 750), and from
Ar. *Pol. Ath.* c. 42. It was probably instituted in the year 336 B.C.; the
earliest inscription dealing with ἔφηβοι dates from 334—3 B.C. At first it
was purely a military organisation. All sons of citizens at eighteen years of
age, after passing a δοκιμασία, were placed under the charge of σωφρονισταί
and κοσμηταί, and trained to military duties. They were maintained at the
public cost, and wore a uniform dress (at first dark, or even black, afterwards white): for the first year they served as a garrison to Munychia or
the Acte of the Peiraeus: in the second, after receiving a shield and a spear
from the State, they patrolled the country or garrisoned the forts. By
degrees the service seems to have become voluntary; the recorded numbers
greatly diminish, and finally strangers are admitted. Naturally it became
more and more restricted to the rich, and the age of entrance was not definitely fixed. In the third and following centuries before Christ the military
and gymnastic exercises are supplemented, and the former ultimately
replaced, by elaborate courses in literature, rhetoric and philosophy; and at
the same time the regular period of study is limited to one year. The
professors, on whose lectures attendance was compulsory, were not paid or
appointed by the State: they were probably selected by the officials, and
remunerated by the fees of their students. There were numerous students'
clubs and reunions, and a common library in the Ptolemaeum, a fragment
of the catalogue of which still exists. Of course the attendance on lectures
was not restricted to the Ephebi: from all quarters students came to complete their education at what thus became the premier University of the
Roman Empire.

Grasberger's *Erziehung und Unterricht im klassischen Alterthume* (Würz-
burg, 3 vols., 1864–81) is a complete storehouse of information.   Bibliography.
Cp. also P. Girard, *L'Éducation Athénienne* (Paris, 2nd ed. 1891),
and his articles *Éducation* and *Ephebi* in Daremberg and Saglio's Dict.; also
Becker-Göll, *Charikles* II. 19–83 and 213–50 (Berlin, 1877); J. L. Ussing,
Erziehung und Jugendunterricht bei den Griechen und Römern (Berlin, 1885);
J. P. Mahaffy, *Old Greek Education* (London, 1881); K. J. Freeman, *Schools of
Hellas* (London, 1907, etc.); E. Ziebarth, *Aus dem griechischen Schulwesen*
(Leipzig, 1909); J. Oehler, *Epigraphische Beiträge zur Geschichte der Bildung
im klassischen Altertum* (Wien, 1909).

VII. 4. BOOKS AND WRITING.

649. THE vehicle by which Greek literature was preserved and transmitted from the earliest times until perhaps the second or
third century after Christ was the papyrus roll. Alike in
respect of form and of material, this was an import from
Egypt, where it had been in use from a very remote time. A detailed
account of the way in which the papyrus was treated in the Egyptian
paper-factories is given by Pliny (*N. H.* XIII. 74 sqq.), but it is obscure
in many points, and has given rise to a great deal of discussion. Without
going into the minuter details of the process, it may be said here that the
material used was the pith of the papyrus-reed (πάπυρος, βύβλος, βίβλος :
botanically *Cyperus papyrus*), cut vertically into slices. In order to make
a sheet of paper, these slices were laid some vertically and others trans-
versely, pressed together, and dried in the sun : unevennesses were then
smoothed or pressed away, and the sheets glued together into a roll.
The writing was arranged in columns, in which the lines of writing
ran parallel to the long side of the roll. Only one side of the paper was
used in books meant for sale. Those written upon both sides (ὀπισθό-
γραφα) were for private use, and were in the nature of rough copies. In
order to read a roll, it, or rather the wooden cylinder on which it was
wound, must be taken in the right hand. It was then opened with the left
hand, and the reader began with the first column : as he proceeded further
and further towards the right, he rolled up with his left hand the portion he
had now read.

The length of the early rolls was very considerable. We are told
of some that were 150 feet long, and would contain the whole *Iliad* or
Odyssey. Clearly this great bulk must have been a grave inconvenience,
and we have evidence that the discomfort of it was felt. The well-known
saying of Callimachus—μέγα βιβλίον μέγα κακόν—alludes to this matter and
to nothing else. Callimachus was speaking, not as a poet or as a literary
critic, but as librarian of the great Alexandrian library, whose contents and
catalogue he arranged. He must have had to deal with enormous masses
of the unwieldy old rolls, and have suffered as much as we do now from
a large folio book without an index. The theory of Birt is that we owe to
Callimachus in a great measure the subdivision of ancient Greek works
into *books*. It is at least clear that from a fairly early period authors were
influenced by the size of the papyrus rolls ordinarily manufactured, and
divided their works into such portions as could conveniently be contained
in single rolls. The manufacture of papyrus had its head-quarters at Alexandria, and all matters relating to its size, quality, and price were carefully
regulated in Roman times. In Pliny's day the standard quantity of a roll
was twenty sheets. The best quality of paper (at first called *hieratica,* but

The papyrus
roll.

subsequently *Augusta*) was about 9½ inches wide, though there was a kind of 'large paper' (*macrocollum*) as much as a cubit wide. The inferior sorts decreased in width, down to about five inches. It should be borne in mind that the slices of pith from the *centre* of the papyrus stalk were alike the largest in size and the best in quality. The papyrus-trade was carried on by the Arabs after their invasion of Egypt in the seventh century A.D., and ceased altogether, it is believed, about the year 950.

650. Side by side with papyrus, another material was in use for several centuries, which was destined entirely to supersede its older rival. This was parchment (*pergamena*) or vellum (*vitu-* *linum*). Rolls of skin were used by the Egyptians in quite early times, though rarely in comparison with papyrus : and the Jews probably employed skins throughout their history for the reception of their sacred books, as indeed they do at the present day. Herodotus, too, tells us that the Ionian Greeks wrote upon skins (διφθέραι), and Diodorus Siculus speaks of the διφθέραι on which the ancient records of Persia were inscribed. The place which has given its name to parchment—Pergamum —was in later classical times the centre of the parchment trade. Pliny quotes from Varro a story that Eumenes II, king of Pergamum (197— 158 B.C.), was forced to use parchment for his library because the Ptolemies, jealous for their own library at Alexandria, forbade papyrus to be exported. The story is not generally believed, but it contains the truth that Pergamum was particularly important in connexion with the development of the use of parchment. From Pergamum the article must soon have made its way in some quantity to Rome; and once at Rome, its diffusion over the whole civilised world was assured. Its superiority to papyrus consisted, firstly in its greater durability, and secondly in the fact that it was procurable in any country, while the papyrus-reed could only be cultivated in one very limited area. For all that, it did not make its way to the front at once. We have no clear evidence as to the comparative value of the two materials. At least we know what the determining influence was which eventually gave to parchment its well-deserved supremacy. It was that of the Christian Church, which, influenced no doubt by the practice of the Jewish Church, chose parchment to write their sacred books upon. As was natural, the Christians soon extended its use, first to the reception of their own theological literature, and then to that of literature in general.

651. The form of the earliest parchment MSS. was naturally that of the roll. We have now to consider the development of the book-form ; an improvement almost comparable in importance to the invention of printing　It is agreed that the book was evolved out of the *tablet*. Single wooden tablets were used in Egypt and in Greece as early as the fifth century B.C., for such purposes as the keeping of accounts, and the writing of models for schoolboys to copy. These tablets were of plain wood, or had a thin coat of glaze. But the more important and more usual form which they took in the Greek and Roman world was that of the set of small tablets which could be carried on the person, and were used for notes and correspondence, or for wills and other legal documents   These were usually of box-wood, covered with wax, on which men wrote with a metal stylus: they were hinged together with rings, and according as they consisted of two or more 'leaves,' they were described as δίπτυχα, τρίπτυχα, etc., or πολύπτυχα.

Take such a set of tablets, and for the inner leaves of wood substitute leaves of papyrus or of parchment, and you have at once something very like the modern book.   Let the further step be taken of using a book so formed for the purpose of transcribing some short literary work, and the thing is done.   The size and bulk of your book can be increased at will. How much more convenient for continuous reading, and more especially for reference, a book is than a roll we do not need to be told : but in the ancient world natural conservatism and the traditions of the book-trade were not overcome at once.   Towards the end of the third century A.D. the supremacy of the book-form was probably assured if not attained.   There were books before that date, and rolls continued to be used for literary works long afterwards : but the former were on the increase and the latter falling off in numbers.

The earliest extant specimens of books must be looked for among recent Egyptian discoveries.   The third-century papyrus-leaf, containing the 'Sayings of the Lord,' is from a book, not a roll: while a parchment leaf with a fragment of the *Melanippe* of Euripides is of the fourth century or earlier.   Of complete books it would not be easy to find earlier examples than the two fourth-century Bibles, known as the *Vaticanus* and *Sinaiticus*.

Alike in books and in rolls the writing was arranged in columns. The reader of a roll would probably find it convenient to have from two to four columns exposed before him at once.   Some of our earliest books bear traces of their descent from the roll in the number of columns which each of their pages shows.   Thus the two famous Bibles mentioned above have respectively four and three columns on a page.   The normal number, however, in MSS. where the lines are of uniform length, is two.   Where they are sense-lines—divided, as the phrase goes, *per cola et commata*, as in the *Codex Bezae*—we find but one column on the page.   The columns were in Greek called σελίδες—a word which originally meant the gangways between the banks of rowers in a trireme.   This was transferred to the spaces between the columns of writing, then to the columns themselves, and finally, when the book-form had ousted the roll, to the pages of the book itself.   Greek papyrus books have not survived outside Egypt save in scanty fragments.

652.   The arrangement of the leaves of ancient MSS. is often important. The construction of the earliest books was essentially the same as that of the most modern ones.   They were composed of a series of quires fastened together, and each quire

Quires of a Book.

consisted of a number of sheets of vellum or papyrus, folded down the middle and placed one inside another.   The most usual number of sheets composing a quire was four, which made eight leaves or sixteen pages, and was called a τετράδιον or *quaternus* (= *cahier* = quire).   We also find quires of six, ten, and twelve leaves.   The number of leaves of which a quire consists is ascertained by looking between each pair of leaves until a string is found passing down the middle of the crease between them.   The sheet in which this string is must be the innermost sheet of the quire, and there ought to be an equal number of leaves on each side of it.   If there is not, the reason must be either that a leaf in the quire was cancelled and cut out by the original scribe, or that it has been subsequently lost.   We can best find out which is the true reason by noticing whether the text of the MS. is continuous throughout the quire.   If a gap in the sense appears between one leaf and the next, we shall be sure that we are dealing with a case of mutilation.

653.   We are familiar with the fact that Egyptian works, notably the *Book of the Dead*, were copiously illustrated. But we have no evidence that the Greeks adopted this fashion in early times.   The first Greek MS. which is illustrated in any way Illustration of Books. is a papyrus of the astronomical τέχνη of Eudoxus, now at Paris, dating from 165 B.C.   It contains some rude diagrams.   Our earliest specimen of real pictures in Greek books is afforded by the illustrated fragments of the *Iliad* in the Ambrosian Library at Milan.   These are 58 pictures cut from a complete MS. of the *Iliad*.   They are themselves as old as the fourth century, and go back to yet earlier models.   The Vienna Dioscorides of the sixth century preserves a remarkable series of pictures of plants and other illustrations.

654.   As to the writing materials ordinarily used by scribes, something must be said.   A number of epigrams in the Palatine Antho-logy (VI. 62—68, 295), mostly late, but all variations on an Writing materials. ancient theme, give lists of the implements in question. They are as follows :

(1) The μόλιβδος, a disc of lead with which lines were ruled; (2) κανών, the ruler which served to keep the lines and columns straight; (3) σπόγγος, the sponge to obliterate mistakes ;   (4) κίσηρις, the piece of pumice to smooth the nib of the pen, and to rub away roughnesses in the paper ;   (5) γλύφανον or σμίλη, the penknife to sharpen the pen ;   (6) μέλαν, the ink, either that of the cuttle-fish, or else a mixture made from oak-galls or the like ;   (7) μελανδόκον (μελανδοχεῖον, etc.), the inkstand ; (8) κάλαμος, the pen, which, as the name shows, was at first a reed, later on exchanged for a bird's quill.   We first hear of the latter in the sixth century, but no doubt it was in use before that.   The metal stylus was only employed for writing on wax tablets.   It is perhaps worth while to add the term ὀμφαλός, which was the name given to the projecting ends—often gilt and decorated—of the cylinder on which a papyrus volume was rolled.

655. As to the methods of storing books, we are not perhaps so well
Libraries, etc.　informed as we are about the books themselves. It is clear
alike from literature and from monuments that the small
collection of an ordinary individual would be contained in a series of
circular boxes in which the rolls stood vertically. Reference to them was
rendered easy by the σίλλυβος, or label of coloured parchment or other
material, attached to the ὀμφαλός of each, on which the title was written.
Larger libraries, such as that found in 1752 at Herculaneum, required to be
accommodated in presses, usually shallow cupboards arranged round the
walls of a room. In these the rolls would lie horizontally on the shelves.
Each press or series of presses would have to be provided with a catalogue.
Callimachus is known to have compiled what are called πίνακες for the
Library of Alexandria ; the work was clearly in the nature of a catalogue ;
and the most probable interpretation is that the catalogue there and elsewhere took the form of a number of wooden tablets, one for each press,
inscribed with the titles of the books contained in that press. The Greek
names for the book-boxes or book-cupboards are not of very common
occurrence. The word βιβλιοθήκη must have originally meant a receptacle
for a small number of books, though its meaning was speedily extended,
and κιβωτός and τεῦχος had also this signification : the things themselves,
however, took firm root at Rome, and survived into later mediaeval times
throughout the West. Of the book-trade in Greece, again, and of the
methods which an author employed to get his works published, we really
know nothing. Judging from what went on at Rome, we should conjecture
that the trade was carried on by men who employed slaves to write from
dictation, and that in this way copies of books were quickly multiplied.
From a passage in Xenophon's *Anabasis* (VII. 5. 14) we gather that there
was an export trade in books from Athens, and that they were packed in
wooden boxes for the purpose.

Th. Birt, *Das antike Buchwesen; Buch und Rolle* ; W. Wattenbach, *Das
Bibliography.　Schriftwesen im Mittelalter*; J. W. Clark, *The Care of Books*;
F. G. Kenyon, *The Palaeography of Greek Papyri*; Sir E. M.
Thompson, *Manual of Greek and Latin Palaeography*.

VII. 5. THE POSITION OF WOMEN.

656. THE position of women in Greece varied, at different periods and
in different States, from a condition of dignity and honour almost equal
with men, to one of subjection and seclusion not unlike that existing among
Oriental nations. The earliest notices of Greek women are found in
Women in　Homer. Both in the *Iliad* and in the *Odyssey* the wives
Homer.　and daughters of chieftains are treated with respect and
have much freedom of intercourse with men. Penelope holds
court at Ithaca in the absence of her husband, and is respected even by

the insolent wooers, who do as they will with the slaves of the household.
It appears to be understood that though Telemachus acts as his mother's
guardian, the sovereignty of Ithaca will pass to the suitor whom she accepts.
Hecuba at Troy and Arete in Phaeacia keep the house in royal dignity
and are the friends and counsellors of their husbands; the latter is perhaps
even more than this, since Odysseus is advised to secure her goodwill first
of all; she joins in the conversation in the hall on equal terms with Alcinous.
Nausicaa, their daughter, goes through the city with only her handmaids
attending her, and her behaviour to Odysseus is a pattern of frank and
natural courtesy. Helen again, attended by her two ἀμφίπολοι, goes openly
through the streets of Troy and mixes with Priam and the elders upon the
wall; when restored to Menelaus after her ten years' sojourn at Troy, she
resumes her place at his side without loss of credit or position. This honour
paid to women does not however extend to those who are slaves either by
birth or by the fortune of war. Andromache, a king's daughter whose
husband falls in defence of his city, can look forward to no better fate than
to become the property of her captor, to be beaten with spear-shafts and
sent to herd with the slave-women, to stand at the loom and bear the pitcher
for a foreign mistress (*Iliad* VI. 450–465). In practice, it seems, the fortune
of a captive might be easier than this. Chryseis and Briseis are held in
honour in the Greek camp; Tecmessa is raised above her servile state by
the favour of her master, Ajax. And the lot of slave-women, though hard,
was not necessarily cruel; Eurycleia, the nurse of Odysseus, occupies a
position of trust, and the αἰδοίη ταμίη of the palace might be a slave.
Though monogamy was the universal custom in Homeric Greece, and there
is no instance of a royal harem such as that maintained by Priam in Troy, un-
wedded connexions with women were not considered disgraceful to either party.
Odysseus is the accepted lover of Calypso and Circe; and Penelope has no
reproaches to her husband for his unfaithfulness (cf. Eur. *Androm.* 213 ff.).

657. Marriage was the rule for all, men as well as women. Parents
could dispose of their children of either sex in marriage. A
widow was expected to marry again if of marriageable age. Marriage
in Homer.
We find no mention of divorce. There were restrictions on
the marriage of those connected by blood or affinity, and in regard to
degrees of kinship many distinctions were observed which reflect primitive
laws of marriage. But there are instances (*Il.* v. 412, *Od.* VII. 66) of
marriage with an aunt or niece. The wife came into her husband's hand
by purchase. A sum of money or a present of other valuables, gold, silver,
oxen, houses, slaves, etc., passed from the husband to the family of
the bride. This payment was no doubt originally a compensation to the
father for the loss of his daughter's services. The Greek term for it is ἔδνα,
ἔεδνα. Sometimes the price was remitted by the father of the bride. Sometimes there was also a contribution from the family of the bride, to furnish
her outfit and provide the marriage feast, *e.g.* Andromache and Penelope
are ἄλοχοι πολύδωροι (*Il.* VI. 394, *Od.* XXIV. 294). It is easy to see how a

gift on both sides to the married couple might supersede the ancient form
of sale, and thus give rise to the custom of a dowry in the usual sense of
property passing with the wife from her family.

658. In Hesiod woman occupies a subordinate position. A wife is
counted in the *Works and Days* (as in the Tenth Com-
mandment) with a house and an ox (405); but later it is
stated that "a man wins nothing better than a good wife, and,
again, nothing worse than a bad one" (702, 703), a generalization which
attests her importance in the home. The discrepancy between the pictures
of Homer and Hesiod may be partly explained by the consideration that
Homer, to please his courtly audience, draws kings and warriors, heroes of
romance like the paladins of mediaeval epic, while Hesiod describes the
manners of the country folk as he knew them, and adds no romantic colour
to the truth.

Hesiod's idea of woman.

659. In the sixth century the instances of Sappho and Corinna and
the traditions about their lives point to a freer and more
equal intercourse with men than we find existing at a later
date. But the notices of women in the lyric poets are few,
and are chiefly in praise of the conventional seclusion, the 'home-keeping'
habit (Theognis ἐχθαίρω δὲ γυναῖκα περίδρομον, Phocylides οἰκονόμος τ'
ἀγαθὴ καὶ ἐπίσταται ἐργάζεσθαι). Equal and happy marriages must have
existed in all states of society, and we do not need the authority of Greek
poets to assure us that 'nothing is sweeter or better than when a wife
loves her husband till old age, and the husband his wife, and there is
no strife between them'; or on the other hand, that a man who married
a rich woman might find himself the servant of her fortune. The development of civilization among the Ionian Greeks was probably affected by
the neighbourhood of Oriental nations.

Women in the lyric poets.

660. At Sparta, and generally among the Dorian nations, a greater
freedom was enjoyed by women than among the Ionians.
Young people of both sexes could meet each other without
restraint. Girls were present at athletic contests in the stadium, to which
matrons were not admitted. They wrestled, boxed and ran races, sometimes
even with young men. The object of the law permitting this, according to
Xenophon, was to provide, not slaves to sit at home and spin, but mothers
of brave men. This freedom is said not to have had any bad moral results;
the chastity of Spartan women was generally acknowledged. It should however be remarked that Aristotle (*Pol.* II. 1269 *b*) speaks of the licence and
parade of the Spartan women, produced by defect of the laws, as having been
a blot upon the institutions of the city from the first. They live (he says)
in every kind of unrestrained luxury. Plato too (*Laws* 780, 781) uses
similar language; and Euripides (*Androm.* 595 ff.) says that no Spartan
girl, even if she wished it, could ever be modest. Yet the idea that a noble
progeny was the aim of marriage so far prevailed that in certain cases
married persons exchanged partners, and some women had more than one

Sparta.

husband and household. Only one instance of a similar licence to a man is recorded, that of King Anaximandridas. Marriage at Sparta followed the fiction of a violent seizure: and for some time the married couple met only in secret. The wife was not merely, as in Athens, a superior housekeeper. She was called δέσποινα, as in Homeric times, and the credit of her husband depended in part upon her conduct. Many instances are given of the devotion of Spartan women to their husbands. The wife and mother was expected to be not only a careful housewife, but a patriot, and to sympathise with all that made Sparta great. 'Return with your shield or upon it,' 'If your sword is too short, add a pace,' and many like sayings are characteristic of the Spartan women; and the mothers whose sons fell at Leuctra were thought more happy than those who received the survivors on their return. Daughters often shared equally with sons in the settlement of property by will, or even received a larger share. Dowries were also large. Hence it came that in the fourth century B.C. nearly half the land in Laconia was owned by women. Daughters were given in marriage at their father's will, as universally in ancient time; the king had the assignment of orphan heiresses to the kinsman who had the best claim. (For the special rules of marriage and inheritance at Gortyn see § 480.)

661. Generally speaking, in Greece marriage was a matter of convenience. The motives which inclined men to marry were such practical considerations as the welfare of the state, the provision of children to perpetuate the race and carry on the religious observances of the family, the acquisition of a responsible and efficient housekeeper. The preliminaries were settled by the parents of the parties, care being taken to choose a wife of respectable origin, and in most cases of similar fortune. The wife was usually younger than the husband. Aristotle and Plato recommend the years from thirty to thirty-seven for the man, and sixteen to twenty for the woman, as most suitable. Few girls remained unmarried. This fact sharpens the tragedy of such figures as Antigone and Electra, "the Unmated." The first step towards marriage was the solemn ἐγγύησις or betrothal by the κύριος, i.e. the father or other person standing in loco parentis to the woman. (ἐγγυᾶν is said of the parents, ἐγγυᾶσθαι of the husband.) In the terms of the ἐγγύησις was included the amount of the προίξ (money in settlement) and φερνή (personal ornaments and outfit). In all Greek cities it was easy for a man to divorce (ἐκπέμπειν, ἀποπέμπειν) his wife; and in the case of adultery he was bound by law to do so. No legal process was necessary beyond the presence of witnesses. The law only took cognisance of the wife's property, which, with the custody of herself, was vested in her nearest male relation or κύριος. Both at Athens and at Sparta a wife could lawfully leave (ἀπολείπειν) her husband, and take her property with her to her κύριος. Infidelity, or ill-usage, on the part of her husband, was a ground for the ἀπόλειψις of the wife. In leaving her husband, she had to make a written statement to the archon; whose general duty it was to protect the interests of married women, and who kept a register of divorces.

Marriage and divorce.

662. At Athens the wife's dowry—i.e. what she brought with her, whether Legal position outfit (φερνή) or property in settlement (προίξ)—did not, of women at according to Greek ideas, become the husband's property. Athens. The husband had to give security (ἀποτίμημα) for it, usually in real property (ἔγγειος οὐσία). He had the administration and enjoyment of it during his married life, and if the wife predeceased him, till his death (if she left children) or remarriage; in either of these events it went to her children, or if she had none, reverted to her guardian (κύριος): and accordingly the husband could not alienate or mortgage it, and in certain cases might have to account for it. During widowhood, the dowry was administered by the widow, if she remained in her husband's family (μενούσης ἐν τῷ οἴκῳ); but her sons received their portion on attaining their majority, subject to a claim for alimony (σῖτος); the daughters had no claim, if there was a son. If the widow married again, her property went from the estate of the first husband to that of the second. If her husband divorced her, her dowry reverted to her κύριος, or the husband paid interest on it at 18°/₀ and provided alimony in addition. In all matters respecting the property of married women, the intention of Greek law appears to be to preserve property in families as far as possible, and principally with a view to prevent the extinction of families, and so the disuse of family *sacra*. A father, having no male heirs, might bequeath his property, with his daughter (who would be called ἐπίκληρος), to anyone that he chose, such person being bound to marry the daughter (if necessary divorcing his own wife), or to forego the inheritance. And if a father, having a daughter but no male heirs, died intestate, the nearest relation could claim the daughter: if the claim was disputed (ἀμφισβητεῖν), a trial (ἐπιδικασία, διαδικασία) was held by the archon, who adjudged (ἐπιδικάζειν) the ἐπίκληρος, according to the laws. If she was already married, she might have to leave her husband and marry the claimant; for in such a case the wishes of the persons concerned were not regarded if they conflicted with the legal disposition of the property. Women at Athens were subject to other disabilities besides those attaching to property. They could not (e.g.) give evidence (μαρτυρεῖν) in a court of law, though in certain cases they were capable of taking an oath upon a challenge (πρόκλησις); nor be parties to a contract.

663. Irregular unions with ἑταῖραι were common at all times, and were not looked upon as discreditable. Some of these women, as, Ἑταῖραι and for example, Lais, Phryne, etc., the ἑταῖραι μεγαλόμισθοι, lived Παλλακαί. in great splendour by themselves or two or three together. Others were maintained by their lovers: the largest class were slaves, who often practised the art of music (αὐλητρίδες and κιθαρίστριαι) and were hired to play and dance at wine-parties. These women were kept by their owners in separate lodgings, or private πορνεῖα. The lowest class of all (πόρναι) were to be found in the public πορνεῖα. Another class, of whom Aspasia is the most famous instance, led irregular but not dissolute lives, and according to Greek ideas were almost without reproach. Such women were sometimes highly educated and held *salons* frequented by all the wits of the day. Married men as well as bachelors frequented the company of ἑταῖραι; and without much blame, provided that they did not neglect their wives, or outrage public decency. Concubines (παλλακαί) occupied a place between wives and ἑταῖραι. The relation was recognised by law and the children born, if the mother was a citizen (ἀστή), were free (ἐλεύθεροι), but not legitimate (γνήσιοι), *i.e.* they were not members of the father's family and φρατρία. The father could, if he chose, legitimise them (ποιεῖσθαι). Παλλακαί had no dowry (προίξ)—but in a case where the κύριος of a young woman gave her to a citizen ἐπὶ παλλακίᾳ, as happened in poorer families, some kind of settlement was made to protect her from being turned away without maintenance.

664. Once married, the woman was expected to live at home and give no trouble. She had to keep the house, to have custody of all the household stores and valuables, to govern the large establishment of slaves, to direct the women slaves in their work, spinning, weaving, etc. Her position, in its powers and limitations, has been compared with that of the mistress of a large establishment in the Slave States of North America before the Civil War. That these responsibilities were not light, or lightly regarded, is shown by Xenophon's enumeration in the *Oeconomicus* of the duties awaiting the young wife of Ischomachus, and by passages in the *Lysistrata* and the *Ecclesiazusae* of Aristophanes where the women cite their domestic efficiency as an incontrovertible proof of their ability to administer public affairs (*Lys.* 495; *Eccl.* 211–2, 236). But the wife's principal duty was to breed citizens to keep up her husband's house, and to educate the boys till the time came for them to go to school, and the girls till they were married. The best woman, says Pericles, is she of whom her neighbours know least for good or evil report. Xenophon says "it is not so good for a woman to be out of doors as in" (*Oec.* VII. 30), and the evidence of Athenian oratory and comedy points the same way. Her limit, says Menander, is the house door:

(Athens: (1) women at home.)

$$\pi\acute{\epsilon}\rho\alpha\varsigma\ \gamma\grave{\alpha}\rho\ \alpha\mathring{\upsilon}\lambda\epsilon\iota\circ\varsigma\ \theta\acute{\upsilon}\rho\alpha$$
$$\mathring{\epsilon}\lambda\epsilon\upsilon\theta\acute{\epsilon}\rho\alpha\ \gamma\upsilon\nu\alpha\iota\kappa\grave{\iota}\ \nu\epsilon\nu\acute{\circ}\mu\iota\sigma\tau'\ \circ\mathring{\iota}\kappa\acute{\iota}\alpha\varsigma.\ \text{(Frag. 546, Kock.)}$$

Wives were present at their husbands' meals. The wife sat on a chair (καθέδρα), the husband reclined on a sofa (κλίνη). Of social intercourse between women and men not of their own family hardly a trace is to be found, except in the case of Cimon's sister Elpinice, who was noted for her independence of mind. Men, except the father of the house and a few near relations, did not enter the γυναικωνῖτις; and it was not decorous for a woman to speak to any man in the street.

665. There were occasions on which women might appear out of doors without losing reputation, and married women had some duties and amusements outside the house. They sometimes went marketing, attended by a servant, and paid visits to one another at luncheon time (ἄριστον) and in the morning or afternoon. They

(Athens: (2) women abroad.)

could resort occasionally to the public baths; a fragment of an Attic vase in the Louvre shows a women's swimming-bath, possibly the well-house of the Enneacrounos. They were admitted to the theatre when tragedies were performed. They took part in certain religious services and processions; in some, such as the ἀρρηφορία and the Panathenaic procession, even unmarried women took part. These were also admitted to παννυχίδες, a common occasion for lovers' meetings in the New Comedy (cf. Cic. de Legg. ii. xiv). In Terence's Andria it is the presence of a young girl at a funeral which starts the plot in motion. The evidence of inscriptions does something to modify the impression that women had no life outside the family. Records of dedications, priestesses and religious associations prove that religion offered some scope for activity. At Aspendus a woman held the office of δημιουργός (cf. Pauly-Wissowa, s.v.). In a humbler social rank women commonly engaged in trade; a list of forty-six freedwomen provides thirty-five weavers, one shoemaker, one cobbler, and there are also keepers of general stores, sellers of frankincense, sesame and tow. Readers of Aristophanes will remember the widowed garland-seller in the *Thesmophoriazusae* and the redoubtable landlady in the *Frogs* (cf. also *Lys.* 457–8). The wives of poor men, as in the East, were unable to live in entire seclusion; and the conditions of country life lead everywhere to greater freedom.

666. There is little evidence that women were discontented with their cloistered life. Euripides has much to say in the *Medea* (cf. esp. vv. 213–251) of the hardship of domestic imprisonment; but he puts his criticisms into the mouth of Medea, hardly a typical wife and mother, and it is probable that her views would have been repudiated by the majority of women, who had no wish for the freedom enjoyed by women whose reputation for σωφροσύνη stood lower. Nor can time have hung heavy on their hands. Domestic work, which included grinding as well as baking, and the entire manufacture of the family's clothes, must have occupied much of every day, and when this was done there were amusements to pass the hours of leisure—conversation, telling stories, dancing (cf. Ar. *Lys.* 408–410), games such as ball (σφαῖρα), swing (αἰώρα), dolls (δαγῦδες, κοραί), knucklebones (ἀστράγαλοι), morra (διὰ δακτύλων), draughts (πεττεία), etc., and the care of pet animals (θρέμματα). In the well-known dialogue of the Syracusan women (Theocr. *Id.* xv), and in the Mimes of Herodas, seven of which portray women, it must be remembered that the women are Dorians, and that so much freedom might have seemed in bad taste at Athens. But the Hellenistic age showed everywhere a wider range of freedom for women, possibly in part a consequence of the conquest of Greece by the Macedonians, a people who seem to have retained something of the Homeric simplicity, and who, in the royal house at least, allowed their women considerable latitude.

667. It has been argued that the sentiment entertained towards women underwent a considerable change in the period covered by Greek literature, that, in short, it was not till the Hellenistic age that women inspired love in the modern sense of the

Amusements of women.

Sentiment about women.

term. It is true that romantic attachment between men and women does not receive special attention before the fourth century B.C. But it seems incredible that up to that time men were attracted to women only by sensuality or by matrimonial prudence. Hesiod, Archilochus, Semonides of Amorgos, Aristophanes, belittle woman as a "necessary evil," but it is unreasonable to look for sentiment in satire, and greater names may be set on the other side. Homer's pictures of Helen, and still more of Andromache, do not suggest a lack of chivalry: it is noticeable, for instance, that Hector in his parting is more concerned about his wife than about his little son; and the laments of the three women at the end of the *Iliad* bespeak, albeit incidentally, keen sympathy and understanding. Simonides has an equally sympathetic touch in the fragment about Danae. Stesichorus is credited with a romantic love-story, which is lost. In Pindar's ninth Pythian ode Apollo falls in love with the spirit of Cyrene, "this maiden with a heart which no toil can subdue, and a mind that no fear can overwhelm," no less than with her beauty. Aeschylus's Clytemnestra cannot be cited in evidence since hers is confessedly ἀνδρόβουλον κέαρ, but there are touches in his portrait of Io in the *Prometheus* which forbid one to place him with the indifferent. Sophocles could not have created his Antigone and Electra, still less his Deianeira and Tecmessa, had he never cared to study woman for her own sake. Euripides, who demonstrated in many plays a deep interest in woman's character, seems also to have painted a picture of romantic love in the lost *Andromeda*. Even Aristophanes, who in his later years took woman for his favourite laughing-stock, has enough insight and sympathy to lay his finger on the tragedy that war can be to her (cf. *Lys.* 596–7). It seems as though the apparent change of attitude were due less to a real change of feeling than to a change of taste. In Homer his "great good breeding," in fifth-century writers their preoccupation with really more important matters, masked or diverted their power to portray romantic passion. Convention, not insensibility, was the barrier. Euripides broke down convention here as elsewhere, and opened the way, which was made easier by the weakening of restraint observable everywhere in the Hellenistic civilization, to the full display of romantic sentiment which characterizes the New Comedy, Apollonius Rhodius, Theocritus, and the epigrammatists of the Anthology.

Becker-Göll, *Charikles*; Smith's *Dictionary of Greek and Roman Antiquities*, s.v. Matrimonium, Thesmophoria, etc.; Daremberg, Saglio and Bibliography. Pottier, *Dictionnaire des Antiquités grecques et romaines*, s.v. Matrimonium, etc.; Baumeister, *Denkmäler des klassischen Altertums* (list of articles on 'Leben und Sitten' on p. 2184); J. P. Mahaffy, *Social Life in Greece.* Cf. also G. Lowes Dickinson, *The Greek View of Life*; E. F. M. Benecke, *Women in Greek Poetry* (London, 1896); P. Gardner and F. B. Jevons, *Manual of Greek Antiquities* (London, 1895); Gustave Glotz, *Ancient Greece at Work* (London, 1926); P. E. Legrand, *Daos* (Paris, 1910); Helen McClees, *A Study of Women in Attic Inscriptions* (New York, 1920); A. E. Zimmern, *The Greek Commonwealth* (London, 1922, 3rd edition).

VII. 6. DRESS

668. OUR knowledge of prehistoric dress is based mainly on archaeo-logical evidence derived from the excavations in Crete and
Prehistoric Dress. on the Mainland of Greece. There are representations of men and women in frescoes (from Cnossus, Phaestus, My-cenae, Tiryns, Thebes) and on sealstones, there are statuettes in stone,

Fig. 140. Reconstructed drawing of Terracotta Statuette from Petsofa, Crete.

terracotta, bronze, faience, and ivory, and there are also jewels and other articles of personal adornment.

There are naturally variations in dress, worn for religious or ceremonial occasions, like the "sacral knot" (Fig. 142), or for sport. The men on the Hagia Triada sarcophagus wear cloaks of peculiar cut which may be animal skins, but in any case are worn for cult purposes. The women in the "Toreador" fresco from Cnossus wear the men's loin-cloth for the sport of bull-baiting. The principal article of male dress (Fig. 143) seems to have been a loin-cloth of varying shape, often dipping to a point or curve in front or back or both, and usually worn with a tight girdle and boots, buskins, or sandals. There is little change in this costume throughout the Middle

Fig. 141. Fresco of woman from the Palace of Hagia Triada.

and Late Bronze Age, but Tiryns frescoes of Late Helladic III date show some men wearing sleeved tunics. This has been held to indicate a difference in dress at this period between Crete and the Mainland.

The women's dress on the other hand shows a distinct change between Middle Minoan I and III. To the earlier date belong the clay figurines from Petsofa and Giouchtas. These wear a one-piece dress with a high Medici collar and sleeves reaching to the elbow (Fig. 140). At the waist it is held in by a rolled sash falling with two long ends down the centre of the skirt front where they probably covered a placket. On the head a high peaked cap was worn. Later by Middle Minoan III the costume became

Fig. 142. Fresco of girl from
Cnossus wearing "sacral knot."

Fig. 143. Fresco of Cupbearer
from Cnossus.

more elaborate with the progress of fashion (Figs. 141, 144, 145), and usually included: (1) a head-dress of varying shape; (2) a tight-fitting bodice which leaves both breasts exposed (on one fresco fragment, *c.* 1500 B.C., a vest may be indicated), stiffened by "bones" in front and fastened by a curved

pin with an ornamental knob; (3) a girdle; (4) a double apron cut high
on the hips with the back and front of approximately equal length; (5) a
skirt of bell shape cut with considerable flare so as to fit the hips closely
and give ample width at the feet. In the cut and decoration both of skirt and
bodice a good deal of originality was shown. The materials were most probably linen and wool, since silk and cotton were not then known. There

Fig. 144. 'Snake goddess' (faience statuette, restored) from Cnossus.

is strong evidence that much of the material used both for men and women
was ornamented with inwoven patterns of considerable variety (Figs. 141,
143). Bodices, aprons, skirts and loin-cloths were frequently bordered with
a narrow edging, possibly a beaded band or a woven braid. (Tapestry woven
ornament and robes occur in xviiith-dynasty Egypt.) Certain designs which
followed the shaped edges of a skirt or bodice can only have been added

after the garments were cut, by direct or applied embroidery in wool or linen.
Women's skirts might be varied in style by the use of flounces (Fig. 145),
usually pleated and applied to a foundation, or by tucks or cords, running
horizontally. The effect of divided skirts apparent in some representations
(Fig. 141), especially on gems, is probably due to the wearing of a skirt of
thin material, perhaps weighted by flounces or applied ornament, without
petticoats. The scale pattern (Fig. 145) frequently seen in the frescoes,
particularly on the Mainland, probably represents overlapping rosettes of
gold or silver leaf, such as have been found in large numbers in the tombs
of Mycenae. Similarly some of the ornamental borders may have been
formed by embossed bands of thin gold. On the Mainland in Late Helladic
III tombs small buttons of steatite are numerous and at all periods constant
use of jewellery was made, necklaces, rings, engraved sealstones, pins,
bracelets, armlets, frontlets, and diadems. For these gold and silver,
semi-precious stones like amethyst, crystal, amber, carnelian, and onyx,
faience, coloured glass, and ivory were employed. Both men and women
wore their hair long, sometimes twisted or coiled, sometimes elaborately
dressed in the shape of long waves and ringlets as in the Tiryns frescoes
(Fig. 145).

669. The Homeric poems took their characteristic shape in the period
of transition from the use of bronze to that of iron. The
'Age of Homer,' more recent than anything that can be
called Minoan or Mycenaean, was an age when the great
cities of which the poet sang were heaps of ruins and when men of a
different race were dominant. In Homeric story the garments of a household were woven by the lady of the house and her maidens. Athena
herself was pre-eminent in this art. The garments, each made as a thing
separate and complete in itself, were a valuable possession and took a
high place in the enumeration of the treasure of a house. The material
of which they were composed would seem in many cases to be wool,
sometimes linen.

Homeric dress.

The chief under-garment of men in Homer was the χιτών, apparently a
sewn shirt-like garment not fastened by pins and probably
made of linen as its glossiness is insisted upon. Under
armour men probably wore a kind of jerkin of rough wool
or leather to prevent abrasions of the skin. The outer garments of the
men in Homeric times comprised wraps made of the skins of animals
or of wool. These, the χλαῖνα, λώπη, etc., were oblong pieces of stuff
folded shawl-wise over the χιτών. They were early varieties of the ἱμάτιον
of historic times and were 'contrived a double debt to pay,' serving as bed-
coverings as well as clothes. To this class belong the σισύρα, the βαίτη and
others of the historic period.

Dress of men in Homer.

The χιτών, both of wool and linen, seems to have been of two kinds.
That worn by Menelaus was short, but the Ionians were specially mentioned as ἑλκεχίτωνες. A girdle was worn with the short variety; the trailing

kind seems to be ungirdled, a custom preserved down to historic times
for solemn occasions.

Women in Homer seem also to have confined themselves to two kinds
of garments, one under, one upper. They wore as an under-   Dress of
garment the πέπλος, probably the equivalent of the 'Dorian'   women in
chiton of later Greece (Figs. 146, 150). As distinguished   Homer.

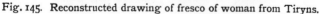

Fig. 145. Reconstructed drawing of fresco of woman from Tiryns.

from the sewn chiton of the men it was a piece of stuff fastened with pins.
It was probably left open at one side and without sleeves, as the white
arms of the women are mentioned. It was evidently long; ἑλκεσίπεπλος
is an epithet of the Trojan dame. The women's outer wrap was a veil-like

piece of stuff, κρήδεμνον, καλύπτρη. This was no doubt an oblong piece of fine woollen or linen material thrown on and off at will.

670. In the dress of the Historic period in Greece we find the ἐνδύματα and ἐπιβλήματα forming the chief classes of garments, with the subdivisions of the Dorian and the Ionian modes. For literary evidence as to the dress of these times we must rely especially on the statements of Thucydides concerning the men's garments and of Herodotus concerning those of the women.

Dress of historic times.

Thucydides notices (1) the oldest period when armour was universally worn—a fashion surviving in the historian's own day only in the wilder parts of Greece; (2) the succeeding period when flowing robes of Oriental fashion were the mode, and (3) the 'present fashion' (*circa* 431 B.C.) of simple woollen garments of the Dorian kind. In the first period the armour may have been worn over a leather or woollen

Thucydides on the dress of the men (i. 6).

Fig. 146. Dorian chiton open at the side[1].

Fig. 147. Women wearing the Ionian chiton.

[1] Figs. 146, 148, 149, 150, 151, 152, 153 are reproduced from F. Studniczka, *Beiträge zur Geschichte der altgriechischen Tracht*, by permission of Carl Gerold's Sohn Verlag.

χιτών as we gather from Homer. The second period recalls the Ἰάονες ἑλκεχίτωνες of Homer when long trailing robes of linen in the Ionian mode were worn. The third period witnesses the practical and useful revival of the short woollen χιτών—called 'Dorian,' which had been pre-served from early times among such Dorian people as the Spartans, and was eagerly adopted throughout Greece in the burst of Hellenic patriotism and the reaction against things Oriental that set in with the victories over the Persians. But at the same time the long Ionian robes were not altogether discarded, but worn as a dress for religious and ceremonial occasions and by certain functionaries as flute-players, charioteers, etc.

Herodotus (v. 87) gives an account of the Athenian women changing their Dorian garments for the Ionian dress, a sewn garment requiring no pins.

When we come to the more valuable evidence of the monuments we may conclude that in historic times the earlier form of women's dress was generally of a sewn kind, while after the Persian wars (490—479 B.C.) the Dorian or pinned kind appears (Figs. 146, 148, 150, 151). In Athens, probably about the first half of the sixth century B.C. the Ionian kind came into vogue (Fig. 147, 153) and was worn contemporaneously with the Dorian till about the time of the Persian wars. Then, when anything savouring of Orientalism fell into disfavour, the Dorian fashion was more generally worn: although even then, the Ionian garment does not seem to have been absolutely discarded by women any more than by men. *Evidence of the monuments.*

671. It is now time to describe in detail, from the evidence of the monuments, the garments worn near or next the skin—the ἐνδύματα of historic times—the Dorian and the Ionian chiton both of men and women. As the difference between these garments for both sexes is but trifling they may well be considered together. *Garments of historic Greece.*

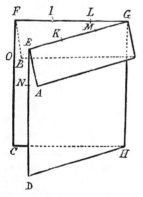

Fig. 148. Scheme of the open
Dorian chiton.

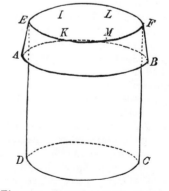

Fig. 149. Scheme of the closed
Dorian chiton.

The 'Dorian' or woollen chiton of the women (corresponding in the main with the πέπλος of Homer) was composed of a large square piece of material *ABCD* (Fig. 148), which in the direction *AD* and *BC* was about a foot longer than the height of the wearer, and in the direction *BA*, *CD* as wide as the span from tip to tip of the hands with the arms stretched out to their greatest extent; *e.g.* for a woman of 5 ft 6 in. tall, the size would be about 6 ft. 6 in. × 5 ft. 6 in. To form the chiton this piece is taken and the upper edge of it folded over (ἀπόπτυγμα, διπλοΐς, διπλοΐδιον) about the depth of the space from the neck to the waist *AE*, *BF*. Then the whole piece is doubled at *GH* and the lengths *FG*, *EG* are divided into three. It

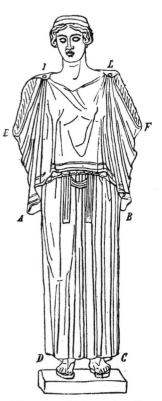

Fig. 150. Girl wearing the closed Dorian chiton.

is generally assumed that these were three equal parts, but in practice, this leaves too much for the neck. The Greeks of a later period (200—168 B.C.) got over this defect by introducing 'gathers.' In the earlier period a pleated fold was introduced in the middle section *KM* and may have been secured by a pin. The points *I*, *L*, *K*, *M* being taken the garment is folded round the body, these points are made to correspond and are fastened together on the shoulders by pins. Thus one side of the garment, *GH*, is closed and the side *AED*, *BFC* is left open (Fig. 148). After putting on the chiton the wearer stands with extended arms and a girdle is passed round the waist from behind, the superfluous length being pulled up through the girdle and allowed to hang over it in a kind of bag (κόλπος). The open side was frequently closed by sewing or pins either partially at *DN*, *CO* (Fig. 148) or wholly (Figs. 150, 149). Sometimes the piece of apoptygma falling down the back was drawn over the head veil-wise.

Another way of dealing with the square of material is to omit the folding over of *AE*, *BF* and to take points parallel to *IL*, *KM* in the upper edge of the unfolded stuff, thus having no apoptygma, and then to draw the whole superfluous length through the girdle. Or the piece folded over at *AE*, *BF* may be so deep that no girdle is required, since there is no extra length left to be drawn through it. A third method, which goes by the

name of the 'peplos of Athena' is given in Figs. 151, 152.   In that
case the girdle is put on outside a larger apoptygma than in Fig. 148,
and no hanging κόλπος is drawn up.   The 'Dorian' chiton was made of
fine wool.   The sleeve was formed, as desired, by placing buttons or pins
at intervals from *IKLM* downwards to the elbow.   Elaborate girdlings of
extra cords crossed on the breast and attached to the waist girdle are often
shown in Art.   It is not always easy to distinguish sharply on monuments
between the closed Dorian chiton and the Ionian variety.   A large class of
examples seems to fall somewhere between the two.   These may have
been adapted for artistic purposes and not necessarily be an exact
reproduction of the dress of daily life.   The distinctive feature of the
'Dorian' chiton consists in the pins seen on the shoulders.   From this
feature it received the name περονατρίς.

The Dorian chiton for men was on the same lines as that for
women, but not so wide and reaching only to the knee or
calf.   It had no διπλοΐς.   The part below the girdle was   Dorian chiton
sewn together, the upper part was connected on the shoul-   of the men.
ders by fibulae or buttons.   Slaves and workmen only fastened it on
one shoulder, ἐξωμίς, ἐτερομάσχαλος χιτών.   The original pin used for
the fastening of garments among primitive peoples was made from the

Fig. 151.   From the Varvakeion
statuette.

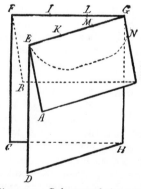

Fig. 152.   Scheme of the peplos
of Athena.

small bone of an animal's leg, hence its name 'περόνη' or 'fibula.'   This
was next introduced in metal, mounted with a bronze head and decorated
with balls of bronze.   The point may have been bent back to prevent it

from slipping out, and from this bending back the developed form of 'fibula,' of which the modern 'safety-pin' is the lineal descendant, may come.

672. The Ionian chiton was entirely without pins, being a sewn garment very like a sleeved night-gown made of linen (Fig. 153).

The Ionian chiton.

The piece of material required is about a foot less in height than for the 'Dorian' chiton. It may consist of two pieces, one for the front and another for the back, or of one piece double the size of these and folded. The sewing to close the seams follows the dotted lines (Fig. 153). The distance from A to B being half the full span of the wearer, a long hanging sleeve is obtained (Fig. 147). The girdling is on the same principle as for the 'Dorian' chiton, the superfluous length forming a kolpos. This garment was the same both for men and women. The long chiton remained as the dress of men of middle life and was also used by younger men on solemn or religious occasions. The material of the 'Ionian' chiton is a finely crinkled kind of linen, elastic in nature, similar to a stuff still woven by Greek peasants. It is finished with a selvage, not a hem, and from its elasticity

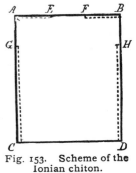

Fig. 153.   Scheme of the Ionian chiton.

would close round the neck of the wearer, after the head had been inserted. The chiton, in its varieties, is sometimes cut short so as only to reach the knee for women when active exercise is desired. Iris, Artemis and the Amazons are so attired in Art. In Sparta, from their twelfth year men wore, winter and summer, as an only dress the 'τρίβων,' i.e. the small oblong coarse mantle of the Doric tribes. This was also worn in Athens as a special dress for active military service, but it was considered boorish for fashionable persons to wear it. The women of Sparta seem to have gone abroad in a short chiton only.

The ζώνη is an important feature of the women's dress in Homer. In Art the height at which the girdle is set is a fair guide to the date of the monuments. In archaic Art it is placed at the line of the waist. About 450 B.C. it goes slightly below this, as in the dress of the maidens of the Parthenon frieze. By degrees it is placed higher till, as time goes on, it reaches the arm-pits. Ladies inclined to stoutness restrained the exuberance of their figures by a broad band (στρόφιον) worn under the chiton.

The girdle.

673. The class of ἐπιβλήματα for men and women in historic Greece comprises all outer garments of the shawl or wrap class. The chief of these is the ἱμάτιον, worn both by men and women In shape it is a large square or oblong, varying in size according to taste and weather. Women often drew it over the head as a covering, and in deep grief muffled the face

Outer garments of both men and women in historic times.

with it.   The general rule for its arrangement in classical times for both
men and women seems to have been as follows :—One corner of the piece

Fig. 154.   Sophocles in the Lateran, Rome.

of stuff is folded or gathered up and grasped by the hand, pulled over the
left shoulder from the back, tucked in securely and held firmly between the
body and the left upper arm pressing against the ribs.   Then with the right

hand the mantle is pulled out across the wearer's back by its right-hand top corner, opposite the corner already secured, till the lower edge of the garment hangs about half-way across the calf of the leg. Then the wrap is brought round over the right side of the body, ἐπιδέξια ἀναβάλλεσθαι ἐλευθέρως, when two ways of disposing of the right-hand corner are possible, viz.:—(1) If the right hand and arm are wanted to be free, the mantle is brought under the right shoulder, drawn across the chest and the end thrown over the left shoulder. (2) In the way considered more suitable for honourable citizens, the mantle is brought over the right arm and shoulder (the arm being bent at the elbow), so that only the right hand appears in a sling-like fold in the front, and then the end is thrown over the left shoulder (Fig. 154). Weights of lead or clay were affixed to the corners of garments to keep them in position. The correct adjustment of the ἱμάτιον was considered an index to a man's character. Judged from the monuments, women often drew the outer folds of the himation over the head as a hood or veil and passed the garment over instead of under the right shoulder. When worn by ladies the ἱμάτιον often bears the name ἀμπεχόνη or φᾶρος.

A narrow, doubled ἱμάτιον, put on cloak-wise from the back, appears on archaic vase-paintings. The χλαμύς, a wrap for men in active work, originated in Thessaly as a rider's cloak worn over armour. From the fifth century it was universal in Greece as the dress of young men serving in the cavalry or for active daily life. It was a short, light, oblong mantle, the corners square or rounded, fastened with a clasp in front or on the shoulder. Women wore a pretty variety of the χλαμύς, the δίπλαξ, a square of stuff doubled and clasped cloak-wise.

674. Children seem as a rule to have worn miniature editions of the dress of their elders. Girls wear the 'Dorian' or 'Ionian' χιτών, while boys wear the short χιτών only or are muffled closely in large ἱμάτια. Frequently in Art boys are depicted without any clothes at all. Infants were closely swaddled, Italian fashion, and wore conical caps.

Dress of children.

In Greek Art foreigners are generally represented as wearing ἀναξυρίδες and long sleeves. These long sleeves to the wrist are also, in the case of women, the mark of the slave.

Dress of foreigners.

675. The men's garments appear to have been made both of wool and linen—the former for the generally worn Dorian, the latter for the less used Ionian style. For all their clothes women seem to wear thinner and lighter materials than men whether in wool or linen. The muslins of Amorgos are mentioned in Attic comedy and the garments of Cos were specially delicate and transparent. These were probably not worn by dignified matrons except in the strict seclusion of their homes. In early art and up to the time of the Persian wars a soft crinkled crape-like material, presumably of linen, with a selvage edge, is used for women's garments. After the time of Pheidias this

Materials.

disappears and a plain surfaced stuff finished with a hem takes its place. Besides wool and cotton, βύσσos, an expensive material, woven doubtless as in modern Taranto from the silky thread of the Pinna shell, was used for veils and the like. Silk was spun and woven at Cos but was extremely dear in Alexandrian times and may have been imported. Garments depicted on Greek vases are often elaborately fringed and embroidered. The χιτών and ἱμάτιον of the men seem to have been white or neutral in tint as a rule. Workmen and field-labourers wore brown. The women's clothes were much more gay in tone, white, saffron, red, blue and green, and are shown as in Art, often with check patterns and devices of animals, birds and stars introduced. Colours of materials.

676. The hair of the men in Homeric times is long. Thucydides mentions the long hair of the Athenians, with the ornament in the form of the τέττιξ. He may allude to a fibula or clasp of that form, or may mean that the heavy braid of hair hanging down the back was bound round and round with gold till it resembled the ringed body of the tettix (tree cricket). The long hair of athletes in Greek art is so bound, or plaited in one or two long tails and wound round the head. From the time of the Persian wars the more convenient custom of short hair prevailed in Greece for men. The younger gods at this time appear in art without beards. A boy on reaching manhood generally dedicated his long locks of hair in the temple of a river-god. In early times full beards were worn. The Macedonian victors introduced the fashion of shaving, but the short beard is often found in Athenian art of Macedonian times. The beard was proverbially, also, the mark of the philosopher. Foreigners generally wear both a beard and a moustache in Greek art. The hair of the women was dressed in many elaborate styles, waved, plaited and crimped. Young girls wore theirs loose and flowing. Hair-pins of gold and other materials are found in women's graves. As a woman's head-dress, the 'Greek fillet' wound several times round the head is proverbial. The στεφάνη or circlet of metal, the σφενδόνη (or sling), the ἄμπυξ, a circlet used to keep the hair-net secure, and the σάκκος or bag-net were all adjuncts of hair-dressing that may be studied on the coins of Syracuse. Hair.

677. When walking about the city near home no hats or caps seem to have been worn by either sex, indeed in the case of the women their elaborately-dressed hair would have suffered from any weight greater than a light veil or the corner of the ἱμάτιον drawn over the head. On journeys women sometimes, as appears from the statuettes found at Tanagra, wore a coquettish variety of the men's πέτασος, i.e. the flat felt hat with flaps at the back and front and over the ears. This hat, with the χλαμύς or cloak, was the usual attire of young men in Greece for hunting or travelling. Artisans or fisher folk wore the πῖλος, a conical cap of felt or leather. Charon, Hephaestos and Odysseus wear it in Art. Umbrellas are found in Greek Art, but do not seem, so far as Coverings of the head.

can be judged, to have been used as a protection against rain. They are often carried by an attendant.

678. In their houses the Greeks seem to have gone barefoot, especially in summer. Out of doors they wore the σανδάλιον or ὑπόδημα, a simple sole tied on by thongs of leather passing between the toes. For hard country walking and for hunting the sole was set round with leather somewhat in modern fashion; interlaced thongs arising from this 'upper' were bound round the leg as high as the calf. These were the ἐνδρομίδες. The κόθορνος was also a high boot reaching to the middle of the leg with very thick soles. As worn by tragic actors, its heels served to add height to the figure. The ἐμβάς was a kind of felt shoe worn by the poorer classes and by such rough country-folk as the Boeotians. On entering a house it was customary for everyone to uncover the feet. Shoes were left at the door when paying calls, as nowadays in the East. Women seem to have adopted the περσικαί or slippers of the East, according to Aristophanes.

Coverings of the feet.

679. From what has been said it will be inferred that, judged by modern standards, Greek dress of the classical period was of a very scanty sort, consisting as it did of squares of material draped about the body. Garments so adjusted can only have remained in position in repose, and must have been very troublesome in active life. But quiet dignity was a sign of high breeding among the Greeks. If the climate of Greece was in ancient times at all what it is to-day there must have been many stormy days when additional wraps would be necessary and no doubt were worn. Philosophers and persons affecting an extreme simplicity of dress and manners usually wore a himation only without any other garment summer or winter. Male slaves and persons doing hard manual work wore the short woollen chiton alone. Anyone wearing the χιτών alone was reckoned as being γυμνός, the term not necessarily implying absolute nudity but meaning simply 'lightly clothed.' Women indoors seem to have been content with the χιτών only, throwing on the ἱμάτιον when out of doors. As to the generally scanty clothing we can only assume that exposure of the body in the case of men was not considered in the same light as by us, and remember that the climate was a southern one and that the women lived almost entirely separate from the men and did not share in their pursuits.

Conclusion.

Prehistoric Dress:—A. Evans, *Palace of Minos*, I–III, 1921–1930; A. J. B. Wace, *A Cretan Statuette in the Fitzwilliam Museum*, 1927; G. Rodenwaldt, *Tiryns*, II, 1912; D. Mackenzie, *B.S.A.* XII, pp. 233 ff.; J. L. Myres, *B.S.A.* IX, pp. 356 ff.; *Monumenti Antichi*, XIII, 1903, pp. 59 ff., Pl. X.

Classical Dress:—F. Studniczka, *Beiträge zur Geschichte der altgriechischen Tracht*, Vienna, 1886; J. Boehlau, *Quaestiones de Re Vestiaria Graecorum*, Weimar, 1884; W. Müller, *Quaestiones Vestiariae*, Göttingen, 1890; J. C. B. Mohr, *Lehrbuch der griech. Privatalterthümer*, Freiburg, 1882; Friederich, *Die Tracht bei Homer*, Erlangen, 1856; Maria Millington Evans, *Chapters on Greek Dress*, Macmillan, 1893; *Jahrbuch des Kaiserlich Deutschen Archäologischen Instituts*, Band XI. 1896, p. 19, article by A. Kalkmann; E. B. Abrahams, *Greek Dress*, Murray, 1908; M. Bieber, *Griechische Kleidung*, Berlin, 1928; G. M. A. Richter, *Silk in Greece* (American Journal of Archaeology, Vol. XXXIII, pp. 27 ff.).

Bibliography.

VII. 7. DAILY LIFE, ITS SURROUNDINGS, EMPLOYMENTS
AND AMUSEMENTS.

A. TOWN LIFE.

680. WE cannot draw any rigid line between town and country life in Greece in early times. There, as elsewhere, those employed in tilling the fields lived together in villages for the sake of greater security, and went out to their work, often a considerable distance away. It will, however, be more convenient to treat the employments and amusements of the town apart from those of the country, as well as to describe separately the conditions and surroundings of the two. A Greek town was as a rule placed in a position which was a compromise between various conflicting advantages. In the first place it must *General* *aspect and* be near some fertile plain, which could supply the food of *arrangement* the community; then it must be, if possible, within reach *of a Greek* *town.* of the sea, which was from the earliest times the chief medium of communication and commerce; at the same time it must be secure from attack, whether by land or sea. Hence we find it is usually clustered round some isolated rocky hill, which served as the dwelling-place of the king in early times, and was extensive enough to shelter his subjects, and often their flocks and herds as well, in times of danger. It is usually at such a distance from the sea that it could not be surprised by a sudden raid of enemies or pirates. Such an arrangement necessitated a harbour town, usually some three or four miles distant; as in the case of Athens, Megara, Corinth, Argos, and other cities. The practice of surrounding the lower town as well as the citadel with a wall was almost universal in later times, and is probably to be associated with the growing importance of the people. In many cases the citadel ceased to be regarded as a fortress, and became the centre of public worship, containing the most sacred shrines and the most valuable dedications; this was especially the case with the Acropolis at Athens. At the same time the city was in some cases, at Athens and Megara for example, connected with the harbour town by long walls, and thus made practically unassailable by land so long as it kept control of the sea.

681. As the palace had been the centre of life for the subjects and vassals of a king, so the agora became in later times the *The agora.* centre of life for the citizens. The influence of this change upon the position of temples and other religious buildings is mentioned above (§ 417). In most old towns the agora was in some convenient and accessible spot in the midst of the city; it was usually of irregular shape, being at first without any definite boundaries, and becoming gradually shut in by the porticoes, law-courts, and other public buildings that grew up around it.   In the case of towns which were deliberately planned out, we find a square or oblong agora, surrounded by regular porticoes; such was known as the Ionic agora, and was prevalent in the rich Ionic cities of Asia Minor; but this form was unusual on the mainland of Greece, except in the case of towns, like Megalopolis, which were founded at a late date.   The agora was originally the place of public meeting for the citizens, as well as the market-place; it was filled with temporary stalls and booths for traders, which could be cleared away on emergency. Parts of it were assigned to different trades, and called after the goods sold there; and a large town, such as Athens, had smaller special markets besides the chief one.   In addition to the agora or agorae, the temene or precincts of temples would be the chief open spaces in a town; these were rigorously protected from encroachment either by walls or by boundary stones.

682.   Apart from such open spaces the houses were closely crowded together and the streets were narrow.   One recently ex-

Houses and streets.

cavated at Athens, which was certainly an important thoroughfare, and possibly the main road from the agora to the Acropolis, is only about 15 feet wide.   Hence the streets of an ancient town must have had a very mean appearance, especially as the private houses usually showed blank walls on the outside; of course a street that ran beside sacred precincts or public buildings was more imposing, especially if it were bordered by dedications, as was the Street of the Tripods at Athens.   The temple with its adjacent temenos, and also the normal private house are described elsewhere (§§ 417, 710); but it must be remembered that a great part of the dense population of ancient cities cannot have commanded the space necessary for such arrangements.   In early times the possession of a hearth and home of his own was probably a necessary qualification of a citizen; but house property, not for occupation but for investment, is a regular institution in classical times; such property was often in the form of συνοικίαι, or common dwelling-places for the poor; such a συνοικία was under the charge of a man called the ναύκληρος, who looked after the tenants, collected their rent, and acted as steward to the owner.   Those who had no civic rights could not acquire landed property, and so were obliged to hire the houses or rooms in which they lived; and probably the poorer citizens, who had mortgaged or lost their property, were often reduced to the same manner of living.

683.   Town life was mostly divided between political duties, society,

Town life. Divisions of the day.

and recreation—except of course in the case of those engaged in commerce, and artisans and others who were classed together by the Greeks as βάναυσοι.   The day was divided into three portions in early times; cf. *Il.* XXI. 111 ἔσσεται ἢ ἠὼς ἢ δείλη ἢ μέσον ἦμαρ. The later division implies that the frequenting of the agora (πλήθουσα ἀγορά), whether for business or conversation, was the most important condition of daily life. If there was a political assembly, or if a man was serving on a jury, or if there was a great religious festival, everything else had to give way to the event of the day; but on ordinary occasions the course of an Athenian citizen's life seems to have been much as follows. He rose about dawn, or earlier, if necessary, and washed either with the help of a slave, who poured water from a jug over a basin, or at one of the public fountains in the streets. He also took his ἀκράτισμα (§ 692). Then he took exercise, at home or in the gymnasia, or paid calls, until it was time for him to go to the agora. This early part of the day was commonly referred to as πρωΐ. Then came the time known as πλήθουσα ἀγορά, which lasted till about noon. This, as the name implies, was the time when the market was frequented, when business was done, and when news was discussed or conversation on more serious subjects was carried on. In bad weather people would congregate in the porticoes that surrounded the agora, and even in the shops; in winter, those were most popular which required a fire, such as smithies or the furnaces of baths. Boys and young men, who as a rule avoided the agora itself, were also in the habit of loitering about the shops. At mid-day (μεσημβρία) the agora became deserted (ἀγορᾶς διάλυσις); it was usual to take a meal of some sort, though this was not of a formal character, nor was it necessary to go home for it. Probably many people contented themselves with buying some of the food usually hawked about the agora, and ate it on the spot, or in a convenient shop. The practice of a siesta at mid-day, now so universal during hot weather in Southern Europe, appears to have been regarded with as much disfavour in Athens of the fifth and fourth centuries as by Hesiod; it was about mid-day probably that places of resort such as the barbers' shops (κουρεῖα) were most frequented, and also the λέσχαι, which corresponded in some ways to a modern café, in others to a club; while the early afternoon was spent in the gymnasia or the baths. So the time was passed until the approach of sunset brought the hour of the evening meal (δεῖπνον), which was more of a formal and social function, and was usually taken either at home or at the house of a friend. In most cases this meal was probably a moderate one, and the habit of early rising seems to imply an habitually early bed-time. But on special occasions, a banquet might be followed by a drinking-bout (συμπόσιον), and by entertainments or conversation that lasted far into the night, or even, as the famous Symposium of Plato, till the next morning. It was probably an unusual thing to pursue any serious employment after the evening meal; but a few studious and literary people worked late at night, and such a practice was probably necessary to those whose whole day was taken up with political and social duties. Technically speaking, the day ran from sunset to sunset. The night had divisions as well as the day; for military and naval

Divisions of the night.

purposes it was divided into watches; generally it was considered as consisting of three portions; cf. *Il.* x. 253

$$\pi\alpha\rho\acute{\omega}\chi\eta\kappa\epsilon\nu \ \delta\grave{\epsilon} \ \pi\lambda\acute{\epsilon}\omega\nu \ \nu\grave{\upsilon}\xi$$
$$\tau\hat{\omega}\nu \ \delta\acute{\upsilon}o \ \mu o\iota\rho\acute{\alpha}\omega\nu, \ \tau\rho\iota\tau\acute{\alpha}\tau\eta \ \delta' \ \acute{\epsilon}\tau\iota \ \mu o\hat{\iota}\rho\alpha \ \lambda\acute{\epsilon}\lambda\epsilon\iota\pi\tau\alpha\iota.$$

These parts were called ἕσπερος or περὶ λύχνων ἁφάς, μέσαι νύκτες, and ὄρθρος. The divisions were not of course accurate either in the case of the night or of the day; time was reckoned by sundials or by the length of the shadow thrown by a vertical staff, and later by a water-clock. The twelve divisions of the day were known to Herodotus as a Babylonian invention; but they were not in practical use, nor was the word ὥρα applied to them until Roman times.

B. COUNTRY LIFE—AGRICULTURE, ETC.

684. The circumstances of country life in Greece were to a great degree dependent upon social and political conditions. We have already noticed how closely town and country life were connected in early times; the constant risk of invasion, when all the inhabitants had to take refuge within the walls of the towns, and the great number of independent cities, each with its little area of cultivated ground around it, tended to perpetuate these primitive conditions. A concentration (συνοικισμὸς) such as that of Attica, attributed to Theseus, would of course tend to cut off a class residing in the city from the country people, and factions like those of the coast, the mountain and the plain seem to indicate local sympathies; but they were over-ridden by Cleisthenes' redistribution of the demes; every citizen, whether of a town or country deme, had equal political rights, and came to Athens to exercise them; and the policy of Pericles, by which the whole country was left deserted to the invading enemy, and all the population concentrated behind the walls of Athens and the Peiraeus would not have been possible if a country life was recognised as a distinct profession. In his famous speech Pericles refers to country houses as an ἐγκαλλώπισμα πλούτου, which the owners must be ready to give up. Some men, indeed, like Xenophon when he settled at Scillus, lived altogether the life of a country gentleman; but such exclusion from political life was exceptional, and was regarded as reprehensible. Even Xenophon's Ischomachus was often to be met in Athens. Country houses probably did not differ essentially from town houses, except that they were less cramped for space, and included store-rooms and farm offices. Farms were mainly worked by slave labour, the stewardess (ταμία), who had charge of the household goods, being an important functionary both in Homeric and in historical times; a foreman (ἐπίτροπος) also was necessary to supervise work in the master's absence. It was possible, by closing a door, to separate the apartments of the male and the female slaves; but it does not follow that there were two separate courts ; sometimes the women's quarters were in a kind of tower that could be closed (Dem. *in Euerg.* 53).

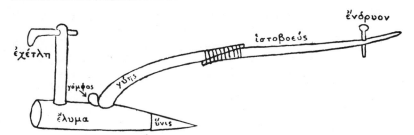

Fig. 155. Hesiod's plough—*Works and Days*, 427—436.

Fig. 156. Ploughing; from a vase by Nicosthenes.

685. The chief agricultural products of Greece were, as they are now,
Agriculture.   corn and wine and oil.   The plough was generally used for
breaking up the ground.   Hesiod's description of a plough
(Fig. 155) (ἄροτρον) would probably apply to historical times, and all its parts
can easily be recognised on vase paintings (Fig. 156).   It might be either
πηκτόν, pieced together, or αὐτογυές, a natural trunk of a tree with a branch
growing out of it that would serve for the lower part of the pole.   In either
case it would have a plough-tail added by which it could be guided.
Oxen were generally used for draught; the system by which they were
fastened to the yoke, and the yoke fixed by thongs (μέσαβον) and a ring
(κρίκος) to a peg (ἔνδρυον) inserted in the end of the pole was the same as
in a waggon or chariot.   Hesiod also gives instructions for making a waggon
(ἅμαξα, Att. ἅμαξα).   The usual digging instrument was the mattock.

Of the cereals, barley (κρίθος) and wheat (σῖτος) are most commonly
mentioned.   Harvest time in Greece is from April to May in the plains,
and about a month later in the mountainous regions.   Corn was cut with the
sickle (δρέπανον), and then bound into sheaves.   Thrashing was usually
done by means of cattle treading out the corn, and winnowing followed,
with the help of a shovel (πτύον) on a breezy day.   Another winnowing
instrument was the fan or basket (λίκνον).

686.   Vines in Greece are now almost exclusively dwarf plants, requiring
no supports, except when they are grown for shade on pergolas.
Vines, olives,   This was probably the case in ancient times also; for there
fruit.   is usually no indication of trellises and other supports on
vase-paintings, where vine branches frequently appear.   The Italian custom
of training vines on trees was not usual in Greece.   The vintage comes in
September, about the beginning of the month in the plains, towards the
end of it in the hills.   The grapes were picked in baskets, and trodden
in wine presses (ληνός), of which some ancient specimens still survive.
They consist of a cemented floor, surrounded by low walls, and sloping
towards one side, where there is an outlet leading into a sunk vessel.
The wine was then stored in jars (πίθοι) to ferment.   (For the use and preservation of wine see § 691.)   Olives were gathered in late autumn.   They
were first crushed (θλάω) beneath a heavy stone wheel which worked in
a circular trough, and then they were put in baskets, and squeezed
(ἐκπιέζω) beneath a long wooden lever, or sometimes, in later times, a
screw press.   Remains of these have been found in Asia Minor and
Cyprus.   Many kinds of fruit were grown, the commonest being figs,
apples, and pomegranates.

687.   Fruit trees imply the existence of orchards, and vegetable gardens
Gardens.   must also have existed both for private use and for the
supply of the market, though doubtless the ancient Greeks,
like their modern successors, depended to a great extent upon the wild
herbs that grow freely on the hills, and that are eaten both cooked and
raw.   The demand for flowers, especially for making wreaths, must also

have necessitated extensive flower-gardens. The distinction between gardens for the production of what was required for the house or the market and pleasure-gardens probably did not exist in early times; the earliest pleasure-gardens seem to have been laid out about temples and springs; they were often sacred to Aphrodite, as the κῆποι at Athens. It was not until the Hellenistic age that the custom began of laying out gardens in towns around houses; this practice was attributed to the influence of Epicurus. But the variety and artificiality ascribed to the *ars topiaria* of the Romans was only gradually developed, partly, perhaps, under oriental influence.

688. Cattle, sheep, goats and pigs were all kept for food, and sheep and goats for milk also. Cheese was commonly made, but not butter. Pasturage such as we are used to hardly exists in **Pasturage and hunting.** Greece, and the duty of the shepherd is to lead his flocks over the mountains, to crop what herbage can be found. Poultry and eggs also formed a staple article of food, and must have been supplied by farms. The chief amusement of country life was hunting, in which dogs were so essential as to give the sport its name (κυνηγετεῖν). Hares were coursed on foot with dogs, and driven into nets, and the same process was used for small deer. Boars were also hunted on foot with a spear. Birds, especially the smaller kind, were usually snared with nets. The bow was of course generally used for shooting game of all sorts; the λαγωβόλον or throwing stick was also used as a missile.

C. FOOD AND DRINK, MEALS, COOKING, AND ENTERTAINMENTS.

689. It appears at first sight that the Greeks of Homeric times were much more used to meat diet than their successors. At the feasts of the heroes whole sheep, pigs, and oxen are cut up **Food in Homer;** and devoured; and the custom is shared by the common **abundance of meat.** people also, *e.g.* by Eumaeus in the *Odyssey*, though it would appear not only extravagant but coarse and brutal to a later Greek. Fish is caught and eaten in the time of Homer, but only by those who can get nothing better; a reduction to a fish diet is regarded as a painful strait, in great contrast to the ideas of later times. Bread is eaten with the meat, and barley meal is sprinkled over it before cooking; but we do not hear much of vegetables—except onions, which are eaten with wine. Meat, however, seems to be the main article of food. In later Greece, on the other hand, farinaceous food, in some form or other, is always regarded as the essential thing, and what **Later cus-** is taken with it, whether meat, fish, cheese or other vege- **tom; farina-** tables, is called ὄψον; in fact the history of this word, which **ceous diet and** originally meant boiled meat, but was later specially applied **ὄψον.**

to fish, and even to a flavouring like salt, is an indication of the change of custom.

690. Attica did not grow enough grain for its own consumption, and consequently the command of the Hellespont was essential to Athens, in order to secure the supply from the regions round the Black Sea. The meal used was mostly of wheat and barley; the former was, of course, the usual material for making bread (ἄρτος); the latter was often made into a kind of porridge. The bread also was either made with yeast or without; in the latter case it was probably made in thin cakes; but the more elaborate process was usual in refined society. Broth made of various kinds of beans and pulse was also much eaten. Such vegetable food, together with cheese (cheese made from ewes' or goats' milk), dried fish (τάριχος) such as was imported at Athens in large quantities, fresh fish (from the small fish called ἀφύη to the tunny (θύννος)), oysters and other shell-fish, olives, and other vegetables, figs and honey, probably formed the usual diet not only of the poorer classes, but also of well-to-do people. Meat

Meat from sacrifices.

was only eaten on the occasion of a sacrifice, in fact, the Greeks had no other word for an animal killed for food than ἱερεῖον, a victim for sacrifice. But the frequent religious festivals gave an opportunity to all classes to enjoy this luxury; and nothing prevented a rich man from offering sacrifices as often as he pleased, and feasting himself and his friends; while the parts of a victim which were the perquisite of the priest must usually have been sold by him to less wealthy customers. Game was also eaten by those who could obtain

Game, fish, etc.

it, whether by hunting themselves or by purchasing it; but this also was probably a luxury for special occasions rather than an article of daily food. The thrush and the hare—the latter still extraordinarily good in Greece—were the favourite dishes. Sausages made of blood and tripe were, as we know from Aristophanes, hawked about in the market, and so were commonly eaten by the poorer classes. Among the luxuries specially affected by richer people, beside game, lambs, and kids, were superior kinds of fish, for example eels from Lake Copais. Fish, indeed, was the luxury most affected by gourmets.

691. The Greeks usually regarded milk as the most primitive drink, but

Drinks, milk, etc.

did not make any extensive use of it; the milk used for cheese or other purposes was, as it is still in Greece, that of sheep or goats, that of cows being regarded as unwholesome. Butter was practically unknown, except for medicinal purposes, olive oil being universally used for cooking. To drink milk neat (ἄκρητον) is described in Homer as intemperate. The usual drink of all classes was wine, which

Wine.

was, then as now, made in almost all parts of Greece, though some places naturally had a higher reputation than others. The greatest quantity of wine was exported from the islands of Rhodes, Thasos, Samos, Lesbos, Cos and Chios. After the store-vats (πίθοι) were opened, at the festival of the πιθοιγία in early spring, it was transported, sometimes in skins (ἀσκός), sometimes in amphorae (ἀμφορεύς), of which the stamped handles, as well as the plaster stopping, served as the brand of the wine, and attested its origin and year of vintage. Age was of course a recommendation to wine; but it does not appear that the Greeks kept their wine so long as was usual among the Romans and is the custom among ourselves. Theocritus speaks of a wine four years old as if it were exceptional (VII. 147, XIV. 16); and it is quite possible that old wine (παλαιὸς οἶνος) may have often meant, in ancient, as in modern Greece, no more than two or three years old; in fact, anything but last year's vintage. Great care was taken in the preparation of wine for the table. It was always mixed with water immediately before serving; the most usual proportion appears to have been two of wine to three of water; but it varied very much according to the character of the wine and the taste of the drinkers; it was often cooled with snow in hot weather. Sometimes wine was boiled, which was supposed to make it less intoxicating; sometimes it was made into a sort of 'cup' by the addition of myrrh and other spices. The colours and characters of the various Greek wines seem to have been about the same as at the present day; they may be classified according to colour as black or red (μέλας, ἐρυθρός), white (λευκός) and yellow (κιρρός), or according to taste as dry, harsh, light, or sweet (αὐστηρός, σκληρός, λεπτός, γλυκύς).

An inferior kind of wine, drunk by slaves and peasants, was made by pouring water on the grape skins and squeezing them again, after the first juice had been pressed out; this was called δευτερίας or στεμφυλίτης. Pliny states also that the Greeks modified their wine by the addition of clay, marble, salt, or sea-water; some of these processes may be analogous to the modern custom of putting gypsum in wine to clear it; resin or pitch seems to have been sometimes put in wine, as is now the custom in many districts of Greece. Beer (ζῦθος) was known to the Greeks, but regarded as a barbarian product, and very rarely drunk by them.

Honey was used for all purposes for which we now use sugar, to sweeten both food and drink. The honeys of Hymettus **Honey.** and of Hybla were especially famous in ancient times; and both retain to the present day their characteristic flavour of wild thyme.

692. The names and times of the various meals in Greece at different periods are matters of some dispute and difficulty; the reason lies mainly in the fact that the tendency of meals to be **Times of** shifted to a later hour operated then as now, and that δεῖπνον, **meals.** like our dinner, was transferred from a mid-day to an evening meal. It followed as a natural result that the ἄριστον, which in Homeric times was usually taken early in the morning, came to be eaten at mid-day; the Homeric δόρπον or supper disappeared, as with us; and the breakfast, taken immediately on getting up, was the ἀκράτισμα, a piece of bread dipped in undiluted wine. This was, naturally, taken at home. The ἄριστον was a more or less informal meal like our lunch; busy people might eat it in

the agora, or wherever they happened to be, while more luxurious people went home for it; and in later times it became a sumptuous entertainment, as appears in the New Comedy; but the δεῖπνον was regularly eaten

Fig. 157. Greek banquet; from a vase by Duris.

either at home or at a friend's house; this was probably in earlier times the only meal at which elaborate cooking and serving was provided, and at which company was usually entertained.

Cooks. While rich men employed professional cooks of their own, a Sicilian corresponding to a French chef of to-day, it was customary for the masters of less pretentious households to hire their cook in the market when they were buying their provisions for a dinner-party. On ordinary occasions, and for the ἄριστον, the mistress of the house, assisted by her slaves, usually saw to the provision and the preparation of the food.

693. When a man had no guests, his wife might dine with him, seated on a chair while he reclined on a couch. The dinner (δεῖπνον) **Entertain-** was regularly served to guests in a room devoted to the **ments.** purpose, and called the ἀνδρών. Representations of banquets are common on vases (Fig. 157), and give a good notion of how they were arranged. The guests reclined upon couches, often long enough to hold two or occasionally three; each had his left arm and shoulder propped on pillows, his right being free to help himself to food or wine. The food was served upon small movable tables, usually square in earlier times, later three-legged and round. When the guests entered their sandals were removed and their feet washed by slaves; then they took their places, either as they chose or as the host bade them. Water was poured by a slave over their hands, and then a separate table was brought in for each pair of guests, with the dishes forming the first part of the dinner disposed upon it. These were usually of a very simple character in Athens, in contrast to the more luxurious diet of the Ionians and Sicilians, and were chosen for giving variety of flavouring to the bread with which they were eaten rather than as forming themselves a substantial meal. They were served cut into small pieces, so that knives were not required; nor were forks or spoons generally used, solid morsels being picked up delicately with the fingers, according to a recog- **Manner of eating.** nised etiquette, and sauces or other liquids being sopped up with a piece of bread (μυστίλη); bread-crumb (ἀπομαγδαλιά) was also used to clean the fingers, and afterwards thrown to the dogs.

694. Then these tables were removed, and others substituted, with fruit, cakes, and other dainties for desert (δεύτεραι τράπεζαι). The end of the dinner was marked by a libation of unmixed **Symposia.** wine (σπονδὴ ἀγαθοῦ δαίμονος) which corresponded to grace after meat; and then usually followed the after-dinner drinking-party (συμπόσιον). The wine was formally mixed and prepared in the presence of the company, usually in three craters, and a libation was first poured from each, (1) to the Olympian gods, (2) to the Heroes, and (3) to Zeus Soter. This religious process was, like other sacrifices, frequently accompanied by the flute; it thus afforded a pretext for the introduction of flute girls at banquets, though the practice was continued for the amusement of the guests.

Where conversation did not suffice for the entertainment of the company, they played games such as capping verses and asking riddles (σκόλια and γρῖφοι) or others requiring manual skill such as cottabus (κότταβος), which was played in many different ways; the **Cottabus.** essential thing always was the discharge of the 'heel-taps' (λάταξ, λατάσσειν) of a bowl of wine at some mark. For this purpose an open bowl (κύλιξ) without a raised rim had to be used; it was suspended by its handle on one finger, and its contents discharged by a sudden swing. The variety of the game depended upon the mark that was used. Sometimes it was merely a bowl or disc set up on a stand like a candelabrum; sometimes smaller bowls were floated in a larger one, and had to be filled; sometimes there was a scale which descended when properly hit, and struck an object below, often a little figure called μάνης. Not only was correctness of aim required, but the sound with which the λάταξ struck the bowl or other object was a sign of skill, and was also taken as an augury, especially in love-matters, a name being pronounced with the throw. The game is frequently represented on vases. Such amusements were often supplemented by the entertainments of hired performers. Later in the evening, the revels were sometimes diversified by the invasion of other parties (κῶμοι, κωμάζειν), or the guests sallied out to make similar incursions upon their friends.

695. This description applies mainly to a banquet at a private house; to this the host invited his guests, but it was no unusual thing **Common** for others to drop in uninvited, and the invitation was **banquets.**

usually a short and informal one. Banquets were often held also at
times of sacrifice or other festal occasions, such as marriages; at some of
these women might be present, being seated together. Such banquets were
often held (especially by those who had small houses) in the sacred precincts, where dining-rooms were sometimes provided. It was a common
practice also, both in the case of sacred banquets and of others, for the
guests to contribute each his own share, either in money or in food (ἔρανος).
These banquets varied in character, from the solemn feast of a religious
association to a mere picnic by the sea-side, such as was a favourite
diversion at Athens and elsewhere (ἀκτάζειν).

Public dinners were an institution in many towns. At Athens the
Prytaneis for the time being and certain other privileged
persons were fed daily in the Prytaneum; but it is not to
be supposed that, except on extraordinary occasions, such as
the entertainment of ambassadors, this implied anything like a modern
civic dinner. At Sparta the common dinners for all citizens (συσσίτια)
were notorious for their simple and frugal fare, which included the famous
black broth; those present reclined on wooden couches; while the
Cretans even kept to the severer custom of sitting at table.

*Public
dinners.*

D. EXERCISE, GAMES, BATHS.

696. Physical exercise (γυμναστική) was an essential part of the life
of all free Greeks, and to it a considerable part of the day
was devoted. It took place, for the most part, in buildings
especially made for the purpose, called gymnasia, which
were originally of a simple character, but grew in luxury and splendour
until they became the elaborate structures of Hellenistic and Roman
times. The essential requirements were a smooth space for wrestling
(παλαίστρα), running and jumping, and rooms where men and boys could
leave their clothes (ἀποδυτήριον), rub themselves with oil (ἐλαιοθέσιον),
sprinkle themselves with sand (κονιστήριον), and have a cold bath afterwards (λουτρόν). To these might be added accommodation for spectators
and for resting; such accommodation usually took the form of long
porticoes surrounding a court, and giving protection from sun, rain, and
wind. Such was the gymnasium of the best times in Greece; sometimes,
as at Sparta, a piece of level ground beside a river sufficed. As to the
arrangements of the numerous gymnasia in Athens we have but little
evidence[1]. In addition to the rooms above mentioned, there were usually
a central hall (ἐφηβεῖον), and a tennis-court (σφαιριστήριον). The exercises
of the gymnasium were varied in nature; some of them being merely for

*Physical
exercise.*

---

[1] Gymnasia have been found at Olympia, Epidaurus, Troezen, Eretria, Priene, and
elsewhere; they are mostly of the Hellenistic age, and are provided with water, bath-
tubs, and foot-baths.

the sake of the physical exercise itself, while others partook more of the nature of games (see below), and others again were athletic in the narrower sense—that is to say competitive—such as running, leaping, wrestling, etc. These are spoken of more in detail in describing the great athletic festivals in which the competition ultimately culminated.

697. Among the Greeks games did not usually, as with us, form an essential part of physical education, although some of them were doubtless calculated to improve the strength or agility of those who took part in them. It followed that most of them were left to boys, or sometimes girls, and that grown men usually restricted themselves to more purely athletic exercises. This of course applies mainly to active games, not to cottabus and such other pastimes as were usually indulged in after a feast. Games with a ball were common at all times. The example of Nausicaa will occur to everyone; a σφαιριστήριον was provided for the maidens (ἀρρηφόροι) who had to live on the Acropolis at Athens; and in later times a kind of tennis **Games with ball, etc.** was recommended as a gentle exercise for elderly men. There is however no clear evidence in ancient times for any games with conventional and elaborate rules such as exist at the present day, though something of the sort may be implied by the game called by Pollux ἐπίσκυρος, in which the boys were marshalled into three lines. Other recorded ball-games do not seem to imply more devices than any boy might invent for himself, such as high catch (οὐρανία), catching on the bounce (ἀπόρραξις), making a feint of throwing (φαινίνδα), and so on. A kind of forfeit seems to have been combined with these and other games, the usual penalty being that the worsted competitor had to carry the victor on his back (ὄνος and βασιλεύς). Other pickaback games are represented on vases, the carrier being sometimes blindfolded, and having then to kick a stone.

Hoops were commonly used by children, and ring-stick was also played. Knuckle-bones (ἀστράγαλοι) were used much as at the present day; they were also marked with figures to serve as dice. Cubical dice (κύβοι), as well as these, were most frequently used for gambling and for casting lots, where we should toss up a coin. A more intellectual game was a kind of draughts, πέσσοι, a game preferred by older men; but though representations of the game and the board on which it was played have been found, its rules are still obscure; the ἱερὰ γραμμή, from which the pieces (λίθοι) were only moved in the last extremity, was in this game, whence came the saying τὸν ἀφ᾽ ἱερᾶς κινεῖν; from this game also came the proverb πάντα λίθον κινεῖν, sometimes wrongly translated 'to leave no stone unturned'; it evidently means 'to bring all one's reserves into action.' For the game of cottabus see § 694.

698. Baths have already been referred to as a necessary adjunct of gymnasia; they also existed, at least as early as the fourth century, as separate buildings, some being public, some **Baths.** private. But elaborate baths, such as are familiar in Rome, were unknown

in Greece during the best period; and we even find in the fifth century a
feeling that warm baths are effeminate. But during the Peloponnesian
War a change of sentiment seems to have taken place, and in the fourth
century the custom of taking warm baths seems to have become practically
universal. Baths (πύελοι) also existed in private houses, usually for the use
of women. In the bathing scenes represented on vases (Fig. 158), the vessel
containing the water is usually a basin mounted on a stand; sometimes

Fig. 158. Scene in a public bath; from a vase.

water is poured from a jug by an attendant over a crouching figure.
Similar scenes are represented also in the case of women's baths; and a
representation occurs even of a women's swimming bath (κολυμβήθρα).
Douches were also obtained from the water flowing out of the lions' heads
that discharged the water from a spring or aqueduct. The chief requisites
for a bath were the oil-flask (λήκυθος), the sponge, and the strigil (στλεγγίς,
ξύστρα), which each bather brought with him; he also paid a small fee to
the attendant (βαλανεύς).

E. TRAVELLING.

699. A habit of travelling appears to have been prevalent in Greece at
all periods, especially among men. It was, indeed, neces-
Causes of
travel.   sitated by the religious and social conditions of Greek life.
The comparatively small distances that separated the various
Greek cities, and the ties of friendship that connected at least their chief

families, made such a habit both convenient and agreeable. The common religious festivals offered frequent occasions for travel (see §§ 421 ff.). Political missions also had considerable influence; such commissioners were often ten in number, and any citizen was eligible to the office. These missions also frequently implied a visit to foreign lands. The amount of travel undertaken for commercial purposes must also have been considerable. Military campaigns also led men, whether as citizen-soldiers or as mercenaries, to see much of the world.

700. Travelling in Greece, and to a great extent outside it also, was greatly facilitated by the custom of guest-friendship. Such a connexion between families living at a distance from one another might often be accidental in its origin, but was strictly observed, and also hereditary. We find it already *Entertainment of travellers.* fully recognized in Homeric times, and ratified by an interchange of gifts. In the historical period it was amplified into the system of proxeny; the πρόξενος was the official host of a State, and his functions included hospitality as well as many of the duties of a modern consul; in return he was awarded both honours and substantial privileges by the State whose citizens he entertained. The duty of entertaining the stranger, who was regarded as under the special protection of Zeus Ξένιος, was also recognized in all ages. But the claim to entertainment thus belonging theoretically to every traveller would naturally be liable to abuse upon frequented routes and in populous cities, and consequently other accommodation was required. In the great centres of religious festivals such as Olympia, and also more especially in sacred precincts like Epidaurus where patients slept as part of the healing rite, porticoes were provided for the shelter of visitors. Elsewhere it was usual for travellers to resort to an inn (πανδοκεῖον); but the accommodation provided in such places appears to have been very poor. If a man of any social position had to stay in a town where he had no friends, he usually carried his bedding with him— a precaution by no means unnecessary, if we may judge from the realistic enquiries Dionysus makes of Heracles in the *Frogs*, as to ὅπου κόρεις ὀλίγιστοι. Food of the simplest description only was provided by the hostess (πανδοκεύτρια); and if a guest required anything more, he bought it for himself in the market, and brought it to the inn to be cooked. The attendance of a slave while travelling was therefore usual; and, as luxury increased, a rich man would not travel without a train of attendants.

701. The means of travel in Greece were to some extent prescribed by the nature of the country. The sea presented by far the easiest and most obvious means of transport, not only to the *Means of travel.* islands or more distant countries, but even to other places on the mainland, since a short sail would often save a long and laborious journey over rough roads and mountainous passes. But the comfort of a sea passage, especially in rough weather, left much to be desired. In the best ages of Greece there was nothing like cabin accommodation

on ships, though rich men in the Hellenistic age may have imitated the
luxurious yachts of the Ptolemies; but even then the ordinary traveller
had nothing like privacy or comfort on a ship. On land, the traveller
might either go on foot, on horseback, or in a chariot or cart; φορεῖα,
litters, were only occasionally used before Hellenistic times, mostly for

Fig. 159. Travelling; Dionysus disguised as Heracles, and the slave Xanthias
with pack, on a donkey or mule. Scene from *The Frogs*, on a vase.

invalids. In the first two cases he would usually be accompanied by a
slave with his baggage on a packhorse or a donkey. The roads in ancient
Greece consisted as a rule merely of tracks worn over the land; in rocky
regions—and most regions in Greece are rocky—two parallel grooves were
cut for the wheels of vehicles to run in. Traces of such grooves may be
found throughout Greek lands. The chariots and carts were consequently
built with large wheels and high bodies. The horses having to pick their
way over the rough track probably never went at more than a walk,
except when they came to a piece of level plain; and the nature of the
country and of the roads must have imposed the same pace upon riding
horses also, as it does to the present day, except in the case of very
sure-footed beasts which keep up a kind of amble over rough and smooth.
Mules as well as horses were extensively used, and are indeed preferable
for every purpose in mountainous country. Both women and older men
usually drove when on a journey in a kind of travelling cart (ἀπήνη). And
the frequent reference in Greek authors to the use of such vehicles along
what now appear to be impossible tracks is a constant source of surprise
to those familiar with modern Greece. The drive of Telemachus and

Peisistratus from Pylos to Pherae, and thence in a single day to Sparta is perhaps the strangest instance, and might be supposed to show the poet's ignorance of the country; whatever identification of the sites be accepted, both the distance and the character of the roads make such a performance improbable; but journeys in a wheeled vehicle such as that of Laius from Delphi to Thebes or of Clytemnestra and Iphigeneia from Mycenae to Aulis seem not to be regarded as unusual. The only explanation seems to be that the travelling carts were built extremely light, and could go wherever a sure-footed beast could walk. Perhaps in some cases a track such as has been described would enable a cart to mount places now thought inaccessible without a regularly engineered road. It is however possible that such roads may have existed to a greater extent than is here suggested, and have disappeared as completely as the Roman roads that superseded them in some places.

Becker-Göll, *Charikles* (Becker, *Charicles*, English translation, antiquated); Iwan von Müller, *Die griechischen Privataltertümer*, being Vol. IV. A. 3 of his *Handbuch der klassischen Altertums-* Bibliography. *wissenschaft*; H. Blümner, *Die Privataltertümer*, being Vol. IV. of Hermann's *Lehrbuch der griechischen Antiquitäten*; Baumeister, *Denkmäler des klassischen Altertums* (list of articles on 'Leben und Sitten' on p. 2184); Schreiber-Anderson, *Atlas of Classical Antiquities*; Mahaffy, *Social Life in Greece*; T. G. Tucker, *Life in Ancient Athens*; P. Gardner and Jevons, *Manual of Greek Antiquities*.

VII. 8. HOUSE AND FURNITURE.

702. OUR knowledge of the houses of Ancient Greece is derived from literature and from excavations. For the prehistoric age we have considerable evidence from actual remains, which, Sources of however, with few exceptions such as the palace of Cnossus, knowledge. are little more than ground plans. The Homeric descriptions give us a later stage, the archaeology of which is for the present a difficult problem. For the central period of Greek History there is less information, partly because the social life of the people existed mainly outside their houses and literary references to domestic arrangements are often not too clear, partly because, except for a few small houses in Athens, no houses of the period have been excavated. For the Hellenistic period we have a full description by Vitruvius, which, however, is by no means free from difficulties of interpretation, and important discoveries, especially at Priene and Delos, show us the walls of rooms still standing to a considerable height, the decoration of which is in many cases in good preservation.

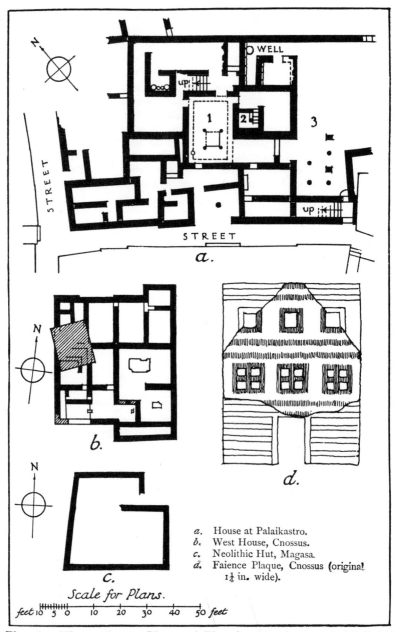

a.   House at Palaikastro.
b.   West House, Cnossus.
c.   Neolithic Hut, Magasa.
d.   Faience Plaque, Cnossus (original
       1¼ in. wide).

Scale for Plans.

feet 10 5 0   10   20   30   40   50 *feet*

Fig. 160. **Minoan Houses, Plans and Elevation** (after the *Annual of the British
School at Athens*, Vol. VI. Pl. VII; Vol. VIII. pp. 15, 17, Figs. 8, 9; Vol. IX. Pl. VI;
Vol. XI. p. 263, Fig. 2).

703. We may make three divisions of the prehistoric houses found in Greek lands, those in Crete and the islands, those in South-Eastern Greece with kindred types elsewhere, and those in North-Eastern Greece. In Crete and the islands *The pre-historic house in Crete.* the primitive house was probably a one-roomed rectangular hut with a flat roof, similar to a modern peasant's hut. The earliest examples are huts of the neolithic age, one at Magasa near Palaikastro (Fig. 160 *c*) and others at Cnossus. The former is rectangular with a stone foundation, which probably carried a superstructure of mud-brick strengthened by rough timbers. One interesting feature is that it has already two divisions, an outer porch-like room and an inner living-room, but the houses may not have been all of a uniform type. At all events two early Cycladic round hut-shaped boxes from Melos and Amorgos show that round huts were known in the Cyclades. The supports on which they stand should not be taken as meaning that they represent lake-dwellings. They are merely the legs of the vases, for it is unlikely that lake-dwellings existed in Crete and the Cyclades. No actual round huts have yet been found, unless the Early Minoan circular ossuaries in Crete are an indication of their existence. Mackenzie has shown that the oval house at Chamaizi is merely a variation of the ordinary more developed Minoan house, and not an independent type.

704. The earliest Minoan houses are those at Vasilike, which date from the later Early Minoan age, and even these are of rather an elaborate type like the houses of much later date (Middle and Late *Minoan houses.* Minoan) excavated in towns such as Gournia and Palaikastro. The small Late Minoan houses are rectangular (Fig. 160 *b*). There are many rooms which are all small and usually intercommunicate, but except in the larger houses no clear design is discernible. The larger houses (Fig. 160 *a*) to judge by the remains of staircases and the evidence of some faience plaques (Fig. 160 *d*) from Cnossus had at least one other storey above the ground floor. They consist of a large number of small rooms, among which a bathroom (Fig. 160 *a*, 2) frequently occurs, often arranged along the side of a court (Fig. 160 *a*, 3). In the centre of the house (Fig. 160 *a*, 1) in order to give light to the living rooms of the ground floor there is a light-well, a central space open to the sky and surrounded by a verandah, the roof of which was supported by four pillars at the angles.

705. The palaces at Cnossus, Phaestus, Mallia, and Hagia Triada are elaborations of the ordinary house plan. That at Cnossus (Fig. 161) is grouped round a large central court (12) which *The Palace at Cnossus.* has an altar in the centre. At the north end of the court is the public entrance to the palace connecting with a paved roadway, and to the west of this entrance lies the 'theatral' area (probably used for ceremonial receptions) with long tiers of steps on two sides. To the south of the central court is another entrance, a columned porch approached by a causeway which carried the main road from the south to the palace. From this a long gallery (4) leads to the north into a west porch and court (5, 6)

beyond the magazines. On the west of the central court lies what may be called
the official and religious part of the palace. Here is the throne room (14)
with the stone throne still *in situ*, where kings of the house of Minos probably
sat in judgment. In the centre of the block opposite the altar of the central
court and on the first floor was the great palace shrine of the snake goddess.
On the ground floor fronting the court was a small shrine with wings similar
to that shown in the reconstructed fresco (see Fig. 22, § 298). The same

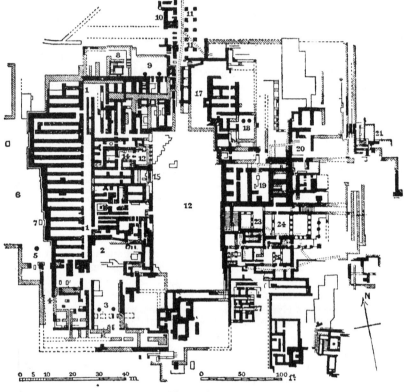

Fig. 161. The Palace at Cnossus.

block, too, has yielded great stores of inscribed tablets, many of which seem
to be inventories of royal stores or tribute. These may be connected with
the long gallery of magazines (Fig. 161, 1) which lies at the back of this
block. Here still stand long rows of store jars where the royal tithes of oil,
wine and corn could be kept; and let into the floors of the magazines and
galleries are stone-lined cists which served as supplementary stores. The
corridors were lighted, when necessary, by torches stuck in the pyramidal
holders which can still be seen. Over the small rooms about the throne

room there was an upper floor reached by staircases and, where necessary, the rooms of the ground floor were lit by light-wells. Above the magazines there was a great hall, approached apparently by a broad staircase leading up from the south propylaea (3). To the east of the central court lies the domestic quarter of the palace, which contained three stories approached by the great staircase (22) rising against the middle of the east side of the court. On the ground floor here are the rooms to which are applied the names 'The Queen's Megaron' (25), 'The Hall of Colonnades' (23) and 'The Hall of Double Axes' (24), all lit by light-wells. Connected with these are (26) bathrooms, latrines and an elaborate system of drainage. Here too is a small chapel, 'The Shrine of the Double Axe,' for the private devotions of the inhabitants of the palace. It is very noticeable that none of the rooms except 'The Hall of Double Axes' can really be called large. Of what appears to have been the Great Palace Hall, north of the 'Domestic Quarter,' only the basement spaces remain. The splendid high-reliefs of painted stucco seem to have been derived from this Hall.

706. In the Cyclades, to judge by the evidence from Phylakopi in Melos, the usual house was a two-roomed building. There was a small outer room and a larger inner or living room. *The Cyclades.* Sometimes, especially in the later houses, the two rooms have separate entrances and do not intercommunicate. The palace at Phylakopi is not of the Cretan, but of the mainland type, like those at Tiryns and Mycenae. The presence of Helladic and not Minoan megara in the Third Late Minoan period in Melos, and at Phaestus, helps to emphasize the supremacy of the mainland after the fall of the Cretan thalassocracy.

In South-Eastern Greece there are some circular neolithic hut foundations at the Argive Heraeum, but the earliest houses are in the Early Helladic settlement at Zygouries, consisting of small dwellings set close together and separated by narrow, crooked alleys. No house is of the megaron type, and the main element *South-Eastern Greece, Early and Middle Helladic.* is a long room with a central hearth and an entrance through a porch at one end. They are related to the Early Minoan houses in Crete and to Early Cycladic houses in Melos, and like them often have a smaller side chamber opening off the main room. The plans are rectangular. The walls were of crude brick on a low stone base and there were flat roofs of brushwood and reeds resting on wooden beams and covered with clay. Middle Helladic houses which have been found at several sites including Thermus and Olympia were similarly constructed, and were usually long and narrow with one apsidal end. The interior was divided into three chambers, a vestibule, a main room, and a store room occupying the apse.

707. To the Late Helladic age belong the palaces at Tiryns and Mycenae and the houses at Mycenae and Korakou. The palace at Tiryns (Fig. 162) shows three periods all of the third Late *Late Helladic, Tiryns.* Helladic age, and the last and greatest period dates from the late 13th century B.C. The ground plan is excellently preserved, and splendid

examples of the painted stucco decorations of its walls and floors have been found. The palace area occupies the highest or southern part of the citadel, and is entered by a large propylaeum on the east, which is approached by a road leading direct from the great gate in the wall. The large propylaeum, faced on both sides by two columns *in antis*, leads into a forecourt (A); and from this a smaller and similar propylaeum leads into the courtyard proper (B) which contains an altar. Facing the altar, and directly to the north, is the entrance to the principal megaron (C). This has a porch faced by two columns *in antis*, behind which is another room entered by three doors and serving as an ante-chamber to the main room beyond. The

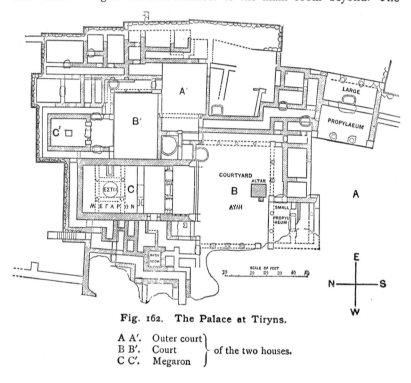

Fig. 162. The Palace at Tiryns.

A A'.   Outer court ⎫
B B'.   Court   ⎬ of the two houses.
C C'.   Megaron   ⎭

hearth was in the centre of this latter room, and round it stood four pillars supporting the roof. To the west of the main hall are many small rooms, including a bathroom. To the east is another and smaller megaron (C') which has two courts (A', B') in front of it, and a number of small rooms on its eastern side. It was formerly thought that the larger megaron was that of the men and the smaller was that of the women, but quite apart from other serious objections to this view later excavations have proved that they are two separate megara or palaces within the same area and of different dates, the larger and later (late 13th century B.C.) being that of the king and the smaller and earlier that of his heir or grand vizier. At Mycenae and at Phylakopi only one megaron was found. Palaces of this type are essentially different from those of Crete. On the mainland and, apparently, also at Troy, even as early as the second city, the megaron type is found, a large central hall of uniform plan with a forecourt and a few smaller rooms attached to it. The likeness of the Trojan palace to those in Argolis may point to early Asiatic influence in Greece. The Cretan palaces are labyrinths, long galleries of small store rooms and complexes of comparatively small-sized living rooms of varying shapes in one or more stories, grouped under one roof on the sides of a central court. The private houses of the Late Helladic III period are in type simple versions of the megaron.

708. In Northern Greece the evidence from the few house-plans so far known does not go to show that there was any uniform type at any period. At Orchomenus in the first stratum the huts were round, and their structure was of mud-brick or Northern Greece. wattle and daub on a low stone foundation. In the second stratum at Orchomenus the huts are oblong with one apsidal end, and in the third stratum no complete house has been found, but enough has been discovered to show that the houses were rectangular and had a courtyard and more than one room. In the first Thessalian period (§ 295) at Tsanglı and Sesklo rectangular huts have been found which had a superstructure of mud-brick and timber on a low stone base. In the second Thessalian period the houses found at Sesklo and Dimeni are of a megaron type. There is a porch with two columns *in antis*, and from this a narrow door leads into the main room, the roof of which was supported by two or three wooden posts in the centre. Behind this was a smaller back room, in which constructions resembling ovens were found. In the third period at Rakhmani an oblong hut with one apsidal end was found, and at the same site an exactly similar house of the fourth period was excavated, while at Rini there is a hut with two apsidal ends also of the fourth period. Lastly, at Lianokladi, in the same period, a house somewhat similar to the megaron type was found.

709. Of the various types of houses described above, the megaron type as at Tiryns, though presumably anterior in date, corresponds best, though not exactly, with the Homeric house. The Homeric House. The essential parts of a house, according to the Homeric poems, are the court (αὐλή) having in the centre the altar of Ζεὺς Ἑρκεῖος and the hall (μέγαρον) with a central hearth (ἑστία, ἱστίη, ἐσχάρα) surrounded by the columns supporting the roof (cf. *Od.* VI. 307). The court served as a farmyard, and was surrounded by sheds which were used as workshops, such as mills for grain, and as rooms for the male slaves, and seem to have included stables as well. The court had a great gate leading into the street, and on its south side was the hall (μέγαρον) itself. Directly against the court was a portico (αἴθουσα), so called because it was the place for sunning one-self (*Od.* IV. 297, 302). Between this and the hall proper was an ante-room (πρόδομος). The great hall behind this was the living room of the family, and also the bedroom of its lord and his wife (*Od.* III. 403), while guests

slept in the porch (*Od.* III. 399, IV. 302). It is only in the palace of Odysseus that there were separate women's quarters, which lay behind the hall and were apparently connected with it by a side door (ὀρσοθύρη). There were store rooms and work rooms for the female slaves, but it was a common practice for the lady of the house to bring her work and attendants into the hall as Penelope did. A separate bedroom for the master and mistress of the house existed in Odysseus' palace, and there seems to have been one in the house of Menelaus as well (*Od.* IV. 121). From the hall a narrow passage (λαύρη) led past it to the rooms behind, as seems to have been the case at Tiryns. The rooms at the side probably included a bathroom—a bath was always offered to a guest on arrival (*Od.* I. 310, III. 464, IV. 48)— for it is here that we find the bathroom at Tiryns. Other rooms included a treasury (θησαυρός), which was in the upper storey of Odysseus' palace. A second storey seems to have been common, but little is known of its arrangements or position, though from the account of Odysseus' palace the upper storey seems to have been the favourite place for Penelope to sit. At all events, it does not seem to have been above the hall. The hut of Eumaeus (*Od.* XIV. 5 ff.) gives a picture of the peasant's house. This had a court serving as a farmyard with stalls round it, and on one side the house itself, consisting of a porch (πρόδομος) and an inner room to live and sleep in, which contained the hearth. This arrangement suggests that of some of the private Late Helladic III houses at Korakou.

710. The Greek house of historical times differs in many respects from the Homeric palace, but it is probably to be regarded as an independent development from the same original and simple type. This type consists of an open court, surrounded by chambers and also, in more elaborate examples, by a cloister; and having, usually on the side facing south, a large recess or open hall, which served as an ante-room to the principal living room. This recess was called the προστάς or παστάς, and is frequently referred to. The aspect of a house was regarded as a matter of the greatest importance, because, as Xenophon makes Socrates say (*Mem.* III. 8. 9), 'in a house facing south the sun shines right into the παστάς'; and he also recommends that 'the parts facing south (*i.e.* on the N. side of the court) should be built high, to catch the winter sun, and that those facing north (*i.e.* on the S. side of the court) should be built low, so as not to catch the cold winds.' These instructions bring home to us the difference between a Greek and a modern house; while we think of the external aspects, and the windows that face outward on each side, a Greek regards a house from inside, and thinks of the various sides that face into the court in the middle. The outside of the house was probably, in most cases, contained by mere blank walls. There is no doubt that the Court corresponds to the Court of Homeric times (αὐλή); the same word is applied to it *e.g.* Plato, *Protag.* p. 311 A; and sacrifices were made in it at the altar of Ζεὺς Ἑρκεῖος (Id. *Rep.* 328 C). If, as we have seen reason to suppose, the παστάς and principal room correspond to the αἴθουσα and μέγαρον, we should expect the room to contain the ἑστία, but we have no

House of historical times.

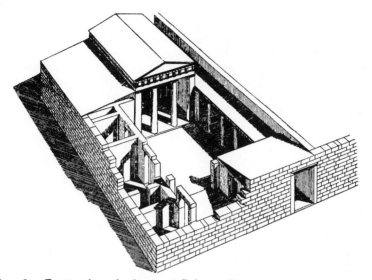

Fig. 163. Restoration of a house at Priene. (Reproduced by permission from Wiegand and Schrader, *Priene*, Fig. 299.)

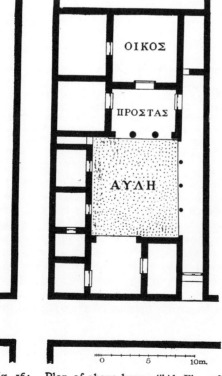

ΟΙΚΟΣ

ΠΡΟΣΤΑΣ

ΑΥΛΗ

Fig. 164. Plan of above house (ibid. Fig. 298).

certain evidence as to this. Since it was most important that the παστάς should face south, while the conditions of situation, especially in towns, often necessitated a front door facing in some other direction, the παστάς was sometimes at the side of the court. The excavations at Priene, which have laid bare the plan of an ancient town with remarkable completeness, show houses which usually conform to a regular type, as may be seen from the plan and restoration here given (Figs. 163, 164, 166). They consist of an open court, with a principal room, usually on the north, faced with a columned porch or ante-chamber; the other principal rooms were usually beside this, and smaller rooms, for slaves or storage purposes, were placed round the

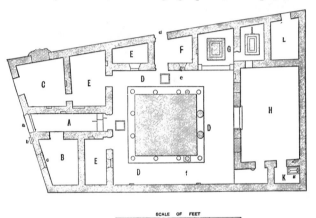

Fig. 165. House on Delos (Rue du Théâtre), (after *Bulletin de Corresp. Hellénique*, xix. Pl. V).

(This description follows in the main that given by the excavator, M. L. Couve.) A. Passage of entrance (θυρωρεῖον). B. Porter's lodge. C. Shop with two doors at corner of street. D. Peristyle, or court (αὐλή), with mosaic. E, E. Chambers, probably for domestics, etc. F. Well of staircase, leading to upper floor. G. Exedra with mosaic floor and drain. H. Large reception room (ἀνδρών), with mosaic. I. Winter dining-room, with mosaic. K. Small chamber. L. Detached room or shop. *a.* Front door. *b.* Niche for lamp. *c.* Window. *d.* Side-door. *e.* Well. *f.* Opening into cistern. *g.* Marble trough.

court. The original plans of these houses may date from the laying out of the city in the fourth century B.C., though many of them were modified later. The Delos houses (Fig. 165) mostly date from the second century or so, and mostly show a later modification such as we find also at Priene, the court being surrounded by a colonnade on all sides; but in the plan of a Delian house here given the larger size of the columns in front of the principal room seems to show that they once belonged to a portico in front of it such as we see at Priene. A curious feature in several of the Delian houses is an exedra opening off the court and well sheltered; this may have served as a sitting room. The house at Priene (illustrated above, Fig. 164) was subsequently joined to another house, presumably to form a γυναικωνῖτις and ἀνδρωνῖτις as described by Vitruvius, and shows also a modification of plan, such as we see at Delos (Fig. 166). Most of the houses at Delos and Priene had an upper storey, containing the more private apartments. The large room which is a feature in most of the Delian houses probably served for the entertainment of guests, and so may be identified as the ἀνδρών.

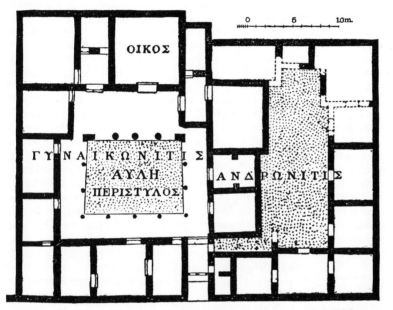

Fig. 166. Plan of House at Priene. (Reproduced by permission from Wiegand and Schrader, *Priene*, Fig. 316.)

711. So far we have been concerned mainly with the simplest form of house, consisting of a single court and surrounding rooms. Such was probably the usual form of house in the fifth and fourth centuries. Vitruvius, who describes in detail the plan of a large house of Hellenistic age, calls the court, with the παστάς and surrounding chambers, into which the front door opens by a corridor (θυρωρεῖον), the γυναικωνῖτις; to this, he says, was added a richer peristyle, surrounded by larger chambers; this peristyle had a separate entrance, and was in every way more sumptuous; it was called the ἀνδρωνῖτις, and was intended for the entertainment of male guests. Its peristyle was often loftier on the side facing south. It is

House of Hellenistic times.

not to be supposed that all these sumptuous arrangements were to be found in houses of the fourth century—much less in the fifth. Demosthenes (*Olynth.* 3. 25) says that the great men of the fifth century were so frugal in their private life that 'even if you knew which was the house of Aristides or Miltiades or other famous men of old, you would see that it made no pretensions beyond its neighbours.' But the elaborate entertainments given by a rich man like Callias (Xen. *Conviv.*; cf. Plato, *Protag.*) imply correspondingly extensive accommodation; and it was probably considered necessary in the fourth century for a man of any position to have special rooms for entertainment. The women usually had separate quarters, shut off by a door called the μέταυλος or μέταυλος θύρα. Into these they retired at night, and also when guests were present; but at other times they occupied the αὐλή. Sometimes the women's rooms were above the men's; for we hear of a man who exchanged quarters with his wife, and gave her the ground floor while he took the first storey (Lysias, *de Caede Eratosth.* 11. 3). Euripides mentions a suite of rooms with a separate entrance for guests (ξενῶνες, *Alc.* 543). Poorer people must have been content with only a room or two, or a portion of a house (συνοικίαι, see § 682). Over-crowding in cities was at least as bad then as now, and many people must have had to dispense with what seemed to their richer contemporaries the decencies or even the necessities of life. Beyond the main features, we know but little of the parts of a house; the same confusion as in earlier times exists in the application of the word θάλαμος, which is sometimes the whole women's quarters, sometimes the best bedroom; this and the ἀμφιθάλαμος are placed by Vitruvius on either side of the pastas.

712. The material of which houses were built was usually sun-dried brick. Even the palace at Tiryns was made of this; and what is preserved is, for the most part, the stone foundation on which the walls stood. It was very easy in the fifth century to dig through the wall of a house. We hear that the Plataeans concentrated their forces in this way without appearing in the street (Thuc. 11. 3); hence also the common word for a burglar, τοιχωρύχος. The walls were probably, at least in the better houses, covered with stucco on the inside. At Tiryns and Mycenae we find the stucco adorned with fresco paintings: the practice of painting the walls came in again towards the end of the fifth century; Alcibiades employed for this purpose the painter Agatharchus, whom he kidnapped and forced to do the work. Socrates complains of the custom, saying that 'pictures and decorations in a house deprive us of more pleasures than they can give' (Xen. *Mem.* 111. 8. 10). But it became more and more prevalent in later times. Relief ornament in stucco was also common; in Delos we find stucco imitating courses of stone, and also artificial marbling, evidently a cheap substitute for marble panelling. Columns, doors, and other structural parts were commonly of wood in early times, though of course marble came to be substituted in more sumptuous

(margin note beside § 712:) Materials of houses.

houses.   The roof was often flat, and so supplied a vantage-ground in street fights; it was generally of hardened mud, as now frequently in the East; but tile roofs were also common, and the tiles served as convenient missiles.   The floor was usually of hardened earth in early times; thus

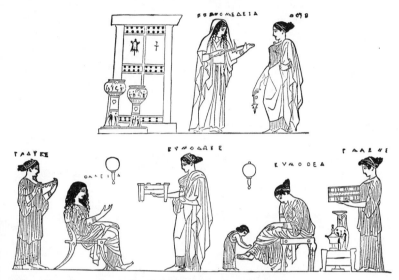

Fig. 167.   Scene in a Greek house, showing furniture, etc.; from a vase.
[*The scene is continuous on the vase.*]

a trough could be dug in it for the axes in the Hall of Ulysses (*Od.* XXI. 120).   Both paving stones and plaster floors are found in early buildings. A floor of pebbles set in cement is found in houses as early as the fifth century in Athens.   In Hellenistic times these floors had elaborate patterns, and developed into mosaic at Alexandria.

713.   Greek houses were probably very bare of furniture, according to our notions.   Beyond beds and couches, chairs, stools, foot-stools, and small portable tables, they do not seem to have had anything that we should call furniture—except chests in which to store clothes and valuable articles.   All kinds of vessels or utensils were either laid on the floor or hung on the walls.   When any things were required, for instance washing appliances, a slave probably brought them and held them during use.   The contents of a country house are thus enumerated and classified by Xenophon (*Oecon.* 9. 6);—implements of sacrifice, women's clothes and ornaments for festivals, men's clothing for festivals and war, mattresses and coverlets for the women's quarters and for the men's, women's shoes, men's shoes, weapons, implements for spinning, for grinding corn, for cooking, bathing utensils, kneading troughs, table

Furniture and vessels, etc.

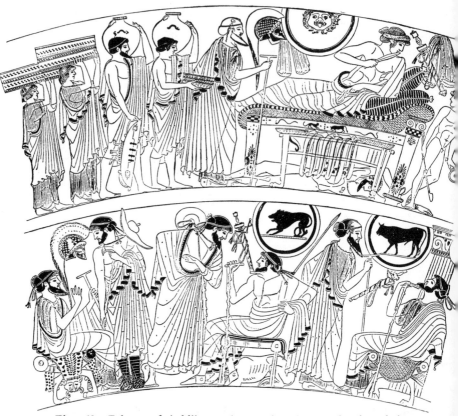

Fig. 168. Priam and Achilles, and scene in a house, showing chairs,
couch, table, etc.; from a vase.

service. The way in which Ischomachus describes how he and his wife
sorted all these and assigned to each class a special place in the house
seems to imply that no proper fittings or appliances were usually provided
for their storage.   In fact, a Greek house would probably have appeared
untidy and disorganised, if judged by a modern western standard, though
doubtless a good housewife introduced order into the chaos.   The majority
of the articles above classified do not call for detailed notice here; but it
is a disputed question how far we are to consider the well-known Greek
painted vases as articles of household furniture and use.   Many may have
been especially made either for export or for dedication; but the representation, in household scenes painted on the vases, of similar painted vases
in actual use, seems to place beyond a doubt the fact that they were sometimes so used, and the inscriptions referring to drinking on cylixes also

imply that they were for use.   It is probable, however, that metal vessels were also extensively used for table service, and these were of silver or even of gold in the more luxurious houses.

For the prehistoric house see the list of books on p. 260.

For the house of historical times see the authorities quoted on p. 649; and also B. Rider, *The Greek House*; Winckler, *Wohnhäuser der Hellenen*; Lange, *Haus und Halle*; J. Chamonard, *Le Quartier du Théâtre* (T. Homolle and others, *Exploration Archéologique de Délos*, Fasc. VIII); Wiegand and Schrader, *Priene*; J. L. Myres, *Journal of Hellenic Studies*, XX. 'On the plan of the Homeric House'; E. A. Gardner, *Journal of Hellenic Studies*, XXI. 'The Greek House'; A. von Gerkan, *Griechische Städte-anlagen*; D. M. Robinson, *Excavations at Olynthus*, II.

Bibliography.

VII. 9. MEDICINE.

714.   Of Greek medicine before the sixth century B.C. we should know little, almost nothing, were it not for the *Iliad* and the *Odyssey*.   In the long course of Aegean civilization medicine may have contained the following elements : (*a*) fetish medicine; (*b*) demon medicine, which may have reached Eastern Europe from the Accadians; (*c*) theurgic, or 'temple medicine,' which may have had its origin in Egypt; and (*d*) a rough but not inconsiderable knowledge of surgery, learned for the most part in the battlefield and owing little to a study of anatomy.   This fourfold system was rolled back, though not vanquished, by the more scientific medicine of Hippocrates and, later, of Alexandria.   It used to be assumed that scientific medicine sprang full-grown from the head of Hippocrates, for whom the way had been prepared by the Ionic schools of philosophy, and especially by Heracleitus.   However the names of a large number of physicians before Hippocrates are given in the so-called Aristotelian MS. of Menon; and older medical treatises are referred to in the Hippocratic collection.   The disciples of Pythagoras are said to have dissected animals.   His chief medical disciple was Alcmaeon of Crotona, the Father of Greek Medicine.   The works of Alcmaeon are lost, but he exercised great influence upon Empedocles, Democritus and Anaxagoras (§ 720).   There is material in the so called 'Edwin Smith Papyrus,' written in hieratic about 1700 B.C., which suggests an Egyptian paternity for some elements in Greek scientific medicine.   The matter is still *sub judice*.

Theurgic medicine knew many gods and heroes also, such as Cheiron, Asclepius, Podaleirius and Machaon; yet it rose far higher than the fetish medicine of the Etrusco-Romans: indeed Paeon, Apollo (in his medical attributes), Eileithyia and Hygieia soon paled before the worship of Asclepius, which seems to have originated in Thessaly, and not to have

Medicine in general.

reached Athens till about 420 B.C. In Homer Asclepius was a mortal chieftain, who seems to have had the root of science in him. Like Achilles he was a disciple of Cheiron; and in his turn taught medicine to Podaleirius and Machaon, chieftains of his own rank and kind. We may note that for the pestilence Calchas had no concern with medical remedies.

715. The apotheosis of Asclepius came later, and many temples were raised to him. We have record of about one hundred; those best known to us by their surviving relics were in Cos, Pergamum, and Epidaurus. Recent excavations in Cos have brought to light remains of an Asclepian temple with cells, the base of a statue, and the foundations of a well-house. If Tricca was the most ancient of the medical temples, Epidaurus was the largest, and the mother of many such health-resorts in Greek lands. These Asclepieia, whither, as to hospitals or spas, the sick were gathered together, were situated in places of fine air, pure water, and exhilarating scenery. In or near some of them were medicinal springs. There, beside religious rites, other physical and moral influences—such as the drama, games, social amusements, diet and gymnastics, and, perhaps, a few drugs—were brought to bear upon the sick in mind or in body, as they are to-day at Harrogate or Aix-les-Bains. At these resorts the effects of 'Airs, Waters, and Places,' and of regimen, as well as those of mental exaltation, diversion or repose, were keenly observed by the positive Greek mind, and the results of these more natural methods quickly distinguished from those of priestly ritual.

Temple medicine.

716. At some of these resorts were medical schools, of which those of Ionian tradition, such as Cos and Cnidus, are best known to us. There were also ancient schools of medicine in Rhodes, and in Magna Graecia, Sicily and Cyrene. The school of Cnidus seems to have been of a dialectic and speculative bent; that of Cos laid stress rather on careful bedside observation, and on the study of atmospheric, telluric, and other external conditions. The recorded doctrines of the Greek physician were very often erroneous but not often unscientific. His recognition of disease as a perversion of normal function, his vigilant reserve, his subordination of his art to the indications of nature, and his reliance on the *vis medicatrix naturae* were in accordance with the best practice of modern times. The medicine of Plato (*Timaeus*), though far from Hippocratic, was not quackery or superstition.

Medical Schools.

Aristotle, the son of a court physician, owed much to Diocles of Carystus; and was destined to hold a perennial ascendancy over medicine, almost to our own day. If we may judge by the evidence of Celsus, the sane and natural method of Hippocrates prevailed until and probably throughout the Alexandrian period; after this period it gradually gave way to a medicine of tradition, formulas and logical categories. On the other hand Hippocratic medicine knew little of anatomy, the study of which was not pursued with success until Alexandrian times, its foremost exponent being Herophilus. Physiology, the science of living function, developed by Erasistratus in

Alexandria, was founded upon experiment by Galen (d. A.D. 200), but on his death fell into oblivion.

717.   That, as is generally stated, rational medicine was an offshoot of theurgic (temple) medicine is not true; the modern visitor to Epidaurus may readily observe that the temple ritual was but a part,   Rational and by no means an overwhelming part, of the splendid   medicine. apparatus built up by the managers, lay and sacerdotal, of these health-resorts. The temple methods may have been engrafted upon an ancient stem of secular medicine, Ionian or mainland, an alliance not inconvenient in a people so little superstitious or priest-ridden as the Greeks; but in all probability professional and sacerdotal medicine were distinct. In Homer no sick Greek or Trojan was carried off to a temple. Herodotus avoids the supernatural origin of disease. Celsus gives honour to Hippocrates for the separation of medicine from philosophy, but he is silent as to any connexion of medicine with religion.

718.   Of the means used by the priests in the cure of disease we know little precisely, but much may be supposed. By pomp, splen-   Treatment dour, and ancient enchantments, the senses were captured   at Temples. and the springs of nervous energy unsealed; sorceries and impostures, which find their way into all great rituals, may have entered more or less into their system. And of such inspirations and suggestions the physicians probably availed themselves, directly or indirectly: it is supposed that mesmerism was a potent means in the hands of the priesthood; that patients were subjected to hypnotic suggestion we know with some fulness. In the age of Hippocrates even sceptical enquirers harboured some belief in the super-natural origin of disease, a belief that is denounced in the noble work *On the sacred disease*. It is certain that dreams took a considerable part in the treat-ment of the sick, and that their value as means of 'suggestion,' and even of diagnosis, was recognised down to the time of Galen. 'Incubation,' or 'temple-sleep,' was practised in the Greek temples, as in the Egyptian, under the hands of the priests. In the fatal illness of Alexander his generals had recourse to it on his behalf. Incubation was by no means peculiar to the temples of Asclepius; it was practised at many other shrines, as of Apollo, Aphrodite and Hera; and in later times. It is said, on slight evidence, that a course of rational medicine preceded the incubation. The suppliants in crowds—the sexes were not segregated—their imaginations previously exalted by imposing rites, lay for sleep in the precincts by night. If, as we hear, some were sleepless, the priests took care no doubt that they should see visions and hear prophecies nevertheless. In such visions the tame snakes kept in the temples played some part; this we infer from the *Plutus* of Aristophanes, from some of the inscriptions from Epidaurus, and from other testimony. Like the Delphic priestess, the priest of Asclepius also may have kept himself informed on the private concerns of the suppliants, at any rate of the more eminent of them. A picture of an Asclepian temple as a centre of idle gossip is yielded by the *Mimes* of Herondas. The whole system of

Apolline religion may be regarded as an Ionian revolt from nature cults, gloomy obscure and Corybantic, which then, as in other times and places, enslaved the thought and debased the passions of man. We may dwell rather on the therapeutical results obtained indirectly by rational means, and by the preparation for the vigils; this seems to have consisted in baths, fasting, purgation, anointings and even bleeding: measures which had their vulgar advantages. On a larger scale, and more persistent method, these trainings, dietetics, gymnastics, mineral waters, sea-baths and the like, fell in with the work of the physicians, and with the Greek cult of the body. Fees were paid at the end of the course.

Besides gold and silver certain peculiar votive offerings were made in the Asclepieia, as still in many modern temples, which bore rude witness to the cures. Some were pictorial or glyptic representations of diseased parts; or, especially in the case of internal maladies, written records. It has been alleged, though on a misapprehension, that the clinical knowledge of the physicians was founded on these records, and was thus handed down in the medical schools. In the Hippocratic collection the *Coan Prenotions* and the first book of *Prorrhetic* are said to have been compiled from such sources, and even some of the *Aphorisms* also; though it is possible that parts of the earlier aphorisms came, with the aphoristic style, from Egypt. Votive tablets could have had no such value, unless dictated by the physician; indeed there is some evidence that the practice of taking clinical notes originated with the physicians.

719. That Hippocrates—by which name we are wont to designate the most eminent of about eight Greek physicians who bore

Medical guilds. it—was of the Asclepiadae, certainly does not prove that he was of the stem of Asclepius. By the time of which we are speaking the Asclepiadae had become what, in our own day, we call a College or Guild. In early times Greek medicine seems to have been the inheritance of certain families, much as with Celtic and Anglo-Saxon medicine (*Iliad* IV. 211). The brotherhood of blood had given place to the brotherhood of a corporation. In the *Iliad* with the Greeks before Troy, many of the craft were held in the highest esteem (XI. 506), and some of them, at any rate, were illustrious, even kingly persons. The field anatomy of Homer is by no means contemptible; he directs no strokes at random, and the heroes knew when a stroke was mortal or not (IV. 185 and 190). Nor was medical practice all surgery. Medicinal herbs belong to our earliest tradition. In the *Odyssey* Eumaeus speaks of an ἰητήρ κακῶν in a context which suggests that even then physicians travelled from place to place, offering welcome service; Nestor's wife Agamede 'knew all drugs' (*Il.* XI. 740). It is said that doctors were introduced into the Spartan army by Lycurgus, where they had a special camp. In the Hippocratic collection there are chapters on the surgery of war. Epameinondas had physicians with his forces at Mantinea; and Xenophon speaks, more than once, of doctors in attendance upon the army: there were eight at least with the Ten Thousand.

Of the constitution of the medical guilds we have some precious evidence in the Oath known as 'of Hippocrates,' the date of which in its surviving form is variously estimated from the fifth century B.C. to the third century A.D. From it we infer that novices were initiated solemnly, and adjured to walk in the steps of masters who held up before their eyes noble examples of honour, integrity, obedience to the laws, secrecy, and loyalty to the interests of the patients under their care. We can scarcely doubt that this oath owes its weight, austerity and dignity to an ancient and honourable tradition of medical independence and responsibility.

720. Physicians of the school of Croton seem to have been regarded as the leaders of the profession in Hellas, and, a hundred years before Hippocrates, one of them, the celebrated *Hippocrates.* Democedes, practised in Aegina, in Athens and in Samos. Hippocrates (born *c.* 460 B.C.) was of Cos—the Mecca of medicine. The Coan School was flourishing in the sixth century. In the name of Hippocrates stands a large body of treatises; some, such as the *De aere, locis, et aquis,* bear the stamp not only of a great and individual mind, but also of a mind positively scientific in bent and habit; others are class-books and collections, more or less rude, of notes and aphorisms, in many instances significant of a true growth of natural knowledge such as we attribute to Ionia; others again, if we may judge by their doctrines, are of Cnidian rather than of Coan origin. Some of the books are earlier than Aristotle; and in many treatises an older body of doctrine is assumed, and even quoted. Of some sixty works under the master's name, not more than six can be from his hand; indeed there is little better evidence to connect even these with the great Hippocrates than the internal evidence that they sprang from the mind or minds of individual genius, and the presumption that the doctrines of a teacher so venerated would be preserved. Neither Plato nor Aristotle refers to him as an author. Moreover since in the 'Menonian' notes of Aristotle certain highly speculative opinions on the πνεῦμα seem to be attributed to Hippocrates, the personal authenticity of particular works in the collection is still more obscured. Those opinions however are more characteristic of Diocles, who was known as the 'alter Hippocrates.' Many works bearing the name of Hippocrates were doubtless documents of the School, current under the leader's name; others, not properly of the canon, nor indeed of the same school of thought, were gathered into the collection more or less accidentally. Their various origin is proved by many inconsistencies of anatomical and other detail, as well as of doctrines and style. It is quite certain that many works of the 'Hippocratic Collection' are of a date later than Hippocrates himself.

721. Of the practice of the Greek physicians we know little. Some of them were attached, as teachers, to the schools. We know that eminent physicians were elected as public physicians, *Private and Public practice.* and were 'called' to the cities, or were sent for by this tyrant or that, as Democedes by Polycrates, and detained about his person for large reward. It seems probable that Thales, who lived at the time of the Milesian factory in Egypt, studied in that country; and as Hippocrates, like other philosophers, is known to have travelled widely, it is suggested that he visited Egypt. Physicians on their travels were consulted on the way, and probably, after the manner of the Sophists, delivered lectures. We read indeed of 'peripatetic physicians', and some historians have interpreted the peripatetic as the practising physician, contrasting him with the physician of the closet; for Greek medicine does not smell of the lamp.

Certain physicians were settled officially in the cities; they were elected by the assembly, and received salaries, not, or not only, from the civic treasury but from a poll-tax. In Athens there were at least six public physicians. Democedes held an office of this kind in Aegina and afterwards in Athens. In ancient Greece anyone might practise privately, but for civic service guarantees were required   Thus apprenticeships and schools arose; and probably there was a register. Midwives and 'wise women' abounded (v. Eur. Hipp. 293), but no woman could be recognised as a physician. The salaried medical officers guarded the public health, combated epidemics, and may have given instruction in dietetics and training. Their presence was required at games and festivals. The public physicians were not forbidden to take fees from private persons, but they rarely did so; ordinarily they attended all persons gratuitously, including strangers visiting the city. The 'Oath of Hippocrates' seems to contemplate private practice almost exclusively. We may note that in it the title of Asclepiad does not occur. The public physicians were men of distinction and dignity; generally speaking, their remuneration seems to have been in corn to the value of 500—700 drachmas per annum, with house and orchard, liberal civic immunities, and many honours. The Greek physicians of this period gave freely to the poor and to the stranger not only of their skill but of their substance.

722. The physicians kept offices or shops supplied with a large variety of surgical and other instruments, dressings for wounds, and drugs, of which last there was a customary but not an official list (see § 100). In these offices, and also by druggists (φαρμακοπῶλοι), medicines were dispensed by the single dose or in larger quantities. Moreover to these medical homes, which grew into hospitals, patients were often removed for closer observation, or for special treatment. There was a public Ἰατρεῖον also in every large city, kept up out of the taxes or rates. Slaves were employed as assistants and dispensers. The physicians had also cases fitted with medical and surgical appliances which they carried with them on their travels. Lofty in ethical standard and pure of all charlatanry as was the school of Hippocrates, too often, in later centuries at any rate, medical practice degraded into a trade; and these offices, like barbers' shops in later times, became places of call, not always to the honour of the profession. Indeed we are told that in ancient Greece, as in mediaeval Europe, elegant and well-dressed physicians were wont to rely rather on personal attractions

Treatment.

than on scientific acquirements; and that others descended even to the level of quacksalvers and criers of medical wares in the markets. In Egypt specialism in medicine had been carried to the absurdest extremes. To the Greeks our unscientific dichotomy of medicine and surgery was unknown, probably inconceivable; but we learn from the 'Oath'—which is, perhaps, late—that cutters for stone were specialists; so were oculists and dentists. Graver operations were a perilous undertaking; and probably, in ancient Greece, as certainly in many later centuries, local practitioners were wont to entrust them to peripatetic craftsmen, who took care to disappear before the issue of their work could be known.

We have seen then that medicine, as a natural science and rational practice, enjoyed in ancient Greece a peculiar independence of the hierophant and the philosopher. The school of Hippocrates was a school of watchful observation of nature, though not of experimental verification; a school devoted to description of diseases—chiefly of the acuter kinds, and of these chiefly the fevers—as orderly sequences of symptoms classifiable under certain types; and also to the study of constitutional proclivities, but not of accurate details or subtler distinctions, which at the time was scarcely possible. It was a school of careful observation of external but not of inward causes, nor of the local seats of disease; for of course pathology was rudimentary. In therapeutics it was a school of vigilant waiting upon nature, and of the use of physical means such as diet, waters, fresh air, and gymnastics; not of violent interference by bleedings, by drugs, or by empirical specifics. Its honourable motto was ἰατρὸς ὑπηρέτης τῆς φύσεως. Surgery, by this direct and natural study of facts, attained a degree of positive excellence which even to this day is admirable.

723. After the Hippocratic period, under the Macedonian supremacy, medicine, though high in court favour, languished, like other Later intellectual pursuits, to rise again with the marvellous Greek development. fecundity in Alexandria, under the Ptolemies; especially under Ptolemy Soter. The two chief figures among the Alexandrian physicians are Herophilus and Erasistratus, under whom not only descriptive anatomy advanced but also the conception of local seats of disease. Herophilus was a pupil of Praxagoras of Cos, who seems first to have taught the clinical use of the pulse. For physiology however little was done till it sprang into life from the brain of Galen. The great epoch of Alexandria was not long; medicine began to lose the broad and sane example of Hippocrates and broke up into sects, dependent in part upon scholastic philosophies; and in practice polypharmacy and the lower forms of empiricism increased. Many of the chief schools of medicine were at this time in Asia Minor; as in Pergamum, Ephesus, Tralles, Miletus. In the second century A.D. Greek medicine prevailed in Rome, after it had been long defied by Cato and his followers. Asclepiades, a Bithynian, the friend of Cicero and Crassus, was the first eminent Greek physician in Rome. By Tiberius the office of Court Physician was established, and we must not refrain from mentioning here the great

Latin name of Celsus. In Galen (*ob.* 200) Greek medicine found its culmination and its eclipse. This extraordinary man, the founder of physiology by the true way of the experimental method, a prodigy of learning, and only too copious and ingenious a philosopher, stood eminent on the abyss which in after time swallowed up medicine and all natural science for more than a thousand years.

The only complete modern text and translation of the Hippocratic Collection is

Bibliography.   Emil Littré, *Oeuvres complètes d'H.*, 10 vols., Paris (1839–1869). A critical text is appearing in the *Corpus Medicorum Graecorum* (Teubner, Leipzig) The most important works are treated by W. H S. Jones and E. T. Withington in the *Loeb Classical Library.* Francis Adams, *The Genuine Works of Hippocrates*, London (1849), is still valuable. For references to early Greek medicine in classical writings see H Poschenrieder, *Die platonischen Dialoge in ihrem Verhältnisse zu den hippokratischen Schriften*, Landshut (1882) and *Die naturwissenschaftlichen Schriften des Aristoteles in ihrem Verhältnis zu den hippokratischen Sammlung*, Bamberg (1887). For MSS. see H. Diels, *Die Handschriften der antike Aerzte*, Teile i, ii, Berlin (1905). From the vast recent literature on the Hippocratic problem we select: F. Spaet, *Geschichtliche Entwickelung der Hippokratischen Medizin*, Berlin (1897); C Friedrich, *Hippokratische Untersuchungen*, Berlin (1899); M. Wellmann, *Die Fragmente der Sikelischen Aerzte Akron Philistion und Diokles*, Berlin, 1901 (radical); W. H. Roscher, *Die Hebdomadenlehren der Griechischen Philosophen und Aerzte*, Leipzig, 1906 (fanciful at times); A. Nelson, *Die Hippokratische Schrift* ΠΕΡΙ ΦΥΣΩΝ, Upsala (1909); W. A. Heidel, "Hippocratea" in *Harvard Studies in Classical Philology*, Camb., Mass. (1914); "Conception of Nature among Pre-Socratics," *American Academy of Arts and Sciences* (1910); T. Gomperz, "Die hippokratische Frage" (radical) in *Philologus*, Leipzig (1911); E. Nachmanson, *Erotianstudien*, Upsala (1917); C Singer, *Greek Biology and Greek Medicine*, Oxford (1922); R. O. Moon, *Hippocrates and his Successors*, London, 1923 (conservative); E. Wenkebach, *Untersuchungen über Galens Kommentare zu den Epidemien des H.*, Berlin (1925); W. H. S. Jones, *The Doctor's Oath*, Cambridge, 1926 (differs from views expressed above); a Bibliography of the excavations at Cos is in K. Sudhoff, *Kos und Knidos*, Munich, 1927. For recent Bibliography of ancient medicine see E. Kind, in *Bursians Jahresbericht über die Fortschritte der klassischen Altertumswissenschaft*, Leipzig, 1919.

VIII. CRITICISM AND INTERPRETATION.

VIII. 1. DIALECTS.

724. THE word *dialect* is applied in two senses which require to be kept distinct. The first of these is its use to indicate the particular form of a language spoken by the inhabitants of a given place at a given time; the second is its use in the phrase *literary dialect*, by which is meant the particular form of language in which some particular work or works of literature are presented to us. A literary dialect often does not correspond exactly to the dialect of any particular place, but contains many forms and constructions drawn from various sources, especially earlier literary works, some of which may have been composed in dialects similar but not identical. — *Spoken and literary dialects.*

The ancient Greek world showed all the conditions likely to produce great diversity of dialects among its people. The tradition of different families, of separate descent from Aeolus, Dorus, and Ion, was widespread; the multitude of independent States, mother-cities and colonies, kept separate by the sea and by difficult mountains, with their rivalries tending to become stronger than their friendships, was sure to develop dialectic differences. These differences are shown to some extent by the extant literature, but more fully by the large number of ancient inscriptions. Many States had no literature of their own; and there was a tendency for literature in certain styles to create a mixed artificial dialect, not spoken in any part of Greece but widely intelligible to educated persons. — *Diversity of dialects in Greece.*

725. The language of the pre-Hellenic population of Greece is known only from proper names, chiefly names of places, which cannot be analysed into known Greek elements. Herodotus, also, says (I. 57) that in his time some Pelasgians still spoke a non-Greek tongue in certain settlements in Chalcidice and on the Hellespont. Both of these arguments, however, must be used with caution. As yet archæology alone has revealed to us the Greece of times earlier than Homer. The numerous records of earlier ages which have recently been discovered in Crete are not yet deciphered; and from the fact that, in the Greek of historical times, we cannot find etymologies for all the names of persons and places, which have been handed down from an earlier age, we cannot draw the certain conclusion that these names are therefore of an origin which is not Greek. Moreover, Herodotus himself could not distinguish clearly between the Pelasgians and the later population of Greece, for elsewhere (VII. 94) he tells us that the Pelasgians — *Language of the pre-Hellenic people.*

of Achaia in the Peloponnese changed their name to Ionians. This
name they took from Ion, the son of Xuthus, after Danaus and Xuthus
had come to the Peloponnese. The islanders also, who were afterwards
called Ionians, and the Aeolians were, he says, once called Pelasgians.
If the name of the Pelasgians means, as some think, the People of the
Plain, or, as is more probable, the Sea-folk, from the weak stem of πέλαγος
and the ethnic suffix -κοι (*Πελασγ-κοί becoming Πελασγοί as *μίγ-σκω
becomes μίσγω), it is not necessary to assume that all the communities
called Pelasgian were of the same racial origin, and both statements of
Herodotus may be correct.

726. In considering dialects, the points to be taken into account are
Dialectic differences. sounds, grammatical inflexions, syntax and vocabulary. Of
most importance are the sounds used by each dialect; the
other features generally confirm the results attained by a
consideration of the sounds alone. Here we are of course not bound to
assume that the same symbol indicates the same sound in different dialects;
no doubt the symbols were differently pronounced in different parts of
Greece and even in the same part at different times. The chief points in
regard to sounds are: (a) in vowels, the retention of ā or its change to η; the
results of contraction, especially of εε and oo; the methods of 'compensation,' e.g. in the syllable which was originally ονς; (b) in consonants, the
treatment of the original spirants y, s, w, especially the last, and the extent
to which original guttural sounds were retained or changed to corresponding
palatal, dental, or labial sounds; (c) the accent. In inflexions, we find
dialectic differences in the use of dual forms, in the relations of -μι to
-ω verbs, and in several case-forms where the differences are sometimes
really due to rules relating to sounds. In syntax we find dialects differing
from each other, e.g. in the cases employed after εἰς and ἐν, and especially
in regard to the elaborate rules for the use of moods with and without the
particle ἄν, which seem to have been mainly the work of Ionic and Attic.
In vocabulary striking differences sometimes occur, e.g. λάω 'wish' was
one of the commonest words in Doric, but it was unknown to Ionic and
Attic. No dialect was stable; all suffered changes, and these changes
nearly always tended in the direction of that κοινὴ διάλεκτος which ultimately became the language of the Greek world.

727. The old classification of the Greek dialects into Aeolic, Doric,
Classification of dialects. Ionic, and Attic is in the main sound, though 'Aeolic'
is used rather vaguely if it includes every dialect not
covered by the other three-names. But the different dialects
are not in all respects sharply contrasted one with another. Some peculiarities are common to Doric and Ionic, others to Attic and Boeotian
and so on. Thus in Euboean (Eretrian), Boeotian, and Attic, certain
classes of words show -ττ- where other dialects have -σσ-; Attic and
Boeotian πράττω, Eretrian πρήττω. Yet Eretrian is Ionic not Attic, as η
shows, and Boeotian is a mixed dialect intermediate between Aeolic and
Doric. Again, medial t before a following i passes into s in Lesbian,

Cyprian, Arcadian, Ionic, and Attic. Thus in Arcadian and Cyprian the preposition ποτί appears as πός; the form προτί, its equivalent in meaning, similarly passes into πρός in Lesbian, Ionic, and Attic. Sound changes no doubt passed sometimes from one dialect to its neighbours. Thus the change of final ς to ρ, which characterises Elean, appeared later in Laconian (the similar change in Euboea was independent of this); the change of a medial σ between vowels into ℎ and its consequent loss is found only in the later Elean, to which it must have come from Laconian and Argive. The particle ἄν is characteristic of Ionic and Attic, κα has approximately the same value in the Doric dialects; in Thessalian, Lesbian and Cyprian κε or κεν appears. Both ἄν and κεν are found in the literary dialect of Homer; in Arcadian the same value is attached to καν, possibly a confusion between the earlier κεν and the Doric κα rather than a combination of κε with ἄν. Others explain εἰκαν as εἰ κ' ἄν or εἰκ (like οὐκ beside οὐ) ἄν.

Many authorities divide the Greek dialects into two groups: (1) the Ionic, including only Ionic and Attic; (2) the non-Ionic, including all other dialects. Against this classification it may be urged that both historically and morphologically Aeolic may claim closer connexion with Ionic than with Doric, so that a classification into Doric and non-Doric would be at least equally plausible. The earliest inscription found in Attica dates probably from the eighth century B.C., others on vases belong to the seventh century: the earliest Dorian known is from the rock inscriptions of Melos and Thera, which go back at least to the seventh century B.C. Ionic not later than the first part of the sixth century B.C. has been found in Paros, Miletus, and elsewhere. Aeolic of Lesbos, however, though represented in the early literature by Sappho and Alcaeus, has no representative of an early period amongst inscriptions, and inscriptions form a much better record of a dialect than literary works which have been copied again and again and the manuscripts of which are separated by many centuries from the date of the authors.

728. Closely akin, however, to the dialect of the Aeolic inscriptions are two dialects in which no literature is preserved but which, having been long isolated by geographical position and historical causes, have preserved a form of the Greek language that, in many of its features, is undoubtedly very archaic. These dialects are Arcadian and Cyprian. Arcadian was recognised by the ancients as the last remains of the ancient Aeolic spoken in the Peloponnese in pre-Dorian times and, according to tradition, Paphos in Cyprus was founded by Agapenor, an Arcadian, and his followers who, on their return voyage from Troy, were carried to Cyprus by stress of weather. Strabo points to the name of the promontory Ἀχαιῶν ἀκτή as conclusive proof of the truth of the tradition. All connexion between Arcadia and Cyprus had long been broken before authentic history begins, and therefore characteristics which the dialects possess in common may be regarded as dating from the age when Cyprus was colonised. The vocabulary of Cyprian is of an archaic cast often resembling that of the Homeric

poems. The exact forms of Cyprian are sometimes uncertain, because as late as the fourth century B.C. it continued to be written, not in the Greek alphabet, but in a syllabary of about 55 characters which (1) could not indicate a separate consonant like *p* though it had symbols for *pa, pe, pi, po, pu,* (2) did not distinguish between breathed, voiced, and aspirated consonants, so that π, β, φ are all represented by the same symbol, (3) did not mark the presence of a nasal before another consonant, so that it is not certain whether the acc. pl. of -o- stems ended in -ονς or -ος, and forms like τάνδε are written in the syllabary *ta-te,* (4) made no distinction between long and short vowels. Arcadian and Cyprian agree in changing final -o to -υ as ἀπύ, γένοιτυ, etc., both have the gen. sing. of masculine ā stems in -αυ for -αο (extended later in Arcadian of Tegea to feminine stems), both have locatives used for datives in o and ā stems (this is much more developed in Arcadian than in Cyprian), both have the third person plural in -νσι; ἐν appears as ἰν, and ἀπύ and ἐς (for ἐξ) govern the locative or dative not the genitive. Arcadian has δ or ζ for the original guttural sound which in Attic is β; δήλομαι, Attic βούλομαι; ζέλλω, Attic βάλλω. It changes the verb-ending -ται into -τοι.

Examples*.

(1) Arcadian, from a Tegean building contract probably of third century B.C.: εἰ δὲ ἄν τις τῶν ἐργωνᾶν¹ ἢ τῶν ἐργαζομένων ἐπηρειάζεν² δέατοι³ ἰν τὰ ἔργα ἢ ἀπειθῆναι τοῖς ἐπιμελομένοις ἢ κατυφρονῆναι τῶν ἐπιζαμίων⁴ τῶν τεταγμένων, κύριοι ἐόντω οἱ ἐσδοτῆρες τὸμ μὲν ἐργάταν ἐσδέλλοντες ἐς τοῖ ἔργοι⁵, τὸν δὲ ἐργώναν ζαμιόντες ἰν ἐπικρίσιγ κατάπερ⁶ τὸς ἐπισυνισταμένος ταῖς ἐσδοκαῖς⁷ γέγραπτοι.

¹ =contractor. ² infinitive. ³ =δοκῇ. ⁴ =ζημιῶν. ⁵ ὄντων οἱ ἐκδοτῆρες τὸν μ. ἐ. ἐκβάλλοντες ἐκ τοῦ ἔργου. ⁶ =κατ τάπερ. ⁷ =τοὺς ἐναντιουμένους ταῖς ἐκδοχαῖς.

(2) From the Arcadian Orchomenus (locally Erchomenos). A treaty of union, in the fourth century B.C.

ὤμοσαν Ἐρχομίνιοι τάδε· ἀψευδήων ἀν¹ τὰν συροικίαν τοῖς Εὐαιμνίοις πὸς τὰς σύνθεσις, νεὶ τὸν Δία τὸν Ἄρηα, νεὶ τὰν Ἀθάναν τὰν Ἀρήαν, νεὶ τὸν Ἰνυάλιον τὸν Ἄρηα· οὐδ᾽ ἀν ἐξελαύνοια τὸς Εὐαιμνίος οὔποτε, οὐ τὸν Δία τὸν Ἄρηα, κτλ.

¹ 'I will be true': ἀψευδήων possibly a subj. followed by an opt. ἐξελαύνοια, as in Homer. Others take both as opt. ἐξελαύνοια is more archaic than the ordinary ἐξελαύνοιμι. Though this is the first occurrence of the form, the formation had been long postulated by comparative philologists.

(3) From a Tegean decree of proxeny: ἦναι δὲ αὐτοῖ ἴνπασιν γαῦ, οἰκίαυ¹, ἀσυλίαν, ἀσφάλειαν καὶ ἰν πολέμοι καὶ ἐν ἰράναι.

¹ =ἔγκτησιν γῆς, οἰκίας.

(4) Transliterated from a bronze plate at Idalion in the Cyprian syllabary. Date probably about the middle of the fifth century B.C. ὄπι σις κε τὰς Ϝρέτας¹ τάσδε λύσε̄, ἀνοσίγα Ϝοι γένοιτυ· τάς κε ζᾶς² τάσδε κὰς τὸς κάπος τόσδε οἱ Ὀνασικύπρων παῖδες ἔξονσι³ αἰϜεί.

¹ =ἐάν τις ῥήτρας. ² =γᾶς (χωρία). ³ fut. with κε as often in Homer.

* In the texts given in this chapter all examples of ι which in modern printed Greek literary texts is "subscript" are printed on the line.

(5) Transliterated from an inscription in the Cyprian syllabary (there is also a Phoenician text) at Idalion. Date about 380 B.C.

ἰν τοι τετάρτοι ϝέτει βασιλέϝος Μιλκιγάθōνος τὸν ἀνδριγάνταν¹ τόνδε κατέστασε ὁ ϝάναξ Βαάλραμ ὁ Ἀβιδμίλκōν τō Ἀπόλλōνι τō Ἀμύκλōι, ἀπ᾽ ὄι ϝοι τᾶς εὐχōλᾶς ἐπέτυχε² ἰν τύχαι ἀζαθᾶι.

¹ = ἀνδρίαντα.　　　² From whom he obtained the fulfilment of his prayer.

729. True Aeolic was the dialect of Lesbos; the dialects of Boeotia and Thessaly (except the southern part, which early became _Aeolic._ Dorian) were akin to it. The common characters are a tendency to υ for ο (ου for ω in Thessalian, υ for οι in Boeotian), the use of adjectives for patronymics, and a tendency to labialise dentals in certain words which originally had a guttural sound: πέτταρες for τέτταρες, Βέλφαιος, adj. to the Thessalian form for Δελφοί, φήρ for θήρ. These dialects also affect, like Homer, dat. pl. in -εσσι, and decline the perfect participle like a present (cp. the Homeric κεκλήγοντες).

Lesbian and Thessalian agree further in using double liquids or nasals where assimilation has taken place, while other dialects lengthen in some form the preceding vowel: χέρρες (χεῖρες), βόλλα (βουλή), ξέννος (originally ξένϝος). Both also tend to inflect contracted -ω verbs with -μι forms, ὄρημι, etc. and their prepositions show apocope. Lesbian is characterised by ψίλωσις, a loss of the rough breathing which is shared by Asiatic Ionic, and by βαρυτόνησις, a uniform throwing back of the accent except in prepositions. Lesbian also has -αις for earlier -ανς, or -αντς, as ἀκούσαις ptcp., παῖσα (πᾶσα), δίκαις acc. pl., and so μοῖσα, λιποῖσα, στρατάγοις acc. pl., ἔχοισι 3rd pl.

Example.

Lesbian, from an inscription of the fourth century B.C., at Mytilene: τὸν κέρναντα¹ τὸ χρύσιον ὑπόδικον ἔμμεναι ἀμφοτέραισι ταῖς πολίεσσι, δικάσταις δὲ ἔμμεναι ταῖς ἄρχαις² παίσαις ταῖς ἐμ Μυτιλήναι. αἰ δέ κε καταγρέθηι τὸ χρύσιον κέρναν ὑδαρέστερον θέλων, θανάτωι ζαμιώσθω. αἰ δέ κε ἀπυφύγηι μὴ θέλων ἀμβρότην³, τιμάτω τὸ δικαστήριον ὄττι χρὴ αὐτον πάθην ἢ κατθέμεναι.

¹ = κίρναντα.
² δικάσταις, ἄρχαις, acc.　　　³ = ἁμαρτεῖν.

The remains of Sappho and Alcaeus are usually given in the MSS. with the non-Aeolic accentuation, and other specially Aeolic features have to be restored by the editors, on the general testimony of ancient grammarians. The dialect of these poets became the type for the form of lyric poetry represented by them and influenced the Ionian Anacreon and also the choral poetry of the Dorians. The following passage of Sappho with the text corrected as in Smyth's _Greek Melic Poets_, p. 27, may serve as an example of the early Lesbian poetry. Many more fragments of these poets have been published in recent years; see especially vol. x. of the Oxyrhynchus Papyri (1914), pp. 20 ff., from papyri of the second century A.D.

Sappho to Alcaeus :

αἰ δ' ἦχες ἔσλων ἴμμερον ἢ κάλων,
καὶ μή τι ϝείπην γλῶσσ' ἐκύκα κάκον,
αἴδως κέ σ' οὐ κ[ατ]ῆχεν ὄππατ'
ἀλλ' ἔλεγες περὶ τῶ δικαίω.

Thessalian agrees with Boeotian in changing -ντο of 3rd plural into -νθο and η into ει. Thessalian has also ει for αι in verbal endings, and -οι and occasionally even in prose -οιο for the ending of the genitive in -o stems.

Examples.

(1) Thessalian, a lead tablet found at Dodona, from the town of Mondaea in the north of Perrhaebia :

Δὶ Νάωι καὶ Διώναι ἐπικοινᾶται Μονδαιατᾶν τὸ κοινὸν περ τοῖ ἀργύρροι τᾶς Θέμιστος.

(2) From a reply of Larissa to Philip V of Macedon, 214 B.C.; Philip's letter in the ordinary Greek of the period, which is the occasion of the document, is quoted and repeated in *Oratio obliqua* in Thessalian. In its use of imperfects in indirect discourse Thessalian is more like Homer than Attic.

Πετραῖος καὶ Ἀνάγκιππος καὶ Ἀριστόνους, ὡς ἀπὸ τῆς πρεσβείας ἐγένοντο, ἐνεφάνιζόν μοι, ὅτι καὶ ἡ ὑμετέρα πόλις διὰ τοὺς πολέμους προσδεῖται πλεόνων οἰκητῶν. ἕως ἂν οὖν καὶ ἑτέρους ἐπινοήσωμεν ἀξίους τοῦ παρ' ὑμῖν πολιτεύματος, ἐπὶ τοῦ παρόντος κρίνω ψηφίσασθαι ὑμᾶς ὅπως τοῖς κατοικοῦσιν παρ' ὑμῖν Θεσσαλῶν ἢ τῶν ἄλλων Ἑλλήνων δοθῆι <ἡ> πολιτεία.

Πετραῖος καὶ Ἀνάγκιππος καὶ Ἀριστόνοος, οὺς ἀτ τᾶς πρεισβείας ἐγένονθο, ἐνεφανίσσοεν αὐτοῦ, πόκκι καὶ ἁ ἀμμέουν πόλις διὲ τὸς πολέμος ποτεδέετο πλειόνουν τοῦν κατοικεισόντουν· μέσποδί κε οὖν καὶ ἑτέρος ἐπινοείσουμεν ἀξίος τοῖ πὰρ ἀμμὲ πολιτεύματος, ἐτ τοῖ παρεόντος κρεννέμεν ψαφιξάσθειν ἀμμέ, οὺς κε τοῖς κατοικέντεσσι παρ ἀμμὲ Πετθαλοῦν καὶ τοῦν ἄλλουν Ἑλλάνουν δοθεῖ ἁ πολιτεία.

Boeotian shows, like the Boeotian people, a certain leaning towards the Dorian. Its marks are ου for υ (merely because υ in Boeotian remained οο as in *moon* and did not become *ü* as in Attic), ει for η, αε (at Tanagra) or η or ει for αι, οε or υ for οι, ι for ει, ττ for σσ, δ initially, δδ medially for ζ.

Examples.

(1) On a Cantharus. Apparently of the fifth century B.C.

Μογέα δίδοτι τᾶι γυναι|κὶ δῶρον Εὐχάρι | τεὐτρετιφαντō κό|τυλον ὅς χ' ἄδαν πίε.

Though not so written, the inscription, apart from the first word, falls into two iambic trimeters.

(2) From a decree of the Boeotian League (about the end of the third century B.C.) found in the precinct of Amphiaraos at Oropus.

Χαροπίνω ἄρχοντος, μεινὸς Πανάμω, ἐπεψάφιδ(δ)ε Διδύμμων Ἐπαρμόσστω Ὀποέντιος. Δαμόκριτος Τιμογένιος Ὠρώπιος ἔλεξε· Δεδόχθη τῦ δάμυ· πρόξενον εἶμεν κὴ εὐεργέταν τῶ κυνῶ Βοιωτῶν Κλεόφαντον Κλεοφῶντος Χαλκιδεῖα κὴ

αὐτὸν κὴ ἐγγόνως, κὴ εἶμεν αὐτοῖ κὴ γᾶς κὴ ὑκίας ἔππασιν[1] κὴ ϝισοτέλιαν κὴ
ἀσφάλιαν κὴ ἀσουλίαν κὴ πολέμω κὴ ἰράνας ἰώσας[2] κὴ κατὰ γᾶν κὴ κατὰ
θάλατταν, κὴ τὰ ἄλλα πάντα καθάπερ κὴ τῦς ἄλλυς προξένυς κὴ εὐεργέτης.

<blockquote>[1] = Attic γῆς καὶ οἰκίας ἔγκτησιν.　　　　　　[2] = οὔσης.</blockquote>

(3)　From Thespiae.　Date towards the end of the third century B.C.

τοῖς μὲν πεπιτευόντεσσι[1] κὴ πεποιόντεισσι τὰ ἐς τὰς προρρείσιος ἤ κα
βείλωντη[2] τᾶς αὐτᾶς μισθώσιος ἐσσεῖμεν αὐτῦς ὑπογράψασθη παριόντεσσι αὐτοῖς·
ὁπόττα δέ κα ἀπίτευτα ἴωνθι[1] ἐνβᾶση[3] τὰν ἀρχὰν καθ' ἅ κα φήνειτη αὐτῦς σύνφορον
εἶμεν.

<blockquote>[1] πεπιτευόντεσσι Meister explains as 'irrigating' (πιτεύω connected with πίνω, πιπίσκω); ἀπίτευτα ἰωνθι 'are not irrigated.'　　[2] = Attic βούλωνται.　　[3] Transitive.</blockquote>

730.　Ionic and Attic agree in opposition to the other forms of Greek
speech in having η for ᾱ, ει and ου for εε and οο and also for ⎫ Ionic.
ε and ο in compensatory lengthening, σι for τι; ϝ is not in ⎭
ordinary use; ᾱο tends to become ηο in Ionic, εω in Attic: in neither is the
particle κε or κα found.　Ionic as distinguished from Attic has ρη, ιη, contracts εο into ευ (as later do many other dialects) and οη into ω, and tends
to lose the aspirate, which seems to have been entirely dropped in the
Ionic of the Asiatic coasts and adjacent islands.　Ionic has no dual.　Other
points of difference are exemplified by the Ionic δέκνυμι, νηῦς, γίνομαι, ξεῖνος,
μοῦνος, ὦν for οὖν, σήμερον, πρήσσω.

Slight differences are found between the dialects of Asiatic Ionic,
the Cyclades, and Euboea with its colonies; αο for αυ and εο for ευ
characterise the Ionic of the Asiatic cities and their colonies; Euboea
retains ϙ and the rough breathing which survives also in the Cyclades.
In Asiatic Ionic ι- stems have the gen. in -ιος, elsewhere their gen. is
in -ιδος.　In Asiatic Ionic Herodotus (I. 142) distinguishes four varieties,
which were at least in part occasioned by mixture with Carians and other
peoples who preceded the Greeks in Ionic lands.

Examples.

(1)　Asiatic Ionic, from a late copy of an inscription of a guild of
singers at Miletus.　The original was dated by the year when Philtes son of
Dionysius was grandmaster (αἰσυμνήτης) of the guild, and this we learn from
a list still preserved was 450–449 B.C.　The passages (a) and (b) were of
different dates:

(a)　ὅταν στεφανηφόροι ἴωσιν ἐς Δίδυμα ἡ πόλις διδοῖ ἑκατόνβην τρία
ἱερῆια τέλεια· ἑβδομαίοισιν δὲ δύο τέλεια καὶ χὸν τὸμ παλαιὸν ὁρτῆς ἑκάστης.

(b)　τῶι κήρυκι ἀτελείη ἐμ μολπῶ(ν) πάντων καὶ λάξις σπλάγχνων ἀπὸ
θυῶν ἑκαστέων καὶ οἶνο φορῆ ἐς τὰ ψυκτήρια τέλεσι τοῖσ' ἑωυτō.　The herald is
to be free from all dues in the guildhouse, to have a share in the meat of
all sacrifices, and the right to have his wine (which came from the guild
cellar) taken at his own expense to the cool places where the guild feasted.

(2)　From an Erythraean decree of proxeny (about 355 B.C.).

ἔδοξεν τῆι βουλῆι καὶ τῶι δήμωι· Μαύσωλλον Ἑκατόμνω Μυλασέα εἶναι
εδεργέτην τῆς πόλεως καὶ πρόξενον…καὶ ἀτέλειαν καὶ προεδρίην· ταōτα δὲ εἶναι
αōτῶι καὶ ἐκγόνοις.

The Eretrian dialect had the peculiarity of changing σ into ρ. This change was most common in the middle of words between vowels, but occurred according to Plato also at the end of words. The only instance in an inscription however is ὅπωρ ἄν, where the second word is closely connected with the first.

Example. From a decree of proxeny (about 411 B.C.).

ἔδοξεν τεῖ βολῆι Ἡγέλοχον τὸν Ταραντῖνον πρόξενον εἶναι καὶ εὐεργέτην καὶ αὐτὸν καὶ παῖδας καὶ σίτηριν εἶναι καὶ αὐτῶι καὶ παιρὶν ὅταν ἐπιδημέωριν καὶ ἀτελέην καὶ προεδρίην ἐς τὸς ἀγῶνας ὡς συνελευθερώραντι τὴμ πόλιν ἀπ' Ἀθηνάων.

Ionic was the chief literary dialect from the seventh to the middle of the fifth century B.C. The Elegiac and Iambic poets used the language of their native cities with some Epic forms intermingled especially in Elegiac. The language of Herodotus was called μεμιγμένη or ποικίλη by the ancient grammarians who name him also Ὁμηρικώτατος, as being influenced to a greater extent than earlier writers like Hecataeus by the epic style and diction. Probably a large number of the uncontracted forms like ποιέει in Herodotus are due to later copyists. He has, however, forms like ἑωυτοῦ which are not found in inscriptions (the only certain example is given above in the inscription from Miletus) nor in earlier Ionic writers. It is remarkable that the forms κῶς, κότερος, etc., which are regular in Herodotus and found also in Iambic poets do not occur in inscriptions, the only exception being the form ὁκοῖα published in 1906 from an inscription of the fourth century B.C. It seems that the literary dialect represented in the inscriptions did not correspond closely to the spoken language—it manifests none of the distinctions between the different varieties of Asiatic Ionic which Herodotus notices—and that Herodotus adopted forms like κῶς, etc., from the spoken dialect. In Timotheus' *Persae* (about 400 B.C.) an Oriental from Celaenae, who speaks Greek very imperfectly, uses κῶς while attempting to express himself in Ionic (Ἰάονα γλῶσσαν ἐξιχνεύων). Being regarded as vulgar, these forms are not found in the medical writings attributed to Hippocrates, who, though his school was in the Doric island of Cos, employed Ionic in his writings as being the literary dialect of his day, and was followed in this by later medical writers. The mimes of Herodas are probably artificial in their dialect—they too belong to Cos but date from the Alexandrian period—; artificial also are the *De deo Syriae* of Lucian, and the *Indica* of Arrian.

731. The earliest inscription found in Attica is upon a wine goblet (οἰνοχόη) given as a prize, which dates probably from the eighth century B.C. (see Fig. 179). It consists of an hexameter and three additional words, the form of the last two being doubtful. As commonly in very old inscriptions, the writing runs from right to left.

Attic.

ΝΟΤΝΑΠ ΝΟΤΣΕΧΡΟ ΝΥΝ SΟΘ
ΝΙΜ ΝΑΚΕΔ ΟΤΟΤ ΙΕΖΙΑΠ ΑΤΑΤΟΛΑΤΑ
(ὃς νῦν ὀρχηστῶν πάντων ἀταλώτατα παίζει | τοῦτο δεκᾶν μιν.)

As Attica took no prominent part in Greek history till the latter part of
the sixth century its dialect probably had undergone little change for a long
period. With the development of commerce came a great influx of strange
words, so that the author of the earliest work in the Attic dialect—the
treatise on the *Constitution of Athens*, formerly attributed to Xenophon,
but dating from about 425 B.C.—remarks that while every other Greek
land preserves its own dialect, the language of Attica is full of words drawn
from all quarters. From the speech of Lysias against Theomnestos we
learn that the vocabulary of Attic had changed very much since Solon's
time. The old forms in -οισι and -ασι, -ησι, -ηισι, for the dative plural
died out in the course of the fifth century B.C., though some forms in -ασι
and -ησι like θύρασι, 'Αθήνησι survived as adverbs.

Within Attic itself there were differences, the city dialect differing from
the rustic and the cultivated language from both. In Aristophanes' *Clouds*
872 Socrates remarks on Pheidippides' pronunciation of κρέμαιο. The vase
inscriptions show us the vulgar dialect, which differs in many respects
from the dialect which appears in the literature.

It is probable that Attic was the most difficult of the Greek dialects
owing to the number of particles and the subtlety of their use. We learn
from Cicero that the true Attic accent was difficult to acquire, Theophrastus
the philosopher being detected by a market-woman as a foreigner after he
had resided many years in Athens, though he belonged to the neighbouring
Euboea. From the speech against Eubulides which is attributed to
Demosthenes, we learn that this accent was also very easy to lose.
Thoucritus, who had been taken a prisoner in the Decelean war, and sent
to Epeirus as a slave, on his return to Athens many years afterwards was
unable to recover the Athenian pronunciation; hence later his son was in
danger of losing the franchise as being the son of an alien. Solon had
long before referred in his poems to the same fact:

ἀνήγαγον πραθέντας...γλῶσσαν οὐκέτ' 'Αττικὴν | ἱέντας.

The works of the earlier Athenian writers are not in the spoken but in
a literary dialect. The verses of Solon were influenced by the existing
lyric poetry of Greece. In his elegiacs some epic forms are found; in his
iambics a considerable number of Ionisms : δουλίην, τρομευμένους, ποιευμένους,
αἰδεῦμαι, δοκέω (but contracted in pronunciation). In tragedy the choral
odes imitated the Doric lyric poetry but only so far in form as to change η
to a, though in vocabulary and metrical structure much was drawn from this
source. In the iambic portions some forms are certainly Doric. As Aristotle
tells us (*Poetics* 3) it was urged amongst other arguments in support of
their claim to be the originators of both Tragedy and Comedy that they
used δρᾶν when the Athenians used πράττειν. It is noticeable that none
of the Ionisms found in Solon's iambics occur in Tragedy, and if Tragedy
had its beginnings amongst Dorians, the persistence with which particular
dialects were assigned to particular forms of literature would easily account
for the presence of occasional Dorisms.

One feature common to Tragedy and to Thucydides is the use of -σσ- for -ττ-, the latter characterising the Attic dialect of all ages. That this was a literary mannerism is shown by the fact that none of the orators save Antiphon uses -σσ-. In only one speech (περὶ τοῦ χορευτοῦ) does Antiphon use -ττ-. The Thucydidean πράσσω, ἔλασσον, forms in -αται, ξύν, etc., were not in use in the Attic of the period, and a considerable element in Thucydides' vocabulary was also strange to the ordinary spoken tongue. The so-called 'old Attic,' therefore, does not agree with the Attic inscriptions, but arises under the literary influence of Ionic.

It was not till 403 B.C. that the Athenians officially adopted the Ionic alphabet and with it the spelling of Greek words which is now customary. In the older alphabet ε was used for η and for ει arising from contraction or compensatory lengthening as well as for ε, ο was used for ω and ου arising like ει above, as well as for ο, while ξ and ψ were represented by χσ and φσ respectively, and the rough breathing by H.

Examples.

(1) From a decree of the beginning of the fifth century B.C. regarding the mysteries at Eleusis:

σπονδὰς εἶναι τοῖσι μύστεσιν καὶ τοῖς ἐπόπτεισιν καὶ τοῖς ἀκολούθοισιν καὶ χρήμασιν τὸν ὀθνεῖον καὶ Ἀθεναίοισιν ἅπασιν...τὰς δὲ σπονδὰς εἶναι ἐν τεῖσι πόλεσιν οἳ ἂν χρôνται τôι ἱεροῖ, καὶ Ἀθεναίοισιν ἐκεῖ ἐν τεῖσιν αὐτεσι πόλεσιν.

(2) From the treaty of alliance between Athens and Leontini in 433 B.C.:

ἐπ' Ἀφσεύδôς ἄρχοντος καὶ τες βολες ἑι Κριτιάδες ἐγραμμάτευε, ἔδοχσεν τει βολει καὶ τôι δέμôι...Τὲμ μὲν χσυμμαχίαν εἶναι Ἀθεναίοις καὶ Λεοντίνοις καὶ τὸν ὅρκον δôναι καὶ δέχσασθαι.

732. The most artificial of all literary dialects has been reserved for this place because traces of all the spoken dialects which precede may be found in it. This is the epic dialect found first in the *Iliad* and *Odyssey*, later in Hesiod, and retained permanently as the dialect of epic and elegiac poetry. Even in the earliest times it is not a uniform dialect, the *Odyssey* differing in some respects from the *Iliad* and both from Hesiod. Differences may be detected also between the main body of the *Iliad* and *Odyssey* and those parts which ancient or modern research has identified as later additions or interpolations. Still more remote from the Homeric style is that of the early Ionic philosophers, who adopted the epic hexameter because a prose style had not yet developed. Late writers like Apollonius Rhodius are simply imitators of Homer and many of their forms are incorrect.

In the Homeric poems the great mass of forms is Ionic, whence Homer is often described as old Ionic. There is, however, a considerable Aeolic element, the presence of which can be explained only by supposing that the poems, Ionic as we have them, were founded on earlier poems in Aeolic, a process to which many parallels in other literatures could be adduced. To this Aeolic element belong forms like ταλαύρινος, καλαῦροψ, εὔαδε, where ϝ has coalesced with a previous vowel into a diphthong, πίσυρες of different quantity from the Ionic τέσσερες, case-forms like 'Ατρείδαο beside 'Ατρείδεω, ἄνδρεσσι beside ἄνδρασι. At the period when the earliest parts of the poems were composed, Ionic was no doubt more like Aeolic than it was in historical times. The change of ᾱ to η must have taken place after Ionia was colonised, for the Greeks of Cyprus knew the Medes as Μᾶδοι, the older form, while the Ionians, also taking over the word in this form, have converted it into Μῆδοι. We have no evidence how early ϝ disappeared from Ionic, but it was entirely lost in historical times, while Aeolic retained it. It is required for the scansion of Homer, but the old scansion might have gone on after the pronunciation changed, just as in English *an University, such an one* are still written, though in present-day pronunciation both *University* and *one* begin with a consonant, rendering the *n* of the article unnecessary. The genitive in -οιο, which survives sporadically in Thessalian, was an archaism in Homer's time, for it is used specially in stereotyped phrases : διέπρησσον πεδίοιο, etc.

On the other hand many of the Homeric forms became modernised, so that the greatest critic of antiquity, Aristarchus, thought that Homer must have been an Athenian. These modifications sometimes took place contrary to the metre, ἕως and τέως being written where the metre clearly requires ἧος and τῆος. The forms of the contracting verbs ὁρόω, ὁράᾳς, and some noun-forms like φόως for φάος suggest that the earlier forms had been contracted to ὁρῶ, ὁρᾷς, φῶς and again expanded to suit the metre by doubling the resulting vowel-sound. Other forms which indicate Attic influence are οὖν (all dialects except Attic write ὦν), τέσσαρες not τέσσερες, μείζων not μέζων, etc.

733. The other dialects of the Greek world may be grouped together as Doric, though there are considerable differences between the Doric of Locris, Phocis, Achaia and northern Elis and that of the other Dorians of the Peloponnese and of the Dorian islands and colonies in the East and West. The characteristics which mark off Doric from Aeolic and Ionic are : -μες in 1st per. plural : αε contracting into η : locatives in -ει : aorist and future in -ξ- : infinitives in -εν, and λάω used for 'wish.' Doric had a special form of accentuation which is very imperfectly known.

(*a*) Laconian. In the language of the Spartiates, from about 450 B.C., σ between vowels becomes ʜ as in μῶἁ for Μῶσα (Μοῦσα); θ later became σ; *dy* is represented by δδ instead of ζ, μύσιδδε in Aristophanes' *Lysist.* 94 for μύθιζε. The vocabulary has many peculiar words, ὠβά, βουαγός, etc. The modern dialect (Tzakonian) of S.E. Peloponnese is found to retain several features of the old Laconian.

Example.

From an inscription dating from before 400 B.C. In the old Laconian alphabet without η and ω.

> Δαμόνον ἀνέθεκε 'Αθαναία[ι] Πολιάχοι
> νικἁας ταυτᾶ 'ἀτ' οὐδὲς πέποκα τὸν νῦν.

Doric.

The Laconian lyric poets Terpander, Alcman, Thaletas, Tyrtaeus, were not natives of Laconia and their language is influenced by Aeolic. Laconian forms are also found in the treaty of Thuc. v. 77, and in Aristoph. *Lysistrata*, though possibly not accurate in all respects.

Kindred forms of dialect are known from long inscriptions found at Heraclea in Magna Graecia (about 300 B.C.) with dat. pl. in -ασσι, πρασσόντασσι, and at Andania in Messenia (about 70 B.C.) which shows 3 pl. subj. in η, τίθηντι, etc.

(*b*) The dialect of Argolis and Aegina (down to the expulsion of its Doric inhabitants in 431 B.C.) retained νς like Cretan. Later Argive adopts from Laconian the change of σ between vowels into the rough breathing.

Examples.

(1) On a bronze tablet, probably of the early fifth century B.C. :

ἁ δὲ βōλὰ ποτελάτō ἀντιτυχόνσα¹, αἰ δέ κα μέ, αὐτοὶ ἔνοχοι ἔντο ἐνς Ἀθαναίαν.

¹ ' Let the council for the time being take proceedings for recovery.'

(2) Found in Aegina near the temple of Aphaia in 1901. Before 600 B.C. :

[ἐπὶ Κλ]εοίτα ἱαρέος ἐόντος τάφαιαι ʽτῖ‍ϙος [ἐποι]έθε χϙ̄ βōμὸς χōλέφας (=καὶ ὁ ἐλέφας) ποτεποέθε. | [καὶ τōρϙο]ς (=τὸ ἕρκος) περι[ε]ποιέθε.

(3) An inscription from Troezen of late sixth or early fifth century illustrates the adoption of Epic phrases in Doric.

Πραξιτέλει τόδε μνᾶμα ϝίσον ποίϝεσε θανό[ντι
τ]οῦτο δ' ἑταῖροι σᾶμα χέαν βάρεα στενάχοντες
ϝέργον ἀντ' ἀγαθōν κ̄επάμερον ἐξετέλεσ(σ)α[ν.

The inscriptions from Asclepius' temple at Epidaurus show a later, more ordinary Doric, with ποί for πρός, and, in the poems of Isyllus, a mixture of dialectic forms.

(*c*) Corinthian : its early form preserved ϙ, ϝ after consonants (Δϝεινία, ὄρϝος), and wrote χσ, φσ for ξ, ψ. A very similar dialect was naturally used in Sicyon, Corcyra and Syracuse.

Examples.

(1) ϙόραχς. Ποτειδᾶνός εἰμ' ἀϙοιτις. Περαιεόθεν ἵϙομες.

(2) A Corcyrean tomb-inscription, probably of the sixth century B.C. :

Σᾶμα τόδε Ἀρνιάδα Χάροπος· τὸν δ' ὄλεσεν Ἄρε̄ς
βαρνάμενον¹ παρὰ ναυσὶν ἐπ' Ἀράθθοιο ῥʹοϝαῖσι
πολλὸν ἀριστεύϝοντα κατὰ στονόϝεσ(σ)αν ἀϝυτάν.

¹ =μαρνάμενον.

(*d*) Syracusan is probably given with fair accuracy in the fragments of Epicharmus and Sophron. The only prose author of note is Archimedes, the writer on mathematics and physics, whose Doric has suffered a good deal in transcription.

Examples.

(1)　From Epicharmus' 'Ελπὶς ἢ Πλοῦτος (Frag. 35):

ἕρπω δ' ὀλισθράζων τε καὶ κατὰ σκότος
ἔρημος· αἲ κα δ' ἐντύχω τοῖς περιπόλοις,
τοῦθ' οἷον ἀγαθὸν ἐπιλέγω τοῖς θεοῖς, ὅτι
οὐ λῶντι πλεῖον ἀλλὰ μαστιγοῦντί με.

(2)　From·the fragments of Sophron: ἔτι μεθὲν ἁ καρδία παδῆι. Ἡρακλῆς τεοῦς κάρρων ἦς. ἐκπεφάναντί τεος ταὶ δυσθαλίαι.

The dialect of Theocritus in the Bucolic idylls is often said to be mainly Syracusan of the third century B.C. In some of the idylls however, as II. and VII., where the scene is laid in Cos, the dialect is as likely to be the Doric of that island, in which Theocritus spent some years. In Theocritus there are also many Aeolic forms: Μοῖσαι, ἔχοισα, νίκημι, etc., no doubt derived from the Aeolic lyric school. His dialect is therefore to some extent artificial, and, according to the MSS., is not consistent with itself even within the same idyll. The language of Isyllus, whose poems are among the inscriptions found at Epidaurus, shows that this inconsistency may be original, and not due to the carelessness of copyists.

(e)　Cretan is now well known from the long and important Gortyn inscription. Here νς is kept (except when final before an initial consonant), there is no φ or χ, θ appears, for ζ we find δ, δδ medially, and final consonants are regularly assimilated to the initial consonant which follows.

Examples.

(1)　From the Gortyn inscription, not later than the fifth cent. B.C.:

ἆς κ' ὁ πατὲδ δόει, τὸν τὸ πατρὸς κρēμάτōν πὰρ υἱέος μὲ ὀνēθθαι μēδὲ κατα-θίθεθθαι. ἄτι δέ κ' αὐτὸς πάσεται ē ἀπολάκει, ἀποδιδόθθō, αἲ κα λēῖ (= ἕως ἂν ὁ πατὴρ ζώῃ), τῶν τοῦ πατρὸς χρημάτων παρ' υἱέος μὴ ὠνεῖσθαι μηδὲ κατατίθεσθαι. ἄττα δ' ἂν αὐτὸς πάσηται (= κτήσηται) ἢ ἀπολάχῃ, ἀποδιδόσθω, ἐὰν λῇ).

(2)　From a Cnosian decree of proxeny at Delos (about 150 B.C.): ἦμεν δὲ αὐτοῖς καὶ ἔγκτησιν γᾶς καὶ οἰκίας καὶ ἀσφάλειαν πολέμω καὶ εἰρήνας καὶ καταπλέονσι ἐς τὸς Κνωσίων λιμένας κὺι ἐκπλέονσι.

(f)　In close relationship to one another stand the islands of Melos and Thera and the colony of Thera, Cyrene. The inscriptions on the rocks of Thera are amongst the oldest Greek inscriptions, dating from at least the seventh cent. B.C. The writing is from right to left, and there is no φ, χ, ξ, or ψ in the alphabet. In recent years many long inscriptions of both the early and the Roman periods have been found at Cyrene.

Examples.

(1)　From Thera. Πρακσίλαι με Θ'αρυμαϙ'ος ἐποίε.

(2)　From an ancient law on matters sacred at Cyrene:

αἰ δέ κα [νύμφα κατίασσα¹ τὸ νυμφήιον] μιᾶι,² καθαραμένα αὐτὰ καθαρεῖ τὸ ἱαρὸν καὶ ἐπιθυσεῖ ζαμίαν βοτὸν τέλευν. The words in brackets occur elsewhere in the Inscr.

¹ = Att. κατιοῦσα. ² A new 2 aor. pass. from μιαίνω: ἐμίαν, cf. the fut. μιασεῖ (3rd sing.).

(*g*) Rhodian had infinitives in -μειν, *e.g.* ἐσίμειν for εἰσιέναι, and characteristic words like κτοῖνα, township ; μάστρος, official.

Examples.

(1) A decree of Ialysus, third cent. B.C. :

ἔδοξε τοῖς μάστροις καὶ Ἰαλυσίοις· ὅπως τὸ ἱερὸν καὶ τὸ τέμενος τᾶς Ἀλεκτρώνας εὐαγῆται, ἐπιμεληθήμειν τοὺς ἱεροταμίας ὅπως στᾶλαι ἐργασθέωντι τρεῖς...θέμειν δὲ τὰς στάλας μίαμ μὲν ἐπὶ τᾶς ἐσόδου τᾶς ἐκ πόλιος ποτιπορευομένοις, μίαν δὲ ὑπὲρ τὸ ἱστιατόριον.

The most important colony from Rhodes was Agrigentum, the dialect of which has the same characteristics.

(2) Τύχα ἀγαθά. ἦ τυγχάνοιμί κα ἐμπορευόμενος ὅπυς κα δοκῆι σύμφορον ἔμειν καὶ ἀγων τῆι κα δοκῆι ἅμα τᾶι τέχναι χρεύμενος. (*v.l.* ἀμάται, Schywzer.)

734. As has been already mentioned the Doric dialects to the north of the Corinthian gulf, and their offshoots in Achaia and northern Elis, differ considerably from ordinary Doric. By some they are made a separate group under the name of the North-western dialects. They contain no literature. The older forms of these dialects are uncouth and difficult : αρ constantly appears for ερ, as in ϝάργον for ἔργον, πατάρα for πατέρα ; στ appears for σθ in verbal terminations, λυσάστω, etc. ; consonant stems have the dative plural in -οις, ἀγώνοις, etc. ; pres. participles passive of verbs in -εω end in -είμενος, -ήμενος, καλείμενος ; ἐν is used for εἰς. In Delphian a fossilised ablative case is found : ϝοίκω = οἴκοθεν.

Northern Doric.

Examples.

(1) Locrian. From an inscription of the fifth century B.C. giving regulations for a colony to Naupactus (δείλομαι occurs for βούλομαι as δήλομαι does in the Doric of the Peloponnese and islands) :

ἐν Ναύπακτον κα(τ) τόνδε ἀπιϝοικία...ὅσστις κα τὰ ϝεϝαδεϟότα[1] διαφθείρει τέχναι καὶ μαχανᾶι καὶ μιᾶι, ὅτι κα μὲ ἀνφοτάροις δοκέει, Ὁποντίον τε χιλίόν πλέθαι καὶ Ναϝπακτίον τὸν ἐπιϝοίϟὸν πλέθαι, ἄτιμον εἶμεν καὶ χρέματα παματοφαγεῖσται[2].

[1] pft. ptcp. of ἀνδάνω. [2] be confiscated.

(2) From the regulations of the phratry of the Labyadai at Delphi ; about the end of the fifth cent. B.C. :

ταγευσέω[1] δικαίως κατὰ τοὺν[2] νόμους τᾶς πόλιος καὶ τοὺς τῶν Λαβυαδᾶν περ τῶν ἀπελλαίων καὶ τᾶν δαρατᾶν[3]·...ὅρκος· ὑπίσχομαι ποὶ τοῦ Διὸς τοῦ πατρώιου· εὐορκέοντι μέμ μοι ἀγαθὰ εἴη, αἰ δ' ἐφιορκέοιμι ϝεκών, τὰ κακὰ ἀντὶ τῶν ἀγαθῶν.

[1] I will perform the duties of ταγός (head or manager of the affairs of the phratry).
[2] τοὺς with -ς assimilated to following ν.
[3] ἀπελλ. sacrifices at a Delphic festival called ἀπελλαί. δαρ. a sacrifice for the young men and maidens.

The older Elean inscriptions are found at Olympia : they show ζ for δ, δ for ζ, ρ for final ς.

(3)　From a Treaty of early sixth cent. B.C. :

ἁ ϝράτρα τοῖς ϝαλείοις. Πατρίαν θαρρὲν καὶ γενεὰν καὶ ταὐτὸ· αἰ ζέ τις
κατιαραύσειε¹, ϝάρρὲν², ὂρ ϝαλείο³· αἰ ζὲ μἐπιθεῖαν τὰ ζίκαια ὂρ μέγιστον τέλος
ἔχοι καὶ τοὶ βασιλᾶες, ζέκα μναῖς κα ἀποτίνοι ϝέκαστος τοῖ Ζὶ Ὀλυνπίοι.

The precise purport of this inscription is disputed. The most plausible
explanation of this clause is to take Πατρίαν as the name of a person who
is to be protected against sacrifice intended to do him hurt by the
magistrates, these being subject to a penalty for neglect of this duty.

　　¹ =καθιερεύσειε in form, like κατεύχοιτο in meaning.
　² i.e. ἔρρειν=φεύγειν in meaning.　　　　³ ὡς Ἡλείου (ὄντος).

(4)　Decree of third cent. B.C. : ἦμεν δὲ καὶ ἀσφάλειαν καὶ πολέμω καὶ
εἰράναρ καὶ γᾶρ καὶ βοικίαρ ἔγκτησιν καὶ ἀτέλειαν καὶ προεδρίαν ἐν τοῖρ
Διονυσιάκοιρ ἀγώνοιρ.

The later inscriptions of Locris, Phocis, and Elis are much less uncouth
and difficult. Under the influence of the Aetolian league in the third and
second century B.C., a kind of literary dialect for official documents grew
up, founded on the characteristics of this group, and through it the dative
of consonant stems in -οις spread to other parts of Greece.

(5)　A fragment of an Achaean sumptuary law :

Δαματρίοις τὰς γυναῖκες μήτε χρυσίον ἔχεν πλέον ὀδελοῦ ὀλκάν, μηδὲ λωπίον
ποικίλον, μήτε πορφυρέαν, μήτε ψημυθιοῦσθαι, μήτε αὐλῆν. Εἰ δέ κα παρβάλ-
ληται, τὸ ἱερὸν καθαράσθω ὡς παρσεβέουσα.

(6)　From an axehead found in South Italy (from an Achaean colony) :

τᾶς Ἕρας ἱαρός ἐμι τᾶς ἐν πεδίοι· Ϙυνίσκος με ἀνέθεκε ὄρταμος¹ ϝέργον δεκάταν.

　　¹ =ὁ ἄρταμος, 'the slayer of the sacrifice,' or simply =μάγειρος.

735.　The literary dialect of the great choral poets Stesichorus, Ibycus,
Pindar, Simonides, Bacchylides was in the main Doric,
though interspersed with Epic and Aeolic elements. Pindar's　　Dialect of
language has no relation to his native tongue, Boeotian, and　　the choral
Simonides and Bacchylides were Ionians from Ceos. Stesi-　　poets.
chorus, who was of Himera, a town founded by a mixed colony of Ionians
from Zancle and Dorians from Syracuse, was the originator of the literary
dialect which, with its mixture of Doric and Epic elements, was henceforth
regarded as that appropriate to choral poetry. That Aeolisms are not
found in his scanty fragments is hardly sufficient reason for attributing
their introduction only to his successors. As the poems were sent to all
parts of the Greek world to be sung on festal occasions, it is clear that a
dialect with very marked local characteristics like Boeotian would have
been an unsuitable, because an unintelligible medium. In the long fourth
Pythian, written for Arcesilaus of Cyrene, a Dorian prince, there are many
Epic forms but no special Aeolisms. In Bacchylides and Simonides there
is a larger Ionic element than in Pindar. Variations in dialect apparently
were often utilised for euphony ; thus Bacchylides uses φήμα and ἀδμήτα
instead of the pure Doric φάμα, ἀδμάτα, in order to avoid repetition of the
same sound, but admits ἄδματοι where the ending is different.

The only Doric prose besides Archimedes of Syracuse is the philosophical prose of the Pythagorean school of Southern Italy, preserved in numerous fragments by later writers. Part of a Doric treatise on rhetoric has recently been discovered in Egypt.

736. As soon as Greece passed beyond the stage of small independent States the dialects began to decay, although it was many centuries before they ceased to be the speech of the common folk. The existence of the Athenian empire tended to develop a common dialect between Athens and her allies, but the fall of Athenian power in 404 B.C. prevented the immediate completion of the process. During the fourth century, however, Greek soldiers of fortune became more numerous, and served for longer periods abroad. The effect of foreign residence upon the language of an educated man may be studied in the works of Xenophon, whose writings in both vocabulary and syntax often differ from Attic. Amongst the orators Hypereides seems to have been the greatest innovator. The Macedonian conquest greatly accelerated the levelling of the Greek dialects. Attic was adopted as the court language of Macedonia, and Attic formed the basis of the dialect which now became coextensive with Greek civilization. Foreign writers living at Athens, like Aristotle and Theophrastus, form the link between the Attic dialect and the κοινή, though both of these authors aimed at Attic diction. The first writer in the new dialect, whose works are preserved on a large scale, is Polybius, who shows the -ττ- and -ρρ- of Attic in such forms as ἡττήθησαν, ἐξέταττε, κατατεθαρρηκότων. The κοινή generally, however, has -σσ- not -ττ-. It is represented in the official papyri of Egypt under the Ptolemies, and in the inscriptions of Pergamum in a form closely resembling the language of Polybius. In vocabulary and construction it contains other elements than Attic, part at least being derived from Ionic. Alongside the formal language thus represented there existed a spoken idiom much farther removed from Attic. Of this the best representative in literature is the language of the Greek New Testament. Under the Roman Empire a literary reaction against the κοινή set in, and writers attempted to imitate the Attic of the best period. The greatest success in this movement was achieved by Lucian, who also made a study of the Ionic dialect. This revival was necessarily founded upon the book language, as were also the Aeolic epigrams of Balbilla, an attendant upon Hadrian's Empress. Neither Lucian nor Balbilla is of value for dialect study, but they show that at this period an antiquarian interest was taken in the dialects, which by this time in many places were almost or altogether extinct.

The κοινὴ *διάλεκτος.*

For further details with regard to dialect characteristics see Giles, *Short Manual of Comparative Philology*, Appendix B (with a selection of inscriptions), or the special works by Buck, *Introduction to the study of the Greek Dialects* (Grammar, selected inscriptions, glossary), 2nd ed. 1928, and Thumb, *Handbuch der griechischen Dialekte* (1909). A complete treatise by Bechtel for the whole of the dialects except Attic appeared in three volumes (1921-4). The best earlier work is Hoffmann's *Die griechischen Dialekte*, of which

Bibliography.

three volumes dealing with Arcadian, Cyprian, Thessalian, Asiatic Aeolic and the phonology of Ionic have been published. Meister's revision of Ahrens, *De Graecae Linguae dialectis*, stopped short after two volumes containing Thessalian, Asiatic Aeolic, Boeotian, Elean, Arcadian and Cyprian had been published. Prof. H. Weir Smyth published an elaborate work on Ionic in 1894 (Clarendon Press) There is a handy selection of dialect inscriptions edited by Solmsen (Teubner), an admirable and much larger volume (*Dialectorum Graecarum exempla epigraphica potiora*, Schwyzer, 1923), and many new volumes of the Berlin *Corpus* (*Inscriptiones Graecae*) have now appeared, the important dialect material of which is collected also in the *Sammlung der griechischen Dialektin-schriften* (1884—1915), edited by H. Collitz and F. Bechtel with the help of many other scholars. This collection includes in the index volume recent discoveries of importance, and also valuable grammars of the various Doric and Ionic dialects compiled by Hoffmann and others. The characteristics of Attic as shown in inscriptions will be found most conveniently in Meisterhans' *Grammatik der attischen Inschriften* (ed. 3 edited by E. Schwyzer). The *Lexicon Graecum Suppletorium* (2nd edition), by Herwerden, is useful for words not recorded in the ordinary dictionaries. The new edition of Liddell and Scott will incorporate most of this material.

VIII. 2. EPIGRAPHY.

737. GREEK Epigraphy may be conveniently defined as the study of documents inscribed or incised on permanent material, such as stone or metal, or occasionally wood, though the latter Definition and scope. has rarely survived except in Egypt. It therefore includes the inscriptions upon coins, gems, seals, rings, weights, stamps, and like objects; and in the case of pottery, it is usually taken to include graffiti scratched with a sharp point, and even painted inscriptions which are made before firing as part of the design of a vase, but not written documents (ostraka), in which pot-sherds are merely used as a material to write on instead of papyrus. On the other hand, documents incised with a stilus on wax, usually spread on wooden panels, are generally considered, from the character of the writing, to belong to the domain of palaeography. It follows that epigraphy is mainly concerned with the simpler and more monumental forms of the letters, though cursive forms occasionally intrude, especially in later inscriptions. As regards date we may exclude from consideration inscriptions of a later time than that of the fall of the Byzantine Empire (A.D. 1453); for classical literature indeed the interest ceases with the second century A.D. As regards language we may exclude documents written in a Greek character but in a non-Hellenic dialect, *e.g.* the half-barbaric inscriptions of Asia Minor (*Aspendus*, etc.), the Cretan (of *Praesos*, etc.) and the Celtic inscriptions. On the other hand the language of the Cypriote inscriptions is Greek, but the script is syllabic, not alphabetic, and non-Hellenic. Yet one more limitation: epigraphical interpretation in the fullest extent presupposes an encyclopaedic knowledge; in the narrower sense here to be understood the science of the

written characters and of the written formulae of Greek monumental literature constitutes the proper domain of Greek Epigraphy.

738. Down to about the end of the fifth century B.C., there was no common alphabet recognised by all the Greek States, but each had its own local variety; and though there were certain elements in common to all, there were also differences in the form of letters, in their significance and in alphabetic order. The common elements are most of them—though not all—to be found in early Phoenician inscriptions; and therefore it has

Fig. 169.   Clay tablet with incised writing found at Cnossus.

commonly been held, both by Greeks themselves and by modern epigraphists, that the various forms of Greek alphabet were derived from the Phoenician. A new aspect has been given to this problem by Sir Arthur Evans' discovery of a system of writing used in Crete during the second millennium B.C. (Fig. 169). This system is entirely independent of the hieroglyphic or other scripts known to have existed at an earlier date in Egypt and Asia, and appears to be derived from an earlier hieroglyphic system in Crete itself. There has been found in Crete, in addition to these, an example of a different system, with symbols impressed by a sort of type, on a terracotta disc from Phaestus (Fig. 170). It has been conjectured, partly because of a certain resemblance to the Hittite hieroglyphs, that this disc was imported from Asia Minor. None of these scripts has been satisfactorily deciphered as yet; the Cretan documents mostly consist of tablets of clay, incised and then baked. Most of them seem to be of the nature of inventories or accounts; it is not known whether the script was used for

Fig. 170. Clay disc with impressed characters found at Phaestus.

literary purposes. In addition to these Cretan discoveries, signs of a similar nature have been found scattered over various regions around the Mediterranean basin, though it is often by no means certain what, if any, was their syllabic or alphabetic value. There existed therefore, at the time when the Greek alphabet was in course of development, an abundant repertory of signs, many of them already adapted in various systems to the

G. A.

No.	Phoenician Names	Greek numerals
1	Aleph	1
2	Beth	2
3	Gimel	3
4	Daleth	4
5	He	5
6	Vau	6
7	Zayin	7
8	Cheth	8
9	Teth	9
10	Yod	10
11	Kaph	20
12	Lamed	30
13	Mem	40
14	Nun	50
15	Samekh	60
16	Ayin	70
17	Pe	80
18	Tsade	(900)
19	Qoph	90
20	Resh	100
21	Shin	200
22	Tau	300
23		400
24		500
25		600
26		700

The table also presents the alphabetic character forms for the following local alphabets (columns): Chalcis & col., Elis, Corinth, Athens, Paros &c., Miletus, Crete, Thera, Moab, Baal Lebanon. The Greek letter equivalents heading the columns are: α, β, γ, δ, ε (or η), F, ζ, η or ', θ, ι, κ, λ, μ, ν, ξ, ο (or ω), π, ρ, ϙ, ρ, σ, τ, υ, φ, χ, ψ.

Table of Phoenician and early Greek local alphabets.

phonetic expression of language.   The Phoenician was one of these systems ; and it seems probable that to the Phoenicians must be assigned the credit of first inventing a purely alphabetic system of writing, at least as far as the consonants are concerned, only the three long vowels *a, i, u* being also represented.   The Greeks improved on this by adopting separate symbols for the five chief vowel sounds, and in some cases also for the long vowels *e* and *o*.   In doing this, they used to a considerable extent the same set of symbols as were used by the Phoenicians, and in the same alphabetic order, the symbols used for vowels being those which in Phoenician appear as the 'breaths' aleph, he, yod, ayin, with the addition of *u*, probably a modification of vau.   The table on p. 690 shows the Phoenician alphabet, and a selection of typical early Greek local alphabets.

739.   It will be seen from the table that, so far as the first 22 letters are concerned, the various local Greek alphabets strongly resemble the Phoenician, though they preserve many forms that seem more primitive in character than any Phoenician   Local Alphabets. inscriptions that are known to us.   The numeral order of the letters, as given in the third column, shows a similar alphabetic order; and this is confirmed by various early abecedaria which have been found, *e.g.* Fig. 173. To the 22 letters all add Y, and many also the signs Φ X Ψ, all of which exist in the Cretan script; but some of the earliest alphabets do not possess these signs, and those that do vary in their use of them ; Ω, which is probably differentiated from O, is found only in the Ionic and its derivatives.   The most probable explanation of these facts seems to be that the Greek alphabet was not derived from any form of Phoenician that is known to us, but either from some more primitive form of Phoenician or from some more primitive system from which the Phoenician was also derived; and that various local groups of alphabets supplemented this system, to meet their requirements, from some common sources, making varied use of what was borrowed.   The main variation was between the eastern and western groups, of which the former used the symbols Φ, X Ψ, for *φ, χ, ψ*, in the order given, while the latter, as may be seen in the last two columns of the table, used them in the order Φ, Ψ, X and with the significance *φ, χ, ξ*.

EASTERN GROUP. A (1). *Ionic.* This contains all the letters of the Greek alphabet now in use, including ω.   It is found on the earliest inscriptions of Miletus, and at Naucratis.   Later it was universally adopted ; see § 740.

A (2).   *Cities on the coast of Asia Minor with colonies.*   The ancient alphabet of Teos, Colophon, Rhodes is thought to be that of the inscriptions engraved (*circa* 590 B.C.) by Greek mercenaries on the colossal figures at Abu Simbel in Egypt (see Fig. 176).   It is Ionic *minus* Ω and with Ｈ standing for the *spiritus asper* (but not in Fig. 176), as well as for a long vowel, the use to which it is limited in Ionic.   It has also the *koppa*.

44—2

B. *The Islands of the Aegean:* (i) *Thera* (see Figs. 172, 174), *Melos and Crete* (see Figs. 175, 177). These have no non-Phoenician signs[1]; they have crooked *iota*, σ in the form of *san*, *e*-sounds denoted by Ε and Η which stands for both *spiritus asper* and η, while in Crete complete *psilosis* or absence of aspirate prevails. (ii) *Paros, Siphnos, Thasos, Delos, Naxos* (see Fig. 178), *Ceos.* All these have Λ for γ as in Attica, and a peculiar form C for β[2]. Except in Ceos, they retain *koppa*. They all have φ, Χ but no ψ; Η in Paros, Siphnos, Naxos = *spiritus asper*; and they are all characterised by peculiarities in the representation of the *e*-sounds. In Paros, Siphnos, Thasos, Delos the values of the *o*-symbols are strangely reversed: Ο = ω, Ω = o, ου.

C. *The Mainland of Hellas: Attica* (see Figs. 179, 180), *Argos, Corinth* (see Figs. 181—183) *and its colonies, Phlius, Sicyon, Megara and its colony Selinus, and Aegina.* These occupy a position intermediate between the Eastern and the Western division and are eclectic. They have the non-Phoenician signs φ, Χ and, except in Attica and Aegina, ψ (in Attica represented by φϟ, as ξ is by Χϟ), with their Eastern values. *Koppa* is in use in the earliest period[3]. Η is *spiritus asper* and not η. *Digamma* is present except in Attica[4].

WESTERN GROUP. D. *States of Northern Greece.* E. *States of Peloponnesus.* The alphabets are characterised by the use of Υ = χ (Fig. 184, *Achaia*, Fig. 185, *Elis*) and Χ = ξ. Ω is absent; ψ in Ozolian Locris and on coins of the Arcadian Psophis has a special symbol, ✳.

---

[1] But in Thera and Melos, in a few archaic inscriptions, Υ occurs, with the value however of ξ, while ϟ is denoted by Ξ. Further Χ = χ appeared before Μ = σ disappeared.

[2] Local varieties of β occur also in Thera (Fig. 174), Melos (where at a certain period C = o, ου), Crete (Fig. 175), Corinth, where Β = ε, η (Figs. 182, 183), Megara.

[3] An archaic Attic vase-inscription (Fig. 180) contains crooked *iota*.

[4] ναϝυ[πηγός], ἀϝυτάρ (sixth century B.C.) and αὐϝο-, assigned to the fourth, are probably not of Attic origin.

TRANSCRIPTION OF TEXTS ON p. 693.

171. (*Naucratis*) ὦ ˙πόλλω, σοῦ εἰμί.
172. (*Thera*) Ῥηξάνωρ. Ἀρχαγέτας. Προκλῆς. Κλεαγόρας Περαιεύς.
173. (Vase from Formello) α β γ δ F ε ζ h θ ι κ λ μ ν [ξ] ο π [san] ϙ ρ σ τ υ ξ φ χ.
174. (*Thera*) Ἄβρωνος ἠ<ε>μί.
175. (*Gortyn*) ...λεβῆτας Fὲξ τον....
176. (*Abu Simbel*) Βασιλέος ἐλθόντος ἐς Ἐλεφαντίναν Ψαμ(μ)ατίχου, | ταῦτα ἔγραψαν τοὶ σὺν Ψαμματίχῳ τῷ Θεοκλ(έ)ος | ἔπλεον · ἦλθον δὲ Κέρκιος κατ|ύπερθε, υἷς ὁ ποταμὸς | ἀνίη · ἀλ(λ)ογλώσσ(σ)ους δ᾽ ἦχε Ποτασιμτώ, Αἰγυπτίους δὲ Ἄμασις. ἔγραφε δ᾽ ἀμὲ Ἄρχων Ἀμοιβίχου καὶ Πέλεκος Οὐδάμου.

Fig. 171.

Fig. 172.

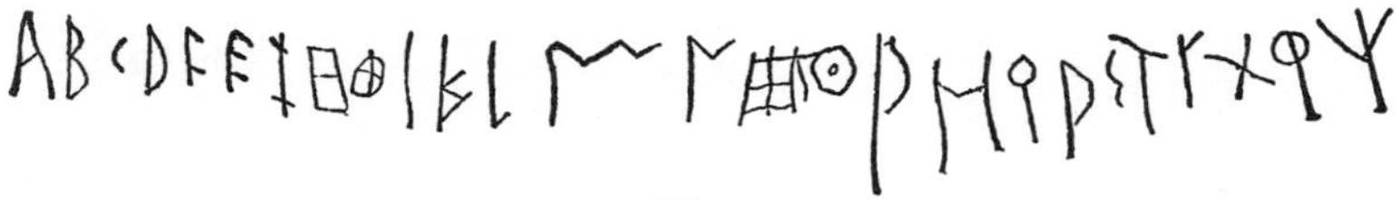

Fig. 173.

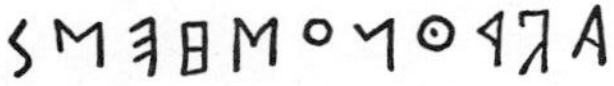

Fig. 174.

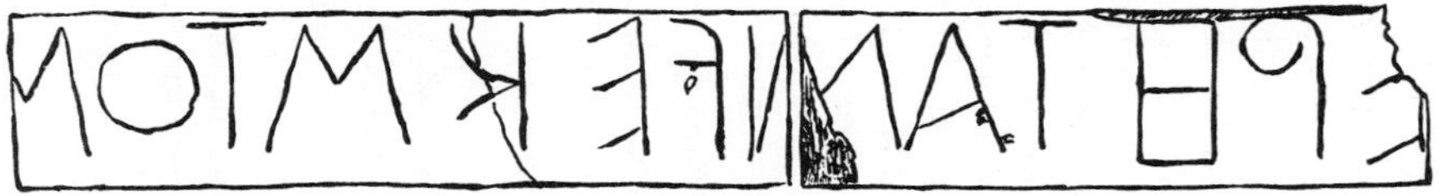

Fig. 175.

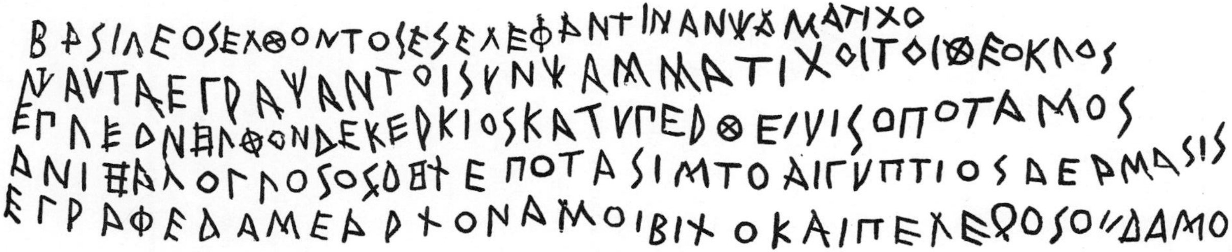

Fig. 176.

For transcription see p. 692.

Ϝ or Ϲ = *digamma* is nearly always present. Ε and Ο represent all the *e*- and *o*-sounds respectively, and Ϻ or Η is *spiritus asper*, which however is entirely absent from Elean inscriptions; see Fig. 185 (ὅρτιρ = ὅστις).

740. The Ionic alphabet (Fig. 186) gradually supplanted the epichoric alphabets. At Athens in the archonship of Eucleides Further de- 403 B.C. it was decreed that in future all public acts should velopment of be engraved in the Ionic characters, which had in private the Ionic alphabet. documents been in use for some decades previously. With-

in a very few years all the other States which used non-Ionic alphabets followed the lead of Athens. Some of them may even have set the example of reform to Athens. But the Ionic alphabet itself underwent changes, especially after the third century B.C., as regards the form of individual letters; they were altered sometimes by way of simplification, sometimes by way of elaboration or embellishment. Thus Α might appear as Ꙇ, Λ, Λ̇, Λ̣ (*i.e.* with *apices*), or might revert to a more ancient form as Α or Λ; Ε became Ϲ ; Ι became Ζ; Θ become Θ and Θ; Ξ became Ξ, Σ, Σ̄, Ζ etc.; Π became Π, ΤΤ, Π; Σ became Σ, Ϲ, Ϲ; Φ in Attica for a considerable portion of the fourth century B.C. appears as +, and at various times as Ϙ, ≠, Φ, Φ; Ω became ω, ɯ, etc. The forms in fact more and more assimilated themselves to the cursive forms in use in MSS. and especially papyrus MSS., in which *e.g.* are found in use more early examples of 'lunated' forms of σ (Ϲ) than appear on stones[1]. The use of these later forms of the Ionic letters came in gradually; thus Σ is found in the second century B.C., Ζ not till nearly the beginning of the first; but in the period of the empire we find not only an occasional recurrence to archaic forms, but also an indiscriminate

[1] Lunated σ appears sporadically on Old Attic boundary-stones.

TRANSCRIPTION OF TEXTS ON p. 695.

177. (*Gortyn*) ...τὸν ἀνπαντόν, καὶ μὴ ἐ|πάνανκον ἤμην τέλλεν [τὰ τῶ | ἀν]παναμένω καὶ τὰ κρήμα|τ᾽ ἀναιλ(ῆ)θαι ἄτι κα κατα[λίπη|ι ὁ ἀν]πανάμενος· πλίυι δὲ τὸν | ἀνπαντὸν μὴ ἐπικωρῆν. [Αἰ δ᾽ | ἀπο]θάνοι ὁ ἀνπαντὸς γνήσια | τέκνα μὴ καταλιπών, πὰρ τὸ[νς τῶ ἀνπ]αναμένω ἐπιβάλλονταν|ς ἀνκωρῆν τὰ κρήματα. Αἰ δ[έ κα | λῇ ὁ ἀνπανάμενος, ἀποϜειπ|άθθω κατ᾽ ἀγορὰν ἀπὸ τῶ λά[ω ᾧ ἀπα]γορεύοντι, καταϜελμέν|ων τῶν πολιατᾶν· ἀνθέμ[ην δὲ | δέκ]α [σ]τατήρανς ἐδ δικαστ|ήριον.

178. (*Naxos*) Νικάνδρη μ᾽ ἀνέθηκεν ᾽[ε]κηβόλῳ Ἰοχεαίρῃ, ϙούρη Δεινο|δίκεω τοῦ Ναξίου, ἔξοχος ἀλ(λ)έων, Δεινομένεος δὲ κασιγνήτη, | Φράξου δ᾽ ἄλοχος μ....

179. (*Athens*) ὃς νῦν ὀρχηστῶν πάντων ἀταλώτατα παίζει, τοῦτο δεκᾶν (?) μίν.

180. (*Athens*) [Εἴτ᾽ ἀστό]ς τις ἀνὴρ εἴτε ξένος | ἄλ(λ)οθεν ἐλθών,
    Τέτ(τ)ιχον οἰκτίρα|ς, ἄνδρ᾽ ἀγαθὸν παρίτω:
'Εν πολέμῳ | φθίμενον, νεαρὰν ἥβην ὀλέσαν|τα·
    Ταῦτ᾽ ἀποδυράμενοι νεῖσθ᾽ ἐπὶ πρᾶγμ᾽ ἀγαθόν.

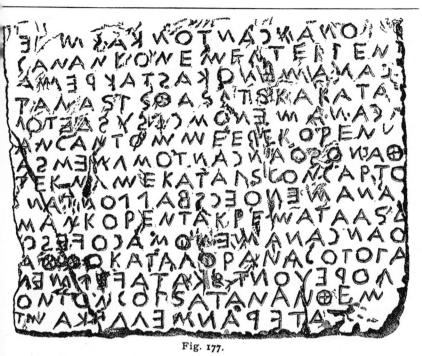

Fig. 177.

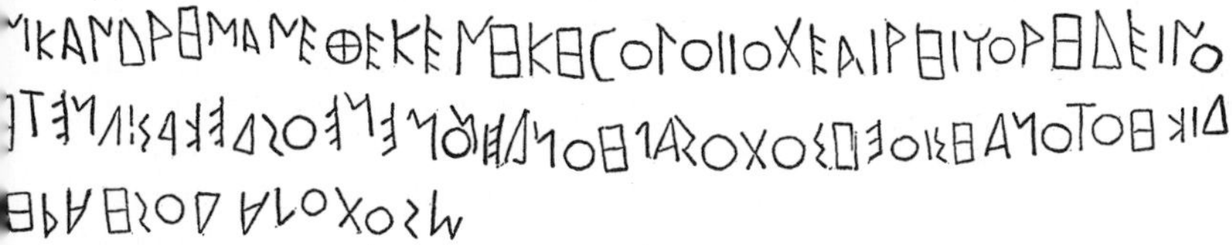

Fig. 178.

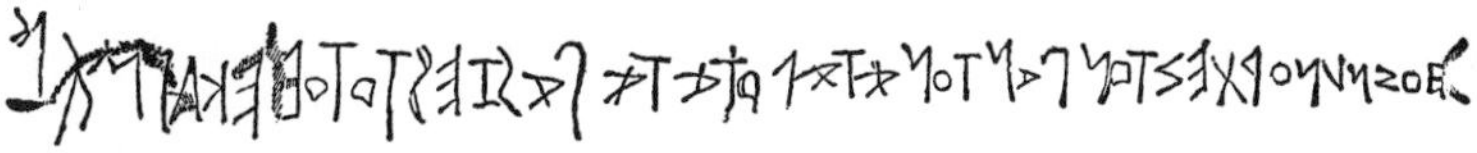

Fig. 179.

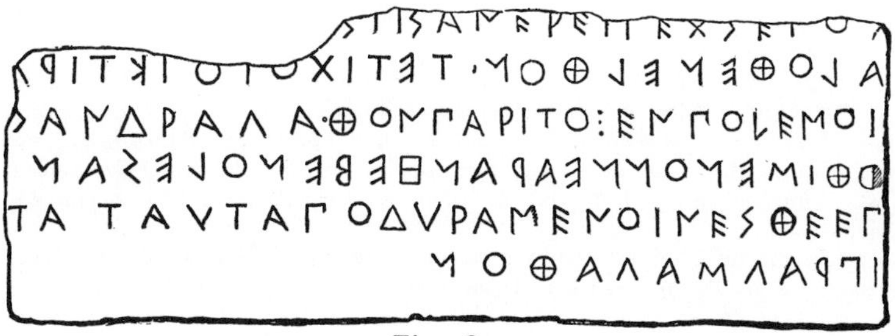

Fig. 180.

For transcription see p. 694.

use of forms of different periods even on the same inscription: one Attic inscription, I.G. III. 1, 1197 (A.D. 238—244), has no fewer than six forms of α.

741. At first Greek writing, like Phoenician, appears to have been invariably from right to left or 'retrograde' (ἐπὶ τὰ λαιὰ ἐκ

Systems of writing.

δεξιῶν, Paus. v. 25, 9) (see Figs. 171, 174, 175, 179, 184). Then followed a transition period, that of the βουστροφηδόν style (winding as one ploughs with oxen), in which the first line is 'retrograde' and the second left to right, and so on (ἀπὸ τοῦ πέρατος τοῦ ἔπους ἐπιστρέφει τῶν ἐπῶν τὸ δεύτερον ὥσπερ ἐν διαύλου δρόμῳ (*ib.* v. 17, 6) (see Figs. 177, 178, 185). By the beginning of the fifth century B.C. the later or left to right style had taken root and it is rare to find a βουστροφηδόν inscription after 500 B.C. Frequently, and especially in Attic inscriptions after Eucleides, the letters though read horizontally are arranged also in vertical lines (στοιχηδόν), a peculiarity obviously of great importance for restoring lacunae.

742. The use of **compounded letters**, as NE = NE,

Ligatures, Abbreviations, Compendia, Stenography.

HK = HK, seems to have owed its origin in the main to the encroachment of cursive combinations upon the lapidary style. Examples at Athens in the centuries before Hadrian are very rare and even in the centuries following are not common, while in the cursive inscriptions of the Byzantine period the use of them is very extensive. **Abbreviations** are found sporadically even in the earliest times, *e.g.* Ἀπόλ(λ)ωνος Λυκ. (= Λυκείου) εἰμί, Θεάγεος Ρύπθ (?) (*Metapontum*, before 500 B.C.), occasionally in the fifth century, *e.g.* τριή. (= τριήραρχος) on a list of dead (*Attica*). In the period from Eucleides to Augustus they are common enough, *e.g.* Ἀλωπ. (= Ἀλωπεκῆθεν), but in Attic decrees not till quite late in this period. In the imperial period regular abbreviations, such as Τι=Τιβέριος, of personal names, and Καλ=Καλανδῶν, were frequent.—

Compendia are rare before Augustus, as Π = πρεσβύτερος; afterwards the use of them is frequent.—A mutilated inscription, apparently of the fourth century B.C., found on the Acropolis, appears to give directions for a system of **stenography**. A portion of it has been restored as follows

TRANSCRIPTION OF TEXTS ON p. 697.

181. (*Corinth*) ...ε F ζ h θ ι κ λ μ ν ο π ξ ϙ ρ *san* τ...
182. (*Corinth*) Ζεύς.
183. (*Corinth*) Ἀνέθηκε τῷ Ποτειδᾶνι.
184. (*Achaia*) τἀθάνᾳ Φιλλὼ Χαρμυλίδα δεκάτα[ν].
185. (*Elis*) l. 2 [ἰα]ρομάοι αἱ μὰ πεν... l. 3 αἴ τιρ μαῖτο χρήεστ[αι], l. 4 ...θαι Ὀλυνπίᾳ, αἱ ζα... l. 5 ...ον αἴ τιρ ταῦτα πα[ρβαίνοι] l. 6 ὁ θεοκόλο[ρ ὄρτιρ τόκα θεοκο[λέοι, ἀποτίνοι κα...] l. 7 [τοῖ] Ζὶ Ὀλυνπίοι λατρα[ἴώμεν....] l. 8 [τοῖ Ζ]ὶ Ὀλυνπ[ί]οι τοὶ ζ....
186. (*Samos*, on a solid bronze votive hare, now in the British Museum) τῷ Ἀπόλλωνι τῷ Πριη(ν)ῆϊ μ' ἀνέθηκεν Ἡφαιστίων.

Fig. 181.

Fig. 182.

Fig. 183.

Fig. 184.

Fig. 185.

Fig. 186.

For transcription see p. 696.

(ll. 14—28): τῶν] δ᾽ ἀφώνων ἡ [μὲν εὐθ]εῖα καὶ βρα[χεῖα γρα]μμὴ [το]ῦ φωνήεντος [κάτω μὲν] τεθεῖσα δύ[ναται δέλτ]α, [ἐπάνω] δὲ ταῦ, [πρὸς δὲ] τεῖ τελευτεῖ νῦ· [μετεώρ]α δ᾽ ἐπὶ τὴν ἀρχὴν [μὲν π]ροσηγμένη πεῖ, [πρὸς δὲ] τεῖ τελευτεῖ μῦ· [κατὰ δὲ τὸ μέ]σον πρὸς [μὲν τ]ὴν ἀρχὴν προση[γμέ]νη βῆτα, [πρὸς δὲ τεῖ τελευτεῖ ψεῖ.] Thus, e.g. ⌐ = δι, ⌐ = πι, ⌐ = διπ, etc. (Note that the orthography ει = η is found in Attic inscriptions as early as 380 B.C.)

743. Separation of words by spaces is not found in inscriptions before the Roman period. Generally in Attic inscriptions punctua-
Punctuation. tion (if employed at all) is effected by the sign : or :, but the usage is very capricious and frequently appears to have no connexion with grammatical construction, e.g. on a Locrian inscription I.G.A. 321 : Λοϙρὸν τὸν : Ὑποκναμίδιον and καταλείπον:τα. Numeral signs are frequently separated from the rest of the text by two or three dots placed on the right and the left of them. Abbreviations, and at Athens proper names also, are often followed by two dots. Various other devices are found in different districts and later times.

744. To denote cardinal numbers in classical and post-classical times
Numeral (demonstrably from 454 to about 95 B.C.) the following
signs— symbols were in use in Attica: | = 1, ⌐ = 5, Δ = 10, H = 100,
'acrophonic.' X = 1000, M = 10,000 and multiplication was expressed by symbols like ⌐ or ⌐ = 50, ⌐ = 500, ⌐ = 5000, ⌐ = 50,000. Units of measure and money were represented by T = τάλαντον, M = μνᾶ, ⌐ or ⌐ = στατήρ, ⊦ = δραχμή, | = ὀβολός, ℂ and ⊃ = ἡμιωβέλιον, T = τεταρτημόριον, X = χαλκοῦς. T, M and ⅀ could be united with the symbols for 5, 10, 50, 100, etc., by ligatures. When no other symbol is given, drachmae are to be understood. For 5 obols the symbol is not ⌐, which might be con-founded with drachmae, but |||||. As examples may be taken Δ⊦⊦ = 12 drachmae; TTT = 3 talents; ⌐TXXX⌐HH⌐ΔΔΔ⌐⊦⊦||||ℂ = 11 talents, 3787 drachmae, 4½ obols. In countries, e.g. Boeotia, in which the Western variety of epichoric alphabets prevailed, Ψ would take the place of X. Thus at Orchomenus (where the fuller symbol ⊢E = ἑκατόν) Ψ|⌐⊢E⊢E⊢E▷▷||| = 5823; and numerous other varieties are found as, e.g. at Troezen ℂ = 1 drachma, ⌐ = 10; at Argos and Nemea ◯ or ⊙ = 10, · = 1; at Epidaurus — = 10, · = 1; thus

XXX⊟⊟ = = = — : : : · ||||| = 3277 drachmas, 5 obols.

For ordinal numerals (marks of date, etc.) there are in the classical period no special symbols.

On the other hand, as early as the fifth century B.C. we find objects
numbered consecutively by the letters of the alphabet in
Alphabetic. order : thus the tickets of the ten panels of heliasts at Athens were marked Α to Κ (Ϛ being omitted), and ὅρος Κ = the 10th boundary-stone. A familiar example of this use of the later alphabet is seen in the num-

bering of the books of the *Iliad* and *Odyssey*. This system, however, could only be of limited application, since it did not provide for any numbers beyond 24. The system usually found in Greek MSS. and classical texts uses 27 signs—the complete Ionic alphabet, including the obsolete signs Ϝ or Ϛ , Ϙ or ϙ, and Ͳ or ͳ (see table on p. 690); these fall into three complete and equal categories, α—θ representing units, ι—ϙ tens, and ρ—ͳ hundreds. It may be inferred from the presence of these three obsolete symbols that the system must have been invented at least as early as the sixth century B.C. in Miletus; but the earliest epigraphic evidence for its use is found in the fourth century B.C., on alabaster vases from the Mausoleum at Halicarnassus, *e.g.* ϒΝΔ = 754, ΣϘΓ = 293. In Athens the usage does not occur until the first century B.C. The thousands are distinguished by a diacritical sign on the left, which in unambiguous cases may be omitted; thus 'Α or ͵Α = 1000. Fractions are represented by special symbols in the acrophonic system; other examples are too uncertain to call for notice here.

745. The grammatical constructions are as a rule simple and free from intricacy. Where they depart from rule there is hardly anything which might not find its parallel in the literary language. Nor is this statement seriously qualified by the occurrence of such variations as ἐπαινεῖν and ἐπιμελεῖσθαι followed by the dative in Attic inscriptions, by the use of ἐν with the accusative in Delphian, the use of ἐξ with the dative in Arcadian and Cyprian, or the use in Elean of the optative with κα and of the subjunctive in an imperatival sense (κ᾽ ἔα = ἂν εἴη for ἔστω, ἀνατεθᾷ = ἀνατεθῇ for ἀνατέθητι). In the non-Attic dialects in fact there is nothing, in the absence of contemporary literary documents, to show that the syntax of the inscriptions is not that of the corresponding spoken and written dialect.

Syntax of inscriptional language.

746. Inscriptions are (1) dated, (2) undated. In dated inscriptions the date of origin or engraving is expressly mentioned in formulae varying with the political circumstances of the Grecian States. As a general rule every independent canton or State dated its public documents according to the term of office of its highest political or State officials; as *e.g.* at Athens by the mention of the eponymous Archon, at Gortyn of the eponymous Κόσμος, in Aetolia by the name of the Στρατηγός and so forth. In some cases we have a continuous list of such officials, as of Attic Archons from 480 to 291 B.C. The date within this period, when the Archon's name in an inscription survives, is immediately determinable, except where there happen to be two Archons of the same name. Inscriptions dated by the reign of a King do not always give the exact year of the reign. The oldest inscriptions in which the year of the reign is specified are those of Mylasa. In the case of Roman Emperors the date may be inferred (1) from the *tribunicia potestas*, (2) the number of the consulate, (3) the abdication. The reckoning

Determination of date.

by Olympiads (from 776 B.C. to Ol. 294 = A.D. 400), common in the historians, is rarely found in inscriptions. Occasionally in votive offerings Olympian victors give the number of the Olympiad in which they won. In the Hellenistic and Roman periods we find a large number of local eras, known for the most part only by coin-inscriptions. Nearly all of these eras belong to Asia Minor. Their starting-point is the grant of autonomy, incorporation in the Roman Empire, organisation as a Roman Colony, the visit of an Emperor, etc. Some eras have reference to events of general history, others to occurrences in the local history of individual towns, especially the institution of games or festivals. The reckoning by Indictions or taxation-periods of 15 years which is found in Oriental inscriptions begins with 1 September 5509 dating from the Byzantine era of the creation = A.D. 313. But for exact chronological purposes it is of little use, because only the year and not the period of the Indiction is given. The Christian era is almost unknown to the Byzantines. In the few inscriptions in which it is found (C.I.G. 8689, 8759) it appears as an addition to the Byzantine date.

In **undated inscriptions** the date is determined (1) by the various contents of the documents, as, *e.g.*, the names of historically known persons; (2) by the dialectic forms, *e.g.*, the presence or absence in Attic of the older dative plural of *a*-stems in -σι (ταμίασι), the use or disuse of patronymic adjectives in Boeotian, as Ἀμινίας Τιμώνιος for Τίμωνος; (3) by official formulae, which were subject to change from time to time : *e.g.*, in Attic decrees the name of the ἄρχων ἐπώνυμος appears for the first time in 433 B.C.; in and after 349 B.C. the name of the proposer is followed by that of his father and his deme; (4) by the written character : *e.g.* the use or disuse of the βουστροφηδόν style, the use of an epichoric or of the Ionic alphabet, the use or disuse in Attic of Ϛ, of Ο for ου (after about 353 B.C.), of Ε for ει (after about 276 B.C.), the use of ligatured letters, the use of Ζ, Φ, Μ, Π, Σ, Ω for the older Ι, Θ, Μ, Γ, Ϛ, Ω ; (5) by the form and architectural character of the stones themselves, sculptures in relief, the form and artistic style of inscribed vases, etc.; lastly (6) by the peculiar circumstances of the place of discovery, as the depth of the strata of earth at Naucratis.

747. Decrees. The Attic documentary style supplied the pattern to a large number of the other Greek States. A typical Attic decree from about the middle of the fifth century to 376 B.C. would contain the following elements: (A) The preamble. This consists of (*a*) the introductory formula : ἔδοξε τῇ βουλῇ καὶ τῷ δήμῳ (or τῇ β. or τῷ δ. alone); (*b*) the name of the 'prytanising' tribe : Κεκροπὶς (Ἐρεχθηΐς, etc.) ἐπρυτάνευεν; (*c*) the name of the Secretary of the Tribe : Μνησίθεος ἐγραμμάτευεν; (*d*) the name of the President of the Ecclesia : Εὐπείθης ἐπεστάτει; (*e*) the name of the eponymous archon (frequently omitted) : ὁ δεῖνα ἦρχεν; (*f*) the name of the proposer : Καλλίας εἶπεν. After 375 B.C., gradually, more specification in the names and more exactness in the dating were introduced. The character of the assembly and the place (ἐκκλησία ἐν———, βουλὴ ἐν———)

Classification and formulae of inscriptions.

and the nature of the decree (δήμου ψήφισμα, βουλῆς ψ.) might be noted. Cf. for the preamble, I.G. II. 1, 247, a decree of 306/5 B.C. : Θεοί. | Ἐπὶ Κοροίβου ἄρχοντος ἐπὶ τ|ῆς Οἰνεῖδος δεκάτης πρυτανε|ίας [or πρυτανευούσης], εἰ (= ῇ) Πάμφιλος Θεογείτονο|ς Ῥαμνούσιος ἐγραμμάτευεν· | Μουννυχιῶνος ἕνει (= ἔνῃ) καὶ νέᾳ ἐ|μβολίμῳ, ἐνάτει (= -ῃ) καὶ εἰκοσ̓τ|εῖ (= -ῇ) τῆς πρυτανείας· ἐκκλησία· | τῶν προέδρων ἐπεψήφιζεν Πύ|θιππος Πυθίωνος Μαραθώνιο|[ς] καὶ συμπρόεδροι· ἔδοξεν τῷ δήμῳ· Στρατοκλῆς Εὐθυδή|μου Διομεεὺς εἶπεν· ἐπειδὴ κτλ. Note that formula (e) is replaced by a heading with the name of the archon, the prytanising tribe (b) has its numerical order specified ; formula (d) gives way to the phrase τῶν προέδρων κτλ. and marks the transference of the ἐπιψήφισις from the epistates of the prytanes to a chief, elected by lot, of the nine πρόεδροι or representatives, one from each 'non-prytanising' tribe. Further, the day of the month (in this case an intercalary day, ἐμβόλιμος) and the day of the prytany are specified. Lastly, this inscription belongs to the period dating from 307/6 B.C., when the two new tribes, Antigonis and Demetrias, were added to the existing ten, and the duration of prytanies, increased from ten to twelve, *approximately* coincided with the limits of the several months. After the statement of (B) motives, introduced by ἐπειδή, there follows, between the preamble and the substance of the measure or law, (C) the transition-formula : (τύχῃ ἀγαθῇ) δεδόχθαι (rarely ἐψηφίσθαι) τῇ βουλῇ or τῷ δήμῳ. This in a large number of decrees was *probouleumatic*, *i.e.*, marks the decree as having been drafted and approved by the Senate before being submitted to the Ecclesia, and then (D) the actual words of the proposition or decree or bill or treaty in the infinitive construction. Amendments (E) or appendices proposed by the Ecclesia are introduced as follows : ὁ δεῖνα εἶπε· τὰ μὲν ἄλλα καθάπερ τῇ βουλῇ (sc. ἔδοξεν) or καθάπερ Ἀντικλῆς (sc. εἶπεν) τὰς δὲ εὐθύνας Χαλκιδεῦσι κατὰ σφῶν αὐτῶν εἶναι ἐν Χαλκίδι κτλ. Lastly (F) follow directions concerning the engraving, choice of material, grant of costs, the boards, officials or fund upon which the payment devolved, the limit of cost and other provisions for publishing or executing copies of the document.

Honorary decrees, including decrees conferring the title of πρόξενος or εὐεργέτης, form a very large class of their own, and in no other department of Epigraphy does the influence of the Attic style make itself more widely felt than in the drafting of these honorary decrees. In the fifth century the framework was very simple ; the introductory formula was immediately followed by the substance of the decree : ἐπαινέσαι τὸν δεῖνα, sometimes with the motive briefly added and an enumeration of the honours conferred. In later times, after the mention of the proposer, there followed (1) a statement of motive, introduced by ἐπειδή and tending to become more and more prolix and tedious ; (2) a 'hortative' section, *e.g.* ὅπως ἂν οὖν καὶ οἱ ἄλλοι ἅπαντες εἰδῶσιν ὅτι ὁ δῆμος ἐπίσταται χάριτας ἀποδιδόναι κτλ. ; (3) the transition formula : δεδόχθαι κτλ. ; (4) the expression of thanks and the grant of various privileges ; *e.g.* προεδρία, ἀτέλεια, γῆς τε καὶ οἰκίας ἔγκτησις, ἀσυλία κατὰ γῆν καὶ κατὰ θάλατταν, etc.

748. In form there is frequently not much difference between the inscriptions known respectively as **Honorary, Dedicatory** and **Sepulchral**, and it is not always possible to decide to which category an inscription belongs. The simple nominative is found on the statue-bases of distinguished men in the earlier time, *e.g.* Λυκοῦργος ὁ ῥήτωρ; in dedications, as Ἡγεμὼν ἀρχηγέτης, to whom the dedication was made; and on tombstones the name of the deceased, as Κλεῖτος; after Eucleides, with the name of the deme added, as Βλέπιος Ἀθμονεύς; or the father's name as well, *e.g.* Φίλων Καλλίππου Αἰξωνεύς. Or the name may be in the genitive, as Ἡρώδου τοῦ Ἀττικοῦ—Ἀπόλλωνος Ἀγυιέως Προστατηρίου—Ἀριστίωνος; or the dative, as θεῷ Σεβαστῷ—Ἀθηνᾷ Πολιάδι; or the accusative, as Τιβέριον θεόν (*honorary*); the vocative as: Μόσχε Μόσχου, χαῖρε (*sepulchral*). Expansions may be as follows: Ἡ πόλις Μάρκῳ Οὐλπίῳ Εὐβιότῳ (*hon.*)—Δήμητρι καὶ Κόρῃ Φάβιος Δαδοῦχος (*ded.*)—Ἡ μήτηρ τῇ θυγατρί (*sep.*); the datives depend upon ἀνέθηκε, ἀνέστησε, ἐποίησε or the like, either expressed or understood. Sometimes the motive is added, *e.g.* (*hon.* or *ded.*) ἀρετῆς ἕνεκα—εὐχῆς χάριν—γυμνασιαρχήσαντα; μνείας or μνήμης χάριν (*sep.*). The source of expenditure may be specified, as ἐκ τῶν ἰδίων προσόδων; or the authorisation, as ψηφισαμένης τῆς πόλεως καὶ τοῦ δήμου; or the executive, as ἐπιμελουμένης τῆς Ἐρεχθηίδος φυλῆς; or the date may be given, as ἐπὶ τοῦ δεῖνος ἄρχοντος. In tomb-inscriptions the age of the deceased may be mentioned, *e.g.* βιώσας ἔτη δεκατρία; or the manner of death, as: λοιμῷ θανούσης, or a consolatory maxim added, as εὐψύχει· οὐδεὶς ἀθάνατος. Sometimes tombstones were erected during lifetime; hence the addition (in the imperial period), ζῇ, ζῶσι. Tomb inscriptions are often written in verse, from the sixth century B.C. onward; in later times they are more elaborate. Sepulchral monuments might be commended to the protection of the community or the gods: τούτου τοῦ μνημείου ἡ γερουσία κήδεται—παραδίδωμι τοῖς καταχθονίοις θεοῖς τὸ ἡρῷον φυλάσσειν. More or less elaborate curses might be imprecated on desecrating persons: κακῶς τε ἀπολέσθαι αὐτοὺς καὶ γένος. Akin to these are curses (*devotiones*) inscribed for the most part on leaden plates, *e.g.* ἀνατίθημι Δάματρι κτλ....τοὺς ἐπ' ἐμὲ ἐλθόντας καὶ μαστιγώσαντας κτλ....μὴ ἐξαλύξαιεν.

749. Property might be indicated by the simple genitive, as—Πανός—Ἀπόλλωνος πατρῴου. On an epistyle we find ἐπεσκευάσθη ἐκ τῶν δημοσίων χρημάτων, ἐπιτροπεύοντος Αἰλίου Ὁμούλλου. Inscriptions in prose and poetry giving the name of the artist or sculptor of a statue or other work exhibit a great variety of style; the most common is that represented by, *e.g.*, Κρησίλας ἐπόει, Ἀριστίων μ' ἐποίησεν, Πυθαγόρας Σάμιος ἐποίησεν. More than 500 such inscriptions have been collected containing the names of a large number of sculptors, many of them not otherwise known, and of various nationalities.

750. The **Ephebic** inscriptions form a distinct category in Athens, ranging from the third century B.C. to the third century A.D. They consist, with a varying measure of complexity, (1) of Ephebic inscriptions. decrees laudatory of the Ephebi (youths between eighteen and twenty years of age, who were entered on the ληξιαρχικὸν γραμματεῖον or register of the deme and were undergoing military training), and one or more of their numerous officers and trainers (παιδοτρίβης, ὁπλόμαχος, ἀκοντιστής, τοξότης, ἀφέτης, γραμματεύς, ὑπηρέτης), (2) of lists of Ephebi, (3) decrees in honour of Ephebi alone.

751. As a type of **Public Accounts** may be taken inscriptions recording the transference of the treasure in the Pronaos of Athena from one set of treasurers to their successors. The Annual Accounts of transactions covered a *penaeteris*, or period of four annual Magistrates, etc. magistracies (ἀρχαί). The preamble ran thus: Τάδε παρέδοσαν αἱ τέτταρες ἀρχαί, αἳ ἐδίδοσαν τὸν λόγον ἐκ Παναθηναίων ἐς Παναθήναια, τοῖς ταμίασιν (= ταμίαις), οἷς ὁ δεῖνα ἐγραμμάτευε. οἱ δὲ ταμίαι, οἷς ὁ δεῖνα ἐγραμμάτευε, παρέδοσαν τοῖς ταμίασιν, οἷς ὁ δεῖνα ἐγραμμάτευε. Ἐν τῷ Προνηΐῳ (*here follows the inventory of treasures*). Ἐπέτεια (*additions during the year*) ἐπεγένετο ἐπὶ τῶν ταμιῶν, οἷς ὁ δεῖνα ἐγραμμάτευε (*here follows the inventory*). The transactions of the second, third and fourth years were similarly described. Under this head the long temple accounts of Delos are the completest of their kind. We have also a long series of documents which give the details of the property handed over by the Overseers of the Dockyards (ἐπιμεληταὶ τῶν νεωρίων) to their successors. Types of formulae are: Τάδε παρελάβομεν καὶ ἀπελάβομεν σκεύη κρεμαστὰ ἐν νεωρίοις—Σύμπαν κεφάλαιον ἀργυρίου οὗ εἰσεπράξαμεν καὶ κατεβάλομεν ἀποδέκταις (*here follows the sum*)—Οἵδε τῶν τριηράρχων τῶν ὁμολογησάντων ἐν τῷ δικαστηρίῳ καινὰς ἀποδώσειν τριήρεις καὶ τοὺς ἐμβόλους ὀφείλουσι τεῖ πόλει, τὰς δὲ ἀποδεδώκασιν (*here follow names*). An inscription containing an architect's specification for the erection of the 'Arsenal of Philo' in the Peiraeus enables us to restore almost stone for stone a building of which not a vestige remains.

From the **Tribute Lists** we learn the long array of States which were subject to Athens in the latter half of the fifth century B.C. The amount of the tribute paid by each is arrived at by multiplying by 60 the percentage (μνᾶ ἀπὸ ταλάντου) paid as ἀπαρχαί to Athena. After the introductory clauses—Αἵδε τῶν πόλεων τῶν παρὰ τῶν Ἑλληνοταμιῶν, οἷς ὁ δεῖνα ἐγραμμάτευε, ὑπὸ τῶν τριάκοντα ἀπεφάνθησαν ἀπαρχαὶ τῇ θεῷ ἐπὶ τοῦ δεῖνος ἄρχοντος—comes the list of States arranged under the categories Ἰωνικὸς φόρος, Ἑλλησπόντιος φόρος etc., with subsections such as—Πόλεις αὐταὶ φόρον ταξάμεναι—Πόλεις ἃς οἱ ἰδιῶται ἔταξαν.

A **Subscription List** might be headed thus: Οἵδε ἐπέδωκαν εἰς τὴν ἐπισκευὴν τοῦ ἱεροῦ καὶ κατασκευήν...κατὰ τὸ ψήφισμα ὃ ὁ δεῖνα εἶπεν. Lists of soldiers on service (chiefly from Official name-lists. Boeotia) might begin: τυὶ (= τοὶ) πρᾶτον ἐστρατεύαθη (= ἐστρατεύνται), followed by the names. In a list of the fallen in battle,

461—460 B.C. the names are preceded by the heading : Ἐρεχθηΐδος οἵδε ἐν τῷ πολέμῳ ἀπέθανον ἐν Κύπρῳ, ἐν Αἰγύπτῳ κτλ....τοῦ αὐτοῦ ἐνιαυτοῦ. A very large category is that of the Choragic and Agonistic inscriptions or lists of victors in contests. A common formula is, e.g., Αἰγηῒς ἀνδρῶν ἐνίκα, Εὐαγίδης Κτησίου Φιλαΐδης ἐχορήγει, | Λυσιμαχίδης Ἐπιδάμνιος ηὔλει, Χαρίλαος Λοκρὸς ἐδίδασκε, | Εὐθύκριτος ἦρχε.

752. It is more difficult to classify according to their formulae
legal documents, such as Leases, Contracts, Deeds of
Legal docu- Sale, State Loans, Donations, Deeds of Manumission,
ments, etc.
etc. Examples are: (1) τὴν γῆν τὴν ἐν Δήλῳ τὴν ἱερὰν ἐμίσθωσαν καὶ τοὺς κήπους κτλ. (Amphictyons in Delos); (2) Ἀγαθῇ τύχῃ· ἐπρίατο Θειογείτων..., χρυσῶν τριακοσίων. Βεβαιωτὴς..., μάρτυρες... (Amphipolis); (3) τοὶ πολέμαρχοι...ἀνέγραψαν καθὼς ἐποείσανθο τὰν ἀπόδοσιν τῶ δανείω τῶν Νικαρέτας κὰτ τὸ ψάφισμα τῶ δάμω (Orchomenus); (4) Θεός, τύχα· Σάωτις δίδωτι Σικαινίᾳ τὰν ϝοικίαν καὶ τἆλλα πάντα· δαμιοργὸς..., πρόξενοι... (Petilia); (5) ἐπρίατο ὁ Ἀπόλλων ὁ Πύθιος παρὰ Σωσιβίου Ἀμφίσσεος ἐπ᾽ ἐλευθερίᾳ σῶμα γυναικεῖον, ᾧ ὄνομα Νικαία κτλ. (Delphi : an act of sale to the deity which was equivalent to a manumission of the person sold).

From Gortyn, in Crete, we have a twelve-column-long βουστροφηδόν inscription (see §§ 475 ff. : for a specimen of the text see Fig. 177) containing provisions of private law relating to slavery, divorce, property, inheritance, adoption, and other topics ; and fragments of inscriptions of a more archaic type apparently anterior to the use of coined money, the calculations of value being made in λέβητες (see Fig. 175), and τρίποδες.

Inscriptions on **boundary stones** are of various types, e.g. Ὅρος Λακεδαίμονι πρὸς Μεσσήνην—Δεῦρε Παιανιῶν τριττὺς τελευτᾷ, ἄρχεται δὲ Μυρρινουσίων τριττύς. A peculiar category is formed by stones marking property and inscribed with the terms of a mortgage or a dowry : Ὅρος χωρίου πεπραμένου ἐπὶ λύσει τῷ δεῖνι—Ὅρος οἰκίας ἐν προικὶ ἀποτετιμημένης τῷ δεῖνι.

Corpus inscriptionum Graecarum (C.I.G.), 1828–77. Inscriptiones Graecae
Bibliography. (I.G.), vols. I—XIV. (some volumes not yet completed) ; viz. I—III.
(C.I.A.) Atticae, IV. Argolidis, V. Arcadiae, Laconicae, Messeniae,
VI. Elidis et Achaiae, VII. Megaridos et Boeotiae, VIII. Delphorum, IX. Graeciae
Septentrionalis, X. Epiri Macedoniae, XI. Deli, XII. Insularum Maris Aegei,
XIII. Cretae, XIV. Siciliae et Italiae &c. Inscriptiones Graecae antiquissimae (not
Attic), Roehl. Greek Inscriptions in the British Museum, Newton and Hicks.
Selections and Manuals. Cauer, Delectus inscrr. graec. propter dialectum
memorabilium, ed.² ; Solmsen, Inscrr. graecae ad inlustr. dialectos selectae ;
Hicks and Hill, Greek Historical Inscriptions ; Dittenberger, Sylloge inscrr.
graecarum and Orientis graeci inscrr. selectae ; Collitz, Sammlung der griech.
Dialekt-Inschriften ; Kirchhoff, Studien z. Gesch. des griechischen Alphabets, ed.⁴
1887 ; Roberts, Introduction to Greek Epigraphy, Pt. I. and (with E. A. Gardner)
Pt. II. ; Reinach, Traité d'Épigr. grecque (incorporating Newton's articles on
Gr. inscrr.), 1885 ; Larfeld, Griech. Epigraphik and Hdbch. d. gr. Epigr. ;

E. A. Gardner, *Inscriptions* in Encyclopaedia Britannica, 14th edition; O. Kern, *Inscriptiones Graecae* with photographic facsimiles. Meisterhans, *Gramm. d. att. Inschriften*, ed.[3] 1900; Michel, *Recueil d'Inscriptions grecques*. There are also numerous collections of inscriptions selected with reference to special subject-matter; *e.g.* Dareste, *Inscriptions Grecques juridiques* ; Loewy, *Inschriften gr. Bildhauer*, and a rapidly increasing series of local collections, *e.g.* of Cos, Boeotia, Crete, the coast of the Euxine; also the official publications of the inscriptions from excavations, such as Olympia, Pergamon, Delos, Delphi, etc. For epitaphs, Kaibel, *Epigrammata Graeca, ex lapidibus collecta.* For numeral systems, Tod, *Ann. British School at Athens*, XVIII. 1911–12, pp. 98–132.

VIII. 3. PALAEOGRAPHY.

753. PALAEOGRAPHY seeks to read, date and place writings in ink on papyrus, parchment or paper, occasionally on sherds or wax.
Epigraphy deals with inscriptions upon stone or metal. The　Definition.
distinction is less superficial than it looks. The forms of written letters, similar at first to those of inscriptions, developed more swiftly and with few exceptions the difference is maintained until the Byzantine engravers of inscriptions took to imitating the work of scribes. The subject-matter also of written documents except a few legal papyri receives little direct illumination from inscriptions.

754. Changes in writing are mainly produced by laziness; in his desire to save trouble the scribe slurs over the forms of　Changes in
letters so that they tend to resemble each other, or runs　writing: book
them together so that it is hard to distinguish them or　and cursive
employs abbreviations themselves subject to degradation.　hands.
This tendency is counteracted by the reader's demand for clearness, generally met by reverting to an older type of script, sometimes by differentiating similar letters through an exaggeration of their characteristic features. A third element, the desire for the writing to look beautiful, on the whole makes for clearness except when it produces excessive uniformity, the scribe as it were forcing all the letters into one mould so that they should not spoil the regularity of his line or page.

These three forces differ in relative strength with the contents or purpose of the writing. In rough copies or documents of ephemeral interest, receipts and the like, the writer goes as fast as he can, often too in deeds with their regular formulae which he is tired of repeating. In such hands the forms of letters change in every generation, whereas in books much more concern for legibility is shown and the changes are extremely slow. Among running or cursive hands some are those of ordinary citizens, others those of legal scriveners, others the styles elaborated in government

offices and written perhaps as carefully in their way as the book-hands. So
the books may be in absolutely cursive hands when a work has been copied
out by an amateur perhaps for his own use; usually we find them transcribed in hands which, however difficult to us through bad preservation
or our want of familiarity with their peculiarities, were as plain as print to
cotemporaries and generally aim at a pleasant appearance; while at any
rate from the first century A.D. we have magnificent scripts written with the
very highest skill. It looks as if these ornamental styles were in earlier
times reserved for Homer, afterwards mainly for bibles or liturgical books.

755. Different materials encourage different sorts of pen-stroke in
the quick writer and set different artistic ideals before the
Influence of calligrapher. On stone letters tend to be separately made
Material. up of independent strokes or scratches of the chisel with
few curves and are generally irregular; while the pen makes curves and
joins independent strokes and even letters together and in time there
comes a feeling for uniformity of height. In the Timotheus papyrus
(Fig. 187, *c.* 330 B.C.) the irregular epigraphic forms have not succumbed
to the soft material, and the books of the third century have not yet
settled down to the typical papyrus hand, yet fourth century cursive must
certainly have grown out of any such awkwardness, for a long development
lies behind such a hand as Fig. 188 (255 B.C.).

Papyrus with its tender surface and thin substance encouraged a light
quick stroke though a heavier style was not impossible. This heavier
manner became general when about the fourth century A.D. scribes took
to parchment and in time realized its possibilities, for it is often difficult to
make very fine lines upon it, while it shows up thick strokes to perfection.
The adoption of paper had little effect upon the forms of letters except
that the cheaper material tempted scribes to use less care upon it.

756. In outline the story of Greek writing is simple and this
simplicity makes it hard to date specimens of any but a
Uncial and few varieties. From the fourth century B.C. till the eighth
Minuscule. or ninth A.D. the book-hand changes very slowly and
often harks back to earlier styles. The letters are *majuscules, i.e.* capitals
nearly all contained between two parallel horizontal lines with only one or
two projecting above or below; almost from the beginning the rounded
Є, C, Ѡ had superseded the angular E, Σ, Ω so this hand is usually
called *uncial* upon the analogy of a Latin majuscule hand in which several
of the letters have rounded forms. Parallel with this runs the cursive; we
can trace most of its continuous development though its changes are very
rapid and its varieties innumerable, only the earliest and latest could be
given here (Figs. 188, 192): from about the fourth century A.D. some letters
become distinguishable by growing tall or developing tails: this classes it
as a *minuscule* hand in which the bodies of the letters are between two
lines but parts of them may project more or less to reach other two lines
above and below. When in the eighth or ninth century the uncials had

become too thick and clumsy, varieties of the cursive regularized and applied to the writing of vellum books superseded the uncials. About the same time materials for following the course of the everyday writing fail us and until the Renaissance we have but the minuscule book-hand.

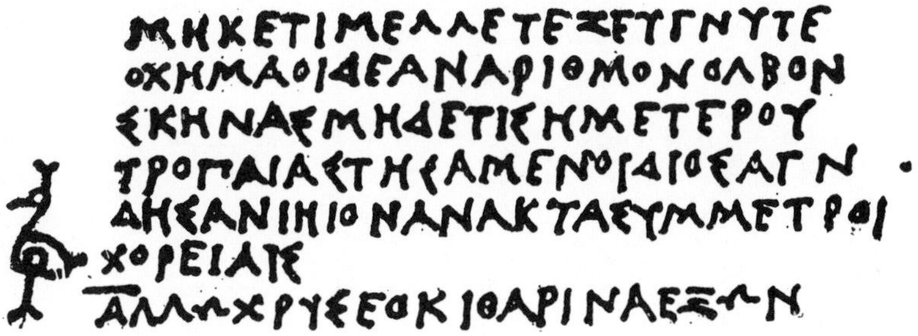

μηκετι μελλετε ζευγνυτε — —
οχημα οι δε αναριθμον ολβον — —
σκηνας μηδε τις ημετερου — —
τροπαια στησαμενοι Διος αγυ[οτατον — — — εκελα-
δησαν ιηιον ανακτα συμμετροι — —
χορειαις
αλλ ω χρυσεοκιθαριν αεξων.

Fig. 187. Timotheus of Miletus, *Persae*, late fourth cent. B.C. *New Pal. Soc.* 22. Slightly reduced. About half each line is shown[1].

757. Fig. 187 shows a book-hand still very like an inscription, note the A with horizontal stroke, B with a big head, square E, small I Θ Ξ and O, the epigraphic I and Σ, and Ω on its **Ptolemaic Writing.** way to the Ⓦ form. The writing is in very long uneven lines and the columns trend away to the left: it may not be the work of a professional. The bird is a glorified *coronis* marking with a *paragraphos* the beginning of the *sphragis* or *coda* of the *nomos*. Book-hands in the third century show the same characteristics in a less degree. Meanwhile the cursive had by 255 B.C. reached the state shown on Fig. 188. Note the forms assumed by α, β, δ, η, λ, μ, ν, τ, υ, φ and ω: the result is an almost continuous line along the top of the writing above which only ν and φ project. This line is characteristic of the Ptolemaic period.

The same sort of feeling comes out in the Ptolemaic book-hand, especially in broad hands with angular letters such as the Bacchylides MS. (Fig. 189), note the shallow topped μ and υ; Ξ too is made in three separate strokes, but it must be allowed that very similar hands went on until the

[1] This and the following transcriptions make the facsimiles intelligible by modernizing the letters, dividing the words, supplying hyphens and capitals and resolving abbreviations, but in punctuation, accentuation etc. they reproduce their originals.

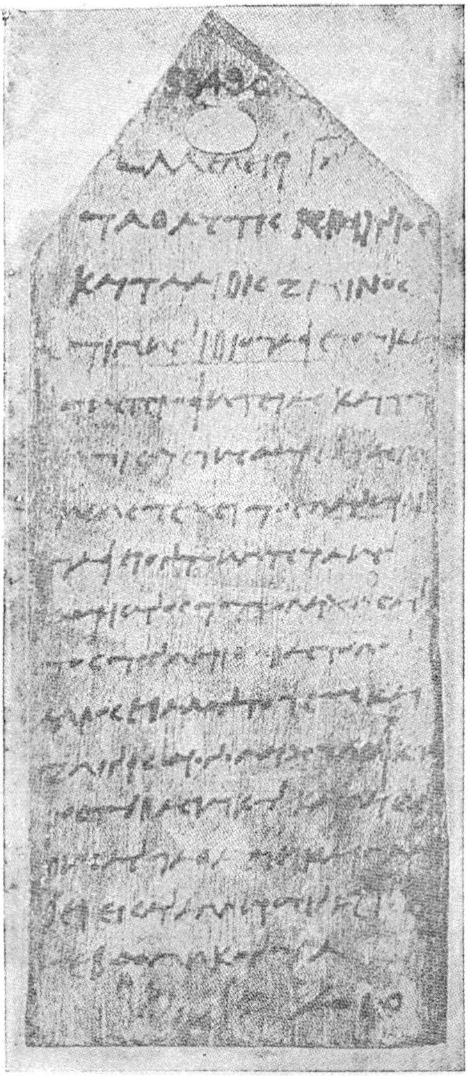

1 (ετους) λα επειφ Ῑη

Ταθαυτις Ζμινιος

και Τααιβις Ζμινος

τιμην ιβιοταφειου και

5 της προφητειας και του

ημισους της δωριαιας γης

ης μετεχει το επανω ιβιο-

ταφειον το ημυσυ δ ην

Δωριωνος του τοπαρχησαν-

10 τος τον περι Θηβας τοπον

α προσεβαλοντο τεως και

Ζμινις δι Ονομαρχου πρακτο-

ρος των βασιλικων και παρεκ-

βησαν Ταθαυτει και Τααι-

15 βει εις αναπληρωσιν ├ Ῡξι

├ εβδομηκοντα.

[Demotic line.]

Fig. 188. Wooden money-bill for 70 drachmas, half the price of burying an ibis, 255/4 B.C., *Pal. Soc.* II. 142. ├=drachma; ∟ is an Egyptian symbol for a year: επειφ is a month's name.

second century A.D.　Parallel with it we find a rounded hand which fore-
shadows the commonest fashion in Roman times, *e.g.* the philosophical works
recovered from a library at Herculaneum and usually put about 50 B.C.

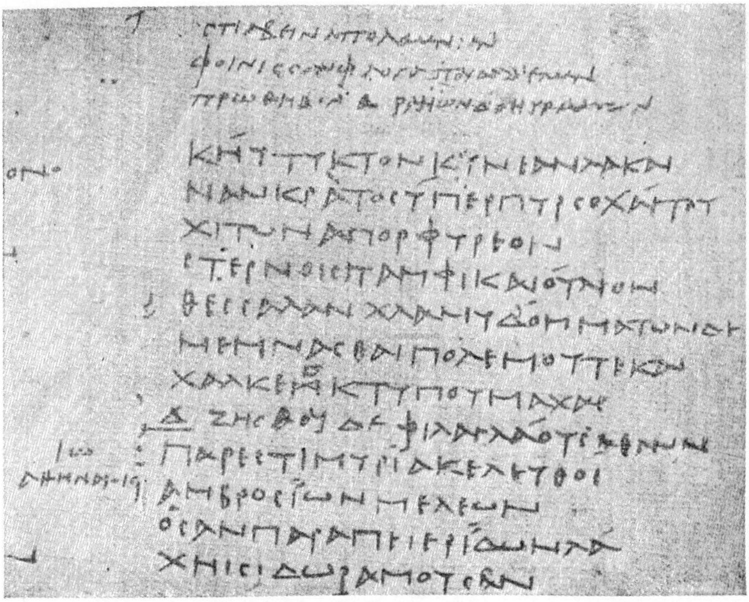

55	**7**	στιλβειν απο Λαμνιαν
		φοινισσαν φλογα· παιδα δ' εμεν
		πρωθηβον· αρηϊων δ' αθυρματων
50		κηυτυκτον κυνεαν Λακαι-
		ναν κρᾶτος ὑπερ πυρσοχαίτου·
		χιτωνα πορφυρεον
		στερνοισι τ αμφι και ούλιον
	))	θεσσαλαν χλαμυδ'· ομματων δε
		μεμνασθαι πολεμου τε και
		χαλκεοκτυπου μαχας
60		' διζησθαι δε φιλαγλάους Αθανας
	Ιω	ˌ παρεστι μυρία κελευθος
	Αθηναιοισ	' αμβροσίων μελεων
		ὸς αν παρα πειερίδων λά-
		χηισι δωρα μουσᾶν.

Fig. 189.　Bacchylides (xvii. 50—xviii. 4), first cent. B.C.　Note the three lines
left out after l. 54 and written by a Roman hand (c. 100 A.D.) in the top
margin; also the accents, breathing, *coronis* with *paragraphos*, punctuation, diaeresis and short marks, *v.* Jebb, *Bacchylides*, Pl. I.

758. This roundness also appears in the Roman cursive marked also by certain peculiar shapes, *e.g.* of η (ϒ) and ε (ʎ). In such a hand is written not only the usual letters and deeds but most of the 'Αθηναίων Πολιτεία. More books have survived from about 100 A.D. than from any other period and they show a great variety of style. There are a few scraps of MSS. in which each letter was carefully made and a standard set up fit for the great vellum bibles : also a fashion for sloping writing, formerly supposed to mark quite a late date, had come in, and the rather archaic broad straight-lined style had not quite gone out; meanwhile the commonest was the rounded book-hand. As these four styles ran parallel for about three centuries it is not in the obvious differences that we are to seek criteria for dating but in occasional cursive forms that a copyist has allowed to creep in when off his guard, or in an indefinable similarity of stroke that the trained eye sees in the work

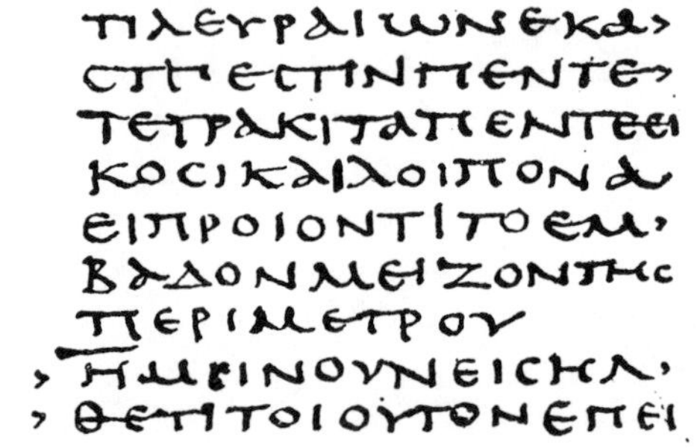

Roman Book-hand.

πλευραι ων εκα-
στη εστιν πεντε
τετρακι τα πεντε ει-
κοσι και λοιπον α-
ει προιοντι το εμ-
βαδον μειζον της
περιμετρου
᾽ ημ[[ε]]ιν ουν εισηλ-
᾽ θε τι τοιουτον επει

Fig. 190. Commentary on the *Theaetetus*, second cent. A.D. Schubart, *Pap. Gr. Berol.* 31.

of each age whether in the cursive or the book-hand : but this is very subjective and the more formal the hand the less there is to go by. To the second century A.D. are referred the earliest vellum books, though we have documents on skins going back to 195 B.C. The example of a good rounded hand in which the letters are made very freely and skilfully is from perhaps the most handsome roll extant; though mutilated it is 20 ft. long and 1 ft. wide; the columns, 8 in. high, leave 1½ in. margin above and 2½ in. below and have only about 17 letters in the line : note the *paragraphos* and the > used as quotation marks on the left and to fill up lines on the right (Fig. 190).

In the fourth century the cursive hand assumes what has been called the Byzantine form, that is to say it gets a look suggesting the Greek writing to which we are accustomed; it is often written with a mannerism aiming at decorativeness or dignity.

In the fourth or fifth century we may place the victory of vellum and of the book over the roll. The supersession of papyrus was not instantaneous; we have parts of MSS., sometimes in book form, for another four hundred years (one or two, *e.g.* fragments of Menander, are of importance), and documents as late as 996 A.D., but it is likely that outside Egypt it gave way more quickly.

759. Our oldest great vellum book, the codex Vaticanus of the Bible, was probably written in the second half of the fourth century and the next, the codex Sinaiticus, about the year 400. The four columns to a page give it a roll-like effect but the writing is a little heavier than that of any but rather exceptional papyri. The *paragraphos* and short line of letters mark the end of what we call a paragraph, and further the first letter of the next encroaches a very little upon the margin: the Vaticanus offers less help to the reader and its writing is lighter, also it uses fewer contractions.

Vellum Uncial.

πολιν λεγομενη(ν)

Ναζαρετ'· οπως

πληρωθη το ρηθε(ν)

υπο δια των προφητω(ν)

„ οτι Ναζωραιος

" κληθησεται :

Ζ　εν δε ταις ημερε(*for* αι)s

Γ　εκειναις παραγει(*for* ι)-
　　(νεται)

Fig. 191.　Codex Sinaiticus, c. 400 A.D.　Note the stroke for ν and the diminished letters at the ends of lines, the apostrophe to mark the unusual ending of Ναζαρετ, the reading υπο for δια in the margin, the quotation marks and the misspellings. Ζ and Γ are numbers of sections.

From the fourth to the ninth century vellum uncial was the chief vehicle of literature, but classical MSS. are few; scribes were busy upon theology and law. The vertical strokes became thicker and in P, Y, Φ and Ψ longer while the horizontal or sloping strokes of Γ, Δ, Є, Z, K, Π, C and T acquire heavy dots or serifs at their ends: codex Alexandrinus of the Bible shows a tendency in this direction and is put in the fifth century, as the great example of this style, a Dioscorides at Vienna, can be set about 513 A.D. A belated specimen, the earliest Greek MS. dated in its subscription, is of 800 A.D. The sixth century seems the age of gospels written in very big letters with gold and silver ink upon purple vellum. Less ambitious books were often in sloping uncials and in the ninth century this slope became fashionable even for large writing: we have such a MS. actually dated

862 A.D. and one or two must be earlier, while there are several in the tenth century. The slope and height of the letters tended to narrow them and the curves in Є, O, C, Φ, Ꞷ become pointed: the uncials on Fig. 193 are not tall enough to show this well, those on Fig. 194 exhibit a vertical form often used for headings and marginalia. Breathings and accents are first universally applied in the ninth century MSS. whether uncial or minuscule. Towards the end of the tenth century upright uncials come in again and after the eleventh the letters recover their broad or round forms, but by this time the style has become very artificial and is reserved for liturgical books.

760.　By the eighth century the uncial had become too magnificent or too clumsy for ordinary use and efforts were made, as it **Adaptation of cursive to books.** seems independently one of another, to adapt for books the cursive of ordinary life. Fig. 192 shows what this had reached by 605 A.D.; later specimens are too full of abbreviations to be generally intelligible.

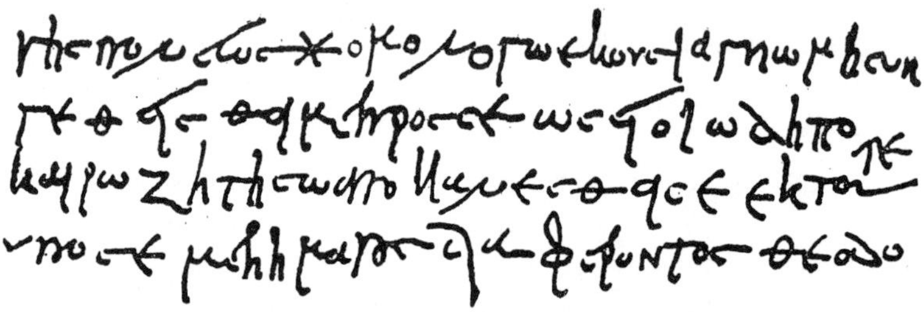

της πολεως χ(αιρειν)· ομολογω εκουσια γνωμη συν-
τεθεισθαι με προς σε ως ει οιωδηποτε
καιρω ζητησω αποβαλεσθαι σε εκ του
υπο σε μενημματος διαφεροντος θεοδο(σακιου).

Fig. 192.　Lease of a house, 605 A.D.　Schubart, *Pap. Gr. Berol.* 47.

If we compare with this the minuscule on Fig. 193 we see that the shapes of α, β (not shown but like *u*), ϵ, ϵι, η, ι, κ, λ, μ, σ, υ, φ are quite peculiar and very similar to each other: in other letters the specimen of cursive does not show the typical cursive forms.

The hand in Fig. 193 is an unsuccessful variant represented by only one or two MSS. and these are very hard to date: logically they precede the ordinary minuscule, but the form of the uncial heading and the use of paper for this MS. makes it hard to put it earlier than the ninth century. The text is very troublesome to read and the slope is ugly: besides the forms noticed above observe γ, θ, ν: the last, though so familiar to us, we shall not meet again until the fourteenth century.

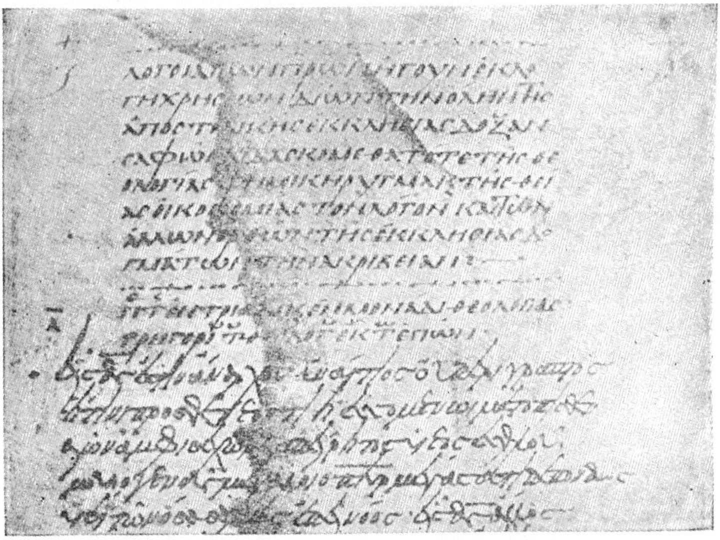

λοροι ἁΓιων π(ατε)ρων ἡΓογν εκλο-
Γη χρηcεων Δι ὡν την ὅλην τηc
ἁποcτολικηc ἐκκλhcιαc ΔοΖαν
cαφῶc ΔιΔαcκομεθα το τε τηc θε-
ολοΓίαc φημι κηργΓμα κ(αι) τῆc θεί-
αc οἰκονομίαc τὸν λόΓον και των
ἀλλων ὀρθῶν τῆc ἐκκλhcιαc Δο-
Γμάτων τὴν ακριΒεῖαν :—

πε(ρι) τ(ηc) ἐν τριἀΔι κ(αι) ἐν μονἀΔι θεολοΓιαc :—
ΓρηΓορι(ογ) τ(ογ) θεολοΓ(ογ) ἐκ τω(ν) ἐπῶν.

εἶs θ(εο)s ἐστιν ἄναρχos, ἀναίτιos ὃν περίγραπτόs
ἤ τινι προσθεν ἐόντι, ἤ ἐσσομενωι μετοπισθεν
αιῶν’ ἄμφιs εχων (καὶ) ἀπείρητos ὑιεos εσθλοῦ.
μουνογενοῦs μεγάλοιο π(ατ)ηρ μέγαs, ὅν τι πεπονθωs
ὑιεί, τῶν ὅσα σαρκόs, ἐπεὶ νόos· εἶs θ(εο)s ἄλλοs.

Fig. 193.   Codex Vaticanus 2200.   Theological verses, ninth cent.(?).

761. The successful variety of minuscule is much superior.   It must go back to about 800 A.D. as the oldest dated example is of 835 A.D.   We can follow continuously the changes in this *Older Minuscule.* hand until the seventeenth century.   It is divided into three main periods, the older until about 975, the middle from then till about

1200 and the later coming down to about 1500 after which we need not descend.

In the MS. from which Fig. 194 is taken the gospels written in uncials are intermixed with a commentary in minuscules of the early style. All the letters except θ, χ and an alternative λ have their own forms far removed from the uncial: when once these are mastered and such ligatures as αγ, ει, εσ, σπ, στ, νν and νσ have become familiar, reading is very easy as there are but few abbreviations at any rate in the texts. The breathings are rectangular and with the accents put on most accurately. On MSS. in such a hand or in one not quite so elaborate the text of most classical authors mainly rests. The period is generally regarded as closing about 975 when scribes took to letting the letters hang from the ruled line instead of standing upon it. A little before this a sloping hand had come in not quite so formal as the upright but almost as well written.

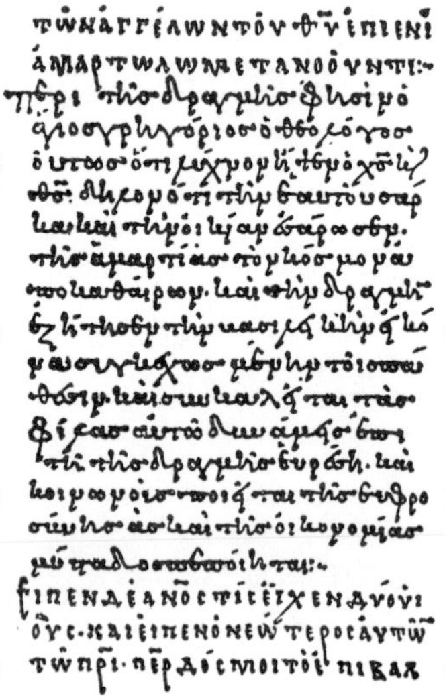

τῶν ἀγγέλων τοῦ θ(εο)ῦ ἐπι ἐνὶ
ἀμαρτωλῳ μετανοοῦντι :—
Περὶ τῆς δραγ(for χ)μῆς φησὶν ὁ
ἅγιος γρηγόριος ὁ θεολόγος
5 οὕτως, ὅτι λύχνον ἦψεν ὁ χ(ριστο)ς κ(αὶ)
θ(εο)ς. δηλονότι τὴν ἑαυτοῦ σάρ-
κα καὶ τὴν οἰκίαν ἐσάρωσεν.
τῆς ἁμαρτίας τὸν κόσμον ἀ-
ποκαθαίρων. καὶ τὴν δραγμην(ν)
10 ἐζήτησεν τὴν βασιλεικὴν ἐικό-
να συγκεχωσμένην τοῖς πά-
θεσιν. καὶ συνκαλεῖται τὰς
φίλας αὐτῶ δυνάμεις ἐπὶ
τῇ τῆς δραγμῆς ἑυρέση. καὶ
15 κοινωνοὺς ποιεῖται τῆς ευφρο-
σύνης ἂς καὶ τῆς οἰκονομίας
μύσταδος πεποίηται:—
Εἰπεν δὲ αν(θρωπ)ος τίς ἔιχεν δύο ύἱ-
οὺς· καὶ ἐιπεν ὁ νεώτερος ἀγτῶ(ν)
20 τῶ π(ατ)ρι· π(ατ)ερ δός μοι τὸ ἐπιβαλ(λον)

Fig. 194. Cod. Monacensis (Cod. X. Evan.), c. 900 A.D. Notice many slips of spelling due to modern pronunciation.

762. In the middle period and henceforward the letters hang from the line, the breathings are not only square but rounded, especially the soft one, often too no clear distinction is made between them, and the abbreviations are much more frequent in the text. Also the uncial forms which seem to have been consciously avoided at first in the older style begin to find their way back in great numbers and new ligatures are devised. Further a slope is

Middle Minuscule.

decidedly commoner and the letters are not formed with the same extreme
care : and yet many MSS. of this period, especially gospels, are hard to
distinguish from older work, the scribe only betraying himself at the ends
of lines or at the bottoms of pages. This middle style shades off into the
next and the limit must be arbitrary ; 1204, the date of the fourth crusade
disastrous to the Greek world, answers to a time when the change for
the worse is very noticeable. Fig. 195 is a characteristic example of the
eleventh century. The rough breathing is square but the soft rounded ;
there are many abbreviations, the uncial н, к, λ, м, n, π, T, φ, ω appear
beside or instead of the cursive forms and a few more lines would probably
yield ᴧ, в, г, ᴧ, ε, c and the like. It has also a slope, but the writing cannot
be called careless.

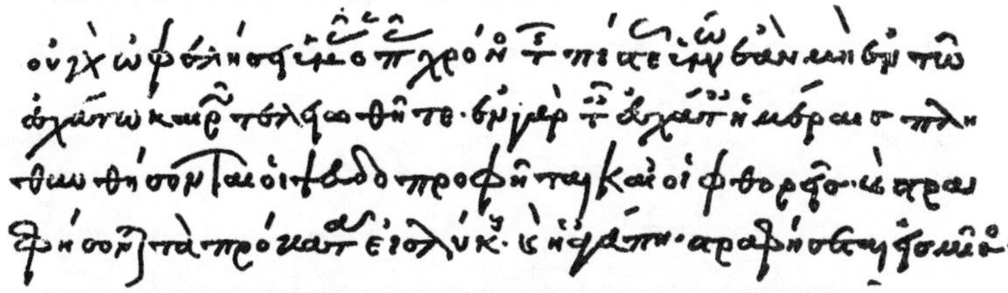

οὐ γ(ὰρ) ὠφελήσει ὑμ(ᾶς) ὁ π(ᾶς) χρόν(ος) τ(ῆς) πίστε(ως) ὑμῶν ἐὰν μὴ ἐν τῷ
ἐσχάτῳ καιρ(ῷ) τελειωθῆτε· ἐν γὰρ τ(αῖς) ἐσχάτ(αις) ἡμέραις πλη-
θυνθήσονται οἱ ψευδοπροφῆται καὶ οἱ φθορεῖς· (καὶ) στρα-
φήσοντ(αι) τὰ πρόβατα εἰς λύκ(ους)· (καὶ) ἡ ἀγάπη στραφήσεται εἰς μῖσο(ς).

Fig. 195.　Teaching of the Twelve Apostles, 1056 A.D.

763.　Fig. 196 stands just on the borderland between this period and
the text is quite archaistic, but the capricious forms
in the commentary (six different forms of ϵ), the numerous　　Late
abbreviations, the careless breathings and the accents made　　Minuscule.
in one with the letters (l. 6) betray its late date.

The same caprice goes on increasing ; in Fig. 197 we have a by no
means extreme example of the late period during which every letter has at
least two forms current, one minuscule and one uncial, and each of these
often a tall and a short variety besides perhaps several special shapes when
entering into ligatures, many of which are many of them new. The abbreviations may be as frequent as ever, and a trick comes in of making quasi-
abbreviations by writing some letters above others. In all this it is
difficult to trace any logical development as each scribe had his own
peculiar style, often founded on an ancient model or quite eclectic :
MSS. written for Italian humanists are generally rather neater ; their forms,
even the most complicated, were imitated by the printers with astonishing

fidelity. It was not till the nineteenth century that they got rid of the ligatures ୪ (ου) and ϛ (στ). Our distinction between σ and ς is all that remains of the alternative forms; in other cases either the cursive or the uncial has prevailed.

764. Assigning a MS. to a particular locality is even more difficult than

Placing MSS. dating it. In the papyrus period nearly everything comes from Egypt, we have just evidence enough to infer that in other parts of the Greek world the book-hand was much the same whereas

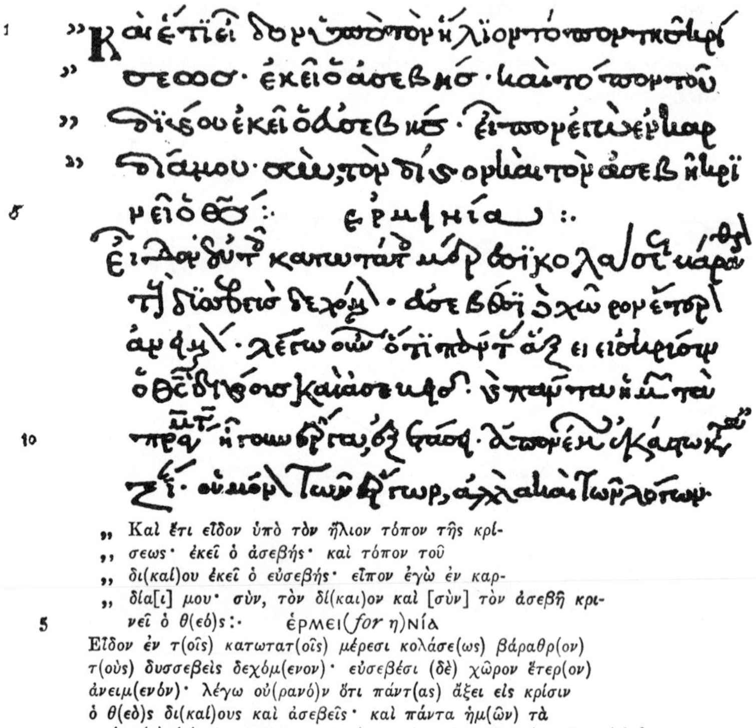

```
 „ Καὶ ἔτι εἶδον ὑπὸ τὸν ἥλιον τόπον τῆς κρί-
 „ σεως· ἐκεῖ ὁ ἀσεβής· καὶ τόπον τοῦ
 „ δι(και)ου ἐκεῖ ὁ εὐσεβής· εἶπον ἐγὼ ἐν καρ-
 „ δία[ι] μου· σύν, τὸν δί(και)ον καὶ [σὺν] τὸν ἀσεβῆ κρι-
 5   νεῖ ὁ θ(εό)ς:·     ἑρμει(for η)νία
   Εἶδον ἐν τ(οῖς) κατωτατ(οῖς) μέρεσι κολάσε(ως) βάραθρ(ον)
   τ(οὺς) δυσσεβεῖς δεχόμ(ενον)· εὐσεβέσι (δὲ) χῶρον ἕτερ(ον)
   ἀνειμ(ενόν)· λέγω οὐ(ρανό)ν ὅτι πάντ(ας) ἄξει εἰς κρίσιν
   ὁ θ(εό)ς δι(και)ους καὶ ἀσεβεῖς· καὶ πάντα ἡμ(ῶν) τὰ
10   πράγμ(α)τ(α) ἤγουν ἔργα, ἐξετάσει· ἀπονέμ(ων) ἑκάστω[ι] κ(α)τ' ἀ-
   ξί(αν)· οὐ μόν(ον) τῶν ἔργων, ἀλλὰ καὶ τῶν λόγων.
```

Fig. 196. Commentary on Ecclesiastes, 1203 A.D. Cav. Lietzm. 34.

the cursives show peculiarities. Some of the vellum uncials are incontestably Egyptian, others may have come from there, there are rather few of the earlier ones which certainly came from elsewhere. Later, as is natural, Constantinople is the centre from which most of our extant MSS. seem to have come: even when there are indications of a book having been written in some province no difference in style enables us to pick out other MSS. from the same region.　　Only in the Greek districts of S. Italy there seems to have been a special school, but its produce is almost exclusively theological.　　The fact is that Greek was not widely enough spread to encourage great local variations.　　Greek as written in Western Europe by scribes more used to Latin script can hardly be reckoned as true Greek, the forms showing more and more Latin influence until knowledge of Greek dies out in the tenth century.　　Greek scribes working in Italy in the fifteenth and sixteenth centuries brought their native hands with them.

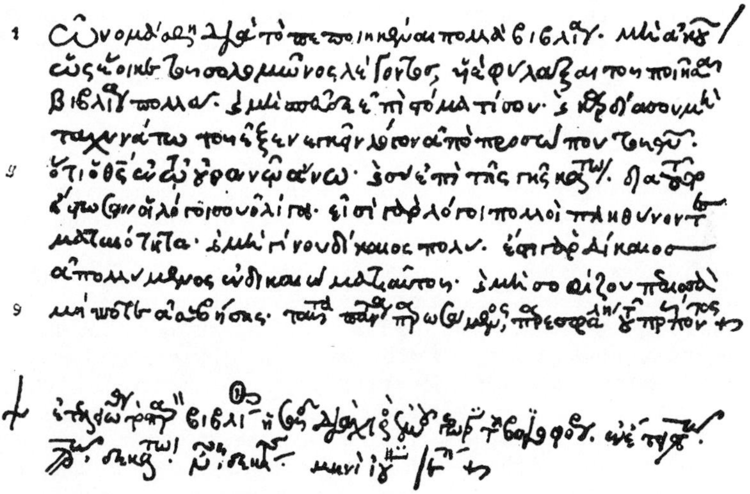

1　ὠνομάσθη διὰ τὸ πεποιηκέναι πολλὰ βιβλία· μὴ ἀκου(ων)
　ὡς ἔοικε τοῦ σολομῶνος λέγοντος, υἱὲ φύλαξαι τοῦ ποιῆσαι
　βιβλία πολλά· (καὶ) μὴ σπεῦδε ἐπὶ στόματί σου· (καὶ) καρδία σου μὴ
　ταχυνάτω τοῦ ἐξενεγκεῖν λόγον ἀπὸ προσώπου τοῦ θ(εο)ῦ·
5　ὅτι ὁ θ(εό)s ἐν τῷ οὐρανῷ ἄνω· (καὶ) σύ ἐπὶ τῆς γῆς κατω. διὰ τοῦτο
　ἔστωσαν οἱ λόγοι σου ὀλίγοί· εἰσὶ γὰρ λόγοι πολλοὶ πληθύνοντες
　ματαιότητα· (καὶ) μὴ γίνου δίκαιος πολύ· ἔστι γὰρ δίκαιοs
　ἀπολλύμενος ἐν δικαιώματι αὐτου· (καὶ) μὴ σοφίζου περισσὰ
9　μὴ ποτε ἀσεβήσῃς· ταῦτα πάντα παρωσάμενος παρεσφάλη τοῦ πρέποντοs†
　†ἐτελειώθ(η)τὸ παρ(ὸν) βιβλίον ἡ σουιδ(ᾶ) διὰ χειρὸ(s) ἐμοῦ γεωργ(ίου) τοῦ βαιοφορ(ου) ἐν ἔτει,ϛ᷍ῷ
　℈ῷ δεκατωι ('Ι)ν(δικτιῶν)ος δεκάτ(ης) μηνὶ ιουν(ίῳ) ιεη†

Fig. 197.　Suidas, 1402 A.D.　Pal. Soc. I. 181.

765.　Abbreviations were rare in most papyrus books, almost confined to ‾ signifying ν at the end of a line.　In a few MSS. we find a system of adding ´, ‵, or ’ to each letter to represent the commonest words or syllables beginning with it, e.g. τ́ = των, τ̀ = την,

Abbreviations.

$\tau' = \tau\eta s$, or $\kappa' = \kappa a i$, $\kappa` = \kappa a \tau a$. In cursive documents words are *suspended*, *i.e.* only the first or the beginning letters are written and then to indicate that the word is incomplete there may follow a transverse stroke or the last letter written is above the line: this upper letter may be a characteristic one of the omitted part of the word. Special signs are also used for words which often occur (*e.g.* Ⳑ = year and ⊦ = drachma on Fig. 188).

With Christianity came in a new system called *contraction* probably having its germ not in a desire to save time or space, but in the Jewish reverence for the name of God: it consisted in leaving out the middle of a word but giving the beginning and the ending, the latter changing with the flexion or even admitting derivative terminations, *e.g.* the Vatican bible has $\overline{\Theta C} = \theta\epsilon\acute{o}s$, $\overline{KC} = \kappa\acute{v}\rho\iota\sigma s$, $\overline{\Pi N A} = \pi\nu\epsilon\hat{v}\mu a$, $\Pi\overline{H}P = \pi a\tau\acute{\eta}\rho$, $O\overline{Y}NOC = o\mathring{v}\rho a\nu\acute{o}s$, $A\overline{NOC} = \mathring{a}\nu\theta\rho\omega\pi\sigma s$, $\overline{\Delta\bar{A}\Delta} = \Delta a\nu\epsilon\acute{\iota}\delta$, $I\overline{H}\Lambda = \mathrm{Ἰ}\sigma\rho a\acute{\eta}\lambda$, $I\overline{\Lambda H M} = \mathrm{Ἱ}\epsilon\rho\sigma\nu\sigma a\lambda\acute{\eta}\mu$, $\overline{IC} = \mathrm{Ἰ}\eta\sigma\sigma\hat{v}s$, $\overline{XC} = X\rho\iota\sigma\tau\acute{o}s$, $\overline{YC} = v\acute{\iota}\acute{o}s$, $M\overline{H}P = \mu\acute{\eta}\tau\eta\rho$: in later MSS. are some variations of these and contractions for $\sigma\omega\tau\acute{\eta}\rho$ and $\sigma\tau a\nu\rho\acute{o}s$ were added but in Greek there are only these fifteen *nomina sacra*, as they are called. They are marked by a stroke over, a sign used in all times of Greek writing to distinguish letters taken in some abnormal sense, *e.g.* numerals and even sometimes proper names.

With the vellum minuscule appears a complete system of abbreviation, at first hardly allowed in the text but soon used equally in text and notes; it is made up of survivals from the haphazard papyrus use, of the *nomina sacra*, and of a full set of signs for the different syllabic endings borrowed from a shorthand in which a few whole books are preserved. At first these signs are made accurately and though troublesome are not really difficult, but in the careless MSS. of later periods they lose their shapes and are mixed up with breathings, accents and overwritten letters. The best way to learn these signs is to work through facsimiles provided with transcripts, even the few here given would if carefully read teach most of them; the tables in the manuals of palaeography are useful for reference though often disappointing.

766. In early MSS. words are not divided, in cursive hands there may be an unconscious division and the minuscules help a little more but often they are very misleading, a new word beginning in the middle of a ligature: sometimes in uncials at difficult places or after words with unusual endings a comma or apostrophe is put in, usually not by the original scribe. Accents and breathings are sporadic in papyri, being commonest in the epic or lyric poets (Fig. 189). From the eighth century they are universal in uncials and minuscules. Double accents often distinguish the particles $\mu\grave{\epsilon}\nu$ and $\delta\grave{\epsilon}$: double dots or lines are often a help in picking out ι or ν. Spelling is good in Greek MSS. except for itacism, *e.g.* $\epsilon\iota$ for $\bar{\iota}$ or ϵ for $a\iota$ (Fig. 194) and great uncertainty as to mute iota: if put in this is adscript until about 1200, afterwards it is subscript.

Accents,
Punctuation,
etc.

Punctuation is most haphazard except in the best minuscules but even in uncials the end of a paragraph in our sense is marked by a horizontal stroke called *paragraphos* under its last line; often the new paragraph begins in the line, perhaps there is a slight gap before it, sometimes the first whole line in a paragraph begins with a bigger letter even though it does not begin a word. Codex Sinaiticus (Fig. 191) already forestalls the modern way of leaving the last line of the paragraph unfilled up and emphasizing the first letter of the next: so emphasized the letter quickly develops into an ornamental capital. Ends of metrical divisions are marked by a *coronis* or hook with the paragraphos, and this may take fanciful shapes especially at the end of a book. Other marks denote quotations, give references to marginal notes or statements of alternative readings often with $\digamma^{P}=\gamma\rho\acute{\alpha}\phi\epsilon\tau\alpha\iota$, or to places into which omitted matter should be inserted (Fig. 189) a fruitful source of textual error, or finally merely fill up ugly spaces at the end of a line (Fig. 190).

767. Beginning with 800 A.D. Greek scribes took to dating their work almost always by the Byzantine reckoning which put the creation at Sept. 1, 5508 B.C. To find the date of, *e.g.* Dated MSS. Fig. 197 subtract 5508 from 6910, result 1402: had it been written between Sept. 1 and Dec. 31 we should have subtracted 5509. The indiction, which is also often mentioned, is a fifteen year cycle beginning in 312 A.D., but we are only given the number of the year in the cycle, so unless we have further data the indiction is no help. Tables of these and other chronological elements are in Gardthausen.

Sir E. Maunde Thompson's *Introduction to Greek and Latin Palaeography*, Oxford, 1912, is the best summary in English, but most of its matter is contained in his *Handbook*, London, 1906. Bibliography. V. Gardthausen's *Griechische Palaeographie*, 2nd ed., Leipzig, 1911–13, is the standard reference book. Cheap facsimiles are, for papyri, W. Schubart, *Papyri Graecae Berolinenses*, Bonn, 1911 (6s.), for vellum MSS. P. F. de Cavalieri et J. Lietzmann, *Specimina Codicum Graecorum Bibl. Vat.* Bonn, 1910 (6s.), mostly theological. Fr. Steffens, *Proben aus griechischen Handschriften*, Trier, 1912 (7s. 6d.), gives a very varied selection. The great series for reference is that of the *Palaeographical Society*, London, 1873-94; *New Pal. Soc.*, 1903– . See also Sir F. G. Kenyon, *Palaeography of Greek Papyri*, Oxford, 1899. The tables in Ts'ereteli, *Abbreviations in Greek MSS.*, St Petersburg, 1904, can be used although the text is in Russian.

VIII.   4.   TEXTUAL CRITICISM.

768.   TEXTUAL criticism has for its sole object to determine as nearly
as possible the words written by the author of the original
text, wherever the reading has become corrupt or doubtful.
In the case of a modern printed text which is known
to have been revised by the author himself, textual criticism has
no place, unless it be in the detection of misprints.   There is a textual
criticism of Shakespeare, owing to the conditions under which the plays
were first printed : there can be none of Tennyson.   The textual critic
must constantly keep in view the simple and single aim of his work.

Office of textual criticism.

769.   The MSS. of an ancient author are our primary witnesses as to
what he wrote.   We look, then, in the first place, to the
actual testimony which they bear, without asking, as yet,
what degree of antecedent credibility belongs to this or
that manuscript.   The intrinsic probability of a reading is relative simply
to the original author of the text, and has nothing to do
with the transcriber of the MS.   We ask, if there is a
doubt :—' Is this what the ancient author is likely to have
written here ? '   In judging this question, we have regard to the general
characteristics of his diction and of his thought, and to the particular
context.   This test may not seldom suffice to warrant a negative decision :
we can pronounce, with tolerable certainty, that such or such a reading is
impossible.   On the positive side, however, such a test will more rarely be
decisive.   The appeal is to our own conception of the author's style and
mind, and of the context.   Different conclusions may be reached by
equally competent judges.   Two things especially should be remembered.
(1) ' Homer sometimes nods '; even the best authors do not always write
worthily of themselves.   Lapses from felicity of style, from clearness,
from consistency, or even (through carelessness) from correct grammar,
may occur now and then in the best writings.   A critic with the requisite
gifts might be able here and there to suggest some verbal change which
would be a real improvement.   The better of two words or phrases in a
given place, however clearly its superiority can be shown, will not necessarily be that which the author used.   (2) In making a choice between
two or more variants, the simple test of intrinsic fitness will lead us to

Internal evidence of readings.

Intrinsic probability.

prefer that reading which best corresponds with our view of the author's intention. But it may happen that we see only a part of his intention. The reading which we reject may have been preferred by him because it expressed some element of thought or feeling which we have failed to seize. These are two general sources of error to which judgment by intrinsic probability is liable. There are others special to particular moods or tendencies in the individual critic.

But the internal evidence of readings supplies a further test of a wholly different kind, which can often be applied as a check on intrinsic probability. Suppose that, in a given passage, several different readings are found: *e.g.* one MS., **Transcriptional probability.** or group of MSS., has γελῶν, another τελῶν, a third πεδῶν: which of these readings is best fitted to account for the existence of the other two? This question, it will be seen, has nothing to do with the intrinsic fitness,—the comparative merit,—of the readings themselves. It is concerned solely with their transmission by copyists. On the hypothesis that reading *a* is the original one, can we suggest how it came to be corrupted into readings *b* and *c*? This is what has been called the test of 'transcriptional probability.'

770. In applying this test, large help can be derived from experience. It is known that certain causes of corruption in the written tradition of classical texts were at work from an early date,—as early, indeed, as the age of the classical writers themselves. These causes may be brought under two **Known causes of corruption in MSS.** general heads:—I. changes due to mere error on the part ot copyists, which are by far the more frequent: II. changes deliberately made.

I. The sources of accidental error in transcription are so various that any attempt to enumerate and classify them must be very incomplete. But it is useful to note some of the **Accidental errors.** causes which operate most frequently. (1) Letters are confused through some partial resemblance of form: as A, Δ, Λ: C, Є, Θ, O: Γ, Π, T. ΛΛ is read as M, or *vice versa* (as in Soph. *Ant.* 436 ἅμ’ was corrupted to ἀλλ’): ΛΙ or ΑΙ is read as N: K, as ΙC (so that, *e.g.*, ἐκ becomes εἰς), or *vice versa* (Σκύφον for Σίσυφον in Athen. 500 B). As so much of ancient copying was purely mechanical,—done by men who simply transcribed the words which they seemed to see before them, without thinking of the sense,—errors due to this cause are often very gross: *e.g.* in Thuc. VI. 74 § 2 (where the reference is to the Athenian army in Sicily) our MSS. have:—ἀπελθόντες ἐς Νάξον θρᾶκας (or θρᾶικας, θράκας, θρακας) σταυρώματα περὶ τὸ στρατόπεδον ποιησάμενοι αὐτοῦ διεχείμαζον. Here ΘΡΑΚΑΣ arose from ΟΡΑΚΑΙ, *i.e.* ὅρα καὶ,—ὅρα (which is actually found in one of the scholia on the passage) being itself a corruption of ὅρια. We must read, then, ὅρια καὶ σταυρώματα ('enclosure and palisade'). And the fact that ΚΑΙ became ΚΑC is the more intelligible if the corruption occurred in the Ptolemaic age, since one form of the Ptolemaic sigma (as seen, *e.g.*, in the new papyrus of Bacchylides) resembles Ɩ with a small curve at the top. Numerals were especially liable to corruption from this cause; *e.g.* Ϲ (5) might be confused with Θ (9), or Ο (70): Γ (3) with Π (80), etc.

(2) Abbreviations of common words, such as καί, θεός, ἄνθρωπος, πατήρ, etc., were often sources of error. The *Commentatio Palaeographica* of F. J. Bast (appended to G. H. Schaefer's edition oı Gregorius Corinthus, Leipzig, 1811) contains a systematic and copious treatment of this subject, and, generally, of the errors arising from confusion of letters or syllables, whether in majuscule or in minuscule writing.

(3) Letters or syllables might be wrongly joined or disjoined: *e.g.* τριήρεσι ν′ (50) might be read as τριήρεσιν: ἐνόν as ἔν ὄν. In Thuc. VIII. 46 § 2 τάδ᾽ εἶναι became τὰ δεινά.

(4) The influence of the immediate context has been a fertile source of error in transcription. (i) The same word or phrase occurs twice, perhaps, within a comparatively small space: the scribe's eye wanders to the second place where it stands, causing him to omit the clause or sentence in which it first appears. (ii) The scribe wrongly repeats some word or phrase, mentally associating it with some other word or phrase which really occurs twice. (iii) Or, thinking of a phrase which has just occurred, he assimilates another phrase to it; as in Isocr. or. 1 § 3 some MSS. have ὅρκοις (instead of γάμοις) ἐμμένειν, due to a preceding ὅρκοις ἐμμένων. (iv) The grammatical form of a word (case, mood, etc.) is wrongly assimilated to that of a neighbouring word. (v) A word is accidentally omitted through its resemblance to the termination of the word next before it, or to the beginning of the word next after it: *e.g.* ἄν, ἐν before or after -αν, -εν.

(5) An explanatory 'gloss,' written by some reader in the margin or above the line, is erroneously substituted by a copyist for the genuine reading; as in Aesch. *Ag.* 282 our MSS. have ἀγγέλου, the true ἀγγάρου being preserved only in *Etym. Mag.*: or is added to it; as in Thuc. VII. 58 § 3, after the words νεοδαμώδεις δὲ τοὺς ἄλλους καὶ Εἵλωτας, our MSS. have the gloss, δύναται δὲ τὸ νεοδαμῶδες ἐλεύθερον ἤδη εἶναι.

(6) Confusion of sounds must be reckoned among the occasional sources of error in MSS., though its operation was limited. There can be no doubt that in later antiquity the *librarii* sometimes employed dictation; a MS. was read aloud, and copied by several scribes simultaneously. The same practice probably survived, to some extent, in the earlier Byzantine age. In the later Greek pronunciation, ει, η, ι, οι, υ were sounds closely alike (as they still are); αι and ε, ω and ο, were hardly distinguishable. After nasals, π and β, τ and δ, κ and γ were similar. This cause, however, tended rather to mere mis-spelling than to larger or deeper corruptions. Madvig assumes it when in Plut. *Pelop.* 23 he suggests σὺν οἷστισιν instead of συνίστησιν: an ingenious, though not a probable emendation.

(7)　Erroneous transposition occurs under various conditions. (a) If the genuine order of words be a rhetorical or a poetical one, it is frequently changed into the more natural and usual order; often, probably, through mere inadvertence, the scribe having glanced at a whole phrase in the book which he was copying, without noting the sequence of the words. Innumerable examples of this occur in the texts of poets, being proved by the violation of metre. Thus in the newly-found papyrus of Bacchylides, which is as old as *circa* 50 B.C., we find in ode XIV. [XV. ed. Kenyon] v. 47, ἆρχεν λόγων δικαίων instead of the genuine λόγων ἆρχεν δικαίων. (b) Again, it may have happened that a scribe has accidentally omitted a word, or a clause, or a whole sentence : he, or a corrector, afterwards supplies it in the margin : a later copyist then restores it to the text, but in a wrong place. When, in the MS. of a poem, a verse or small group of verses has been incorrectly transposed, such a process will sometimes account for the fact. Larger dislocations of a text may occur through the leaves of a MS. having become deranged.

II.　But the MSS. of the classics had also been liable, from ancient times, to changes deliberately made. (1) The texts of the classical poets were peculiarly exposed to such changes, owing to the influence of oral recitation. A rhapsode, a chorus-leader, or an actor might add some words or verses, and these might pass into the books. Thus in Pindar *Olymp.* II. 26 f., after φιλεῖ | δέ νιν Παλλὰς αἰεί, our four best MSS. add φιλέοντι δὲ Μοῖσαι, words which, as the scholia attest, Aristophanes of Byzantium pronounced spurious, but which were first banished from the text by the Byzantine critic Demetrius Triclinius (*circa* A.D. 1300—1325). In *Iliad* XXIV. 45, after οὐδέ οἱ αἰδώς, stands the verse, γίγνεται, ἥ τ' ἄνδρας μέγα σίνεται ἠδ' ὀνίνησιν,—interpolated, as Aristonicus remarked, from Hesiod *Op.* 318, 'by some one who thought the sense defective' (because the verb for αἰδώς, viz. ἐστί, is understood). With regard to the dramatic texts, alteration or interpolation by actors is well attested. That cause of corruption was already active in the fourth century B.C. : it was in order to check it that, on the proposition of the orator Lycurgus, a standard copy of the three great tragic masters was made at Athens *circa* 330 B.C. Ancient scholia sometimes expressly attribute a false reading to the actors : thus on Eur. *Med.* 909 f., εἰκὸς γὰρ ὀργὰς θῆλυ ποιεῖσθαι γένος | γάμους παρεμπολῶντος ἀλλοίους πόσει, the scholiast says that 'the actors write' ἐμοῦ instead of πόσει. See also the scholia on Eur. *Med.* 85, 228, 356, 379 ; *Phoen.* 264 ; *Andr.* 6.

(2)　In the Alexandrian and Roman ages, revisers of texts sometimes altered the reading, in order to make it, as they thought, clearer or more correct. Thus Galen (vol. xvii. 2, p. 110 Kühn), commenting on a passage in the Ἐπιδήμια of Hippocrates, says : τῆς παλαιᾶς γραφῆς οὔσης ταύτης, ἐπὶ τὸ σαφέστερον αὐτὴν μετατεθείκασι πολλοὶ τῶν ἐξηγητῶν. In the Φαινόμενα of Aratus, verse 693, Ἵππος δ' Ὑδροχόοιο μέσον περιτελλομένοιο, the astronomer Hipparchus (*circa* 150 B.C.) states that μέσον was the reading of 'all the copies' known to him; but his contemporary, the commentator Attalus, had changed it to νέον, which is found in all our MSS. So, too, in v. 713 Attalus had changed λήγοντι to ἀνιόντι.

(3) It would seem, too, that the order of words was sometimes deliberately altered by revisers, with a view to making it more lucid or effective. Thus in the *Codex Vaticanus* of Thucydides, which from VI. 92 to the end of VIII not seldom exhibits an order of words peculiar to itself, there is sometimes reason to suspect such licence.

(4) Mutilations and gaps, dating from a very early time, existed in many of the texts which had come to the Alexandrians. An editor sometimes attempted to supply what was missing. A traditional instance is that of Apellicon (*circa* 100 B.C.), who, in editing the damaged MSS. of Aristotle, εἰς ἀντίγραφα καινὰ μετήνεγκε τὴν γραφήν, ἀναπληρῶν οὐκ εὖ (Strabo p. 609).

771. Such are some of the principal causes of corruption, accidental or

Such an analysis is helpful:

deliberate, which in the course of centuries have affected the transmission of the classical texts. Account has to be taken of one or more of them when a question of 'transcriptional probability' arises. That is, when we have to choose between two or more traditional readings, the knowledge of such facts may enable us to explain how the reading which we adopt can have generated that (or those) which we reject. Or if only one reading has come down, and that one is manifestly corrupt, such knowledge may guide the endeavour

but it is necessarily incomplete.

to correct it. But no appeal to experience will enable us to frame exhaustive categories of transcriptional error or licence. It is impossible to draw up a list of the motives which might lead to wilful change, or of the accidents which might lead to blunders: the organs of the tradition were not machines, but men.

Limited validity of critical canons.

Hence those general rules which have been called 'canons of criticism,'—founded mainly on observed forms of error or of licence,—should be used with a due sense of their limited validity. To take a familiar example, one of Griesbach's canons of New Testament criticism,—'Prefer the harder reading,'—is valid in most cases (though not necessarily in all) where a transcriber has deliberately altered the reading which he found; since a frequent motive of such change was a wish to make the sense clearer. But it is obviously not valid in a case of accidental error, since the result may be a reading which (if intelligible at all) is 'harder' than the true one.

772. Intrinsic probability, coupled with transcriptional, will sometimes

Internal evidence of documents.

suffice to establish or condemn a reading, or to decide the choice between variants: it may be possible, *e.g.*, to say at once, 'this word, ΟΛΟΝ, cannot conceivably be right; manifestly it is a corruption of ΟΔΟΝ.' But it will frequently happen that these tests fail. The choice may lie between two readings, each of which is intrinsically suitable; and we may be unable to perceive either how reading *b* could have arisen from *a* through error, or why anyone who found *a* in his text should have deliberately changed it to *b*. In such a dilemma there is, however, a further test which will often help us; it is still derived from the internal evidence of readings, but involves a new application of that evidence. The general character of a witness has a bearing on the credibility of any particular deposition which he makes. The general character of a manuscript may aid us in   General weighing the value of its testimony with regard to a par-   character of ticular reading. There are two MSS., A and B: comparing   a MS. them wherever they differ, we find that the number of readings which are either certain or highly probable is much larger in A than in B. The superiority of A in general trustworthiness may then be taken into account in those cases where a choice between the reading of A and that of B is more difficult. It is true, and must always be remembered, that B may be the worse copy on the whole, and yet in a particular case may have chanced to preserve a true reading which A has lost; such an occurrence is not, indeed, very rare: still, the general character of A will warrant a general presumption in its favour. This is the ground of the rule, ' Knowledge of documents should precede final judgment upon readings.'

773. Every manuscript has peculiarities of its own. The idiosyncrasy of the scribe appears in traits of handwriting; in a proneness   Every MS. to certain kinds of error, and comparative immunity from   has traits others; in a bias of thought or taste which has influenced   peculiar to his work where he had two or more variants before him,   itself. and had to choose between them. Such peculiarities can be learned only by close and continued study of the particular MS.; but to learn them is an essential part of the textual critic's business. It is none the less essential when the ancient work happens to be extant in only one MS.; as is the case with the orations of Hypereides, the fables of Babrius, the mimes of Herodas, the odes of Bacchylides, the Ἀθηναίων Πολιτεία. An intimate acquaintance with the general characteristics of the solitary witness is needed in gauging the chances that a particular reading is corrupt, and in attempting to amend it. On the other hand, the task of comparing MSS. in respect to their general trustworthiness becomes excessively complex and difficult when the number of MSS. is large. In such a case it is of the first importance to enquire whether, and how far, the genealogy of the MSS. can be traced.

774. The genealogical method of studying MSS. rests on considerations of a simple kind. That it was almost entirely neglected   Genealogy down to comparatively recent times, is not, however, very   of MSS. surprising. The MSS. of the classics are scattered through the libraries of Europe. Before the days of railways few scholars had the means of consulting all the best MSS. of a given author, or of procuring accurate collations. Nor were those processes known by which facsimiles can now be produced. It may be added that, from the later period of the

Renaissance down to the early part of the last century, there was a tendency
to regard conjectural criticism as a free exercise of scholarship and ingenuity, to be cultivated for its own sake, rather than simply as a remedy
to be used only in the last resort, after a careful but baffled scrutiny of
the actual data furnished by the MSS.

The varying written copies of a text handed down through centuries
are not ultimately independent of each other. They are descendants of
a common original, now lost. If we knew all the facts, we could construct
an accurate stemma of their descent. The more nearly we can approach
to doing so, the better shall we be able to sift the spurious readings from
the genuine.

775. In tracing the genealogy of MSS., the general principle is that
identity of reading implies identity of origin. Suppose that
there are twenty MSS. of an ancient book, and that in a
given passage they are divided between two readings ; nine
of them, let us say, have ἔχει, and eleven have παρέχει. This fact shows
that a common ancestor of the nine had the one reading, and a common
ancestor of the eleven had the other. The variation carries us back to
the point at which two lines of transmission diverged. But, again, of the
nine, four in another place have ἀργόν, and five have ἀγρῶν : this indicates
a point, lower down in the transmission, at which the immediate ancestors
of the two smaller groups diverged from the common ancestor of the nine.
Hence this general rule :—In a comparison of variants, the larger arrays of
MSS. represent the earlier divergences ; the smaller arrays represent the later.

Mode of tracing genealogy.

776. This assumes that the different lines of descent have remained
independent of each other. But a disturbing element comes
in where mixture has occurred ; *i.e.* where a copyist has
had two or more MSS. before him, and has followed sometimes one, and
sometimes another. In the 'mixed' MS. C the texts of A, B, etc., are
thus interwoven ; and, it may be, in such an intricate manner that they
cannot be disentangled. The best help in such cases is afforded by
'conflate' readings, formed by the blending of two variants. *E.g.* one
MS., A, has εὑρὼν ταῦτα, and another, B, λαβὼν ταῦτα : if C has εὑρὼν καὶ
λαβὼν ταῦτα, there will usually be a presumption that this reading is the
latest of the three, and is due to mixture.

Mixture.

777. The simplest application of genealogy in sifting readings is where
it can be shown that, among the extant MSS. of an ancient
text, one is the MS. from which all the rest have been
derived. If there are twenty of these MSS., then nineteen
have no independent value for the purpose of determining
the original reading ; since, wherever they vary from their
parent, the twentieth MS., the variation must be due either to error or to
conjecture. Thus it has been shown that one of the extant MSS. of
Lysias, *Palatinus X*, is the parent of all the other extant copies (except
those which contain only the spurious *Epitaphios*). But great caution is

Case in which one extant MS. is the parent of all the rest.

necessary in examining the alleged proofs of such a relationship; a clear demonstration of it must be obtained before it is admitted. One extant MS. may be greatly superior to all the others. It may be a plausible theory that any sporadic good readings in the other MSS. are merely felicitous conjectures; yet one or two minute facts may suffice to prove that those others are not all mere transcripts of the best MS.; and, if so, they retain their claim to be treated as independent witnesses. Thus some eminent critics at one time held that the Laurentian MS. of Sophocles (L) is the source of all the others : it is decidedly better than all the rest; all the greater corruptions of the text found in L are present in the rest; while, when some minor fault in L is corrected in one or more of the other documents, the correction usually appears to be such as might have been made by an intelligent grammarian or scribe. Yet there are some small pieces of evidence which refute that opinion. It will suffice here, for the purpose of illustration, to notice one of them. Verse 800 of the *Oedipus Tyrannus* is absent from the text of L (written in the first half of the eleventh century), and has been added in the margin by a later hand, which experts refer to the end of the thirteenth or the early part of the fourteenth century. But this verse stands in the text of all the other MSS., including at least one (Vat. a) which belongs to the late twelfth or early thirteenth century, and which therefore cannot have derived the verse from L.

778. Suppose, again, that there are a dozen extant MSS. of a text, *a, b, c, d, e, f, g, h, i, k, l, m*. A comparison of their readings shows that they may be divided into two sets or 'families,' one consisting (say) of the seven *abcdefg*, and the other of the five *hiklm*. The seven are descended from one lost MS., X; the five, from one lost MS., Y. A further scrutiny shows that the family of seven falls again into three smaller sets, *ab, cde, fg*; these smaller sets being derived respectively from three lost MSS., *a, β, γ*, descendants of X. Similarly the family of five falls into two smaller sets, *hi* and *klm*, derived respectively from two lost MSS., δ, ε, descendants of Y. We will suppose, further, that there is no evidence of *mixture*, either between the families descended from X and Y respectively, or between the smaller sets within either family. The stemma will then stand as follows, O being the lost archetype from which X and Y are derived :—

Partial reconstruction of a lost archetype.

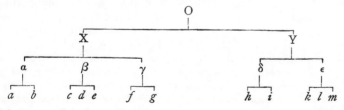

(1) A reading in which all the twelve MSS. agree must have been that of O. (2) If all the seven descendants of X have one reading, and

all the five of Y have another, then the genealogical evidence does not
enable us to decide which was the reading of O. The fact that seven
MSS. are arrayed on one side, and only five on the other, is immaterial;
so also is the fact that on one side there is a consent between three
smaller sets, and on the other side a consent between two only; since
each larger family comes from a single ancestor. (3) Next, let us suppose
that the descendants of X (or of Y) are divided among themselves. The
representatives of γ (f and g) are found dissenting from those of α and β
(*ab*, *cde*), and agreeing with the representatives of δ (*hi*) and ϵ (*klm*). Is
the reading of X to be inferred from the representatives of α and β, or
from those of γ? The answer is, from those of γ: because (excluding the
hypothesis of mixture or of accidental coincidence) the agreement of γ
with δ and ϵ can be explained only by supposing that γ has preserved the
reading common to X and Y, which was also, therefore, the reading of O.
The readings of *abcde* (representatives of α and β) may then be left aside.
The advantage of the genealogical method in such a case is twofold:
(i) the work is simplified by the elimination of certain variants; and
(ii) it becomes possible to infer some readings of O besides those in
which all its descendants agree.

779. But it may happen that the genealogical relations between MSS.
are too obscure to afford ground for the application of such
a method. This may occur through complex mixture
between different lines of transmission. In such a case

*Evidence of
groups, not
genealogical.*

there may be another resource, of a kind intermediate between the
evidence derived from the known character of a single document, and the
genealogical evidence of families. Suppose that there are five MSS., A, B,
C, D, E. The history of their lineage is not clear: we cannot say (*e.g.*) that
ABC form one family, descended from one common ancestor, while DE
form another. A comparison shows, however, that certain good readings
are common to the group ABC, but are not found in D and E. This
indicates that, so far as those readings are concerned, some good MS. was
one element of ancestry common to A, B and C; though that ancestry may
in other respects be diverse or mixed, and though, in regard to the great
bulk of the text, neither A, nor B, nor C may have much claim to trust.
Here there is an application, indeed, of the genealogical principle that
identity of reading implies identity of origin. But the application is
limited in such a way that the resulting evidence is not properly genealogical. It is merely the internal evidence of documents; collected, however, not from documents taken singly, but from groups of them.

The authority of a manuscript depends on pure descent from a good
ancestry. In a conflict of manuscript testimony, the mere
number of MSS. on either side proves nothing: this is
obvious. But it is perhaps easier to forget that the age of
a MS. does not necessarily prove anything. Suppose, for

*Inconclu-
siveness (a) of
mere number,
and (b) of age.*

example, that a manuscript, A, was copied in the eleventh century from a good archetype; A is now lost, but we have a copy of it, *a*, made in the fifteenth century. Another MS., B, was copied in the eleventh century from a corrupt archetype, and is extant. The fifteenth century *a* will be of higher authority than the eleventh century B.

780. The testimony of the MSS. can occasionally be supplemented from other ancient sources. (1) Quotations in ancient writers furnish one of these sources : *e.g.* the citations of Dionysius of Halicarnassus from Thucydides and the orators must be counted among the witnesses for the text of the passages quoted. The critical use of such aid is Documents in supplement of MSS.
(1) Ancient quotations. subject, however, to certain considerations. (i) When an ancient writer quotes only a few words or sentences from an older prose-writer, or a verse or two from a poet, it would appear that such quotations were often made from memory, and were sometimes inaccurate; it cannot be doubted that such is the case (*e.g.*) in regard to some of the quotations made by Aristotle from Tragedy. (ii) The longer citations, such as those of Dionysius from prose-writers, were doubtless, as a rule, transcribed by the quoting writer from his texts. But it would not always be safe to assume that the text of his citation, as it has come to us, is precisely that which he wrote out. Thus Dionysius, in his essay on Thucydides (c. 26), quotes a famous passage of some length from book VI. (c. 69 § 4— 72 § 1). A later transcriber of Dionysius, when he came to that citation, may have turned to a contemporary text of Thucydides, compared the citation with it, and made some corrections. The general presumption may be, more or less, against such an occurrence; but it is a possibility which has to be borne in mind.

(2) The older Greek scholia, dating from the Alexandrian age, are commentaries, or fragments of such, made on texts which, in some cases at least, must have been purer than those of (2) Scholia. our MSS. Hence these scholia sometimes preserve, or indicate, true readings which our MSS. have lost. Thus in the *Philoctetes*, v. 954, our MSS. have αὖ θανοῦμαι: a scholium preserves the true reading, though only as a variant; γρ. ἀνανοῦμαι. Again, in the *Antigone*, v. 117, our MSS. have the corrupt φονίαισιν: the scholiast does not, indeed, mention the true reading (φονώσαισιν), but he clearly indicates it by his paraphrase, ταῖς τῶν φόνων ἐρώσαις λόγχαις. The older Homeric scholia, on the *Iliad* especially, are the chief sources of what we know as to the readings of Aristarchus and other Alexandrian critics. The worth of the scholia varies much in relation to different authors; but there is scarcely any classical Greek writer of the first rank, in prose or in verse, on whose text, where it is corrupt, some light may not occasionally be gained from the older scholia. The later scholia, written chiefly by grammarians of the Byzantine age, seldom have any value for textual criticism. It may be added that, in using scholia, there are certain warnings which it

is well to remember. (i) The paraphrases by which the scholiasts interpret difficult words in the text are often loose, and sometimes very inaccurate. Such a paraphrase may seem to suggest that the reading in the text, on which the scholiast was commenting, varied from the reading (or readings) of our MSS. But great caution should be used in drawing such an inference. Before assuming an old variant, we must feel quite sure that the scholiast's paraphrase could not possibly be intended to represent the general sense (as he took it) of our text. (ii) Similar caution should be observed in concluding from a scholiast's language that his text was more concise than ours, because his paraphrase seems to ignore something which we read. Interpolations have often been rashly assumed on this ground. (iii) The word or words, taken from the text, which form the λῆμμα ('lemma') of the scholium may not always be precisely the words which stood in the text as the scholiast had it: they may have been adjusted to a variant text by a later transcriber of the scholium.

(3) Old translations sometimes come into account as witnesses where a reading is doubtful. Thus in Cicero's version (*Tuscul.* 2. 8) of a passage in the *Trachiniae* (vv. 1046—1102), the first verse, *O multa dictu gravia, perpessu aspera,* shows that his text of that verse was the same as that of our MSS., ὦ πολλὰ δὴ καὶ θερμὰ καὶ λόγῳ κακά: though it is probable that the second καὶ was originally κοὐ. As a general rule, however, the translations from the Greek classics made by ancient Latin writers are not sufficiently close to be of much service for textual criticism. The Latin versions made in the period of the Renaissance, being as a rule more literal, are more useful for that purpose, though (as might have been expected) they seldom presuppose a text better than that of our MSS. Thus the Latin translation of Thucydides made in the fifteenth century by Laurentius Valla is commonly cited as one of the witnesses for the text. In VII. 16 § 2, for instance, all our better MSS. have εἴκοσι τάλαντα ἀργυρίου, a sum which the context shows to be much too small: Diodorus XIII. 8 makes it '140' talents. But Valla has *centum viginti,* and so is an authority for adding the words καὶ ἑκατὸν after εἴκοσι.

(3) Old translations.

781. The best and oldest of our classical MSS. exhibit many errors and defects which must already have existed in their archetypes. Such faults are anterior in their origin to any documents which we possess or can reconstruct: many of them probably date from a time very near to that at which the autograph was written. The recently-found papyrus of Bacchylides is of eminent rank, in respect to antiquity, among extant MSS. of the Greek classics: it is presumably of the first century B.C.: but, when it was written, Bacchylides had been dead for some four hundred years: and though the MS. is, on the whole, of a good class, the text already abounds in mistakes and corruptions.

Errors anterior to our documents.

782. It has sometimes occurred that a primitive error in the MSS. has been happily corrected by a transcriber, whose correction has displaced the traditional reading in one or more of the MSS. Suppose, *e.g.*, that we find two variants, κλῆρον and καιρόν. Genealogical evidence may prove conclusively that κλῆρον was the reading of a lost ancestor from which all our MSS. are descended. But it may be equally plain that κλῆρον is not right; the word may be decisively condemned by its intrinsic unfitness. Transcriptional probability, on the other hand, points to καιρόν having arisen from κλῆρον: and yet intrinsic probability strongly favours καιρόν: it suits the context so exactly that it is presumably the true reading. In such a case we infer that καιρόν is a successful emendation (whether conscious or unconscious) by a transcriber.

Emendation traceable in MSS.

783. If the only reading, or each of several readings, which our documents supply is seen to be impossible, then the remaining resource is conjectural emendation. Before a conjecture can be regarded as even probable, it must satisfy the two primary tests which we apply to doubtful readings of MSS.: (1) it must be intrinsically suitable: (2) it must be such as to account for the corrupt reading or readings in the transmitted text. There is, however, one important difference between the method of applying these tests to a conjectural emendation, and that of applying them to variants in MSS. We accept the variant which best satisfies the tests; but we require that the conjectural emendation shall satisfy them absolutely well. The conjecture does not rise from probability to certainty, or approximate certainty, unless its fitness is exact and perfect. So far as the greater classical texts are concerned, most, if not all, of the self-evident corrections have long ago been made; and also, probably, a very large proportion of those which, though not self-evident, admit of demonstrative proof. The problems which remain for the textual critic must often be insoluble (without new data) under the conditions imposed upon him : *e.g.* he may possibly have hit upon a true emendation, and yet be unable to explain how the corruption arose; since we cannot account for all the impulses of scribes, or for the whole chapter of accidents which might befall MSS. in the course of centuries. The fault most often committed in the use of conjectural emendation has been to use it prematurely. Corruptions have frequently been assumed with singular levity,—as if, indeed, for the mere sake of exercising divinatory art,— where a more thorough and sympathetic study of the author's language and thought would have shown that the text is sound. Textual criticism is never safe except in alliance with thorough interpretation. Another very common form of rash conjecture has consisted in suspecting interpolation wherever the text contains a word or phrase which, though unobjectionable, is not indispensable. There are probably few good writers, ancient or modern, whose text could not be grievously mutilated

Modern use of conjecture.

by revising it on the assumption that the author never used a superfluous word.

784. When the materials for judgment on doubtful readings are set forth in an 'apparatus criticus' subjoined to a text, clearness and simplicity are consulted by omitting all needless details, such, *e.g.*, as mere mis-spellings or false accents (unless they have some special significance). A very short note may tell much, if the characteristics and relationships of the principal MSS. have been stated in the preface, with due explanation of the symbols employed. The following note, taken from C. Hude's critical edition of Thucydides (1890), will serve as an example: it is on the words in VII. 87 § 2, τῶν νεκρῶν ὁμοῦ ἐπ᾽ ἀλλήλοις ξυννενημένων.

ξυννενημένων C (ut vid.) Eg₂ ξυνενημένων AF ξυνενη + μένων G ξυνενηνεγμένων BMc₂

This note is to be read in the light of the editor's preface. The better MSS. of Thucydides fall into two families, each descended from a single lost ancestor. One family consists of C, *Laurentianus*, of the early 10th century, and G, *Monacensis*, of the 13th century, which closely agrees with C, yet is not a mere transcript of it. The other family consists of A, *Italus* (now at Paris), of the 11th or 12th century; B, *Vaticanus*, of the 11th (very closely related to A); F, *Augustanus*, and E, *Palatinus*, both of the 11th, and less near to A than B is; E, indeed, often agrees with the MSS. of the other family. M, *Britannicus* (in the British Museum), a MS. of the 11th century, shows 'mixture' of both families, and is full of corrections. We can now interpret the note just quoted. ξυννενημένων 'seems' to have been the original reading of C: the qualifying 'ut videtur' is added, because the second hand in that MS. (c₂), which changed it to ξυνενηνεγμένων, has blurred what the first hand wrote. G, the other MS. of the same family, originally had ξυνενη + μένων (where + means that a letter has been erased); but the second hand, g₂, has added a second ν after ξυν-. Of the other family, one MS., E, has ξυννενημένων, and two others, AF, have ξυνενημένων. The agreement between members of both families makes it certain that the reading of the archetype from which the common ancestor of both families sprang was ξυννενημένων or ξυνενημένων: probably the former, to judge from the traces in C. But, at some early point at all events in the transmission, the loss of the second ν in ξυννενημένων led a transcriber to conjecture ξυνενηνεγμένων, the reading of B and M, which a later hand has imported into C. Thus the reading ξυννενημένων, which is intrinsically far the better, is confirmed by genealogical evidence, and, in its mis-spelt form, also accounts for the variant ξυνενηνεγμένων.

It is often possible to simplify the apparatus by using a single symbol for a whole group of MSS. Thus Hude's note on the word ὃν in Thuc. VIII. 66 § 3 runs thus:—

ὃν D et ex ci. *Ps.* ὃ ἦν L (del. e₂) ὅσον ἦν γρ. G₁, sed ltt. σον del. g.

Here 'L' denotes the consent of all the seven better MSS., A, B, C, E, F, G, M. By 'D' is meant 'one or more of the inferior MSS.' The first hand in each of the seven better MSS. wrote the corrupt ὃ ἦν: but in one of them, E, the second hand (e₂) struck the words out. The first hand in another (G₁) noted ὅσον ἦν as a variant (γρ.); but another hand in G (g) changed ὅσον back into ὅ. The true reading, ὄν, occurs in D (probably through a scribe's conjecture), and was also conjectured by Aemilius Portus ('Ps.'), the author of a Latin version published in 1594.

785. Two principal causes may be assigned for the great progress made in recent times by textual criticism. The first cause has been the closer and deeper study of palaeography. **Conclusion.** The second has been the application, aided by that study, of rational and thorough methods in examining the relationships of MSS. to each other. Textual criticism has become an art, guided, within certain limits, by definite general principles. More often and more confidently than of old, it can challenge strict reasoning on its results. But we must not exaggerate the degree in which textual criticism can approach to the character of an exact science. Its technical aspects must not lead us to forget the more humane and literary elements which the work involves. If that work is to be good, it requires not only special knowledge and sound method, but also a power of entering into the ancient author's mind, a feeling for the shades of his expression, a capacity for weighing nicely-balanced probabilities, a tact which can guard rules of general validity from hardening into rigid formulas. For the subject-matter of textual criticism is the play of human thought and emotion in creating literature, and the subsequent play of human agency, or of chance, in defacing it.

The student may also consult Cobet, *Variae Lectiones* (Leyden), 2nd ed. 1873, and *Novae Lectiones* (Leyden), 1858; J. N. Madvig, **Bibliography.** *Adversaria Critica* (Copenhagen), 1871–3, esp. Book I. of Vol. I.; and F. W. Hall, *Companion to Classical Texts* (Oxford), 1913.

VIII. 5. METRE.

786. Metre exists wherever words are arranged in a regular or recurring
rhythm. This rhythm can be achieved by different methods.
Quantitative Verse. Most modern verse depends on the regular repetition of
accent, that is the loudness or intensity with which a syllable
is spoken. But the Greeks based their metre on quantity, that is the time
which a syllable takes to pronounce. Syllables were divided into long and
short, and it was assumed that a long syllable took twice as long to pronounce as a short. No doubt there must have been some forcing of natural
quantity to secure this relation, but the Greek language fortunately possessed
syllables which were naturally either long or short. The regular arrangement
of long and short syllables made the metre, and as these syllables can be
arranged in many different ways, there was a correspondingly great variety
of metres. Of the influence of accent Greek verse shows no trace. Spoken
Greek certainly possessed a pitch accent, but this was neglected in verse and
need not be considered in connection with it.

787. Syllables become metre when they are arranged in symmetrical
Feet: groups. The single group is called 'foot', πούς, and groups
Classification are arranged into a whole or line called στίχος. Where one
of Feet. combination is continuously repeated the metre is called
monostich, where two, distich etc. Feet are distinguished from each other
according to the position in them of long and short syllables, and to this
distinction we owe the names of familiar feet such as dactyl (– ᴗ ᴗ), anapaest
(ᴗ ᴗ –), iamb (ᴗ –), trochee (– ᴗ) etc. When feet belonging to any of these
classes are combined in simple homogeneous series, they produce the
simplest and most easily recognizable metres. Feet however were classified
not merely by the arrangement in them of long and short syllables but by the
proportion in them of long syllables to short. Assuming that a long syllable is
the equivalent of two short, this method of classification is simple and natural.
First we may consider those feet where there is one long syllable and one
short. Both in iambs and trochees this is the case, and these feet were called
ἐν διπλασίῳ λόγῳ because the iamb (ᴗ –) provides the ratio 1 : 2, ᴗ | ᴗ ᴗ, and
the trochee (– ᴗ) provides the ratio 2 : 1, ᴗ ᴗ | ᴗ. Second are those feet where
there are two short syllables to one long, *i.e.* dactyls and anapaests. These
are called ἐν ἴσῳ λόγῳ because the dactyl (– ᴗ ᴗ) provides the ratio 2 : 2,
ᴗ ᴗ | ᴗ ᴗ, and the anapaest (ᴗ ᴗ –) provides the same. Thirdly comes the
class of feet ἐν λόγῳ ἡμιολίῳ, containing cretics (– ᴗ –) and paeons (– ᴗ ᴗ ᴗ or
ᴗ ᴗ ᴗ –), where the relation is 3 : 2 or 2 : 3. This classification was recognized
by the Greeks and was of great importance. Their metrical practice allowed
a considerable amount of substitution of one foot for another. Thus in the

epic hexameter spondees are freely substituted for dactyls. But generally the foot substituted must be in the same time as that whose place it has taken. So a spondee, being of the same proportion 2 : 2 as a dactyl, can take its place.

788. The Greeks tended even in prose to avoid collisions of vowels between word and word (*hiatus*), and in verse this avoidance became almost a rule. Short vowels might stand before other vowels, but only on condition that they were elided and not reckoned. In Homer *hiatus* is fairly frequent and is an indication of the earlier character of his verse. Archilochus seems sometimes to have allowed it, and it may be found in the tragedians. But on the whole it is avoided. In Pindar there is only one certain case (*Isth.* I. 16); there is none in Bacchylides. Homer allows it in two forms. He both keeps a long syllable short in hiatus (Πηληιάδεω | ᾿Αχιλῆος) and shortens a long vowel or diphthong before another vowel (ἄνδρα μοῖ | ἔννεπε). Except in small closely-knit lyric stanzas the avoidance of hiatus is not observed in the final syllable of a στίχος or line. Here it is freely permitted because of the metrical break or pause which follows. The same pause could also generally be used to fill up the time of the verse if it ended with a 'short' syllable when the metre strictly required a 'long,' and so the final syllable is ambiguous (*anceps*) in quantity and can be either long or short.

Hiatus and Syllaba Anceps.

789. All Greek metres, with the possible exception of the iambic tri-meter, seem originally to have been sung or chanted. So ultimately they owe their character to music. The simple metres must have been sung to a simple chant, the more complicated owe their complications to the varying music and movements of the old μολπή, the song accompanied with music and dancing. But while the second class must always have been dependent on the music and the dancing for its precise character, the first class seems early to have lost any such dependence and to have developed separately as poetry divorced from music. In consequence recited verse is both freer and simpler than choric verse. Being no longer tied to an accompaniment, it can allow certain licences, and having no tune to emphasize its character, it has to maintain its pe-culiarities as a verse.

Sung and Recited Verse.

790. To this class belongs the oldest known type of Greek verse, the dactylic hexameter in which the epics were composed. It had a foot of 4 times (*dactyl*, – | ∪ ∪, 2 : 2) and a verse of six feet. In any of the six the two short syllables might be replaced by one long, though this is comparatively rare in the fifth foot, and obligatory in the sixth foot with the freedom of *syllaba anceps*. The dactylic hexameter is in no sense primitive and implies a long history before itself. It seems to have grown from the songs sung by a wandering people cut off from its traditional μολπαί. Its ancestor may have been a shorter dactylic verse, such as survived for different uses in the dactylic trimeters, tetrameters and pentameters of Lesbian poetry. In the final stage the

Dactylic Hexameter. Its origin and character.

hexameter may have been formed by the combination of a dactylic tetrameter with a dactylic dimeter catalectic such as

ἄνδρα μοι ἔννεπε, Μοῦσα, πολύτροπον
ὃς μάλα πολλά

Of such an origin the hexameter keeps traces in its partiality for a break
after the fourth foot and its avoidance of spondees in that foot. The ancestor
of the hexameter was almost certainly sung, and for Homer ἀείδειν is still
the word for poetic recitation. Traces of this singing survive in the free
admission of hiatus and in the apparently light-hearted treatment of certain
quantities. These features, noticeable in recitation, would be less marked
when sung. But as we have it, the hexameter is not a sung verse, or if sung,
it was not sung to anything that we might call a tune. Though it carries
traces of its origin, the hexameter has a marked individuality of its own.
Each line is a unity separated from preceding and succeeding lines. For
this reason we seldom find a break after the trochee of the fourth foot, as
such a break might indicate that the line was finished before it actually was.
For similar reasons the line is never hypermetric, and a break after the
third foot is avoided. The caesura, whether in the third or fourth foot, is
a necessary result of the finished form. It was dictated by the exigencies of
recitation which demands that the reciter of a long line should have time to
take breath.

791. Half-way between the recited hexameter and the varieties of sung
verse comes the elegiac couplet. This first appears in the
seventh century B.C. associated with the names of Callinus
and Archilochus. It is a variation of the epic hexameter in
the direction of lyric poetry. The origin of the name is uncertain. It may
be of foreign origin, or it may be derived from the cry ἒ λέγε ἒ λέγε ἔ. It was
certainly used for funereal inscriptions, but the earliest examples are martial.
So its origin remains unknown. Its construction is first an ordinary dactylic
hexameter and then a pentameter formed on a different principle. This
pentameter falls into two equal parts, and the division between them is
marked by the end of a word. So strictly speaking, the pentameter is not
five feet but 2½ feet followed by 2½ feet. In the second part spondees may
not be substituted for dactyls. The line may perhaps be considered as two
dactylic trimeters catalectic whose catalexis is due to the expression of grief
or other emotions. The two halves are closely connected, and the whole is
one στίχος, not two. So the last syllable of the first half may not be *anceps*,
hiatus is not allowed at all at the division, and elision is extremely rare.

Elegiac
Couplet.

792. The Iambic Trimeter or *Senarius* consists of six feet, each an
iamb. The Greeks regarded it as consisting of three dipodies
and called it a trimeter

∪ – ∪ – | ∪ – ∪ – | ∪ – ∪ – |

Its origin is almost certainly Ionian. It first appears in the
middle of the seventh century, written by Archilochus, and it

Iambic
Trimeter.
Caesura:
Resolution of
Syllables.
Porson's Law.

reached its full popularity in the work of the Attic tragedians. It is, as Aristotle calls it, λεκτικώτατον τῶν μέτρων and well suited to the dramatic passages of tragedy. As the line consisted of three dipodies, the first syllable of each dipody was regarded as *anceps* and could be either short or long:

$$\sigma - \cup - \mid \sigma - \cup - \mid \sigma - \cup \sigma \mid$$

or if we prefer to speak of feet, the first, third and fifth feet may be spondees. An essential feature of the iambic trimeter is its use of the *caesura*. The normal place for this is after the fifth syllable, that is after the first syllable of the third foot, as in

θεοὺς μὲν αἰτῶ τῶνδ' ἀπαλλαγὴν πόνων　(Aesch. *Ag.* 1)

but it is also found after the first syllable of the fourth foot, when it is often preceded by a break in the second foot, as in

γυναικὸς ἀνδρόβουλον ἐλπίζον κέαρ.　(Aesch. *Ag.* 11)

It may even come at the end of the third foot, especially if there is an elision to ease the pause as in

ὦ μοῖρα δυστάλαιν' ἐμή τε καὶ τέκνων.　(Eur. *H. F.* 456)

On the whole these rules are observed. The exceptions, in cases in which there is no reason to suspect textual corruption, are few but commoner in Aeschylus than in Sophocles or Euripides. As the Iambic Trimeter was a recited line, it was allowed a certain freedom in the resolution of syllables. In Archilochus only one resolution is allowed in a line:

κλαίω τὰ Θασίων, οὐ τὰ Μαγνήτων κακά　(fr. 20)

but this strictness was not maintained, and eventually in Euripides we find

πενία δὲ σοφίαν ἔλαχε διὰ τὸ δυστυχές.　(fr. 641)

Still the admission of resolution was not entirely haphazard. When the second long syllable of the first, third or fifth foot was resolved, the result would be $- \cup\cup$, a group of syllables of dactylic form. This was admitted only in the first and third feet, not in the fifth. Again, when resolution took place and the three syllables were divided between two words, the rule was that the two syllables which stood for the long should be in the same word as in

$$\cup \cup$$
Σκύθην ἐς οἶμ|ον, ἄβα|τον εἰς ἐρημίαν.　(Aesch. *P. V.* 2)

Lastly, an anapaest was admitted only in the first foot, and even then the three syllables must be in the same word as in

$$\cup \cup - \mid$$
ποταμῶν τε πηγαὶ ποντίων τε κυμάτων　(Aesch. *P. V.* 89)

though an exception was made for proper names:

$$\mid \cup\cup - \mid$$
ἐμοὶ μὲν οὐδεὶς μῦθος, Ἀντιγόνη, φίλων.　(Soph. *Ant.* 11)

G. A.　　　　　　　　　　　　　　　　　　　　　　　　47

Finally, the spondee in the fifth foot was curiously restricted by what is called Porson's Law—that is, when a line ends in a cretic (– ◡ –), the preceding syllable must either be short or a word of one syllable connected closely with the word that follows. There are exceptions to this rule, but many are open to question. In the remainder either the last five syllables go very closely together in sense or the words are bound together by elision:

$$ἃ\ μοι\ προσελθὼν\ σῖγα\ σήμαιν'\ εἶτ'\ ἔχει. \quad (\text{Soph. } Phil.\ 22)$$

793. The iambic verse of Greek comedy is based on the same principles as that of tragedy but is allowed far more licenses. The caesura is often neglected, Porson's Law is not always observed, resolution is allowed in any foot except the last. The Satyric plays seem to have approximated far nearer to the tragic than to the comic style, but Porson's Law is neglected both by Euripides (*Cyc.* 210, 681) and by Sophocles (*Ichn.* 333, 344).

Iambics in Comedy and Satyric plays.

794. Another familiar metre of tragedy is the Trochaic Tetrameter, which according to Aristotle (*Poet.* 4) was the predecessor of the iambic trimeter. Its character and origin must be closely allied to that of the iambic trimeter, as both are in the same time, but the Greeks regarded the two as of widely different character. The trochaic tetrameter consists of two pairs of trochaic dipodies

Trochaic Tetrameter.

$$– ◡ – ◡\ |\ – ◡ – ◡\ |\ – ◡ – ◡\ |\ – ◡ ◡ ʌ\ |$$

of which the last is catalectic. There is a marked break after the second dipody; the fourth, eighth, and fifteenth syllables are *ancipites*, and the twelfth also is *anceps*, but subject to Porson's Law. Tribrachs are readily admitted and anapaests in the second, fourth and sixth places. Beyond this few resolutions are admitted even in comedy. The verse is used strictly by Aeschylus and freely by Euripides (*Phoen.* 592 ff.). Attic Comedy did not treat it very freely, and its easier treatment comes from Epicharmus. From him it passed to Menander and Roman comic drama.

795. The Anapaest is the converse of the dactyl, ◡ ◡ –, but its time is the same: it is 2 : 2, ◡ ◡ | ◡ ◡. Its origin must be a march-rhythm, as it is to be found in the ἐμβατήρια of Tyrtaeus and the songs for the exit and entrance of the chorus in the Attic theatre. The short syllables accompany the raising of the foot (ἄρσις) and the long syllable its setting down again (θέσις). Two anapaests accompany two steps and make one βάσις. Hence the μέτρον was thought of as two anapaests, and anapaests like iambs are scanned κατὰ διποδίαν. The most familiar form of anapaestic verse is that used for the πάροδος of the Chorus in drama, and similar passages elsewhere are built on the same rules. In these we find groups of anapaestic dimeters ending with a catalectic line called *paroemiacus*:

Anapaests.

$$◡ ◡ – \quad ◡◡ – | ◡ ◡ \quad – \quad ◡◡ –$$
$$μαλακαῖς\ ἀδόλοισι\ παρηγορίαις$$

$$◡◡ – \quad ◡◡ – \quad | \quad ◡ ◡ – –$$
$$πελάνῳ\ μυχόθεν\ βασιλείῳ. \quad (\text{Aesch. } Ag.\ 95\text{–}96)$$

These lines are continuous. There is no hiatus between them or *syllaba anceps*, but certain liberties are allowed. At times a line of two anapaests varies the structure. Dactyls and spondees may be substituted at any part of the line, but a dactyl may not precede an anapaest and the *proceleusmaticus* (◡ ◡ ◡ ◡) is not allowed. There is also a longer anapaestic line, favoured by Aristophanes when writing a parabasis, and hence called Ἀριστοφάνειον. It is a tetrameter composed of an acatalectic and a catalectic dimeter:

◡ ◡‒ ◡ ◡‒|◡ ◡‒ ‒ ‒ || ‒ ‒ ◡ ◡‒|◡ ◡ ‒◡ ||

ὅτ᾿ ἐγὼ τὰ δίκαια λέγων ἤνθουν καὶ σωφροσύνη νενόμιστο. (*Clouds* 962)

There is a regular diaeresis after the fourth foot, and the seventh foot is not a spondee though spondees are freely admitted elsewhere.

796. The anapaest belongs essentially to sung and not to recited verse, but in its use it approximates nearer to the freedom of the dactylic hexameter or the tragic iamb than to the stricter measures of lyric poetry. We may now consider those lyric measures which resemble it in being based on the aggregation of similar feet but differ from it in other ways. This class as a whole was known as μέτρα μονοειδῆ, metres constructed homogeneously from feet of the same character. Much lyric and choric verse is of this type. The main homogeneous metres follow the main type of feet. Purely dactylic systems are not common in lyric poetry, but they were used by Stesichorus and a good example can be seen in Aristophanes' 'Song of the Clouds' (*Clouds* 275 ff.). They were naturally influenced by Homeric usage, but in lyric dactyls spondees are comparatively rare and the trochaic caesura is avoided.

Μέτρα μονοειδῆ.
Dactyls:
Ionics:
Trochees:
Paeons:
Dochmiacs.

Far commoner is the *Ionic*. In its regular form it is either 'a maiore' (‒ ‒ ◡ ◡ ‒ ‒ ◡ ◡) or 'a minore' (◡ ◡ ‒ ‒ ◡ ◡ ‒ ‒). It was considered μανιῶδες and suited to excitement or frenzy, but it is usually a stately enough metre. Its simplest form can be seen in Corinna:

μάκαρας δ᾿ αὐτίκα Μώση   ◡ ◡ ‒ ‒ ◡ ◡ ‒ ‒

φέρεμεν ψᾶφον ἔταττον   ◡ ◡ ‒ ‒ ◡ ◡ ‒ ‒

Here no resolution or substitution is allowed. It is used by Aeschylus to describe the march of Xerxes (*Pers.* 65 ff.). Perhaps its licentious name is due to Anacreon who created the metre called after him by a simple anaclasis, transposing the fourth and fifth syllables in an octosyllabic line:

φέρ᾿ ὕδωρ, φέρ᾿ οἶνον, ὧ παῖ   ◡ ◡ ‒ ◡ ‒ ◡ ‒ ‒

This form of anaclasis was freely used by Aeschylus in his ionics (*Supp.* 1025, *P.V.* 399 ff., *Ag.* 709 ff.). He also syncopates (*i.e.* omits a syllable) an ionic into ◡ ◡ ‒ in lines like

◡ ◡ ‒
ζυγὸν ἀμφιβαλὼν αὐχένι πόντου.   (*Pers.* 72)

Aeschylus is said to have learned the secret of this verse from Anacreon. If so, he greatly widened its scope and made it appropriate to uses alien to its original wild or mournful character. Aristophanes uses this metre strictly and Euripides freely with resolution of syllables.

Trochaic verse is sometimes used in the choruses of Greek tragedy as in Aeschylus:

$$τίς ποτ' ὠνόμαζεν ὧδ' \quad -\cup-\cup-\cup-$$
$$ἐς τὸ πᾶν ἐτητύμως \quad -\cup-\cup-\cup- \quad (Ag.\ 681-2)$$

but it is seldom found in this simple form. One form of variation is the use of syncopation, that is, the omission of a syllable:

$$-\ \cup-\ ^\wedge\ |-\ \ \cup\ -\ \cup|\ -\cup-$$
$$δέξομαι\ Παλλάδος\ ξυνοικίαν\ (Eum.\ 916)$$

and another is the substitution of a spondee for a trochee:

$$-\quad-$$
$$ῥυσίβωμον\ Ἑλλάνων\ ἄγαλμα\ δαιμόνων\ (Eum.\ 920).$$

In many of its characteristics trochaic verse is very like iambic, and sometimes it is impossible to say which of the two metres is employed (*e.g.* Aesch. *Eum.* 924).

A *paeonic* foot may be $-\cup-$ (cretic), or $-\cup\cup\cup$ (first paeon) or $\cup\cup\cup-$ (second paeon). This is the metre of the Delphic Hymns:

$$-\ \cup\cup\cup\ |\ -\cup-|\ -\ \ \cup-|\ -\cup\cup\cup|-\ \cup-\ |$$
$$μέλπετε\ δὲ\ Πύθιον\ χρυσοχαίταν\ ἕκατον\ εὐλύραν.$$

Its origin is unknown, but it may be derived from trochaic verse, the second long of a trochaic dipody being lightened to answer to a light footfall in the dance, $-\cup\cup\cup$ taking the place of $-\cup-\cup$. The metre seems to have been used chiefly in supplications, as Aeschylus uses it in *Supplices* 418 ff., and it is the basis of Pindar's Second Olympian Ode. But it is also used freely by Aristophanes and by Sophocles in the Ἰχνευταί.

Finally there is the *dochmius*. This foot is described as an ὀκτάσημος ῥυθμός and was regarded as divided in the ratio 5 : 3 or 3 : 5. The normal form is $\cup--\cup-$, but each of the long syllables may be resolved and both the short syllables may be 'irrational,' that is, actually long, if counting as as short. The regular arrangement is

$$\cup\ -\ \ -\ \ \cup-|\ \ \cup\ --\ \ \cup\ -$$
$$τὶ\ χρίμπτει\ βοάν·\ ποτᾶται,\ βρέμει\ δ'\ (Aesch.\ Sept.\ 84)$$

but we find lines like

$$-\ \ \cup\cup\ \cup\cup\ \ \cup-|\ \cup\ \cup\ \ \cup\ -\ \cup-$$
$$ῥεῖ\ πολὺς\ ὅδε\ λεὼς\ πρόδρομος\ ἱππότας\ (ib.\ 80).$$

In practice dochmiacs are used in tragedy for intense feelings of distress or suspense, and as such they are used in Aristophanes' parodies of tragic style. Their origin is unknown, but perhaps they are derived from an iambic tripody $\overset{\smile}{-}-\cup-\cup-$ whose third syllable has been suppressed. When this syllable was dropped the total time became eight χρόνοι and the foot became 'askew,' δόχμιος.

797. Opposed to the μέτρα μονοειδῆ, in which one type of foot is used, are the μέτρα ἐπισύνθετα in which different types of feet are combined. The possibilities of such combination are enormous, and here it will be possible only to mention some main types. The simplest is that where a line in one metre is followed by a line in another. Archilochus, for instance, combines iambs and dactyls:

Μέτρα ἐπισύνθετα.
Glyconics:
Choriambic
Dimeter:
Dactylo-
Epitrites.

$$\cup \; - \cup -- \; - \cup - \; \cup \; - \; \cup -$$
πίθηκος ἤει θηρίων ἀποκριθεὶς

$$- \; \cup \; \cup \; - \; \cup \cup -$$
μοῦνος ἀν᾽ ἐσχατίην

or places a trochaic phrase after a group of four dactyls:

$$- \; - \; - \; \cup \cup \; - \cup \cup \; - \cup \cup \,| \; - \cup - \; \cup \; - \; -$$
τοῖος γὰρ φιλότητος ἔρως ὑπὸ καρδίην ἐλυσθείς.

But usually the interrelation of feet is more complex than this. On the one hand there is the strictly lyrical poetry of Sappho, Alcaeus and Anacreon, where the possibilities of variety are limited by a short stanza, and on the other hand there is the choric ode of Alcman, Pindar and Bacchylides, where there is no necessary limit to length and great variety is possible.

A popular metre of great importance was the Glyconic. As used by Anacreon this was

$$- \; - \,| \; - \; \cup\cup \,| \; {-}\cup - \; {\wedge} \; |$$
ξανθὴ παῖ Διὸς ἀγρίων

and it is most simply explained as a spondee, dactyl, trochaic dipody catalectic. The last syllable is always long, the second may be short and there is no hiatus between lines of the same stanza. Anacreon normally makes a stanza of three such lines followed by a Pherecratean

$$- \; - \,| \; - \; \cup\cup \,| \; - \; -$$
δέσποιν᾽ Ἄρτεμι θηρῶν

consisting of spondee, dactyl, spondee. This combination is very common and found in many choruses of tragedy (*e.g.* Aesch. *Ag.* 383–384, *Choeph.* 619–22). Sappho builds up different types of lines from a glyconic basis. Sometimes she inserts a dactyl

$$- \; \cup \; \cup$$
μέμναισθ᾽, οἶσθα γὰρ ὥς σε πεδήπομεν

or prefixes a cretic:

$$- \; \cup \; -$$
νῦν δὲ Λύδαισιν ἐμπρέπεται γυναί-.

Alcaeus increases the line by inserting one or more choriambs:

$$- \; \cup\cup-$$
λάβαν τῶ ξίφεος χρυσοδέταν ἔχων

$$- \; \cup \; \cup \; - \; - \; \cup \cup \; -$$
μηδὲν αλλο φυτεύσῃς πρότερον δένδριον ἀμπέλω.

Glyconics are combined with other types of feet in tragic choruses. Sophocles combines them with dactylic series (*O.C.* 676), and with trochees (ib. 669). He sometimes removes the first syllable and makes them 'acephalous' (*O.T.* 1195). In the second chorus of the *Agamemnon* Aeschylus combines them with syncopated iambics. They are even made to form part of still more complicated metrical patterns as in Pindar's First Olympian which begins with the simple combination

$$\cup - - \cup \cup - \cup -$$

ἄριστον μὲν ὕδωρ, ὁ δὲ

$$- \cup - \cup \cup - -$$

χρυσὸς αἰθόμενον πῦρ.

Another simple form of verse is that used by Corinna in *The Daughters of Aesopus* and called the Choriambic or Polyschematist Dimeter. This is an octosyllabic verse in which the last four syllables must be a choriamb but the first four can be filled variously:

$$\times \times \times \times - \cup \cup -.$$

This is evidently a primitive form of song-metre, but it is important because it was developed in various forms for choric poetry. Euripides uses it sometimes quite simply (*Orestes* 807 ff.), sometimes with an admixture of glyconics and pherecrateans (*I.A.* 206 ff.) or anapaests (*Cyc.* 50 ff.). It is an important element in some of Pindar's Odes, sometimes used simply as in

τὸν εὐεργέταν ἀγαναῖς

ἀμοιβαῖς ἐποιχομένους (*Pyth.* ii. 24),

more often in combination with other feet such as iambs (*Pyth.* vii) or a mixture of different feet (*Paean* i).

In these cases the metres of complicated choric songs are developed from simpler schemes common in lyric verse. But a favourite metre of Pindar's seems fitted only for the large scale of the great ode. This is the *dactylo-epitrite*. It is based on dactyls and the *epitrite*, $- \cup - -$. The dactyls however are usually arranged in series as a *prosodiac* $- \cup \cup - \cup \cup - (-)$. The relation of dactyls to epitrites, both in number and position, is extremely varied, and the results are correspondingly diverse. Sometimes the dactylic series is extended by a dactyl (*Pyth.* iv. 4), sometimes reduced by one (*Pyth.* iv. 20). Other variations are common. Cretics are occasionally admitted by syncopation for epitrites, the first syllable of an epitrite is sometimes resolved (*Pyth.* iv. 8) and often anacrusis is employed in the prosodiac, giving $- - \cup \cup - \cup \cup -$. This metre is employed by Bacchylides with the same rules.

798. The possibilities of metrical combinations are so numerous that they cannot be considered here, but most when analyzed will be found to fall into quite simple elements. The varieties must to some extent be due to varieties in musical accompaniment, but as almost all the music is lost, no explanation on these

Other Varieties.

lines can be given. Other difficulties arise from the nature of the problem. Though separate feet can be known in isolation, sometimes when feet are combined it is hard to see what is what. Trochees, for instance, easily become indistinguishable from iambs, and the combination of dactyls or anapaests with spondees easily produces a choriambic effect. In such cases a general rule is impossible, and each instance must be judged on its merits.

799. Both in strictly lyric verse and in choric verse lines are formed into a larger unity of stanza or strophe. With the lyric poets this may be of two, three or four lines. Each stanza is built on precisely the same metrical plan, and such divergences as are allowed are those allowed to the particular metre used. In choric poetry there are different arrangements. One form of stanza may be used throughout as in Alcman's *Partheneion* or some of Pindar's Odes (*Pyth.* xii, *Isth.* viii). Or the stanzas may be grouped in pairs. Then the two members of a pair correspond metrically, but have no necessary relation to any other pair of the same poem. This is the normal arrangement in tragic choruses. An abnormal case is that of the great Κομμός of the *Choephoroe* where we find the arrangement a b a ‖ c b c ‖ d e d ‖ f e f g g ‖ h h i i. Different from any of these is the triadic structure invented by Stesichorus. In this we have a corresponding pair of strophe and antistrophe followed by an epode on a different plan, though usually involving the same metrical elements. The structure is repeated throughout the poem, all strophes and antistrophes being built on the same plan and all the epodes corresponding with each other. The earliest example of this is Ibycus' ode to Polycrates, but it is the method employed by Pindar in the majority of his Epinician Odes and even in his Dithyrambs. The degree of metrical correspondence secured between parallel sections of an ode varies somewhat with different authors. Pindar is very strict. He hardly allows even resolution of syllables without maintaining it in the same place throughout a poem. He is however freer in his other metres, such as cretics, than in his dactylo-epitrites. Aeschylus too avoids anomalies. Euripides however and, to a less degree, Sophocles both allow certain licenses in the admission of resolved and even irrational syllables.

(margin note: Stanza and Strophe.)

W. R. Hardie, *Res Metrica*, Oxford 1920. W. Headlam, *J.H.S.* Vol. xxii (1902), pp. 209–227. P. Maas, 'Griechische Metrik,' in *Einleitung in die Altertumswissensch.* I. Band, 7 Heft, Berlin 1923. K. Rupprecht, *Einführung in die griechische Metrik*, Munich 1924. O. Schroeder, *Vorarbeiten zur griechischen Versgeschichte*, Berlin 1908; *Nomenclator Metricus*, Heidelberg 1929. G. Thomson, *Greek Lyric Metre*, Cambridge 1929. J. W. White, *The Verse of Greek Comedy*, 1912. U. von Wilamowitz-Moellendorff, *Griechische Verskunst*, Berlin 1921.

(margin note: Bibliography.)

VIII. 6. HISTORY OF SCHOLARSHIP.

800. THE History of Greek Scholarship falls into five periods, (1) the *Alexandrian, c.* 300—1 B.C., (2) the *Graeco-Roman, c.* A.D. 1—330, (3) the *Byzantine*, from the founding of Constantinople in A.D. 330 to *c.* 1350, (4) the *Italian Renaissance*, from *c.* 1350 to the death of Leo X in 1521, (5) the *Modern* period, including the subsequent history of scholarship in Italy, and in France, the Netherlands, England and Germany, and extending to the present day.

Division of periods.

801. Greek Scholarship was fostered in Alexandria under the rule of the earlier Ptolemies. Under Ptolemy Soter, Demetrius of Phalerum gave the first impulse towards the formation of public libraries in the capital of Egypt (*c.* 295). Under Ptolemy Philadelphus (285—247), learning found a home in the Museum and in the Libraries of Alexandria. The Museum and the larger Library was in the royal quarter NE of the city, while the smaller Library was in the SW quarter, near the Serapeum. The first six Librarians were Zenodotus, Apollonius Rhodius, Eratosthenes, Aristophanes of Byzantium, Apollonius the 'Classifier,' and Aristarchus.

Alexandrian period.

Zenodotus, the pupil of Philetas of Cos (300), compiled a Homeric glossary and shortly before 274 produced the first scientific edition of the *Iliad* and *Odyssey*. In this edition, which was founded on numerous MSS., each of the two poems may perhaps have been divided into 24 books; spurious lines marked by a marginal obelus. It was succeeded by a recension executed with taste and judgment by the epic poet, Rhianus. As Librarian, Zenodotus classified the epic and lyric poets, while Alexander Aetolus dealt with the tragic, and Lycophron with the comic poets (*c.* 285).

Zenodotus.

It is sometimes supposed that the successor of Zenodotus as Librarian was the poet Callimachus (*fl.* 260). He certainly produced a classified catalogue, in which the authors were arranged under the heads of dramatists, epic and lyric poets, legislators, philosophers, historians, orators and rhetoricians, and miscellaneous writers, with a brief biography of each author, and, in the case of plays, the date of their production. To the school of Callimachus belonged Eratosthenes, Aristophanes of Byzantium and Apollonius, the author of the *Argonautica*, whose rivalry with Callimachus at last compelled him to leave Alexandria and settle in Rhodes (*c.* 260). He accordingly became known as Apollonius *Rhodius.* He succeeded Zenodotus as Librarian.

Callimachus.

Apollonius Rhodius.

Eratosthenes, the successor of Apollonius Rhodius, was a man of vast and varied learning. He was the founder of astronomical geography and of scientific chronology, and was the first to assume the name of φιλόλογος. A work on the Old Attic Comedy was regarded as his philological masterpiece.

Eratosthenes.

Eratosthenes was succeeded (195) by the greatest philologist of antiquity, Aristophanes of Byzantium, the first of the Librarians who was not a poet as well as a scholar. He reduced accentua- Aristophanes of Byzantium tion and punctuation to a definite system. He also added to the obelus a variety of critical symbols, which he used in his recension of the *Iliad* and *Odyssey*. He further edited Hesiod's *Theogony*, Pindar, Euripides and Aristophanes ; established a scientific system of lexico- graphy ; wrote on grammatical ' analogy,' as contrasted with ' anomaly '; drew up lists of the ' best authors'; and composed introductions to the dramatists, excerpts from which are still extant. He died in 180 B.C.

He was succeeded, as Librarian, by Apollonius, 'the Classifier,' whose successor Aristarchus, in the form of commentaries alone, Aristarchus. wrote 800 volumes, apart from special critical treatises. His extensive learning embraced history and geography, mythology and chronology. Besides commentaries on the early Greek poets, he produced two critical editions of the *Iliad* and *Odyssey*. He placed the study of grammar on a sound basis, and was the founder of scientific scholarship. The date of his death is *c.* 144 B.C.

Among his numerous pupils was Apollodorus of Athens and of Pergamum (*fl.* 140 B.C.), the author of a work on Chronology beginning with the fall of Troy and ending in 119 B.C., Apollodorus. and also of 24 books on Mythology, the substance of which was borrowed freely by later writers. Between 100 and 50 B.C. appeared the first Manual of Mythology, the lost work of an unnamed author, which was largely used by Diodorus and Hyginus and in the extant ' Bibliotheca ' of Pseudo-Apollodorus.

The tradition of Aristarchus was maintained at Alexandria by his pupil Ammonius (*c.* 145), and (*c.* 30 B.C.) by Tryphon, who was celebrated as a specialist in Greek Grammar. A dis- Ammonius. tinguished pupil of Aristarchus, Dionysius Thrax (born Dionysius Thrax. *c.* 166 B.C.), was the author of a work on Grammar, which remained the standard text-book for more than 1300 years.

The most versatile and most industrious of all the successors of Ari- starchus was Didymus Chalcenterus (*c.* 65 B.C.—A.D. 10), who taught at Alexandria and perhaps also at Rome. He Didymus. was reputed to have written some 3500 volumes, including works on lexicography which were the source of much of the learning of later ages. In his work on Homer, probably preceded by that of Aristonicus, he aimed at restoring the lost recension of Aristarchus, and considerable fragments of his restoration are still extant. He also commented on Hesiod, Pindar and Bacchylides ; on Eupolis, Cratinus and Aristophanes ; and on Thucydides and the Attic Orators. The age of original com- mentaries was already over ; and it was reserved for Didymus to sift the remains of the past and to preserve all that was worth preserving for the future.

Grammar had meanwhile been studied by the Stoics, as a necessary part
of a complete system of dialectic. Chrysippus (*c.* 280—
c. 206), besides other grammatical works, wrote on 'anomaly,'
being the first to use that term in a grammatical sense. 'Anomaly,' as
opposed to 'analogy,' was also maintained as a leading principle in
grammar by the Pergamene Librarian, Crates of Mallos, who
in this, and also in the allegorical treatment of Homer, was
opposed to his great contemporary, Aristarchus. He was
probably responsible for drawing up the classified lists of authors in the
Pergamene library, founded by Eumenes II (197—159 B.C.), in which the
leading writers of prose, especially the orators and the critics of Art, had a
prominent place, just as the poets had in the lists of the Alexandrine
librarians. His accidental detention as an envoy in Rome shortly after
the death of Ennius (169 B.C.) led to his inspiring the Romans with an
interest in the study of Literature.

The Stoics.

Crates of Mallos.

Towards the close of the Alexandrian period, the contents of the larger
library at Alexandria are said to have been destroyed by fire while Caesar
was being blockaded in the royal quarter of the city in 47 B.C. If so, it
was in partial compensation for this loss that Antonius presented Cleopatra
with the library of the Pergamene princes.

802. The Graeco-Roman period begins with the name of Dionysius of
Halicarnassus, who lived at Rome for at least 22 years, from
B.C. 30 to B.C. 8. We are here concerned with his rhetorical
writings alone. They may be arranged in chronological
order as follows :—(1) *The First Letter to Ammaeus*, valuable
in connexion with the history and criticism of the public
speeches of Demosthenes ; (2) *De Compositione Verborum*,
on the different kinds of oratorical prose ; (3) *De Oratoribus Antiquis*, on
the styles of Lysias, Isocrates and Isaeus, and (later) on Demosthenes and
Dinarchus ; (4) The *Epistola ad Pompeium*, with strictures on Plato ;
(5) Three books *De Imitatione*, surviving in fragments only ; (6) The
treatise *De Thucydide*, with a severe criticism on his style ; and (7) The
Second Letter to Ammaeus, a fuller exposition of c. 24 of (6). The *Ars
Rhetorica* bearing his name belongs to the age of the Antonines. Among
the Greek writers later than Aristotle, he is a leading representative of
aesthetic criticism. In a degenerate age he aims at reviving a true standard
of Attic prose ; and, in pursuit of that aim, tries the extant speeches of the
Attic orators by the test of a strictly critical inquiry. In such inquiries his
name is associated with that of his friend Caecilius of
Calacte (a pupil of the Pergamene rhetorician, Apollodorus),
who wrote on the characteristics of the 'Ten Orators,' and
on other rhetorical subjects. His lost treatise περὶ ὕψους (' on elevation of
style') is mentioned by the author of the extant treatise of
perhaps the first cent. A.D., bearing the same name and
erroneously ascribed to ' Dionysius or Longinus.' The object

Graeco-Roman period.

Dionysius of Halicarnassus.

Caecilius of Calacte.

Anon. περὶ ὕψους.

of the extant work is to point out the essential elements of an impressive style which, avoiding all tumidity, puerility, affectation and bad taste, finds its inspiration in grandeur of thought and intensity of feeling, and its expression in nobility of diction and in skilfully ordered composition.

In the next century, Apollonius Dyscolus (*c.* A.D. 130) was the founder of scientific Syntax; his four books on Syntax are still extant, besides other grammatical works. In the opinion of Priscian, Apollonius Dyscolus. he is 'grammaticorum princeps,' and shares with his son the distinction of being 'maximus auctor artis grammaticae.' His definitions of the parts of speech show a marked advance on those of his predecessors and are adopted by Priscian and by subsequent grammarians. His son Aelius Herodianus (*fl. c.* A.D. 160) was one of the Herodian. most celebrated grammarians of antiquity. His great work on Prosody, and many of his other grammatical writings, are only known to us through excerpts in later authorities, but his book on peculiar or anomalous forms (περὶ μονήρους λέξεως) is still extant.

803. Among the early lexicographers and compilers of collectanea may be mentioned Juba II, king of Mauretania (*fl.* 25 B.C.), the author of a work on the stage accepted as an authority by Athenaeus Early lexico-graphers, etc. and Pollux; Pamphilus (1st cent. A.D.) the compiler of a vast work περὶ γλωσσῶν, abridged by later writers and then lost; Herennius Philon of Byblus (A.D. 64—141), author of a work on cities and their celebrities, used by subsequent lexicographers; Hephaestion, whose 48 books on metre have only survived in an epitomised form in his own ἐγχειρίδιον; his younger contemporary, Athenaeus of Naucratis (A.D. 190), who in the varied contents of the 15 books of his extant work quotes at least 700 authors who would otherwise have been unknown to us; the Atticists, Aelius Dionysius (*fl.* A.D. 117), Pausanias (*c.* 160, not the traveller), Moeris and Phrynichus; Harpocration (2nd cent.?), the lexico-grapher of the Attic Orators; and Pollux of Naucratis (*fl.* 180), the author of an ὀνομαστικὸν of Attic words and phrases, arranged according to subjects. Among rhetoricians we have Hermogenes of Tarsus (A.D. 170), the author of an important text-book, and Cassius Longinus (*ob.* A.D. 273), whose *Rhetoric* is imbedded in that of Apsines, and who was the pupil of Plotinus, the preceptor of Porphyry and the minister of Queen Zenobia at Palmyra.

804. In the Byzantine period our first name is that of the rhetorician Libanius (*c.* A.D. 314—*c.* 393), who taught at Athens, Con-stantinople and Antioch, and is the author of numerous Byzantine period. works in imitation of Demosthenes, together with a Life of that orator and Arguments to his speeches. The name Libanius. of Hesychius is borne by two lexicographers, (1) Hesychius Hesychius. of Alexandria (probably cent. 5, A.D.), the compiler of an ex-tant Greek lexicon founded on a lost work by Diogenianus (*fl.* A.D. 117); (2) Hesychius of Miletus (cent. 6), the author of a list of persons famous

for learning, a work derived in part from Aelius Dionysius and Herennius
Stephanus of Philon, and surviving only in excerpts. The geographical
Byzantium. lexicon of Stephanus of Byzantium (*c.* A.D. 500), originally
in 60 books, exists in the form of an abstract drawn up by Hermolaus
(*fl.* 527—65).

Choice passages from many writers have been preserved in the
Byzantine *Florilegia*, the earliest of which is the Anthology of
Stobaeus. Stobaeus (*c.* 480), including selections from more than 500
writers. Similar service has been rendered to scholarship in the *Bibliotheca*
Photius. or *Myriobiblon* of Photius (*c.* A.D. 820—891), giving an
account of 280 volumes, and preserving fragments of Hecataeus, Ctesias, Theopompus, Diodorus and Arrian. Another work of Photius
connected with Greek scholarship is his *Lexicon*, the only MS. of which, the
codex Galeanus, now in the Library of Trinity College, Cambridge, was
twice transcribed by Porson and published by Dobree. Among the pupils
of Photius who was Patriarch of Constantinople was Arethas, Archbishop of
Caesarea. One of the important MSS. copied under the orders of the latter
was the Patmos MS. of Plato, now in the Bodleian (A.D. 895).

In the tenth century the emperor Constantine Porphyrogenitus (A.D.
912—959), besides composing independent works, caused an Encyclopaedia of History to be drawn up, in which many extracts from earlier
historians (esp. Polybius) have been preserved. To the same age we may
ascribe the Greek Anthology compiled by Constantine Cephalas (*fl.* 917)
and preserved in the *Anthologia Palatina*. In the last quarter of the same
Suïdas. century (*c.* 976) we may place the Lexicon of Suïdas (Σουΐδας),
which is a combination of a lexicon and an encyclopaedia,
the best articles being those on the history of literature. It is founded on
earlier lexicons and on scholia; also on the historians, and on biographical
material collected by Hesychius of Miletus and by Athenaeus.

In the eleventh century the most notable name is that of Psellus
Psellus. (1018—1078), a scholar of varied attainments who lectured
on Homer and on Plato, and whose voluminous writings
include not only a history of A.D. 976—1077, but also a poem on Greek
dialects, a brief description of the surroundings of Athens and a list of
Athenian forensic phrases containing an extract from Aristotle's *Constitution
of Athens*, c. 21 § 4.

To the twelfth century, and to a revival of the influence of Photius, we
may ascribe the principal part of the lexicon which its first
'Etymologi- editor printed with many interpolations in 1499 under the
cum Magnum. name of the *Etymologicum Magnum*.

The same century is also marked by the name of Tzetzes (*c.* 1110—
Tzetzes. *c.* 1180), the author of the *Chiliades*, a didactic poem on
literary and historical topics extending over 12,674 lines of
accentual verse and displaying a vast amount of miscellaneous reading.
Among his other works are allegories on the *Iliad* and *Odyssey* in 10,000

lines, hexameter poems on *Antehomerica*, *Homerica* and *Posthomerica*, and scholia on Hesiod and Aristophanes. He is proud of his rapid pen and his remarkable memory, but he is for the most part dull as a writer and untrustworthy as an authority.

A far more memorable name in the same century is that of Eustathius, whose philological studies at Constantinople precede his tenure of the archbishopric of Thessalonica from 1175 to *Eustathius.* *c.* 1192. Of his *Commentary on Pindar* the only part preserved is a valuable preface on lyrical and Pindaric poetry, on the poet's life, and on the Olympic games and the pentathlum. His next work was on *Dionysius Periegetes*, followed by his extant *Commentary on the Iliad and Odyssey*. That on the *Iliad* is twice as long as that on the *Odyssey*; both are preceded by literary introductions, and include many *Gregorius* excerpts from earlier writers. Another learned ecclesiastic *Corinthius.* was Gregorius, archbishop of Corinth (*c.* 1200), author of an extant work on Greek dialects.

The scholars of the age of the Palaeologi (A.D. 1261—1453) have less in common with Photius and Eustathius than with the humanists of the Italian renaissance. Thus, Maximus Planudes (*c.* 1260— *Planudes.* 1310) was familiar with Latin, and besides many other works, paraphrased 'Aesop' in Greek prose, compiled historical and geographical excerpts, often of importance for textual purposes, and by abridging and rearranging the Anthology of Constantine Cephalas (*fl.* 917), formed the collection of Greek epigrams known as the *Anthologia Planudea*. His pupil Manuel Moschopoulos (*fl.* 1300) is best known as the *Moschopoulos.* author of a catechism of Greek Grammar which successively formed the foundation of the Grammars of Theodorus Gaza, Constantine Lascaris and Melanchthon. Among his contemporaries were *Thomas* Thomas Magister, author of an extant 'Selection of Attic *Magister.* nouns and verbs,' and Theodorus Metochites (*ob.* 1332), one *Theodorus* of the most learned men of his age, whose excerpts from *Metochites.* more than 70 philosophers and historians are often of textual importance.

The foremost textual critic of the later Byzantine age was Demetrius Triclinius (early in the 14th cent.). He had considerable knowledge of metre, and he expounded and emended and *Triclinius.* not unfrequently corrupted the texts of Hesiod, Pindar, Aeschylus, Sophocles, Euripides (three plays) and Theocritus. His Scholia on Aeschylus and Hesiod (*c.* 1316—1320) still exist in his own handwriting.

805. Most of our manuscripts belong to the Byzantine period, and very few to any earlier time. Among the earliest are the *Persae* of Timotheus (*c.* 350 B.C.); the fragments of the *Antiope* of *Manuscripts.* Euripides, and the *Phaedo* of Plato (250 B.C.) and of *Iliad* XI. 502—537 (240 B.C.) in the Petrie Papyri, 1891; the Louvre fragment of Euripides, *Medea* 5—12 (2nd cent. B.C.), the Harris *Iliad* 18 and the Bankes *Iliad* 24 (1st and 2nd cent. A.D.), the Herculanean papyri of Epicurus and Philodemus (*c.* 50 B.C.), the papyrus of Bacchylides (*c.* 50 B.C.), the Mariette

papyrus of Alcman (1st or 2nd cent. A.D.), the papyri of Aristotle's
Ἀθηναίων πολιτεία (c. A.D. 100), Hypereides (2nd cent. B.C.—2nd cent.
A.D.), Isocrates' *de Pace*, and Herondas (1st—2nd cent. A.D.), the Berlin
fragment of the *Melanippe* of Euripides (3rd—4th cent.), the Marseilles
fragment of Isocrates' *ad Nicoclem* (3rd cent.), the Ambrosian MS. of the
Iliad, the Vatican MS. of Dio Cassius, and the fragments of Menander,
of the *Phaëthon* of Euripides, and of the *Birds* of Aristophanes (all of
5th—6th cent.). Most of the later MSS. owe their preservation to the fact
that they were removed from Greek lands to Italy during the Revival
of Learning. The best MSS. of Homer are now in Venice; of Hesiod
and Herodotus, in Florence; of Pindar, in Rome, Florence, Milan and
Paris; of Aeschylus, Sophocles and Apollonius Rhodius, in Florence;
of Euripides, in Venice, Florence and Rome; of Aristophanes, in Venice
and Ravenna; of Thucydides, in Florence, Rome, Munich and London;
of Demosthenes and Plato, in Paris; and of Aristotle, in Venice, Rome
and Paris.

    Explanatory comments in the margins of manuscripts or between the
lines of the text, are known as *Scholia*, and their authors as
Scholia.   *Scholiasts*. Except in the case of later writers like Tzetzes,
Moschopoulos and Triclinius, their names are seldom known. The *Scholia*
have been the means of preserving fragmentary remains of ancient commentaries. Among the earliest are those on Alcman, in which Pamphilus
(1st cent. A.D.) is named. The most important are those on the *Iliad*,
which record for us the readings of Aristarchus and other Alexandrian
critics, and even of pre-Alexandrian texts. Much in the earlier *Scholia* on
Pindar, Aeschylus, Sophocles, Euripides and Aristophanes is ultimately due
to Didymus. There are also important *Scholia* on Thucydides, Plato,
Aeschines and Demosthenes, the last partly by Ulpian (early in 4th
cent. A.D.), and by Didymus (published from a papyrus in 1904).

    806. During the Byzantine period Greek was little studied in the West
of Europe, except for ecclesiastical and diplomatic purposes,
Western   especially in connexion with negotiations between the Church
Europe.   and Empire in the West and the Church and Empire in the
East. From the eighth and ninth centuries to the age of the Renaissance, it
still survived as a living language in the extreme south of Italy. The knowledge of Greek, which possibly passed from Gaul to Ireland in the sixth
century, was brought back to Frankland by the Irish monks, who founded
the monastery of St Gallen in the early part of the seventh (614). Greek
was studied at Canterbury under the Greek archbishop Theodore of Tarsus
(d. 690), and the Irishman known as 'John the Scot' was capable of
producing for Charles the Bald (845) a literal rendering of 'Dionysius the
Areopagite.' Plato was hardly represented in the West except by Latin
versions of the *Phaedo* and *Timaeus*. The knowledge of Aristotle, which
was at first confined to translations of part of the *Organon* by Boëthius, was
extended to the whole of the *Organon* after 1128. In and after 1150,
Latin versions of Arabic renderings of Aristotle reached Europe from the

Arabs in Spain. The study of Aristotle's *Physics* and *Metaphysics*, proscribed at Paris in 1215, was permitted in 1255; and the renderings from the Arabic were in course of time superseded by renderings from the Greek, such as those of the *Politics* and other works of Aristotle, which were executed in 1272—81 by William of Moerbeke at the instance of Thomas Aquinas (d. 1274). The current translations of Aristotle were keenly criticised in 1272 by Roger Bacon, whose own knowledge of Greek is exemplified in his recently published *Greek Grammar* (1902). In and after the fourteenth century the mediaeval dependence on the authority of Aristotle was gradually weakened, and the transition from the Middle Ages to the Renaissance was attended by a general widening of the range of classical studies and, in particular, by a renewed interest in Plato.

807. The soil of Italy was prepared for the reception of Greek culture by the influence of Petrarch (1304—1374). He learnt a little of the language from a Greek monk named Barlaam (1342); and, in 1353, exactly a century before the fall of Constantinople, received from that city a MS. of Homer, which he set beside his MS. of Plato, sighing at the thought that, in both cases, the Greek text was to himself a sealed book. At his promptings Boccaccio (1313—1375) learnt Greek, and caused a pupil of Barlaam, Leontius Pilatus, to be appointed the first teacher of Greek in Florence (1360—63). For the use of Boccaccio and Petrarch, Pilatus prepared a Latin translation of Homer; while Boccaccio himself wrote a text-book of Greek mythology.

The Italian Renaissance.
Petrarch.
Boccaccio.

Even before the dispersion caused by the fall of Constantinople (1453), many teachers of Greek found their way into Italy. Manuel Chrysoloras (*c.* 1350—1415), who had visited the West as an imperial envoy, was invited to Florence in 1396 and taught Greek for three years, having among his pupils the eminent humanists Guarino, Filelfo, Poggio, Leonardo Bruni, Marsuppini and Traversari. He also taught Greek at Pavia (*c.* 1400), there producing a literal rendering of the *Republic*. He died at the Council of Constance in 1415. Georgius Gemistus Plethon (*c.* 1355—1450), born at Constantinople, lived for a long time on the site of Sparta. In his old age he lectured on Platonism in Florence (1439), and prompted Cosimo de' Medici to found the Platonic Academy which, through Ficino and Pico della Mirandola, influenced the thought of Italy, and, through Reuchlin and Melanchthon, even that of Germany.

Greek Immigrants.
Chrysoloras.
Plethon.

Bessarion (1403—1472), born at Trapezus, was a pupil of Plethon in the Peloponnesus, and took part in the Council of Florence (1439), joined the Church of Rome, became a Cardinal and Patriarch of Constantinople, was nearly elected Pope in 1471, and died at Ravenna in the following year. He translated the *Memorabilia* of Xenophon and *Metaphysics* of Aristotle, and bequeathed to Venice a vast number of Greek MSS. which formed the foundation of the famous Library

Bessarion.

of St Mark's. Theodorus Gaza (*c.* 1400—75) left Thessalonica in 1430 and
probably reached Italy in 1438. He taught Greek and learnt

Theodorus Gaza.

Latin at the celebrated school of Vittorino da Feltre at
Mantua, became the first Professor of Greek at Ferrara in
1444, and went to Rome in 1451, to take part in the great scheme of
Nicholas V for translating the principal Greek Classics into Latin. On
the death of the Pope (1455), he went to Naples, withdrew in 1458 to an
Abbey on the coast of Lucania, was recalled to Rome after 1464, and on
the death of his patron Cardinal Bessarion (1472) finally retired to
Lucania where he died in 1475. He translated parts of Aristotle and
Theophrastus into Latin and Cicero *de Amicitia* and *de Senectute* into
Greek. His Greek Grammar, the first modern manual to include Syntax,
was used as a text-book by Budaeus in Paris and by Erasmus at Cambridge.

Georgius Trapezuntius (1395—1484), born in Crete, reached Venice
c. 1430, taught Greek and learnt Latin under Vittorino,

Georgius Trapezuntius.

visited Padua and Vicenza, and went to Rome in 1440.
He was compelled to leave Rome owing to faults of temper,
and, after his return to Venice, was involved in further trouble by
the publication of his comparison between Plato and Aristotle, to the
advantage of the latter (1458). He wandered from place to place, and
died at a great age in 1484. His numerous translations were only of
moderate value, but his Latin handbooks to Greek earned him the reputation of being a sound grammarian.

Johannes Argyropoulos (1416—1486) of Constantinople was in Padua
as early as 1441. In 1456 he was invited to Florence,

Argyropoulos.

where he lived under the patronage of the Medici for fifteen
years, leaving in 1471 for Rome, where he died at the age of 70. He
was the ablest of the Greek immigrants, and was highly esteemed as a
translator of Aristotle; he also lectured on Thucydides. Among his pupils
was Constantine Lascaris; his lectures were attended at Florence by
Politian, and at Rome by Reuchlin.

Demetrius Chalcondylas (1424—1511), who left Athens for Rome in
1447, taught Greek at Perugia in 1450, at Padua from 1463

Chalcondylas.

to 1471, at Florence from 1471 to 1491, and at Milan from
1492 to his death. He showed much insight (not unmixed with caprice) in
the emendation of Greek texts. He is best known as the editor of the
editio princeps of Homer (Florence, 1488), followed by that of Isocrates
(Milan, 1493), and Suïdas (*ib.* 1499).

All the above teachers of Greek had reached Italy before the fall of
Constantinople (1453). Among those who arrived after that

Constantine Lascaris.

event was Constantine Lascaris (1434—1501), who probably
stayed in Corfu for two or three years after the fall of his
native city. From 1460 to 1465 he taught Greek at Milan, being tutor to
the princess Hippolyta Sforza; he afterwards went for about a year to the
court of her father-in-law, Ferdinand I, at Naples; and finally settled at

Messina from 1466 to his death in 1501. One of his pupils at Messina
became famous as Cardinal Bembo. His Greek Grammar was the first
book printed in Greek (Milan, 1476).

His namesake Janus Lascaris (1445—1535) was born at Constantinople,
and, after its fall, was taken to the Peloponnesus and to
Crete. On reaching Venice he was sent to study Latin   Janus
                                                          Lascaris.
at Padua, at the charges of Cardinal Bessarion, who died
in 1472. He taught Greek with great success at Florence, and visited
the East twice in quest of MSS. for Lorenzo de' Medici (*ob.* April, 1492).
From Mount Athos he brought as many as 200 Greek MSS. He was afterwards in high favour at the court of France, was its envoy at Venice
(1503—8), and was placed by Leo X at the head of a school for Greek
youths at Rome (1516). With Budaeus, he aided Francis I in forming
the Library at Fontainebleau. He finally returned to Rome, where he died
in 1535. His reputation mainly rests on his five *editiones principes*, all
printed in Greek uncials with accents :—Greek Anthology, 1494 ; Callimachus, Euripides (four plays), *c.* 1494 ; Apollonius Rhodius, and Lucian,
1496. He also published the ancient Scholia on the *Iliad* (1517) and on
Sophocles (1518).

Marcus Musurus (*c.* 1470—1517) was a pupil of Janus Lascaris in
Florence, *c.* 1486. After revisiting his home in Crete, he
returned to Italy, and remained in or near Venice from 1494   Musurus.
to 1515, being Professor of Greek at Padua (1505—9) and in Venice
(1513). In 1516 he was invited to Rome as Professor of Greek, and, in
recognition of his Greek elegiac poem on Plato, was appointed Archbishop
of Monembasía, but died of the plague before starting for his diocese.
During his stay at Venice, he aided Aldus (1450—1515) in producing the
editiones principes of Aristophanes (1498), Plato (1513), Athenaeus and
Hesychius (1514), and Pausanias (1516). He also assisted in the *editio
princeps* of the '*Etymologicum Magnum*' (1499). He is described by
Erasmus, who met him in Rome, as *gente Graecus, eruditione Graecissimus.*

808. The interest taken in Greek by the earlier Italian humanists,
Petrarch and Boccaccio, has already been noticed (§ 807).
In the year of Boccaccio's death (1375) Coluccio Salutato   Italian
                                                              humanists.
was appointed Chancellor of Florence and promoted Greek
learning by persuading Chrysoloras to accept the Chair of Greek (1396).
The most enthusiastic pupil of Chrysoloras was Leonardo
Bruni of Arezzo (1369—1444), who translated several of the   Leonardo
                                                               Bruni.
speeches of Demosthenes and the Lives of Plutarch, part of
Plato, and the Oeconomics, Ethics and Politics of Aristotle. Poggio
(1380—1459) is best known as the discoverer of important Latin MSS. at
St Gallen and elsewhere, about 1415—7. His contemporary
Cyriacus of Ancona (*c.* 1391—1450) was an unwearied   Cyriacus of
                                                         Ancona.
traveller and an enthusiastic collector of ancient inscriptions
in Greece and Italy.

While Greek refugees, such as Theodorus Gaza and Georgius Trapezuntius, learnt their Latin under Vittorino, some of the foremost scholars of
Italy visited Greek lands on purpose to learn the language.   Thus Guarino
of Verona (1370—1460) lived for five years (1403—8)
Guarino.   in the household of Chrysoloras at Constantinople, and
afterwards taught in Florence, Venice, Verona and Ferrara, was interpreter at the Council of Ferrara (1438), and also translated parts of
Strabo and Plutarch, besides commenting on Aristotle and editing, with a
Latin version, the Accidence of Chrysoloras.   Similarly the
Aurispa.   Sicilian Aurispa (*c.* 1370—1459) visited Constantinople in
1422—3, learnt Greek and returned to Venice with 238 MSS., mainly of
Classical authors, having already sent to Niccolo de' Niccoli, the industrious
collector of MSS. at Florence, the important MS. of Aeschylus, Sophocles and
Apollonius Rhodius, now known as the *Codex Laurentianus* (cent. x).
Lastly, Filelfo (1398—1481) spent seven years as a Secretary
Filelfo.   of Legation at Constantinople, returning with a large supply
of Greek MSS. (including at least 40 authors[1]), and spending the rest of his
long life as Lecturer in Greek and Latin at Venice, Florence, Siena, Milan
and Rome.

809.   Among eminent Italians who learnt their Greek in Italy may be
named Traversari (1386—1439), one of the foremost in the
Traversari.   literary circle of Florence, a writer of learned letters in
excellent Latin, and the translator of Diogenes Laërtius ; Laurentius Valla
(1407—57), the elegant Latin scholar who translated Hero-
Laurentius
Valla.   dotus, Thucydides and two-thirds of the *Iliad* ; Campanus
(*c.* 1427—77), the translator of Plutarch's *Lives* ; Perotti
(1430—80), the translator of Polybius ; Ficino (1433—99), the translator
of Plato and Plotinus ; and, lastly, one of Ficino's pupils,
Ficino.   Politian (1454—94), who translated *Iliad* 2—5 into Latin
Politian.   hexameters at the age of 16, and afterwards counted among
his pupils Reuchlin, Grocyn and Linacre.

The year of the death of Ficino was that of the birth of the greatest
Greek scholar of Italy, Petrus Victorius of Florence (1499—
Victorius.   1584), who edited Aeschylus (1557) and Sophocles (1547),
and the *editio princeps* of the *Electra* of Euripides (1545), and who also
produced elaborate commentaries on the *Ethics, Rhetoric, Poetics* and
Politics of Aristotle, and displayed vast stores of critical learning in
the 38 books of his *Variae Lectiones* (1538, etc.).   His younger contemporary, Robortello (1516—67), Professor at Padua and
Robortello.   elsewhere, edited Aeschylus (1552) and Callimachus (1555),
and, in his classical studies, paid special attention to metre and to chronology, besides laying the foundations of a theory of criticism in his work *de
arte seu ratione corrigendi antiquos libros* (1557).   Since his time most

---

[1] List in Symonds, *Revival of Learning*, p. 270[1].

of the best work of Italian scholars, except Corsini's *Fasti Attici* (1744—56), has been concerned with Latin rather than with Greek, and in both mainly with Archaeology.

810. Greek Scholarship was transmitted from Italy to France (1) through the Italian humanists Gregory Tifernas and Jerome Aleander, who were appointed to lecture in Paris in 1456 and 1508 respectively; and (2) through Janus Lascaris, who was in the French diplomatic service from 1495 to 1525. Among his pupils he counted Budaeus (1467—1540), who published his memorable *Commentarii linguae Graecae* in 1529. The learned printer Robert Estienne or Stephanus (1503—59) produced his Eusebius in 1544, his Greek Testament in 1546, and the works of Dionysius and of Dio Cassius on Roman History in 1546—8. His son Henri Estienne (1528—98), who is best known for his Greek *Thesaurus* (1572), and for his Plato (1578), was a pupil of Turnebus (1512—65), who as Greek Professor and as Director of the Royal Press in Paris produced editions of Aeschylus, Sophocles and the Ethics of Aristotle. Dorat (*c.* 1504—88) edited the *Prometheus* in 1549. The fame of Lambinus (1520—72), who spent nine years in Italy, and of Muretus (1526—85), who lived there from 1563 to his death, rests mainly on their Latin scholarship, though Lambinus translated the *De Corona* of Demosthenes, and the *Ethics* and *Politics* of Aristotle. The same is partly true of J. J. Scaliger (1540—1609), who passed the last 16 years of his life as Professor at Leyden. Before his call to that University in 1593, his most famous work (apart from editions of Latin authors) was his *De emendatione temporum* (1583); and, after that event, his *Thesaurus temporum*, including a masterly edition of the Eusebian and other chronicles (1606). His strength lay in a remarkable capacity for textual criticism, in a clear historic conception of antiquity as a whole, and in the concentration of vast and varied learning on important works.

Next to Scaliger, the most learned scholar of his time was Casaubon (1559—1614), who was Professor at Geneva, Montpellier and Paris, and spent the last four years of his life in England. His emendations are fewer than those of Scaliger, but they are more certain. He produced a masterly treatise on the Greek satyric drama and on Roman satire (1605); and his editions of Greek authors include Aristotle, the *Characters* of Theophrastus, Polybius, Strabo and Athenaeus. Salmasius (1588—1653), like Scaliger, left France for Leyden in 1631, a quarter of a century after his discovery of the Greek Anthology of Cephalas in the Palatinate Library at Heidelberg (1606), but only two years after the publication of his greatest work, that on Solinus (1629). Guyet's criticisms on Hesiod and Hesychius, those of Petavius on Aratus and on chronological subjects, and Viger's work on Greek idioms (1627), can only be named in passing.

France.

Budaeus.

R. Stephanus.

H. Stephanus.

Turnebus.

Lambinus.

Scaliger.

Casaubon.

Salmasius.

48—2

Henri de Valois, *Valesius* (1603—76), did much for the elucidation of
Harpocration (publ. 1682). Du Cange (1610—88), besides
his great Lexicon of late Latin (1678), published a similar
work on late Greek (1688) and an edition of the Byzantine
historians (1680); while Montfaucon (1655—1741) laid the
foundation of the study of Greek MSS. in his *Palaeographia
Graeca* (1708), and also produced in 15 folio volumes a vast work on
Greek and Roman Antiquities (1719, 1724). Strassburg was the home
not only of Brunck (1729—1803), editor of Sophocles, but
also of Schweighaeuser (1742—1830), editor of Herodotus,
Polybius and Athenaeus. Herodotus was translated by
Larcher (1726—1812); the Homeric Scholia were published
by Villoison (1753—1805); Greek Palaeography minutely
studied by Bast (1771—1811), and the *ed. princeps* of Babrius produced
by Boissonade (1774—1857). Thurot (1823—82) and Bar-
thélemy Saint-Hilaire (1805—1895) did good service for
Aristotle; Graux (1852—82) showed the highest promise as a palaeo-
grapher; and Egger, in the course of his far longer life
(1813—85), was the author of an Essay on the History of
Criticism in Greece (1849), and of Lectures on the History of Hellenism in
France (1869).

811. In the Netherlands the earliest name of note is that of
Erasmus (1466—1536), who was born at Rotterdam, but
who in his intellectual activity is more closely connected
with France, England, Italy and Germany than with the land
of his birth. He lectured in Paris in 1496 and visited
England in 1497; on his return, spent ten years in France, Italy and the
Netherlands, took his doctor's degree at Turin (1506), and lived with
Aldus Manutius in Venice, during the reprinting of his *Adagia* (1508). He
returned to England in 1510, was appointed Lady Margaret Professor of
Divinity and Greek Lecturer at Cambridge, and went to Basel in 1514, where
he published his Greek Testament in 1516, his treatise on Latin and Greek
pronunciation in 1528, the first complete edition of Aristotle in 1531, and
the *ed. princeps* of Ptolemy in 1531, and where he died in 1536.

Between 1530 and the foundation of the University of Leyden in
1575, the only important name connected with Greek
scholarship is that of W. Canter (1542—75). His *Euripides*
(1571) was the first in which the metrical responsions between *strophe* and *antistrophe* were clearly marked.

In the Second Period (1575—1650), Lipsius (1547—1606) was famous
as a Latinist, and was succeeded by Scaliger, who was
Professor at Leyden from 1593 to 1609. Gerhard John
Voss (1577—1649) produced a work on the Greek historians (1623); and
his contemporary Meursius (1579—1639) showed great learning in Greek antiquities. It was in his early years alone that

Margin notes:
Valesius.
Du Cange.
Montfaucon.
Brunck.
Schweig-
haeuser.
Villoison.
Boissonade.
Egger.
The
Netherlands.
Erasmus.
First period.
Canter.
Second period.
Meursius.

Scaliger's pupil, Daniel Heinsius (1581—1655), edited Greek authors. Salmasius, professor at Leyden from 1631, only edited Greek writers of minor importance. Though he had discovered the *Anthologia Palatina* in 1606, it was the *Anthologia Planudea* alone that was known to Grotius (1583—1645) and was translated by him into Latin verse.

In the Third Period (1650—1750) Joh. Friedrich Gronovius (1611—71) was great as a Latin scholar; his son Jacob (1645—1716) published his Polybius in 1670, the *ed. princeps* of Manetho 　Third period. in 1689, and the *Thesaurus* of Greek Antiquities in 1697— 　J. Gronovius. 1702. Nicolaus (son of Daniel) Heinsius (1620—81) was a Latinist. Graevius (1632—1703) edited Hesiod (1667), and also produced a posthumous edition of his son's Callimachus (1697). To the latter work an extensive collection of the Fragments and a new recension of the Epigrams was contributed by Bentley, with a prolix commentary by Bentley's friend, Spanheim (1629—1710), then Prussian minister in London, who is best known for his treatise on the importance of numismatics (1664). In this period, which was also that of Bos and Küster and of Bergler and Duker, by far the foremost Greek scholar in Holland was 　Hemsterhuis. Hemsterhuis (1685—1766), the restorer of Greek learning in that country. He edited Pollux at an early age (1706) and was incited to remedy his defective knowledge of Greek metre by Bentley's criticism of his immature work. He also edited Lucian (completed by Reitz, 1743—1746), and the *Plutus* of Aristophanes (1744). His colleague Wesseling (1692—1764) edited Diodorus (1746) and Herodotus (1763).

The Fourth Period (from 1750 to the present day) opens with the name of Valckenaer (1715—85), who edited the *Iliad* (1747), the *Phoenissae* (1755) and the *Hippolytus* of Euripides with a 　Fourth period. Diatribe on the Fragments (1768), also the Bucolic Poets 　Valckenaer. and the Fragments of Callimachus (1781); while, in another Diatribe (printed 1806), he exposed the forgeries of the Alexandrian Jew, Aristobulus. Ruhnken (1723—98), whose first *Epistola* 　Ruhnken. *Critica* was on the Homeric Hymns and on Hesiod (1749), and his second on Callimachus and Apollonius Rhodius (1751), is celebrated as the editor of the Platonic lexicon of Timaeus (1754) and of the *ed. princeps* of the Homeric Hymn to Demeter (1780). He did much for the Greek grammarians and for Hesychius. He was also the author of a critical history of the Greek Orators (1768), and the discoverer of the lost *Rhetoric* of Longinus (1765). He is described by F. A. Wolf as *criticorum princeps*. His life was written by Wyttenbach 　Wyttenbach. (1746—1820), the unwearied editor of Plutarch's *Moralia* (1795—1821). The list closes with the great name of Cobet 　Cobet. (1813—89), editor of Lysias (1863) and Diogenes Laertius (1850), and author of the *Variae Lectiones* (1854), the *Novae Lectiones* (1858), and the *Miscellanea Critica* (1876).

Cobet's distinguished contemporary, Madvig (1804—86), belongs to
Denmark, and is mainly famous in connexion with Livy

Denmark.

and Cicero and Latin Grammar; his Greek scholarship is,

Madvig.

however, well represented in his Greek Syntax (1847), and
also in part of his *Adversaria Critica* (1871—84).

812. The revival of Greek learning in England was due to Selling,
prior of Canterbury (d. 1494), who studied Greek under

England.

Politian in Florence, and to Linacre, who accompanied

First period.

him on his next visit to Italy, attended the lectures of

Linacre.

Politian and Demetrius Chalcondylas at Florence, and became acquainted with Hermolaus Barbarus in Rome (1485).
Linacre produced a Latin rendering of the 'Sphere' of Proclus and of
certain treatises of Galen; at his instance Grocyn, Lily and W. Latimer
learnt Greek in Italy and inspired Oxford with an interest in Greek
literature (1491). Grocyn, Linacre, Colet, and More are lauded by Erasmus
in a letter written in London in Dec. 1499. Erasmus lectured on Greek in
Cambridge (1510—3); and, after his departure, the interest in that language
was sustained by Bullock and Croke of King's, by Thomas Smith of Queens',
and by John Cheke and Roger Ascham of St John's.

In the First Period after the revival of Greek learning in England
(1485—1570), Linacre and Ascham represent the imitative, elegant and
tasteful type of scholarship characteristic of the Italian scholars of the
Renaissance. The Second Period (1570—1700) is marked

Second period.

by industrious erudition rather than by special attention
to the form of the classical languages. In this period was produced the

Elizabethan
translators.

remarkable series of Elizabethan translations, including
North's *Lives* of Plutarch (1579), Chapman's *Homer*, and
Plutarch's *Moralia* by Philemon Holland, the 'Translator-

Savile.

General' of his age. Sir Henry Savile edited Chrysostom
(1613) with the aid of Downes, 40 years Professor of Greek

Selden.

at Cambridge; Selden published the *Marmor Parium*

Gataker.

(1628); Thomas Gataker was the first Englishman who produced, in his Marcus Aurelius, an original commentary on any

Milton.

classical work (1652); while Milton not only studied Euripides,
Pindar, Aratus, and Lycophron with the eye of a critic, but
also sketched in his 'Tractate of Education' an encyclopaedic course of
training in Greek literature (1644). During the Civil War Duport continued lecturing on Theophrastus at Cambridge, and translating the Book
of Job into Homeric hexameters. In 1660 he was succeeded as Professor
of Greek by Isaac Barrow; Thomas Stanley's *History of Philosophy*
appeared in 1655—60, his Aeschylus in 1663; and Bishop Pearson's
comments on Diogenes Laërtius in 1664. Thomas Gale published
some of the Greek mythologists, and Iamblichus *de Mysteriis* (1678);
John Hudson, Thucydides (1696) and Josephus (1720); and John Potter,

Lycophron (1697) and the 'Antiquities of Greece' (1699). About the close of the period Joshua Barnes edited Euripides (1694), Anacreon (1705) and Homer (1711); and H. Dodwell published his   Barnes.
treatise *de Cyclis Veterum* (1701) and his *Annales Thucydidei*   Dodwell.
et Xenophontei (1702).

The Third Period (1700—1782) begins with Bentley (1662—1742), the founder of classical criticism, and with the 42 years of his tenure of the Mastership of Trinity College, Cambridge.   Third period.
In his *Letter to Mill* (1691) he had published the first-fruits of   Bentley.
his study of the Greek dramatists. In 1696 he collected the Fragments of Callimachus. In a masterly Dissertation published in 1697, and enlarged in 1699, he had proved the spuriousness of the '*Letters of Phalaris.*' In 1710 he emended Philemon and Menander; in 1722 he revised Nicander, and in 1732 and 1734 was busy with Homer, having discovered as early as 1713 that many of the metrical peculiarities of the Homeric poems were due to the lost *Digamma.* Among Bentley's friends were John Taylor, editor of Lysias, and Markland, editor of several plays of Euripides. Among those who came under his influence were Dawes, the student of Attic moods and tenses; Toup, the editor of 'Longinus'; Tyrwhitt, the commentator on the *Poetics*; Musgrave and Heath, the able critics of the Greek tragic poets; and (above all) Porson, who was first drawn towards critical research by Toup's *Longinus*, and who regarded Dawes and Bentley as his great masters in the art of criticism.

The literary activity of Porson (1759—1808), who was Fellow of Trinity (1782—92) and Professor of Greek at Cambridge (1792—1808) was mainly limited to the 20 years between 1782   Fourth period.
and 1803. His emendations of Aeschylus appeared in 1795;   Porson.
his first edition of the *Hecuba* of Euripides in 1797 (ed. 2, 1802), followed by the *Orestes, Phoenissae* and *Medea.* He advanced the study of Attic Greek by elucidating many points of idiom and usage, by establishing the laws of tragic metre, and by the emendation of texts.

Among Cambridge scholars, Twining (1734—1804) translated the *Poetics* of Aristotle; Dobree (1782—1825) did much for the criticism of the Attic orators; Monk (1784—1856) wrote the   Greek scho-
Life of Bentley, and edited several plays of Euripides. Five   lars at Cam-
plays of Aeschylus were produced by C. J. Blomfield (1786—1857), and the bridge.
whole by Samuel Butler (1774—1840). B. H. Kennedy (1804—89), his successor as Head Master of Shrewsbury, edited the *Agamemnon* and the *Oedipus Tyrannus*; and Shilleto (1809—76), Demosthenes, *De Falsa Legatione*, and Thucydides I, II. Blakesley (1808—85) edited Herodotus; W. H. Thompson (1810—86), the *Gorgias* and *Phaedrus* of Plato; E. M. Cope (1818—69), the *Rhetoric* of Aristotle, J. W. Donaldson (1811—61) completed K. O. Müller's *Greek Literature* and edited Pindar; and Charles Badham (1813—84), parts of Euripides and Plato. The best work of F. A. Paley (1816—88) was his Aeschylus; he also edited Euripides, Hesiod, Theocritus and the *Iliad.* T. S. Evans (1816—89) as well as

Kennedy and Shilleto, showed special ability in Verse Composition. W. G. Clark (1821—78) wrote on the Peloponnesus and edited Shakespeare. H. A. Holden (1822—96) edited Aristophanes and parts of Xenophon and Plutarch; and Churchill Babington (1821—89), the *ed. princeps* of four speeches of Hypereides. Sir Richard Jebb (1841—1905), the able author of the 'Attic Orators,' and of an Introduction to Homer, Lectures on Modern Greece, and on Greek Poetry, and monographs on Erasmus and Bentley, was distinguished as the editor of Sophocles and Bacchylides, and as the translator of Theophrastus. His genius in Classical Composition was exemplified in his 'Translations into Greek and Latin Verse.' He was Professor of Greek at Glasgow (1875—89) and Cambridge (1889—1905), M.P. for the latter University, and President of the Hellenic Society. A. W. Verrall (1851—1912), by his editions of the *Oresteia* and the *Medea*, and by his Essays, promoted an intelligent appreciation of the literary merits of Aeschylus and Euripides. S. H. Butcher (1850—1910) expounded Aristotle's *Poetics*.

At Oxford, Routh (1755—1854) edited the *Euthydemus* and *Gorgias* of Plato; Elmsley (1773—1825) the *Acharnians* of Aristo-
Greek scholars at Oxford. phanes, and several plays of Sophocles and Euripides; Gaisford (1779—1855) the *Poëtae Graeci Minores*, Herodotus, Stobaeus, Suïdas and the *Etymologicum Magnum*; Liddell (1811—98) and Scott (1811—87) produced a standard Greek Lexicon; Chandler (1828—89) a standard work on Greek Accents; George Rawlinson (1815—1903) translated Herodotus; Jowett (1817—94) translated Plato, Thucydides, and the *Politics* of Aristotle, and Pattison (1813—84) wrote the 'Life of Casaubon' and Essays on Scaliger. D. B. Monro (1836—1905) produced a 'Homeric Grammar' and an edition of *Odyssey* XIII—XXIV; I. Bywater (1840—1914), a commentary on Aristotle's *Poetics*.

The foremost of the English Historians of Greece have been Grote (1794—1871) and Thirlwall (1797—1875). Mure (1799—
Historians of Greece. 1860) wrote a work on Greek Literature, and Fynes-Clinton (1781—1852) the *Fasti Hellenici*.

In Classical Topography and Archaeology we must only mention Stuart and Revett's *Antiquities of Athens* (1762—1816);
Greek archaeologists. E. Dodwell's *Tour in Greece* (1819); Leake's *Topography of Athens* (1821), *Travels in the Morea* (1830) and *Northern Greece* (1835); the works of Fellows on Lycia, of Pashley and Spratt on Crete, and of Bunbury on Ancient Geography. Sir Charles Newton (1816—94), the discoverer of the Mausoleum of Halicarnassus, was one of the principal founders of the Hellenic Society (1879) and the British School of Archaeology at Athens (1886).

813. An interest in Greek scholarship was transmitted from Italy to Germany by Rudolf Agricola 1443—85, who spent seven
Germany. years in Italy and specially studied the philosophy of Aristotle,
Reuchlin. and by Reuchlin (1455—1522), who visited that country in 1482, 1490, 1498, and published his Greek Grammar in 1506.
Melanchthon. The Grammar of Melanchthon, the *praeceptor Germaniae*

(1497—1560), was first printed in 1518. Melanchthon and his biographer Camerarius (1500—74) translated some of the speeches of Demosthenes. In the next generation, Sylburg (1536—96)   Sylburg. edited Aristotle, Pausanias and Clement of Alexandria, as well as the *Etymologicum Magnum.*

In the eighteenth century, J. A. Fabricius of Hamburg (1668—1736) supplied in his *Bibliotheca Graeca* (14 vols. 1705—28)   Fabricius. important materials for the history of Greek Literature ; Damm of Berlin (1699—1778) produced lexicons to Homer and Pindar; and Reiske of Leipzig (1716—74) edited the Greek Orators, Dionysius of Halicarnassus, and other important works.   Reiske. The science of Classical Archaeology was founded by his contemporary Winckelmann (1717—68), who lived at Rome 1755—68 and published his History of Ancient Art in 1764. The founder   Winckelmann. of scientific Numismatics was Eckhel of Vienna (1737—98),   Eckhel. whose *Historia Numorum* was published in 1792—8. Winckelmann's friend Heyne (1729—1812), for thirty years   Heyne. prominent as a professor at Göttingen, edited Virgil, Pindar and the *Iliad*, and wrote much on ancient Art. Among Heyne's pupils were Jacobs (1764—1847), translator of Demosthenes and editor of the Greek Anthology ; Schneider, the Greek lexicographer (1750—1822); Matthiae, the Greek grammarian (1769—1835), and Dissen (1784—1837), editor of Pindar and the *De Corona.*

A new era was begun by F. A. Wolf (1759—1824), who was Professor at Halle (from 1783) and at Berlin (from 1807). In 1782   F. A. Wolf. —92 he edited Plato's *Symposium*, Hesiod's *Theogony* and the *Leptines* of Demosthenes, and in 1795 produced his famous *Prolegomena* to Homer. Among his pupils were not only August Boeckh and Immanuel Bekker, but also Heindorf (1774—1816), editor of part of Plato ; Schleiermacher (1768—1832), translator of the whole ; Passow (1786—1833), the Greek lexicographer ; and Bernhardy (1800—75), the editor of Suïdas and author of important Histories of Greek and Roman Literature.

Classical Philology, as understood by Wolf, was soon divided into two great fields of research, cultivated by separate groups of scholars :— (1) the *grammatical and critical* school, concerned mainly with the grammar, the textual criticism and the interpretation of the Classics ; and (2) the *historical and antiquarian* school, dealing mainly with the mythology and archaeology, the political and legal institutions and the comparative philology of the ancient world.

The head of (1) was Gottfried Hermann (1772—1848), 50 years Professor at Leipzig, who did much for the text of the Greek   G. Hermann. Tragic poets. His pupil Lobeck of Königsberg (1781—   Lobeck. 1860) commented on the *Ajax* of Sophocles, edited Phrynichus, and dealt with the Greek Mysteries in his Aglaophamus. Lobeck's successor Lehrs (1802—78) made his mark by his   Lehrs.

works on Aristarchus and Herodian, and on the Scholia to Pindar.
Meineke.   Meineke (1790—1870) distinguished himself as a critic of the
Greek Comic poets and of Alexandrian literature, besides
editing Strabo and Athenaeus. His son-in-law Bergk (1812
Bergk.   —81) is best known as editor of the *Poëtae Lyrici Graeci*.
Bergk's contemporary Ahrens (1809—81) devoted himself to the Greek
dialects ; Schneidewin (1810—56), with Leutsch, to the *Paroemiographi*,
also to the Lyric Poets and Sophocles. The *Poëtae Scenici Graeci* were first
produced in a single volume in 1830 by W. Dindorf (1802
W. Dindorf.   —83), who also edited the Homeric Scholia and Demos-
thenes, and joined in revising the Paris edition of the Greek *Thesaurus*.
Nauck.   Nauck (1822—92) published texts of Homer, Sophocles,
Euripides and (above all) a collection of the *Tragicorum
Graecorum Fragmenta*.

Bekker (1785—1871) collated more than 400 manuscripts, and produced
a vast series of carefully edited texts, including Plato, the
Bekker.   Attic Orators, Aristotle (with the Index by Bonitz), Thucydides, Homer (with the *Scholia* to the *Iliad*), several Greek lexicographers, besides Dio Cassius and many of the Byzantine
Lachmann.   historians. Lachmann (1793—1851) is famous as an editor
not only of Lucretius, but also of the Greek Testament, and as author of a
critical treatise on the *Iliad* (1837). Ritschl (1806—76), of
Ritschl.   Bonn and Leipzig, besides his distinction as editor of
Plautus, was the author of a masterly monograph on the Alexandrian
libraries. Among Greek Grammarians may be mentioned Buttmann (1764
—1829), Thiersch (1784—1860), Krüger (1796—1874), and
Grammarians;
Demosthenic   Kühner (1802—78) ; among Demosthenic scholars, G. H.
and Aristote-   Schaefer (1764—1840), Voemel (1791—1868), Rehdantz
lian scholars.   (1818—79), Sauppe (1809—93), and the historian, Arnold
Schaefer(1819—83); and among Aristotelian scholars, Brandis (1790—1867),
Spengel (1803—80), Bonitz (1814—88), Bernays (1824—81), Susemihl (1826
—1901), Vahlen (1830—1912). / Usener (1834—1905) is best known for
his *Epicurea*.

The historical and antiquarian School begins with Niebuhr, the
historian of Rome (1776—1831). Boeckh (1785—1867),
Boeckh.   whose main achievement in pure scholarship was his edition
of Pindar (1811—22), produced a monumental work on the Public
Economy of Athens (1817), followed by his *Corpus Inscriptionum Graecarum* (1825—40) and by important metrological and chronological works,
closing with a general survey of the whole field of classical
Welcker.   philology. Welcker (1784—1868) wrote on the Epic Cycle
and on Greek Tragedy, as well as on Greek Archaeology and Mythology;
K. O. Müller (1797—1840) on Aegina and Orchomenus,
K. O. Müller.   on the Dorians and Etruscans, on the Archaeology of Art
Schömann.   and on the Literature of Greece. Schömann (1793—1879)
edited Isaeus and wrote on Greek Law and Constitutional

Antiquities; K. F. Hermann (1804—55) on Greek Antiquities; and
Preller (1809—61) on Mythology. Jahn (1813—69)　K. F. Her-
did much towards making classical archaeology an exact　mann.
science. Side by side with Mommsen (1817—1903), the　Jahn.
historian of Rome, we must name Ernst Curtius (1814—96),　E. Curtius.
the historian of Greece, the writer on the topography of Attica and the
Peloponnesus, and the inspirer of the exploration of Olympia.　G. Curtius.
His brother, Georg Curtius (1820—85), produced important
works on the Greek Verb and on Greek Etymology and was a leading
representative of the School of Comparative Philology　Holm.
founded by Bopp (1791—1867). The History of Sicily and
of Greece was the life-long theme of Adolf Holm (1830—90).　Bursian.
The History of Classical Philology in Germany has been written by the
author of the 'Geography of Greece,' Conrad Bursian (1830—83).

In this brief outline of the History of Greek Scholarship in Greek lands,
as well as in Italy, France, the Netherlands, England and Germany, many
notable names have unavoidably been omitted: further information may,
however, be found in the authorities quoted below.

General bibliography in Hübner's *Bibliographie der klassischen Alterthums-*
wissenschaft, ed. 2, pp. 1-139, 1889. Bibliographies of the special　Bibliography.
literature of the several parts of the subject in J. E. Sandys,
History of Classical Scholarship (with chronological tables, and with 86 illustrations) in three volumes, (i) from the Sixth Century B.C. to the end of the Middle
Ages, 2nd ed., 702 pp., 1906; (ii and iii), from the Revival of Learning to the end
of the Nineteenth Century, 1021 pp., 1908. Outlines (with bibliographies and
'loci classici') in A. Gudeman, *Grundriss zur Geschichte der klassischen Philo-*
logie, 2nd ed., 260 pp., 1909; see also W. Kroll, *Geschichte der klassischen Philo-*
logie, 152 pp., 16mo., 1908, Otto Immisch, *Wie studiert man klassische Philologie?*
1909, and J. E. Sandys, *Short History of Classical Scholarship*, pp. 455, 1915.
Among books dealing with definite portions of the subject, or with individual
scholars, may be mentioned:—On the history of the science of language,
H. Steinthal, *Geschichte der Sprachwissenschaft bei den Griechen und Römern*,
2 vols. (2nd ed., 1891). For the Alexandrian period, Susemihl's *Geschichte der*
griechischen Litteratur in der Alexandrinerzeit, 2 vols. (1891-2). For the period
ending A.D. 400, Gräfenhan, *Geschichte der klassischen Philologie* (1843-50).
For the Byzantine period, Krumbacher in Iwan von Müller, IX. (I), ed. 2, 1897.
For the Revival of Learning, G. Voigt, *Die Wiederbelebung des classischen*
Alterthums (ed. 3, 1894); J. A. Symonds, *Revival of Learning* (ed. 3, 1897); and
R. C. Jebb, in *Cambridge Modern History*, I. (1902), 532-84; also J. E. Sandys,
Harvard Lectures on the Revival of Learning (1905). For the History of Greek
Scholarship in France, Egger, *l'Histoire d'Hellénisme en France* (1869), Mark
Pattison's *Essays* I. (1889), and *Life of Casaubon* (ed. 2, 1892); in Holland,
L. Müller, *Gesch. der class. Philologie in den Niederlanden* (1869); in England,
Jebb's *Erasmus* (1890), *Bentley* (1882), and *Porson* (in *Dict. Nat. Biogr.*); on
Sir Richard Jebb, as Scholar and Critic, A. W. Verrall, on pp. 427-87 of *Life*
and Letters (1907). For its History in Germany, Bursian's *Gesch. der class.*
Philologie in Deutschland (1883), and also, for the earlier period, the second half
of Geiger's *Renaissance und Humanismus in Italien und Deutschland* (1882).

I. INDEX OF PERSONS, DEITIES AND RACES[1].

The numbers refer to the sections.

Abantes 39
Achaeans 33 ff., 38 ff., 112 f., 128, 634; of the Pelopon-
nese 30
Achilles 38; Tatius 235
Acragas 379
Acusilaus 134, 165
Adeimantus 244
Adonis 99, 409
Aeacus 38 f.
Aelian 54, 68, 73, 228, 282
Aelius Dionysius 803; Hero-
dianus 204, 802; Theon 221
Aenesidemus 276
Aeolians 27, 37, 110, 117, 150
Aeschines 32, 178, 494
Aeschylus 50, 155 ff., 159, 635
Aesop 47
Aethiopians 33 f.
Aetolians 430
Africanus, Sextus Iulius 106
Agatharchus 712
Agathias 196 ff.
Agathocles 588
Ageladas 320
Agesander 341
Agesilaus 466
Agias of Troezen 144
Agis III 472
Aglaophon 348
Akaiwasha 38
Alcaeus 150, 387, 729
Alcamenes 321, 326, 406
Alcibiades 456, 710
Alciphron 226
Alcmaeon of Crotona 714
Alcmaeonidae 109, 445
Alcman 151, 733
Alexander I 39; the Great
125, 282, 310, 332 f., 582 f., 587, 601, 718; of Aphro-
disias 266
Alexis 164
Alyattes 315
Alypius 389
Ameinocles 617

Ammon 546
Ammonius 801
Amoebaeus, actor 567
Amphiaraus 395, 414
Amphilochus the Athenian 93
Amyclas of Heraclea 280
Anacreon 136, 146, 150
Anaxagoras 135, 239, 280
Anaximander 165, 237
Anaximandridas 660
Anaximenes 165, 237, 281, 626
Andocides 173; vase painter 361 ff.
Androdamas of Rhegium 474
Andronicus of Rhodes 266
Antenor 316
Antidotus 350
Antigonus 125; Doson, Go-
natas 126, 271; Monoph-
thalmus 520; sculptor 337
Antimachus of Colophon 147
Antinous, marble relief of 344
Antiochus Epiphanes 311; of Ascalon 277
Antipater of Sidon 196
Antiphanes 164
Antiphilus 352
Antiphon 172, 280
Antisthenes 238, 243
Antonius Diogenes 234
Apelles 331, 346, 351
Apellicon 770
Aphaea 320
Aphrodite 57, 82, 89, 323, 327 ff., 395, 409
Aphthonius 221
Apollo 44, 52, 89, 128, 314 f., 319 f., 323, 327 ff., 330, 389, 396, 403, 420 f., 435, 546
Apollodorus 164; of Athens 106, 203, 349, 801
Apollonius 341; Dyscolus 204, 802; Rhodius 189, 731; of Perga 282; (en-
graver) 382 a

Appianus of Alexandria 39, 213
Aratus 126; poet 193, 282
Arcadians 37
Arcadius 204
Arcesilas 276
Arcesilaus 343, 735
Archelaus of Priene 341
Archermus of Chios 314 ff.
Archilochus 42, 46, 90, 94, 149, 155
Archimedes 282, 622, 733
Archytas of Tarentum 280 f.
Archytas (mus.) 388
Arctinus of Miletus 144
Ares 411
Arete 663
Arethusa 71
Argives 37 f., 112
Arion 36, 155
Aristander 328
Aristarchus 136, 201 ff., 282, 801
Aristeides, Publius Aelius 223; artist 350; of Ceos 474
Aristides Quintilianus 390 f.
Aristippus 243, 271
Aristobulus 100
Aristonophus 615
Aristophanes 47 f., 64, 98, 159, 162 f., 368; of Byzantium 136, 201 f., 770
Aristotle 42, 44 f., 46 ff., 52 ff., 64 ff., 71 ff., 81 ff., 97, 111, 129, 185, 239, 245, 247, 255 ff., 279 ff., 281, 335, 383, 716
Aristoxenus 384, 388 ff.
"Armenoid" 34
Arrian 86, 217, 730
Artemis 304, 310, 315, 325, 327, 395, 404
Artemon 604
Aryandes 582
Asclepiades, of Samos 196; physician 723
Asclepius 24, 107, 328, 395, 414, 714 ff., 719

[1] The indexes contain no references to the Chronological Tables.

II. INDEX OF PLACES.

III. INDEX OF SCHOLARS AND MODERN WRITERS.

IV. INDEX OF GREEK WORDS AND PHRASES.

ὁ κσένιος at Gortyn 478, 746
κόσσυφος 52, 71
κότερος, κῶς, etc. not found on inscriptions 730
κότινος 94, 422
κότταβος 694
κοτύλη=τρύβλιον and ἡμίνα 573
κουκούφα 55
κουνάδι (=κυνίδιον) 47
κουρεῖα 683
κοῦρμι 91
κοχλίας (πωματίας) 83; (screw) 281
κόχλος 83
κόψιχος 52
κράγγων 81
κραμβασπάραγος 96
κράμβη 96
κράνεια 94
κρανοποιοί 558
κρᾶσις δι' ὅλων 273
κρέξ 60
κρήδεμνον 669
κρήματα 480
κριθή 91
κρῖθος 685
κρίκος 685
κρίμνον 91
κρίνον λευκόν 90; (πορφυροῦν) 90; (ἡμεροκαλλές) 90
κριός, κριὸς ἄγριος 46
κροκή 554
κροκόδειλος, χερσαῖος 67
κρόκος 90, 102
κροκυδίζω 554
κρόμμυον 98
κρόταλον 638
κρούω 554, 557
κρυπτεία 532
κτείς 84, 554
κύαθος 569, 572
κύαμος 92; ὁ Αἰγύπτιος 92
κύανος 556
κυβερνήτης, κυβερνητήρ 611
κύβοι 279, 697
κυδωνέα 94
κυδώνιον 94
κύκλοι 560
κύκνος 61; κύκνοι (naut.) 616
κύλιξ 694
κύλισις 641
κύλλαρος 81
κῦμα, κυμάτιον 306
κύμινδις 51
κύμινον 98
κυμινο-πριστο-καρδαμο-γλύφος 98

κυνέη 589
κυνηγετεῖν 688
κυνόσβατος 94
κυπάρισσος 88
κύπειρος 105
Κύπρια 144
κύπρινος 73
κύριος 264; legal representative of a minor, etc. 493, 633, 661 f.
κύρτος 74
κύτινος 94
κύτισος 93
κύφαι 81
κύψελος 52
κύων 47, 243
κωλακρέται 443, 518
κωμάζειν 694
κώμη 161, 264, 432
κῶμος 161, 694
κωμῳδία 161
κώνειον 101
κωνοφόρα 87 f.
κώπη 611; κῶπαι θρανιτικαί 622
κωρυκώδη 87

λάβραξ 71
λαγίδιον 44
λαγωβόλον 413, 688
λαγώς 44; ὁ θαλάττιος 83
λαῖαι 554
λαιός 52
Λακεδαιμόνιοι, οἱ 465; τὸ κοινὸν τῶν Λακεδαιμονίων 472
λαμπαδηδρομίαι 515
λαμπυρίς 77
λαμψάνη 96
λάπαθον 96
λάρος 62
λάταξ, λατάσσειν 44, 694
λαύρη 709
λαχανηρά 96
λάω 726
λέβητες 475, 752
λεγόμενα 428
λείριον 90
λειχήν 90
λεκιθοπωλίδες 560
λεκτόν 272
λέξις 171, 185; εἱρομένη, κατεστραμμένη 172; λιτή or ἀφελής 174
Λεοντοφόρος, ἡ 622
λεπάς 83
λεπίς 556
λεπορίς 44
λέσχαι 683
λευκαία 103

λευκερωδιός 59
λεύκη 87
λευκόϊον 90
λευκόλινον 103
λευκὸς χρυσός 581
λεύκωμα 499
λέων 47
ληκυθοποιοί 558
λήκυθος 634, 698
λῆμμα 780
ληνός 686
ληξίαρχοι 460; ληξιαρχικὸν γραμματεῖον 451
λῆξις 499
λῃτουργίαι 515
λιβανωτίς 89
λίγδος 556
λιθάργυρος 556
λιθόδενδρον 85
λίθος, τρητός 611; λίθοι, pieces in a game 697
λίκνον 632, 685
λιμνόστρεα 84
λίνον 103
λιποταξίου (γραφή) 482
λῖς 47
λιχανός, μέσων, ὑπάτων 389
λιχάς 570
λογεῖον 425
λογιστής 449, 453, 458
λογιστική 278
λογογράφος 165, 167, 172, 506
λογοποιός 165 f.
λόγος (divine Reason) 237; in physics 273; Ἄδικος of Aristophanes 163; ψιλός 165; λόγοι of Demosthenes 177; λόγοι = definitions 248
λογῶδές τι μέλος 384
λουτρόν 696
λουτροφόρος 633
λοχαγοί 456, 597
λόχος 597
λυγίζειν 641
λύγξ 47
λύγος 89
λύκιος, λύκειος 396
λύκος 47
λύκος ὁ ξανθός 47
λύρα 152, 391, 645
λυρικός 150
λυχνίς 90
λύχνων ἁφαί 626
λώπη 669
λωποδύται 496
λωτός 87; (τρίφυλλος) 93

μάγαδις 391